ARCHAEOLOGY

THIRD EDITION

THIRD EDITION

David Hurst Thomas

American Museum of Natural History

Australia • Canada • Mexico • Singapore • Spain
United Kingdom • United States

WADSWORTH
THOMSON LEARNING™

Publisher: Earl McPeek
Acquisitions Editor: Brenda Weeks
Product Manager: Julie McBurney
Project Editor: Angela Williams Urquhart
Art Director: Carol Kincaid
Production Manager: Darryl King

Cover Design: G.A. Caldwell
Cover Images: Courtesy American Museum of Natural History
Cover Printer: Phoenix Color
Compositor: TechBooks
Printer: R.R. Donnelley, Willard

About the cover: The photographs document a century of archaeological excavations by the American Museum of Natural History at Pueblo Bonito (1896–1899), Gatecliff Shelter (1970–1978), Hidden Cave (1979–1980) and St. Catherines Island (1974–present).

Printed in the United States of America
1 2 3 4 5 6 7 05

For more information about our products, contact us at:
Thomson Learning Academic Resource Center
1-800-423-0563

For permission to use material from this text, contact us by:
Phone: 1-800-730-2214
Fax: 1-800-730-2215
Web: http://www.thomsonrights.com

Library of Congress Catalog Card Number: 97-80982

ISBN: 0-15-501369-6

Asia
Thomson Learning
60 Albert Street, #15-01
Albert Complex
Singapore 189969

Australia
Nelson Thomson Learning
102 Dodds Street
South Melbourne, Victoria 3205
Australia

Canada
Nelson Thomson Learning
1120 Birchmount Road
Toronto, Ontario M1K 5G4
Canada

Europe/Middle East/Africa
Thomson Learning
Berkshire House
168-173 High Holborn
London WC1 V7AA
United Kingdom

Latin America
Thomson Learning
Seneca, 53
Colonia Polanco
11560 Mexico D.F.
Mexico

Spain
Paraninfo Thomson Learning
Calle/Magallanes, 25
28015 Madrid, Spain

This book is dedicated to LSAP(T),
colleague, companion, advocate, and mother of my son.
And, most significantly, she's still my very best friend.

Preface

People who like this sort of thing will find this the sort of thing they like.

Book review by Abraham Lincoln (1809–1865)

Archaeology, Third Edition, is a user-friendly, but not dumbed-down, introduction to archaeology—what it is, who does it, and why anybody should care about archaeology.

This book departs, in a few ways, from the standard textbook. For most archaeology texts, the approach is fairly encyclopedic and dispassionate.

But I can't do it that way. Little about archaeology is impersonal to me, and my biases are clearly reflected here, as they were in the two previous editions of this book.

To be sure, modern archaeology is a specialized and complicated academic discipline. Today's archaeology has plenty of concepts, several bodies of theory, and a huge array of analytical methods—and these are things I'd like you to understand. But archaeology is more than method and theory. It's also dust and discouragement, and I want you to know something about that part as well.

Many, perhaps most, archaeologists tend to write about their life's work in narrative as dry and stuffy as the caves they often excavate. I don't see why archaeological writing needs to be like this. Archaeologists don't talk like that in real life and many even enjoy what they do, although you'd never know it from the literature. Archaeology should be fun and satisfying.

Because of this perspective, you'll find that these pages will reflect something of my own personality. In the first chapter, for instance, I narrate the history and development of Americanist archaeology. Because the lives and interests of individual archaeologists can be as revealing as the archaeology itself, I'll give you a brief life history of eight well-known American archaeologists. The selection is personal, reflecting my own mind-set and background. Other archaeologists would doubtless choose others to personify different values. This is what I mean about the largely personal slant.

Don't be humble. You're not that great.

Golda Meir (1898–1978),
Israeli politician

You'll also find that the text proceeds largely by example, several of which are drawn from my own archaeological experience. I'll tell the tale of how Gatecliff Shelter was discovered, a fairly subjective sketch designed to show you something of what archaeology really feels like. I'll take you along with us as we search for a lost sixteenth/seventeenth-century Franciscan mission in

Georgia's fabled Sea Islands. This search not only illustrates the growing importance of high-tech remote sensing approaches, but it also tries to impart something of the flavor of getting out there and actually doing the archaeology.

So now you're forewarned: What follows is an anti-encyclopedia. It's a personalized and admittedly idiosyncratic interpretation of what's up in contemporary Americanist archaeology.

Scientists are not mere knowledge-acquisition machines; they are guided by emotion and intuition as well as by cold reason and calculation.

Paul Horgan, staff writer, *Scientific American*

How This Book Evolved

This is a brand new, 18-year-old book.

The first edition of *Archaeology* was published in 1979. It provided an overview of what was then called the *new archaeology* (and today is better termed the *processual agenda*). The first edition was unique in a couple of ways. For one thing, it was written from a first-person perspective. I just couldn't see why archaeology needed to be presented as deadly dull and lifeless.

I may have my faults, but being wrong ain't one of them.

Jimmy Hoffa (1913–1975?),
American labor leader

Beyond this, the first edition reflected the times in which it was written. The 1970s and 1980s were at once stimulating and confusing—not unlike today. Many archaeologists could see little but conflict and chaos: loud arguments about how best to understand the past, with little agreement on much of anything.

I bluntly disagreed with this position. The "new archaeologists" had an unfortunate habit of rejecting all that had gone before. I believed (and still believe) that the discipline of archaeology develops by selective accretion—adding newer developments in method and theory to the solid base of what our predecessors accomplished. I saw my role as textbook author to be one of cutting through the hype and self-serving bluster, to demonstrate how the various pieces—"new" and traditional—fit together into a workable discipline of archaeology.

Archaeology was not practiced exclusively by idiots before 1962 (or 1950 or 1935).

Albert Spaulding (1914–1990), archaeologist

The processual agenda had three sequential goals. Archaeologists must first *establish cultural chronology*—define the spatial and temporal framework with which to organize the specifics of the archaeological record. The intermediate goal was to *reconstruct past lifeways,* to define the recoverable aspects of past human existence: settlement pattern, population density, technology, economy, organization of domestic life, kinship, maintenance of law and order, social stratification, ritual, art, and religion. In effect, archaeologists working at this intermediate goal were pursuing "the anthropology of the dead." The ultimate goal in archaeology was to transcend the specifics of chronology and lifeway to *define the cultural processes* behind past and present behaviors. So-called *processual archaeology* sought to uncover the timeless and spaceless law-like generalizations that would help us understand modern society and how it came to be. Explaining this sequential, overarching framework in processual archaeology was my major objective in the first edition of *Archaeology.*

If I have seen a little further it is by standing on the shoulders of Giants.

Sir Isaac Newton (1642–1727), physicist and mathematician

But after nearly a decade, *Archaeology* began looking a little frayed around the edges. The discipline had changed, and a new edition was clearly in order. In 1989's *Archaeology,* Second Edition, I replaced out-of-date and "moribund" sections with fresher examples that demonstrated current archaeology in action.

Although the second edition maintained the basic processual agenda as an organizing framework, I made several significant additions, upgrading the discussions of historical archaeology and Cultural Resource Management ("applied archaeology"), explicitly confronting the changing roles of women in archaeology, and adding three new chapters on archaeological field methods.

Archaeology, Second Edition, remained an anti-encyclopedia with a personal (often first person) tone and examples often drawn from my own experiences and interests, grounded in the mainstream processual agenda. Neverthless, in 1989, I did take note that some archaeologists had begun framing alternatives to the processual agenda. The so-called *postprocessual critique* attacked the basic premises of processual archaeology. For one thing, the postprocessual critics rejected the processual search for universal laws, arguing instead that such "laws" supposedly governing human behavior simply do not exist. Postprocessual critics also pointed out the inadequacies of "an explicitly scientific approach," emphasizing instead the subjectivity involved in all archaeological interpretation. Some of the more extreme postprocessualists even argued that there is no real past at all: The past is merely a subjective construction in the present. Ecological and "systemic" views of the past were similarly rejected as a "robotic view of the human past." Postprocessual critics favored developing more empathetic and humanistic approaches, which give priority to human thoughts, decisions, and other highly subjective elements.

Archaeology's postprocessual critique rejected the evolutionary, antihistorical, objective, science-based, and ethical neutrality of the processual agenda. Instead, postprocessual archaeologists emphasized empathetic approaches, multiple pathways of belief. They questioned how "value-free" archaeology really is: Do archaeologists discover "a real past" or do they "construct" that past based on present-day experiences and biases? For what political purposes do archaeologists interpret the past?

Archaeology, Second Edition, explored several of these postprocessual approaches, particularly within the realm of historical archaeology (where the presence of documentary evidence made the subjective, humanistic approaches more productive). The processual agenda continued to provide a relatively consistent and relatively coherent framework for understanding the past. I continued to argue that "archaeology is anthropology or it is nothing." I still believed that the diverse archaeological approaches fit into the single set of three stepwise and sequential objectives mentioned before: construct cultural chronology, reconstruct extinct lifeways, and define cultural processes. I continued to teach that "the canons of established scientific methods" provide the best way to understand the human past. In the second edition of *Archaeology,* the processual agenda remained intact, but the postprocessual critique had clearly begun to make inroads.

So Why a Third Edition?

Any jackass can kick down a barn, but it takes a good carpenter to build one.

SAM RAYBURN (1882–1961), SPEAKER OF THE HOUSE

Today, the field of Americanist archaeology has changed so dramatically that it is difficult to know where to begin. This time around, I found my basic text required modification from top to bottom. Neither the original processual agenda nor the subsequent postprocessual critique were sufficient to explain what's going on in modern Americanist archaeology. Although it's not an easy story to tell, I'm enjoying the diverse and yet eclectic theoretical blend that characterizes contemporary archaeology.

The "processual agenda" and "postprocessual critique" stand as important historical milestones in a complex dialogue about how to encounter the human past. Both were historical events, firmly grounded in specific places and particular times. But most of the underlying issues—science and humanism, objectivity and empathy—have concerned thoughtful archaeologists for more than a century.

Archaeology is about facts; if you want the truth, go next door to the philosophy department.

INDIANA JONES, FICTIONAL ARCHAEOLOGIST (IN THE MOVIE *INDIANA JONES AND THE LAST CRUSADE*)

For years, archaeology has been buffeted by a number of "theoretical schools," each claiming for itself a privileged status in defining what constitutes adequate explanation in archaeological research.

It is no longer useful—nor even possible—to pick Americanist archaeology apart into such tidy subdivisions. Americanist archaeology is today neither processual nor postprocessual: It usefully employs modified versions of both. The vast majority of those practicing Americanist archaeology fall somewhere toward the middle: There are very few hard-core processualists or die-hard postprocessualists around these days. The surviving parts of processual and postprocessual archaeologies comprise what is today our approach to the past.

Archaeology, history, and anthropology appear as increasingly arbitrary partitions of the necessary elements of comprehensive understanding.

ANDREW SHERRATT, ARCHAEOLOGIST (ASHMOLEAN MUSEUM, OXFORD UNIVERSITY)

So it is that today's Americanist archaeology is best characterized as multiple paths leading toward an understanding of the past. Archaeologists today wrestle with several important questions: To what extent do we "discover" an objective past? Or, are we "creating" alternative pasts from the same data? What is the proper mix of humanism and science in archaeology? What social responsibilities does the archaeologist have to properly use the past in the present? Each of these questions has been around for a century, and no clear-cut resolution appears on the horizon.

This is a strength, not a weakness. Learning to live with mutually irreconcilable views about the past is not an easy thing, but it's the only way that archaeology will survive in the upcoming millennium.

What's New in This Edition?

My concern now is to find cases and inventions, gathering them as they occur to me. . . . Therefore you will not wonder nor will you laugh at me, Reader, if here I make such great leaps from one subject to the other.

LEONARDO da VINCI (1452–1519), PAINTER, SCULPTOR, ARCHITECT, ENGINEER, AND SCIENTIST

Here are some of the new features that have been added to the third edition.

New emphasis on the rapidly evolving relationship between archaeologists and Native American people. These discussions illustrate the dynamic (and sometimes contentious) relationships between native people and the archaeologists who wish to study them. Evolving linkages highlight the increasing importance of newer, multicultural modes of explaining and understanding the American past.

New integration of scientific and humanistic approaches in archaeology. Although some believe that it's necessary to choose sides—either be a scientist or be a humanist—I hope to convince you that the choice isn't really necessary. Modern archaeology spans a broad philosophical spectrum, with both scientific and humanistic strategies contributing significantly to modern archaeological theory.

Emphasizes the increased importance of cognitive archaeology. In recent years, a so-called "cognitive revolution" has swept across Americanist archaeology. Concerned with defining an "archaeology of the human mind," cognitive archaeologists pursue a broad agenda, seeking to understand the importance of ritual and religion, symbolism and iconography, and the development of human consciousness.

Focuses attention on the rapidly growing field of historical archaeology. More than a dozen specific case studies are introduced to illustrate why the field of historical archaeology has become one of the most vital aspects of Americanist archaeology. These examples demonstrate how (and why) historical archaeologists have taken a major role in crafting archaeological theory for the future.

Underlines the increased participation by women in archaeology. Several sections have been added to demolish misleading Hollywood stereotypes—to illustrate how the fallacies of Indiana Jones are being replaced by the realities of Indiana Joans. In several places, we demonstrate how feminist archaeology is changing our perception of gender in the past.

Accentuates the importance of applied archaeology. America has come to recognize that her common cultural heritage is under threat from the demands of contemporary life. Two new chapters show how archaeologists throughout the Americas have assumed a very practical role in modern society, helping to preserve our common cultural heritage. Here, we emphasize the role of archaeologist as manager of cultural and heritage resources, informing students about the broad range of employment possibilities in archaeology and stressing the role of conservation archaeology as a practical extension of the more traditional academic and museum-oriented archaeologies. In the final chapter, we present several new directions in "applied" archaeology, including *forensic archaeology,* the rediscovery and reintroduction of ancient agricultural technologies, and some ethical difficulties in "taking archaeology public."

Includes a new chapter on the archaeology of African America. This important addition (1) shows the factual and theoretical basis for a rapidly developing new direction in archaeology (especially in urban America), (2) details how local communities are actively participating in archaeology to learn about their own past, and (3) emphasizes how the new brand of "grassroots" archaeology is available to anybody interested in participating—even avocational archaeologists and kids.

Emphasizes the importance of remote sensing as a nondestructive way of learning about the past. We examine in detail the increasingly sophisticated technology that is enabling archaeologists to find where sites are, what they contain, and how the remains are articulated—all without disturbing the site. Remote sensing technology is rapidly becoming a cost-effective way of doing archaeology in a noninvasive, nondestructive manner.

Emphasizes new developments in archaeology at the molecular level, showing how human diets are being reconstructed from human bones through the analysis of isotope levels and the extraction analysis of ancient DNA.

Adds dozens of In His/Her Own Words *boxes.* These first-person excerpts broaden the focus of my own largely first-person approach and also emphasize the importance of seeking multiple voices and explanations about the past.

The graphics have been significantly upgraded. We've spent considerable time and effort gathering some neat photographs of *real people doing real archaeology.* Although some archaeologists do indeed look like movie actors, most don't. As you look through these pictures, you might be surprised to see what real archaeologists look like.

Everything is explicitly tied into the Internet. Throughout these pages, you'll find dozens of *Archaeology on the Internet* boxes that provide on-line amplification of subjects I'm discussing in the text—"virtual tours" of sites being considered in the text, FAQs (Frequently Asked Questions) about theoretical or methodological advances, more complete discussions and/or bibliographies, relevant professional and avocational groups, and places to find the newest developments in Americanist archaeology.

To improve readability, we have streamed the bibliography. I've deleted bibliographic references from the body of the text and acknowledge my sources in a lengthy bibliographic essay at the end of the book. Thus, without interrupting the flow of the narrative, I can credit those whose work was used directly and also acknowledge those who helped inform and shape my own reporting and writing.

Each chapter now begins with a Preview and ends with a comprehensive Summary.

The new What's in a Name? *features discuss the importance of respecting the wishes of various constituent groups for self-identification.*

A new chapter on ethical concerns in archaeology. The final chapter looks in depth at the complex issue of "Who Owns the Past?," a storyline developed throughout this entire book. It also focuses on the profound implications of the *Native American Graves Protection and Repatriation Act*—NAGPRA for short.

A new feature entitled Archaeo-Mythbusters. These boxes are designed to explode some of the more humorous modern myths about archaeology and archaeologists.

> *From the moment I picked up your book until I laid it down, I was convulsed with laughter. Some day I intend to read it.*
>
> GROUCHO MARX (1895–1977), HUMORIST

Who Helped Out?

Despite the personal flavor of these pages, don't think that the book was completed by a single pair of hands—no book is. Many people helped, and I must include several words of thanks.

The overall presentation was vastly improved by a contingent of top-notch colleagues and friends who provided advice and critical reviews of the manuscript. I am particularly grateful to Paul Goldstein, Steve Lekson, and Janet Spector, each of whom slogged through the entire revised draft and contributed measurably to the final product. For input on the various Internet links, I thank Joelle Clark, Network Subcommittee E-Mail Coordinator for the Public Education Committee of the Society for American Archaeology.

I also gratefully acknowledge timely and sometimes detailed assistance from Sumru Aricanli, Larry Babits, Mary Beaudry, Richard Burger, Lewis Binford, Michael Blakey, Ama Badu Boakyewa, Rob Bonnichsen, Bruce Bradley, Jane Buikstra, Robert Carneiro, Catherine Cameron, Margaret Conkey, Cheryl Claassen, C. William Clewlow, the late Don Crabtree, Jay Custer, Phil Da Vita, William Davis, Kathleen Deagan, Jeffrey Dean, Rob

DeSalle, Robert Elston, Clark Erickson, T. J. Ferguson, Kent V. Flannery, Don Fowler, Anne Fox, George Frison, Ervan Garrison, Joan Gero, Diane Gifford-Gonzalez, Dean Goodman, Martha Graham, Donald K. Grayson, David Grimaldi, Marvin Harris, Christine Hastorf, William Haviland, Brian Hayden, Richard Holmer, Robert L. Humphrey, the late Cynthia Irwin-Williams, Gregory Johnson, William Kelso, Thomas King, Stephen Kowalewski, Charles Lange, Clark Spencer Larsen, Robert Leonard, Mark Leone, Randall McGuire, Frank McManamon, Scotty MacNeish, David B. Madsen, William Maples, Joyce Marcus, Alexander Marshack, George Miller, Paul Minnis, Craig Morris, Michael J. O'Brien, James O'Connell, Christopher Peebles, Kathy Place, Stephen Plog, William Rathje, Elizabeth Reitz, Thomas Riley, John Rick, Anibal Rodriguez, Nan Rothschild, Irwin Rovner, Michael Schiffer, Enid Schildkrout, Payson Sheets, Theresa Singleton, Stanley South, Janet Spector, Charles Spencer, William Tallbull, Anya Taylor, Mark Taylor, W. W. Taylor, Ian Tattersall, Ruth Tringham, Donald Tuohy, Patty Jo Watson, John Weymouth, Joe Ben Wheat, and Mary Whelan. Each contributed worthwhile suggestions, which I often followed. Although the finished product remains my own, I gratefully acknowledge the help of these people for improving the ideas and sharpening the focus.

Several others in the American Museum of Natural History also deserve thanks. Margot Dembo handled innumerable editing chores, and my confrere Lorann S. A. Pendleton spent endless hours helping with the background research. Rachel Goddard and Jason Sherman read the entire draft. Niurka Tyler cheerfully helped out with dozens of details. I also thank the newer members of our research staff, Eric Powell and Cheryl White, who also contributed their advice and assistance.

I gratefully acknowledge the library staff of the American Museum of Natural History, beginning with the incomparable director, Ms. Nina Root. I also thank Tom Baione, Kathy Burek, Donald Clyde, Arthur Cook, Mary DeJong, Daryl Gammons, and Mary Stock. We also appreciate the help from the American Museum of Natural History Photography Studio staff, especially Craig Chesek, Jackie Beckett, and Denis Finnin.

I am also grateful to the crew at Harcourt Brace—Bryan Leake, Brenda Weeks, Cathy Richard, Carol Kincaid, Darryl King, and Angela Williams Urquhart. Dennis O'Brien generated much of the artwork illustrating this volume, and I also gratefully acknowledge the contributions of the late Nicholas Amorosi and Diana Salles, both of the American Museum of Natural History.

D. H. T.
St. Catherines Island, Georgia
November 1997

Brief Contents

Contents

A Note About Human Remains

This book discusses, in several places, important new frontiers of bioarchaeological research. But we also recognize the need to deal with human remains in a respectful and sensitive manner. Several Native American elders have requested that we refrain from publishing photographs or other depictions of American Indian human remains. In specific response to this request, no such images appear in this book. Should other groups express similar concerns, these requests will be addressed in further editions as appropriate.

Chapter 1

Meet Some Real Archaeologists

PREVIEW This book is about two things: what archaeologists want to learn and how they learn it. This task is more complex than it might appear. Today, there are dozens of ways to do good archaeology. To understand the range of acceptable archaeological methods, we will at times look at the extremes. One extreme is largely scientific, the other is largely humanistic. One extreme is mostly objective, the other is mostly subjective. One extreme is heavily ecological, the other is heavily ideational. Sometimes these approaches can coexist, sometimes they clash.

As we go along, we will assign names to these extreme views (archaeologists *love* to name things). But for now, the names are inconsequential. What is consequential, however, is that you understand that opinions differ about what constitutes "good archaeology." This difference of opinion is certainly tolerable and may even be a good thing. This book will try to teach you about today's archaeology and explain why at present there are multiple views about past events and what they really mean. An understanding of these multiple views comes, quite naturally, only by examining the past. Where else could an archaeologist turn? This first chapter begins by looking at how contemporary archaeology evolved. This done, we will explore the meaning of today's archaeology and how each part articulates with the rest.

> *I just like the challenge that prehistory seemed to give, the mystery of it, and finding out about people—why they think the way they do, and what makes history.*
>
> MARGORIE F. LAMBERT (1910–), ARCHAEOLOGIST (SCHOOL OF AMERICAN RESEARCH)

Archaeological objects vary. So do archaeological contexts. Deciphering meaning from objects in context is the business of archaeology. In fact, today we have so many complex techniques for doing so, that it has become impossible for anyone to know and understand them all. No matter how hard we might study, we will never learn all there is to know about archaeological theory and technique. New techniques appear each year, and—alas—with each advance, each individual archaeologist becomes relatively less knowledgeable. In truth, archaeologists are learning more and more about less and less.

The same is true of field techniques. Archaeological fieldwork is becoming so refined that many of us now regret portions of our earlier research: We threw too much away. This is nothing new. Archaeologists in 1923 did not save charcoal. Why should they? Who knew that in 1949 a physicist named Libby would perfect a method of dating lumps of charcoal? Archaeologists did not collect pollen samples in the 1930s because nobody knew how to reconstruct extinct past environments from microscopic pollen grains. In my first field class, I was told to chuck out all the animal bone that

> *Archaeology is a collection of different, often contradictory and competing ways of doing the same thing, and of different goals being met in similar ways.*
>
> ROBERT C. DUNNELL, ARCHAEOLOGIST (UNIVERSITY OF WASHINGTON)

was not "identifiable" (whatever that meant). Today, by trying to save all bone, we are learning about hunting strategies, butchering patterns, seasonality, and even the sex-age characteristics of bygone animal populations. Soil from archaeological sites is now a gold mine of information. We have recently discovered that archaeological sites are often littered with ancient hair. It turns out that human and animal hair is amazingly durable, capable of surviving for thousands, maybe even hundreds of thousands, of years. We now realize that important clues about the past—such as the ancient DNA preserved in hair samples—can easily be missed unless you're specifically looking for it.

Archaeologists are justly proud of their microscopic techniques. No clue from the past is too minor to escape scrutiny. We are afraid to throw anything away; indeed, entire sites are occasionally brought back to the laboratory and "excavated" under a microscope.

But there is a danger lurking in these procedures, and that danger is *myopia,* losing sight of the forest for the trees. This book does not view archaeology through a microscope; rather, it uses just the opposite: a macroscope. Instead of magnifying the minutiae of archaeology, our macroscope will merge particulars in search of overall patterns. Archaeology consists of hundreds, maybe thousands, of tiny pieces. Sometimes the pieces seem so varied that they no longer fit together. Yet viewed another way, they seem to define a single picture. What you see depends largely on where you stand.

That is one problem: fitting the diversified techniques, concepts, and strategies of archaeology into a meaningful whole. There is a second problem: What does this framework tell us? Can it stand alone, or does it somehow tie into a yet larger whole?

So we are left with this: What are archaeologists? What are scientists? What are humanists? What are anthropologists? When each question has been answered, we will be in a position to assess what contemporary archaeologists are up to. Then we shall find out how they do it. But first, a word about archaeology's past.

The Western World Discovers Its Past

Most historians ascribe the honor of "first archaeologist" to Nabonidus (who died in 538 B.C.), the last king of the neo-Babylonian Empire (to understand just what "B.C." and the other calendrical abbreviations mean, see *A.D./B.C./B.P. . . . Archaeology's Alphabet Soup*). A sincerely pious man, Nabonidus's zealous worship of his gods compelled him to rebuild the ruined temples of ancient Babylon and to search among their foundations for the inscriptions of the earlier kings. For this reason, Nabonidus is known to modern history more as an antiquarian than an administrator. In fact, we are indebted to the research of his scribes and the excavations by his subjects for much of our modern picture of the Babylonian Empire. Though nobody would call Nabonidus an "archaeologist" in the modern sense of the term, he remains an important figure for one simple reason: *Nabonidus looked to the physical residues of antiquity to answer questions about the past.* This may seem

A.D./B.C./B.P. . . . *Archaeology's Alphabet Soup*

Throughout this book—and, in fact, almost anything written by real archaeologists—you will encounter a blizzard of stand-alone capital letters: A.D., A.C., B.C., B.P., and a host of others. Let me try to clear the air right away by providing you with some concise definitions of the most commonly used abbreviations:

B.C. ("before Christ"): For instance, 3200 B.C.

A.D. (literally *anno Domini*, meaning "in the year of the Lord"): Indicates that a time division falls within the Christian era. Archaeologists generally place the "A.D." *prior to* the numerical age estimate—you should say "A.D. 1560" rather than "1560 A.D." By the way, the earliest A.D. date is A.D. 1; there is no A.D. 0 because this year is already denoted by 0 B.C. and double numbering is not allowed.

A.C. ("after Christ"): Basically the same as A.D., except that it's written A.C. 1560 (with the abbreviation written *before* the number). This usage is confusing, and hardly anybody uses it anymore. Neither do we.

B.P. ("before present"): Many archaeologists feel more comfortable avoiding the A.D./B.C. split altogether, substituting the single "before present" age estimate (with the calendar year A.D. 1950 arbitrarily selected as the zero point). By this convention, A.D. 1560 becomes 390 B.P.

R.D. ("relative date"): An age estimate derived by tree-ring studies when the specific sequence cannot be correlated with a known calendrical age; Chapter 7 discusses how such dates can be converted to absolute estimates.

Note that all the abbreviations used so far are *capital letters* (for example, 3200 B.C.). Just in case you're not confused enough, you may also run into a date written in *lower case*, such as 3200 b.c. This is a special convention applied by some to denote that the particular date was derived by radiocarbon methods (presented in Chapter 7), and hence reflects "radiocarbon years" rather than "calendar years." So the term "3200 b.c." would be read "3200 *radiocarbon years* before Christ." I find this usage confusing, and won't employ it here.

Today, if you are not confused, you are just not thinking clearly.

IRENE PETER

like a simple step, but it contrasted sharply with the beliefs of his contemporaries, who regarded tradition, legend, and myth as the only clues to the past.

Archaeology's family tree has an unsavory branch as well, because the looters and grave robbers of antiquity contributed greatly to the archaeological legacy. Unlike Nabonidus, untold generations of mercenaries were attracted by the promise of easy riches through the looting of tombs and other ancient storehouses.

Too often, the early-twentieth-century Egyptologists found, to their dismay, that they had been "beaten to the punch" by looters and vandals. Sometimes the bodies were barely cold before the grave goods were purloined. H. E. Winlock, then director of New York's Metropolitan Museum expedition to Dier el Bahri, found episode after episode in which the ancient Egyptians had rifled the graves of their own rulers. When the Twenty-first Dynasty (ca. 1090 B.C.) mummies of Hent-Towy and Nesit-Iset were discovered, for instance, Winlock and his associates thought they were perfectly intact. But closer examination revealed that the mummies had been unwrapped before interment and the valuable metal pectoral hawks and finger rings

Archaeology is rather like a vast, fiendish jigsaw puzzle invented by the devil as an instrument of tantalising torment, since:
a) it will never be finished
b) you don't know how many pieces are missing
c) most of them are lost forever
d) you can't cheat by looking at the picture

PAUL BAHN, ARCHAEOLOGIST

Ethnocentrism: The belief that one's own ethnic group is superior to all others.

stolen. This deceit could only have been the work of the very undertakers commissioned to prepare the mummies for the hereafter. The pilfering from Egypt's royal tombs has continued for millennia, and, in fact, much of the popular appeal of Egyptology is matching modern wits with those of the ancient architects of the tombs, who tried every trick imaginable to outfox looters, both ancient and modern.

Despite contributions in other fields, the classical Greeks did little to further the aims of modern archaeology. The ancient Greeks for the most part held that the way to understand themselves was to study themselves. What others did was irrelevant. Socrates, for instance, was concerned primarily with his own thoughts and those of his contemporaries; he showed marked disdain for the languages and customs of "barbarians" (by whom he meant all non-Greeks). The Romans, of course, traced their intellectual ancestry to the heroes of Greek legend; they imitated Greek protocol; and they shared in the pervasive Greek **ethnocentrism.** The ethnographies written by Greek historians Herodotus and Tacitus stand virtually alone in their concern with non-Greek and non-Roman customs and values.

Pre-Renaissance writings did little to foster the development of archaeological inquiry, but the Renaissance changed all this. It has been suggested that the major contribution of the Renaissance–particularly in Italy–was the distinction between the present and the past. Classical Greeks and Romans recognized only the most remote past, which they reified in myth and legend. Because the Europeans of the Middle Ages likewise failed to distinguish between themselves and the ancients, it fell to Renaissance scholars to point up the differences between classical and medieval times.

Petrarch, perhaps the most influential individual of the early Renaissance, defined an intellectual tradition that continues to be important in today's archaeology. Beyond his considerable talents as poet and linguist, Petrarch also provided strong impetus for archaeological research. To him, the remote past was an ideal of perfection, and he looked to antiquity for moral philosophy. But in order to imitate classical antiquity, one must first study it. In a real sense, Petrarch's approach led to a rediscovery of the past by those in the Western European intellectual tradition. Petrarch's influence can best be seen in the work of his close friend Boccaccio, who wrote extensive essays on classical mythology, and also in that of Giovanni Dondi, who is generally credited with the first systematic observations on archaeological monuments.

But it remained for the fifteenth-century Italian antiquarian Ciriaco de' Pizzicolli to establish the modern discipline of archaeology. After translating the Latin inscription on the triumphal arch of Trajan at Ancona, he was inspired to devote the remainder of his life to studying ancient monuments, copying inscriptions, and generally promoting the study of the past. His travels ranged from Syria to Egypt, throughout the islands of the Aegean, and finally to Athens. When asked his business, Ciriaco is said to have replied, "Restoring the dead to life," which today remains a fair definition of the everyday business of archaeology.

The antiquarian spirit was also alive and well in Great Britain. In fact, a group of eminent British historians and students of the classics formed an antiquarian society as early as 1572. The emphasis of this and later societies was to record and preserve the national treasures, rather than indiscriminately to acquire curios and objets d'art. Of course, many private collectors were still concerned only with filling their curio cabinets, but the goal of British antiquarianism was to map, record, and preserve archaeological ruins. By the late eighteenth century, a healthy interest in classical antiquities was perceived as an important ingredient in the "cultivation of taste" among the European leisure classes, hence the term *antiquarian.*

Archaeological research to this point proceeded mostly within the tradition of Petrarch, concerned primarily with clarifying the picture of classical civilizations. This lore was readily digested by the eighteenth- and early-nineteenth-century mind because it was in basic agreement with the religious teachings of the time. The Bible remained a natural access point into the understanding of classical cultures.

Boucher de Perthes found Paleolithic handaxes like this in the Somme River gravels.

A problem arose, however, when very crude stone tools were discovered amidst the ancient gravels of England and continental Europe. About 1836, Jacques Boucher de Perthes, a controller of customs at Abbeville (France), began to find ancient axeheads in the gravels of the Somme River. Along with those tools, he also found the bones of mammals long extinct. To Boucher de Perthes, the implication was obvious: "In spite of their imperfection, these rude stones prove the existence of [very ancient] man as surely as a whole Louvre would have done."

But few contemporaries believed him, in part because of prevailing religious thought. That is, in the early nineteenth century the orthodox opinion held that human beings had been on earth for roughly 6,000 years. Theological scholars, who had studied the problem of the Creation in marvelous detail, simply refused to concede that there had been sufficient time for people to have coexisted with animals of extinct form. Paley's *Natural Theology* (1802) explained the matter something like this: The earth was created according to a splendid design, not unlike a fine watch; God was the ultimate watchmaker, and he had deliberately placed people on his earth in about 4000 B.C.

Actually, this chronology had been suggested before. In 1642, Dr. John Lightfoot, master of St. Catharine's College and vice-chancellor of Cambridge University, published a treatise with the delightful title *A Few and New Observations on the Book of Genesis, the most of them certain, the rest probable, all harmless, and rarely heard of before.* Lightfoot's later, slightly refined chronology concluded that "heaven and earth, centre and circumference, were created all together in the same instant and clouds full of water . . . this took place and man was created by the Trinity on October 23, 4004 B.C. at nine o'clock in the morning."

We may perhaps see in these dates and time a prejudice of a Vice-Chancellor for the beginning of an academic year and the beginning of an academic morning, but, at least, Lightfoot did provide an exact and absolute chronology which must have been very comforting.

GLYN DANIEL (1914–1986), ARCHAEOLOGIST

By this reckoning, of course, there was zero probability of an extensive human antiquity; there simply wasn't enough time. Therefore, the thinking went, Boucher de Perthes must be mistaken—his rude implements must be something other than human handiwork. Some suggested that the "tools" were really meteorites, and others felt that the stones must have been produced by lightning, or elves, or fairies. One seventeenth-century scholar even suggested that the chipped flints were "generated in the sky by a fulgurous exhalation conglobed in a cloud by the circumposed humour," whatever that might have meant.

But customs officials have never been known for their reserve, and Boucher de Perthes stuck to his guns. More finds were made in the French gravel pits at St. Acheul, and similar discoveries turned up across the Channel in southern England. The issue was finally resolved when the respected British paleontologist, Hugh Falconer, visited Abbeville to examine the disputed evidence for himself. A procession of esteemed scholars followed Falconer's lead, until finally, in 1859, a paper was presented to the influential Royal Society of London supporting the claims of Boucher de Perthes. In no time, several powerful natural scientists declared their support.

The year 1859 turned out to be a banner year in the history of human thought: Not only was the remote antiquity of humankind accepted by many, but Charles Darwin published his influential *On the Origin of Species,* which suggested the process by which modern people had arisen from those ancient ancestors.

The floodgates now open, British archaeology billowed out in two rather divergent courses. One direction became involved with the problems of remote geological time and the demonstration of long-term human evolution. Other scholars, following the tradition of Petrarch, continued their course of classical studies, focusing particularly on the archaeology of ancient Greece and Rome. This philosophical split continues into modern times.

Sustained European contact with the Americas opened yet another option for prehistoric studies. Fairly early in the game, it became clear that in sheer antiquity, American archaeology would never rival the European finds: The New World was indeed new. Beginning with Columbus's triumphant return to Europe in 1493, several vexing issues cropped up. How could regions such as the Valley of Mexico and Peru boast fantastic riches, while many other places—such as the North American West—seemed relatively impoverished, even primitive? When did people first arrive in the New World? Where had these migrants come from, and how did they get there?

Archaeology in Canada and the United States began as the study of the prehistory of the American Indian. It was generally assumed that Indian cultures had been static prior to the arrival of Europeans and that they had a shallow time-depth; hence archaeological finds were intepreted in terms of what was known about the ethnography of tribes that had lived in the same area in historic times.

BRUCE G. TRIGGER, ARCHAEOLOGIST (MCGILL UNIVERSITY)

Enormous confusion and speculation immediately arose. There was, for instance, the "Lost Tribe of Israel" scenario, which emphasized alleged Native American–Semitic similarities. And the fabled Island of Atlantis was seriously proposed by some as the ancestral homeland of the Native Americans. Even voyaging Egyptians and Vikings were cited as hypothetical proto-Americans.

The mystery deepened with each new discovery of American ruins. How, for instance, does one account for the thousands of prehistoric earthen mounds that dot North America east of the Mississippi? Once-prevalent racist theories generally assumed that Native Americans were simply incapable of constructing such monuments, and much debate during the eighteenth and nineteenth centuries centered on the mythic Mound Builders, who had mysteriously vanished before the arrival of Columbus.

Investigators gradually came to realize the considerable continuities that existed between the unknown prehistoric past and the Native American population of the historic period. As such knowledge progressed, profound differences between European and American archaeology became more apparent. While the Europeans wrestled with their ancient flints—without apparent modern correlates—American scholars came to realize that the living Native Americans were indeed relevant to the interpretation of archaeological re-

WHAT'S IN A NAME?

American Indian or Native American?

Last year, as I was telling my son's third grade class what it's like to be an archaeologist, a small (but adamant) voice of protest came from the back of the room.

"How come you keep saying 'Indians'? Don't you know they want to be called 'Native Americans'?"

She had a good point. Many people are confused about these terms. In fact, my Native American colleagues tell me this happens all the time—people correcting them when they say "Indian," as if the term has somehow become a dirty word.

Names will always be important, but some are more important than others. Let's look at the Native American/American Indian issue in a bit more depth.

The word *Indian*, of course, is a legacy from some fifteenth-century European sailors, who mistakenly believed they'd landed in India. The term *American* derives from the first name of another European sailor. As Suzan Shown Harjo points out, the term *Vespuccidners* could just as easily have been applied to native inhabitants of the land Columbus "discovered."

Many Indian people will also point out the ambiguity in the term "Native American." Although I'm not an American Indian, I am a *native American* (because I was born in Oakland, California). According to the dictionary, if you're born here, you're a native.

Most indigenous people of North America today recognize the garbled logic behind all such terms. Most simply accept the imprecision, and use such terms as *American Indian*, *Canadian Native*, *Native American*, *Indian*, and *Native* interchangeably; we will do so throughout these pages.

Of much greater concern to most Indian people is the tribal name. Many Navajo people, for instance, now wish to be known as *Diné* (a traditional name meaning "The People"). The terms *Lakota* and *Dakota* are generally preferred over *Sioux* (which is a French variant of an Ojibwe or Chippewa word meaning "enemy"). When discussing particular tribes, we will, whenever possible, use the term preferred by the particular tribe in question.

Do not be discouraged about what is or is not correct, only mindful of what is or is not respectful. The basic rule, as it applies to all human relations, is simply to ask Indians how they would like to be addressed and referred to, and to respect their responses.

SUZAN SHOWN HARJO (CHEYENNE/HODULGEE MUSCOGEE), PRESIDENT, THE MORNING STAR FOUNDATION

mains. In the crass terms of the time, to many Europeans, the Native Americans became "living fossils," accessible relics of times long past.

So it was that New World archaeology became inextricably wed to the study of living Native American people. While Old World archaeologists began from a baseline of geological time or classical antiquity, their American counterparts began to develop an anthropological understanding of Native America. The **ethnology** of American Indian people not only became an important domain of Western scholarship in its own right, but the increased understanding of Native American lifeways quickly helped unravel questions such as the peopling of the New World.

Ethnology: That branch of anthropology dealing chiefly with the comparative and analytical study of cultures.

Let me stress another important point here. As Europeans refined the archaeology of Europe, they were studying their own ancestors (Angles, Celts, Balts, Slavs, Huns, and so forth). But New World archaeology was basically a matter of Euro-Americans digging up somebody else's ancestors (mostly those of the Native Americans). This important difference explains several

When we go back to the history of antiquarianism and archaeology . . . we all have our heroes, our founder fathers of a faith which has become well established and world-wide.

GLYN DANIEL

defining elements of New World archaeology:

1. why racist, anti–American Indian theories dominated nineteenth-century Americanist archaeology,
2. why European governments enacted antiquity legislation decades before North American governments did so (because Europeans were taking care of their own ancestors' sites), and
3. why many contemporary Native American people still distrust conventional Western scholarship to interpret their past.

We will return to each theme in the pages to follow.

Founders of Americanist Archaeology

Now we are ready to begin looking more closely at how Americanist archaeology is currently practiced. Here, we will draw upon Robert Dunnell's useful term *Americanist* to denote the kind of archaeology that has developed in association with anthropology in North America. Although many other terms have been used—"scientific archaeology," "anthropological archaeology," and, too often, just "archaeology"—I prefer the phrase **Americanist archaeology** because it is the most descriptive, yet least pejorative. Let me also emphasize that archaeologists working in the Americanist tradition can (and do) practice their craft around the world.

Americanist archaeology: The brand of archaeology that evolved in close association with anthropology in the Americas; it is practiced throughout the world.

Archaeologists typically ignore biography.

JANET D. SPECTOR, ARCHAEOLOGIST (UNIVERSITY OF MINNESOTA)

If you want to get across an idea, wrap it up in a person.

RALPH BUNCHE (1904–1971), DIPLOMAT

The history of Americanist archaeology (all history, really) is a commingling of tradition and change. Here, we meet with a few of the more traditional figures, people who illustrate how archaeology was practiced during their lifetimes. This section is evolutionary. Then we shall discuss two people whose skepticism helped define contemporary archaeology; in a sense, that section is revolutionary. Finally, we look at one of our better-known contemporary archaeologists, a person who has contributed to the theoretical diversity that characterizes Americanist archaeology on the eve of the twenty-first century.

But first a warning: These eight archaeologists were deliberately selected to make some specific points. Other authors would undoubtedly choose different people. But provided you understand that my selections were made in fairly arbitrary fashion—and largely for effect—I make no apologies. Each person represents a critical stage in the growth of Americanist archaeology, and the career of each has a message.

Thomas Jefferson (1743–1826): America's First Prehistoric Archaeologist

The European Renaissance, which began in the fourteenth century and lasted well into the 1700s, produced a breed of scholars known for their prowess across a prodigious range of topics. Aptly known as *Renaissance men,* these cultivated gentlemen embodied the essence of intellectual and artistic excellence for their time. Although Thomas Jefferson postdates the Renaissance period in a chronological sense, his varied accomplishments place him well within the tradition of the Renaissance thinker.

Not only did the author of the Declaration of Independence later become the third president of the United States, he was also described by a contemporary as "an expert musician (the violin being his favorite instrument), a good dancer, a dashing rider, and proficient in all manly exercises." Jefferson was an avid player of chess (avoiding cards), an accomplished horticulturalist, a distinguished architect, and a connoisseur of fine French cooking.

Thomas Jefferson, archaeologist.

These accomplishments aside, one of Jefferson's lesser-known achievements interests us here. Thomas Jefferson's curiosity about the origins of Native Americans illustrates the initial stage of Americanist archaeology. Fascinated by Indian lore since boyhood and trained in classical linguistics, Jefferson, often dubbed the "father of American archaeology," believed that the Native American languages held valuable clues to the origins of the people. Jefferson personally collected linguistic data from more than 40 tribes and wrote a long treatise on the subject. Reasoning largely from his linguistic studies, Jefferson sensed an Asiatic origin for the Native Americans. But unlike his contemporaries, he was not content to restrict his speculation to armchair theorizing. Always a man of action, he tested his notions on some hard data.

Jefferson's contribution to Americanist archaeology was presented in the only book he ever published, appearing in a limited French edition in 1784 and in a widely distributed American edition in 1787.

Notes on the State of Virginia dealt, in part, with the aborigines of Virginia. Jefferson listed the various Virginian tribes, relating their histories since the settlement of Jamestown in 1607 and incorporating a census of Virginia's current Native American population. As noted earlier, the origin of American Indians had been a compelling topic of speculation since the time of Columbus and probably even before. The Spanish explorer de Soto correctly surmised that many of the mounds he found in the New World served as foundations for priestly temples, but his astute observation was soon lost in a flood of fanciful interpretation. Racist attitudes prevalent in late-eighteenth-century America had fostered the conception of the mythical Mound Builder People, who allegedly constructed the impressive monuments throughout the Americas before they either mysteriously vanished or underwent a profound degenerative process, rendering them smaller and less intelligent than modern Europeans.

To Jefferson, solving the problem of Native American origin required a dual strategy: to learn as much as feasible about contemporary Indian culture and also to examine their prehistoric remains. He argued emphatically that contemporary Native Americans were in no way mentally or physically inferior to the white races and rejected all current racist doctrines explaining their origins. He correctly reasoned that Native Americans were wholly capable of having constructed the prehistoric monuments of the United States.

Then Jefferson took a critical step: He proceeded to excavate a burial mound located on his property. Today, such a step seems obvious, but few of Jefferson's contemporaries would have thought of resorting to bones, stones, and dirt to answer intellectual issues. Contemporary eighteenth-century scholars preferred to rummage through libraries and archives rather than dirty their hands with the hard facts from the past (for some excerpts from Jefferson's own writing, see *Excavating a Burial Mound in Virginia* in Chapter 17).

I think that this is the most extraordinary collection of talent, of human knowledge, that has ever been gathered together at the White House—with the possible exception of when Thomas Jefferson dined here alone.

President John F. Kennedy (addressing a group of Nobel Prize winners)

Highly imaginative nineteenth-century artist's conception of an ancient Indian battle mound.

Written in the flowery style of the time, Jefferson's account provides quite an acceptable report of his investigation. First he describes the data—location, size, method of excavation, stratigraphy, condition of the bones, artifacts—and then he presents his conclusions: Why did prehistoric peoples bury their dead in mounds? He first notes the absence of traumatic wounds, such as those made by bullets or arrows, and also observes the interment of children, thereby rejecting the common notion that the bones were those of soldiers who had fallen in battle. Similarly, the scattered and disjointed nature of the bones militates against the notion of a "common sepulchre of a town," in which Jefferson would have expected to find skeletons arranged in more orderly fashion.

Jefferson surmised, quite correctly, that the burials had accumulated through repeated use and saw no reason to doubt that the mound had been constructed by the ancestors of the Native Americans encountered by the colonists. Today, nearly 200 years after Jefferson's excavations, archaeologists would modify few of his well-reasoned conclusions.

Thomas Jefferson's primary legacy to archaeology is the fact that he dug at all. By his simple excavation, Jefferson elevated the study of America's past from a speculative, armchair pastime to an inquiry built on empirical fieldwork. As a well-educated colonial gentleman, Jefferson understood the importance of exposing speculation to a barrage of facts. The "facts" in this case lay buried beneath the ground, and that is precisely where he conducted his inquiry.

Unlike his contemporaries, Jefferson did not dig to obtain exotic curios for his mantel but initiated his excavations to answer specific, well-formulated problems. He collected his data in as systematic a manner as possible and then drew carefully reasoned inferences from his fieldwork. Jefferson thereby pioneered the basics of archaeological reporting: recording his finds in meticulous detail, to be ultimately published for scrutiny by interested scholars.

People have a strong tendency to simply forget how much we've learned about the past. As new knowledge becomes part of the generally accepted mainstream of knowledge, we don't think about it anymore. It is knowledge for which most contemporary archaeologists can't take credit, and it is knowledge that apparently begins to fall into the category of always having been known.

JAMES N. HILL (1934–1997), ARCHAEOLOGIST

C. B. Moore (1852–1936): A Genteel Digger

Clarence Bloomfield Moore was born into an affluent family of Philadelphia socialites. After receiving his B.A. degree from Harvard University in 1873, Moore followed the social circuit, rambling through Europe and joining safaris into exotic Africa. By 1892, however, Moore found the well-to-do socialite lifestyle to be shallow, meaningless, and boring. Somewhere along the line, Moore was introduced to American archaeology and, at age 40, he was transformed from gentleman socialite into gentleman archaeologist.

Smitten by his new pastime, he purchased a specially equipped flat-bottomed steamboat, which he christened the *Gopher*. Moore set off to explore the seemingly endless waterways of America's Southeast, excavating the major archaeological sites he encountered. Particularly drawn to the hundreds of burial and temple mounds, Moore enlisted the services of Dr. Milo G. Miller as secretary, physician, and colleague.

C. B. *Moore.*

From the outset, Moore's annual archaeological campaigns were models of organization and efficiency. Aboard *Gopher,* Moore and Miller conducted preliminary investigations so likely sites could be located and arrangements could be contracted with landowners; actual excavations began in the spring. Moore hired and supervised the workmen and kept the field notes. As human skeletons were located, Dr. Miller conducted paleoautopsies on the spot, examining the bones in the field to determine sex, age, probable cause of death, and any unusual pathologies. The summers were spent cleaning and repairing the finds and then photographing and analyzing the collection. Moore prepared detailed excavation reports for publication and distributed the more unusual artifacts to major archaeological institutions.

Moore's first investigations concentrated on the shell middens and the sand burial mounds sprinkled along the Gulf Coast of Florida. Gradually, year after year, Moore worked his way around to Florida's eastern shore and eventually to the Sea Islands of coastal Georgia and South Carolina. In 1899, Moore returned to the Gulf Coast, traveled up the Alabama River, and examined the coast of northwest Florida. He excavated literally dozens of archaeological sites on each expedition.

Finally, in 1905, Moore paused on the Black Warrior River, Alabama, to excavate intensively the ruins appropriately known as Moundville. Working with several trained assistants and a crew numbering 10 to 15, Moore explored the large temple mounds to examine the human burials and unearth spectacular pieces of pre-Columbian art. Moore concluded that Moundville had been a prominent regional center. He further surmised from the varied art forms that the ancient people of Moundville worshiped the sun, and that motifs such as the plumed serpent and eagle suggested strong ties with contemporaneous Mexican civilizations.

C. B. *Moore's paddle-wheeled quarterboat* Gopher *docked along the* Tombigbee River, Mississippi.

By 1916, Moore concluded that the *Gopher* had explored every southeastern river then navigable by steamer. In fact, once a sandbar was removed, Moore promptly piloted the *Gopher* up the newly navigable Chocktawatchee River in northern Florida. He had truly exhausted the resources available for riverboat archaeology. Of course, archaeological techniques have improved markedly since Moore's time, and many a contemporary archaeologist wishes that Moore had been somewhat less thorough: He left so little for the rest of us.

Nels Nelson (1875–1964): America's First-Generation "Working" Archaeologist

Whereas C. B. Moore was born into a wealthy family, Nels Nelson grew up on a poor farm in Jutland, Denmark. Although first a farmhand, and a student only in his spare time, he did stumble onto the James Fenimore Cooper novels—*The Last of the Mohicans* and *The Deerslayer*—while still quite young and became fascinated with the lore of the Native Americans. Several of his relatives had already emigrated to America, and in 1892 Nelson's aunt in

Nels Nelson with an array of Dutch archaeological artifacts.

Minnesota sent him a steerage ticket to New York. On his way westward, he worked at a number of jobs (including driving a six-mule team and butchering hogs) and finally saved enough money to enroll in Stanford University, where he studied philosophy by day and took odd jobs at night to pay his expenses.

Quite by accident, someone invited Nelson to attend an archaeological excavation in Ukiah, north of San Francisco, and he was hooked. The dig apparently rekindled the same fascination with Indian lore he had first experienced while reading the pages of Cooper. Nelson immediately enrolled in all the archaeology courses available at the University of California.

Nelson's M.A. thesis was an archaeological survey of the shell middens surrounding San Francisco Bay. He later boasted that according to his pedometer, he had walked more than 3,000 miles during his reconnaissance, and had recorded 425 prehistoric shell mounds. His report discussed the location of these sites relative to available natural resources, listed the animal bones found in the shell heaps, and pondered the ecological adaptation implied by such a bayside lifeway. Urban sprawl has today destroyed all but a handful of these once obvious sites, and Nelson's map, originally published in 1909, remains an irreplaceable resource to modern archaeologists interested in central California prehistory.

Then, in 1912, the American Museum of Natural History in New York City launched an archaeological campaign in the American Southwest, and Nelson was engaged to oversee this influential research program. Nelson's stratigraphic excavations in New Mexico proved to be a breakthrough in archaeological technique. In his next few years, Nelson broadened his experience by excavating caves in Kentucky and Missouri, and more shell mounds in Florida. In 1925, Nelson accompanied an American Museum expedition to Central Asia; his North American and European fieldwork continued until his eventual retirement in 1943.

Nels Nelson typifies the state of Americanist archaeology during the first quarter of the twentieth century. Although receiving infinitely better archaeological training than did his predecessors, such as C. B. Moore, Nelson nevertheless learned largely by firsthand experience. Archaeology was still in a pioneering stage, and no matter where Nelson turned, he was the first archaeologist on the scene. In large measure, his first responsibility was to record what he saw, then to conduct a preliminary excavation where warranted, and finally to proffer tentative inferences to be tested and embellished by subsequent investigators. Nelson also typified the new breed of early-twentieth-century museum-based archaeologists. Nelson strongly believed that the message of archaeology should be brought to the public in books, popular magazine articles, and, most of all, interpretive displays of archaeological materials.

Today, Nels Nelson is best remembered in archaeology for his contributions to stratigraphic technique. Nelson's 1912 excavations in the Galisteo Basin of New Mexico are generally acknowledged as the first significant stratigraphic archaeology in the Americas. At that time, the cultural chronology of the American Southwest was utterly unknown, and Nelson's painstaking excavations and analysis of the pottery recovered provided the first solid chronological framework.

Nels Nelson (far left) having lunch with other archaeologists and paleontologists at Castillo Cave (Spain) in 1913.

A. V. "Ted" Kidder (1886–1963): Founder of Anthropological Archaeology

Although he was born in Michigan, the life and career of Alfred V. Kidder revolved about the academic community of Cambridge, Massachusetts. Kidder's father, a mining engineer, saw to it that young Alfred received the best education available. First enrolled in a private school in Cambridge, Kidder then attended the prestigious La Villa, in Ouchy, Switzerland, after which he registered at Harvard. Kidder soon joined an archaeological expedition to northeastern Arizona, exploring territory then largely unknown to the Anglo world. The southwestern adventure sealed his fate.

When Kidder returned to Harvard, he enrolled in the anthropology program and in 1914 was awarded the sixth American Ph.D. specializing in archaeology—and the first with a focus on North America. Kidder's dissertation examined prehistoric Southwestern ceramics, assessing their value in reconstructing culture history. Relying on scientific procedures, Kidder demonstrated ways of deciphering meaning from archaeology's most perplexing debris, the lowly potsherd. Urging accurate description of ceramic decoration, he explained how such apparent minutiae could be used to determine relationships among the various prehistoric groups. Kidder argued that only through controlled excavation and correlative analysis could inferences be drawn about such anthropological subjects as acculturation, social organizations, and prehistoric religious customs (see *The Pan-Scientific Approach to Archaeology* by A. V. Kidder).

Each age has its archaeology, in which the interpretation owes as much to the interests and prejudices of the interpreter as to the inherent properties of the data.

COLIN RENFREW, ARCHAEOLOGIST (CAMBRIDGE UNIVERSITY)

In 1915, the Department of Archaeology at the Phillips Academy in Andover, Massachusetts, embarked on a multiyear archaeological project. The project leaders were seeking an appropriate site large enough and of sufficient scientific merit to warrant such a research commitment. Largely because of his anthropological training, Kidder exemplified the new breed in archaeology, and he was selected to direct the excavations. After evaluating

IN HIS OWN WORDS

The Pan-Scientific Approach to Archaeology by A. V. Kidder

Archaeologists are often portrayed in the media as latter-day hermits who trudge off into the wilderness to conquer the secrets of the past. But in fact, contemporary archaeologists never work alone, as archaeological sites contain information too diverse, too varied for any single scholar to analyze. Teamwork is a requirement of all modern archaeology, but the team approach to archaeology is hardly new. Kidder fully anticipated modern trends with his "pan-scientific" approach at Chichén Itzá (Yucatán, Mexico) in the 1920s:

In this investigation the archaeologist would supply the Prehistoric background; the historian would work on the documentary record of the Conquest, the Colonial, and the Mexican periods; the sociologist would consider the structure of modern life. At the same time studies would be made upon the botany, zoology, and climate of the region and upon the agriculture, economic system, and health conditions of the urban and rural, European mixed and native populations. It seems probable that there would result definite conclusions of far-reaching interest, that there would be developed new methods applicable to many problems of race and culture contacts, and that there would be gained by the individuals taking part in the work a first-hand acquaintance with the aims of allied disciplines which would be of great value to themselves, and through them to far larger groups of research workers.

the possibilities, he decided on Pecos Pueblo, a massive prehistoric and historic period ruin located southeast of Santa Fe, New Mexico. Kidder was impressed by the great diversity of potsherds scattered about the ruins and felt certain that Pecos contained enough stratified debris to span several centuries. In all, Kidder excavated at Pecos for ten summers.

The excavations at Pecos were consequential for several reasons. Kidder became the first archaeologist in America to test Nelson's stratigraphic method on a large scale, and he went beyond the pottery to make sense of the artifact and architectural styles preserved at Pecos. His intensive artifact analysis, done before the advent of radiocarbon dating or a tree-ring chronology, established the framework of Southwestern prehistory, which remains intact today.

Kidder then joined the Carnegie Institution of Washington as director of the Division of Historical Research. Attracting several of his southwestern colleagues to work with him, Kidder launched an aggressive archaeological program to probe the Mayan ruins of Central America. Kidder directed the Carnegie's Mayan campaigns for the next two decades, arguing that a true understanding of Mayan culture would require a broad-based plan of action with many interrelated areas of research. Relegating himself to the role of administrator, Kidder amassed a staff of qualified scientists with the broadest possible scope of interests. His plan was a landmark in archaeological research, stressing an enlargement of traditional archaeological objectives to embrace the wider realms of anthropology and allied disciplines. Under Kidder's direction, the Carnegie program supported research by ethnographers, geographers, physical anthropologists, geologists, meteorologists, and, of course, archaeologists.

Kidder even proved the potential of aerial reconnaissance, by convincing Charles Lindbergh, already an international figure, to participate in the Carnegie's Mayan program. Early in 1929, Lindbergh flew Kidder throughout British Honduras, Yucatán, and the Petén jungle of Guatemala. Beyond discovering new ruins, the Lindbergh flights also generated a wealth of previously unavailable ecological data, such as the boundaries of various types of vegetation. Today, the interdisciplinary complexion of archaeology is a fact of life. But when Kidder proposed the concept in the 1920s, the prevailing attitude still reflected the one-person/one-site mentality.

A. V. Kidder.

In addition to his substantive Mayan and Southwestern discourses, Kidder helped shift Americanist archaeology toward more properly anthropological purposes. Unlike many of his contemporaries, Kidder maintained that archaeology should be viewed as "that branch of anthropology which deals with prehistoric peoples," a doctrine that has become firmly embedded and expanded in today's Americanist archaeology. To Kidder, the archaeologist was merely a "mouldier variety of anthropologist." Although archaeologists continue to immerse themselves in the nuances of potsherd detail and architectural specifics, the ultimate objective of archaeology remains the statement of anthropological universals about people.

James A. Ford (1911–1968): A Master of Time

James A. Ford is the last archaeological forefather to be considered here. Born in Water Valley, Mississippi, Ford's major research interest centered on the archaeology of the American Southeast. While Ford was attending Columbia, Nels Nelson retired from the Department of Anthropology at the American Museum of Natural History, and Ford was chosen as the new assistant curator of North American archaeology.

James Ford came of age during the Great Depression, part of an archaeological generation literally trained on the job. As the Roosevelt administration came to realize that jobs must be created to alleviate the grim economic conditions, crews of workmen were assigned labor-intensive tasks, including building roads and bridges, and general heavy construction. One obvious make-work project was archaeology, and literally thousands of the unemployed were set to work excavating major archaeological sites. This program was, of course, an important boost to Americanist archaeology, and data from government-sponsored, depression-era excavations poured in at a record rate. In fact, materials from the 1930s excavations are still being analyzed and published.

Ford worked Poverty Point, the Louisiana site explored 40 years earlier by C. B. Moore. After completing his initial mapping and reconnaissance, Ford launched a series of stratigraphic excavations designed to define the prehistoric sequence. His overall objective was to read in human terms the meaning of the Poverty Point site, a goal considerably more ambitious than that of C. B. Moore, who dug primarily to unearth outstanding examples of artwork. Ford continually asked, What does archaeology tell us about the people? To Ford, Poverty Point represented more than a fossilized ceremonial center, and he attempted to recreate the social and political networks

IN HIS OWN WORDS

The Goals of Archaeology by James A. Ford

The study of archaeology has changed considerably from a rather esthetic beginning as an activity devoted to collecting curios and guarding them in cabinets to be admired for their rarity, beauty, or simple wonder. Students are no longer satisfied with the delights of the collector and are now primarily interested in reconstructing culture history. In recent years methods and techniques have progressed rapidly, and there are indications which suggest that some phases of the study may develop into a truly scientific concern with general principles. This trend seems to be due more to the kinds of evidence that past human history offers than to any planned development. For centuries the perspective of the study of history was narrowed to a listing of battles, kings, political situations, and escapades of great men, an activity which is analogous to collecting curios and arranging them in cabinets. Such collections are fascinating to those who have developed a taste for them, but they contribute little towards the discovery of processes which are always the foremost interest of a science. The evidence that survives in archaeological situations has made it impossible to study prehistory in terms of individual men, or even in terms of man as an acculturated animal. When the archaeologist progresses beyond the single specimen, he is studying the phenomena of culture.

I join a number of contemporaries in believing that archaeology is moving in the direction of its establishment as a more important segment of the developing science of culture than it has been in the past. This does not mean that such objectives as discovering chronological sequences and more complete and vivid historical reconstructions will be abandoned; rather these present aims will become necessary steps in the process of arriving at the new goal.

responsible for this colossal enterprise. In this regard, his approach typified the overarching anthropological objectives of mid-century Americanist archaeology (see *The Goals of Archaeology* by James A. Ford).

The unprecedented accumulation of raw data during the 1930s created a crisis of sorts among Americanist archaeologists: What was to be done with all these facts? Ford and his contemporaries were beset by the need to synthesize and classify and by the necessity to fabricate regional sequences of culture chronology. Unlike Nelson, Kidder, and the others working in the American Southwest, Ford did not have access to deep, well-preserved refuse heaps; southeastern sites were more commonly shallow, short-term occupations. To create a temporal order, Ford relied on an integrated scheme of surface collection and classification.

Ford earlier refined techniques to order sequentially the various stages of pottery development. This technique of sequential ordering is known as *seriation*. Later, we will develop the principles behind seriation, but the central idea is simple: By assuming that cultural styles (fads) tend to change gradually, archaeologists can chart the relative popularity of pottery decoration through time. Generally, a given pottery style is introduced at one specific locality. Its popularity gradually spreads throughout the region until the first type is successively replaced by another style. Thus, at any particular time, the available ceramic assemblage reflects the relative proportions of the available pottery styles. By fitting the various short-term assemblages into master curves, Ford developed a series of regional ceramic chronologies. Although sometimes overly simplistic, Ford's seriational technique was sufficient to establish the baseline prehistoric chronology still in use in the American Southeast.

Ford then synthesized his ceramic chronologies into patterns of regional history. When C. B. Moore was excavating the hundreds of prehistoric mounds throughout the Southeast, he lacked a system for adequately dating his finds. Using seriation along with other methods, Ford helped bring temporal order to his excavations, and he rapidly moved to synthesize these local sequences across the greater Southeast. He proposed the basic division between the earlier Burial Mound Period and the subsequent Temple Mound Period, a distinction that remains in use today.

James A. Ford making a plane table map at Boca Escondida, north of Veracruz (Mexico).

Americanist Archaeology at Mid-Century

The biographies of these five forebears provide a sense of Americanist archaeology's past. Thomas Jefferson's archaeology was drastically different in manner from that of, say, James Ford. Still, each person made a distinctive contribution to modern archaeology and each was clearly one of the very best among his contemporaries. These five careers define a colorful continuum, and some meaningful trends are evident.

Perhaps the most striking contrast is that brought out by comparing the scholars as individuals. Americanist archaeology began as a pastime of the genteel rich such as Thomas Jefferson and C. B. Moore, who purchased *Gopher* and personally financed his own fieldwork. Not until the days of immigrant Nels Nelson could a "working-class" scholar hope to penetrate the archaeological establishment.

You will also note, of course, that women are virtually invisible in most discussions on the early history of Americanist archaeology. Women were, in fact, contributing, but they were excluded from traditional communication networks, so this contribution is more difficult to find (see Mary Ann Levine's discussion of this point in *Archaeology's Unrecognized Working Women*).

Through the years, archaeology developed into a professional scientific discipline. C. B. Moore was among the first generation of full-time professional archaeologists. As practicing specialists, some archaeologists from Moore's time and later have been affiliated with major museums and universities; others have joined the private sector, working to protect and understand America's long-term cultural heritage. This institutional support not only encouraged a sense of professionalism and fostered public funding, but such public repositories also were required to care for the archaeological artifacts recovered. The twentieth-century Americanist archaeologist is not a collector of personal treasure: All finds belong in the public domain, available for exhibit and study.

We can also see a distinct progression toward specialization in our five target archaeologists. So little was known about archaeology in the eighteenth century that a single scholar such as Jefferson could control all the relevant data. But by the late nineteenth century, so much archaeological information had already accumulated that no single scholar could hope to know

IN HER OWN WORDS

Archaeology's Unrecognized Working Women by Mary Ann Levine

Although women are absent from much of the literature on the early history of Americanist archaeology, they have been contributing to the development of archaeology for over a century. In the 1880s, female anthropologists began to hold marginal positions in museums. Women participated in anthropology as loosely affiliated field workers who were generally unpaid but permitted to publish in museum proceedings, or as financial patrons for particular museums. For example, Mary Hemenway (1820–1894), a philanthropist, donated the substantial collection of materials unearthed by the Hemenway Southwestern Archaeological Expedition to Harvard's Peabody Museum. As possibly the first avowedly scientific research into that area's prehistory, Hemenway's Expedition helped establish the Southwest as a distinct culture area. Zelia Nuttall (1857–1933), a Mesoamerican archaeologist, acted as an honorary assistant at Harvard's Peabody Museum and frequently published through that institution. Her most significant contribution to Americanist archaeology centers on having rediscovered and authenticated several codices and manuscripts. Both women were members of the Women's Anthropological Society of America (est. 1885), an organization established as an alternate to the sexist practices of the all-male Anthropological Society of Washington.

While their contributions to archaeology differed, Mary Hemenway and Zelia Nuttall had much in common. Neither woman carried out extensive fieldwork nor received formal training in archaeology. They both contributed to archaeology as single women and they were both sufficiently affluent to make their chosen careers possible. Women such as Hemenway and Nuttall were active in Americanist archaeology prior to World War I and made notable contributions to the development of the discipline, but their involvement was limited and circumscribed. Male organizations such as the Anthropological Society of Washington marginalized women from the mainstream of professional life in anthropology. The first generation of women in Americanist archaeology were excluded from both formal and informal networks of communication and were afforded few career opportunities.

The next generation of female archaeologist includes women born early in the twentieth century who launched their careers in the inter-war years, the 1920s and 1930s. Beginning in the 1920s, the range of professional pathways for women in archaeology widened while the education opportunities and socioeconomic backgrounds of women expanded. Although women in this second generation also faced sizable obstacles to advancement and recognition, they achieved greater visibility in academic and museum settings.

Women were awarded Ph.D.s for their research in cultural anthropology as early as 1914, but it was not until the 1930s that women earned doctorates in anthropology for their research in archaeology. The 1930s also witnessed female archaeologists securing academic posts for the first time.

MARY ANN LEVINE is assistant professor of anthropology at Ithaca College, Ithaca, New York.

everything relevant to Americanist archaeology. Although C. B. Moore became the leading authority on Southeastern archaeology, he knew relatively little about the finds being made by his archaeological contemporaries in Peru, Central America, and even the American Southwest. By the mid-twentieth century, archaeologists like Ford were forced to specialize in specific localities within limited cultural areas. Today, it is rare to find archaeologists with extensive experience in more than a couple of specialized fields.

Possibly the greatest change, however, has been the quality of archaeologists' training. Although Jefferson was broadly educated in science, literature, and the arts, his archaeology was wholly self-taught and largely a matter of common sense. Although Harvard-educated, Moore was untrained in archaeology; his fieldwork was still based on personal trial-and-error methods. Nelson and Kidder, among the first professionally trained Americanist archaeologists, studied under America's most prominent archaeologists. From then on, Americanist archaeologists were almost without exception well versed in anthropology. As the chronological problems were solved, archaeologists such as Ford used this anthropological training to transcend mere chronology to explicate cultural contexts and functions. Although Ford personally contributed to the refinement of local chronologies, he also participated in research programs designed to define settlement patterns and to reconstruct prehistoric social environments. Such was the state of Americanist archaeology at mid-century.

Revolution: Archaeology's Angry Young Men

The previous sections chronicled the development of traditional Americanist archaeology. A succession of hardworking, intelligent archaeologists—the Moores, Kidders, and Fords—symbolize the mainstream thinking of their day. The technology, assumptions, explanations, and speculation of Americanist archaeology evolved along an unbroken progression. But archaeology also grew by revolution. Beginning in the 1940s, a succession of scholars challenged such orthodox archaeological thinking, urging explosive change and demanding instantaneous results. Two such crusaders have been particularly influential in shaping modern archaeological thought.

If you want to make enemies, try to change something.

Woodrow Wilson (1856–1924), 28th President of the United States

Walter W. Taylor (1913–1997): Moses in the Wilderness

Educated first at Yale and then at Harvard, Walter W. Taylor completed his doctoral dissertation late in 1942. After returning from overseas military service, he published in 1948 an expanded version of his dissertation as *A Study of Archeology.* It was a bombshell. Greeted with alarm and consternation by the archaeological community, the book was no less than a public call for revolution. Bourgeois archaeologists—the orthodox fat cats—were blasted, assailed, and berated by this wet-behind-the-ears newcomer. Few liked Taylor's book, but everybody read it.

Taylor launched a frontal attack on the elders of Americanist archaeology. This assault was particularly plucky, as Taylor was himself a rank beginner, having published little to establish his credentials as an archaeologist, much less a critic. Undaunted, he lined up the archaeological establishment in his sights and then let them have it between the eyes.

A Study of Archeology blasted A. V. Kidder, among others. What offended Taylor most was Kidder's alleged two-faced attitude, saying one thing yet doing another. Kidder repeatedly maintained that he was an anthropologist who had specialized in archaeology. Taylor probed Kidder's end products to determine how well his deeds conformed to his stated anthropological objectives and boldly concluded that there was no conformity. He could find in

I am not young enough to know everything.

Oscar Wilde (1854–1900), poet, wit, and dramatist

Walter W. Taylor during his archaeological survey of Coahuila (Mexico) in 1937.

Kidder's research no cultural synthesis, no picture of life at any site, no consideration of cultural processes, no derivation of cultural laws—no anthropology at all.

These were serious charges, considered to be blasphemy by most archaeologists of the time. But Taylor supported his case with a vivid dissection of Kidder's published record. Kidder's research at Pecos, New Mexico, and elsewhere in the American Southwest was said to be full of "apparent contradictions," merely "description for its own sake." Taylor claimed that Kidder was incapable of preparing a proper site report, much less of writing the anthropology of the prehistoric Southwest.

Taylor then turned to Kidder's prestigious research into the archaeology of the Maya and, once again, accused him of failing to live up to his own goals. Granting that Kidder began his investigations with anthropology in mind, Taylor concluded that somewhere along the line Kidder went astray. Commenting that "the road to Hell and the field of Maya archeology are paved with good intentions," Taylor deduced that the Carnegie Institution, under Kidder's direction, "has sought and found the hierarchical, the grandiose. It has neglected the common, the everyday." Kidder had been blinded by the "pomp and circumstance" of Classic Maya archaeology, disregarding the pedestrian world of real people. To hear Taylor tell the story, Kidder not only botched his own research but also misdirected the explorations of literally dozens of archaeologists working under his aegis.

High time it is, that the younger generation stops sneering at its predecessors.

CARLETON S. COON (1904–1981), ANTHROPOLOGIST

In 1948, Taylor was indeed archaeology's angriest young man, panning the "comparative" or "taxonomic" approach to archaeology. Kidder and several other luminaries were accused of classification and description for their own sake. Claiming to be anthropologists, they failed to do anthropology (at least according to Taylor). Though careful not to deny the initial usefulness of a comparative strategy, Taylor urged archaeologists to get on with the proper business of anthropology: finding out something about people. Chronology, to Taylor, was merely a stepping-stone, providing a foundation for more anthropologically relevant studies of human behavior and cultural dynamics.

Conjunctive approach: As defined by Walter W. Taylor, finding the explicit connection of archaeological objects with their cultural contexts.

Walter W. Taylor's prescription was his so-called **conjunctive approach** to archaeology. By *conjunctive,* Taylor emphasized the interconnection of archaeological objects with their cultural contexts. Whereas comparative scholarship emphasizes relationships among archaeological sites, the conjunctive perspective would shift the emphasis to a particular cultural entity. Taylor attacked Kidder's Mayan research on this basis: He believed that Kidder was preoccupied with comparing things—temples, glyphs, fancy potsherds—among sites and that he had failed to decipher what goes on within any single Maya site. According to Taylor, Kidder merely skimmed off the sensational, the spectacular, the grandiose (and forgot all about the people who made up the Maya population).

Idealism is what precedes experience; cynicism is what follows.

DAVID T. WOLF

A conjunctive approach would scrutinize the minutiae of a single Maya center, attempting to write a comprehensive ethnography of the Maya people who once lived there. In effect, Taylor urged archaeologists to forsake the temples for the garbage dumps. Messy business, this conjunctive archaeology, but Taylor contended that this was the only way for archaeologists to achieve their anthropological goals.

Going beyond the specifics of Maya archaeology, Taylor proposed reforms by arguing for a conjunctive approach in all archaeology. Archaeologists must quantify their data (trait lists are rarely useful); they must test hypotheses and progressively refine their impressions (too often initial observations were taken as gospel); they must excavate less extensively and more intensively (too many sites were just "tested" then compared with other remote "tests" with no effort to detect patterning within sites); they must recover and decode the meaning of unremarkable food remains (the bones, seed hulls, and rubbish heaps were too often shoveled out); they must embrace more specialties in the analysis of finds (zoological, botanical, and petrographic identifications were too often made in the field and never verified); and they must write more effective site reports (too often only the glamorous finds were illustrated, with precise proveniences omitted).

Lewis R. Binford excavating at Mission Santa Catalina (Georgia).

In perusing Taylor's propositions nearly six decades after they were written, I am struck by how unremarkable they now seem. Where is the revolution? Today's archaeologists do quantify their results; they do test hypotheses; they do excavate intensively; they do save food remains; they do involve specialists in analysis; and they do write detailed site reports.

But archaeologists did not do these things routinely in 1940, and this is what Taylor was sputtering about. Taylor's suggestions of 1948 embody few surprises for today's student, testimony to just how far archaeological doctrine and execution have matured since Taylor wrote his *A Study of Archeology.*

Lewis R. Binford (1930–): Visionary With a Message

Taylor had the aims but not the tools.

LEWIS R. BINFORD

American archaeology's second angry young man is Lewis R. Binford. After a period of military service, Binford enrolled in 1954 at the University of North Carolina, wanting to become an ethnographer. By the time he moved on for graduate education at the University of Michigan, however, Binford was a confirmed archaeologist (see *The Challenge of Archaeology* by Lewis R. Binford).

As a young professional, Binford was a man on the move—literally. He first taught a year at the University of Michigan, then moved on to the University of Chicago, to the University of California at Santa Barbara, down the coast to UCLA, on to the University of New Mexico, and landed at Southern Methodist University (in Dallas). During his travels, Binford met the brightest of an upcoming generation of archaeologists (and we shall meet many of them later in this book).

The mid-1960s was a hectic time for archaeology. Waves of social alienation and political confrontation were rolling across the nation, baby-boom demographics inflated university enrollments, and archaeology was firmly embedded in the intellectual climate of the times. This revolutionary spirit derived in part from the general anxiety that permeated university campuses during the Vietnam War era. Things must change: not just war and poverty and racism and oppression, but also the academic edifice itself. Scholarship must become relevant; older concepts must give way to fresh perceptions. Such was the social environment in which Binford's ideas took hold. Without the revolutionary spirit and social upheaval of the mid-1960s, I believe that

If you ain't the lead dog, the scenery never changes.

BUDDY RYAN, FOOTBALL COACH

IN HIS OWN WORDS

The Challenge of Archaeology by Lewis R. Binford

As I was riding on the bus not long ago, an elderly gentleman asked me what I did. I told him I was an archaeologist. He replied: "That must be wonderful, for the only thing you have to be to succeed is lucky." It took some time to convince him that his view of archaeology was not quite mine. He had the idea that the archaeologist "digs up the past," that the successful archaeologist is one who discovers something not seen before, that all archaeologists spend their lives running about trying to make discoveries of this kind. This is a conception of science perhaps appropriate to the nineteenth century, but, at least in the terms which I myself view archaeology, it does not describe the nature of archaeology as it is practiced today. I believe archaeologists are more than simply discoverers.

Archaeology cannot grow without striking a balance between theoretical and practical concerns. Archaeologists need to be continuously self-critical: that is why the field is such a lively one and why archaeologists are forever arguing among themselves about who is right on certain issues. Self-criticism leads to change, but is itself a challenge—one which archaeology perhaps shares only with palaeontology and a few other fields whose ultimate concern is making inferences about the past on the basis of contemporary things. So archaeology is not a field that can study the past directly, nor can it be one that merely involves discovery, as the man on the bus suggested. On the contrary, it is a field wholly dependent upon inference to the past from things found in the contemporary world. Archaeological data, unfortunately, do not carry self-evident meanings. How much easier our work would be if they did!

In science the credit goes to the man who convinces the world, not to the man to whom the idea first occurs.

Francis Darwin (in Eugenics Review)

Binford's archaeology would have taken on a rather different, perhaps less aggressive configuration.

An extraordinary lecturer, Binford rapidly assumed the role of archaeological messiah. His students became disciples, spreading the word throughout the land. Binfordians preached a gospel with great appeal in the 1960s. Archaeology does have relevance to modern problems; archaeology must transcend potsherds to issues of cultural evolution, cultural ecology, and social organization; archaeology must take full advantage of modern technology; archaeology must become more systematic, using uncompromising logic and more sophisticated, quantitative techniques; archaeology must be concerned with the few remaining preindustrial peoples in order to scrutinize firsthand the operation of disappearing cultural adaptations. As Binford's movement gained momentum, nothing was considered sacred in the traditionalist paradigm of archaeology. As Binford himself characterized these early years, he and his colleagues were "full of energy and going in all directions at once."

New archaeology: A label commonly associated with Lewis R. Binford and his students, emphasizing the importance of understanding underlying cultural processes; today's version of the "new archaeology" is sometimes called the *processual agenda.*

Binford and his students—and their students—became the primary agents of change in Americanist archaeology during the 1960s. The phrase **new archaeology** became associated with their way of interrogating the past. The battle plan for the new archaeology was set forth in a seminal series of articles published through the 1960s and early 1970s. Binford asked why archaeology had contributed so little to general anthropological theory. His answer was that in the past material culture had been simplistically interpreted.

WHAT'S IN A NAME?

The Various New Archaeologies

New archaeology . . . that precious and prissy phrase.

GLYN DANIEL

The term *new archaeology* requires some qualification, because several brands of archaeology have, at one time or another, labeled themselves "new." At least three new archaeologies have surfaced over the past century.

The First New Archaeology: In 1917, anthropologist Clark Wissler published an article entitled "The New Archaeology," emphasizing the revolutionary implications of the stratigraphic excavation techniques developed by Nels Nelson and others (discussed in more detail in Chapter 8).

A *Second New Archaeology*: During the early 1950s, a second new archaeology arose, stressing the importance of scientific methods—particularly radiocarbon dating—on archaeology. Before this time, archaeologists relied heavily on stylistic analysis of artifacts, which led them to suggest various migrations and diffusion of traits to explain culture change. After radiocarbon dating of various significant artifacts, then conventional human history was overturned in favor of a scientifically based new archaeology.

The Most Recent New Archaeology: This new archaeology is explicitly associated with the work of Lew Binford and his colleagues. In this case, the name derived from a 1959 article in *Science* magazine—entitled, of course, "The New Archaeology"—published by Joseph Caldwell.

To avoid confusion, we'll generally use the term *processual agenda* to designate the "new archaeology" of the 1960s and 1970s.

Too much attention had been lavished on the artifacts of shared behavior, as passive traits that "blend," "influence," and "stimulate" one another. Echoing Taylor, Binford proposed that artifacts be examined in terms of their cultural contexts.

Binford underscored the importance of precise, unambiguous scientific methods. Archaeologists must stop acting like passive receptors, waiting for the artifacts to speak up. Archaeologists must formulate pointed questions (hypotheses); these hypotheses must then be tested on the remains of the past. Binford argued that because archaeologists always work from samples, they should acquire data that make the samples more representative of the populations from which they were drawn. He urged archaeologists to stretch their horizons beyond the individual site to the scale of the region; in this way, an entire cultural system could be assessed. Such regional samples must be generated from research designs based on the principles of probability sampling. Random sampling is commonplace in other social sciences, and Binford insisted that archaeologists apply these procedures to their own specific research problems.

Binford's strictly methodological contributions were gradually amplified by projects designed to demonstrate how the approach fosters the comprehension of cultural processes. Intricate statistical techniques were applied to a variety of subjects, from the nature of Mousterian (some 50,000 years old) campsites to the patterning of African Acheulian (hundreds of thousands of years old) assemblages. These investigations were critical because they em-

Kathleen Deagan digging at Bas En Saline (Haiti), *thought to be the site of* La Navidad, *established by Christopher Columbus on Christmas Eve,* 1492.

broiled Binford in factual, substantive debate. Not only did he advocate different goals and new methods, but he also related to field archaeologists through these substantive controversies—he argued about specifics, not just theory. Binford presented an extended consideration of post-Pleistocene human adaptations and conducted his own ethnoarchaeological fieldwork among the Nunamiut Eskimo, the Navajo, and the Australian aborigines.

In true Taylor-like fashion, Binford lambasted archaeology's principals, accusing them of retarding progress in the discipline. And yet his reception was quite different from Taylor's. Whereas *A Study of Archeology* languished on the shelf, Binford was hailed as "the father of the new archaeology." Taylor was the harbinger of impending change, but Binford was the architect of that change.

Binford and his students set off a fire storm that quickly spread throughout the archaeological community. A 1970s generation of new graduate students and young professionals was greeted with the admonition: Are you a new archaeologist, an old archaeologist, or what? Make up your mind!

A principle is never useful or living or vital until it is embodied in action.

MANLY HALL

Today, the new archaeology of the 1960s has become the orthodoxy of the 1990s, transformed into what is termed the *processual agenda.* In several subsequent chapters, we explore the tenets of this position, and also examine how yet another wave of archaeological criticism—the so-called *post-processual critique*—finds fault with Binford's approach and suggests some alternative directions.

Kathleen A. Deagan (1948–): Neither Angry nor a Young Man

It wouldn't be any fun if the solution to every problem were obvious.

ISABEL KELLY (1906–1984), ANTHROPOLOGIST

Struggles twixt new and old make interesting history indeed, but this is not a history book. This book is about the methods, techniques, assumptions, and goals of contemporary archaeology. But before grappling with these issues, let me introduce one more archaeologist, someone who embodies the diversity and animation that is archaeology today.

IN HER OWN WORDS

The Potential of Historical Archaeology by Kathleen Deagan

Historical archaeology today is actively contributing to a variety of problems and disciplines. From its emergence as a recognized area of research in the 1930s, the field has advanced from being essentially a set of techniques providing supplemental data for other disciplines, through being an anthropological tool for the reconstruction of past lifeways and the study of cultural process, to being a means of discovering predictable relationships between human adaptive strategies, ideology, and patterned variability in the archaeological record.

Certain aspects of historical archaeology should be particularly noted as having the potential for making contributions not possible through any other discipline. The contributions result from historical archaeology's unique ability to simultaneously observe written statements about what people said they did, what observers said people did, and what the archaeological record said people did. Inconsistencies and inaccuracies in the records of the past provided by written sources may be detected and ultimately predicted. Insights into past perceptions of human conditions provided by such written sources may be compared to the more objective archaeological record of actual conditions in the past in order to provide insight into cognitive processes. The simultaneous access to varied sources of information about the past also allows the historical archaeologist to match the archaeological patterning of a given unit against the documented social, economic, and ideological attributes of the same unit in order to arrive at a better understanding of how the archaeological record reflects human behavior. The unique potential of historical archaeology lies not only in its ability to answer questions of archaeological and anthropological interest, but also in its ability to provide historical data not available through documentation or any other source. [Correcting] the inadequate treatment of disenfranchised groups in America's past, excluded from historical sources because of race, religion, isolation, or poverty, is an important function of contemporary historical archaeology and one that cannot be ignored.

No archaeologist represents contemporary Americanist archaeology better than does Kathleen Deagan, currently a curator and formerly chair at the Florida Museum of Natural History. An archaeologist specializing in Spanish colonial studies, Deagan received her doctorate in anthropology from the University of Florida in 1974. Like her mentor, Charles H. Fairbanks, Deagan is pushing the frontiers of traditional historical archaeology, pioneering the archaeological investigation of disenfranchised groups.

Kathleen Deagan is best known for her long-term excavations at St. Augustine (Florida), continuously occupied since its founding by Pedro Menéndez in 1565. As pointed out by signs sprinkled throughout the town, St. Augustine is the oldest European enclave in the United States (complete with the "oldest pharmacy," "oldest house," "oldest church," and so on). Deagan's research here dates back to her graduate student days, her doctoral dissertation neatly straddling the traditionally discrete studies of historical archaeology, ethnohistory, and anthropology (see *The Potential of Historical Archaeology* by Kathleen Deagan).

Deagan addressed the processes and results of Spanish-Indian intermarriage and descent, a topic dear to the hearts of many anthropologists and ethnohistorians; the fact that people of such mixed descent (***mestizos***) constitute nearly the entire population of Latin America brought this issue to the forefront long ago. Similar processes took place in Spanish Florida, but the Hispanic occupation left no apparent *mestizo* population in La Florida, what

Mestizo: A person of mixed blood (particularly used to denote mixed European and Native American ancestry); the female form is *mestiza*.

Archaeological Sources on the Internet

The Society for American Archaeology maintains an important Web site.
http://www.saa.org

Archaeological Institute of America provides information about meetings, publications, and issues.
http://csaws.brynmawr.edu:web2/aia.html

Archaeology Magazine on the Internet
http://www.he.net/~archaeol/index.html

You Could Look It Up specializes in books for sale related to anthropology and archaeology.
http://www.polaris.net/~millerj2

Information and review of archaeology Web sites:
http://www.lib.uconn.edu/~lizee/WebRev/archonw3.html
http://medoc.gdb.org/best/stc/usda-best.html

See **MediaFinder** for listings of print media and catalogs (many of which relate to archaeological interests).
http://www.mediafinder.com/

The WWWorld of Archaeology
http://www.he.net/~archaeol/wwwarky/wwwarky.html

Deagan calls "America's first melting pot." Accordingly, when she began her doctoral research, virtually nothing was known about such early race relations in North America.

Deagan hypothesized about how the *mestizo* population fit into this colonial setting. Given the nature of the unfortunate interactions that characterized eighteenth-century Florida, she expected the burdens of acculturation to have fallen most heavily on the Indian women living in Spanish or *mestizo* households. Because no *mestizo* people survive here, the tests for her hypothesis were necessarily archaeological. If her hypothesis is true, then acculturation should affect mostly the Native American women's activities visible in the archaeological record (food preparation techniques, equipment, household activities, basic food resources, child-related activities, and primarily female crafts such as pottery manufacture). Moreover, male-related activities (house construction technology and design, military and political affairs, and hunting weapons) should show less evidence of Indian infusion.

To explore these processes, Deagan began in 1973 a series of archaeological field schools at St. Augustine. This long-term, diversified enterprise excavated sites representing a broad range of income, occupation, and ethnic affiliation. Hundreds of students have learned their first archaeology at St. Augustine, where a saloon still sports an aging placard celebrating the years of "Digging With Deagan."

It was not long before her explorations into Hispanic–Native American interactions led Deagan to the Caribbean, where between 1980 and 1985, she headed interdisciplinary excavations at Puerto Real, the fourth oldest European-style New World city (established in 1503). As she steadily moved back in time, Deagan's research eventually led her literally to the doorstep of Christopher Columbus.

In northern Haiti, Deagan apparently discovered La Navidad, the earliest well-documented point of contact between Spanish and Native American people. On Christmas Eve, 1492—following two nights of partying with local Taino Arawak Indians—Columbus's flagship *Santa Maria* ran aground. He abandoned ship, moved to the *Nina,* and appealed to the local Native Americans for help. This disaster left the explorers one boat short. When Columbus sailed home with his world-shattering news, he left 39 unfortunate compatriots behind, protected by a small stockade built from the timbers of the wrecked *Santa Maria.* Returning a year later, Columbus found the settlement burned, his men killed and mutilated.

Columbus soon established the more permanent settlements of La Isabela and Puerto Real—sites of the first sustained contact between Europeans and Native Americans—and Deagan is also conducting field excavations there. Having a population of nearly fifteen hundred people, La Isabela was home to soldiers, priests, stonecutters, masons, carpenters, nobles, and warriors. Although this first Columbian town lasted only 4 years, an instant compared with the entire period of Hispanic–Native American contact, several critical events took place here: the first intentional introduction of European plants and animals; the first expedition into the interior; and the first Hispanic installation of urban necessities, such as canals, mills, streets, gardens, plazas, ports, ramparts, roads, and hospitals.

Society for American Archaeology Bulletin
http://www.sscf.ucsb.edu/SAABulletin/index.html

Journal of Field Archaeology
http://jfa-www.bu.edu

Archaeology on Film is an electronic database of critical film reviews.
http://www.sscf.ucsb.edu/anth/videos/video.html

World Archaeological Congress Home Page hosts an international forum dealing with ethics, protection, conservation, new technologies, education, and archaeological impacts on indigenous peoples and their countries.
http://wac.soton.ac.uk/wac/

National Archaeological Database provides inventories of 120,000 archaeological projects, including guidance on compliance with NAGPRA.
http://cast.uark.edu/other/nps/nadb

The World-Wide Web Virtual Library: Archaeology, on the University of Connecticut Archaeological Home Page, provides the most comprehensive links to archaeological stuff throughout the world.
http://www.lib.uconn.edu/ArchNet/

The biological effects of the Columbian exchange soon overtook La Isabela. European and Native American alike suffered from dietary deficiencies, an excessive work load, and contagious disease. Influenza struck during the first week, affecting one third of the population. When Columbus ordered the settlement abandoned in 1496, fewer than three hundred inhabitants were left. Deagan extended her research to investigate daily life in the initial colonial period, including the ways in which European colonists coped with their new and largely unknown New World environment.

Beyond the new directions in historical archaeology, Deagan's research demonstrates the degree to which contemporary Americanist archaeology is played out in the public arena; she creates headlines wherever she works. Newspapers around the world chronicle her success, and her research was featured in consecutive years in the pages of *National Geographic* magazine. Deagan has shown extraordinary skill and patience with the onslaught of well-meaning reporters.

Media types seem astonished that such a successful archaeologist can also be female. Here is how a reporter from the *Florida Times-Union* described her: "Kathleen Deagan balanced on one foot in the parking lot: 'You lose all pride in this profession, changing your clothes in a parking lot,' she said with a wry grin.... Wind swirled through the parking lot and tousled her blond hair.... It would be Archaeology A-Go-Go."

Melodramatic coverage like this plagues archaeology these days, but Deagan overlooks the chatter because such reporting has a far more serious side. Archaeologists can no longer afford isolationist ivory-towerism. One way or another—whether through federal grants, state-supported projects, tax laws, or private benefaction—archaeology depends on public support for its livelihood.

Decades ago, Margaret Mead recognized the importance of taking the work of anthropologists to the public, and she spent considerable effort keeping anthropology alive in the print and electronic media. Today, archaeology enjoys unprecedented press coverage, and archaeologists like Deagan know that without such publicity, Americanist archaeology will have no future.

Beyond her appeal to the press, Deagan's research and publications have helped establish historical archaeology as a viable subdiscipline in the field of anthropology. Although awash in time-specific details and artifacts, she is ultimately addressing the general processes behind the particulars: the sexual and social consequences of Spanish-Indian intermarriage, the demographic collapse and biological imbalance resulting from Old World/New World interchange, and the processes behind the disintegration of traditional cultural patterns. Although her data are documentary and archaeological, Deagan is confronting issues of anthropological relevance.

SUMMARY The origins of archaeology can be traced to Nabonidus, the sixth-century B.C. Babylonian king who looked at the physical residues of antiquity to answer his questions about the past. Since then, archaeologists have continued "to restore the dead to life." New World archaeology has been inextricably wed to the study of Native Americans, who provided endless clues for those concerned with America's more remote past. Americanist archaeology evolved in the work of such scholars as Thomas Jefferson and C. B. Moore who, though lacking formal anthropological training, applied sound principles of scientific research to problems of America's past. No longer the pastime of genteel rich males, twentieth-century Americanist archaeology has become a specialized discipline, requiring intensive training not only in techniques of excavation but also in ethnology, classification, geology, and the philosophy of science. The gradual evolution of Americanist archaeological thought has been stimulated by a few revolutionary archaeologists, most notably Walter W. Taylor in the 1940s and Lewis R. Binford in the 1960s. Archaeology's "angry young men" urged their colleagues to stick by their anthropological guns, to attempt to define the processes operative behind the specifics of the archaeological record.

Chapter 2

Anthropology, Science, and the Humanities

PREVIEW In this chapter, we will place archaeology within the dynamic worlds of anthropology, science, and the humanities. Each has its own distinctive approach and each is relevant to modern archaeology.

We begin with the basic, anthropological perspective–an outlook that the human condition is best understood from a holistic, all-encompassing view of humanity. You will also learn about *culture* and why it is important that culture be viewed in several different ways. Finally, you will learn about the major trends in anthropological thinking. Some anthropologists employ an *ideational strategy,* emphasizing the importance of ideas, symbols, and mental structures in shaping human behavior. Other anthropologists follow an *adaptive strategy,* isolating technology, ecology, demography, and economics as the key factors.

We then look at the knotty question of just what is archaeology: A science? One of the humanities? Both? Neither? The question is more than semantic because it conditions the very way archaeologists approach the past. If you are a scientist, you probably believe that there is a real world "out there" that can be known more or less objectively. But suppose you believe that archaeology is fairly subjective and that our knowledge of the past depends largely on who's doing the observing. If so, then you probably don't like conventional science very much; you're probably a humanist. We look at each viewpoint as it applies to archaeology.

Although some believe it is essential to choose sides–*either* be a scientist *or* be a humanist–this chapter should convince you that the choice isn't really necessary. In practice, Americanist archaeology spans a broad philosophical spectrum. Although we explore the extremist positions, you will probably be most comfortable on the more realistic middle ground. That's where most of those in Americanist archaeology find themselves today.

In the mid-1950s, Philip Phillips published a memorable article concluding that "archaeology is anthropology or it is nothing." More than any single statement, this mantra came to characterize mainstream Americanist archaeology for the next three decades.

The mantra is no longer true.

Americanist archaeology is many things, and some of them remain anthropological. But today's archaeology has a diverse tool kit. Many tools still come from anthropology and we'll talk about those now. Some tools are borrowed from elsewhere.

I went to the University of Chicago for a while after the Second World War. I was a student in the Department of Anthropology. At that time, they were teaching that there was absolutely no difference between anybody. They may be teaching that still. Another thing they taught was that nobody was ridiculous or bad or disgusting.

KURT VONNEGUT, JR., AUTHOR

There is no other field that does what we do [in anthropology]—that tries to bring together the social, cultural, linguistic, and biological aspects of being human.

LAURA NADER, ANTHROPOLOGIST (UNIVERSITY OF CALIFORNIA, BERKELEY)

Anthropology: The study of all aspects of humankind, extant and extinct, employing an all-encompassing holistic approach.

What's an Anthropological Approach?

Everyone knows what anthropologists do: They study native people and fossils and chimpanzees. Anthropologists grin from the pages of *National Geographic* magazine and make chit-chat on "The Tonight Show." Anthropologists are Richard Leakey, Jane Goodall, and Don Johanson. Some people think that Stephen Jay Gould is also an anthropologist.

But few seem to know what anthropologists actually do, what anthropologists share, what makes them anthropologists at all. This is because, as scholarly disciplines go, **anthropology** is tough to pin down.

Anthropologists run in so many different directions at once, it's often difficult to find the common thread. In fact, anthropologists sometimes get so involved with the minutiae of their own deliberations that they themselves forget what they are.

So what makes an anthropologist an anthropologist?

The answer is deceptively simple: What all anthropologists share is a perspective, an outlook. Anthropologists believe that the best understanding of the human condition can arise only from a global and comparative approach. It is not enough to look at any single group—Americans, Chinese, Balinese, or *Australopithecines*—to find the keys to human existence. Neither is it enough to look at just one part of the human condition, as do economists, historians, political scientists, and psychologists. Looking at part of the picture only gives you just that—part of the picture.

What holds anthropology together is its dogmatic insistence that every aspect of every human society, extant or extinct, counts. For a century, anthropologists have tried to arrive at the fullest possible understanding of human similarities and diversity. Because of this broad-brush approach, anthropology is uniquely qualified to understand what makes humankind distinct from the rest of the animal world.

This is not to say that all anthropologists study everything: Margaret Mead never excavated an archaeological site and Richard Leakey never interviewed a native Athabascan speaker. The Renaissance anthropologist—the individual who does everything—has long since passed into folklore. Today, nobody can hope to do everything well.

Anthropologists are highly individual and specialized people. Each of them is marked by the kind of work he or she prefers and has done, which in time becomes an aspect of that individual's personality.

MARGARET MEAD (1901–1978), ANTHROPOLOGIST

So anthropologists specialize, and archaeologists are clever enough to draw something useful from each brand of anthropologist. Before examining how modern archaeology articulates with the rest of anthropology, we first must see just what anthropology is and how anthropologists have carved up the pie of human existence.

Kinds of Anthropologists

Biological anthropology: A subdiscipline of anthropology that views humans as biological organisms; also known as *physical anthropology*.

The basic division within anthropology concerns the very nature of human existence. There are four primary fields of study, which fall under the general umbrellas of **biological anthropology**, which deals with humans primarily as biological organisms, and **cultural anthropology**, which views humans as "the animals of culture." Although these are not wholly independent divisions, they do bisect the range of humanity into manageable domains of study.

Cultural anthropology: A subdiscipline of anthropology that emphasizes nonbiological aspects—the learned social, linguistic, technological, and familial behaviors of humans.

Biological Anthropologists

Modern *biological anthropologists* (also known as *physical anthropologists*) pursue a number of aspects of human biology. One major concern is the biological evolution of humans. How did the modern species *Homo sapiens* come into being? An intricate family tree has been pieced together by physical anthropologists over the past century, working largely from fossil evidence and observation of living primates.

A second major focus of modern physical anthropology is the study of human biological variability. No two human beings are identical, even though we all are members of a single species. The study of inherited differences has become a strategic domain of scientific investigation and also a matter of practical concern for educators, politicians, and community leaders.

A recent study by the American Anthropological Association looked into the future of biological anthropology by asking the chairs of various anthropology departments how the future looked to them. Most thought that biological anthropology would grow over the next 25 years. The spectacular recent fossil finds, the progress in studying human DNA, the expansion into forensic and medical studies, and advances in evolutionary anthropology have all given biological anthropology perhaps the most visible academic and public profile within anthropology's traditional four fields.

Today, roughly 12 percent of anthropology Ph.D. degrees are awarded in biological anthropology. This indicates that, although biological anthropology remains a fairly small subfield of anthropology, it has demonstrated a remarkable ability to adapt to changing technologies and an increasingly diverse academic environment.

Cultural Anthropologists

Physical anthropologists approach humanity from a distinctly biological perspective. The rest of anthropology, which deals with human beings as *cultural* animals, is conventionally divided into three parts: archaeology, linguistic anthropology, and cultural anthropology (also sometimes called *sociocultural* anthropology).

Cultural anthropologists describe and analyze the culture of human groups in the present and relatively recent past. By questioning and observing people throughout the world, they try to evaluate how diverse cultural elements intermesh and change in contemporary human societies. Conventionally, cultural anthropologists who describe present-day cultures on a firsthand basis are termed *ethnographers.* The comparative study of multiple cultures is usually termed *ethnology.* Roughly half the Ph.D.s in anthropology are awarded to cultural anthropologists.

The twenty-first century should be anthropology's century: so many of our strengths are needed, so many of our values resonate with the future.

James Peacock, cultural anthropologist (University of North Carolina)

Anthropology on the Internet

The Net contains a wealth of information of interest to anthropologists; here's a very small sampling:

AnthroNet, maintained by graduate students at the University of Virginia, provides a large set of Internet connections of interest to all brands of anthropologists.
http://darwin.clas.virginia.edu/-dew7e/anthronet/

Anthropology Resources on the Internet provides a comprehensive listing of anthropological sources.
http://nitehawk.com/alleycat/anth-faq.html

The Center for Anthropology and Science Communications lists discussion groups, fieldwork opportunities, databases, and bibliographies.
http://pegasus.acs.ttu.edu/-wurlr/anres.html

The World-Wide Web Virtual Library: Anthropology
http://www.usc.edu:80/dept/v-lib/anthropology.html

American Anthropological Association
http://www.nas.edu:70/1/cwse/discipline/Anthropology

Chicago Anthro Exchange answers frequently asked questions (FAQ).
http://www.lib.uchicago.edu/LibInfo/SourcesBySubject/Anthropology/CAE

WEDA (the Worldwide Email Directory of Anthropologists) is a keyword search index to the e-mail addresses of most subdisciplines of anthropology.
http://wings.buffalo.edu/academic/department/anthropology/weda/

Anthropological Resources on the World Wide Web, run by the Undergraduate Association at the University of California, Berkeley, provides links to anthropological resources on the Web.
http://server.berkeley.edu/AUA/#Guide

Anthropological linguists, who constitute the third of anthropology's four major fields, concentrate on a more specialized cultural component—language. They evaluate linguistic behavior in considerable detail: how sounds are made, how sounds create languages, the relationship between language and thought, how linguistic systems change through time, the basic structure of language, and the role of language in the development of culture. The field of linguistic anthropology is shrinking; in 1990, linguistic anthropology accounted for only 2 percent of all Ph.D.s in anthropology, a decline from 7 percent in 1970.

This book is concerned with a fourth kind of anthropology—**archaeology.** Most archaeologists also attempt to understand human culture, but their technology and field methods differ radically from those of ethnologists and linguists. Because archaeologists commonly study extinct cultures, they work at somewhat of a disadvantage. Lacking living, breathing informants, archaeologists have formulated a powerful array of techniques for gleaning relevant information from the material remains of the past. As we will see, these methods sometimes give archaeologists information that living, breathing informants probably never would have told them.

The future of archaeology is bright indeed. The study by the American Anthropological Association, mentioned earlier, discovered several probable trends in the archaeology of the future. The results may surprise you. Although no firm figures are available, archaeology accounts for about one quarter of anthropology's total graduate enrollment. When questioned, many chairs of anthropology departments felt that archaeology is today the most lively, exciting, and attractive program in anthropology. One chair called archaeology "the subfield most likely to promise jobs to graduating anthropology students." Another was sure that archaeology "will continue as a kind of university showpiece." This current excitement is due, in part, to the dazzling assortment of new

Archaeology: The study of the past through the systematic recovery and analysis of material remains.

ways to explore the past (such as the remote sensing techniques considered in Chapter 5).

Many of those questioned felt that Americanist archaeology in the next quarter-century will continue to expand, especially in such areas as historical archaeology, reconstruction projects, and various heritage-management programs (especially those in the private sector). Many universities recognized that archaeology provided an excellent way to collaborate with other schools, and most felt archaeology would continue to make significant contributions to the overall mission of anthropology.

Later on, we shall see how archaeologists are employing new tools for understanding the past. For now, however, we will stick to the tried-and-true techniques that archaeologists share with other cultural anthropologists

Human Origins Chat Room includes current theories, news, and issues pertaining to human evolution.
http://www.gu.edu,au/gwis/hub/chat/hub.anthrochat.html

Yahoo—Science: Anthropology and Archaeology includes a searchable, clickable index to books, companies, events, institutes, journals, museums and exhibits, and organizations.
http://www.yahoo.com/Social-Science/

Anthropology/Archaeology Information and Software
ftp://neosoft.com:/pub/users/cclaird/sci.anthropology

Anthropology Resources, from the Australian National University, provides clickable access to various anthropological resources around the world.
http://sosig.esrc.bris.ac.uk/Subjects/anthro.html

The World-Wide Web Virtual Library: Anthropology is an index to many anthropology department home pages throughout the world.
http://www.usc.edu/dept/v-lib/anthropology.html

Nicole's AnthroPage links to anything anthropological, including universities, museums, anything in print, software, specific cultures, addresses, home pages, jobs (both paid and volunteer), scholarships and grants, and subject scans on all four subareas of anthropology and their various specialties.
http://www.wsu.edu:8000/~i9248809/anthrop.html

Anthropological Resources on the World Wide Web by Anita Cohen-Williams is a massive and clickable guide to resources, institutions, labs, associations, societies, and journals for all the subdisciplines of anthropology, as well as palynology and museums.
http://server.berkeley.edu/AUA/resources.html

The Culture Concept in Anthropology

A dozen distinct academic disciplines purport to study culture (or at least cultural behavior): economics, sociology, linguistics, political science, history, cultural geography, psychology, and so forth. "Classical" historians, for instance, might investigate Greek culture, Roman culture, or Byzantine culture; their interest centers on the cultural characteristics of each particular society. One does not expect, however, to find classical historians discoursing on the general nature of culture, for if they did, they would cease to be classical historians; they would have become anthropologists. It is this generalized, overarching conception of culture that traditionally formed the central theme melding so many diversified (and sometimes conflicting) concerns into a singular, collective anthropological perspective. As we will see in the next chapter, some of this solidarity within the anthropological community has weakened in recent years.

Cultural Anthropology on the Internet

Cultural Anthropology: An Internet guide
http://gpu2.srv.ualberta.ca/~slis/guides/canthro/anthro.htm

Information Sources:
http://www.lib.duke.edu/anthro.html

Anthropology Internet Sites: Plenty of links and an excellent visual archive
http://www.brown.edu/Departments/Anthropology/sites.html

What Is Culture?

Surprisingly little general agreement exists among anthropologists about just what is culture. Nearly 50 years ago, A. L. Kroeber and Clyde Kluckhohn compiled more than two hundred distinct definitions of culture, proposed by as many anthropologists and social scientists. Since that time, the number of definitions of culture must have tripled.

Fortunately for us all, archaeologists need not be overly concerned with culture's ultimate definition. But we must recognize something about how human culture works and how anthropologists go about studying it. Suppose we begin with the classic definition offered by Sir Edward Burnett Tylor (the person considered by many to be the founder of modern anthropology). Tylor's (1871) definition of culture appeared on the first page of anthropology's first textbook:

As a University of Chicago graduate student, I encountered the anthropological culture concept not long after my commitment to a particular form of Protestantism, as a matter of personal faith and belief, had faded away. So it perhaps is not surprising that during my pre-M.A. period I concluded culture was a crucial tenet of anthropological faith.

PATTY JO WATSON, ARCHAEOLOGIST (WASHINGTON UNIVERSITY)

> Culture . . . taken in its wide ethnographic sense is that complex whole which includes knowledge, belief, art, morals, law, custom, and any other capabilities and habits acquired by man as a member of society.

Culture in Tylor's sense is *learned,* incorporated in a society's general body of tradition. Although this definition provides a proper baseline from which to investigate past cultural behavior, Tylor's formulation is too general. We must find a way of pinning down this broad definition by asking precisely how one goes about perceiving cultural behavior, both in the present and in the past.

Three Views of Culture

Culture is a little like dropping Alka-Seltzer into a glass—you don't see it, but somehow it does something.

HANS MAGNUS ENZENSBERGER

Idiolect: The reflection of individual variation; the way in which an individual speaker pronounces his or her language or practices his or her culture.

Language: The overall manner of speaking that reflects general shared speech patterns.

Archaeologists use culture in three basic ways. In order to understand what each kind of culture is—and how each perspective differs from the others—we will employ a simple analogy to the workings of language, itself a subset of all cultural phenomena. The rather simple principles involved in language can tell us something about the more complex principles involved in general human culture.

Language consists of three components: the **idiolect,** the language (or dialect) per se, and the system of communication. No two speakers of a language pronounce every linguistic element in precisely the same way. Each speaker has a personal idiolect, which is how we can identify specific voices on the radio or the telephone. But linguists postulate that an overall manner of speaking—what we call **language**—transcends and orchestrates all the idiolects within a speech community. Although each individual speaker pronounces the language in a distinctive manner, the pervasive linguistic structure consists of shared speech patterns within a community. Language, in other words, is a generalized model that individuals only approximate to a greater or lesser extent.

The third aspect of language, the **system of communication,** explains why languages exist at all. People speak because they have some message to communicate: Please pass the oatmeal; go to your wickiup; do you have tickets for the football game? Each is a message communicated by language. Furthermore, an entire repertoire of hand gestures, facial expressions, body language, and even manner of dress and hair length amplifies the system of purely verbal communication. Most modern languages also rely on a written language to further enhance communication.

System of communication: The underlying rationale of language, namely to communicate information among individuals.

So it is that linguists recognize a strategic contrast between language itself and language as a vehicle of communication. Language is shared behavior, and speech communities are defined on the basis of these collective speech patterns. Individual speakers, however, occupy different positions in the chain of communication: People do not share a system of communication; they participate in it. Speakers join in the system differently. For this reason, we carefully distinguish the medium (human language) from the function it serves (human communication). Communication is why language evolved, but the reverse is not true.

Society in its full sense . . . is never an entity separable from the individuals who compose it. No individual can arrive even at the threshold of his potentialities without a culture in which he participates. Conversely, no civilization has in it any element which in the last analysis is not the contribution of the individual.

RUTH BENEDICT (1887–1948), CULTURAL ANTHROPOLOGIST

The Potlatch: Culture at Three Levels

This linguistic analogy provides some insights into culture in general. Just as linguists define three linguistic components (idiolect, language, and a system of communication), so too can cultural phenomena be said to have three components. The cultural idiolect is an individual's version of his or her culture. Like linguists, cultural anthropologists can either focus on the role of the individual, or sort through apparently chaotic individual behavior in pursuit of the more communal cultural threads.

Nineteenth-century Kwakwaka'wakh people who practiced the **potlatch** are far from mainstream Western culture, and have kept generations of anthropologists busy observing, participating, and describing. These are culture's shared, modal aspects.

Potlatch: Among the nineteenth-century Northwest Coast Native Americans, a ceremonial involving the giving away or destroying of property in order to enhance status.

But culture, like language, has a third component, the underlying system. Shared language exists to provide a system of communication among people, and shared culture serves a similar function. Leslie White (a noted general anthropologist) pioneered the investigation of cultural systems, and archaeologists have reworked White's reasoning to suit the study of extinct cultural systems. Following White's lead, archaeologist Lewis Binford defined the cultural system as a set of repetitive articulations among the social, technological, and ideological aspects of culture. These three facets are not genetic—they are, in White's terminology, *extrasomatic,* meaning "outside the body," or learned.

Social, technological, and ideological perspectives together comprise the nonbiological (cultural) mechanisms through which human populations handle their biological and derived needs. This view of the cultural system emphasizes the structural elements basic to human adaptation, and de-emphasizes the aggregates of "cultural traits" that happen to be shared.

Newittee (1881, British Columbia), a Kwakwaka'wakh (Kwakiutl) settlement and scene of potlatch ceremonies. The signs on the door read "Boston. He is Head chief of Arweete. He is true Indian. Honest. He don't owe no trouble to white man" and "Cheap. He is one of the head chiefs of all tribes in this country. White man can get information." By this time, Kwakwaka'wakh leaders were heavily engaged in commerce with white traders.

Binford's point was this: People do not share a cultural system—they participate in it. More precisely, one behaves in a way that reflects, and is governed by, the underlying cultural system. How one participates is at least partly determined by one's place in the society, often expressed through intricate sets of statuses and roles.

These important points can be illustrated by the well-known case of rivalry *potlatch* practiced by several late-nineteenth-century tribes throughout the Northwest Pacific Coast of Canada and the United States—and best documented for the Southern Kwakwaka'wakh of Vancouver Island. The post-contact potlatch consisted of competitive feasting, during which ambitious, status-hungry men battled one another for social approval by hosting massive, often opulent feasts. Kwakwaka'wakh protocol dictated that the more food one gave away, the greater the prestige that would be accrued. Potlatch feasts were considered successful only when the guests had "eaten themselves under the table" and crawled groaning into the forest, only to vomit and return for more.

The competitive feasting extended far beyond simple gluttony. Late-nineteenth-century potlatching culminated in the outright destruction of property—not only food but also clothing, money, pieces of art, and even entire houses. The logic was this: The more goods destroyed, the greater the host's prestige would be. The guest chief belittled the host's efforts and eventually held a return potlatch manifesting his own superior means and hence superior status.

Potlatches proceeded according to strict, culturally dictated "rules." One person functioned in the role of host, inviting neighbors to his village for the feasting and festivities. The host parceled out gifts of varying degrees of worth: boxes of candlefish oil, baskets of berries, stacks of blankets, animal skins. As each gift was presented, the guests responded with a great degree of (culturally prescribed) dissatisfaction. They were being insulted by the host's generosity. Some guests served in the roles of "speaker" or "artist," and dancers assumed a variety of traditional poses, such as that of cannibal dancer, bear dancer, and food dancer.

The potlatch contains all three cultural components previously defined. The observer would initially be overwhelmed by the cultural idiolects. Each costume and mask is unique; every dancer has his or her own style; each speaker renders a personal touch. This idiosyncratic behavior reflects a degree of culturally prescribed variance from group standards.

Viewed in another way, the potlatch is a piece of shared, modal behavior. All Kwakwaka'wakh share an implicit belief in the institution of the pot-

WHAT'S IN A NAME?

Who Are We? by Gloria Cranmer Webster

We are not the Kwakiutl, as the white people have called us since they first came to our territory. The only Kwakiutl . . . are the people of Fort Rupert. Each of our village groups has its own name. . . . The language we speak is Kwakwala. The name Kwakwaka'wakh refers to Kwakwala speakers and accurately describes who we are. To call all of us who live in a specific cultural area "Kwakiutl" is like calling all indigenous people of the Americas "Indians." No longer is either acceptable.

GLORIA CRANMER WEBSTER (Kwakwaka'wakh) is a historian and former director of the U'mista Cultural Centre (Alert Bay).

latch, and that is why they participate. Males have certain culturally prescribed roles, and so do females. By the same token, most Americans share a belief in the ballot box, a knowledge of American English, and the use of cash. In this sense, the potlatch consists of communally shared cultural beliefs.

Human societies are everywhere complex, for living at peace with ourselves requires a vast multiplicity of rules.

ISAAC ASIMOV (1920–1992), WRITER

The potlatch also served an adaptive function within the fabric of Kwakwaka'wakh culture. But what could be adaptive about the wholesale destruction of personal property or the flurry of personal indignities exchanged over potlatch fires? The question "Why potlatch?" has confounded generations of observers. Anthropologists versed only in the shared behavior view of culture could not see beyond the burning blankets and flaming candlefish oil. These destructive and wasteful cultural practices were viewed as "quaint." Fifty years ago, anthropologist Ruth Benedict termed this culture **Dionysian**, accentuating the violent, frenzied aspects: "The final thing they strove for was ecstasy."

Dionysian: Being of a frenzied or orgiastic character (after Dionysus, the Greek god of wine (also called Bacchus).

A rather different interpretation of the potlatch arose after investigators looked beyond the potlatch's obvious visual effects into its systemic functions. What ecological, technological, and economic purposes were being served by such odd (to us) cultural behavior? Could the potlatch serve any useful function? Some anthropologists answer yes.

First, the competitive feasting between local groups may have actually increased overall regional productivity. People seem to work harder when personal prestige is at stake, and such regionalized banquets and revelry might have helped distribute goods and services between villages, thereby overcoming the effects of failures in local production. Had each Northwest Coast village been totally independent, then the failure of salmon to run up a particular stream could have been locally disastrous. Through the potlatch system, however, the less fortunate villages were invariably invited to several potlatches hosted by their more prosperous neighbors. Although the visitors were required to endure seemingly endless barbs and slights, they departed with full bellies. In effect, the less fortunate Kwakwaka'wakh traded prestige for sustenance. All else being ecologically equal, this year's luckless should have had ample opportunity to redeem their lost status when their neighbors fell on hard times.

A lot of people have heard about the Kwakiutl. We're probably the most highly anthropologized group of Native people in the world.

GLORIA CRANMER WEBSTER

But what if some villages sustained a continued subsistence catastrophe? There is some suggestion that the potlatch helped shift population from less

Artist's rendering of a late-nineteenth-century Kwakwaka'wakh [Kwakiutl] potlatch ceremony (painting by Will Taylor*).*

productive to more productive villages: Economically prosperous villages could "boast" of (and demonstrate) their affluence at the potlatch ceremonies, thereby inducing guests to leave their impoverished situations and join the wealthier, more ecologically stable village.

People do not necessarily consciously construct such cultural systems to fulfill their needs. It is an aspect of culture that may function without people being aware of its doing so.

To summarize, human culture can be trisected into three distinct domains of analysis: the idiolect, the body of modal values, and the underlying cultural system. In the potlatch we can see all three ingredients. Whereas most anthropologists concede the existence of all three elements, there is remarkably little consensus on how to conceptualize these complex cultural components. Before narrowing the scope to archaeology, we shall look more closely at the mainstreams of current anthropological thought.

The Emic Versus the Etic

The concept of culture provides the baseline from which all anthropology begins. But culture is hardly a monolithic concept, and, as you might expect, anthropologists who investigate culture tend to emphasize one aspect over another.

Emic: A term referring to anthropological concepts and distinctions that are somehow meaningful, significant, accurate, or "appropriate" to the participants in a given culture.

The dichotomy between *emic* and *etic* approaches is critical. The term **emic** is applied whenever anthropologists employ concepts and distinctions that are somehow meaningful, significant, accurate, or "appropriate" to the participants in a given culture. The potlatch ceremony, discussed earlier, has a complex series of emic "rules" about how individual Kwakwaka'wakh persons should act during attendance. Emic research into potlatching might attempt to identify the categories and rules required to think and behave like a Kwakwaka'wakh attending a potlatch. Emic statements–the "native's point of view"—can be approached from either a scientific or an empathetic perspective.

Anthropologist Marvin Harris has defined an opposite research strategy that relies on **etic** categories, based on concepts and distinctions that are meaningful and appropriate to the community of scientific observers. Etic observations of the same potlatch ceremony might enumerate participants, their relationship to one another, the quantities and values of goods exchanged and destroyed, and the prevailing ecological and economic conditions at each participating village. Such etic observations would not necessarily be familiar or understandable to the Kwakwaka'wakh participants, and such statements could neither be verified nor negated by comparison with native categories. Successful etic statements, expressed in the vocabulary of science, can be verified only when independent observers using similar operations agree that a given event has transpired.

Both emic and etic data are useful, and the comparisons of emic and etic versions of culture provoke some of the most meaningful debates in anthropological inquiry.

Kwakwaka'wakh (*Kwakiutl*) *chief holding potlatch copper* (Fort Rupert, 1984).

Ideational Versus Adaptive Research Strategies

It is likewise useful to understand another major dichotomy in anthropological thought. Baldly stated, an **ideational strategy** focuses on ideas, symbols, and mental structures as driving forces in the shaping of human behavior. Alternatively, an **adaptive strategy** isolates technology, ecology, demography, and economics as the key factors defining human behavior.

Neither viewpoint implies "always"; both seek only to discriminate causes that "tend to" produce observed effects. Both ideational and adaptive strategies allow for the interplay and interaction between the mental and the material. The ideational approach maintains that sociocultural phenomena are best understood in terms of mental ingredients, while adaptivists feel that sociocultural differences are better understood by defining relevant materialistic parameters.

Etic: Applied to concepts and distinctions that are meaningful and appropriate to the community of scientific observers.

Ideational strategy: The research perspective that defines ideas, symbols, and mental structures as driving forces in shaping human behavior.

Adaptive strategy: A research perspective that emphasizes technology, ecology, demography, and economics in the definition of human behavior.

Culture as Adaptation

Several points must be made about the adaptive view of culture. Concern is primarily with "culture as a system"—with the cultural idiolect and shared aspects of culture secondary. It is the cultural system that articulates human communities directly with their ecological settings: technology, modes of economic organization, settlement patterns, forms of social grouping, and political institutions.

Technology is the hero of our piece.

LESLIE WHITE (1900–1975), ANTHROPOLOGIST

Culture can be viewed principally in adaptive terms, in a sense analogous to natural selection: "Man is an animal and, like all other animals, must

Man shapes himself through decisions that shape his environment.

RENÉ DUBOS, BACTERIOLOGIST

maintain an adaptive relationship with his surroundings in order to survive. Although he achieves this adaptation principally through the medium of culture, the process is guided by the same rules of natural selection that govern biological adaptation." Cultures in this sense function in dynamic equilibrium with their ecosystems. When deviations occur in environment, demography, or technology, the effects will spread throughout a cultural system.

Adaptive prime movers are those elements of technology, subsistence economy, and social organization most closely tied to production. This materialist view contrasts sharply with the ideational perspective. Although there is a certain amount of disagreement as to how cultures actually adapt, all cultural adaptationists agree that economics (in its broadest sense) and its social correlates are in most cases primary. Ideational systems are secondary.

The people who say: "You are what you eat" have always seemed addled to me. In my opinion, you are what you think, and if you don't think, you can eat all the meat in Kansas City and still be nothing but a vegetable.

RUSSELL BAKER, JOURNALIST

Culture as Ideas

According to anthropologist Roger Keesing, the basic theme of the ideational approach to anthropology is simple: "The realm of ideas, the force of symbols is centrally important in shaping human behavior." Culture in the ideational sense refers primarily to the complex sets of perceptions, conceptual designs, and shared understandings that underlie the way people approach life. Culture, in this sense, is principally what humans learn, not what they do or make. This perspective on culture emphasizes cognition: ideas, thoughts, and shared knowledge. Ideational culture does not encompass material belongings or performance.

Ideational views of culture suggest that one cannot comprehend human deportment without postulating a *cognitive code* for behavior. Much of what we perceive in the world, and hence endow with meaning, does not exist in the physical world at all. It exists only in the mind's eye. The ideational theorist insists on "getting inside the informant's head."

Our life is what our thoughts make it.

MARCUS AURELIUS (A.D. 188–217), ROMAN EMPEROR

Current Theoretical Approaches in Archaeology

So you see that the anthropological tool kit contains a great variety of conceptual perspectives. Today, there is no general agreement—either within archaeology or in anthropology at large—about which tools are best. Within Americanist archaeology, epic struggles between "materialism" and "idealism," and between interpretive "emics" and explanatory "etics" have dominated the theoretical stage for the past two decades. This is basically a disagreement about which tools are best for the job.

Many archaeologists in America believe that culture and the human past should be seen in systemic, scientific, materialistic, behavioral, relatively objective, explanatory, and etic perspective. So viewed, cultural behavior is a phenomenon basically driven by demographic, technological, economic, and ecological processes. Culture is largely independent of history and the ultimate job of archaeologists is to seek timeless and spaceless generalizations about the human condition. A couple of decades ago, this perspective dominated Americanist archaeology, and many continue to follow this view.

As this work progresses, materialist and idealist approaches in anthropology are likely to find more common ground through a more thorough interpretation of culture and ideology as systems which mediate between actors and environments than the construction of behavioral alternatives.

BENJAMIN ORLOVE, CULTURAL ECOLOGIST (UNIVERSITY OF CALIFORNIA, DAVIS)

Many other archaeologists, however, express indifference to what people ate or how they earned a living. Taking the alternative perspective, these archaeologists see culture from a basically symbolic, ideational, humanistic, mental, relatively subjective, interpretive, and emic viewpoint. Cultural behavior is driven by the realms of values, aesthetics, rules, beliefs, religions, and symbols. Culture depends heavily on an understanding of historical events; general laws of human behavior do not exist. This view looks beyond subsistence to seek the intrinsic meaning of artifacts and the roles they once played in the social environment.

Some contemporary archaeologists even believe that the concept of culture is itself irrelevant to understanding human behavior. They suggest that many cultural patterns can be more effectively explained in terms of broad biological principles, such as the drive to pass on one's genes to the next generation. Some feel that anthropology should be subsumed under biology if a real theory of human behavior is to be developed.

Right now, it is unnecessary to assign names to these diverse and somewhat extreme approaches to the past (although plenty of such names exist). But as the story of Americanist archaeology unfolds, we will, in several subsequent chapters, look in more detail at each of these theoretical perspectives and explore the theoretical diversity that presently characterizes Americanist archaeology.

The most important thing is how much you learn after you already know it all.

EARL WEAVER, BASEBALL MANAGER

What's a Scientific Approach?

Science has evolved into an elegant and powerful way of allowing people to understand the workings of the visible world and the universe beyond. The goal of scientific theory building in archaeology is to develop theories that can be criticized and evaluated, to be eventually modified or even replaced by other theories that better explain the archaeological data.

Science (from the Latin "to know") refers, in its broadest sense, to a systematic body of knowledge about any field. The pursuit of such knowledge is commonly termed "pure science," to distinguish it both from so-called *applied science* (the practical application of scientific knowledge) and from *technology* (through which such applications are achieved).

Science: The search for universals by means of established scientific methods of inquiry.

Although the era of modern science is generally considered to have begun in the Renaissance, the origins of scientific thought extend far back in human history. The archaeological record of the world has preserved examples of early scientific reasoning: astronomical observations, treatment of disease, calendrical systems, recipes for food and drink. Upper Paleolithic cave paintings and carvings in bone or stone are often cited as early examples of systematizing knowledge.

The real purpose of scientific method is to make sure Nature hasn't misled you into thinking you know something you don't actually know.

ROBERT PIRSIG, AUTHOR

The seventeenth-century Italian physicist and astronomer Galileo is commonly credited with initiating the scientific revolution that led directly to the universal laws of physics enunciated by Isaac Newton. During the next cen-

Aristotle could have avoided the mistake of thinking that women have fewer teeth than men by the simple device of asking Mrs. Aristotle to open her mouth.

BERTRAND RUSSELL (1872–1970), MATHEMATICIAN AND PHILOSOPHER

tury came discoveries as diverse as the atomic theory of matter and various electromagnetic and energy theories. Darwin's nineteenth-century consideration of evolution added a biological component to the overall scientific picture.

Today, the world of pure science is generally divided into two classes: the physical sciences (including physics, chemistry, and geology) and the biological sciences (such as botany and zoology). Some crossover takes place in the so-called interdisciplinary sciences, for instance, biochemistry (which attempts to understand life processes in terms of chemical substances and reactions). The social and behavioral sciences are also examples of interdisciplinary approaches to science. *Anthropology* is commonly considered to be a generalizing social science, along with economics, sociology, psychology, and political science.

Science as a Method in Archaeology

The problem of creativity, of the source of fruitful theories and the questions that they generate, is not solved by scientific methods. Despite the high hopes of some fierce sciencemongers, there are no clear and certain methods of producing good ideas; scientific method is concerned with the process to follow once the question has been asked.

ALBERT SPAULDING (1914–1990), ARCHAEOLOGIST

The beginnings of a scientific approach to archaeology can be traced to a time when people stopped viewing the past as myth. They no longer thought of the past as merely another kind of story, but as something that left physical residues that could be retrieved and studied in order to find answers about antiquity.

Later in this chapter, we will examine how the Greek poet Homer described the Trojan War in his *Iliad.* Until a little more than a century ago, most people familiar with the *Iliad* considered the story to be pure fiction, lacking any foundation in fact. But it was the power of this "myth" that led directly to the discovery of the archaeological site of Troy. Heinrich Schliemann applied the principles of science to Homer's specific geographical descriptions, which became clues that led him to the actual, historical location of Troy.

When defining *scientific method,* most people employ two key concepts: *objectivity* and *testability.*

As scientists, archaeologists pride themselves on their ability to present analytically their aims, procedures, and results for full public inspection. Science is a public undertaking requiring that objectives be plainly and honestly stated, research procedures constantly reassessed, research methods explicitly described, and observer bias monitored.

Objectivity: The attempt to observe things as they actually are, without prejudging or falsifying observations in light of some preconceived view of the world—reducing subjective factors to a minimum.

Testability: The degree to which one's observations and experiments can be reproduced.

Scientific methods in archaeology are often misunderstood because **objectivity** can never be complete. Objectivity is the scientific ideal, but the reality of science is what ethnographer A. L. Cerroni-Long has recently termed "a messy, bumbling, all-too-human affair."

The methods of science are neither a preordained gift from the gods nor a way to foolproof the results. Science is a human activity, conducted by culture-bound human beings. Because of this, conclusions can be swayed by the prevailing worldview, emphasizing the importance of some observations over others. Scientists–in archaeology as elsewhere–employ judgment when selecting which theories to explore.

Then there is **testability.** From a scientific perspective, the more testable a theory is, the greater the chance that it will lead to new insights. The main characteristic of "testability" is, of course, *refutability* (often called *falsifiability*)—the privilege of being wrong.

Although observations are, of course, guided to some degree by an observer's theories, the obstinate empirical quality of the real world also enters the picture. It determines that there will be agreement on observations by independent observers, in both daily life and in scientific research. This all occurs, of course, within a specific cultural context; it remains entirely possible that "independent observers" from a radically different culture might disagree about the supposed "empirical qualities of the real world."

It is quite true that the facts do not speak for themselves, but a conclusion that therefore there are no facts is a crashing non sequitur. *Facts and theories go hand-in-hand in the development of explanations of the way the world works.*

ALBERT SPAULDING

Questions become "scientific" (1) if they are concerned with the publicly detectable properties of things and (2) if the result of observations designed to answer the question cannot be predetermined by the biases of the observer.

Today, theoretical archaeology can be viewed along a continuum, with theories ranging from completely nontestable to highly testable. Most theories fall somewhere in between.

In science, it does not matter where the questions come from. What matters is that they contain implications that can be examined by objective methods.

How Science Explains Things: The Maize Maze

It seems odd, but science in archaeology is better done than discussed. Archaeologists have been performing some pretty fair science, but only recently have they begun discussing their science in any detail. Consider, for example, how scientific methods were used to look for the origins of plant domestication in the Americas.

The philosophers of science are allowing themselves, it seems to me, to become involved in a series of debates which, although they purport to be about the nature of explanation in archaeology, in reality sometimes bear little specific relation to the subject matter of archaeology as such. One sometimes almost feels that they are, in fact, earning a living taking in each other's washing.

COLIN RENFREW, ARCHAEOLOGIST (CAMBRIDGE UNIVERSITY)

Enter "Scotty" MacNeish

Shortly after World War II, Herbert Dick (then a graduate student at Harvard) excavated a site in southwestern New Mexico named Bat Cave. The site yielded the typical prehistoric material culture from that area—projectile points, pottery vessels, shell beads, basketry, sandals, and so forth—and it also served up an unexpectedly primitive form of corn.

The archaeological contexts suggested that these stubby little corncobs were between 4,000 and 5,000 years old—the oldest and most primitive corn yet discovered. Later that same year, another archaeologist, Richard "Scotty" MacNeish, discovered similar specimens in the caves of Tamaulipas, not far below the Mexican border. Over the next few years, additional northern Mexican excavations recovered no corn older than about 5,000 years. Searching for more ancient evidence of plant domestication, MacNeish traveled far to the south, into Guatemala and Honduras. Although he found no ancient corncobs, he did stumble on fossil corn pollen in strata dating about 3000 B.C.

Given these baseline data, MacNeish contemplated his next move. Corn was apparently no older than 3000 B.C. in either the United States or

Richard "Scotty" MacNeish excavating at the North Mesa site, near Las Cruces (New Mexico).

Guatemala. MacNeish reasoned that if any older corn existed, it should be found somewhere between the two areas, probably in southern Mexico. This preliminary assumption was supported by intensive genetic studies conducted by MacNeish's colleague, Paul Mangelsdorf, indicating that corn had probably been domesticated from a highland grass. Putting these two pieces together, MacNeish decided that the best place to look for early domestication was in the uplands of southern Mexico.

To test his speculative theory, MacNeish made some specific predictions that could be tested in the field. Studying maps of southern Mexico, he narrowed his search to two prime targets. He first explored Oaxaca, which was quickly rejected: no early corn to be found there. MacNeish then turned to his second choice, the Tehuacán Valley of Puebla State, Mexico. Because corncobs generally survive best in deposits protected from moisture, he looked inside dry caves and overhangs. After personally delving into 38 such caves, MacNeish tested Coxcatlán Cave, which yielded six tiny corncobs more primitive than any previously discovered. Subsequent radiocarbon dating suggested that these cobs were about 5,600 years old, a full 500 years older than any other corn yet discovered.

These finds bolstered MacNeish's theory about the origins of corn in southern Mexico and also fostered an understanding of the processes that conditioned our early human relationships to domesticated plants and animals.

The Scientific Cycle in Action

Scientific method: Accepted principles and procedures for the systematic pursuit of secure knowledge. Established scientific procedures involve the following steps: Define a relevant problem; establish one or more hypotheses; determine the empirical implications of the hypotheses; collect appropriate data through observation and/or experimentation; compare these data with the expected implications; and revise and/or retest hypotheses as necessary.

Beyond its contributions to our knowledge of maize domestication, MacNeish's investigation also clearly demonstrates the essential components of the **scientific method** as they apply to archaeology:

1. Define a relevant problem.
2. Establish one or more hypotheses.
3. Determine the empirical implications of the hypotheses.
4. Collect appropriate data through observation and/or experimentation.
5. Compare these data with the expected implications.
6. Revise and/or retest hypotheses as necessary.

Like many archaeologists, MacNeish used other terms to describe his procedures. But in actual practice he followed this scheme rather closely. Such procedures characterized much archaeological research over the past century. Yet only during the past two decades have archaeologists begun to talk about these methods in any detail.

Let us review how these steps translate into actual scientific research. The first task is to define a relevant question and translate it into an appropriate hypothesis. The idea here is to get beyond the specifics of the known facts. To understand how hypotheses are derived, suppose that the "known facts" were a swarm of simple points drawn on a graph. Hypothesis formation is the process of drawing a single line to describe these points. There are, of course, an infinite number of hypotheses (lines) that can be drawn to account for the facts (the data points). The scientist must first examine the possible theories and select the most likely—that is, the most probable—for actual testing. On the graph, the most credible lines pass through every point, and many such curves could be drawn. Most people feel that if the points tend to fall in linear fashion, then a straight line will form the simplest hypothesis to describe the known data.

Such hypotheses are generated through *induction,* an inductive argument working from the specific to the general; in this sense, the conclusion of an inductive statement contains more information than the premises do. The facts as known serve as premises in this case, and the resulting hypothesis not only accounts for these known facts but also predicts properties of unobserved phenomena.

Inductive reasoning assumes that if something is true in a limited number of observed cases, it will also be true in similar, but unobserved, examples. The probability of being correct thus increases with the number of cases observed. Political opinion polls are an example of inductive reasoning.

Inductive reasoning: Working from specific observations to more general hypotheses.

No rules exist for induction (any more than there are rules for thinking up good ideas). Some hypotheses are derived by enumerating the data, isolating common features, and generalizing to unobserved data that share these common properties. At other times, archaeologists turn to analogies, relatively well understood circumstances that seem to have relevance to poorly understood cases. But equally common is the simple application of good sense. Judgment, imagination, past experience, and even guesswork all have their place in science. It does not matter where or how one derives the hypothesis. What matters is how well the hypothesis accounts for unobserved phenomena.

It is, of course, entirely possible that several hypotheses will apply to the same data, just as several lines can be drawn through the points on a graph. In practice, scientists generally work their way systematically through the various possibilities, testing them one at a time. This method of *multiple working hypotheses* has long been a feature of scientific methods. To distinguish among the various options, most scientists assume that the simplest hypothesis will tend to be correct. Thus they begin with the simplest hypothesis and see how well it holds up against some new data. If it fails the test, they then will try the next least complicated hypothesis, and so on.

Remember MacNeish's hypothesis about plant domestication? He began his research with a careful assessment of the known facts—the finds at Bat Cave and Tamaulipas, the reconnaissance in Guatemala and Honduras, and the available genetic information. These were, in a sense, his graph points to be accounted for. MacNeish could have come up with any number of hypotheses to explain these facts: Corn could have been domesticated simultaneously all over Mesoamerica in 3000 B.C.; corn could have been domesticated independently in both the north and the south at the same time (3000 B.C.); corn may not have been domesticated in Mesoamerica at all but, rather, traded from somewhere else, such as South America or even Mesopotamia. These are just a few of the infinite number of possible hypotheses that could be cited to explain the archaeological facts. By choosing the hypothesis he did, MacNeish was selecting the simplest of the available possibilities. But

A hypothesis may be simply defined as a guess. A scientific hypothesis is an intelligent guess.

ISAAC ASIMOV

An early phase of MacNeish's excavation at Coxcatlán Cave in the Tehuacán Valley (Mexico).

regardless of which hypothesis is initially selected, none is accepted until it survives further, independent observations. Mere induction does not lead to scientific acceptance.

Once the hypotheses are defined, the scientific method requires their translation into testable form. Hypotheses can never be tested directly because they are general statements, and one can test only specifics. The key to verifying a hypothesis is simple: You don't. What you verify are the logical consequences of hypotheses.

Deductive reasoning is required to uncover the logical outcomes. A deductive argument is one for which the conclusions must be true, given that the premises are true. Such deductive arguments generally take the form of "if . . . then" statements: *If* the hypothesis is true, *then* we will expect to observe the following logical outcomes. Bridging the gap from *if* to *then* is a tricky step.

Deductive reasoning: Reasoning from theory to account for specific observational or experimental results.

Bridging arguments: Logical statements linking observations on the static archaeological record to the dynamic behavior that produced it.

In the "harder" sciences, these bridging arguments derive directly from known mathematical or physical properties. In astronomy, for instance, the position of "unknown" stars can be predicted using a long chain of mathematical arguments grounded in Newtonian physics. The classic deductive method begins with an untested hypothesis and converts the generalities into specific predictions based on established mathematical and/or physical theory (the **bridging arguments**).

But how do archaeologists bridge this gap? Where is the "well-established body of theory" that allows us to transform abstract hypotheses into observable predictions?

When MacNeish translated his general hypothesis into testable propositions, he was assuming that several bridging arguments existed (although like many archaeologists, he did not make these assumptions explicit). Experience told MacNeish that unburned corncobs can be preserved for millennia in an arid cave environment but rapidly decompose when exposed to moisture. So, MacNeish figured, we should concentrate the search on dry caves and skip the river bottoms. Reasoning like this provided a "bridge" between the logical expectations and the archaeological record. Since the geneticists surmised that maize had been domesticated as a highland grass, MacNeish decided to confine his search to the highlands. Here is another bridge into the archaeological record, based this time on genetic theory.

The really valuable factor is intuition.

ALBERT EINSTEIN (1879–1955), PHYSICIST AND PHILOSOPHER

In truth, modern archaeology is almost bereft of explicit theory. The bridging arguments necessary for determining the logical outcomes of hypotheses are generally seat-of-the-pants statements, and archaeological inference is hampered by this lack of precision. Today, the development of *middle-range research* is a significant direction in archaeology (and Chapters 3 and 10 discuss these developments in detail). We should add, somewhat parenthetically, that test implications can also be derived through induction, based on known prior probabilities of the various hypotheses. But for now, we shall keep things simple and consider only the deductive case.

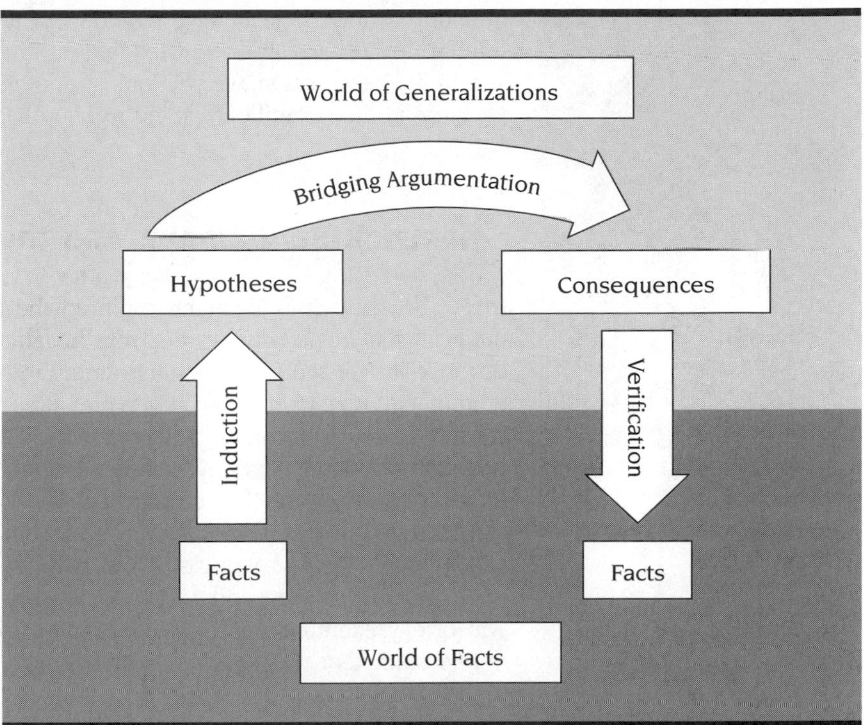

Major steps in the scientific cycle.

The final operation in the scientific cycle is actually to test the implications. For MacNeish, this step required additional reconnaissance in archaeologically unknown regions of southern Mexico. These new data were then evaluated, and had his projections not been verified, his hypothesis would have been rejected. As it turned out, excavations in the Tehuacán Valley failed to reject MacNeish's hypotheses. Hence, MacNeish's preliminary notions on plant domestication survived an empirical test.

No such simple experiment can ever completely validate any hypothesis, and more intensive inquiry is generally required to increase credibility. Scientific methods are not really designed to prove anything; instead, the aim is to eliminate the untenable hypotheses. MacNeish's work at Tehuacán generated new data ready for synthesis into new and more refined hypotheses (which in turn had to be tested). Scientific progress actually requires a pyramiding of verified hypotheses into a hierarchy of more generalized laws.

The process we have sketched is commonly called the *scientific method.* But I prefer the more accurate designation of *scientific cycle* because it emphasizes the reiterative, repetitive nature of the inquiry. A scientific cycle begins in the world of facts. Through the process of induction, these facts are probed, and hypotheses are invented to account for what is already known. But because hypotheses are general declarations, they cannot be tested against further facts until they are translated into their logical consequences, through the judicious use of bridging arguments. The final step, verification, returns to the world of facts.

The scientific cycle thus begins and ends with facts. But these new facts themselves will suggest new hypotheses, and, once again, inductive reasoning will lead from the world of facts to the world of abstraction, thereby

Heinrich Schliemann.

initiating a new cycle of investigation. As a method, science implies a continuing upward spiral in knowledge.

In the next section, we will look at another example showing how the simple steps in the scientific cycle led to one of archaeology's greatest discoveries.

Heinrich Schliemann and the New Siege of Troy

In 1875, Heinrich Schliemann captured the imagination of the world by announcing that he had discovered Troy, the fabled city in Homer's *Iliad.* Dispelling 2,000 years of doubt, Schliemann announced that not only had Homer been a marvelous epic poet—which everyone already knew—but also he had been a reliably accurate historian. Schliemann's claim has since been subjected to a century of scientific scrutiny, and contemporary archaeology has verified that he was basically correct. Schliemann really did find ancient Troy.

Despite his mercurial manner and a compulsion to overstate his theories, Schliemann's historic work at Troy truly established the scientific protocols now standard at thousands of contemporary archaeological excavations. We will briefly examine the Trojan excavations because they illustrate how scientific methods actually work in archaeology.

Homer Was Putting Us On, Right?

Science is nothing but developed perception, integrated intent, common sense rounded out and minutely articulated.

GEORGE SANTAYANA (1863–1952), PHILOSOPHER, POET, AND NOVELIST

The great confusion began with Homer, considered the world's first and perhaps greatest poet—although there is some speculation that "Homer" is actually a composite of several anonymous epic poets. We will probably never know.

But we do know that the Trojan War he describes in his two most famous works, the *Iliad* and the *Odyssey,* was real. It took place sometime during the twelfth century B.C., when Troy was an affluent regional capital. Troy was located just east of the Aegean Sea and formed the backdrop for the central plot of the poems.

Here is what Homer had to say: So magnificent were the towers and walls of Troy, that Greek tradition ascribed their construction directly to the hands of Poseidon and Apollo. On the summit of the Acropolis stood the palace of King Priam, and nearby were those of Hector and Paris. A single road led from the Trojan plain through the Scaean Gate into the heart of Troy.

The Greeks invaded Troy to recover Helen, who had been carried off by Paris, son of King Priam. Agamemnon arrived at Troy with 100,000 men in 1,186 ships. After the Trojans refused to return Helen, the Greeks held Troy under siege for a decade. The impasse was finally broken by Greek treachery: The Greeks pretended to retreat, leaving only a giant wooden horse, which the Trojans triumphantly hauled inside their walled city. The wooden horse was, of course, packed with Greek soldiers. Once inside the walls, they opened the gate to let in more Greek soldiers and all proceeded to sack and incinerate a defenseless Troy.

Scholars have speculated for millennia about the location of the Trojan fortress. Ancient Greek tradition suggested that the ruin at *Hissarlik* in northwest Anatolia (Turkey) was the actual site of Troy. The classical Greeks believed that Hissarlik had been periodically reoccupied, burying all traces of Troy beneath dense layers of later debris.

The tongue of man is a twisty thing, there are plenty of words there of every kind.

HOMER (NINTH–EIGHTH? CENTURY B.C. IN THE ILIAD)

But Demetrios, a Greek historian of the second century B.C., questioned Hissarlik as the real Troy. He felt that the geography was all wrong. Although the ruin at Hissarlik fronted a large plain, Demetrios felt that it would have been impossible for the Greeks to have landed on the Aegean shore and then to have crossed the Scamander Plain to do battle at Hissarlik. The modern shore must have been submerged in Trojan times.

Demetrios saw a second problem with Hissarlik. At one point in the *Iliad,* Homer described how, on the final day of fighting at Troy, Hector remained alone outside the city walls to confront the feared Greek warrior Achilles. Homer described in great poetic detail how the Trojans watched helplessly as Achilles chased Hector three times around their besieged capital. Thus ended the life of noble Hector, dragged into the sunset, head bobbing, from behind the chariot of Achilles. Thus also ends the *Iliad.*

Demetrios refused to believe that Homer would have fabricated such a critical moment. Demetrios apparently traveled to Hissarlik and personally judged the topography to be unsuitable for such a chase.

Demetrios thus rejected Hissarlik on two grounds: Achilles could not have chased Hector around Hissarlik three times, and the modern Plain of Scamander had been a deep-water bay during Trojan times. Demetrios's conclusion was endorsed two centuries later by the influential Greek historian Strabo.

Other Greek scholars soon began to question the historical veracity of Homer's epics. Through the next 15 centuries following the evaluation by Demetrios, suspicion increased that Troy was merely a myth. During the eighteenth and early nineteenth centuries, skepticism grew until few scholars accepted the reality of Troy, the Trojan War, and even Homer himself.

By the nineteenth century, those few enthusiasts who still believed in Troy at all favored a small ruin near the town of *Burnarbashi,* also in western Anatolia (Turkey). Although the ruins at Burnarbashi were unpretentious, these scholars felt that Homer had taken poetic license to transform a nondescript mountain community into the royal city of Troy.

Schliemann and the Scientific Cycle

Such was the situation when Heinrich Schliemann first tackled the problem of locating Troy. When Schliemann was a boy, his father had read to him of the Trojan War, and the ancient heroes captivated Schliemann from the start. He eventually taught himself ancient Greek so that he might enjoy Homer in the original. The more he read, the more he came to believe that Troy, the Trojan War, and the episodes chronicled by Homer must be true. But what had become of Troy? Surely it was too breathtaking, too monumental simply to have evaporated.

The essential point in science is not complicated mathematical formula or ritualized experiment. Rather the heart of science is a kind of shrewd honesty that springs from really wanting to know what the hell is going on!

SAUL-PAUL SIRAC

Schliemann began his quest for Troy in 1860, and in his search we can trace the development of scientific methods of archaeology. I shall recount the excavations of Schliemann in the idiom of modern science, not because Schliemann thought in these terms (for surely he did not), but, rather, to emphasize the logical structure of his explorations, which mirror today's scientific guidelines almost to the letter.

Remember that the scientific cycle begins with hypothesis formation, inducing a tentative conclusion sufficient to account for the known, specific facts. At this stage, there are no rules; induction is the province of the genius, of the creative mind. In the search for Troy, the inductive process evolved over 2,000 years. Three hypotheses had come to dominate mid-nineteenth-century scholarship:

Hypothesis A: Burnarbashi is the authentic ruin of Troy.

Hypothesis B: Hissarlik is the authentic ruin of Troy.

Hypothesis C: There is no authentic ruin of Troy because the *Iliad* is poetic fiction.

Keep in mind that scientific methods are not designed to prove anything; they only eliminate untenable hypotheses.

Hypotheses A and B can be tested outright because the archaeological sites of Burnarbashi and Hissarlik can be physically examined for Trojan ruins. The third hypothesis—that Troy never existed—cannot be tested because no observations can ever verify or disprove this theory. Hypothesis C thus becomes attractive only after all the other possibilities become untenable on the basis of the data at hand.

The second step of the scientific cycle deduces explicit and testable outcomes from each alternative hypothesis. Such outcomes are commonly stated as "if . . . then" statements: *If* Burnarbashi is the true site of Troy, *then* we should find . . . . *If* Hissarlik is the true site of Troy, *then* we should find . . . . Each declaration is followed by a series of logical outcomes, test implications to be verified or rejected by independent physical evidence.

Here we have multiple working hypotheses. The first hypothesis (Burnarbashi) has precisely the same logical consequences as does the second hypothesis (Hissarlik), because all the hypotheses derive from a single source, Homer's *Iliad.* The site conforming best to these outcomes should be the actual location of Troy. If neither site conforms, then Hypothesis C will become more tenable; maybe Troy is poetic fiction after all. It is, of course, also possible that a third (unknown) site is really Troy; in this case, all three hypotheses would be incorrect.

Schliemann worked out in great detail the test implications for ancient Troy from specific passages in the *Iliad.* We can summarize Schliemann's expectations for ancient Troy in the following eight propositions:

I. *Troy was a spacious, opulent city.* Schliemann expected to encounter this wealth in the form of precious metals. (This is why he was so often accused of treasure hunting.)

II. *Troy should provide ample evidence of imposing temples and other royal architecture.*

III. *The Trojan citadel must be surrounded by substantial fortifications.*

IV. *It must have been possible for Achilles to chase Hector thrice around the city.*

V. *Troy had two springs—one hot, one cold—located near the former Scaean Gate, the only exit from the city.*

VI. *Troy was located near the Aegean Sea.*

VII. *Troy was erected on a lengthy plain, site of the former Trojan battlefield.*

VIII. *The Scamander River (and tributaries) must flow between Troy and the Aegean coast.*

In effect, these hypotheses rested largely on two criteria: (1) the actual ruins of the Trojan citadel (Propositions I–III), and (2) the precise topographic setting surrounding the ruins (Propositions IV–VIII).

The final step in the scientific cycle is verification—bringing new evidence to bear upon the test propositions and seeing which, if any, of the hypotheses survive. In the search for Troy, such independent facts must derive from physical proof: Homeric poetry nurtured the hypotheses, but did not provide data against which to test these ideas.

Schliemann journeyed to Turkey in 1868 to examine firsthand the various ruins and to look for the Trojan landscape. He climbed the summit overlooking the village of Burnarbashi. He also visited Hissarlik, a 100-foot-high **tell** rising above the Scamander Plain. Schliemann agreed immediately with the ancient Greeks that Hissarlik must indeed be the Trojan ruin. His initial, gut-level hunches arose not from hard scientific evidence but from his intuitive grasp of the situation. Such insights are reserved for the finest fieldworkers of any generation. Good intuition cannot be taught.

Tell: An artificial mound created by the accumulation over centuries of stratified layers of disintegrated mud-brick walls and cultural debris. This term is most commonly used to describe the mounds that were once Near Eastern settlements.

Schliemann was hardly the first to visit the Scamander Plain searching for Troy with a dog-eared copy of Homer, trying to read clues from the landscape. What set Schliemann apart from earlier travelers was his demand for a more intensive review than merely touring the countryside. Not content simply to amble across some ancient ruins, Schliemann intended to excavate these ruins systematically. He planned to catalog all finds according to stratum and to draw and map the ruins as they were unearthed. Photographers would document his excavations to provide proof to a skeptical world.

Schliemann is the progenitor of modern archaeological methods because of his hardheaded appreciation of real data. He elevated the research of the past from speculative fancy to the realm of solid fact. Schliemann felt one could not—and should not—argue theories without finding the physical proof. He was a romantic, to be sure. But his step-by-step, methodical guidelines propelled him far beyond his contemporaries, to establish the modern canons of scientific thinking in archaeology.

Cycle 1: Schliemann Starts Digging

Although personally favoring Hissarlik, he felt obliged to address the Burnarbashi theory first. After scrutinizing the mountainous landscape, Schliemann undertook limited excavations at Burnarbashi in 1868 and 1871. The results, published by Schliemann in *Troy and Its Remains* (1875), can be summarized according to the preceding eight test propositions.

His excavations at Burnarbashi established that Propositions I through IV—that Troy must have been a rich complex citadel, surrounded by intimidating fortification walls—were not present. The excavations revealed the modest debris of a casual circuit wall. The village debris was thin, implying only a short-term occupation, probably by just a few inhabitants. And the chronology seemed wrong. Burnarbashi was probably a minor, short-term fortress.

Then Schliemann turned to the springs at Burnarbashi (Proposition V), found previously. Upon investigation, they did not have hot and cold running water; they were over half an hour's travel from Burnarbashi and were not visible from the citadel. Schliemann thought it unlikely that Homer would describe these distant springs as "under the wall along the public way."

The final test implications dealt with the topography of the immediate area and in each case, after point-by-point comparison with Homer's description, Burnarbashi was found wanting.

Schliemann thus completed this first round of scientific investigation by rejecting the theory that Burnarbashi could be ancient Troy. The ruins were wrong, the dating was wrong, the springs were wrong, the topography was wrong, Burnarbashi was wrong. End of Cycle 1.

What had Schliemann actually proved? Schliemann's preliminary work at Burnarbashi proved exactly nothing. Cycle 1 succeeded only in eliminating one competing hypothesis: Burnarbashi was not likely to have been Troy.

Cycle 2: Schliemann's Campaign of 1870–1873

So it was that Schliemann began large-scale excavations at Hissarlik in 1870. It has been said that Schliemann's first seasons at Troy were "more a rape than a scientific examination." Though this is no doubt true from the perspective of contemporary excavation technology, the Trojan excavations were exemplary for their day. The early work was not without gross blunders, as Schliemann subsequently readily admitted, but that hardly justifies accusing him of ignoring methods that evolved decades later.

The Schliemanns (Heinrich and Sophia) supervised a horde of inexperienced local workmen, the crew averaging 150 men per day. Initially convinced that Homeric Troy lay in the basal stratum of Hissarlik, Schliemann began an enormous north-south trench, in places reaching 50 feet deep before penetrating primary soil. This master trench emerged as the heart of Schliemann's strategy, and nothing was allowed to stand in its way. Using picks, shovels, wheelbarrows, and even battering rams and great iron levers, the workmen tore out all walls, structures, and foundations in order to find the earliest occupation. Schliemann detected four distinct strata, which he called "nations," of which the basal stratum was presumably Homeric Troy.

In 1872, however, Schliemann was forced to change his interpretation of the Hissarlik stratigraphy. Now convinced that Homeric Troy lay in the second rather than the first stratum, Schliemann identified the adjacent structure as the palace of Priam because the terra-cotta vases found inside the "palace" were so well made. A silver vase was discovered nearby, further convincing Schliemann that he had indeed found King Priam's ancient dwelling.

Hopes were high when Schliemann returned to Hissarlik in the spring of 1873. While probing through the dust and rubble, Schliemann spied a "large

Engraving from Schliemann's description of Troy, showing the Trojan buildings of Hissarlik during excavation.

copper article of most remarkable form, which attracted my attention all the more as I thought I saw gold behind it." Dismissing the workmen, he and his wife Sophia excavated one of archaeology's most famous treasures.

Below the copper "shield" (which proved later to be a basin) lay a copper cauldron, a silver jug, a globular gold bottle, and two gold cups. Further digging revealed more cups and vases of precious metals, lances, daggers, axes, knives, two gold diadems, and four gold earrings. On top of these lay 56 more gold earrings and 8,750 small gold rings, perforated prisms and dice, gold buttons, six gold bracelets, and more gold goblets.

"Priam's treasure," as it became known, further convinced Schliemann that Homeric Troy lay on the second, rather than the basal, level of Hissarlik. Schliemann regretted this shift in context, because "unfortunately, in 1871 and 1872, [I] destroyed a large portion of the [second] city, for I at that time broke down all the house-walls in the higher strata which obstructed my way." Then as now, archaeology remains a science that destroys its own data, and today's field methods stress the importance of analysis proceeding hand in glove with excavation strategy.

In his report of the Hissarlik excavations, published in 1875, Schliemann boasted to the world that he had indisputably discovered the ruins of Homeric Troy:

> I have excavated two-thirds of the entire city; and, as I have brought to light the Great Tower, the Scaean Gate, the city wall of Troy, the royal palace, . . . I have also made an exceedingly copious collection of all the articles of the domestic life and the religion of the Trojans; and therefore, it is not to be expected that science would gain anything more by further excavations.

On what did Schliemann base such claims? To examine his reasoning, we must return to the initial eight test propositions for Troy:

Propositions I through III were overwhelmingly verified. As predicted, Schliemann had discovered fantastic wealth, ruined temples, public architecture, and an impressive fortification wall. With regard to Proposition IV—that Achilles could have chased Hector thrice around the hill—Schliemann's excavations suggested that Homeric Troy was 37 feet lower than the present surface of Hissarlik. Furthermore, during the continuous occupation, the ridge would have gained in both height and breadth. Thus, even allowing for Homeric hyperbole, Schliemann concluded that the size of Hissarlik would not preclude the epic chase.

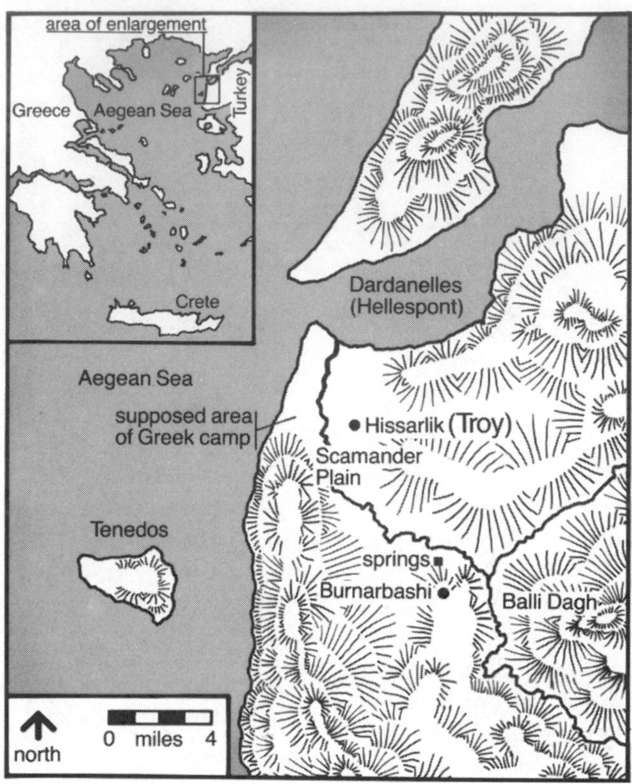

Map showing the location of Hissarlik in Anatolia (Turkey).

The topographic propositions (VI–VIII) also seemed to square with the modern Scamander Plain. In his initial campaign at Troy, however, Schliemann could not answer the ancient criticism of Demetrios, namely, that the Aegean had once formed a bay on the current alluvial plain. Schliemann also failed to locate a spring near his "Scaean Gate." Schliemann's excavation clearly implicated Hissarlik, not Burnarbashi, as the site of ancient Troy. Not all the predictions were verified, but Hypothesis B fared considerably better than did Hypothesis A.

Still, Schliemann's publication of the Trojan campaign received mixed reviews. A few raved that "the question is now decided forever. On the hill of Hissarlik Dr. Schliemann has uncovered the ancient palaces of Troy." But most scholars, particularly those trained along more traditional lines, thought that Schliemann's work fell far short of his claims. While granting that he had unearthed a significant early civilization, most authorities were critical of his methods and conclusions. At one point, Schliemann was even accused of salting his own site with silver and gold (he was, after all, a well-to-do man). Few scholars would allow any close connection between the artifacts of Hissarlik and the antiquities described in the *Iliad.* The architectural evidence was declared equivocal. In fact, Schliemann's bold, even audacious correlations between the *Iliad* and archaeology became at times an open joke in both the public press and closed scientific circles. All in all, the 1875 publication convinced few, and Burnarbashi remained the most fashionable nominee as Homer's Troy (if indeed it existed at all).

Cycle 3: Schliemann Wins

> [*Schliemann*] *found a whole series of ancient towns, one on top of the next, until he reached the one he believed was Homer's Troy. This feat gave rise to the adage "if at first you don't succeed, Troy, Troy again."*
>
> Paul Bahn, archaeologist

Criticism often leads to further research and refined hypotheses, and the adverse critiques of *Troy and Its Remains* spurred Schliemann to rise once again to the defense of Hissarlik. Schliemann's second Trojan excavations comprise the third loop in his scientific cycle. The first round tested and rejected the Burnarbashi hypothesis. The initial excavations at Hissarlik, the second loop in the cycle, produced ambiguous results, as Schliemann's critics were quick to point out. In order to verify the still untested implications and thereby respond to his critics, Schliemann commenced his campaign of 1878–1879.

The new excavations had two clear-cut goals. First, expose the ruins of the fortifications and of the large building in the second level, near where the treasure had been found. Several additional treasure hoards were found—10

IN HER OWN WORDS

The Hidden Contributions of Sophia Schliemann by Cynthia Irwin-Williams

Within the field of antiquarianism/archaeology in nineteenth century Europe and America, what was the role and contribution of women? To follow the lead of the principal recent chroniclers and historians of archaeology, the apparent answer is "none-at-all." Neither Daniel [1976] in his massive history of archaeology nor Willey and Sabloff [1980] in their treatment of New World archaeology mention a single contribution by a woman archaeologist before World War I.

Sophie Schliemann, wearing the golden diadem, earrings, and necklace she recovered as the "Treasure of Priam" at Hissarlik (Troy).

In fact, however, there were early women pioneers. For the most part they gained entrance to the field and limited public recognition as the wives and daughters of the famous archaeologists of the time. Best known among these was Sophia Schliemann, wife of Heinrich Schliemann. Their story reflects something of the climate of the time. In 1869, at age 47, after amassing a fortune from profiteering during the Civil War, Schliemann decided to divorce his "unsuitable" first wife and to marry a Greek girl specifically to help him in his lifelong passion to find and excavate the lost city of Troy. He selected the photograph of 27-year-old Sophia Engastromenos from a collection of photographs presented to him, and proceeded to court and marry the girl in three weeks. He then tutored her rigorously in the arts, history, geography, philosophy and archaeology, so as to prepare her to be his helpmate for his long awaited expedition to Hissarlik in Turkey, which he believed was the site of Priam's Troy. Their work together there led to a tremendous growth of interest in archaeology and prehistory. Throughout, although thoroughly overshadowed by her flamboyant husband, Sophia was recognized as the more diligent, careful, and perseverant of the two. What records were made of the excavations were largely the result of her efforts.

CYNTHIA IRWIN-WILLIAMS (1936–1990) was research professor, Quaternary Science Center, Desert Research Institute of the University of Nevada (Reno).

in all—and the collection of ceramics and material culture was dramatically increased. The 1878–1879 excavations showed even stronger support for Propositions I through III. There could be little doubt that Hissarlik was rich enough to have been Homeric Troy.

The greatest single achievement of science in this most scientifically productive of centuries is the discovery that we are profoundly ignorant; we know very little about nature and understand even less . . . .

LEWIS THOMAS (1910–1995), AUTHOR

The second goal represented a critical departure from Schliemann's earlier approach. On his return to Hissarlik in 1878, Schliemann brought with him a battery of consulting scientists to conduct a broad-based ecological study of the Trojan plain—its topography, geology, flora, and fauna. This broad-based, naturalistic approach to the Trojan Plain culminated in Schliemann's discovery of the much-disputed springs and washing troughs. Lying in an ancient rock channel at the foot of Hissarlik, the springs suggested

No one is more convinced than I am that anthropology has profited by being born within the scientific tradition. . . . My conviction is simply that today the scientific and humanist traditions are not opposites nor mutually exclusive. They are supplementary, and modern anthropology handicaps itself in method and insight by neglecting the work of the great humanists.

RUTH BENEDICT

continuous use from early Mycenaean (thirteenth century B.C.) into Roman times (900 B.C.–A.D. 500). Hence Proposition V was also verified by the 1878–1879 fieldwork.

Schliemann summarized his second campaign in *Ilios: The City and Country of the Trojans* (1880), published in German, English, and French. This volume, while still failing to silence his most vociferous critics, conclusively confirmed Schliemann's claim that he had found Homeric Troy.

The shortcomings of Schliemann's excavation technique need not detain us. Of course Schliemann should not have ripped out walls indiscriminately; in fact, he unknowingly dug right through the most likely candidate for Homeric Troy. Surely he was rash to apply unfortunate and judgmental terms like "Priam's treasure" and the "Scaean Gate." Perhaps we can excuse Schliemann as a "pioneer" who, like all pacesetters, must be forgiven occasional errors in execution and judgment.

Schliemann's self-assertiveness irritated many, past and present, but without such characteristics, he never could have forced himself—or his archaeology—to the attention of the learned world. As modern archaeologists are tempted to label their methods new, or revolutionary, they ought to check the writings of Schliemann. He may have gotten there first.

What Archaeology Is Not: The Evils of Scientism

Scientism: An exaggerated and mistaken trust in the methods of science to yield absolute Truth.

Philosophers of science don't agree on too many things. But one statement comes close to getting blanket approval: If there's one thing to avoid, it's an affliction called **scientism**—the rigidly held belief that there is a single, monolithic method for doing science. Scientism holds out the (false) promise that, if scrupulously followed, *the* scientific method will guarantee the successful path to Truth. Scientistic approaches are wrong.

Philosophers of science recognize that science can be pursued in several different ways. And regardless of how defined, scientific methods provide no guarantee that they produce the absolute truth. Science is, after all, only a Western perspective and the comparability to non-Western worldviews remains open to question.

In recent years, some archaeologists have advocated an *anti-science* position—the wholesale rejection of scientific methods in archaeology. The argument often goes like this: Since archaeology is not precise in the sense of the physical sciences, then the methods of science are inappropriate (and/or harmful) when applied to things archaeological. Such attacks on scientific methods are commonly directed at the exaggerated, scientistic caricature of science.

Labeling a theory "scientific" because it follows some definition does not in itself render the theory any more deserving of confidence.

JAMES A. BELL, PHILOSOPHER OF SCIENCE (UNIVERSITY OF SOUTH FLORIDA)

Science gives no ironclad assurance that application of its methods will necessarily result in the absolute, final truth about anything. Rather, scientists claim only that scientific methods provide the means for distinguishing, more or less, whether the evidence favors the validity of some hypotheses. Scientific methods do not assume that such subjective conditions as human motives, emotions, and dispositions are causally irrelevant.

The most ferocious anti-science rhetoric seems to come from those with a faulty understanding of the way contemporary science really works. It seems likely that few in the raucous anti-science minority have actually practiced any science themselves. Modern social scientists no longer believe in either absolute truth or absolute objectivity. Today, most philosophers of science recognize that science is part of culture, not outside it. Values, properly factored in, can be productive, not contaminating.

Science teaches, above all, to doubt and to be ignorant.

MIGUEL DE UNAMUNO, PHILOSOPHER

What's a Humanistic Approach?

Virtually all modern archaeologists, to one degree or another, subscribe to the basics of science. We all believe in careful scholarship, in generalizations backed by firm data, in honesty, in full consideration of negative evidence. Archaeologists do not follow a set of logical rules based on formal principles, but rather they are free to use creative imagination to solve problems of interest.

[Anthropology is] the most humanistic of the sciences and the most scientific of the humanities.

U. LEONARD MOSS

But archaeologists are not automatons and they are not emotionally neutral data-gathering machines. Archaeologists commonly have political opinions and sometimes these perspectives are reflected in their archaeology. At times, archaeologists make moral or ethical judgments about the past (and particularly about its use in the present). This occurs because archaeologists are historically situated; they are products of their era. But many also bring a humanistic perspective to their understanding of the past. In this section, we will look at an example of how an archaeologist can be both a scientist and a humanist.

So what do we mean by **humanism?** In general, humanists tend to emphasize the dignity and worth of the individual. Humanistic-style inquiry begins with an important premise—that all people are rational beings, possessing a capacity for self-realization through reason. Unlike the purely scientific approach, which stresses objectivity and independent testing, humanists also believe that the value of their contributions lies in precisely the opposite direction—in the fact that their work is intuitive, synthetic, and idiosyncratic. By employing more *subjective* methods, humanists stress reality as perceived and experienced. The result of a humanistic study is heavily conditioned by a researcher's personal mental characteristics or attitude.

Humanism: A doctrine, attitude, or way of life featuring human interests or values. In general, a humanistic approach tends to reject supernaturalism and stress the individual's value, dignity, and capacity for self-realization through reason.

The humanist side of anthropology is most obvious in its concern with the languages, values, and artistic achievements of other cultures. Ethnographers spend long periods living with the people they study, and they share both joys and sorrows. They cannot, and should not, be dispassionate about the people whose trials and tribulations they share.

In practice, then, Americanist archaeology spans a broad philosophical spectrum. To understand the sweep of opinion that characterizes today's archaeology, we begin by defining the extremist positions, which far exceed ordinary practice. Once these questionable outer limits are defined, it will be possible to work our way inward, toward the more realistic middle ground.

In retrospect, I believe my archaeological goals were basically humanistic rather than scientific. I was using archaeological methods to produce history and sometimes used simple scientific methods toward that end, but the ultimate goal was always history or perhaps ethnographic history.

GEORGE I. QUIMBY, ARCHAEOLOGIST (UNIVERSITY OF WASHINGTON)

Without the continued grounding in the empirical that scientific aspects of our tradition provide, our interpretive efforts may float off into literary criticism and into particularistic forms of history. Without the interpretive tradition, the scientific tradition that grounds us will never get off the ground.

ROY A. RAPPAPORT, ANTHROPOLOGIST (UNIVERSITY OF MICHIGAN)

It may be fair to say that the primary distinction between scientific and humanistic approaches revolves around the issue of objectivity. If you believe that archaeology is "mostly objective," then you probably lean more toward the scientific side. You probably think that there's a fairly clear separation between the observer and what is being observed—the "observed" being the "facts" of the archaeological record, which tend to have an inherent connectedness and regularity (which you might term "laws"). You probably believe that there's a world out there that can be known more or less objectively.

But if you say no, that archaeology is "mostly subjective," then you're probably more comfortable with the humanistic perspective, which maintains that the observer and the observed cannot really be separated—that our knowledge of the archaeological record mostly depends on who's doing the observing. You probably don't like conventional science very much and are more comfortable with those who do literary criticism and philosophy. You're probably what is called an *interpretivist* (or, perhaps, a *postmodernist*—much more about all this later). You probably believe that what we know about the archaeological record is itself a product of today's social forces—the product of how archaeologists relate to the archaeological record.

Science and humanism have been the two wings of the anthropological bird. Without both of them, working together, the bird doesn't fly.

E. N. ANDERSON, ANTHROPOLOGIST (UNIVERSITY OF CALIFORNIA, RIVERSIDE)

Today, fewer archaeologists than ever are interested in making people choose sides, in name-calling one another into a frenzy. The watchword today is "pluralism"—accepting that archaeological reality may come in many shapes and sizes.

Adolph Bandelier: Scientific Humanist or Humanistic Scientist?

I have known many scholars and some heroes, but they seldom come in the same original package.

CHARLES LUMMIS (1859–1928), AUTHOR AND EDITOR

To show you how this works, let me introduce Adolph Bandelier, another pioneer in American anthropology. Although Bandelier lived and worked a century ago, we can clearly see in his lifework the proper relationship between scientific and humanistic perspectives in anthropology.

The son of a Swiss army officer (and Russian aristocrat), Adolph Francis Bandelier came to America at the age of 8, growing up in Highland, Illinois. Although fascinated by the history and ethnography of American Indians, Bandelier seemed destined for a life dominated by his family businesses of banking and mining. As his fortieth birthday approached, he bitterly wrote that his life was "dreary and annoying . . . a life of mental slavery."

Then, through a remarkable set of circumstances, his life did an about-face. He was hired by the newly founded Archaeological Institute of America and immediately sent westward, where he would help establish the foundations of archaeological, ethnological, and early historical inquiry in the American Southwest.

How long this drudging day and night will last till it carries me to the grave or the insane asylum, I cannot tell.

ADOLPH BANDELIER (1840–1914), ARCHAEOLOGIST

Bandelier colorfully combined romanticism with a factual approach to history. Always the explorer, Bandelier traveled thousands of miles, unarmed and ill-equipped, on foot and horseback, working under the most adverse conditions. At one point, Bandelier was erroneously reported dead at the hands of Geronimo and his Apache warriors in southern Arizona. Here is a man who literally read his own obituary.

The "Scientific" Bandelier

Bandelier reached New Mexico in the late summer of 1880, and within days he began investigating the huge abandoned pueblo at Pecos. He knew the basics of Pecos history from his documentary research. Founded sometime in the distant past, Pecos Pueblo had grown to 2,000 inhabitants by the time Coronado passed through in 1540. It was a flourishing trade center, straddling the border between the farming Pueblo world to the west and the buffalo hunters of the High Plains. Out of Pueblo country came traders carrying turquoise, pottery, maize, cotton blankets, and marine shells (imported from the Pacific Coast). And hunters (such as the Comanche) came to Pecos from the Plains, bringing with them bison meat, fat, and winter robes of tanned hides, flint cores for tool making, and wood for bows. The hunters usually arrived about harvest time, camping nearby for several months before returning home. After a Franciscan mission was established at Pecos, the native population began dying out. The site was completely deserted in 1838, when a handful of Pecos survivors joined their linguistic relatives at Jemez Pueblo.

I am dirty, ragged, and sunburnt, but of best cheer. My life's work has at last begun.

ADOLPH BANDELIER (SHORTLY AFTER ARRIVING AT PECOS PUEBLO)

Given this sketchy background, Bandelier correctly concluded that the lengthy and well-preserved archaeological record at Pecos could provide an important baseline to long-term cultural development in the American Southwest.

A self-trained scientist, Bandelier immediately busied himself in the details of his new profession. At Pecos, he meticulously mapped the extensive ruins, measuring wall thickness and room dimensions, collecting samples of artifacts and building materials (which he shipped to Harvard's Peabody Museum). Bandelier believed in careful, standardized description and hired a photographer to record the current condition of the site. His report, published the following year, contained a wealth of historical and archaeological evidence gleaned from his own observations.

Bandelier with his usual thoroughness and accuracy, described the ruins [at Pecos] as they were at that time, and included a most valuable series of measurements of the house-mounds, the church, and the surrounding defense wall. . . . While his work was not accompanied by excavation, which would, of course, have solved many of the problems that puzzled him, Bandelier arrived at remarkably accurate conclusions.

ALFRED V. KIDDER

After finishing his research at Pecos, Bandelier switched his focus to ethnography. He began working at Santo Domingo Pueblo, a Keresan-speaking village on the banks of the Rio Grande, where he continued to accumulate factual, firsthand information: kinship and linguistic terms, building and room dimensions, characteristics of local pottery. But Bandelier had much to learn about the proper conduct of ethnographic research, and within a couple of weeks, he had worn out his welcome. After he was "starved out" (his term), Bandelier relocated across the Rio Grande where he was welcomed by the people of Cochiti Pueblo.

Apparently taking his Santo Domingo experience to heart, Bandelier quickly made numerous friends among the Cochiti people, who shared with him details of their customs and beliefs. He witnessed several religious ceremonies, made notes about daily life, and recorded the Keresan language, myths, stories, legends, and origin tales.

My relations with the Indians of [Cochiti] are very friendly. Sharing their food, their hardships, and their pleasures simple as they are, a mutual attachment has formed itself, which grows into sincere affection. . . . On the whole they are the best people the sun shines upon.

ADOLPH BANDELIER

Three weeks into his stay, the governor of Cochiti guided Bandelier on a horseback tour of numerous nearby archaeological sites. When they arrived at the site of Tyuonyi (chew-*ohn*-yee), Bandelier was dumbstruck; in his

Adolph Bandelier.

ever-present diary, Bandelier wrote that Tyuonyi was "the grandest thing I ever saw." The Cochiti told him that they had once lived at Tyuonyi before moving to their present location. Something in Bandelier resonated deeply with this place, and Bandelier would return to Tyuonyi time and again, exploring the surrounding mountains, excavating in the ruins, and sometimes living in the nearby caves of "this Stone Age of the past." Reflecting Bandelier's strong attachment to the area, President Woodrow Wilson, in 1916, would officially designate Tyuonyi and the surrounding valley the "Bandelier National Monument."

Bandelier would spend the next decade of his life exploring and describing nearly 400 major archaeological ruins throughout the American Southwest and northern Mexico. His *Final Report* describing this fieldwork—published in 1890–1892 by the Archaeological Institute of America—is an 800-page monument to Bandelier's single-minded obsession with accurate description and nit-picking detail.

Distancing himself from "any theoretical discussions or speculations," Bandelier attempted instead to record "as far as possible, the lay of the land in each case, in connection with its aboriginal remains, and such rays of light as documentary history and Indian tradition may shed upon them."

These cautious words were written by Bandelier-the-scientist—observer, recorder, and communicator. A century later, Bandelier's *Final Report* remains an extraordinary source of baseline information about the archaeology of the American Southwest.

We anthropologists are always seeking to portray reality. Fiction can sometimes reveal inner truths more clearly and succinctly.

ROBERT ALVAREZ, ANTHROPOLOGIST (ARIZONA STATE UNIVERSITY)

The "Humanistic" Bandelier

Bandelier was fanatical in his pursuit of knowledge about Native American cultures, but he never allowed his enthusiasm to shake his scientific detachment. Still, his interests extended beyond simply writing lofty scientific treatises to be read and digested by perhaps a few dozen specialists.

Beyond his purely scientific responsibilities, Bandelier was deeply concerned about the popular perception of American Indians. He was particularly annoyed with the wildly successful writings of James Fenimore Cooper—the first great American writer of fiction. In his five-volume *Leatherstocking Tales* (1823–1841), Cooper celebrated both the American wilderness and the basic frontier life that played out there. Like many romantic authors of his day, Cooper believed that science, art, and European social institutions corrupted humankind from its natural, or primitive, state, which was morally superior to the civilized state.

I was prompted to perform the work by a conviction that however scientific works may tell the truth about the Indian, they exercise always a limited influence upon the general public; and to that public, in our country as well as abroad, the Indian has remained as good as unknown.

ADOLPH BANDELIER (IN HIS PREFACE TO THE DELIGHT MAKERS)

Cooper idealized the American Indian as a heroic yet sadly vanishing species. The so-called noble savage was a mythic portrayal of non-European cultures as having an innate natural simplicity and virtue that was being corrupted by European civilization. Cooper's novels looked back on American Indians with nostalgia and romanticism.

In *The Last of the Mohicans* (1826), for instance, Cooper appropriated the name of "Uncas" to personify his title character. Although a historical figure—a seventeenth-century chief of the Mohegan (Mohican) people—the fictionalized Uncas was transplanted and sanitized into a "good Indian," a noble and loyal friend of the Euro-American. Cooper convinced generations of Americans that with the death of the fictional Uncas, the Mohican people became extinct.

Although motivated by compassion, Cooper knew precious little about Indians—and much of what he did know was either badly distorted or outright false. *The Last of the Mohicans* was a premature epitaph. In truth, the Mohegan people survive today, a few hundred still residing in their homeland—in and around the town of Uncasville (in southeastern Connecticut). Several thousand more people with some Mohegan ancestry live elsewhere in the United States.

Bandelier's 1890 *archaeological survey at* Pecos Pueblo (*New Mexico*).

*We have . . . unsettled the Romantic School in science, now the same thing must be done in literature on the American aborigine. . . . It remains to show that Fennimore [*sic*] Cooper's Indian is a fraud. Understand me: I have nothing personal in view. Cooper has no more sincere admirer than I am, but the cigar-store red man and the statuesque Pocahontas . . . pervert the public conceptions about our Indians.*

ADOLPH BANDELIER

Bandelier detested inaccuracy and romantic sentimentality. He ridiculed Cooper's superficial knowledge of real American Indians and stewed about the impact the "cigar-store red man" was having on the American public. In the late 1880s, as Bandelier was preparing the manuscript describing his scientific explorations, he hit upon a new idea.

Bandelier decided to write his own novel—accurate in its portrayal of American Indians, yet written in an engaging, accessible style that would appeal to the general public. In a book he called *The Delight Makers,* Bandelier drew upon his profound knowledge of ethnographic and historical facts—what he called "the sober facts"—to create a rich description of Pueblo life projected back into the past.

The Delight Makers is a story about the pre-European-contact Keresan people living at Tyuonyi, the archaeological site that had so captivated his imagination. In the title role as "Delight Makers" are the **Koshare**, a kind of Keresan clown and members of a powerful secret society.

Koshare: Ritual clowns in Rio Grande Pueblo society. *Koshare* is a Spanish term denoting those who perform comic relief between acts of formal European plays. Among Keresan Pueblo people (as at Cochiti) these sacred clowns are called *Ku-sha'li*.

The story begins on a sparkling June day at Tyuonyi in A.D. 1450 (about a century before the Spanish explorer Coronado would pass through the area). Okoya, an adolescent boy, is confronted by his younger brother, Shyuote, who complains about the older boy's cynical attitude toward the Koshares. This worries Okoya, since he has confided these inner thoughts only to his mother (who shares his feelings, but must be still, since her husband—Okoya's father—is a Koshare and Shyuote is pledged to become one himself in adulthood).

The conflict and doubt about Koshares escalates into accusations of witchcraft and supernaturally induced sickness. The dissidents perform their own rituals—a form of Keresan "black magic"—but little happens except that the much-needed rain does not fall. Navajo intruders side with the anti-Koshare forces and threaten to murder the grandfather (the war chief). As

IN HIS OWN WORDS

Bringing Tyuonyi's Past Alive by Adolph Bandelier

Here are brief excerpts from the first and last chapters of *The Delight Makers*:

The Keres of Cochiti declare that the tribe to which they belong, occupied, many centuries before the first coming of the Europeans to New Mexico, the cluster of cave-dwellings, visible at this day although abandoned and in ruins, in that romantic and picturesquely secluded gorge called in the Keres dialect Tyuonyi, and in Spanish "El Rito de los Frijoles" [meaning "bean creek"].

These ruins, inside as well as outside the northern walls of the cañon of the Rito, bear testimony to the tradition still current among the Keres Indians of New Mexico that the Rito, or Tyuonyi, was once inhabited by people of their kind, nay, even of their own stock. But the time when those people wooed and wed, lived and died, in that secluded vale is past long, long ago. Centuries previous to the advent of the Spaniards, the Rito was already deserted. Nothing remains but the ruins of former abodes and the memory of their inhabitants among their descendants. These ancient people of the Rito are the actors in the story which is now to be told; the stage in the main is the Rito itself.

The language of the actors is the Keres dialect, and the time when the events occurred is much anterior to the discovery of America, to the invention of gunpowder and the printing press in Europe. Still the Rito must have appeared then much as it appears now—a quiet, lovely, picturesque retreat, peaceful when basking in the sunlight, wonderfully quiet when the stars sparkled over it, or the moon shed its floods of silver on the cliffs and on the murmuring brook below.

"Umo,—'grandfather!'"

"To ima satyumishe,—'come hither, my brother,'" another voice replied in the same dialect, adding, "see what a big fish I have caught."

It sounded as though this second voice had issued from the very waters of the streamlet.

Pine boughs rustled, branches bent, and leaves shook. A step scarcely audible was followed by a noiseless leap. On a boulder around which flowed streams of limpid water there alighted a young Indian.

He was of medium height and well-proportioned. His hands and feet were rather small and delicate. He carried his head erect with ease and freedom. Jet-black hair, slightly waving, streamed loose over temples and cheeks, and was gathered at the back in a short thick knot.

And so Bandelier's tale begins. Four hundred and eighty-five pages later, it ends this way:

---

the Koshare search for evidence of heresy, antagonism within the Keresan community at Tyuonyi intensifies. When the grandfather's scalped corpse is found, a revenge-driven blood feud breaks out with the neighboring (Tewa-speaking) Pueblo group (when, in fact, it was Navajo interlopers who did the deed). As the Pueblo people fight it out, the Navajos destroy Tyuonyi. But thanks to Keresan heroism, many escape. The story ends when the fugitives begin building a new village (see *Bringing Tyuonyi's Past Alive* by Adolph Bandelier).

The material that Bandelier gathered in his 490 pages, each scientific detail embedded in a well-constructed story, is absolutely enormous. There is scarcely a book in which the modern reader can find so much lore presented so readably.

C. W. Ceram (1915–1975), literary critic and author

Nor, I should add, so accurately.

Barbara A. Babcock, anthropologist (University of Arizona)

Although well aware of the Indians' plight, Bandelier refused to write a melodrama about a sadly vanishing lifestyle. Exactly because of the disasters brought about by Euro-American contact, Bandelier staged his novel in the twelfth century, to emphasize the richness and complexity of purely Pueblo cultural life. Bandelier's Indians were complicated human beings—neither the pawns of their basest instincts nor romanticized noble savages.

Bandelier knew his protagonists well: He met them all while living among Pueblo people for nearly 8 years. Although fiction, *The Delight Makers* proceeded according to a strict narrative formula. All accounts of the south-

After twenty-one long and it may be tedious chapters, no apology is required for a short one in conclusion. I cannot take leave of the reader, however, without having made in his company a brief excursion through a portion of New Mexico in the direction of the Rito de los Frijoles.

It is a bare, bleak spot, in the centre of the opening we see the fairly preserved ruins of an abandoned Indian pueblo. There are still in places three stories visible. The village forms the usual quadrangles. In the ruins of the dwellings over four hundred cells [rooms] are still well defined, so that the population of this communal village must formerly have reached as high as one thousand souls.

Over and through the ruins are scattered the usual vestiges of primitive arts and industry,—pottery fragments and arrow-heads. Seldom do we meet with a stone hammer, whereas grinding slabs and grinders are frequent, though for the most part scattered and broken. We are on sacred ground in this crumbling enclosure. But who knows that we are not on magic ground also?

We might make an experiment. Let us suffer ourselves to be blindfolded, and then turn around three times from left to right. One, two, three! The bandage is removed. What can we see?

Nothing strange at first [but] a change has taken place in our immediate vicinity, a transformation on the spot where stood the ruin. The crumbling walls and heaps of rubbish are gone, and in their place newly built foundations are emerging from the ground; heaps of stone, partly broken, are scattered about; and where a moment ago we were the only living souls, now Indians move to and fro, busily engaging.

Some of them are breaking the stones into convenient size. The women are laying these in mortar made of the soil from the mesa, common adobe. We are witnessing the beginning of the construction of a small village. Farther down, on the edge of the timber, smoke arises; there the builders of this new pueblo dwell in huts while their house of stone is growing to completion. It is the month of May, and only the nights are cool.

These builders we easily recognize. They are the fugitives from the Rito.

And now we have, though in a trance, seen the further fate of those whose sad career has filled the pages of this story. We may be blindfolded again, turned about right to left; and when the bandage is taken from our eyes the landscape is as before, silent and grand. The ruins are in position again; an eagle soars on high.

The circular ruin of Tyuonyi (New Mexico).

western landscape and ecology are accurate, based on Bandelier's firsthand observations. The architecture of archaeological sites is also precise, based on the same painstaking measurements, fieldnotes, and photographs that Bandelier would publish in his strictly scientific *Final Report.* For dialogue, he employed the Keresan language (as spoken at Cochiti).

In true humanistic fashion, *The Delight Makers* stressed the value of the individual, the dignity and

Bandelier on the Internet

Bandelier National Monument Homepage
http://www.nps.gov./band/

capacity for self-realization, the joys and sorrows of everyday Pueblo life. But although he was writing fiction, Bandelier's scientific side required that he return to Cochiti, time and time again, to confirm and reconfirm each detail. And, as modern ethnographers agree, most of Bandelier's "sober facts" have subsequently been reconfirmed.

The descriptions of manners and customs, of creed and rites are from actual observations by myself and other ethnologists, from statements of trustworthy Indians, and from a great number of Spanish sources of old date.

ADOLPH BANDELIER

The Delight Makers would never compete with the action-packed plots hatched by James Fenimore Cooper, and Bandelier's stilted Victorian prose is somewhat tedious by modern standards. But over the decades, the novel came to be recognized as an important piece of late-nineteenth-century literature, a classic of both science and literature. The original publishers, Dodd, Mead and Company, recently reported that Bandelier's book was the longest-running title the company ever had in its inventory. *The Delight Makers* remains in print today, more than a century after its original publication.

In Bandelier, we see both scientific and humanistic approaches to archaeology. In fact, it is impossible to classify Bandelier as either a scientist or a humanist because, clearly, he was both. Although a few contemporary archaeologists continue to debate the tiresome "science versus humanities" issue, most would agree with Bandelier that modern archaeology is—and must be—a mixture of both approaches.

I divide scientific and humanistic approaches by method: Scientific approaches build knowledge that is external and cumulative while humanist approaches seek knowledge that is internal and historical. The former depersonalizes, the latter is highly personal. The two are compatible and co-exist in each of us (think of Leonardo, artist and scientist). The matter is in the mix.

STEPHEN H. LEKSON, ARCHAEOLOGIST

For decades, mainstream archaeology has prided itself in the ability to straddle the fence between scientific and humanistic perspectives. Kathleen Deagan's archaeology at St. Augustine and in Haiti has been supported by both the National Science Foundation and the National Endowment for the Humanities. Like Deagan, many archaeologists have found it advantageous from time to time to switch emphasis away from the science side and lean a little toward a humanistic view Some archaeologists have even been known to twist their research around to the point that the National Endowment for the Arts could be asked to help. In a very practical sense, then, many archaeologists have found it useful to avoid doctrinaire ideological positions.

SUMMARY Anthropologists believe that a true understanding of humankind can arise only from a holistic, all-encompassing perspective. The biological anthropologist views people chiefly as biological organisms, whereas the cultural anthropologist analyzes people as creatures of their culture. Archaeology, as a branch of cultural anthropology, is deeply concerned with the concept of culture, the learned body of tradition that ties a society together. Cultural phenomena can be divided into three major domains of study. The cultural idiolect reflects an individual's cultural expression. Then there is the overall shared (modal) aspect of culture, which exists both mentally and as observable behavior. Third is the cultural system, the underlying structural basis for a society's adaptation to environment. These three aspects of culture are reflected in different ways by various schools of anthropological thought.

[The Delight Makers] *will always be a standard—the most photographic story yet printed of the life of the prehistoric Americans.*

CHARLES LUMMIS

Contemporary anthropological thinking can be characterized by two major strategies of research. The ideational strategy deals with mentalistic, symbolic, cognitive culture. Viewed in a reflexive sense, material culture is an instrument to create meaning and order in one's world. The contrasting adaptive strategy in anthropology emphasizes those aspects of culture that most closely articulate with the environment, technology, and economics. This infrastructure is seen as ultimately conditioning the character of both structure and superstructure. Archaeologists draw upon both ideational and adaptive perspectives and no single anthropological school dominates contemporary archaeology.

For more than a century, archaeology has been firmly grounded in a scientific perspective, which provides an elegant and powerful way of allowing people to understand the workings of the visible world and the universe beyond. The goal of scientific theory building is to develop theories that can be criticized and evaluated, to be eventually modified or even replaced by other theories that better explain the archaeological data. The scientific method relies heavily on the twin concepts of objectivity and testability. All archaeologists believe in certain scientific fundamentals: in honest and careful scholarship, in generalizations backed by firm data, and in full consideration of negative evidence.

But many archaeologists also believe in humanism, in the dignity and worth of the individual. Humanistically inclined archaeologists look for holistic syntheses of the cultural patterns of the past. For decades, archaeologists have prided themselves on their ability to straddle the fence between scientific and humanistic perspectives.

Chapter 3

Levels of Archaeological Theory

PREVIEW This chapter is important because it sets out the theoretical baseline for the rest of the book. *Low-level* theory is required in order to make relevant observations about the archaeological record. This is how archaeologists get their "data," their "facts." Theory at the *middle level* is what links these archaeological data to human behavior. Sometimes archaeologists generate their data by conducting controlled experiments, sometimes by doing ethnoarchaeology, by making observations of ongoing, observable behavior to see how it is translated into the archaeological record. Finally, there is *high-level* (or *"general"*) theory, which provides the overarching framework for understanding the human condition. General theory applies to all intellectual inquiry about human beings; it is not restricted to archaeology. We will concentrate on two specific kinds of high-level theory—*cultural materialism* and *postmodern interpretivism*—and see how these general research strategies translate into specific activities that archaeologists do. I understand that many students are put off by obscure discussions of various "-ologies" and "-isms," but it's important that you understand these basic theoretical points. I try to minimize the jargon, and hope that in the coming chapters, you will recognize the importance of understanding these basic theoretical concepts.

Science is facts; just as houses are made of stone, so is science made of facts; but a pile of stones is not a house and a collection of facts is not necessarily science.

HENRI POINCARÉ (1854–1912), NINETEENTH-CENTURY MATHEMATICIAN

Theory is a term we have used very little so far, but it is important nevertheless. Social scientists use the word *theory* in a number of different ways. In one usage, a theory is an untested explanation that would probably be false if ever properly tested. We might speak of Erich Von Dähniken's goofy *Chariots of the Gods* theory, in which he argues that the major cultural advances on earth have resulted from visitations by extraterrestrial beings. Many archaeologists would call this "theory" an improbable and untested generalization. In this sense, *theory* is a put-down, almost a dirty word.

Theory also refers to a general set of untested principles or propositions—theory as opposed to practice. Thus a new invention to harness solar energy might work "in theory" (that is, on paper) but would require extensive field testing before one could decide whether it was a successful design. If the solar device functioned as expected, the theory would be valid; if the device failed, the theory would be held invalid.

Although both usages are common, neither has much to do with archaeological theory. Instead, we will define theory at three fundamental levels: low, medium, and high. These are critical distinctions because the rest of this book will be organized in terms of these three sequential levels of archaeological theory.

Archaeology on the Internet

Erich Von Dähniken's outlandish "Chariots of the Gods" theory states that ancient astronauts are responsible for the achievements of the earth's ancient civilizations: http://wheel.ucdavis.edu/~btcarrol/skeptic/vondanik.html

Skeptic's Dictionary also addresses the errors and misrepresentations in Von Dähniken's claim: http://www.dictionary.com/skeptic/dict18.htlm

Low-level theories are the observations that emerge from hands-on archaeological fieldwork. Although you may be accustomed to thinking of such observations as data or facts, we will see why even the baseline facts of archaeology are themselves really theories.

Middle-level theory links archaeological data with the relevant aspects of human behavior that produced them. This is a critical transition because it moves from the archaeologically observable (the "facts") to the archaeologically invisible (human behavior in the past). Middle-level theory building involves both methodological and substantive applications. One *methodologically oriented* example is *experimentation,* when archaeologists make their own stone tools, attempting to understand which specific stoneworking techniques (human behavior) create specific kinds of flake scars on stone tools (archaeologically observable data). Another methodological example is *ethnoarchaeology,* in which archaeologists observe aspects of ongoing, observable culture to learn how certain behaviors are translated into the archaeological record.

Facts are stupid until brought into connection with some general law.

Louis Agassiz (1807–1873), zoologist

Middle-level theory building also involves *substantive applications*—archaeologists applying principles drawn from general theory (discussed later in this chapter) to explain specific datasets from the archaeological record. For instance, an archaeologist might test competing hypotheses regarding the origins of agriculture against cross-cultural data from archaeological explorations in several parts of the world. Because this exercise attempts to link specific archaeological data with behavior patterns that may have produced them, this is an instance of middle-range theory building as well.

Finally, there is *high-level* (or *general*) theory building. Theory at this level provides the overarching framework for understanding the human condition. General theory is not specific to archaeology, but rather applies to intellectual inquiry in general. Such theory attempts to interrelate concepts, not account for specific observations; theory at the general level is sometimes called "research strategy." Some would suggest that general theory resembles a religious creed or dogma because it can never be directly confirmed or falsified; others would counter that general theory embodies an empirical method of testing itself, which religion does not. Here, we introduce the two major research strategies that are most relevant to modern Americanist archaeology.

Low-Level Archaeological Theory

All too frequently, methodology-theory-practice discourses get lost in abstraction and become divorced from archaeological reality altogether. To avoid this problem, we will begin our discussion of low-level theory in

Facts are the world's data. Theories are structures of ideas that explain and interpret facts.

STEPHEN JAY GOULD, PALEONTOLOGIST (HARVARD UNIVERSITY)

archaeology by looking at some real archaeological data. The idea is to keep this discussion firmly grounded, basically down to earth.

We will introduce archaeological theory, beginning at the lowest level, in the context of real archaeological objects. To keep things simple, I will, from time to time, talk about some specific objects recovered in my own excavations. Two sites in particular—Gatecliff Shelter and Mission Santa Catalina—will crop up frequently.

Gatecliff Shelter (Nevada) is a prehistoric cave in the American Desert West, where people gathered beneath the shallow overhang for more than 7,000 years. I discovered Gatecliff in 1970, and throughout the 1970s, our interdisciplinary team excavated the microstratigraphic deposits in the cave. Gatecliff provides a good example of how things work in archaeology.

The second archaeological case study, *Mission Santa Catalina de Guale,* is located in the Sea Islands, off the coast of Georgia. Here, a Franciscan mission was founded among the Guale Indians in the late 1500s, and for more than a century Santa Catalina defined the northern Spanish frontier along the eastern seaboard. It was overrun by British troops in 1680. I began searching for this lost mission site in 1978, the same year we finished digging at Gatecliff. Three years later, we discovered Santa Catalina and have been digging there ever since.

Gatecliff was discovered by old-fashioned, dogged fieldwork; we found Mission Santa Catalina using modern sampling theory and "hi-tech" remote sensing. The Gatecliff excavations were "vertical"—in some places nearly 40 feet deep—but nowhere at Santa Catalina have we dug deeper than 6 feet. The cultural deposits at Gatecliff were stacked up within a floor area of about 300 square feet, whereas Mission Santa Catalina sprawled across a dozen acres. Buried within Gatecliff Shelter were several thousand stone tools, weighing more than a ton; all the stone artifacts from Santa Catalina would easily fit in a single shoe box. Only three pieces of pottery turned up at Gatecliff, but ten thousand sherds so far have been cataloged from Santa Catalina.

The list of contrasts grows, but my point is simple: Having spent two decades excavating at Gatecliff and Mission Santa Catalina, I have yet to excavate any important data from either. In fact, I dug up no data at all.

What Are Archaeological Data?

Let us not underrate the value of a fact; it will one day flower into a truth.

HENRY DAVID THOREAU (1817–1862), WRITER

Why would any right-thinking archaeologist waste half a career digging holes that produced no archaeological data? Am I feebleminded or just jinxed?

Neither, I hope. I found no data at Gatecliff or Mission Santa Catalina because archaeologists do not excavate data—anywhere. Rather, they excavate objects. Gatecliff Shelter and Mission Santa Catalina surrendered overwhelming artifact collections, thousands upon thousands of archaeological objects. But neither the physical sites nor the archaeological objects they contained are data.

Data: Relevant observations made on objects that then serve as the basis for study and discussion.

Data arise only from observations made on such objects. Each observation is specifically designed to answer one or more relevant questions: How old is this part of the site? Who were the people? What language did they speak? Was the ancient climate similar to that of today? Why did they choose to live in this particular spot? What did they eat? What kinds of social groups were present? Where did they go? Each question may require a different set of observations, giving rise to several batches of dissimilar data. But remember that quite different observations can often be made on exactly the same objects.

The hallmark of today's archaeology is the precept that the objects of the past can (and must) be viewed from multiple perspectives. Gatecliff and Mission Santa Catalina provide recurring points of reference, and we use the objects from these two sites—plus many, many others—to illustrate differing perspectives on the past.

More than anything else, today's archaeology is flexible and broad-based. Sometimes we ask questions about time; we also consider human adaptation; we may ask about religion and social organization; sometimes we might inquire about mind-set and cognitive structure; sometimes we operate as relatively objective scientists, while at other times a more subjective, humanistic approach is more suitable. The theoretical perspective may vary widely, but the objects remain the same.

What, Exactly, Is Gatecliff Shelter?

Gatecliff is a collection of archaeological objects. The cultural objects—the **artifacts**—are made of chipped or ground stone, bone, plant fibers, tanned hides, shells, and turquoise. Archaeological sites contain other objects not made by humans, those relating to the natural environment, and archaeologists term such things **ecofacts.** Prehistoric pollen grains are ecofacts; so are food bones and piñon nut hulls.

Artifact: Any movable object that has been used, modified, or manufactured by humans.

Ecofact: Plant or animal remains found in an archaeological site.

Corncobs are borderline: To dirt archaeologists, cobs are ecofacts simply because they aren't artifacts; but to specialists in ethnobotany, corn is decidedly an artifact because it was produced by deliberate domestication.

So Gatecliff Shelter is a collection of archaeological objects. But it is more than that. We see collections of archaeological objects in every small-town saloon in the West. Sometimes the assortment is no more than a handful of arrowheads in a cigar box. More aesthetically minded collectors arrange their brightly colored arrowheads in decorative shadow boxes.

These frames are filled with prehistoric ancient artifacts, but the gin mills are not prehistoric archaeological sites. The reason for this is simple: The artifacts are merely isolates, objects displayed in a modern context. When we dug Gatecliff, we discovered prehistoric implements and ecofacts where they were discarded by their makers. The artifacts were **in situ**—in place. The artifacts had an ancient context.

In situ: A term referring to the position in which an item is initially encountered during excavation or survey.

Low-Level Theory Building

Now that we have some real archaeological things in mind, we can return to the issue of theory building in archaeology.

Low-level theory begins with archaeological objects, then generates some relevant "facts" or "data" about these objects. Some data consist of physical observations. For example, *artifact 20.2/4683 is (a) made of obsidian, (b) 21.5 mm long, and (c) weighs 2.1 grams.* This statement contains three pieces of

I'm a realist, not an idealist. I never had a thesis, I just took the facts and let them fall where they may.

Esther Goldfrank, Archaeologist

data—observations made on the same archaeological object. Other data might be contextual. For example, *artifact 20.2/4683 found in unit B-5, 56 cm below the surface.* This observation places this artifact into a three-dimensional coordinate system (as discussed in Chapter 6).

An infinite number of observations can be made on any single archaeological object: distances, angles, weights, color readings, chemical compositions, manufacturing techniques, and so forth. But in practice, of course, archaeological data consist of a relatively standardized series of descriptive observations. At this level, archaeological data should be relatively objective and, if possible, reproducible by independent observers. Several subsequent chapters will show, in some detail, how archaeologists build their data into reliable cultural chronologies.

Low-level archaeological theory also addresses the data generated from ecofacts. Animal bones, for instance, are often recovered in archaeological contexts. Beyond the standard contextual data generated during excavation, these bones are commonly identified as to taxa (Is it a deer bone or a bunny bone?) and to body part (Is it a vertebra or a toe bone?). Data are also generated about the bone's condition (Is it broken or whole? Are butchering marks evident? Is it burnt?).

Overall, the important dimensions of low-level generalizations are the classical ones in archaeology: time, space, and form. Low-level theory does not refer to the archaeological record in terms of human behavior. Theory at this level only demonstrates the existence of regularities to be explained, rather than attempting to explain those regularities.

Theory at the Middle Level

The past can be understood only through the present.

ALBERT SPAULDING (1914–1990), ARCHAEOLOGIST

Archaeological theory at the middle level (sometimes called the middle range) addresses both substantive and methodological questions. In both cases, however, *middle-level theory* links some specific archaeological data with the relevant aspects of human behavior that produced it. At this middle range, we make a critical transition because we move from the archaeologically observable (the low-level theoretical "facts") to the archaeologically invisible (relevant human behaviors in the past). How, you might wonder, does this transition actually take place?

First of all, remember what the archaeological record is: It is the contemporary evidence left by people of the past. Strictly speaking, the archaeological record is comprised only of static objects—the artifacts and ecofacts that survive into today. The dynamic behavior that produced or interacted with these archaeological objects is long gone.

Archaeologists conducting such methodological research at the middle range spend time studying situations in which archaeologically relevant behavior is still taking place, fashioning the theoretical tools by which past material culture can be translated. Methodological theory building at the middle range has proven to be an extremely productive research area, involving ethnoarchaeology, modern material culture studies, and experimental archaeology. Each topic is discussed in some detail in later chapters.

One methodologically oriented field is *experimental archaeology.* Archaeologists sometimes conduct controlled experiments in which they manufacture their own stone tools. Here, they are studying specific stoneworking techniques to learn how human behavior is translated into specific archaeologically observable evidence (such as flaking scars, breakage patterns, and leftover flake by-products). Experimental archaeologists also conduct intensive studies of pottery manufacture, house-construction methods, and hunting techniques and technology, to name but a few.

Middle-range research can also be conducted as *ethnoarchaeology,* in which archaeologists observe ongoing, present-day cultural contexts to see how behavior translates into the archaeological record. Several examples of such middle-range theory building are discussed in Chapters 4 and 10.

General Theory in Archaeology

High-level (or *general*) *theory* provides archaeologists with an overarching framework that structures the way we view the world. General theory is not specific to archaeology; it applies to all intellectual inquiry about the human condition. Some general theory is heavily scientific, some is not. Some general theory stresses environmental adaptation, some does not. Some general theory emphasizes strictly biological factors; some involves only cultural causality; some theory combines the two approaches.

When all think alike, no one thinks very much.

WALTER LIPPMANN (1889–1974), AUTHOR AND HISTORIAN

General theory attempts to interrelate higher-level concepts, not to account for specific observations. It is not open to direct empirical verification or rejection; people tend to believe in a particular body of general theory for highly personal reasons. This is why high-level theory is sometimes called one's "research strategy": Your general theoretical leanings influence how you view humanity, how you structure your questions about the present and the past, and how you interpret the answers you receive to these questions. General theories vary in the degree to which testable propositions can be derived from them. But general theory is never right or wrong: It is either an appropriate way to answer questions, or it is not—and everyone gets to judge what is meant by "appropriate."

Understanding Archaeology's Primary -isms and -ologies

Archaeologists subscribe to a broad range of research strategies, and an exhaustive discussion of such diverse views would take a long time. Since our purpose here is merely to tell you something about the role of high-level theory in archaeology, we will sketch only the two most prevalent strategies—cultural materialism and postmodern interpretivism.

There are many roads to truth.

PAUL S. MARTIN (1900–1980), ARCHAEOLOGIST

Just doing this is not quite enough, however. Remember what I said earlier: "General theory is not specific to archaeology; it applies to all intellectual inquiry about the human condition." This means that we must also look at how these general research strategies translate into the practice of actual, down-to-earth, dirt archaeology.

The new circumstances under which we are placed call for new words, new phrases, and for the transfer of old words to new objects.

THOMAS JEFFERSON (1743–1826), THIRD PRESIDENT OF THE UNITED STATES

Specifically, then, the concluding part of this chapter will:

present the basics of *cultural materialism* (a general research strategy) and sketch its importance to the processual agenda in Americanist archaeology.

discuss the overall premises of *postmodern interpretivism* and show how it is translated into archaeology's *postprocessual critique.*

We will cover considerable ground in a relatively short space. Keep in mind that we are presenting here only the overall theoretical framework within which today's Americanist archaeology operates. Each topic will be much more fully developed in later chapters.

High-Level Theory: Cultural Materialism

The most coherent adaptive approach in anthropology is termed *cultural materialism,* a movement with roots extending back at least a century. But today, cultural materialism is largely associated with Marvin Harris (now professor of anthropology at the University of Florida), who gave it its name. The cultural materialist strategy attempts to explain the evolution of differences and similarities in the global repertory of sociocultural systems.

The Premises of Cultural Materialism

Cultural materialists begin from the scientific premise that knowledge is acquired through public, replicable, empirical, objective methods. Such scientific research allows us to formulate theories to explain cultural differences and similarities. Rival theories are judged by the same criteria, based on their power to predict and to admit independent testing. By explicitly embracing a scientific framework, cultural materialists reject humanist and aesthetic theories that attempt to explain culture on nonscientific grounds. More than this, cultural materialism posits that environmental, technological, and economic factors—the material conditions of existence—are the most powerful and pervasive determinants of human behavior.

Marvin Harris.

Cultural materialism focuses on behavioral events, which must be distinguished from mental events because they are observed in such different ways. They cannot be understood using the same set of criteria. Human behavior is available to the scientific community in a form that can be observed, measured, photographed, and objectively described. Human thought, the events of the mind, can be observed only indirectly. Although distinct relationships exist between behavior and thought, these associations must be demonstrated and not assumed.

Although behavior has its *emic* component—the subject's perception of what has transpired—cultural materialists prefer to concentrate on the *etic* component, the observable outcome of human behavior. Within these guidelines, cultural materialistic research covers a rich array of topics: the origin and evolution of sex and gender roles, warfare, origins of dietary patterns and food avoidance, and settlement and demographic trends, to name just a few.

Cultural materialists use the term *infrastructure* to denote those elements considered most important to satisfying basic human needs: the demographic, technological, economic, and ecological processes—the modes of production and reproduction—that are assumed to lie at the causal heart of every sociocultural system. Specifically, it is the *etic behavioral infrastructure* that mediates a culture's interactions with the natural and social environment.

Put another way, the infrastructure embraces the etic and behavioral components of production and reproduction modes:

> *Mode of production:* The technology and practices employed for expanding or limiting basic subsistence production (especially food and other energy production), given the restrictions and opportunities that provide for a specific technology to interact with a habitat.
>
> *Mode of reproduction:* The technology and practices employed for expanding, limiting, and maintaining population size (specifically, demography, mating patterns, fertility, natality, mortality, nurturing of infants, medical controls, contraception, abortion, infanticide).

At the next level, the sociocultural subsystem is made up of those interpersonal relationships that emerge as behavior: social organization, kinship, economics, ethics, and military and political organizations. This sociocultural subsystem is today subsumed by the term *structure,* with the following etic, behavioral components (*Hint:* If you are wondering how these various processual views came to be, *sit tight:* We revisit these issues in some detail in Chapters 13 and 15):

> *Domestic economy:* The organization of reproduction and basic production, exchange, and consumption within camps, houses, apartments, or other domestic settings: family structure, domestic division of labor, domestic socialization and enculturation, age and sex roles, domestic discipline, hierarchies, and sanctions.
>
> *Political economy:* The organization of reproduction, production, exchange, and consumption within and between bands, villages, chiefdoms, states, and empires: political organizations, factions, clubs, associations, corporations, division of labor, taxation, tribute, political socialization and education, class/caste and urban/rural hierarchies, discipline, police/military control, warfare.

Finally, the term *superstructure* refers to values, aesthetics, rules, beliefs, religions, and symbols. Expressed in etic behavioral terms, superstructure is manifested as art, music, dance, literature, advertising, religious rituals, sports, games, hobbies, and even science.

Cultural Materialism on the Internet

Cultural Materialism, an introduction:
http://msumusik.mursky.edu/~felwell//http/cult.htm

Review of Cultural Materialism:
http://anatomy.su.oz.au/danny/book-reviews/

Failure of Cultural Materialism, a critique from the University of Texas at Arlington:
http://www.uta.edu/english/apt/homepage/papers/crisis.html

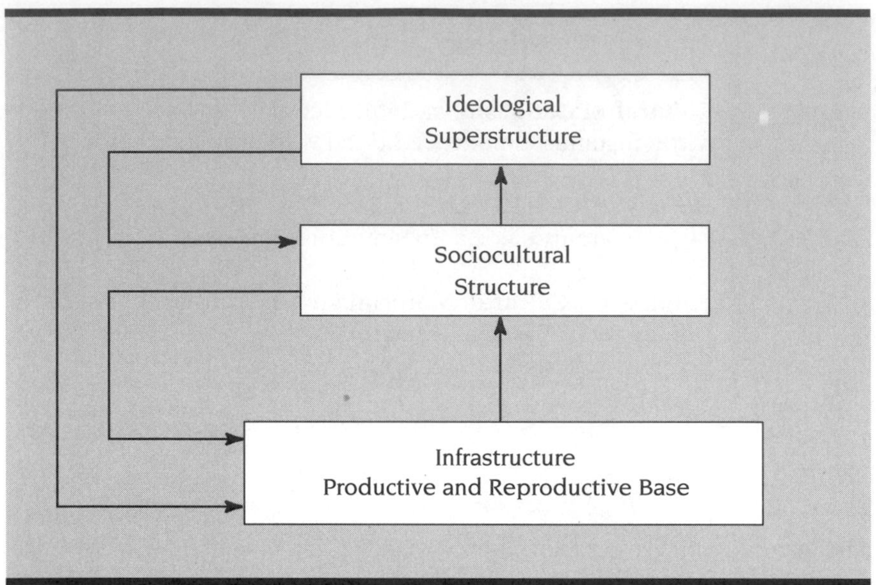

How the cultural materialist views causality.

The Principle of Infrastructural Determinism

Distinguishing cultural materialism from other approaches is the *principle of infrastructural determinism,* which has two facets: (1) human society strives to optimize the costs and benefits for those genetically derived needs most important to the survival and well-being of human individuals (sex, sleep, nutrition, vulnerability to stress, and so forth); these occur primarily in the etic behavioral infrastructure; and (2) such infrastructural changes determine changes in the rest of the sociocultural system.

Though clearly interrelated, the three sectors listed in the preceding section influence one another differentially, and cultural materialists assign priority to the modes of production and reproduction. Technological, demographic, ecological, and economic processes become the independent variable and the social system is the dependent variable. Domestic and political subsystems (the structure) are considered to be secondary; values, aesthetics, rituals, religion, philosophy, rules, and symbols (the superstructure) are all tertiary. The modes of production and reproduction tend to foster quite distinctive ideological systems. Farmers think differently than hunter-gatherers, who view the world differently than industrialists. *To the cultural materialists, infrastructure is the key to understanding the growth and development of all culture.*

Such causality is considered to be probabilistic, however, with feedback between components. Some sociocultural traits in every society arise from arbitrary, idiographic events. As scientists, cultural materialists look past the "exceptions" to seek overarching generalities that can be tested and refined. Stating that structure and superstructure are causally dependent on infrastructure does not mean that determinations are transmitted in a single direction; as Leslie White put it, the influences are *reciprocal* but not necessarily *equal.* No component is a passive recipient. Without input from domestic, political, and ideological subsystems, the observable modes of production and reproduction would have evolved differently.

Cultural materialists prefer to use the term *research strategy* rather than *general theory,* but the outcome is largely the same. Cultural materialists believe that their program is better than any of the ideational options in conforming to the canons of acceptable scientific explanation. Their strategic principles can be discredited only in light of alternative principles that produce better and more scientifically acceptable theories.

The Processual Agenda: Cultural Materialism at Work in Archaeology

Processual archaeology is the strategy of cultural materialism applied to the past. Here, we use the broad term **processual agenda** in a fairly specialized way. It includes the new archaeology of Lewis Binford and others, but it also extends to the evolved brand of processualism practiced by a large segment of Americanist archaeologists today.

Processual agenda: The view that explains social, economic, and cultural change as primarily the result of internal dynamics ("processes"). Materialistic conditions are assumed to take causal priority over ideational factors in explaining change.

For now, it is important only that you understand the basics of the processual agenda, and how it differs from the *postprocessual critique,* briefly introduced at the end of this chapter. These two conflicting approaches define what contemporary Americanist archaeology is all about: Neither, by itself, is sufficient to explain what today's archaeologists are up to. In several later chapters, we discuss general theory in archaeology in considerably more detail.

Processual archaeology grew out of dissatisfaction with the increasingly sterile cultural-historical and largely descriptive archaeology of the 1950s. Processualists correctly noted that these descriptive approaches were inadequate to explain how cultures operated in the past. The chronology-building tools perfected in cultural-historical archaeology were retained, but the rest was rejected in favor of what can be called the processual agenda.

The processual agenda has several key characteristics:

Processual archaeology emphasizes evolutionary generalizations, not historical specifics: In the processual agenda, history tends to be viewed as the opposite of science, as descriptive rather than explanatory. The processual agenda is scientific, not historical. The focus is on regularities and correlations. Processual archaeology explicitly associates itself with the generalizing social sciences, such as economics, political science, sociology, and ethnology.

Just as Darwin's theory of natural selection defined the mechanism of biological evolution, archaeologists can define theories that condition the progressive evolution of culture. This evolutionary perspective assumes—takes as a "given"—that people's actions are the immediate determinants, but specific human decisions and specific historical sequences are not of particular interest or significance in their own right.

An interest in developing evolutionary theory directed the processual agenda away from ideology and toward the approach of cultural materialism, emphasizing demographic pressure, the role of hydrological systems, marketing networks, and conflict over limited resources as the forces driving cultural evolution.

Processual archaeology seeks universal laws: The ultimate goal of processual archaeology is to produce law-like generalizations that could be useful for understanding modern society. As processual archaeology matured, the interest in defining the laws of human behavior expanded from general theory to include middle-range research as well.

Explanation in processual archaeology is explicitly scientific: Initially, the processual agenda championed the view that predicting events (even those in the past) is equivalent to explaining them. Procedures in processual archaeology depended on deductive models grounded in the "hard" sciences and emphasized the importance of absolute objectivity. More recent formulations stress the interplay between induction and deduction and the relative objectivity of observations.

Processual archaeology attempts to remain objective and ethically neutral: Processual archaeology tries to provide positive evidence about the past. Such knowledge is highly specialized and has created generations of archaeological specialists, each knowing a specific field, but that knowledge is deliberately disconnected from the present. Politics of the present have nothing to do with the ancient past. Archaeology should avoid subjectivity and not be used for modern political purposes. Processual archaeology is not interested in passing moral judgments on people of the past.

Processual archaeology defines culture as humanity's extrasomatic means of adaptation: In processual archaeology, the culture concept squarely focuses attention on the key elements of environment, technology, ecology, and economy. Religion and ideology are "epiphenomena"—cultural add-ons with little long-term explanatory value. Thus the processual agenda is in complete agreement with the principle of infrastructural determinism.

The processual agenda views culture from a systemic perspective: Because culture provides the nonbiological system through which people adapt to their environments, processual archaeology could tap into a much larger body of established external theory (often called "general systems theory"). The theoretical premise here is that various complex entities—thermostats, computers, glaciers, living organisms, even sociocultural entities—can be viewed as systems comprised of multiple interacting parts. Depending on the application, the general rules governing all systems (such as positive feedback, negative feedback, and equilibrium) could explain the behavior of the major parts of any particular system—regardless of the specifics of that system.

Processual archaeology deals with etic phenomena: While not denying that people have their own cultural views, processual archaeology defines culture in *etic* terms only, strictly from the perspective of the outside observer.

I'd guess that well over half of today's practicing American archaeologists are pursuing the processual agenda, in one form or another (although many of these same archaeologists also agree with aspects of the *postprocessual critique,* as detailed in the rest of this chapter). This implies that these same archaeologists are practicing cultural materialists (although many would probably not admit it). Cultural materialism appeals to archaeologists for two obvious reasons. First, the cultural materialistic strategy emphasizes technology, economy, environment, and demography—all aspects of human existence that leave relatively clear-cut evidence in the archaeological record. Almost by default, Americanist archaeologists have for decades concentrated on precisely the same factors that cultural materialism holds as primary.

Equally important, cultural materialism needs archaeology. In several of his most important writings, Marvin Harris calls for archaeological support of his theories of human behavior. Harris urges archaeologists to throw off the constraints imposed by current ethnographic theory. Cultural materialism is important to archaeology in part because archaeology is important to cultural materialism. Not all general research strategies—particularly those with an ideational philosophical bent—see archaeology as particularly relevant to their interests.

High-Level Theory: Postmodern Interpretivism

Consensus has become an outmoded and suspect value.

Jean-François Lyotard, postmodernist

Postmodern interpretivism is a world apart from the cultural materialism we just discussed. The differences between the two research strategies are deep and profound. Each general theory has produced its own archaeological offspring. As we have seen, the general research strategy of cultural materialism directly informs what we have called the *processual agenda* in Americanist archaeology. For the rest of the chapter, we will concentrate on the other primary research direction in Americanist archaeology, what we are calling the *postprocessual critique,* a direct intellectual outgrowth of the general research strategy known as postmodern interpretivism.

Our explication of this theoretical chain goes as follows: To understand archaeology's postprocessual critique, you must first appreciate the impact of postmodernism on the general field of anthropology; and in order to understand how postmodernism works, you must first know something about *modernism,* against which postmodern interpretivism has so strongly reacted.

What Is Modernism?

Most scholars would trace the roots of modernity to the Enlightenment of the eighteenth century, when thinkers tried to develop objective science and universal standards for morality and law. It was a period of great optimism, of scientific discoveries that would enable humanity to dominate the perversities of nature and enjoy freedom from want and from the arbitrariness of natural catastrophe.

Modernism thus began as an attempt to demystify and desanctify knowledge—a way of liberating human beings from the oppressive traditions of myth, religion, and superstition. Thinkers of the Enlightenment attempted to do this by appealing to the ideas of linear progress, absolute truth, rational planning of ideal social orders, and the standardization of knowledge (and how it is produced).

Artists, writers, architects, composers, poets, and philosophers all occupied a very special position in the modernist worldview: The role of the modern artist was to define the secular essence of humanity. Frank Lloyd Wright—perhaps the greatest of the modernist architects—argued that one must not only comprehend the spirit of the age, one must also initiate

Postmodernism on the Internet

Postmodern and Cyberculture:
http://www.academic.marist.edu/1/postmod.htm
http://146.19.2.3/~alquier/cyber/post_cult.html

Postmodern Culture is a journal that lists its tables of contents, prize competitions, and talk archives:
http://jefferson.village.virginia.edu/pmc/contents.all.html

Why I Am Not a Postmodernist is an essay by Edward R. Friedlander, M.D.:
http://worldmall.com/erf/postmod.htm

the process of changing it. Particularly in architecture, so-called creative destruction became an integral element of modernism—destroying the ancient, tradition-bound buildings that tied us unnecessarily to the past.

What Is Postmodernism?

I cannot remember exactly when I first encountered the term postmodernism. I probably reacted to it in much the same way as I did to the various other "isms" that have come and gone over the past decades, hoping that it would disappear under the weight of its own incoherence. . . . But it seemed as if the clamor of postmodernist arguments increased rather than diminished with time. . . . In recent years [postmodernism] has defined the standards of debate, defined the manner of "discourse," and set parameters on cultural, political, and intellectual criticism.

DAVID HARVEY, GEOGRAPHER (JOHNS HOPKINS UNIVERSITY)

The postmodern movement arose in the 1960s as an intellectual antidote to the perceived excesses of modernism. Postmodernism has been described as a "sea change," a dramatic shift in perception that has forever changed our cultural, political, economic, and artistic outlooks. The consequences of the postmodern critique on contemporary thinking—including the way archaeologists view the past—are difficult to overemphasize. Before turning to the direct archaeological implications, we must begin with a brief look at some of the basic tenets of postmodern thought.

With its roots in the Enlightenment, modernism was very much about optimism and the pursuit of a better future. But twentieth-century reality—particularly the two world wars, the death camps, and the continued threats of nuclear annihilation—shattered many people's confidence in the modernist agenda. A suspicion arose that the dreams of the Enlightenment had been transformed from solutions for human emancipation to a world that somehow oppressed nearly everyone. To many, the modernistic rationality of the Enlightenment became the logic of domination and tyranny.

The postmodern movement arose as an attempt to strip away the prospect of such oppression by concentrating instead on social fragmentation and instability. The emphasis on decentralization and anarchy makes postmodernism itself a difficult concept to define, because of the way in which postmodern culture views the use of language.

Given this definitional ambiguity, it is easier to view postmodernism in terms of its vigorous and negative reaction to modernity, to what went before. In Table 3.1, we set out some of the fundamental contrasts between the two positions, characterizing an admittedly complex series of relations as simple polar opposites. Rather than analyze Table 3.1 in terms of line-by-line comparisons, it's better simply to scan the two columns and pull out an impression, an overall flavor of each outlook.

If your impressions are like mine, you will come away with something like this:

> *Modernist thinking* embodies a systematic, clinical, single-minded approach, emphasizing linear progress and goal-oriented behavior, ultimately seeking a carefully crafted finished product.
>
> *Postmodernist thinking* embodies an emphathetic, playful, dissociated series of approaches, emphasizing multiple and sometimes fragmented pathways toward indeterminate, decentralized, transitory performances.

We are now in the process of wakening from the nightmare of modernity, with its manipulative reason and fetish of the totality, into the laid-back pluralism of the post-modern. . . . Science and philosophy must jettison their grandiose metaphysical claims and view themselves more modestly as just another set of narratives.

TERRY EAGLETON, LITERARY CRITIC

In general, postmodern thinking shows an intense distrust of the universals and generalizations that provide the keystone to modern scientific reasoning. Although not entirely anti-scientific, postmodernists put down deterministic, rigidly causal methods, praising instead such new developments as mathematical models that emphasize indeterminacy (such as catastrophe and chaos theory).

TABLE 3.1
Some Binary Contrasts Between Modernism and Postmodernism

Modernism	Postmodernism
purpose	play
design	chance
hierarchy	anarchy
mastery	exhaustion
finished work	performance/happening
creation	deconstruction
centering	dispersal
selection	combination
master code	idiolect
determinacy	indeterminacy
trade union	individualism
ethics	aesthetics
centralization	decentralization
single task	multiple task
scientific rationality	pluralistic otherness
function	fiction
permanence	ephemerality
time	space

Postmodernism castigates the imperialism of a modernity that presumed to speak for "the other" (colonized peoples, indigenous groups and minorities, religious groups, women, the working class) with a unified voice. The ideas of postmodernist thinkers held special appeal for the various social movements that sprang up in the 1960s, including feminists, gays, ethnic and religious groups, and those seeking regional autonomy. The idea here is that each group has a right to speak for itself, in its own voice, and to have that voice accepted as authentic and legitimate. Such **pluralism** is an essential premise of postmodernism.

Postmodernism swims, even wallows, in the fragmentary and the chaotic currents of change as if that is all there is.

David Harvey

Pluralism: A theory that multiple kinds of ultimate reality exist. A pluralist society is one in which members of diverse ethnic, racial, religious, or social groups continue to participate in their traditional culture or special interest.

With their distrust of the general, postmodernists have put down broad interpretive schemes like those of Karl Marx on modern communism or those of Sigmund Freud on psychoanalysis. Rejecting the idea of progress, postmodernism abandons all sense of historical continuity and memory, instead taking bits and pieces of the past quite eclectically and mixing them all together.

Deconstruction: A Tool of Postmodern Thought

Deconstruction is a term borrowed from literary criticism to describe a primary research tool, if it may be called that, in postmodern thinking. The term was coined by French philosopher Jacques Derrida in the 1960s to describe his efforts to expose the abstract and implicit assumptions behind the so-called objective and systematic search for knowledge. Deconstruction minimizes the authority of the "cultural producer" and creates an opportunity for popular participation and democratic determination of cultural values.

Deconstruction: A philosophy of trying to understand how meaning is constructed by writers, texts, and readers.

Deconstruction is less a general philosophical position than a theory about language and literature that developed in the 1970s. The works of Derrida have converted a number of U.S. academics, and Americans have

Deconstruction on the Internet

http://130.179.92.25/Arnason_DE/Derrida.html
http://wc3.webcrawler.com/select/philos.36.html

established different schools of deconstruction—feminist deconstruction, for one. But the basic principles of the theory are the same for all.

What most characterizes deconstruction is its notion of *textuality,* a view of language as it exists not only in books, but in speech, in history, and in culture. For the deconstructionist, language is much more than just words—either written or spoken. The world itself is "text." Communication directs humanity and creates human reality. Meaning is nested in multiple ways, one of which is language. Yet, upon close examination, words seem to have no connection with reality or ideas.

The Enlightenment is dead, Marxism is dead . . . and the author does not feel very well either.

NEIL SMITH

Related to textuality, the concept of *intertext* refers to the broader cultural background, the context that permeates the text with countless conventions and codes. This intertextual weaving has a life of its own. Given the hidden linkage of a text to its cultural and social intertext, the content and meaning of the text are, essentially, indeterminate. Texts, therefore, are unreadable, and the practice of interpretation may be defined as misreading.

The search for truth is silenced by answers which have the weight of undisputed authority.

PAUL TILLICH (1886–1965), THEOLOGIAN AND PHILOSOPHER

Thus whatever we write connotes meaning we could not possibly intend. Our words cannot say what they mean because the perpetual interweaving of texts and meanings is beyond our control. This explains the deconstructionist impulse to look inside one text for another, to dissolve or build one text into another. To a deconstructionist, meaning also includes what is left out of a text, and what is silenced by it.

The Internet has been called a postmodern dream. Because it has no center, the Internet can thus have no margins. The "authorial presence" is erased, replaced by the pandemonium of millions of newly empowered authors. Some have claimed that the Internet "acknowledges" the constructed nature of reality, self, and "the other," creating a level playing field for all participants. The Internet is "postmodern" in the sense that it is a dramatic challenge to governmental and other controls over what we see, hear, read, and think.

Deconstruction has been attacked by some as unintelligent, as philosophical restlessness, as the death of communication. Nevertheless, since the 1970s it has been the leading school of literary criticism in the United States. Deconstruction has also extended far beyond philosophy and literary theory. The techniques and ideas of deconstruction are today employed by scholars in history, sociology, educational theory, linguistics, art, and—as we see next—anthropology.

There's a Chinese curse that says, "May you live in interesting times." And, unfortunately, I'm afraid that's what's happening now in anthropology.

ROBIN FOX, SOCIAL ANTHROPOLOGIST (RUTGERS UNIVERSITY)

Postmodern Interpretive Anthropology

As the seeds of postmodern, deconstructionist thinking blew through the intellectual establishment, they fell on particularly fertile ground in the world of cultural anthropology. After all, the world had changed considerably since the beginning of anthropology. Colonial powers no longer dominate, the so-called primitive has disappeared, the geopolitical landscape has become violent and hostile to anthropologists, funding is more difficult to find, university and institutional priorities have shifted. For many, the post–Vietnam War era created a kind of "anthropological identity crisis."

A postmodern call to action has occurred, and many social theorists have welcomed the chance to steer anthropology away from its roots in the "natural science of society." Sometimes calling themselves "interpretive" anthropologists, they have embraced the postmodern critique, rejecting all causal viewpoints in favor of a quest for understanding different worldviews, symbol systems, values, religions, philosophies, and systems of meaning. Interpretive anthropology has left behind all notion of overarching theories or systematic research on "the other." In its place was proposed a close consideration of such issues as contextuality and the meaning of social life to those who enact it. Instead of looking for regularities, postmodern anthropology seeks to explain the exceptions.

Scientific thought is now an archaic mode of consciousness surviving for a while yet in degraded form.

Stephen Tyler, postmodern anthropologist (Rice University)

This means that specific ethnographic situations can only be fully appreciated in their specific historical contexts. Ethnographic particulars have to be firmly situated into a broad framework of both time and space. There are no timeless and spaceless generalizations.

Particularly useful have been deconstructionist methods originally devised in theology for interpreting religious texts, today applied by anthropologists to understand cultural phenomena. Those employing textual analogies emphasize the use of empathic rather than scientific method, the use of personal intuition to understand the inner lives of others—their attitudes, expectations, experiential meanings, and other affective and spiritual elements.

We once had in our department a biological anthropologist who said that the diverse belief systems in cultures could all be explained by endocrinology.

Bradd Shore, symbolic anthropologist (Emory University)

Many contemporary ethnographers believe that their task has become to analyze a culture in the way a literary critic would read a book or poem. The goal of discovering scientific truth about a culture is rejected in favor of composing interpretations about the "other" culture that are elegant and convincing. According to one postmodern critic, ethnography is not an empirical account, it is a species of fiction.

Anthropology in the postmodern world has found itself enmeshed in the cross-cultural attempt to strip away surface forms of knowledge in order to explore truths formerly buried and concealed. Deconstructionism was considered appropriate here because it got away from notions such as "what the culture was really like," to focus instead on hidden intentions and unexpressed biases of the ethnographer/author. Many cultural anthropologists have turned away from traditional "scientific" ethnography to embrace instead the tenets of postmodernism: All truth is relative; all perceptions are mediated by one's cultural and sexual identity.

There always was a certain amount of divisiveness [in anthropology], but now it's like Yugoslavia.

Clifford R. Barnett, applied anthropologist (Stanford University)

Many anthropologists have adopted a *reflective* viewpoint, moving away from the so-called objective natural sciences. The very concept of objectivity—a reality somehow knowable in a concrete sense—is alien to postmodern thinking, which holds that everything knowable is inherently subjective. Instead of traditional science as a method of discovery, postmodern anthropologists rely on "reflection."

If this is accepted, then science becomes merely one of many ways of telling a story about the world around us. Some have gone so far as to argue that scientific methods are merely tools used by the privileged to oppress

[Human evolution is a] sexist and racist storyline created by Western white men. . . . There is a great deal of wild theorizing about men hunting and women gathering, when it's hard to tell the male [hominid] bones from the female to begin with.

Jane Collier, cultural anthropologist (Stanford University)

the weak. Some anthropologists even oppose the term *evolution* because they feel it implies a hierarchy in which some cultures are considered "primitive."

Although some anthropologists have always thought such things, the postmodern movement attracted a large following in cultural anthropology. At the extremes of anthropological theory, the pro- and anti-scientific positions hardened. Among some anthropologists, the gap has become so broad, according to bioanthropologist Vince Sarich, that "you can dismiss someone's argument simply by calling them a 'scientist.'"

Archaeology's Postprocessual Critique: Postmodern Interpretivism at Work

The *postprocessual critique* is the strategy of postmodern interpretivism applied to the past. This new way of viewing the archaeological past arose largely in Great Britain and Europe, a direct outgrowth of mainstream postmodernism. Under the leadership of Ian Hodder of Cambridge University, this distinctly postmodern brand of archaeology emerged during the 1980s. Although they were somewhat premature in calling themselves *postprocessual archaeologists,* this energetic and vocal band of scholars took up the banner of postmodernism and attacked the premises of processual archaeology full force.

As we have just seen, postmodernism rejects the systematic, clinical, single-minded approach of modernism. With respect to archaeology, the postprocessual critique similarly rejects the etic, evolutionary, anti-historical, objective, science-based, ethically neutral approach of the processual agenda. *Postmodernist interpretivism* emphasizes instead empathetic approaches, multiple pathways of belief, which produce sometimes indeterminate products. The postprocessual critique seeks a similar approach to the archaeological record.

> *If the . . . scientists of the "new" archaeological paradigm saw themselves as the ultimate social planners, discovering laws of cultural evolution that would lead us knowingly into the twenty-first century, we post-processualists have more modest aims. We can predict neither the past, nor the future; in fact, we claim not really to know the past at all. Rather, we tell stories about it and discover stories told by generations of scholars.*
>
> PHILIP L. KOHL, ARCHAEOLOGIST (WELLESLEY COLLEGE)

As with the general modern/postmodern dichotomy, it is difficult to define precisely the processual/postprocessual division. Here, we will use the term *postprocessual critique* to characterize this ideationally oriented brand of archaeology that today enjoys huge popularity on both sides of the Atlantic. Although processual archaeology has hardly been driven into extinction (as the somewhat premature *"post-"* would imply), the postprocessual critique has fundamentally changed the way the world views archaeology and has shaped the direction of contemporary Americanist archaeology.

In later chapters, we explore the general theoretical trends in archaeology in some detail. For now, it is sufficient to highlight areas of disagreement. It is important that you understand the differences between the processual and postprocessual perspectives because in the next several chapters, we will explore numerous cases as illustrations of these very different ways of approaching the archaeological record.

Some very different intellectual developments have emerged in recent years, in general featuring the relativism characteristic of the "postmodern" school of thought seen most notably in anthropology and literary studies. In choosing to term their approach "post-processual" the leading practitioners of this trend in archaeology are pronouncing a judgement which some commentators have found to be a shade arrogant in its assumptions.

Colin Renfrew, archaeologist (Cambridge University)

The postprocessual critique rejects the cultural evolutionary generalizations: The postprocessual critique has argued that cultural evolution's sometimes racist views of the past have developed because of reliance on the (Western) notion of "progress."

The postprocessual critique rejects the processual search for universal laws: Consistent with postmodern interpretivism, the postprocessual critique holds that such universals of human behavior simply do not exist. Scientific explanations are inadequate for understanding the past because historical circumstances are downplayed in the search for universals.

Postprocessualists also claim that processualists have demonstrated a remarkable ignorance of what contemporary historians actually do. They argue that the processualists have not advanced beyond the grossest and mostly outdated caricatures of history as a particularizing, idiographic discipline.

The postprocessual critique rejects explicitly scientific methods: Postprocessual critics point out, quite correctly, that much of the early processual literature smacked of scientism—of rigidly adhering to rote rules of evidence and interpretation. As it turns out, the processualists tied themselves to a brand of science that most philosophers of science had found to be inadequate. Moreover, many involved in the postprocessual critique have shown a manifest distrust of science in any form (particularly during the earliest years of the critique).

Scientific methods of study tend to demean the culture of others, as well as the others themselves, by measuring, comparing, objectifying, and denaturing them.

Mark Leone, historical archaeologist (University of Maryland)

The postprocessual critique rejects the processual emphasis on objectivity and ethical neutrality: To understand the past, many postprocessual archaeologists argue, one must develop an empathetic, particularistic approach to it. So-called *empathetic explanations* of the past consider not only human thoughts and decisions, but also such highly subjective elements as affective states, spiritual orientations, and experiential meanings. Empathetic approaches assume that the inner experience of humanity is worthy of study both for its own sake and as a clue for interpreting the human past.

Some in the postprocessual critique argued for the position of extreme relativism: There is no real past; it is merely a construction in the present. They point out the lack of truly objective data in any science (including archaeological science) because data and theory can never be considered to be truly independent. Today, most postprocessual archaeologists have backed away from this extreme position, preferring archaeological interpretations that are situated historically in both past and present.

The postprocessual critique rejects the processual view of culture as an extrasomatic means of adaptation: As you will remember from earlier discussions, the processual approach followed Leslie White's concept of culture as an

Archaeology and the Modern/Postmodern Dialogue

Archaeology enjoys a strange relationship with postmodernism. In this chapter, we have explored the degree to which postmodern thinking has permeated archaeological method and theory. But in a curious way, archaeological thinking has also played a role in shaping the core of the modern/postmodern dialogue. The story goes like this:

Alan Sokal, a physicist at New York University, once wrote a manuscript suggesting, among other things, that "physical 'reality' . . . is at bottom a social and linguistic construct." In other words, Sokal was suggesting that the postmodern condition impacts even physics, the hardest of the "hard sciences." Another NYU professor, Andrew Ross, liked Sokal's manuscript and published it in *Social Text*, a postmodern journal he co-edits.

The problem is that Sokal's article was a parody, a devastating put-on that, he believed, illustrated the degree to which the postmodern critics had lost any sense of intellectual standards. After all, if they'd publish this stuff—suggesting (among other things) that gravity was simply "a linguistic and social construct"—they'd believe anything! Ross was roundly ridiculed for gullibility and, by extension, postmodern theorists were red-faced for their apparent rejection of gravity-as-reality.

Curiously, although they taught at the same university, Sokal and Ross had never met. Here's how *The New Yorker* magazine reported their first encounter, onstage anchoring a forum debating the relative merits of various scientific and postmodern perspectives:

Sokal is a boyish, bespectacled man, with a physicist's haircut and mischievous look in his eye. Ross is a brooding Scotsman, with matinée-idol features and a certain dark charm. The two men considered the weighty issue of intellec-

The aim of archaeology is not to secure knowledge of the past for its own sake but to secure knowledge of the past that is socially responsible in the present.

IAN HODDER, POSTPROCESSUAL ARCHAEOLOGIST

"extrasomatic means of adapting"—postprocessualists point out that because all scientific inquiry is "situated" within the culture of the scientist, the *extrasomatic* view of culture must be accepted simply as a self-evident truth. How, they ask, can this bald assertion be tested objectively and independently?

The postprocessual critique further rejected all strictly ecological interpretations. This group began searching for a way to discover an interpretive system that would (1) not rigidly preassign chronological or causal priority to economy, demography, technology, and ecology and (2) incorporate internal societal diversity, human initiative and enterprise, and ideology in theories of cultural change.

The postprocessual critique rejects the systemic view of culture: Postprocessual archaeologists view culture basically as comprising four elements: (1) the mental, symbolic (*emic*) elements, (2) the material culture per se, (3) social behavior, and (4) the recursive relations among the first three. In this case, artifacts become full participants in the cultural process. In this postmodern view, artifacts are not just objectifications of culture, they *are* culture itself.

In addition, the overall "systems" approach, a central tenet of the processual agenda, has been ridiculed by postprocessual archaeologists as "the robotic view of the human past." Postmodern views in general distrust such "deterministic" perspectives that reduce the individual human being to the *tual standards from behind a conference table in a large, crowded lecture hall, looking directly at each other only once, when Sokal offered Ross a glass of water and Ross, understandably suspicious of his colleague's offer, declined. It was Sokal's point that some people . . . had let their allegiance to postmodernism muddle their thinking. He gave as his example an archaeologist who asserted that there was no incompatibility between the position of scientists who had evidence that Native Americans came to North America across the Bering Strait more than ten thousand years ago and the position of Indians who believed that their ancestors arose, fully formed, from a subterranean spirit world. Sokal said that the positions were incompatible, and asked which one was true. His question seemed entirely reasonable, at least until the postmodernists in the audience began to pick it apart.*

"On whose authority should we be forced to ask your question?" someone at the back asked Sokal.

At this, Sokal appeared puzzled, and so Stanley Aronowitz, the City University sociology professor . . . stepped in. . . . "He's asking whether the framing itself is subject to interrogation."

"I don't understand," Sokal responded, a little exasperated. "These are two theories that are mutually contradictory."

"Oh, no," someone else chimed in. "The question is, Should the question be answered?"

Sokal was on unfamiliar ground now, and things were getting worse, because just then Andrew Ross leaned across the table, breaking his brooding silence.

"Why would you choose a question that would put on trial Native Americans?" he said, seizing the upper hand. "Why, then, in a polarizing way, are we asked to decide this question?"

Sokal was interested in an answer to this question. But it was dawning on him that the audience was chiefly interested in questioning the question, and in the questions raised by the questioning—not just about Indians but surely about gravity as well—and if you looked very closely you could see that the little look of mischief in his eye had vanished.

demeaning status of a historical droid, not significantly different from conditioned laboratory rats.

Some postprocessualists point out that the systemic view does not account for the unequal distribution of power within complex societies, then or now–the dominance by specific individuals or small elites, even when some interests are maladaptive for the society at large.

All of the fashionable adjectives . . . contextual, symbolic, postprocessual, and so on . . . are in my interpretation ornamentation for some fundamentally sound recommendations for progress in prehistoric ethnography as part of a scientific cultural anthropology.

Albert Spaulding (1914–1990), archaeologist

The systemic view of human society suggests a coordinated, uniform "organism" responding only to environmental pressures. To many postprocessualists, a society is comprised of conflicting individuals, groups, families, and classes, whose goals are not necessarily identical and whose interests and actions are commonly in conflict with the "adaptive" success and "functional" needs of the cultural system as a whole.

The postprocessual critique shifts the focus to the groups within societies that interact with one another, from the individual and household level through the community and even region. Structured in this way, archaeology views historical change as the result of "external" factors (such as changing environments or population growth) plus various "internal" factors (specifically the relations within and between various social groups). This perspective allows for internal social dynamics as a significant engine of change, rather than merely a passive agent in systemic change instituted from the "outside."

We have met the enemy, and they are partly right.

ANTHONY CAMPOLO

The postprocessual critique rejects the processual emphasis on etic phenomena: Reversing the adaptive stance of processual archaeology, the postprocessual critique is based on a mentalist (*emic*) view of culture, emphasizing the role of artifacts as important symbols of social interaction.

This brief outline sets out some, but hardly all, of the basic premises of the postprocessual critique. Although the distinction between the processual and postprocessual approaches will be discussed in greater detail in subsequent chapters, a few additional points deserve mention here.

Whereas the processual agenda saw itself as an integral part of anthropology, the postprocessual critique argues that because archaeology is uniquely qualified to study material culture, archaeology should be central to a new arena of social theory—quite apart from anthropology. Those involved in the postprocessual critique thereby proposed a rather different academic alignment: *Archaeology is archaeology and archaeology is history—but archaeology is not anthropology.*

The frustrating thing about postprocessual archaeology [is that] it's reptilian. You try and get a handle on it and it's like a snake—it slithers away or changes in color.

MICHAEL BRIAN SCHIFFER, ARCHAEOLOGIST (UNIVERSITY OF ARIZONA)

The postprocessual critique, which is highly critical of middle-range theory building, argues that observations of present human behavior cannot readily be transferred back into the past by reference to any postulated system of laws. The relevance of one observation to another has to be established by a network of local understandings. Another important strand of the postprocessual critique includes explicitly feminist concerns about the past, and how the past has been applied to the present. Feminist critiques played little role in the processual agenda (although they could have).

Postprocessualists are dissatisfied with archaeology's long-term infatuation with matters of subsistence; they suggest shifting focus to look instead at the intrinsic meaning of artifacts and the roles they once played in the social environment. To postprocessual archaeologists, it is the culturally created symbol systems that distinguish human beings from all other creatures.

The central topics of the postprocessual critique—gender, power, ideology, text, discourse, rhetoric, writing, structure, history, and the role of the individual—have come to dominate some areas of archaeology. You should be aware, however, that a large segment of Americanist archaeology continues to pursue the scientific, ecological, and evolutionary agenda of processual archaeology.

Was Adolph Bandelier a Postmodernist?

In the rest of this chapter, we explore how the various processual and postprocessual concerns coexist today within the framework of contemporary Americanist archaeology. Several important points will emerge, one of them being the term *coexist* itself. Modern archaeology is neither fully processual nor completely postprocessual—it is a complex mixture of both. Various archaeologists put the often contradictory pieces together in different ways, but it is clear that mainstream Americanist archaeology draws heavily on both processual and postprocessual inputs. We return to this important point later in this chapter.

You should also understand that both processual and postprocessual concerns have deep roots extending far back in the history of archaeology. In Chapter 2, I presented Heinrich Schliemann as the primary example of archaeologist-as-scientist. Although Schliemann might have seemed to be a curious choice, I deliberately selected him to make one simple point: Working more than a century ago, Schliemann employed all the fundamentals of modern scientific inquiry (at least as they apply to the practice of archaeology). There is a tendency to think that a concern with the proper practice of science in archaeology was somehow invented with the processual agenda of the late 1960s. The truth is that the canons of science were with us long before the new archaeology came along, and Schliemann's single-minded search for Troy neatly illustrates the point.

Now, I wish to draw a similar parallel with respect to archaeology's postprocessual critique. When reading about postmodern, postprocessual archaeology, the temptation is to think in terms such as new, pioneering, trailblazing, and innovative. A certain freshness and spontaneity exist in the postprocessual critique, which has shaken off the heavy-handed materialism that dominated processual archaeology of the 1970s and 1980s.

But caution is required here. Many of the key ideas contained within the various postprocessual critiques have been kicking around archaeology and anthropology for a long time. For instance, as discussed in Chapter 15, the interplay of neo-evolutionism and anti-evolutionism has been part of a major dialogue for a century. Although the formalized postprocessual movement in archaeology has been with us only since the 1980s, anti-evolutionary sentiment in America can be traced to the writings of Franz Boas during the early 1900s.

Just as Heinrich Schliemann illustrated the deep roots of scientific inquiry in archaeology, we now return to another important nineteenth-century archaeologist—Adolph Bandelier—to make a parallel and related point: Many of the essential concerns evident in postmodern viewpoints (at least so far as they relate to Americanist archaeology) have been with us a very long time.

The Delight Makers: Deconstructing the Noble Savage

Bandelier, you will remember from the preceding chapter, was a late-nineteenth-century archaeologist and ethnographer who conducted pioneering research in the American Southwest (and elsewhere). He believed in objective, standardized, and authoritative description. He recognized the value of hard facts and spent much of his career recording such evidence from firsthand archaeological and ethnographic observation. Bandelier was, to be sure, a scientist at heart—a "modernist" in the sense of the discussion earlier in this chapter.

Barbara Babcock, an ethnographer and literary critic, argues that in *The Delight Makers,* Bandelier clearly demonstrates his basic postmodern outlook. Recognizing how little science actually filtered out to the general public, Bandelier was appalled at what he believed to be a "long and popular tradition of ignorance concerning the Native American." Wishing to transcend the world of science and objectivity, Bandelier wrote a novel in which he candy-coated "the sober facts" of Pueblo life into readable fiction, thereby hoping to reach the larger, nonscientific public.

Published in 1890 in both German and English, Die Köshare *or* The Delight Makers *was the first novel written about Pueblo Indians and is still one of the best—and the only full-length—published accounts of ritual clowning. The novel is rarely read . . . and is generally regarded as a quaint, if informative, document in the history of Keresan anthropology.*

BARBARA A. BABCOCK, ANTHROPOLOGIST (UNIVERSITY OF ARIZONA)

Beyond the much-repeated words insatiable, indefatigable, and encyclopedic, it is difficult to characterize either the man or his works. [Bandelier] was a complex and contradictory personality: at once condescending toward the poor benighted savages, while living with and loving them "as a brother," enthralled with the complexities of their culture; at once aristocratic, aloof, and confident, yet extremely sensitive to and desirous of the friendship of others.

BARBARA A. BABCOCK

But in what sense is *The Delight Makers* postmodern?

First is the matter of shifting literary narrative styles and perspectives. Most of *The Delight Makers* uses standard narrative techniques. Bandelier is the all-knowing author who reveals the thoughts of each character, bringing readers into the story through the authorial ability to jump backward and forward at will—through time and through the text. Bandelier drew on his years of firsthand experience in the American Southwest in his lengthy and detailed descriptions of the landscape and ecology. He also included plenty of solid archaeological detail about the ancient sites depicted, drawing directly from his own technical reports. In his introduction to *The Delight Makers,* Bandelier emphasizes the descriptive accuracy of his book. Make no mistake about it, he says, this is not the romanticized American wilderness à la James Fenimore Cooper. This is the *real* American West as personally experienced and related by Adolph Bandelier.

The Delight Makers also contains ample ethnographic description—the social practices, ceremonies, religious practices, beliefs, and customs—all, once again, observed and recorded by Bandelier himself. But when describing the Pueblo people, Bandelier grants himself considerable poetic license. Bandelier steps out of his role as scientific observer to portray Pueblo life from the inside, from the (*emic*) perspective of the participants.

But Bandelier also feels free to interrupt his own story with asides about nature, the human condition, or general characteristics of "The Indian" ("The reader will forgive a digression . . . ," "This tradition was told me by . . . ," and so forth). By jumping in—as first-person author—Bandelier shifts scenes, elaborates on the actors' motives, and makes his own reflexive comments (". . . the title of our story is now before us fully represented, arrayed in its appropriate dress . . .").

Babcock highlights Bandelier's full-blown postmodern penchant for "deconstruct[ing] stereotypes of the savage, past and present. Whatever its faults, all of his work is distinguished by an overriding concern with cultural relationships." In *The Delight Makers,* Bandelier employs both the authoritative tone of the ethnographer and the insider view of the Cochiti Indian. In good postmodern fashion, Bandelier strikes up a dialogue between himself (Anglo-American ethnologist) and his Cochiti friends (the "informants"). At this level, *The Delight Makers* is an attempt to unseat the romantic and inaccurate images of James Fenimore Cooper's "noble savage." Bandelier felt obliged to step out of his role as objective scientist and bring something of the texture and complexity of real American Indian lifeways to the greater American public.

[The Delight Makers] *failed to attract the audience it was intended for, the public at large. . . . Bandelier had taken the adventure out of the Old West; he had written about the enemy, the Indians, as if they were real (that is, white) people struggling in a muddled social world rather than mythical creatures grazing in a long-extinct forest.*

STEFAN JOVANOVICH [INTRODUCTION TO THE DELIGHT MAKERS, 1971 EDITION]

As it turned out, Bandelier's book did not achieve its aim, and Anglo-America would continue to romanticize and fictionalize native people. Even on the eve of Bandelier's death, in 1914, filmmakers would initiate an entirely new, if equally specious, presentation of Native American culture—the Hollywood Indian. Native people still are fighting to debunk and deconstruct some stereotypes of Indian life that Bandelier fought so hard against.

Bandelier: A Nineteenth-Century Scientist "in Full Ritual Undress"

In good postmodern fashion, Bandelier attempted to use his own intimate knowledge of the past to influence the geopolitical landscape in which he lived, to educate the broader public about the "true" nature of Native Americans.

At a deeper level, however, Babcock suggests that *The Delight Makers* did much more. Another side of Bandelier was motivated by affective, reflective concern with himself as observer. He was deeply disturbed by something he saw at Cochiti, and, according to Babcock, *The Delight Makers* was his attempt to "come to terms" with the bizarre reality he observed as scientific ethnographer.

Three Koshares at San Juan Pueblo (New Mexico).

Throughout his life, Bandelier was entranced by the "hideous, often obscene clowns or jesters [who] endeavor to provoke merriment by performances which deserve decided reprobation." The so-called *Koshares,* Pueblo ritual clowns, have been maligned and misunderstood by non-Indians since the Spanish arrived in the American Southwest. For years, whenever the general "outsider" perception of Pueblo society emphasized the serious, pacific parts of the culture, the subject of Pueblo clowns was left undiscussed in public. More recent ethnographers describe Koshares as "nearly naked black and white apparitions with corn husk horns, creating a Pandemonium of disorder and delight."

Bandelier was neither the first nor the last Anglo observer to be unsettled by the Koshare, but he was perhaps the most accurate and the most honest.

Barbara A. Babcock

Although he earnestly wished to bring the "real" Indian to the American public, Bandelier did not know what to do with the Koshares he had observed at Cochiti. He was confused by the Koshares and conflicted in his response to them. Year after year, Bandelier returned to Cochiti to observe what he once called those "disgusting creatures . . . in full ritual undress."

Elsewhere, Bandelier would write:

> During [the dancing] the skirmishers kept acting around them. One of [the Koshares], who was particularly fond of rolling in the dust, was at last dragged about and through the lines [of dancers] by his companions till he was completely naked. There an exhibition of obscenity hard to describe took place. [Numerous sexual acts were] performed to greatest perfection . . . to the greatest delight of the spectators (certainly over a hundred), men, women, girls and boys. . . . I was terribly ashamed, but nobody seemed to take any concern about it. . . . The naked [Koshare] performed masturbation in or very near the center of the plaza, alternately with a black rug and with his hand. Everybody laughed. I went home.

Well, white man . . . you think [our ritual] business is vulgar, but it means something sacred to us. . . . If this were evil we would not be doing it. You are supposed to be an educated man, but you better go back to school and learn more about Pueblo life.

Hopi clown responding to an Anglo observer not unlike Bandelier

At once disgusted and intrigued, Bandelier was repulsed by the Koshares and their lewd conduct. In the decades since Bandelier, anthropologists have termed Koshares "among the most powerful of ritual personages, mediating between the worlds of the spirits and worlds of the living." For Bandelier, these scandalous Pueblo clowns destroyed the boundary between sacred and secular, between dignified and obscene. Although he would grant the Koshare

IN HER OWN WORDS

The Multiple Voices of Adolph Bandelier by Barbara A. Babcock

I am getting tired of these many conflicting conventions. In the end, I shall go my own way without consulting anybody at all.

ADOLPH BANDELIER

Bandelier was neither the first nor the last Anglo observer to be unsettled by the Koshare, but he was perhaps the most accurate and the most honest. Given Bandelier's initial reaction to these "disgusting creatures," which was reiterated year after year with every clown performance, one wonders why he gave the Koshare the title role in his novel, or why, given his interest in a scientific rather than a romantic portrait of the Indian, he wrote a novel at all.

*What he never says, but what I would like to suggest is that [*The Delight Makers*] was a 7-year imaginative effort to come to terms with that which was most alien, most other. In contrast to his "scientific" writing, fiction gave him the license to indulge in wish fulfillment, to create a very different cultural world that all the research in the world could not put back together or enable him to enter, and to talk about himself in relation to that Otherness.*

The Delight Makers *is something of a monstrous jumble held together by an authorial presence. Bandelier's basic narrative technique is one of complete omniscience, revealing the thoughts of one character after another, being several places at the same time, and moving forward and backward in time and space. Much of the narrative is composed of third-person description and dramatic dialogue, but the author is not at all adverse to intruding in the first-person plural to shift the scene, comment on the characters, their thoughts and actions, ask a rhetorical question, or make reflexive remarks about his own narrative.*

The Delight Makers's *melange of past and present, them and us, author and audience, art and science in assorted styles and codes culminates in the last chapter in something of a grand finale.*

Fortunately for us, nobody told Bandelier about scientific and novelistic conventions or that his audience wasn't supposed to see backstage. If they did, he ignored them. In contrast to the majority of folkloristic and anthropological studies, here self and work, representation and reflection, fact and fiction, product and process, knowing and being are not separated, but engaged in a continuous dialogue. They always are, in any interpretive act, but given the screens of objectivism that have been thrown up in the years since The Delight Makers, *we are rarely privy to the real process of understanding an Other.*

What is even rarer, given the fact that most interpretations of clowning end up negating their subjects, is that without knowing or intending, Bandelier does what he describes.

*If Pueblo clown performances can be summed up in a few words, they are motley—a comic dialogue constructed of bits and pieces of cultural debris. Like the Koshare, Bandelier is attempting to translate and interpret between worlds and to establish a dialogue between the knowns and the unknowns, be they present or past, self and other, or science and art. [*The Delight Makers*] is as a whole a dialogue, composed of many overlapping and intercalated dialogues, written in a language of motley.*

And, just as a clown performance is an exercise in metacultural commentary and interpretation, so, too, is The Delight Makers, *and part of that story is a deconstruction of the stereotypes of the Indian and of the fictions of ethnographic interpretation.*

Self and Other, after all, are the oldest and most ubiquitous pair of clowns.

BARBARA A. BABCOCK is professor of cultural studies at the University of Arizona.

the title role in his novel *The Delight Makers* (or, in the original German, *Die Köshare*), it is clear–to Bandelier and many others–the Koshares inspired terror and awe as well as delight.

Babcock suggests that Bandelier wrote *The Delight Makers* over a 7-year period of observing, trying to "come to terms" with the Koshares he saw. In his scientific writings, Bandelier remained precise and literal. But in his novel, Bandelier could let his imagination run free, allowing him to confront a fictional Other in a way denied him in the immediate world of Cochiti ceremonialism.

The result, originally written in 1890, is a highly empathetic, postmodern document (see also *The Multiple Voices of Adolph Bandelier* by Barbara A. Babcock).

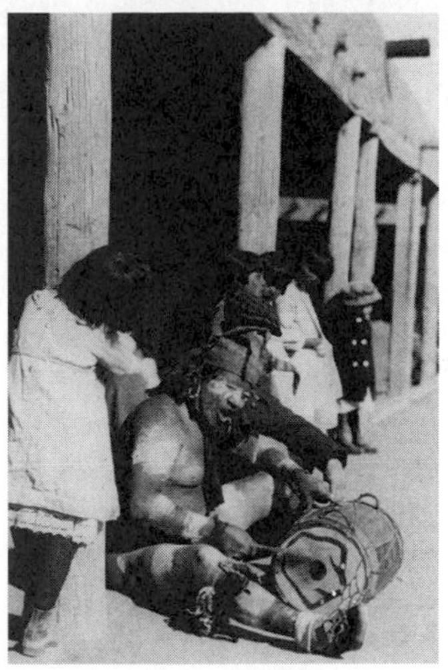

Koshare clown drumming at San Ildefonso Pueblo (New Mexico).

Archaeology at the Millennium: Defining a Middle Ground

Let me close this discussion by emphasizing that the "processual agenda" and the "postprocessual critique" are really polar extremes of a highly complex dialogue about the way in which archaeologists encounter the human past. Much of this chapter tried to show you how the processual agenda and postprocessual critique came to be. Both were historical events, each firmly grounded in specific places and particular times. But, as the examples of Heinrich Schliemann and Adolph Bandelier amply demonstrate, the issues raised by science, humanism, objectivity, and empathy have concerned thoughtful archaeologists for more than a century.

Archaeology is a common theoretical hat-rack for all our parochial hats.

David L. Clarke (1938–1976), archaeologist

The processual agenda was an episode in the history of archaeology that had a demonstrably positive effect on archaeological theory and practice. But it was also characterized by "wretched excesses," as obvious as its accomplishments. Even some of the strongest advocates of processual archaeology recognized the problems of ignoring ideology and of pushing cultural materialism beyond its limits.

Few modern archaeologists seek to reduce the past to the mechanical application of naive positivism dressed up as scientific procedure. Nor do they wish to abandon the criteria of testability and falsification in favor of simple speculations about the unrecorded purposes of knowledgeable actors who participated in a past—or to participate in an archaeology where anyone's opinion is as good as anyone else's. Mainstream Americanist archaeology is proud of its track record of successful research into important segments of the human past. Archaeologists are continuing to employ scientific empirical methods to explain human behavior. But they also understand the importance of forging an empathic linkage between past and present.

There is far greater continuity between processual and postprocessual archaeology than the various proponents, opponents, or commentators on these approaches have yet admitted. . . . Unfortunately, academic disciplines do not always, not necessarily, advance. Sometimes, they get sidetracked or structured around false problems.

Philip L. Kohl

Postprocessual concerns are also with us, but this so-called anarchic vision has generally mellowed. Most advocates of postprocessual objectives today accept the need for scientific procedures, guarded objectivity, and a rejection of the position "anything goes."

Today, it is no longer useful—nor even possible—to sunder Americanist archaeology into such tidy subdivisions. Modern Americanist archaeology is neither processual nor postprocessual: It embodies modified versions of both. The vast majority of those practicing Americanist archaeology fall somewhere toward the middle: There are very few hard-core processualists or die-hard

IN HIS OWN WORDS

On Multiple Perspectives in Archaeology by Robert W. Preucel

Current archaeological research resists being neatly dichotomized into a simple contrast between processual and postprocessual programs. There is a considerable diversity of approaches among practicing archaeologists today. It would seem that part of the postmodern condition is learning how to live with mutually irreconcilable views about the past. This does not imply that there was no real past, but rather that there are multiple perspectives that we can adopt to study the past in the present and that the perspectives that we favor depend upon our specific research interests. Our interests may be to explain change in prehistoric diet by measuring the ratios of different isotopes in bone, to understand the shifts in production and social organization in terms of structural transformations in material culture, or even to expose the cultural biases that we bring to our interpretation through a critique of ideology. Each of these approaches can and should have a place within a scientific archaeology for the simple reason that they make qualitatively different kinds of contributions to our knowledge base. To borrow a metaphor from the philosopher Charles Sanders Peirce, a strong archaeology is one that weaves different theoretical perspectives into a multistranded cable that can be used to join the past to the present in meaningful ways.

ROBERT PREUCEL is an associate professor of anthropology at the University of Pennsylvania.

I have always regarded a materialist outlook as being more productive of an understanding of human behavior than any other approach. . . . Yet I have never found that ecological determinism, neo-evolutionary theory, or cultural materialism provide satisfactory explanations of the full range of variation found in human behaviour or of the various complexities of concrete sequences of cultural change. Throughout my career I have sought to reconcile a materialist approach with efforts to account for the historical diversity that characterizes the archaeological record.

BRUCE TRIGGER, ARCHAEOLOGIST (MCGILL UNIVERSITY)

postprocessualists around these days. Processual and postprocessual archaeologies are better understood as complementary and mutually reinforcing.

Archaeologists are today wrestling with several questions: To what extent do we "discover" an objective past? Or are we "creating" alternative pasts from the same data? What is the proper mix of humanism and science in archaeology? What social responsibilities does the archaeologist have to properly use the past in the present? Each of these questions has been around since Bandelier's day, and no clear-cut resolution appears on the horizon.

For years, archaeology has been buffeted by a number of "theoretical schools," each claiming for itself a privileged status in defining what constitutes adequate explanation in archaeological research. Much of the so-called communication consists of polemical claims to pioneering and exclusive sources of truth. Today, mainstream archaeology has tired of such claims to the "exclusive" highway to truth.

At present, most archaeologists share a dissatisfaction and discontent with the current state of archaeological theory and practice. No grand theoretical synthesis has emerged to replace the extremes of the processual agenda or the postprocessual critique. Instead today's Americanist archaeology is best characterized by multiple paths toward understanding the past. There is simply too much theoretical diversity; too many approaches are being applied in the attempt to understand the human past. This isn't bad, just difficult to characterize.

Maybe, as archaeologist Robert Preucel has suggested, this may simply be the result of the postmodern condition—learning to live with mutually irreconcilable views about the past (see *On Multiple Perspectives in Archaeology* by Robert W. Preucel).

"The Literature" of Archaeology and How to Use It

PUBLISH, v. In literary affairs, to become the fundamental element in a core of critics.

AMBROSE BIERCE, JOURNALIST AND WRITER

In this book, I attempt to provide a succinct, up-to-date synthesis of Americanist archaeology, drawing here and there from my own experience. But no single archaeologist knows more than a fraction of what's significant through firsthand involvement.

This is why we have "the Literature"—the books, journals, bulletins, essays, reports, and newsletters that contain our collective wisdom about the past. Each of us learns by reading what others have done (as you are doing right now). This is why scholars are told to "publish or perish." This is why my employer, the American Museum of Natural History, tells me, "It's not science until it's published." This is why to accuse an archaeologist of "not knowing 'the Literature'" is to deliver a telling blow indeed.

"The Literature" of science can be overpowering, and even veteran scholars despair at the avalanche of new journals and alternative publication outlets springing up each year. The *New York Times* estimated recently that 40,000 scientific journals roll off the presses annually, inundating the scientific readership with more than a million new articles. The *New Republic* magazine—using the term *publishing mania*—estimates that sociologists alone generate more than 2,400 articles each year. Recent surveys show that the majority of scientific articles go virtually unread. Even more alarming are signs that time-honored quality controls in science are breaking down as tales of research fraud and deception haunt current headlines.

As in the scientific world at large, contemporary archaeologists face a dilemma: Whereas we all rely on the printed word, none of us can read everything (or even most things). The problem is doubly difficult for students, who must not only learn the archaeology but also learn how to learn the archaeology. Anyone serious about understanding contemporary Americanist archaeology, however, must soon leave the relative comfort of the textbook to encounter "the Literature." Rather than clutter the text with specific citations, I have a bibliographic essay for each chapter. These essays are grouped together toward the end of the book. Here, I acknowledge the key sources on which my discussion is based and provide a selective guide to additional relevant material, both classic and contemporary. Where appropriate, I have annotated and rank-ordered the list. Consulting some of these primary published sources and searching for the newer information available on the Internet is the best way to learn more about what archaeology is and what archaeologists do.

SUMMARY Archaeological theory is defined at three basic levels. *Low-level theory* involves the observations that emerge from archaeological fieldwork; this is how archaeologists get their "data," their "facts."

Middle-level theory links archaeological data with the human behavior that produced it. Such theory is required to move from the archaeologically observable (the "facts") to the archaeologically invisible (human behavior in the past). Middle-level theory building involves both methodological and substantive applications. Methodologically oriented research programs include *archaeological experimentation* and *ethnoarchaeology;* in both cases archaeologists observe how certain ongoing behaviors are translated into the archaeological record. Middle-level theory building also involves *substantive applications to the past,* as when archaeologists apply principles drawn from general theory to explain specific datasets from the archaeological record.

High-level ("general") theory provides the overarching framework for understanding the human condition. General theory applies to intellectual inquiry in general; it is not specific to archaeology. General theory attempts to interrelate concepts, not account for specific observations. In this sense, general theory is somewhat akin to a religious creed or dogma because it can never be directly confirmed or falsified. This is why theory at the general level is sometimes called a "research strategy." This chapter explored the two major research strategies in modern Americanist archaeology: the processual agenda and the postprocessual critique.

Chapter 4

Doing Fieldwork: Surveying for Archaeological Sites

X never, ever marks the spot.

INDIANA JONES (IN INDIANA JONES AND THE LAST CRUSADE)

PREVIEW Now the fun begins. In the next three chapters, you will get a glimpse of what it's like actually to do archaeology. For many of us—myself included—fieldwork is why we became archaeologists in the first place. This said, there are two important warnings that every introduction to archaeological field technique should begin with:

- There is no "right" way to look for and excavate sites (but there are plenty of wrong ones).
- Nobody ever learned how to do proper archaeological fieldwork from a book (including this one).

Despite recent advances, archaeological fieldwork remains as much craft as science. All we can do here is to look at some common techniques, some archaeological standards and conventions, and, perhaps most important of all, what it feels like to participate in an archaeological exploration.

Every archaeologist addressing a general audience will, sooner or later, be asked the same question: How do you find your sites? *How do you know where to dig?*

There are as many answers as archaeologists. Some **archaeological sites** have been known for centuries—they were never lost. The mythical locations of other sites have been handed down through the generations, preserved in oral and written traditions. For example, the site of Tula in northern Mexico was finally identified as the prehistoric Toltec capital by tracing and testing Aztec traditions. Sites are sometimes deliberately discovered in large-scale systematic surveys, during which entire valleys or islands are scanned for the remains of previous habitation. But some of the best archaeological sites in the world were found by accident. Hard work and luck help, too.

Archaeological site: Any place where material evidence exists about the human past. Usually, the term *site* refers to a concentration of such evidence (although an isolated artifact find is sometimes called a "site" as well).

Here, we will explore some of the ways to find sites. Where possible, we let archaeologists speak for themselves about their own experiences. Many archaeologists—and, once again, I include myself here—feel that it's much more fun to find the sites than it is to dig them. To see what archaeological survey feels like, take a look at *What Archaeological Survey Was Like in 1907,* by A. V. Kidder, and *Finding a Place to Dig—That Old "MacNeish Luck,"* by Scotty MacNeish.

IN HIS OWN WORDS

What Archaeological Survey Was Like in 1907 by A. V. Kidder

In the first chapter, we mentioned Ted Kidder's baptism into Southwestern archaeology. Here is Kidder's own account of the way in which he and two fellow Harvard undergraduates were instructed to conduct their archaeological survey through the mesas and canyons of the Colorado Plateau:

Thursday, July 4th [1907]: Up, as usual in this country at four, to take advantage of the delicious hours of the early morning and forenoon. At ten or eleven the heat of the day comes on and lasts till after four. We pitched our tent, as this is to be our headquarters for some time, unpacked our duffle-bags and with Mr. Hewett started up the mesa that separates the canyons of the McElmo and the Yellow Jacket. It is usual, he told us, to find sites on mesas that overlook the junctions of important drainages, so we walked out along its flat sage-brush covered top. Near the tip we found a partly fallen zig-zag wall set with a tower. It extended clear across the mesa, defending the end. Mr. Hewett predicted a pueblo on the protected tip and, sure enough, this lay a bit further out. It was entirely gone except for the butts of a few walls.

My diary says very little of what we look out upon. I think I was dazed by that view, my first of such a vast desolation; naked red rock below and all about, mesas, pinnacles, ragged canyon walls, sheer cliffs. I must, too, have been a bit overcome by what Mr. Hewett so casually told us we were to do. He waved an arm, taking in it seemed, about half the world, "I want you boys to make an archaeological survey of this country. I'll be back in three weeks."

So much for explicit research designs (but they sure did find plenty of neat new sites).

Archaeologists are the cowboys of science.

Bumper sticker spotted outside archaeology meeting in Albuquerque, New Mexico

Twenty-year-old Ted Kidder (right) and Jesse L. Nusbaum conducting an archaeological survey at Mesa Verde (Colorado) in 1907.

Good Old Gumshoe Survey

It's not what you find, it's what you find out.

David Hurst Thomas

Let me begin with a brief recap of my own experiences in finding Gatecliff Shelter, Nevada. In several places throughout this text, we will return to excavations at Gatecliff as an example of how Americanist archaeology actually

IN HIS OWN WORDS

Finding a Place to Dig—That Old "MacNeish Luck" by Richard S. MacNeish

See first of all, and argue afterwards.

Jean Henri Fabre (1823–1915), entomologist and naturalist

When I began to organize my thoughts about survey techniques is difficult to pin down exactly. . . . I spent that first season in Mexico in Tamaulipas (1945–1946) mainly on reconnaissance. I can't remember thinking very profoundly about what I was doing, but I must have learned how to do something right for I did discover over two hundred new sites. Probably it was during the 1949 cave digging season in the Sierra de Tamaulipas that I began to think about my technique for finding good preceramic sites, in Meso-America. Gradually, however, it occurred to me that the reason I was being so successful was that I was constructing hypotheses about ancient settlement patterns, subsistence systems, and paleoecologies and then testing these hunches in the field by good hard survey work—which meant not only looking where I thought a site might be but also checking areas where our hypotheses indicated that probably there were no sites. For example, I speculated that in the dry Canyon Diablo sites from preceramic food collection times were probably to be found near water sources—ancient or modern—high enough above them to stay out of the way of flash floods (thus above the high terraces) but not so high that the inhabitants could not get to the water source in a half-hour or less. Survey showed that open sites in this position were most often on the high terraces at potential game crossings, game lures (springs or salt licks), game lookouts, or some other special spot, perhaps where wild foods could be harvested. Often even if there were no bare ground showing artifacts, I did a little digging just to test my hypothesis. About half of the time I found sites.

Even better than the open sites were cave sites in a similar position. Because of the hypothetical seasonally nomadic nature of the ancient inhabitants, caves were likely to be stratified with layers of one occupation on top of previous ones. I also learned to predict which kinds of caves in these strategic positions probably had plant preservation, deep stratigraphy, and abundant artifacts. I had to take into account such factors as the size and shape of the cave and ask whether the back sloped downward in such a manner so that there would be more deposits the deeper one dug; whether the roof was blackened by fire; whether the cave faced away from the direction from which the storms came; what kinds of artifacts and how many occurred on the talus slope; whether the cave floor soil was dry and ashy; whether there were stalactites or stalagmites or other evidence of water in the cave. Thus the "MacNeish luck" in finding good caves was, in fact, not luck at all.

Richard S. MacNeish is director of research at the Andover Foundation for Archaeological Research.

---

works in practice. But before we could excavate Gatecliff, we had to find it. And the process of discovery is what this chapter is all about.

And luck does play a very large part in the life of an archaeologist.

Ivor Noël Hume, archaeologist (Colonial Williamsburg Foundation)

My experiences at Gatecliff Shelter are probably typical of contemporary Americanist archaeologists. We found Gatecliff through a fortunate combination of happenstance, hard work, and trial-and-error. James O'Connell calls the process "gumshoe survey," probably because such rudimentary archaeological reconnaissance closely resembles detective work: Set out a problem, get some leads, track them down, and, if you're fortunate, you crack the case. In archaeology, "cracking the case" can mean turning up just the right site to answer a question that's bothering you. This is precisely how we found Gatecliff Shelter.

At the time, I was a graduate student at the Davis campus of the University of California, supporting my doctoral fieldwork by conducting archaeological field schools. We offered green, untrained students the chance to join our fieldwork in the Reese River Valley of central Nevada. The students paid for the summer's research through their enrollment fees. They also supplied the physical labor. In return, I taught them what I could about archaeological fieldwork. The trade seemed fair enough. I progressed in my doctoral research, and they acquired training and credits toward graduation.

The summer was taken up doing "systematic archaeological survey," a technique we discuss later in the chapter. Basically, it involved mapping and collecting archaeological stuff from the ground. While the so-called "surface survey" was going well, it was necessary for us to check our findings against the kind of data you get only from excavating buried sites, such as caves or deep trash deposits. Although we tried everything, we never could seem to find good places to dig. It was frustrating.

As it turned out, we eventually found exactly what we were looking for—a very deep cave site with great stratigraphy and plenty of archaeological stuff buried inside; we called it Gatecliff Shelter. And while I would love to tell you about the elegant research strategy we designed to find Gatecliff, the truth is that we just lucked into it.

But it's still worth telling the story, I think, because it illustrates the way that great archaeological sites are found—as windfalls for those fortunate enough to be in just the right place at the proper time. It also helps to know what you're looking for.

So here's how we found Gatecliff Shelter.

At the end of our first field session in Reese River, we assembled the crew for steak dinners in the nearby town of Austin (Nevada). In the high desert, "nearby" meant taking a dusty ride for an hour or more, but the push seemed worth it. We relaxed, gnawed T-bones, and spun rattlesnake and stuck-truck stories into the morning hours.

Austin is a pocket-sized Nevada mining town with fewer than 250 citizens, a picturesque little desert dive, which has attracted its share of attention. In his epic journey across backroads America, *Blue Highways* author William Least Heat Moon wrote, "I liked Austin . . . a living ghost town: 40 percent living, 50 percent ghost and 10 percent not yet decided."

But above all, Austin is small-town America, and when two dozen grubby archaeologists come to town for steaks and beverages, word soon gets around. When our waitress politely inquired who was in charge and somebody pointed to me, she told me about her husband, a mining geologist who had prospected the Western mountains for 40 years. There are few places Gale Peer had not been. So when we met, I asked him about any archaeological sites he might have seen. We were hoping to find a local cave or rock shelter with some stratified cultural deposits, in order to check our Reese River findings.

The simplest way to find sites is to ask somebody who knows where they are. . . . Be aware that the most important sites are not found by archaeologists at all—instead they are found accidentally by farmers, quarrymen, construction workers, or aerial photographers.

PAUL BAHN, ARCHAEOLOGIST

Mr. Peer indeed knew of such a cave—over in Monitor Valley, a dozen miles east of Austin. He had not been there in years, but the details were fresh in his mind. "You take the main dirt road south in Monitor Valley, then turn west, up one of the side canyons. I don't remember which one. As you drive along, oh, let's see, maybe ten or fifteen miles, there's a large black chert cliff. It goes straight up. A thousand feet or so. At the bottom of the cliff is a cave. Some time, a long time ago, the Indians painted the inside of the cave. There are pictures of people and animals, plus a lot of writing I don't understand. Top of the shelter's caved in. Maybe in an earthquake. There's not much of the cave left. Drive out there when you get a chance.

I'd like to know what's in that cave." He sketched a map on his business card. He remembered exactly where the cave was relative to the canyon, but he was not sure exactly which canyon. I stashed the card in my shirt, and thanked him for the tip.

Simply walking around the countryside in the hopes of stumbling on an archaeological site is good exercise, but the rewards are likely to be small unless the searcher knows what to look for and approximately where to find it.

IVOR NOËL HUME

This is the essence of gumshoe survey—just hanging out in bars and gas stations, listening to those who know more about the landscape than you do. I hoped that Mr. Peer's advice was as good as his memory seemed to be. Maybe this was the deep cave site I'd been looking for. But of course I had heard of a dozen similar caves, all of which proved uninteresting when investigated.

The season ended, the students went their various ways, and I resumed my graduate studies. But throughout that academic year I kept remembering Mr. Peer's cave. At times I felt like dropping everything, hopping into a pickup truck, and taking off for Monitor Valley. But the classroom sometimes seems to get in the way of an archaeological education, and my graduate student commitments kept me from breaking away, even for a weekend. Besides, I consoled myself, the mountains of Monitor Valley reach 11,000 feet, and the October snowfall can last until late spring. Even if I knew where it was, the cave would probably be snowed in until May. So I plugged along, working on the summer's artifacts, every now and again reflecting on a make-believe cave somewhere in the Nevada backwoods.

Summer finally arrived, and once again I rounded up undergraduates to help out at Reese River. With the necessary state and federal excavation permits in hand, we drove to central Nevada, scouting out new campsites and hoping to find the cave that Mr. Peer had spoken of nearly a year before. We knew that the rock shelter must be in a canyon—but which one? We had 15 canyons to choose from.

Beginning at the southern end of Monitor Valley, we drove up and down each side canyon, working our way slowly northward. The roads were rough, and the weather was no ally. We were snowed into one campsite for 3 days—and it was June! Then the sun showed up and melted the snow, washing out the only road. At times it took all our concentration to remember why we were there.

Still, there was this cave. . . . Mr. Peer seemed too astute a geologist and observer of nature simply to have imagined a rock shelter covered with prehistoric paintings, and we kept looking. Each canyon had potential. We would see something, stop the truck, skitter up the hillside. But each time, it turned out to be a shadow, an abandoned mine shaft, or just a jumble of boulders. The cave with its rock art eluded us.

After a week of this we came to Mill Canyon, just the next one on the list, with no greater potential than the previous 10 canyons we had combed. The road was a little worse than most, and we had to inch down a steep ridge into the rocky canyon. Even in four-wheel drive, our truck lurched downslope, on a path so steep it seemed barely glued to the mountainside. Finally, as we started up the flat canyon bottom, a brooding black cliff loomed ahead. The scarp was riddled with small caves and rock shelters.

Gatecliff Shelter (Nevada) as it appeared when first recorded in 1970.

And sure enough, the caves were empty, unless you counted the occasional coyote scat, owl pellet, or packrat midden. The cliff face was nearly a half-mile long, and we became more and more discouraged as we moved upcanyon, scanning each small alcove for pictographs. Finally, only one section remained to be inspected, where the black cherty formation was swallowed up beneath the alluvial Mill Canyon bottomland. We saw a dim shadow near the bottom, but a dozen similar shadows had been just that—shadows.

The paintings were not visible until we crawled into the mouth of the cave. There they were, just as Mr. Peer had said a year before: small human figures, painted in red and yellow pigments. On the other wall were cryptic motifs in white and black. And, yes, the roof had caved in years before. Half the floor was buried beneath tons of chert. One boulder would have dwarfed the pickup we had left in the canyon.

I scoured the shelter floor, looking for artifacts, animal bones, pieces of basketry. Anything. But no matter how hard I looked, there was nothing remotely suggesting that prehistoric people had lived here. We had the rock art, of course, but pictograph caves sometimes have no habitation debris at all.

Retrieving some digging gear from the truck, we carefully excavated a small test pit in the floor of the cave. Old World archaeologists sometimes call these exploratory excavations *sondages.* I always like the ring of that word—what class. In Nevada, we just call them test pits. Anyway, we set out a small square, 50 centimeters on a side, and I scraped away the rocks and rat dung with my favorite Marshalltown trowel. An old-time archaeologist once told me about digging in a cave just like this. "It smelled brown," he recalled.

We dug through the afternoon, taking notes and measuring artifacts. We finally stopped armpit deep when I could no longer reach the bottom of the test pit. It was a pretty meager haul: several pieces of broken bone, a few of them charred, and a dozen stone flakes, probably debris from resharpening stone knives or projectile points. Not exactly treasure, but we knew that at least one prehistoric flintknapper had paused here to ply his craft. Still we were disappointed. The rock art already spoke of the occasional prehistoric visitor. We were looking for something more.

Across the sagebrush campfire that night our small crew assayed the finds. The rock art was neat; only two similar sites were known in the central Great Basin. The stones and bones were suggestive enough, but the shelter seemed hardly the deep site we had hoped for all year. The deposits were maybe 2 or 3 feet deep, and the strata probably jumbled. People had most likely dug storage pits, cleared bedding areas, and scooped out fire hearths in there for centuries. It probably had stratigraphy like most desert caves, so jumbled that they looked as though they had been rototilled. At best, our test pit results were borderline.

As it turned out, we were wrong about this site, which we eventually called Gatecliff Shelter, after a local geological formation. The site came to dominate my archaeological life for more than a decade. The prehistoric deposits were not a few feet deep, as I had initially thought. Gatecliff turned out to be 40 feet deep, maybe the deepest rock shelter in the Americas. The strata were also not mixed as I first feared. Over the millennia, the shelter had been inundated every so often by flash floods. The surging waters laid down thick layers of mud, forming an impenetrable cap of rock-hard silt. This flooding occurred at least a dozen times, stratifying the deposits into horizontal "floors."

Gatecliff had what textbooks—including this one—describe as "layer-cake stratigraphy." The shelter had been occupied for much longer than the past few centuries, as I had thought at first. Gatecliff was old, at least 7,000 years

Robert Bettinger trowel-excavating in the first test trench at Gatecliff Shelter.

old, as radiocarbon dating would later establish. The sediments also contained ample evidence about the past environments of Monitor Valley.

After I began working at the American Museum of Natural History in New York City, I convinced the museum to dispatch five major field expeditions to Gatecliff Shelter. More than 200 people helped excavate the site over the years. The National Geographic Society supported part of the fieldwork and prepared an educational film about the site. The society also wrote a book about our excavations at Gatecliff. The *New York Times* and *The New Yorker* magazine published stories about Gatecliff. Then there was television and radio. Even a United States congressman became involved in the struggle to preserve the site. Gatecliff Shelter was decidedly on the map.

And that was how we found it. Our experience was not unusual. Many of the archaeological sites discussed in these pages were found in just this manner. Throughout the various chapters on fieldwork, several seasoned archaeologists will share briefly their experiences doing archaeological survey: Florence Hawley Ellis on her experiences digging in Chaco Canyon in the 1920s; John Hyslop surveying the 14,000-mile-long Inka road; Ted Kidder on his first archaeological survey in the American Southwest; Scotty MacNeish looking for caves in Mexico. Although their experiences were as different as they could be, they all illustrate how archaeologists find a place to dig.

Archaeology Is More Than Just Digging Sites

Gatecliff Shelter turned out to be a marvelous place to dig (and we talk about those excavations in Chapter 6). MacNeish found some extremely important buried cave deposits in Mexico, and his excavations there are detailed later. Even the rough-and-ready survey by Kidder and his young colleagues recorded some sites that, once excavated, would prove critical in our understanding of Southwestern archaeology.

We are as much gainers by finding a new property in the old earth as by acquiring a new planet.

Ralph Waldo Emerson (1803–1882), essayist and poet

But as John Hyslop worked his way along the Inka Road, he wasn't looking for a place to dig. Although excavation would have been possible at many of the places he recorded, Hyslop knew that his Inka Road survey would, in itself, produce a huge quantity of valuable details about ancient road

IN HIS OWN WORDS

Exploration Archaeology on the Inka Road by John Hyslop

No archaeologist can ever organize a completely prepared expedition to survey an Inka road. The uncertainties lend spice to exploration archaeology, and from them arise some of the survey work's greatest rewards as well as headaches.

JOHN HYSLOP

Five hundred years ago, the Inka Empire—precontact America's largest state—was welded together by a massive road system more than 14,000 miles long. As the Inka Empire extended its authority over millions of subjects, most of them had seen firsthand one or more of the fabled Inka roads. The Inka Road was their bond to the authority of the state, an overwhelming and enduring symbol of this highland Andean empire. The road network was stupendous, one of Native America's greatest achievements.

Until recently, our knowledge of Inka roads was largely anecdotal. Even the most scholarly considerations were written by those who had spent little time "on the road," maybe occasionally walking a readily accessible splinter of the road or sometimes glimpsing longer stretches through the window of a four-wheel-drive vehicle—but little else.

Such was the state of knowledge until the late John Hyslop came along. Hyslop initiated his Inka Road Project as a concerted attempt to document in detail this remarkable archaeological feature. Over the years, Hyslop personally covered about 5 percent of the known Inka road system—no easy feat, considering its length.

Here, let us listen to the measured words of an archaeological veteran who spent years of his life experiencing the Inka Road—up close and very personally.

John Hyslop and his team surveying a broad stretch of the Inka Road.

The objective of the Inka Road Project was to survey a number of road segments throughout the Andes to collect comparable data on many aspects of the road system—among them, the nature and placement of roadside sites, environmental effects on trajectory, and the types of road construction. For some scholars, this scope was disturbingly wide. The scheme's strong point was that it allowed an archaeological survey to establish a data bank about many parts of the Inka road system, which, in its entirety, is far too large for any individual to see even over a lifetime.

The broadly based field data are perhaps the greatest strength of the project. On the other hand, the desire and need for a large sample of Inka roads was the project's greatest weakness when funds were sought to finance it. More than one referee opposed funding, judging it impossible to carry out a project over such a broad area. The panel of the National Science Foundation *denied funds to the project on this basis and recommended "a very intensive study" in "a small region where preservation of provincial construction is good." The panel's well-intentioned advice reflected the position that an archaeological project by defin-*

building and engineering: evidence of building and maintaining bridges, location of trailside shrines and storage areas, artifacts associated with various stretches of road, variability in width and grade, and so forth. In fact, Hyslop wrote an important book, *The Inka Road System,* based strictly on his survey results–without ever digging at all.

This is an often forgotten point about archaeological reconnaissance. Sometimes archaeologists survey to find good places to dig (this is why we *ition takes place at a specific site, or within a limited geographic area. It is noteworthy that the majority of support came from sources where no panel of archaeologists was used to judge the potential of the project, but rather where one person was struck by the project design's uniqueness and was willing to bet that an unusual project might have special results.*

One of the most important decisions of the preinvestigation preparations concerned what form of transportation would be used. In general, the use of four-wheel vehicles for road survey is impractical since they usually cannot go where the Inka roads go. They are utterly useless on the steep gradients of the Andean slopes and are too wide for the narrow passages found on the many road segments with earth slides and eroded surfaces. Vehicles were used only where the Inka road passed over flat, hard-surface terrain (the Atacama Desert and the high plateau of Lake Titicaca).

Expeditions in the Andean highlands or slopes used pack animals. If possible, horses and mules for riding were rented; when they were unavailable, the archaeologists walked and donkeys carried the gear.

Expeditions in highly indigenous areas of the Andes probably could not function well without coca leaves, since giving them is a common and expected form of gratitude for help or favors. Also, expedition participants found the leaves' gentle effect a pleasant relief when climbing at high altitudes.

Most archaeologists are trained with an anthropological perspective. Their lack of historical training often causes considerable deficiencies when they investigate protohistorical remains such as those of the Inka Empire. They have difficulties in locating and evaluating the related evidence from the early historical sources, and even have difficulties reading sixteenth-century Spanish. Road survey should not be attempted by archaeologists who are unwilling to become part-time historians.

The modern scientific training received by archaeologists has probably never been better. However, with it has come a lack of respect for the achievements of some of the explorers and travelers of the past several centuries. A general ignorance or disregard of earlier descriptive sources has led many modern archaeologists to claim discoveries, or miss discoveries, that were already reported decades ago.

I have been surprised how few North American or Andean archaeologists have any solid training in expedition techniques. Even archaeologists with years of fieldwork experience have rarely if ever undertaken exploration work in truly isolated areas. Exploration archaeology cannot be learned from most archaeologists. One must seek out people who have traveled over long distances in isolated areas.

Successful expedition archaeology requires that local guides and communities be treated with the utmost respect. Without their aid, most expeditions in isolated areas could not be successful, since these people supply the animals, knowledge of the route, and often the lodging. The local peoples' tendency to be generous with their time and liquor, particularly with the arrival of archaeologists from far away, tends to hinder the objectives of the survey. The ability to decline or manage festive hospitality and diplomatically to proceed with the work is one of the most important arts of successful Andean survey. It cannot be learned from books, and is sometimes risky business.

JOHN HYSLOP (1945–1993) was a senior scientific assistant at the American Museum of Natural History.

were looking for a place like Gatecliff Shelter). But in many other cases, the archaeological survey is an end unto itself, a way of generating important archaeological data on a regional scale. In the following sections, we will examine a few ways developed by archaeologists to systematize the survey process. As you will see, sometimes archaeologists can learn a great deal without ever having to dig at all.

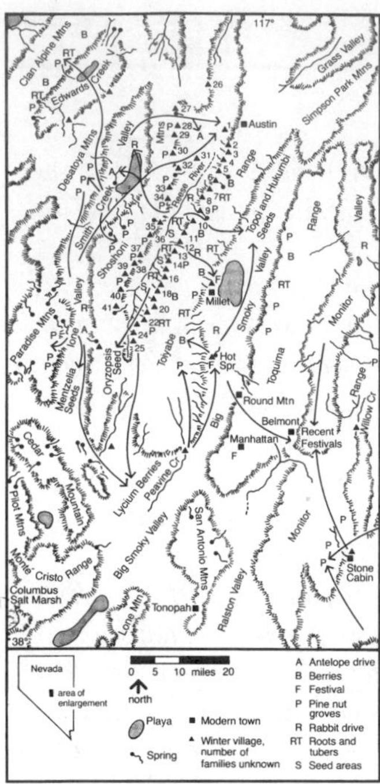

Julian Steward's reconstruction of the seasonal round of the Western Shoshone and Northern Paiute people (Nevada), projected for the mid-nineteenth-century period.

The Fallacy of the "Typical" Site

We have seen the various ways in which culture can be viewed. Although "shared culture" is useful for defining time-markers, the modal definition of culture has some severe limitations. Taking something as "modal" or "typical"—be it an artifact, a cultural component, or an entire site—is a dangerous practice, and this is why many archaeologists today are employing the systematic regional survey as a way of understanding the overall range of variability in the archaeological record—not just focusing on the "normative" or "typical."

To see why this is so, take a look at the graphic rendering of the seasonal round of the Western Shoshone and Northern Paiute people of the central Great Basin. This map, produced by ethnographer Julian Steward, charts the cultural landscape of these people who survived by collecting seasonally ripening plant foods, supplemented to some degree by hunting.

This ecological adaptation depended on a meticulous, exacting exploitation of Great Basin microenvironments. Because they practiced no true agriculture, the Shoshone and Paiute people traveled from one habitat to another to harvest the local wild crops as they became available. Nuts of the piñon tree, a staple Shoshonean resource, ripened in the late fall and often provided enough food for the winter. Buffalo berries and currants also became available in the low foothills about this time. Indian ricegrass seeds were usually ripe during the summer months, and so camp was moved from the piñon forest to the flat valley floor in late spring. Many other local foods were utilized in the same cyclical fashion. Because of their intimate relationship with the natural environment, the Western Shoshone and Northern Paiute people were able to work out a solid economic subsistence cycle from these resources.

Look closely at the pattern for the Reese River Valley, near the top of the map. The numbered triangles in the Toiyabe and Shoshone ranges are winter villages, inhabited seasonally to exploit the ripening piñon nuts. Other kinds of sites (denoted by letters) occur lower, along the Reese River, and these localities were established in the summer to gather seeds and roots and to catch rabbits and occasionally hunt antelope. Satellite sites were established for ceremonial purposes and, in the upland areas, to gather berries and hunt bighorn sheep.

This reconstruction is based on what Western Shoshone and Northern Paiute people told ethnographer Steward between 1925 and 1936. Because most of the mapped sites had been abandoned sometime in the nineteenth century, Steward's informants were often recalling events that had not occurred for 50 years. Yet despite the large amount of information that was irretrievably lost, a staggering amount of complexity remained, and the figure demonstrates how intricate and complex a seasonal round the native people had actually practiced.

You can observe a lot just by watching.

Yogi Berra (1925–), baseball player and coach

This map also illustrates the *fallacy of the typical site.* Suppose that an archaeologist had the opportunity to locate and excavate just one of Steward's Western Shoshone sites. Which one to choose? Winter village sites are of interest because they represent the lengthiest occupation and probably contain remains of a great variety of activities. But winter village sites are almost always located on windswept ridges, and all that is preserved are stone tools and ceramics.

Or would it be better to seek out one of the small upland shelters where hunters briefly camped while pursuing bighorn sheep? The preservation in these shelters is often good, and the chances are excellent for finding remains of sandals, snares, and even pieces of bows, arrows, and fire-making apparatus. But these small shelters represent only a minor portion of the overall Shoshone pattern. Women were probably not included in such small hunting parties, and men conducted only a limited range of activities. Perhaps one might choose to excavate a seed-gathering camp, an antelope drive, or a place where women gathered lycium berries.

The difficulty is clear: No matter which site is selected, a great deal will be missed. No single Shoshone site is sufficient to demonstrate the total range of cultural variability. One cannot just dig here or there, because there is no typical site.

Let us take this difficulty one step farther. Suppose you decided to excavate a piñon-gathering camp in the Toiyabe Range. You would probably end up reconstructing a lifeway like this:

- The economy of that site was based on harvesting piñon nuts.
- The camp contained between one and two dozen people.
- The men made lots of stone tools and repaired their weapons.
- The women spent a great deal of time collecting piñon nuts and preparing them into meal, sewing hide clothing, and making basketry.

These inferences are all quite likely, given the enormous amount of ethnographic information available about Shoshone lifeways, and the strong connections between the ethnographic and archaeological records in this part of the world. You are probably correct, based on what you excavated.

But now suppose that I decided to conduct some fieldwork of my own in the same area, but chose to excavate the scene of a *fandango* (or "festival," denoted by "F" on Steward's map). My reconstruction would probably suggest a grouping of 200 to 300 people who subsisted on communal hunting of jackrabbit and antelope, and who spent a great deal of time dancing, gambling, and "living off the fat of the land." And, based on what we know about Western Shoshone lifeways, I would be correct as well.

In other words, you would have reconstructed a hardworking society composed of small social groupings (extended families), whereas I would have seen a more exuberant society living in large aggregations and particularly concerned with rite, ritual, and feasting.

In truth of course, both kinds of sites were produced in the course of a single year, as part of the seasonal round of the Western Shoshone people. The point is simple: Neither site can be taken as typical.

The remainder of this chapter will discuss the modern methods by which contemporary archaeologists deal with the variability evident at the regional level.

The Importance of Surface Archaeology

Traditionally, archaeologists anxious to examine past adaptations have attempted to find deep, stratified sites with a high degree of preservation. Caves such as Gatecliff Shelter and the Mexican sites excavated by MacNeish are particularly fruitful in this regard. Plant and animal remains can be carefully excavated and analyzed using methods discussed in Chapter 11.

But archaeologists do more than dig deep sites. Archaeology is where you find it, and many archaeologists are looking to the ground surface itself as an important source of information about the past. In some places, important archaeological remains have simply lain on stable ground surfaces rather than becoming buried by sand, silt, and gravel. In regions that have been spared the plow, archaeologists have the unparalleled opportunity of collecting artifacts literally where they were dropped, often thousands of years ago.

Not only do those surfaces offer the possibility for studying ancient lifeways, but they also represent adaptations different from the more traditionally excavated sites. Surface sites were once largely ignored, as they lacked the contextual relations (stratigraphy) necessary for establishing cultural chronologies. But time–space sequences, while always important, are only part of the puzzle. Surface sites provide unique data regarding past human–land relationships. In the next section, we consider briefly the surface archaeology of the Reese River Valley in central Nevada, an illustration of how archaeologists have approached their survey data from a regional perspective.

Surface Archaeology at Reese River

Earlier, I mentioned fieldwork at Reese River that ultimately led to the discovery of Gatecliff Shelter. At the time, we were conducting a regional randomized sample of the surface archaeology evident at Reese River. Let me explain a bit more about that project, because it illustrates a very different approach to archaeological field reconnaissance.

In the late 1960s, computer hardware was complicated and cumbersome. Archaeologists were only beginning to think about applying computers to archaeological problems. We had decided to investigate the Western Shoshone seasonal round—the one discussed earlier.

This seasonal round required the aboriginal groups to schedule their itinerary to exploit locally varied flora and fauna. But this relatively high mobility created an archaeological record that was extensive—distributed mostly as surface scatters rather than as buried, stratified deposits. Before we could take to the field, it was necessary to consider more closely how such an archaeological record was formed and what it should look like when encountered. To do this, we developed a computer simulation predicting the archaeological record of this area. This simulation projected a series of archaeological expectations for the Reese River Valley. Then, instead of looking for a couple of sites to excavate, we developed a way to sample the entire region.

The mere formulation of a problem is far more often essential than its solution.

Albert Einstein (1879–1955), physicist

Predicting artifact distributions in the archaeological record is tricky business. Rather than attempting to deal by hand with all the variability involved, we programmed a relatively primitive computer to take the ethnographic data, monitor projected environmental variations, and then predict attendant artifact frequencies across the landscape.

Without going into the details of the computer simulation—which today is badly outdated—let me just explain briefly what we were trying to accomplish. First, we marshaled all the environmental data we could find regarding the behavior of wild plants and animals, and then coded these data for input into the campus mainframe computer. We then wrote a FORTRAN program with our interpretation of how the historic-period Shoshone collected wild plants and hunted animals.

The computer constructed an imaginary (mathematical) archaeological record. The computer told us that if the weather were just so, if the plants responded in a certain way to this weather, if the Shoshone gathered certain plants and killed certain animals, then their archaeological sites should look like this. In effect, we programmed a computer to project what it could about extinct Shoshone cultural ecology, ultimately translating these findings into things that archaeologists could recover in the field.

Thus we had some hypotheses based on the extensive ethnohistoric documentation of the Western Shoshone people. But was this documentation accurate? Did it tell the whole story? Had different patterns existed prior to Euroamerican contact? How had subsistence patterns changed over the long term?

Now it was time to test these notions against some archaeological field data. This is what we were doing when we found Gatecliff Shelter—spending 6-week summers climbing 12,000-foot mountains and walking along saltbrush flats looking for archaeological artifacts. We were trying to see whether the ethnohistoric documentation, translated through a computer simulation, had indeed succeeded in forecasting the archaeological record.

Wanted: Some Relevant Archaeological Data

So here is the question: We had projected what the archaeology of an entire valley should look like. But how do you dig an entire valley?

The answer to this question is twofold, and the first part is easy: You don't dig at all. Because so many sites in the Great Basin are not buried and because this is a desert where the vegetation is sparse, most things lying on the surface can easily be seen as you walk along. All you need to do is to spot them, plot their location in your fieldnotes, and pick them up.

So, once we recognized the importance of surface archaeology, the task became one of defining a workable strategy for doing archaeology without digging. To be relevant to our questions, the archaeological data must satisfy three basic criteria.

First, all elements of the annual round must be represented; it is not enough to generalize from a single site. Because these people moved from place to place every year, information from any single site (even a place like Gatecliff Shelter) can tell only a small part of the story.

In addition, the area to be surveyed was huge, and we could not hope to survey an entire seasonal round. So we needed to sample. But capricious and biased sampling can lead the archaeologist astray in assessing the significance of the various sites. We felt that the single best way to ensure unbiased results in such situations was through judicious use of *probability sampling theory.*

To conduct such a probability sample, you first choose the *sampling elements* that are the objects of study. In many cases, these elements are archaeological sites, in the traditional sense. All these elements taken together form a set of all possible elements, the *sampling universe.* Each element is assigned a consecutive number from 1 to *N,* and the numbers are randomly selected so that each has an equal probability of selection, $1/N$. In this manner, a subset, called the *sample,* of the *N* elements is chosen, so that each member of the universe has an equal chance of inclusion.

In addition to providing relatively unbiased samples, randomized procedures have the added benefit of providing data that can be analyzed statistically. On the other hand, because statistical analysis generally requires a random sample, archaeologists who accept a biased sampling design will immediately and unnecessarily tie their own hands.

Finally, the research design must provide for meaningful *negative evidence.* In addition to telling archaeologists what activities took place, such data must indicate which activities did not occur in a particular area or biotic community. The requirement for negative evidence, only recently recognized as relevant to archaeological research, imposes severe yet necessary qualifications on fieldwork.

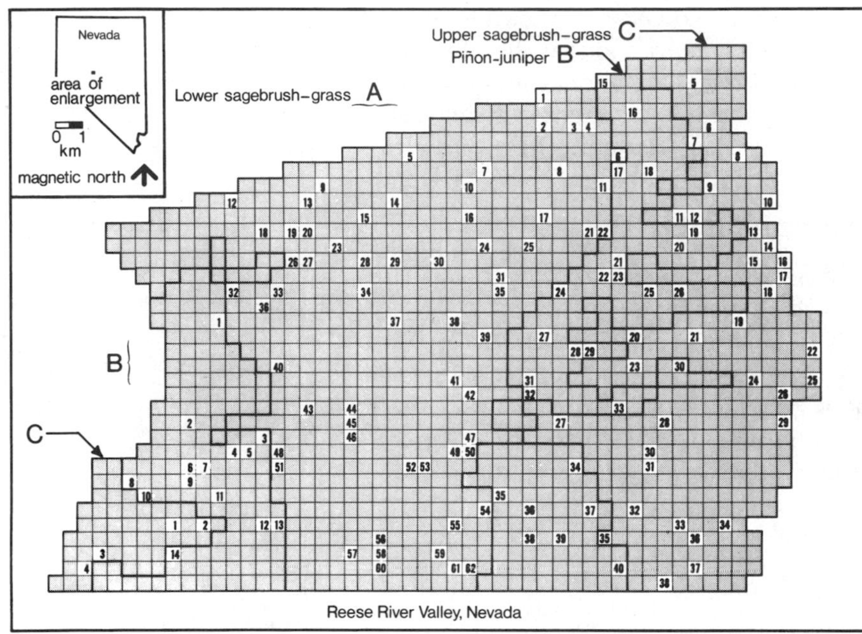

Grid sampling scheme for the central Reese River Valley *(Nevada). Each square is 500 meters on a side; a 10 percent random sample was surveyed in the field.* Note *each of the three major "strata," which correspond to modern plant communities.*

An Appropriate Research Design

We selected the upper Reese River Valley of central Nevada as the area that best satisfied the preceding prerequisites. The Reese River is a lazy little stream less than 15 feet wide, which originates about 40 miles south of Austin, Nevada. Flowing northward between the Shoshone and Toiyabe mountain ranges, the Reese finally empties into the Humboldt River. The valley itself is about 15 miles wide and more than 100 miles long. For survey purposes, a cross section was selected to provide a suitable universe, which, you will remember, ought to enclose roughly the area of an annual seasonal round of the historic Shoshoneans. The overall study area comprised a tract of land about 15 miles wide by about 20 miles long.

The valley floor in this area lies about 6,500 feet above sea level and is at present dominated by sagebrush shrubs. The piñon-juniper belt, so critical to winter forage, starts at about 7,000 feet and reaches 8,500 feet elevation, covering the low flanks of the mountains. Thick stands of buffalo berries, currants, ricegrass, and a host of other native foods also grow in the montane forest belt. Above 8,500 feet, trees yield again to low sagebrush. The mountain peaks, some of which tower over 11,000 feet, are tundralike, practically devoid of vegetation. A riparian zone consisting of willow, aspen, and cottonwood is found along all montane streams, as they gradually wind their way toward the Reese River.

These life zones of the Reese River Valley were clearly defined and easily discerned in the field. Four life zones were isolated for study: lower sagebrush-grass, piñon-juniper, upper sagebrush-grass, and the riparian zone, including both upland stream margins and the immediate vicinity of the Reese River.

The real challenge was to design a field strategy fitting our minimum requirements. Note first that Steward's ethnographic summary of historic period settlement pattern for Western Shoshone people basically avoided the site concept entirely; Steward spoke of gathering areas, hunting areas, pine nut groves, and so forth. Following Steward's summary quite literally forced us away from the traditional concept of the "archaeological site" and toward a so-called "nonsite" sampling strategy.

This "nonsite" imperative became the first major requirement of the research design. At the outset, we had some problems with logistics, figuring out exactly how to go about the actual sampling. We had been heavily influenced by Lew Binford's early work, which demonstrated the advisability of probability sampling at the regional level. But "advisability" is one thing, feasibility is quite another. At the time, I could find no substantive application of such regionwide sampling that actually put Binford's ideas into practice.

After considerable experimentation in a barley field near Davis, California, we found that 500-meter quadrats were relatively easy to plot on the ground and then to search for archaeological remains. Thus the 500-meter square formed the observational sampling unit of the Reese River survey. This turned out to be a fortunate choice and has proved to be relatively useful throughout much of the Desert West and elsewhere. In areas of higher artifact density, the size of the quadrat can be reduced.

These considerations in the early phases of the Reese River research led us to devise a *nonsite stratified quadrat approach* to sample design. The study area (termed the *universe*) is selected to include an entire seasonal round. In the central Great Basin, this universe is a single valley system, situated between the north-south mountain ranges.

The universe is then gridded into a series of large squares (*tracts*), which are each considered as a sample element. Every tract will be completely searched for all visible remains of prehistoric subsistence activities. In this case, archaeological sites per se could not serve as elements, because we did not know beforehand how many of what kinds of sites were involved in this particular valley. This universe was circumscribed on aerial photographs and divided into about 1,400 tracts, each of them 500 meters (about one-third of a mile) on a side. Each tract was numbered, a slip of paper with each number dropped into a hat, and a 10 percent random sample was selected. Each

Science is nothing but perception.

PLATO (427 B.C.?–347 B.C.?), PHILOSOPHER

tract was considered as a sampling element in this study. Economic considerations—time and money available, scope of the project, estimated unit variability, and so forth—determined how many tracts can be selected. The sampling fraction is expressed as n/N.

The actual fieldwork consisted of locating each of the 140 tracts of the sample on the ground and then surveying the entire 500-meter square for signs of human occupation. All artifacts and waste chippage, whether an isolated find or part of a dense concentration, were mapped, cataloged, and collected. The most efficient survey unit was a team of six archaeologists, mainly instructors and students from the universities of California (Davis) and Nevada. Each crew could survey one or two such tracts daily, depending on accessibility and local terrain. This sampling design minimized bias by forcing archaeologists to look in *every* topographic locale, even those unlikely to have archaeological remains. It is not enough to say that people could not possibly have lived in a particular situation, for such statements are colored by the archaeologist's preconceived ideas and are unacceptable in scientific research. The random survey established (within statistical sampling error) precisely which types of localities were or were not occupied, with little bias or ethnocentrism involved.

Generating the Data

The Reese River fieldwork took about 4 months to complete, with a field crew varying in size from 23 to 45 people. Approximately 3,500 artifacts were recovered from the surface of the 140 tracts. But we still had amassed no data—what we had were just objects. The *data* were generated by observing a large series of attributes on each artifact, which were then computer-coded and analyzed (by criteria explained in Chapter 9).

The primary aim of the analysis was to evaluate the presence of consistent artifact assemblages that corresponded to the ancient exploitation of the life zones. Areas of extensive hunting, for example, were expected to exhibit a distinctive assemblage: spent projectile points, butchering tools, and flaking debris resulting from resharpening rather than from primary artifact manufacture. Habitation areas, on the other hand, ought to have reflected residential activities such as tool manufacture, clothing preparation and repair, and cooking; they should have had remnants of house foundations, campfires, ritual paraphernalia, and the like. These projections were based on the available ethnographic and historic documentation, but the middle-range linkages were tentative and not as well defined as one might wish.

Results at Reese River

Still, based on the randomized fieldwork and analysis, we attempted a first-order synthesis of the archaeology of the Reese River Valley for the past 7,000 years. In a strict sense, the Reese River ecological pattern held only for the Reese River locality, but further research at Gatecliff Shelter and elsewhere in central Nevada confirmed that these patterns existed well beyond the survey area.

The Reese River settlement pattern contained two major areas of residence. The *shoreline settlements* consisted of a series of large sites located at permanent water sources within the lower sagebrush-grass zones. The artifact assemblage suggested that the economic focus was on the wild grass and root crops that ripen in the late spring and early summer. These shoreline settlements consisted of massive linear scatters of artifacts—often a couple of miles long—that paralleled the flowing water. In this context, the "site" was anywhere along the river or stream, for no specific village areas were consistently reoccupied. These campsites were probably situated near scattered caches of harvested summer seeds, and the only structures were mere brush windbreaks and sunshades. The waste chippage indicates that much of the stone tool manufacture took place in the summer camps. The seed diet was doubtless supplemented by rodents and rabbits, both of which could be easily hunted on the nearby flats.

The other primary focus of habitation, the *piñon ecotone settlement,* was located in the dense stands of piñon and juniper trees, generally on long, low ridges that finger onto the valley floor. This "edge effect" is a rather common ecological adaptation that allows exploitation of dual life zones—in this case, the piñon belt and the nearby valley floor. These sites are also linear scatters of artifacts and chippage, but unlike the shoreline settlements, the piñon ecotone sites consisted of more densely concentrated artifact clusters. Potential areas of habitation were more limited than those along the river, because only a few suitable flat-topped ridges exist in the area. The piñon sites were occupied just after the fall pinecone harvest and only if the nut crop of the immediate area had been successful. In other years, the winter village had to be relocated to some more distant portion of the forest where the piñon nuts were available. The artifact inventory of these sites indicates that most hide preparation and clothing manufacture took place during the winter encampments. Deer and mountain sheep probably supplemented the diet of piñon nuts. Houses consisted of domed wickiups, sometimes surrounded by stone circles and covered with piñon tree bark or juniper boughs. These houses were often placed in shallow pits up to 18 inches deep. Although only about five families could live on each ridge top, there might have been several such villages within a one-mile radius.

In addition to the habitation sites, the remains of several special-purpose localities were mapped. On the flat valley floor several butchering assemblages were recovered (knives, scrapers, and resharpening flakes), apparently resulting from communal hunting of both jackrabbits and antelopes. Scattered about in the same area were additional artifacts (knives and grinding stones) that resulted from the women's seed-gathering forays. Evidence was also recovered that suggested that deer and mountain sheep were hunted in the piñon belt and also in the high, more barren mountains that flank the Reese River. All these *task-group assemblages* represent short-term, ancillary subsistence activities undertaken by small groups of relatives working out of the more permanent habitation sites.

Some Implications

This extended example has been presented as a case study to show how archaeologists, working at a regional level, attempt to reconstruct an extinct lifeway. The initial step was to establish a local cultural chronology and then to impose the chronological controls necessary for further investigation. Some

The Global Positioning System: A New Way for Archaeologists to Find Themselves

A nifty new piece of technology is revolutionizing the way archaeologists conduct site surveys. The *Global Positioning System* (GPS) is a space-based way to find out—very quickly and very accurately—where you are standing on the surface of the earth. This is particularly important if you are standing on an archaeological site because you can then plot the site's precise position.

This has not always been possible. In doing our survey in the Reese River Valley, for instance, we spent much of our time trying to find out where, exactly, we were. In setting up our 500-meter squares, we established a *datum* corner by estimating our position on aerial photographs, then using a Brunton compass mounted on a photographer's tripod and chaining the quad boundaries with 100-meter ropes. This system was not only cumbersome and time-consuming, but it was also misleading. We lost much of our alleged accuracy when transferring distance from the aerial photographs to the uneven ground surface. The Reese River Valley is an extremely vertical place, and some of the 500-meter grids covered nearly a kilometer in elevation. So what were we measuring: 500 meters along the actual ground surface or 500 meters as measured on an aerial photograph?

GPS technology has changed all that. A simple hand-held unit—costing less than $500—now provides 24-hour, three-dimensional positioning to suitably equipped users anywhere on or near the surface of the earth.

The GPS consists of 24 satellites (21 active and 3 spares) that circle the earth in 12-hour orbits, evenly distributed around the earth at an altitude of about 11,000 nautical miles. These orbits repeat the same ground track (as the earth turns beneath them) once each day. Each satellite carries a computer and a very accurate atomic clock.

The Master Control facility, located at Falcon Air Force Base in Colorado, calculates each satellite's orbit a week or so into the future, predicts various ionospheric conditions over that time, and then uploads this information into the satellite's computer. This way, the satellite can tell where it is in the sky at any given microsecond during the week. It transmits its position and the current time continuously.

The GPS receiver held by somebody—in this case, an archaeologist on the ground—listens to signals from either three or four satellites at a time and triangulates a position fix using the interval between the transmission and reception of

specific research objectives were then outlined and an archaeological strategy framed to gather the relevant data. In the Reese River case, the more conventional approach of excavating a few large stratified sites such as Gatecliff Shelter would not have answered the questions under consideration. A research design based on the systematic random sampling of an entire valley was therefore devised (see *The Global Positioning System: A New Way for Archaeologists to Find Themselves*).

The regional approach did indeed shed light on past human adaptations in the Reese River Valley. But as happens with all such fieldwork, many additional questions were raised. We began by assuming that the prevailing cultural and environmental chronologies were essentially correct. Although this assumption proved generally true, the Reese River work highlighted the need for finer-grained chronological studies, based on stratified site excavation. This is why we dug Gatecliff Shelter.

The settlement patterning observed in Reese River also raised the question of regional variability. And throughout the 1970s, we conducted a conthe satellite signal. Any given receiver tracks more satellites than are actually needed for a position fix. Thus, if one satellite becomes unavailable, the receiver knows exactly where to find the best possible replacement.

The Global Positioning System is funded and controlled by the U.S. Department of Defense. Although thousands of civilians also employ GPS throughout the world, the system originated, and continues primarily, to provide continuous, worldwide position and navigation data to the U.S. and allied military forces. But legitimate commercial and scientific applications were recognized early in the system's development, and it was decided to allow free access to GPS signals within certain constraints.

GPS receivers are capable of providing position information with an error of less than 25 meters. But this accuracy is normally "degraded" to about 100 meters due to so-called Selective Availability (which should really be called "Selective Unavailability"). This prevents any hostile military power from using the GPS as a free, super-accurate, preinstalled targeting computer. The U.S. military "dithers" the satellites by inserting random errors into the information being broadcast. Such Selective Availability is normally on, but was switched off during the Gulf War and during the invasion of Haiti (presumably because the military didn't have enough military receivers to go around).

If more mapping accuracy is required, then signals arriving at your receiver can be compared with signals received simultaneously at another location whose exact coordinates are known. The difference between these two sets of data—known appropriately as "Differential GPS"—yields a location accurate to within 0.5 meter to 20 meters. Even greater accuracy—to within one centimeter—is possible by further analyzing the satellite message after capture.

Beyond its obvious archaeological implications, GPS technology has already found many new applications in the everyday world. By combining GPS with current and future computer mapping techniques, we will be better able to identify and manage our natural resources. Vehicles are already being manufactured with navigation systems that allow the driver to avoid congested freeways and find more efficient routes. Ship and airline travel is becoming safer because of the enhanced navigation in all weather conditions.

siderably more comprehensive program of regional archaeology in the vicinity of Monitor Valley and Gatecliff Shelter. Also because of lessons learned in Reese River, we realized the importance of setting up a middle-range research framework, to understand the processes through which the archaeological record of such areas is created. In the next stage of work at Monitor Valley, considerable effort was spent looking at formation processes and middle-range research.

Some Sampling Considerations

The archaeological fieldwork at Reese River depended heavily on the theory of random error, so we should now look at such considerations in more detail. Archaeologists are becoming more and more aware of how important it is to think through their sampling procedures. They have always dealt with

GPS on the Internet

An Overview of GPS is provided as part of The Geographer's Craft, Department of Geography, University of Texas, Austin:
http://www.utexas.edu/depts/grg/gcraft/notes/gps/gps.html

Frequently Asked Questions About GPS:
http://vancouver-webpages.com/peter/gpsfaq.txt

samples, of course, but the recent trend has been toward drawing samples in accordance with the accepted principles of probability. Several sources discuss archaeological sampling procedures, and the discussion here is intended only to highlight some of the more important aspects.

The first key sampling concept is that of population. In general usage, *population* refers to a group of living organisms of a single species that is found in a circumscribed area at a given time; this is a biological population. Cultural anthropologists also commonly use the term *cultural population* to denote a specific society, and archaeologists are often heard speaking of "ancestral Pueblo populations" or the "Shoshone-speaking population." Proper sampling, however, requires that we adopt a more restricted statistical usage for the term *population.*

Statisticians use the term *population* to refer not to physical objects (people, lemurs, or artifacts) but, rather, to observations made on these objects. The difference is both subtle and important. Shoshone Indians could comprise a biological or sociocultural population, but they could never be a statistical population. Only a set of related variates—such as stature, body weight, daily caloric intake, or presence of the Rh blood factor among Shoshone Indians—could comprise a statistical population. A **statistical population** consists of an arbitrarily defined set of observations of interest. Statistical populations thus differ from "populations" in the common usage.

Statistical population: A set of counts, measurements, or characteristics about which relevant inquiries are to be made. Scientists use the term *statistical population* in a specialized way (quite different from "population" in the ordinary sense).

Some populations may consist of a finite number of variates, such as the stature of all living Shoshone Indians. But population can also be defined to include not only the stature of all living Shoshone but also of all Shoshone who lived in the past, and even of those who will live in the future. So populations can also be infinite. It would be troublesome indeed for an anthropologist to attempt to interrogate, measure, observe, or photograph the entire physical population of living Shoshone. And if the statistical population were defined to include Shoshone of all times and all places, complete observation would be impossible. Because of this, most statistical populations are incompletely observable: Physical anthropologists can never hope to measure the cranial capacity of *Australopithecus robustus,* and archaeologists can never measure the length of every Clovis point.

This is why archaeologists nearly always deal with samples. A *sample* is defined as any subset of a statistical population, whether randomly, haphazardly, or capriciously selected. The objective behind probability sampling is to obtain samples that were selected from the statistical population with a known probability.

No single best way exists to select a sample, as too many practical and logistical matters enter into the decision. In the Reese River example, the physical population included 1,400 tracts of land, each of which was 500 meters on a side. Each tract contained archaeological objects, and each of the archaeological objects could be observed in a number (an infinite number) of ways. Thus in the single physical population, we could define an infinite number of statistical populations. This is why it is important to specify the research objective before taking the sample.

One objective at Reese River was to find the density of archaeological objects, say, projectile points, such as are discussed in Chapter 9. Because it was impractical to find the density of points in each of the 1,400 squares, we elected to measure that density in only 140 squares and then to extrapolate to the entire statistical population. Such an estimate can be unbiased only if it is taken from a sample in which every element had an equal probability of selection. In this case, the probability of selecting any individual tract was exactly 1 to 1,400.

Nonsite Archaeology: Up the Creek Without a Site?

Relatively little archaeology had been done in the central Great Basin when we began working there in the 1960s because archaeologists had not yet come to grips with the predominantly nonsite character of such regions. True, we spent a decade digging Gatecliff Shelter in this area, but even this 40-foot-deep site had very little potential based on its surface appearance. Spectacular dry caves and Early Holocene lakeside occupations are rare, and the multiroom pueblo is absent. In part because of this, some of archaeology's most desirable artifacts—basketry, fluted points, and painted pottery—are almost nonexistent in this area. By mid-century standards, this area seemed to have very little archaeological potential, particularly because archaeologists were trapped in the pervasive site-specific mind-set.

Still, this area is extremely rich in prehistoric archaeological remains. But these assemblages rarely occur in buried contexts, and they are rarely concentrated in convenient "sites." Most artifacts are simply lying on the surface, and, until recently, archaeologists thought they were important only as signposts for places to dig, as a way to prospect for the "real" archaeology.

Precisely the same assemblages can be considered from a site-specific context, a nonsite context, or (preferably) from both perspectives. Only the research framework differs. Gatecliff Shelter—an archaeological "site" in the conventional sense—illustrates this point.

And yet for many purposes, Gatecliff Shelter is not a site at all. More realistically, Gatecliff is a composite of 16 relatively independent sites that happen to be stacked one on top of another, inside a chert and dolomite overhang in Mill Canyon, Nevada. Had each horizon been deposited as a surface scatter, several—but perhaps not all—would undoubtedly have qualified as sites by the traditional definition (which is, admittedly, fairly arbitrary).

So what is Gatecliff Shelter: 1 site, 10 sites, or 16 sites?

Today, we realize that the archaeological record need not simply be viewed as Easter eggs, scattered about the landscape awaiting discovery. For administrative purposes, Gatecliff can be viewed as a single site. In terms of cultural chronology, it is convenient to think of Gatecliff as one site within which six millennia of human prehistory are recorded. But in spatial analysis on a regional scale, it is much more useful to isolate horizontal segments of Gatecliff Shelter as analytical units. It is irrelevant whether or not these subsegments are themselves sites.

Nonsite archaeologists did not invent a new archaeological record—the objects and their contexts remained the same. What distinguished nonsite archaeology from its more traditional site-specific counterpart was the modification of the archaeologist's perspective. Rather than recovering archaeological objects from 10-centimeter levels inside 1-meter excavation squares, the *nonsite* perspective began to perceive pattern and process on a scale of kilometers and hectares.

Plow zone: The upper portion of a soil profile that has been disturbed by repeated plowing or other agricultural disturbance.

Archaeologists have also come to realize that **plow zones** can contain significant spatial information, even after repeated plowing. Archaeological data generated from surface and plow zone assemblages can (and do) provide systematic, quantifiable information at both local and regional levels. As we shall see later, such data can point to growth patterning within sites, identify discrete areas of activity, and distinguish places where people lived from places used only during daytime. Combined with excavation-derived data, "surface" materials can contribute to our understanding of changing land use patterns through time, dating components across entire regions and determining intrasite relationships.

The problem was the concept of the archaeological site. For years, "sites" remained unchallenged as primary existential entities. They had always been archaeology's "proper" units of observation. But over the past two decades, several archaeologists have begun to question seriously whether the site is really a useful abstraction. *Surface archaeology* has become a respectable venture, and archaeologists have developed a body of powerful techniques to cope with this record. Correspondingly, the concept of *nonsite archaeology* is now widely used around the world.

How to Find a Lost Spanish Mission (Part I)

Having discussed the importance of the nonsite concept, let us return to the issue of archaeological sites and how to find them. In the following example, I want to tell you something about Mission Santa Catalina, a site lost somewhere in Georgia's Sea Island for more than 300 years. I had the good fortune of leading the team that rediscovered this lost Franciscan mission. The story of how we did it shows yet some other ways that archaeologists are learning about the archaeological record, this time drawing on space-age technology.

Aerial view of St. Catherines Island *(Georgia).*

But first, a word of background about this little-known chapter of American colonial history. At its seventeenth-century zenith, Spanish Florida had three dozen Franciscan missions, each a satellite settlement heavily dependent on the colonial capital at St. Augustine. To the west lived the Timucuan, Apalachee, and Apalachicola Indians; to the north, toward St. Catherines Island, lay the province of Guale. Although a dozen sixteenth- and seventeenth-century missions once existed in the present state of Georgia, not one such mission site had been identified archaeologically when we began our search for Santa Catalina.

Like many historians and archaeologists before us, we felt that the lost mission of Santa Catalina lay along the western margin of St. Catherines Island, a 1,400-acre tract 50 miles south of Savannah. Unique among the so-called Golden Isles, St. Catherines Island has not been subdivided and suburbanized. The Georgia-based, not-for-profit St. Catherines Island Foundation owns the island and strictly regulates a comprehensive program of research and conservation. This enlightened and progressive land management policy ensured that Mission Santa Catalina was not destroyed beneath the crush of condos and fast-food joints that typify too many of the southern barrier islands.

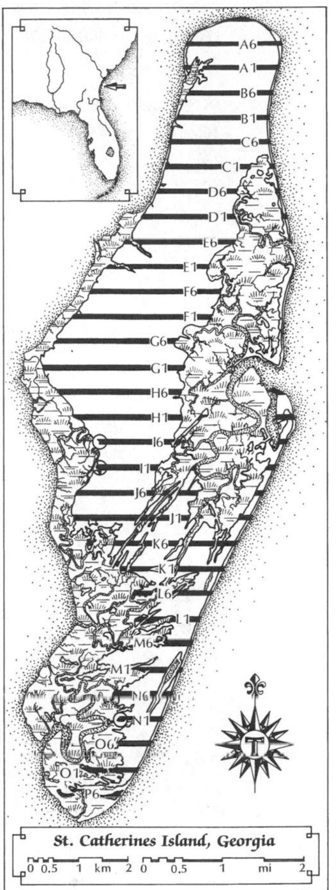

Systematic transect research design used to derive a 20 percent regional randomized sample on St. Catherines Island (Georgia). Occurrences of sixteenth- and seventeenth-century Spanish ceramics have been circled.

A Randomized Transect Approach

In 1974, when I first visited St. Catherines Island, the combined French, English, and Spanish historic documentation supplied only vague geographic clues; and although several first-rate archaeologists had previously worked on the island, none had successfully located this important mission site.

Virtually uninhabited, St. Catherines Island is today blanketed with dense forest, briar patches, and almost impenetrable palmetto thicket. When we began our search for Santa Catalina, I was overwhelmed by the huge area involved. We knew so little that I could not overlook any portion of St. Catherines Island.

By its nature, archaeological fieldwork is slow and tedious—and nobody could (or should) excavate an entire island—so we began by random sampling. Using the same theoretical base employed in our Reese River samples, we worked out a method requiring that the archaeological team walk a series of 31 east-west transects, each 100 meters wide. Our crews attempted to follow a specific compass heading without deviating from the survey transect. This randomized approach forced us to look into the most unlikely, inaccessible places (even when we didn't expect to find anything).

Taking a lesson from statistical survey theory, we began our search by random sampling. Using a *transect sampling strategy,* we took a 20 percent randomized sample of the archaeology of St. Catherines Island, looking for, among other things, the lost mission of Santa Catalina de Guale.

Theory is fine, but practical random sampling in archaeology is hardly easy because it forces you to look in the most improbable, difficult places. Such fieldwork is much like the old "beeline hike" I learned in Scouts: Follow your compass heading, and walk through, over, or under any obstacle. If a tree lies across your path, go over it. If you run into a palmetto and briar patch, crawl through it. No need to worry about yellow and black spiders hanging from the live oaks (it's uncool to gag or squeal while inhaling a web). And don't give rattlesnakes and cottonmouths a second thought (that's why we gave you the snake guards). And above all, do not divert from your transect.

Systematic archaeological survey on St. Catherines Island (Georgia).

Our survey turned up 135 mostly unrecorded archaeological sites, ranging from massive shell middens to isolated shell scatters. We investigated each site with two or more 1-meter-square test units, in all excavating more than 400 such test pits. Viewed from the air, the island began to look like Swiss cheese, except that the holes were square.

Controlled survey sampling told us that sixteenth- and seventeenth-century Spanish ceramics occurred only at 5 of the 135 archaeological sites,

Fieldwork requires both men and women to really get a whole picture.

Ruth Bunzel, anthropologist (Columbia University)

all but one along the western perimeter of the island. The ruins of Mission Santa Catalina almost certainly lay buried in a target area the size of 30 football fields along the southwestern margin of the island.

But 30 football fields is still a huge area to dig with dental pick and camel hair brush. Moreover, although our confidence was growing, we were forced to admit almost complete ignorance of what we were looking for. Did Santa Catalina survive merely as heaps of sixteenth- and seventeenth-century garbage? Or could we realistically hope to find evidence of buried buildings as well? Clearly it was time to scratch the surface.

A Power Auger Approach

Looking around for better ways to find the needle hidden in this haystack, we learned from Kathleen Deagan about her successful search for sixteenth-century St. Augustine. She and her students used a gasoline-powered post-hole digger and excavated hundreds of round holes. Following her lead, we did the same on St. Catherines Island. With this noisy, nasty machine, two people can dig a 3-foot-deep hole in less than a minute. The power auger throws up a neat doughnut of dirt, to be hand-sifted for artifacts (for another application of this approach, see *How Kathleen Deagan Found Old St. Augustine*).

Once the field testing was complete, we identified all materials recovered and plotted the distribution in a series of simple dot-density maps. Since then, a number of readily available computer programs have greatly assisted the data conversion process. But even using the hand-plotted maps, the power auger data allowed us to focus further field evaluation on a single 100-by-100-meter square in the overall sampling grid for St. Catherines Island. Although this area contained absolutely no additional surface evidence to distinguish it from the surroundings, it contained the remarkably well preserved ruins of Mission Santa Catalina de Guale.

In effect, the simple and expedient auger testing narrowed our search area from 30 football fields to a target zone smaller than 3 acres. Although we found broken Guale Indian pottery almost everywhere we dug in that area, diagnostic mission-period artifacts were largely restricted to a single, well-circumscribed area. By 1981, we had defined this 100-meter-square area as the most probable location for the central mission complex.

In the next chapter, we complete the Santa Catalina story by showing how space-age technology helped find the invisible mission site. By using a combination of proton magnetometers, ground-penetrating radar, and soil resistivity techniques, we could pinpoint actual buildings inside the mission complex—before we ever excavated them.

Squares, Rectangles, or Circles: Which Is the Best Research Design?

Archaeologists select their samples by literally dozens of strategies. When we gridded the Reese River area into 500-meter squares, we were using a quadrat sample technique. This method, derived from quantitative sampling in plant ecology, has been used in several archaeological applications.

How Kathleen Deagan Found Old St. Augustine

I do not seek, I find.

PABLO PICASSO (1881–1973),
PAINTER AND SCULPTOR

Working with historians and town planners in 1976, Kathleen Deagan set out to find the exact boundaries of sixteenth-century St. Augustine, founded in 1565. The problem was that St. Augustine had been continuously inhabited since prehistoric times, and the presumed sixteenth-century settlement lay sandwiched between prehistoric occupational debris and four centuries of later debris.

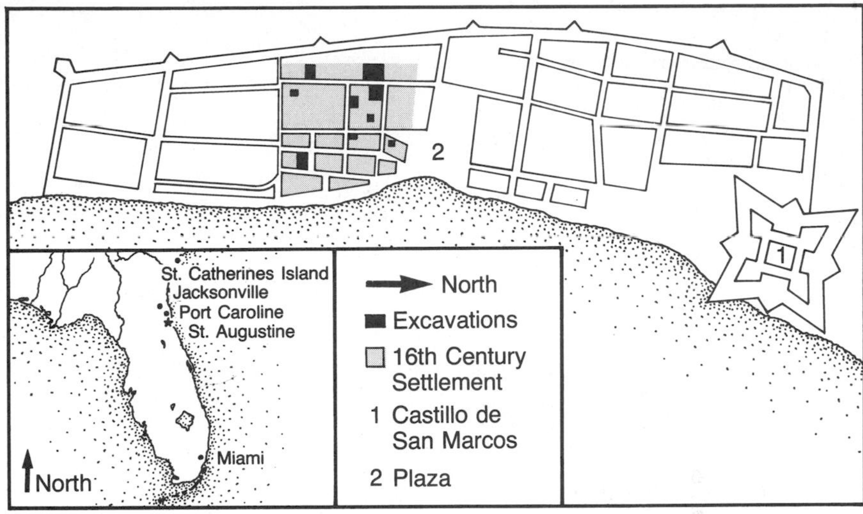

Historical continuity in St. Augustine (Florida). The shaded area shows the extent of the sixteenth-century occupation, superimposed on the street plan of the walled eighteenth-century St. Augustine (which remains virtually identical to that in the city today).

By comparing modern street plans with existing sixteenth-century maps, project historians nominated a nine-block area to the south of the town's central plaza as reflecting the original settlement's layout. Some 600 power auger holes were drilled along a systematic grid throughout downtown St. Augustine to test this hypothesis.

To do this, Deagan used a "modified systematic sampling strategy," in which auger tests were drilled along a 5- and 10-meter grid system, tied into existing street corners. The auger proved a particularly efficient tool for digging through driveways, parking lots, and shell middens. The survey technique was a relatively fast, inexpensive, reliable, and fairly nondestructive method of gathering information needed for the long-term inventory of St. Augustine's cultural and historical resources.

One potential problem was that the presumed sixteenth-century town lay in a highly developed downtown section. Fortunately, St. Augustine is acutely aware of its unique history, and residents were intensely interested in helping to learn more about the "oldest city." The power auger technique was pivotal here, for it caused minimal disturbance to both the archaeological record and the modern citizenry. Nonetheless, gardens and lawns were temporarily uprooted; sections of St. Augustine's streets were occasionally removed; and the local schoolchildren had to give up their playground for a season, giving Deagan and her crew time to test the property.

As it turned out, the sixteenth-century artifacts clustered exactly where the historians had predicted. Deagan then initiated a program of excavation to refine these preliminary town boundaries and to probe the households of the early Spanish settlers as they adapted to life in their New World.

Two archaeologists muscle a gasoline-powered soil auger into the ground, looking for subsurface evidence of sixteenth-century St. Augustine.

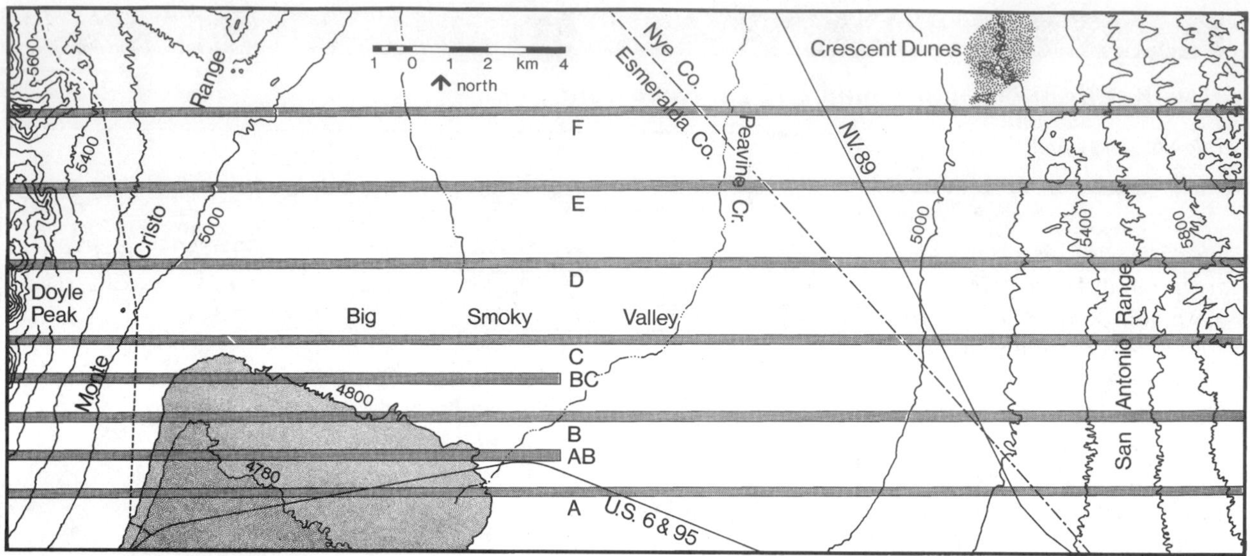

Transect sampling method used at Pleistocene Lake Tonopah (Nevada). Each transect is 150 meters wide, and the shaded portions at the lower left show approximate lake levels during the late Pleistocene period. An adaptation of this survey strategy was used in the search for Mission Santa Catalina.

In describing our search for Mission Santa Catalina, we presented another popular method of archaeological sampling, the transect technique. Instead of using square sampling units, the transect method defines long linear units. Teams of archaeologists can thus survey in long, straight lines. Transect sampling is often easier than quadrat sampling because access time is minimized; the team simply walks from point A to point B without having to travel throughout the region in a checkerboard fashion. There also is some evidence that transect samples tend to be statistically more efficient than quadrat samples.

The map above shows how transect sampling works. In this case, we wanted to find out how archaeological sites were distributed along the margins of Pleistocene Lake Tonopah, about 100 miles south of Reese River, Nevada. Some 12,000 years ago the lake was full, and the shoreline stood at about 4,800 feet above sea level. Presumably, the early inhabitants in this valley would have lived near the beach line. But as the climate became hotter and drier, Pleistocene Lake Tonopah began to shrink. One thing we wanted to learn at Lake Tonopah was how later Paleo-Indian groups changed their settlement pattern in response to the receding beach levels.

Lake Tonopah is now completely dry, and the area could have been gridded and sampled like Reese River. But because we were mainly concerned with the relationship of cultural materials to fossil beach terraces, it made more sense to run a series of east-west transects across the dry lake, laid out so as to intersect the known beach terraces perpendicularly.

The Lake Tonopah example differs in another important way from the Reese River sampling design. You will remember that at Reese River the 1,400 sampling tracts were divided into homogeneous strata (based on modern life zones), and a 10 percent sample was selected within each stratum. Technically speaking, the Reese River design was a *stratified random quadrat sample.* At Lake Tonopah the climate had changed so drastically that contemporary environmental strata were less important, and so they were not included in the sampling strategy.

The universe of transects is really a large series of 150-meter-wide strips running across dry Lake Tonopah because we wanted to obtain an overall picture. For reasons of time and budget we decided to select a systematic sample. A random method of selection would have had us number every strip and then select random numbers to define which strips would become transects in the sample. In a *systematic sample selection,* only the first sampling unit is selected at random, and the remaining transects are chosen at intervals to complete the predetermined sampling fraction. There are statistical advantages and disadvantages to both sampling schemes. At Lake Tonopah we selected a systematic transect sample because we thought it would give us the best overall coverage of the zones in question.

Several other options exist for sampling designs in archaeology. In fact, it is easy to be led astray by the theoretical and statistical advantages of one sample design over another. At least as important as the abstract statistical characteristics of each design are the practical archaeological considerations, and archaeologists should never feel tied to any single sampling strategy. Random quadrats were used at Reese River because I wanted to know the distributions of artifacts and sites within discrete life zones. Systematic transect sampling was employed at Lake Tonopah in order to provide clear-cut data on the relationships between archaeological sites and the Pleistocene beach terraces.

One final example should underscore the point that archaeologists must be flexible in designing their samples. While digging Gatecliff Shelter we needed to conduct a regional sampling operation in order to examine additional components of the seasonal round; Gatecliff represents only a fraction of the overall pattern of the seasonal round. So we devised a method of sampling the surrounding Monitor Valley. One key question was to find how the sites related to water.

Water can occur on the landscape in a number of ways. In the Reese River Valley, water was a *linear* resource, concentrated in streams that flowed year-round out of the mountains and into the Reese River, which ran south to north. At Pleistocene Lake Tonopah, water was a *circular* resource contained in a massive lake basin.

Monitor Valley presented yet a third option for distribution of water. With a few exceptions, Monitor Valley lacked the permanent streams of the Reese River area, and the dry lake in Monitor Valley was never an important Pleistocene lake. Water occurred primarily in springs that bubbled forth, flowed a short distance, and then disappeared. That is, water at Monitor Valley was neither circular nor linear—it was a *point* resource.

In order to compare how water-determined settlement patterns vary among valleys, we needed to sample the archaeological sites of Monitor Valley. Our survey area contained a total of 30 permanent springs, each of which seemed to hold potential for prehistoric exploitation. From our work at Reese River we knew that prehistoric inhabitants tended to camp about 450 meters from their water source. At Reese River, we examined this distribution by walking linear strips along stream courses. But the Monitor Valley water was concentrated at single points, small springs scattered throughout the Toquima Mountains.

So we devised a sampling design to look at the relationship of sites to these springs. Neither quadrats nor transects seemed appropriate for sampling

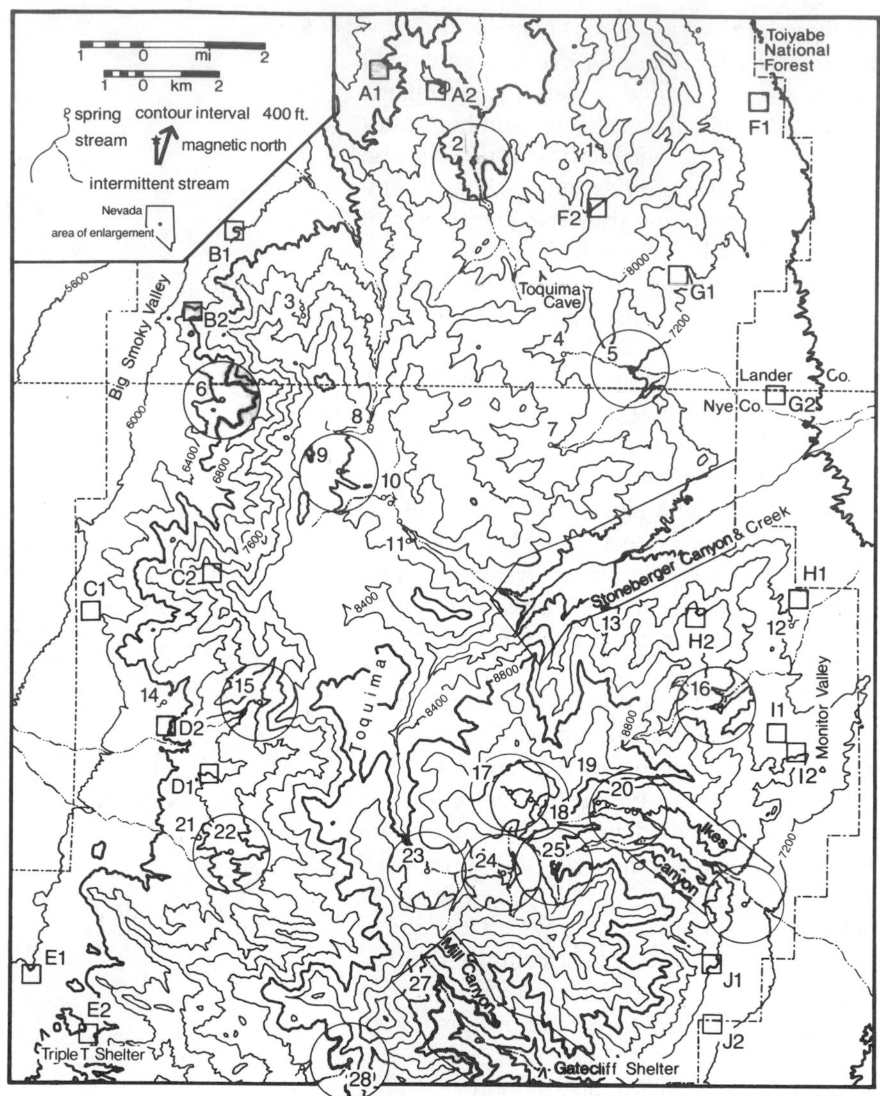

Circular and square sampling units used in the upland survey of the Toquima Range, near Gatecliff Shelter (Nevada).

these springs. We elected to use a circular sampling unit in Monitor Valley: Each spring was considered a point, and so we surveyed the surrounding area using a radius of 1,000 meters. That is, we looked for all sites within 1,000 meters of water. But we did not have time enough to survey all 30 springs, and so we numbered them 1 through 30 and selected a 50 percent random sample. These 1,000-meter-radius circles were then completely surveyed in order to locate, map, and collect all the associated sites. The Monitor Valley survey was also concerned with sites located away from water (that is, more than 1,000 meters from a spring). We thought there would be few such sites, but as a control, we overlaid a 500-meter grid system (like that used at Reese River) and drew another random sample for survey. In this way we were forced to look even where we thought there would be no sites.

These three examples point out the importance of fitting the sampling scheme to the topography and the questions being asked. The basic sampling unit at Reese River was the 500-meter-square quadrat; the unit at Pleistocene Lake Tonopah was a 150-meter-wide transect; and the sampling unit in Monitor Valley was a 1,000-meter-radius circle. The Reese River and Monitor Valley samples were selected randomly, and the Lake Tonopah sample, while randomized, was determined systematically. The sampling fractions also differed: Reese River, a 10 percent sample; Monitor Valley springs, a 50 percent sample; and Lake Tonopah, a 7.5 percent sample.

Do not be misled into thinking there is a single best sampling scheme. There is not.

In fact, as the next section on the Valley of Oaxaca survey suggests, you may not want to "sample" at all. There are times when you might just want to look at the whole thing.

The Valley of Oaxaca Archaeological Survey

The central plaza at Monte Albán (Oaxaca, Mexico).

For more than a century, explorers and archaeologists have celebrated the monumental ruins at Monte Albán (*moan*-tay-al-*bahn*), overlooking Oaxaca (wa-*ha*-kuh) City in the highlands of southern Mexico. Literally "white mountain," Monte Albán is an extraordinary concentration of pre-Columbian architecture atop an artificially flattened mountain summit.

Beginning in 1931, Alfonso Caso and several other Mexican archaeologists undertook 18 field seasons of excavation. They determined that Monte Albán was founded shortly after 500 B.C., the mountaintop settlement reaching its maximum physical size around A.D. 700.

Along the edge of the plaza, which covered nearly four football fields, rose low masonry pyramids. Stepped platforms at either end hid tombs and served as foundations for palaces and temples, a complex of buildings that housed the ruling families and also provided formal spaces for these rulers to meet with high-ranking government officials and ambassadors from afar. Nearby was a ballcourt for ritual ball games, which were important throughout Mesoamerica. The main plaza served as the center of government for the city and the region.

Caso's Monte Albán project explored more than 170 tombs in the vicinity of the sprawling central plaza, the perimeter of which was decorated with carved stone monuments depicting sacrificial victims, killed, and sometimes mutilated, by the rulers of Monte Albán.

The discoveries in Tomb 7 grabbed headlines around the world. Sometime during the decline of Monte Albán, a very powerful leader had been buried in a tomb constructed earlier. Inside was one of Mesoamerica's greatest treasures: gold, shell, turquoise, jet, crystal, and carved jaguar bones. This was one of the richest caches ever discovered in the New World.

Today, many tourists travel to Oaxaca to view firsthand the partially restored ruins of Monte Albán, and local Aeromexico flights sometimes circle the site, dipping wingtips so the passengers can catch an aerial view of the fabled sacred city of the **Zapotecs.**

Zapotec: The cultural and linguistic group centered in Oaxaca, southern Mexico, from pre-Columbian times to the present day.

But the potential of Oaxacan archaeology was hardly exhausted by the excavations at Monte Albán. Spectacular as it may be, Monte Albán is only a single site. In 1971, another team of archaeologists undertook a decade-long regional survey to determine how Monte Albán fit into the regional landscape of Oaxaca. They began with a complete mapping of Monte Albán, estimating a total population between 25,000 and 30,000 people. The archaeological reconnaissance project soon expanded into a complete and systematic survey of the hinterlands—covering the entire Valley of Oaxaca.

The main players–Richard Blanton, Gary Feinman, Laura Finsten, Linda Nicholas, and Stephen Kowalewski–selected this area for several good reasons. First, the cultural chronology for the Valley of Oaxaca was fairly well understood–a critical factor for anybody designing a regional survey. The physical land conditions were also conducive to the regional surface survey: The land surface over the past 3,000 years had been relatively stable (meaning that most sites remained visible from the surface) and vegetative ground cover was relatively thin and sparse. Furthermore, settled villages were established in the Valley of Oaxaca beginning about 1500 B.C., creating huge quantities of archaeological debris–readily datable remains that could be observed simply by walking along.

The Valley of Oaxaca Settlement Pattern Project established a set of systematic protocols to ensure that data were collected in standardized format. The survey crews consisted of three or four trained people, each familiar with the basic ceramic sequence of the area. They covered all terrain in the survey area by systematically walking 25 to 50 meters apart while searching for archaeological materials. Unlike some regional survey projects, the Valley of Oaxaca research design called for the surveyers to walk in a zigzag pattern, checking all suspicious features along either side of the survey line. Through a series of related geological studies, interpretation of aerial photographs, and field inspection of geological cuts, the researchers determined where soil erosion or buildup had occurred (thereby modifying the dimensions of the sites encountered).

As Stephen Kowalewski has learned from his experiences in Oaxaca and the red clay country of Georgia, this survey strategy ensures an up-close appreciation of "alluviation, erosion, mesquite thickets, manzanillo thickets, palmetto thickets, copperhead thickets, pine forests, precipices, cities and their dumps, salt marshes, mean dogs, and meaner land owners." The idea here is fairly simple: to find *everything archaeological,* by looking even in places where nothing is expected to be.

Sites were usually recognized from surface scatters of potsherds and/or building stones. Once found, sites were plotted on aerial photographs and mapped by the crew leader, while others took notes and made sherd collections. Time-diagnostic sherds were analyzed on-site, enabling the crew to map the distribution of each archaeological phase separately while still in the field.

In the course of 10 years, five field seasons were spent on the Oaxaca archaeological survey. A total of about 830 square miles was completely searched, resulting in about 2,700 places being recorded as containing archaeological remains. But these field-numbered "sites" were not very meaningful units because they often lumped together numerous components, each with its own distinctive temporal span and spatial distribution. These 6,353 components, defined and mapped right in the field, became the basic units of analysis for the Valley of Oaxaca survey. For each such unit, the investigators recorded 97 substantive variables such as environmental zone, soil characteristics, degree of erosion, predominant vegetation, current land status, present irrigation (if any), artifact types, and building materials. In addition, the survey teams located 2,000 pyramidal mounds, 9,000 residential terraces, and 124 tombs. Overall, the Valley of Oaxaca personnel feel satisfied that they found most occupations, even the small ones, in this huge area.

Zapotec pottery sculpture of Lightning (Cociyo) with four receptacles for his companions—Clouds, Rain, Wind, and Hail.

The massive database from the Oaxaca survey has enabled archaeologists to understand the nature of ancient Zapotec society. Using the number of size-specific components and also the variable ceramic densities, for instance, it has been possible to estimate human population sizes through time and develop a quantitative model of settlement location and land use. These models have, in turn, helped archaeologists understand the dynamics behind the evolution of America's ancient civilizations. We will discuss these developments later; for now, let's look specifically at the archaeological survey methods employed.

The Case for Full-Coverage Survey

The Valley of Oaxaca survey employed the so-called full-coverage technique, an alternative to the random sampling designs discussed earlier. The full-coverage survey technique, developed in a decade-long archaeological survey project in the Valley of Mexico, involves large-scale, 100 percent reconnaissance of an archaeological region. Many specific research designs exist for such surveys, but the single common denominator is the systematic examination of contiguous blocks of terrain, surveyed at a uniform level of intensity.

By *region,* most archaeologists usually mean something ranging anywhere from a few dozen to several thousand square miles. As Jeffrey Parsons points out, this is not entirely a semantic matter: Define too large a region, and a satisfactory survey becomes too expensive. Define too small a region, and you will end up with an incomplete view of the cultural system you are trying to understand.

Basically, the question of "How big?" depends on what the project is trying to find out. To answer this question correctly requires the ability to estimate—*before the survey starts*—the expected spatial limits of the system being studied, so that the overall scope of the survey region (or subregions) can be adequately defined as early as possible (see *What Does "Full-Coverage" Survey Mean?* by Jeffrey Parsons).

The full-coverage approach seems most appropriate to those areas (1) with a highly visible archaeological record, and (2) where the topography is not too formidable. Arid or semiarid environments are ideal for both full-coverage and sampling strategies because of the optimal surface visibility.

When these conditions are not met, rigorous survey methods can become too expensive. For the same reason, full coverage of regions is most appropriate when the main objective involves finding relatively large, dense concentrations of artifacts—that is, those places where the nature of ancient residential patterns is reasonably clear from the surface evidence. Many of these same strictures apply to the randomized sampling methods discussed earlier.

Obviously, you can do better archaeology based on 100 percent coverage than on 10 percent. That is not the issue. The more appropriate question is this: When is the expense and effort of full-coverage survey justified?

IN HIS OWN WORDS

What Does "Full-Coverage" Survey Mean? by Jeffrey Parsons

What is full coverage for one archaeologist could well be something less for another. For example, in the Valley of Mexico I have generally been comfortable with equating full coverage with the practice of walking every accessible open area at intervals of 30–50+ meters. On the other hand, some workers in other areas have advocated a much closer survey interval. The latter would certainly be less comfortable than I with the notion that my own work represents full coverage.

One way around this conflict, of course, is to consider what you are looking for, the surficial visibility of the archaeological features you are concerned with, and the topographic configuration of your study area. Take, for example, my own field experience in central highland Mexico, central highland Peru, northern Guatemala, and southern Michigan. In highland Mexico, the combination of gently sloping terrain, frequent shallow plowing, and a highly visible archaeological record offers a near-ideal combination for effective survey of the sort I have described. In central Peru the surficial archaeological record is generally quite visible (at least for most ceramic periods), but the rugged topography often excludes large areas of steep slope from effective observation, and usually requires compromising field tactics as well. In the Peten forest of northern Guatemala, only sizable platforms and standing architecture are visible, and even then such features become apparent only if you literally walk into or across them. Finally, in southern Michigan, surficial evidence of prehistoric occupation is generally much more subtle, and surveyors must usually look very carefully for small, diffuse scatters of lithic debris in plowed areas. For unplowed or forest areas, surface remains are rarely present.

Without further belaboring the obvious, it should be apparent that there can be no absolute standard for full-coverage survey. Survey tactics must be designed on a case-by-case basis, where the particular characteristics of specific regions and the principal concerns and interests of a particular investigator have to be carefully dovetailed.

JEFFREY PARSONS is the curator of Latin American archaeology, Museum of Anthropology, University of Michigan.

Full-coverage survey seems to be clearly desirable in the following situations:

- when the fieldwork is directed toward understanding complex settlement systems and explaining their changes through time
- for exploring site function and intersite relationships
- for addressing questions regarding human and environmental interactions at a regional scale (that is, beyond the range of single, face-to-face communities)
- for understanding the interactions of sets of communities and lower-scale settlement units

The full-coverage regional survey is a way to define change and continuities in social and ecological networks, operating above the relatively small scale of the individual and the local community.

SUMMARY This chapter addressed the basic question: How do you know where to dig? Archaeological sites are found in several different ways and there is no single formula. Many of the archaeological sites discussed here were found by a combination of luck and hard work. Others were discovered as part of a systematic regional reconnaissance, called archaeological survey. This chapter describes the experiences of several field archaeologists, illustrating the different ways that archaeologists find a place to dig.

But many archaeologists are not actually seeking a place to excavate. Sometimes the reconnaissance itself produces sufficient information for understanding the archaeological record; this was the case with John Hyslop's survey of the Inka Road in South America. Hyslop conducted his pioneering study without ever digging at all.

Hyslop's research illustrates an aspect of the regional approach that has become a major theme in American archaeology. Focusing on the relationships between people and the land, settlement pattern archaeology transcends the single site in order to determine the overarching relationships among the various contemporaneous site types used by societies. The regional approach thus precludes assuming single sites as somehow typical of a given culture. Instead, the emphasis is on variability among sites within the settlement pattern.

In such places, important archaeological remains have simply lain on stable ground surfaces rather than becoming buried by sand, silt, and gravel. In regions that have been spared the plow, archaeologists have the unparalleled opportunity of collecting artifacts literally where they were dropped, often thousands of years ago.

Sometimes, these areas are sampled using one or more probability-based sampling designs to minimize bias in recovering settlement pattern data. Sometimes these archaeological surveys record the distribution of archaeological sites. In other cases, the concept of archaeological "site" is not used at all, particularly when archaeological artifacts are distributed across broad areas.

Sometimes, the so-called full-coverage technique is a better alternative than these random sampling designs. The full-coverage survey technique involves large-scale, 100 percent reconnaissance of an archaeological region. Many specific research designs exist for such surveys, but the single common denominator is the systematic examination of contiguous blocks of terrain, surveyed at a uniform level of intensity.

Chapter 5

Doing Fieldwork: Remote Sensing as Noninvasive Archaeology

It's kind of fun to do the impossible.

Walt Disney (1901–1966), film producer

PREVIEW Generations of archaeologists have longed for a way to peer beneath the earth's surface, for some magical X-ray machine that would let us learn from archaeological sites without actually having to dig them up. Today, that dream has almost come true.

In this chapter, we look at the increasingly sophisticated remote sensing approaches that are being used in today's archaeology. It often is indeed possible, before excavation, to find where the sites are, what they contain, and how they are articulated.

Sometimes, we can learn these things without having to dig at all. Remote sensing technology is a cost-effective way of doing archaeology in a noninvasive, nondestructive manner. Remember, remote sensing is simply one more way of generating archaeological data. But in this case, archaeologists are making their counts, measurements, and observations on objects and features that have not yet been excavated.

Modern archaeology has much in common with modern medicine. It was not long ago that a slipped disk or blown-out knee—both common archaeological ailments—meant immediate and sometimes radical surgery. And surgery was often more painful than the injury itself. Although your knee joint bounced back pretty quickly after the cartilage was removed, it took months for the muscle tissues and nerves to recover from the 10-inch-long incision required to get at the injured area. Here was a classic case of the cure being almost worse than the disease.

Modern medical technology has changed all that. CAT scan and MRI technology today allow the physician to map in detail afflicted areas without any nasty "exploratory" surgery or damage to the patient. And when surgery is warranted, techniques like arthroscopy and laser microsurgery permit physicians to trim, cut, excise, and repair even gross damage with only the slightest incision. Today's *noninvasive* medicine minimizes tissue damage and surgical intervention.

Americanist archaeology is undergoing a parallel revolution. In the good old days, archaeologists simply blasted away at their sites, leaving ruined ruins in their wake. For example, the earliest excavations at Colonial Williamsburg were conducted by architectural historians who used an extraordinarily destructive method known as *cross trenching,* digging parallel trenches a shovel blade in width and throwing up the dirt on the unexcavated space between. The strategy was designed to disclose foundations for restoration, but the workmen paid little attention to the artifacts and none whatsoever to the stratigraphy encountered. To archaeologists at mid-century, the greatest technological revolution was the advent of the backhoe as a tool of excavation.

Americanist archaeology today views its sites differently. A new conservation ethic suggests that we dig less, and save more of our archaeological remains for the future. Equally important has been the development of noninvasive technology for doing relatively nondestructive archaeology. Using the archaeological equivalents of CAT scan and ultrasound, archaeologists can now map subsurface features in detail—without ever excavating them. And when it does become necessary to recover samples, we can execute pinpoint excavations, minimizing damage to the rest of the site. The idea is to leave large parts of our sites unexcavated, as a legacy for our archaeological grandchildren, who doubtless will possess methods, theories, and technology we cannot even imagine (see *Remote Sensing the Sacred*).

Data at a Distance

Some purists would restrict the term *remote sensing* to mean only applications of *photogrammetry*—to those devices not in direct contact with the ground.

However, when archaeologists use the term *remote sensing*, they generally mean the total array of techniques used in geophysical observation. In this broad sense, **remote sensing** technology includes not only the various forms of aerial photography, but also such land-based techniques as proton magnetometry, soil resistivity, ground-penetrating radar, and so forth. Each of these methods relies on some form of electromagnetic energy—it might be raw electricity, light, heat, or radio waves—to detect and measure some characteristics of an archaeological target. Most of these techniques were initially designed to measure geophysical features on the scale of several yards or even miles. Yet to be most effective in archaeology, such operations must be scaled down to the order of inches and feet.

Remote sensing: The application of methods that employ some form of electromagnetic energy to detect and measure some characteristics of an archaeological target.

Today, many archaeologists have come to rely on remote sensing technology as a "space-age" way to learn about the past. In 1982, radar aboard the space shuttle penetrated the Saharan sands, revealing the presence of previously undiscovered ancient watercourses. A generation of archaeologists has since been mapping out these so-called radar-rivers and the desert towns they once served (see *Geographic Information System (GIS): Mapping a New Frontier*).

In Chapter 13, we will see how the use of Landsat satellite imagery has been used to plot subtle vegetation changes in Central America. Working with archaeologist Joyce Marcus, remote sensing specialists have found that some distinctive linear patterns of xeric vegetation are actually ancient Maya roads, the existence of which Marcus had predicted 20 years earlier (but she lacked any way to test her hypothesis—until now).

Ideally, we should have an X-ray machine which would allow us to locate and formally evaluate the range of variation manifest in cultural features.

Lewis R. Binford, archaeologist (Southern Methodist University)

Remote Sensing the Sacred

Many Plains Indians groups once used, and continue to use, medicine bundles to store sacred objects important for various curing rituals. Individually owned and carefully guarded, these sacred bundles often have a definite set of rules, songs, and rituals associated with them. Most medicine bundles contain a smoking pipe and tobacco; they may also contain a wide variety of sacred items including animal bones and skin, unusually shaped rocks, bunches of sweetgrass, beads, bells, and so forth. In the hands of someone properly trained, medicine bundles seem capable of effecting some remarkable cures.

Tribal tradition and museums have on occasion clashed over the ownership of these culturally charged sacred objects. In recent years, some tribal elders have asked museums to return certain key bundles considered to be critical for the modern performance of Native American religion. Some museums have agreed to do this; others have refused.

Such interactions will always require sensitivity of all parties involved, but remote sensing technology has recently provided an intriguing solution to the issues of sacredness and scholarship. Here's one example where high-tech methods have offered a resolution satisfactory to all parties concerned.

In 1987, a Pawnee tribal member donated a family-owned medicine bundle to the Kansas State Historical Society with the request that it be cared for, studied, and exhibited. This particular bundle held great cultural significance for Pawnee people because during a nineteenth-century battle at Massacre Canyon, a young Pawnee girl was sent out of the family lodge by her father with this sacred bundle tied to her back. It has re-

Guided almost literally to the find spot by Landsat data, paleoanthropologists found fossil hominid teeth in Ethiopia's Great Rift Valley that were more than 3.7 million years old—at the time, among the oldest remains of the species *Australopithecus afarensis.* The satellite data served somewhat like a navigation tool, allowing investigators to study fault and drainage patterns to pinpoint the kind of geological structures that would warrant tedious on-the-ground foot searching (which is still necessary to find the fossils).

The promise of remote sensing is awesome. In this chapter, we explore several ways in which archaeologists are gathering their data at a distance. We begin with a firsthand example of how this technology tells us things we just can't know in any other way.

How to Find a Lost Spanish Mission (Part II)

You will remember from the preceding chapter that we used both transect survey and power auger testing to narrow down the location of Mission Santa Catalina to a 1-hectare (2.6-acre) area on St. Catherines Island, Georgia. So-called Quad IV was a totally undistinguished piece of real estate, covered by typical scrub palmetto and live oak forest. The only evidence of human occupation was a little-used field road for island research vehicles. Although aboriginal shell scatters could be seen here and there, Quad IV betrayed absolutely no surface clues to what lay below.

mained in family hands ever since—until it was donated to the Historical Society.

Following standard curatorial procedures, the museum staff cleaned and conserved the bundle. The curator in charge was anxious to learn as much as possible about this well-documented and highly significant bundle. Although the donating Pawnee owner granted permission for it to be opened for study, other Indian people objected.

Recognizing the sensitivity of the situation (and also the likelihood that the bundle had not been opened within the last century), the museum staff proposed an alternative. Rather than opening it to inventory and identify the contents, why not use remote sensing techniques instead?

Everyone involved agreed and, employing a specialized technique known as *computerized axial tomography*, personnel of the Kansas State Historical Society X-rayed and precisely identified the bundle's contents: a woven grass mat, bundles of sticks or reeds, leather pouches, a raccoon penile bone, 8 bird skulls with associated wing and leg bones, a large talon, 11 metal bells, a possible human scalp, and some glass beads. The bird bones could even be identified to species (pigeon hawk, Swainson's hawk, and marsh hawk).

This innovative and sensitive use of noninvasive remote sensing technology fostered cooperation and goodwill, balancing the sometimes conflicting interests of Native American and scientific communities. At the request of the Pawnee donor, the bundle is currently on display at the Pawnee Indian Village Museum near Republic, Kansas.

And, significantly, the bundle has yet to be opened.

At this point, we shifted our field strategy once again, switching from preliminary subsurface testing to noninvasive, nondestructive remote sensing. Choosing the right method depends on what you expect to find. What, exactly, were we looking for? For more than a century, Santa Catalina had been the northernmost Spanish outpost on the eastern seaboard, and this historical fact implied considerable size and permanence. The seventeenth-century mission must have had a fortified church, some buildings to house the soldiers and priests, plus enough granaries, storehouses, and dwellings for hundreds of Guale Indian neophytes.

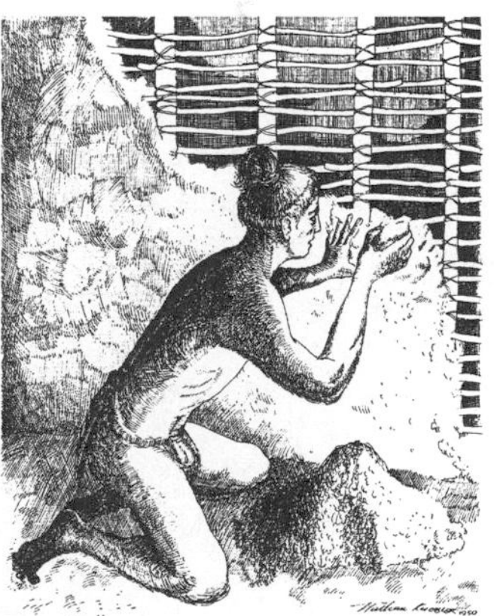

Artist's reconstruction of the wattle-and-daub technique used to build Mission Santa Catalina. The upright wattlework is being "daubed" (plastered) with a mixture of marsh mud and organic fibers.

We reasoned that the mission buildings were built by a *wattle-and-daub* technique. Freshly cut timbers were probably set vertically along the walls and reinforced with cane woven horizontally between the uprights. This sturdy wattlework was then plastered ("daubed") with a mixture of marsh mud, sand, and plant fibers (probably Spanish moss). Roofs were thatched with palmetto.

So constructed, wattle-and-daub buildings are biodegradable. Left to nature, the roof will go first; if it does not burn off, the thatch will either blow away or simply rot. And once directly exposed to the weather, mud and twig walls will simply wash away. Archaeologists seeking such a dissolved mission would soon be out of business.

But if we were lucky—and many archaeologists would secretly rather be lucky than good—the mission buildings would have burned, firing and hardening the daub walls, like a pot baking in a kiln. Fired daub, nearly as

Geographic Information System (GIS): Mapping a New Frontier

Archaeologists use maps all the time: maps to plot site distributions, maps to plot artifact distributions within sites, maps showing how primary-secondary-tertiary political centers hook up, remote sensing maps that suggest what archaeological features might lie buried beneath our feet.

In this book alone, we've used a dozen maps, each one showing you some aspect of the archaeological record that cannot be illustrated in any other way.

Geographic information is basic to archaeology, and, to a large degree, the way we represent that information conditions how we view the past. Maps show where things are, and how they relate to other things. The more complex the archaeological data, the more complex the map.

And therein lies the problem. In their traditional form, maps are static and difficult to update with new information. Traditional maps are also inflexible, and sometimes so specialized, map-reading experts are required.

All that has changed with the advent of **Geographic Information System (GIS),** a high-tech computer program designed to store, retrieve, analyze, and display cartographic data. GIS lets you view information—practically any kind of geologically related information—as a map. Every GIS consists of three primary components: a powerful computer graphics program used to draw a map, one or more external databases that are linked to the objects shown on the map, and a set of analytical tools that can be used to graphically interpret the externally stored data, for example, by showing objects or regions that meet certain criteria in different colors or shadings. Satellite imaging technology is a kind of GIS. Although all GISs are ultimately mapping programs, all mapping programs are not necessarily GISs.

In true GIS format, the earth's various features are not depicted visually—as they would be on standard two-dimensional maps—but as information (or data). Although such stored data contain all the information of a conventional map, computer storage allows for the data to be manipulated in numerous ways. After appropriate manipulation, the computer-stored data can be

Geographic Information System (GIS): A computer program for storing, retrieving, analyzing, and displaying cartographic data.

indestructible as the ubiquitous potsherd, thus became a key in our search for Santa Catalina.

But how do you find chunks of fired daub buried beneath a foot of sand? It turns out that the marsh mud used in daub plaster contains microscopic iron particles. When intensely heated, the particles orient toward magnetic north—like a million tiny compass needles. To pinpoint these magnetically anomalous orientations, we relied upon a *proton precession magnetometer.* The theory behind this device is a bit complicated, but the principle is simple: Magnetometers measure the strength of magnetism between the earth's magnetic core and a sensor controlled by the archaeologist. If hundreds of these readings are taken across a systematic grid, a computer plotter can generate a magnetic contour map reflecting both the shape and the intensity of magnetic anomalies beneath the ground surface.

Many subsurface anomalies are archaeologically irrelevant magnetic "noise"—interference from underlying rocks, AC power lines, or hidden iron debris. The earth's magnetic field fluctuates so wildly on some days that the readings are meaningless, and electrical storms can hopelessly scramble mag-

displayed (in printed or other form) showing common features like roads, rivers, and mountains as they would appear on a more conventional paper map. But, significantly, these same data can also be summarized into tables and graphs.

A GIS stores its data in a structured format (known as a *spatial database*). Sometimes, GIS data are stored as highly accurate points, lines, and polygons; this method is preferred in urban applications involving legal boundaries. A GIS can also store information in more generalized grid form, as a regular matrix of cells; data stored in this manner are used for statistical analysis, remote sensing applications, and computer-simulation modeling.

Often several different kinds of data from the same area are stored separately as "themes." Vegetation, rivers, contour elevations, and archaeological sites might, for instance, each be stored in separate themes, or overlays. These various kinds of data can be combined and analyzed in many different ways.

GIS technology is useful to anyone who needs to interpret or display large quantities of data on a spatial or geographic basis: governments (for tracking land usage, utilities, real estate parcels, and emergency response planning), businesses (for interpreting demographic data), and scientists (for arraying the distribution of geological formations, soils, plants, animals—and archaeological remains).

Today, GIS is being used by fire and police departments to route emergency vehicles to accident scenes. Urban planners use it to find the most convenient locations for stores, roads, and public facilities. Land management agencies are attempting to balance the sometimes conflicting needs of development and conservation with GIS-based planning. Medical researchers use it to track the sources of epidemics.

GIS applications caught on quickly with some archaeologists, its seductive technology far outstripping any archaeological need for such maps. But today, GIS is transcending its bandwagon phase, and archaeologists around the world are working with GIS programs of all kinds.

netometer readings. Even minor interference such as the operator's wrist watch or eyeglasses can drive a magnetometer crazy.

But when everything works just right, the magnetometer provides the equivalent of an areal CAT scan, telling archaeologists what is going on beneath the earth's surface. Many archaeological features have characteristic magnetic signatures—telltale clues that hint at the size, shape, depth, and composition of the archaeological objects hidden far below. Shallow graves, for instance, have a magnetic profile vastly different from, say, a buried fire pit or a wattle-and-daub wall.

We worked with Ervan Garrison (now of the University of Georgia) and a magnetometer team from Texas A&M University. As they were packing up their field equipment, to work up the data in their lab, they shared a couple of hunches, based strictly on their raw magnetometer readings: "If we were y'all, we'd dig in three places: here, over yonder, and especially right here." We took their advice, exploring each of the three magnetic anomalies in the few days remaining in our May field season. One anomaly—"especially right here"—turned out to be an iron ring. Excavating further, we came upon

GIS on the Internet:

Plenty of information available; here's a little bit:

Some General GIS Sites:
http://info.er.usgs.gov/research/gis/title.html
http://www.frw.ruu.nl:80/nicegeo.html
http://www.blm.gov/gis/hotnews.html

Frequently Asked Questions About GIS:
http://fatboy.larc.nasa.gov/gisfaq.html

another ring and more below that. At about 9 feet down, we hit the water table. Digging underwater, we finally encountered a well-preserved oak well casing.

Archaeologists love wells because, like privies, they can be magnificent artifact traps. After removing the bones of an unfortunate fawn (which had long ago drowned), we found an array of distinctive Hispanic and Guale Indian potsherds and a metal dinner plate dropped (or tossed) into the construction pit. All artifacts were typical of the sixteenth and seventeenth centuries. We had indeed found Mission Santa Catalina, and we pressed on to see what else the magnetometer might have turned up.

Our second magnetic anomaly—the one "here"—was a small mound. We thought at first it might be a grave or tomb. But after removing the overburden, we came across a burned daub wall that, as it fell, had crushed dozens of Spanish and Guale domestic artifacts: imported tin-enameled glazed cups, painted ceramic dishes, a kitchen knife, and at least two enormous pots for cooking or storage. Charred deer and chicken bones littered the floor, and dozens of tiny corncobs were scattered about. This time, the magnetometer had led us to the kitchen (or *cocina*) used by seventeenth-century Franciscan friars at Santa Catalina.

Finally, we began digging the "over yonder" anomaly, which proved to be a linear daub concentration more than 40 feet long, obviously the downed wall of yet another, much larger mission building. Here excavations turned up none of the everyday implements and debris so common in the scorched kitchen. Instead we found human graves, the first of more than 400 Christianized Guale Indians buried here.

The search was over. We had discovered the church, the paramount house of worship at Santa Catalina de Guale. Our magnetometer survey had given us trustworthy directions to the buried daub walls and iron barrel hoops. Even without computer enhancement, the magnetometer had taken us to the very heart and soul of Mission Santa Catalina.

Since the discovery of Santa Catalina, we have spent a decade excavating the church ruins. The lateral church walls were constructed of wattle and daub that, when encountered archaeologically, consisted of a densely packed linear rubble scatter; this is what the magnetometer "saw" in Quad IV. Beneath the nave and sanctuary of the church we discovered the cemetery, where approximately 400 to 450 Christianized Guale Indians had been interred. These bones have much to tell, and technology is becoming available to help unravel their story. In Chapter 12 we discuss how such skeletal materials are being used in a new, *biocultural* approach to the past.

The search for Santa Catalina illustrates the maturation in Americanist archaeology. Rather than rip into the site with trowels and shovels—much less

Ervan Garrison and Deborah Mayer O'Brien looking for Mission Santa Catalina (on St. Catherines Island, Georgia) using a proton magnetometer. She is holding the "sensor," and he is recording magnetometer readings.

backhoes and front loaders—we, like many archaeologists, first drew on today's technological arsenal, which includes dozens of noninvasive, nondestructive techniques to assess the archaeological record. Remote sensing is simply another way to gather archaeological data, in this case data from unexcavated objects, features, and buildings. That these things still lie buried beneath the ground has become largely irrelevant.

High-Altitude Imagery

The first well-documented application of remote sensing methods in archaeology took place in 1891, when a British archaeologist tied a camera to a crewless balloon to get better pictures of the site he was digging in India. Since then, archaeologists have used an array of aerial techniques—at first balloons and airplanes, more recently the space shuttle and satellites—to sense their sites "remotely."

Perhaps the most famous early application of remote sensing methods was by none other than Charles Lindbergh, the famous American aviator-explorer. Two years after his nonstop transatlantic solo flight, Lindbergh undertook "goodwill tours" throughout Mexico, Central America, and the West Indies. Working closely with archaeologist A. V. Kidder, Lindbergh

Aerial photograph of Pueblo Bonito (New Mexico) *taken in* 1929 *by* Charles A. Lindbergh.

photographed important archaeological ruins at Chichen Itza (Mexico) and Tikal (Guatemala). He also did extensive photographic reconnaissance at Chaco Canyon, New Mexico. As it turned out, these innovative photographic records have proven invaluable to archaeologists working in these areas today. As we see in the following section, archaeologists—armed with new knowledge and more advanced technologies—can find in these 1920s photographs traces of the past that would have astonished even Lindbergh, who took the pictures. Here's an example of how it works (see *Airborne Archaeology: The Shippee-Johnson Expedition of 1931*).

The Ancient Roads of Chaco Canyon

Despite such early promise, many archaeologists were slow to recognize the potential of photogrammetry as a systematic research tool. Many felt that the things they were studying were too small to be observed aloft. That misconception changed dramatically with the discovery of the ancient Anasazi road system connecting Chaco Canyon with its hinterlands. Although proto- and early Anasazi people lived in pit houses, between A.D. 700 and 1000 the ancestral Puebloans began constructing their distinctive multiroom apartment complexes that would give their descendants, the Pueblo Indians of New Mexico, their name.

Charles Lindbergh *and* Anne Morrow Lindbergh *in* 1929, *examining flight photographs they have just taken of pueblo ruins.*

About A.D. 900, the Anasazi of northwestern New Mexico generated a sustained burst of cultural energy in Chaco Canyon, a place that still amazes: hundreds of contiguous rooms made of beautifully shaped and coursed stonework, three or four stories high, forming huge sweeping arcs. Within its 30-odd square miles, the canyon contains more than 2,400 archaeological sites: nine full-blown towns (the "Great Houses"), each with hundreds of rooms.

Between A.D. 1050 and 1300, something happened. During these so-called classical times, two distinct kinds of sites appeared. Throughout the Anasazi area, numerous smaller pueblo sites dotted the landscape. But in Chaco Canyon and a few other places on the Colorado Plateau, huge sites were built. Pueblo Bonito (the Spanish name for *Beautiful Town*), in Chaco

Canyon, reached five stories into the sky and housed a thousand people. America would not witness a larger apartment building until the Industrial Revolution of the nineteenth century. Pueblo Bonito, like each of these Great Houses, was centrally located amidst a cluster of smaller sites, defining a "community." By A.D. 1100, the large, formal ancestral Pueblo towns had sprung up.

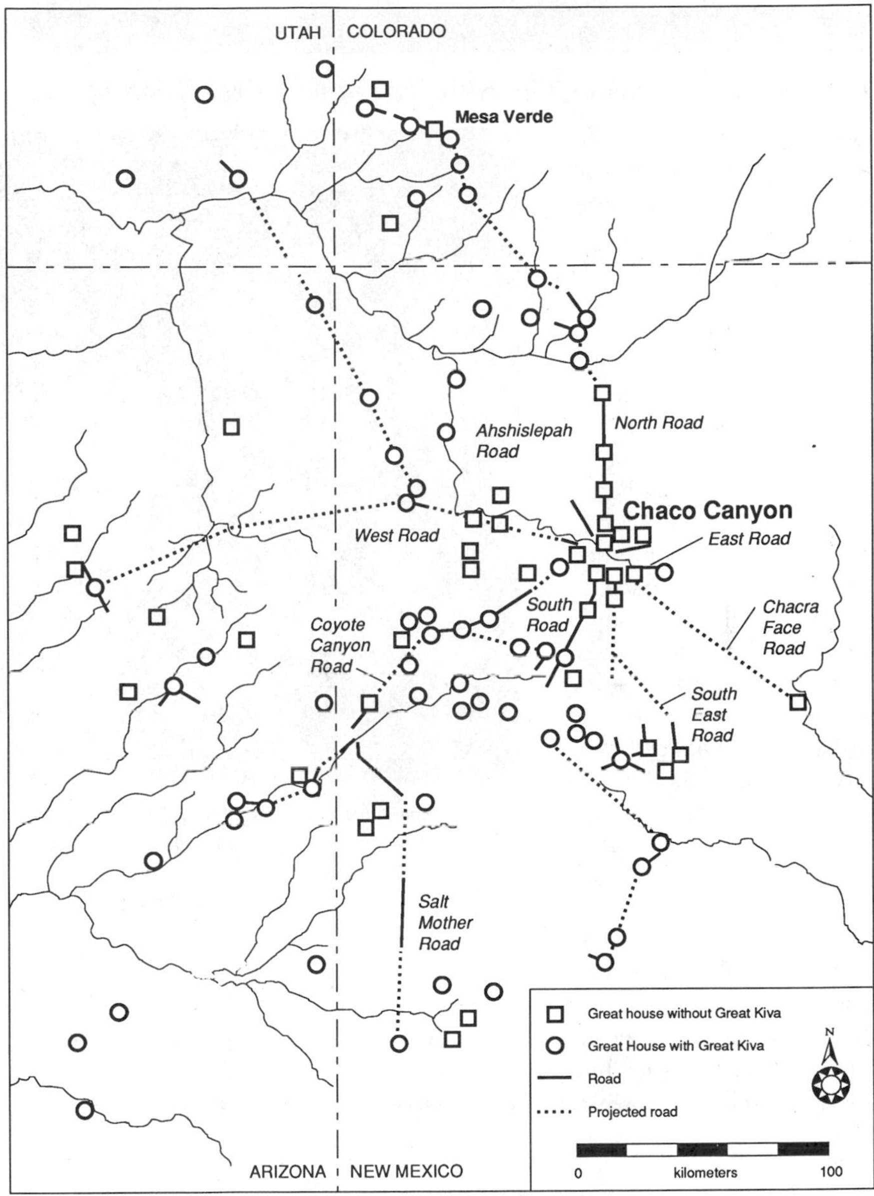

Schematic diagram of Chaco road system as it may have appeared by A.D. 1050.

In 1970–1971, archaeologist R. Gwinn Vivian was mapping what he thought was a series of ancient Anasazi canals in Chaco Canyon. As he began excavating, Vivian realized that this linear feature was like no canal he'd ever seen. Instead of being U-shaped, the Chaco "canal" was obviously a deliberately flattened and carefully engineered roadway. Although some archaeologists working in Chaco had speculated about possible roads, they lacked the technology to trace these possibilities more than a mile or two, and their ruminations were buried deep inside voluminous fieldnotes, unavailable to Vivian.

Vivian described his curious find to Thomas Lyons, a geologist just hired to experiment with remote sensing possibilities in Chaco Canyon. Together, Vivian and Lyons started looking at the available aerial photographs from the area. One set, taken in the 1960s, was compared with a 1930s series, taken before grazing was permitted at Chaco National Monument.

The more they looked, the more they saw—unmistakable traces of a prehistoric road network. New flights were commissioned and road segments were field-checked against the aerial photographs. By early 1973, more than 80 miles of prehistoric roads had been confidently identified in the Chaco area. By the end of the same year, identification had been extended to over

Airborne Archaeology: The Shippee-Johnson Expedition of 1931

Geologist Robert Shippee and ex-Navy pilot (and accomplished aerial photographer) George Johnson teamed up in 1931 to document the spectacular archaeology of both highland and coastal Peru. This was the first time that an aerial perspective was used to observe the Andes and the way people had transformed them. Today, this tradition is continued by satellites and space shuttle flights that relay up-to-date digital images of the same areas back to earth.

Aerial photograph taken during the Shippee-Johnson expedition of 1931. It shows the prehistoric irrigation system of the Pisco Valley (Peru). The surface evidence of this extensive feature has been entirely destroyed since then, but this photograph provides archaeologists with a remote sensing guideline of where to find the subsurface evidence still preserved there.

Massive changes have taken place in the Peruvian landscape since the Shippee-Johnson images were taken. Sites and extensive Inka irrigation systems have been bulldozed to clear land for agricultural fields. Although clearly visible on the 1930s photographs, all on-the-ground traces of these ancient constructions have disappeared. Today, archaeologists are using the hundreds of surviving Shippee-Johnson images to explore this disappearing archaeological record.

200 miles of the network. Amazingly, the Lindbergh photographs of Chaco Canyon taken in the 1920s actually show the famous Chacoan roads. But nobody recognized them as such in the photos until 1971, when archaeologists had a clue of what to look for.

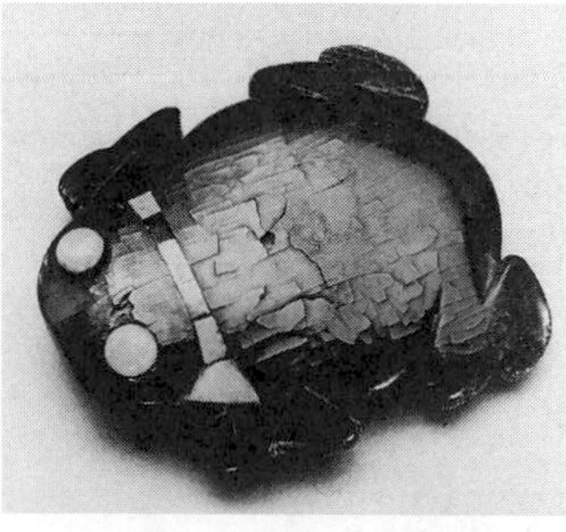

Jet and turquoise frog effigy excavated from Pueblo Bonito in 1897.

Today, analysis of aerial photographs has revealed more than 400 miles of ancient roadways radiating out from Chaco Canyon. On the photos, the roads appear as narrow, dark lines running through the surrounding landscape. The roads are sometimes completely invisible at ground level because they are merely shallow depressions only a couple inches deep and 25 to 35 feet wide. Often they turn suddenly in angular doglegs and are occasionally edged by low rock berms. The roads are littered with potsherds.

WHAT'S IN A NAME?

Anasazi *or* Ancestral Pueblo?

For more than 60 years, archaeologists have used the word *Anasazi* to denote the last prehistoric (ca. A.D. 200–1600) culture centered on the Four Corners area of northwestern New Mexico, northern Arizona, southwestern Colorado, and southern Utah. The Anasazi people are generally considered to be ancestors of the modern Pueblo groups in New Mexico and the Hopi people of northwestern Arizona.

But over the past several years, a number of Pueblo people have expressed concern over use of this term. Why, they ask, should their ancestors be known by a non-Puebloan (Navajo) term meaning "ancient enemy"? Although a number of substitute terms have been suggested, many archaeologists today prefer the term "ancestral Pueblo" to "Anasazi."

The matter is far from settled. Here, we'll use both terms, more or less interchangeably.

The longest and best-defined roads, probably constructed between A.D. 1075 and 1140, extend more than 50 miles outward from Chaco Canyon. In places the Chacoans constructed causeways, and elsewhere they cut stairways into sheer cliffs. The generally straight bearings suggest that the roads were laid out—"engineered"—prior to construction, although archaeologists still argue about exactly how this was done.

Why would the Chaco people build arrow-straight roads running hundreds of miles into the surrounding desert? This elaborate road system covered more than 100,000 square miles. Why are the roads so wide, so straight? What were they used for?

Maybe the well-built Chaco roads operated like a lower-case version of the amazing Inka road system. Like the Inka roads, the Chacoan roads could have served for communication as well as transport. Several related mesa-top signal stations have been found near Chaco that provided for line-of-sight communication—presumably by smoke, fire, or reflected light.

In both cases, the Inka and the Chaco roads tied far-flung regions together, moving the goods and people required to build and maintain extensive public works. The roads themselves may also have become symbols of authority, linear banners proclaiming affinity and cooperation, signifying participation in a system whose importance exceeded the mere sum of its parts.

Whatever the answer, it is clear that archaeologists had walked over the remains of the Chaco road system for decades without recognizing what remained to be discovered. It was just a matter of getting a new perspective, of starting to sense data "remotely."

A Soil Resistivity Approach

Not all remote sensing technology flies over the ground. Soil resistivity survey monitors the electrical resistance of soils in a restricted volume near the surface of an archaeological site. Perhaps partially because of its relatively

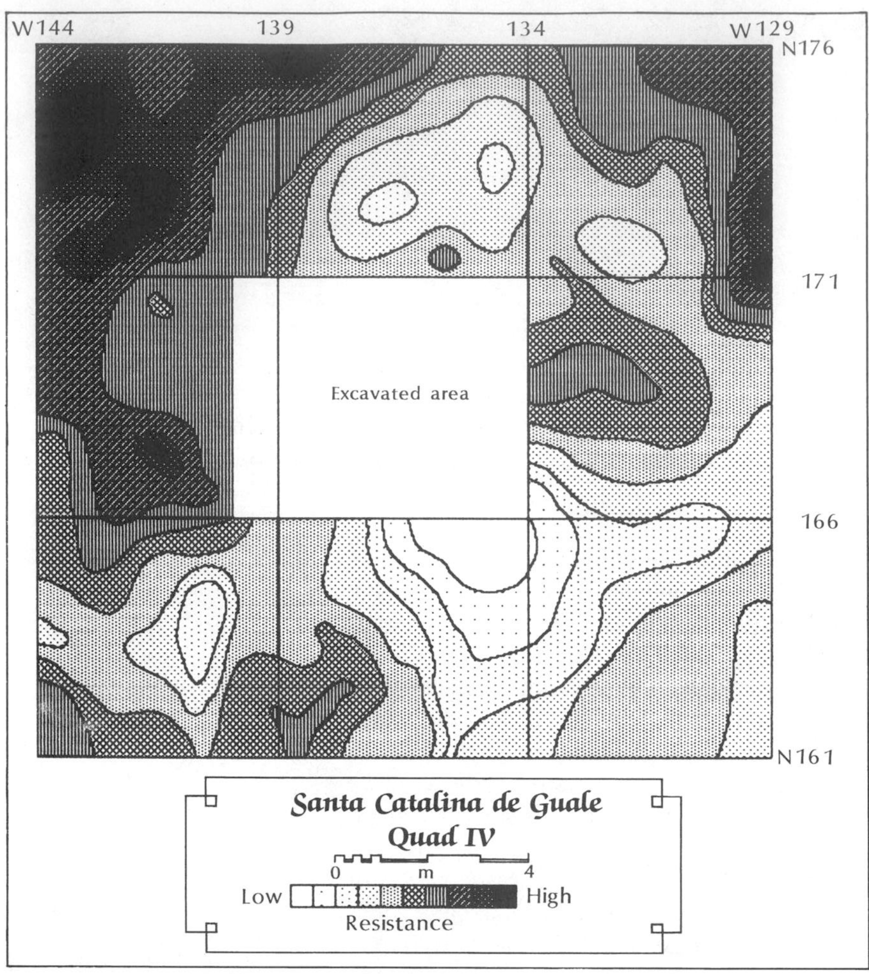

Soil resistivity contour map from Mission Santa Catalina (Georgia). The top of this map is oriented toward magnetic north; the buried kitchen building appears as a large square outline, oriented at 45° off north.

low cost, soil resistivity survey has become a popular technique of geophysical prospecting over the past three decades.

The degree of soil resistivity depends on several factors, the most important of which is usually the amount of water retained in the soil—the less water, the greater the resistance to electrical currents. Compaction such as occurs in house floors, paths, and roads tends to reduce pore sizes and hence potential to retain water; this registers as high resistance. In effect, when electricity is sent through the soil, buried features can often be detected and defined by their differential retention of groundwater (and hence their differential resistance to electrical charge).

The aggregation of fill in pits, ditches, and middens will also alter resistivity. Foundations or walls, particularly those in historic-period sites, generally have greater resistivity than surrounding soil, while the generation of humus by occupation activity increases the ion content of the soil, reducing resistivity.

To illustrate how soil resistivity survey actually works in archaeology, we return to our search for Mission Santa Catalina. After the initial discovery and pilot resistivity survey, Mark Williams and the late Gary Shapiro returned to St. Catherines Island to conduct a more comprehensive resistivity study.

Soil resistance was measured by setting four probes in line at 1-meter intervals, each probe inserted to a depth of 20 centimeters. When an electrical current was passed between the probes, the electrical conductivity (the opposite of resistivity) was recorded between the two center probes. In this way, readings were consistently taken on east-west grid lines at 1-meter intervals (each 20-meter line resulting in 21 readings). The line was then advanced 1 meter north or south, and another 21 readings were taken. This procedure resulted in a gridded array of resistance values as in the figure above, recorded in the field on graph paper and eventually transferred to computer disks. Locations of trees, backdirt piles, roads, and other features that might influence earth resistance were also charted.

One of the preliminary resistivity surveys was conducted in a test square straddling a 5-by-5-meter test of Structure 2 at Santa Catalina, initially located by the proton magnetometer survey. From our test excavations, we knew that this building was probably the *cocina* (kitchen), but we had no idea of the building's configuration. The figure shows the resistivity diagram of this area, clearly identifying the margins of the unexcavated building. Our recent excavations have conclusively confirmed the accuracy of the soil resistivity diagram.

A Ground-Penetrating Radar Approach

Yet another "active" method of geophysical prospecting is ground-penetrating radar. Although this method tends to be rather expensive, its cost is offset to some degree by its speed. But neither operating the radar equipment nor interpreting the results is simple, and the assistance of trained specialists is always required.

Ground-penetrating radar was first developed in 1910, but a significant peak in relevant articles coincided with the *Apollo 17* lunar sounding experiment in the early 1970s. Today, ground-penetrating radar techniques are commonly employed by environmental engineering firms to aid in selecting routes for proposed rights-of-way; to find buried rock or deep swamp deposits; to investigate foundations; in mineral studies; to search for peat, lignite, and coal; in siltation studies; to locate and identify caverns in limestone; in making groundwater studies; and to investigate ground pollutants.

Ground-penetrating radar operates as an echo-sounding device, transmitting energy over a frequency band. Radar pulses directed into the ground reflect back to the surface when they strike targets or interfaces within the ground (such as a change of stratum, interface between soil and rock, presence of groundwater or buried objects, and void areas). As these pulses are reflected, their speed to the target and the nature of their return are measured. The reflection time of the signal can provide useful information about the depth and three-dimensional shape of buried objects.

By using transducers of various dimensions, it is possible to direct the greatest degree of resolution to the depth of specific interest. A pulsating electric current is passed through a bow-tie shaped antenna, inducing electromagnetic waves that radiate toward the target and return in a fraction of a microsecond to be recorded. The dimensions of this transducer influence the depth and detail that are desired in any specific archaeological application.

As the antenna is dragged across the ground surface, a continuous profile of subsurface electromagnetic conditions is printed on a graphic recorder. The location and depth of subsurface targets can be inferred from, and tested against, this graphic record.

Ground-Penetrating Radar on the Internet:

Some General GPR Sources:
http://www-gpi.physik.uni-karlsruhe.de/pub/workgroup6
http://www.treasurenet.com

ARCHAEO-MYTHBUSTERS

The Great Wall Is the Only Mortal Creation Visible From the Moon, Right?

We've all heard this one. Whenever anybody mentions the Great Wall of China at a cocktail party, it won't be long before somebody chimes in: "You know, the Great Wall is the only humanmade object on earth that's visible from the moon."

The title of this fable—"the Great Wall is the only mortal creation visible from the moon"—is actually quoted directly from the editorial page of the *New York Times* (March 8, 1983). It appeared right after the report that archaeologists had discovered "62 hitherto unknown miles of the Great Wall" (which was true).

Great Wall of China.

Groundwater can pose a problem in such studies because it changes the relative permeability of most soils. Soils are good reflectors when they are associated with steep changes in soil water context, as occurs in coarse materials. Unsorted soils, such as moraine deposits, will have a broad and varying capillary zone, and thus no clear reflection. Ground-penetrating radar is generally ineffective over saltwater, in penetrating some clays, and at depths of more than about 30 meters below the surface. The maximum depth of penetration depends on the conductivity of the overlying deposit. Deep profiling by ground-penetrating radar requires more expensive equipment and more highly trained personnel than do the other geophysical prospecting technologies currently used in archaeology.

Radar seems to work best when the soil resistivity is high, as in well-drained soils and those with a low clay content. Subsurface wells, foundations, cellars, voids, cavities, and well-defined compacted zones, such as house floors, are known to provide clear radar echoes. Ground-penetrating radar equipment is relatively portable. It may be transported on a handcart as the transmitter/receiver is dragged across the earth's surface.

Fortunately, 12 days later, the *Times* corrected its slip-up (also on the editorial page):

> Writing about China the other day, we innocently repeated what turns out to be an old savant's tale—that the Great Wall is the only mortal structure visible from the moon.
>
> Challenged by a sharp-eyed reader (see Letters), we decided to check with higher authority, the Apollo astronaut Buzz Aldrin. He says that from the moon, he never saw the Wall, and doesn't think any human could.
>
> "You have a hard time even seeing continents," recalled Mr. Aldrin. . . . "I guess where this all got started was on the Gemini flights, much closer to earth, when astronauts were able to identify man-made structures, maybe including the Great Wall."
>
> Chastened, we passed this along to McGraw-Hill, publisher of our source, "The Great Wall of China," whose foreword by Jacques Gernet of the Collège de France proclaims that the Wall is "the only man-made structure that can be seen from the moon." It's still a big wall but that's an extraterrestrial tale. (*New York Times*, March 20, 1983)

That "sharp-eyed reader" was Arthur N. Waldron, a researcher in Princeton University's Asian Studies Department, whose letter to the editor read in part:

> You say the Great Wall is "the only mortal creation visible from the Moon." This idea is at least 60 years old, and it is often repeated, even in learned articles. It isn't true.
>
> No communication with manned spacecraft makes mention of the Wall, and in any case, a few calculations demonstrate the idea's absurdity. According to my friend Dr. Alta Walker of the U.S. Geological Survey, seeing the Wall from the Moon is like seeing a popsickle [*sic*] stick from 384 kilometers.

Where does all this stuff come from?

By the time we conducted our intensive radar study at Mission Santa Catalina, we had already completed the magnetometer and soil resistivity surveys, and excavations were being conducted in the church, kitchen, and friary. We were also using shallow test trenching to determine the extent and configuration of the associated area containing Guale Indian houses.

Historical documents suggested that Santa Catalina had been fortified as a precaution against British attack, so we thought that a stockade and moat complex might have been constructed to protect the Spanish buildings immediately adjacent to the central plaza. Yet, despite 3 years employing other remote sensing prospecting and limited excavations, we had failed to locate any trace of defensive fortifications at Santa Catalina. Thus, our immediate objective for the ground-penetrating radar survey was a search for fortifications, such as palisades, bastions, or moats encircling the central mission zone.

We used the existing grid system, having cleared brush and palmetto from the transect lines before our survey. Initially, a number of systematic north-south transects were run at 20-meter intervals, followed by a series of east-west transects. Obvious anomalies were hand-plotted on the gray scale computer output, and additional transects were run across these target areas. Significant anomalies were plotted on the ground by means of pin flags. We then ran a third set of transects at a 45-degree angle, to intercept buried anomalies in a perpendicular fashion.

By this point, we had become such great believers in, and advocates of, remote sensing technology that we worried about extending our excavations into areas not first surveyed geophysically. Remote sensing is not very effective in partly excavated areas, and we were troubled about the potential information loss should the site be excavated "blind," without benefit of a remote sensing survey. The complete ground-penetrating radar survey of Santa Catalina had thus become mandatory simply to stockpile potential information that would be lost during the excavation process.

The general objective of the ground-penetrating radar research was to establish a baseline library of radar signatures for Santa Catalina. We now have comprehensive sets of such profiles, suitable for comparison with both the results of excavation and the projections obtained from other means of geophysical survey.

We also accomplished our specific objective: The test excavations, guided by radar profiles, led directly to the discovery of the palisade and bastion complex encircling the central buildings and plaza at Santa Catalina. Although this defensive network could surely have been located by extensive test trenching, the radar approach proved to be considerably more cost effective and less destructive than conventional archaeological exploration.

In effect, we saturated a 2.6-acre area with several methods of remote sensing. Then we began extensive excavations to compare the efficacy and results of each method against the in-ground archaeological evidence. Once the excavations are finished, we will comprehensively compare magnetometer, resistivity, and ground-penetrating radar methods against the facts as uncovered by excavation.

Cerén: The New World Pompeii?

Remote sensing studies work best when instrumentation and imagery are calibrated to local conditions and when extensive field verification studies can be conducted. Such a situation exists at the site of Cerén, located in the Zapotitlan Valley of El Salvador (just northwest of the capital city of San Salvador). The Zapotitlan Valley is surrounded by large volcanoes and cinder cones, all of which are either currently active, or soon to be.

The Cerén site was discovered in 1976 by a bulldozer operator as he was attempting to level a platform on which to build some grain storage silos. When he noted that his bulldozer blade had uncovered the corner of a deeply buried building, this workman did a remarkable thing: Instead of just plowing ahead, he stepped down, looked around, and, when he found some old-looking pottery buried in the building, stopped work and notified the National Museum in San Salvador. Unfortunately, when a representative of the museum arrived 3 days later, he dismissed the find as very recent construction and gave the heavy equipment operator his blessing to continue working. As an unfortunate result, several other ancient buildings were bulldozed.

Adobe columns and flooring of Structure 1 at the Cerén site (El Salvador). This Maya house was buried instantaneously in about A.D. 590 by nearly 20 feet of volcanic ash from the nearby Loma Caldera. When archaeologist Payson Sheets and his crew excavated this house, they found all artifacts left in place. Even the thatched roof had been preserved.

Two years later, when Payson Sheets and his students from the University of Colorado arrived to conduct a survey of the Zapotitlan Valley, townspeople told them of the unusual find, and showed them where some of it remained. Sheets saw some adobe columns protruding from the disturbed area and expected to find bits of plastic and newspaper eroding out of the ruined building. Even when he found some Classic Period polychrome Maya pottery (thought to date A.D. 500–800), he still assumed that the building was modern—the thatch roof was almost perfectly preserved, even though it was buried beneath 16 feet of volcanic ash.

But after a few hours of careful excavation, Sheets found lots of ancient Maya artifacts—without any historic-period material turning up at all. Writing about his experience later, Payson Sheets noted that he "began to perceive two very different possibilities: (1) I was on the brink of a massive professional embarrassment if I prematurely announced the find of these structures as prehistoric, and they turned out to be recent, or (2) they were in fact prehistoric, and therefore the site is of extreme importance." The whole issue turned, of course, on dating. Sheets carefully collected some of the buried roof thatch for radiocarbon analysis. When the results of the tests came back, he no longer worried about embarrassing himself professionally—all the thatch samples (and therefore the buried houses as well) were 1,400 years old.

Today, the Zapotitlan Valley find, known as the Cerén site, clearly dates to the Classic Maya Period. The entire village had been instantaneously buried in about A.D. 590 by up to 20 feet of volcanic ash from the nearby Loma Caldera. Because the ash had cooled off considerably by the time it hit, nearly all the ancient agricultural features and cultural artifacts were miraculously preserved—crops still in the field, orchards, a central public plaza surrounded by Classic Period adobe houses with artifacts left exactly as buried, and even the ancient Maya farmers' footprints. Although other sites have been proposed as the "Pompeii of the Americas," Cerén certainly remains one of the leading contenders.

So completely did the volcanic ash cover the area that nothing of Cerén remained visible on the ground surface. How could Sheets map something that was buried beneath 20 feet of volcanic debris?

Payson Sheets and his colleagues turned to ground-penetrating radar as a way to see what lay below the surface. The depositional conditions at Cerén

Ground-penetrating radar unit collecting data on subsurface stratigraphy at the Cerén site (El Salvador). The sending-receiving antenna is attached to the rear of the oxcart. Inside the oxcart are the oscilloscope, instrumentation tape recorder, graphic recorder, and gas-powered generator.

were almost ideal for remote sensing. The overlying volcanic ash contained relatively little clay and there was only minimal soil formation. One of the radar antennas, using 80 MHz frequency radar energy, could penetrate more than 7 meters deep; but this long wavelength would only resolve buried features greater than 1 or 2 meters in diameter. However, when a 300 MHz antenna was employed, and the maximum depth was reduced to 5 meters, then features as small as 45–50 centimeters could be delineated.

But these radar antennas are unwieldy and difficult to pull over rocky terrain. And to make matters worse, much of the ground surface at Cerén was a functioning maize field. When we ran into comparable problems during our own radar surveys of Mission Santa Catalina, we loaded the radar equipment onto the bed of a pickup truck, and drove slowly along, taking radar readings as we drove.

Faced with the same difficulty, Sheets and his team employed a more local solution. They loaded their ground-penetrating radar system into the back of an oxcart, the most common mode of transport in rural El Salvador, first introduced by the sixteenth-century Spanish colonists. This imaginative solution worked quite well, although it was an incongruous sight—a wooden cart laden with hundreds of pounds of high-tech radar equipment, pulled by slowly plodding oxen through a Salvadoran cornfield.

The entire ancient landscape at Cerén was mapped and reconstructed from the GPR results (and verified with numerous test pit and block excavations). The population density of the buried zone was surprisingly high. On the day it was buried, Cerén was a prosperous farming village with closely packed domestic, civic, and religious buildings constructed on elevated platforms, with all intervening space between them taken up by agricultural crops.

Because of its extraordinary preservation, the Cerén site is one of the most important places in Central America for studying ancient land-use practices. GPR mapping has proved to be a cost-effective method for discovering buried houses—some of which were excavated, the rest preserved for the future. By carefully working out the various radar signatures from the excavated houses, remote sensing and associated computer-modeling techniques allowed these pre-Columbian houses to be precisely mapped even though unexcavated (see also *High-Tech Wizardry: Discovering the Thousand-Year-Old Footpath at Arenal,* by Payson D. Sheets and Thomas L. Sever).

The Emperor's Secrets Are Buried: No Digging Allowed

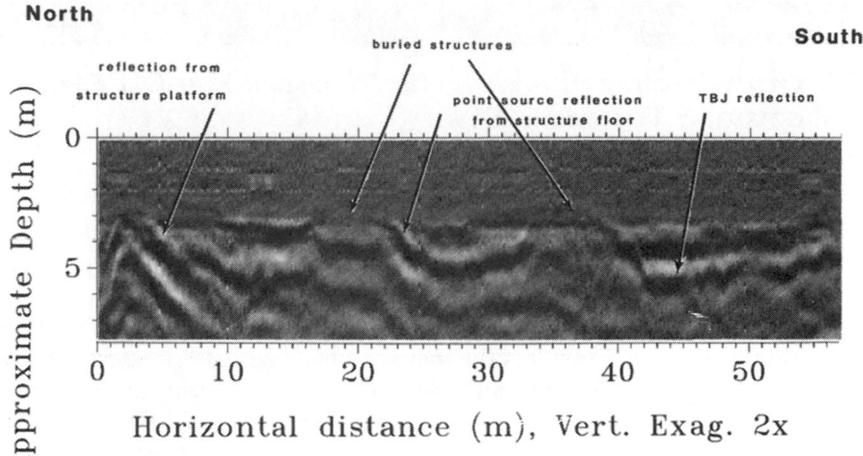

Ground-penetrating radar profile across three buried structures at the Cerén site.

Ground-penetrating radar today is being applied around the world. In Japan, for cxamplc, this technology, together with more conventional archaeological discoveries, is threatening to upset the political applecart.

The interpretive sign at the Nishitonozuka mound, placed there by the Imperial Household Agency of the Japanese government, officially declares that it is the tomb of a sixth-century empress. This designation is meaningful because this site is today revered as an important religious shrine.

But archaeologists working outside the fenced-off area, in the moat surrounding this huge keyhole-shaped mound, have found sherds of a distinctive funerary-style pottery suggesting the tomb may actually have been built 1,600 years ago—making it a century older than the sign says. Now, in many places, a disparity of a century in dating would not be a big deal. But in Japan, where the ceramic chronology is highly refined, a single century can make quite a difference.

Every professional knows that this is not the empress's tomb. The Government just does not acknowledge our findings.

HIROAKI MATSUMOTO, ARCHAEOLOGIST

So the official government position says one thing, the newly found potsherds another. But are the sherds actually associated with the mound, or are they later fill that accumulated in the moat? Any competent archaeologist could resolve the problem with a few carefully placed test pits. Numerous contemporary mounds—but not those of the royal family—have been excavated, and they are known to contain grave goods such as weaponry, household items, and jewelry—all items that could be dated fairly accurately.

The problem is that archaeologists are not allowed to dig. A specific directive from the Imperial Household Agency states that this mound and the 455 other royal tombs it seeks to protect contain the remains of emperors, empresses, and other royal relatives—no digging allowed.

Artist's reconstruction of the buried structures at the Cerén site. The domicile (Structure 1) appears in the center, with the workshop on the right, and the storehouse on the left.

The official governmental position follows the tradition

IN THEIR OWN WORDS

High-Tech Wizardry: Discovering *the* Thousand-Year-Old Footpath *at Arenal* by Payson D. Sheets and Thomas L. Sever

Payson Sheets and Tom Sever experienced their own sort of "aha!" experience as they looked at satellite imagery of the Lake Arenal region in northwestern Costa Rica, where they were working at the time. This place receives an average of 14 feet of precipitation a year, resulting in a dense tropical rainforest, which renders the archaeological record almost invisible. Not only does the dense vegetation obscure things, but volcanic ash, deposited from at least 10 explosive eruptions over the past 4,000 years, blankets the landscape. The chances of finding any significant surface indication of the archaeological record here is about zero—at least when you're standing on the ground.

But, as Sheets and Sever found out, there is new technology to explore the hidden archaeological record, even in the ash-covered rainforest of Costa Rica:

One morning in the spring of 1985 we were leafing through some infrared aerial photographs of the Tilaran area of northwestern Costa Rica. We were familiar with the territory and could easily correlate most locations on the photos with places we knew at ground level.

What surprised us was an odd, twisting line. It began near an ancient cemetery, headed straight downhill, made a wide-angle bend around an enigmatic prehistoric rockpile, crossed a stream, headed uphill, and made another bend around another enigmatic rockpile. Because it ran straight across hills and valleys, linking archaeological sites such as cemeteries, villages, and sources of stone, we suspected it was not a natural feature, but perhaps a prehistoric road.

The only way to be sure was to excavate. The next day we hired three local workers and dug three trenches across the area in question. We discovered that volcanic ash had fallen there in A.D. *1000 and 1500, but that earlier ash layers had been eroded away as the prehistoric "line" formed. Excavation and examination of these layers indicated that the feature was not a road, but a footpath, an erosional feature. The rockpiles beside the path were probably piles of construction stone that had been left behind for use in burials at the cemetery.*

The infrared photographs had revealed a footpath created over time, more than 1,000 years ago, and then buried by an act of nature. Such a thing had never before been detected by remote sensing and then confirmed by field excavations.

As archaeology becomes more regional, remote sensing can contribute more to the understanding of the prehistoric impact of people on the environment—whether these impacts take the form of cities, roads, agricultural fields, or even little footpaths in a tropical forest.

Our experience strongly suggests that when combined with sophisticated data analysis and field verification, remote sensing may be as revolutionary in archaeology today as was the introduction of radiocarbon dating in the 1950s.

PAYSON D. SHEETS is professor of anthropology at the University of Colorado (Boulder) and THOMAS L. SEVER is senior research scientist at the Earth Resources Laboratory, NASA, Stennis Space Center, Mississippi.

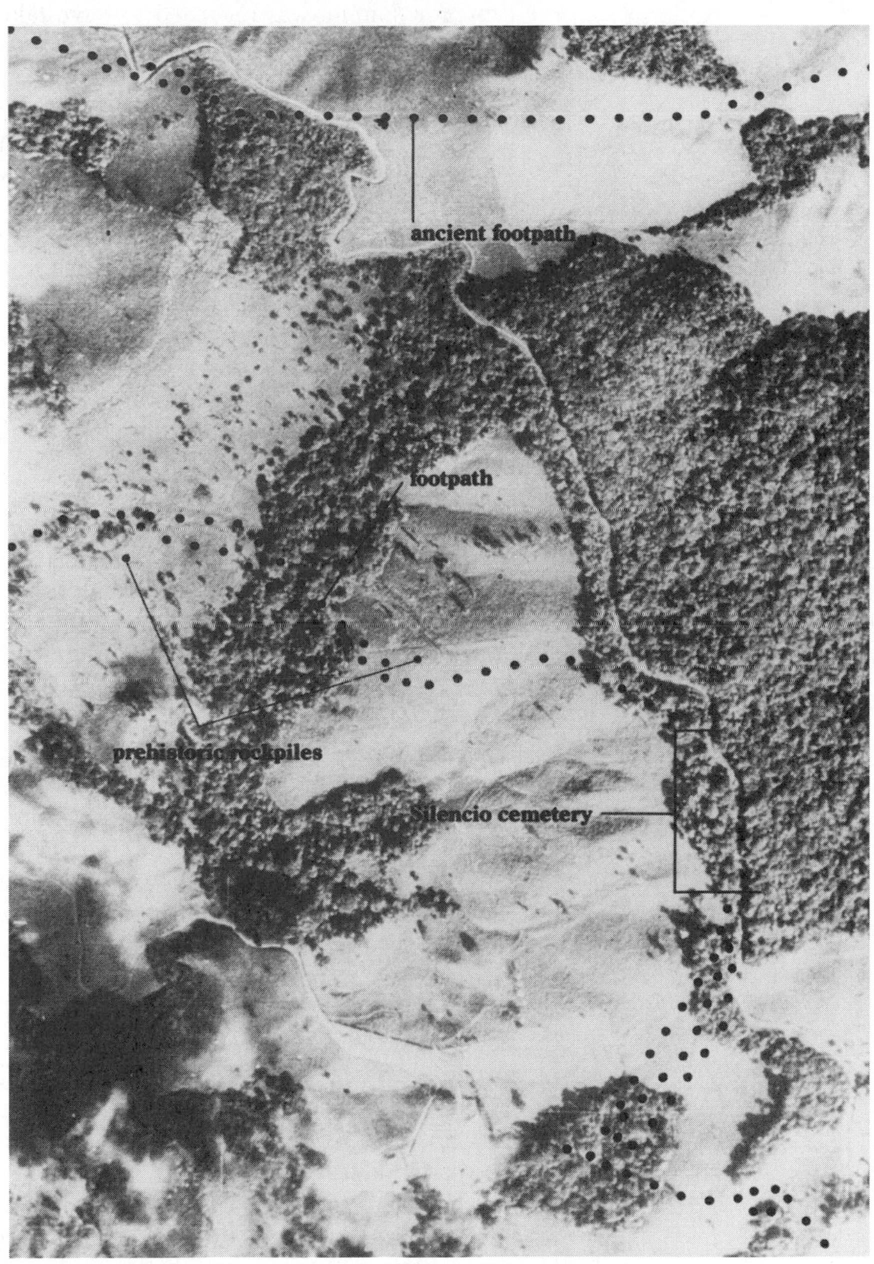

Aerial photograph showing the relationship of ancient footpaths and cemetery at Arenal. The various ancient rockpiles were accumulated as building materials for tombs or retaining walls.

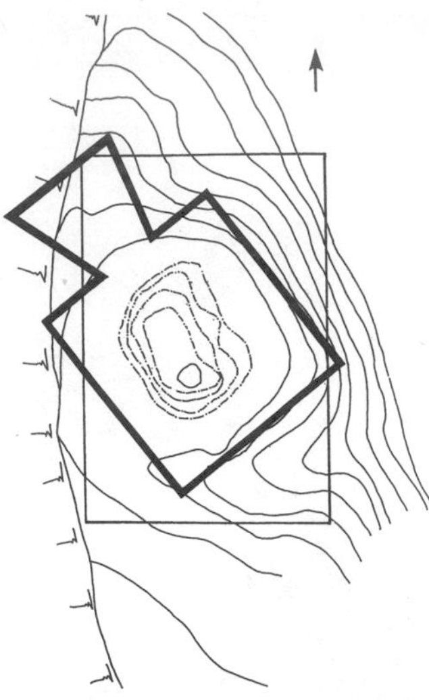

Topographic map of the Kanmachi Mandara keyhole burial mound (Japan).

that Japan's imperial family line stretches back unbroken for more than 2,500 years—making it the world's oldest continuously reigning monarchy. The imperial family's claim to the throne relies on ancient historical sources saying the line descends directly from the Sun Goddess; the first Emperor, Jimmu, was recorded to have taken the throne on February 11, 660 B.C.

But the historical records allegedly documenting this unprecedented line of succession are kept in secret government files. Fifty years ago, a historian named Sokichi Tsuda was convicted of insulting the dignity of the royal family when he questioned whether the first nine emperors were actual historical figures.

Today, most Japanese historians view the first 10 to 15 emperors as purely mythical, and they believe that the royal line actually began in the fifth or sixth century A.D. Some even suggest that the earliest emperors may have had Korean blood coursing through their royal veins—a heresy to many modern Japanese nationalists. The Imperial Household Agency continues to refuse any archaeological exploration of the mounds because, they claim, it would desecrate the graves of the emperor's ancestors—who remain the objects of worship and veneration.

But critics charge that political motivations lie behind the ban on excavation. Those who oppose archaeological investigations have a vested interest in perpetuating the myth of the unbroken line and the mystique of the imperial throne.

Each year, a delegation of archaeologists petitions the Imperial Household Agency for permission to explore the mounds of questionable age. And each year, according to Masayoshi Mizuno of Nara University, the answer is always the same: There is no answer.

So how can scholars conduct valid historical research on these off-limits mounds? Dean Goodman (Geophysical Archaeometry Laboratory, University of Miami Japan Division) and Yasushi Nishimura (Archaeological Operations, Nara National Cultural Properties Research Institute) believe that remote sensing technology may be the answer. Goodman and Nishimura have recently been conducting ground-penetrating radar studies to determine the internal configuration of such "official" royal tombs.

The Kanmachi Mandara keyhole burial mound, in Ishikawa Prefecture, is one of the protected mounds. It is believed to date to the early Kofun period, roughly A.D. 30–350 (toward the early end of the "official" claim to the throne). It has a square rear mound with burial remains and a triangular frontal extension. Because of its relatively small size, the ancient mound was not initially recognized as such by road engineers, and the triangular section was partly destroyed by a road.

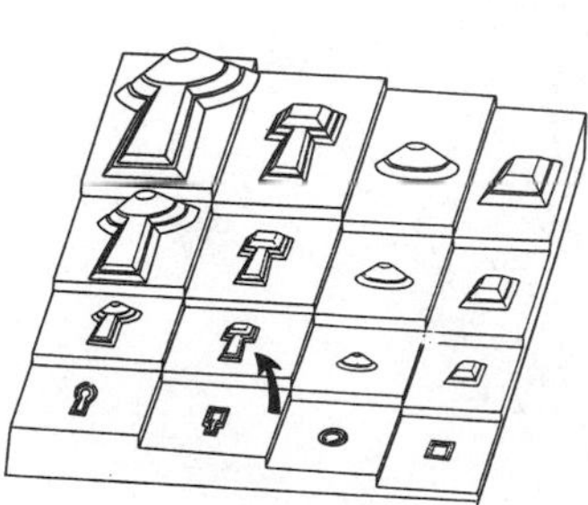

The rank of the Kanmachi Mandara burial mound within the general hierarchy of the Japanese mound-building sequence (as shown by the arrow).

The intact part of this mound is protected by Japanese cultural property law—no digging allowed. But nondestructive remote sensing is permitted and was done to determine the location and shape of the burial area contained within and also to learn something about its structural design.

A series of parallel radar profiles—called "time slices"—were run through the Kanmachi Mandara burial mound. A *time slice* is an analytical method for synthesizing the various radar passes at a specific vertical level. Time slices can be made at various radar-scan depths, creating remotely sensed site plans for these depths below the ground surface—and all based strictly on nondestructive data.

Using the time-slice technique, at a projected depth of about .5 meters below the ground surface of the Kanmachi Mandara burial mound, a remarkable pattern appeared. By looking at the internal structural data, one sees the general orientation and location of the coffin remains clearly evident as the large central anomaly.

To determine even more detail, a second radar survey was run across the coffin area, this time at a 90-degree angle. From this second radar perspective, it seems clear that a large burial pit was first excavated, into which a clay foundation was set to anchor the wooden coffin containing the deceased and various grave goods. This foundation originally sloped upwards to encase the lateral sides of the coffin, which by now has probably deteriorated.

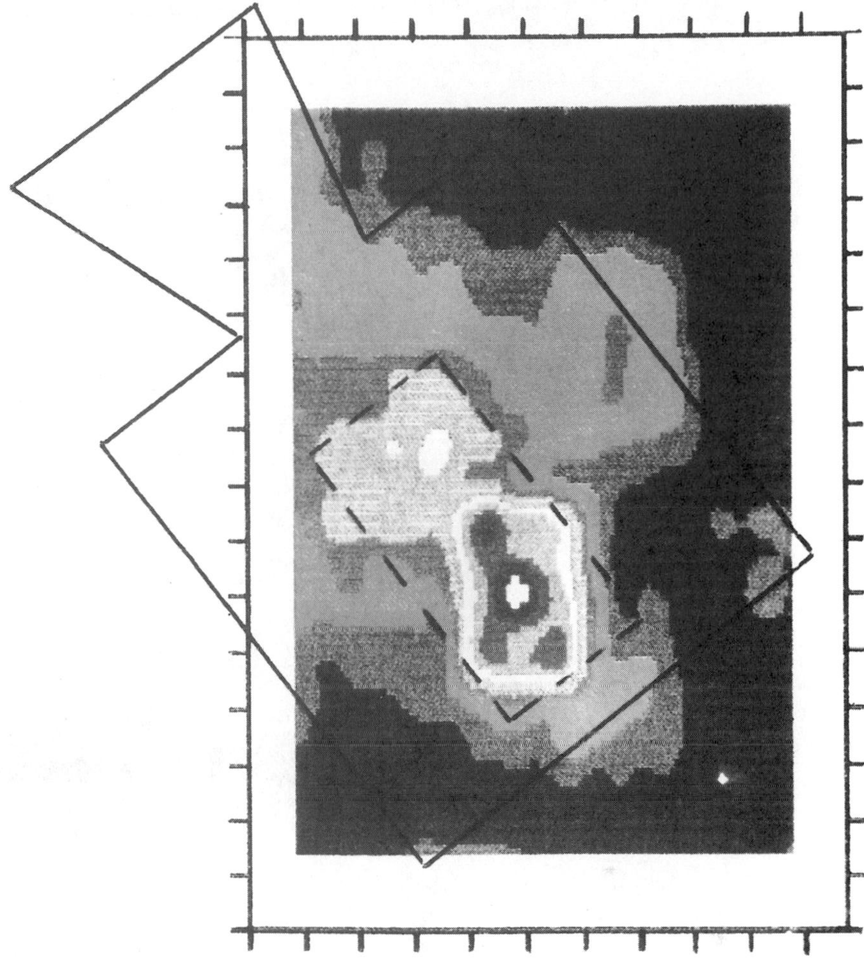

A "time slice" of the Kanmachi Mandara burial mound, generated by ground-penetrating radar. The large central anomaly (the whitish area) is believed to be the central tomb; the dark area inside that is probably the coffin remains.

These ground-penetrating radar results tell us a great deal about the internal structure of the unexcavated Kanmachi Mandara keyhole burial mound and, if excavation were permitted, the various radar-generated site plans could be used to pinpoint relatively small test excavations to obtain samples for radiometric dating.

But since such excavations are not permitted, archaeologists are limited to the relatively general internal site plans—intriguing in their own right, but not of sufficient resolution to shed any significant light on the highly controversial longevity of Japan's imperial family.

The Potential of Noninvasive Archaeology

A striking parallel exists between the development of remote sensing in today's archaeology and the birth of "nonsite," surface archaeology three decades ago. In both cases, the nature of meaningful data has changed, as is vividly illustrated by recent developments in the field of Maya archaeology.

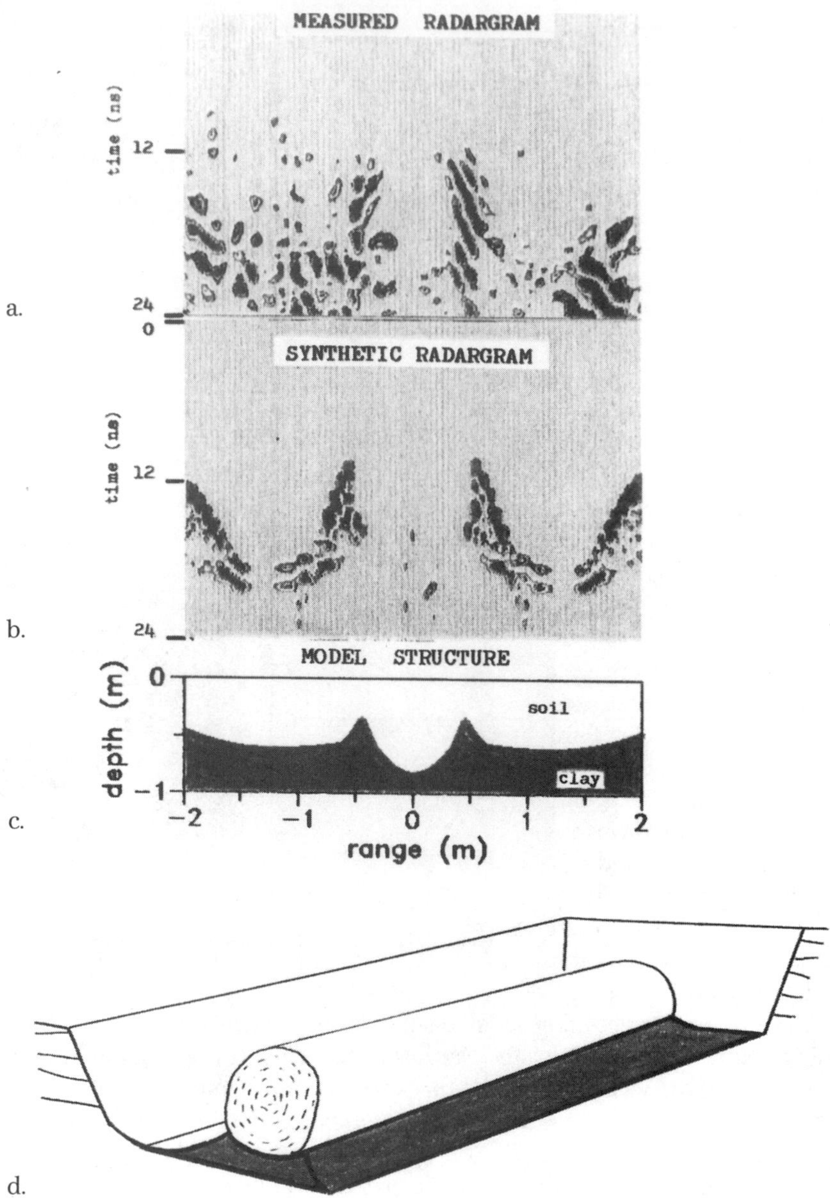

Ground-penetrating radar cross section through tomb area of the Kanmachi Mandara keyhole burial mound; a *shows the actual radar results,* b *and* c *are models abstracted from these results, and* d *is a reconstruction of the coffin region, showing a clay bed supporting a since-eroded coffin.*

After years of debate about the foggy relationship between urbanism and Classic Maya subsistence, investigators tried using airborne synthetic aperture radar to penetrate the forest cover. Investigators mapped and spot-verified an extensive system of previously unknown canals that drained a truly impressive segment of the Mayan lowlands. An entirely new avenue of inquiry was opened. Although the issues of Classic Maya subsistence can hardly be settled by remote sensing, such technology without question has generated a fresh perspective, creating data inherently different from that obtained through more conventional techniques of excavation and terrestrial survey.

Remote sensing can lead us to new ways of defining traditional concepts in archaeology, provided that we work out unambiguous relations between the things still buried and the reasons we know they are there. Doing this requires that we construct the requisite linkages between the more traditional archaeological concepts—walls, structures, and features—and the way that they are perceived ("remotely") by the sensors of geophysical machinery.

Remote sensing technology can give archaeologists a cost-effective means of making a noninvasive, nondestructive assessment of the archaeological record. In the early developmental stage, the emphasis has necessarily been on technology, but for such technology to pay off in archaeology, the hardware must be thoroughly integrated into the mainstream theoretical fabric of working archaeology. Newer developments in geophysical technology and field technique cannot be viewed merely as refined ways of generating traditional archaeological data.

Remote sensing can act as a bridge between the empirical record of geophysical technology and theory building in archaeology. Archaeologists are now building a baseline library of geophysical signatures for key archaeological sites. They are not only comparing the results between geophysical survey and actual excavation; they are also examining the efficiency of the various geophysical media. Although preliminary, such exercises should ensure that in the future, at places like Mission Santa Catalina, destructive exploratory groping can be avoided. Subsurface research designs can be guided instead by a sequence of unambiguous, nondestructive geophysical signatures.

The use of remote sensing technology also makes archaeologists look once more at the nature of their data. "Empirical observation" in yesterday's archaeology was conducted by "tactile sensing"—you-know-what-something-is-after-you've-dug-it-up-and-can-hold-it-in-your-hand. Although archaeologists working in this framework soon fill up their empty museum cases and storerooms, they are often confused about what archaeological data really are. As discussed earlier, archaeological data are not the objects or things that archaeologists acquire. Rather, archaeological data are the counts, measurements, and observations made on these recovered objects. There can be no archaeological data in this sense until an archaeologist observes them. Data cannot exist passively. Archaeological data are deliberately generated (sometimes decades after objects are recovered from their contexts). Remote sensing is simply one more way of generating archaeological data. But in this case, archaeologists are making their counts, measurements, and observations on objects and features that have not yet been excavated.

So What's Holding Remote Sensing Back?

The enormous potential of noninvasive, nondestructive archaeology is recognized by many. But the actual number of archaeologists employing remote sensing technology in their everyday research is still relatively limited.

So what's holding remote sensing back? I believe that several factors have kept remote sensing from living up to its advance billing, at least in archaeology. For one thing, remote sensing has rarely been given a fair chance, which reflects a general lack of commitment in the archaeological community. Many of us have overheard practicing field archaeologists toss off the throw-away line: "Oh, we tried resistivity (or magnetometers, or ground-penetrating radar) once, but it didn't work"—the implication being that they won't waste their time doing *that* any more. Let me suggest some reasons for this.

Remote Sensing Has Relatively High Start-Up Costs

Even setting aside the cost of the machinery and software, many archaeologists seem to be put off by the added burden—measured in time, knowledge, and access—required to conduct remote sensing studies as part of their routine fieldwork. Few are willing to pay the up-front costs necessary to use remote sensing in any more than cursory fashion.

Today's generation of student archaeologists can prove invaluable here, because even as novices, many already possess computer and analytical skills unheard of even among the younger generation of practicing field archaeologists. Indeed, great opportunities exist for those wishing to break into a hot new field in archaeology.

Remote Sensing Is Boring

Or, as geophysicist John Weymouth puts it, "mind-numbing." While this is surely true, to be fair, one must also ask: What about archaeological fieldwork isn't? Have you tried screening dust for 6 weeks? What about drawing topographic maps? Or processing flotation samples? Or recording stratigraphies? Each of these activities, taken in isolation and conducted at length, can be tedious and boring—just ask the person who does it.

But should we stop screening sites just because it's monotonous to stand at a screen all day? Should archaeologists stop making site maps just because it's tiring to hold a stadia rod? What about walking in straight lines on systematic surveys?

What separates geophysical methods from the rest of archaeological tedium is that screening, map making, and walking transects has become part of field archaeology's *minimum acceptable standard.* Remote sensing is not considered in that league (at least not yet).

Why?

Augmenting the Available Perspectives

Part of the problem lies with our still-limited perspective of what archaeological things really are. The conventional archaeological approach to fieldwork is still to pursue a single-point version of the "truth"—as in "ground truth." Look, for instance, at how remote sensing is conducted today. First you get some geophysical instruments, then you conduct a systematic survey across a suspected area of archaeological significance, and finally you evaluate the results. But, we are always cautioned, one must be wary of taking the geophysical evidence at face value *because remote sensing results must always be ground-truthed.*

That expression, *ground truth,* is revealing. Not only does it conjure up the traditional affinity between archaeologists and the earth—real dirt archaeology—but "ground truth" underscores the prevalent notion that "it isn't true unless it's found in the ground . . . it isn't real unless you can dig it up."

Nobody should quibble with the importance of confirming the results of geophysical survey through controlled excavation. But the implied methodological sequence betrays a misunderstanding of what archaeological data are all about.

This misapprehension may explain why so few remote sensing studies are now conducted in archaeology. This approach conflicts with the current overarching perception of archaeological data: what data are, and how you get them.

Suppose instead that we approach the archaeological record from multiple directions simultaneously. While we surely do not reject excavation as a way to gather knowledge about the past—I still spend months each year conducting "conventional" excavation—it may be that the past is best addressed by considering fresh, multiple perspectives as well.

To see how this might work, look at what we have said in the last couple of chapters about regional archaeology. For years, archaeologists relied on "things dug up." But then, using some of the techniques discussed here, archaeologists are learning to understand things from a regional context.

The objects remained the same. What distinguished regional archaeology was the attempt to redefine the scale of observation. Rather than excavating 10-centimeter levels inside 1-meter squares, projects like the Oaxaca, St. Catherines Island, and Reese River surveys all encouraged a shift in scale: We began to perceive pattern in terms of kilometers and hectares. The shift to archaeology at the regional scale required retooling a conceptual base specifically designed to keep theory apace with field technique—by using methods and concepts independent of those employed in archaeological excavation. The acceptance of "nonsite" archaeology is one such advance. The newly recognized value of surface and plow zone archaeology is another example of how archaeology, viewed at a regional scale, changed our conception of what archaeological data are.

Similar perceptual and conceptual shifts will be required before remote sensing can fully contribute to archaeological research. Remote sensing is another way of generating perfectly respectable archaeological data. But in this case, archaeologists are making their counts, measurements, and observations on objects and features that have not yet been excavated. If this view were to proliferate, not only would remote sensing studies benefit, but so would several other aspects of archaeological inquiry.

Today's archaeology is fully capable of applying such shifting perspectives to the various databanks of the past—whether the data are derived from sites, from regions, or from geophysical prospecting. Historically, "empirical observation" too often defined an archaeology that was conducted by "tactile sensing." The physical artifacts were viewed as comprising the "hard data" of archaeology.

Much of the ambivalence toward remote sensing on the part of the archaeological profession can be attributed directly to this basic, shared perception of archaeological data. Archaeologists still too often mistakenly believe that the process of excavation somehow reveals the "truth"—the way it really was.

SUMMARY Americanist archaeology is undergoing a revolution. In the days of Schliemann and C. B. Moore, archaeologists simply blasted away at their sites, leaving wrecked ruins in their wake. To archaeologists at mid-century, the greatest technological revolution was the advent of the backhoe as a tool of excavation.

Today, we view archaeological sites in a radically different manner. Part of this new conservation ethic reflects the definition of archaeological remains as nonrenewable resources. But equally important has been the development of noninvasive technology for doing relatively nondestructive archaeology. Using the archaeological equivalents of the CAT scan, archaeologists can now map subsurface features in detail without ever excavating them. And when it does become necessary to recover samples, we can, like the orthopedic surgeon, execute pinpoint excavations, minimizing damage to the rest of the site.

This chapter presented several remote sensing techniques: proton magnetometry, high-altitude imagery, soil resistivity, and ground-penetrating radar. These are just a few weapons in today's high-tech arsenal, which includes a dozen noninvasive, nondestructive techniques to assess the archaeological record.

Chapter 6

Doing Fieldwork: Why Archaeologists Dig Square Holes

PREVIEW Ask most people what archaeologists do, and they'll tell you this: "They dig." And that's right. Despite what we have seen in the preceding two chapters about archaeological survey techniques and remote sensing technology, digging up old stuff remains at the heart of archaeology—and probably always will.

We warned earlier about the problems of learning archaeological field techniques from a book (even this one): You can't do it. But in these next three chapters describing common archaeological field methods, we do hope to show you how fieldwork is done and what it really feels like. Archaeological excavation is really something special, as anybody who has ever participated in a dig will tell you. I joined my first archaeological expedition as a college junior. From that day on, I was hooked. These days, it is much easier to participate in an excavation, and anybody with even a casual interest in archaeology ought to give it a try.

When I excavate sites and touch things that have lain untouched for centuries, I know why I am an archaeologist.

JANET D. SPECTOR, ARCHAEOLOGIST (UNIVERSITY OF MINNESOTA)

In Chapter 4, we talked about the discovery of Gatecliff Shelter. Although sometimes electrifying, finding sites like Gatecliff is only the beginning. Our excavation strategy and tactics evolved dramatically as we learned more about the site and its potential.

Excavated sites are the archaeologist's bread and butter.

LEWIS R. BINFORD, ARCHAEOLOGIST (SOUTHERN METHODIST UNIVERSITY)

We began with two simple test pits dug the same year we found the site. From day one, we wanted to learn two things: how long people had used Gatecliff Shelter and whether the buried deposits could tell us about the human chronology of the region. These two questions were clear-cut, and so was our fieldwork. Our earliest excavation strategy was vertical, designed to supply, as expediently as possible, a stratified sequence of artifacts and ecofacts associated with other potentially datable materials.

Like most archaeologists, I dig "metrically" in typically 1-meter squares. There is, of course, a minimum size in such exploratory soundings: Squares much smaller would squeeze out the archaeologists, and larger units are overly destructive (and too time-consuming).

Test pits tend to be quick and dirty, particularly because they must be excavated "blind," without knowing what stratigraphy lies below. Nevertheless, even in test pits, archaeologists must maintain three-dimensional control of the finds: the X axis (front to back), the Y axis (side to side), and the Z axis

Archaeology is the only discipline in ancient studies which to attain its ends is required to destroy its evidence. Once excavated, a site must be reconstructed from literary evidence, notebooks, diaries, and published reports, aided if available by drawings and photographs. From this fact derives the importance of archaeology.

WILLIAM M. CALDER III

Archaeologists excavating inside Hidden Cave (Nevada). *Without the quartz-halogen landing lights (evident on the left-hand side of this photograph), the excavation area would be pitch black.* Note *also the respirators and hard-hats—often required equipment for working inside such enclosed cave environments.*

(top to bottom). This is why archaeologists dig square holes. Provided the sidewalls are kept sufficiently straight and perpendicular, excavators can use the dirt itself to maintain horizontal control on the *X* and *Y* axes by measuring directly from the sidewalls. As test pits deepen, however, the sidewalls may start sloping inward, cramping the digger and biasing the measurements. Field archaeologists call these sloppy pits "bathtubs"—decidedly bad form.

What about vertical control? At Gatecliff, we dug test pits in arbitrarily imposed 10-centimeter levels. Everything of interest—*artifacts, ecofacts,* soil samples, and so forth—was kept in separate level bags, one for each 10-centimeter level. The *Z* dimension for each level was usually designated according to distance below the ground surface: Level 1 (surface to 10 centimeters below), Level 2 (10 to 20 centimeters below), and so forth.

Excavation procedures vary widely, depending on the stage of excavation, the nature of the deposit, and the impulse of the archaeologist in charge (remember, digging is perhaps still as much craft as science). Because they are so small, test pits are often dug by trowel (rather than by shovel), maintaining a horizontal working surface. Deposit is scooped into a dust pan, dumped into a bucket, then carried off-site for a closer look.

The test pits told us that Gatecliff Shelter warranted a closer look, and we returned the next year to do just that. The site was divided into a 1-meter grid system, oriented along the long axis of the shelter. We assigned consecutive letters to each north-south division and numbered the east-west division. By this method, each excavation square could be designated by a unique alphanumeric name (just like Bingo—A-7, B-5, and the ever-popular K-9). The east wall of the "7-trench"—so named because it contained Units B-7 through I-7—defined a major stratigraphic profile, a vertical section against which all artifacts, features, soil and pollen samples, and radiocarbon dates were correlated.

Datum point: The zero point, a fixed reference used to keep control on a dig; datum points are established in both vertical and horizontal planes.

Feature: The nonportable evidence of technology. Usually refers to fire hearths, architectural elements, artifact clusters, garbage pits, soil stains, and so on.

A *vertical datum* was established at the rear of the shelter. For all on-site operations, this single **datum point** was arbitrarily designated as zero. All site elevations from this point on were plotted as "*x* centimeters below datum." Then, using an altimeter and a U.S. Geological Survey topographic map, we determined the elevation of this datum point to be 2,319 meters (7,607 feet) above sea level; today, we might use some high-tech, satellite-driven technology like GPS to determine this (see *The Global Positioning System: A New Way* *for Archaeologists to Find Themselves* in Chapter 4).

All archaeological **features**—fire hearths, artifact concentrations, sleeping areas, and the like—were plotted on a master site map, and individual artifacts found **in situ** were plotted in three dimensions. All fill was first carefully troweled, then passed outside the cave for screening (as discussed later in this chapter); artifacts and ecofacts found in the screen were bagged by stratigraphic or **arbitrary level.** Field notes at this stage were kept by individual excavators in bound, graph paper notebooks. Good field notes record everything, whether or not it seems important at the time. Depending on the nature of the site (and the stage of excavation), field notes can either be taken "formless" or recorded on specific unit-level forms, with precise categories defined for each kind of necessary information.

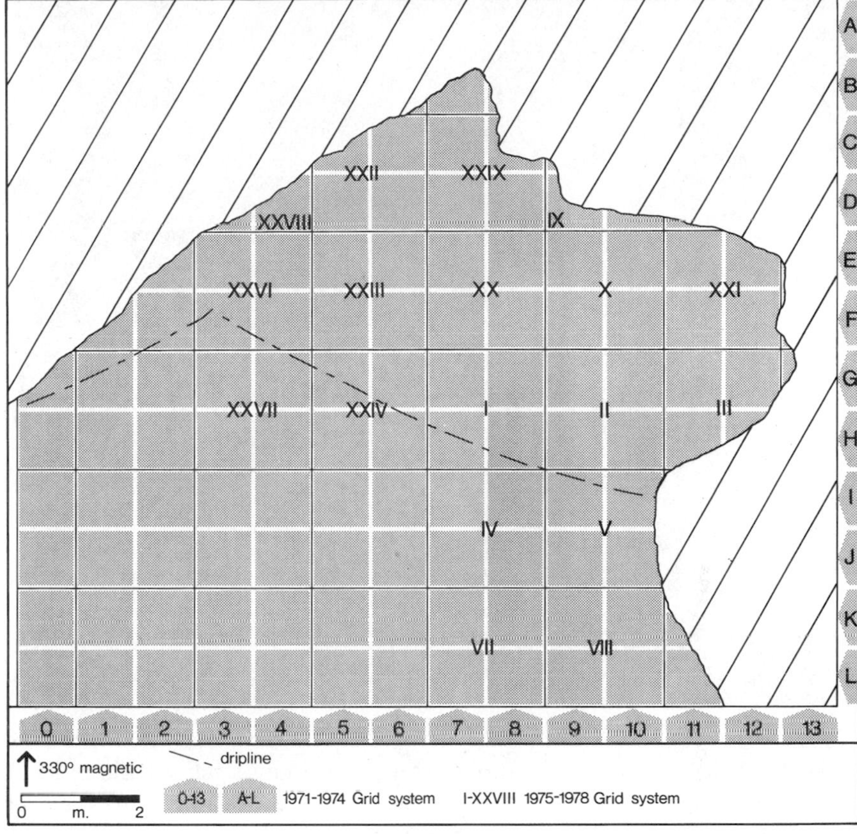

Plan view of the two grid systems used at Gatecliff Shelter. The alphanumeric (numbers and letters) system defined 1-meter excavation squares used in the first four seasons. Roman numerals designate the 2-meter squares used later, when large horizontal exposures were excavated.

At this stage, we were looking primarily for change through time. At Gatecliff, this meant looking for key time-sensitive artifacts to be grouped into temporal types, which (as discussed in Chapter 9) enabled us to place previously undated archaeological contexts into a meaningful sequence as we excavated. Laboratory work subsequently tested these preliminary field hypotheses, what geologists call their "horseback correlations."

The *vertical excavation strategy* is a deliberately simplified scheme designed to clarify chronology. As emphasized throughout this book, archaeologists concentrate on the shared aspects of culture when attempting to chart culture change along a temporal axis. Although this strategy blurs much of the complexity in the archaeological record, it can be justified for these initial temporal aims.

By the end of our fourth field season, our major strata-trench had reached a depth of 9 meters below the ground surface. We knew a good deal about Gatecliff. In Chapter 8, for instance, we will discuss how the master stratigraphic sequence was worked out and how the dozens of radiocarbon dates provided us absolute dates for each stratum. We had successfully defined the cultural sequence of Gatecliff Shelter, but our vertical excavation strategy had also left us with a series of extremely steep and hazardous

In situ: A term referring to the position in which an item is initially encountered during excavation or survey.

Arbitrary level: The basic vertical subdivision of an excavation square; used only when easily recognizable "natural" stratification is lacking.

Excavating the basal strata at Gatecliff Shelter using the bucket brigade method. At this point, the deepest units reached about 40 feet below the ground surface.

sidewalls. Even though the excavation was stairstepped downward to minimize these sidewalls, the sheer verticality of the site made it dangerous. Change was clearly in order, both conceptually and logistically.

Gatecliff Shelter held potential far beyond mere chronology. Remember that establishing cultural chronology is only archaeology's first objective; our early excavations amply demonstrated that Gatecliff could make useful contributions to paleoethnographic objectives as well. Several stratigraphic units contained short-term, intact occupational surfaces, and the remaining excavations at Gatecliff concentrated on the spatial distributions within these key stratigraphic units.

My fieldwork was a picnic with a purpose.

DOROTHY KEUR (1904–1989), ARCHAEOLOGIST

As we shifted away from chronological objectives, we also shifted our digging strategy. We began looking beyond the modal aspects of culture to view things as part of the overall cultural matrix. In other words, the focus moved from the when and where to the more elusive what. Viewed in this manner, digging mine shafts becomes inappropriate. Culture in the broader sense embraces the structural elements basic to adaptive and ideational aspects, rather than merely aggregates of functional traits that happen to be shared. The paleoethnographic approach requires looking at the interrelationships among artifacts, waste debris, cultural features, and cave walls. We must understand what activities took place, not just which artifacts were deposited.

The tactics required to pursue paleoethnography likewise change, sometimes radically. With the stratigraphy suitably defined, extensive vertical sections were no longer necessary, and we concentrated on opening entire living surfaces simultaneously. The cultural lenses at Gatecliff were slowly excavated by hand, with thicker stratigraphic units removed in arbitrary 10-centimeter levels. Exposing living floors proceeded more slowly than had the previous vertical excavations, and excavators were instructed to recover and map all artifacts in situ. Features were screened separately, and flotation samples were retained for laboratory processing. Significant debitage scatters were plotted, as were concentrations of bone and other artifacts. The excavated deposits were then placed in buckets and carried to the screening area where they were passed through 1/8-inch screens, and as before, artifacts missed by the excavators were saved along with all fragments of chippage and bone.

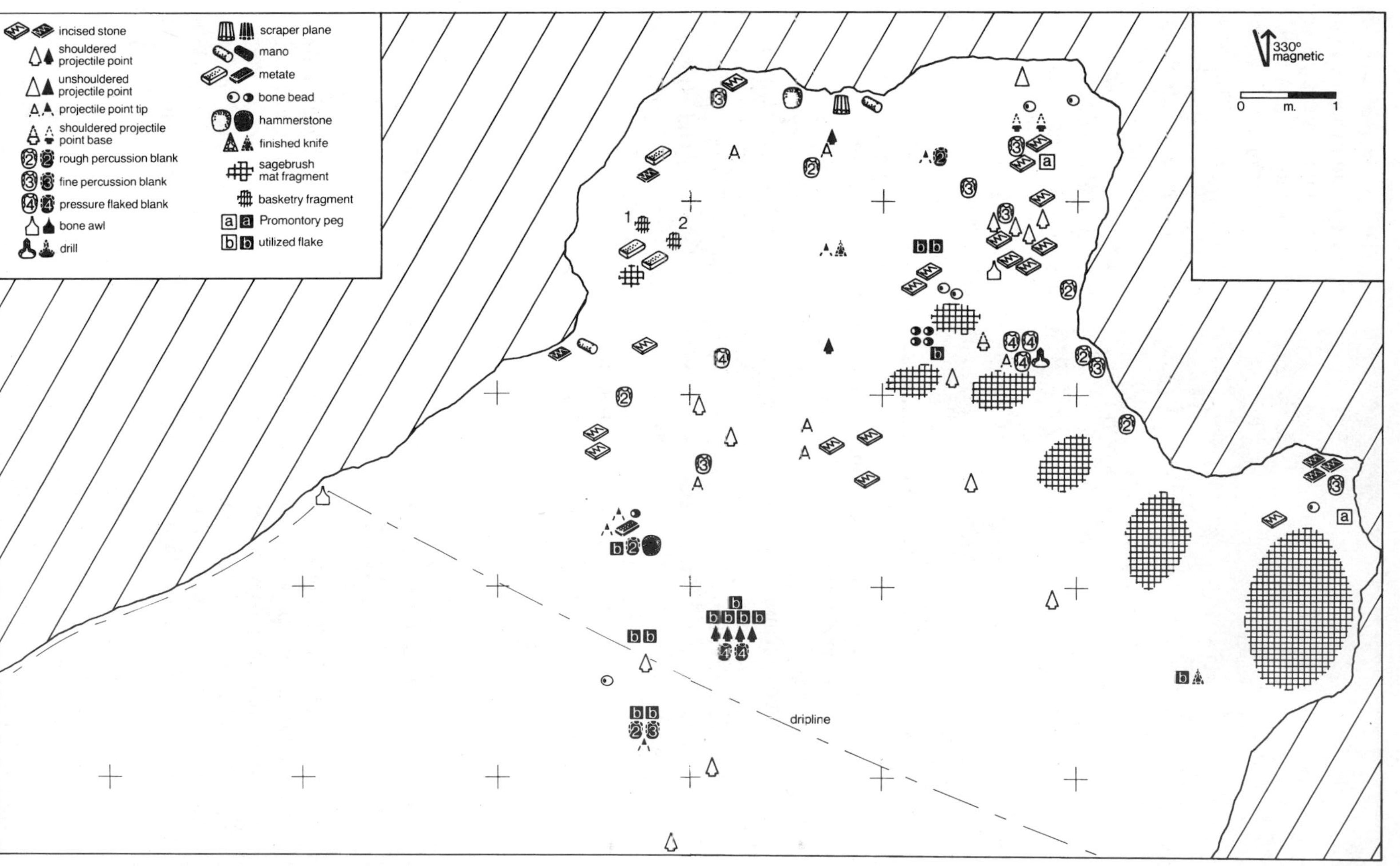

A *"living floor map" showing the distribution of artifacts and hearths on* Horizon 2 (*deposited in about* A.D. 1300).

Artist's reconstruction of the horizontal excavation strategy to expose living surfaces at Gatecliff Shelter. The archaeologist in the foreground is troweling a small test exposure. Those in the background are using a transit and stadia rod to map features on this surface.

The horizontal strategy required significantly more control within contemporary stratigraphic units. A single crew chief took excavation notes for the entire site at this point (rather than having individual excavators do it, as before). Three-dimensional data were transferred to site notebooks, and living floor maps were plotted for each surface at the time of the excavation. A single excavator was assigned to each 2-square-meter unit, and all artifacts, features, and large ecofacts were plotted onto the large-scale living floor maps. Since then, sophisticated computer-driven systems have been developed to assist in piece-plotting objects on living surfaces.

Archaeological sites with such deep, stratified deposits are rare, and excavating such middens poses certain problems to the excavator. In a similar situation, Don Fowler once cleared a 15-foot-high profile at a cave in eastern Nevada. It took 2 days to clean the section for final drawing and photography, and just as workers began to make the final sketch, an Air Force jet screamed overhead. The resulting sonic boom triggered the collapse of the stratigraphic profile and also a fusillade of angry letters of protest from the archaeologists. But like Humpty Dumpty, there is no piecing together a collapsed stratigraphic profile.

Some Rules and Principles Guiding Archaeological Excavation

The major flaw in inferential arguments based on excavated data is the assumption, always implicit, that the absence of evidence is evidence for absence.

MICHAEL BRIAN SCHIFFER, ARCHAEOLOGIST (UNIVERSITY OF ARIZONA)

Our Gatecliff Shelter excavations covered the basics of archaeological excavation: stratigraphy, recovery, provenience. Although the strategies are universal to archaeology, the tactics are site specific. For example, ancient Pueblo sites in New Mexico, containing well-defined room clusters, must be excavated very differently from a high-altitude cave in Nevada. Peeling off sequential levels in a Maya temple in Guatemala differs radically from excavating through seemingly homogeneous shell midden deposits in Georgia. Underwater archaeology uses a host of techniques and equipment totally alien to terrestrial contexts.

Field Archaeologists dig up rubbish, Theoretical Archaeologists write it down.

PAUL BAHN, ARCHAEOLOGIST

Still, certain considerations transcend the site-specific context, and the rest of this chapter addresses the more universal characteristics of archaeological fieldwork.

Sifting the Evidence

The deepest stratigraphic sounding at Gatecliff Shelter. The archaeologists are making detailed maps of strata evident in the vertical sidewalls. Standing about 40 feet below the modern ground surface, they are pointing to strata deposited about 7,000 years ago.

No matter how carefully you excavated, it is impossible to see, map, and recover everything of archaeological interest. This is why archaeologists today use fine-screen sifters to find things that hand excavation misses.

Archaeologists agree that Marshalltown makes the only trowel worth owning. But when it comes to sifters, all agreement evaporates. Because most archaeologists manufacture their own screens, the design and workmanship vary from dig to dig. Some screens are suspended from tripods; others have two legs. Some are mounted on rollers, and others are driven by gas engines. When we dug Alta Toquima Village (Nevada) at 12,000 feet, we invented a "backpacker" design for our screens.

Junius Bird was a crusader in screening archaeological deposits. In the mid-1950s, he and James Ford published articles describing their views on how sifters should work. When I first met Junius, he had just returned from visiting a dig in the American Northwest and was livid about the dinky little screens being used on such an important site. He later wrote an article describing how these sifters wasted a million dollars.

The story went like this:

> The sifters utilized while I was at this excavation were the small box type on rollers moving back and forth on a fixed frame. These were set within and at the mouth of the shelter in close proximity to the excavators, subjecting them to windborne dust and dirt as they worked. The capacity of each box was small; sorting for artifacts and other materials had to be done on the wire within the boxes, then these had to be lifted from the frames to be emptied. Later most if not all of the sifted dirt and trash had to be removed to other locations.

A *few of the innumerable sifter designs used by archaeologists.*

This procedure seemed both cumbersome and extremely time-consuming. The excavators were racing against time because a dam was being constructed to flood the entire site. Bird argued that had "proper" sifting and recovery methods been used, the site could have been entirely excavated "with greater accuracy long before there was any risk of flooding." But the excavations fell seriously behind schedule, and the waters were rising daily. To buy some time, the Army Corps of Engineers constructed a massive (and expensive) coffer dam around the unexcavated deposits. Unfortunately, because the engineers had overlooked the nature of the underlying deposits, the dam failed, actually siphoning in water and flooding the remaining unexcavated site. This, according to Bird, is how the wrong sifters cost the taxpayers a million bucks.

Modern archaeologists spend plenty of time thinking about sifters and how they facilitate archaeological excavation. There is near-universal agreement that sifters of some sort are necessary on all terrestrial sites. Even into the 1970s, the occasional archaeologist in America could still be caught simply troweling or shoveling the deposit, sorting through the loosened matrix for artifacts, and then tossing the dirt on a spoil pile. Today, we recognize that simply too much archaeological material is lost when the deposit is not screened; in fact, some deposits contain such minute remains that even sifting is inadequate, in which case, a more precise recovery technique (such as flotation, discussed next) should be used.

Screen size affects what is recovered. For my M.A. thesis project, I built a three-decker screen with superimposed layers of 1/4-inch over 1/8-inch over 1/16-inch mesh screens. The idea was to find out how screen size affects the recovery of animal bones in archaeological sites. We found that the then standard 1/4-inch mesh is entirely adequate when the midden contains only bones of large animals such as bighorn or bison, but significant numbers of medium-sized animals, such as rabbits and rodents, are lost through the 1/4-inch gauge. A 1/8-inch mesh screen is recommended whenever the faunal assemblage includes these smaller mammals. In fact, significant amounts of small mammal bones are even lost through 1/8-inch screens! When one is concerned with recovering animals the size of, say, pack rats or small birds, a flotation method of recovery is strongly recommended. The nature of the archaeological debris must be carefully considered before selecting a method of excavation.

Nothing has such power to broaden the mind as the ability to investigate systematically and truly all that comes under thy observation in life.

MARCUS AURELIUS (121–180), ROMAN EMPEROR AND PHILOSOPHER

Flotation

In some archaeological sites, like the upper parts of Gatecliff Shelter, the deposits are sufficiently protected from moisture so that plant remains simply dry up and can be recovered by screening. But in more humid climates, plant remains generally are preserved only when they have been burned and carbonized. The most common method of recovering such plant remains is **flotation**, a technique that has become standard at most (if not all) digs during the last few decades.

Flotation: The use of fluid suspension to recover tiny plant and bone fragments from archaeological sites.

Several procedures exist for "floating" archaeological samples, but all of them do basically the same thing. Dirt does not float, but burned seeds, bones, and charcoal do. By using water (or chemical) flotation, archaeologists can float most ecofacts (and even some artifacts) out of samples of archaeologically recovered dirt.

In one of the earliest applications, Stuart Struever floated soil samples from 200 features attributable to the Middle Woodland component at the Apple Creek site, Illinois. The samples were hauled to nearby Apple Creek, where they were placed in mesh-bottomed buckets and then water-separated by students who worked midstream. Over 40,000 charred nutshell fragments, 2,000 carbonized seeds, and some 15,000 identifiable fish bones were collected in this manner. Standard dryland excavation techniques would have missed most.

While excavating at Salts Cave in Kentucky, Patty Jo Watson and her associates were not blessed with a nearby stream, so they improvised. The sediments to be floated were placed in double plastic bags and carried outside the cave. The samples (weighing a total of 1,500 pounds) were spread in the shade to dry. Two 50-gallon drums were filled with water, and the dry samples were placed in metal buckets whose bottoms had been replaced with window screen. The buckets were submerged in the 50-gallon oil drums, which had been filled with water. After a few seconds, the investigator skimmed off the charcoal and carbonized plant remains that had floated to the surface, using a small scoop made from a brass carburetor screen. Both the debris that floated to the top (the "light fraction") and the stuff that sank (the "heavy fraction") were placed on labeled newspaper to dry once again. The

Patty Jo Watson (left) and Louise Robbins operating a flotation device constructed in a 55-gallon drum. Carbonized seeds and other plant remains are recovered as they float to the surface.

ARCHAEO-MYTHBUSTERS

You Gotta Watch Out for That Mummy's Curse, Right?

We've all seen this one in the tabloids, the comic strips, and on late night movies—yet another archaeologist is snuffed after messing with the supernatural. It's a wonder enough survive to write the textbooks. . . .

Believe it or not, the "Curse of the Mummy" still comes up sometimes in cocktail conversation about archaeology. Its origin, I suppose, can be traced to the supposed curse that protected King Tutankhamun's tomb in Egypt.

It all started when Lord Carnarvon, well-heeled sponsor of Howard Carter's discovery of Tut's tomb, died unexpectedly in 1923. At the precise moment of Carnarvon's death, it is said, all the lights of Cairo blacked out. Egyptian authorities failed to find any reason for the mishap. The mystery was compounded when Lord Carnarvon's son swore that at that same instant, at the moment of his father's death, Carnarvon's favorite dog yelped in sorrow, then himself dropped dead. Conan Doyle, creator of Sherlock Holmes and believer in the occult, then chimed in to assure the world that a "Pharaoh's Curse" had indeed struck Carnarvon down.

Newspapers around the globe carried the story. One even directly quoted the specific curse, written in hieroglyphs over the entry to Tut's tomb: *They who enter this sacred tomb shall swiftly be visited by wings of death*. The world began a death watch on other participants in the Tutankhamun expedition.

Then, when a tourist who had visited the tomb was killed by a Cairo taxicab, near hysteria broke out. Throughout the world, collectors of Egyptian antiquities packed up their treasures and shipped them off to startled curators of Egyptology.

Although many believed Conan Doyle's unearthly solution, others looked for more rational explanations—maybe deadly bacteria, waiting patiently inside ancient tombs to strike down the disrespectful. Or perhaps Carnarvon had pricked himself on something inside the tomb—maybe an ancient arrowhead armed with a poison so potent that it endured for 3,000 years. Who would be the next victim of the Mummy's Curse?

Police Officer George LeBrash thought he was the one. In September 1979, while guarding the King Tut traveling exhibition in San Francisco, Officer LeBrash suffered a stroke and then requested $18,000 in disability payments, claiming that his stroke was job-related because King Tut had lashed out at him for disturbing his rest. But San Francisco Superior Court Judge Richard P. Figone didn't buy the curse story and threw the case out.

Good story, this mummy's curse stuff. But Judge Figone was right—it's just a story. The facts of the allegedly Tut-related deaths have been scrupulously researched, and the truth is that nobody even remotely associated with the King Tut excavations died under "suspicious" circumstances. Lord Carnarvon died of blood poisoning caused by an infected mosquito bite. Howard Carter, famed discoverer and excavator of Tutankhamun's tomb, lived into his mid-sixties and died of natural causes—16 years after he opened the tomb. Even the hieroglyphic "curse" itself above Tut's tomb is a phony: No such inscription exists—some newspaper reporter just made it up.

But rumors persist even today. In the late 1970s, as the "Treasures of Tutankhamun" exhibition triumphantly toured the United States, the then Lord Carnarvon was questioned on NBC television about the curse. Replying that he "neither believed nor disbelieved it," he quickly added that he would "not accept a million pounds to enter the tomb of Tutankhamun in the Valley of the Kings."

Later that same evening, according to the *Daily News*, Lord Carnarvon dined in an apartment high above Manhattan. As he admired the view, all the city lights suddenly flickered and went out. By candlelight, Carnarvon turned to his hosts, reportedly with a straight face, and growled, "It is again the curse of Tutankhamun."

Kenneth Feder, an archaeology professor, keeps track of what today's college students think about such things. In 1984, Feder found that 12 percent of his students believed that King Tut's curse "actually killed people." When he repeated the same question to his students a decade later, he found that the proportion of "believers" in Tut's curse had jumped to 24 percent.

If current trends hold, then by the year 2074, fully 100 percent of Feder's students would believe that the curse placed on King Tut's tomb "actually killed people."

That prospect, I can assure you, is monumentally more chilling to the world of archaeology than any curse a mummy might conjure up.

"OK, let's see ... That's a curse on you, a curse on you, and a curse on you."

I have seen yesterday.
I know tomorrow.
A real inscription on the tomb of Tutankhamun

IN HIS OWN WORDS

Who Really Dug Guilá Naquitz? by Kent V. Flannery

My discussion of Americanist archaeology tends to focus on the research of individual personalities. Although this approach is designed to bring archaeology alive, the emphasis on individuals also glosses over the critical role of teamwork in all phases of archaeological investigation. In the following, Kent Flannery imparts some of the camaraderie and harmony that accompanied the excavations at Guilá Naquitz (Oaxaca, Mexico):

The real excavators of Guilá Naquitz Cave, in Oaxaca, Mexico (clockwise from lower left): Ambrosio Martínez, Alfredo Sosa, Genaro Luis, Pablo García, Felix Sosa, Don Juan Martínez, Eligio Martínez, Angel Sosa, Carlos Pérez, Ernesto Martínez, and Kent Flannery.

Guilá Naquitz (Site OC-43) was discovered on January 26, 1966. Part of the following month was spent converting the old ox cart trail from Mitla to Díaz Ordaz into a road that would allow us access to the Rancho El Fuerte caves by means of our 4-wheel-drive pickup truck. We returned to Guilá Naquitz on April 14 with a larger crew. [I] and [Chris] Moser were joined by Silvia Maranca, and the crew of Mitla workmen was increased to 10. This group of Zapotec-speaking Mitleños was the heart and soul of our project and should be considered the real excavators of Guilá Naquitz. . . . Their patience, intelligence, careful attention to detail [were] indispensable to our success, and their unflagging high spirits and sense of humor kept us continuously entertained.

Somehow our Ford pickup, "El Caballito Blanco," made it up the boulder-strewn slopes of the mountain every morning, and we dismounted in a wind-deflated gully below the cave. Somehow all the equipment made it up the cliff, including the 10-gallon garrafón of drinking water that Don Juan would entrust to no one else. Once at the

sediments at Salts Cave yielded carbonized remains of hickory nuts and acorns, seeds from berries, grains, sumpweed, chenopods, maygrass, and amaranth.

Today, flotation is not an expensive or even a particularly time-consuming process. Flotation techniques can (and should) be fitted to the local requirements. At Mission Santa Catalina, we used a converted 55-gallon drum, and one person could process dozens of samples each day. Some elaborate power-driven machines are available for separating specimens chemically.

cave, Moser would tether his faithful watchdog on the talus to keep out any stray goats that wandered away from their herders on the slopes below us.

Over the sound of trowels and paintbrushes, an interminable shaggy-dog story would be told in Zapotec by one of the excavators. Inevitably, the punch line would be in Spanish, *but this was little consolation to those of us who had not understood the preceding* 1,500 *words. The frequent inclusion of lines such as, "Confiésame, Padre, porque yo he pecado," made it clear that many stories involved priests and confessionals, but the sins were confessed in Zapotec to the accompaniment of high-pitched laughter. Though we gradually picked up the minimum vocabulary necessary to describe the archaeological deposits, we never really deciphered any of the stories.*

Nor did the entertainment cease at lunchtime. Out of the hamper came tortas, fruit, and other goodies prepared by Lupe *back at the* Posada La Sorpresa, *along with a dozen hard-boiled eggs. No, make that eleven hard boiled eggs. The twelfth was "the egg of the day," a raw one indistinguishable from the others, which had been slipped into the basket by* Eligio Martínez. *Tension mounted as we all began to crack and peel our eggs, and we waited to see who would get the egg of the day. Finally there would come a crack, a sickening squish, and an epithet in English or Zapotec. Eventually, Moser began cracking his egg on Eligio's head as a precautionary measure.*

One memorable lunchtime there came an ear-splitting whoop, and seconds later one workman emerged from the shadow of the cliff holding the tattered remnants of what had once been his shirt. Everyone knew what had happened: One of the screen operators had captured a scorpion and cut off the last segment of its tail, leaving it harmless but alive and very angry. Approaching one of the trowelmen as he hunched over his lunch, he had pulled his comrade's collar away from his neck and suspended the creature over the resulting opening by holding its tail between his fingers. As the trowelman looked up, the last he saw was an obviously live scorpion plummeting down between his shoulder blades and his shirt. Now most of the workmen were on the ground, helpless with laughter. "It's the only way," one of them giggled, "we can get him to change that old shirt."

No one ever lost his temper at such times, not even the victim. He simply waited; he knew his turn would come, and probably sooner than his tormenter expected.

Through the long afternoons, our crew of Mitleños became better and better at following the cultural stratigraphy of the cave. They knew each living floor intimately, remembering what had been found in it and in which square, and had their own code name for each. Zone C, with its soft white ash, was referred to as leche en polvo, *"powdered milk." Zone D, with its granular brown matrix of burned oak leaves, was referred to as* el Nescafé, *"instant coffee." Zone E was simply* yusu *(Zapotec for "sand"). We were constantly amazed at the near-photographic memory our trowelmen displayed for the squares they had dug and the retrospective comments they made that were confirmed by field notes from weeks before.*

It was with some sadness that we closed the excavation on May 10, 1966. Guilá Naquitz had been a great site, a joy to excavate, with remarkably clear stratigraphy and excellent preservation throughout. Beyond that, it had been a colorful experience shared with a group of people none of us would ever forget.

Kent V. Flannery is the James B. Griffin Distinguished University Professor and curator of environmental archaeology at the University of Michigan, Ann Arbor.

But technology is not the issue. What is important is that for decades archaeologists meticulously saved, cataloged, and identified all scraps of bone but ignored plant remains. The resulting skew led archaeologists to overemphasize hunting aspects and ignore the gathering component altogether. Now that flotation techniques have come into their own, archaeologists are placing proper emphasis on the gathering of wild and domesticated plant foods.

Full-scale excavations at the convento (friars' housing) at Mission Santa Catalina (Georgia). Archaeologists in the foreground are mapping finds within the horizontal grid system and those in the mid-ground are excavating using the "shovel-skimming" technique. All excavated dirt is screened in the gasoline-powered sifters evident in the background.

Provenience: The location in which something was found. In archaeological excavation, most recovered artifacts and ecofacts are assigned a provenience within a three-dimensional reference system. The horizontal coordinates are assigned by a grid system, the vertical dimension by a datum point.

Automating the Excavation

From test pit through full-scale excavation, archaeologists must maintain exact records of the three-dimensional **provenience** of the objects being recovered. At Gatecliff, we piece-plotted artifacts by removing each item separately and assigning a unique number to it. Level maps were prepared for each surface, and the artifacts were plotted in each unit. In general, the most time-consuming part of the provenience-assigning process is measuring three-dimensional coordinates. At the beginning of an excavation, the coordinates are measured with levels and tape measures. As excavation techniques increase in complexity, so does control over provenience, generally requiring specialized surveying equipment such as a **transit.** Measurements are always recorded to the nearest centimeter. Because of human error and the difficulty of keeping straight sidewalls, such measurements are probably not more accurate than ±5 centimeters.

Fortunately, archaeologists are not alone in their need to measure things, and we are able to apply increasingly sophisticated engineering and computing technology to our excavations. Not only does such automation free archaeologists from much routine drudgery—to spend more time actually excavating—but the increased accuracy provides an extraordinary degree of quantitative control.

Working at the famous site of La Quina (France), Harold Dibble developed an automated method of on-site recording. At the heart of the system is a *theodolite,* a surveying device that contains a built-in electronic distance meter. At La Quina, artifacts occurred in well-defined living surfaces, each littered with thousands of stone tools. Using traditional methods (like those I described for Gatecliff Shelter), Dibble and his team recorded 2,000 tools and bones in one field season. But during the next season, by using the theodolite, he cut the measurement time by 60 percent (recording 7,000 items in one field season).

Dibble's system works like this: While one excavator works the theodolite, another holds a small prism reflector at various points on the tool or

The Legend of the Marshalltown Trowel

The archaeological record is usually first encountered at the tip of the trowel, an object dear to the hearts of field archaeologists. Although archaeologists rarely endorse individual products, trowels are an exception.

As every archaeological veteran knows, there is only one kind of trowel, the *Marshalltown*, named after a town in Iowa. What makes the Marshalltown so legendary? For one thing, the handle is welded, not riveted. Nobody likes a wobbly trowel blade. The steel is also high quality and holds a good edge. It comes in a variety of sizes and lasts a lifetime. There is simply no substitute.

Plenty of folklore surrounds the Marshalltown trowel. When Kent Flannery delivered the Distinguished Lecture to the American Anthropological Association in 1981, he called it "The Golden Marshalltown: A Parable for the Archaeology of the 1980s."

People often personalize their trowels. Some archaeologists square off the ends, others prefer a rounded point; Bill Rathje and Mike Schiffer (both of the University of Arizona) once recorded seven kinds of "technofunctional, use-wear, and stylistic variability" in Marshalltown trowels. When digging in forested areas, some even cut a notch in the edge, to trim back the roots. And you can always tell whether the owner is left- or right-handed, just by looking at the wear pattern on the trowel blade. People like to hang onto their trowels, often carving their initials in the handle.

Most archaeologists sharpen their trowels. In fact, I've had crew members who spent more time in trowel maintenance than in excavation. In California, there was once an archaeologist who used juvenile delinquents as excavators. They got so involved with macho trowel sharpening, they'd sneak up and secretly slit their supervisors' Levis, from cuff to belt loop.

Some well-worn Marshalltown trowels.

Writing for the *National Geographic* in 1967, distinguished archaeologist Emil Haury expanded the Marshalltown lore. He told the story of how, returning to reexcavate the Hohokam village of Snaketown after an absence of three decades, his seminar class at the University of Arizona presented him with a "good-digging token," a silver Marshalltown bearing the inscription from Shakespeare's *Julius Caesar*: "You are not wood, you are not stones, but men." Haury unpacked his graven trowel at Snaketown, where "standing in the old village, I hurled the shining trowel into the air. Jones Williams, a 72-year-old Pima who had been with me on Hohokam adventures before, turned the first spade of earth at the place where it landed. And, sure enough—that proved to be the least productive spot in the whole village! I gave up the business of magic and went back to the hardheaded work of excavation."

bone. The theodolite's built-in distance meter emits a laser beam that bounces off the prism and returns to the instrument. These measurements are then computed into the familiar *X, Y,* and *Z* coordinate system.

Transit: A surveying device capable of measuring horizontal and vertical angles and horizontal distances.

This procedure is fast, simple, and cost effective. The total cost for the system is less than $20,000. Each measurement takes about 5 seconds, and is accurate within ±5 millimeters. This system is so efficient that the La Quina crew began taking several measurements on each item, so the in situ orientation was also recorded. The same is done for features such as hearths and roof fall, eliminating the need to prepare the tedious "end-of-level" maps that eat up so much time on a dig.

The theodolite transmits these data to a small computer, together with data on the kind of object being measured, the stratigraphic provenience, and the initials of the excavator. A small printer immediately produces a tag that is attached to the artifact for its trip to the field laboratory.

Dibble has also worked out software allowing him to quickly manipulate and retrieve his La Quina data. This program graphically displays the color-coded artifacts across the site, from a variety of perspectives. It will immediately produce living surface maps, but skips the laborious hand-plotting and drafting stage entirely.

Such technology changes rapidly, and archaeologists are increasingly using laser-based surveying instruments, global positioning, and GIS mapping technologies to speed up the excavation process (as discussed previously). But note this: Nothing in the new technology is actually new to archaeological excavation procedures—these are simply better ways of recovering archaeological objects and recording them in the three basic dimensions.

Archaeologists commonly proceed by trowel and error.

ANONYMOUS

Archaeology's Conservation Ethic: Dig Only What You Must

Of course we are all destroyers; that's the name of the game.

IVOR NOËL HUME, ARCHAEOLOGIST (COLONIAL WILLIAMSBURG FOUNDATION)

Archaeologists have traditionally protected their excavations against vandals and pothunters. On my first job in archaeology, we were forced to post a 24-hour guard (armed, appropriately enough, with bow and arrow) to protect the open excavation units from looters and treasure seekers. At Gatecliff, we tediously backfilled the site by hand every year, to protect the archaeology from the curious public, and the public from the dangers of open-pit archaeology.

On St. Catherines Island, the problem is somewhat different. The only visitors are scientists, who realize the research value of archaeological sites and leave the excavations untouched. It is thus possible to open a few test units on several sites, return to the laboratory to process the finds, and then come back to the more promising sites for more intensive excavation.

But the luxury of research freedom highlights today's responsibility for site conservation. Archaeology is a destructive science, ruining its sites in the very process of excavation. Sites can be excavated only once, and so it is imperative to do things right. On strictly research projects—like our work at Mission Santa Catalina—the sites are not threatened by outside incursions, and one must adopt an enlightened and conservative strategy of excavation. Many archaeologists vow never to excavate more than half of a site not threatened by development or erosion. Whatever the rule, responsible investigators start with a suite of questions that are generally asked by all, plus additional questions specific to each excavation. The trick is to excavate no more than necessary to answer such questions, leaving as much intact as possible for later investigators, who undoubtedly will have more enlightened questions to ask and superior techniques with which to find the answers.

When in doubt, preserve!

WALTER W. TAYLOR (1913–1997), ARCHAEOLOGIST

And, as we have seen, remote sensing technology and archaeological survey techniques sometimes provide archaeologists with low-impact ways of learning without digging at all.

How Do People Learn How to Dig?

From the outset, I have emphasized the importance of hands-on experience in archaeology. There is no substitute for personal field experience, and no textbook or classroom exercise satisfactorily simulates the field situation. Learning to excavate means getting your hands dirty. It all boils down to going on a dig, and there are three ways to do this.

Most archaeologists get their first taste of fieldwork by enrolling in an organized archaeological field school. Major universities and colleges offer such opportunities, sometimes on weekends but more often during the summer session. Field schools are conducted on virtually every kind of archaeological site, and living conditions vary from pup tents to relatively plush dormitories. Many instructors require only a passing classroom familiarity with archaeology, whereas others accept only relatively advanced graduate students (see *How Can I Get on a Dig?*).

It is increasingly possible to join a dig as a volunteer or intern. Several branches of the federal government and many large research projects rely on nonpaid participants to supplement the paid staff. A number of overseas excavations rely almost exclusively on volunteers who pay for their own transportation, and exchange their on-site labor for room and board. Over the years, I have directed nearly a dozen such sessions at both Gatecliff Shelter and Mission Santa Catalina.

Avocational ("amateur") archaeological societies also offer numerous opportunities to excavate. In many cases, these nonprofessional groups are well trained and adequately supervised. The best ones coordinate their own excavations with ongoing professional-level research. But some caution is advised here. Current ethical standards discourage private collectors from digging up artifacts. In many instances, "pothunting" is illegal, and recent legislation has made it easier for the courts to crack down on looters. Although most archaeological societies discourage illegal and unethical destruction of archaeological sites, a few outlaw groups still sponsor "digs" for the sole purpose of obtaining artifacts. If you have any question about the integrity of an archaeological society, I suggest that you contact a local university, government agency, or museum to clarify the situation. As a rule of thumb, you might ask two key questions: What professionally trained archaeologists are involved in the excavations, and what happens to the artifacts once they have been dug up? If no responsible archaeologist is involved, and/or if the artifacts end up in private hands, steer clear of the dig.

Fieldwork opportunities vary from year to year, and you should obtain the most current information before making plans. And having supervised a dozen such digs, let me enter a personal plea: Before signing on with any expedition or field school, be certain you know what you are getting into.

Extreme care is required when exposing fragile artifacts. Here, Tormod Christensen is exposing a beaded necklace at Mission Santa Catalina by slowly removing the sand overburden—grain by grain.

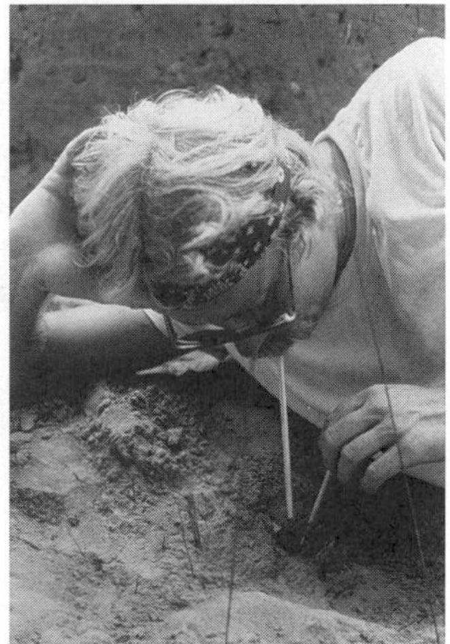

How Can I Get on a Dig?

Dozens of opportunities occur each year for the inexperienced to join up with a dig, but people are often puzzled about where to begin. Here are some useful contacts:

Clearinghouses

The Archaeological Institute of America annually publishes the *Archaeological Fieldwork Opportunities Bulletin*, a comprehensive guide to excavations, field schools, and special programs with openings for volunteers, students, and staff throughout the world. This publication is to introduce both the student and the amateur archaeologist to the experience of actual excavation or survey and is available each year on January 1. Current price is $9 for AIA members and $11 for nonmembers, plus $4 for shipping and handling for the first copy and $.50 for each additional copy. All orders must be prepaid in U.S. dollars or by an international money order. Send orders and make checks payable to Kendall/Hunt Publishing Company, Order Department, 4050 Westmark Drive, Dubuque, IA 52002; or call (800) 228-0810 or (319) 589-1000.

Earthwatch is a nonprofit membership organization that, since 1972, has mobilized over 40,000 people to spend from 1 to 3 weeks assisting noted scientists and scholars on projects that range from coral reef surveys to archaeological digs. Earthwatch members receive bi-monthly *Earthwatch* magazine, featuring in-depth articles on leading science issues of the day as well as a complete expedition catalog. Earthwatch, Mt. Auburn St., P.O. Box 403, Watertown, MA 02272; (800) 776-0188; fax: (617) 926-8532; Internet: info@earthwatch.org.

Smithsonian Institution, Smithsonian National Associates, Research Expedition Program, Suite 4210 L'Enfant Plaza SW, Washington, DC 20560; (202) 357-1350.

University of California Research Expeditions Program allows the general public to join small University of California research excavations around the world; no experience necessary. Partial student and teacher fellowships available. University of California, Desk K5, Berkeley, CA 94720; (415) 642-6586.

Archaeology Abroad Service (31–34 Gordon Square, London, WC1H 0PY, UK) publishes a list of digs three times a year; about 500 places in 15 countries are advertised. The bulletins also contain information on British schools and institutes of archaeology abroad together with scholarships available.

Current Archaeology publishes its Directory of British Archaeology in the spring of each year; a recent directory listed over 500 names, addresses, and telephone numbers for organizations in British archaeology. Copies of this are available free to those who send a stamped, addressed envelope to Current Archaeology, 9 Nassington Road, London NW3 2TX, UK.

Passport in Time Clearinghouse (P.O. Box 18364, Washington, DC 20036) is a program in which volunteers work with archaeologists in the National Forest Service on a variety of projects.

Foundation for Field Research, P.O. Box 2010, Alpine, CA 91001; (619) 445-9264.

Several museum and independent travel groups offer specialized travel packages to archaeological sites, often with professional archaeologists as guest lecturers. Although few offer hands-on possibilities, several visit ongoing excavations; be certain to find out the exact itinerary before joining up. A partial listing is available in *Natural History* magazine.

Some Sources on the Internet

Archaeological Fieldwork Server is a first-rate way to find current information.
http://durendal.cit.cornell.edu/TestPit.html

Preserve/Net is a national listing of internships.
http://www.preservenet.cornell.edu/pnetopp.htm

The Society for American Archaeology provides fieldwork opportunities.
http://www.saa.org

Internship and Fieldwork Listings Nationwide.
http://minerva.acc.virginia.edu/~career/intern.html

ArchNet: University of Connecticut Anthropology Department World-Wide Web Virtual Library: Archaeology.
http://www.lib.uconn.edu/archnet

David L. Carlson, associate professor of anthropology, Texas A&M University, provides an excellent Internet service entitled *Frequently Asked Questions About a Career in Archaeology in the* U.S., which includes an up-to-date section on archaeological fieldwork opportunities; some of the information from this FAQ is incorporated below.
http://www.museum.state.il.us/ismdepts/anthro/dlcfaq.html

Some Specific Suggestions

Crow Canyon Archaeological Center allows nonexperienced participants to join excavation teams working on thirteenth-century Anasazi pueblos. Adult programs of a week or more are available June through October. Crow Canyon Archaeological Center, Dept. AM, 23390 County Road K, Cortez, CO 81321; (800) 422-8975.

Anasazi Heritage Center, Bureau of Land Management, 27501 Highway 184, Dolores, CO 81323; (303) 882-4811.

The Center for American Archaeology conducts educational research programs for junior and senior high school students, college students, and the nonprofessional, and separate workshops for teachers. Kampsville Archaeological Center, P.O. Box 366, Kampsville, IL 62053; (618) 653-4316.

Institute for Minnesota Archaeology, 3300 University Avenue, S.E., Suite #202, Minneapolis, MN 55414; (612) 627-0315.

Other Tips About Archaeological Fieldwork

Amateur archaeological organizations, frequently assisted by the state archaeologist, often conduct summer or weekend excavations and hold meetings to discuss the results of their work. Usually these societies are regional or state organizations. Affiliation with these organizations can provide a student or an avocational archaeologist with valuable training in excavation and publication. To locate your local or regional archaeological society, contact the anthropology department of a nearby university.

The federal government publishes a brochure, *Participate in Archeology,* that lists books and videos on archaeology (available from the Publication Coordinator, Archeological Division, National Park Service, P.O. Box 37127, Washington, DC 20013-7127).

Archaeological excavation is physically taxing, and field camps can be socially intense. Neither you nor the dig will benefit if you are unable or unwilling to participate fully. If you have specific questions, by all means talk to the archaeologist in charge before making a commitment. Do not get in over your head.

SUMMARY Despite recent advances, archaeological excavation remains as much craft as science. Here, we looked at some common techniques, some archaeological standards and conventions, and, perhaps most important of all, what it feels like to be on a dig. Diverse excavation strategies represent different assumptions and different objectives. In a vertical strategy, designed largely for chronological control, artifact provenience generally means little more than stratigraphic placement; the exact location within a given stratum is analytically irrelevant.

But in a horizontal strategy, designed to explore the conditions of past lifeways, the context of artifacts and ecofacts within excavation strata becomes critical; artifacts found in situ are commonly plotted relative to one another on living floor maps. When an excavator misses an artifact—and it turns up in the screen—a significant piece of information has been lost because it can then be located only within the excavation square.

Modern archaeologists spend plenty of time thinking about recovery techniques, and both mechanical sifters and flotation devices are commonplace. From test pit through full-scale excavation, archaeologists maintain exact records of the three-dimensional provenience of the objects being recovered, and computer-assisted equipment is now available for this purpose.

It's hard to overemphasize the importance of hands-on experience in archaeology. There is no substitute for personal field experience, and no textbook, computer simulation, or classroom exercise satisfactorily simulates the field situation. Learning to excavate means getting your hands dirty. It all boils down to going on a dig. Numerous sources provide information on current fieldwork opportunities in archaeology.

Once I discovered there was such a thing as archaeology, I just never looked back.

H. Marie Wormington (1914–1994), archaeologist

Chapter 7

Chronology Building: How to Get a Date

It has taken the planet Earth 4.5 billion years to discover it is 4.5 billion years old.

GEORGE WALD, BIOCHEMIST AND NOBEL LAUREATE

PREVIEW The next three chapters address a single problem—how archaeologists get a grasp on *time.* This chapter is all about dating archaeological sites—a topic of great interest to most archaeologists. Here, you will find a broad range of dating techniques: tree-ring dating, radiocarbon dating, thermoluminescence dating, and several others. In fact, when archaeologists get together, one of the first things mentioned is often the "neat new dates" just back from the lab.

But what you don't hear so much—and you should—is exactly what these dates mean. The radiocarbon lab takes a chunk of an old, dead tree and figures out how long ago that tree died. By itself, this lab date tells you almost nothing of interest about your site. When a particular tree died becomes important only when its death is somehow related directly to some human event of interest—such as roofing over a pueblo room. Only if you can establish that this particular tree was cut down to build the roof, do you have something of archaeological interest. Demonstrating the validity of such associations is really the key issue in archaeological dating. It's important to keep this point in mind while you read this chapter: The physics and chemistry behind dating technology are not unimportant, but it's the deep-down archaeological associations that make it all work.

The Fourth Egyptian Dynasty lasted from 2680 to 2565 B.C. The Roman Colosseum was constructed between A.D. 70 and 82. In the seventeenth century, Dr. John Lightfoot proclaimed that God created the entire earth in 4004 B.C., at precisely 9 A.M. on October 23. Each date represents the most familiar way of expressing chronological control—the **absolute date.** Such dates are expressed as specific units of scientific measurement: days, years, centuries, or millennia, but no matter what the measure—Lightfoot computed his estimate by projecting biblical life spans—all absolute determinations attempt to pinpoint a discrete, known interval in time.

Absolute dating: Dates expressed as specific units of scientific measurement, such as days, years, centuries, or millennia; absolute determinations attempt to pinpoint a discrete, known interval in time.

Archaeologists also measure time in another, more imprecise manner by establishing the **relative date.** As the name implies, relative duration is monitored not through specific segments of absolute time but, rather, through relative relationships: earlier, later, more recent, after Noah's flood, prehistoric, and so forth. Although not as precise as absolute dating, relative estimates are sometimes the only dates available. Taken together, both forms of dating, absolute and relative, give archaeologists a way of controlling the critical dimension of time.

Relative dating: Dates expressed relative to one another (for instance, earlier, later, more recent, after Noah's flood, and so forth).

Tree-Ring Dating

Tree-ring dating (dendrochronology): The use of annual growth rings in trees to assign calendar ages to ancient wood samples, especially those from archaeological sites.

Like many of archaeology's dating techniques, **tree-ring dating** (also called **dendrochronology**) was developed by a nonarchaeologist. The first systematic dendrochronologist was A. E. Douglass, an astronomer inquiring about the effect of sunspots on the earth's climate. Douglass began with the knowledge that trees growing in temperate and arctic areas remain dormant during the winter and then burst into activity in the spring. In many species, especially conifers, this cycle results in the formation of well-defined concentric growth rings.

Because each ring represents a single year, it should be a simple matter to determine the age of a newly felled tree: Just count the rings. Douglass took this relatively common knowledge one step farther, reasoning that because tree rings vary in size, they may preserve information about the environment in which individual trees grew. Because environmental patterning affects all the trees maturing there, these regular patterns of tree growth (that is, ring width) should fit into a long-term chronological sequence.

A. E. *Douglass, pioneer in dendrochronology.*

Douglass began his tree-ring chronology with living specimens, mostly yellow pines near Flagstaff and Prescott, Arizona. He would examine a stump (or a core from a living tree), count the rings, then overlap this sequence with a somewhat older set of rings from another tree. But the dead trees and surface snags went back only 500 years or so. Beyond this point, dendrochronology had to rely on the prehistoric record.

Fortunately for him, Douglass worked in the American Southwest, where arid conditions enhance preservation. By turning to archaeological ruins, Douglass began mining a vast quarry of tree-ring data. Sampling ancient beams and supports, he slowly constructed a prehistoric "floating chronology," spanning several centuries but not tied into modern samples. Douglass

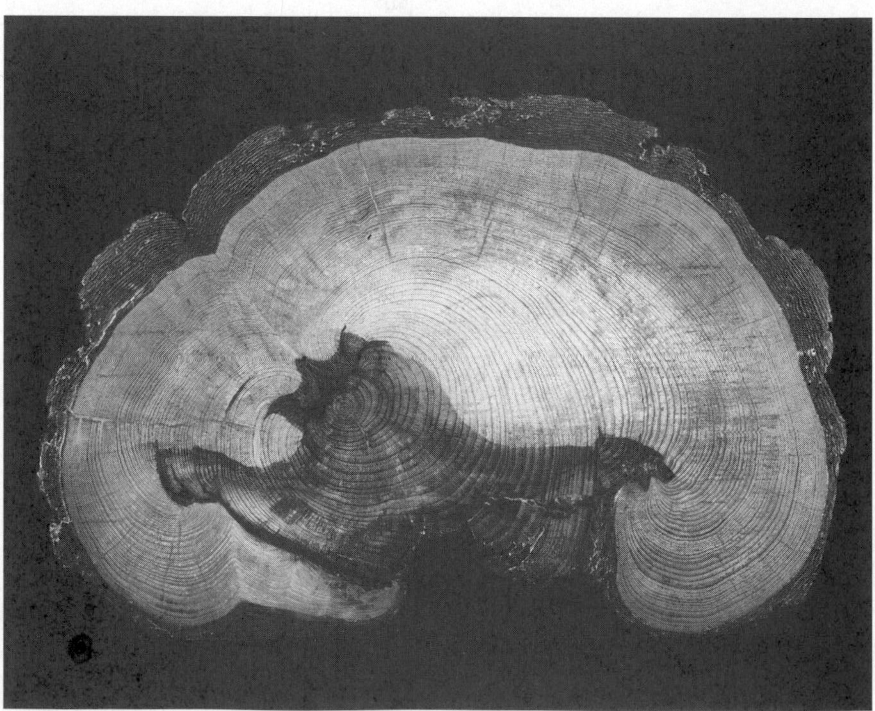

This cross section of a ponderosa pine shows a detailed record of the tree's 108-year life span. Each year is represented by a "tree-ring," and evidence of fire scars is also preserved.

could use his floating sequence to date various ruins relative to one another, but the hiatus between prehistoric and modern sequences meant that his chronology could not be correlated with the modern calendar.

Douglass was therefore forced to work with two separate sequences. The absolute sequence permitted him to date with precision those ruins later than about the fourteenth century A.D. The second, relative sequence dated archaeological sites only in relation to one another, and this older sequence was expressed in purely arbitrary numbers followed by the designation R.D. (relative date).

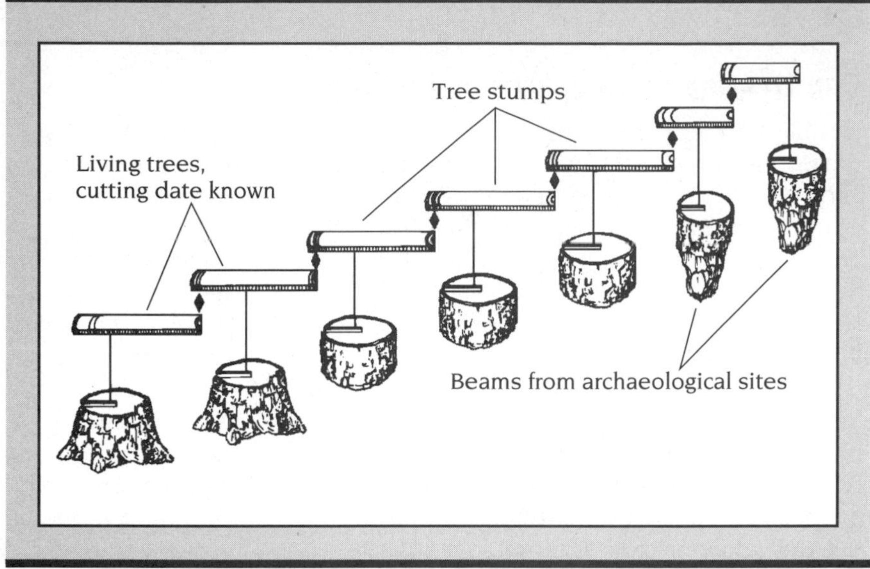

This schematic diagram shows how a tree-ring chronology is built up, working from known-age living trees (lower left) to older archaeological samples.

Thus arose "the gap," an unknown span of time separating the ancient, prehistoric sequence from the known, historically grounded chronology. It took years, but "the gap" was finally bridged (see *Gap Hunting in the American Southwest*)—Southwestern archaeology finally had its reliable, year-by-year dating tool.

Year-by-Year Chronology Becomes a Reality

Not only has tree-ring dating spread worldwide, but the methods also have become increasingly sophisticated. In August 1927, Douglass traveled to Betatakin, an extensive cliff dwelling in northeastern Arizona. Douglass collected two dozen samples that placed the construction of Betatakin within a decade of A.D. 1270. Accuracy to this degree was stunning back then—and still is, compared with every other technique.

But contemporary archaeology requires even more from its dating techniques. Jeffrey Dean of the University of Arizona's Laboratory of Tree-Ring Research spent 2 months collecting further samples from Betatakin in the 1960s. The important thing was to find samples with the bark still attached; in such "cutting" samples, you can be sure that the outer ring surviving in the sample was really the outer ring when the tree was alive; if not, then your "tree-ring" date does not actually date the felling of the tree. The total collection now represents 292 individual beams, and modern tree-ring technology documents the growth of Betatakin literally room by room.

Betatakin Cave was first occupied about 1250 by a small group that built a few structures that were soon destroyed. The occupation was probably transient, the cave serving as a seasonal camping spot for men traveling to plant fields at some distance from their home.

The actual village site at Betatakin was founded in 1267, when three room clusters were constructed; a fourth cluster was added in 1268. The

Gap Hunting in the American Southwest

Establishing a valid year-by-year chronology in the Southwest was delayed for a while by "the gap," an unknown span of time separating the ancient, prehistoric sequence from the known, historically grounded chronology. In the 1920s, a number of major institutions, including the National Geographic Society, the American Museum of Natural History in New York, and the Carnegie Institution of Washington, launched ambitious expeditions to locate logs from the pesky undated interval. The "gap hunters," as they were known, experienced little initial success. Each sequence was occasionally extended a year or two, but the void persisted. The problem was that Pueblo peoples had built their substantial sites at Mesa Verde, Chaco Canyon, and elsewhere during the relative part of the sequence. After these sites were abandoned, the tree-ring trail evaporated. Some (unknown) time later, the "postgap" sites were occupied—after the Spanish arrived in the Southwest.

Perhaps the contemporary Hopi towns could help, as people had resided there during gap times. Striking a deal with the Hopi, the gap hunters started poking holes in the roof beams at Old Oraibi. Although they stretched the historic sequence back to A.D. 1260, the gap lingered.

Finally, in 1929, the Third National Geographic Society Beam Expedition came across the ruins at Showlow, a modern village in east-central Arizona and an unappetizing place to dig, amidst a disarray of pigpens and corrals. Morale sagged; the laborers were offered a bonus of $5 for anybody finding a specimen with 100 rings or more. At last, the excavators happened on a charred log fragment, which was routinely preserved in paraffin and labeled HH-39. With his intricate knowledge of tree-ring patterning, Douglass realized that sample HH-39 neatly bridged the gap. It was a breakthrough in American archaeology.

All that work, and here was the answer: The last year of the relative sequence was A.D. 1284. The sequences were united, creating impressive headlines in the pages of *National Geographic*. Almost overnight, Douglass was able to tell Southwestern archaeologists when their most important sites had been built: Mesa Verde was erected between A.D. 1073 and 1262, Pueblo Bonito in Chaco Canyon between A.D. 919 and 1130, the Aztec ruin between A.D. 1110 and 1121, plus dozens of others.

Ironically, when HH-39 was added to the picture, the gap hunters discovered that the former absolute and relative sequences actually overlapped by 49 years. Apparently a long period of drought during the thirteenth century had formed rings so minute that they had been previously overlooked. There had been no gap at all! The data had been there since the earlier expedition to the Hopi town of Oraibi, but it took a specimen like HH-39 to clarify the sequence.

next year, a group of maybe 20 to 25 people felled several trees, cut them to standardized length, and stockpiled the lumber, presumably for future immigrants to the village. Additional beams were stockpiled in 1272, but none was used until 1275, which signaled the beginning of a 3-year immigration period during which more than 10 room clusters and a kiva were added. Population growth at Betatakin slowed after 1277, reaching a peak of about 125 people in the mid-1280s. The village was abandoned sometime between 1286 and 1300 for unknown reasons.

Tree-ring dating obviously has tremendous potential to provide absolute dates for archaeological sites, subject to one important limitation (shared with all other dating methods): There must always be a clear-cut association between the datable specimen and the definable cultural behavior. At Betatakin,

Betatakin, a cliff dwelling in Tsegi Canyon (Arizona).

Dean assumed that the wood was timbered during site occupation, as using dead trees or beams from abandoned structures provides erroneously ancient dates.

Tree-ring dating can be applied to many, but not all, species of trees. The most commonly dated species are piñon pine, ponderosa pine, Douglas fir, juniper, and white fir. Limber pine, bristlecone pine, and the giant sequoia have also been extensively studied. Even sagebrush is (sometimes) datable.

Matching unknown specimens to the regional master key can be a slow, laborious process requiring an expert with years of experience. Gradually, more automated means such as correlation graphs have been devised, and computer programs have been attempted (based on the statistical theory of errors). To date, no truly successful computer program is available because computers are unable to handle the problem of false and missing rings. Skilled dendrochronologists can still date samples much faster than any computer.

Dendrochronology also has potential for providing climatic data. Assuming that tree-ring width is controlled by environmental factors such as temperature and soil moisture, it is possible to reconstruct past environmental conditions by examining the band widths. Although tree metabolism is complex, great progress has been made in such ecological reconstructions. In the American Southwest, for instance, detailed models today exist telling us how much rain fell in the spring of the year A.D. 1088. Tree-ring data also demonstrate that catastrophic floods occurred in A.D. 1358. These very detailed climatic reconstructions have become extremely impressive, providing archaeologists with fine-grained paleoenvironmental chronologies—provided they

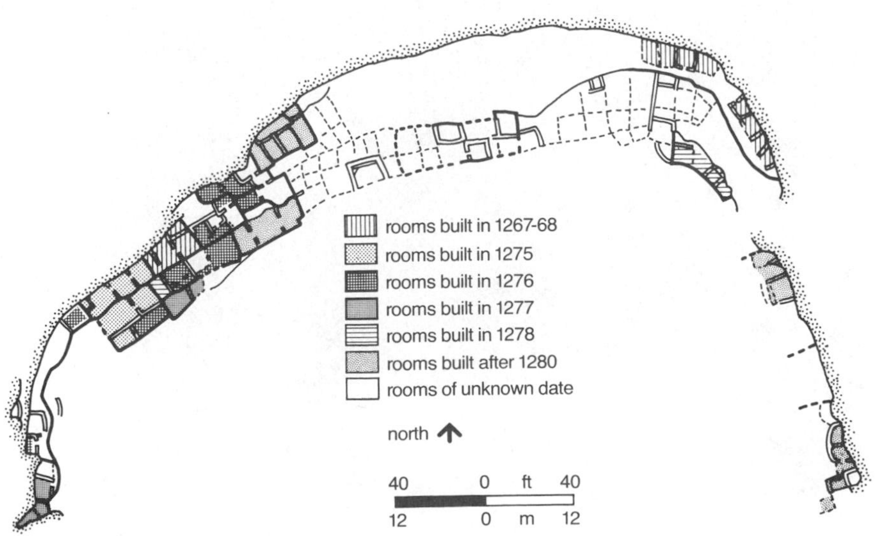

Floor plan of Betatakin and the construction sequence inferred by Jeffrey Dean from the tree-ring evidence.

Dendrochronology on the Internet:

Laboratory of Tree-Ring Research (University of Arizona) provides history and bibliography, plus links to software for the manipulation and analysis of tree-ring research: http://www.ltrr.arizona.edu

Internal Tree-Ring Data Bank, provided by NOAA Paleoclimatology Program and World Data Center for Paleoclimatology, is the most useful single collection of tree-ring data in the world, providing data from more than 1,000 sites across five continents: http://www.ngdc.noaa.gov/paleo/treering.html

work in an area with a workable dendrochronological sequence.

But even lacking such automated means, dendrochronological sequences have been developed in many areas, including the American Southwest, Alaska, the American Arctic, the Great Plains, Germany, Great Britain, Ireland, Turkey, Japan, and Russia. In the next section, we look at how tree-dating has been productively applied to Viking Age archaeology in Scandinavia.

Dating a Viking Queen

The most dramatic discovery in Viking archaeology took place in 1904, when a large burial mound at Oseberg was excavated not far from Oslo, Norway. Buried inside was an incredibly well-preserved Viking ship; after it was excavated, this 1,000-year-old Viking treasure was triumphantly paraded through the streets of Oslo.

The Oseberg ship was an amazing piece of nautical design: lightly built, shallow of draught, and highly maneuverable. Riding like a swan on a wave, the 22-meter-long vessel could be either sailed or rowed with ease. In fact, a fairly similar "sister ship" (previously excavated from a burial mound at nearby Gokstad) had already been replicated and sailed across the Atlantic in 1892, to commemorate the 400th anniversary of the Columbian "discovery" of America. As the Scandinavian crew convincingly demonstrated, the Vikings were fully capable of sailing to America several centuries before Columbus's celebrated voyage.

The most dramatic discovery in Norwegian archaeology came in 1904, with the excavation of the Oseberg Viking burial ship, just outside Oslo.

Richly carved from stem to stern, the Oseberg ship served as the coffin of a Viking queen, who had been buried inside, surrounded by an astonishing array of personal furnishings—an unprecedented collection of Viking-age art, including several carved beds, sleighs (replete with mythical monster heads), oil lamps, kitchen ware, tools, and equipment for weaving and spinning. The queen's grave goods revealed many aspects of the daily life of Viking royalty.

But when was the Oseberg ship buried? Until very recently, the find could be dated only by stylistic evaluations of the decorated wooden artifacts recovered in the excavations. In his initial analysis, Norwegian archaeologist Haakon Shetelig assigned them to the "Early Oseberg Style," thought to date around A.D. 800. Later, based on a reexamination of several Irish artifacts recovered at Oseberg, Shetelig changed his mind, moving the age of Early Oseberg Style to between A.D. 820 and A.D. 830; for him, this meant that the Oseberg burial must have taken place in about A.D. 850 or later (a revision that was, and still is, generally accepted).

Ferocious lion's head wooden sculpture found inside the Oseberg ship.

But then as now, such stylistic dating remains subjective. In attempting to refine these dates, the Radiological Dating Laboratory in Trondheim (Norway) processed a radiocarbon date on oak wood from the grave chamber in the Oseberg ship. The result was 1190 ± 60 radiocarbon years B.P. (which, as discussed later in this chapter, converts to a calendar age of A.D. 880, with a range of A.D. 780–960). Although these radiocarbon results obviously bracket the stylistic dating of A.D. 850 or so, they also demonstrate that the error margin involved in radiocarbon dating is much too gross to help refine the already fine-grained Viking age stylistic sequence.

Recognizing this, archaeologists Niels Bonde and Arne Christensen recently proposed that tree-ring dating might pin down the true age of the Oseberg burial more precisely. This intriguing possibility arose because, over the past couple of decades, several master chronologies have been built up for oak trees growing in southern Scandinavia. This means that when local "floating chronologies" can be matched against the master sequence, it is possible to tree-ring date specific archaeological sites and features.

It is instructive to see how these dates were obtained, because a series of assumptions and arguments of relevance are required to bridge the gap between the tree-ring dates and the past event of interest.

The original Oseberg ship, now on display at Oslo's Viking Ship Museum (Norway).

What, exactly, was being dated at Oseberg?

Bonde and Christensen were specifically interested in establishing the age of the *queen's burial* inside the Oseberg ship; the date of the ship's construction could well be somewhat older than the funerary event.

What samples were appropriate for tree-ring dating?

Certain problems plague all attempts to use ship's timbers for tree-ring dating. For one thing, there is usually some doubt about

ARCHAEO-MYTHBUSTERS

Vikings Wore the Horned Hats, Right?

Whether in comic strips, airline advertisements, or National Football League helmets, it's easy to spot the Vikings. They're the guys with horns sticking out of their hats, right?

Wrong. The pedestrian truth is this: Despite centuries of digging up Viking sites, archaeologists have never found the slightest evidence for such a helmet. Nor are they mentioned in the Viking sagas or the runic inscriptions. Horned helmets are also conspicuously absent from all Viking art, which has survived in great abundance. So far, judging from everything we know, zero evidence exists that Viking helmets *ever* had horns protruding from them.

Actually, when you think of it, horned helmets would be a pretty stupid thing to wear in battle. In hand-to-hand combat, the last thing a warrior needs is two handy levers by which any foe within arm's reach could unhelm him with ease.

Sure, Vikings sometimes wore headgear. Various Viking-age carvings and rune-stone inscriptions show warriors wearing a protective skull cap made of heavy bull's hide. They also occasionally donned conical or ridged metal helmets, sometimes even fitted with face-guards to protect the eyes and nose.

But horns? No evidence so far.

Still, such factual details haven't restrained the generations of artists, poets, and composers in their uninhibited celebration of the ancient Scandinavian past. Singers in mid-nineteenth-century productions of Richard Wagner's opera *The Ring of the Nibelung* sported major horned headgear. Before long, an assortment of plumed, winged, and horned Viking helmets cropped up in art and literature. Even the Valkyries—the female supernaturals who escorted dead warriors to Viking heaven—often were depicted wearing horned hats.

So where did the myth of the Hagar-horns come from? Who knows? But somehow, through the ages, the image of the horned helmet became an unquestioned icon of the Viking Age—ask any Minnesota Vikings fan. And as with so many myths, the lack of even a shred of supporting evidence seems to make no difference in the mind of the true believer.

---

just where the Viking shipbuilders obtained their supplies. Since ships are highly mobile, they could be built anywhere within their cruising range; in fact, evidence from one Viking ship recovered near Roskilde, Denmark, shows it was constructed from trees harvested in the vicinity of Dublin, Ireland. Obviously, the southern Scandinavian dendrochronological sequence would not be appropriate for dating Irish trees.

Dating a ship's construction is also complicated because of the distinct possibility that wood for shipbuilding was seasoned prior to being used in construction. If such seasoning lasted several years, then the "cutting dates" would provide a misleadingly early "construction date" for the ship itself.

Therefore, these investigators shifted their attention to the wood samples contained within the Oseberg ship. Plenty of wooden artifacts were buried

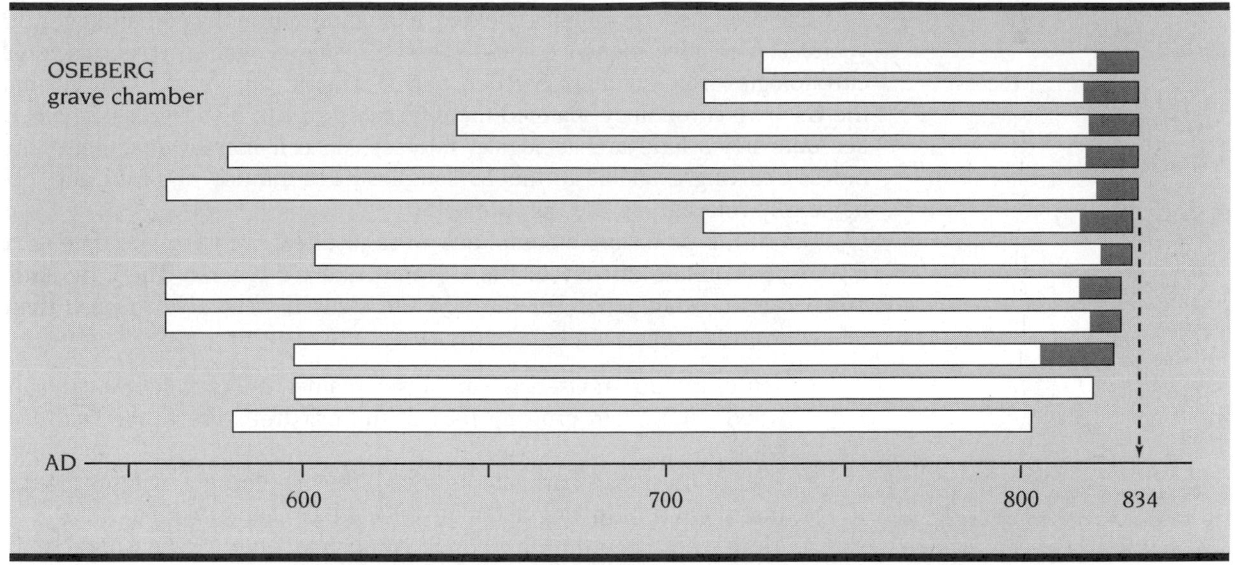

Bar diagram showing the position of the dated tree-ring samples from the Oseberg Viking ship burial, plotted against the A.D. time scale.

here and many of these could, perhaps, be dated by tree-ring methods. But in nearly all cases, the assumptions required to date these artifacts were as difficult as those necessary for the ship itself.

This is why Bonde and Christensen decided to concentrate their investigation on the grave chamber itself, the small, wooden "tent" erected amidships to contain the Viking queen's corpse. This was the only construction that could be specifically tied to the burial itself.

What assumptions were required?

Even after deciding what should be sampled, several important assumptions were required before the tree-ring dating could be conducted.

Specifically, the investigators assumed that the oak trees used to build the funerary enclosure were felled shortly before construction of the grave chamber. This assumption was warranted, in part, by experiments showing that newly cut trees are considerably easier to work with hand tools than seasoned oak. It also seemed reasonable because the burial chamber was crudely constructed of rough-hewn planks and posts. The masterful hand of the shipbuilder was nowhere to be seen, suggesting that the burial chamber was built as part of overall mound construction and was never meant to be seen; it was built only to be quickly buried.

Investigators also assumed that the felling site was not far from the intended location of the burial mound. If so, transport of timber probably took only a matter of weeks, or maybe even days. This meant that the dendrochronological dates for the burial chamber should quite accurately reflect the age of the funeral itself.

This determined, the investigators took 12 dendrochronological samples from the gables, uprights, and planks of the Oseberg burial chamber. This was done by sawing off cross sections from each sample; these sections were replaced after the tree-ring analysis.

The 12 Oseberg samples yielded a floating chronology spanning 299 years. This relative sequence could then be matched against master regional chronologies from southern Sweden and Denmark. The results showed that the Oseberg chronology spanned the interval from A.D. 536 to 834. The earlier date holds little archaeological interest (since it merely documents the oldest tree ring available in the 12 samples); this interior ring was not "behaviorally relevant" to the burial event.

But, if the preceding assumptions were justified, then the late date—A.D. 834—should relate directly to the Oseberg queen's funeral. Then, by additional careful examination, Bonde and Christensen were able to push their results even farther.

1. Ten of the dozen Oseberg samples contained intact *cambium* (or "sapwood"—the outer, growing part of the oak tree, directly beneath the bark).
2. Half of these had bark still attached, thus confirming, without doubt, that the A.D. 834 ring actually reflected a reliable "cutting date."
3. Moreover, since the bark rings comprised only "early wood," they must have been cut fairly early in the growing season of the year A.D. 834.
4. Because of the brief growing season at these northern latitudes, "early" could only mean "summer."

This chain of inference led Bonde and Christensen to their final conclusion: *The Oseberg grave chamber was built during the summer of A.D. 834, probably in August.*

As at Betatakin, this is phenomenal precision in archaeological dating. This example is important because it demonstrates not only the amazing potential of tree-ring dating but also the necessary caution with which such investigations must proceed.

Once established, such precise dating not only pinpoints when the Oseberg burial mound was constructed, but it also enables archaeologists to refine stylistic chronologies for the artifacts contained inside. Assuming that these artifacts were not intrusive—that is, that they were not introduced into the mound *after it was built*—then the method provides a firm date *before which* the artifacts must have been crafted.

As the Oseberg ship burial amply demonstrates, dendrochronology will always enjoy a precision unsurpassed in the arsenal of archaeological dating methods. But of course, tree-ring dating can be applied only in certain limited contexts.

Radiocarbon Dating

What is time? If no one asks me, I know. If I try to explain it to someone asking me, I don't know.

SAINT AUGUSTINE (354–430), EARLY CHRISTIAN LEADER

In 1949, a physical chemist named Willard F. Libby announced to the world that he had discovered a revolutionary new radiocarbon (carbon-14) dating technique. The world apparently agreed and handed Libby the Nobel Prize in chemistry for his breakthrough. The earliest radiocarbon dates worked on organic materials younger than about 30,000 years. But more recently, technical refinements have extended the effective range of the C-14 method to over 75,000 years.

Kinds of Carbon

Like many great discoveries, the basic principle behind radiocarbon dating is deceptively straightforward. Cosmic radiation produces neutrons, which enter the earth's atmosphere and react with nitrogen to produce the "heavy" carbon isotope carbon-14.

$$N^{14} + \text{neutron} = C^{14} + H$$

Carbon-14 is "heavy" because its nucleus contains 14 neutrons, rather than carbon's more common load of 12. The extra neutrons make the nucleus unstable and subject to gradual (radioactive) decay. Libby calculated that after 5,568 years, half of the C-14 available in a sample will have decayed; this is termed the **half-life** of C-14. Whenever a neutron leaves a C-14 nucleus, a radioactive (beta) particle is emitted, and the amount of radioactivity escaping can be measured by counting the number of beta emissions per gram of carbon.

Half-life: The time required for half of the C-14 available in an organic sample to decay.

$$C^{14} = B- + N^{14}+$$

These fundamentals established, Libby proceeded to convert the fact of radiocarbon decay into a chronometric tool. Once again, back to basics: Plants and animals are known to ingest atmospheric carbon in the form of carbon dioxide throughout their lives. When an organism dies, no more carbon enters its system, and that which is already present starts its radioactive decay. The rate of beta emissions from the dead organism indicates the C-14 to C-12 ratio, which is an indicator of the amount of time since the C-14 started decaying. This is how you figure out roughly how long ago that organism died.

Once you ask the question, where is the carbon-14, and where does it go, it's like one, two, three, you have [radiocarbon] dating.

WILLARD F. LIBBY (1908–1980), CHEMIST

Radiocarbon decay is, strictly speaking, a random process, as nobody can ever predict exactly which C-14 molecule will decay. It is an actuarial matter, like a life insurance table (nobody knows who will die this year, but it's a dead certainty that a certain number will).

What the Radiocarbon Laboratory Can Tell You

We ran 47 radiocarbon determinations on charcoal from Gatecliff Shelter, and these samples illustrate how contemporary archaeologists actually use the radiocarbon method. The procedure is fairly simple: Collect appropriate samples in the field, correlate them with the known stratigraphy, and submit selected samples to a commercial radiocarbon laboratory. Radiocarbon dating is not cheap. Current rates run about \$200 to \$250 per sample for a "standard" sample (and perhaps twice that if specialized processing is required).

Nobel Prize winner Willard Libby with extraction apparatus in the Radiocarbon Laboratory at the University of California, Los Angeles.

The radiocarbon lab reports a date like this:

UCLA-1926A 5200 ± 120 radiocarbon years B.P.

This is an actual date, from charcoal found in Hearth A on Horizon 12 at Gatecliff Shelter. The first designation records the laboratory and sample number: University of California (Los Angeles) Radiocarbon Laboratory sample number 1926A. The second part—5200—estimates the age of the sample in radiocarbon years B.P., the latter an abbreviation for "before present" (arbitrarily defined as the year A.D. 1950). Keep in mind that the sample was

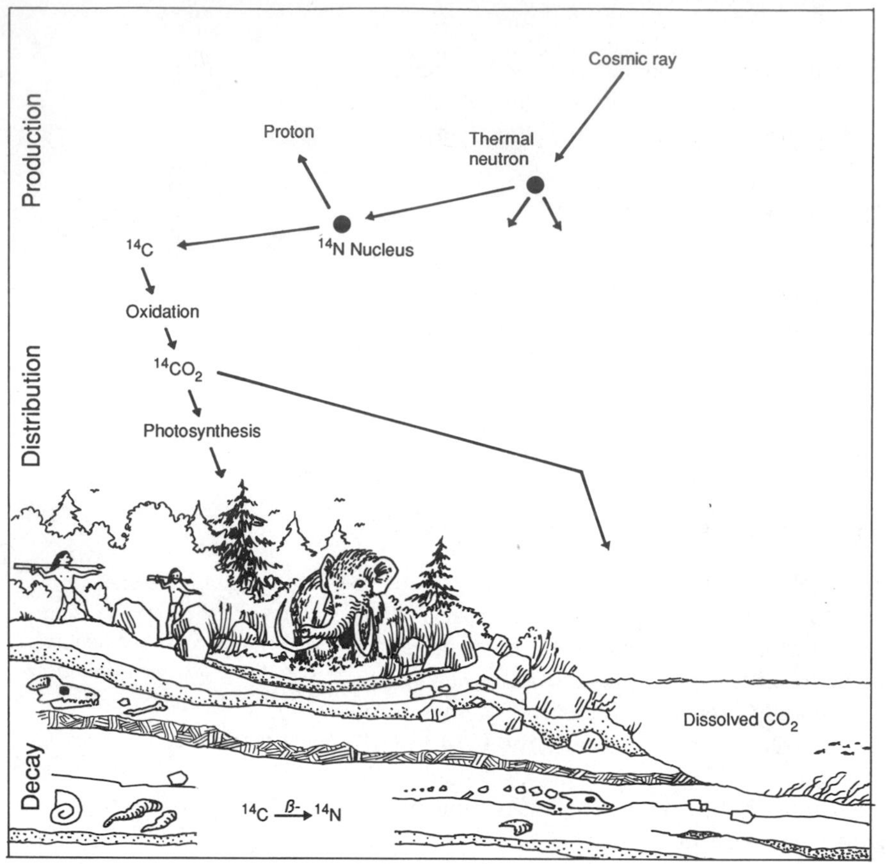

This reconstruction shows the theoretical basis of radiocarbon dating. The natural production of C-14 is a secondary effect of cosmic-ray bombardment in the earth's upper atmosphere. Most of the C-14 is then absorbed into the oceans, but a small percentage becomes part of the terrestrial biosphere. Normal metabolic processes maintain an equilibrium of C-14 content in living organisms. Once the plant or animal dies, however, metabolism ceases, and the proportion of C-14 begins to decrease. Measuring the progress of such random decay provides the basis for modern radiocarbon dating.

measured in radiocarbon years, not calendar years. As we will see, radiocarbon dating has certain biases, and the laboratory date must be "corrected" to reflect actual calendar years. In short, the radiocarbon lab at UCLA told me this: A tree died 5,200 radiocarbon years before A.D. 1950, and charcoal from that tree turned up on Horizon 2 at Gatecliff Shelter.

Can You Handle the Uncertainty?

So far, so good. But remember that the lab report attaches a "±120" to the age estimate. This *standard deviation* estimates the consistency (or lack of it) between the various "counting runs" performed at the laboratory. This statistical appendage, read as "plus or minus," is the standard deviation (or "sigma"), a projection of the error in the estimate. Because of their random, statistical nature, radiocarbon dates cannot be precise. Some samples, like this one, generate relatively minor inaccuracy (only 120 years, more or less). But sometimes C-14 determinations involve larger errors—up to several hundred years—and the plus-minus factor warns the archaeologist about this unusually high degree of uncertainty.

The standard deviation expresses the range within which the true date probably falls. In UCLA-1926A, the number "5200 (radiocarbon years)" estimates the actual age of the sample (which, of course, remains unknown); the standard deviation estimates the range of error. We know from statistical theory that a 2-in-3 (67 percent) chance exists that the true date falls within one "sigma." Specifically, by both adding and subtracting 120 from the age estimate, we will find the probability to be 67 percent that the true age of UCLA-1926A falls between 5,080 (*minus* 120) and 5,320 (*plus* 120) radiocarbon years B.P.

Because random probabilities are involved, we can never be absolutely certain that the true age falls into this interval, but the chances are good (2 in 3) that it does. If you want to be more certain, try doubling the standard deviation. In this case, there is a 95 percent chance that the actual date falls within ±2 sigmas. The chances are 95 in 100 that the true age of UCLA-1926A falls within 2 sigmas = ±2(120) = ±240 years—that is, between 4,960 and 5,440 radiocarbon years B.P.

Sometimes truth comes riding into history on the back of error.

REINHOLD NIEBUHR (1892–1971), THEOLOGIAN

The standard deviation must never be omitted from the radiocarbon date, because without it one would have no idea how accurately the sample was actually measured. Statistical theory provides simple methods to test whether two radiocarbon determinations are the same or different.

Tree Rings Incite the Second Radiocarbon Revolution

Radiocarbon dating relies on a number of key assumptions, perhaps the most important being that the radiocarbon level—that is, the ratio between carbon-12 and carbon-14—has remained constant in the earth's atmosphere. Libby assumed this when developing the method, but we now know that this assumption is not valid. That is, levels of atmospheric carbon-14 have shifted somewhat over the past millennia. The first investigator to find fault with the atmospheric assumption was H. L. De Vries of The Netherlands. De Vries cut several beams from historic buildings and determined the exact age of the wood by counting tree rings. When he later dated the known-age specimens by radiocarbon assay, he found the C-14 contrast to be 2 percent higher than expected for the known-age wood. Scientists at the time generally dismissed the work, as the errors De Vries discovered were relatively small, just barely outside the limits of expected error.

But the specter of larger errors finally inspired radiocarbon specialists to look more closely into the problem. This joint investigation was conducted by laboratories in Copenhagen, Heidelberg, Cambridge, New Haven, Philadelphia, Tucson, and La Jolla. In one landmark study, Hans Suess of the University of California at San Diego (La Jolla) analyzed wood from bristlecone pine trees. Native to the western United States, bristlecones are the world's oldest living organisms, some living up to 4,600 years. Working from live trees to ancient stumps, investigators had already extended the bristlecone tree-ring sequence back nearly 8,200 years (by the tree-ring technique we just discussed). Suess radiocarbon-dated dozens of known-age samples and compared the results obtained by each method. It was clear that there were significant fluctuations in the atmospheric C-14 concentrations. The assumption of C-14 stability was false, rendering the hundreds of previous radiocarbon determinations in error. Although dates younger than about 1500 B.C. were not too far off, comparison with the tree-ring data showed that more ancient radiocarbon dates could be up to 700 years too young.

Bristlecone pine, the world's oldest living organism.

The fluctuations in carbon-14 appear to be worldwide because the earth's atmosphere is so well mixed. Once a gas is released into the atmosphere, it becomes evenly distributed throughout the entire global atmosphere within a few years. Hence the discrepancy between tree-ring and radiocarbon ages, first noted by De Vries, must be independent of geographic origin. When radiocarbon dating was first introduced, Egyptologists told Libby that his dates did not square with the historically derived dynastic chronology. Libby attributed this disparity to experimental error, but now that we know that the effect is due to differential production of atmospheric C-14, it is possible to "correct" for these errors. Several international conferences have been held on the problem, and several correction tables were constructed to enable archaeologists and others to "correct" their own dates. More recently, these tables have been incorporated into a series of readily available computer

Radiocarbon Calibration on the Internet:

The CALIB Program is discussed on the University of Washington ftp site or you can write the Quaternary Isotope Lab, c/o Ms. Paula Reimer or Dr. Minze Stuiver, University of Washington, Seattle, WA 98195. Internet addresses are:
ftp://ftp.u.washington.edu/pub/user-supported/
pjreimer@u.washington.edu
minze@u.washington.edu

The Oxford University Calibration Program (OxCal) can also be downloaded:
http://info.ox.ac.uk/departments/rlaha.oxcal/oxcal_h.html
An e-mail distribution list is also available at:
orau@vax.ox.ac.uk

programs, each easily run on a desktop PC. The most popular such program, named CALIB, was written at the Quaternary Isotope Laboratory, University of Washington. Another calibration program, known as CAL15, was prepared by the Centre for Isotope Research, University of Groningen, The Netherlands. The third such program, OxCal, was devised at Oxford University. Considerable research continues on calibration issues, and these state-of-the-art radiocarbon age calibrations are unlikely to be the last (see *How to "Calibrate" Raw Radiocarbon Dates*).

Most regional sequences are unaffected by the correction factors. As long as all dating is by radiocarbon, the various subareas will remain in identical relationships, the only change being in the absolute dating. American cultural sequences, for example, remain intact, although all appear slightly older in absolute time. The Old World, however, is less fortunate because of disparities in dating techniques. In areas where writing was invented quite early, historic records provide firm chronology, over some 5,000 years. Radiocarbon dates for the Fertile Crescent and Egypt were corrected and supplemented by independent historical records. Western European chronologies, however, lacking historical evidence, were arranged strictly according to radiocarbon determinations. Over the years, Old World data have been almost universally interpreted as indicating that the early traits of civilization, such as metallurgy and monumental funerary architecture, were originally developed in the Near East, only later diffusing into the "culturally retarded" European area. The peoples of the Near East were considered the inventors and the barbaric Europeans the recipients.

The bristlecone correction changed much of that. Colin Renfrew has compared the process to a "temporal fault line." Most European chronologies are now placed several centuries earlier, but the classical Greek and Near Eastern chronologies remain unchanged. Stonehenge, formerly considered to be the work of Greek craftsmen who traveled to the British Isles in 1500 B.C., clearly predates even the Mycenaean civilization; Renfrew now refers to Stonehenge as the world's oldest astronomical observatory. These "corrected" radiocarbon dates suggest that Europe can no longer be viewed as a passive recipient of cultural advances from the Mediterranean heartland. Monumental temples were built on Malta before the pyramids of Egypt. The elaborate British megalithic tombs now appear to date a full millennium before those in the eastern Mediterranean. It is no longer possible to believe that agriculture moved from Asia into Europe. Although diffusion of cultural traits remains an important process, the recalibration in some cases reverses the direction of the arrow. In other instances the whole concept of a "cradle of civilization" seems irrelevant. The impact of the second radiocarbon revolution is clear in most recent discussions of European prehistory.

Accelerator Dating: The Third Radiocarbon Revolution

Radiocarbon dating has recently undergone a third revolution. But unlike the second one—which caused some to write off the technique entirely—this upheaval has no downside.

Archaeology tends to be viewed as an odd science by some because it progresses through unique and unrepeatable experiments. This is partially true. Digging remains our primary "experimental" method, and every excavation destroys the stratigraphic association of archaeological objects. For rare or unique finds, it is simply impossible to confirm the discovery by repeating. Maybe this is why archaeologists are always feuding with one another.

The recent development of the **accelerator mass spectrometric (AMS) technique** for radiocarbon dating drastically reduces the quantity of datable material required. When a Geiger counter is used to monitor the beta-ray emissions, several grams of organics are required. But because the new accelerator technology counts the proportion of carbon isotopes directly, the sample required is only a few milligrams.

Accelerator mass spectrometric (AMS) technique: A relatively new method of radiocarbon dating that counts the proportion of carbon isotopes directly (rather than using the indirect Geiger counter method), thereby dramatically reducing the quantity of datable material required.

Armed with the new technology of radiocarbon dating, archaeologists have already begun to "redo the experiment." In some cases, this research has fundamentally changed our perception of the human past. AMS radiocarbon dating allows investigators to date the individual amino acid fractions extracted from partially fossilized bones and has already been used to date the earliest skeletal materials in the New World. For years, George F. Carter has argued from geomorphological evidence that humans have been in the New World for at least 50,000 years. His views sharply contradicted the conventional wisdom, which holds that humans crossed the Bering Strait no more than about 25,000 years ago. Carter was particularly vocal about some human skeletal remains found near San Diego, California. He identified five bones that he thought were especially ancient, and Jeffrey Bada (Scripps Institute of Oceanography) processed them using a problematical dating technique based on amino acids, with the following results: 26,000 years; 6,000 years; 28,000 years; 44,000 years; and 48,000 years. These dates strongly supported Carter's assertions of humans' long inhabitation of the New World. If accurate, Bada's amino acid determinations would become the oldest direct dates available for New World humans, at least doubling the time conventionally accepted.

However, many archaeologists were skeptical, not only about the extreme age, but also about the accuracy of the amino acid technique. Until very recently, the skeletons in question could not be directly dated by radiocarbon because too much bone would have been destroyed in the process. But direct AMS radiocarbon dating has conclusively demonstrated that these skeletons are considerably later. Many range between 3,000 and 5,000 years in age, and the oldest is no more than 11,000 years old. The technique of amino acid dating of bone is no longer used (but see later in this chapter for an adaptation of this technique on ostrich eggshells).

The dating revolution has affected everyday archaeology. In 1924, M. R. Harrington and L. L. Loud excavated a cache of a dozen extraordinary duck decoys, long ago buried in the dusty depths of Lovelock Cave (Nevada). Although they almost certainly were manufactured in prehistoric times, the desert aridity had preserved these singular artifacts in near-mint condition.

How to "Calibrate" Raw Radiocarbon Dates

Let us explore the correction factors for two radiocarbon dates processed on charcoal recovered from Horizon 4 at Gatecliff Shelter:

Example A: (GAK-3611) 1730 ± 90 radiocarbon years B.P.

Example B: (GAK-3612) 2020 ± 90 radiocarbon years B.P.

In this case, the initial letters tell us that the samples were processed at the Gakushuïn Laboratory, Japan.

There are actually two different ways for applying the same conversion factors. Because each method illustrates an important principle regarding tree-ring corrections in radiocarbon analysis, I shall work through an example using each technique.

The Graphic Method

The tree-ring calibration curve (above, right) relates radiocarbon ages to their calendrical equivalents. Several such curves are available, depending on the time-range of interest.

The conversion of raw radiocarbon years to calendar years is not difficult:

1. Draw a horizontal line through the radiocarbon age to be converted.
2. Draw a vertical line through the intercept of the first line and the calibration curve (the center line).
3. The tree-ring–corrected calendrical age (expressed in years A.D./B.C.) is read on the bottom axis, and the corrected age B.P. appears at the top.

For Example B from Gatecliff (shown here), the raw date of 2020 B.P. corresponds to a "corrected" calendrical date of about 35 B.C. (read at the bottom of the graph) or about 1985 B.P. (at the top). It's as simple as that.

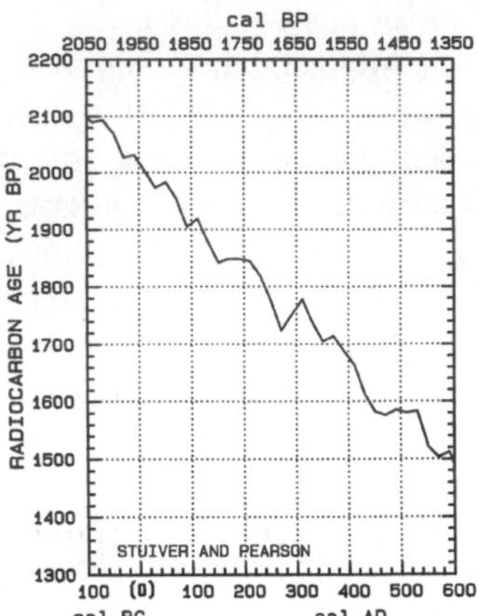

Tree-ring calibration curve.

Example A (not shown here) is a bit more complex because it crosses the tree-ring curve not just once but three times: at A.D. 255, A.D. 280, and A.D. 315. This blip is caused by atmospheric fluctuations in C-14, and so we cannot tell which age is reflected by the raw laboratory result. Accordingly, we must consider all three.

Although tree-ring dating provides absolute results, the derivation of these correction factors involves random errors, and one must also correct the ± factor at the end of the date. This correction could also be done using the graphic method, but there is a much easier method for doing this.

The PC Computer Method

The same conversion can be effected another way, by applying new computer software, readily available on the Internet and easily installed on most personal computers.

Here's the computer printout for GAK-3611, based on the widely employed CALIB computer program (produced by investigators at the

Cleverly crafted from tule reeds twisted to simulate the body and head of a duck, some had plain tule bodies and others were adorned with paint and feathers. As artifacts, the decoys are striking. Even *Sports Illustrated* extolled the creativity and craftsmanship of these prehistoric duck hunters.

But nobody knew how old the decoys were. The excavators assigned the artifacts to an ill-defined "Late Period," and over the next five decades, various

University of Washington). Note that such computer processing allows more precise computations than does the curve fitting and also avoids the problem of interpolating between fixed intervals (as we had to do with the ±90 error factor).

CALIB allows investigators to average radiocarbon dates across several samples. Remember that the raw determinations for Examples A and B differed by only 290 radiocarbon years. Should—for whatever reason—we wish to collapse these two determinations, it is a simple matter to pool the counting runs. The new, uncorrected composite date is 1875 ± 64.1 radiocarbon years B.P. (and the appropriate tree-ring–corrected dates are also appended). By pooling these two dates, the error rate decreases from ±90 to ±64.1 radiocarbon years (reflecting the increased number of counting runs on a "single" sample). Note that such pooling removed the problem of multiple crossings.

Regardless of which method is used, the tree-ring correction factors tell us that the raw dates from Gatecliff Shelter were too old, and they allow more accurate comparison with absolute calendar age.

```
                         UNIVERSITY OF WASHINGTON
                           QUATERNARY ISOTOPE LAB
                    RADIOCARBON CALIBRATION PROGRAM REV 3.0.3
      Stuiver, M. and Reimer, P.J., 1993, Radiocarbon, 35, p. 215-230.

 Calibration file(s): INTCAL93.14C
 Listing file: C14FIL.TXT

GAK-3611

Radiocarbon Age BP   1730  ± 90                      Reference(s)
 Calibrated age(s) cal AD 268, 274, 334          (Stuiver and Pearson, 1993)

  cal AD/BC  age ranges obtained from intercepts (Method A):
   one Sigma**    cal AD 229 - 420
   two Sigma**    cal AD 87 - 101  113 - 542

   Summary of above:

   minimum of cal age ranges (cal ages) maximum of cal age ranges:
    1í    cal AD 229 (268, 274, 334)  420
    2í    cal AD 87 (268, 274, 334)  542



References for datasets used:
Stuiver, M and Pearson, GW, 1993, Radiocarbon, 35, 1-23.

Comments:
éThis standard deviation (error) includes a lab error multiplier.
** 1 sigma = square root of (sample std. dev.»+ curve std. dev.»)
   2 sigma = 2 x square root of (sample std. dev.»+ curve std. dev.»)
[ ] = calibrated with linear extension to calibration curve
0* represents a "negative" age BP
1955* denotes influence of bomb C-14
For cal yrs between 5500-5190 BC an offset of 25 years is possible.
NOTE:  Cal ages and ranges are rounded to the nearest year which
       may be too precise in many instances.  Users are advised to
       round results to the nearest 10 yr for samples with standard
       deviation in the radiocarbon age greater than 50 yr.
```

Sample desktop computer output from the CALIB *program for the tree-ring conversion of radiocarbon date* GAK-3611 *from Gatecliff Shelter.*

archaeologists studied the unique decoys and guess-dated their age. Although estimates ranged from 500 B.C. to the historic period, conventional wisdom among Great Basin archaeologists held the decoys to be about 2,000 years old.

The Lovelock Cave originals were curated at the Museum of the American Indian (Heye Foundation) in New York City. In 1969, L. Kyle Napton (California State University, Stanislaus) and Robert F. Heizer (University of

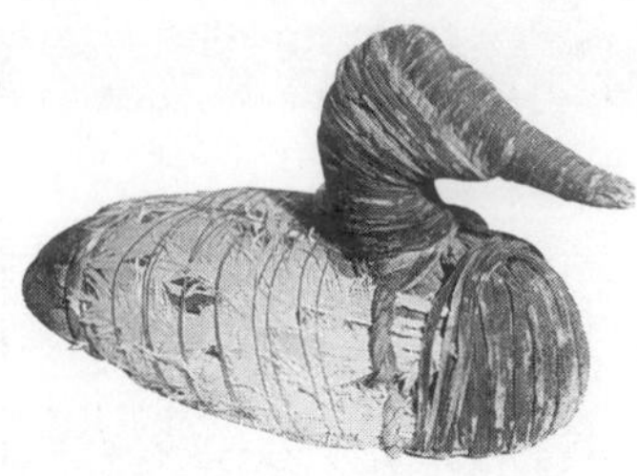

Ancient duck decoy from Lovelock Cave (Nevada). The AMS-based radiocarbon method has determined that this artifact was made about 2,000 years ago.

California, Berkeley) secured a large enough chunk from one of the decoys to submit for conventional radiocarbon dating. Incredibly, the irreplaceable sample was lost by the radiocarbon laboratory (giving a new meaning to the term *laboratory error*). Although Napton tried to obtain additional samples, he realized that samples adequate for conventional radiocarbon dating would unacceptably damage the unique artifacts.

Then came radiocarbon's "third revolution" to the rescue. Knowing that extremely small samples could be dated, Don Fowler (University of Nevada) obtained permission to remove such samples from the Lovelock decoys. Under watchful curatorial eyes, he gingerly snipped off tule tidbits from inside two decoys. The priceless clippings, each the size of your little fingernail, were submitted for processing by the new University of Arizona accelerator mass spectrometer (AMS) facility.

The two statistically consistent AMS radiocarbon dates came out to be 2080 ± 330 and 2250 ± 230 radiocarbon years B.P. Taking into account the plus-minus factor, the dates overwhelmingly confirmed the previous conventional estimates: The Lovelock decoys are about 2,000 years old. But without the advent of AMS dating, we would still be wondering.

AMS dating has been used on a wide variety of cultural materials, but no application has received greater popular attention than when radiocarbon technology was used to determine whether the famous **Shroud of Turin** was an ancient hoax. For the answer, see *Is the Shroud of Turin the Burial Cloth of Christ?*

Shroud of Turin: A sheet of twill-woven linen cloth on which appears a pale sepiatone image of the front and back of a naked man about 6 feet tall; pale carmine stains of blood mark wounds to the head, side, hands, and feet. The shroud has been claimed to be the actual cloth in which Christ's crucified body was wrapped.

Obsidian Hydration

Obsidian—volcanic glass—has been fashioned into stone tools for millennia. As anyone who has ever fractured an obsidian nodule is well aware, the resultant razor-sharp flakes can be chipped into a host of handy artifacts: knives, scrapers, drills, projectile points, and so forth. Obsidian artifacts are found in archaeological sites on every continent except Australia and one day may rival ceramics as archaeology's most useful artifact for controlling time.

Obsidian: Volcanic glass often used as raw material for the manufacture of stone tools.

Two geologists working for the U.S. Geological Survey, Irving Friedman and Robert Smith, first started looking into the potential of obsidian as a timemarker in 1948. Friedman and Smith knew that obsidian is a fairly "dry" rock, containing only about 0.2 percent water. But when a piece of obsidian is fractured and the fresh surface is exposed to the environment, water is absorbed into the new surface. The absorption, or *hydration,* process continues until the obsidian reaches approximately 3.5 percent water, the saturation point. These zones, or rims, of hydration are more dense than the unhydrated inside, and the hydrated zone has different optical properties. Whenever obsidian is broken, the hydration process begins from scratch on the fresh surface. This much is simple geophysics, but Friedman and Smith propelled this knowledge into archaeological relevance by reasoning that the degree of hydration observed on an archaeological artifact could measure how long it had been since that surface was created by the flintknapper.

Time is nature's way of keeping everything from happening at once.

WOODY ALLEN, ACTOR AND AUTHOR

Some Rocks Are Wetter Than Others

Obsidian Hydration on the Internet:

Obsidian Hydration Analysis Service Home Page:
http://www.pacific.net:80/~ohas/

Northwest Research Obsidian Studies Laboratory:
http://www.peak.org/~skinncr/obsidian.html

The principle behind **obsidian hydration dating** is as clever as it is austere: The longer the artifact surface has been exposed, the thicker the hydration band will be. By making certain that the datable surfaces were only those exposed by deliberate flintknapping, obsidian hydration can be taken as a direct indicator of age.

Obsidian hydration dating: The technique of dating obsidian artifacts by measuring the microscopic amount of water absorbed on fresh surfaces.

To measure how much hydration is present, the artifact must be cut and a microscopic thin section prepared. To do this, a small wedge is removed from the edge of the artifact by making intersecting cuts with a diamond-impregnated saw. This section is then ground thin on a lapidary machine and affixed to a microscopic slide with Canada balsam. The obsidian wedge is ground once again, this time to less than 50 microns thick. The slide is finally ready for microscopic analysis, using a polarizing light source.

Obsidian hydration dating is simple, rapid, and cheap: Ten obsidian hydration dates may be run for the cost of a single radiocarbon determination. Students can be readily trained to prepare obsidian hydration samples, and several laboratories are currently in operation for such dating. But obsidian dating is hardly without difficulty. After examining about 600 specimens, Friedman and Smith discovered that the rate of hydration is not uniform throughout the world. Of the several variables that seem to influence the hydration rate, atmospheric temperature seemed to be paramount. Once a sufficient number of global samples were analyzed, the investigators constructed a world map describing the correlation between climate and hydration rates.

The origin (and hence chemical composition) of obsidian samples is another major factor in determining hydration rate. Donovan Clark, then a graduate student at Stanford University, analyzed hundreds of obsidian artifacts from five prehistoric California sites and compared the hydration rims with known radiocarbon determinations of the sites. Clark found that central California obsidian hydrates at slightly more than 1 micron per thousand years. Thus, by comparison with radiocarbon dating, Clark suggested a means of converting obsidian hydration from a simple rim thickness (measured in microns) to an actual age estimate (in years).

Photomicrograph, taken at 490×, with arrows indicating the obsidian hydration band (or "rim") that is 4.2 microns thick. This specimen is from Mono County, California.

Estimating Absolute Age With Obsidian Hydration Dating

A study by Frank Findlow and his colleagues illustrates how the obsidian hydration technique is used to date specific flows. The Government Mountain–Sitgreaves Peak obsidian flow is one of the most heavily exploited in the American Southwest. Obsidian from this area ranges from gray to shiny black in color, and the matrix is free of inclusions. Its excellent fracturing qualities probably account for its wide distribution by trade throughout Arizona and southern Utah.

ARCHAEO-MYTHBUSTERS

Is the Shroud of Turin the Burial Cloth of Christ?

Accelerator dating is still a relatively new technology, but the effects have already reached far beyond standard archaeological inquiry. Antiquarians and musicians, for instance, are turning to AMS technology to detect fakes: Is this really a Stradivarius violin?

The newest radiocarbon revolution grabbed headlines around the world when AMS dating was applied to the famous *Shroud of Turin*, thought by many to be the actual cloth in which Christ's crucified body had been wrapped. Although the Roman Catholic Church never officially proclaimed the shroud to be Christ's burial cloth, neither did it discourage that belief. Three million of the faithful filed past the shroud when it was last displayed in the Cathedral of St. John the Baptist in 1978. Many believed they had looked into the face of Christ. What did they see?

The shroud itself is an unspectacular sheet of twill-woven linen cloth, slightly more than 14 feet long and a yard wide. On this appears a pale sepia-tone image of the front and back of a naked man about 6 feet tall. Pale carmine stains of blood mark wounds to the head, side, hands, and feet. Believers took the shroud to be a true relic of Christ's Passion. But critics since the fourteenth century have been equally convinced that the shroud is a cruel, if clever, hoax. Studying the Shroud of Turin became a scholarly and scientific discipline on its own.

The mystery only deepened when teams of scientists from the Air Force Academy, the Los Alamos laboratory, and several other research centers examined the shroud in detail, photographing it under ultraviolet and infrared light, bombarding it with X rays, peering at it microscopically. To the delight of many, the high-tech scientists could not come up with a clear conclusion either way. Creationists immediately asked why the United States government should support places like the Smithsonian Institution when scientists cannot even explain how such an "obvious fraud" was perpetrated? The implications for science in general (and archaeology in particular) were enormous, and the debate raged on.

For nearly 40 years, scientists had argued that radiocarbon dating could definitively determine

Obsidian from the Government Mountain–Sitgreaves source was recovered in 10 archaeological sites, ranging in age from about 1500 B.C. to historic times. After the samples were prepared for microscopic analysis and the hydration bands were read, the results were synthesized into the following rate of hydration:

$$Y = 43.58 + 158.16\,(x^2 - x)$$

where Y is the date (in years B.P.) and x is the hydration value in microns.

A few examples will illustrate how this hydration equation is used to date archaeological sites. Awatovi (Arizona) is a large Hopi city abandoned in A.D. 1630. Findlow and his associates dated 10 Government Mountain obsidian artifacts recovered from the latest occupation at Awatovi. The hydration rims averaged 1.8 microns thick, leading to an estimated age of

$$Y = 43.58 + 158.16\,(1.8^2 - 1.8) = 271 \text{ years B.P.}$$

This age converts to a calendar date of about A.D. 1680, in fairly close agreement with the historically dated abandonment of Awatovi.

whether the Shroud of Turin dates to the time of Christ. Unfortunately, conventional radiocarbon methods would have destroyed a handkerchief-sized piece of the shroud, and church authorities rejected all such requests. But since the new AMS method of radiocarbon dating necessitates destruction of only a minuscule sample of linen—easily removed from unobtrusive parts of the shroud—the Pontifical Academy of Sciences agreed in 1984 to such dating.

After years of squabbling about the ground rules, three laboratories (at the University of Arizona in Tucson, the British Museum in London, and the Swiss Federal Institute in Zurich) finally received a postage-stamp-size piece of the shroud, plus control specimens of various ages. Only British Museum officials, who coordinated the research, knew which specimen was which. When the owner of the shroud, Pope John Paul II, was informed of the outcome, his response was simple: "Publish it."

And publish it they did. In October 1988, a gathering of ecclesiastical and technological specialists hosted a news conference at which Anastasio Cardinal Ballestrero, archbishop of Turin, solemnly announced that all three laboratories agreed that the flax plants from which the linen in the shroud was made had been grown in medieval times—between 1260 and 1390—long after the death of Jesus.

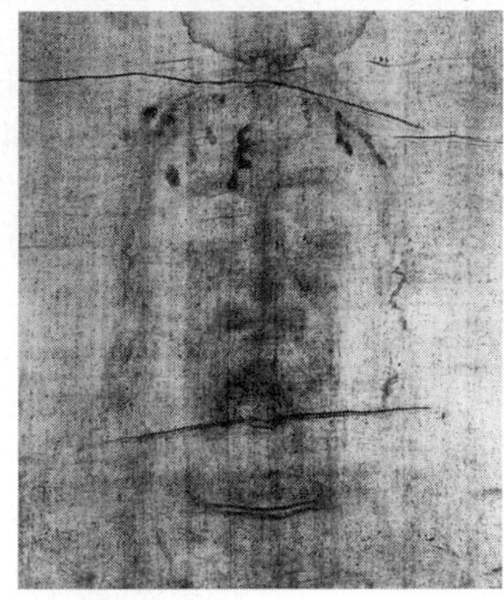

Shroud of Turin.

Although a certain degree of mystery still surrounds the shroud, particularly since nobody can explain how such an image was created using Middle Ages technology, one thing is clear: Radiocarbon dating's "third revolution" unambiguously resolved this controversy that spanned five centuries. The Shroud of Turin could not possibly be the authentic burial cloth of Jesus.

This same procedure was used to date Stratum 3 at site CS-184, also in Arizona. The average rim thickness was 5.2 microns, which converts to an absolute age of 3,498 years B.P. In this case the obsidian hydration value agrees closely with the date estimated by the radiocarbon method.

Several factors conspire to render the future of obsidian hydration dating somewhat clouded: differential hydration rates for different obsidian sources, artifact reuse, short-term temperature fluctuations, and variable amounts of available moisture. It is known, for instance, that obsidians of different composition can hydrate at different rates. In studying obsidians from the central Mexican highlands, Joseph Michels found that green rhyolitic obsidian hydrated almost three times as fast as did the gray rhyolitic obsidian. That is, even under uniform temperature conditions, the green obsidian hydrates at a rate of 11.45 millimicrons per millennium, whereas the gray obsidian hydrates at a rate of only 4.5 millimicrons per thousand years. Fortunately, this differing composition was obvious by superficial inspection, but the problem of differing rates is compounded when seemingly identical obsidians are of different composition. A number of

The Shroud on the Internet:

The Shroud of Turin Home Page has the latest on the shroud:
http://www.cais.com/npacheco/shroud/turin.html
http://205.177.10.11/npacheco/shroud/turin.html

investigators are currently working on the physiochemical separation of various obsidian sources.

As long as the restrictions are kept in mind, obsidian hydration does provide a useful technique for dating archaeological sites. Even the best dating technique cannot be used without some restrictions and caution.

Thermoluminescence Dating

A weak but measurable flash of light is emitted whenever prehistoric ceramics, tiles, bricks, or figurines are ground up and intensely heated. But if you repeat the experiment on the same sample, no flash will occur; the sample will just glow.

This difference is due to *thermoluminescence.* The fabric within ceramics traps energy inside its internal microscopic lattice, and when the sample is heated, the stored energy is released as light. Simplified, it works like this: Nuclear radiation always exists within the ceramic fabric, and radioactivity constantly bombards everything else inside the sherd. Although most of the nuclear energy dissipates as heat, some electrons are knocked away from their parent molecules. Most electrons eventually return home, but a few runaways keep bouncing around inside the ceramic lattice. In their wanderings, the malcontents will eventually encounter imperfections in the lattice. When this happens, they are "trapped." As time passes, an increasing amount of energy is stored in this way.

But heating the lattice to 500° C or so precipitates a jailbreak. Maverick electrons are allowed to slip their bonds, becoming free once again to wander. This release creates the flash of light, called the *thermoluminescent* (or TL) signal. Firing a pot in a kiln creates a *time-point zero,* effectively setting the TL clock at zero. When samples are reheated under laboratory conditions and the intensity of the light emissions is measured, it is possible to gauge the elapsed duration between the two episodes of heating.

Schematic representation of the process of "time-zero" setting in the thermoluminescence dating of pottery.

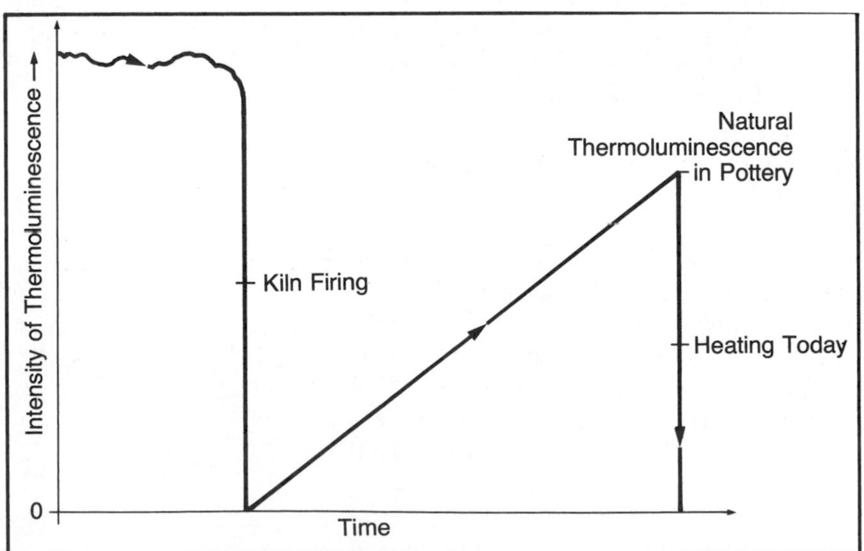

Actually computing the age of ancient ceramics or figurines is considerably more complicated than this, requiring a number of additional procedures, cautions, and assumptions. Still, a number of relatively reliable dates have become available, and TL dating is now extensively used to date archaeological deposits, detect fakes in art collections, and even date burned flint artifacts.

Radiocarbon on the Internet:

Radiocarbon Homepage is provided by *Radiocarbon*, the main internal journal for research articles: http://packrat.aml.arizona.edu/

Radiometric Dating of Potassium

Many rocks, including volcanic minerals, contain traces of potassium, which, like carbon, occurs naturally in several isotopic forms. One of these, known as potassium-40, decays slowly and regularly into an inert, stable gas (argon-40). By comparing the relative proportions of these potassium and argon isotopes in an archaeologically relevant sample, it is possible to derive a radiometric clock for measuring the passage of time. Again, as with radiocarbon dating, the principle is simple: The more argon-40 in a sample relative to potassium-40, the older must be that sample.

So far, so good, but how can one express such relative age estimates in more absolute terms? This initial datum for radiocarbon dating is the death of the absorbing organism since C-14 acquisition ceases with death. Fortunately, volcanic rock provides a comparable method for "zeroing out" the potassium-argon clock. During all major volcanic eruptions, the temperature is so high that all gases—including argon-40—are driven out of the microscopic rock crystals. Such episodes in effect set the potassium-argon clock to zero because all argon-40 present must have accumulated since the last major volcanic eruption.

Potassium-argon dating involves assumptions similar to those of radiocarbon analysis. There must have been no argon trapped at the time of formation (that is, all argon must be the direct result of potassium decay), and all argon must be retained in the rock structure without absorption by the atmosphere. It is known that some rocks, such as mica, tend to leak argon, and so care must be taken in deciding which rock types to subject to potassium-argon dating.

Potassium-argon dating: An absolute dating technique that monitors the decay of potassium (K-40) into argon gas (Ar-40).

This is why archaeologists love to find ancient sites in association with volcanic deposits. If fossils, for instance, are found just below a layer of volcanic ash, the potassium-argon method will provide a minimum age estimate for the tools and fossils contained in the archaeological stratum.

The archaeological potential of potassium dating is more limited than that of radiocarbon because the K-Ar time range is so great (as much as several billion years). Rarely are archaeological deposits old enough. But some critically important early sites in Africa have been successfully dated by the K-Ar method. The late Glynn Isaac, for instance, discovered a mass of broken bones strewn across a 20-foot area in the badlands of Kenya. Scattered among the bones (mostly hippopotamus) were remains of stone tools, including flakes and a few pebble choppers. The so-called KBS site is embedded in volcanic **tuff**, and pumice cobbles within the tuff have been dated at 2.61 ± 0.26 million years by means of the potassium-argon technique.

Tuff: A geological term for the rock formed from consolidated volcanic ash.

Archaeology on the Internet:

RLAHA Home Page (Research Lab for Archaeology and Art History) develops applications of scientific methods for the study of the past, including radiocarbon, thermoluminescence dating, materials analysis, stable isotope, DNA, and ground-penetrating radar: http://info.ox.ac.uk/departments/rlaha/

Homo erectus: A human ancestor who lived in Africa, Asia, and Europe between 2 million and 500,000 years ago. These so-called "erectines" walked upright, may have used fire, and often made stone tools in the Acheulean tradition.

Acheulean: An early stone tool industry that appeared more than 500,000 years ago in Africa, Europe, and Southwest Asia. Acheulean technology involved the first use of regular bifacial flaking, producing hand axes as well as flakes and other cores. The culture is named after the site of St. Acheul, in northern France.

Argon-argon dating: A high-precision method for estimating the relative quantities of argon-39 to argon-40 gas.

Potassium-argon dating was also used to estimate the age of ***Homo erectus,*** one of our intermediate human ancestors. For decades, investigators generally believed that *Homo erectus* evolved exclusively in Africa. The earliest fossils are slightly less than 2 million years old; over the next 500,000 years or so, an early **Acheulean** stone tool culture developed, characterized by large, tear-shaped hand axes. Then, sometime after 1.5 million years ago, these *Homo erectus* pioneers began moving out of Africa into other parts of the Old World.

Thus fossil hunters were shocked in 1971, when Garniss Curtis, then of the University of California at Berkeley, used potassium-argon methods to date the sediments associated with the *Homo erectus* fossil from Mojokerto, Java. Because Java is a long way from Africa, most investigators thought that the Mojokerto skull should be much younger than a million years. But Curtis estimated that the fossilized infant's skull from Mojokerto was nearly twice that age—1.9 million years old. This extraordinarily ancient age was rejected by most paleontologists, who were convinced that the only humans in the world prior to 1 million years ago lived in Africa.

Both these early dates and the dating technique itself came under criticism. Although potassium-argon dating had been around for decades, the laboratory methods were still somewhat cumbersome. In the laboratory, a given sample of crystals is first split into two subsamples. One of these is dissolved in acid, then passed through a flame; the wavelengths of light emitted allow estimation of the amount of potassium-40 in the sample. The other sample is heated directly, and the amount of argon-40 gas released is measured. This two-sample process increases the potential for error and contamination because there is twice the opportunity for things to go wrong.

Potassium-argon dating also requires several grams of volcanic crystals in order to process a single age estimate. While most of these crystals probably derive from the eruption that covered the fossil, the possibility always exists that other crystals, from volcanic eruptions millions of years older, may have become mixed in, thereby creating a date that vastly overestimates the age of the fossil in question.

Curtis has since teamed up with Carl Swisher of the Institute of Human Origins in Berkeley to develop a new method to date the age of key volcanic deposits. The so-called **argon-argon** method was specifically designed to avoid the contamination problems inherent in the earlier technique. The volcanic crystals to be dated are first irradiated. When a neutron penetrates the potassium nucleus, it displaces a proton, converting the potassium into argon-39, an "artificial" isotope not found in nature. The minute quantities of artificially created argon and naturally occurring argon-40 can then be measured in a single experiment. Because there is no longer a need to split the sample, the argon-argon method produces superior results, even from tiny samples. This high-precision method also allows investigators to focus on single volcanic crystals, which can be dated one by one; thus any older contaminants can be discarded.

In 1992, Curtis and Swisher returned to Java to collect additional samples to be dated with the new argon-argon method. With some white volcanic pumice obtained from the matrix inside the braincase of the Mojokerto fossil, Swisher returned to Berkeley. Within a few weeks, he proclaimed that the new dates were equally ancient—1.8 million ± 40,000 years. The researchers also tested additional sediment samples from another Java site where *Homo erectus* fossils had been found. The results, yielding an age of about 1.6 million years, confirmed the initial Mojokerto fossil date derived from the now "old fashioned" potassium-argon dating method.

Although these dates remain controversial—many paleontologists continue to doubt that *Homo erectus* could have left Africa so early—it is clear that new high-precision dating techniques such as the argon-argon method will be increasingly important in evaluating the fossil evidence in the years to come.

Dating Ancient Ostrich Eggshells

One of anthropology's Big Questions is this: When and how did anatomically modern people arise? Did modern *Homo sapiens* arise through gradual, global evolution? Or did modern humans evolve relatively recently and in one place (Africa), then expand throughout the world, displacing less successful forms? Currently, both positions are hotly defended.

But there is a problem. For years, archaeologists interested in dating the origins of anatomically modern humans have been confounded by a lack of relevant dating techniques. Specifically, an irksome gap exists between the effective ranges of commonly used dating techniques, particularly the radiocarbon and potassium-argon techniques. As we have seen, the *maximum* reliable age for radiocarbon dating is about 40,000 years and the *minimum* reliable age of K-Ar dating is roughly 200,000 years before present. The disparity between 40,000 and 200,000 years is hence a "gap" within which fall many of the important hominid fossils and their associated artifacts from Africa and the Near East. Until more precise dating was possible within this gap, little solid progress seemed likely in resolving the origins of anatomically modern people. Fortunately, a relatively new dating approach has bridged, or even closed, this gap between fossil dating methods.

This welcome resolution arose from a rather commonplace observation: African ostrich eggshell fragments litter archaeological sites throughout Africa and the Middle East, reaching as far as China and Mongolia. Sometimes, as in many northeastern African sites, eggshell fragments comprise the only identifiable faunal element (usually because all the bones have decayed away). Human use of ostrich eggs ranges in age from extremely ancient (1.8 million years at Olduvai Gorge) to the historic period. This extraordinarily broad range in time and space can be directly attributed to the importance of ostrich eggs to human populations: The contents were often used for food and the eggshells were ready-made water containers. And, for the last 30,000 years, people have crafted eggshell fragments into ornamental beads.

Eggshells are organic by-products, of course, meaning that they contain carbon. For years, archaeologists dated archaeological eggshells using standard radiocarbon methods. But because the maximum age range of radiocarbon is about 40,000 years, the older ostrich eggshells—and in many cases, the archaeological sites with which they were associated—remained undated. This was unfortunate because many of the ostrich eggshell-bearing sites contained key hominid fossils, which, accurately dated, could shed considerable light on the origin of anatomically modern humans.

Wouldn't it be nice to be able to date those older eggshells? In theory, at least, that should be possible because ostrich eggshells contain proteins (amino acids), which are known to decompose through time. Therefore, if one could estimate the proportion of the eggshell protein that had decomposed and relate that percentage to a calendrical scale, it should be possible to estimate the time elapsed since that eggshell was formed.

Archaeologist Allison Brooks and her colleagues at George Washington University and elsewhere have recently devised a new way to date the amino acids contained in ostrich eggshells. Not only does this method expand the range of datable materials, but it promises to extend the range considerably beyond that of the current radiocarbon method.

Amino acids are protein compounds found in all living organisms. These compounds exist in two forms, which are mirror images of one another (and can be distinguished from one another only by their refractive properties). When placed under a polarized light, one molecule bends light to the left; the mirror-image compound bends the same light to the right. Such left-handed compounds are called L-isomers (*lepto* is Greek for "left"). The right-handed amino acids are called D-isomers ("D" standing for *dextrorotation* [right-hand bending] of the polarizing light).

Most of the proteins in living organisms are left-handed. When the organism dies, the protein molecules begin to flip over, more and more of them converting to the right-handed form. Geophysicists have converted this reaction to a dating technique. Because living forms contain primarily L-isomers and fossil materials have mostly D-amino acids, the D:L amino acid ratio can be used as a measure of absolute age. The chemical reaction responsible for this change from L- to D-amino acids is called **racemization.**

Amino acid racemization: A dating technique of organics that utilizes postmortem changes in proteins to estimate age at death.

There is, of course, a catch. In order to use amino acid decomposition to estimate the age of an organic compound, it is first necessary to know the temperature history of that sample—both the temperature during which the sample was formed and also the temperature of the surrounding matrix (prior to archaeological excavation). Sometimes, the past temperature of an archaeological stratum can be derived from other materials buried in that stratum. Obsidian hydration, for instance, would provide one such cross-check. In other cases, on-site sensors are employed to determine the modern sediment temperatures. But sometimes, it is necessary simply to estimate the ancient temperatures of the archaeological sediments in question.

This temperature estimate is critical in establishing the range of eggshell dating. Allison Brooks and her coworkers, for instance, estimate that at normal sediment temperatures in the tropics and subtropics, the age range of eggshell amino acid should extend from modern times back to about 200,000 years. But in colder climates, the racemization rate slows down, meaning that in northern China and Mongolia, amino acid dating of eggshells could be accurate for up to a million years.

To be certain that their temperature estimates were reasonable, Brooks first explored a relatively recent archaeological site in the Kalahari Desert, in southern Africa. Various eggshell samples were easily datable using standard radiocarbon methods. Then she used the new amino acid dating method to date another eggshell fragment from the same strata. The dates obtained from the radiocarbon and amino acid methods corresponded so closely that the investigators decided that their dating experiment had potential.

So they moved to another site, this time at the other end of Africa, in the Sahara Desert of southern Egypt. They collected archaeological eggshell fragments from the site surface, using on-site sensors to estimate the effective temperatures. They then dated the fragments using both radiocarbon and racemization methods and found, as before, a satisfactory agreement between the two techniques. They moved to other archaeological sediments in the same area, comparing their new amino acid dates with stratigraphic ages obtained through other conventional techniques. Once again, the new method was able to mimic results obtained from established dating methods.

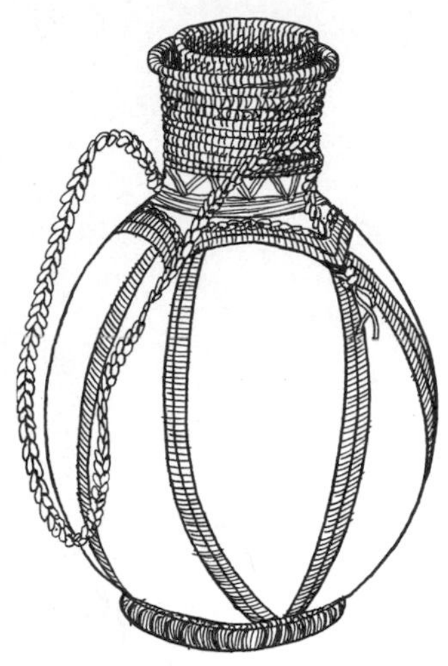

Ostrich eggshell converted into a pot (Cameroon, Africa).

A Brief Warning About Arguments of Relevance

We have considered several current methods of obtaining chronometric dates for archaeological sites—and many more are currently available—but one important issue has yet to be addressed. In the section on dendrochronology, for instance, I said that tree-ring dating provides absolute dates for archaeological sites. Although this is true, it points to an important issue not yet discussed.

Archaeological sites can never be dated by simple equivalences. For example, a tree-ring cutting date provides the year, such as A.D. 1239, that a particular tree died. I also said that the UCLA radiocarbon laboratory dated 5,200-year-old tree charcoal in Horizon 2 at Gatecliff Shelter. By themselves, these dates tell us exactly nothing about archaeology. A dead tree assumes archaeological importance only when its death is somehow relevant to a human behavioral event of interest, such as the roofing of a pueblo room. The same argument applies to archaeology's other dating methods, which really only tell us when a clam died, or a piece of obsidian was broken, or a particular rock was heated.

In every case, the event dated must be demonstrated to be contemporaneous with a behavioral event of interest—building a boat, cooking a meal, or killing a deer. The demonstration of association is a key issue in archaeological dating, and the general topic of *arguments of relevance* will be considered in more detail later.

SUMMARY Contemporary archaeologists are equipped with a powerful battery of techniques that can be used to date objects of the past. *Tree-ring dating* (dendrochronology) enables archaeologists to establish the precise year of death for many species of trees commonly found in archaeological sites. When properly correlated with known cultural events, these "cutting dates" can often pinpoint the exact occupation history of a site.

Radiocarbon dating is a physiochemical technique that monitors the degree of radioactive emission from organic specimens. During life, all plants and animals ingest atmospheric carbon (including C-14), and after they die, they cannot absorb any more C-14. Through the continuing process of radiocarbon decay, these C-14 molecules break down at a steadily decreasing rate. By determining the current rate of C-14 breakdown, one can estimate the length of elapsed time since the death of a plant or animal. Recently, physicists discovered that the atmospheric level of radiocarbon has changed somewhat over the last several millennia. Many archaeologists thus now "correct" their radiocarbon dates using an absolute chronology based on the radiocarbon dating of bristlecone pine samples of known age. New advances in accelerator-based radiocarbon methods permit archaeologists to use extremely small samples, vastly stretching the potential of the method.

Obsidian hydration is a microscopic technique that measures the amount of water absorbed into the freshly broken surface of an obsidian artifact or piece of waste chippage: The older the artifact is, the greater the degree of hydration.

Potassium-argon dating is an absolute technique that monitors the decay of potassium into argon gas. It involves assumptions similar to those of radiocarbon analysis. There must have been no argon trapped at the time of formation (that is, all argon must be the direct result of potassium decay), and all argon must be retained in the rock structure without absorption by the atmosphere. A variant of this technique, *argon-argon dating* is a high-precision method that dates single volcanic crystals, thereby eliminating important sources of potential contamination.

The maximum reliable age for radiocarbon dating is about 40,000 years and the minimum reliable age of K-Ar dating is roughly 200,000 years before present. A relatively new dating technique, *amino acid racemization,* spans this critical gap by dating fragments of ostrich eggshells (which are commonly found in sites throughout Africa, the Middle East, and China).

Keep in mind that, by themselves, these various dating techniques tell us nothing about cultural activities. Dendrochronology, for example, can estimate only when a certain tree died; obsidian hydration tells us only when a certain piece of obsidian rock was fractured. In each case, the event being dated must be demonstrated to be coeval with a behavioral (cultural) event of interest.

Chapter 8

Chronology Building: How to Understand Stratigraphy

To find old sites, you must look in old dirt.

Jonathan O. Davis (1948–1990), geoarchaeologist

PREVIEW Archaeology commonly borrows methods, techniques, and theories from nonarchaeological fields. We saw this in the preceding chapter on dating techniques, which were heavily borrowed from chemistry, physics, geochemistry, and elsewhere. In later chapters, we shall also draw on the expertise of zoologists, botanists, and molecular biologists, to name just a few.

Geology has been a particularly useful mine for good ideas. It was geologists who first pulled together the major principles of **stratigraphy**. This chapter dwells on two extremely important stratigraphic principles—the concepts of superposition and index fossils—which have been critical in our understanding of how the archaeological record has been put together.

Stratigraphy: An analytical interpretation of the structure produced by the deposition of geological and/or cultural sediments into layers, or strata.

Nicolaus Steno (1638–1687) initially formulated the **law of superposition.** Simply stated, *Steno's law* tells us that in any pile of **sedimentary rocks** undisturbed by folding or overturning, the strata on the bottom must have been deposited first. On a broader scale, this principle, almost preposterously simple, holds that—all else being equal—older deposits tend to be buried beneath younger ones. This canon facilitates the correlation of various geological exposures such as cliffs, stream valleys, and drill cores.

But geological correlation has its limits. It is impossible, for instance, to correlate geological exposures at the Grand Canyon directly with the White Cliffs of Dover in England. Ever resourceful, our geological colleagues dreamed up a second principle, the index fossil concept, which assisted worldwide correlation.

This second concept is a bit more involved. In the early nineteenth century, a British surveyor named William Smith (1769–1839) began collecting data from geological strata throughout England. Smith gradually became enraptured by the **fossils** he found in various canals and vertical exposures. As he grew to understand the regional geology, he recognized that different exposures of the same stratum contained comparable fossils. Smith eventually became so knowledgeable that when somebody showed him a fossil, he could guess the stratum from which it had come.

Smith's French contemporaries were making similar discoveries. While mapping the fossil-rich strata surrounding Paris, Georges Cuvier

Law of superposition: The geological principle stating that in any pile of sedimentary rocks that have not been disturbed by folding or overturning, each bed is older than the layers above and younger than the layers below; also known as *Steno's law*.

Sedimentary rock: Rock formed from the weathered products of preexisting rocks that have been transported, deposited, and turned once again to stone.

Fossil: A remnant, impression, or trace of an organism from the past that has been preserved in the earth's crust.

Geology gives us a key to the patience of God.

JOSIAH GILBERT HOLLAND (1819–1881), EDUCATOR AND WRITER

(1769–1832) and Alexandre Brongniart (1770–1847) discovered that certain of their fossils were restricted to specific geological formations. After applying the law of superposition to arrange the strata in the proper chronological sequence, they then organized their fossil collection into the appropriate stratigraphic order. French fossil assemblages, it turned out, varied systematically according to the age of the parent strata. Cuvier and Brongniart then compared their fossils with modern species and discovered, as expected, that fossils characterizing later strata more closely resembled modern forms than did those of more ancient strata.

Stratum: More or less homogeneous or gradational material, visually separable from other levels by a discrete change in the character of the material being deposited or by a sharp break in deposition (or both).

Index fossil concept: A theory that proposes that strata containing similar fossil assemblages will tend to be of similar age. In archaeology, this concept enables archaeologists to characterize and date strata within archaeological sites using "diagnostic" artifact forms.

Fossils contained in a geological **stratum** thus became a clue to the relative age of the deposit. This is the **index fossil concept:** Rocks containing similar fossil assemblages must be of similar age. Obviously there are exceptions to both the index fossil concept and the law of superposition, but these two principles enabled geologists around the globe to correlate their stratigraphic sections into master chronologies. Both principles are likewise important as guideposts for interpreting the human record of the past.

In the first chapter, we examined Thomas Jefferson's eighteenth-century excavations in Virginia—generally acknowledged as the first application of stratigraphic principles to archaeology. Jefferson's firsthand stratigraphic observations enabled him to reconstruct the various stages in the construction of the site he was exploring, suggesting its probable use as a burial feature. As it turns out, the stratigraphic techniques for analyzing archaeological sites have changed very little since Jefferson's time. The technology, of course, is vastly improved, but the bedrock philosophy is basically unchanged. Let me show you what I mean.

Fossil Footprints at Laetoli: The Law of Superposition in Action

Primitive spelling bees

Laetoli: Important hominid fossil site in Tanzania. *Laetoli* (also sometimes spelled "Laetolil") is the local Masai name for a red lily that grows throughout the area.

Mary Leakey was one of the world's most famous fossil finders. She scoured East Africa, seeking archaeological evidence of the earliest human ancestors who once lived there. With her esteemed husband, Louis Leakey, she electrified the world with finds that included the celebrated *Zinjanthropus* skull from Olduvai Gorge in northwestern Tanzania. To many, Mary Leakey's discovery of the "Zinj" cranium in 1959 heralded a new age, the beginning of modern paleoanthropological research in East Africa.

But here, nearly two decades later, as she stood staring at the ground in a place called **Laetoli** (lay-*toe*-lee), it was Mary Leakey's turn to be shocked. As she dug down slowly, just below the surface of the Serengeti Plain, she found ancient footprints—hundreds of them—as clear as if they had been cast in fresh concrete. As always, she had been looking for fossils, any scrap of bone or tooth from which she might infer something about behavior in the remote human past. But here, at Laetoli, she found that early behavior was itself fossilized, right beneath her feet.

At some time in the remote past, a nearby volcano must have erupted, blanketing the landscape around Laetoli with a lens of very fine volcanic ash. Then a light rain must have moistened the ash layer without eroding it, turning it into a thin slurry that hardened like concrete. Various animals moved across this wet surface, apparently on the way to a nearby water hole: spring hares, birds, buffaloes, pigs, a saber-tooth tiger, and baboons—each leaving dozens of footprints in the gooey trackway. Before long, the ash layer dried, freezing the footprints in an enduring, rock-hard land surface.

But not only birds and four-legged mammals had been there. At one point, a pair of very early hominids also strolled across the landscape. More than five dozen individual human footprints clearly demonstrate a human-like gait—fully bipedal with a stride and balance similar to our own. Across a distance of about 80 feet, two of our ancestors walked side by side, one larger than the other, close enough to touch one another. Were they mother and child? Male and female? One species or two? Almost everyone familiar with the evidence has one opinion or another, but the implications were clear.

Jonathan O. Davis studying the stratigraphy along the western exposure at Gatecliff Shelter (Nevada).

If the evidence could be trusted—and if the presumed ancient age could be firmly established—Mary Leakey realized that these footprints would shatter one of paleoanthropology's most cherished concepts. For decades, specialists in human evolution had argued that upright posture—a preeminent human characteristic—must have arisen in response to tool use. After all, if you're going to make and use stone tools, it makes sense to have your hands free. But if Leakey was correct in her guess-dating of these, the world's oldest human footprints, they implied that our most ancient human ancestors

The famous hominid footprints at Laetoli (Tanzania, Africa).

They are the most remarkable find I have made in my entire career. . . . When we first came across the hominid prints I must admit that I was skeptical, but then it became clear that they could be nothing else. They are the earliest prints of man's ancestors, and they show us that hominids three-and-three-quarters million years ago walked upright with a free-striding gait, just as we do today.

MARY LEAKEY (1913–1996), PALEOANTHROPOLOGIST

Keep your eyes on the stars and your feet on the ground.

THEODORE ROOSEVELT (1858–1919), 26TH PRESIDENT OF THE UNITED STATES

Get your facts first, then you can distort them as you please.

MARK TWAIN (1835–1910), WRITER AND HUMORIST

Let us not underrate the value of a fact; it will one day flower into a truth.

HENRY DAVID THOREAU (1817–1862), WRITER

were walking fully upright for more than a million years prior to the appearance of the oldest stone tools in the area. This was *big news!*

Let's Start With the Facts

The fossil footprints were contained in the upper portion of the so-called *Laetolil Beds,* within a geological subunit known as Tuff 7. The actual footprints were found near the bottom of the Tuff 7 formation in what Mary Leakey called, appropriately enough, the *Footprint Tuff.* But to determine the age of the footprints, it is necessary to place this key geological stratum within its appropriate stratigraphic context.

The geological investigation was spearheaded by Richard Hay from the University of Illinois, Urbana-Champaign. Over a period of 6 years, Hay worked out the complicated geological sequence at Laetoli, which can be summarized in the following generalized stratigraphic column:

Ngaloba Beds: sheetwash and mudflow deposits containing volcanic ash, pebbles, and cobbles

Olpiro Beds: volcanic tuff layers, maximum thickness about 20 feet (*Olpiro* is the name of a nearby village.)

Naibadad Beds: volcanic tuff layers, generally 35–50 feet thick

Ogol Lavas: a series of distinctive lava flows and ash deposits; in places, 750 feet deep (*Ogol* is the Masai word for "hard rock.")

Ndolanya Beds: sedimentary deposits generally 60–75 feet thick; appear to be windblown

Laetolil Beds: the basal stratigraphic unit, consisting of a complex series of compressed volcanic ash, in places more than 500 feet thick (*Note:* The name of the site is spelled "Laetoli"; the basal formation is called the "Laetolil" Beds.)

Hay clearly understood that the canons of good scientific fieldwork require that such primary data be published in detail to allow anybody to compare these field data with others recorded elsewhere. In the final report on Laetoli, these descriptions run to more than 25 pages. Any qualified geologist would have generated comparable primary data.

But once these basic descriptive data are recorded, the objective shifts to interpretation. From evidence preserved on the surface of the Footprint Tuff, it was clear that the footprints had been buried rapidly, soon after they were formed. This accounts for their extraordinary state of preservation.

Geologists working at Laetoli could also infer something about the season in which the footprints were laid down. There was, for instance, no evidence of grasses at the base of the ash lens. This meant that the grass had probably been grazed off, leading the excavators to suggest that the eruptions took place during the dry season. But toward the middle of the Footprint Tuff, there is evidence that this surface was gently rained upon—actual raindrop impressions occur along with the footprints. Then, toward the upper part, widespread erosion occurs, which is attributed to full-blown rainy season downpours.

Therefore, the excavation team at Laetoli concluded, the Footprint Tuff must have been deposited over a short span of time, probably only a few weeks, beginning near the end of the dry season and lasting into the rainy season. This is an amazingly detailed reconstruction, based strictly on the available geological evidence.

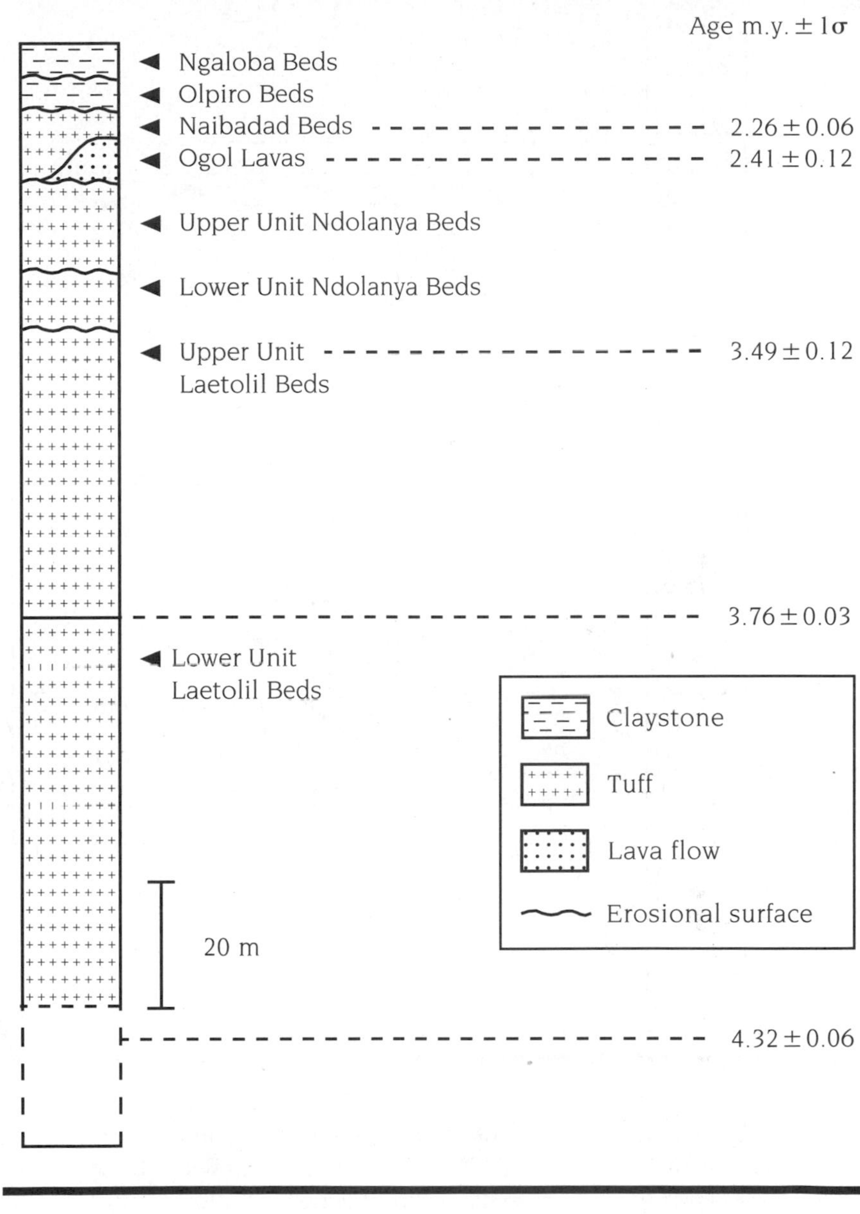

The major stratigraphic profile at Laetoli.

Fine, but How Old Are the Footprints?

Here the geological law of superposition comes to our immediate aid. Steno's law holds that, all else being equal, older deposits lie at the base of the stratigraphic profile.

So we work from the bottom up. The Laetolil Beds lie beneath the Ndolanya Beds: This is a geological fact. The law of superposition applied to this stratigraphic fact *suggests* that the Laetolil Beds *should be* older than the Ndolanya Beds: This is geological interpretation. Similarly, because the Ogol Lavas lie above both the Laetolil and Ndolanya beds, these lavas should be younger still. And so forth. Because they lie uppermost in the stratigraphic column at Laetoli, the Ngaloba Beds should be the most recent of all. In each case, the law of superposition provides the interpretive key to unlock the *relative* stratigraphic sequence at Laetoli.

But to understand the age of the hominid footprints, we must move from relative to absolute dating methods. In the preceding chapter, we introduced the basics of *potassium-argon dating,* which was used to pin down the date of the famous footprints at Laetoli.

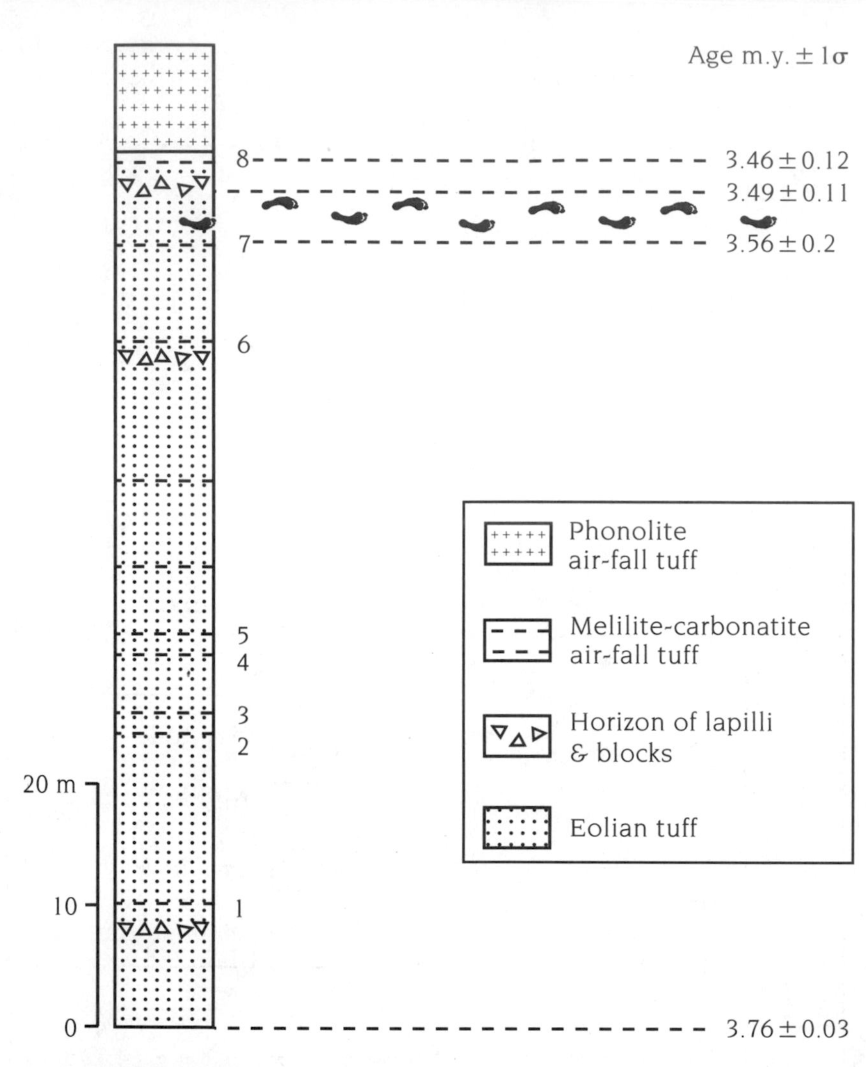

Detailed stratigraphic profile of dated tuff horizons within the upper unit of the Laetolil Beds.

Beginning in 1975, Leakey and her research team began working with Robert Drake and Garness Curtis, geologists from the University of California (Berkeley), who processed a series of potassium-argon dates on samples from the major stratigraphic units recognized in the Laetoli area. The oldest date, from the base of the Laetolil Beds, is 4.32 ± 0.06 million years. The youngest date is 2.26 ± 0.06 million years, from near the top of the stratigraphic column (in the Naibadad Beds). The dates of intermediate age (between 3.76 million and 2.41 million years) occur from strata sandwiched in the middle of the stratigraphic column. Note particularly how this suite of dates follows in precise stratigraphic order, from most ancient (at the bottom) to most recent (at the top). In this case, absolute dating technology confirms the stratigraphic sequence inferred from Steno's law.

The stratigraphic profile sets out results of additional potassium-argon dating conducted on specific tuff horizons within the Laetolil Beds. This sequence is important because, you will remember, the Footprint Tuff occurred near the bottom of Tuff 7 in the Laetolil Beds. In the more detailed stratigraphic section, the various numbered tuff horizons are dated by four K-Ar dates, ranging in age from 3.76 million to 3.46 million years. As with the site as a whole, the dates within the Laetolil Beds fall into perfect stratigraphic order.

Finally, we can answer the single most important question at Laetoli: *The fossil hominid footprints (located near the bottom of Tuff 7) must be somewhere between 3.76 ± 0.03 million and 3.56 ± 0.2 million years old.*

This depositional sequence, inferred entirely from the stratigraphic column, provides the basic chronological sequence at Laetoli; and the law of superposition was the key that unlocked the stratigraphic sequence.

Nothing in the interpretation by Hay departs radically from that arrived at by Thomas Jefferson in 1784. Though it is true that modern scientists have more precise and sophisticated technology, I am confident that had he been able to travel to Laetoli, Thomas Jefferson would have applied the principles of stratigraphy in exactly the same way that Leakey and Hay did.

Reconstruction of the early humans (Australopithecus afarensis) *who made the 3.5-million-year-old footprints at Laetoli. Although the fossil-based proportions are accurate, many of the details (such as hair density and distribution, sex, skin color, form of the nose and lips, and so on) are entirely conjectural.*

Unlocking the Stratigraphy at Gatecliff Shelter

Laetoli was, of course, an archaeological site—one of the world's most famous. Because of the peculiar circumstances of the Laetoli footprints—no artifacts, no household refuse, no construction debris—the basic contexts surrounding the Footprint Tuff were geological, so the principle of superposition could be applied directly.

But the human hand is involved more directly in most archaeological sites, creating stratigraphy that can be considerably more complicated to interpret. Gatecliff Shelter was one of these cases, and the stratigraphic profile encountered there illustrates some of the quandaries involved in the workaday archaeological situation.

During our first three seasons at Gatecliff, I recorded and interpreted the Gatecliff stratigraphy myself. Drawing upon my somewhat limited classroom training in geology, soil science, and microstratigraphy, I drew and described the gross stratigraphy. This master profile served as the major descriptive device throughout the excavations.

As the field season wound down, it became clear that Gatecliff was too complex for me to continue the geological interpretation. This is not unusual in archaeology. On small-scale digs, archaeologists must often cover all the bases, from stratigrapher to photographer, from engineer to camp cook. But as the operation expands, specialists must be recruited to take over selected aspects. The trick is for an archaeologist to recognize the critical line separating flexibility from irresponsibility.

It may undoubtedly be said that strata have been always forming somewhere, and therefore at every moment of past time Nature has added a page to her archives.

SIR CHARLES LYELL (1797–1875), GEOLOGIST

Whatever their degree of statistical rigor, social scientists build their knowledge on the sands of interpretation.

LOUIS A. SASS

Geology on the Internet:

U.S. Geological Survey maintains an excellent homepage:
http://www.usgs.gov/education/

See also their learning Web page:
http://www.usgs.gov/learnweb/index.html

At Gatecliff, I was in danger of crossing over that fine line, so we soon arranged for some experienced Great Basin geologists to join the team. Although each had somewhat different ideas—and some rather heated debates took place—the diversity fostered a better overall interpretation of the stratigraphic column.

In the course of a decade, we had exposed a remarkably well stratified profile, more than 40 feet deep, spanning the last 7,000 years. Gatecliff Shelter has textbook stratigraphy, and that is why I discuss it here.

The Gatecliff profile resulted from a complex interplay of natural and cultural factors. The master stratigraphy demonstrates how two very different kinds of deposits resulted from each set of processes. The thin dark levels (such as those numbered 9, 11, and 13) are living surfaces, or cultural horizons. Each dark horizontal band represents a single campsite. The 16 cultural horizons occurred as the result of human habitation, and these surfaces contain the fire hearths, broken stone tools, grinding slabs, flakes, food remains, and occasional fragments of basketry and cordage. In Chapter 9, we discuss how material culture from each horizon at Gatecliff can be used to define time-markers, which in turn are useful for dating other sites. Chapter 14 discusses how the patterning of these artifacts on each floor allows the reconstruction of the activities that occurred on each living surface.

But what makes Gatecliff so unusual is that living surfaces were capped by sterile, noncultural layers of purely geological origin. After the excavation was finished, we divided up the Gatecliff profile into a sequence of 56 geological strata: layers of more or less homogeneous or gradational sedimentary material, visually separated from adjacent layers by a distinct change in the character of the material deposited (see Table 8.1).

Some strata, such as 2, resulted from small ponds that occasionally formed at the rear of Gatecliff Shelter. The pond water acted as a sink for windblown dust particles, which settled out as finely laminated silts. Other strata, such as 8, consist of coarser sediments grading from gravels at the bottom to fine sand silts at the top. Apparently, the ephemeral stream flowing in front of Gatecliff Shelter occasionally flooded and coursed through the shelter. The water of such flash floods would first deposit coarse sediments such as pea-sized gravels. As the water's velocity diminished, its carrying capacity decreased, and smaller particles were deposited. Finally, when the water slowed, the tiniest silt particles would cap the stream deposits. Such floods occurred several times throughout the 7,000 years of deposition at Gatecliff, and each time the previous occupation surface was immediately buried. When the inhabitants returned to Gatecliff, they thus lived on a new campsite, separated from the previous one by as much as 2 feet of sterile alluvial sediments.

Fifty-six such depositional strata were stacked up inside Gatecliff. Here is how we described one stratum at Gatecliff (evident at the bottom of the master stratigraphy):

Stratum 22, Rubble:
Angular limestone clasts, charcoal firepit, and baked area at top, somewhat churned into the underlying silty top of Stratum 23. Maximum thickness 50 cm. on the southwest pile and formed continuous layer up to 15 cm. thick in eastern parts of excavation, but was discontinuous elsewhere. Almost as voluminous as Stratum 17, the top was about −4.85 m. on the southwestern pile and ranged from −5.50 to −5.30 m. elsewhere, and its bottom was about −5.30 m. in the southwest corner, −5.35 m. in the Master Profile, and −5.32 m. in the present excavation. . . . Stratum 22 was deposited by gradual accumulation of roof fall and talus tumbling over the shelter lip between 5,250 and 5,100 years ago. Stratum 22 was called GU 6R-74 in the field and contained cultural Horizon 14.

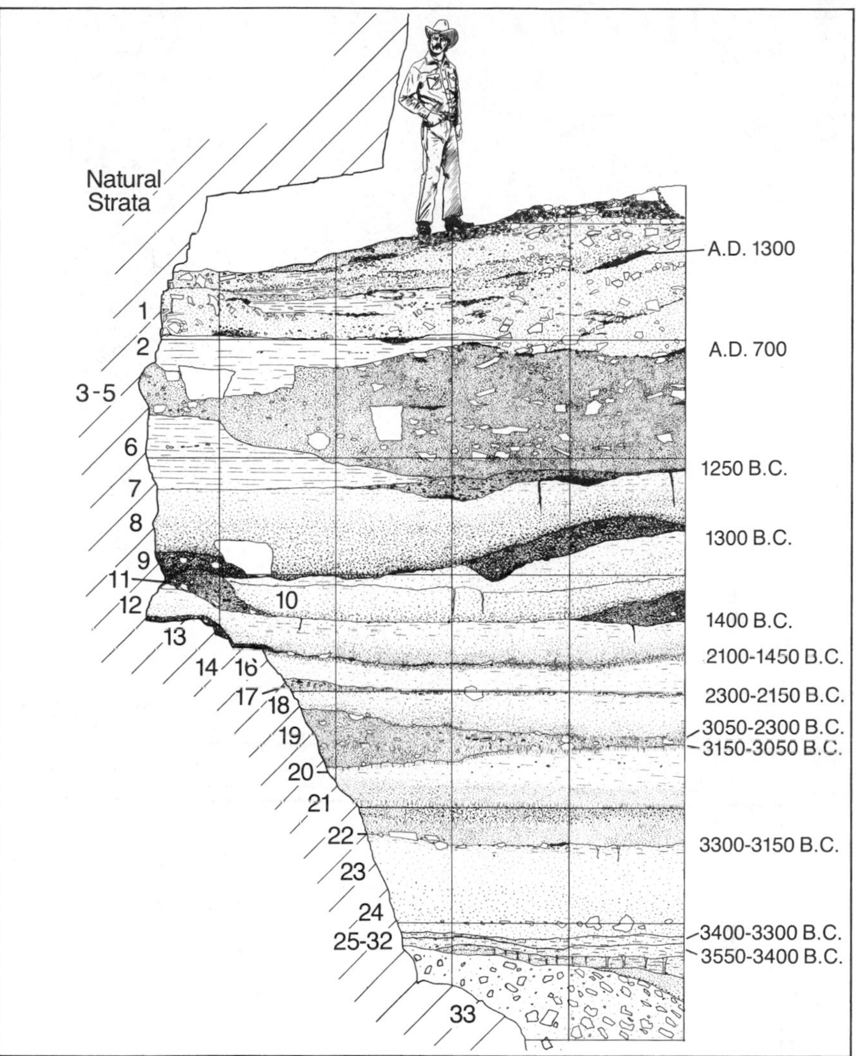

The master stratigraphic profile from Gatecliff Shelter. The standing figure is exactly 6 feet tall and the grid system shows 1-meter squares. Only the upper 33 of the 56 stratigraphic units show in this particular profile.

Several important points can be made with reference to Stratum 22 at Gatecliff.

Note the detail of description. Exact depths are given relative to a central-site datum point, arbitrarily assigned a zero value of 0.0 meters. (Actually, the Gatecliff datum is 2,319 meters [7,606 feet] above sea level.) When paired with our horizontal grid system, these arbitrary elevations document the exact configuration of each geological stratum.

Each geological term is sufficiently well defined so that geologists who have never visited Gatecliff can still understand what Stratum 22 looked like. Note also how we separate such descriptions from our interpretation. This way, others can use our data to make their own assessments (disagreeing with us, if they wish). Geoarchaeologists sometimes use the term *stratification* to refer to the physical layers in a site, reserving *stratigraphy* for the geoarchaeological interpretation of the temporal and depositional evidence.

Daily it is forced home on the mind of the geologist that nothing, not even the wind that blows, is so unstable as the level of the crust of this Earth.

Charles Darwin (1809–1882), naturalist, evolutionist

You can also see how we dated Stratum 22. Forty-seven radiocarbon dates were processed on materials from Gatecliff, and four dates were avail-

TABLE 8.1

Part of the Physical Stratigraphy of Gatecliff Shelter

Stratum	Soil	Nature of Deposit	Field Designation	Cultural Association	Age (C-14 yr. B.P.)	Date (C-14 yr. A.D./B.C.)
1	S-1	Rubble	GU 14	Horizons 1–3	0–1250 B.P.	A.D. 700–present
2		Sand and silt	Upper GU 13	—	1250 B.P.	A.D. 700
3	S-2	Rubble	Part of GU 12	Part of Horizon 4	1250–1350 B.P.	A.D. 600–700
4		Sand and silt	GU 13 & GU 12 Silt	—	1350 B.P.	A.D. 600
5	S-3	Rubble	Part of GU 12	Parts of Horizons 4, 5, 6	1350–3200 B.P.	1250 B.C.–A.D. 600
6		Sand and silt	GU 11	—	3200 B.P.	1250 B.C.
7		Rubble	GU 11 & GU 10R	Horizon 7	3250–3200 B.P.	1300 B.C.–1250 B.C.
8		Sand and silt	GU 10	—	3250 B.P.	1300 B.C.
9		Rubble	GU 9R	Horizon 8	3300–3250 B.P.	1350 B.C.–1300 B.C.
10		Sand and silt	GU 8 A&B	—	3300 B.P.	1350 B.C.
11		Rubble	GU 7R	Horizon 9	3400–3300 B.P.	1450 B.C.–1350 B.C.
12		Sand and silt	GU 7	—	3400 B.P.	1450 B.C.
13		Rubble	6 Living Floor	Horizon 10	4050–3400 B.P.	2100 B.C.–1450 B.C.
14		Sand and silt	GU 5 Silt	—	4050 B.P.	2100 B.C.
15		Rubble	Part of GU 5	—	4100–4050 B.P.	2150 B.C.–2100 B.C.
16		Sand and silt	Part of GU 5	—	4100 B.P.	2150 B.C.
17		Rubble	GU 4	Horizon 11	4250–4100 B.P.	2300 B.C.–2150 B.C.
18		Silty sand	GU 3	—	4250 B.P.	2300 B.C.
19		Sand and rubble	GU 2	Horizon 12	5000–4250 B.P.	3050 B.C.–2300 B.C.
20	S-4	Silt and clay	GU 1A	Horizon 13	5100–5000 B.P.	3150 B.C.–3050 B.C.
21		Sand and silt	GU 1 & GU 7–74	—	5100 B.P.	3150 B.C.
22		Rubble	GU 6R–74	Horizon 14	5250–5100 B.P.	3300 B.C.–3150 B.C.
23		Gravel, sand, and silt	GU 6–74 & GU 5–74	—	5250 B.P.	3300 B.C.
24		Rubble	GU 4R–74	Horizon 15	5350–5250 B.P.	3400 B.C.–3300 B.C.
25		Silt	GU 4–74	—	5350 B.P.	3400 B.C.
26		Rubble	GU 3R–74	Horizon 16	5500–5350 B.P.	3550 B.C.–3400 B.C.
27–29		Silts	GU 3A–74	—	5500 B.P.	3550 B.C.
30		Sand	GU 3B–74	—	5500 B.P.	3550 B.C.
31		Rubble	GU 2R–74	—	5700–5500 B.P.	3750B.C.–3550 B.C.
32		Fine sand and silt	GU 2–74	—		
33		Fine sand and silt	GU 12–76, GU 1–78 & GU 1–74	—		
34		Silt and very fine sand	GU 2–78	—		
35		Rubble	GU 3R–78	—		
36		Silty medium sand	GU 3–78	—		

SOURCE: Thomas, 1983b, Table 3.

able from this particular stratum. This information, combined with the added radiocarbon evidence from adjacent strata, allowed us to estimate that Stratum 22 was laid down between about 5,250 and 5,100 years ago.

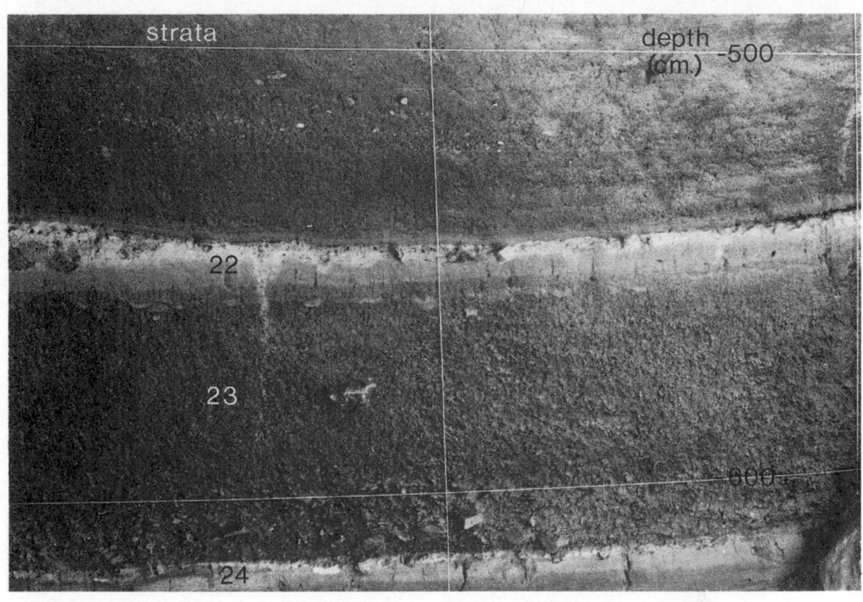

Close-up of Strata 22–24 at Gatecliff Shelter.

Other strata at Gatecliff provided different clues to help date the site. Stratum 55, near the very bottom of the site, contained an inch-thick lens of sand-sized volcanic ash *(tephra),* fragments of crystal, glass, and rock once ejected into the air by a volcanic eruption. Not discovered until the last week of the last field season, the tephra was indistinct, mixed with the cobbles and rubble of Stratum 55. In the laboratory, the late Jonathan O. Davis, one of our geologists and a leading expert on the volcanic ashes of the American West, confirmed that this ashy deposit was Mount Mazama ash. When this mountain in the Oregon Cascades blew up 6,900 years ago, it spewed out 11 cubic miles of pumice and related materials; the caldera formed by the Mazama explosion now contains Crater Lake. The Mount St. Helens eruption in 1980 was a cherry bomb in comparison. The prevailing winds, coupled with the force of the explosion itself, carried Mazama ash across the western United States. Wherever the ash settled out, it created a "marker-bed" (see also Chapter 11, where we discuss the pollen grains included within the Mazama ash). **Tephrochronology** has become a valuable tool for dating sites in volcanically active areas. When Davis found the Mazama ash at the bottom of Gatecliff, we had a critical, independent check on the largely radiocarbon-derived chronology at Gatecliff, and so we knew that Stratum 55 must be 6,900 years old.

Tephrochronology: The analysis of undisturbed volcanic ash (*tephra*) deposits with the aim of constructing a temporal sequence.

In truth, I am not certain whether I would have recognized the volcanic ash at the bottom of Gatecliff. At Mummy Cave (Wyoming), near Yellowstone National Park, the excavators confused the thin layers of Mazama ash with wood ash; the important tephra lens was later recognized under the microscope. Fortunately, the Mazama tephra at Gatecliff was instantly recognized by Jonathan Davis. Both cases highlight the importance of having specialists work on-site, during excavation.

Gatecliff is like a giant birthday cake. The sterile strata are the layers and the cultural horizons are the icing capping each layer. Both strata and horizons contained datable artifacts and ecofacts that could be used to reconstruct the human events and environmental background.

Tephrochronology on the Internet:

Northwest Research Obsidian Studies Laboratory provides an overview of trace element characterization studies, including volcanic glasses: http://www.peak.org/~skinncr/bio2_0.html

Several of these studies will be introduced later. But the important point is that such objects would be relatively useless in archaeology were it not for the stratigraphically controlled contexts in which they were recovered.

The Index Fossil Concept

Geologists proposed the law of superposition rather early in the game, in 1669! But fossils did not become a worthwhile tool for geological correlation until much later, during the early nineteenth century. Whereas an archaeologist like Thomas Jefferson could apply principles of superposition to his excavations, his successors had to wait nearly two centuries to learn—once again from geologists—how the index fossil concept might make human artifacts useful tools in dating archaeological sites.

Diagnostic Artifacts: Archaeology's Version of Index Fossils

Nels Nelson, one of archaeology's forefathers extolled in the first chapter, is generally credited with one of the very first uses of the index fossil concept in stratigraphic archaeology in the Americas. In 1912, the president of the American Museum of Natural History, Henry Fairfield Osborne, sent Nelson on a tour of European archaeological sites to bone up on the most recent methodological innovations (and also, not coincidentally, to round up collections of artifacts to be displayed in New York). While at Castillo Cave in Spain, Nelson participated for several weeks in excavating tightly stratified Paleolithic remains. Like Gatecliff Shelter, the Castillo grotto held deposits roughly 45 feet thick, with 13 archaeological strata ranging from Paleolithic times through the Bronze Age. Nelson was staggered by the fine-scale stratigraphic divisions possible at Castillo, and he eagerly looked for similar sites on his return to the American Southwest the next year.

But in his initial stratigraphic excavations in the Galisteo Basin (south of Santa Fe, New Mexico), Nelson was bitterly disappointed. It turns out that the trash heaps of the Southwest tend to be badly jumbled, not at all like the crisp strata found in European caves. Although he tested several sites, Nelson's **middens** either contained too short a time span or had been riddled by prehistoric grave digging.

Midden: Refuse deposit resulting from human activities, generally consisting of soil, food remains such as animal bone and shell, and discarded artifacts.

Nelson finally came across the stratigraphy he was seeking at Pueblo San Cristobal (ironically, the site where he had been working for the past three seasons). As he returned to San Cristobal in 1914, Nelson was determined to try out a new stratigraphic method.

Selecting an area with minimal disturbance, Nelson isolated a block of debris measuring 3 feet by 6 feet wide and nearly 10 feet deep. Clearly the midden had accumulated over a long interval, and several discrete kinds of pottery were buried here. But there was still a problem because the greasy black midden lacked the sharp stratigraphic divisions Nelson had seen in the Paleolithic caves of Europe. How do you dig stratigraphically without perceptible strata?

General view across Nels Nelson's excavations at San Cristobal (New Mexico). The 700-year-old walls of this huge pueblo are clearly evident. Note also that no screens appear anywhere; sifting of archaeological deposits did not become standard archaeological practice until almost 50 years after this picture was taken.

Not one to be easily deterred, Nelson did the next best thing: He created his own stratigraphy. First dividing his test block into 1-foot vertical sections, Nelson dug each level in the way he had learned to dig the strata in Europe, accurately cataloging the sherds recovered by level. To Nelson, the only difference was that the Castillo Cave strata were readily discernible, whereas the "stratigraphy" at San Cristobal was arbitrarily imposed as 12-inch levels. Apparently mistrusting his workmen to maintain proper controls, Nelson later noted, "I performed this work with my own hands, devoting fully three days to the task." Imposing arbitrary levels on nonvisual stratigraphy seems almost pedestrian today, but in 1914, Nelson's stratigraphic method was a dazzling and revolutionary innovation, immediately seized by New World archaeologists as a fundamental of excavation.

Given these arbitrarily imposed divisions, Nelson could apply the principles of superposition to look for culture change within a midden column. All else being equal, the oldest trash should lie at the bottom, capped by more recent accumulations. Even though the dense midden lacked tangible stratigraphy, Nelson began to search for time-markers in the form of diagnostic pottery types. The concept is precisely that of the index fossil, developed a century before by geologists Cuvier and Brongniart. Just as geologists learned to distinguish certain extinct life-forms as characteristic of various rock strata, so too could archaeologists use diagnostic artifact forms to characterize (and hence date) strata across archaeological sites.

So it was that Nels Nelson applied the index fossil concept to the prehistoric ceramics of San Cristobal. Pottery was a natural choice, as sherds were the most common cultural debris and Nelson knew that ceramic styles varied considerably across the American Southwest. More than 2,000 sherds turned up in the 10-foot test section at San Cristobal. First grouping the sherds into obvious stylistic categories, Nelson then plotted their distribution according to depth below the surface (see Table 8.2). Column 1 contained the frequency of corrugated pottery, the most common everyday cooking ware. Because the relative frequency of corrugated sherds remained fairly constant throughout the occupation of San Cristobal, Nelson rejected Column 1 as a potential index fossil. Column 2 tabulated the frequencies of "biscuit ware," a dull whitish-yellow pottery that Nelson felt was traded into San Cristobal from someplace else. But these frequencies did not change markedly

Nels Nelson's experimental stratigraphic excavation at San Cristobal Pueblo (New Mexico). The white markers indicate arbitrary 1-foot levels by which the deposits were carefully removed.

throughout the stratigraphic column either, and so biscuit ware also was rejected as a potential time-marker.

Nelson then turned to the three remaining kinds of pottery—which he termed Types I, II, and III—and discovered, just as Cuvier and Brongniart had with their French fossils, that certain forms were associated with specific stratigraphic levels. The most ancient levels at San Cristobal contained a predominance of black-on-white painted pottery (Nelson's Type I). Type I sherds were most numerous at and below the 8-foot mark and only rarely recovered above 7 feet. Type II pottery—red, yellow, and gray sherds ornamented with a dark glaze—occurred most commonly at and above the 7-foot mark.

This evidence meant that Type I sherds are "diagnostic" of the 8-foot-and-below strata and the Type II sherds characterized the upper deposits. The Type III pottery (three-color glazed ware), though rather rare at San Cristobal, appeared only in the uppermost levels of Nelson's column. This made sense, as three-colored wares were still being made when the Spaniards arrived in New Mexico in the sixteenth century.

Creating simulated stratigraphy was a brilliant stroke, and remains today the preferred method of excavation whenever visible stratigraphic units are absent. Nelson's arbitrary levels made possible the definition of three important time-markers (archaeology's equivalent to index fossils). Not only did he document the specific ceramic changes at San Cristobal, but the presence of these pottery types elsewhere provided clues to the age of undated archaeological deposits (Chapter 9 discusses further how pottery types function as time-markers).

TABLE 8.2

Potsherd Frequencies From Pueblo San Cristobal, New Mexico

Depth Below Surface	Corrugated Ware (1)	Biscuit Ware (2)	Type I (black-on-white) (3)	Type II (2-color glaze) (4)	Type III (3-color glaze) (5)
1st foot	57	10	2	81	5
2nd foot	116	17	2	230	6
3rd foot	27	2	10	134	3
4th foot	28	4	6	93	0
5th foot	60	15	2	268	0
6th foot	75	21	8	297	1?
7th foot	53	10	40	126	0
8th foot	56	2	118	51	0
9th foot	93	1?	107	3	0
10th foot	84	1?	69	0	0
Total	649	83	364	1,283	15

SOURCE: Nelson 1916, p. 166.

Kidder Does Nelson One Better

Pecos on the Internet:

The National Park Service provides general visitor information on Pecos National Historical Park: http://www.nps.gov

Nels Nelson thus blazed the trail, but it remained for A. V. Kidder to put Nelson's stratigraphic method on the map. Kidder visited with Nelson at the San Cristobal dig and shortly thereafter adapted Nelson's technique for use at his own large-scale excavations at Pecos Pueblo, less than 25 miles to the southeast. From his earlier research, Kidder surmised that, like San Cristobal, the early Pecos sequence was characterized by black-on-white pottery, followed by a later phase in which glazed ceramics predominated. The last of these, the Glaze 5 period, arose sometime before the Spanish conquest and survived until nearly 1680.

By 1915, Kidder had located several rich deposits laid down during the later phases, but the early black-on-white period was poorly represented. Kidder resolved the next year to uncover the earliest Pecos occupation. Unlike modern searchers—who can call on nondestructive, noninvasive remote sensing techniques—Kidder dug a series of long exploratory trenches, cut at intervals of 100 feet or so. Finding almost no refuse on the gaunt west slope of Pecos—probably owing to the fierce prevailing west winds that still buffet the Pecos valley—Kidder shifted his trenching to the leeward side of the ruin. Just inside the defensive perimeter, Kidder located a series of chambers with razed walls rising less than 18 inches. When only black-on-white rubbish was found stacked against these walls, Kidder knew he had found the earliest dwelling at Pecos. Here indeed lay the founding settlement, the nucleus of Pecos Pueblo. Burials interred in the black-on-white rubbish comprised the first Pecos cemetery. The succeeding Glaze 1, 3, and 4 walls were built south of this early occupation, and they in turn were swamped by tons of Glaze 5 and 6 rubbish.

A. V. Kidder supervising excavations at Pecos Pueblo (New Mexico).

Kidder's Pecos investigations verified Nelson's techniques again and again. By carefully following the course of the various trash heaps

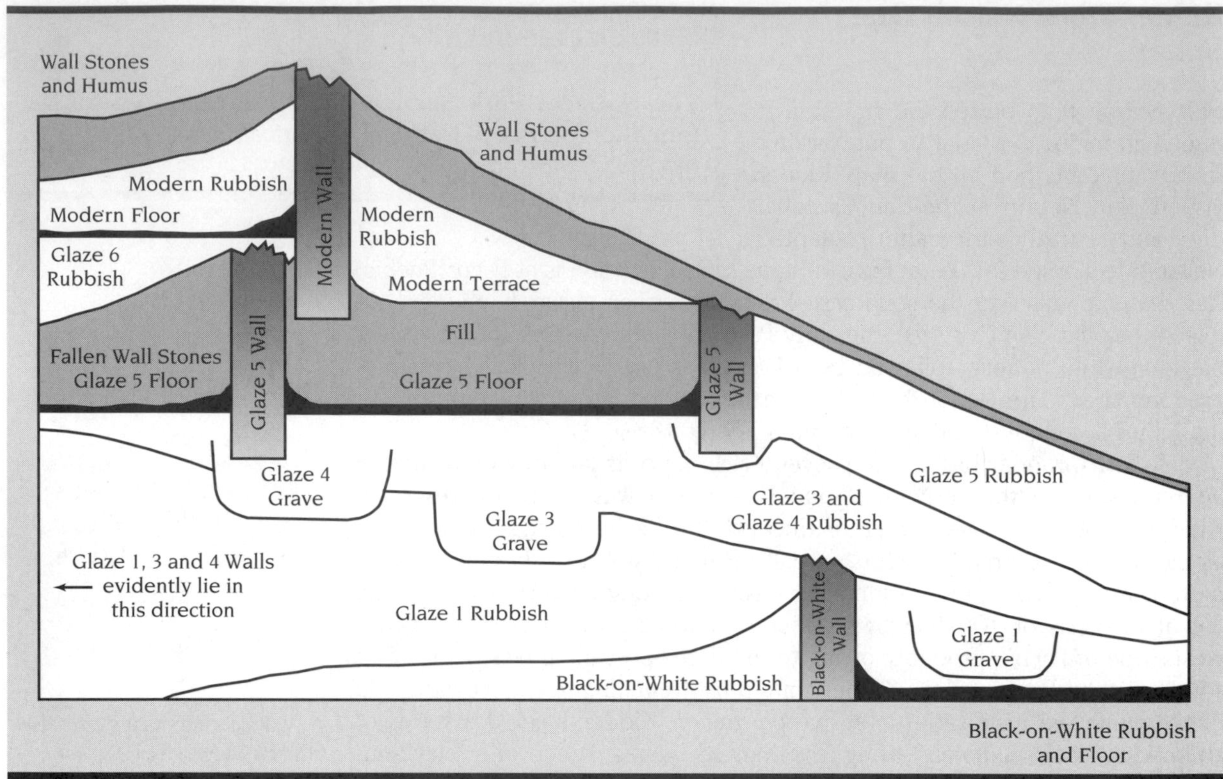

Kidder's cross section of Pecos Pueblo, showing walls, burials, and ceramics.

characterized by the time-marker sherds, Kidder reconstructed the several centuries of habitation at Pecos Pueblo. And when walls or burials were encountered, they could be dated by applying the index fossil concept to the associated midden.

Reverse Stratigraphy at Chetro Ketl

I don't live in the past. The past lives in me.

THOMAS BURR OSBORNE (1859–1929), BIOCHEMIST

This chapter introduces two geological principles, each adapted by archaeologists attempting to establish chronological controls in their sites. The law of superposition suggests that—all else being equal—each stratum is older than the layers above and younger than the layers below. An index fossil concept highlights diagnostic life-forms (or artifact types) that—all else being equal—are associated with a specific span of geological time.

We explored several archaeological cases in which these principles worked quite nicely. In the 3.5-million-year-old footprints at Laetoli, the 40-foot stratigraphic section at Gatecliff Shelter, and the deep trash midden deposits at San Cristobal and Pecos Pueblo, "all else" really did seem to be equal.

Dedication to anthropology is like dedication to one's religion; it is a way of life.

FLORENCE M. HAWLEY (1906–1991), ARCHAEOLOGIST

But what happens when all else is *not* equal? What if the archaeological evidence doesn't fall into the neat categories suggested by Steno's law and the index fossil concept?

Chaco on the Internet:

Chaco Culture National Historical Park is administered by the National Park Service, which provides a general information home page:
http://zuni.chaco.com/park/brochure.html

Indian Ruins of the Southwest is a catalog of information about archaeological sites and museums in the Four Corners area, including a general discussion of Anasazi culture:
http://www.coolworks.com/gorp/resource/archael/indruin.htm

Such difficult cases crop up with some regularity in archaeology; there are times when "established principles" just cannot be taken at face value. These tricky situations require all the training, ingenuity, and common sense that an archaeologist can muster.

This is just what happened to Florence Hawley, one of the first women awarded a Ph.D. in archaeology (University of Chicago, 1934). For a decade before receiving her doctorate, Hawley spent her weekends and summers learning to excavate from some of the best archaeologists in the world. So skilled did she become in archaeological fieldwork and laboratory analysis that shortly after finishing her M.A. thesis (on Anasazi ceramic complexity in the American Southwest), she was hired to teach at the University of Arizona (in 1928, at an annual salary of $1,500!). In addition to her teaching duties, Hawley found time to enroll in A. E. Douglass's first class in dendrochronology, where she learned firsthand the potential and the frustrations of tree-ring dating.

Florence Hawley was thus a rare scholar, with professional expertise in archaeological excavation, laboratory analysis of ancestral Pueblo ceramics, and dendrochronology. Hawley decided to take up a long-term research program in Chaco Canyon, in northwestern New Mexico. As Robert and Florence Lister have emphasized, this was a most fortunate choice: "Chaco Canyon offered an ideal laboratory for training students because of the dense concentration of Anasazi civilization within its walls. Isolated from campus distractions, a select few were free to focus upon proper methods of excavation and sharpen their reasoning powers by mentally re-creating a past milieu from the surviving random scraps of archaeological information."

Hawley was soon drawn to the massive ruins of Chetro Ketl (*chee*-tro-*kettle*), along the northern wall of the canyon. Containing more than 500 rooms, this three- and four-story D-shaped pueblo had been explored by a number of archaeologists, but it remained for Hawley to put the pieces together (see *Fieldwork 1920s-Style at Chetro Ketl,* by Florence Hawley Ellis).

Drawing on her rare expertise in tree-ring dating, Hawley began by collecting 565 samples from the more than 5,000 wooden beams used to build Chetro Ketl. By correlating the tree-ring evidence with the various styles of stone masonry, Hawley was able to define four major construction periods, beginning in A.D. 945 and continuing until A.D. 1116.

But she was less successful in correlating these tree-ring dates with stylistic elements observed on the painted pottery. Although Hawley spent the following winter trying to build a more comprehensive picture of ceramic change in Chaco Canyon, she was dissatisfied with the emerging ceramic chronology. Hawley returned to Chaco Canyon again and again, spending the next summers excavating in the huge refuse heap to the east of Chetro Ketl—archaeological deposits that reached nearly 20 feet deep in places.

Florence Hawley Ellis (right) supervising University of New Mexico's 1964 field school at Chaco Canyon (New Mexico).

IN HER OWN WORDS

Fieldwork 1920s-*Style at Chetro Ketl*, by Florence Hawley Ellis

It was 1928. [She was 22 years old.] At Chetro Ketl we were 60 miles from the railroad; mail came only when our truck went for provisions. If summer storms struck, everyone gathered along the steep-sided but usually dry Chaco arroyo to watch the return of the heavy vehicle through a tumbling torrent. Pushing might be necessary. Telephone connections between the little Chaco trading post and Crownpoint (administrative center and boarding school for the Eastern Navajo Reservation) finally were put in, the line being on the top wire of 40 miles of ranch fencing. When a cow leaned against that fence, the phone went out.

A canvas bag of water was delivered to each occupant of the two-party tents every morning. Those who could not scrub teeth, underwear, and their persons in the single gallon must carry their own water. On weekends we washed our hair and then our jeans in a scant bucket of well water and finally used what remained to settle the sand of the tent floor. Then, virtuously clean, we could drop in to the post to watch the trader dicker for rugs, still sold by the pound, from Navajo women who with equal care took out their credit in flour, lard, sugar, Arbuckle's coffee, sometimes a small bag of hard candy, and perhaps a payment on some item of pawn hung back in the closet. If we were hungry we could do as the Navajo did: Buy a can of tomatoes and a box of soda crackers. The trader opened the can and furnished the spoon; the consumer perched on the high counter to swing his heel and enjoy the treat.

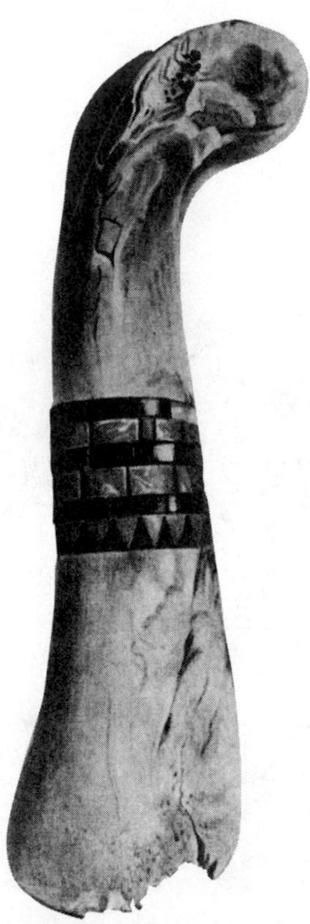

Deer bone spatula inlaid with turquoise and jet (from Chaco Canyon).

Hawley recognized that two kinds of strata were present. Beginning at the bottom, she defined Strata 1 and 3 as household debris: daily sweepings containing ash, charcoal, and potsherds heaped in small, overlapping mounds. After examining comparable dump deposits in modern pueblos, Hawley decided that these deposits must have accumulated basketful by basketful, as trash was thrown out of individual homes. These strata looked like the daily dumpings.

By contrast, Strata 2 and 4 consisted of a mass of refuse, with a generalized gray color signaling a general mixing of ash and charcoal throughout. Although these strata also consisted of stone, ash, and charcoal debris, they lacked the laminations and outlines of small basketloads.

In effect, everything was wrong. The latest strata and the most recent pottery seemed to turn up near the base of the trash mound. This material seemed to have been removed en masse from some abandoned section of the pueblo, perhaps to make way for a new building to be constructed on the site of a more ancient dumping area.

But Hawley stewed about this interpretation: "The suggestion looked far fetched, however, for this would place half the mound as re-dumped material. . . . Briefly put, part of the dump was upside down." Clearly some independent evidence was required to sort out the confusing strata at Chetro Ketl.

Here is where Hawley's training in dendrochronology came in handy. "Fortunately we were accustomed to tree-ring work in this area, and although small chunks of charcoal occurring in a dump had never before been tried out for dates, we had saved them from our strata tests." The problem with this technique was obvious: Beams used to support the masonry usually retained at least some of the outer bark, ensuring that the latest tree ring (the outermost "cutting" ring) actually dates the death of the tree—and thereby reflects when the timber was harvested for construction.

But the odd bits of charcoal recovered from the trash heap at Chetro Ketl, averaging only about an inch in diameter, rarely retained the critical cutting ring (and thus did not directly date when the tree was harvested). In these cases, an arbitrary number of missing rings was added (indicated by Hawley as "+30 ca. rings" or "+ca. 4 rings," etc.). In addition, because the bits were so small, only about 20 percent of the charcoal recovered could be accurately dated by the dendrochronological method.

Unhappily we can scarcely say that it is obvious that "the objects at the base of an undisturbed midden must be older than those at the top." Into every ointment there is some fly.

FLORENCE M. HAWLEY

Still, by paying strict attention to all these sources of error, Hawley matched tree-ring patterns on these unlovely charcoal lumps to the known dendrochronological sequence. Eventually, Hawley was able to create an entirely new level of accuracy in dating the stratigraphic sequence at Chetro Ketl (moving from top to bottom):

Stratum 4: secondary fill dating from the late A.D. 900s, moved to present location between A.D. 1119 and 1222

Stratum 3: another lens of daily sweepings, dating between A.D. 1090 and 1119

Stratum 2: mostly older, twice-moved debris redeposited from elsewhere (The tree-ring dates suggest the trash was initially created about A.D. 900, then moved to its present location between A.D. 1088 and 1090.)

Stratum 1: short-term deposition, apparently consisting entirely of daily sweepings from a 4-year period (between A.D. 1084 and 1088)

So that was that: Independent evidence confirmed that the stratigraphy at Chetro Ketl was indeed upside down. Why upside down? Decades later, archaeologist Steven Lekson and others found out that the "trash midden" Hawley was excavating at Chetro Ketl was actually a deliberately constructed *architectural* feature. These large earthen platforms have since been recognized at several of the major sites in Chaco Canyon, including Pueblo Bonito. Small wonder the stratigraphy was all messed up: The "trash" was actually fill, deliberately hauled in for building purposes.

Hawley, of course, did not know that the ancient Chacoans built mounds; she, like all other archaeologists of her day, thought mound construction was restricted to the various moundbuilding cultures in the midwestern and eastern United States. But she did know that these deposits were not simply discarded trash middens. Using her carefully developed techniques, Hawley not only unraveled the complex stratigraphy of this unusual deposit, but she established an entirely new application for tree-ring dating. She also eloquently demonstrated the need for care and caution when applying geology's grand principles to the complexities of archaeological stratigraphy.

Horizontal Stratigraphy

The overriding concern of geologists like Steno, Smith, and Cuvier was verticality—how sedimentary beds stack up on one another. But more recent geological investigation has also looked at diversity within a single stratum. The

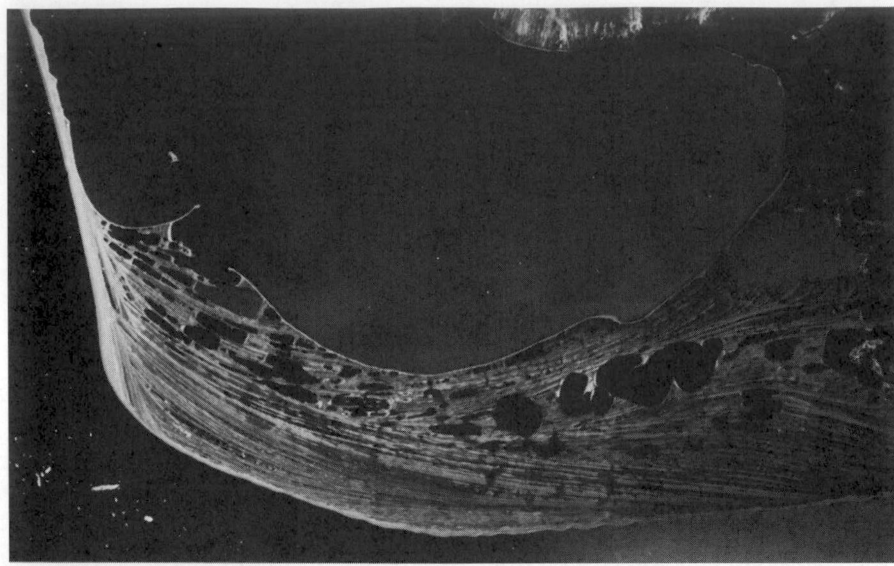

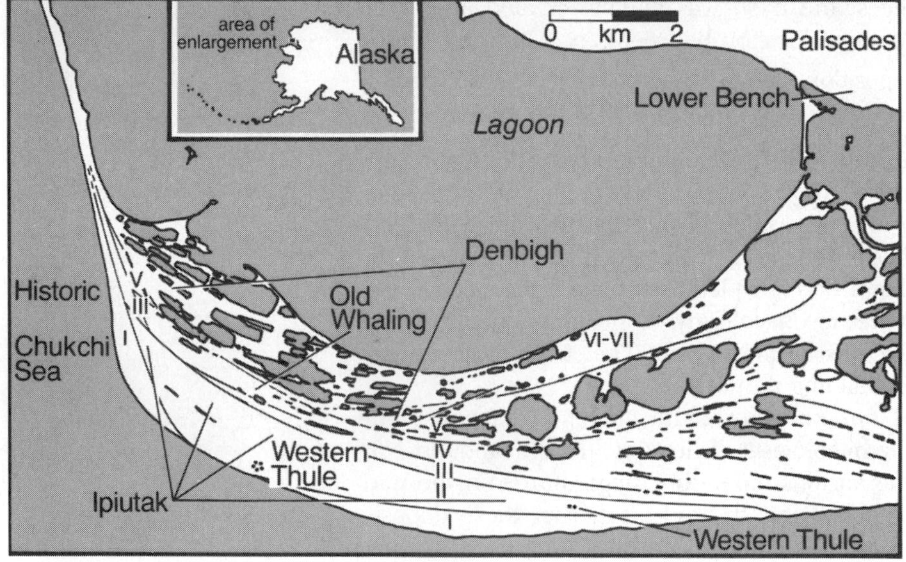

Aerial photograph and sketch map showing beach ridges at Cape Krusenstern (Alaska). The most recent beaches appear at the bottom and the oldest beaches appear on top, toward the lagoon. Segment numbers I to VII correspond to Beaches 1 through 104, as discussed in the text.

paleogeography of certain stratigraphic units is extraordinarily well known. The oil-rich Permian Basin of west Texas, for instance, is known to have formed, in part, as stream deposits and elsewhere as back-reef, quiet-water lagoons. Stratigraphy obviously has a horizontal dimension.

Cruising Cape Krusenstern

Archaeologists are also aware of "flat stratigraphy," and this is why temporal variability can sometimes be expressed horizontally. Archaeology's most dramatic example of horizontal stratigraphy can be found at Cape Krusenstern, a beach formation northeast of Nome, Alaska. An aerial photograph of Cape Krusenstern discloses that the cape is not a single beach at all but, rather, 100 secondary dune ridges that merge to create a peninsula extending far into the Chukchi Sea. The modern shoreline, designated as Beach 1, is a protracted, relatively flat surface made of coarse sand and gravel. Behind this most recent beach is an older shoreline (Beach 2), which has become stranded and landlocked. As you walk away from the Chukchi Sea, you will encounter 114 such relic beach terraces, most of them covered by a protective rind of grassy sod.

J. L. Giddings began investigating the archaeology of Cape Krusenstern in 1958, and he spent four seasons excavating beneath the frozen sod. Eventually, he dug up house pits, human burials, artifact caches, tent sites, and entire settlements of the peoples who once lived on Cape Krusenstern. The Krusenstern ruins are as tightly stratified as the sediments of Gatecliff Shelter or the trash heaps of Pueblo San Cristobal. But rather than finding campsites stacked one on top of another, Giddings discovered that Cape Krusenstern sites are stratified side by side. One important corollary to the general canons of vertical stratigraphy thus applies to beach terraces such as Krusenstern.

Krusenstern on the Internet:

Cape Krusenstern National Monument, administered by the National Park Service, is available for visitation: http://www.nps.gov/noaa/index.html

The principle of horizontal stratigraphy is not complex: On any series of uneroded beach surfaces, the younger stratum will be seaward, the older inland. The modern Krusenstern beach contains house pits of very recent Eskimo who camped there within the past century. Five beaches or so inland are multiple-roomed, deeply entrenched house ruins of an ancestral pre-Eskimo culture called Western Thule. The artifacts and distinctive pottery found inside these houses pinpoint the Western Thule sites to an age of about A.D. 1000. Farther inland, about Beach 35, are the large square pit houses and clusters of shallow summer lodges constructed by the Ipiutak people, a society known for its expertise in carving ivory. Some 15 beaches behind the Ipiutak sites, nearly a kilometer from the modern sea, are the hearths and tent sites of the Choris people, characterized by large spear points remarkably like those used to hunt extinct forms of bison on the western American Plains.

Beach 35 also contains a ruined settlement of deep, multiple-roomed winter lodges, along with a few scattered summer settlements. Giddings coined the term "Old Whaling" culture to emphasize the profusion of whale bones scattered in and about these houses. Farther back, on Beach 78, are the hearths of the culture known as the Denbigh Flint complex, and even more ancient tent sites were found on Beach 104.

In all, the Cape Krusenstern archaeological sequence spans at least 5,000 years. Not only is the archaeology enlightening, but it also provides valuable clues to interpreting the geological processes evident there. Studies of the ocean sediments indicate that the modern beach is built of gravels that are slowly shifting southward along the coast, moved along by persistent longshore currents. But the beachfront of Krusenstern has switched direction at least six times, changing some 20 to 32 degrees each time. Some geologists attribute this change to the prevailing wind's shifting directions, coupled with a slight rise in sea levels. Giddings, however, argues that because the early Denbigh Flint sites have never been washed over by water, sea levels could not have risen more than a meter or so over the past 5,000 years.

This is one case, finally, in which archaeologists can begin to pay back their enormous debt to the geological profession, because archaeological sites provide the best fine-scale chronological control for geological research. The horizontal stratigraphy evident on the beach ridges of Cape Krusenstern holds promise as an ideal laboratory for future geological studies of shifting sea levels and sea currents.

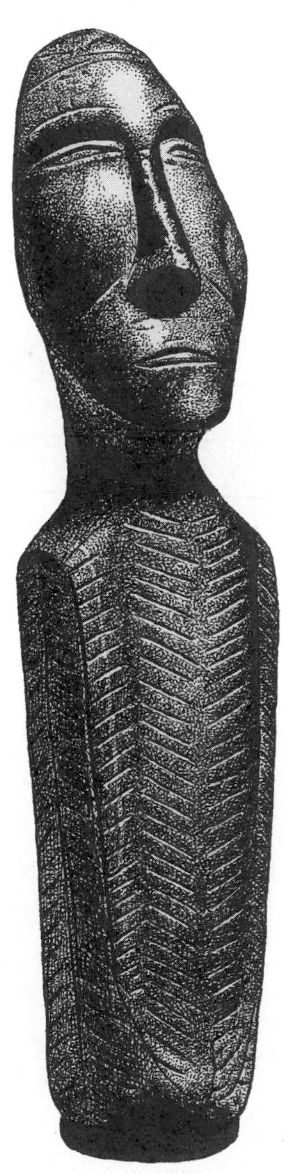

Walrus ivory human figure from the Bering Strait, ca. 200 B.C.–A.D. 100 (*Punuk Island, Alaska*).

Dating Beach Ridges in the Sea Islands

The principle of horizontal stratigraphy has also been applied in the continental United States by archaeologist Chester DePratter and his geological colleague James Howard. Together, they have been using archaeological dating (primarily of ceramics) to document rates of growth and erosion on

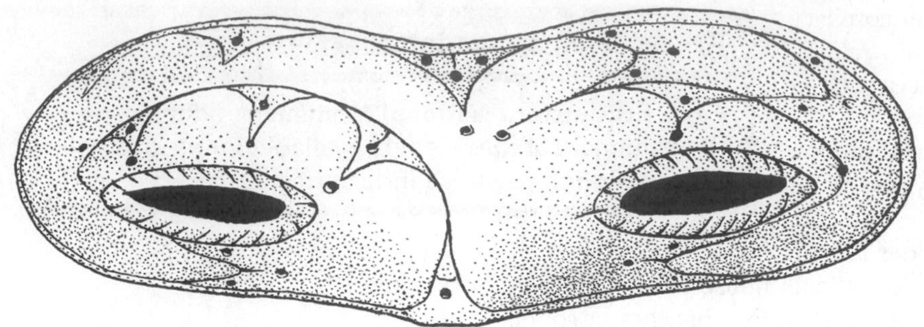

Ivory snow goggles, ca. A.D. 500–1200 (*Bering Strait, Alaska*).

the Georgia coastline. Unlike Giddings's work at Krusenstern, the challenge here is basically geological: How did the Georgia Sea Islands originate, and to what extent are they being modified by ongoing erosion? Both deposition and erosion have formed a number of beach dunes along the margins of islands such as St. Catherines. Geologists have long wished to document how these islands change but lack a reliable method of dating the beach lines.

Once again, archaeology returns a favor to geology. Native Americans prospered on the Georgia Sea Islands for the past 4,000 years, their ecological adaptation closely linked to the shallow marine habitat. Shell heaps dot the beach lines of coastal Georgia, just as Eskimo and earlier sites accumulated on the Alaskan shorelines. Ceramic styles changed rapidly during this interval, and archaeological sites can be dated with some accuracy from the potsherds contained in the shell middens. The two independent factors—(1) growing shorelines and (2) rapidly changing pottery styles—result in a fine-grained chronology that permits geologists to measure the growth of the Georgia Sea Islands.

This island chain is progressively growing seaward. When the aboriginal occupation commenced 4,000 years ago, the shoreline must have been several hundred meters from the modern beaches. As on Cape Krusenstern, people adapted to the sea tend to leave archaeological sites clustered along the then current shoreline. As younger beach ridges develop, people move. The oldest archaeological sites are, of course, found on the oldest beaches, and the more recent dunes contain the more recent archaeological sites.

The distribution of prehistoric pottery thus dates the antiquity of sand dunes. In a pilot study on Tybee Island (near Savannah, Georgia), DePratter and Howard demonstrated that their methods work.

The earliest pottery on the Georgia coast, and also in North America, is fiber-tempered St. Simons ware, a pottery type found on Tybee Island only some 3 miles from the modern shoreline. Because the archaeologists are certain that St. Simons pottery is more than 3,000 years old, geologists can safely conclude that the shoreline was about 3 miles inland at 1000 B.C. St. Simons pottery cannot be found any closer to the modern shoreline because the seaward beaches had not yet formed. The next oldest kind of pottery, known as Deptford, occurs up to 2 miles off the present beach line, but no closer; therefore, the 500 B.C. shoreline must have been about 2 miles inland from the current beach. During the Wilmington–St. Catherines phases (some 850 years ago), the shoreline was about a mile inland, and the pottery of the protohistoric Irene phase is found much closer to the present beach. The geological processes continue, of course, and future archaeologists will be able to date the late-twentieth-century shoreline from the Coke bottles and beer can poptops that litter today's beaches.

This is an excellent use of the principle of horizontal stratigraphy. It is necessary, of course, to have a detailed cultural chronology, for without a radiocarbon-dated ceramic sequence the beaches could not be dated. It is also fortunate that the Georgia coastline was heavily populated in the past. Furthermore, the coast has been tectonically inactive (a good thing, as earthquakes would have disrupted the gradual development of beach dunes). Finally, because the Sea Islands are relatively undeveloped, most archaeological sites remain undisturbed and, in fact, undiscovered. Remember also that horizontal stratigraphy is fallible. One can never rule out the possible reoccupation of ancient beaches and terraces by later cultures.

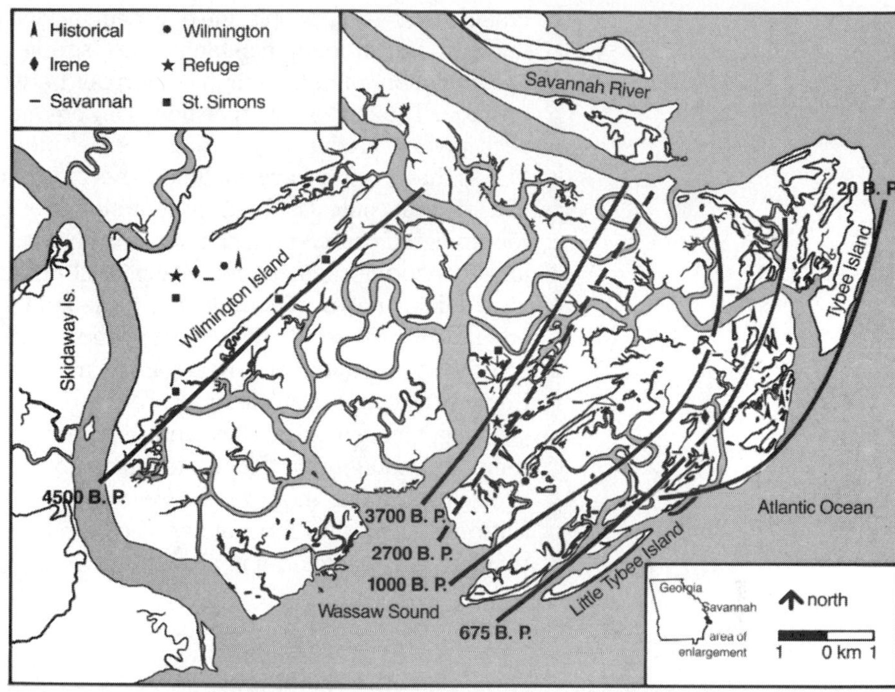

Chester DePratter and James Howard used the distribution of potsherds to reconstruct the age of ancient beach lines on Wilmington and Tybee islands (Georgia).

These last two studies underscore the shifting relationship between archaeological and geological science. Archaeology began as a parasitic science, borrowing concepts, techniques, and methods from the "hard" sciences. But thanks to research at places like Cape Krusenstern and the Georgia Sea Islands, the borrowing has now become reciprocal. Geophysics gave birth to radiocarbon dating; archaeologists use C-14 dating to establish ceramic chronologies; geologists can now employ C-14–verified pottery types to date previously undatable geological surfaces. Archaeology still has its scientific debts to pay, but pioneer studies such as these suggest that the balance may soon be redressed.

SUMMARY Archaeologists—like most other scientists—love to pirate useful techniques and concepts from other disciplines. When dealing with stratigraphy, they have relied on two essential geological principles. The law of superposition holds that (all else being equal) older geological strata tend to be buried beneath younger strata, and the index fossil concept states that strata containing similar fossil assemblages must be of similar age. Exceptions exist, but these principles have enabled geologists around the world to correlate individual stratigraphic sections into master chronologies.

Archaeologists commonly use the law of superposition to unravel complex sequences of stratification within archaeological sites. Most of the stratigraphic record in sites, such as burial mounds, results from deliberate cultural activities; people have systematically deposited strata as cultural features. But in many habitation sites, stratigraphy results from accidental accumulation, often a complex interplay between natural and cultural deposition. The law of superposition is an organizing principle through which such diverse archaeological sites can be interpreted and correlated.

Archaeologists have modified the index fossil concept for use in archaeological contexts. Changing ceramic patterns, for example, become clues for stratigraphic interpretation and correlation. The methods of establishing and monitoring such cultural change will be discussed in the next chapter.

A final means of correlation, horizontal stratigraphy, can be applied whenever successive cultural occupations are spaced along a systematically changing landscape. Beach lines are particularly good candidates for horizontal cultural stratigraphy. Whenever a shoreline is progressively growing, archaeological sites tend to be arrayed along a spatial (and hence temporal) continuum: Older sites occur on inland beaches, and the later sites cluster along more recent (seaward) surfaces. Horizontal stratigraphy not only establishes the validity of cultural sequences but also is an independent way to determine absolute rates of beach deposit and erosion.

Chapter 9

Chronology Building: Low-Level Archaeological Theory in Action

PREVIEW Everyone knows what an *artifact* is—something that's portable and has been either used or modified by people. At one point, archaeology was almost totally artifact oriented—archaeological sites were viewed as little more than mines in which to prospect for more artifacts. Gradually, archaeologists have shifted objectives, realizing that understanding the person behind the artifact is more compelling than the artifact itself. Today's archaeology has turned from simply filling museum cabinets to discovering how people of the past actually lived.

To do this, archaeologists have developed sometimes sophisticated methods linking artifacts with the human behavior that produced them. At the most fundamental level, artifacts must be accurately described; then they can be classified into meaningful categories. In this chapter, we look at how archaeologists classify artifacts into *temporal types*, using a specialized form of the *index fossil concept,* discussed previously.

Here, we emphasize in particular the short-cut view of culture that archaeologists employ when building their chronologies. We use this so-called *modal view of culture* both in classifying artifacts and also in building the larger, regional-level chronologies that tie together individual archaeological sites.

Chronology is at the root of the matter, being the nerve electrifying the dead body of history.

BERTHOLD LAUFER (1874–1934), ARCHAEOLOGIST

Archaeology's major contribution to anthropological theory is its time perspective. Although many ethnologists study cultural evolution and cultural change, if they were to restrict themselves to ethnographic testimony, their studies would remain shallow, short term, and perfunctory. The same holds true for human ecology. It is marvelous to examine the adaptive nuances of an existing human group, but this study takes on broader significance only when one can determine how such an adaptation came to be, an understanding that generally requires an archaeological perspective.

Paradoxically, time is archaeology's double-edged sword. Before archaeologists can explore what ancient life was like, the archaeological record must first be partitioned into appropriate segments of time and space. Ethnographers have it relatively easy because they operate within a single time interval—the present. Of course, many ethnographers also employ historical documents; but so-called ethnohistorians are limited to the time frame for which written records are available.

Consider the difficulties, however, in monitoring time at a major archaeological site, such as Gatecliff Shelter, Nevada. Radiocarbon evidence tells us that people have lived intermittently at Gatecliff for at least 7,000 years. How many different occupations were there? Five? Ten? Seven thousand? This is no mere exercise in typology and classification. Any discussion of a cultural system must necessarily assume that all the so-called components of this system actually existed at the same time. Suppose you're reconstructing a prehistoric trade network. If you suspect a series of interrelated trading stations—Group A trades with Group B, Group B passes goods on to Group C, Group C returns something to Group A—you are obviously assuming that Groups A, B, and C must have been contemporary. How else could they have been trading partners?

The idea that time can vary from place to place is a difficult one, but it is the idea Einstein used, and it is correct—believe it or not.

RICHARD FEYNMAN

One of archaeology's cardinal principles is this: Whatever else you intend to do, you must first have a firm grasp on time. Archaeologists have long realized that you must know the when and the where before contemplating the how, the who, the what, and especially the why. Defining a temporal framework generally involves two related procedures: dating the physical remains and contexts and classifying the archaeological objects to reflect these temporal categories.

Chronology and the Concept of Culture

Americanist archaeology relies heavily on the concept of culture. In one sense, archaeologists deal with culture as would any other social scientist: Culture has three components (cultural idiolect, shared culture, cultural system), and each constitutes a necessary domain of study. But in another sense, the problems confronting archaeologists differ markedly from those facing anthropologists who specialize in, say, ethnographic or linguistic scholarship. Archaeologists lack living informants, making certain aspects of cultural belief and behavior of the past inaccessible. But—almost as if to compensate for this void—archaeologists have access to a world of material remains, adding a time depth and overarching perspective inconceivable in ethnographic or linguistic inquiry.

The diversity of archaeological data has spawned a host of innovative tactics. Each of culture's three domains requires specialized treatment to bridge the gap between lofty concepts and practical guidelines for use in actual archaeological research. Here, we shall consider in detail two of the three cultural components, shared culture and the cultural system.

Simplicity, simplicity, simplicity! I say, let your affairs be as two or three, and not a hundred or a thousand; instead of a million count half a dozen, and keep your accounts on your thumbnail.

HENRY DAVID THOREAU (1817–1862), WRITER

Looking at Shared Culture

You're a lucky archaeologist—the first one in an archaeologically unexplored territory. As you look around, you find the ground littered with the remains of objects produced by societies ranging from simple to industrial. Even though the long-term history of this area is wholly unknown, it seems clear that this hodgepodge of archaeological objects represents several different things: different times, different materials, different tool functions, different technologies, different conditions of preservation, different degrees of looting, and so on. The cultures you will be dealing with—from fairly recent to historical to truly ancient—seem to contain the whole range of human variability, all wrapped up in an archaeological record that you get to unravel.

If you're lost in all this variability, you are in good company. Similar problems have faced archaeologists for centuries. Where to begin? What to collect? What to leave behind? What to look at? What to ignore?

Here's a clue: *The archaeologist's first responsibility is to simplify.* Generations of our archaeological forebears found it unrealistic, even preposterous, to try to cope simultaneously with all the variability that turns up in even the simplest batch of archaeological objects. Cultural things are just too complicated.

So the first assignment for you, the archaeologist, is to reduce the observed variability to manageable proportions. If you can control just a few key variables, then eventually you can move on to trickier aspects of the archaeological record.

Fine, you might say to yourself—simplify. But just how does such elementary simplification take place? As in life itself, compromise will be required.

Because nobody can deal simultaneously with the three major aspects of culture—idiolect, shared culture, and the cultural system—you must narrow things down to what's important. That was the first clue. Here's a second one: *Before you can do anything else, you must control your archaeological data through time and across space.*

Now, here's another clue. Over the years, archaeologists learned that time can best be controlled by provisionally adopting a simplified, purposefully streamlined concept of culture. More formally, this final clue can be stated like this: *Temporal and spatial variability is best reflected by the shared, modal aspects of culture.* It is difficult to overemphasize how important this simple conclusion has been—and still is—to practicing archaeologists.

This is important. When an archaeologist sets out to monitor spatio-temporal change, most of the cultural complexity can, provisionally, be skipped. Put yet another way, so long as you just want to divide the observed archaeological record into manageable segments of time and space, both the cultural idiolect and the cultural system can be momentarily overlooked.

Why, you might well ask, should time (and space) be easier to figure out by looking at shared culture?

One answer might be that you've got to start somewhere (and there is some truth to that). Another reasonable answer is that shared, modal culture is among the most conspicuous elements of the archaeological record (this is also generally true). But a more satisfying explanation derives from the fundamental characteristics of time and space as rudimentary variables.

Take a look at the figure on the next page, which shows how fiber-tempered ceramics change through time and space along the Georgia coast. Later, we say much more about this ceramic complex, and what it tells us about the people who made and used the pottery. But for now, concentrate on the way this figure handles the variables of time and space. Following general archaeological convention, such charts render time vertically. This reflects the way that most archaeologists think: earlier at the bottom, later at the top. It's easy to

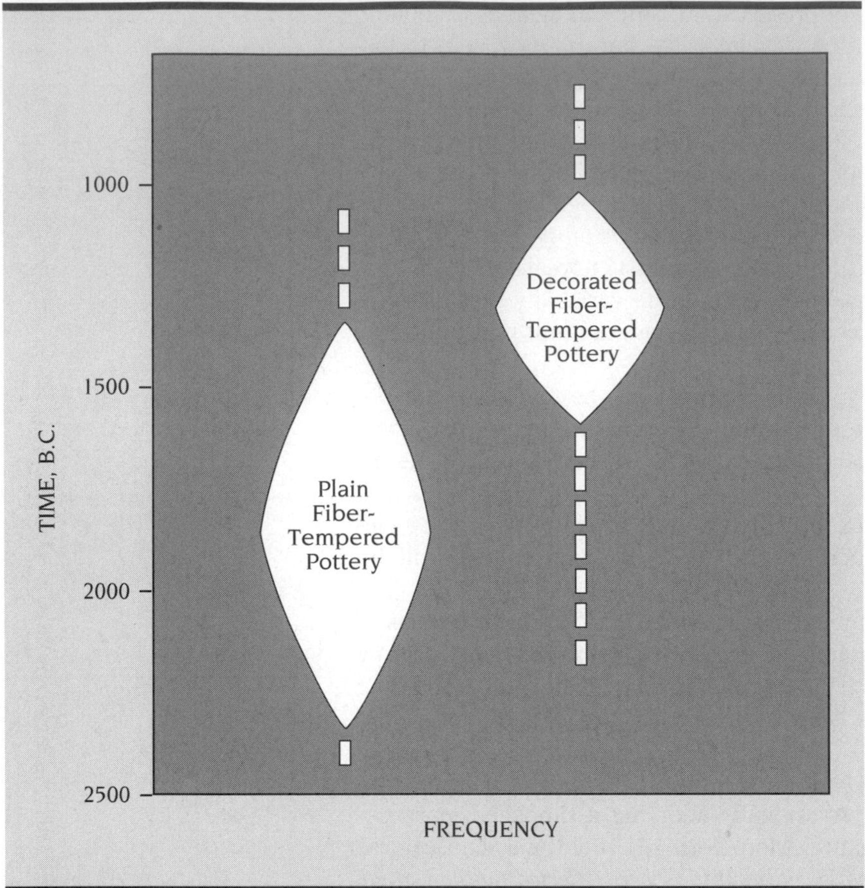

Hypothetical changes in relative frequency of fiber-tempered potsherds from archaeological sites along the Georgia coast.

see why this works; as time passes, things tend to stack up. When enough things have accumulated, the older ones will generally be toward the bottom, the later ones at the top. Earlier, we examined the law of superposition in some detail; note how the figure reflects this principle by displaying time vertically, with the early end of the sequence at the bottom of the chart. The horizontal axis shows the abundance of some shared cultural characteristic: the kind of pottery, the method of manufacturing stone tools, the way houses are built, the motifs painted on cave walls.

Once we arbitrarily elect to fix on temporal variation, we are free to disregard temporarily the why and what in favor of the when and where. Never mind, for the moment, *why* a particular cultural ingredient becomes more or less popular or *what* its function was. At this point, it is sufficient to recognize that things change through time. Temporarily ignoring the *why* and *what* allows archaeologists to nominate any aspect of material culture for analysis, regardless of how it articulates with the cultural system.

For precisely this reason, archaeologists sometimes seem hung up on some very trivial things: what kind of rim people once put on their pots, how people once chipped notches into their spear points, whether they sewed their moccasins along the side or along the top. Archaeologists working with this initial strategy are merely seeking an effective way to monitor change through time (and space). *Why* these cultural items change can be answered later.

Defining North America's Earliest Pottery

The card-player begins by arranging his hand for maximum sense. Scientists do the same with the facts they gather.

Isaac Asimov (1920–1992), writer

Archaeologists believe that the oldest pottery in North America occurs in the southeastern United States, mostly along the coasts of Florida, Georgia, and South Carolina (and also inland up the principal waterways such as the Savannah River). These distinctive pots (and the sherds they break into) are easy to recognize. The whole pots are generally bowl-shaped, with thick walls and flaring lips.

The most distinctive thing about North America's oldest pottery is its *temper*—the tiny pieces of "foreign matter" mixed into the moist clay to keep the vessels from cracking when fired. Potters, both ancient and modern, use a wide variety of tempering materials—sand, shell fragments, even ground-up potsherds.

The earliest Native North American potters used plant fibers, usually grass or shredded palmetto fiber. Why they chose organic fibers over sand or seashells we may never know. But literally hundreds of thousands of these very early potsherds have been recovered, and we know that using fiber as temper was a cultural decision followed almost without exception for a long period of time.

How long? On the basis of radiocarbon evidence, we now know that these earliest pots were first made about 2500 B.C. and they seem to have died out about 1000 B.C., when potters gave up fiber in favor of coarse grit and sand for tempering their pots. This is an important generalization because it means that whenever these distinctive fiber-tempered potsherds are found in undisturbed primary contexts, the age of these deposits can be guess-dated between 2500 B.C. and 1000 B.C.—based strictly on the ceramic association. This is a critical first step in defining a cultural chronology for the coastal Southeast.

We can refine our elementary chronology a bit further by looking at some other attributes. The earliest fiber-tempered pots are plain, without decorations of any kind. But then, about 1500 B.C. or so, potters started decorating their vessels with simple designs carved in before the pots were fired—small circles (probably made with a reed), simple cross-hatching, and interlocking frets. There's not an archaeologist alive who knows for sure why the first design was added or exactly what that particular motif signified to the potter.

But we can be fairly certain when these pots were manufactured. Whenever a decorated fiber-tempered pot or potsherd is found in primary undisturbed archaeological contexts, we can justifiably hypothesize that the contexts date between 1500 and 1000 B.C. We might be wrong, of course, but that becomes our first guess.

Look what we've done: Fiber-tempered pottery in the ancient American Southeast has been defined as an *archaeological time-marker.* We can show how this works by plotting some hypothetical frequencies of fiber-tempered sherds against the time-scale in the accompanying figure. At the bottom (early) part of this chart, at about 2500 B.C., are the plain, undecorated sherds. As time went by, such sherds became increasingly widespread. By about 1500 B.C., decorated sherds start showing up and increase in frequency until about 1100 B.C. After this, fiber-tempered sherds of any kind become progressively rarer, until they finally disappear from the archaeological record altogether.

This is precisely how archaeologists build their cultural chronologies, using the minute details of material culture to divide up a longer span of time. As we shall see, time-sensitive objects like potsherds can commonly be grouped into "temporal types," and such time-markers help archaeologists to fit new, undated sites into an established time sequence.

Artifacts themselves are not important—it's the information they can provide about cultures and about people.

H. MARIE WORMINGTON (1914–1994), ARCHAEOLOGIST

As we discuss later, the next step in chronology building involves synthesizing several such temporal types into larger divisions called *cultural phases.* For now, it is only important that you generally understand how archaeologists go about anchoring various cultures securely in time.

Fiber-Tempered Ceramics and the Modal Concept of Culture

Fiber-tempered ceramics also show how archaeologists use the *modal concept of culture.* If you are an expert in ancient ceramics, you can literally make hundreds of scientific observations on a single potsherd. Judiciously applied, however, the modal concept of culture narrows things down considerably.

Take the pottery of, say, the Georgia coast. When you're building a chronology, you ask simply: *What changes through time and across space?*

We begin by eliminating the constants. All pottery is made of clay, for instance, so that observation tells us nothing about chronology. All pots have been heated and fired, and so "firing" is another constant. By examining enough archaeological collections, you will begin to perceive sometimes subtle dissimilarities.

We already saw, for instance, that the earliest pots seem generally to be tempered with vegetable fiber. The later ones were tempered with sand, or ground-up potsherds. Temper is thus a useful variable for monitoring temporal variability. Because the earlier fiber-tempered pots are plain and the later ones are ornamented, surface decoration becomes a second variable well suited to partitioning time. And so on.

But why do pots made after 1500 B.C. tend to be decorated? Why wasn't quartz grit used for temper before 1000 B.C.? Why don't fiber-tempered pots have outcurving rims? Do certain decorative motifs occur only in ceremonial contexts?

These are all interesting questions, each of which might tell us something about the people who lived for the last 4,500 years along the Georgia coast. But these additional questions must be ignored for the moment because they are not germane to this initial, chronological stage of our analysis.

The important point here is to begin with a deliberately simplified scheme and gradually build the approach to deal with multivariate cultural complexity. It is sufficient at the outset to isolate time-markers and to define some tentative cultural phases. These initial phases are not inviolate; they are working hypotheses that will probably be modified in light of additional information.

The modal concept has a simplified view of reality. People began making plain, fiber-tempered pots about 2500 B.C. We do not know why; we only know when. About 1500 B.C., potters began decorating their pots. We do not know why they did that either, but the change gives us a way to monitor temporal context in our archaeological sites. Once the sites are suitably ordered, using such basic criteria, we might begin to explain why these changes occurred. But we cannot explain before we explicate, and the modal concept of culture is the first step along the path.

The exact meaning of any particular object for the living group is forever lost, and the real significance of any object in an ethnological sense has disappeared by the time it becomes a part of an archaeologist's catalogue of finds.

JAMES B. GRIFFIN (1905–1997), ARCHAEOLOGIST

Thus by restricting focus to modal behavior—the shared aspects of culture—archaeologists chart cultural changes along a temporal scale. These changes can then be plotted on a map to determine spatial variability. This is how archaeology derives its basic analytical units.

Not all culture changes, of course. Culture change is an extremely complicated business, and the modal conception effectively sets aside the question of why. Initially, it is enough to document that a change has occurred. Chances are that the change will be apparent only across a restricted range of archaeological objects. Suppose you dig a site with 100 classes of objects: potsherds, chipped-stone dart points, grinding slabs, bone awls, and so on. Ninety-five of these items remain constant through time. The modal concept of culture—defined by what most people do or believe—allows you to ignore the 95 percent of the stable cultural inventory to concentrate on the critical 5 percent that has changed. The modal concept of culture is only a heuristic, and not an explanatory, device.

With this background, we can now look specifically at the way in which archaeologists classify the material culture they recover.

Types of Types

Archaeology's basic unit of classification is termed a type. Be careful here because *type,* like *culture* and *personality,* is an everyday word appropriated by anthropology and reassigned a specific, nonintuitive meaning. Artifact **types** are idealized categories created by the archaeologist to make sense of past material culture.

Type: A class of archaeological artifacts defined by a consistent clustering of attributes.

Although archaeologists excavate specimens, they analyze types. Rather than poring over each of the thousands of individual items recovered on a dig, archaeologists usually abstract them into a certain number of carefully selected typological categories. Artifact types come in all shapes and varieties, and the naked word *type* must never be applied without an appropriate modifier. One must always describe precisely which type of type one is discussing.

The same objects can, of course, be classified in many ways. Think about a familiar set of modern artifacts, say, a workshop of woodworking tools. Carpenters classify their tools by function—hammers, saws, planes, files, drills, and spokeshaves. But when insuring a carpenter's workshop, the insurance agent uses another set of classifications, sorting these same tools into new categories such as "flammable" and "nonflammable" or perhaps according to replacement value: "under $10," "between $10 and $25," and so on. Should the carpenter relocate, the furniture movers will group these same tools into another set of divisions such as "heavy" or "light," "bulky" or "compact," or perhaps (if you're lucky) "fragile" and "nonbreakable."

Emphasis in archaeology is gradually shifting . . . from things to what things mean.

A. V. Kidder (1886–1963), ARCHAEOLOGIST

The point here—and the crux of archaeological classification in general—is this: Each classification must be formulated with a specific purpose in mind. Archaeology has no general, all-purpose classification; the more classifications the better. Irving Rouse urged archaeologists to ask continually, "Classification—for what?"

Most intellectual problems are, ultimately, problems of classification and nomenclature.

S. I. Hayakawa, SEMANTICIST AND POLITICIAN

Morphological Types

Modern observers exploring the range of material remains left by an extinct group will encounter many unfamiliar, even meaningless, artifacts. To make

Morphological type: A descriptive and abstract grouping of individual artifacts whose focus is on *overall* similarity rather than specific shape or function.

sense of the past using these remains, the first analytical step is to describe the artifacts carefully and accurately by grouping them into **morphological types.**

Emil Haury, an eminent Southwestern archaeologist, drafted one such description in his report on Ventana Cave, Arizona:

> *Discs*–Of the twenty-four stone discs, twenty-two are centrally perforated. They were all made of schist, from 36 to 75 mm. in diameter and averaging 8 mm. in thickness. The customary way of producing them was by breaking and then smoothing the rough corners by abrasion. . . . Only one was well made. . . . Drill holes are bi-conical and not always centrally placed. Two were painted red. Next to nothing is known about these discs.

Inanimate objects are classified scientifically into three major categories: those that don't work, those that break down, and those that get lost.

RUSSELL BAKER, JOURNALIST

Haury did not even speculate what the discs were used for. But he did illustrate and describe them in enough detail so that contemporary and future colleagues can visualize the artifacts without having to view them firsthand. Such bald description is the primary function of a morphological type (often termed a *class* in archaeological literature).

Morphological types have a second basic property: They are abstract. Types are not artifacts but are composite descriptions of many similar artifacts. Accordingly, every morphological type must encompass a certain range of variability: Several colors may have been applied; the quality of manufacture might vary; absolute size usually fluctuates; and so forth. Walter Taylor called this abstract quality an *archetype* to emphasize the elusive "ideal form" implicit in every morphological type.

Damn description, it is always disgusting.

LORD BYRON (1788–1824), POET

Tabletop Typology at San Cristobal

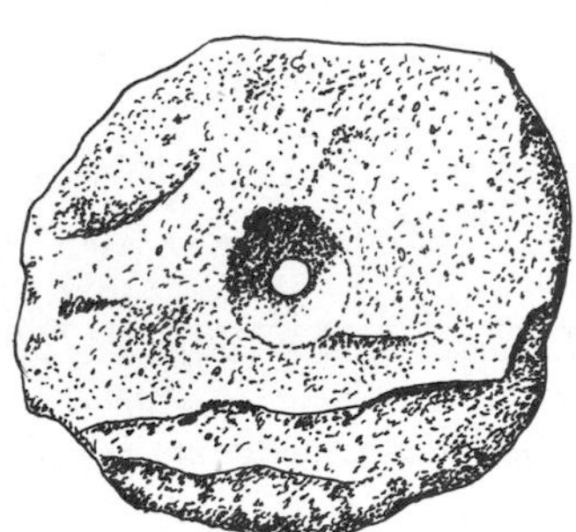

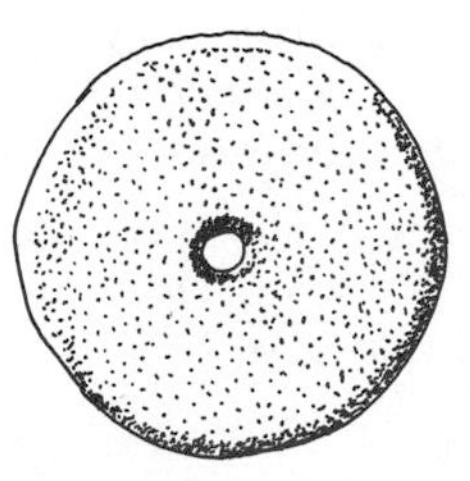

Two prehistoric stone discs excavated from Ventana Cave (Arizona).

To see how archaeologists create their types, we shall return to Nels Nelson's work at San Cristobal Pueblo in New Mexico's Galisteo Basin. I stressed earlier that Nelson's method of stratigraphic excavation was a critical step in the history of archaeology. But Nelson also advanced the thinking about how best to classify material culture. Remember that Nelson recovered over 2,000 potsherds in his 10-foot controlled section at San Cristobal. Earlier, I said simply that he sorted these sherds into five types and then plotted them stratigraphically. But I deliberately did not tell you how he arrived at these types (and I hope this bothered you). How did Nelson know there were five kinds of pottery at San Cristobal? Why not fifteen? Or fifty-five?

Put yourself in Nelson's boots. The date is 1914 and you have just invested several years excavating prehistoric pueblo ruins throughout the American Southwest. Because absolute dating techniques have not yet been invented and little relevant scientific literature exists, it all really boils down to your innate powers of observation. Approaching the trash heap at San Cristobal, you know certain basic facts about Southwestern ceramics. In your travels through New Mexico and Arizona, you have seen some prehistoric pottery with ornamental indentations; other wares were painted, and still others were glazed. But these are merely impressions, more perceived than explicit. During your 3 days of excavating at San Cristobal, you accurately peeled off arbitrary 1-foot sections, bagging the ceramics from each artificial horizon. Your workmen hauled these level bags into your rude field laboratory, washed the sherds, and laid out the collections on a creaking, makeshift table. What now?

What Nelson did was simple: He turned his senses loose, trying to absorb what he called "basic characteristics." Admitting that his procedures were "no doubt arbitrary," he just sorted things out on the table, trying to ignore frivolous differences and focusing on the major trends. One by one, he grouped similar sherds together into individual stacks.

Then he assigned a descriptive name to each pile. The first stack contained 649 pieces of unpainted pottery with rough surface corrugations. Nelson described the "leading characteristics" in the following way:

1. *Form, Size, etc.*: Normally a jar, spherical body, short neck, flaring rim; occasional shoe or bird-shaped pots with knobs suggesting wings and tails; bowls uncertain. Sizes range from miniature to medium, approaching large.
2. *Surface Finish:* Plain coil of primary and sometimes apparently secondary origin; indented coil (fingernail or sharp implement being used) with occasional effort at ornamental effect. Coiling and indenting often obscured either by wear or by "wiping" during process of manufacture. Some specimens of later times show evidence of a micaceous wash.
3. *Paste Composition:* Gray colored clay, more or less tempered with coarse sand or crushed rock. Vessel walls are thin and brittle, the latter fact being due probably to constant use over the fire.

Not great prose perhaps, but such baseline descriptions still form the foundation of archaeological classification, seven decades later.

Moving down the table, Nelson's second stack contained 83 sherds of so-called *biscuit ware,* a "peculiar kind of pottery, which can be detected even by the touch." One by one, Nelson worked his way through the piles of pottery until the "types" on Table 8.2 had been described and plotted.

Typology to Nelson was a matter of judgment, experience, and feel. Biscuit ware was "peculiar"; Type I pottery was "decidedly pleasing." In looking over the Type III sherds, he noted that "the new type of ceramics has gained in diversity of form and general adaptability, but it has lost not a little in decorative elegance." In more current terminology, Nelson defined a series of morphological types. Also called "descriptive," these divisions are designed to reflect an artifact's overall, superficial appearance. Morphological types usually deal in broad generalities rather than specific traits, simultaneously embracing a wide range of properties–length, width, weight, material, color, shape, and volume, just to name a few.

Archaeologists derive scant comfort from the fact that over and above the certainties of death and taxes, they are blessed with the additional constant of a seemingly limitless quantity of sherds to classify.

Prudence M. Rice, archaeologist (Southern Illinois University)

Taxonomy in archeology should be viewed as a system of working hypotheses which may be changed as the evidence warrants and opinion changes.

Walter W. Taylor (1913–1997), archaeologist

Typology: The systematic arrangement of material culture into types.

If You Can't Measure It, Is It Real?

The analyses by Nelson and Haury were grounded in what was called earlier the *modal concept of culture.* Establishing types at this level attempts only to group like with like. Nelson concentrated on the most flagrant differences among the stacked-up potsherds on the table. Even had he known about the cultural idiolect and the cultural system, Nelson would have declared both (temporarily) irrelevant. Forget for now the complex issues of why pottery

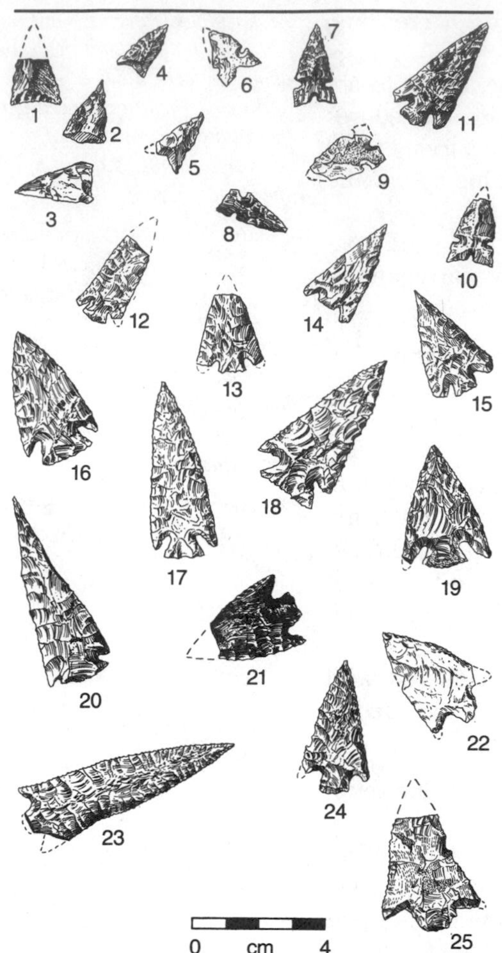

An unsorted batch of stone projectile points recovered at Gatecliff Shelter (Nevada).

changes, how the pottery was made, or what different kinds of pottery were used for. Interesting issues perhaps, but they can be resolved only during a later stage of analysis.

To look more deeply into how the modal concept of culture works in archaeology, remove yourself from Nelson's boots and pretend to be me. You have just spent a good chunk of the 1970s enlisting more than 300 people to help excavate a Nevada rock shelter that turned out to be 40 feet deep. Literally tons of artifacts were recovered. Once washed and cataloged (to preserve contextual information), the artifacts lie mounded in your lab—just like Nels Nelson's San Cristobal potsherds. Where to now?

Your first job, before anything else, is to describe what you found. Not only will such description form the basis of all further analysis, but it will provide your archaeological colleagues with the data necessary to ask their own questions of your artifacts.

Archaeologists generally begin by creating morphological types and later incorporating these preliminary groups into special-purpose types. The initial sort is often fairly informal, sometimes just separating superficially similar artifacts into piles on the laboratory table. This is what Nelson did in 1914, and exactly what I did with the Gatecliff artifacts. Ignore the extraneous variables like stratigraphy, time depth, cultural affiliation, even provenience for now. The main concern here is to reduce the complexity by looking for simple patterns.

Most artifacts are sorted several times. The first sort is usually general, often conducted in the field. On most sites, excavators create separate "level bags" for each kind of artifact and ecofact recovered. Potsherds are bagged separately from the bones and from the stone tools. On historic-period sites, European ceramics are commonly separated from pottery of aboriginal manufacture. Kinds of stone tools are also distinguished: chipped stone artifacts in one bag, flaking debris in another, and broken grinding slabs in individual boxes to keep them from crushing everything else.

> *Time will soon destroy the works of famous painters and sculptors, but the Indian arrowhead will balk his efforts and Eternity will have to come to his aid. They are not fossil bones, but, as it were, fossil thoughts, forever reminding me of the mind that shaped them. . . . Myriads of arrowpoints lie sleeping in the skin of the revolving earth. . . . The footprint, the mind-print of the oldest men.*
>
> HENRY DAVID THOREAU

Once the artifacts are cataloged, laboratory personnel dispatch selected artifacts, ecofacts, and field samples to specialists: artifacts needing first aid and long-term stabilization to the conservation lab, bones to the zooarchaeologist, soil samples to the geoarchaeologist, plant remains to the ethnobotanist, and so forth. Everything else is sorted into rough categories for actual analysis.

Let us consider some of the more than 400 classifiable projectile points recovered at Gatecliff Shelter. (Archaeologists term such artifacts *projectile points,* rather than "arrowheads," because so many of them were actually hafted as darts and spears rather than arrows.) These projectile points were some of the most important artifacts recovered at Gatecliff, and we spent considerable time classifying them. Like Nelson with his San Cristobal sherds, we began by defining some morphological types. And like Nelson, we worried about just how many such morphological types there were. Two? Six? Twenty-five?

If you are looking for a fixed rule for how many types to make, forget it. Defining morphological types has progressed very little since the days of Nelson. Morphological types, I must repeat, are merely descriptive groupings, later to be tested for temporal and/or spatial and/or functional and/or technological significance. The point here is simple: Just get on with it, and then be explicit about what you have done.

Lithic Studies on the Internet:

ArchNet-Lithics provides a guide to the specific and general in lithic studies, for example, a New England projectile point guide, bibliography of projectile points, exhibits on quarry, functional analysis, lithic technology: http://www.lib.uconn.edu/ArchNet

Each point in the sample is unique. But if you are any kind of observer at all, you should be able to distinguish some important similarities and differences among them. The points at the top of the accompanying figure, for instance, are smaller than those at the bottom. Another difference is in how the points are notched for hafting:

Some (like numbers 7, 8, and 9) are notched from the side.

Numbers 14 and 15 are notched from the base.

Points at the bottom are notched from the corner.

Those in the upper left-hand corner are not notched at all.

Differences like size and notch position are called **attributes** in archaeology, and they form the basis of morphological classification. Nelson looked at several different attributes on his San Cristobal sherds: the kind of paint, the surface texture, and the color and pattern of the design. No regulation governs the number of attributes people observe; use as many as seem appropriate. Morphological types are created in dozens of ways, based on as many criteria and attributes. How you do this rests solely on your best judgment as an archaeologist.

Attribute: An individual characteristic that distinguishes one artifact from another on the basis of its size, surface texture, form, material, method of manufacture, and design pattern.

I already mentioned two attributes for the Gatecliff points: size and notch position. These two attributes, as we shall see, are sufficient to create workable morphological types. But it is insufficient simply to say "size" and "notch position." To define adequate attributes, I must explain precisely what is meant by the terms, so that you can make identical observations.

Take size. We all know what size means, and it can be observed in several ways. Measure the length of a projectile point, and you know something about its size. The width measurement also reflects size. Or you can weigh something to find its size. You can even drop it in a cup of water; the amount of fluid displaced will tell you its volume. So what size are we talking about?

Over the years, I have found that *weight* is the best way to measure the size of a projectile point, although it is necessary to estimate the original weight of broken specimens. The lightest point in our Gatecliff sample weighs only 0.4 grams (about the weight of a common paper clip) and the heaviest, more than 5 grams (about the same as a nickel).

So weight was the first attribute I used to define my morphological types. If you look closely, you will see that the weights on Table 9.1 are patterned, with certain natural breaks in the distributions, defining three projectile point sizes in this collection:

A stone arrowhead is as convincing as a steam-engine.

HENRY BROOKS ADAMS (1838–1918), HISTORIAN

Small points: weight less than 1.0 gram (less than a standard business card)

Medium points: weight between 1.0 and 2.5 grams (the weight of a dime)

Large points: weight over 2.5 grams

Some variability arises naturally among projectile points because they are manufactured by a subtractive technology. Flintknappers cannot fix their mistakes; they must simply work around errors, creating more variability in the finished product than is evident in, say, an additive technology like ceramic manufacture.

By and large, however, the three size categories suitably reflect breaks in the distribution of weights. At least the weight groups are replicable; if you were to visit my laboratory, you would come up with the same weights and the same categories (within a small and definable measurement error). It is important that your "small points" are the same as mine.

The second attribute is notch position. Among the small points (numbers 1 to 10), some have notches and others do not. Two categories are hence apparent: small unnotched points and small side-notched points. I am hardly

Cottonwood Triangular projectile point.

Desert Side-notched projectile point.

TABLE 9.1

Attributes for Gatecliff Projectile Points

Specimen Number	Weight in Grams: Actual	Weight in Grams: Estimated Total	Proximal Shoulder Angle
1	0.8	(0.9)	—
2	0.8	0.8	—
3	0.9	0.9	—
4	0.4	0.4	—
5	0.8	(0.9)	—
6	0.3	(0.4)	200
7	0.8	0.8	180
8	0.5	(0.6)	180
9	0.6	0.7	180
10	0.7	(0.8)	190
11	2.3	2.3	100
12	1.1	(1.5)	100
13	1.2	(1.4)	95
14	1.5	1.5	85
15	2.5	2.5	80
16	4.1	4.1	110
17	3.5	3.5	120
18	3.9	3.9	130
19	3.5	3.5	120
20	4.1	(4.2)	150
21	2.3	(2.8)	80
22	3.3	(3.4)	85
23	5.2	(5.5)	80
24	2.7	2.7	100
25	4.4	(5.5)	60

the first archaeologist to note this distinction, and the literature of Great Basin archaeology refers to these two morphological types in this way:

Cottonwood Triangular points (nos. 1–5)
Weight: less than 1.0 gram
Notching: absent

Desert Side-notched points (nos. 6–10)
Weight: less than 1.0 gram
Notching: present (and from the side)

Rosegate series projectile point.

One of archaeology's small rewards is that we get to name our discoveries (but never after ourselves). Archaeological convention dictates that the point types receive first and last names. The first name generally refers to the site (or region) where they were first distinguished. The last name describes some obvious morphological characteristic. "Desert Side-notched" points were named in the late 1950s by M. A. Baumhoff and J. S. Byrne. "Desert" refers to their general distribution throughout the arid West, and "side-notched" tells us something about their appearance. Similarly, "Cottonwood Triangular" points were first recognized at the Cottonwood Creek site in Owens Valley, California. These points look triangular because they have no notches.

Points 11 through 15 are medium sized (weighing between 1.0 and 2.5 grams) and have notches creating a small base (or *stem*).

Rosegate series (nos. 11–15)
Weight: between 1.0 and 2.5 grams
Notching: present

The term *Rosegate* is an amalgam, a combination of "Rose Spring," a site in southeastern California, and "Eastgate," a small overhang near Eastgate, Nevada. Originally, two different point types were defined, one named after each site, but during the investigation, we could find no significant difference between the two, and so we combined them. In this case, we modified the naming convention somewhat: The first term still denotes the place(s) of discovery, but because "Rosegate" combines two former types, it is termed a "series" (a higher-order category).

Elko Corner-notched point.

The larger points are more complicated. Numbers 16 through 25 weigh more than 2.5 grams. Whereas some have expanding bases, others have contracting bases. But expanding and contracting are ambiguous terms, and on given points, archaeologists often disagree about just which stems expand and which contract.

Look at point 24: I call this stem *contracting,* but you might think that it is *expanding.* Who's right?

Who knows? Our types can be whatever we say, as long as each of us is consistent in defining the terms. Terminological difficulties like this are easily avoided with a little forethought.

I look at it this way: The *stem* is created by the notch, a slit added so that the point can be tied more easily to a shaft. The edge of this notch forms an angle with the major axis of the point, and angles are interesting because they can be accurately measured: Draw an imaginary line along the notch of

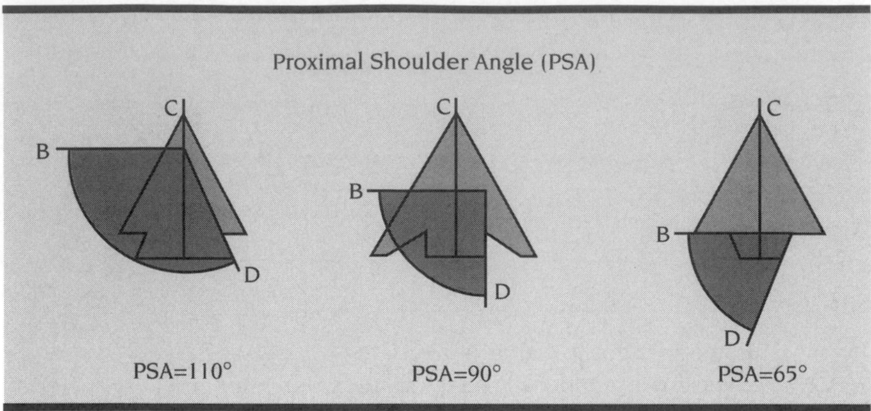

How to measure proximal shoulder angle (PSA) on a projectile point.

the point, and compute the angle between that line and the cross axis of the point. Sounds a bit complicated, but the accompanying figure shows what I mean. Angles like this are usually measured using polar grid paper, with a measurement error of about ±5°. This is called the *proximal shoulder angle* because this side of the notch is nearest ("proximal to") the point shaft.

Table 9.1 lists the proximal shoulder angles for the ten large points from Gatecliff Shelter. Now the difference between expanding and contracting stems is apparent: Points 16 through 20 have angles greater than about 110°, and points 21 through 25 have angles smaller than that. On this basis, I define the following morphological types:

Elko Corner-notched points (nos. 16–20)

Weight: greater than 2.5 grams

Proximal shoulder angle: greater than (or equal to) 110°, and less than (or equal to) 150°

Gatecliff Contracting Stem points (nos. 21–25)

Weight: greater than 2.5 grams

Proximal shoulder angle: less than 100°

Gatecliff Contracting Stem point.

Elko points were initially recognized at sites in Elko County, Nevada, and I first defined Gatecliff points—obviously—at Gatecliff Shelter. As morphological types, they differ only in basal form, as described by the angle measurements. All 25 points have been grouped by type. This example, while purposely simplified, demonstrates the first step in projectile point classification. Although a number of additional attributes were necessary in dealing with the more than 400 points found at Gatecliff, the fundamental procedures are the same.

We need more rather than fewer classifications, different classifications, always new classifications, to meet new needs.

J. O. Brew (1906–1988), Archaeologist

To many, these names and measurements are mumbo jumbo. But such mumbo jumbo makes up the world of archaeological facts. Although it is boring to memorize endless names—and archaeologists are forever trying to rename everything—dealing with these five descriptive names is five times better than coping with 25 individual artifacts. And this is the function of morphological types.

Temporal Types in Prehistoric Archaeology

Temporal type: A morphological type that has been shown to have temporal significance; also known as a *time-marker* or *index fossil.*

Remember the earlier caution (under *Types of Types*): "The naked word *type* must never be applied without an appropriate modifier." I said this because archaeologists use this term in many ways, and it is essential to distinguish which type of type is meant.

So far, we have dealt strictly with *morphological types,* defined for baseline descriptive purposes. We now turn to a second, more important type, the *temporal type* (or *time-marker*). As the name implies, **temporal types** help archaeologists monitor change through time. Previously, we used the term "index fossil" to relate this notion to the geological concept of stratigraphy. In an archaeological context, both terms—*temporal type* and *index fossil*—refer to diagnostic artifact forms that enable archaeologists to characterize and date strata within archaeological sites.

Nelson's *Type I pottery* (*Santa Fe Black-on-White:* A.D. 1200–1350).

Perhaps without knowing it, you already took the first step toward defining a workable set of time-markers by grouping the individual artifacts into morphological types. The next step is to see which of the morphological categories has significant temporal associations. If morphological type B occurs only in strata dating between A.D. 500 and 1000, then this descriptive type can be elevated to the status of a temporal type. This promotion is useful because when artifacts belonging to temporal type B turn up in undated contexts, the dates A.D. 500 to 1000 become the most plausible hypothesis.

Nelson's *Type II pottery* (*Rio Grande Glaze, two-color:* A.D. 1300).

Southwestern Ceramic Time-Markers

Nels Nelson's San Cristobal ceramic typology illustrates the process. Step 1 was to sort the 2,300 sherds into five piles. After naming each category, he published concise descriptions so that other archaeologists could see how the classification was defined. Nelson then turned to the stratigraphic distribution of each morphological type. Two such types—corrugated and biscuit ware—were distributed throughout the 10-foot section. Nelson concluded that these categories were useless for chronological purposes, and so he put them aside. But the frequencies of three other types changed markedly through the stratigraphic profile at San Cristobal, and he devoted considerable time to discussing the temporal significance of his Types I, II, and III.

Nelson's *Type III pottery* (*Rio Grande Glaze, three-color:* A.D. 1300).

Procedures haven't changed much since 1914, but the terminology has. In the modern idiom, the five piles of potsherds were morphological types, basically descriptive hypotheses to be tested against the stratigraphic record. Only three morphological types (Types I, II, and III) passed the test. Because of their demonstrated stratigraphic significance, Nelson elevated them to the status of temporal types. When sherds of these three types were found in new, undated contexts, the San Cristobal stratigraphic associations suggested further temporal hypotheses for testing.

And these hypotheses have indeed been tested. Nelson's Type I, the early black-on-white pottery, is now known as Santa Fe Black-on-White (note the parallel conventions for naming ceramic and projectile point types: place name first, followed by key description). Tree-ring dating suggests that Santa Fe Black-on-White was first made about A.D. 1200, remaining popular until about A.D. 1350. Nelson's Types II and III (the two-color and three-color glazed pottery) are now placed in a ceramic series called Rio Grande Glaze (a series is a higher-level category, grouping together several similar temporal types). Rio Grande Glaze ceramics show up in sites dating about A.D. 1300, the later types running into the historic period. In short, Nelson's temporal hypotheses have been wholly confirmed and refined by techniques not yet invented in 1914.

Nelson's *Type IV pottery.*

Gatecliff Projectile Points as Time-Markers

The Gatecliff Shelter point typology works in the same way. The morphological types that we derived are really just hypotheses waiting to be tested. Some may have temporal significance; others may reflect the different ways in which projectile points were broken and repaired; and some may even mirror divisions among social groups. But before behavioral life can be breathed into these formal categories, they must be comprehensively tested against independent data. To show how this works, we shall concentrate on temporal differences.

As noted earlier, the stratigraphy of Gatecliff Shelter looks like a huge layer cake stacked 40 feet high. Geology's law of superposition tells us that, all else being equal, the oldest artifacts will lie at the bottom, with later artifacts showing up progressively higher in the stratigraphic column. The Gatecliff deposits thus provide extraordinary temporal control over the past 7,000 years. We can plot the vertical distribution of the more than 400 classifiable projectile points from Gatecliff Shelter (note that additional types were required to classify the entire Gatecliff collection).

Look at the sharp stratigraphic differences evident on the accompanying figure. All the Desert Side-notched and Cottonwood Triangular points occurred in the uppermost part of Gatecliff Shelter. The Rosegate series points were found in slightly older strata; Elko points are older than this, and Gatecliff points older still. Because 47 radiocarbon dates were available to date the geological sequence at Gatecliff, it was possible to assign the following time ranges to each category:

Desert Side-notched: post–A.D. 1300

Cottonwood Triangular: post–A.D. 1300

Rosegate series: A.D. 500–A.D. 1300

Elko Corner-notched: 1500 B.C.–A.D. 500

Gatecliff Contracting Stem: 2500 B.C.–1500 B.C.

With this critical step, our morphological types have become temporal types. Each time similar points are found in undated contexts, we now have a clue (a hypothesis, really) to their time of manufacture.

Note what's happened here. (1) Individual artifacts were initially grouped strictly on formal criteria; all that mattered for morphological types was what the artifacts looked like. (2) These morphological categories were then tested against totally independent evidence, the layer-cake stratigraphy and the ladder of 47 radiocarbon dates available from Gatecliff Shelter. (3) All five morphological categories were significantly restricted in time, and so they were elevated to the status of temporal types.

Not every morphological point type from Gatecliff made the grade. The frequencies of some morphological types (especially the larger, concave base points) did not change significantly through time, and these types flunked the test for graduating to the level of temporal type. Maybe somebody, eventually, will demonstrate that concave base points are indeed time-markers in the Great Basin; but until that demonstration, these types remain merely "morphological," without temporal significance.

A related issue emerges here. Throughout these pages, I stress the nature of archaeological data—data are not objects, data are observations made on objects—and the point typology from Gatecliff illustrates this principle. Using a series of formal attributes (weight, distal shoulder angle, and so forth), we grouped the individual Gatecliff artifacts into morphological types, each a hypothesis to be tested against independent temporal data. But note that our "independent" data—the datable context of each point inside Gatecliff Shelter—were merely other observations made on the same objects that we used to derive the initial hypothesis. Because formal attributes are autonomous relative to context, the criterion of independence holds, and so the test is valid.

The goal of all inanimate objects is to resist man and ultimately defeat him.

RUSSELL BAKER

This principle is critical to archaeology. Hypotheses (even simple ones like time-markers) need continual testing. We should never become too comfortable with our "verified" hypotheses. Even without lifting a shovel, we can refine the Gatecliff chronology in several ways. Why not measure the microscopic hydration rim on each obsidian projectile point? This would give us an independent age estimate. Some points still have hafting sinew adhering to the base. Why not use the new accelerator technology to radiocarbon-date these fibers? Here would be another independent estimate of age. Both tests elicit more data without requiring more objects. This is one reason why well-curated museum collections are important research tools, enabling scientists of the future to generate new data from old objects.

Although critical to archaeology, time-markers have distinct limitations. As I have stressed before, archaeology proceeds with its initial objective—establishing cultural chronologies—only by making an admittedly simplistic assumption. The deliberately simplified "modal" concept of culture focuses attention on only shared aspects; the rest is temporarily ignored.

Now you can see why that simplifying assumption was necessary. Temporal types were defined for Gatecliff Shelter based on this modal definition. Never mind (for now) what the artifacts mean—we care only whether they change through time. As a result, some first-rate time-markers were discovered at Gatecliff.

We have paid a price to find our time-markers. Although we now know that Desert Side-notched and Cottonwood Triangular points postdate A.D. 1300, much ignorance remains. Why should two morphological types exist simultaneously? Are two social groups living at Gatecliff in the post-1300 time period?

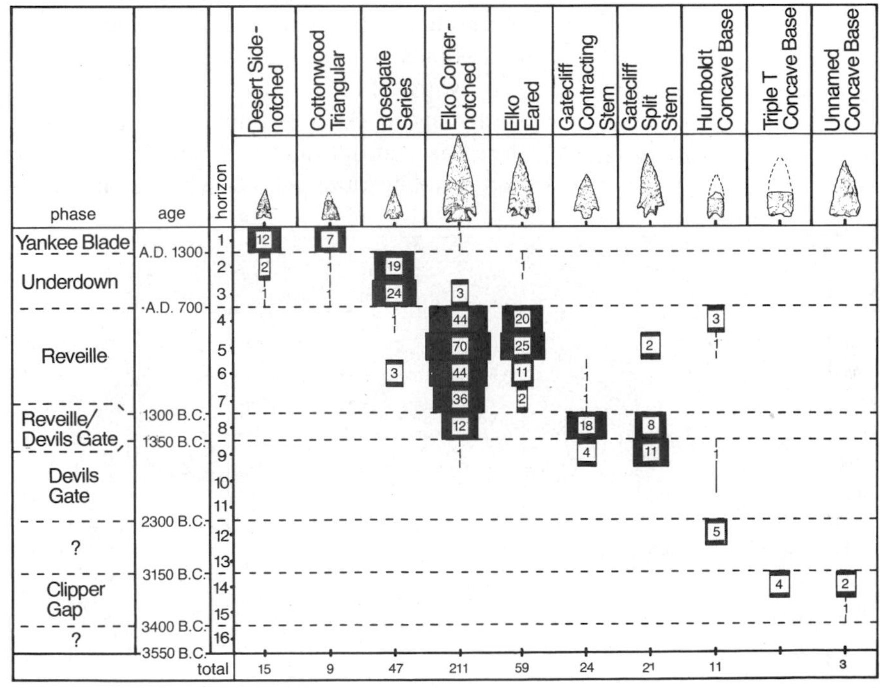

Relative proportions of selected projectile point types across the stratigraphic units of Gatecliff Shelter. Note how one or two extremely abundant temporal types seem to dominate most horizons.

Seriation on the Internet:

Analytical Software/BASP provides plenty of statistical aids for archaeologists—including seriation:
http://www.lib.uconn.edu/ArchNet/software/Base/basp.html

Evolution, Transmission, and Seriation is a series of papers arguing for evolutionary explanations in archaeology (seriation included):
http://www.emergentmedia.com/archy/saa/theory.html

Are Desert Side-notched points designed for hunting bighorn, whereas Cottonwood points are for rabbits? Are Cottonwood points really for "war arrows," left unnotched so that they cannot be pulled out once lodged? Or perhaps the difference is technological: Could the Cottonwood Triangular points be unfinished, intended to be later notched (and thereby becoming Desert Side-notched points)? These guesses are hypotheses at present untested.

Seriation

Seriation: A temporal ordering of artifacts based on the assumption that cultural styles (fads) change and that the popularity of a particular style or decoration can be associated with a certain time period. The fattest part of the cluster is the central part of the fad.

One powerful upshot of the typological concept is **seriation**, a technique that permits archaeologists to place stylistic periods into a relative chronological sequence. Unlike absolute dating procedures such as radiocarbon and dendrochronology, seriation works strictly with qualitative, relativistic ordering.

Seriation implicitly assumes that people are fickle: Sometimes styles change; sometimes new technologies arise. Most such new ideas are slow to catch on, with only a few pioneers participating in the fad. But fashions have a way of becoming chic in one group, eventually replacing earlier vogues, and then gradually falling into disuse.

Seriation curves often assume a characteristic form. In the example presented here, new lighting technologies are gradually introduced, flourish for a while, and then slowly disappear. In the mid-nineteenth century, most houses in Pennsylvania were illuminated by candles and oil lamps; only a few households had gas lamps. But over the next 50 years, more and more families switched to gas lights. Those who could not afford such installations started using kerosene lamps (made possible by the growing petroleum industry in Pennsylvania and elsewhere). By the turn of the century, gas lights had virtually disappeared. Then along came another invention, electricity, and incandescent light bulbs started lighting the houses of Pennsylvania in increasing numbers. By 1940, "everybody" had electric lights, the gas and kerosene lamps fading into nostalgia.

Seriation diagram showing how methods of artificial illumination changed in Pennsylvania between 1850 *and* 1950.

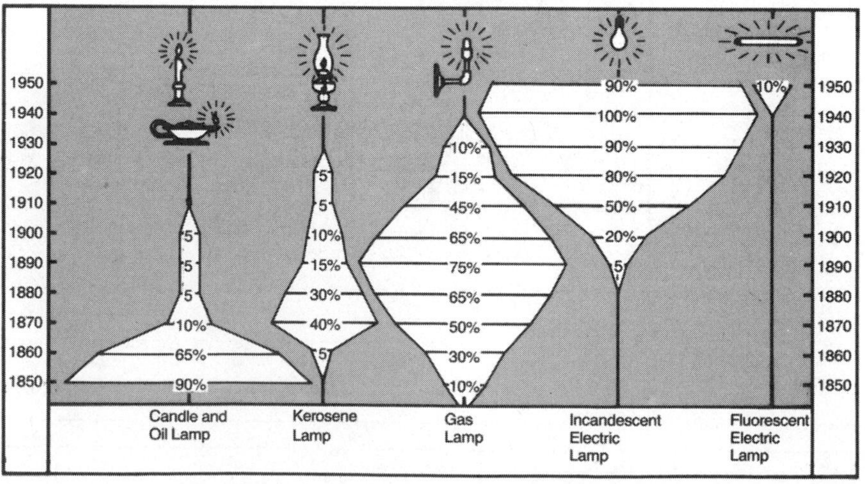

The shape of such popularity curves, which struck archaeologist James Ford as somehow "battleship shaped," established the basis for seriation. By arranging the proportions of temporal types into lozenge-shaped curves, one can determine a relative chronological sequence. The classic late nineteenth-century example of such ordering was made by Sir Flinders Petrie, who examined the contents of hundreds of Egyptian graves. After studying the ceramics, Petrie "seriated" the pottery styles in time simply by looking at the characteristics of the handles.

Seriation is a deceptively simple technique, the unnecessarily abstruse discussion of which has become an embarrassment to quantitative archaeologists

William H. Marquardt, archaeologist (Florida Museum of Natural History)

This same phenomenon is evident in Nelson's sherd counts from San Cristobal Pueblo. When San Cristobal was first built, ceramics were most commonly decorated with black-on-white painting. Moving up Nelson's stratigraphic column, two-color glaze rapidly takes over in popularity, with black-on-white embellishment fading out. Near the top of the column, three-color pottery comes into use. The town dump at San Cristobal faithfully preserved these ceramic fads, helping archaeologists date the prehistoric sites of the American Southwest.

The sands and silts inside Gatecliff Shelter acted similarly, preserving such proportional patterning in the projectile points. Above, we found that Elko Corner-notched points were vertically distributed across the strata at Gatecliff Shelter in near-perfect, "battleship-shaped" fashion. The other types are similarly distributed, but the smaller sample sizes tend to mask the battleships.

Artifacts tend to "seriate" in stratified deposits. This principle of seriation has been adapted by archaeologists to create a relative dating technique that works in the absence of stratified deposits.

Take a look at the percentage frequency chart concocted by James Ford to demonstrate west-to-east changes in ceramic surface texture from many different sites across the American Southeast. To do this, pottery is first washed, cataloged, and classified; then the percentages of each type are calculated across the relevant provenience units. The percentages are signified by horizontal bars on long, narrow strips of graph paper, "like slats of a venetian blind," and held together with paper clips. The strips are "arranged and rearranged in relation to one another until the clearest patterning appears." Each of the strips is a provenience unit, and the idea is to move things around until you create the smoothest (most battleship-shaped) curves. The prin-

Cultural-historical archaeology in action. James Ford's 1952 presentation of unimodal curves representing pottery type frequencies, with illustrations of vessels of each type also on the chart. Here, Ford attempted to correlate the ceramic sequences from northeast Texas, Louisiana, and Florida.

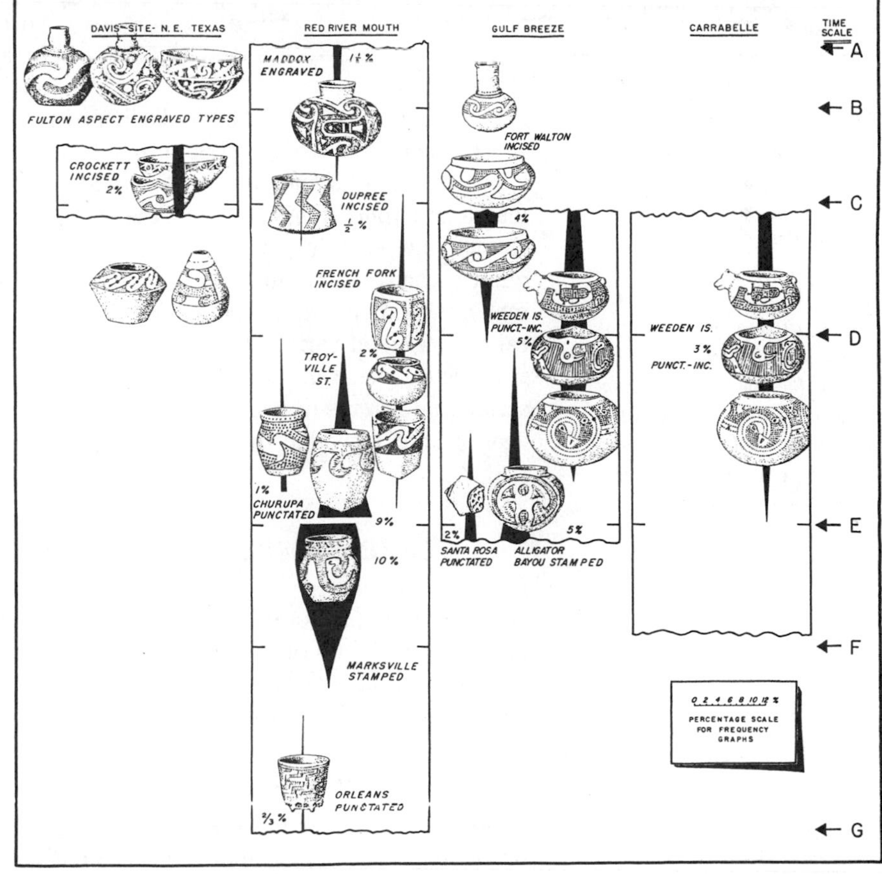

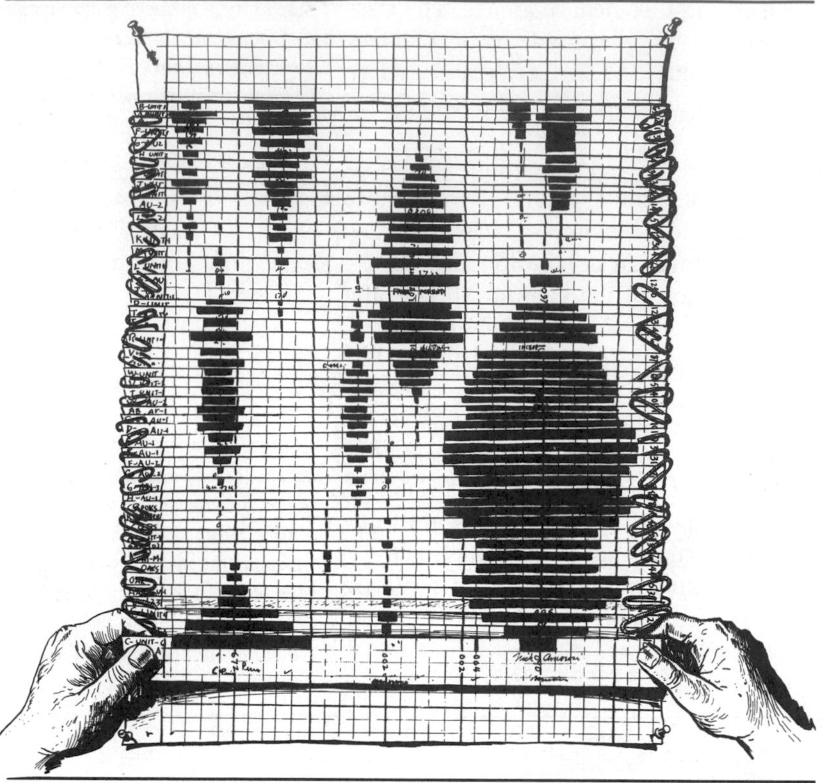

This is how seriation diagrams were once constructed—literally by hand. Frequencies of temporal pottery types were computed by percentage, then drawn on individual strips, which were moved up and down until a series of "battleship-shaped" curves emerged. Seriation theory says that the smoothest diagram is the "most likely" temporal sequence. Today, this tedious and subjective procedure has been replaced by computer programs.

ciples of seriation suggest that the smoothest sets of curves are likely to indicate the correct temporal order for the various proveniences.

The drawing shows how the process works. In fact, the drawing has itself become an archaeological artifact. When researching the first edition of this book two decades ago, I discovered the original in an art file outside my office at the American Museum of Natural History. It was drawn more than 30 years ago by the late Nicholas Amorosi, who for decades illustrated artifacts at the American Museum. This "hands-on" demonstration of seriation has become a classic in the literature of archaeology. Those hands actually belonged to Nick. Virtually every elementary discussion of seriation uses it (including this one). The original piece-by-piece seriation diagram being illustrated was turned into a museum exhibit at Marksville, Louisiana—rusting paper clips and all!

It should be obvious that seriation, like the other typological tools discussed here, rests squarely on the modal definition of culture. All seriation diagrams implicitly assume that the observed variability is due to temporal change; that is, only the shared aspects of culture (styles) are reflected in frequency change through time. Of course this assumption will be incorrect in many cases, because artifact frequencies often reflect functional, technological, and societal variability as well. When too much nontemporal variability is reflected, the collections simply do not seriate very well. But the fact that seriation diagrams do work so often indicates that the modal concept is once again useful, provided that one realizes the limitations.

Time-Markers in Historical Archaeology

Over the years, historical archaeologists have developed an impressive number of dating techniques suitable for historic-period artifacts. The same basic principles of classification apply to prehistoric and historic-period archaeological sites, but the specific procedures vary somewhat.

Pipe Stem Dating

Changing technology has created a vast array of time-marker artifact types in historical archaeology: Before 1830, for example, the fiber of the metal ran crosswise to the axis of a nail; after that, the fibers ran lengthwise. Nineteenth-century glass often had a purplish cast (caused by sunlight reacting with magnesium oxide, but magnesium was no longer added after World War I). Examples proliferate endlessly.

Historical archaeologists have been particularly clever in finding increasingly fine-grained ways to partition time on their sites. One classic way to date colonial-period American sites was developed at mid-century by J. C. "Pinky" Harrington. Clay tobacco pipes changed form markedly in the seventeenth and eighteenth centuries, and broken fragments turn up by the hundreds on many archaeological sites of this period. Everybody recognized that clay pipes held great potential as time-markers: They were manufactured, imported, smoked, and thrown away, all within a year or so. Some people studied changes in pipe bowl shape. Others observed that stem thickness also changed through time. Stem length bore a direct relationship to period of manufacture: starting with 6- to 8-inch pipes in the early seventeenth century and extending to the long "church warden" pipes of the early eighteenth century. The trend then reversed itself, ending in the short-stem pipes made during the nineteenth century.

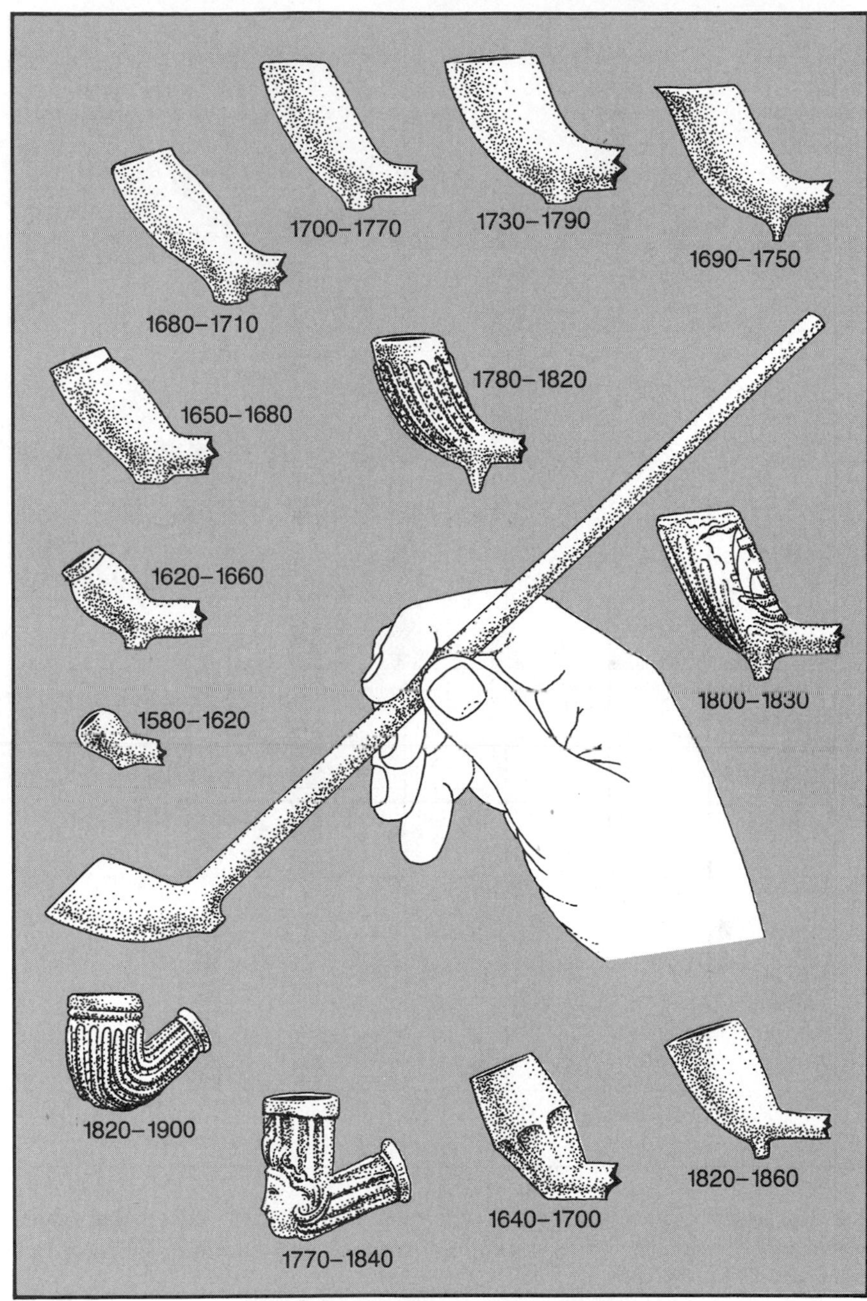

Simplified evolutionary sequence of English and American clay smoking pipes.

Each method has merit, but the same problem plagued each one because the fragile clay pipes rarely survived in a condition sufficiently complete to allow fruitful analysis. While working with the pipe collection from Jamestown, including some 50,000 small chunks of broken stems, Harrington observed that the early pipe stems seemed to have relatively large bores, which became smaller in the later specimens. Following up on this, Harrington measured the stem hole diameters for a series of 330 known-age pipes from

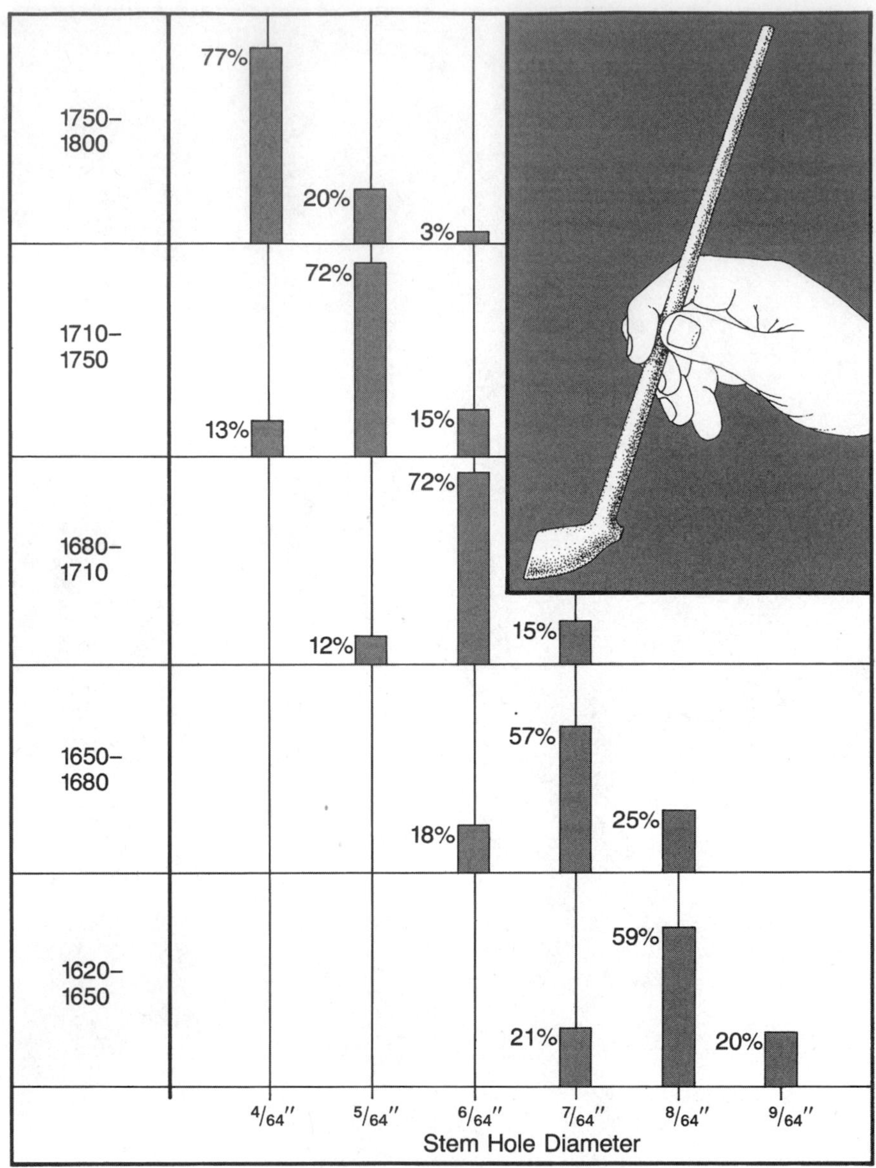

J. C. Harrington's diagram showing how he used pipe stem hole diameters to date archaeological sites.

Jamestown and Colonial Williamsburg (Virginia) and Fort Frederica (St. Simons Island, Georgia).

It turned out that inside diameter did change through time, and systematically at that. The resulting pipe stem chronology began in 1620 and lasted through 1800. Harrington divided this period into five cultural periods. Best of all, the technique was simple and cheap. As Harrington put it, "In making use of this dating device, the first requirement is a 39-cent set of drills; the second is common sense."

Fifteen years later, Lewis Binford decided Harrington's method was "clumsy" and reworked the original data to derive a statistical regression formula for estimating age from the size of pipe stem holes:

$$Y = 1931.85 - 38.26X$$

where X is the mean stem bore for a sample of pipe fragments and Y is the projected mean date. Archaeologists have debated the pros and cons of pipe stem dating ever since, many investigators ignoring Harrington's original cautions and "commonsense" strictures.

Documentary Evidence to Define Time-Markers

Nothing about the pipe stem example differs from procedures used in prehistoric archaeology. Harrington began with empirical observation, tested his notions against known-age controls, and then formulated his time-markers; Binford simply codified the estimates. But in many cases, those working on historic sites have a decided advantage over those studying prehistoric remains because historical archaeologists also have access to documentary evidence that can help create even more exact temporal divisions.

One particularly handy method has been the study of period paintings to learn more about ancient artifact forms. When Kathleen Deagan was researching the shapes of Hispanic bottles used in the New World, for instance, she was dismayed to find that although green and clear glass littered sixteenth-century sites, not a single complete bottle from this period survived anywhere in Florida and the Caribbean. But rather than simply give up, she temporarily turned art historian because bottles, it turns out, are frequently depicted in sixteenth-century Spanish art, such as *The Last Supper* by Juan de Juanes. Such paintings provide rare clues to unknown forms of Hispanic bottles, and Deagan was able to construct a chronological sequence of bottle forms abstracted largely from such paintings.

The Last Supper *by Juan de Juanes (ca. 1550). The bottle forms evident in paintings like this assist historical archaeologists in building temporal types.*

Noël Hume considered the role that paintings can play in reconstructing British colonial artifact forms. One particularly illuminating source is William Hogarth, an eighteenth-century English artist whose paintings, drawings, and engravings depict a vast spectrum of everyday, domestic artifacts of the time. Look at Hogarth's well-known tavern orgy scene from his series *The Rake's Progress,* done in 1735. Here, our roving rake sprawls in Rose Tavern, charmed and robbed by an obliging cadre of trollops, awash in artifacts of their day: chairs, clothes, caps, a watch, drinking glasses, plates, a sword, candlesticks, and so forth. Working from an enlargement of this print, the observant historical archaeologist should be able to learn plenty about artifact styles typical of the first third of the eighteenth century, right?

Scene III (The Rose Tavern scene) from The Rake's Progress *series by William Hogarth, engraved 1735.*

Perhaps, but historical archaeologists have learned to be cautious in evaluating the historical accuracy of surviving documents and commentary. Some paintings seem to be as accurate as photographs. Historical archaeologists have concluded, for instance, that most artists in the Dutch and Flemish traditions are

Colonial America on the Internet:

Jamestown: Recreation of America's First English Colony:
http://www.williamsburg.com/wol/tour/james/james.html

Jamestown Rediscovery, with emphasis on recent archaeology and fieldwork opportunities:
http://www.apra.org

Williamsburg has information on guided tours and more:
http://www.williamsburg.com/wol/tour/tour.html

Ft. Frederica National Monument:
http://pigpen.itd.nps.gov/fofr

relatively trustworthy in rendering both people and objects faithfully. At least these artists sat directly across from the subjects they painted.

But Hogarth is a problem because his own writings suggest that most of his creations came from memory, often assembled from sketches squirreled away in his files. Sure enough, when specialists study the orgy scene, they find that his rendering of everyday items is suspect: The brickwork is unrealistic; the scimitar-shaped knife wielded by the young lady is all wrong; and the bottles are about 30 years too early for the period of the drawing. Hogarth had learned how to draw a bottle during his early life, and kept on drawing that type, ignoring the changes that had taken place in the intervening years. Noël Hume concluded that "in all probability, therefore, having drawn, say, a rat trap two or three times, Hogarth knew what a rat trap looked like and thenceforth extracted it from his memory 'prop room'

Some of the sixteenth-century bottle forms found in archaeological sites throughout the Caribbean.

whenever he needed it. Consequently, every trap he drew looked more or less the same, no matter whether it had been outmoded by new and better rat traps developed later on in his life." This case underscores the general point that historical archaeologists must be discriminating when dealing with documentary evidence.

TPQ Dating

Regardless of how they are established (from ceramics or otherwise), such date ranges form the backbone of chronology in historical archaeology. They are used in two basic ways: to define a temporal cutoff point or to estimate a central temporal tendency. Let me explain how each works.

Kathleen Deagan and Joan Koch excavated an important cemetery named Nuestra Señora de la Soledad in downtown St. Augustine. They first classified the sherds into the various ceramic types commonly found on Spanish American sites. One such type is named Ichtucknee Blue on White. The last part describes the surface decoration, but "Ichtucknee" comes from the Ichtucknee River in north central Florida, where John Goggin first recognized the type based on specimens salvaged from Fig Springs. The estimated age of Ichtucknee Blue on White ceramics ranges between A. D. 1600 and 1650.

Each grave pit can then be dated according to the associational concept of ***terminus post quem* (TPQ)**, defined as the date after which the object must have found its way into the ground. At Soledad, the TPQ indicates the first possible date that the latest-occurring artifact could have been deposited in that grave pit. So when a sherd of Ichtucknee Blue on White turned up in the grave fill at Soledad, excavators knew that this grave could not have been dug before 1600 (the date after which the sherd must have found its way into the ground). Had the same grave pit contained a sherd of, say, San Luís Polychrome (with an associated age range from 1650 to 1750), then the TPQ date would have to have been revised to 1650. This is how TPQ dating works.

***Terminus post quem* (TPQ):** The date after which a stratum or feature must have been deposited.

In practice, the TPQ dating at Soledad was not that precise. But when combined with the correlative excavation data and documentary evidence about site usage, the TPQ estimates enabled Deagan and Koch to group the Soledad burials into three culture periods: seventeenth-century Spanish (TPQ: pre-1700), eighteenth-century Spanish (TPQ: pre-1762), and eighteenth-century British (TPQ: post-1762). Once this classification was established, they could look for cultural differences and similarities among burial assemblages. The Spanish-period burials were mostly shroud wrapped, whereas the British used coffins. The Spanish crossed the arms over the chest, whereas the British were interred with arms along the sides. Spanish burials were oriented toward the east, British toward the west, and so forth.

TPQ estimates the date after which the grave must have been dug (or, technically, after which it was filled in). This estimate is the earliest possible date, given the accuracy of the known date range.

Ichtucknee Blue on White plate: A.D. 1600–1650.

Mean Ceramic Dates

Some disagreement exists about the utility of *terminus post quem* ceramic dating in historical archaeology. Many, such as Kathleen Deagan, find the concept to be useful in providing a valid baseline for site chronology. Noël Hume has even declared that *terminus post quem* procedures provide "the cornerstone of all archaeological reasoning."

Other archaeologists, such as Stanley South, are less enthusiastic about TPQ dating. They point up a number of complicating factors: Seventeenth-century Anglo-American sites are relatively rare, and less is known about the ceramic associations; status differences influence relative ceramic frequencies; and so forth. Some archaeologists argue that such a slight connection exists between the date of manufacture and the date of deposition of a ceramic type on historic sites that any attempt to date a site on the basis of pottery-manufacturing dates is subject to gross error.

Mean ceramic date: A statistical technique devised by Stanley South for combining the median age of manufacture for temporally significant pottery types.

Stanley South has derived a provocative method to minimize these perceived problems. South's **mean ceramic date** approach emphasizes the average age, shifting the emphasis away from beginning and end dates for ceramic wares, emphasizing instead the mid-range (*median*) date. Working from information in Noël Hume's *A Guide to Artifacts in Colonial America,* South constructed a model based on selected ceramic types, defined by attributes of form, decoration, surface finish, and hardness plus the temporal dates assigned by Noël Hume for each type, as shown in Table 9.2.

Seventy-eight specific ceramic types were included in South's formulation. Canton porcelain, for instance, has a known range of dates between 1800 and 1830. The median date for this type is thus (1800 + 1830)/2 = 1815. Bellarmine brown, salt-glazed stoneware with a well-molded human face ranges in age from 1550 through 1625; the median date is 1587.

The mean ceramic date pools this information across a feature (or an entire site) to determine the median date of manufacture for each time-sensitive sherd and then averages these dates to arrive at the mean occupation date implied by the entire collection. Table 9.3 shows how the mean ceramic date is computed for the cellar fill in the Hepburn-Reonalds Ruin in Brunswick, North Carolina. Available historic records revealed that the building was probably still standing in 1734 and burned in 1776; the *median historic date* is thus (1734 + 1776)/2 = 1755. South's mean ceramic date came out to be 1758.4, only 3.4 years later than the median historic date. Moreover, the pipe stem date for this site is 1756, so substantial agreement exists among all three sources. In fact, South has found that the mean ceramic dates seldom deviate from a range of ±4 years from the known median historic date. Such agreement is nothing short of remarkable.

Stan used to come up to Colonial Williamsburg with boxes full of sherds. He wanted to know about the types and dates of all kinds of ceramics, and I did my best to help him. I think that was when he was working on that formula. You know, the one that gives you a date you already know.

Attributed to Ivor Noël Hume, archaeologist (Colonial Williamsburg Foundation)

The mean ceramic date relies on two central assumptions: (1) that ceramic types are roughly contemporary at all sites at which they occur, and (2) that the mid-range date of manufacture approximates the modal date of popularity. These are, of course, some fairly large assumptions.

Mean ceramic estimates are not limited to British colonial sites. South expanded the method to Spanish American sites throughout the New World. Other investigators have tinkered with the mean ceramic dating procedure, attempting to apply it to nineteenth-century Anglo-American assemblages, English wine bottles, and even Native American pottery, in the American Southwest and elsewhere. Others have tried to take this research one step farther by looking for the factors responsible for creating discrepancies between mean ceramic dates and their documentary equivalents.

TABLE 9.2

Some Ceramic Types Used to Construct Mean Ceramic Dates in Seventeenth-Century Anglo-American Sites

Type Number	Date Range	Median Date	Ceramic Type Name and Page Reference
			Porcelain
5.	c.1800–1830	1815	Canton porcelain (262).
7.	c.1790–1825	1808	Overglaze enameled China trade porcelain (258, 261).
26.	c.1660–1800	1730	Overglaze enameled Chinese export porcelain (261).
31.	c.1745–1795	1770	English porcelain (137).
39.	c.1660–1800	1730	Underglaze blue Chinese porcelain (257).
41.	c.1750–1765	1758	"Littler's Blue" (119–23) (on white salt-glazed stoneware, porcelain, and creamware).
69.	c.1574–1644	1609	Chinese porcelain, underglaze blue, Late Ming (257, 264).
			Stoneware
Brown			
1.	c.1820–1900+	1860	Brown stoneware bottles for ink, beer, etc. (78–79).
46.	c.1700–1810	1755	Nottingham stoneware (Lustered) (114).
52.	c.1700–1775	1738	Burslem "crouch" pale brown stoneware mugs.
53.	c.1690–1775	1733	Brown salt-glazed mugs (Fulham) (111–13).
54.	c.1690–1775	1733	British brown stoneware (excluding 1, 52, 53) (112–114).
66.	c.1620–1700	1660	Deteriorated Bellarmine face bottles (one example dated to the 1760s) (56–57).
74	c.1550–1625	1588	Bellarmine, brown salt-glazed stoneware, well-molded human face (55–57).
75.	c.1540–1600	1570	Rhenish brown-glazed sprigged, mould-decorated, Cologne-type stoneware (277–79).
Blue, gray			
44.	c.1700–1775	1738	Westerwald, stamped blue floral devices, geometric designs (284–85).
58.	c.1650–1725	1668	Sprig molding, combed lines, blue and manganese decorated Rhenish stoneware (280–81).
59.	c.1690–1710	1700	Embellished Hohr gray Rhenish stoneware (284).
77.	c.1700–1775	1738	Westerwald chamber pots (148, 281).
White			
16.	c.1740–1765	1753	Moulded white salt-glazed stoneware (115).
24.	c.1765–1795	1780	Debased "Scratch blue" white salt-glazed stoneware (118).
30.	c.1755–1765	1760	Transfer printed white salt-glazed stoneware (128).
34.	c.1744–1775	1760	"Scratch blue" white salt-glazed stoneware (117).
40.	c.1720–1805	1763	White salt-glazed stoneware (excluding plates and moulded) (115–17).
41.	c.1750–1765	1758	"Littler's blue" (119–23) (on white salt-glazed stoneware, porcelain, and creamware).

SOURCE: South 1977a, Table 31, p. 210.
Used by permission of the author and Academic Press.

Basic Units of Regional Archaeology

Americanist archaeology has adopted a relatively standardized framework for integrating the kind of chronological information just discussed into a larger, regional scale. This regional infrastructure was initially set out by Harvard archaeologists Gordon Willey and Philip Phillips in their influential book entitled *Method and Theory in American Archaeology,* published in 1958. Although nomenclature varies somewhat from region to region, the basic Willey–Philips framework remains the most generally accepted system in the Americas.

TABLE 9.3

Using the Formula With Ceramics From the Brunswick Hepburn–Reonalds Ruin

Ceramic Type	Type Median (X_i)	Sherd Count (f_i)	Product
22	1791	483	865,053
33	1767	25	44,175
34	1760	32	56,320
36	1755	55	96,525
37	1733	40	69,320
43	1758	327	574,866
49	(1750)	583	1,020,250
44	1738	40	69,520
47	1748	28	48,944
53,54	1733	52	90,116
56	1733	286	495,638
29	1760	9	15,840
		1960	3,446,567 ÷ 1960 = 1758.4

The mean ceramic date formula $Y = \frac{\sum_{i=1}^{n} X_i f_i}{\sum_{i=1}^{n} f_i}$ $Y = \frac{3,446,567}{1960} = 1758.4$

SOURCE: South 1977a, Table 32, p. 220.
Used by permission of the author and Academic Press.

We have already seen how to derive *temporal types* (such as the two kinds of fiber-tempered pottery): You group individual artifacts into relatively homogeneous categories, then test them against independent data (such as site stratigraphy, correlation with other known sites, and direct dating of the artifacts themselves). These groups of artifacts that can be shown to change systematically and observably through time are then called *time-markers*.

The next analytical step is to see how the time-markers themselves cluster to reflect site chronology. The first critical unit in the synthesis is called a *component* (defined earlier as a culturally homogeneous unit within a single site). "Culturally homogeneous" is the buzzword here, the line separating homogeneous and heterogeneous often existing only in the excavator's mind. Many archaeological sites contain only a single component; that is, the artifact assemblage is essentially homogeneous (with respect to time) throughout the entire site. Most archaeological sites contain more than one component.

Because defining archaeological components rests on the intangible factor of cultural homogeneity, there can be no firm rules. In some sites, such as Gatecliff Shelter, the strata are strikingly obvious from the stratigraphic profile. As we discussed earlier, Gatecliff contains numerous strata of sterile, noncultural silts, separating the deposits into discrete living floors. These various surfaces can then be kept distinct (as individual components) or grouped together on the basis of shared similarities. Gatecliff contained five distinct cultural components, each incorporating one to six living surfaces. At other sites, the archaeological deposits are often found to be churned and mixed. Although components still exist, they bleed stratigraphically one into another without visible breaks. In such cases, components must be isolated analytically, without the assistance of obvious physical stratigraphy.

Components are thus site specific. But components from several sites must usually be analytically combined to define the master regional chronology. The next analytical step is the **phase:** similar components as manifested at more than one site. The phase has become the practicable and intelligible unit of archaeological study, defined by Gordon Willey and Philip Phillips as "an archaeological unit possessing traits sufficiently characteristic to distinguish it from all other units similarly conceived . . . [and] spatially limited to the order of magnitude of a locality or region and chronologically limited to a relatively brief interval of time."

Phase: An archaeological construct possessing traits sufficiently characteristic to distinguish it from other units similarly conceived; spatially limited to roughly a locality or region and chronologically limited to a relatively brief interval of time.

Like the component, the phase concept is encumbered by weasel words like "sufficiently characteristic," "similarly conceived," and "relatively brief interval." No matter how hard archaeologists try, some degree of wishy-washy imprecision lingers, and decisions still rely heavily on simple familiarity with the archaeological data at hand.

At Gatecliff Shelter, we recognized five components, each defined by shared similarities. The latest of these began about A.D. 1300 and lasted until Anglo-American contact, about 1850 in central Nevada. The other components were similarly defined, each composed of different kinds of artifacts, and spanning other episodes of time.

When talking only about Gatecliff, the analytical unit remains the component. But actually we excavated nearly a dozen sites in Monitor Valley and several of these sites contained a late assemblage similar to that recognized at Gatecliff. At the site level, these assemblages comprise a component. At a regional level, similar contemporary components are synthesized into a phase, which we named *Yankee Blade* after a nineteenth-century silver mine in nearby Austin.

The following figure diagrams the relationship between component and phase. Three archaeological sites have been tested within a region, and, as is often the case, no single site contains the complete cultural sequence: The first site has components A and B; the second site contains a new component called C; and the third site has components A and C but lacks component B. By analyzing the temporal types shared among the components and comparing the absolute dates, a regional sequence of phases can be constructed from evidence at these three sites.

The phase becomes archaeology's basic unit of areal synthesis. To ensure that the phase concept remains viable in practice, the definition is left purposely vague. Phases can be as short as a few generations, especially in areas where the chronology is based on dendrochronologically controlled painted ceramics. The length of the phase depends in part on the kind of archaeological remains involved and also on our contemporary knowledge of these remains. Well-studied areas tend to have shorter phases.

The phase concept allows archaeologists to treat time, actually a continuous variable, as if it were a discrete set of points. The overall Gatecliff Shelter sequence lasted for about 7,000 years, and "years" are a perfectly viable way to think of time. But "years" can create difficulties in archaeological sites. We found it better to view Gatecliff in terms of five components, one stacked on another.

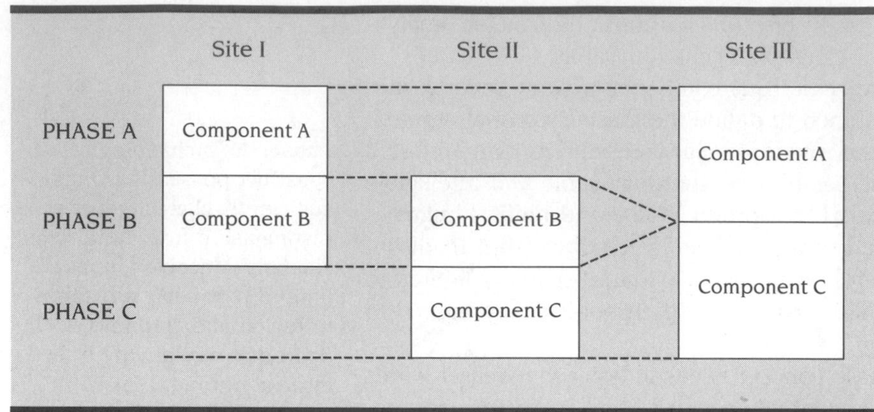

Relationship of archaeological sites to the analytical concepts of "component" and "phase."

Each component has an associated array of dates and a set of characteristic artifacts. Gatecliff components can be compared with components at other nearby sites, and a regional chronology can be constructed. Using the phase as our smallest unit, we can establish regional contemporaneity. Strictly speaking, two events can never be truly "contemporary," even if we measure time in millimicroseconds. Time has no intrinsic units, and the smallest subdivision can always (at least in theory) be subdivided.

The job of archaeology's phase concept is to impose a set of minimal units on time, and the phase is that minimal unit. When we discuss the Yankee Blade phase, we are treating the time span from A.D. 1300 to A.D. 1850 as if it were an instant. By definition, two components of the Yankee Blade phase are simultaneous, provided that "simultaneous" is understood to last 550 years. As knowledge of the Yankee Blade phase expands, we may be able to distinguish divisions within the phase. It might be possible, for instance, to distinguish an early Yankee Blade component from a late Yankee Blade component. When this happens, the initial phase is segmented into *subphases*. This increasing subdivision reflects the amount of research accomplished on each phase and underscores the degree to which our knowledge of the archaeological record is a contemporary phenomenon.

Culture Chronology Versus Culture History

Archaeology's initial *chronological* aim makes two assumptions:

1. Variability not attributable to time (and/or space) is irrelevant.
2. Temporal variability is best isolated by monitoring only shared cultural behavior.

In *chronological* analysis, the archaeologist addresses only the isolated segments of the archaeological record that differ across time and/or space. This assumption is simplistic, to be sure, for the archaeological record contains plenty of nontemporal, nonspatial variability. But it is precisely this complexity that leads us to simplify. For chronological purposes, any source of variability other than temporal or spatial is random noise and temporarily irrelevant.

Let us look at the case of Shoshone pottery to make one final point. Such ceramics appear suddenly in many parts of the Desert West about A.D. 1300, and the Shoshone people are known to have made similar pottery until about 1860. Shoshone brownware pottery thus implies certain limits: time

(A.D. 1300–1860), space (the Desert West). Note that the early boundary (A.D. 1300) is only an estimate derived from radiocarbon dating, whereas the late date (1860) is based on historical documentation. The initial 1300 date is thus subject to considerably more error than is the termination date. Such is often the case with time-markers, but this disproportionate error will cause no particular difficulties so long as we recognize it.

Its temporal parameters suitably estimated, Shoshone pottery becomes a useful time-marker in the chronology of the Desert West. Sites containing lots of these potsherds can be tentatively assigned to the A.D. 1300–1860 interval (subject, of course, to independent verification by suitable dating techniques).

But Shoshone pottery, taken as a time-marker, leaves many more questions unanswered. What about the origins of the Desert West ceramic complex? Was this post-1300 pottery introduced as the result of a migration of Shoshone-speaking peoples? Did the idea of pottery simply spread across the Desert West? Or did the peoples of the Desert West independently invent the idea of pottery?

These are not easy questions, and answering them requires a thorough understanding of the local cultural history. Is it possible to document a population movement across the Desert West at A.D. 1300? If so, where did these newcomers come from? And what happened to the pre-1300 inhabitants of the Desert West? What conditions would allow the replacement of one group of hunter-gatherers by another group? Are there signs of warfare in A.D. 1300? Did the climate change to render the pre-1300 adaptation untenable, thereby enabling the Shoshone to invade the Desert West? Could it be that a ceramic-using population moved into the Desert West and intermarried with the previous inhabitants? Did the ecological adaptation somehow change to make ceramic vessels more efficient after A.D. 1300? Were the vessels actually manufactured in the Desert West, or were they traded in from neighboring ceramic-manufacturing areas? If so, what did Desert West peoples trade for the ceramics, and why did this exchange begin only after A.D. 1300?

Data-free questions like this can pile up without apparent end. The point here—and a compelling point indeed—is that the mechanics of cultural change cannot be understood strictly by looking at time-markers. By definition, we base our time-markers on selected aspects of shared culture; time-markers deliberately ignore most of what is cultural. Obviously, questions such as diffusion, migration, and independent invention are complex, reflecting changes in the underlying cultural systems. Time-markers, grounded only in shared behavior, are patently inadequate for unraveling the mechanics of cultural systems.

Thus it is that we distinguish between cultural chronology and cultural history:

- A *cultural chronology* documents a temporal and spatial change in selected artifacts.
- A *cultural history* documents what people actually did.

Cultural chronology does not equal cultural history.

The time-marker Shoshone pottery tells us that distinctive potsherds occur in archaeological deposits dating from A.D. 1300 to 1860 across the Desert West. But viewed as a time-marker, Shoshone pottery tells us nothing

. . . for a time the term culture history not only fell into disuse but also was almost an obscenity, not to be mentioned in mixed company.

JESSE D. JENNINGS (1909–1997), ARCHAEOLOGIST

about why pottery was introduced in 1300. For some reason, one segment of the Desert West cultural system changed, and people began using (if not manufacturing) pottery. This complex issue can be studied only by pursuing related shifts in the lifeway, drawing evidence from the settlement pattern and demography, cultural ecology, social organization, and religion. If one posits that the pottery was introduced through the people's physical migration, then a second cultural system must be examined, the system operative in the area from which the newcomers migrated.

Cultural history cannot be understood either by using time-markers or through the modal definition of culture alone. A systematic perspective is required. Time-markers document only changes in shared material culture (as reflected by selected kinds of artifacts); they do not tell us why such changes have occurred.

This warning is repeated several times throughout the text. It is a critical point that speaks to the very objectives of archaeology. You cannot study the more sophisticated aspects of the human past until you have a chronology, and your chronology must be based on the modal concept of culture. Once your chronology has been thoroughly refined and repeatedly tested, then you are free to explore the rest of culture—provided you redefine the basic units of analysis. Do not confuse the initial, chronological objectives of archaeology with the later, more sophisticated aims to be considered further on in this book.

Shoshone ware ceramic vessel.

SUMMARY Archaeology's major contribution to anthropological knowledge is time. Although many ethnologists study cultural evolution and cultural change, if they were to restrict themselves to ethnographic testimony, their studies would remain shallow, short term, and perfunctory. Only through an archaeological perspective can episodes of both short- and long-term cultural change be satisfactorily explored.

Not all culture changes, and the modal concept of culture—defined by what most people do or believe—allows you to ignore the large proportion of the stable cultural inventory to concentrate on the critical small percentage that deviates through time. The modal concept of culture attempts only to describe what changes; it does not explain why that change has taken place.

Artifacts are the material cultural remains of human activity. The *type* is the basic unit of artifact analysis, an idealized construct that allows archaeologists to transcend individual artifacts to consider more generalized categories. The *morphological type* reflects the overall appearance of a set of artifacts, emphasizing broad similarities rather than focusing on specific traits. Morphological types are descriptive, enabling the archaeologist to summarize large sets of individual artifacts into a few ideal categories.

The *temporal type* serves a more specific function, to monitor how artifacts change through time. Temporal types are best defined through stratigraphic analysis, by using the index fossil concept.

Seriation is a relative chronological method that also enables archaeologists to follow systematic artifact change through time. Seriation operates on the implicit assumption that stylistic change tends to begin gradually and then to pick up speed as the style catches on. After this peak of popularity, the frequency of the style tapers off gradually, until it disappears entirely. Thus relative popularity takes on a characteristic "battleship-shaped" curve when plotted on a seriation diagram.

Historical archaeologists have been particularly clever in finding increasingly detailed ways to partition time on their sites: dating small fragments of tobacco pipe stems, evaluating evidence for time-markers in period paintings, and extracting a mean occupation date by averaging ceramic dates of manufacture across entire assemblages. But despite such differences—and the precise results they produce—the basic procedures and assumptions behind artifact classification differ little between historical archaeology and archaeology in general.

The next analytical step is to see how the time-markers themselves cluster to reflect site chronology. The first critical unit in the synthesis is called a *component,* a culturally homogeneous unit within a single site. Components are site specific, but similar components at different sites can be synthesized into *phases,* which are archaeological units of internal homogeneity, limited in both time and space. In general, phases comprise the basic archaeological building blocks for regional synthesis.

Chapter 10

Middle-Range Research: Ethnoarchaeology and Experimental Archaeology

PREVIEW To this point, we have explored how archaeologists locate and excavate their sites, and some of the ways they construct cultural chronologies. All these activities fall into what we call low-level archaeological theory.

Now it is time to move up the theoretical scale a notch, to see how middle-range research is conducted in modern archaeology. We begin with a look at the various natural and cultural processes that combine to create the archaeological record. Low-level theory enabled us to generate data from the statics of this record. Now, using theory developed in middle-range research, we can begin to relate these data to past human behaviors. Here, we see how *ethnoarchaeologists* study the way modern behavior is translated into the archaeological record—among the !Kung of Botswana and the Nunamiut people in Alaska—and also how the garbage that each of us discards daily is being incorporated into the archaeological record of industrial North America. Each study contributes, in its own way, to our theoretical knowledge at the middle range.

There is another way to do this: by experimentally recreating the necessary conditions and looking for the linkage between systemic and archaeological context. Known as *experimental archaeology,* this research has the same middle-range objectives as ethnoarchaeology. But ethnoarchaeologists work within a functioning behavioral system—experimental archaeologists do their middle-range research through controlled and directed replication. Although sometimes involving newer, high-tech methods, experimental archaeology is not itself new; many of these questions have been around a long time, and so have experimental archaeologists.

Behavior is the first thing to go when you're dead.

LARRY MARTIN, PALEONTOLOGIST

Simply stated, the archaeological record is the contemporary evidence left from prehistoric or historic cultures. These are the static remains of past dynamic behavior. Both natural and cultural factors have impinged on these remains to such a degree that the archaeological record is rarely a direct reflection of past behavior. There are three key components to the archaeological record.

Michael Brian Schiffer in the Laboratory of Traditional Technology at the University of Arizona.

First, as we have already seen, *the archaeological record is a contemporary phenomenon.* Although the objects and their contexts might have existed for centuries or millennia, observations and knowledge about those objects and contexts remain as contemporary as the archaeologists who do the observing.

The second significant point is that although created through dynamic behavior, *the archaeological record itself is static, dead, lifeless, and noninformative.* Michael Schiffer of the University of Arizona has brilliantly clarified this critical realization. Schiffer began with the key distinction between *archaeological* and *systemic* contexts. The artifacts, features, and residues with which archaeologists deal once were part of an ongoing, dynamic behavioral system. Arrowheads were manufactured, used for specific tasks, often broken, sometimes repaired, and then lost or deliberately discarded. Potsherds were once part of whole pots, which were manufactured and decorated according to prescribed cultural criteria, used for utilitarian or ceremonial functions, and then either broken or deliberately discarded, perhaps as part of a rite or ritual. Food bones are the organic residues resulting from a succession of activities—hunting, butchering, cooking, and consuming. While these materials are being manufactured and used, they exist in their **systemic context.** These items are part of the actual behavioral system.

Systemic context: Cultural materials within an existing, ongoing behavioral system; they are being handled or at least observed by real, living people.

By the time such materials reach the archaeologist's hands, they have long ceased to participate in this behavioral system. The artifacts, features, and residues encountered by archaeologists were recovered from their **archaeological context**, interacting only with the natural environment. Although these natural conditions still remain dynamic and interactive, the cultural milieu has become static and noninteractive. It is common, of course, for items to move back and forth between contexts. During the archaeological

Archaeological context: Cultural materials that are no longer participating in a behavioral system; these artifacts, features, and residues exist only in the archaeological record.

excavation at Gatecliff Shelter, for instance, artifacts were removed from their archaeological contexts and placed into the systemic contexts of the 1970s. In effect, doing archaeology is part of today's systemic context.

Formation Processes That Create the Archaeological Record

Perhaps how it comes to be is really more distinctive than what it is.

ALFRED L. KROEBER (1876–1960), ANTHROPOLOGIST

To this point, we have perceived the archaeological record as contemporary, yet static and distinct from the behavioral processes that produced it. Our definition of the archaeological record contains a third key attribute: *Because of a variety of intervening factors, both natural and cultural, this record is not usually a direct reflection of past behavior.*

These "intervening factors" are what condition the archaeological record as we know it today. Before archaeologists can meaningfully encounter the archaeological record, they must grasp the important transformations that wrenched the objects, features, and residues from their behavioral interactions and deposited them into the static record we encounter today. Once again, we are indebted to Michael Schiffer for defining an appropriate framework for understanding the transformational processes, both cultural and noncultural, that create the archaeological record.

Schiffer has defined cultural processes as those "processes of human behavior that affect or transform artifacts after their initial period of use in a given activity." For our purposes, it is sufficient to distinguish among four distinctive cultural transformations that directly influence the creation of archaeological sites: deposition, reclamation, disturbance, and reuse.

Depositional Processes

Depositional process: The transformation of materials from a systemic to an archaeological context. Such processes are directly responsible for the accumulation of archaeological sites, and they constitute the dominant factor in forming the archaeological record.

Cultural deposition transforms materials from a systemic to an archaeological context. In contrast, **depositional processes** are the operations directly responsible for the accumulation of archaeological sites.

Cultural deposition processes are relatively easy to study, and they constitute the dominant factor in forming the archaeological record. For example, when a pottery vessel is broken and discarded on the trash heap, it has ceased to function in the behavioral system and becomes incorporated in its new archaeological context: This is cultural deposition. Similarly, when an individual dies and is buried, the physical being has been transformed from a systemic to an archaeological context.

Depositional processes need not involve deliberate discard or ritual; one major depositional process is the simple loss of still useful artifacts. In this case, the transformation from systemic to archaeological context is accidental, involving artifacts that are still capable of performing tasks in the behavioral system. Archaeologists are generally quite familiar with cultural deposition processes because such processes are directly relevant to conventional archaeological interpretation. In Chapter 8, we mentioned the law of superposition, the most general statement governing depositional processes in archaeology.

Other principles governing cultural deposition are more complex. Size, for instance, has been found to have a major influence on the way items are deposited in the archaeological record. One study of discard behavior was conducted on the campus of the University of Arizona. Small items (those less than 4 inches in overall dimensions) had been discarded almost independently of the location of trash cans, but larger items almost always found their way into trash cans when they were available. A number of specific "transforms" can be related to the deposition of faunal materials, artifacts, and ecofacts.

Reclamation Processes

Somewhat more elusive is the **reclamation process.** As the name indicates, this is the transition of cultural materials from the archaeological back into the systemic context. It is not uncommon to find evidence that archaeological artifacts have been scavenged for reuse by both nonindustrial and industrial peoples. Whenever a discarded projectile point is resharpened, a potsherd picked up and used to scrape hides, or an old brick reused in a new fireplace, reclamation has occurred. The act of archaeological excavation is itself reclamation: Artifacts are removed from their archaeological contexts and integrated into the functioning behavioral system of the archaeological profession. A common and recurring problem when dealing with surface sites is to recognize and account for previous collecting on that site.

Reclamation process: The transition of cultural materials from the archaeological record back into the systemic context, such as the scavenging of archaeological artifacts for reuse by both nonindustrial and industrial peoples. The act of archaeological excavation is itself reclamation.

We know, for instance, that when people collect artifacts from the surface of a site, the larger, more complete artifacts generally are the first to be picked up. If either scientific collection or unethical "pothunting" continue, the remaining complete artifacts will be removed, along with the smaller, harder-to-find ones. After sufficient collecting pressure, all that is left is a scatter of barely recognizable bits and pieces. Archaeologists oblivious to the ongoing reclamation processes would probably produce differing (systemic) interpretations for the same site, depending on the stage of previous collecting at which they encounter the site. Unlike cultural deposition, reclamation has received relatively little attention from archaeologists until very recently.

Disturbance Processes

The first two cultural formation processes pertain to the transference of materials *between* archaeological and systemic contexts. But the archaeological record is also heavily conditioned by transformations *within* the archaeological and systemic contexts. Disturbance changes the contexts of materials within the archaeological site itself. Examples include such diverse cultural mechanisms as dam building, farming, and heavy construction. Although the **disturbance process** has few direct implications for systemic contexts, the modification (and, indeed, preservation) of archaeological sites is a major and pressing problem facing modern archaeology.

Disturbance process: Changing the contexts of materials within the archaeological site itself.

Reuse Processes

The final relevant cultural mechanism is reuse, or the transformation of materials through successive states in the behavioral system. The **reuse process**

Reuse process: The transformation of materials through successive states within the behavioral system.

moves a single object through a series of different behavioral settings. Potsherds, for example, are sometimes ground up to be used as temper in manufacturing new vessels, and broken arrowheads are rechipped into drills and scrapers.

A host of noncultural formation processes also influences the archaeological record. The natural environment affects cultural materials, in both systemic and archaeological contexts: microscopic and mechanical decay; churning by rodents and earthworms; geological events such as volcanic eruptions, earthquakes, and flash floods.

A complex suite of natural and cultural transformations interact to create each unique archaeological site, and they must be recognized in order to project contemporary meaning onto our observations of the past. So viewed, the archaeological record is a "distorted" reflection of the structure of past cultural systems. These distortions occur as the result of both cultural and noncultural processes, and the regularities in such processes are of major concern to contemporary scholars studying the archaeological record.

Throughout the rest of this chapter, we shall see how (and why) archaeologists are conducting "actualistic" studies to learn more about the systemic contexts in which the archaeological record is initially formed. From conducting fieldwork among native people to digging up their own garbage, these archaeologists are trying to define the dynamics that link behavior to the static archaeological record.

Middle-Range Research: What Is It?

Remember from Chapter 3 that archaeologists employ *theory* at three basic levels. *Low-level theories* are the observations that emerge from basic archaeological fieldwork, the actual "data" or "facts" of archaeology. In the preceding few chapters, we have seen how these data are generated.

At the opposite end of the theoretical spectrum is *high-level* (or *general*) *theory,* the broad, overarching research strategies that condition archaeological theory. The research strategy of cultural materialism, for instance, informs what has become the *processual agenda* for doing Americanist archaeology. An alternative viewpoint, the *postprocessual critique,* arose from the general postmodern interpretivist research strategy. As we will see, processual and postprocessual viewpoints differ sharply in how they approach and interpret the archaeological record. Neither general perspective is either right or wrong. They are simply contrasting ways of viewing the world.

Middle-range research: Investigation aimed at linking the static data from the archaeological record with the dynamic processes that formed it.

Here, we see how the high- and low-level theoretical extremes are brought together. By conducting so-called **middle-range research,** archaeologists are generating the knowledge necessary to relate the world of archaeological facts to the world of general behavioral theory. We shall consider several ways to do this, using ethnoarchaeology, experimental archaeology, and the heralded "Garbage Project" as examples of how archaeologists study the processes of site formation.

Before doing this, however, we will look more closely at why theory at the middle range is necessary. Why, after all, is it so difficult to match the archaeological facts with the behaviors that produced it? This is archaeology's so-called linkage problem.

The Linkage Problem

Facts never speak for themselves; facts are known, and the mission of science is to use these facts to generate universal statements called *theories.* In reality, the facts of archaeology are contemporary observations made on the material remains of the past. Archaeology requires external input from today's behavioral world in order to bridge the gap between these contemporary observations and past behavior.

Geologists face a similar problem. The geological record, like that of archaeology, consists of only two things: the objects and the relationships among them. A "geological fact" is an observation made by a contemporary geologist on objects from the geological record. Since rocks do not speak, how do geologists advance from their contemporary observations to meaningful pronouncements about the remote geological past? This obstacle was addressed long ago by pioneering geologists. The modern science of geology is said to have begun largely through the efforts of James Hutton. An eighteenth-century medical doctor and gentleman farmer, Hutton formulated a simple principle that provided the very cornerstone of modern geology. Hutton's principle, called the **doctrine of uniformitarianism**, asserts that the processes now operating to modify the earth's surface are the same ones that operated long ago in the geological past. It is that simple: *The geological processes of the past and the present are assumed to be identical.*

Doctrine of uniformitarianism: The principle asserting that the processes now operating to modify the earth's surface are the same processes that operated long ago in the geological past.

We know from modern experiments that as today's glaciers move, they deposit distinctive glacial debris, often in distinctive formations (called **moraines**). Thorough study of modern glaciers has convinced geologists that moraines and striations are formed only through glacial action.

Moraine: An accumulation of earth and rocks carried and finally deposited by a glacier.

Suppose a geologist finds moraines and striated rocks in Ohio, California, or New Mexico, where no glaciers exist today. Armed with a knowledge of contemporary glacial processes, the geologist can readily frame and test hypotheses explaining ancient glacial action. This is an important point: *Observation of contemporary, ongoing processes provides the bridging arguments (or linkages) necessary to assign meaning to the geological objects of the past.*

Precisely the same logical stricture applies to archaeology. Archaeologists recover the material remains of past cultural processes. Like geologists, archaeologists can frame hypotheses that account for the formation and deposition of these physical remains. Input from contemporary anthropological observation supplies the bridging arguments necessary to translate general hypotheses into specific, observable outcomes that can be expected to appear in the archaeological record. Anthropology allows archaeologists to bridge this important gap between contemporary observation and relevant statements about past behavior. This is what *ethnoarchaeology* is all about.

Some Bones of Contention

Let me illustrate this relationship more fully with an example. As we shall discuss in Chapter 11, archaeologists often study the abundance and distribution

Ethnoarchaeology on the Internet:

Ethnoarchaeology Bibliography has been compiled by Nicholas David of the University of Calgary: http://www.ucalgary.ca/UofC/faculties/SS/ARKY/nicintro.html

ArchNet—Ethnoarchaeology: http://spirit.lib.uconn.edu/ArchNet

of animal bones to learn about past diets, hunting practices, how animals were domesticated, how animals were butchered, the season in which the hunt or harvest was conducted, and a host of other related issues. This is called **faunal analysis.**

Faunal analysis: The study of animal remains from archaeological sites to illustrate past hunting and dietary practices.

Most of these faunal studies begin with a consideration of the relative frequencies of various animal bones in archaeological sites. When analyzing the bones from Suberde, a seventh-millennium B.C. Neolithic village in Turkey, Dexter Perkins and Patricia Daly observed that the upper limb bones of wild oxen were usually missing. These static facts—contemporary observations—were then interpreted in terms of past human behavior. In this case, the investigators suggested that the relative frequencies of the bones resulted from the way in which the oxen had been butchered: The animals must first have been skinned; then the meat was stripped from the forequarters and hindquarters, and the upper limb bones thrown away. The investigators presumed that the meat was piled on the skin and the lower limb bones were used to drag the hide bearing the meat back home. Calling this the *schlepp effect,* they believed their interpretation explained why the upper limb bones were left at the kill site and the lower limb bones were discarded at the habitation site.

R. E. Chaplin analyzed the bones recovered from a late-ninth-century A.D. Saxon farm in the Whitehall area of London. The facts in this case also suggested a shortage of limb bones, and Chaplin suggested that the limb bones of sheep and cattle disappeared because the carcasses were dressed and exported to market. Chaplin then hypothesized about the marketing and animal husbandry strategies implied by such trade.

Investigators working on American Plains Indian sites also discovered that the upper limb bones of food animals were often missing. When Theodore White analyzed these facts, he decided that the bones must have been destroyed during the manufacture of bone grease from the marrow.

I could cite other examples, but the point is clear. Exactly the same archaeological fact—that habitation sites contain more lower limb bones than upper limb bones—has been construed in three different ways:

1. *Perkins and Daly:* Upper limbs were discarded at the kill site, and lower limbs were hauled with the meat back to the campsite.
2. *Chaplin:* Upper limb bones were selectively butchered and traded to market.
3. *White:* Upper limb bones were pulverized into bone grease and hence destroyed at the campsite.

The relative frequencies of animal bones comprise some real data—these observations are the "facts" of archaeology. But they have been read differently by three teams of archaeologists, each interpretation suggesting dissimilar behaviors that allegedly created these same facts. Which (if any) interpretation is correct?

Here is a problem archaeologists face daily: three competing hypotheses to account for the same body of facts (namely, that lower limb bones were more common than upper limb bones). The initial hypothesis holds that the animals had been butchered away from the habitation area and that some bones were discarded at the butchering locale while others were carried to camp with the meat. Let us term this perfectly reasonable first suggestion H^1. A second hypothesis, H^2, postulates that after butchering, the choice cuts were traded away, which is why the upper limb bones were rarely found at the habitation site. A third proposal, H^3, hypothesizes that the larger bones had been ground into bone grease, thereby increasing the relative frequency of the smaller elements in the archaeological record.

Dozens of additional hypotheses could be framed to explain why upper limb bones were less common than the lower limbs and feet. Perhaps some bones were venerated in a shrine away from the habitation area. Or maybe the larger bones were made into awls and bone pins. Or possibly the largest bones were used as clubs. At this point in the scientific process, one is perfectly justified in using imagination (and genius, if available) to generate worthwhile hypotheses. No rules govern how to get a good idea.

Scientific protocol, however, does stipulate how to select among the competing hypotheses. Let us restrict our attention to the three numbered hypotheses (H^1, H^2, and H^3). Each one is a generalized statement about human behavior. A contemporary archaeologist can never hope to observe somebody butchering a Neolithic wild ox. None of us will ever observe firsthand the making of bone grease by a nineteenth-century American Plains Indian. Those opportunities are gone. Instead, archaeologists must concentrate on finding the material consequences of activities like butchering Neolithic oxen or making bison bone grease.

We do this by constructing a series of logical *if . . . then* statements: If bone grease were manufactured from bison bones, then we should find artifacts X, Y, and Z and physical residues M, N, and O; bones should be distributed in patterns C, D, and E; and specific bone elements (J, K, and L) should be missing. Similarly, to test H^2, we must generate some *if . . . then* statements regarding the trading of meat and bones. We need answers to some very specific questions: Which are the best cuts to trade? How far can meat be transported to be traded before it spoils? Is meat marketed only in the winter months? Are carcasses butchered in special ways so that certain cuts can be traded? Once defined, *if . . . then* statements become bridging arguments that translate general, untestable hypotheses into specific expectations that can be tested using archaeological evidence.

But–I hope you are wondering–how do we know these things? Why do archaeologists surmise that making bone grease requires artifacts X, Y, and Z? And how do we know which bone elements are destroyed in the process? *Hypothesis testing is only as robust as these if . . . then bridging arguments.* If we generate incorrect implications, then our hypothesis testing will be worse than useless, because it will lead us to specious conclusions.

Here is where the notion of *middle-range research* comes into play. Because the facts are incapable of speaking for themselves, archaeologists must provide firm **bridging arguments** to breathe behavioral life into the objects of the past. In an analogy between archaeology and geology, I cited the doctrine of

Bridging argument: Logical statements linking the static archaeological record to the past dynamics that produced it; *middle-range research,* using contemporary observations—mainly through ethnoarchaeology and experimental archaeology—is generally required to define these linkages.

Lewis Binford inspecting an abandoned aborigine camp near MacDonald Downs Homestead, Australia. James O'Connell took this picture as part of his long-term ethnoarchaeological research among Alyawara-speaking aborigines. The melons scattered about are the kind formerly cultivated here when the site was occupied.

uniformitarianism: The processes that now operate to modify the earth's surface are the same processes that operated in the geological past. Precisely the same issues face contemporary archaeologists when they attempt to interpret the material remains of past cultural processes. Archaeologists also must frame hypotheses to account for the formation and deposition of these physical remains and so require bridging arguments to translate the general hypotheses into specific outcomes that can actually be observed in the archaeological record.

Properly formulated, middle-range research links our ideas about the world to the world itself, and attributes meaning to our empirical observations. Middle-range research dictates the way that we perceive the past and is quite different from the research used to explain that past. In this case, defining middle-range relationships requires that we also define the precise relationships between concepts and an appropriate class of empirically observable phenomena. Such a linkage has been extremely important to both past and contemporary Americanist archaeology.

Middle-range linkage has been an important aspect of archaeological inquiry for more than a century. Lewis Binford's call for middle-range studies served largely to focus this research, and even critics of the new archaeology recognized the importance of middle-range research.

Archaeologists interested in learning about middle-range theory cannot restrict their attention to the past. In order to define relevant bridging arguments, archaeologists must observe firsthand the workings of a culture in its systemic contexts, much as geologists defined their processes through contemporary observation. This is why they are turning to living peoples for clues to the interpretation of prehistoric remains. Although people are never considered as data, the insights gained by participation in a functioning society have opened the eyes of modern archaeologists.

In all such research, it is necessary to look around and select the closest available analogies for study. Geologists interested in glacial processes cannot today study firsthand the massive continental glaciers that once draped the North American continent, but they can examine the numerous mountain glaciers that occur at the highest altitudes and the higher latitudes.

Archaeologists are now doing similar things, studying closely the possible analogies in order to understand the processes that condition the archaeological record. Sometimes, it is possible to reconstruct such con-

Middle-Range Research and the Lipschitz

It would be easy to assume, mistakenly, that middle-range research would eventually evolve into a grand edifice, erected on lofty principles and generalizations. Actually, the most useful middle-range research turns out to be fairly prosaic in nature. After all, this research is merely a way of making sense out of empirical chaos, and as such it takes on a decidedly mundane cast.

Consider the case of Tel Yin'am, a late Roman–Byzantine site in Israel. The excavators, Harold Liebowitz and Robert Folk, came upon a paved surface of uniformly sized and closely fit basalt cobbles. Locally occurring basalt had been used in 99 percent of all construction at this site and has, in fact, been used for building throughout the eastern lower Galilee area for millennia.

The Tel Yin'am cobbles were slightly worn on the upper surfaces, but nobody had any idea what this wear patterning meant. Although the excavators could obtain endless empirical data from the paved floor cobbles, they lacked any way of assigning a behavioral meaning to these archaeological facts.

Not far away, in the modern kibbutz of Yavne-el, Moshe Lipschitz and his family have walked out of their front door and across the street for the past 18 years. This modern street is paved, like many in the area, with exactly the same kind of squared basalt cobbles that turned up in the Tel Yin'am excavations. Over nearly two decades the pavement in front of the Lipschitz house had begun to wear in some places but not in others.

This is when Moshe Lipschitz and his paved street became involved in middle-range research. Liebowitz and Folk studied the modern evidence and came up with an "official unit of scuffle," which they called a *Lipschitz*, defined as the wear produced by one family in two decades. One Lipschitz of wear produces distinctive rounded corners on basalt cobbles, with an apparent radius of curvature of about 2 meters.

In adopting the Lipschitz, the investigators cautioned that the constant works only on basalt pavements. Limestone, used occasionally for construction materials, wears more rapidly. There are also differential, but unknown, effects of abrasion caused by animal feet, naked human feet, moccasins, sandals, and leather shoes. Leibowitz and Folk note, wryly, that "this information awaits further research and volunteer scufflers with patience."

Once the Lipschitz had been established, the researchers returned to the archaeological pavement. Because the basalt cobbles at Tel Yin'am had only about one-half Lipschitz of wear, the excavators concluded that "the Tel Yin'am pavement was probably made for a private room; obviously it could not have been for a street or public building."

This little study illustrates how middle-range research can be derived to deal with the everyday empirical and definitional problems in archaeology. Middle-range theory is, after all, where you find it.

ditions experimentally (and we shall discuss several such experiments). In other cases, contemporary human societies can be found that continue to function under conditions that—in a limited way—are analogous to specific circumstances of the past. In *Middle-Range Research and the Lipschitz,* you will see how archaeologists working in Israel involved the inhabitants of the nearby kibbutz of Yavne-el in helping them build a body of locally relevant middle-range theory to interpret the Roman-Byzantine site of Tel Yin'am.

Ethnoarchaeologist James O'Connell leaving camp with a Hadza hunter on a morning foraging trip (dry season, 1986, in northern Tanzania). Conducting a "focal person follow," O'Connell will follow along and keep a record of what the hunter does, particularly how much time is spent acquiring food, kinds and amounts of food collected, and amounts consumed in the field and brought back to camp.

What Is Ethnoarchaeology?

Before the mid-1960s, archaeologists only rarely worked directly with informants (although plenty of them relied on data from ethnographers). Since that time, ethnoarchaeology has become fairly common. Archaeologists have come to realize the importance of establishing a relevant middle-range theory, and the study of living peoples is perhaps the best single way to do so. As archaeologists reached beyond mere chronology, they began to make assumptions about the behavior behind the static archaeological record. Increasingly, such critical assumptions were being tested through firsthand ethnoarchaeological research.

Ethnoarchaeology had a fairly modest beginning. Richard Gould, for instance, was trained as an archaeologist at the University of California and spent months living with the aborigines of Australia and the Tolowa people of northwestern California. Gould was observing the behavior behind the processes that form the archaeological record. Why, he would quiz his informants, are arrowheads made in a particular manner? How does one go about surviving in a harsh environment without benefit of agriculture or industry? Exactly who lives with whom, and what would these houses look like 100 (or 1,000) years from now?

Gould once asked some Tolowa to look at his ongoing archaeological excavations, hoping they could solve some of the puzzles he had encountered. Gould had begun digging under the then standard assumption that habitation areas are best located by looking for surface concentrations of artifacts and midden deposit. But despite repeated digging, he was unable to locate any prehistoric house remains on an otherwise promising site. Seeing his dilemma, the Tolowa informants were quite amused: "The old-timers never put their houses in the garbage dump. . . . They don't like to live in their garbage any more than you would." They pointed, instead, to a steep slope on the edge of the "site." Although this hillside had seemed to Gould an unlikely spot on which to construct a house, he followed their suggestion. After only 20 minutes of digging, he came upon a well-preserved redwood plank house buried only 18 inches below the surface. Gould's Tolowa informants grinned knowingly.

Such are the lessons of ethnoarchaeology.

Ethnoarchaeology: The study of contemporary peoples to determine how their behavior is translated into the archaeological record.

Do the !Kung Have Tool Kits?

One particularly beneficial aspect of middle-range research is that archaeologists are required to take a critical look at some of their baseline assumptions. One such case is the so-called *tool-kit* concept: Writing in the 1970s, archaeologist Robert Whallon wrote that "the aim of such analysis is generally to define 'tool kits,' or clusters of artifacts and other items which occur together on occupation floors as a consequence of having been used together in certain activities. It is hoped that inferences concerning patterns of prehistoric human activity can be made by interpreting these 'tool kits' in terms of their contexts and their position on the occupation floors."

Note the implicit bridging argument here that allows an inference about dynamics from the static archaeological remains: Under ideal conditions, tools found in spatial association on an occupation surface (archaeological context) reflect a single task (systemic context). In fairness, few archaeologists made the bald assumption that tool kits must *always* be found in spatially discrete concentrations (so-called *activity areas*). Most recognized that multiple factors could intervene between the behavioral and archaeological contexts. But if assemblages did turn up in spatially discrete areas at least some of the time, this pattern could be translated into meaningful statements about the behavior that produced the patterning.

It certainly sounds logical enough to infer that tools found together on a **living surface** must have been discarded from a single or a few related tasks. But how do we know this is necessarily so? Just because the bridging argument sounds plausible is insufficient reason. As Lewis Binford notes, "*Plausibility does not render the interpretation true or accurate;* it simply emphasizes the utility of investigating such possibilities."

Living surface: A generic and imprecise term applied to an assumed level of human occupation within an archaeological site; a handy term to use in the field but sometimes tricky to defend later.

Similar reasoning in geology would lead to the interpretation of morainal features as glacial deposits just because the explanation "sounds logical" or "seems plausible." Geologists certainly do not do this. They go out and investigate active glaciers to see whether or not they, in fact, produce moraines. And if so, exactly what do these moraines look like? In other words, geologists have for centuries realized the importance of relating the "facts" of the geological record to systemic, processual contexts. Archaeologists have only recently arrived at this point.

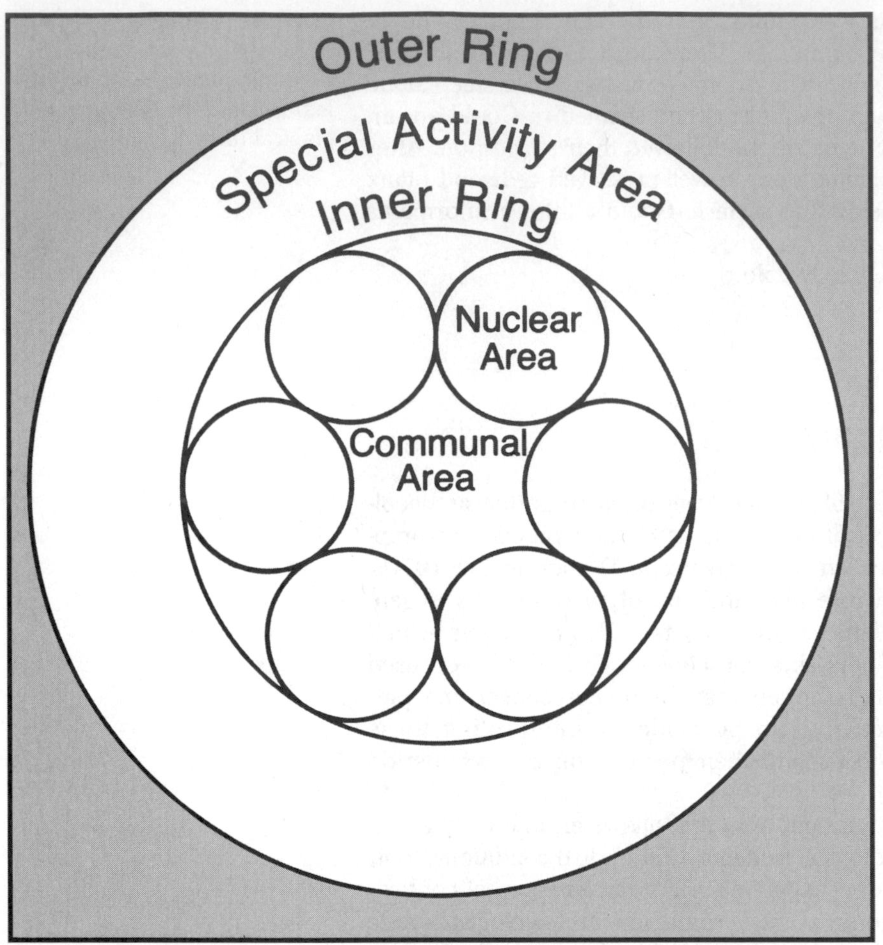

John Yellen's schematic representation of activity area patterning at a !Kung camp.

John Yellen is one who, in the 1970s, began to take a hard look at such "plausible" concepts and assumptions. Although trained at Harvard as an archaeologist, Yellen spent over 2 years in Botswana, studying the behavior and material culture of the !Kung Bushmen. Although he never became fluent in the language, he did learn enough !Kung so that he could dispense with an interpreter and conduct his own direct interviews. Yellen's goal was to draw plans of !Kung campsites in order to provide fundamental data to be used in middle-range theory formation. He was particularly concerned with recording how long each camp was occupied, exactly what activities occurred there, and how these activities were reflected in the archaeological record.

Yellen mapped 16 !Kung camps and was able to make some generalizations. The "typical" !Kung camp is circular in shape, with huts located along the circumference of the circle and entrances facing toward the center. The hut serves primarily as a place in which to store belongings; very few activities actually take place inside it. Only during rainstorms do people sleep in the huts at night. A hearth is located in front of each hut. It provides warmth in winter and a place to cook food and also serves as a focus for domestic activities. In all camps a characteristic amount of debris accumulates around each hearth, including vegetable remains (such as nut shells and fruit and melon skins), bone fragments, and waste products of manufacturing activities (such as bits of ostrich eggshell, bone, wood shavings, and fiber used for making string). A few fist-sized nut-cracking stones are the only items of value left at a campsite when it is abandoned. The most important tools in the !Kung tool kit—iron knives, axes, and adzes—are never left behind, and Yellen found only one such lost tool in over 2 years of research.

!Kung camps are divided into public and private areas. The public portion includes both the center of the camp circle and the space outside it. The primary, or family, area consists of the hearth, the hut, and the space immediately surrounding it. To an individual, space within a !Kung campsite is thus divided into three parts: the area belonging to one's own family, similar spaces belonging to other families, and the communal area shared by all.

These 16 campsites formed a database for Yellen to examine the concept of the tool kit. He was impressed with the number of disruptive factors that conspired to mix and jumble the archaeological context of these sites. The exact area being utilized depends on a number of changing factors, such as the continually shifting pattern of sun and shadow. The huts themselves provide some shade, and in some camps, the charcoal and nut scatters tend to lie to the east and north of the huts, where shade is generally available. In other camps it is more convenient to use the shade provided by trees and shrubs. Thus, the same general areas used for skin drying and the roasting of animal heads are also occupied to take advantage of shade. Children run and play continually, scattering and discarding debris. Some adults maintain their own huts and hearths, but they are dependent largely on others for food. At these huts, occupational debris is either scanty or absent.

Nevertheless, a certain pattern of occupation does emerge for all !Kung camps. Activities do not occur at random, and the by-products of such cultural activities do indeed tend to cluster across the camp spaces. Yellen defines four basic activity areas. The *communal activity area* is characterized by an absence of evidence: Debris never accumulates in this central area. The *nuclear activity area* includes the hut, the hearth, and associated debris; this is the site of most domestic activities. Outside the hut circle one finds a *shade area* and a *special-use area* for drying skins and so on.

What does this evidence tell us about tool kits? Yellen finds little support for the common assumption that artifacts found in similar archaeological contexts must have been involved in similar systemic contexts. The debris from subsistence activities (cooking and preparing vegetable foods) is found scattered about with debris resulting from manufacturing activities, such as making ostrich eggshell beads or poison arrows. There is no spatial separation in the archaeological record because there is no spatial separation in the systemic context. Similarly, the debris from a single activity, such as cracking nuts, can be found in several different places in the !Kung camp. Nuts are usually cracked in the nuclear family context, but people also crack nuts in the shady area outside the hut circle.

Research such as Yellen's early work among the !Kung points up many fallacies in archaeological interpretation, and his notions of camp patterning among the !Kung have been amplified and refined by parallel studies among similar groups elsewhere in the world (in Chapter 14, we shall examine the tool kit and activity area correlates in much greater detail).

Lewis Binford Takes Off for Points North

Ethnoarchaeological inquiry such as this provides the arguments necessary to bridge the gap between observable archaeological contexts and nonobservable systemic contexts. These propositions, by their nature, will apply to systemic contexts both present and past. Ethnoarchaeology is based on the premise that if generalizations cannot cover the contemporary contexts, they cannot be viewed as adequate (see *Why I Began Doing Ethnoarchaeology* by Lewis R. Binford).

IN HIS OWN WORDS

Why I Began Doing Ethnoarchaeology by Lewis R. Binford

In 1967 I received funds to go to Europe for a year to work more closely with François Bordes in Bordeaux. My program for research was the following. If we could not study the chipped stone directly, perhaps we could study faunal remains and the horizontal distributions, on excavated archaeological floors, of both fauna and chipped stone. Then it might be possible to relate variability in the lithics to these other properties of the archaeological sites in question. I worked for a year in France, identifying and plotting all the stone tools and animal bones by anatomical part and by breakage pattern.

Then began the first of a whole series of disillusionments. I performed one correlation study after another—so many, in fact, that I needed a great steel trunk in order to carry all the papers back to the United States. I could tell you cross-correlations between any pair of Mousterian tool-types, between tools and bones, between bones and the drip-lines in cave sites, between almost any type of data you care to name. What I found, of course, was many new facts that nobody had seen before. But none of these new facts spoke for themselves.

My metal trunk was so big and heavy that I decided to return home by boat and that 5-day trip from Le Havre to New York gave me an opportunity for some disconsolate self-reflection. The whole project was obviously a total failure. What had I done wrong? What had I not done that I should have done? Could it really be that archaeologists simply cannot learn anything about the past? Where was I missing the real problem?

By the time we steamed into New York City, just before the New Year of 1969, some of the answers to these problems were suggested, at least in my thoughts. I prepared a research proposal to go to the Arctic in the spring of 1969 to live with a group of Eskimo hunters. My reasons for going there were little more specific at that stage than that it could hardly fail to be a good educational experience. If I was ever to be able to make accurate inferences from archaeological facts, I was convinced that I had to understand the dynamics of living systems and study their static consequences.

Mousterian: A culture from the Middle Paleolithic ("Middle Old Stone Age") period that appeared throughout Europe between about 180,000 and 30,000 years ago (named after the Le Moustier rock shelter in southwestern France). Mousterian artifacts are frequently associated with Neanderthal human remains.

Lewis Binford conducted significant ethnoarchaeological research in the 1970s among the Nunamiut people of Alaska. These people were particularly appropriate to Binford's interest because he had studied reindeer bones on **Mousterian** sites in France and wanted a chance to work with people still hunting reindeer. The Arctic environment was also somewhat similar to the Middle Paleolithic French occupation sites he had studied. But Binford emphasized that "the focus on fauna and my study of the Nunamiut were not research choices made because of an abiding interest in either fauna or Eskimos. My primary interest was in evaluating the utility of certain concepts commonly employed by the archaeologist."

Binford accompanied the Nunamiut hunters on practically all the various kinds of hunting they practice today. He was concerned with recording what the hunters did at each locality and what debris would be left for the archaeologist. Binford was struck by the general lack of correlation between observed activities and the artifacts that were deposited in the archaeological record. He characterized the Nunamiut technology as "almost exclusively curated," meaning that artifacts are reused and transported so much that they are rarely deposited (lost) in contexts that reflect their actual manufacture and use. One problem for archaeologists is that localities that are demonstrably different in behavioral (systemic) terms produce archaeological sites that are almost identical. Differentiation among activities is possible only by means of artifacts, which are very rare and nearly always broken and heavily modified through use. The more that artifacts are curated, preserved, and transported, the less correspondence there will be between the systemic and archaeological contexts of given sites.

Since then, Binford has expanded his ethnoarchaeological fieldwork across three continents. In Australia, he joined O'Connell to study site structure and butchering patterns among the Alyawara Aborigines. He traveled to South Africa to observe firsthand the effect of hyenas and other scavengers on bone assemblages. Binford also returned several times to the Nunamiut, mapping, collecting, and observing the linkages between modern behavior and the archaeological record it creates.

The Garbage Project: The Archaeology of Yesterday's Lunch

Wait a thousand years and even the garbage left behind by a vanished civilization becomes precious to us.

Isaac Asimov (1920–1992), writer

Why wait a thousand years?

William L. Rathje, archaeologist (University of Arizona)

Another example of ethnoarchaeological research is the self-declared Garbage Project. Emil Haury was the senior archaeologist at the University of Arizona for decades. A specialist in Southwestern prehistory, Haury continually taught his students that "if you want to know what is really going on in a community, look at its garbage."

Haury's earthy advice was not lost on his students and colleagues. In 1971 the University of Arizona launched a long-term, in-depth study of just that—garbage. But it must have surprised Haury when he found out which community the Garbage Project decided to study; they were after the garbage of contemporary Tucson.

The Garbage Project was begun by William Rathje, a Harvard-trained archaeologist who had previously specialized in the Classic Maya. Through the Garbage Project, Rathje (now a professor at the University of Arizona) was attempting to apply archaeological methods to the analysis and description of modern societies. Rathje objects to the traditional injunction in archaeology that the lifeways being reconstructed must be extinct. He contends that we still have a great deal to learn about contemporary

Ethnoarchaeologist William Rathje, director of the Garbage Project, with a fresh array of modern artifacts.

Studying garbage, I've learned this about human nature: What we say and what we do are two different things. I could tell you stories . . .

William L. Rathje

lifeways and that a century of archaeological experience with material culture should be brought to bear on relevant issues of modern society.

The Garbage Project has several fundamental goals, each of which we can examine in some detail.

Quantifying Today's Material Record

The archaeology of contemporary society began as a rather bizarre concept, but a considerable amount of such ethnoarchaeological research has been conducted over the past 25 years. Rathje was dissatisfied with available research techniques for dealing with contemporary society, particularly the dependence on interviews and questionnaires. He saw the very act of conducting an interview and administering a questionnaire as a foreign element intruding into the social setting under study. Respondents are continually aware of their status as subjects, and the questions themselves can act as agents of change and bias. Sociology and psychology have become largely the science of administering questionnaires and interviewing informants. Nothing in the training of sociologists or psychologists equips them to deal with actual physical evidence. This is sometimes a problem in traditional ethnography as well.

Archaeologists, of course, have been dealing with mute material evidence for over a century. But why restrict ourselves to behaviors that have become extinct? For over two decades, Rathje has searched for ways to apply established archaeological methods and theory to the analysis of contemporary behavior.

The key term here is *nonreactive.* Whereas conventional questionnaires condition the nature of the response, material culture is static and relatively easy to quantify. Garbage is garbage, discarded without the knowledge that some archaeologist is going to be sorting through it—this is what is meant by *nonreactive.*

Garbage Project archaeologists at the sorting table.

Rathje's ongoing Garbage Project began with a focus on Tucson, an urban community with a population of slightly over 360,000. A strict sampling design ensured the proper correlation with relevant socioeconomic variables. Garbage was picked up from randomly selected households. Nearly 1,000 student volunteers from the University of Arizona sorted the garbage on special sorting tables provided by the sanitation department's maintenance yard

What Garbage Says About Us

As an applied anthropologist, Rathje is always on the lookout to find what the material evidence tells us about ourselves. "Show me a neighborhood's discarded hazardous wastes, and I can tell you its income range."

- Used motor oil, degreasers, and fuel additives (evidence of home car care indicates a lower-income group)
- Lots of wasted paint, stains, and varnishes ("fixer-upper" evidence suggests a middle-income group)
- Leftover pesticides, herbicides, and fertilizers (lots of lawn-care items usually reflects an upper-income group)

in Tucson. As with all archaeological fieldwork, the student workers were required to take the appropriate inoculations, and were given appropriate field equipment, in this case, laboratory coats, surgical masks, and gloves. Students sorted garbage items into about 150 categories under the larger headings of food, drugs, sanitation products, amusement and educational items, communication, and pet-related products. The data were then recorded on forms for computer processing. The standard principles of archaeological classification provided objective, repeatable categories of data retrieval. The Garbage Project has now involved hundreds of students and 60 organizations, recording more than 2 million items from 15,000 household refuse samples. The initial Tucson project has operated continually since 1973, and satellite projects have been launched throughout North America.

University of Arizona archaeologists are hardly the first to snoop in somebody else's garbage can. The most sensational garbage probe occurred some years ago, when A. J. Weberman—a self-proclaimed "garbage guerrilla"—investigated the private lives of celebrities as reflected in their garbage. In one sense, Weberman was following up the same discrepancy that bothered the sociologists—that people say one thing yet often do another. Pop singer Bob Dylan, for instance, proclaimed benign disinterest in popular fan magazines, boasting that he never read what they wrote about him. But when Weberman ransacked Dylan's New York garbage pail, "the many rock magazines wasted Bob's claim that he didn't follow the rock scene."

Dylan, of course, was outraged and reportedly directed his housekeeper henceforth to deliver his trash directly to the sanitation workers. Weberman conducted similar garbage exposés on other celebrities such as boxer Muhammad Ali, playwright Neil Simon, and the late yippie Abbie Hoffman. Rathje terms such tactics "a rip-off, a threat to the conduct of garbage research as a means of quantifying the resource management strategies of population segments."

To combat the adverse publicity that resulted from the Bob Dylan and Muhammad Ali cases, the Garbage Project instituted elaborate safeguards in their collection procedure so as to ensure the complete anonymity of particular individuals and households. The sample garbage is collected by the sanitation department foremen, who are not present when the bags are opened and are denied access to the Garbage Project data. Personal data such as names, addresses, photographs, or financial statements are never recorded and are not analyzed. The Garbage Project field director and/or one senior Garbage Project field supervisor are always present during analysis to ensure that no personal items are examined or saved. Participating students are required to sign pledges against even looking at such personal items. No garbage of any kind is saved; all aluminum is recycled, and the rest of the garbage is sent to sanitary landfills.

Building a Practical Theory of Household Resource Management

The Garbage Project has used its accumulated data to study a number of contemporary social issues, one of them being the rate of alcohol consumption. Years ago, the Pima County Health Department conducted interviews with 1 percent of the households in the city of Tucson. Questions were phrased like this: "On the average, how many cans or bottles of beer does ______ have in a usual week?" The sample was carefully chosen using conventional sociological procedures, and informant anonymity was assured. The health department then published its findings, which were taken by many as an accurate indication of the rate of alcohol consumption in Tucson.

How did the questionnaires stack up against the material evidence? Rathje's garbage volunteers record the presence of beer bottles and cans as part of their routine sorting. They also note the kind and volume of the containers discarded and have even tried to monitor the amount of recycling of aluminum cans.

Rathje points out the discrepancy between front-door answers given to interviewers and back-door behavior as reflected by the actual contents of the trash. Garbage cans don't lie, and the differences from the health department questionnaire were striking. In one tract, only 15 percent of the respondent households admitted to consuming beer, and no household reported drinking more than eight cans in a week. But the Garbage Project data from that same area showed that over 80 percent of the households had beer containers in their garbage pails and that fully 54 percent discarded more than eight cans each week. In fact, these households averaged about two and one-half six-packs each week. Although the details varied among the sampling tracts, the patterning was always the same: significantly heavier beer consumption—in the form of more drinkers and higher rates of drinking—than was reported to the interviewers.

That the interview data are distorted should astound nobody. People simply drink more beer than they own up to. But the degree of distortion is noteworthy, and the analysis of the material remains even provides future interviewers with a means for correcting this inevitable bias. The skewing, it turns out, is also correlated with socioeconomic factors. The low-income Mexican American households typically distorted their interviews by reporting no beer consumption at all. By contrast, although the middle-income Anglo respondents admitted to limited beer consumption, they significantly underreported the amount of beer they actually consumed. These preliminary findings point up future directions not only for garbage research but also for the administration of health questionnaires.

Linking Past to Present

Because we know so little about our own food, we waste it without much thought.

WILLIAM L. RATHJE

The Garbage Project also attempts to compare modern food discard behavior with past trends. Researchers give American householders mixed reviews. On the one hand, the actual waste of food has declined through time. During World War I, the War Food Administration collected large-scale food discard data for United States households (one of the few known precursors to Rathje's Garbage Project). In 1918, households discarded between 25 percent and 30 percent of the total amount of solid food acquired. This compares with only 10 percent to 15 percent food waste in Tucson during the period of the Garbage Project (which may, or may not, represent trends for the entire United States). The decrease in waste is probably linked to increasingly available technology for processing, packaging, storing, and transporting of foods. But although this represents a significant improvement, Rathje points out that it was achieved in a typically American way: by turning to technology to solve our problems.

The Garbage Project data also disclose some surprises about the effectiveness of modern recycling campaigns. The advertising media have given great coverage to campaigns by beverage companies and aluminum factories to recycle aluminum cans; Boy Scouts sponsor newspaper drives to raise money and to save trees; and more Christmas cards are printed on recycled paper each year.

As Rathje puts it, "We think of ourselves today as ardent recyclers." But the facts are otherwise. In 1975, the households of Tucson recycled only 19 percent of all wood fiber; this figure stands in marked contrast to the 35 percent national average that was recycled during World War II. Similarly, studies in a mid-1800s trash deposit in Magdelena, Mexico, show that only broken bottles were discarded, and these had apparently been reused extensively before breakage. In the 1970s, the average Tucson household discarded about 500 whole bottles each year; of these, over 10 percent were made of returnable glass and could have—ideally—been used up to 40 times had they been returned.

Want some more examples of waste?

- Health-conscious America is eating less fat from red meat and slimming down to minimize risk of colon and breast cancer. To do this, people are buying fewer steaks, roasts, and chops (because you can *see* all the fat they contain!). What is bought instead? Mostly sausage, bologna, hot dogs, luncheon meat—products that contain even more fat. But because it's "invisible," it's OK, right?
- Because of a botulism scare, people threw away even slightly dented cans of food. The problem? Only an *expanded* can indicates danger from botulism.
- Garbage Project figures suggest that the citizens of Tucson, Arizona, daily discard $3,000 in coins. But before you quit your day job and

IN HIS OWN WORDS

Garbage and Our Future by William L. Rathje

I wonder sometimes how future generations will see us when they look at our garbage. I interpret the Classic period of the Maya civilization as one of profligate waste, followed by a period of decline. The Maya woke up and discovered resources were in short supply, and they became very efficient very fast—they recycled, they reused. But it was too late.

If we compare our garbage to theirs, I think we can see we're still in a classic phase; that is, we're still discarding tremendous amounts of valuable resources on a daily basis. We have an important opportunity today. We can go into a period of efficiency and pragmatism, and in that way sustain our society in the style to which we've become accustomed for a much longer time.

head for the landfill, remember that your daily haul in coins is embedded in 600 tons of garbage.

Today, any American family's garbage for only a few months would fill an entire room.

Looking at America's Landfills

Shortly after World War II, the "landfill" became the most popular way to dispose of refuse in the United States. Five decades later, more than 70 percent of our garbage—180 million tons annually—is tossed into the 5,500 active landfills across the country. Every man, woman, and child in the United States generates 4 pounds of trash a day—a staggering thought. For most of us, once this trash is dumped in a garbage can, it's gone, off to a landfill someplace. But our landfills are filling up, and the cost of dumping trash is skyrocketing. Little thought has been given to their long-term environmental and societal consequences. Our landfills are nearing full capacity, and few new ones are being approved.

America has precious little idea what's going on in her landfills and how to plan for the future. Our annual trash bill is about 15 billion dollars and rising. No wonder Rathje speaks of a "serious garbage problem." But all is not lost—archaeology to the rescue!

The Garbage Project devised a plan to employ systematic archaeological methods to explore a series of landfills across the United States. To date, the Garbage Project has completed excavations in 15 landfills from California to New York, from Toronto to Florida, recovering and analyzing about 12 metric tons of debris initially deposited between 1952 and 1989.

Perhaps the most impressive excavation took place at the Fresh Kills Landfill on Staten Island, New York City. First opened in 1948, it receives 17,000 tons of refuse daily. Today, the landfill occupies 2.4 billion cubic feet, covering 3,000 acres—25 times the size of the Great Pyramid at Giza. It is one of the largest human-made monuments in the world.

Rathje argues that "if we are making such a large contribution to future generations, we should know exactly what we are bequeathing them. The only way to unlock these entombed secrets is to excavate—with hands-on digging, sorting, analyzing, and even smelling."

How do you dig a landfill? Basically, the Garbage Project employs well-established archaeological methods. For one thing, the various "strata" can be chronologically ordered using newspapers and magazines. Season of deposition can be monitored, for instance, by the presence of pine needles and Santa Claus logos on packaging in "Christmastime" deposits. Telephone books are particularly good stratigraphic markers because everybody receives new ones at the same time and most toss out the old with the next day's garbage. The new findings suggest that decomposition proceeds more slowly than anticipated in recent landfills, suggesting that a revamping of our garbage priorities may be in order (see *Garbage and Our Future* by William L. Rathje).

Landfill exposures were made by backhoe trenches (up to 25 feet deep) and bucket-auger wells, reaching down 100 feet. With their hands-on, archaeological perspective on our trash, the Garbage Project personnel can calculate exactly what's going into America's landfills. When most people think of trash heaps, they think of plastic bags, plastic cups, and disposable plastic diapers. In fact, plastic is what Rathje calls "everybody's favorite villain. . . . We will believe anything bad about plastic." The Garbage Project excavations show that plastic might not be so bad after all. Surprisingly, our landfills contain relatively little plastic, only about 15 percent by volume.

The big culprit, it turns out, is *paper*—packaging, newspapers, telephone books, glossy magazines, and mail order catalogs. Paper takes up fully 40 to 50 percent of American landfills. Despite the growing commitment to local recyling programs, the amount of paper is steadily rising—up from only 35 percent in 1970. And, here's the really bad news: Contrary to popular opinion, paper doesn't biodegrade very well. The Garbage Project has found 40-year-old newspapers, still fully readable.

In fact, **biodegradation** is one of the biggest myths in the trash business. Our landfills are constructed, literally, in the belief that the nasty stuff inside will—sooner rather than later—simply decompose on its own, like some kind of monumental compost heap.

Biodegradation: Decomposition of trash through the action of microorganisms.

Wrong. Very little in our landfills is actually biodegrading. Backyard compost heaps work well, but only when we chop up the organics, add lots of fluids, and regularly churn the whole batch. This process does not happen in landfills: Nothing is chopped up, fluids are often prohibited, and landfill debris is compacted, not churned. The result is that our landfills are incredibly inefficient in terms of biodegradation. Organics will, to be sure, eventually break down, but this is a very, very slow process.

Want to know one of the most common foods preserved in landfills? Hot dogs—those preservatives really work! If you want a 20-year-old hot dog, Rathje's got one.

Most of our knowledge about solid waste disposal and landfill design comes from laboratory experiments, but the inside workings of landfills—what actually happens—have remained almost entirely unknown. Plenty of federal policies regulate landfills, but usually, government planners plan by making "logical assumptions" about what landfills "should" contain.

Rathje doesn't assume; he digs. If we are interested in finding sensible ways to dispose of our trash, doesn't it make sense for us to know *exactly* what is being thrown away? And he has learned that many of the long-held assumptions about America's garbage are just that—rubbish.

The Garbage Project: Neat, *but* Is It *Archaeology*?

The Garbage Project still receives somewhat mixed reviews from Americanist archaeologists. Although many applaud this endeavor as "building middle-range theory" and "constructing a science of material culture," others have expressed concern. Some worry that such nontraditional directions may sap the strength of Americanist archaeology. Others allow that whereas it is "oft-cited" and "innovative," they also ask, "Is it archaeology?"

Here's how the leaders of the Garbage Project recently answered their critics:

Those of us in the Garbage Project define archaeology as the study of the relation between human behavior, attitudes, and artifacts in all times and places. . . . We believe that our research is as much archaeology as the excavation of refuse middens piled up in ancient times in the Near East or during historic times in New England. We are aware, however, that some archaeologists believe that our data are not old enough or that our study of society is too technologically advanced for our research to be called main-stream archaeology. So be it. . . . [We are] content in the certain knowledge that in another 50 years the insides of the landfills we have excavated will meet everyone's criteria for an archaeological site.

Archaeologists have been studying the past for more than 100 years; the archaeology of contemporary landfills in differing sociocultural and physical settings has just started.

To make arrows properly one should smear his face with mud and sit out in the hot sun in a quiet secluded spot. The mud is a precaution against harm from flying chips of glass, possibly also a good luck ritual.

ISHI (CA. 1860–1916), YANA YAHI MAN

So there you have it. The Garbage Project is an important component of middle-range theory building in contemporary archaeology, highlighting the importance of applying archaeological methods to discern modern, ongoing trends. It is so radical that comparable data are almost nonexistent.

Like much of the research at the middle range, the Garbage Project has two basic goals. On the one hand, Rathje and his team are finding out how material remains relate to the behavior that produced them: This is a *methodological* objective. They are also attempting to find workable explanations of specific and recurrent patterns they observe in the archaeological record: This is a *substantive* objective.

Taken together, this is what middle-range research is all about: linking archaeological data with the relevant aspects of human behavior that produced it. Because the ethnoarchaeologists like Rathje work in contemporary society, they can observe this behavior, providing important analytical tools for use on more ancient trash deposits, where the human behavior vanished long ago (see *The Garbage Project: Neat, but Is It Archaeology?*).

Experimental Archaeology as Middle-Range Research

Experimental archaeology: A way to determine the archaeological correlates of ancient technology. Experimental archaeology is an important and popular method of building middle-range theory.

Another way to explore middle-range theory is through **experimental archaeology**, the origins of which can be traced to Saxton Pope, a surgeon at the University of California Medical Center (San Francisco). The poignant story began in 1911, when a beaten and defeated Indian, later named Ishi, was found crouching in a slaughterhouse corral near Oroville, California. His family either had been murdered or had starved, and Ishi himself had lost his will to live. The local sheriff locked him in the jail, as "wild" Indians were not allowed to roam about freely in those days. Through good fortune, Alfred Kroeber, a young anthropologist at the University of California, learned of Ishi's plight and arranged for his release. Kroeber brought Ishi to San Francisco and secured quarters for him in the university museum. From that time until Ishi's death in 1916, Kroeber and his staff taught Ishi the ways of "civilization," and the Indian revealed his secrets of survival in back-land California; clearly Ishi had more to offer.

Ishi soon developed a tubercular cough—which later cost him his life—and was treated daily by Dr. Pope. Over their short association, Pope and Ishi found common ground in their interest in archery. An odd combination: Pope, the urbane physician/scholar paired with the Yahi Indian, hair singed in tribal custom, together shooting arrows through the parks of downtown San Francisco. Pope was a good student, and, after Ishi's death, the doctor continued his research into the almost lost art of archery, studying bows and arrows preserved in museum collections and often test-shooting the ancient specimens.

Pope wrote *Hunting With the Bow and Arrow* in 1923, describing his experiments in archery. The book not only provided baseline information for interpreting ancient finds but also quickly became the bible of the bow-hunting fraternity. Apparently, as many sportsmen as archaeologists were intrigued by the fine points of this nearly extinct art. Now, of course, archery is big business. This is but a single example of how the techniques of a nearly lost survival art were salvaged by timely observation and experimentation.

Ishi (*ca.* 1860–1916), *Yana-Yahi man.*

Love is fleeting, but stone tools are forever.

T-SHIRT SLOGAN FROM THE THUNDERBIRD SITE (VIRGINIA)

Flake: A thin, sharp sliver of stone removed from a core during the knapping process.

Core: A piece of stone that is worked ("knapped"). Cores sometimes serve merely as sources for raw materials; they also can serve as functional tools.

Stone Tools: How Were They Made?

Unlike archery, many other prehistoric techniques died with their practitioners, and experimental archaeologists have been forced to rediscover the lost technology.

Making a stone tool is not easy. Appropriate raw materials—rocks such as flint, obsidian, and basalt—must be located, tested, and collected. Sometimes, it is necessary to heat-treat them to improve "flakability." Then a series of stone **flakes** are knocked off the **core** to create a shaped

"So what's this? I asked for a *hammer*! A hammer! *This* is a crescent wrench! ...Well, maybe it's a hammer. ... Damn these stone tools."

Lithic Technology on the Internet:

Lithic Resources on ArchNet provides catalogs, overviews, references:
http://spirit.lib.uconn.edu/ArchNet/Topical/Lithic/Lithic.html

The New Knappers Anonymous:
http://www.ucs.mun.ca/~t64tr/knap.html

Holland Comparative Lithic Laboratory at the Buffalo Museum of Science contains a variety of information about books, software reviews, and symposia:
http://wings.buffalo.edu/academic/department/anthroplogy/jwa/VIN2/jdhlab.ann.html

tool; sometimes, the already-sharp flakes can be used as tools. Anybody who thinks it's easy to make a stone tool should give it a try—it is not as easy as it might seem. Unfortunately, over the millennia, plenty has been forgotten about the detailed technology required to make good stone tools from a pile of rocks.

Fortunately, a school of dedicated experimentalists has spent years rediscovering some of the virtually extinct technology used to fabricate stone tools. The late Don Crabtree (affiliated with the Idaho State University Museum) began this research by undertaking a series of carefully documented studies to uncover the nature of prehistoric stoneworking. One of Crabtree's many projects was to rediscover the techniques once used to fabricate the *Folsom* spear points discovered at the Lindenmeier site in Colorado. Folsom points, some of the world's most exquisite stone artifacts, were originally made between 10,000 and 11,000 years ago by the **Folsom culture.** Mounted on spear shafts, these artifacts were used for hunting larger, now extinct forms of American bison. Although the spear points are only about 2 inches long, Crabtree counted over 150 minute sharpening flakes removed from their surface.

There are several ways to make a stone tool. The two top diagrams show hand-held techniques of stone-on-stone percussion. At the lower left, an anvil is employed to steady the working surface for added control in flake removal. At the lower right, a bone (or antler) tool is used to remove flakes by direct pressure.

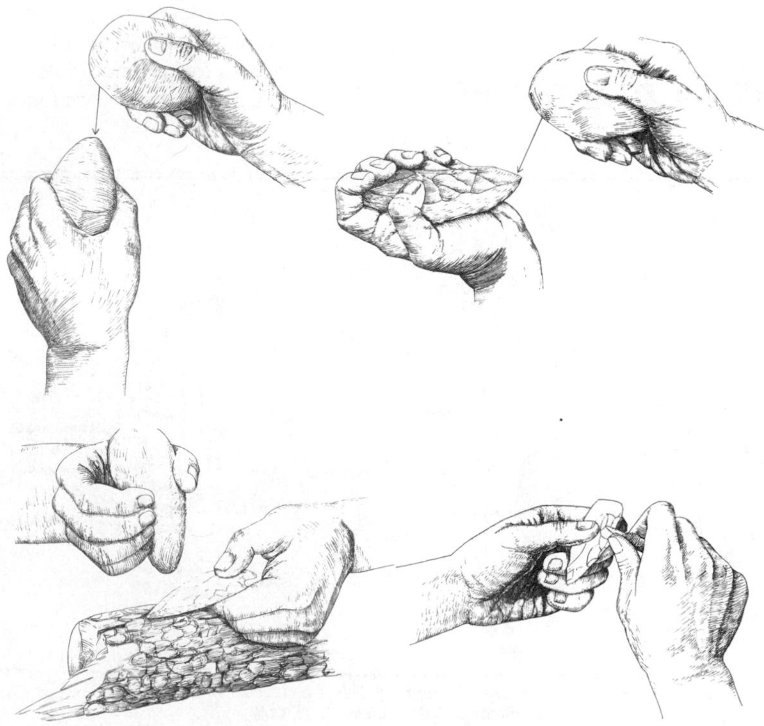

The distinctive property of Folsom artifacts is the **flute** (or channel flake) removed from both sides of the base. Nobody is really sure why these artifacts were thinned in this distinctive fashion, but everybody agrees that fluting is an extraordinary feat of flintknapping—almost impossible to achieve. The technical quality and intrinsic beauty of the Folsom point intrigued Crabtree. Most projectile points can be fashioned in a few minutes (by somebody who has spent years studying the techniques). But making the Folsoms must have required hours, assuming that one understood how to do it in the first place. And in the twentieth century, nobody did.

Archaeologists speculated for years how the flutes were removed. Frank H. H. Roberts, the archaeologist who excavated the Lindenmeier Folsom points, concluded that the channel flakes must have been driven off with a bone or antler punch serving as an intermediary to transfer the blow to the artifact. Interested in flintknapping for most of his life, Crabtree thought about this, tried it out himself, and concluded that Roberts's technique would not work.

So began an experimental period that lasted over 40 years. Crabtree tried every way he could think of to manufacture Folsom replicas. In his published account, he described the 11 different methods he had tried to remove fluting flakes. Most techniques simply did not work: Either the method was impossible with primitive tools or the resulting flute was different from those on the Folsoms. One method succeeded only in driving a copper punch through his left hand.

Crabtree eventually concluded that fluting flakes could be removed in only two ways. In one experiment, he placed an antler shaft on the bottom of the unfinished artifact and then struck the punch with a sharp upward blow. But because placement of the antler punch was critical, this technique requires two workers—not a very satisfactory solution. At one point, Crabtree came across a documentary source describing some long-lost flintknapping techniques once practiced by Native Americans. Particularly interesting were the observations of a Spanish Franciscan friar, Juan de Torquemada, who had traveled through the Central American jungles in 1615:

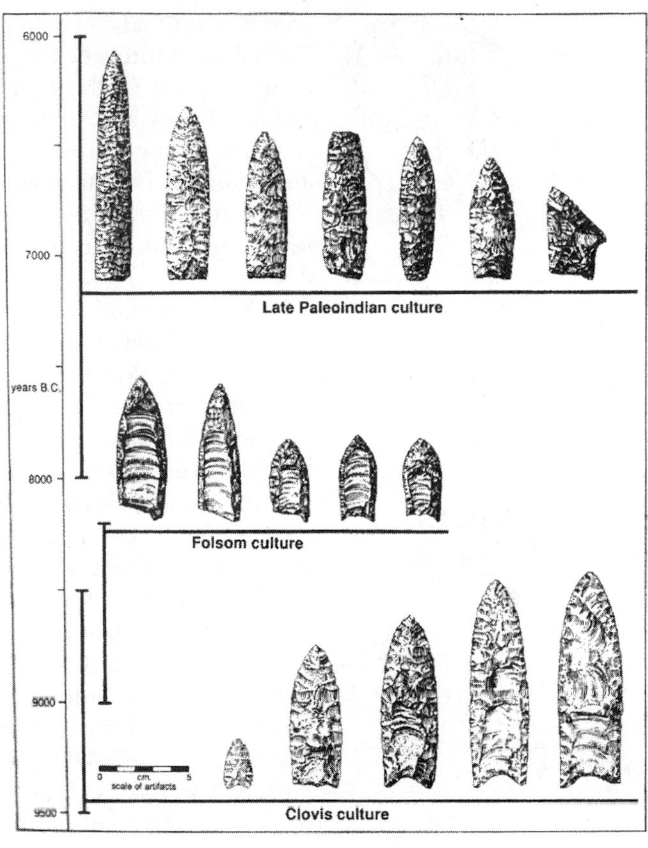

Paleo-Indian projectile point chronology.

Folsom culture: One of the earliest Native American cultures (9000–8200 B.C.), distributed throughout much of North America.

Flute: Distinctive thinning flake or flakes evident on Folsom and Clovis projectile points.

> They take the stick with both hands, and set well home against the edge of the front of the stone, which also is cut smooth in that part; and then they press it against their brest [*sic*], and with the force of the pressure there flies off a knife. . . . Then they sharpen it [the tip of the crutch] on a stone, using a hone to give it a very fine edge; and in a very short time these workmen will make more than twenty knives in the aforesaid manner.

Torquemada was describing how flakes could be driven off a polyhedral core, but Crabtree wondered whether the method might work to produce meaningful results on his Folsom replicas. Crabtree manufactured a chest crutch following Torquemada's descriptions, padding one end and equipping the other with a sharp antler flaker. He tied an unfinished, unfluted Folsom point into a wood-and-thong vise, which he gripped between his feet. Bracing the crutch against his chest, he successfully detached perfect fluting flakes, time after time. The resulting artifacts were almost identical to the prehistoric Lindenmeier Folsom points.

Direct percussion: A flintknapping technique that involves hitting a core (or flake) with a stone (or antler) hammer.

Crabtree's pioneering research unleashed an avalanche of interest in the fluting problem. Henry Irwin was able to detach fluting flakes with **direct percussion**, using wood or stone as a "backstop." J. Jeffrey Flenniken did it

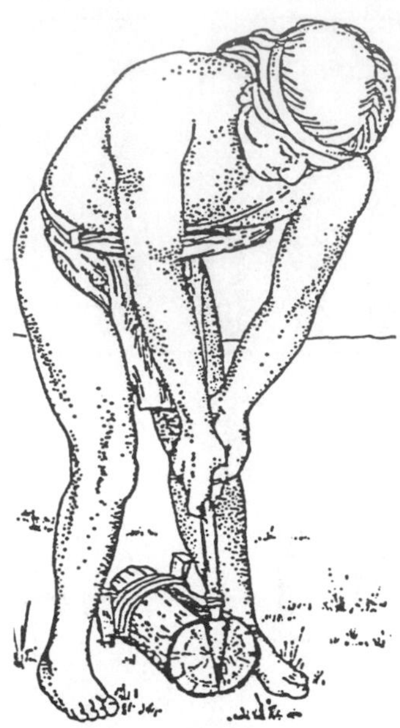

Conjectural reconstruction of the use of a chest crutch to drive off the central "flute" from a Folsom point.

with a modified version of Crabtree's method of indirect percussion. C. Tunnell used **indirect percussion** with a grooved anvil-and-backstop arrangement. Eugene Gryba reported several experiments in which he detached channel flakes with a simple, hand-generated pressure technique (**pressure flaking**). George Frison and Bruce Bradley once dug up a portion of elk antler amidst Folsom point-manufacturing debris at the Agate Basin site in Wyoming; after extensive experimentation, they concluded that channel flakes could be successfully removed with a wood-and-antler lever/fulcrum device.

Which method was actually used in Folsom times? Who knows? I find it fascinating that all these grown scientists are spending so much time knocking rocks and bloodying their fingers to figure out what was common knowledge 10,500 years ago.

Bruce Bradley has recently injected a spiritual tone into the fluting question. Speaking as one of the world's experts on prehistoric lithic technology, Bradley wonders why anybody would bother to do something so tricky in the first place. He thinks that the complex fluting process probably started out as an expedient way to thin the point's base, to make it easier to tie onto the shaft. But as in many human endeavors, once risk of failure increases, so does desire for supernatural assistance.

Bradley thinks that flintknapping became ritualized during Folsom times. After all, many contemporary Native American cultures include projectile points in sacred bundles, believing that stone points have their own spirit, that they can be used to secure supernatural power.

Life was risky in Folsom times. Not only was fluting a tricky business, but so was putting meat on the table day after day. Could fluting one's Folsom points have become an integral part of some prehunt ritual, a way of making a lithic sign of the cross? Bradley thinks so.

Indirect percussion: Use of a punch, placed between the object being flaked (core or flake) and the hammer.

Pressure flaking: Use of a compressor (antler, bone, hardwood, or stone) to apply direct pressure to the margin of a stone flake; fine, flat flakes can be detached with great precision using pressure flaking techniques.

Striations: Microscopic scratches left on stone or bone tools, the result of either manufacture or utilization.

Microwear: Minute, often microscopic evidence of use damage on the surface and working edge of a flake or artifact.

What Does Replicative Experimentation Prove?

But what do all these experiments mean? If Crabtree was right, was Irwin wrong? Or maybe Crabtree was wrong and Flenniken was right? But if Gryba is right, does this mean that Crabtree, Irwin, and Flenniken all were wrong? Considerable confusion exists on this point. A widely distributed review article on anthropological flintknapping suggests a series of "formal procedures" by which such replicative experiments are to be judged: The first step is to identify correctly the techniques involved, which are then controlled for several variables, ultimately producing a "statistically valid sample." Experimental results have even been compared technologically with prehistoric controls as a measure of assessing validity. One over-enthusiastic proponent wrote: "If valid, the replicator has reproduced a tangible aspect of prehistoric human behavior and demonstrated the reality of that behavior."

The results of experimental archaeology cannot be judged in this way. Adventurer and author Thor Heyerdahl once argued that Easter Island had been populated from the east, by Peruvians, rather than by Polynesians from the west. When skeptics told him that the ocean currents made a westward voyage impossible, Heyerdahl took up the challenge and launched his famous (and successful) raft trip aboard the *Kon-Tiki* westward from South America into Polynesia. But what did Heyerdahl prove? Did he "reproduce tangible aspects of prehistoric human behavior" by his raft trip? Did he "demonstrate the reality" of the past? Hardly. The voyage of the *Kon-Tiki* merely demonstrated to the world that such a westward raft trip was *not impossible.*

Although this is a relevant finding, no amount of trans-Pacific bravado will ever *prove* that prehistoric Peruvians floated to Easter Island. This is an empirical matter, requiring archaeological validation.

So too with lithic experimentation. Crabtree demonstrated that it was *not impossible* to use a chest crutch to replicate the Lindenmeier Folsom points. Gryba showed that hand-held percussion could be used to recreate channel flaking. But none of the experimental flintknappers demonstrated conclusively how the Lindenmeier Folsom points were *actually made.* Once again, this is an empirical question, requiring considerable archaeological verification. Like any other scientist, experimental archaeologists should not attempt to think in terms of "right" and "wrong." Replicative experiments do not "demonstrate the reality" of anything; experiments demonstrate only that a given technique could have been used in the past—that it was *not impossible.* So long as these objectives are kept in mind, experimental flintknappers can make significant contributions to the growing body of middle-range research in Americanist archaeology.

Accomplished flintknapper Bruce Bradley uses a bone flaker to remove pressure flakes from a large, corner-notched projectile point. Although he attempts to protect himself with a leather shield, flintknapping is a bloody business and Bradley sports numerous scars from his years of experimental flintknapping.

Stone Tools: What Were They Used For?

Another promising direction of experimental study is to determine the function of prehistoric stone tools. As the stone tools were used in their behavioral contexts, the edges often became damaged and dulled. Tools found in the archaeological record often contain such distinctive edge damage. Sometimes stone knives are found to have minute **striations** or scratches, which often reveal something about how tools were made, and how they were used. Sickles used to harvest grain often acquire a characteristic sheen from abrasion by the silica contained in plant stalks. Tools used for piercing or drilling often have small nicks or polish on the surfaces that protrude. And so on.

Folsom-style spear points manufactured by Don Crabtree. Note particularly the two large "fluting" flakes that were removed from the points at the bottom of the photograph.

The pattern of edge damage (often called **microwear**) on a stone tool is archaeological evidence of some previous behavior. But given only the stone tool, how do we know that the edge damage resulted from a specific action? How, for instance, do we know that the sickle sheen came from harvesting plants rather than from scraping hides? How do we know that the striations on a stone knife came from gritty inclusions contained in meat rather than from cleaning the knife or from putting it into a sheath?

This is an issue requiring a bridging argument to eliminate ambiguity. Archaeologists who use microwear patterns to infer tool function must in each case demonstrate the relationship

Obsidian Blade Technology: Modern Surgery's Newest Ancient Frontier

Damn! That's sharp!

ALL KNAPPERS, SOONER OR LATER
(ACCORDING TO JOHN WHITTAKER)

All experienced lithic technologists have their battle scars. Should you decide to try your hand at flintknapping, it won't be long until you've sliced, diced, mashed, and otherwise trashed your fingers. In his 50 years of flintknapping, the Master, Don Crabtree, slashed himself in about every conceivable way—across his fingers, through the palm, through a fingernail; one flake zipped right through his shoe. He once termed this regularized bloodletting "making a contribution to the lithic blood bank."

One day, while surveying the carnage, he noted that whereas he still had epic scars from jagged-edged flint flakes, the wounds caused by obsidian had healed quickly and were almost invisible. He wondered about that.

Then he saw a friend slice himself while handling some obsidian artifacts Crabtree had just made. The gash bled profusely, and a physician was summoned. But by the time the doctor arrived, some 20 minutes later, the wound had already begun to heal.

A curious soul, Crabtree decided to use an electron microscope to compare some of his obsidian flakes with the sharpest razor blades:

The platinum plus razor blade is the sharpest thing man has ever developed, far sharper than the old surgeon's scalpel. But this platinum plus [razor] blade had a rounded edge at about 750 diameters. Still the obsidian blade is far sharper even at 10,000 diameters. That platinum plus may be like an aerial view of west Kansas, you know—pretty nearly flat. But the obsidian blade can be magnified so many thousand times more and still have been sharp. It fractures right to the last molecule of the matter.

Immediately recognizing the potential of such supersharp instruments for surgical applications, Crabtree worried that "the surgeon who pioneers the use of such blades may be accused of reverting to caveman tactics."

The breakthrough came in 1975, when Crabtree himself faced major surgery. After some debate, he cajoled his surgeon into using obsidian blades Crabtree himself had fashioned:

The first surgery was when I had a rib removed and a lung section. The cut goes from right under the breast there, clear around back under the shoulder blade. So it's about an 18" cut. And you know I hardly have a scar. You have to get the light on it just right to see the sutures. And then I've had abdominal surgery four times, from my sternum down to the pelvis—one time was to remove a blood clot. Then I had bilateral femur arteries of woven dacron tubing put in. . . . And there was no problem with sterilization. A fresh blade comes off sterile.

Crabtree's venturesome surgeon, Dr. Bruce A. Buck, was equally enthusiastic, and he wrote up a laudatory article in the *Western Journal of Medicine*.

The story of Crabtree's successful surgery was picked up by the Associated Press, and a flood of related popular stories soon appeared in *Omni*, *Geo*, *Natural History*, and *Science News*. Not long thereafter, more technical assessments cropped up in medical journals, reporting on successful experimental surgeries and speculating about additional applications.

Everyone was impressed with the "exquisitely sharp" obsidian edge. Obsidian blades are as sharp as the newest diamond scalpels, which, in turn, are 100 to 300 times sharper than steel

between the wear pattern observed (archaeological context) and the act that produced that wear (systemic context). Hundreds of experiments have been conducted to provide precisely this sort of one-to-one relationship between edge damage and tool use.

blades. Experiments showed that the size of the steel cut was not only much larger than the glass cut but also very irregular. Moreover, the steel blade caused considerable tissue translocation, drawing "hamburgerized" tissue into the incision area.

Such medical research cannot proceed without the hands-on assistance of flintknapping archaeologists (for somebody must still be skilled enough to create the blades in the first place). Particularly important has been the involvement of Payson Sheets, an archaeologist who began studying obsidian blade technology for his doctoral dissertation. Acting on a suggestion from Crabtree, Sheets has pioneered research on surgical applications and eventually, in collaboration with an eye surgeon in Boulder, presented a paper at the Welsh Cataract Congress.

Sheets and the surgeon have formed a partnership called Fracture Mechanics Limited and have received a patent to protect their manufacturing process. Another Crabtree associate, Errett Callahan, began another company, Aztecnics, to market obsidian blades.

Payson Sheets tells of one operation in Washington, D.C., in which a physician planned thoracic surgery using an obsidian blade for half the cut and then his favorite steel blade for the rest, hence creating a control situation to study for cutting and healing. Incredibly, he read the X rays backwards—performing his operation on the wrong lung; subsequent surgery on the correct side was done entirely with steel scalpels. Although this unfortunate patient reported considerable discomfort from the steel-cut side, he experienced virtually no pain during recovery from the obsidian cuts.

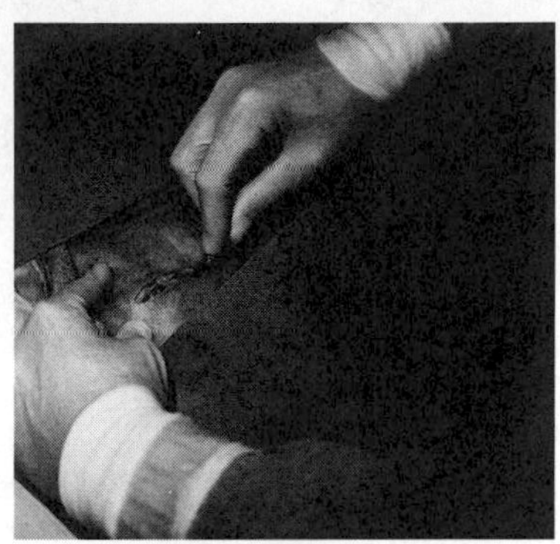

Most people having kidney stone surgery fear "going under the knife." But when faced with this surgical procedure, archaeologist C. William Clewlow decided to "go under the flake," and convinced his surgeon to use obsidian flakes that Clewlow himself had manufactured.

Eye surgeons have used obsidian knives to remove cataracts and to assist in cornea transplants. The sharpness allows for extraordinarily accurate incisions, and because less pressure is required, the eye remains more stationary in the orbit when obsidian tools are used. Obsidian implements have also been successfully used for breast biopsies, bilateral vasectomies, facial plastic surgery, and nerve microsurgery.

Using an ancient technology for modern purposes is another case of the far-fetched turned practical. The roots of modern medical science, for instance, can be traced to the curiosity of a few who conducted clandestine (and illegal) autopsies to determine the nature of human physiology and the causes of disease. The same is true in the thriving fields of computer technology and bioengineering: Both began as simple inquisitiveness, without any thought of a practical application. Without overstating the point, these episodes illustrate the importance of "pure" research. Who knows the direction from which the next angel of enlightenment may descend?

Although microwear studies can be traced well into the nineteenth century, the current trend was established by Sergei Semenov, whose major work, entitled *Prehistoric Technology,* was first published in the Soviet Union in 1957. Semenov documented the results of more than two decades of

Caught in the act! Here's Ruth Tringham, photographed at Catal Höyük (Turkey) while excavating—horrors!!—with a pick-axe. She assures us that she usually uses more delicate tools (such as a trowel) while excavating fragile architectural remains.

experimentation with primitive tools, some studies dating back to the 1930s. He experimented with a variety of techniques to replicate prehistoric stone tools. His major contribution to tool-use scholarship was the definition of three kinds of microwear: polishing, coarse abrasion (such as grinding and striations), and rasping of the edge. Semenov argued that the direction of microscopic striations seems to be the most important key in the discovery of functions of ancient implements.

The translation of *Prehistoric Technology* into English in 1964 spurred a flurry of microwear research throughout the world. One such follow-up study was conducted by Ruth E. Tringham, who studied with Semenov for a year in Leningrad, then moved her experiments to the University College of London and eventually to Harvard University. Tringham and her associates conducted a wide range of experiments in the tradition of Semenov, with some important differences. Although Semenov's work was largely intuitive and unsystematic, Tringham followed rigorous procedures to determine the exact extent and nature of tool wear in a number of different media. She attempted to reproduce working edges and to bring each into contact with a specific material working in a given direction. Her experiments consisted of making tools from British flint and systematically applying tools to a variety of media such as antler, bone, wood, skin, flesh, and plant fiber, carefully maintaining constant direction of force and counting the number of strokes. Some of the tools were hand-held, while others were placed in a haft.

Tringham then looked at the experimental tools under a low-power stereoscopic microscope (the power of magnification varying between 40X and 60X). Photographs were taken to document each stage of wear. Among other things, Tringham found that Semenov's striations were not as universal as he had thought. Striations sometimes appeared slowly during the period of use and sometimes they did not show up at all. Thus, instead of focusing on striations, Tringham concentrated on *microflaking,* the minute edge chipping that occurs as stone tools are used. This approach allowed her to characterize the kind of wear resulting from a variety of functional movements. Cutting, for instance, produced a series of tiny uneven flake scars along both sides of the working edge. Planing, however, produced flake scars only on the surface opposite that in direct contact with the worked material. Boring produced distinct trapezoidal flake scars, especially on the sides of the tool. In addition, edge damage varied with the nature of the materials being worked. Soft materials such as skin and flesh produced only scalar-shaped scars, whereas hard materials such as antler and bone slowly crushed the edges, eventually dulling the tool so that it would no longer cut at all.

Photomicrograph of a scraper from Gatecliff Shelter, manufactured about 400 B.C. *This photograph was taken at low power (about 50× magnification) by a scanning electron microscope. The broad, smooth flaking at the top of the picture results from initial manufacture of the scraper. The small step scars toward the bottom result from edge damage during use, probably from scraping a relatively hard surface (such as antler or bone).*

Tringham's experiments established the value of functional analysis with low-power microscopy, and numerous investigators have followed in this tradition, taking advantage of the relatively inexpensive equipment and rapid rate of analysis.

An alternative approach was pioneered by Lawrence Keeley, who used high-powered microscopy (up to 400X) to test the variables of lithic material, worked material, action, use duration, edge angle, and intentional retouch. The Keeley technique focuses on locating specific *micropolishes* rather than damage to tool edges (*microscarring*).

My experiments in flintknapping have led me to conclude that the making of this point [Folsom] probably took more time, patience, and skill than any other projectile point of comparable size.

DON CRABTREE

Keeley's work is particularly noteworthy because he employed a series of "blind" experiments to test both the accuracy and the repeatability of his technique. The blind tests were conducted at the suggestion of M. H. Newcomer (University of London) who was skeptical of Keeley's ability to determine tool use from microwear analysis. Newcomer used a red deer antler and quartzite hammerstone to manufacture a set of 15 tools of fine-grained black flint from the chalk at Brandon, Suffolk. He then worked on a series of materials–ash and pine, bracken, ox bone and hide, rabbit skin and bone, pork fat, raw and frozen lamb–and replicated a range of simple activities known from ethnographic evidence: scraping, slicing, sawing, boring, chopping, and whittling. Newcomer used the 15 artifacts only in left-handed fashion, being careful not to drop them, step on them, or use them with gritty hands, since "applying this sort of accidental damage would have put the wear analyst at an unfair disadvantage."

Newcomer then turned the artifacts over to Keeley, who knew the ground rules but not the specifics of the experiments. The implements were carefully cleaned using detergent, warm water, and some chemicals. Sometimes an ultrasonic cleaning tank was used to remove extraneous material such as fingerprints and organic deposits from the flint surfaces. Keeley then proceeded to use his high-power method to study each piece. Specifically, he looked at four characteristics: (1) general tool size and shape, (2) type and placement of damage, (3) distribution and orientation of linear wear features (like striations), and (4) location and extent of microscar polish.

How well did Keeley's high-power analysis do in the blind test? Table 10.1 shows some remarkable results. In 14 of 16 interpretations–because the right and left edges of Tool 14 seemed different, they were scored independently–he correctly identified the business end of the tool. Keeley contends that the only mistake should not be held against him. He admits to "simple human error" in the case of Tool 10: There is no doubt in Keeley's mind that had he looked at the right area of the implement's edge, he would have made the correct interpretation of its function. Tool 5, used to scrape raw pig hide for 31 minutes, had no apparent wear, as uncontaminated fat cannot be expected to damage flint.

Keeley's success fell off slightly when he reconstructed tool wear (12 of 16 correct); he felt that this degree of accuracy adequately reflected interpretive possibilities on prehistoric implements. However, when identifying the material being worked (10 of 16 correct), Keeley cried foul. In conducting his butchering experiments, Newcomer had used a wooden cutting board, and Keeley felt that the wood and meat polishes confounded the issue. Similarly, Keeley misread the polish on Tool 7 as bone polish and that on Tool 11 as antler polish. But as it turned out, Newcomer had used extremely well seasoned wood, at least 10 years old.

These blind experiments established the validity of the high-power method of microwear analysis in the minds of many archaeologists, and the techniques have become an important tool in the arsenal available to

TABLE 10.1

Results of Blind Testing in "High Power" Microwear Analysis

Tool No.	Use by Newcomer	Interpretation by Keeley
1	Whittling seasoned ash sapling (2 cm diameter) for 18 min.	Cutting* wood (branch less than 4 cm diameter).
2	Chopping ash sapling (3 cm) on pine cutting board for 21 min.	Chopping wood.
3	Sawing ash sapling (2.5 cm) for 12 min.	Sawing possibly wood.
4	Cutting raw lamb meat on cutting board (see above) for 44 min.	Cutting unknown material, possibly vegetable matter or meat.
5	Scraping fat from raw pig hide for 31 min.	Unused.
6	Whittling seasoned pine for 14 min.	(1) Whittling wood, (2) graving wood or bone (secondary use).
7	Drilling seasoned pine for 10 min.	Graving, planing, and scraping bone.
8	Cutting raw lamb meat on cutting board for 28 min.	Cutting meat.
9	Unused.	Unused.
10	Cutting ox hide on cutting board for 23 min.	Cutting meat (guess)—wrong area of edge thought to have been used: counts as wrong interpretation.
11	Scraping ash sapling (1.5 cm) for 13 min.	Scraping antler (or possibly wood).
12	Cutting frozen lamb meat on cutting board for 23 min.	Cutting or sawing wood.
13	Cutting bracken fern for 26 min.	Slicing unknown material but probably vegetable matter.
14a	Right edge used to skin off rabbit then cut skin into strips.	Cutting meat.
14b	Left edge used to cut forefeet off rabbit at joint.	Cutting meat, cartilage, bone (i.e., breaking joint).
15	Scraping ox bone for 11 min.	Scraping possibly hide, less likely antler.

*In the sense of slicing rather than whittling.

SOURCE: Newcomer and Keeley 1979, Table 1. Reprinted by permission of M. L. Newcomer and L. H. Keeley and Academic Press.

reconstruct prehistoric behavior. Studies such as Keeley's provide direction for a functional analysis of stone tools and also a way to bridge archaeological and systemic contexts. Although microwear analysis continues to be extremely time-consuming, this is an important beginning.

Paleo-Indian: A term applied to late Pleistocene and early Holocene (ca. 13,000–6,000 B.P.) cultural traditions found throughout much of North America.

Clovis culture: The earliest well-established Native American culture, distributed throughout much of North America and dating 9500–8500 B.C.

How Does George Frison Hunt Extinct Mammoths?

Earlier we discussed how experimental archaeologists tried to figure out how Folsom projectile points had been fluted. The Folsom people are classified by archaeologists as **Paleo-Indians**—among the very first people to set foot in America. But the first human footprint in America was not left by the Folsom folks, but probably by their predecessors, those of the **Clovis culture**. The name "Clovis" comes from an important site near Clovis (New Mexico) where Clovis period artifacts were found lying stratigraphically beneath diagnostic Folsom artifacts.

Not only does it predate Folsom, but Clovis is the oldest well-documented occupation of the Americas (consistently dating 9500–8500 B.C.). Although claims for pre-Clovis Americans abound, none of these claims has been satisfactorily substantiated. For now at least, the Clovis culture can lay claim to the title "First American."

So far, about 20 Clovis sites are known with solid stratigraphic associations. The most common bones associated with Clovis points are mammoth, with bison running a distant second. Camel and native American horse may also have been hunted. Even bear and rabbit have turned up in Clovis contexts.

So it seems unlikely that the Clovis people were totally dependent on mammoth hunting for their survival. Few nonagricultural people focus exclusively on a single food source—particularly one so difficult to hunt as an elephant. Perhaps, as one archaeological wag put it, the average Clovis hunter saw a mammoth once in his life, and never stopped talking about it—like some archaeologists.

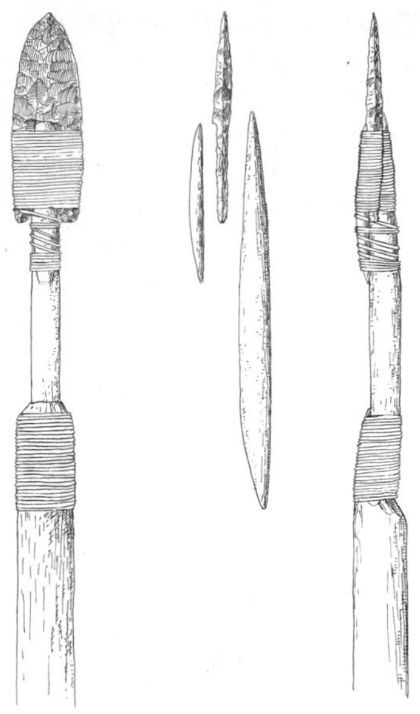

One way to haft a Clovis point onto a spear shaft.

Be that as it may, the fact is that mammoth kills remain the most visible evidence we have of the first Americans. Because they are all we have, archaeologists are always going to dig Paleo-Indian sites and study ancient hunting implements. But these same archaeologists are increasingly hoisting themselves out of the trenches and pushing back from the lab tables, looking for suitable analogies to "see" such ancient behavior patterns firsthand.

Looking at analogies is nothing new in science. Geologists studying glacial processes will never analyze firsthand the massive continental glaciers that once draped the North American continent. But they often study the smaller mountain glaciers that can still be found at the highest altitudes and the higher latitudes.

Archaeologists are now doing the same thing, closely studying the plausible analogies in order to understand ancient behavior patterns. We saw, for instance, the elaborate experimentation that has taken place in the attempt to replicate the distinctive Folsom spear points.

Two huge and carefully crafted Clovis points recovered from the Richie-Roberts site, near Wenatchee (Washington).

But what about studying Clovis hunting practices? Mammoths can no longer be hunted; they have been extinct since Clovis times. So how can science stage a confrontation between a modern hunter and a mammoth? And besides, who would want to?

One archaeologist seems to have found the way. Although a professor and practicing archaeologist at the University of Wyoming, George Frison is also an experienced hunter, and a life-long student of preindustrial hunting practices. Figuring that the best analogy to a mammoth must be the modern African elephant, Frison took off for Zimbabwe, where he conducted extensive experiments on endangered African elephant populations.

Such "experimentation" was possible only because these elephants have multiplied far beyond the carrying capacity of the national parks, forcing game officials to cull the herds. The Zimbabwe Division of Wildlife agreed to carefully supervised experimentation with Paleo-Indian weaponry—provided only dead or dying animals were targeted.

The Clovis projectile point is the first piece of flaked stone weaponry in the world that was well-enough designed to allow a single hunter a dependable and predictable means of pursuing and killing a large mammal such as a mammoth or bison on a one-to-one basis.

George Frison, archaeologist (University of Wyoming)

So there was Frison, Clovis-style replicas in hand, trying to learn what Clovis hunters knew 12,000 years ago. He came away from the experience understanding several things not evident from simply studying archaeological remains.

For one thing, Frison was impressed with the physical strength required to down an elephant with a spear. Frison concluded that hunting elephants is not only dangerous, it's hard work! He knew from looking at frozen Siberian mammoth hides that Ice Age elephants were protected across the vital ribcage area by a hide one-half inch thick. African elephants are built about the same, and it takes an extraordinarily well designed weapon to penetrate such natural protection.

It turns out that Clovis points are not only gorgeous, but they were deliberately made to maximize penetration and minimize breakage. The lateral indentations—the distinctive "flutes"—allowed them to be smoothly and efficiently tied to foreshafts. The point bases were ground smooth, probably to keep them from cutting the shaft bindings.

Atlatl: A throwing stick used as an extension of the arm to propel a dart shaft through the air.

The Clovis point was the business end of a thrusting spear or dart. Paleo-Indian weaponry probably included a throwing stick (**atlatl**), which Frison found gave him a good combination of leverage and distance. The Clovis point was tied with sinew to a bone or wooden foreshaft that, in turn, fit into a long, heavy mainshaft, probably with a carefully designed hole so the foreshaft would fit snugly.

This composite shaft-foreshaft-point construction provided Clovis hunters with a detachable lance head—a sophisticated piece of hunting equipment well suited for killing at close range. When ambushing, tracking, or holding quarry at bay, hunters could make numerous accurate shots at vital nerve centers. Retrieving the lance and inserting another foreshaft with a stone point could be done in seconds—a much safer and more effective technology than trying to carry and manipulate several lances in such a dangerous situation.

Weapons, Frison discovered, become a subtle extension of the hunter's own body. He thinks that Clovis hunters must have spent considerable time making and maintaining the weapons. If the shaft is not perfectly straight, the spear may not transmit the necessary force to the stone point. And even invisible flaws in the stone point can cause a Clovis point to fail at the critical moment—perhaps allowing a prey to escape or exposing the now-unarmed hunter to sudden danger. Clovis hunters must have continually tested and retested their equipment before setting off on a large-scale kill.

California rock art showing ancient hunters carrying atlatls.

Frison's Zimbabwe experience had made him skeptical of earlier reconstructions of Clovis hunting. Traditionally, artists have drawn

Clovis hunters armed with spears, darts, and rocks incapacitating a mammoth trapped in a bog or pit. Barking dogs, women, and children are often pictured in the background, creating a general picture of mayhem and commotion.

Frison thinks this scenario goes against smart hunting know-how. If a healthy mammoth were mired in mud and unable to escape, no band of human hunters would be able to drag it out either. The mammoth would be unbutcherable. The smarter hunter would remain on solid ground, away from crowds, relying on individual prowess and a carefully prepared set of weapons.

SUMMARY Because the "facts" of archaeology are incapable of speaking for themselves, it is necessary for archaeologists to develop middle-range theoretical arguments to breathe behavioral life into them. Archaeological objects have actually existed in two discrete contexts. When these artifacts, features, and residues were created and used, they existed in *systemic contexts*. By the time they reach the hands of the archaeologist, however, the objects have long ceased participating in their behavioral system and have passed into *archaeological contexts*.

Archaeological sites are formed by four basic processes: cultural deposition, reclamation, disturbance, and reuse. Each process has certain regularities, but archaeologists are only beginning to understand the complex mechanisms involved.

Middle-range research links our ideas about the world to the world itself and gives meaning to our empirical observations. Middle-range research dictates the way that we perceive the past. In this case, defining middle-range relationships requires that we also define the precise relationships between concepts and an appropriate class of empirically observable phenomena. Such a linkage has been extremely important to both past and contemporary Americanist archaeology.

One way to supply these *bridging arguments* between archaeological and systemic contexts is to study firsthand the workings of ongoing societies. *Ethnoarchaeologists* study living societies, observing artifacts, features, and residues while they still exist in their systemic contexts. To date, ethnoarchaeological studies have examined, among other things, the processes determining settlement pattern and intrasite patterning, the validity of the tool-kit concept, the mechanisms of artifact curation and reuse, and the social correlates of stone tool manufacture and use. Ethnoarchaeologists are also examining the relationship of material culture to modern industrial society, as illustrated by the Garbage Project at the University of Arizona.

Archaeological formation processes are currently being defined by experimental archaeologists. Whereas ethnoarchaeologists work within a functioning behavior system, the experimental archaeologist attempts to derive relevant processes by means of experimental replication; both share a primary interest in middle-range research. Much of this initial experimental work has concentrated on the manufacture and use of stone tools, although archaeologists are currently experimenting on a wide range of problems, including tool efficiency, processes of site destruction and preservation, and methods of ceramic manufacture. Thor Heyerdahl's epic transatlantic and transpacific voyages can even be considered to be a variety of experimental archaeology.

Chapter 11

People, Plants, and Animals in the Past

PREVIEW Archaeologists have a well-stocked arsenal of methods and techniques available for reconstructing how people made a living in the past. In this chapter, we shall discuss quite a few of them.

We begin with bones, one of the most common archaeological finds. *Faunal analysis* is the identification and interpretation of animal remains recovered in an archaeological context. Such bones not only enable the archaeologist to study ancient hunting methods and dietary practices, but they can often assist in reconstructing the environments in which people have done their shopping. But getting at the meaning behind the bones is neither easy nor straightforward. This chapter will provide you with the basics for understanding what can—and cannot—be done with a bunch of archaeological bones.

Modern archaeologists have also found that plant remains recovered from sites can provide first-rate information about what people ate, what they used for fuel, how wild plants were domesticated, and what past environments looked like.

We have already seen how the study of tree rings provides archaeologists with a trustworthy way of dating specific events of the past—when a certain Pueblo dwelling was built, or when a Viking queen was buried. Tree-ring analysis also indicates something about past climates, the local history of forest fires, and the previous distributions of certain trees.

Tree-ring analysis is just one way—a very important one—to study how people and plants interacted in the past. Archaeological plant remains also tell us about ancient diets: what wild plants people collected, the domesticated crops people grew, and even the roles played by plants in rituals (for example, as funerary offerings). As you will see, these examples reflect both of contemporary archaeology's major research strategies—the processual agenda and the postprocessual critique.

Bones are documents as are potsherds and demand the same scrupulous attention both on the site and in the laboratory.

Sir Mortimer Wheeler (1910–1970), archaeologist

Take a look at the narrative in the box, *Ancient Bison Hunting at Olsen-Chubbuck*. It was written by Joe Ben Wheat, the archaeologist who excavated the Olsen-Chubbuck site in eastern Colorado. During these excavations, Wheat studied the jumble of bones on bones, the occasional stone tool, and the dry sands and silts that formed the ancient arroyo.

Wheat was fortunate to possess the vision to look beyond the bones and rocks: To him, Olsen-Chubbuck was "a picture so complete within itself,

IN HIS OWN WORDS

Ancient Bison Hunting at Olsen-Chubbuck by Joe Ben Wheat

Down in the valley the little stream flowed gently southward. Pleasant groves of trees were heavy with their new burden of early summer leaves. To the north, a small herd of 200 to 300 long-horned bison—cows, bulls, yearlings, and young calves—were grazing in the small valley. A gentle breeze was blowing from the south.

As the bison grazed, a party of hunters approached from the north. Quietly, under cover of the low divide to the west and the steep slope to the east, the hunters began to surround the grazing herd. Moving slowly and cautiously, keeping the breeze in their faces so as not to disturb the keen-nosed animals, they closed in on the herd from the east, north and west. Escape to the south was blocked by the arroyo. Now the trap was set.

Suddenly the pastoral scene was shattered. At a signal, the hunters rose from their concealment, shouting and yelling, and waving robes to frighten the herd. Spears began to fall among the animals, and at once the bison began a wild stampede toward the south. Too late, the old cows leading the herd saw the arroyo and tried to turn back, but it was impossible. Animal after animal pressed from behind, spurred on by the shower of spears and the shouts of the Indians now in full pursuit. The bison, impeded by the calves, tried to jump the gully, but many fell short and landed in the bottom of it. Others fell kicking, twisting and turning on top of them, pressing them below even tighter into the confines of the arroyo. In a matter of seconds, the arroyo was filled to overflowing with a writhing, bellowing mass of bison, forming a living bridge over which a few animals escaped. Now the hunters moved in and began to give the coup de grace to those animals on top, while underneath, the first trapped animals kept up the bellows and groans and their struggle to free themselves, until finally the heavy burden of slain bison above crushed out their lives. In minutes the struggle was over.

One hundred ninety bison lay dead in and around the arroyo. Tons of meat awaited the knives of the hunters—meat enough for feasting, and plenty to dry for the months ahead—more meat, in fact, than they could use. Immediately, the hunters began to butcher their kill. As it was cut off, some of the flesh was eaten raw, but most of the meat was laid on the skin to keep it clean. Some carcasses were wedged well down in the arroyo, and these were too heavy for the hunters to move. The beautifully flaked spear points which had killed these animals went unretrieved. Wherever a leg jutted up, it was cut off, and other accessible parts were butchered; but much remained which could not be cut up.

For many days, the butchering, feasting, preparation of hides, and meat drying went on. In time, however, the meat remaining on the carcasses became too "high" for use, and the hunters had dried as much meat as they could carry; so finally they moved on, leaving the gully filled with bones and rotting flesh.

Several thousand years passed before this last remnant of the arroyo was filled. By 1880, there were no bison left, and the last Indians began to be replaced by White cattlemen. In 1957, the sod was broken for planting; shortly thereafter, the combination of drought and fierce winds that marked the early 1950s began to erode away the upper deposits that had covered the gully. By 1957, the bones that filled the one-time arroyo were once again exposed on the surface.

JOE BEN WHEAT (1916–1997) was a curator at the University Museum, University of Colorado.

whose action was so brief and self-contained, that, except for minor details, one could almost visualize the dust and tumult of the hunt, the joy of feasting, the satisfaction born of a surplus of food, and finally, almost smell the stench of rotting corpses of the slain bison as the Indians left the kill scene."

The Olsen-Chubbuck excavation is a great place to start our consideration of archaeological bones. Not only does this site contain the remains of a remarkably well preserved Paleo-Indian bison kill, but the efforts of Joe Ben Wheat show us a great deal about how archaeologists reconstruct extinct subsistence patterns.

The Special Case of Olsen-Chubbuck

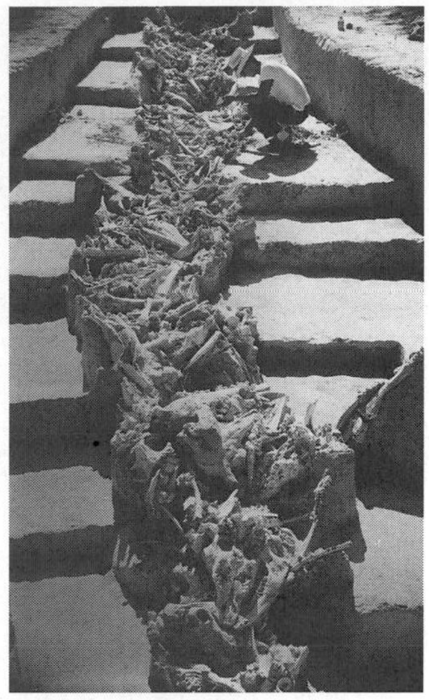

The "river of bones" excavated by Joe Ben Wheat at the Olsen-Chubbuck site (Colorado). The bones were originally buried in a narrow arroyo where the bison were driven and killed. The stairsteps and vertical sidewalls result from Wheat's careful archaeological excavation.

In 1957, Jerry Chubbuck, an avocational archaeologist, was driving through a ranch near Cheyenne Wells, Colorado. He noticed an eroded area with a discontinuous outcropping of large bones protruding from the surface. Upon investigation, he found a Paleo-Indian projectile point and an endscraper. Chubbuck wrote to Joe Ben Wheat describing his find, but Wheat was momentarily occupied on another dig and was unable to inspect the site. Meanwhile, Chubbuck also told Sigurd Olsen about the site. By an odd coincidence, Olsen had, in 1937, found the tip of another ancient spear point near the same spot. At the suggestion of curators at the Denver Museum of Natural History, Olsen and Chubbuck joined together to dig a few test pits into the site.

On the basis of their test findings, Olsen and Chubbuck became convinced of the importance of their site. Once again they contacted Wheat, who first visited the site in April 1958. Despite their enthusiasm for the new find, Olsen and Chubbuck refrained from further excavation so that Wheat could field a crew from the University of Colorado Museum. The summers of 1958 and 1960 were spent excavating at the site. The site was named, incidentally, after the toss of a coin established the sequence of names.

When Wheat first visited the Olsen-Chubbuck site, a deep furrow had been plowed lengthwise through the outcropping of bones. This furrow, coupled with the pits excavated by Olsen and Chubbuck, revealed a "river of bones" lying in a filled-in gulley (or *arroyo*).

Wheat established a baseline to the south side of the bones and then divided the baseline into 2-meter sections, providing the basic units of excavation. His crew began digging the odd-numbered sections, starting from the western end of the site. In this manner they defined the margins of the site, and, at the same time, created profiles of the arroyo and bone bed every 2 meters. Once the profiles had been drawn and photographed, the even-numbered sections could be excavated, exposing the entire bone bed.

The dig team used trowels, various small knives, dental tools, and brushes to excavate the bones and artifacts. Shovels were used only to move backdirt and to trim the sides of the trenches. Each bone and carcass was wholly exposed in place and recorded.

> *What are all those bones* doing *there?*
>
> Pat Shipman, human paleontologist (Pennsylvania State University)

By this time, Wheat realized that the Olsen-Chubbuck excavations had created a big problem: how to analyze the roughly 190 bison that had been killed there? Wheat devised a series of terms to assist in the task. Completely articulated individuals (those so deep in the arroyo as to preclude butchering) were cataloged as *animal units.* Partially butchered skeletons were treated similarly: pelvic-girdle units, rear-leg units, front-leg units, and so on. Each animal unit was drawn and photographed, and the associated artifacts (if any) were also photographed in situ. In addition to the animal units, Olsen-Chubbuck contained more than 4,000 unarticulated, disassociated bones.

The animals ambushed at Olsen-Chubbuck are an extinct form of bison. Modern bison are characterized by short, curving horns, and are known as *Bison bison.* The extinct animals at Olsen-Chubbuck have been identified as *Bison antiquus.* Not only does *Bison antiquus* have nearly straight horns, but the

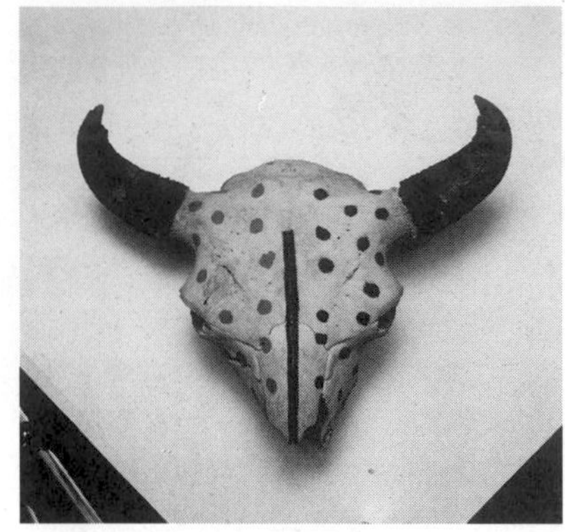

Modern buffalo (Bison bison) *skull painted for* Blackfeet Sundance *ceremony.*

It is necessary not only to have a reasonable explanation for the presence of the elements found but also for the absence of those not found. From here on out the student is on his own.

THEODORE E. WHITE (1905–1970), PALEONTOLOGIST

Olsen-Chubbuck individuals are an average 25 percent larger than *Bison bison.* This means that the adult males at Olsen-Chubbuck weighed about 2,250 pounds, as compared to 1,800 pounds for a modern bison bull and up to 1,000 pounds for the modern females.

Because he so carefully plotted and cataloged the bone bed, Wheat could make certain inferences regarding the herd composition at Olsen-Chubbuck. Both sexes and all ages were represented in the single bison kill. About 6 percent of the bison were juveniles. Most of the young bison appeared to be a month or two old, although a couple of animals could not have been more than a few days old. Reasoning from figures for modern American bison, Wheat estimated that the kill could have occurred as early as April or as late as August, but the evidence points to a time fairly late in the calving season, probably late May or early June. Although he could not count the ones that got away, Wheat estimated that nearly all the herd was ambushed, as 200 is near the optimal modern herd size.

Careful analysis revealed even more details about that late spring day some 10,000 years ago. Wheat's description of the bottommost animals bellowing and ultimately suffocating is supported by the physical data. The lower half of the arroyo contained skeletons of 40 whole or nearly whole animals who became virtually inaccessible as the ambush proceeded. Of these, 15 had been violently twisted on or around the axis of the vertebral column. Many bison had backs broken just behind the rib cage, and the forepart of the animal had rotated up to 45 degrees. Three animals had been completely doubled up into a U-shape, wedged against the sides of the arroyo. Based on orientations of the unbutchered carcasses, it was clear that the herd had been stampeded from north to south.

A very limited array of cultural items was found associated with the Olsen-Chubbuck bones. As you might expect, these were artifacts directly involved in the killing and subsequent butchering of the bison: projectile points, scrapers, and knives. Most striking were the two dozen beautifully flaked spear points found that were directly associated with the bison carcasses. Wheat used this evidence to infer that the hunters had been stationed along the path to the arroyo.

Noting that projectile points were found lodged in the bodies of the lowermost animals in the arroyo, Wheat also concluded that the very first animals into the arroyo had been ambushed. These animals were inaccessible to later butchers and could only have been speared as they were charged by the waiting hunters. Spears were probably heaved at the flanks of the moving herd, striking the lead animals and coercing the herd toward the arroyo. These animals would have tumbled into the arroyo first, precisely where Wheat found them.

The Olsen-Chubbuck site illustrates many of the principles used to reconstruct past lifeways, and stands as a vivid counterpoint to the chronologically oriented studies considered earlier. We know that Joe Ben Wheat excavated Olsen-Chubbuck in order to reconstruct an aspect of the overall lifeway of those ancient bison hunters.

But suppose he had been interested only in chronology. How would his strategy have changed?

Although no contemporary archaeologist would ethically do so, the Olsen-Chubbuck site *could have been excavated* for strictly chronological purposes. The scenario would go something like this. Chronological analysis is grounded in shared, modal behavior. Thus, any part of the site is as useful as any other. Two things are needed if you are interested in chronology only—a decent sample of cultural items, and a satisfactory way to date these artifacts.

The easiest way to do this would be to quickly sink a trench through the bone concentration, basically to determine the stratigraphy. Then lateral trenches could be extended through the densest concentration of bone. In effect, this strategy would be strip-mining the site for time-sensitive projectile points—and several would have been found. Then the bones themselves could be dated by the radiocarbon method.

The results look something like this: "Firstview projectile points date roughly 8200 ±500 B.C." In addition, our mono-minded archaeologist, concerned strictly with chronology, would surely note the presence of the extinct *Bison antiquus,* because these bones are themselves time-markers.

When one is concerned strictly with chronology, it makes little difference where the artifacts come from in a site. Nelson established the relative chronology and stratigraphy at San Cristobal by digging in arbitrary 1-foot units; it mattered not at all where the individual potsherds occurred within each of the 10 levels. Nelson also assumed that the sherds were more or less uniformly distributed across the site at any particular time; it didn't matter where his excavation unit was placed, provided that the stratigraphy was intact, and that the column ran from "earliest" to "latest."

Of course there is not a qualified archaeologist around who would approach either Olsen-Chubbuck or San Cristobal in this manner today. Reconstructing aspects of extinct lifeways is commonplace in today's archaeology—everyone is a paleoethnographer. I emphasize this point because the techniques of chronology building permit certain shortcuts, in both excavation and analysis. These shortcuts—especially applying the modal concept of culture and ignoring horizontal patterning—are justified only in the rarest of cases, when a regional chronology is wholly unknown. And even then, an adequate paleoethnographic strategy can (and does) encompass all the objectives of chronology building and yet preserves the contextual information necessary for reconstructing the details of lifeways long since past.

What's an Archaeofauna?

Faunal materials turn up in two rather different contexts in most archaeological sites. Sometimes archaeologists find food bones and shells roughly where they were butchered or eaten. Such *primary refuse* deposits often provide archaeologists the opportunity to reconstruct the sequence of cultural events that took place here. At a *kill site* such as Olsen-Chubbuck, bones are discovered in more or less the way they were left when the hunters and butcherers left. This is why Wheat spent so much time exposing and mapping the butchered carcasses.

Bones are more commonly found as *secondary refuse,* discarded away from their immediate area of use. For example, although Nelson saved only the ceramics from the San Cristobal trash heap, hundreds of bone scraps

Rocky Mountain bighorn sheep (Ovis).

were also present in this midden, the equivalent of a prehistoric town dump. Today's archaeologist would recover these animal remains, along with the ubiquitous potsherds, and perform a **faunal analysis**.

At Gatecliff Shelter, we recovered more than 60,000 animal bones, mostly bighorn sheep, rabbits, and rodents. Here, the depositional contexts were complex. In some rare cases, the bones seemed to lie almost exactly where they had been dropped after butchery. More commonly, however, the trash bones had been tossed into secondary discard areas near the drip line of the site, away from where people actually lived. There were also plenty of noncultural bones, encountered where carnivores had left them, where small rodents had died inside their burrows, or inside compact little pellets (where owls had spit them out).

Faunal analysis: Identification and interpretation of animal remains from an archaeological site.

The contexts of the faunal materials condition, in large measure, the recovery techniques used in excavating archaeological sites. Primary refuse is commonly mapped in place, the bones individually numbered, and then removed to the laboratory for further study. The isolation of the ancient living surface enables analysts to determine rather accurately the nature and composition of archaeological faunal assemblages. Secondary refuse creates more difficulties because it consists of reworked trash heaps, whose primary contexts have been destroyed. In Chapter 6, we considered various ways of recovering faunal materials from sites. Obviously, recovering tiny fish bones will require a digging strategy different from that for bison bones.

Once the faunal materials have been removed from the ground, the archaeologist must identify and analyze what has been found. Field archaeologists are expected to know, at least in a gross way, what mammal, bird, reptile, and fish bones look like. In addition, there are specialists—the **zooarchaeologists**—who are experts in the analysis of bones recovered from archaeological contexts.

Zooarchaeology: The study of faunal (animal) remains recovered from archaeological sites.

Identifying archaeological fauna is a complex procedure. One must first assign the specimen to a particular part of the body. Is it a rib splinter, part of the pelvis, or a skull fragment? Doing this requires a solid working knowledge of comparative anatomy.

Next the specimens must be identified to taxon (kind of animal). One's success here depends both on the condition of the specimen and the expertise of the analyst. Sometimes, the bones are so fragmentary that they cannot be identified as to species, but only to higher-order groups like family or even class. For instance, one might not be able to tell whether a long bone fragment came from a deer or a bighorn sheep—but it's certainly not a mouse bone. Identification to taxon, therefore, often means simply "narrowing down the possibilities," instead of exact species assignment.

Thousand year-old split twig figurine from the Grand Canyon; it probably represents a bighorn.

When possible, the bones are also identified by sex and age of the animal; sometimes the individual specimens are also measured and/or weighed (depending on the objective of the analysis). Many departments of anthropology have assembled their own comparative faunal collections, so that archaeological specimens can be readily and routinely identified. Often, field archaeologists do a "first sort" before consulting one or more zooarchaeologists to tackle the actual identifications.

Analysis to this point is fairly routine and concerned mostly with the zoological aspects of the bones recovered. But analysis beyond the initial identification stage requires a number of archaeological considerations. Were these bones found in *primary* or *secondary* context? (Hint: If these terms are confusing, it might be a good idea to look back at the definitions in Chapter 10). How were the bones broken? Have the specimens been butchered? Or worked into tools? Has the deposit been disturbed by erosion, or by predators, or by later scavenging? Who (or what) is responsible for the bones being on-site in the first place—cultural or noncultural agents? Questions such as these are critical and sometimes difficult to answer; but understanding the stories contained within the faunal records of any particular site requires a careful, step-by-step consideration of the archaeological contexts within which they were found.

Zooarchaeology on the Internet:

Zooarchaeology Home Page provides extensive links, including online libraries, appropriate field schools, and discussion groups:
http://home.sprynet.com/sprynet/fdirrigl

The Basic Problem: What to Count?

How then do archaeologists proceed beyond mere identification of archaeological bones? In a sense, Olsen-Chubbuck was a special case. The bones themselves were distributed stratigraphically in still-articulated skeletal portions (Wheat's "animal units"), such as forelimbs, hind limbs, and vertebral columns. Animal units can generally be recognized during excavation, and often assigned to taxon and even sex and/or age. At sites like Olsen-Chubbuck, it became a relatively simple matter to determine the number of animals involved (about 190), the sex distribution (about 57 percent female), and even the season of the kill (late May or early June). Looking at the micro-stratigraphic layering of the various stacks of butchering units at Olsen-Chubbuck even allowed Joe Ben Wheat to reconstruct the sequence of steps in the butchery process.

As you might imagine, sites like Olsen-Chubbuck are extremely rare, and the task facing the zooarchaeologist is usually much more difficult. The vast majority of sites contain no articulated bones at all, requiring that archaeologists draw inferences directly from hundreds, sometimes thousands, of isolated bone fragments.

To illustrate some of the problems posed by such sites, let me serve up a piece of my own research, done a long time ago. Early in my archaeological career, I was given the chance to analyze the food bones recovered from Smoky Creek Cave, a small site located in northern Nevada.

In looking over this diverse collection of burnt and broken bones, it was immediately obvious that several species were represented, ranging in size from mice to bighorn sheep. No two bones had been found articulated with one another. After identifying the excavated bones to genus and species, I wanted to see what, if anything, we could say about the overall food intake represented by the bones from Smoky Creek Cave.

But how do you move from bone counts to statements about human diet? Obviously, you can't simply count up the number of bones per species and then work out a simple percentage—clearly a mouse bone should count

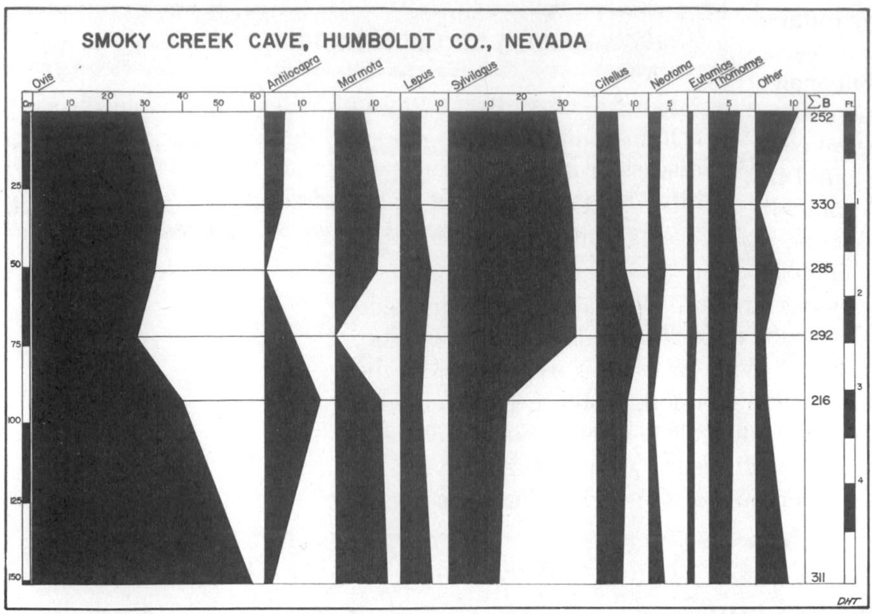

Estimates of the percentage meat intake through time at Smoky Creek Cave (Nevada). The text explains the assumptions that such diagrams require (and why the results are probably wrong).

for less edible meat than, say, a bighorn sheep bone.

To take the vast size difference in these various prey species into account, I multiplied the total raw fragment counts by the meat potentially available from each species. After butchering several experimental animals and working my way through the available literature, I estimated that the average deer provided about 100 pounds of usable flesh per animal. Because jackrabbits contribute only about 3 pounds per individual, one must kill more than 30 rabbits in order to obtain as much meat as is available from a single deer carcass. These elementary cost-benefit relationships would seem to have some implications for prehistoric hunting practices, and I combined the size-adjusted bone frequencies into a chart that provided a rough idea of the relative importance of food animals hunted in the Smoky Creek Cave vicinity.

The diagram above indicates that bighorn sheep (*Ovis*) declined in overall dietary importance during the occupation of Smoky Creek Cave; but the cottontail rabbit (*Sylvilagus*) increased markedly in significance through time. The bottom of the site (about 150 centimeters below the ground surface) dates to about 1000 B.C.; the site was probably abandoned about A.D. 600. This analysis suggests that mountain sheep decreased in importance after about A.D. 1. Whether this change is due primarily to environmental shifts or different hunting patterns, I did not speculate.

These estimates differ from Wheat's estimates in a very important way. At Olsen-Chubbuck, Wheat dealt with actual individuals (the 190 *Bison antiquus*), whereas the Smoky Creek Cave data are just relative counts. When dealing with thousands of isolated bone fragments, one has no way to tell how many individuals were involved. A single bone could represent an entire animal consumed (of which only a single bone was recovered) or only a small part of an animal, perhaps a portion scavenged and brought into the cave by carnivores. The Olsen-Chubbuck estimates provided fairly reliable data about the probable number of calories represented by the meat obtained. But the Smoky Creek Cave estimates can be viewed only relative to one another; they certainly cannot be translated into absolute figures. This approach to the Smoky Creek Cave fauna seemed perfectly reasonable at the time. I even published a professional paper, to show other archaeologists how my scheme worked.

American antelope (*Antilocapra americana*).

The problem is that virtually everything I said about the Smoky Creek fauna is incorrect. Inadvertently I made a number of hidden assumptions, which we now know are untenable. Let's deconstruct the Smoky Creek Cave research to see how far the analysis of bones from archaeological sites has come in the past few decades.

Sometimes truth comes riding into history on the back of error.

REINHOLD NIEBUHR (1892–1971), CLERGYMAN AND THEOLOGIAN

First of all, what—exactly—was I counting? Lacking such obvious analytical units as at Olsen-Chubbuck, the most tempting way to proceed was simply to use raw bone counts as an indicator of relative dietary frequency: If you dig up 100 bighorn bones and only 5 antelope bones, then bighorn must have been 20 times more important than antelope in the diet, right? For years, the raw bone count—the **number of identified specimens (NISP)**—was the standard measure for counting up and comparing archaeological bone fragment frequencies. We now realize that many problems attend the use of such simple counts.

Number of identified specimens (NISP): The raw number of identified bones (specimens) per species; a largely outmoded way of comparing archaeological bone frequencies.

For one thing, we can never be certain whether all the various bone fragments were deposited independently from one another. What if the hundred bighorn (*Ovis*) bones from the bottom of Smoky Creek Cave came from a single disarticulated carcass, whereas each antelope (*Antilocapra*) bone derived from a different individual? In that case, antelope would be five times more abundant than the bighorn. The animals may also have been butchered differently, with some bones becoming highly fragmented (and hence either disappearing from the archaeological record or turning into unidentifiable elements).

My Smoky Creek diagram assumes that each bone recovered from Smoky Creek Cave could be considered as independent. Today, nobody familiar with the formation processes at archaeological sites would accept that assumption.

There are other flaws with NISP as well. Because, for example, various kinds of animals have different numbers of bones, the NISP counts vary from species to species. Because of these and other such difficulties, some archaeologists have turned to another technique of comparing animal frequencies, called the **minimum number of individuals (MNI)** method. Long used in paleontology, this method determines the number of individuals that are necessary "to account for" all the skeletal elements of a particular species found in the site.

Minimum number of individuals (MNI): The number of individuals necessary to account for all identified bones.

Suppose, for instance, that you dig up 100 fragments of bighorn bone from a site. The NISP equals 100, but we saw earlier some of the problems with that measure. What instead is the MNI—the minimum number of individual bighorn required to account for these 100 bone fragments?

To figure this out, you tabulate bone frequency by element (left femur, right tibia, hyoid, and so on) to find the most abundant skeletal element. If four right femurs show up in the 100 bone fragments, then you will know that at least four bighorn are required "to stand behind" the fragments. In this way, archaeologists can reduce large collections of bone fragments into the minimum number of individuals required to account for the bones and also to minimize the problem of interdependence among bones.

Unfortunately, several problems have also arisen in the minimum number of individuals approach. When the bones are highly fragmented, it is entirely possible that the four right femurs are really all fragments from one whole upper leg bone. To eliminate this problem, it is necessary to compare the bone fragments one by one, to see whether two fragments could have come from the same bone. If so, then only a minimum of three individuals are represented.

Moreover, the results depend on how you divide your site. At a place like Smoky Creek Cave—occupied over a relatively long period of time, with poorly stratified deposits—it would certainly be possible to have computed a minimum number of individuals over the entire occupation. But this approach has the unfortunate consequence of reducing hundreds of bone fragments to a very few MNI, sometimes involving a minimum of one or two individuals. This is obviously a poor choice. Sometimes investigators choose to calculate their minimum numbers based on stratigraphic breaks observed during excavation. Once again, however, the minimum number per species depends on how fine one wishes to draw the stratigraphic boundaries.

The minimum number of individuals is also known to be a direct function of the sample size of the stratigraphic units involved: the more strata, the more MNI. Because of this difficulty, the results may not be comparable across sites or even across strata, unless the sample sizes are about the same. In general, the minimum number approach functions best when fine stratigraphic divisions are involved, containing bones that are not overly fragmented.

Yet another problem surfaces with the Smoky Creek Cave analysis. Note the hidden assumption that all bones recovered in our archaeological excavations were deposited directly as a result of human activities. Today, few archaeologists would be willing to so assume.

If you spent tonight in Smoky Creek Cave, you would probably hear the scurrying pack rats that still live there. You probably would not see them, but coyotes, bobcats, and owls also occasionally stop by. By dragging in food bones, by leaving scats or owl pellets, or simply by dying there, each species may have contributed to the faunal remains we encountered in Smoky Creek Cave. All these nonhuman visitors also remove bones, further distorting the faunal record as a reflection of past human activities.

Although at the time, we pondered some of the difficulties in separating "natural" from "cultural" bone, the truth is that the depositional contexts are so complex in places like Smoky Creek Cave that the natural and cultural assemblages may be hopelessly intermixed. Given our knowledge of the processes involved in the formation of the archaeological record in caves and rock shelters, no simple chart relying on *number of identified specimens* can hope to reflect anything close to behavioral reality. The newer taphonomic approaches and the advent of stable isotope analysis point to more fruitful lines of inquiry.

Taphonomy

When I started my studies of vertebrate faunal remains recovered from archaeological sites over 20 years ago, I had no idea what taphonomy was. . . . [Today] taphonomic research has found a home in zooarchaeology, and it is here to stay.

R. Lee Lyman, archaeologist (University of Missouri)

Taphonomy is a synthetic term coined by a Russian paleontologist, I. A. Efremov, combining the Greek words for "tomb" or "burial" (*taphos*) with that for "law" (*nomos*). Generally considered a subdiscipline of paleontology, taphonomy is the study of the processes that operate on organic remains after death to form fossil deposits. As Diane Gifford-Gonzalez has pointed out, taphonomy embraces two distinct but necessarily related lines of investigation.

The first focus is basic middle-range, "actualistic" research: documenting the observable, contemporary processes involved in the transition from behavioral to systemic contexts (observing so-called fossils-in-the-making). The second analyzes the archaeological evidence in light of what is learned through the middle-range studies.

When an archaeologist encounters bones in a site, the first question is usually: Was this animal eaten by people? The answer is sometimes obvious. Joe Ben Wheat knew immediately that Olsen-Chubbuck's "river of bones" resulted from a prehistoric bison drive. And excavators working in the privies and dumps of historic Sacramento had no question that sawed beef bones reflected nineteenth-century meals at taverns and hotels. Sometimes, however, both natural and cultural agents are doubtless responsible for depositing bones in the archaeological record. The picture becomes considerably more complex when dealing with late Pliocene/early Pleistocene sites. In many cases, documenting the presence of hominids depends on faunal evidence, and considerable research has been conducted in the attempt to find whether distinctly human patterns of bone butchery exist.

Only a small part of what once existed was buried in the ground; only a part of what was buried has escaped the destroying hand of time; of this part all has not yet come to light again, and we know only too well how little of what has come to light has been of service for our science.

OSCAR MONTELIUS (1843–1921), ARCHAEOLOGIST

Butchering patterns at Olsen-Chubbuck were distinct. Not only were cut marks evident on individual bones, but still-articulated butchering units such as forelimbs, hind limbs, and vertebral columns could be identified in the field. These stacks of anatomically articulated butchering units at Olsen-Chubbuck allowed excavators to reconstruct the order of steps in the butchery process by invoking the law of superposition. Although "signature" bone piles have some chance of preservation at such kill sites, it is rare that they survive in camps or village sites. Archaeologists cannot simply assume that bone distribution is indicative of butchering techniques or that it is necessarily reflective of social organization.

Taphonomic studies by Andrew Hill and Anna Behrensmeyer suggest that there may be a pattern in the sequence of natural skeletal disarticulation. They studied sequences of skeletal disarticulation across a broad range of African mammals in a tropical savanna environment. The first joint to disarticulate is the forelimb-to-body, followed by caudal vertebrae-to-sacrum and scapula-proximal humerus. The last joints to disarticulate tend to be various vertebrae from one another. Basically, these findings confirm the commonsense perception that more work is required to cut apart tighter joints than looser ones.

Such documented sequences of "natural" disarticulation provide a "baseline" against which to judge the distinctiveness of human butchering practices. By comparing "natural" sequences of disarticulation with the clear-cut cases of butchery by humans at Olsen-Chubbuck, researchers found profound similarities between the two, regardless of the agent of disarticulation. In other words, they found that simple frequencies of disarticulation and articulation of joints in a bone assemblage did not permit archaeologists to infer that hominids had butchered the carcasses.

Reconstructing Human Diet From Animal Bones

Although the preceding discussion is fairly brief, it does highlight some of the major procedures involved in the analysis of archaeological bone assemblages. With these basics, we can proceed to consider some of the primary questions that archaeologists ask of their faunal materials. This discussion covers only the highlights, and ongoing studies will doubtless point up new directions for the analysis of faunal remains.

The Olsen-Chubbuck site was introduced earlier. One major objective of Joe Ben Wheat's analysis was to determine the quantity of meat available to this Paleo-Indian hunting party. Wheat estimated that 190 bison were killed at Olsen-Chubbuck; of these animals, roughly 10 percent were not butchered in any way. Over 6,000 pounds of usable meat were thus wasted. Taking into account the sex and age distribution of the herd, the degree of butchering, and the amount of usable meat per individual, Wheat estimated that the hunters at Olsen-Chubbuck obtained almost 30 tons of usable meat from this single kill. Moreover, roughly 4,400 pounds of tallow and nearly 1,000 pounds of marrow grease would have been available.

How long did this butchering take? Relying on a number of ethnographic accounts describing similar communal bison hunts on the Great Plains, Wheat estimated that approximately 210 person-hours were required for the heavy butchering, and another 15 hours or so for the partly butchered animals. In other words, 100 people could have completed the butchering in about 2.25 hours. Alternatively, a party of 10 could have butchered the entire herd in less than 3 days.

Some additional clues emerge from the Olsen-Chubbuck bone bed. The distribution of the hyoid bones (from near the throat) suggests that many tongues were removed—and presumably eaten on the spot—before or during the early stages of the butchering. Similarly, the distribution of shoulder blades suggests that some animals were butchered early on, to get at the internal organs, the hump, and the ribs. Judging from the distribution of the ribs, these choice pieces were probably cooked immediately and consumed while the remainder of the herd was being butchered. Feasting was a common occurrence among historic Plains tribes, and the evidence suggests that a victory feast was indeed held at Olsen-Chubbuck.

Wheat also notes that even the heftiest bull was wholly butchered. Because the neck meat from these massive animals was generally so tough, it defied chewing even when dried. He suggests that the people working at Olsen-Chubbuck must have been making **pemmican**, which was the only really effective way of using neck meat from bulls.

Pemmican: Concentrated food source consisting of pounded lean dried meat and animal fat.

Joe Ben Wheat thus learned a great deal from his meticulous excavations and equally detailed analysis of the Olsen-Chubbuck archaeofauna. But that knowledge did not come easily. If his estimates are correct—that something close to 250 person-hours of labor were invested 10,000 years ago to butcher these 190 bison—then there's no question that Wheat himself spent more than twice this time figuring out what all those bones meant—not a very cost-effective analysis, but that's the way archaeologists learn things.

What Did Sixteenth-Century Colonists Eat in Spanish Florida?

Archaeologists have also begun to make important contributions to our understanding of faunal remains from historic period sites. As we have seen, historical archaeologists have the advantage of independent documentation that, though often biased, opens up the possibility of building middle-range bridges between the bones themselves and the behaviors they represent.

Zooarchaeologist Betsy Reitz in her laboratory at the University of Georgia.

Elizabeth Reitz and C. Margaret Scarry have found extensive documentation, for instance, to chronicle the subsistence practices in sixteenth-century Spanish Florida. Accounts from St. Augustine and elsewhere emphasize the chronic shortages of some traditional Iberian foods, and the substitution of less-valued New World resources. But significant biases and gaps are known to exist in the documentary base. For example, many important records were lost to deterioration, fire, and storms at sea. Other letters are known to have deliberately exaggerated (or even falsified) the situation to elicit greater support from the Spanish crown, and contradictions in eyewitness accounts are not uncommon.

The main problem, however, with the historic record for Spanish Florida is that it rarely contains the mundane details that archaeologists need. Whereas the contemporary accounts leave little doubt that the Spanish were displeased with their new diet, there is simply no substitute for the physical evidence obtained through archaeological excavation. Reitz and Scarry have synthesized the plant and animal evidence from food remains recovered in excavations at St. Augustine and Santa Elena (South Carolina). These results amply demonstrate the importance of dietary reconstruction in historical archaeology.

As in many such colonial situations, relying on traditional Old World subsistence practices did not work in the new environment. Many key Iberian food crops failed miserably in the coastal Florida environment, and the Spanish settlers were forced to alter their husbandry techniques to incorporate foods that could prosper in the coastal setting.

Lacking any sophisticated ecological knowledge, the settlers had to pass through an early period of adjustment and experimentation. The earliest shipments of livestock to St. Augustine and Santa Elena reflected Iberian food preferences. There was an initial attempt to cater to the traditional preference for mutton, for instance, but sheep raising was unsuccessful in Spanish Florida, primarily because the sheep were unable to defend themselves against wild dogs and wolves, and because they would not reproduce freely. At first, several species, especially marine fishes, filled the gap left by mutton; however, eventually, the meat supply of Spanish Florida shifted to beef and especially pork.

The documentary and archaeological evidence shows that, shortly after their arrival in the New World, the colonists of Spanish Florida attempted to raise their favorite Old World crops, particularly wheat and grapes. But they were quick to note how successfully the Native Americans were growing their own indigenous crops, and soon the Spaniards began to supplement their harvests with maize, beans, and squash. Wild plants were never very important, presumably because the colonists rapidly substituted indigenous crops for traditional ones.

In effect, the Spanish strategy shifted toward an essentially aboriginal subsistence pattern, complemented by those European domesticates that could survive and prosper. Considerably more than half of the meat consumed in St. Augustine and Santa Elena by both Spanish settlers and aborigines derived from wild species, especially deer, sharks, sea catfishes, drums, and mullet. Spaniards also hunted and ate small mammals, such as opossums, squirrels, and raccoons—which they disparagingly termed "the scum and vermin."

The subsistence pattern that emerged at St. Augustine reflected a fusion of the various elements available to the Spanish colonists. Whereas they continued to use Old World livestock, the dietary importance of the various animals shifted significantly. And although they still raised some Old World cultigens, these were mostly fruits and vegetables that supplemented a diet based on domesticated New World plants. Thus, despite adopting many aboriginal items, the St. Augustine diet remained distinctly Spanish. Several Old World plants and animals were still maintained; some of them were even adopted by the Indians, and these food items were still processed through unmistakably Spanish institutions of the slaughterhouse and the marketplace. Occasionally, the rare supply ship from home would provide European delicacies, such as olives, walnuts, and hazelnuts.

St. Augustine was established 70 years after the Spaniards began colonizing the New World, and some valuable lessons had been learned in this interval. Nevertheless, Reitz and Scarry found that significant dietary adaptations were still necessary to cope with the conditions of coastal Florida. These important dietary adjustments took place within the first 40 years of the colonization of Spanish Florida. But once established, the balance remained virtually unchanged for the next two centuries.

The investigation by Reitz and Scarry emphasizes the important shifts in archaeological approaches to diet and subsistence in the past two decades. Now that field strategies in historical archaeology routinely consider the details of screen size, volumetric sampling, water screening, and flotation, investigators are generating an enormously valuable database of fine-grained subsistence data that allow a detailed reconstruction of human adaptations to frontier environments.

Reconstructing Early Californian Cuisine

The Gold Rush frontier in California offered a different set of challenges. The decades following the Civil War saw unprecedented differentiation in lifestyles between the rich and the poor. In the remote outpost of Sacramento, established in 1848, considerable economic wealth was channeled into the hands of the already well-to-do. Although the historical archaeologist has numerous techniques for studying this process of sociocultural differentiation, faunal remains are particularly useful because they are abundant, little subject to "curation" before being discarded, relatively unaffected by loot-

Old Sacramento on the Internet:

http://www.oldsacramento.com

ing, and potentially informative about the daily life across a broad social spectrum.

Peter Schulz and Sherri Gust demonstrated the usefulness of combining historical documentation with faunal data derived from archaeological excavation in their analysis of four late-nineteenth-century sites in Sacramento (California):

> *The City Jail:* Minutes of the City Council indicated that meals were brought to the prisoners already prepared; an 1866 food contract allowed $.30 per chain gang worker and $.18 for other prisoners. Because nearly half of this went for bread, the researchers suspected that only the cheaper cuts of meat were purchased.
>
> *Hannan's Saloon:* Judging from the complete lack of newspaper advertising for this saloon, and the fact that owner Owen Hannan lived in his bar and was never mentioned in the numerous county histories, Schulz and Gust suspected this to have been a low-level establishment.
>
> *Klebitz and Green's Saloon:* The prosperous owners advertised daily in local papers and later expanded their interests to include real estate holdings and a sheep ranch. They paid to have biographies appear in local county histories; moreover, their saloon served as the Sacramento depot for the Bavarian Lager Beer Brewery.
>
> *Golden Eagle Hotel:* This hotel and oyster bar was one of the most highly regarded in the state, advertising in commercial, literary, and travel periodicals throughout the Pacific Coast area and announcing well-to-do guests in the local papers. This establishment occasionally hosted dinners honoring millionaire railroad barons and touring American presidents.

From cheap, assembly-line meals dished out to city prisoners to sumptuous repasts served to California's powerful at the Golden Eagle, these four sites span the range of status in post–Gold Rush Sacramento. Hannan's Saloon was a cut above the jail, but well below the Klebitz and Green saloon.

These inferences derive strictly from historical documentation available for each site: local newspaper accounts, city directories, tax assessment rolls, census schedules, and business license registers. But remember that William Rathje and his colleagues found huge discrepancies between such self-reports and actual out-the-back-door evidence. How do we know that such documents accurately portray nineteenth-century reality?

These four sites were excavated between 1976 and 1980, as part of urban renewal of the original mercantile district of Sacramento. More than 1,500 beef bones were recovered during these excavations. Contemporary accounts indicate that shortly after California's famous Gold Rush, Anglo-American settlers in Sacramento found beef to be more abundant than any other meat. But throughout this period, beef prices varied from extremely expensive for the choicest steaks to relatively cheap for the less desirable shanks and necks.

Using contemporary advertising from the late nineteenth century, Schulz and Gust established retail prices for the various cuts of beef. Although prices were expressed at the time in dollars and cents, the available nineteenth-century documentation is not sufficiently precise to allow an exact price to be assigned to each cut. Instead, Schulz and Gust rank-ordered their data, reflecting a price scale from cheap (shanks and necks) through expensive (steaks cut from the short loin).

In effect, they determined the nineteenth-century "relative cost" of each cut, and these results can be displayed as cumulative curves for each site. The cumulative curve technique is becoming an increasingly popular way of statistically demonstrating trends in nonmetric data. If a faunal assemblage contained an "equal mix" of all beef bones, then a straight line would result on the graph. Expensive cuts cause the curve to bow outward; cheap cuts make the curve sag.

The profile also shows some interesting relationships among the four target sites. The faunal assemblage from the Golden Eagle Hotel contains a disproportionate number of expensive cuts; more than 50 percent of the sample consists of T-bone cuts (derived from the short loin, the most costly portion of the beef carcass). By contrast, the bones from the Sacramento jail are mostly soup bones. Saloons of the day served free lunches to draw customers into the bar. Judging from the bone distributions, the saloon owners used mostly roasts—easy to cook, available in quantity, and ready throughout the day to be sliced by the bartender.

This innovative study demonstrates how food bones can be used to examine dietary differences by social status, at a time before any dietary surveys were taken in the United States. Whereas most archaeological data from the historical period relate to individual households, this study suggests a potential for understanding more about the nature of Victorian urban life by providing quantitative measures not available through documentary evidence alone. In the next sec-

Diagrams showing faunal remains from Gold Rush era Sacramento (California). The upper diagram shows how cows were butchered, ranked according to late-nineteenth-century retail prices. The bottom chart shows beef cut frequencies from four archaeological deposits in Sacramento (plotted as cumulative percentages) with cuts ranked in ascending economic value (expensive cuts to the right).

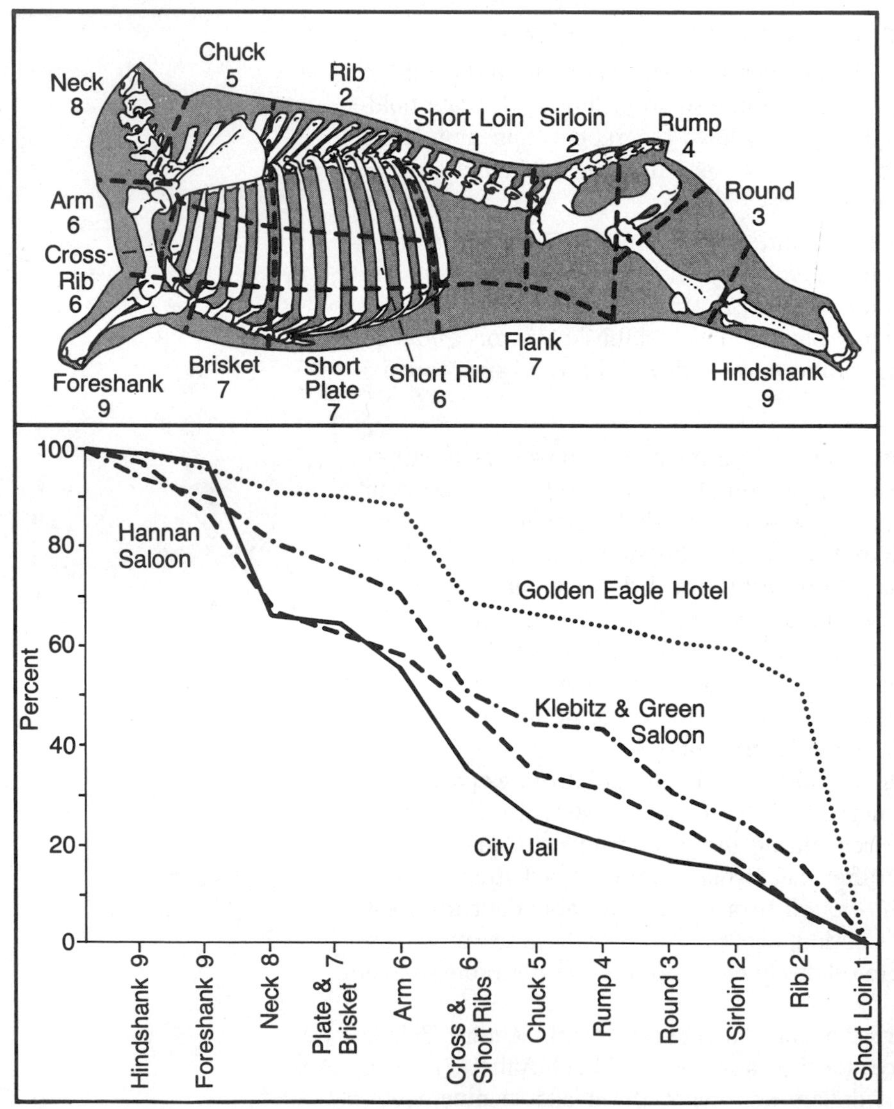

tion, we explore how faunal evidence is being used to reconstruct dietary and economic patterns from a much earlier period, the early civilizations of highland Peru.

The Zooarchaeology of an Early Peruvian Civilization

Although the town of Chavín de Huántar is today just one of a multitude of small district capitals in highland Peru, the archaeological site next to it has taken on an importance analogous to Rome or Jerusalem for specialists in Peruvian archaeology.

George R. Miller, archaeologist (California State University, Hayward), and Richard L. Burger, archaeologist (Yale University)

The site of Chavín de Huántar (cha-*veen*-day-*whan*-tar) is one of the most celebrated ceremonial centers in the Andes. It flourished from about 850 B.C. to 200 B.C., making it one of the earliest civilizations in South America.

Chavín de Huántar is located at an elevation of 10,000 feet above sea level, ringed by snow-covered mountains (with peaks rising over 18,000 feet). Some scholars believe that the establishment of places like Chavín de Huántar may be related to an early form of mountain worship. The initial settlement was a small ceremonial center surrounded by numerous domestic structures, homes to a vigorous highland community. Its location on a key trade route midway between the Peruvian coast and the lowland tropic forest to the east made Chavín de Huántar a natural trade center.

The site has given its name to the world famous Chavín art style, which some believe represents the pinnacle of Andean artistry. Chavín art is characterized by a range of fantastical and representational figures, usually combining the features of humans, snakes, jaguars, caymans (alligators), and birds with intricate geometrical and curvilinear motifs. The most elegant expression of the Chavín style is found in the exquisite stonework of the huge Chavín de Huántar temple complex.

These ceremonial buildings are honeycombed with rooms, passageways, stairways, vents, and drains. The main object of worship, perhaps the earliest oracle at Chavín de Huántar, is a knife-shaped monolith 15 feet tall, set into an interior gallery. The top of the elaborately carved sculpture reached through the ceiling, into a gallery above, where the priests of Chavín de Huántar, acting as the voice of the oracle, spoke to the worshipers below.

Understandably, the mysterious Chavín art style and associated temple architecture have attracted the attention of Andean archaeologists, causing them to slight the study of the mundane aspects of the Chavín lifeway.

What, for instance, did the Chavín people eat? Until very recently, one could only guess at their subsistence by exploring the iconography of the roughly 150 stone sculptures that once ornamented the temple buildings. But studying religious inscriptions is not a very fruitful way to understand everyday diet.

George Miller and Richard Burger advocate a more direct approach to the problem. After all, Chavín de Huántar was not just a ceremonial center. Thousands of people lived in the area and, like people everywhere, they ate things (and threw away the garbage). Why not find the garbage and see what it contained?

The renowned ceremonial center of Chavín de Huántar flourished between about 850 to 200 B.C. It is strategically situated at the confluence of two major rivers.

When Burger first went to Chavín de Huántar, there was no reliable chronological sequence (except for sculptural style), so he conducted a number of basic excavations to bring temporal order to the sites. Subsistence remains were, of course, also encountered in the domestic structures and refuse heaps being excavated around the ceremonial center. In Chapter 12, we will learn how Burger and his colleagues reconstructed the plant portion of the ancient Chavín cuisine. For now, however, let us restrict our attention to the recovered faunal remains—more than 12,000 fragments of discarded food bone.

George Miller had been conducting his own ethnoarchaeological study on South American pastoralists. This experience enabled him to help analyze the remains excavated by Burger at Chavín de Huántar and elsewhere.

The bones were identified, first to body part and then to taxon. Next, using methods introduced earlier, the investigators computed the *minimum number of individuals* for each of the three major cultural phases at Chavín de Huántar. An estimate of "usable meat values" was then derived for each phase by multiplying the MNI figures per phase by the known carcass weight for each taxon.

Let us look at the relative abundance of major food-animal changes through time at Chavín de Huántar.

Early Patterns at Chavín de Huántar

Four kinds of camelids are today found in the Andes. The *llama* was used mostly as a pack animal, and only secondarily for its coarse hair. The *alpaca*

This vessel is made of hammered sheet gold, decorated with Chavín-style geometric designs.

was valued mostly for its fine and abundant fleece. Both of these domesticated species played important roles in religious rituals. *Guanacos,* which were never domesticated, could be obtained only by hunting and were used mostly for meat. The *vicuña,* also a wild species, was hunted mostly for its extremely fine hair.

During the earliest or Urabarriu phase (900–500 B.C.), more than half the estimated available meat came from the so-called camelids (animals of the family *Camelidae*). Although the various Andean camelids are quite difficult to distinguish from bones alone, by metric analysis of living camelids, the investigators believe that most of the larger camelids from the Urabarriu phase must be llamas; stable isotope analysis (considered in Chapter 12) suggests that these early llama herds may have consumed considerable quantities of maize. The smaller camelids seem to be mostly vicuña.

White-tailed deer came in second (representing 31 percent of the available meat). Skunk, big cat (either jaguar or puma), fox (or dog), and guinea pig bones also turned up in small numbers. Some of these rarer animals were probably used as sources for bone tools, rather than for food. In other words, the Urabarriu phase bones strongly suggest a transitional pattern of mixed hunting and experimental herding.

The Later Fauna at Chavín de Huántar

Things changed markedly during the subsequent Chakinani phase (500–400 B.C.). Deer frequencies drop off dramatically during this intermediate phase. Camelid frequencies jump to 83 percent, with llama bones becoming considerably more common than those of vicuña.

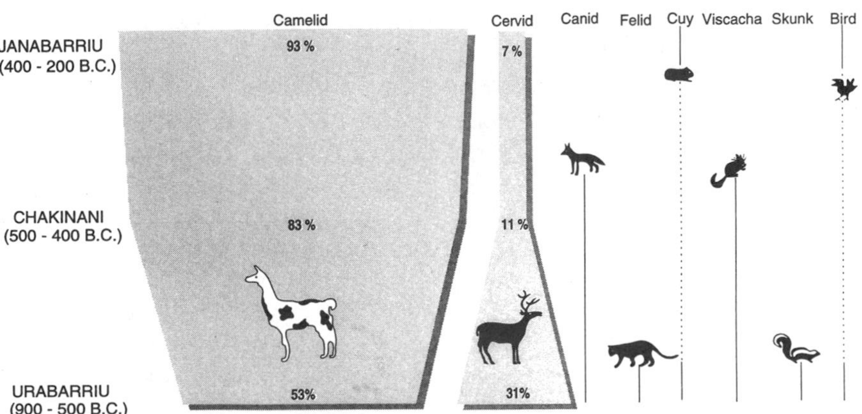

Changing relative abundance of the major animal groups at Chavín de Huántar.

This handsome silver long-haired llama dates from the Inka period.

The large faunal sample from the terminal Janabarriu phase (400–200 B.C.) basically continues this trend: Camelid bones comprise 93 percent of this highly specialized assemblage. During this phase, the rapidly expanding population has virtually abandoned hunting in favor of herding domesticated llamas. This much seems clear.

As noted earlier, Miller and Burger "identified" the bones from Chavín de Huántar in two ways. They recorded, of course, the taxon of each bone: *What kind of animal is this?* But they also noted the differential representation of surviving skeletal parts: *What body part is this?*

The taxonomic changes through time clearly indicated that overall subsistence activities changed markedly at Chavín de Huántar. And by looking at differential representation of body parts, investigators were able to explore the way in which the various animal products were distributed throughout the community.

What they found was a very consistent pattern: The early Urabarriu camelid assemblage consisted mostly of head and foot bones. During the two subsequent phases, however, leg bones become considerably more frequent, with cranial and foot bones becoming rare: *Neat pattern–what does it mean?*

A Brief Look at Camelid Taphonomy

Puna: Native American (Quechua) term for the treeless, windswept tablelands and basins of the higher Andes.

In order to understand the implications of these bone distributions, George Miller conducted a number of ethnoarchaeological studies among contemporary herding communities in the ***puna*** of southern Peru. Interestingly, Miller found that the modern bone refuse mirrored almost exactly the "early" pattern from Chavín de Huántar: plenty of head and foot bones, not many leg bones.

But finding parallel bone distributions still does not explain why the faunal remains are so skewed. The problem remains: *Neat pattern–what does it mean?*

In effect, Miller needed to conduct middle-range research to explain the bone distributions. He began by examining the problem of differential preservation. Archaeologists have known for some time that denser bones survive longer in the archaeological record than do fragile bones. It's basically a matter of chemistry and physics.

To translate this general principle into terms relevant to Andean archaeology, Miller conducted a variety of bone density experiments on camelid bones, to see just which ones tend to survive and which ones disappear. Not surprisingly, he found that the extremely dense foot bones and enamel-covered teeth lasted much longer than the long, hollow leg bones and the relatively porous vertebrae.

Miller then looked at the way in which butchering patterns might create a differential representation of skeletal parts. Basically, the process of modern camelid butchering accelerates the skewing effects already suggested from the bone density studies. Because people commonly break up the leg bones to get at the marrow inside, such long bones commonly enter the archaeological record in fragmentary condition (and hence are more difficult to identify archaeologically). In addition, Miller observed that when dogs gnawed on camelid remains, they tended to consume spongy bones (such as vertebrae) almost entirely, but even repeated gnawing left teeth and foot bones basically intact. In other words, the various processes involved in differential preservation—bone density, butchering patterns, and carnivore gnawing—all operated to bias the modern faunal assemblage in precisely the manner observed from the early deposits at Chavín de Huántar.

But there is another factor at work here, what Miller calls the *ch'arki (jerky) effect.* Today, herders of southern Peru's *puna* preserve the meat of llama and alpaca by alternately drying it out in the intense Andean sun, then freezing it during the cold, high-altitude nights. The product of this freeze-drying process—called ***ch'arki*** in the native Quechua language—has made its way into English as "jerky."

Ch'arki: Native South American (Quechua) term for freeze-dried llama and alpaca meat.

But unlike the overpriced western beef jerky peddled in bars and gas stations throughout the Americas, Peruvian *ch'arki* consists of meat dried on the bone. In general, the bones of the head and feet are cut off in the *ch'arki*-making process and reserved for home consumption by the local herding communities. *Ch'arki* is today one of the major trade items between the highland *puna* herders and those living in the intermontane valleys and along the Pacific coast.

So, if all you have left to examine are the bones, what does *ch'arki* production look like? That is, what are the archaeological implications of *ch'arki*-making?

The pattern depends entirely on where on the landscape you are. If you're in the *puna,* where llama are herded and *ch'arki* is being made, you will find lots of cranial and foot bones. These are the heavy, dense bones (without much meat attached) that nobody wants to drag around the Andes. So they are cut off and discarded, entering the archaeological records of the upland *puna.*

But if you are on the receiving end of the *ch'arki* trade network—in the downhill intermontane valleys and along the coast—then the pattern is just the opposite. The camelid bones you receive from the uplands are those still left adhering to the *ch'arki* chunks. So, your garbage will contain lots of leg bones and vertebrae, but not many skull parts or foot bones.

Given this simple taphonomic patterning based on behavior of modern camelid-herding communities, we can return to the bone assemblages from Chavín de Huántar. Now we are prepared to look at the bones in a more informed manner and address the question: *Neat pattern—what does it mean?*

Understanding the Behavior Behind the Bones

Remember that the faunal remains from the Chakinani (500–400 B.C.) and Janabarriu (400–200 B.C.) phases contained mostly camelid bones—mostly llama and some vicuña, with deer frequencies dropping off markedly from earlier times. The rapidly expanding population at Chavín de Huántar had forsaken hunting in favor of camelid herding. Miller and Burger also found that, whereas camelid assemblage from earlier deposits consisted mostly of head and foot bones, leg bones dominated the later archaeological record, with cranial and foot elements rare.

Pictorial representation of the *ch'arki* effect, an explanatory model of the differential representation of camelid bones between the Andean highlands and lower areas.

Middle-range studies also tell us that three of the major taphonomic factors—differential bone densities, longitudinal fracturing of long bones, and carnivore gnawing—all tend to *decrease* survival of leg bones. Although these factors doubtless influenced the composition of this assemblage, the observed superabundance of leg bones suggests that taphonomy alone will not account for the faunal distributions.

Instead, we must look to the final taphonomic process—the *ch'arki* effect. The ethnoarchaeological findings indicated that the observed late phase pattern at Chavín de Huántar is almost exactly the opposite of what is seen among contemporary alpaca herders living on the *puna*. Obviously, there is some important behavioral difference between the modern community and that of late Chavín times. Let us examine the larger picture to see what that difference might be.

Then and now, the valley floor immediately surrounding Chavín de Huántar is well suited for maize agriculture, but provides poor pasturage. Because llama herding is most effective in the *puna,* it seems likely that the camelids were slaughtered and *ch'arki* prepared there.

Taking the *ch'arki* effect into account suggests a natural flow of exchange. High-altitude herding communities would trade *ch'arki* to the valley residents of Chavín de Huántar. In return, the valley communities would send agricultural products (such as maize) into the mountains, where few crops would grow.

Translated into bones, this means that discarded faunal elements (cranial and foot bones) should turn up at sites in the *puna;* downhill, the imported *ch'arki* would result in mostly upper limb bones and vertebrae entering the archaeological record of domestic dwellings along the valley floors. And this is precisely the pattern observed in the archaeological record of Chavín de Huántar and inferred for the surrounding *puna* sites (for which no faunal samples are presently available).

We can summarize the overall pattern read from the differential faunal distributions. The earliest occupants of Chavín de Huántar used llamas mostly as pack animals, camelid meat being a byproduct from culling the herds. Meat was also obtained by hunting both vicuña and white-tailed deer, probably using the atlatl (which shows up in the iconography at Chavín de Huántar). People living on this valley floor were basically self-sufficient, acquiring their own meat as needed.

The ritual importance of Chavín de Huántar increased through time, and the local community grew in size. The associated increase in agricultural production on the valley floor made hunting of local wild species less productive, and thereafter meat was derived almost exclusively from domesticated llamas. Because the valley floor was poorly suited for llama herding, there was an increased need for long-distance trade with the high-altitude regions. *Ch'arki* was traded in, and agricultural products (among other commodities) were traded out.

The differential distribution of camelid bones thus seems to reflect important economic and social relationships between Chavín de Huántar and surrounding communities. These exchange relationships were probably also reinforced by a shared participation in the Chavín religious cult, both at the massive valley-floor temple and at small shrines located in the various high-altitude villages. With time, the residents of Chavín de Huántar shifted from a generalized economic system with only loose ties to the upland neighbors to a more specialized subsistence pattern that depended heavily on long-distance exchange with the upland herders in the *puna*.

In Chapter 16, we will compare the long-term economic pattern derived here to the symbolic and iconographic systems encoded in Chavín art style, at Chavín de Huántar and elsewhere. Doing the "archaeology of the Chavín mind" tells a story remarkably different from the one we understand on strictly economic grounds. The results of this mind-and-matter comparison are surprising and, to some extent, puzzling.

Studying Ancient Plant Remains From Archaeological Sites

Information about ancient plants is available from several sources. Sometimes, archaeological sites contain large concentrations of easily recognizable plant remains: caches of corncobs, baskets of pine nuts, charred roof beams, and acorn mush adhering to the inside wall of a food bowl.

Plant remains are particularly vulnerable to the biases of archaeological preservation. For years, much of what we knew about ancient plants came from archaeological sites in arid climates, which had a far better chance of preserving **plant macrofossils** for study. The archaeological deposits inside Danger and Hogup caves (in Utah), for instance, consisted almost entirely of plant seeds, hulls, and chaff. In places, virtually no dirt was present, even

Plant macrofossil: Nonmicroscopic plant remains recovered from an archaeological site.

ARCHAEO-MYTHBUSTERS

The Phoenix Phenomenon

Phoenix: A mythical, eagle-like bird, sacred to the ancient Egyptians. At the end of its 500-year life span, the phoenix builds its own funeral pyre, on which it is consumed to ash. A new phoenix then arises out of the ashes, the cycle repeating itself every 500 years. The tale of the phoenix symbolizes immortality and rebirth.

This is how the city of Phoenix got its name: When Anglo settlers arrived in 1867, they were so impressed with the ruins of the abandoned towns and irrigation system built by the ancient Hohokam people, they named their budding settlement *Phoenix*, hoping that their town, like the legendary sunbird, would arise from the ashes.

Archaeology has its own *Phoenix Phenomenon*. It goes like this: Maybe it's possible to grow "truly ancient crops." All we need to do is get some prehistoric seeds, plant them, and, sure enough, they'll sprout. Who knows what secrets of the past will be unlocked from these ancient seeds? Maybe they'll taste great and make somebody a fortune. Maybe they contain long-lost chemical compounds that can cure cancer and AIDS. Maybe they'll feed the world.

It's not difficult to see why the Phoenix Phenomenon has great appeal in today's uncertain world. We've all seen the headlines:

Three-Thousand-Year-Old Tut Bread! Some folks claim to have sprouted seeds recovered from King Tut's tomb (left there as food for the afterlife, you know).

Seven-Hundred-Year-Old Anasazi Beans! A cache of red-and-white spotted beans was reportedly recovered at Gila Cliff Dwelling National Monument (New Mexico) and allegedly C-14 dated to A.D. 1270 "at the latest." As part of the American Bicentennial Commission events in 1976, some were actually sold for a buck a bean. When a national news service picked up the story, orders flooded in from throughout the country. The offspring of other ancient beans, sworn to have been discovered inside prehistoric pots and baskets in southern New Mexico, still sell today for up to $25 a pound.

Claims like this circulate all the time. The problem is that, when investigated, they turn out to be bunk. Gary Nabhan, research director of the nonprofit Native Seeds/Search (of Tucson, Arizona)—bless his soul—has meticulously tracked down dozens of such stories. In each case there was a problem.

Usually, it was a case of simple contamination; modern seeds were somehow mixed with supposedly ancient ones. Very often, the "ancient" context was questionable. Sometimes, the claim was an outright hoax.

Twenty years ago, after looking into dozens of such claims, Nabhan concluded that stories of modern yields from ancient seeds "remain rich in folklore, but poor in facts." Most archaeologists agree—just so many tales of bogus beans and mummy muffins.

But before we completely write off the Phoenix Phenomenon, let us consider the brand-new Case of the Sacred Lotus, a modern blend of religious fantasy, wishful thinking, and scientific fact that shows the Phoenix Phenomenon in a somewhat different light.

The Sacred Lotus plant has long been associated with the Buddhist religion. From the marshy mire (symbolic of its humble origin) it rises, untainted, above the water surface—a symbol of vi-

though the deposits were deeper than 10 feet. From column samples of the fill, investigators were able to reconstruct a picture of the vegetational history and climatic change in the vicinity of both sites. Such studies often highlight the degree to which modern plant distributions can mislead the archaeologist studying the cultural ecology of even the fairly recent past.

tality and purity. The lotus blossom is a popular theme throughout Oriental art and architecture. The oldest well-dated image of Buddha (ca. A.D. 240) shows him seated cross-legged on a lotus throne. Even the Hindu god Vishnu—popularly regarded as the preserver of the universe—holds a lotus blossom in one of his four hands. In Greek legend, the "lotus-eaters" forgot their friends and homes and lost all desire to return to their native land—just from eating the lotus fruit. Today, the Sacred Lotus is still eaten as a delicacy, and the plant is important in traditional Chinese medicine, particularly to strengthen the spleen and to "cultivate the heart."

A great stir arose when a buried deposit of Sacred Lotus fruits was discovered in dry lake sediments at Palantien, China. Adding to the intrigue, historical records suggested that the lake had been drained six centuries ago by a massive earthquake (on February 4, 1484). Many naturally wondered whether the ancient lotus plants could be germinated—and, if so, what powers these spiritual seeds might hold.

A research team from UCLA recently decided to find out by attempting to grow several of these archaic lotus seeds under strict laboratory conditions. It worked. Several sprouted, some yielding fruits even faster than modern lotus plants. And when they flowered, the blossoms of the ancient Sacred Lotus were an intense pink—more brilliant than any of their modern descendants. Perhaps, some suggested, the curative powers of the ancient plants were more intense as well.

But many were skeptical. After all, the previous Phoenix Phenomenon claims were phonies. The Palantien lotus seeds are considered "ancient" only because of their alleged association with a 600-year-old earthquake—plenty of potential for error here. Maybe the A.D. 1484 earthquake is just folklore; maybe the earthquake actually occurred, but had nothing to do with the lake drying; maybe the seeds were deposited after the lake dried up; maybe later seeds were somehow introduced into earlier sediments. Questions like these make most archaeologists queasy.

So the UCLA research team decided to date the newly sprouted lotus seeds directly. Conventional radiocarbon dating was used on three of the lotus plants (after they had sprouted). All three dates turned out to be "old," and the oldest one was really old—1288 ±271 B.P.

Overnight, the 1,288-year-old Sacred Lotus seed from Palantien became the oldest viable seed in the world. When announced, the results made headlines: *Sacred Buddhist Plant Survives the Ages! Hope for Ancient Plants!*

And this time, the headlines had it right. Under just the right conditions, ancient seeds can be sprouted after more than a millennium. Knowing this, scientists are once again seeking to grow the crops of the ancients.

So here is one myth that's not so mythical after all. Maybe the phoenix can, indeed, still rise again.

This sleeping beauty, which was already there when Marco Polo came to China in the thirteenth century, must have a powerful genetic system to delay its aging. It's unbelievable it could sleep for thousands of years and in 4 days a little green shoot emerged.

JANE SHEN-MILLER

Unfortunately for the archaeologist, such plant macrofossils are hard to come by; the Utah samples were preserved only because of the general aridity of the environment. In more humid climates, plant remains generally are preserved only when they have been burned and hence carbonized. The most common method of recovering plant remains is water

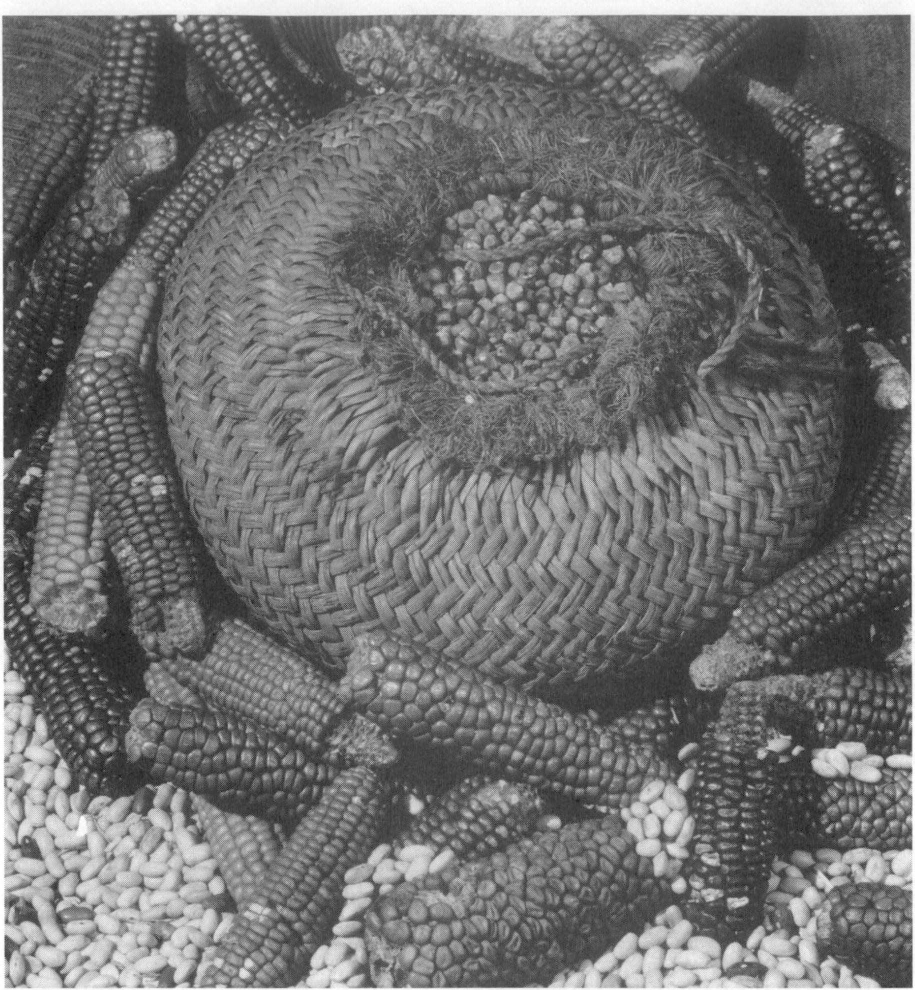

Thousand-year-old basket and ancient maize from Utah. Could these ancient corn kernels be germinated today?

flotation, a technique that has become standard archaeological procedure only within the past couple of decades. Plant remains are also sometimes preserved in unlikely places, such as waterlogged contexts (shipwrecks, mudslides, and wells), sun-dried adobe bricks, wattle-and-daub walls, and ceramics.

Archaeologists also occasionally find plant remains in very curious places, such as inside ancient human stomachs (preserved through mummification, for instance) and in *coprolites* (dessicated human feces); this evidence of past diets is about as "direct" as one could hope for.

Microscopic plant parts are also preserved in many sites; the analysis of plant pollen, for instance, can tell archaeologists a great deal about past climates. *Phytoliths* (microscopic silica bodies contained inside many plants) can also be recovered and analyzed. Evidence of past plant consumption is even preserved inside human bones; by measuring various stable isotope ratios, for instance, it is possible to learn a great deal about past diets.

In this and subsequent chapters, we will examine many of these sources of information about plants of the past, and their relationship to our human ancestors. Traditionally, archaeologists have been much more interested in animals than plants, perhaps because bones are such a conspicuous feature of the archaeological record. But as recovery and analytical techniques have been refined, the study of ancient plant remains has flourished and is today one of the most rapidly growing research directions in Americanist archaeology.

If current trends hold, our knowledge of the ancient plant world will soon catch up with what we think we know about past human interactions with the animal kingdom.

Who Studies Ancient Plant Parts?

In the Americas, an **archaeobotanist** is basically one interested in recovering and identifying plant remains from ancient contexts; interpretations may be cultural or noncultural. But if you're specifically interested in exploring the world of plant–people interactions, you'll probably call yourself a **paleoethnobotanist.**

Regardless of the terminology, people who study ancient plant remains make an important contribution to our understanding of the archaeological record. Throughout this chapter, we will examine some of these insights.

Paleoethnobotany on the Internet:

ArchNet: Botanical Resources/Archives and Catalogues includes a wealth of searchable databases from the U.S. Department of Agriculture; of special interest to anthropologists:
http://spirit.lib.uconn.edu/ArchNet/Topical/Botan/Botan.html

Southwestern Archaeology–Ethnobotany and Paleoethnobotany is an extensive bibliography:
http://seamonkey.ed.asu.edu/swa/ethnobot.html

Native Americans and the Environment contains a huge bibliography on traditional environmental knowledge:
http://www.indians.org/library/subt.html

Newton's Apple provides a neat kid's home page on ethnobotany:
http://ericir.syr.edu/Projets/Newton

Some Applications of Palynology to Archaeology

Palynology, the analysis of ancient plant pollen and spores, has long been one of archaeology's most informative methods for examining prehistoric ecological adaptations. The basics of palynology are not difficult to understand.

Most plants shed their pollen into the atmosphere, where it is rapidly dispersed by both insects and wind action. Pollen grains—microscopic single-celled organisms produced during plant reproduction—are present in most of the earth's atmosphere; a single pine branch can produce as many as 350 million individual pollen grains. Small wonder that pollen grains are also commonly found in archaeological sites.

Determining what these pollen concentrations mean can be quite challenging, but the initial steps in extracting and identifying pollen are rather simple. Sometimes, pollen is recovered by *core sampling,* in which a circular tube is forced downward into a sediment column. Pollen samples can also be taken from the sidewall of test pits or trenches, special care being taken to prevent contaminating the sample with foreign pollen. The outer surface of the excavation profile is first scraped with a trowel (which has been cleaned with distilled water), and 0.2 liter to 0.3 liter of material is then extracted from the sediment and placed in a sterile, uncontaminated container that can be sealed. Samples are often taken at 5- or 10-centimeter intervals—working from the bottom of the column to the top—to provide a continuous record of the pollen rain throughout the period of deposition. Careful stratigraphic drawings are used to correlate the emerging pollen record with the rest of the archaeological remains recovered from these strata. Pollen samples can also be taken from sealed deposits within architectural features (such as ancient floors), and sometimes "pollen washes" are taken from the surfaces of

Archaeobotany: The recovery and identification of plant remains in archaeological contexts.

Paleoethnobotany: The analysis and interpretation of plant remains from archaeological sites in order to understand the past interactions between human populations and plants.

Palynology: The technique through which the fossil pollen grains and spores from archaeological sites are studied.

The study of pollen is . . . a very taxing discipline, and one that gets right up some people's noses.

PAUL BAHN, ARCHAEOLOGIST

Palynology on the Internet:

American Association of Stratigraphic Palynologists, Inc., Home Page:
http://opal.geology.utoronto.ca:80/AASP/

Geosciences, University of Arizona provides a lengthy listing of palynology resources:
http://www.geo.Arizona.EDU/palynology

Palynology and Palaeoclimatology:
http://www.csu.edu.au/landscape_ecology/landscape.html

plant-related, archaeologically sealed artifacts (such as grinding stones). Pollen is occasionally found associated with human burials, on the inside of ceramic vessels, trapped inside the weave of ancient baskets, or even adhering to the working surface of a stone tool. Again, the excavator and collector must be certain that the artifact has been collected from a very recently exposed surface.

Even with these careful procedures, the truth is that good pollen samples are difficult to come by. Most contexts are very problematical, and considerable caution is required in making palynological intepretations.

In the laboratory, pollen grains are isolated from the soil matrix with repeated acid baths and centrifuging. Microscope slides containing the fossil pollen grains are scanned at magnifications between 400X and 1,000X. The individual grains are then identified and tabulated until a statistically significant number have been recorded. Although sample sizes vary, most palynologists feel that 400 to 500 pollen grains are required for statistically significant samples from each slide. It takes a skilled analyst about an hour to obtain a 200- to 300-grain count from a single archaeological sample. These figures are converted to percentages and integrated into a pollen spectrum, indicating the proportional shift between stratigraphic levels within the site. The pollen profiles are then correlated with the known absolute and relative dates for each stratum. The resulting *pollen diagrams* provide several different kinds of data to the archaeologist.

Today, most pollen analysis of archaeological sediments is conducted by specialized laboratories and facilities, on a contract basis. Pollen laboratories charge an average of about $125 to process and analyze a single sample.

One major application of palynology is to reconstruct the character of past environments because pollen percentages that fluctuate through time can reflect changes in prehistoric habitats. The postglacial climatic sequence in Europe, for instance, has been documented from hundreds of individual pollen diagrams. The composite European pollen profile reveals notable fluctuations in the forest cover, as indicated by the changing relative frequencies of hazel, oak, birch, and grass pollen. Once such a regional sequence has been developed (often from noncultural deposits), archaeological samples can be statistically compared with the pollen rain from known extant plant communities. The ratio of tree (*arboreal*) to non-tree pollen, for example, generally indicates the degree of forestation.

Mesolithic: The Middle Stone Age; a period of transition from hunting and gathering to agriculture, featuring settlements based on broad-spectrum wild resource exploitation.

Assessing Human Impacts on Postglacial Forests: Palynology at Star Carr

In one classic study, palynology was applied to Star Carr, a **Mesolithic** site in northern England, occupied about 7500 B.C. The primary pollen diagram from Star Carr plots the relative pollen frequencies determined from small, uncontaminated samples of peats or lake muds. These samples were arranged in stratigraphic order, with the oldest at the bottom. The stratigraphic profile is divided into seven zones, with the human occupation of Star Carr spanning the transition from Zone IV to Zone V. The diagram expresses pollen frequencies as percentages of the total tree pollen; these arboreal pollen frequencies are shown in black, with herbaceous pollen represented by white polygons.

This is one of several pollen profiles available from the Star Carr vicinity. These profiles, coupled with the identification of preserved plant macrofossils, enabled J. D. G. Clark and his colleagues to reconstruct the ecological shifts of the Star Carr landscape.

Zones I, II, and III, from the late glacial period, suggest a park tundra, dominated by **herbaceous** communities, punctuated by dense stands of birch or pine trees. This vegetation lasted until the human occupation of Star Carr, roughly 7500 B.C., when the vegetation abruptly shifted to a birch and pine forest, with the park tundra disappearing altogether. The increasing abundance of hazel pollen in these strata suggests a shift to warmer, woodland conditions. Pollen diagrams from nearby localities likewise reflect an increased warming of climatic conditions during this time.

Herbaceous: Plants (particularly herbs) with little or no woody tissue and usually persisting only for a single growing season.

This pollen evidence provides a glimpse of what the Star Carr landscape must have looked like during Mesolithic times. Note particularly that the pollen diagrams show absolutely no indication of any large-scale

Pollen diagram from geological deposits near the site of Star Carr (England). The human occupation of the site is denoted by the shaded horizontal band.

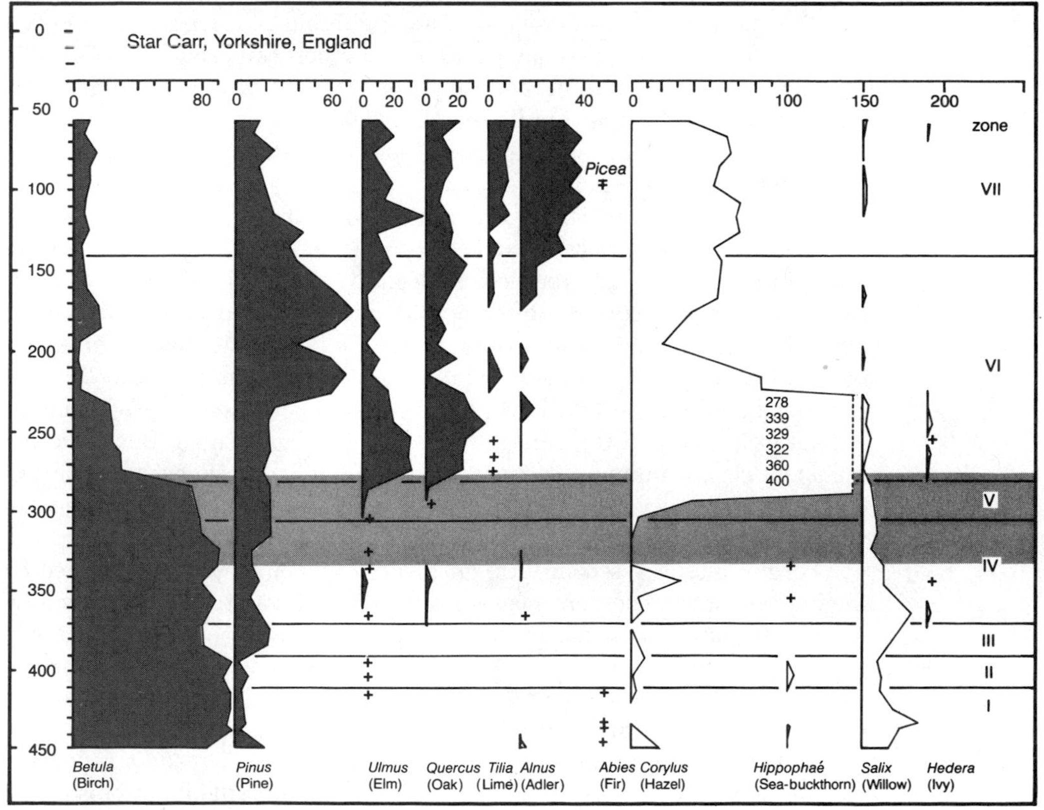

deforestation during the early occupation of Star Carr. The abundant animal remains from these same strata also suggest that whereas the Mesolithic folk took advantage of the rich forest fauna, they left the forest itself virtually untouched.

The overlying Zone VI, deposited after people abandoned Star Carr, indicates that hazel came to dominate the forest cover, with elm and oak also becoming more abundant. This shift reflects the transition from birch woodland to mixed oak forest. Later pollen profiles from this area document the extension of herbaceous plant communities—almost certainly the result of human-caused deforestation.

Past Desert Environments: Palynology at Lehner Ranch

Look at another pollen diagram, the one from the Lehner Ranch site, an important Paleo-Indian site in southern Arizona. Excavations at Lehner in the 1950s yielded several Clovis fluted points, butchering tools, and charcoal in association with mammoth, horse, bison, and tapir remains. The four radiocarbon dates available from the Lehner site average about 11,200 radiocarbon years ago.

Palynologist Peter Mehringer set out to determine the nature of the environment of the early big-game hunters and their prey. Pollen analysis at Lehner is complicated by the repeated cut-and-fill sequences during prehistoric times, and it is difficult to find a single locality at Lehner that contains a continuous and unbroken pollen record.

This diagram is a composite, showing the results of three different pollen profiles, each of which partially overlaps the others. Mehringer's pollen diagram for Lehner Ranch differs notably from the Star Carr profile. Here, the pollen spectrum is dominated by high frequencies of pollen from *composites* (herbs such as ragweed and sagebrush) and *cheno-am* (plants of the goosefoot family and amaranth).

This pattern, which characterizes many postglacial pollen profiles from the southwestern desert area, creates a problem because it masks the presence of the less common (yet more ecologically sensitive) indicators. In order to offset the high frequency of composite and cheno-am pollen, Mehringer applied the technique known as the *double fixed sum.* The black profiles are based on a standard summary for all pollen types identified, with the percentages based on the first 200 pollen grains encountered in each sample. A total of 25 such 200-grain sample counts are represented. But while the dominant cheno-am and composite pollen undoubtedly represent locally occurring species, they are insufficient by themselves for interpreting regional vegetation or climate.

For this reason, a second, 100-grain count was employed (represented by the hatched area). The percentages for the second count were computed by ignoring the high abundance of cheno-am and composite pollen, counting only the other, rarer pollen types. By comparing the results of both counts, one can study both the gross frequencies of the dominants and the presence of the rarer species, which turn out to be the more sensitive ecological indicators.

At Lehner Ranch, the pollen from stratigraphic units i, j, and k reflect the climatic conditions that prevailed during the mammoth-killing episode of Clovis times. Although the pollen frequencies during this period are quite

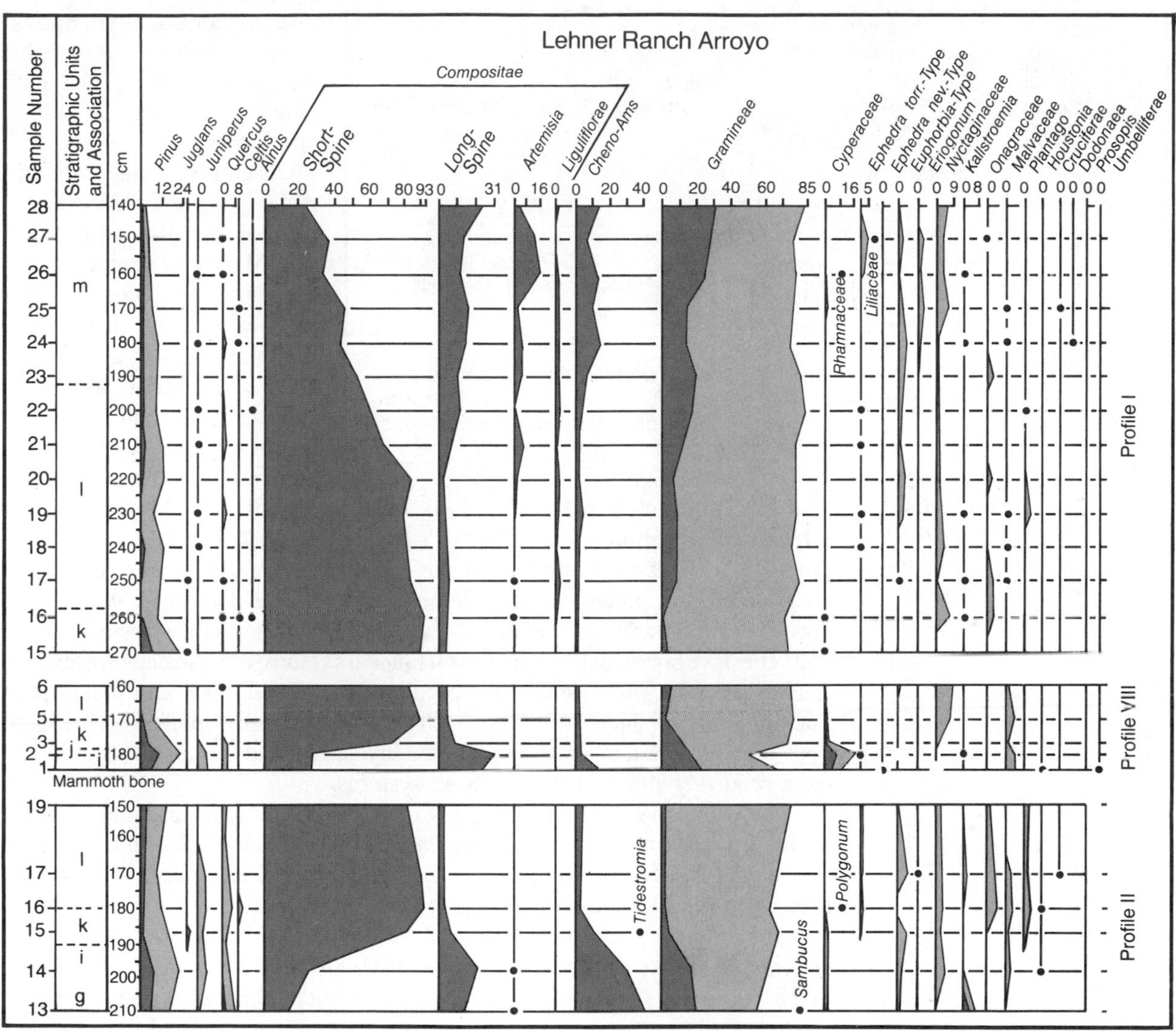

Pollen diagram from the Lehner Ranch site (Arizona).

similar to those in modern samples collected nearby, the slightly greater abundance of pine, oak, and juniper pollen may indicate somewhat more moist or cool conditions before and during the deposition of the lower part of unit k. Somewhat later, in unit l, a gradual shift appears in the composite categories.

Overall, the vegetation represented by the pollen spectra from Lehner Ranch denotes a desert grassland, which today occupies more favored sites nearby. Peter Mehringer and Vance Haynes conclude that the climate at the Lehner site 11,000 years ago was only slightly wetter and cooler than today.

Microchronology of the Mount Mazama Eruption: Palynology at Lost Trail Pass Bog

Remember from Chapter 8 that when Mount Mazama (today's Crater Lake, in Oregon) erupted nearly 7,000 years ago, it spewed volcanic ash throughout

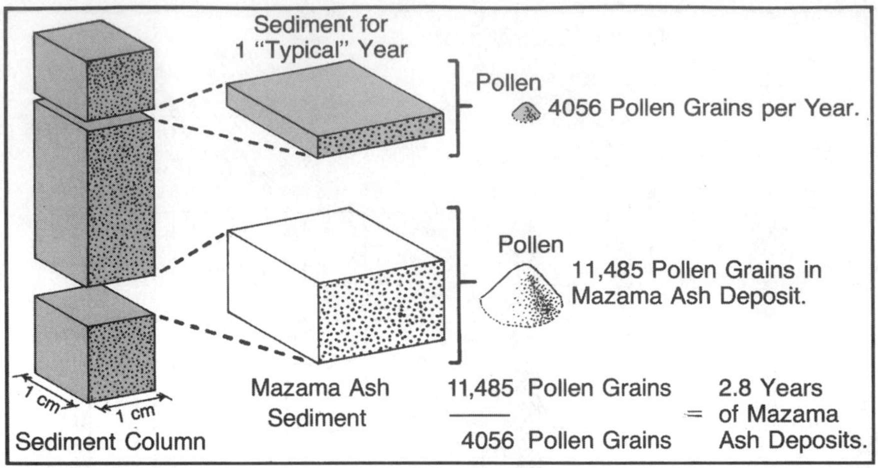

Diagram illustrating how ashfall duration is computed from pollen influx within a 1-cubic-centimeter column of Mazama ash from the Trail Pass Bog site (Montana).

the western United States, even washing into the basal deposits of Gatecliff Shelter several hundred miles away.

Peter Mehringer and his colleagues decided to take a look at the effects of the Mount Mazama ashfall by sampling the deposits at Lost Trail Pass Bog (Montana). Using a sediment core 10 centimeters in diameter, Mehringer and his team extracted a sample of Mazama ash from a depth of 5.1 meters below the bog surface. Lake sediment on either side of the ash was radiocarbon dated at 6700 ±100 B.P. and 6720 ±120 B.P. Clearly the sample dates to the period of the Mount Mazama eruption.

Overall, the pollen diagram demonstrated the ecological impact of this massive eruption. Huge quantities of incoming volcanic ash effectively lowered the lake's productivity at Lost Trail Pass. However, perhaps through a "mulching" effect, the ashfall also produced increased vigor and pollen production in some sagebrush steppe plants. Based on the pollen records for both aquatic and terrestrial species, the investigators concluded these effects were relatively short term in both ecosystems.

But what does "short term" really mean? How long, for instance, did the ashfall from Mount Mazama actually last? To find this out, Mehringer applied the so-called *pollen influx* method of palynology. "Pollen influx," in this context, estimates the number of pollen grains incorporated into a fixed volume of sediments over a particular time. It works like this: Suppose that 1 cubic centimeter of lake sediment containing 100,000 pollen grains was deposited in 25 years. This being so, we know that an average of 4,000 pollen grains were deposited on a 1-centimeter-square surface during each of the 25 years represented by the sediments. The pollen influx of this sample is thus 4,000 grains per year.

We can also turn the relationship around: If we know the pollen influx for a certain volume of sediment, then it is possible to estimate the number of years represented in that same sample.

This reasoning was applied to the Lost Trail Pass Bog samples. First, the depositional time span was determined by running a series of closely spaced radiocarbon determinations. Then the total pollen influx was estimated by adding 100,000 "tracers" (*Lycopodium* spores) to each 2-cubic-centimeter sample before pollen extraction. The ratio of the artificially introduced tracers to the fossil pollen grains permitted the calculation of population estimates for each zone. The actual pollen influx for each stratigraphic zone could be estimated from the average pollen content. The figure above shows that a 1-cubic-centimeter column of the Mazama ash, containing 11,485 pollen grains, must have been deposited in about 2.8 years.

Using this extremely meticulous approach, Mehringer and his colleagues could make several inferences about the conditions under which the Mazama ash fell. Because pine and sagebrush pollen are good seasonal indicators, and they occur in high concentrations with the ash layer, the investigators concluded that volcanic ash from a major eruption of Mount Mazama first fell in the autumn (roughly 6,700 radiocarbon years ago) and continued to fall over the next 3 years.

Palynology of Shanidar Cave: A Cautionary Tale

One of the most dramatic palynological studies in archaeology used sediments recovered from Shanidar Cave, Iraq. This famous site was occupied sporadically over the past 100,000 years. During his fourth season at Shanidar, Ralph Solecki and his crew discovered a Neanderthal skeleton that appeared to have been intentionally buried roughly 60,000 years ago. The bones were extremely fragile, and the entire block was removed in a plaster jacket, earth and all. The box containing Shanidar IV was transported to an Iraqi museum where it remained unopened for 2 years. It was later discovered that the Shanidar IV grave actually contained four individuals—three adults and an infant.

Following routine field procedures, Solecki took soil samples from around and within the area of Shanidar IV. Although he had no specific purpose for collecting the samples, Solecki had learned in previous work on Native American archaeological sites in Ohio that soil samples can provide unexpected

Neanderthal skull as it was being exposed at Shanidar Cave (Iraq). This person was probably [illegible]ed by roof fall inside the cave.

Shanidar Cave on the Internet:

Excellent summary of the burial evidence by Christy Turner:
http://enuxsa.eas.asu.edu/~voegele/bioarchy/erin.html

dividends. Some 8 years later, these soil samples would provide "significant, if not startling results."

Project palynologist Arlette Leroi-Gourhan tested the Shanidar IV samples for pollen and—to everyone's surprise—found pollen preserved in great quantities in the Neanderthal grave site. Microscopic examination of the pollen spores indicated that the matrix around Shanidar IV contained dense concentrations of at least eight species of brightly colored wildflowers, including grape hyacinth, bachelor's button, and hollyhock.

Leroi-Gourhan suggested that the flowers had been woven into the branches of a pinelike shrub, which apparently grew nearby on the Ice Age hillside. She also concluded that the individuals found in the Shanidar IV grave were laid to rest sometime between late May and early July. In other words, this Neanderthal burial took place as a formal interment, showing a degree of deliberate planning and "humanness" that few were willing to grant the Neanderthal community. The pollen evidence at Shanidar caused many to rethink our view of Neanderthal ritual and belief systems.

But once again, one must look more closely at the formation processes involved. Unfortunately, as Charles Miksicek has pointed out, the pollen grains were extracted as an afterthought, and it remains quite possible that the flower pollen grains had nothing to do with the skeletons but were simply contained in the cave sediments, introduced by either natural or other cultural agencies. It is certainly possible that the pollen grains were in the Shanidar Cave before the grave pit was dug. If so, then the secondary botanical remains inside the burial pits have little relationship to the bones (and actually predate them). Because the samples were analyzed without adequate controls from elsewhere in the surrounding deposits and without consideration of the formation processes involved, it is impossible for us to understand what the Shanidar Cave pollen really means.

Looking at Economic Pollen: Palynology at Broken K Pueblo

Once several pollen diagrams from an area have been analyzed and integrated, a regional sequence can be constructed. At this point, pollen analysis can even function as a relative dating technique. That is, an undated site can be placed in proper temporal sequence simply by matching the unknown pollen frequencies with the dated regional frequencies, just as in dendrochronology. In eastern Arizona, pollen analysis has even assisted in the reconstruction of the sequence of pueblo room construction. The regional pollen profile indicates that during the occupation of the Broken K pueblo, from A.D. 1100 to 1300, the relative frequency of tree pollen was decreasing. Through careful excavation, the floors of about 50 rooms were located and pollen samples taken. Samples from room floors are assumed to represent the pollen rain during site occupation. Each room was placed in temporal sequence by measuring the relative frequency of tree pollen (because earlier rooms have higher arboreal pollen counts than do the later rooms).

The sequence of room construction compiled in this fashion corresponded precisely to the sequence based on architectural superposition and soil stratigraphy.

Broken K pueblo provides another example of the utility of palynology. James Hill and Richard Hevly isolated room functions through the analysis of the fossil pollen spectrum. During excavation, they knew that several different sorts of rooms were represented. Many of the rooms contained fire hearths and stone slabs for grinding corn; these were interpreted as habitation rooms, in which daily activities generally were carried out. A second type of room, considered to be a storage facility, was not only smaller than the habitation rooms but also lacking in the artifacts and features involved in food processing. A third type of room, markedly different from the others, was round and completely sunken below the ground surface. Both context and artifact yield convinced the excavators that these rare rooms must have been ceremonial, analogous to the modern pueblo kivas. On the basis of conventional archaeological reasoning, Hill and Hevly discerned three sorts of rooms: habitation, storage, and ceremonial.

What did the pollen from these rooms indicate? Pollen counts from Broken K pueblo were divided into "natural" and "economic" categories, the latter dominated by domestic maize (corn), squash, prickly pear cactus, and other edibles. The economic varieties were assumed to be largely introduced into the deposits by humans, whereas the natural pollen was probably windborne. As expected, the economic pollen was most common in the storage rooms, as the stored crops probably dropped their pollen as they were stacked in the room. Habitation and ceremonial rooms had some economic pollen grains, but in lower frequencies than in the storage rooms. Two kinds of pollen, Mormon tea (*Ephedra*) and buckwheat, were particularly abundant in the ceremonial rooms. It seems likely that, because both species are considered sacred by modern Hopi and Zuni Indians, these species served a similar function in prehistoric ceremonies. By verifying this pattern in the ancient past, the Broken K pollen analysis provides a useful and scientifically valid method for reconstructing the nature of subsistence (and even ceremonial) activities in archaeological sites.

Analysis of Plant Phytoliths

One extremely important method of learning about both wild and domesticated plants is through the analysis of microscopic plant opal phytoliths, literally, "plant stones." **Phytoliths** are formed when the silica ordinarily dissolved in groundwater is carried through plant roots and deposited in mineral form inside the plant, in places where water is used or lost through transpiration. When dead plant material decays, the almost indestructible opal phytoliths are deposited in the ground. Phytoliths have been found in sediments older than 60 million years. Distinctive phytoliths occur in members of the grass family and are also found in such groups as rushes, sedges, palms, conifers, and deciduous trees.

Phytoliths: Tiny silica particles contained in plants. Sometimes these fragments can be recovered from archaeological sites, even after the plants themselves have decayed.

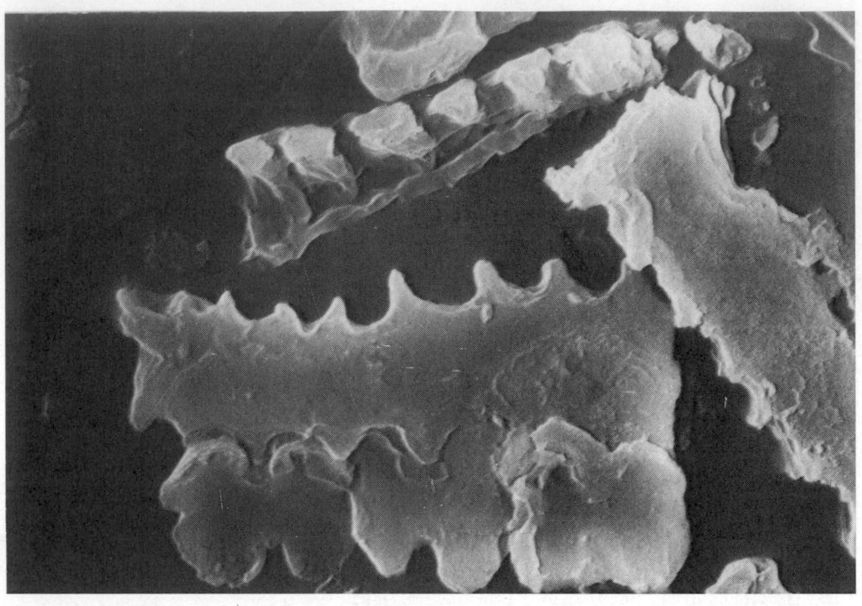

What a phytolith looks like under the microscope.

Phytolith analysis is superficially similar to pollen analysis. Both deal with plant remains at a microscopic level; samples for each are collected in the same way; and the same laboratory can be used for both analyses (in fact, the same sample can be used for both).

But there are differences. Some plants produce pollen but not phytoliths, and vice versa. Different taxa are commonly analyzed by each technique. Although pollen is produced in a single form, phytoliths vary considerably within a single species. Phytoliths are preserved under a wider range of soil conditions than pollen. These critical differences render the methods complementary, and, when taken together, they provide independent sources of data for the paleoethnobotanist.

Although phytoliths have been recognized in archaeological sites for decades, only occasionally before 1970 were archaeological deposits analyzed for phytoliths. Since then, interest in this unusual technique has exploded and, today, the identification and analysis of phytoliths recovered from archaeological sites hold great promise for reconstructing paleoenvironments and for tracking the process of plant domestication.

Considerable progress has been made recently on these taxonomic issues, particularly in the grasses. Phytoliths are being used to study rice, millet, barley, and wheat. Particularly important to Americanist archaeology is Deborah Pearsall's breakthrough in the identification of corn (*Zea mays*) phytoliths, which allowed the introduction date of maize to be pushed back in Ecuador by several millennia. But to truly make a contribution to our understanding of how maize was domesticated, criteria for identifying the phytoliths of teosinte—the probable wild ancestor of maize—must be developed. Recent work using computer-assisted image analysis shows promise for distinguishing wild varieties of teosinte from cultivated primitive maize; similar diagnostics have now been defined for beans and squash.

High-Altitude Archaeology

Phytolith analysis was successfully employed on samples we recovered in the high-altitude excavations at Alta Toquima Village (Nevada). Less than 5 miles south of Gatecliff Shelter, Alta Toquima is located on what is today a cold, wind-swept tabletop, at an elevation of 11,000 feet. About A.D. 1000, a seasonally permanent base camp was established at Alta Toquima. The large number of grinding stones suggested that people were gathering summer-ripening seeds. But the area today supports no grassland; perhaps it never has, or maybe the serious overgrazing by sheep during the historic period eradicated this biotic community.

Flotation analysis did not produce sufficient carbonized plant remains, so we submitted to Irwin Rovner a series of 48 soil samples from the features, interior house floors, cultural middens, and exterior sterile zones at Alta Toquima. We were hoping that the phytoliths, if present, could tell us whether suitable grasslands existed during prehistoric times in the Alta Toquima area.

> **Jefferson's Monticello on the Internet:**
>
> **Monticello Home Page** presents "A Day in the Life," Plan Your Visit," and "Matters of Fact":
> http://www.monticello.org/index.html
>
> **Monticello Main Menu:**
> http://curry.edschool.virginia.edu/~monti/home.html
>
> *See also:*
> **Monticello, Home of Jefferson:**
> http://www.elpress.com/staunton/mnticlo.html
>
> **The Architecture of Thomas Jefferson:**
> http://jefferson.village.virginia.edu/wilson/home.html

Rovner found pine phytoliths in every sample (no great surprise, since Alta Toquima is perched on the upper margin of the limber pine treeline). The exterior samples contained the most abundant amount of pine phytoliths, with considerably less on the interior floors; very little occurred in feature samples. High-altitude festucoid grass phytoliths did occur at Alta Toquima, but in inverse relationship to the pine distribution.

Most of the grass phytoliths occurred in the archaeological features, with little grass outside or elsewhere inside the prehistoric houses. Rovner concluded that during the late prehistoric period, Alta Toquima was inside a pine grove, with the grasses introduced to the site through human transport. This grass must not have been used for flooring, bedding, or roofing. Rovner thinks that the Alta Toquima residents harvested now-extinct grasses, and phytoliths from these foodstuffs ended up in the refuse deposits.

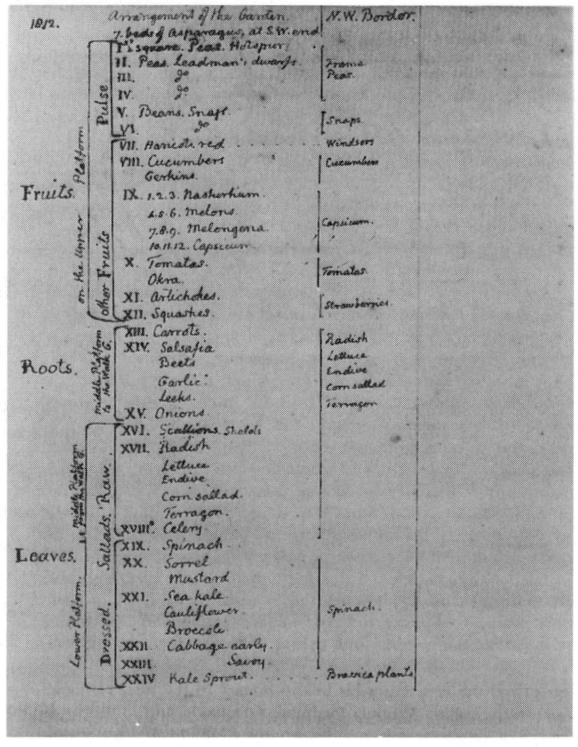
1812. Arrangement of the Garden. | N.W. Border.
7. beds of asparagus, at S.W. end
Fruits. on the Upper Platform. Pulse
I. square. Peas. Hotspur
II. Peas. Leadman's dwarfs | Frame Peas.
III. do
IV. do
V. Beans. Snap | Snaps
VI. do
other Fruits
VII. Haricots. red | Windsors
VIII. Cucumbers | Cucumbers
Gerkins
IX. 1.2.3. Nasturtium
4.5.6. Melons
7.8.9. Melongena | Capsicum.
10.11.12. Capsicum
X. Tomatas. | Tomatas
Okra
XI. Artichokes. | Strawberries.
XII. Squashes.
Roots. middle Platform to the Walk &c.
XIII. Carrots. | Radish
XIV. Salsafia | Lettuce
Beets | Endive
Garlic | Corn sallad
Leeks. | Terragon
XV. Onions
Leaves. Lower Platform. Sallads. Raw.
XVI. Scallions. Shalots
XVII. Radish
Lettuce
Endive
Corn sallad.
Terragon.
XVIII. Celery
Dressed.
XIX. Spinach
XX. Sorrel
Mustard
XXI. Sea kale | Spinach.
Cauliflower
Broccoli
XXII. Cabbage. early
XXIII. Savoy
XXIV Kale Sprout. | Brassica plants

This diary entry, in which Thomas Jefferson lists the vegetables planted in his garden at Monticello (Virginia), helped archaeologist William Kelso determine the exact layout of that garden.

Thomas Jefferson's Elusive Garden

Phytolith analysis has also assisted historical archaeologists in reconstructing the once-elaborate plantings of Thomas Jefferson. Among his other achievements, Jefferson was an avid and astute gardener, employing part of his Monticello (Virginia) plantation as a natural laboratory. One of Jefferson's objectives was to experiment with different kinds of livestock fodder—grasses, clover, alfalfa, and so forth. But whereas Jefferson left numerous drawings, plans, and accounts of the decorative portions of his garden, only a single sketch survives showing the more mundane aspects of Jefferson's

Low-level aerial photograph showing the archaeology of Thomas Jefferson's huge garden at Monticello (upper right), one of the most extensive experimental vegetable gardens of its time. Note particularly the original orchard planting holes (white dots left center) and the western section of the 1809 garden fence postholes (dots extreme left).

garden. The Monticello Foundation has been reconstructing this garden, but will only restore those features whose existence can be confirmed independent of the surviving documentation.

Deciding whether Jefferson really planted fodder fields at Monticello seemed a suitable test for phytolith analysis. Irwin Rovner knew that the site of Monticello was predominantly woodland before Jefferson established his plantation there. If fodder fields actually existed, they should produce phytolith assemblages distinct from the woodland and natural grasses surrounding the plantation.

Archaeologist Scott Shumate collected a series of 19 "blind" samples from various locations in and around Jefferson's garden, some from the projected fodder plots. Rovner, who processed these samples without any knowledge of their provenience, strongly indicated that such discrimination is possible. With the exception of only four individual particles found in scattered samples, all diagnostic grass phytoliths belonged to the projected fodder species. Almost no native grasses turned up in the samples. If this initial sampling proves representative of the rest of Monticello, the procedure can provide significant clues for landscape architects reconstructing the eighteenth-century home of Thomas Jefferson.

Fossil Pack Rat Nests

One increasingly important, if somewhat surprising, source of plant macrofossils is in the ancient nests of wood rats (*Neotoma*) throughout the arid desert West. (Actually, most people call these rodents "pack rats," but the acceptable scientific name is "wood rats"; they're the same critter). These animals drag home extensive quantities of food and nest material; actualistic studies have demonstrated that pack rats do not usually travel more than 100 meters from their nest. Throughout arid North America, these pack rat assemblages are commonly incorporated into rock-hard, urine-impregnated middens. Because the plants contained in the middens must have come from the immediate vicinity of the nest itself, researchers have used pack rat midden analysis to reconstruct detailed environmental chronologies of **Pleistocene** and **Holocene** vegetational change throughout the greater American Southwest.

Pleistocene: The geological epoch beginning about 1.8 million years ago and ending about 10,000 years ago; also known as the Ice Age.

Holocene: The post-Pleistocene geological epoch that began about 10,000 years ago and continues today.

In one study, Philip Wells and Rainer Berger excavated and radiocarbon-dated a number of fossil wood rat nests from the Nevada Test Site (the scene of the highly publicized nuclear test explosions). Their study showed conclusively that the junipers, common throughout southern Nevada, grew as much as 3,000 feet below their present range within the last 12,000 years.

More recently, Robert Thompson and Eugene Hattori analyzed pack rat materials collected in stratigraphic segments from the rear wall of Gatecliff Shelter and from two small shelters in the nearby Gatecliff formation. These midden units were soaked in the laboratory until the pack rat urine was dissolved and then were poured through geological screens, dried, and hand sorted. Selected specimens of juniper twigs, piñon pine needles, twigs and winter buds of quaking aspen, and wild rose twigs were submitted for radiocarbon dating. The dates, ranging from 9520 ±480 B.P. to essentially modern, allowed Thompson and Hattori to devise a chronology of the changing plant communities in the immediate vicinity of Gatecliff Shelter for the past 10,000 years.

The most important finding was that piñon pine was absent from the Gatecliff area until about 6000 B.P. (and this was confirmed by macrofossils found in flotation samples processed on the Gatecliff hearths and also counts of fossil pollen grains in the Gatecliff sediments). This finding is extremely important because it indicates that people arrived in the Gatecliff area well in advance of the piñon pine. Clearly the people visiting Gatecliff before 6000 B.P. relied on plant foods other than the piñon pine, so critical to the economy of the historic Western Shoshone populations of the area.

"Reading the Fuel" in the Ancient Andes

As discussed elsewhere, Americanist archaeology has recently broadened its interpretive framework. For two decades, processual archaeologists emphasized the analysis of "natural" resources—such as plant remains—as a key to understanding how people coped with the ecological and environmental issues of the past. More recently, the postprocessual critique has suggested that archaeologists must set aside their compulsive fixation with the purely physical environment in order to explore how humans in the past constructed the worlds in which they lived.

As is true for the rest of Americanist archaeology, paleoethnobotanists have registered the postprocessual shockwaves. Rather than simply looking at what plant remains can tell us about past economies and ecologies, some archaeologists are exploring how to investigate the social, symbolic, and political dimensions of the relationship between plants and people.

The Upper Mantaro Valley Archaeological Project

To explore how such research might proceed, let us examine a pioneering study in which Christine Hastorf and Sissel Johannessen have analyzed the changing patterns of fuel use in the Upper Mantaro region, in the central Andes of Peru. This high, intermontane valley begins at 3,500 meters in elevation. The intensively settled and cultivated valley floors are surrounded by rocky hillsides, supporting a few rocky fields, but mostly grasses, a few shrubs, and small trees.

Thousands of years of intensive cultivation and herding have undoubtedly changed the character of these upland valleys, but nobody is certain just how. Although some investigators believe that the landscape was originally forested, pollen analysis suggests that this area has been relatively treeless since humans first moved in, several thousand years ago.

The Upper Mantaro Archaeological Project excavated numerous house compounds from six archaeological sites spanning the period A.D. 500–1500. During the Wanka II period, the population of the Upper Mantaro area aggregated into large, walled towns located on protected knolls just above the rolling upland zone. The archaeological evidence suggests that this was a time of considerable intersite tension, with land use probably restricted to areas close to the walled settlements. After the Inka conquest during Wanka III times, the population was relocated into small villages on the valley floor.

Six-liter soil samples were collected and processed from the floors, middens, pits, and hearths encountered in each excavation unit. The more than 900 samples contained thousands of pieces of charcoal and plant fragments, recovered by both dry screening and flotation of the archaeological sediments. The recovered plant remains were classified into three readily observable categories: "grass,"

Bar chart showing the changing composition of fuel remains in the Upper Mantaro region (Peru).

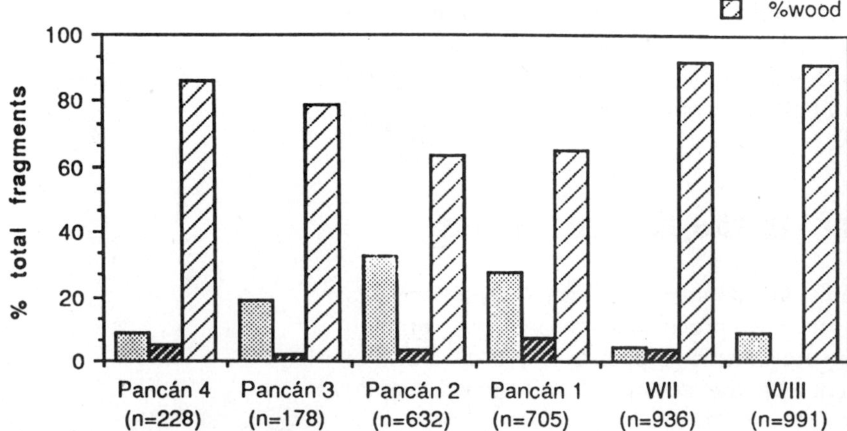

"stem" (small diameter twig fragments), and "wood" (pieces of mature wood). The "wood" category was further subdivided if the tree source could be identified.

The previous diagram sets out the results of the paleoethnobotanical investigation, plotted according to the 1,000-year-long sequence of the Upper Mantaro Valley. Everyone can recognize the trends evident here. First, it is obvious that mature wood is the dominant category throughout the sequence. This trend coincides with the expressed preferences of people living in this area.

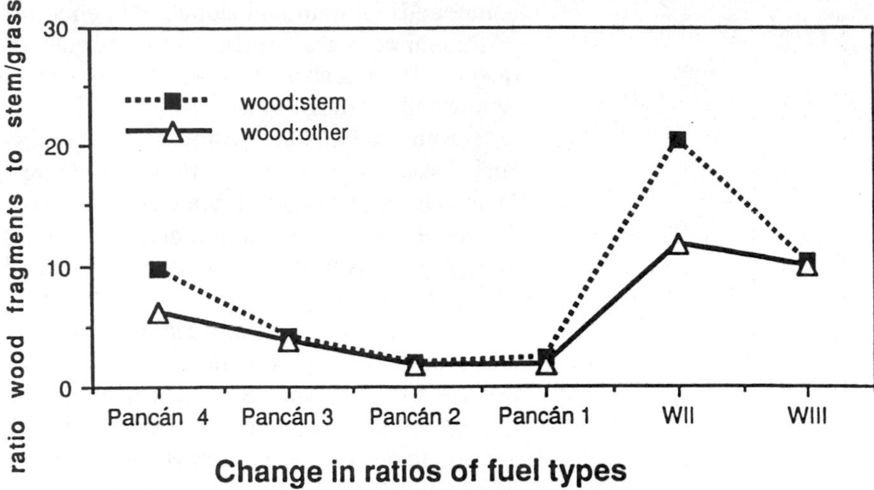

Graph of the changing ratios of wood to other fuel types through time in the Upper Mantaro area of Peru.

Another pattern is also evident: Prior to A.D. 1300 (that is, during the Pancán phases), the relative proportion of mature wood fragments dropped, with a corresponding increase in stem and grass fragments. Then, during Wanka II and Wanka III times, this trend reversed, with stem and grass remains decreasing again. (See graph above.)

Finally, these investigators noted that the species composition of the mature wood shifted somewhat through time. Up to 40 different kinds of wood are present in the Upper Mantaro Valley samples, with no particular taxa being especially dominant. But the most common taxa did change in relative frequency through time. The five most popular wood types during the early Pancán phases (from as yet unidentified trees) dropped out entirely by Wanka II times. And beginning in A.D. 1300 or so, new wood types appeared. One notable example is *Buddleia* (locally called *quishuar*), a high-elevation tree that became the most popular fuel source during Inka (Wanka III) times.

How Can These Patterns Be Explained?

Let us work through the analysis step by step, following the arguments developed by Hastorf and Johannessen. First, we must consider whether the charcoal distributions on our diagram can be attributed to factors other than fuel use. Is it possible, for instance, that we are looking at changing patterns in the use of house construction materials, changing subsistence practices, or perhaps differential plant preservation through time?

Hastorf and Johannessen rejected all these possibilities. They noted that most of the charcoal in these samples seems to have come from fire refuse accumulated over a span of several months or years. Although the possibility exists that some of the charcoal resulted from inadvertent fires (such as accidental burning of thatch roofs and roof beams), the investigators assume that the vast majority of the charcoal recovered reflects intentional fuel use for heating and cooking. They also note that the composition of the house compounds (of mud and stone), the general subsistence remains, and the depositional contents are basically constant throughout the 1,000-year sequence. There is also little reason to believe that rates of preservation changed significantly through time.

From this baseline, Hastorf and Johannessen moved to interpret the charcoal distributions strictly in terms of changing fuel use patterns. Beginning their paleoethnobotanical analysis in fairly standard processual fashion, they first determined whether the archaeological patterning of fuel use revealed long-term shifts in the relationship between these highland people and their environment.

From this strictly economic perspective, the increased reliance on twigs and grasses during the Pancán sequence is just what one might expect in a relatively treeless landscape. Through time, the growing human population and more intensive agricultural land-use patterns should be expected to create conditions of fuel scarcity. It makes sense that, as people denuded their landscape of trees (the best locally available fuelwood source), they were forced to use less desirable, yet more costly sources of fuel (in this case, the small shrubby plants, twigs, and grasses).

But if this is so, then it's difficult to see why this trend should reverse during later Wanka times. Contrary to strictly ecological expectations, the archaeologically recovered plant remains show that the use of high-quality fuels actually *increased* after A.D. 1300.

Perhaps the evidence from settlement pattern archaeology provides a clue. Beginning in Wanka II times, an elite class began social and political consolidation of the area. Maybe this elite mandated some sort of fuel management program, perhaps in the form of tree cultivating, resulting in more available mature wood sources. This scenario is certainly possible, since we know that tree cultivation was practiced during Inka times.

Although tree farming is certainly a rational response to increasing wood shortage, this explanation raises some other difficult questions:

> *Why does the change take place in Wanka II times?* Why not earlier (when the population also increased) or later (when the Inka took over and restructured the location of the production system)?
>
> *Why would cultivation be chosen to alleviate the fuel shortage?* Why not simply go farther afield to gather fuel? Or why not just shift to lower quality fuels?
>
> *And why do certain tree taxa show up during Inka times, when they were absent before?*

Fuel, of course, has an important economic role in Andean life; it is a basic requirement of life. And the increased fuel management/possible tree cultivation explanation provides a workable answer in economic terms, but leaves several questions unanswered.

Moving Beyond Econo-Think

At this point, the investigators decided that it was necessary to explore explanations that moved beyond conventional economic and ecological factors.

They delved into the modern and ethnohistoric records available to document the relationships between Andean people, the upland forest, and traditional fuel sources. Hastorf and Johannessen discovered that this relationship is considerably more complex than a strictly economic perspective might indicate: "Wood and trees in the Andes are much more than fuel; they also have social, symbolic, and political dimensions."

Ethnohistoric sketch of an Inka man linking himself to his in-laws by presenting them with wood and straw fuel at a wake.

Collecting fuel was an important aspect of Andean life during the ethnohistoric period, consuming up to 4 hours each day for some segments of the Inka population. We know from the documentary accounts that logs, kindling, and straw were also important tribute items in the Inka state. And even within households, fuel sometimes had a ritual function similar to food, being exchanged to cement social relations. Wood and straw, for instance, were sometimes provided by brothers-in-law to relatives at a wake.

Trees had important, symbolic connotations in Andean cosmology. Certain sacred trees were planted at administrative sites. Others were symbolically linked with deities. Wood from *quishuar,* mentioned earlier, was burned in large quantities at festivals, and human figures carved of *quishuar* were ritually burned as sacrifices to the divine ancestor of the Inka dynasty. Trees were also symbolically associated with water (the source of life), as well as with women, clouds, winter, and the moon.

From these and other ethnohistoric and ethnographic examples, Hastorf and Johannessen defined "several dimensions of meaning given to planted trees, linking the people to their land and to their ancestors, providing a reason to nurture and plant trees. This gives us a fuller understanding of why an Andean people might plant trees, not just as their fuel source, but as a symbol of the linking reciprocal relationship of a kin group with their land."

Relating Ideology to the Past

As they expanded their focus to include the cultural world of the Andean past, these investigators came to supplement their strictly ecological perspective with a new appreciation of the overarching, "cultural" relationship between ancient Andean people and their environment. Initially, they had viewed such "natural" fuel supplies as basically "passive" entities in the environment, "out there" to be exploited, extracted, and used up by the humans living in this environment. As they broadened their perspective, however, Hastorf and Johannessen came to recognize a dynamic cultural interaction between these ancient Andean people and their resources. They came to redefine their paleoethnobotanical approach as "reading the fuel," reflecting the postprocessual fascination with the archaeological record as a surrogate text, available for "reading."

The postprocessual critique has suggested some new ways of approaching old questions about the changes evident in the paleobotanical record. Why, for instance, did the major change take place in Wanka II times?

Hastorf and Johannessen believe that the ideology associated with the planting of certain trees could have been a factor in establishing the local political consolidation occurring at that time: The tree symbolized family continuity on the land, with the roots symbolizing ancestors and the fruits, the children. A ritual step in contemporary marriage ceremonies is termed "to bring the branch" and involves the bringing forth of ritual offspring. The dramatic increase in the use of *Buddleia* or *quishuar* might thus be attributed to its ritual significance of bringing social groups together into larger entities, rather than simply its mundane use as firewood.

These investigators believe that the act of planting trees—which could be interpreted as a purely economic response to a fuel shortage—was chosen from the other available alternatives due to cultural values concerning the ways in which cultivation and trees functioned as symbols of life and lineage, socially and politically.

Hastorf and Johannessen are careful not to imply that economic factors were irrelevant in this case, but they argue that a purely economic explanation is insufficient to understand the patterning evident in the archaeological record of the Andean highlands.

SUMMARY For the archaeologist, the study of subsistence generally focuses on the way in which people go about feeding themselves. A wide variety of techniques is now available to assist the archaeologist in such subsistence reconstructions. Faunal analysis—the study of animal remains in archaeological sites—can be directed toward a number of relevant objectives. In some cases, the faunal remains provide direct evidence of which species were hunted (or collected) for food, how these animals were captured, and what butchering methods were employed. Some sites can provide clues as to exactly how many animals were killed at a time and how much meat was subsequently consumed (or wasted). Sometimes the reconstruction of hunting practices implies the presence of correlated patterns of social organization, as, for instance, the coordinated bison hunts that occurred on the American Plains.

Plant remains are also powerful sources of data regarding ancient life. Macrofossils (intact plant parts) have been important not only to paleoclimatic reconstruction but also as direct evidence of which plant species were exploited, the season during which these plants were collected, and exactly how the various plant parts were cooked. Flotation is the most commonly used method for recovering plant macrofossils from archaeological sites. Plant microfossils—pollen grains, phytoliths, and spores—are also of interest to archaeologists. Fossil pollen grains can be systematically recovered from archaeological deposits and used to construct a pollen diagram, which plots the changing frequency of pollen throughout the occupational history of the site. Coupled with relevant data on modern plant biogeography, the pollen diagram enables the archaeologist to reconstruct the distribution of prehistoric plant communities and to document how these floral associations have changed through time. A regional pollen analysis can be used as a relative dating technique. The frequencies of pollen types can also serve as clues to the economic functions of specific intrasite areas, such as storage rooms and ceremonial areas.

For decades, archaeological plant remains were used mostly to reconstruct past subsistence practices. But some paleoethnobotanists are moving beyond relatively straightforward ecological interpretations to explore the overarching, "cultural" relationships between ancient people and their environment. Particularly when solidly tied to independent ethnohistorical and ethnoarchaeological documentation, this relatively new direction in analyzing ancient plant remains promises to make a considerable contribution to the ideational objectives of the postprocessual critique.

Chapter 12

Some Bioarchaeological Approaches to the Past

PREVIEW This chapter looks at a relatively new breed of scholar—the bioarchaeologist—someone who feels at home in both biological anthropology and Americanist archaeology. Bioarchaeology is an important new field that specifically examines the human biological component in the archaeological record. Bioarchaeologists study the origin and distribution of ancient diseases, they reconstruct human diets, they analyze the evidence for biological stress in archaeological populations, and they reconstruct past demographic patterns—all by looking directly at the evidence preserved in human tissues. We pay special attention to the very new and flourishing field of *molecular archaeology*—itself a subdivision of bioarchaeology—which is taking advantage of new DNA-related technologies to learn about both the very recent and the ancient human past. Although this chapter is a bit heavy on chemistry and biology, I hope you will agree that the archaeological payoff is well worth the effort.

In Chapter 2, I distinguished between biological and cultural approaches to anthropology, clearly placing the field of archaeology in the "cultural" camp. Like most black-and-white criteria, this distinction is not really as clear-cut as I have led you to believe. But in books like this, one must draw lines somewhere, and so I excluded biological anthropology from our immediate domain of interest. Now it is time to redress the balance.

In truth, archaeologists have a long history of slighting their colleagues in biological anthropology. For years, archaeologists excavating mortuary sites have called in a biological anthropologist to help out with the human bones recovered. However, it was rare for the archaeologists even to invite an osteologist to the site, much less to solicit advice about the best way to go about testing the site and removing the human burials. Although people who did this were biological anthropologists, we used to call them "osteologists" (*oste* = bones, *ologists* = people who study). This made some sense, since **osteology** is that branch of anatomy dealing with bones, and that is what these osteologists did.

Osteology: A branch of anatomy dealing with human bones.

But over the years, the biological anthropologists who helped out on digs came to do more than just study human bones. For one thing, they insisted (correctly) that they should be full-scale members of the archaeological team.

In many cases, they became skilled archaeological excavators themselves, who preferred to excavate personally the bones they would study. These so-called osteologists, then, not only studied ancient bones, but they also knew how to excavate and record such remains as well as the best archaeologist. And very often, their "osteological" studies went far beyond the bones, as when mummified human tissue or human hair turned up. They found that, although it was possible to learn quite a bit about human diet from studying bones, they must also factor in the plant and animal remains recovered from sites, because this was another important source of information that could be used to cross-check results obtained from human bones.

Over the years, as the field of "archaeological osteology" became more specialized, various names have been proposed for those who do it: osteoarchaeologist, human zooarchaeologist, biological archaeologist, and so forth. Here, we will follow Clark Spencer Larsen's self-description of **bioarchaeologist** to describe those who study the human biological component of the archaeological record.

Bioarchaeology: The study of the human biological component evident in the archaeological record.

Paleopathology and Skeletal Analysis

We begin with *paleopathology,* the study of ancient disease (which comprises one of the most challenging branches of bioarchaeology). Although paleopathologists must often be satisfied with identifying a "disease cluster" rather than naming a specific pathogen, the fact that research is limited to dry, bony tissues has not precluded the development of alternative stategies of inquiry.

I am convinced that disease ecology may be important archaeologically, but it's been a damn difficult thing to figure out.

TOM D. DILLEHAY, ARCHAEOLOGIST (UNIVERSITY OF KENTUCKY)

The past two decades have seen significant progress in several directions. First has been the progress toward identifying specific diseases (and disease complexes), from both the diagnosis of skeletal materials and the development of models for disease patterns in specific regions. Another important research direction has been the investigation of "nonspecific" indicators of stress, particularly as caused by nutritional deficiencies and/or infectious disease. Paleopathological researchers have succeeded relatively recently in developing chemical techniques for reconstructing ancient nutritional patterns. The search for diseases of the past is hardly a new enterprise, but some disorders can now be placed in a more reliable biocultural matrix: for instance, the impact of malaria and hyperostosis in eastern Mediterranean regions, the problem of iron deficiency anemia in early-historic New World populations, and the relationship between malnutrition and infectious disease.

One particularly important application has been the study of how increased population density is reflected in the proliferation of specific diseases. Jane Buikstra and Della Cook reported on a pattern of disease in western Illinois fully consistent with a diagnosis of tuberculosis. Although the presence of tubercular-like skeletal lesions is well documented in these mortuary samples, Buikstra suggests that

Paleopathology on the Internet:

Paleopathology Resources facilitates exchange of information, including a database:
http://www.usd.edu/~archlab/paleo.html

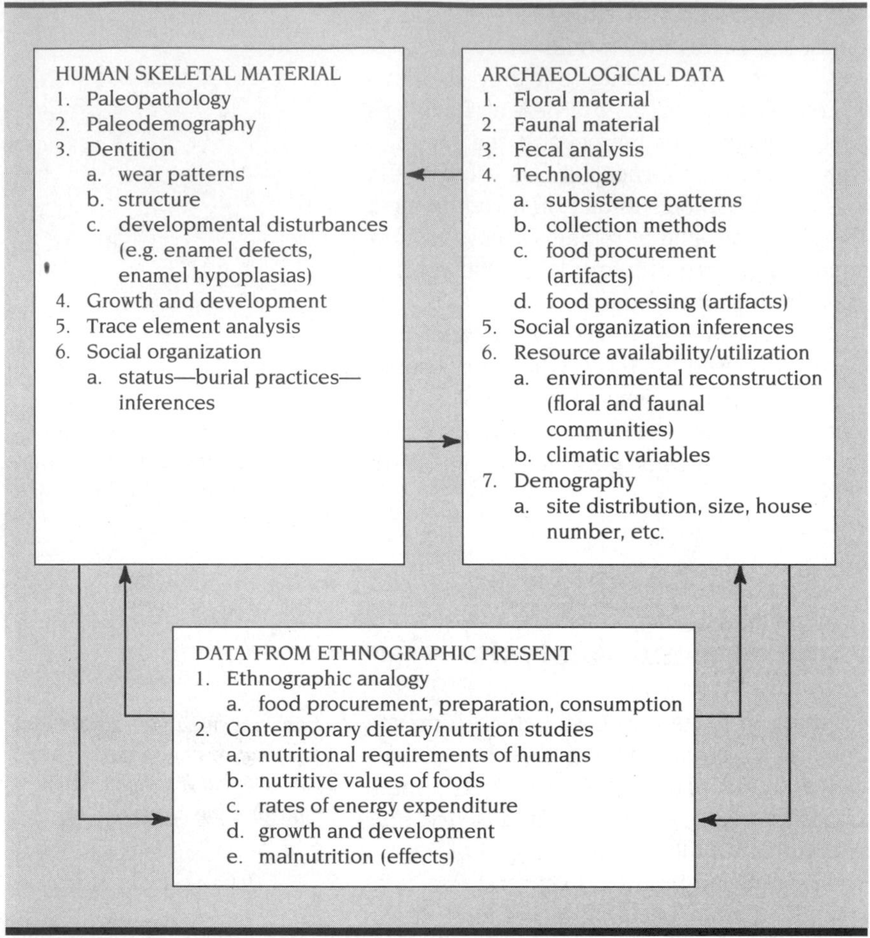

Bioarchaeological interrelationships among human skeletal, archaeological, and ethnographic data.

the responsible pathogen may no longer exist. That is, we are seeing archaeological evidence of a disease that has become extinct.

Reconstructing Diet by Analyzing Stable Isotopes in Human Bones

We already encountered the concept of isotopes in talking about radiocarbon dating (in Chapter 7). Carbon, you will remember, has both stable and unstable isotopes, essentially the same molecule but with differing numbers of neutrons in the nucleus. One stable form, C-12, makes up about 99 percent of the world's carbon; C-13 is also stable but accounts for only about 1 percent. The unstable isotope, C-14, most familiar to archaeologists because of its important implications for dating technology, is extremely rare.

Over the past decade, researchers have established that some kinds of plants differentially absorb these carbon isotopes. The first such "pathway," discovered in experiments with algae, spinach, and barley, converts atmospheric carbon dioxide into a compound with three carbon atoms. This so-called *C_3 pathway* is characteristic of sugar beet, radish, pea, and wheat. A second pathway converts carbon dioxide from the air into a complex compound with four carbon atoms. This *C_4 pathway* includes many plants from arid and semiarid regions, such as maize, sorghum, and millet—the cereal staples of the Americas and Africa. A third *CAM pathway* (an acronym for "crassulacean acid metabolism") is found in succulents, such as cactus.

These findings proved to be critical to reconstructing past diets because we now know that human bone reflects the isotopic ratios of the various plants ingested. Thus, by determining the ratios of carbon (and sometimes nitrogen) isotopes contained in bone collagen, bioarchaeologists can reconstruct the dietary importance of various kinds of plants and animals. Although stable carbon isotope analysis is just emerging from its developmental stage, it has already revolutionized the way in which archaeologists reconstruct prehistoric diets.

Maize in the Tehuacán Valley of Mexico

The use and implications of the stable isotope method can be illustrated by returning to the Tehuacán Valley of Mexico. We previously outlined how Richard MacNeish used direct archaeological methods to reconstruct dietary change throughout the 7,000-year occupation of this highland Mexican valley. Now, with the help of stable isotope analysis, archaeologists have an unusual opportunity to double-check MacNeish's innovative and pioneering work.

The following diagram synthesizes MacNeish's theory about the changing subsistence patterns reconstructed from the Tehuacán Valley excavations. Michael DeNiro and Samuel Epstein analyzed the stable isotopes in samples of human bone from the Tehuacán Valley, in order to provide an independent test of MacNeish's conclusions. They began by converting MacNeish's theory—expressed as changing dietary proportions of plants and animals—into a series of expectations in terms of stable carbon and nitrogen isotope ratios. Basically, this meant that DeNiro and Epstein were required to derive isotope ratios for the various foods that MacNeish recovered archaeologically; this is middle-range research.

They began with the plants, classifying each according to the appropriate photosynthetic pathway. Several of the Tehuacán Valley species used a C_3 pathway; maize is a C_4 plant; and cacti belong to the CAM category. Similar assignments were made for the nitrogen isotopes. Because living plants display a range of isotopic ratios, average values were used as estimates.

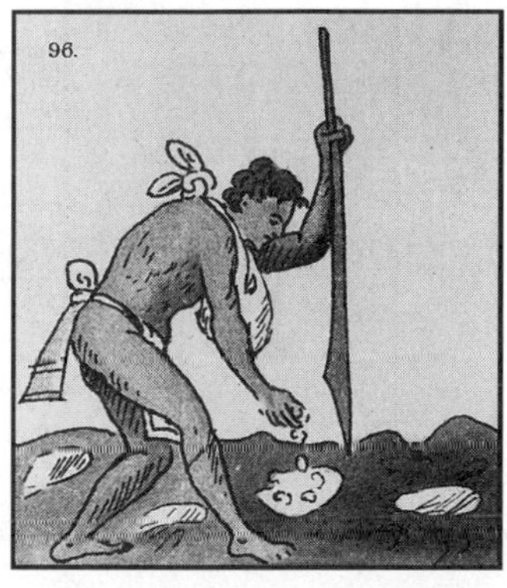

These ethnohistoric drawings, made by sixteenth-century Aztec artists, show traditional methods used to plant maize in the Tehuacán Valley of Mexico.

But the prehistoric Tehuacános also ate meat, and so isotope ratios were required for the various meat sources as well. These results were less satisfactory because DeNiro and Epstein did not know the percentage of C_3 and C_4 plants that these long-dead animals had consumed. It would, presumably, be possible to derive these values precisely using mass spectrometry on the actual animal bones recovered archaeologically; instead, they used a complex, and less satisfactory, "mass balance equation" to derive the animal bone estimates and then combined the plant and animal ratios mathematically by phase.

The diagram also illustrates the stable isotope conversion of MacNeish's dietary reconstruction as the solid line. This curve, in effect, summarizes the logical implications of MacNeish's initial theory, but expressed in stable isotope terms. Actually, because of the relatively primitive state of middle-range research on isotopic correlates, three different conversions were attempted, but only the simplest is discussed here.

DeNiro and Epstein then sampled some of the human bones recovered by MacNeish and his team at Tehuacán. The sample from only 12 burials was relatively small because several potential samples no longer contained enough bone collagen to allow computation of carbon and nitrogen isotope ratios. The bone isotopic ratios were then obtained using mass spectrometry analysis.

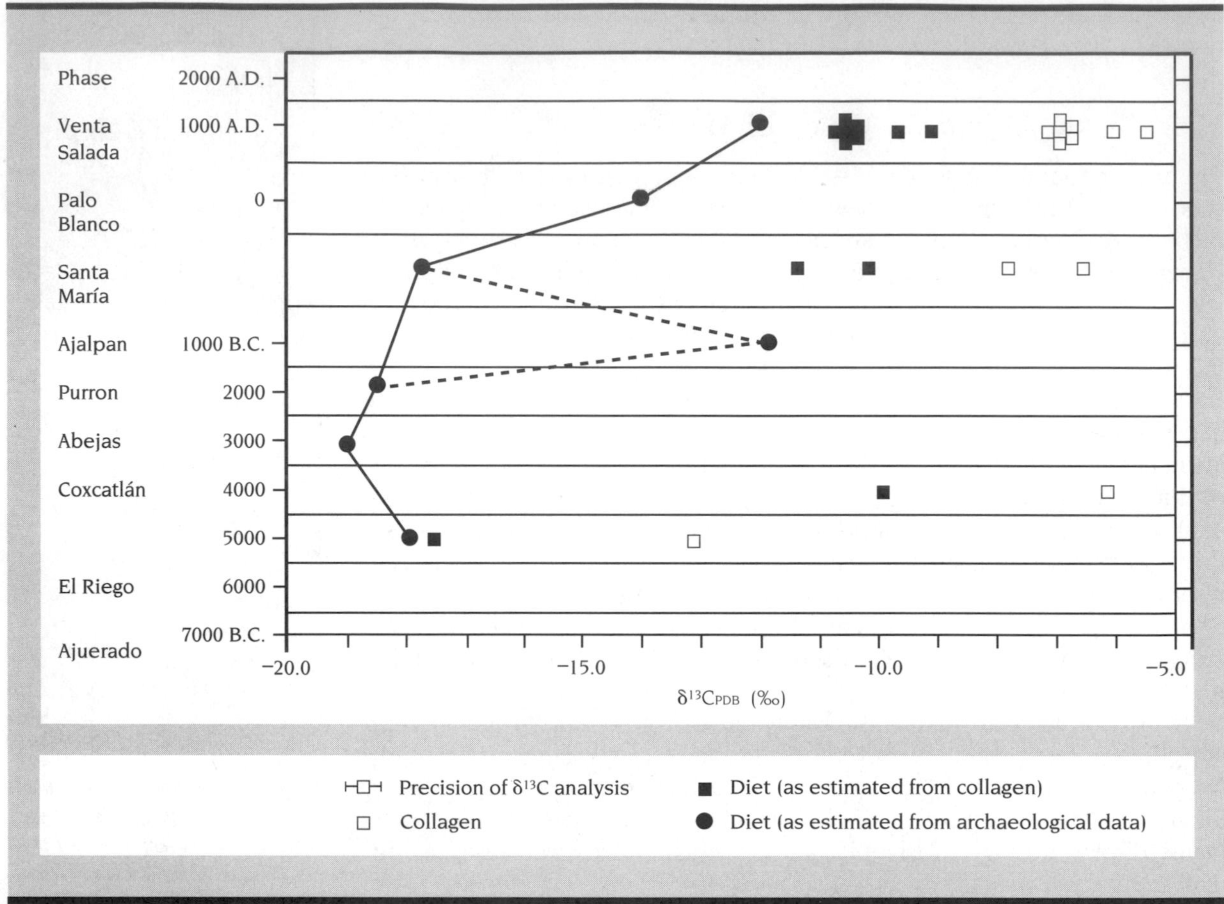

C-13 values of the diets of people living in the Tehuacán Valley, as derived from analyzing stable isotopes in bone collagen. The solid line shows the major trend—an increased reliance on a maize-based diet. The dashed line shows periods for which the data are unreliable.

The diagram compares the new carbon isotope data with expectations from MacNeish's reconstructions. The isotopic findings for the El Riego phase match closely MacNeish's interpretation. At this early phase, the Tehuacános subsisted strictly by hunting and by gathering wild plants–mostly C_3 food–with meat making up slightly over half the diet.

MacNeish's reconstruction suggested that later, between the El Riego and Santa María phases, hunting and wild plant gathering slowly declined in importance as domesticated plant foods assumed greater importance. This process accelerated rapidly during the Palo Blanco and Venta Salada phases as maize became the staple. Specifically, MacNeish thought that during the Coxcatlán and Abejas phases, wild plants comprised about half the diet, domesticated plant materials being of minor but increasing importance (about 20 percent); meat sources remained significant but were proportionately declining (to about 30 percent). MacNeish believed that wild plant consumption continued through the Palo Blanco phase, ending only with the advent of maize farming during the Venta Salada phase.

But the isotopic evidence suggests otherwise. Rather than a gradual introduction of maize agriculture, the isotope ratios in the human bone suggest a dramatic dietary shift toward maize much earlier, between the El Riego and Coxcatlán phases. The isotope ranges suggest that most of the diet during Coxcatlán times and later was supplied by C_4 plants, probably maize.

Although this discrepancy has important ramifications for our understanding of plant domestication in the New World, both dietary reconstructions are plagued with problems. The difficulty in the translation of MacNeish's proportional diagram into its isotopic correlates is a shortcoming of middle-range research that can be overcome only by a better understanding of isotopic fractionation in living plant populations.

Another biasing factor is that MacNeish's reconstruction is based entirely on data from five cave excavations (because these are the best places to find preserved animal bones and plant remains). But the Tehuacán caves were occupied only seasonally, and one wonders how representative these data are of the overall picture of Tehuacán subsistence. After all, sedentary villages were established elsewhere in the valley during the later phases, the cave sites being used in only marginal and specialized ways. In Chapter 4, we also discussed the fallacy of the "typical" site, demonstrating how the results from a single kind of site can be misleading when used to reconstruct overall patterns.

The stable isotope analysis results are thus equivocal. MacNeish's view on Tehuacán Valley subsistence held up only for the earliest part of the sequence (the El Riego phase). For the latter 6,000 years, there remains a discrepancy between MacNeish's archaeological reconstruction and the one suggested by isotopic analysis of human bone. Current evidence does not permit an informed choice between the two alternatives. Perhaps MacNeish underestimated the importance of early agriculture in the Tehuacán Valley. Or perhaps the small sample size and premature assumptions involved in the bone isotope technique make these results suspect. Nevertheless, it is clear that stable isotope determinations will provide an important tool for archaeologists attempting to reconstruct prehistoric diet.

The supernatural being represented on this Chavín-style ceramic bottle had awesome fangs and serpents emerging from the eyes.

Maize in the Chavín Civilization of Peru

Archaeologists have long attempted to explain the subsistence base of the remarkable Chavín culture, Peru's first highland civilization. As you will remember, Chavín de Huántar is an important civic and religious center where Chavín civilization coalesced about 850 B.C. Here, archaeologists have found evidence of clearly stratified social organization and accomplishments in metallurgy, textile manufacture, monumental architecture, irrigation technology, and stone sculpture.

Such achievements require a stable and highly productive subsistence base, both to support the legions of specialized artisans and elite, and also to sustain the thousands of people who supplied the labor necessary to build such temple complexes.

One aspect of the Chavín subsistence base has already been discussed. In Chapter 11, we examined how food bones excavated from domestic and refuse contexts at Chavín de Huántar enabled archaeologists George Miller and Richard Burger to reconstruct the way in which subsistence patterns shifted from hunting of wild animals to dependence on domesticates (mostly llama).

But what about plant foods? In particular, what about maize, known to have played a critical role in the formation of complex societies elsewhere in the Americas? For instance, we looked at the importance of maize cultivation in early Mesoamerican civilization, where it became an important dietary component in a surprisingly short time. We also know that at the time of Spanish contact, maize enjoyed both ceremonial and economic importance in the Inka Empire in Peru.

Many archaeologists believe that maize must have been a major factor in stimulating the development of early, pre-Inka Peruvian civilization as well. Some have argued that the remarkable spread of the Chavín art style was made possible because of its association with a new, improved variety of maize. Others have noted the depiction of maize on early Chavín-style ceramics. Maize kernels have also been recovered in recent excavations at Chavín de Huántar (where maize continues to be one of the most popular local crops today).

On balance, however, the quality of the evidence supporting this position is rather poor. Because of its overtly religious overtones, iconography is not itself a particularly reliable indicator of the subsistence base, and cultivated plants of any kind are rarely depicted in Chavín art. Direct archaeological evidence, in the form of macrobotanical remains, is also unsatisfactory in this case; undoubtedly a broad range of plant crops were consumed at Chavín de Huántar—certainly maize, squash, beans, and potatoes—but poor conditions of preservation have destroyed most of the evidence. And while it is true maize macrofossils were recovered at Chavín de Huántar, the total recovered sample consisted of merely two maize kernels—hardly the stuff on which robust theories are based.

Recognizing the limitations of the archaeological data, Richard Burger and Nikolaas van der Merwe turned to stable carbon isotope analysis as a means of assessing the importance of maize as a staple for the Chavín civilization. The basics of this technique were discussed earlier, but the application of stable isotope analysis to Chavín differs in some important ways from the Mesoamerican example.

The high-altitude environment surrounding Chavín de Huántar precludes the growth of indigenous C_4 pathway grasses. With very few exceptions, all plants involved in the human food chain in the high Andes photosynthesize along the C_3 pathway. But the exceptions are important because maize (a C_4 plant) and prickly pear cactus (a CAM plant) were probably both introduced from Mesoamerica.

This botanical baseline suggests that prior to the introduction of maize into the high Andes, the diet of people like those living at Chavín de Huántar should have been based exclusively on C_3 pathway plants. Because diet composition directly conditions the stable carbon isotope character of human bone, it should be possible to test for a significant presence of maize in past diets. All you need is a decent sample of human bone from the Chavín civilization.

As it turns out, obtaining such bone samples was not an easy matter. Despite the decades of digging at Chavín de Huántar, no tombs have been found from the appropriate time period. Burger and van der Merwe were able, however, to sample four skulls that had been left as votive offerings, along with complete vessels and wild fruit in the fill of an Urabarriu-phase platform (constructed ca. 850–460 B.C.) located about a mile from the main temple at Chavín de Huántar. Another sample was taken from the remains of a young child interred in a niche in a house wall. The investigators also conducted isotope analysis on a control sample of camelid bones (presumably llama) from refuse deposits excavated at Chavín de Huántar.

Despite the variability in the samples, the stable isotope values were remarkably similar: Each bone sample suggests that only roughly 18 percent of the carbon came from C_4 sources (presumably maize). One of the camelid samples, however, was aberrant, with more than 50 percent of the carbon attributable to C_4 sources. This intriguing result suggests that the llama herds may have been fed on maize fodder. Although the results were obtained on very small sample sizes, the findings were supported by additional stable isotope analysis on human bone from a neighboring valley.

The two primary conclusions from this carbon isotope analysis are: (1) maize seems not to have been an important factor in the genesis of highland Peruvian civilization, and (2) maize was not the staple even in fully developed Chavín lifeways. Despite the lack of direct archaeological evidence, it seems certain that C_3 crops, such as potatoes, contributed the bulk of the dietary intake.

This pattern contrasts vividly with the result of isotope analysis from elsewhere in the Americas (including the study from the Tehuacán Valley, considered earlier). It would seem that the central Andes already enjoyed a rich array of indigenous domesticated plants and animals prior to the importation of maize from Mesoamerica. Because these plant foods were locally adapted, they were frost resistant, were capable of sustained production even with limited rainfall, and could be stored for long periods. As a newcomer, maize simply could not prosper in the extreme Andean environments until extensive terracing and irrigation systems had been constructed (as they were during Inka times).

Looking for Indicators of Stress

Another way to look at human diets is through the documentation of generalized stress responses in human hard tissue. Both the causes and the effects of malnutrition are complex and can rarely be traced precisely. Instead, paleopathologists prefer to study the effects of *stress,* defined as any environmental factor that forces the individual or population out of equilibrium.

Stress is a behavioral impact that cannot be observed directly in archaeological skeletal populations. To overcome this problem, Alan Goodman modeled the effects of generalized stress. Past nutritional deficiencies can be inferred from the pattern and severity of the effects of stress on individuals, as well as the distribution of that stress on the contemporary population. This model views the degree of physiological disruption as dependent on both the severity of environmental stressors and the adequacy of host response.

A range of cultural factors—technological, social, and even ideological—can dampen the effect of stress on human populations. A particular

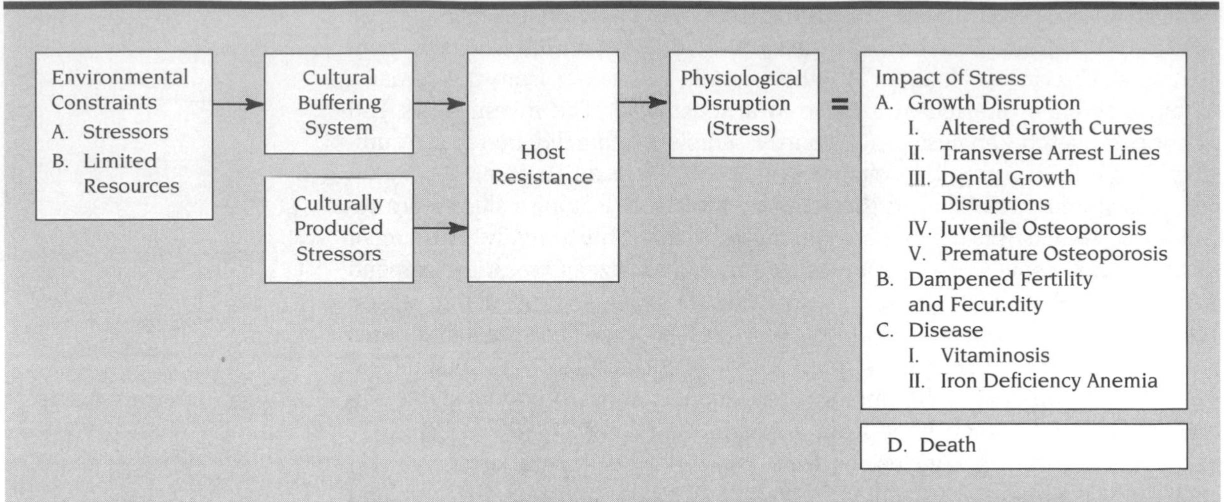

The interaction of environmental, cultural, and biological factors that can enhance or inhibit human nutrition.

nutritional constraint can, for instance, be overcome by (1) changes in technology that broaden (or intensify) the subsistence base, (2) social modifications that effectively distribute food to those in need, or (3) an ideology rewarding and reifying a sharing ethic. Culture likewise can increase stress: Intensifying agricultural production is known to increase the potential for nutritional deficiencies and infectious disease, and relying on monocropping makes populations vulnerable to drought-induced crop failure and protein inadequacies. When insufficiently buffered, stress creates physiological havoc by disrupting growth, decreasing fertility and fecundity, triggering (or intensifying) disease, and, in some cases, causing death.

The human skeleton retains evidence of stress in several ways: As some investigators have put it, "Bone provides a 'memory' of past events and the behavior of its cells up to the point of the individual's death." Numerous methods exist for evaluating the way in which environmental stress affects the growth, maintenance, and repair of the long bones.

Harris lines: Horizontal lines near the ends of long bones indicating episodes of physiological stress.

Harris lines, for instance, are bands of increased bone density—observable on X rays of human long bones. They are often caused by a variety of nutritional stressors, especially severe and short-run dietary deprivation. Harris lines, which generally show up between birth and 18 years of age, have been observed on dozens of archaeological samples and are consistently associated with decreased longevity.

Dental hypoplasias: Horizontal linear defects in tooth enamel indicating episodes of physiological stress.

Another common technique for monitoring physiological stress is the analysis of **dental hypoplasias,** growth arrest lines formed from birth through 6 years. Hypoplasias are often evident from gross examination, although some investigators also look at enamel cross sections. Not only does the presence of hypoplasias betray the presence of environmental stress, but their size also can be measured, allowing estimates of the duration of metabolic stress. Dale Hutchinson and Clark Larsen examined dental defects on a large sample of human skeletal materials from St. Catherines Island, ranging from prehistoric burial-mound populations through the seventeenth-century Christianized Guale Indians buried in the cemetery at Mission Santa Catalina.

They found that the historic-period hypoplasias were wider than those during the precontact period. This pattern strongly suggested that the duration of stress was longer after the European contact, probably reflecting the long-term metabolic stresses associated with the arrival of the Europeans, through the introduction of Old World epidemic diseases and increased health risks overall.

These techniques, when applied to skeletal remains from meaningful archaeological contexts, can be extraordinarily helpful for understanding the effects of nutritional stress among human populations of the past.

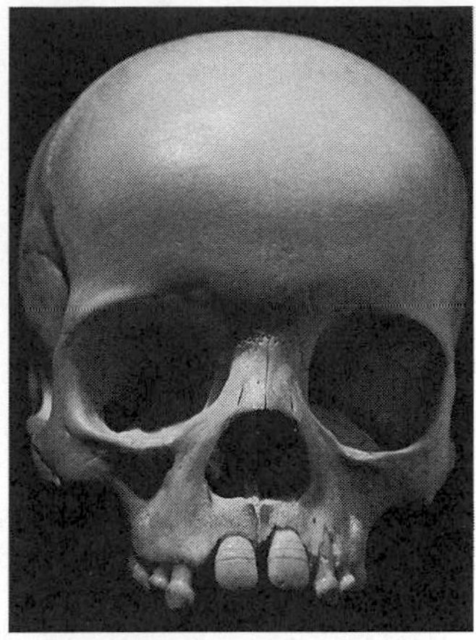

Juvenile cranium showing significant enamel hypoplasias in partially erupted central incisors.

Paleodemography

As with all other archaeological samples, the corpus of human skeletal materials available in the archaeological record contains great potential for understanding the past. Such skeletal populations, however, can carry with them several sources of bias. Extreme caution is required when skeletal populations are taken as representative of the behavioral populations from which they derive. One problem is the differential preservation of human skeletal samples. For example, older bones tend be more badly decomposed, and earlier burials in cemeteries are often disturbed by later interments. Despite such distortions, important conclusions can be drawn about prehistoric population profiles, provided that there are sufficient controls.

A particularly significant skeletal series was recovered by A. V. Kidder when he dug at Pecos Pueblo (New Mexico). More than 2,000 human burials were unearthed, ranging in age from A.D. 1300 to the historic period. When initially analyzed in the 1920s, T. W. Todd crowed that "no other collection surpasses this one for completeness of skeletons, precision of data, and thoroughness of care." The skeletal material from Pecos has been reanalyzed several times, and the changing nature of these analyses reflect the maturation of biocultural analysis.

Charles Mobley attempted to reconstruct the human demography at Pecos by using the raw age data initially published in 1930 and adding earlier prehistoric material from nearby Forked Lightning Ruin. Mortality, survivorship, and life expectancy curves for the Native American samples from Pecos were grouped across the seven chronological periods. Using the mortality curve as an example, we find that the earliest samples—Forked Lightning (A.D. 1150–1300), Pecos Black-on-White (1300–1375), and Glaze I (1375–1425)—exhibit the highest young-child mortality in the Pecos area and the lowest percentage of deaths in the 30- to 50-year age interval. By contrast, the Glaze II, III, and IV (A.D. 1425–1600) samples show relatively fewer child deaths and a higher percentage of deaths in the 30- to 50-year interval (the aberrance of the Glaze V sample was attributed to the small sample size). When compared to other available North American Indian population profiles, this demographic structure suggested to Mobley that the Pecos populations probably enjoyed better than average nutrition and superior hygiene, or perhaps both.

Mobley's study—like all those involving the archaeological record—was grounded in middle-range assumptions. When reanalyzing the same skeletal series from Pecos, Christopher Ruff found that Earnest Hooton had consistently overestimated the ages of the adult sample because of the limited criteria available in the 1920s to estimate age of death from skeletal material. Hooton's criteria also apparently contained systematic biases in the sexing of the Pecos skeletons, resulting in a suggested 60-to-40 male-female adult sex ratio. Ruff thinks that Hooton and Todd were unprepared for the striking robustness encountered at Pecos, and hence they classified some females as males (a worry also voiced by Hooton in 1930). Using modern criteria, Ruff reconstructed a sex ratio much closer to 50-50.

Ann Palkovich has pointed up an additional problem with Mobley's analysis. Only about 30 percent of the Pecos skeletal sample could be assigned to the temporal periods shown on the corresponding figure. Palkovich's statistical analysis shows that this one-third sample does not represent an unbiased sample of the entire archaeological population.

It turns out that infant remains are underrepresented in the ceramically dated samples—perhaps because of cultural preferences at Pecos or a bias in excavation. In any case, this unrepresentative sample strongly suggests that the demographic profiles may be seriously biased.

We dissect this example not to pick on Mobley but, rather, to underscore a general problem: Even relatively rarefied archaeological interpretations—though potentially informative for reconstructing past lifeways and popula-

Mortality curves for various human skeletal samples, plotted by phase, from Pecos Pueblo *(New Mexico).*

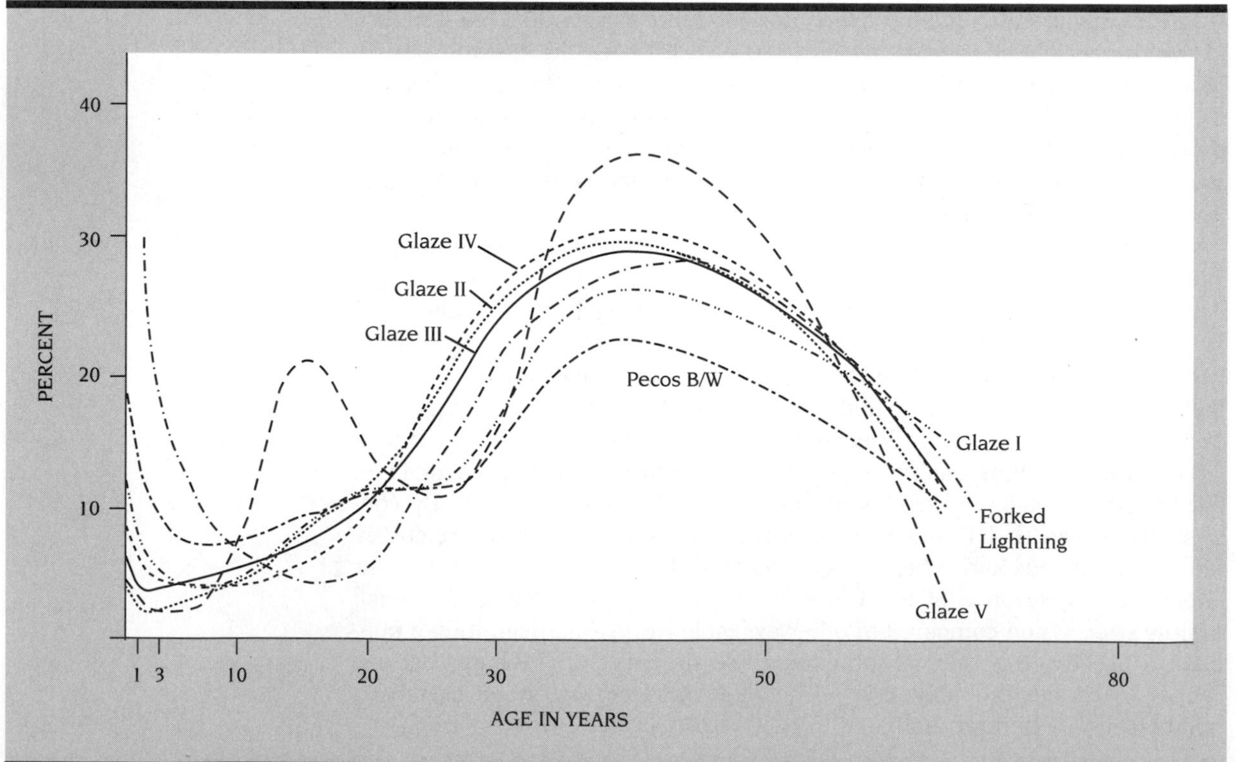

tion dynamics—still depend heavily on the fundamentals of sampling and reliable chronology.

Exploring the Frontiers of Molecular Archaeology

We can now dream of catching molecular evolution red-handed.

ALLAN C. WILSON, BIOCHEMIST

Today's technology permits bioarchaeologists to analyze the past on an entirely different level. Calling upon the most recent developments in the field of genetic experimentation, so-called *molecular archaeologists* can now actually study the past at the level of the individual molecule. Like its counterpart, molecular biology, this newly emergent field addresses the ultimate physiochemical organization of life, focusing particularly on the molecular basis of human inheritance. Although less than a decade old, molecular archaeology has already racked up some spectacular successes, providing unexpectedly precise answers to questions long explored through more conventional approaches.

We begin this discussion with a very recent archaeological application—the use of DNA fingerprinting to track down the long-missing remains of the last Russian Czar and his family. With these basics in hand, we then back up a bit, to examine something of the biological fundamentals behind DNA analysis. Then we look at some of the more recent applications of DNA fingerprinting to the question of our remote human ancestry.

The Case of the Missing Russian Czar

A Russian geologist and a Moscow filmmaker working in 1979 on the outskirts of Ekaterinburg (Siberia) made a bizarre find—a shallow mass grave containing what appeared to be human bone. They reported their discovery to Russian authorities, and in 1992, their find was finally investigated. To everyone's surprise, nine virtually complete skeletons were found, along with 14 spent bullets, some rope fragments, and a shattered jar that had once contained sulfuric acid.

The news was immediately splashed across the headlines. Ekaterinburg was, after all, where deposed Czar Nicholas II had been imprisoned during the Russian Revolution. At midnight, July 16–17, 1918, Czar Nicholas II, the last of the Romanovs, was ordered into the basement, where the royal family and their servants were gunned down by a Bolshevik death squad. One reporter called it "one of the most fateful mass executions in this century."

Great care was taken to dispose of the bodies. According to one account, they were piled on a funeral pyre, then doused with gasoline and set afire. "I stood by to see that not one fingernail or fragment of bone remained unconsumed. Anything of that sort the Whites [pro-Czarists] found I knew they would use as a holy relic." When all was reduced to powder, the ashes were allegedly scattered to the Siberian wind.

At first, the executions were officially defended as an act of revolutionary justice, but because of the outrage from the rest of the world, the massacre soon became an embarrassment to the Russian government. Even the

Formal portrait of Czar Nicholas II and his family, taken 2 years before they were murdered. Such photographs would later provide important evidence about relative heights of each family member to identify their skeletal remains.

house where the Czar and his family had been imprisoned and murdered became a destination for pilgrims from throughout the Soviet Union, attempting to pay homage to the memory of the last Czar. The house was eventually bulldozed, reportedly on direct orders from Boris Yeltsin. Details surrounding the massacre at Ekaterinburg remained a tightly guarded Soviet secret, and the remains of the Czar and his family were never found.

For years, rumors circulated that some, perhaps all, of the Czar's family had somehow escaped. Each of the royal children has had multiple claimants. Even the Czar himself was rumored to be living comfortably somewhere in Poland.

So in 1992, royalty watchers around the world, naturally, wondered the same thing: *Could these bones be those of the murdered Czar Nicholas II and his family?*

Today, thanks to the modern techniques of DNA fingerprinting, we know the answer. Let us examine the Ekaterinburg case in some detail; it illustrates the same DNA-related methods currently being applied by molecular archaeologists to considerably more ancient archaeological remains.

Czar Nicholas II (in 1916).

Looking for the Last Romanov Ruler

Suspecting that the bodies might be those of the royal family, Russian officials invited both national and foreign forensic experts to examine the skeletal remains. Age, gender, stature, and ethnicity were assigned to each skeleton. Additional detailed measurements were taken, the bullets were studied, and dental work was examined. One big problem was that the facial bones appeared to have been deliberately disfigured at death (perhaps, the team speculated, to keep pro-Czarist forces from recognizing the remains, should they be found). Although the skeletons were certainly consistent with those of the Czar and his family, the skeletal identifications remained inconclusive.

Then, in 1993, a British research team, examining some of the Ekaterinburg finds, found traces of DNA still present in the bones. *DNA (deoxyribonucleic acid)* is the characteristic double-stranded molecule in all living cells that encodes specific genetic information. At the time, some courts were beginning to admit

DNA evidence as a way of determining a suspect's guilt or innocence. Although still controversial, DNA fingerprinting did seem to offer a way of establishing whether or not these were the remains of the Romanovs.

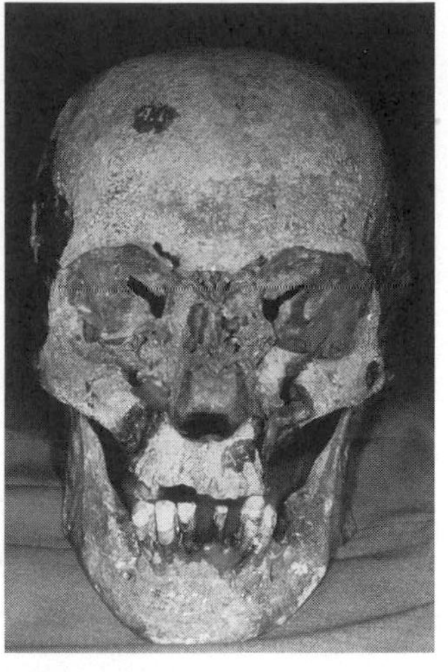

Czar Nicholas II (in 1992).

British Royalty Clinches the Case

Because the Romanovs were royalty, the family bloodlines were well known. Queen Victoria of England—called by some "the grandmother of Europe's royal families"—was the murdered Czarina Alexandra's grandmother. Another of Victoria's granddaughters, Princess Victoria, was the grandmother of Prince Philip, Duke of Edinburgh. Therefore, investigators reasoned, because certain kinds of diagnostic DNA are inherited through the female line, Prince Philip's blood should match that of Queen Victoria, Czarina Alexandra, and all her five children.

In July 1993, Prince Philip agreed to donate a sample of his royal blood, from which DNA was extracted for comparison. But there was still a problem because the degraded 75-year-old DNA from the Ekaterinburg bones was available only in minute quantities. Fortunately, a new laboratory technique—known as *PCR (polymerase chain reaction)*—had just been developed, enabling investigators to create trillions of copies of the degraded DNA (we will explain this process later in this chapter). Enough of the Ekaterinburg DNA was thus available to match against DNA segments from a living relative, in this case, Prince Philip of Britain.

Then, through computer-assisted means, selected small segments of complicated DNA sequence—the "hyper-variable regions"—were matched. Whenever the two sets of DNA match at these critical checkpoints, investigators can be virtually certain that the DNA is the same.

This is exactly what happened: Prince Philip's DNA proved to be a virtually perfect match with that extracted from the bones. Both samples reflected, within a very small statistical error, the distinctive blood of the Romanovs. Just to double-check, the skeleton of Nicholas's younger brother, George, who died at age 28 of tuberculosis in 1899, was exhumed from the royal crypt. Similar DNA testing showed another conclusive match on the other side of the family.

Russian officials accepted the unavoidable conclusion that the bones from the mass grave at Ekaterinburg must indeed be those of the murdered Czar and his family. On February 25, 1996, the Russian Orthodox Feast of Absolution, the royal remains were reburied in the imperial family vault—final resting place of Romanov Czars for three centuries, inside the cathedral of St. Peter and Paul Fortress in St. Petersburg.

A great murder mystery spanning most of the decade is solved.

ARMY LT. COL. VICTOR W. WEEDN (DIRECTOR, DNA LABORATORY, U.S. ARMED FORCES INSTITUTE OF PATHOLOGY)

Beyond any reasonable doubt, the remains are those of Czar Nicholas and his family.

PAVEL IVANOV (DIRECTOR, DNA UNIT, RUSSIAN ACADEMY OF SCIENCES)

Short of the Last Judgment, when the dead shall rise up and be cloaked anew with flesh . . . we may say that the mystery of the Romanovs is solved.

WILLIAM R. MAPLES, BIOARCHAEOLOGIST (1937–1997)

A Little Background on DNA

The Case of the Missing Romanovs demonstrates the very basics of how DNA fingerprinting works in practice. But in order to understand how such forensic techniques are being applied in molecular archaeology, we must explore

DNA was the first three-dimensional Xerox machine.

KENNETH BOULDING (1910–1993), ECONOMIST

a couple of these basics in a bit more detail. Bear with me while I run through a quick overview of how DNA operates as the so-called Code of Life, and how molecular biologists are learning to decipher the code.

How Is DNA Inherited?

Most of our genetic information exists inside the nucleus of our cells; this stuff (called *nuclear DNA*) makes each human being unique, and it's inherited from both parents. But nuclear DNA degrades fairly quickly, and, by the time the human body decomposes, the nuclear DNA has virtually disappeared. You can see why nuclear DNA was not very important in the early studies of molecular biology.

Instead, researchers concentrated on another, more specialized source of DNA—*mitochondrial DNA (mtDNA)*—which is also found inside the cell, but outside the nucleus. Unlike nuclear DNA, mtDNA survives longer, making it much easier to find in ancient sources.

In life, mtDNA exists in two places: in the female ovum and in the tail of the male sperm. But after the sperm fertilizes the egg, the sperm tail breaks off. This means that mtDNA is inherited *only* through the maternal line. If you are female, you will pass along the mtDNA to your children. If you are male, none of the mtDNA will be passed on.

From the mitochondrial point of view, the father's genetics are irrelevant. This means that human lineages (through the female line) remain distinct generation after generation, making it possible to define molecular phylogenies (family trees). This was, in effect, what was being traced in the Romanov case: Queen Victoria passed along her mtDNA to her daughter (without any input from her husband, Prince Albert). The daughter, in turn, passed along her mtDNA to the murdered Czarina Alexandra. Alexandra's five children, also present at the massacre, received their mother's mtDNA, without any input from the Czar. The forensic analysis of the Ekaterinburg bones was based on the royal family tree, *traced strictly through the female line.*

Mitochondrial DNA has another important characteristic for molecular archaeologists. When compared to nuclear DNA, mtDNA evolves fairly rapidly. Even so, the actual changes in the mtDNA code take place only once every 3,000 or 4,000 years. If one is willing to assume that this rate of change has been constant through time, then the degree of divergence between related mtDNA samples can be used to estimate the time elapsed since the various branches of the tree diverged. Obviously, insufficient time has elapsed in the Romanov case to allow for such divergence. Projected on an archaeological time scale, however, mtDNA has assumed considerable importance as a clock for monitoring the movements of human populations in the remote past.

What Is PCR?

So far, so good. Nuclear DNA degrades rapidly and is of little use to the archaeologist. Mitochondrial DNA is more robust, and can actually survive in many archaeological samples. But mtDNA is still a fairly fragile molecule, and ancient DNA survival depends on some rather special conditions of preservation. Even then, ancient DNA generally survives only in extremely small quantities. Initial research on archaeological samples was continually hampered by a lack of suitable surviving mtDNA.

All that changed with an important recent breakthrough in molecular biology, which has partially offset the preservation problem. The *polymerase chain reaction* (usually just called *PCR*) is a laboratory technique for rapidly synthesizing large quantities of a given DNA segment. **PCR** methodology enables researchers to make millions (or even billions) of copies of a very small sample of mtDNA, so that this genetic material can be more readily studied.

PCR (polymerase chain reaction): A method for amplifying a DNA sequence. Because the newly synthesized DNA strands can serve as templates, PCR produces rapid and highly specific amplification of the desired sequence.

Basically, PCR works in two steps. First, it melts down the double-strand DNA helix into two single complementary strands, then it builds up a new second strand from a bath of free-floating nucleic acid bases. This way, a single DNA molecule becomes two, then these two become four, and so on geometrically, until a bucketload of DNA results. The significance for molecular archaeology is that even a single surviving molecule of DNA can be studied—an incredibly important consideration when studying ancient DNA.

Unfortunately, PCR cannot distinguish the ancient DNA under consideration from later contaminants. Modern DNA is all around us, and the problem here is to keep out the skin cells constantly being shed by archaeologists or museum curators as they handle archaeological samples. Dust particles are also a big problem, as are minute amounts of DNA from earlier experiments conducted in the same room. Regardless of where it comes from, if the tiniest piece of modern DNA is introduced during the processing of an ancient DNA sample, the PCR method will multiply both the ancient and the modern DNA over and over again. This means that if you slough off a single DNA cell into the laboratory sample, PCR will blindly reproduce *your* DNA along with the ancient stuff.

This actually happened when one molecular laboratory reported that it had successfully extracted dinosaur DNA from fossil bones. Once it was compared against control samples, however, it was discovered to be modern DNA, somehow inadvertently introduced and multiplied by the PCR technique.

This explains why molecular biologists are fanatical about their laboratory "protocols," specific rules and procedures designed to minimize the possibility of modern contamination: Conduct different experiments in separate rooms, do not allow ventilation systems to connect one PCR laboratory to another, and so forth. This is also why control samples are so important. Sometimes, independent PCR tests are run in different parts of the same lab, as another safeguard against contamination.

In truth, most archaeologists don't care about the details of mtDNA, PCR, or laboratory protocols. It's like radiocarbon dating: Few archaeologists care much about the intricacies of carbon isotopes, but they *love* getting all those neat dates on their sites. In both cases, the importance lies in what the technology has allowed investigators to learn from the archaeological record. We look at this next.

Hair as Data?

People are hair factories. . . . Human remains, once so rare in ancient sites, now appear to be ubiquitous.

ROBSON BONNICHSEN, ARCHAEOLOGIST (OREGON STATE UNIVERSITY)

Archaeologists are often accused of splitting hairs, but now they're doing it, literally. Archaeology has just found a neat new source of data: hair.

Until a few years ago, nobody even thought about looking for hairs while excavating. But today, Robson Bonnichsen (now affiliated with Oregon State University) and his team routinely attempt to recover hair whenever they dig. And they find it, sometimes in great quantities: In dry caves, in wet caves, in permafrost, and in open-air sites, hair seems to be everywhere, once you actually look for it.

Hair is surprisingly durable, and it can enter the archaeological record in several ways. Not just from hair cuts or simple shedding, but also in human feces and even regurgitated stomach contents.

Great care must be taken when recovering ancient hair samples (because crew members can easily contaminate the site with their own hair while they dig). Hair samples are often taken using precisely controlled techniques like those described earlier for pollen sampling. First, scrape down an existing sidewall to remove modern contaminants. Then collect a vertical column of soil samples (either by natural stratigraphic unit or by arbitrary 10-centimeter level); then label, double bag, and carefully seal the samples.

The hair itself is usually separated from the soil matrix by standard flotation, often aided by water softener to break down adhering clay particles. Once recovered, hair provides archaeologists with a wealth of information.

Identification, however, is not easy. After cleaning in the laboratory, the recovered hair must be mounted on microscope slides. Then, at high magnification, such characteristics as color, scale pattern, size, and shape allow investigators to determine the species of animal from which the hair came. Some hair is hollow, and the pattern of air pockets (which look like a string of grapes) can

Prospecting for Ancient DNA

The Romanov case, solved in the early 1990s, relied heavily on the techniques of DNA analysis pioneered by Allan Wilson and his research team at the University of California at Berkeley. In 1984, Wilson and his team became the first to identify genetic materials from old tissue. When they cloned DNA from the 140-year-old skin of *quagga*—a recently extinct, zebra-like African beast—the Berkeley team showed the world that DNA could indeed survive after the death of an organism.

The next year, a Swedish researcher, Svante Pääbo, cloned DNA from a 4,400-year-old Egyptian mummy. This was the first time that PCR techniques had been applied to ancient humans. Not long after, Pääbo pushed the barrier back another 2,600 years into the past by extracting ancient DNA from human brains miraculously preserved at the Windover site in Florida.

Some 7,000 to 8,000 years ago, ancient Native Americans at Windover buried their dead in a spring that flowed through an ancient limestone sink-

tell the skilled investigator whether the hair came from a moose, a caribou, or a white-tailed deer.

The internal structure of human hair reveals the age at death, accurate to about 5 years. Diseases also show up in human hair; leukemia, for instance, can be detected in human hair samples before it shows up in the blood. It is also possible to determine the proportion of meat to vegetal matter in the diet by looking at the phosphate-calcium ratio in human hair.

Detailed examination can also show whether the animal (human or otherwise) suffered from scalp diseases or parasites. It also seems likely that trace elements can eventually be extracted from hair, then evaluated (as in the stable isotope studies of human bone, discussed earlier). If so, these ancient hair samples should provide valuable insights into ancient diet and disease patterns. Hair can also be directly dated (using AMS radiocarbon methods). Hair sometimes contains ancient DNA, which has been recovered from hair shafts less than an inch long. Because this DNA is the same as that recovered from bones and soft tissue, it is possible to use the entire tool kit of molecular archaeology on even tiny samples of ancient hair.

Particularly intriguing is the hair recovered from the Mammoth Meadow site (southwestern Montana), where preliminary identifications have turned up hair from 18 species, including extinct mammoths, caribou, and horses. Human hair was also found beneath a lens of volcanic ash dated to about 11,200 years ago. This is human hair that was shed more than 550 generations ago (perhaps in pre-Clovis times).

Bonnichsen and his team hope that the analysis of these hair fragments may eventually answer some stimulating questions: When did the first Americans initially arrive? In how many waves? What did they eat? What diseases did they have? What animal species did they hunt?

Right now, the potential for ancient hair recovery and analysis seems virtually unlimited.

The only thing that can stop hair falling is the floor.

WILL ROGERS (1879–1935), ACTOR AND HUMORIST

hole. Water levels fluctuated seasonally, with a maximum depth of less than 4 feet. In the soft bottom, deposits were preserved among the several distinct strata of peat—compact, dark brown organic material built up from the partial decay and carbonization of vegetation. The team of archaeologists, headed by Glen Doran of Florida State University, dug into these peat levels, while pumps bailed out the encroaching water. The skeletons were extremely well preserved, some even still held in place by large stakes, probably placed there at the time of burial to keep the bodies from floating to the surface.

The low oxygen level and neutral Ph of such boggy conditions were also perfect for preserving soft tissue. More than 60 well-preserved human brains turned up at Windover, including the one used by Pääbo in his pioneering extraction of ancient DNA. Geneticists were particularly excited about the large numbers involved, because it provided the first chance to examine gene frequencies across an entire prehistoric population. Microbiologists at the University of Florida were surprised to find how little the genetic makeup of the Windover population had changed during the thousand years that the burial ground was used, possibly a sign of ancient inbreeding. If this trend would hold for other early Native American populations, it would suggest that early Indian groups tended to stay put, perhaps explaining the remarkable linguistic diversity in the New World.

The Story of African Eve

The work at Windover signaled the birth of molecular archaeology as a viable way of exploring the human past. However, as spectacular as the 8,000-year-old brains from Windover might be, Wilson's research team at Berkeley had only begun to examine the possibilities in studying ancient DNA.

Wilson and his team collected mtDNA samples from around the world, and compared the human data with that of chimpanzee (as a control). The most striking fact about mtDNA is how much of it we all share. At the molecular level, all living human groups share all but about 0.6 percent mtDNA. As you might expect, humans and, say, chimpanzees share somewhat less; humans and horses share even less, and so forth. The 0.6 percent figure is important because it suggests a way to determine the "relatedness" among all living individuals and groups.

By examining the mtDNA from various modern human populations, Wilson could see what a close-knit species we really are. This was a surprise because mtDNA evolves fairly rapidly. Components of the modern global sample turned out to be remarkably alike—both within geographical populations and between continental groups. The result was a family tree for all of (surviving) humanity. Africa provided the longest branch on the tree, suggesting this is where human mtDNA began to differentiate. Those of African descent showed the most variability among themselves, and also were the most distinct from other populations of the world. Wilson argued that this pattern is precisely what one would expect, if modern humans had descended from a single population in Africa.

These investigators went a step farther, suggesting that all the genetic composition evident in living human populations could be traced to a single ancient African ancestor. Because mtDNA is passed down strictly through the maternal line, this fictive ancestor must have been female. She was quickly nicknamed—what else—Eve, after the biblical first woman and wife of Adam.

Even more controversial than Eve's African origin was the molecular clock that Wilson and his group also derived. Because geneticists are willing to assume that mtDNA changes at a constant rate, the 0.6 percent figure is important for another reason: It provides a relatively precise way to gauge the first appearance and development of human beings. Although this so-called *molecular clock* does not keep perfect time, it does suggest some genetic limits within which human evolution may have taken place.

Wilson's molecular clock suggests that Eve must have lived about 200,000 years ago. If so, then the first descendants of Eve (early modern humans) must have fanned out of Africa to supplant other hominids about this time. This theory, which has come to be known as the "out of Africa" hypothesis, had, it turned out, also been framed independently strictly on the basis of the fossil evidence (although other paleoanthropologists read the same fossils as contradicting the "out of Africa" hypothesis).

To call the Eve hypothesis "controversial" is an understatement. Shortly after Wilson published his results, critics from around the world weighed in. Some found fault with Wilson's family tree for humanity, suggesting that equally plausible alternative reconstructions could point to an Asian origin for humanity. Others charged that the Eve hypothesis was based strictly on modern genetic distributions. It could be tested by using paleo-DNA, extracted from ancient bone, but such research has only begun. And when using ancient DNA, it will be difficult to employ the molecular clock, because it is difficult to tell whether an old specimen is truly the direct ancestor of a present-day species; could it be that modern and ancient DNA sequences merely share an ancestor farther back in time? Some paleoanthropologists reject the genetic-based approach in its entirety, suggesting that debates about human ancestory will be settled by studying fossils rather than molecules.

Regardless of whether the Eve hypothesis survives or itself goes extinct, it is clear that the molecular approach is providing an entirely new perspective from which to view the human past.

Human Origins on the Internet:

Human Origins includes recent finds, an evolutionary/geological timeline, skull study module, and plenty of background:
http://euler.ntu.ac.uk/lsteach/origins.html

Human Origins and Evolution in Africa provides links to prehistoric diet, African prehistory, paleoecology, plus online research tools from the journals *Nature* and *Science*:
http://www.indiana.edu/~origins/

It's over for Eve. . . . I don't think molecular clocks work in this species [humans].

MILFORD WOLPOFF, BIOLOGICAL ANTHROPOLOGIST (UNIVERSITY OF MICHIGAN)

It is a good morning exercise for a research scientist to discard a pet hypothesis every day before breakfast.

KONRAD LORENZ (IN *ON AGGRESSION*)

Tracking the First American

The most consequential, if least dramatic, event in the history of the Americas came when that first human footprint appeared in the New World. Nobody knows exactly when this happened, or where. We do not know what these Paleo-Indians wore, spoke, looked like, or thought. We do not know when they left their Asian homeland or what conditions they experienced along the way.

And yet there remains no reasonable doubt that the first Americans did indeed travel across a land bridge from Asia during the late Pleistocene. As we will see, biology, language, and archaeology all point to an Asian homeland; it is the timing and conditions surrounding their arrival that remain unknown.

Clovis is the earliest cultural complex in the New World, appearing sometime between 11,000 and 12,000 years ago. This relatively conservative estimate remains reasonable because, despite decades of concerted research, no undisputed evidence of a pre-Clovis presence has been uncovered anywhere in the Western Hemisphere.

The antiquity of the first Americans is one of the most controversial issues in American archaeology, and it must be resolved.

DAVID J. MELTZER, ARCHAEOLOGIST (SOUTHERN METHODIST UNIVERSITY)

Tracking the First Americans Through Historical Linguistics

One controversial line of evidence regarding the first Americans comes from linguist Joseph Greenberg of Stanford University, who has reanalyzed the available data from every known American Indian language—a gargantuan task. Like many archaeologists, Greenberg believes that Native Americans arrived in the New World in three distinct groups—Amerind, Na-Dene, and Eskimo-Aleut—each descendants of separate migratory pulses, with the Eskimo-Aleut and Na-Dene populations arriving in relatively recent times.

This reconstruction suggests that the earliest wave of immigrants—the large "Amerind" language family—must have arrived about 12,000 years ago; they were the people of the Clovis complex. These ancestral American Indians spread throughout most of North, Central, and South America. According to Greenberg, virtually all the indigenous languages spoken throughout the Americas derived from this single ancestral language.

But Greenberg's reconstruction has come under heavy fire from his linguistic colleagues. One linguist called this classification "distressing. . . . 'Amerind' is discounted by nearly all specialists." Others worry about the lack of specifics: How, for example, were the individual languages compared? What kinds of statistics were employed? What steps were taken to screen out linguistic similarities due to language contact? And what about the possibility of multilingualism among these groups? Why do linguistic differences necessarily reflect just migration histories?

Lingering questions such as these make many archaeologists wary of accepting the reconstructions of historical linguistics without solid archaeological support.

The Bering Strait theory is tenaciously held by white scholars against the varied migration traditions of the natives and is an example of the triumph of doctrine over facts. . . . If the universities were controlled by the Indians, we would have an entirely different explanation of the peopling of the New World and it would be just as respectable for the scholarly establishment to support it.

Vine Deloria Jr., Philosopher (University of Colorado; Standing Rock Sioux)

But were Clovis people the very first Americans? Numerous sites throughout North and South America offer tantalizing suggestions, but none provides iron-clad proof acceptable to all archaeologists. Many archaeologists believe that it's just a matter of time before solid pre-Clovis evidence turns up. In fact, many modern archaeologists have begun to acknowledge, if sometimes only privately, that Native Americans could easily have arrived as long as 40,000 years ago.

But if that were true, how could we tell?

One answer, of course, is simply to dig more. But other archaeologists, frustrated with the difficulties of finding such early remains, have tried to resolve the issue by resorting to bioarchaeological evidence. Christy Turner, a physical anthropologist from Arizona State University, has conducted extensive studies of variability in human teeth. Focusing on the crown and root areas, Turner discovered that modern and precontact American Indian teeth are most similar to those of northern Asians. Turner postulates an initial migration out of northeast Asia at the end of the Ice Age, followed by two later migrations. A very similar story emerges from recent research on Native American languages (see *Tracking the First Americans Through Historical Linguistics*).

Today, it is possible to contrast the strictly archaeological, linguistic, and dental evidence with an important new source of information—the testimony from mtDNA, which is a sensitive marker for those curious about the number, timing, and age of migrations into the Americas.

Greenberg's language families remain controversial, but geneticists are still fond of using these simple groupings as baseline configurations against which to compare the genetic results. Some molecular archaeologists believe that the initial population moving out of northeastern Asia ran into a severe "bottleneck" as they passed across the Bering Strait into the New World, limiting the molecular diversity in the newly arrived population. This is how the molecular biologists argue that the genetic differences between Asian and Native American populations must generally postdate their separation. Thus the measurement of the genetic distance becomes a valid estimator of the time elapsed since they separated. An initial estimate placed this separation between 21,000 B.P. and 42,000 B.P.

Even as intelligent a man as Vine Deloria Jr. . . . dismisses as "scientific folklore" the discovery that Indians arrived in North America by crossing a land bridge across the Bering Strait. Yet there is solid evidence that people migrated that way from Asia to North America some 20,000 years ago. There is no question that the arguments in favor of scientific inquiry are legitimate. Science has unlocked countless doors, has allowed human beings to see themselves with a clarity not available to our forebears.

N. SCOTT MOMADAY, PULITZER PRIZE–WINNING NOVELIST (KIOWA)

One recent study, conducted at Emory University, analyzed mtDNA samples from living people in seven linguistically related tribes in Central America (the so-called Chibcha speakers). *Assuming* that this homogeneous group separated from other American Indian tribes 8,000 to 10,000 years ago—obviously a whopping assumption—then their mtDNA had mutated at a rate of 2.2 percent per million (working out to 0.0022 to 0.0029 percent per 1,000 years—a very small quantity to gauge accurately).

These same investigators also examined the mtDNA from 18 other tribes from throughout the Americas and, employing the mutation rate derived above, computed how long ago these people had diverged from a common ancestor. The answer turned out to be 22,000 to 29,000 years ago, suggesting a pre-Clovis presence in the Americas.

Critics, however, have pointed out that the Emory study depends on a critical, and unconfirmed, assumption: that all the observed genetic diversity began after these tribes crossed the Bering land bridge into the New World. But suppose the tribes had split up someplace in Asia, prior to arriving in America? If that happened, then the biological clock would have begun ticking prematurely.

Comparisons of genetic similarities and differences in widely separated contemporary American Indian groups strongly suggest that these people share a common genetic ancestor, with an estimated divergence varying between about 15,000 and 30,000 years. Some molecular archaeologists even argued that more than 95 percent of all Native Americans are descended from a single pioneering founder population—perhaps a few families that crossed the Bering Strait together in the late Ice Age. The same genetic evidence suggests that the Eskimo-Aleut and Na-Dene people—today confined mostly to the northern rim of North America—may derive from later migrations out of Asia, perhaps 7,500 years ago.

As was the case with African Eve, we presently lack any kind of final, definitive word about the peopling of the New World. But the preliminary results are sufficiently teasing to suggest that whatever the solution may be, molecular archaeology provides a major new source of data regarding the first Americans.

Ultimately, the question of the antiquity of the first Americans is a strictly archaeological one: Although the ages can be inferred, neither genes nor languages can be directly dated—only sites can.

DAVID J. MELTZER

A Couple of Cautions About Molecular Archaeology

The potential of molecular archaeology is obviously enormous. Even a decade ago, no right-thinking archaeologist could have dreamed up what has already happened. Before we get carried away, however, it is appropriate to pause and consider briefly a couple of implications from all this DNA-related research into the human past.

The Human Genome Project

Human Genome Project: Begun by the U.S. Department of Energy in 1986, this project has three primary objectives: (1) to create an ordered set of DNA segments from known chromosomal locations, (2) to develop new computational methods for analyzing the human genetic map, and (3) to develop new techniques and instruments for detecting and analyzing DNA.

Genome: All the genetic material in the chromosomes of a particular organism.

First, you should be aware of something called the **Human Genome Project.** This is a worldwide research effort to study the structure of human DNA and determine the location of the estimated 100,000 human genes. The DNA of some model nonhuman organisms is also being studied to provide the comparative information necessary to understand how the human **genome** functions. The results are expected to provide the baseline for biomedical science in the twenty-first century. These data should help medical science understand and eventually treat many of the more than 4,000 genetic diseases known to afflict humanity.

Research centers have been established to promote collaboration among diverse disciplines. These centers coordinate investigators at other locations with industrial organizations that want to develop applications of the research results, thereby creating networks of interrelated projects. Meetings and workshops bring together investigators with common research objectives to encourage collaboration, exchange of materials, and use of common starting materials or protocols whenever these are appropriate. The Human Genome Project was initially expected to take about 15 years, at an estimated cost of about $200 million per year. Actual appropriations for the first few years are somewhat below that figure.

Unfortunately, there is also a controversial downside to all this. First, the Human Genome Project aims to sequence "the" human genome, with DNA taken mostly from individuals of European ancestry in North America and Europe. But even brothers and sisters have slightly different genomes, and some scientists have argued that the Human Genome Project should explore the full range of genome diversity within the human family.

Anyone who wishes to cope with the future should travel back in imagination a single lifetime—say to 1900—and ask himself just how much of today's technology would be, not merely incredible, but incomprehensible *to the keenest scientific brains of that time.*

ARTHUR C. CLARKE (IN THE LOST WORLDS OF 2001)

The so-called *Human Genome Diversity Project,* an offshoot of the overall Human Genome undertaking, is an effort by anthropologists, geneticists, doctors, linguists, and other scholars from around the world to document the genetic variation of the human species worldwide. If it proceeds, blood samples would be collected from at least 25 people in each of 500 of the world's ethnic groups. These data, it is argued, would be of enormous assistance to molecular archaeologists, helping to clarify the major human migrations of the past. Such information may help trace the history of specific human populations and of our species as a whole. These samples can also help resolve some fundamental scientific issues about how genetic change takes place in humans. How quickly do humans adapt to changed environments and how is the response made?

The Human Genome Diversity Project has its share of critics. Although many endorse the notion of learning about human diversity, some believe that the research design embodies "typological thinking" by appealing to an archaic sense of human "races." Other critics point up a "colonial aspect" of the Diversity Project: Let's swoop down, collect the blood, and leave. Many charge that this approach ignores the plight of aboriginal peoples, many of whom either verge on outright extinction or are in danger of being wholly absorbed into larger populations. Many anthropologists have argued that "science isn't everything," noting that it is their duty to pay attention to the real-life conditions of the people they study. In a larger sense, some also express the fear that science is in danger of becoming dominated by genetic determinism, thereby losing touch with social and cultural values.

Human Genome Project on the Internet:

There's far too much to list here, but the following is a brief and very arbitrary sampler.

Human Genome Project, overall resources:
http://www.er.doe.gov/production/oher/hug_top.html

Frequently Asked Questions:
http://www-leland.stanford.edu/group/morrinst/HGDP.FAQ.html

Some view this debate in terms of extreme positions. The so-called First World position holds that the genes of the world's plants and animals are part of a common international heritage. As such, the right to financial benefits should go to those clever and ambitious enough to derive commercially viable products from the global genetic repository. After all, it is private industry that must front the research money, without any guarantee of success. And the world will be better off because of the medical breakthroughs involved.

[The Human Genome Project is] a 21st-century technology applied to 19th-century biology. . . . It is simplistic to think that isolated populations can be treated as genetically discrete.

Alan Swedlund, anthropological demographer (University of Massachusetts, Amherst)

Critics have challenged this argument, deriding the Human Genome Diversity Project as the "Vampire Project" because of the delicate legal and ethical issues involved. Whose consent would be required? Who will own the right to the commercial products that will certainly flow from the project? What about the immediate needs of these donor populations, many of whom may soon disappear entirely?

This could be another form of exploitation, only this time they are using us as raw materials.

Leonora Zalabata (spokesperson, Arhuaco people of Colombia)

In a bizarre twist, the United States government has recently issued itself a patent on a foreign citizen. Legally, the government assumed ownership of the genetic material from a Hagahai man from Papua New Guinea (see *Who Owns the Past?*).

Let's Not Get Carried Away

A number of people today are also thinking about the possibility, admittedly remote right now, that such DNA-based research could be used to clone entire ancient organisms. Maybe we could grow ancient crops to feed the world. Maybe we could repopulate the world with extinct species. Maybe we could even bring back our own ancestors. In the *The Jurassic Park Scenario,* we

Who Owns the Past?

The following news release was issued by the Rural Advancement Foundation International (RAFI):

Indigenous Person From Papua New Guinea Claimed in U.S. Government Patent

In an unprecedented move, the United States Government has issued itself a patent on a foreign citizen. On March 14, 1995, an indigenous man of the Hagahai people from Papua New Guinea's remote highlands ceased to own his genetic material. While the rest of the world is seeking to protect the knowledge and resources of indigenous people, the National Institutes of Health (NIH) is patenting them. "This patent is another major step down the road to the commodification of life. In the days of colonialism, researchers went after indigenous people's resources and studied their social organizations and customs. But now, in biocolonial times, they are going after the people themselves" says Pat Roy Mooney, RAFI's Executive Director.

The Hagahai, who number a scant 260 persons and only came into consistent contact with the outside world in 1984, now find their genetic material—the very core of their physical identity—the property of the United States Government. The same patent application is pending in 19 other countries. Though one of the "inventors," [a] resident in Papua New Guinea, apparently signed an agreement giving a percentage of any royalties to the Hagahai, the patent makes no concrete provision for the Hagahai to receive any compensation for becoming the property of the U.S. Government. . . . Indeed, the Hagahai are likely to continue to suffer threats to their very survival from disease and other health problems brought by outsiders. . . .

Linked to the "Vampire Project"

The first-ever patent of an indigenous person comes as an international group of scientists are embarking on the Human Genome Diversity Project (HGDP), which aims to draw blood and

explore the details with specific reference to bringing back the dinosaurs.

You should know that "growing" humans or dinosaurs (or anything else) from DNA samples is science fiction and will remain that for decades to come—possibly forever. Currently, molecular biologists have no idea how to fit together the millions of DNA fragments that can be extracted from living animals (for which the template is known). Extinct life-forms? Not a chance.

The best that can be hoped for is the isolation of a single ancient gene. Such a gene, when introduced into the genetic framework of a living species, might create an animal that could mimic an aspect of an extinct species. If so, then it might become possible to conduct a genetic "test" to determine the function of an ancient gene. But such an experiment would not in any sense preserve or recreate lost species or ecosystems.

Alas, extinction is, and will remain, forever.

tissue samples from as many indigenous groups in the world as possible. While the Hagahai are not specifically mentioned in the draft "hit list" of the HGDP—dubbed the "vampire project" by its opponents worldwide—it has targeted over 700 indigenous groups, including 41 from Papua New Guinea, for "sampling" by researchers. . . .

The Value of Human DNA: Mining Indigenous Communities for Raw Materials

Recent cases have concretely demonstrated the economic value of human DNA from remote populations in the diagnosis and treatment of disease and development of vaccines. Blood samples drawn from the asthmatic inhabitants of the remote South Atlantic island of Tristan da Cunha were sold by researchers to a California-based company which in turn sold rights to its as yet unproved technologies for asthma treatment to German giant Boehringer Ingelheim for U.S. $70 million.

NIH patent claims on indigenous people's genetic material are pursued abroad by the National Technical Information Service, a division of the U.S. Department of Commerce. Ronald Brown, the [late] U.S. Secretary of Commerce, has left no question as to his interpretation of the controversy, stating "Under our laws . . . subject matter relating to human cells is patentable and there is no provision for considerations relating to the source of the cells that may be the subject of a patent application." The Hagahai, and millions of other indigenous people, in other words, are raw material for U.S. business.

RAFI believes that this is only the beginning of a dangerous trend toward the commodification of humanity and the knowledge of indigenous people. Whether human genetic material or medicinal plants are the target, there is scarcely a remote rural group in the world that is not being visited by predatory researchers. Indigenous people, whose unique identity is in part reflected in their genes, are prime targets of gene hunters.

SUMMARY *Bioarchaeology* is the study of the human biological component evident in the archaeological record. This specialty requires expertise in the method and theory of both biological anthropology and field archaeology. Many of the bioarchaeologists discussed in this chapter have years of experience with hands-on excavation of the remains they study.

One branch of bioarchaeology is called *paleopathology,* the study of ancient disease. The search for diseases of the past is hardly a new enterprise, but some disorders can now be placed in a more reliable biocultural matrix: for instance, the impact of malaria and hyperostosis in the eastern Mediterranean, the problem of iron deficiency anemia in early-historic New World populations, and the relationship between malnutrition and infectious disease.

Bioarchaeologists also study past human diets by determining the ratios of carbon (and sometimes nitrogen) isotopes contained in bone collagen; they can thus reconstruct the dietary importance of various kinds of

ARCHAEO-MYTHBUSTERS

The Jurassic Park Scenario

Everyone knows the storyline behind Michael Crichton's *Jurassic Park*, right? An energetic capitalist constructs the ultimate theme park—an entire landscape from the remote past, complete with lots of live dinosaurs: raptors, tyrannosaurs, stegosaurs—the works. Where did the living dinos come from? With his unlimited funds, our tycoon has hired the world's best paleontologists and geneticists to bring these ancient monsters to life—in their own labs. Their logic is simple: Knowing that some very ancient bloodsucking insects are remarkably well preserved in globs of amber, they looked for those that had fed on dinosaur blood. After extracting the ancient DNA from the blood, they amplified it into the whole dinosaur.

This so-called *Jurassic Park scenario* made for a best-selling novel and a blockbuster movie. People around the world became fascinated with the possibility of creating extinct life-forms from ancient DNA—not just dinosaurs, but all kinds of useful and interesting creatures from later times. Even though archaeologists don't deal with dinosaurs—this is an important point that many somehow seem to forget—the possible applications of a Jurassic Park scenario to the archaeological record are limitless.

Of course, *Jurassic Park* is just a fantasy. But Michael Crichton is not just any author, after all; he actually trained as a physician and is pretty familiar with the intricacies of molecular biology. So maybe, just maybe, it won't be long before one of those hotshot biotech firms starts cloning extinct life-forms, right?

I posed this very question to my colleague, Dr. David Grimaldi, a fellow curator at the American Museum of Natural History. Working in our Molecular Systematics Laboratory, Grimaldi and his colleagues actually did the first part of what Crichton wrote about: They extracted ancient DNA from insects encased in amber. Their most famous find was a batch of DNA 20 million to 30 million years old from an extinct termite. Grimaldi and his crew did TV interviews for days.

Then, 8 months later, another team of molecular paleontologists (working at California Poly University) found some older DNA. As I write this, the oldest known DNA comes from a 125-million-year-old amber-encased weevil from Lebanon (thought to be the oldest amber in the world). But maybe by the time you read these words, somebody else will have found even older DNA. Who knows?

Simple time depth is thus not the problem for the Jurassic Park scenario—the ancient DNA is "out there" somewhere. The real problem is technology—how to construct an entire organism from minute DNA fragments preserved in the amber insects. Is it possible to build plants and animals this way? If so, then the molecular archaeologist can really set about "reconstructing the past" in a way never before imagined.

Because of his experience with amber-derived DNA, I asked Grimaldi about all this and he laid out the following step-by-step laboratory protocol for the Jurassic Park scenario, with his own evaluation of the various possibilities:

Step 1. *Get the right stuff.*

Step 1A: To date, ancient DNA has actually been extracted from amber insects only about eight times. Since we know that DNA can be preserved at least 125 million years, going after Cretaceous

plants and animals. Although stable carbon isotope analysis is just emerging from its developmental stage, it has already revolutionized the way in which archaeologists reconstruct prehistoric diets.

Another way to look at human diets is through the documentation of generalized stress responses in human hard tissue. Because the causes and the effects of malnutrition are complex and can rarely be traced precisely,

Period (ca. 135 million to 65 million years) DNA is well within the ballpark. *Verdict: Jurassic Park scenario plausible.*

Step 1B: A number of bloodsucking insects are known to have been preserved in Cretaceous Period amber. There were probably plenty of bloodsuckers dining on dinosaurs. *Verdict: Jurassic Park scenario plausible.*

Step 1C: In the Jurassic Park labs, dinosaur DNA was extracted from the gut of biting flies. But modern flies digest their meal almost immediately. To retain the dino-DNA, the flies would have had to have been encased in amber almost instantaneously after dinner. No such insects have ever been found. *Verdict: Jurassic Park scenario implausible.*

Step 2. *Extract and amplify the* DNA.

Intricate protocols are involved to ensure that ancient DNA has not been contaminated. This is done by comparing the prehistoric DNA sequences with those of living relatives. However, because DNA has never been found in dinosaur bones (at least not yet), nobody has any way of knowing what such DNA would look like, much less control samples to compare with the old stuff. *Verdict: Jurassic Park scenario implausible.*

Step 3. *Convert the* DNA *fragments into a complete genome.*

DNA found in amber insects turns up in only very small pieces; a complete gene in organisms like lizards and humans would consist of thousands of such fragments. So, if these are adequate models for dino-DNA (and nobody knows this), then the tiny pieces found in amber would be too small for creating even a single gene, to say nothing of an entire *genome* (consisting of thousands of such genes). Even if the dino-DNA fragments could somehow be put together, the result would be a developmental monster, with zero chance of making it past the earliest stages of embryo. *Verdict: Jurassic Park scenario implausible.*

Step 4. *Culture the dinosaur.*

Now, even if all the preceding steps could be completed successfully—a technological mind-blower—could we actually grow the dinosaur? This would be the toughest part. At present, it is possible to insert a foreign gene into a surrogate (or "host") organism, where the gene then develops normally—provided the foreign copy isn't too foreign. But at the level of an entire organism, we have no idea how the host genes would interact with the foreign ones. Genes don't simply "develop" on their own; they need intricately orchestrated sequences of events (which in turn depend on numerous unknowns). In short, biology is vastly ignorant about how genetic processes operate at the level of the organism. *Verdict: Jurassic Park scenario implausible.*

Overall, this isn't an encouraging picture. Grimaldi once summed things up like this for the readers of *Natural History* magazine: "*Reconstructing the genome of a dinosaur from base pairs of* DNA *would be like trying to reconstruct* Tolstoy's War and Peace *from a gigantic vat of alphabet soup.*"

So, at least for the foreseeable future, the Jurassic Park scenario remains mission impossible. For an archaeologist, however, this news is not so grim. There's always something to be said for job security.

---

paleopathologists prefer to study the effects of stress, defined as any environmental factor that forces the individual or population out of equilibrium. Harris lines, for instance, are bands of increased bone density—observable on X-rays of human long bones. They are often caused by a variety of nutritional stressors, especially severe and short-run dietary deprivation. Harris lines, which generally show up between birth and 18 years of age, have been observed on dozens of archaeological samples and are consistently associated with a shortened life span.

Another common technique for monitoring physiological stress is the analysis of dental hypoplasias, growth arrest lines formed from birth through 6 years. Hypoplasias are often evident from gross examination, although some investigators also look at enamel cross sections. Not only does the presence of hypoplasias indicate the presence of environmental stress, but their size also can be measured, allowing estimates of the duration of metabolic stress.

Today's technology also permits bioarchaeologists to analyze the past on an entirely different level. Calling upon the most recent developments in the field of genetic experimentation, so-called molecular archaeologists can now actually study the past at the level of the individual molecule. Molecular archaeology, like its counterpart, molecular biology, addresses the ultimate physiochemical organization of life, focusing particularly on the molecular basis of human inheritance. Although less than a decade old, molecular archaeology has already achieved some spectacular successes, providing unexpectedly precise answers to questions long explored through more conventional approaches.

Chapter 13

Understanding the Social Systems of the Past

PREVIEW Here, we approach the study of past social systems in several ways. Beginning with a fairly conventional "anthropological" perspective, we emphasize the way in which the concepts of *social status* and *role* serve to integrate community and nonresidential groups. We then examine how such social statuses are *achieved* and/or *ascribed.* Archaeologists have found this approach to be a fruitful way to chart the origins of social inequity. To illustrate this approach, we turn to a classic study by Christopher Peebles and Susan Kus, who examine community-level inequities through the burials at Moundville, Alabama.

We then shift the emphasis from social roles to social practice. Employing a postprocessual perspective, Randall McGuire relies on the allied concepts of *human agency* and *social power* to examine the ancient Hohokam (Arizona). The contrasts between these approaches employed in the Moundville and Hohokam studies illustrate the broad interpretive range in today's Americanist archaeology.

Finally, we will look at how the sociopolitical dynasty of the lowland Classic Maya was organized. Relying on the research of Joyce Marcus, we see how both *etic* (external, "scientific") and *emic* (internal, "cognitive") approaches can complement one another, even within the same project.

This chapter is about social systems of the past: what they were and how archaeologists find out about them. We begin with ethnologist Walter Goldschmidt's classic definition of **social organization:** "The structure of a society involves two things: first, there is a division into smaller social units, which we call groups; and second, there are recognized social positions (statuses) and appropriate behavior patterns to such positions (roles)." This will be our primary distinction: The *group* is a social subdivision, distinct from the network of *statuses* that define and influence the conduct of interpersonal relations.

Social organization: The way in which a society is structured. It is divided into social units (groups) and also has recognized social positions (statuses), with appropriate behavior patterns prescribed for these positions (roles).

The Nature of Social Groups

Social groups are either residential or nonresidential in character. *Residential groups* consist of domestic families or households, territorial bands, or community-level villages. The residential group is spatial, local, and territorial—consisting of relatively permanent aggregations of people. By contrast, the *nonresidential group* consists of associations formed to regulate some specific aspect of society.

Residential and nonresidential groups have quite different origins and courses of development. Residential groups are physical agglomerations of people; they are truly face-to-face associations. Nonresidential groups, on the other hand, are groups only in the abstract sense, and, as such, they do not necessarily ever convene. The solidarity of nonresidential groups is usually maintained through the use of symbols, such as names, ceremonies, mythologies, or insignias of membership. Their boundaries can be fixed and can sometimes be recognized in the archaeological record (as, for instance, ceramic motifs, rock art patterns, and burial style). In a sense, the residential group functions to regulate discrete spatial matters, whereas the nonresidential group binds these territorial units together.

The Nature of Social Status

Gender . . . is a constitutive element of human social relations, based on culturally perceived and culturally inscribed differences and similarities between and among males and females. .

MARGARET CONKEY, ARCHAEOLOGIST (UNIVERSITY OF CALIFORNIA, BERKELEY), AND JOAN GERO, ARCHAEOLOGIST (UNIVERSITY OF SOUTH CAROLINA)

Status consists of the rights, duties, privileges, powers, liabilities, and immunities that accrue to a recognized and named social position. A single social status is a collection of rights and duties. In our own society, the status of "mother" is determined both by the duties she owes to her son or daughter and the reciprocal responsibilities she can legitimately demand of her children. Similarly, a child owes certain obligations to a parent, and can expect certain privileges in return.

Social status is apportioned according to a number of culturally determined criteria. Nearly all societies categorize their members in terms of their age and their consequent position in the life cycle. Ethnographer Paul Bohannan notes that for African societies the list of male age categories generally runs like this: newly born infant, child on the lap, uninitiated boy, initiated bachelor, married man, elder, and retired elder. The specifics vary from culture to culture, of course, but the underlying principle of age almost always influences one's social standing in the society at large.

Sex is another ubiquitous way in which societies allot status, and it is important here to remember the difference between *sex* and *gender.* As discussed in the next chapter, the term *sex* refers to inherited, biological differences between males and females. *Gender,* a culturally constructed concept, emphasizes such biological differences to varying degrees.

To emphasize the multifaceted meaning of gender, we will follow Margaret Conkey and Janet Spector in distinguishing gender role from gender ideology. *Gender role* refers to the differential participation of males and females in the various social, economic, political, and religious institutions of a given cultural group; such roles describe appropriate behavior for gender categories. *Gender ideology* refers to the culturally specific meaning assigned to terms such as "male," "female," "sex," and "reproduction." Both role and ideology vary considerably from culture to culture and cannot be merely assumed (as in biological determinism).

Another related conditioner of status is kinship. As with sex and age, kinship in a sociocultural sense depends on a biological counterpart but is rarely identical to it. Kinship terms provide cultural labels for the social positions that determine how interpersonal relations are conducted. Ethnographers commonly study social organization through the **kinship** network. The kinship group (or **descent group**) is an organized association of people who are somehow related to one another. Kinship statuses are really just special cases within a society's overall status framework.

Kinship: Socially recognized network of relationships through which individuals are related to one another by ties of descent (real or imagined) and marriage.

Descent group: A publicly recognized social entity that defines its membership on the basis of lineal descent from a real or mythical ancestor.

An obvious yet important point to be made here is that all individuals in a society simultaneously possess several different *social statuses* (sometimes called *social identities*). For example, for a given adult male, "father" is only one of several statuses that are operative. That individual may also be a colonel in the air force, a captain of the bowling team, and a Harvard graduate. Each social position has its own collection of rights and duties. Which identity is currently operating depends on those with whom the individual is interacting. The composite of the several identities maintained by a single individual is termed the *social persona.* It is this encompassing social persona that is reflected in the archaeological record, along with individual status categories such as sex and age.

Margaret Conkey studying Paleolithic rock art deep inside the cave of Le Reseau Clastres in the French Pyrenees.

Role and status are the basic social parameters that define social structure and influence individual behavior and worldview. Sex, ethnicity, age, wealth, power, and religion add up to define individuals and social personae.

Joining a social group requires that one meet a series of culturally prescribed guidelines for "appropriate behavior." For example, such social "rules" will generally govern where a couple lives after they are married and how they are to behave toward particular categories of people. Social organization thus embraces the structure and functions of the groups within a society, including how individual statuses relate to one another. Kinship, marital residence, and descent reckoning all are part of a society's internal organization.

Many human societies are also integrated along status lines. Sometimes these statuses correspond closely to residential or nonresidential groups, but more commonly the status divisions crosscut conventional social groups. The statuses *male* and *female* might, for instance, comprise two separate residential groups, but usually they do not. Similarly, membership in a specific nonresidential group might confer some degree of high status, or it might not.

With this general orientation, let us see how archaeology goes about reconstructing social organizations that functioned in the past.

The Origins of Social Inequality

Societies have developed two rather different ways of assigning statuses—through ascription and through achievement. An *ascribed status* is assigned to individuals at the moment of birth, without regard to innate differences or abilities. Alternatively, a society can provide for statuses to be *achieved,* requiring that an individual possess certain admirable qualities (which are, of course, culturally defined). Rather than being assigned at birth, achieved statuses are left open until filled through competition and individual effort.

Egalitarian Societies

Egalitarian societies: Social systems that contain roughly as many valued positions as there are persons capable of filling them.

The concept of status allows us to leap from the level of the individual to that of the entire society. A society is termed **egalitarian** when the number of valued statuses is roughly equivalent to the number of persons with the ability to fill them. Such societies lack the means to fix or limit the number of persons capable of exerting power; egalitarian societies are therefore characterized by generally equal access to important resources.

The social system of the nineteenth-century Great Basin Shoshone people (discussed in Chapter 4) was generally egalitarian, with leadership taken over by those believed to be the most capable of supervising others. Authority was restricted to a particular, short-term circumstance. A good hunter might, for instance, assume a position of leadership when a group decided to hunt bighorn. Or an accomplished dancer might take charge of the rare communal gatherings (*fandangos*). A gifted talker might keep the villagers informed about the ripening of plant foods in different areas and urge the people to cooperate for the good of the group. The key to leadership here is experience and overall social standing; such social position is *not* inherited in an egalitarian society.

Ranked Societies

A **ranked society** limits the positions of valued status so that not everyone of sufficient talent to occupy such statuses can actually achieve them. Such a social structure embodies an intrinsic hierarchy in which relatively permanent social stations are maintained, with people having unequal access to basic life-sustaining resources. Although the distribution of labor is determined by sex and age in both egalitarian and ranked societies, ranked societies tend to have economies that redistribute goods and services throughout the community. Many tribes of the American Northwest Coast are ranked societies. Localized kin groups—not individuals—control the resources, and major economic goods flow in and out of a finite center.

Ranked society: One in which a hierarchy of social status has been established, with a restricted number of valued positions available.

The categories *egalitarian* and *ranked* define a social spectrum that archaeologists believe can be traced through analysis of material culture. Mortuary remains, for instance, are commonly analyzed in order to examine the workings of extinct social systems. For the past three decades, many archaeologists have made an important assumption when dealing with burial assemblages: *Persons who are treated differentially in life will be treated differentially in death.*

Death, in a sense, is a period of separation and reintegration for both the deceased and those left behind. The dead are separated from the living and must be properly integrated into the world of the dead. Social ties existed between the living and the once-living, and the ceremonial connections at death reflect in large measure these social relations. Archaeologist Christopher Peebles has emphasized the importance of studying human burials as the *fossilized terminal statuses* of individuals. Although these terminal statuses commonly differ from those studied by ethnographers, those models defined archaeologically are thought to be every bit as real as those observable among ethnographic cultures.

Community-Level Inequity: Rank and Status Markers at Moundville

Let us examine the ranking of social status evident at Moundville, one of the best-known and most intensively investigated ceremonial centers in the United States. Sprawling across about 300 acres, Moundville overlooks Alabama's Black Warrior River. Three thousand people once lived at Moundville—an astonishing number. For the next five centuries, no city in the American Southeast would again reach that size.

This complex of two dozen earthen mounds was a bustling ritual center between about A.D. 1000 and 1500. Like most **Mississippian** polities, this maize-based society engaged in extensive trade, and their skilled artists worked in stone, ceramics, bone, and copper. Moundville contains 20 major ceremonial mounds, large flat-topped earthen structures designed to function both as artificial mountains elevating temples above the landscape and as mortuary areas. Moundville had a large central plaza and was protected by a stout palisade.

Mississippian: A widespread cultural tradition across much of the eastern United States from A.D. 800–1500. Mississippian societies engaged in intensive village-based maize horticulture and constructed large, earthen platform mounds that served as substructures for temples, residences, and council buildings.

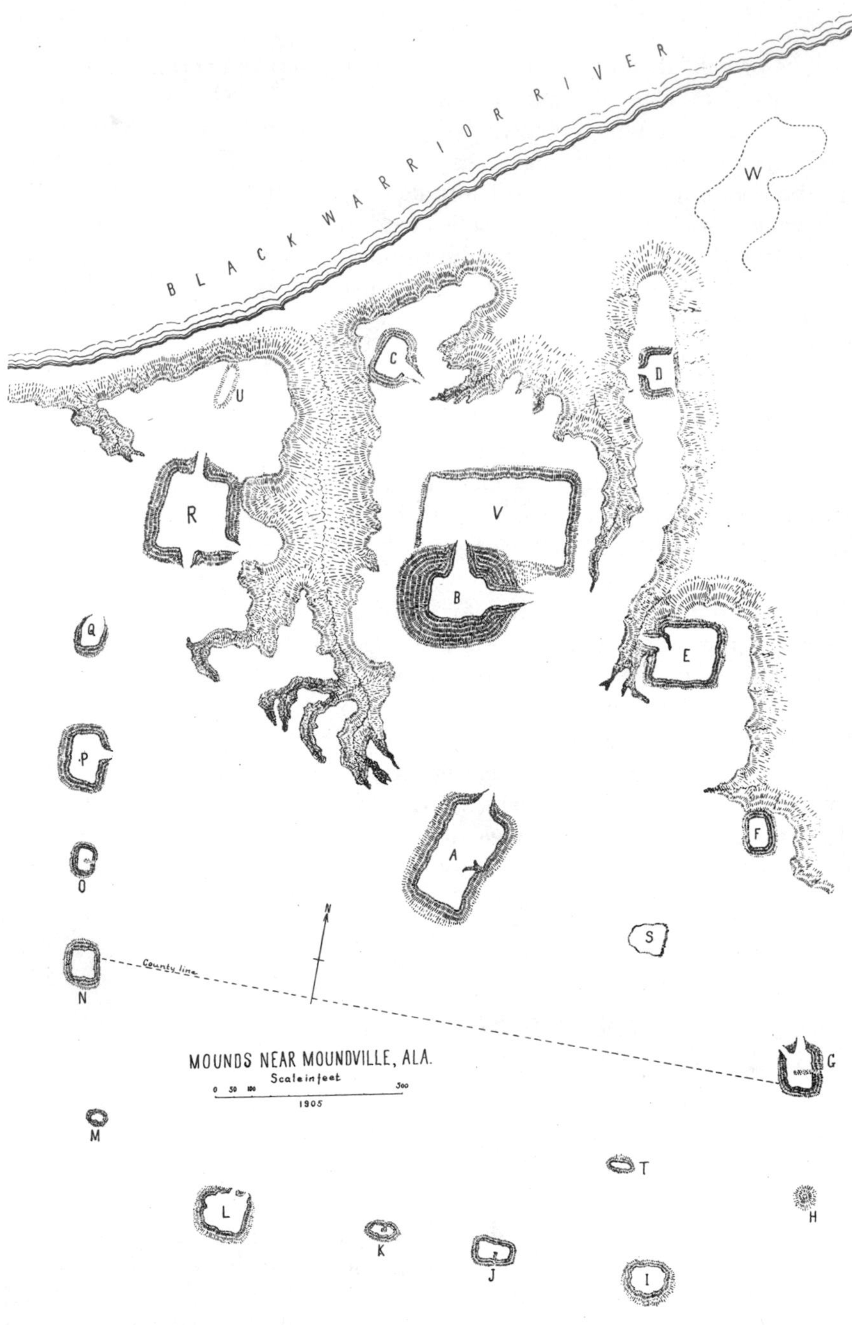

C. B. *Moore's map of* Moundville (*Alabama*).

Moundville was a major participant in the Mississippian tradition, a term referring to the hundreds of late precontact societies that thrived between about A.D. 800 and 1500 (or later) throughout the Tennessee, Cumberland, and Mississippi river valleys. In their heyday, the Mississippian elite presided over breathtaking ceremonial centers (as at Moundville). The Mississippian aristocracy was invested with power by the thousands upon thousands of farming people who lived in smaller palisaded hamlets and farmsteads.

Initial archaeological investigations at Moundville were conducted in 1905 and 1906 by the ubiquitous C. B. Moore (see Chapter 1). Moore excavated both platform mounds and village areas, and although his work is not up to contemporary standards, his basic data are still quite usable. The Alabama Museum of Natural History then excavated at Moundville from 1929 through 1941. Over half a million square feet of the village areas at Moundville were uncovered during this 12-year period, in part by workers in the Civilian Conservation Corps.

More than 3,000 burials have been excavated at Moundville, and they have provided an excellent database for studying Mississippian social structure. This task is complicated by the different methods of excavation employed, but work by Christopher Peebles, Susan Kus, and Vincas Steponaitis clearly indicates that a special kind of "salvage archaeology"—studying museum collections excavated decades ago—can be fruitful indeed.

Local and Supralocal Symbolism

Mississippian Archaeology on the Internet:

National Park Service lists where Mississippian archaeology can be seen firsthand and provides an overview of Mississippian culture:
http://www.cr.nps.gov/seac/misslate.htm

Moundville Archaeological Park Home Page:
http://www.olcg.com/al/atc/central/map.html

Peebles and Kus began their analysis by studying the abundant Moundville grave goods, many of which display the distinctive symbolism characteristic of the so-called **Southern cult.** Also called the *Southeastern Ceremonial Complex,* this huge ritual network was concentrated in three regional centers: Moundville (Alabama), Etowah (Georgia), and Spiro (Oklahoma).

Southern cult: A complex of ceremonial objects that occur in the graves of high-status Mississippian individuals. Ritual exchange of Southern cult artifacts crosscut the boundaries of many distinctive local cultures.

The striking similarities in Southern cult themes, motifs, and media imply more than simple trade networks; a higher degree of social interaction was at work. The conch shell gorgets and cups, the copper plates, the ceremonial axes and batons, the effigy pipes and flint knives found at Spiro and elsewhere contain a distinctive set of Southern cult symbols. The forked eye, the cross, the sun circle, the hand and eye, and the bi-lobed arrow, among others, suggest a shared symbol system that extended beyond the limits of any single Mississippian polity, spreading from Mississippi to Minnesota, from the Great Plains to the Atlantic coast. In addition to small, "expensive" items, Southern cult exchange may have involved critical subsistence resources such as food and salt.

Many of the representations of crosses, hand and eye, sun symbols, serpent, woodpecker, falcon, raccoon, and others, plus ceramics modeled on animal and human forms, continued (in the various forms) into the belief systems of postcontact Native Americans of the Southeast–to their folk tales, myths, and religious observances.

Whatever the Southern cult really was–and archaeologists still debate the point–it crosscut the boundaries of many distinctive local cultures. Peebles and Kus termed the Southern cult artifacts *supralocal* because of their widespread distribution, far beyond the boundaries of Moundville.

They also recognized a second distinctive kind of grave goods, the *local symbols.* These artifacts are specially constructed animal effigy vessels, or parts of animals, such as canine teeth, claws, and shells. The local symbols seem to have functioned as status items within a single site (that is, presumably within a single community), while the supralocal symbols designated the rank of individuals in the overall region.

An image in the southern cult style, pounded in copper. Note par*ticularly the forked eye motif around the eye, which probably represents a symbolic association with either the duck hawk or peregrine falcon, both known for their keen vision and skill as hunters (from Spiro, Oklahoma).*

Each mound at Moundville appeared to have contained a few high-status adults. Grave goods include copper axes, copper gorgets, stone discs, various paints, and assorted exotic minerals, such as *galena* (cubes of natural lead) and *mica* (paper-thin sheets of translucent silicate minerals). Each mound also contained some less well accompanied (presumably lower-status) individuals, furnished with only a few ceramic vessels.

Because each of the Moundville mounds once supported temples, it seems that the high-status burials in the mounds may be specifically associated with those ceremonial structures. The lower-status burials–particularly the infant and isolated skull burials–were probably ritual accompaniments to the high-status individuals.

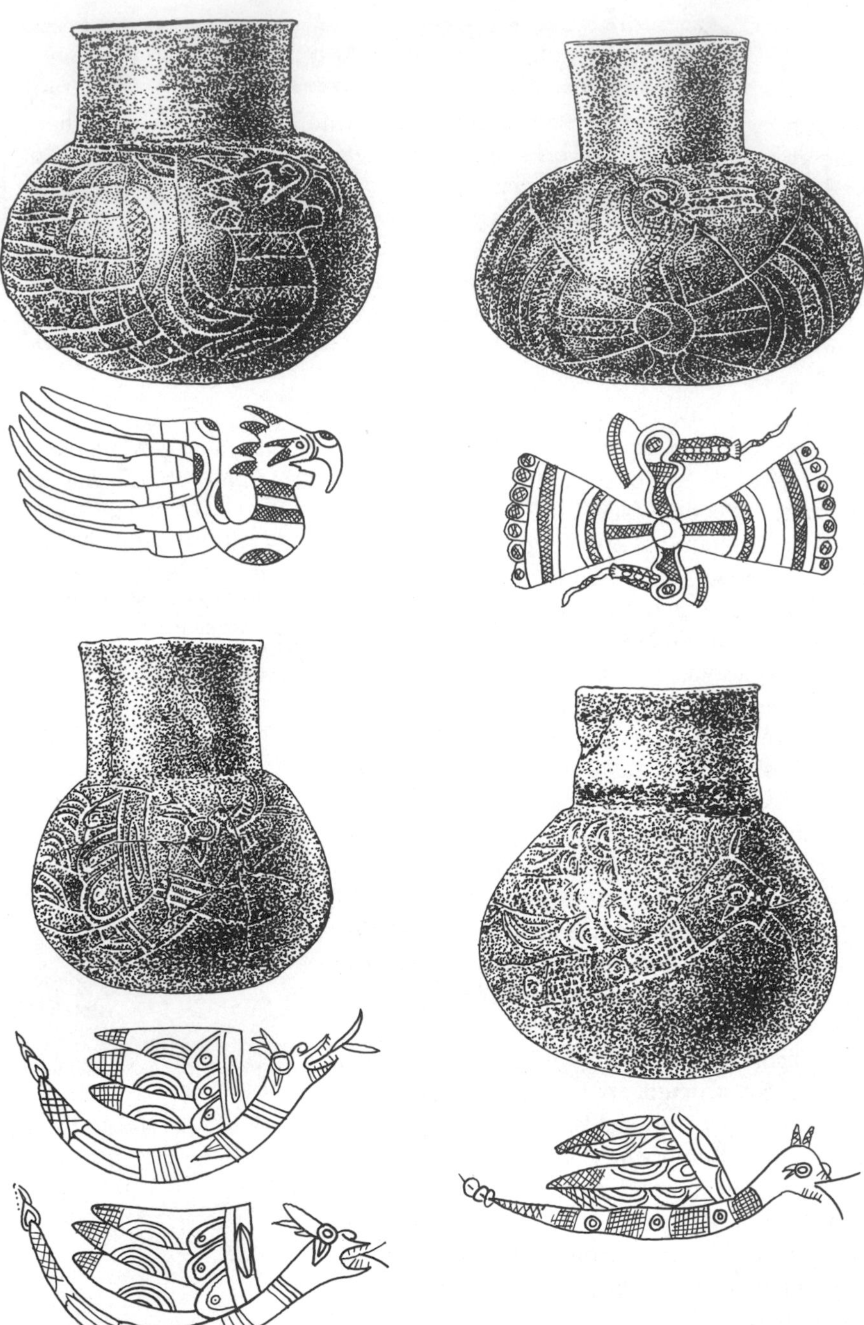

Ceramics recovered by C. B. Moore at Moundville (Alabama).

Only the most elite were accompanied by the supralocal symbols—including ceremonial axes and sheet copper plumes that depict the "eagle being" and the "dancing priest." Presumably these individuals had statuses and reputations recognized throughout the entire Moundville cultural system. By correlating the presence of higher- and lower-status symbols, Peebles and Kus could infer the following about the mechanisms of ranking at Moundville: Social position seems to have been inherited automatically by all family members. This inference is reinforced by the fact that even infants and children—clearly too young to have accomplished anything very noteworthy in life—were buried with lavish grave goods. That is, the most valuable grave goods were buried with truly high-status individuals of all ages and both sexes, implying that status at Moundville must have been assigned at birth. That is, these individuals, because of their parents, were important because of who they were at birth, not what they had done in life.

Two Axes of Social Patterning

On the basis of comparable ethnographic evidence, Peebles and Kus predicted that the Moundville population may have been subdivided along two major social axes, which they termed the superordinate and subordinate.

Unlike the elite discussed earlier, a *subordinate* division in a ranked society consists of a "commoner" class, within which social rank—manifested in certain symbols and the energy expended on mortuary ritual—is based exclusively on age and sex. With respect to age, the older the individual, the

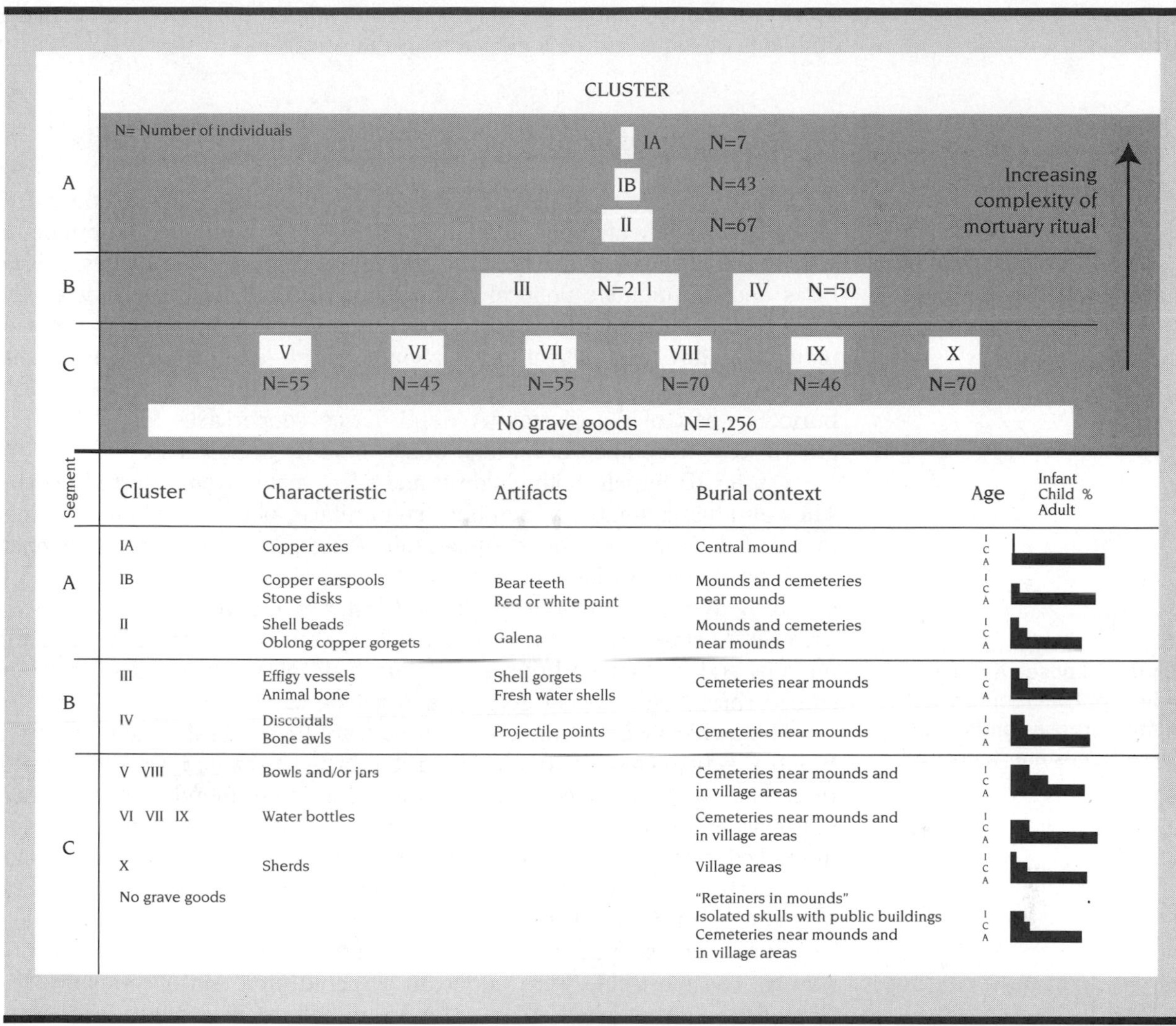

Segment	Cluster	Characteristic	Artifacts	Burial context	Age
A	IA	Copper axes		Central mound	I C A
	IB	Copper earspools Stone disks	Bear teeth Red or white paint	Mounds and cemeteries near mounds	I C A
	II	Shell beads Oblong copper gorgets	Galena	Mounds and cemeteries near mounds	I C A
B	III	Effigy vessels Animal bone	Shell gorgets Fresh water shells	Cemeteries near mounds	I C A
	IV	Discoidals Bone awls	Projectile points	Cemeteries near mounds	I C A
C	V VIII	Bowls and/or jars		Cemeteries near mounds and in village areas	I C A
	VI VII IX	Water bottles		Cemeteries near mounds and in village areas	I C A
	X	Sherds		Village areas	I C A
	No grave goods			"Retainers in mounds" Isolated skulls with public buildings Cemeteries near mounds and in village areas	I C A

Graphic representation of the hierarchial social clusters represented in burials at Moundville.

greater is the opportunity for lifetime achievement, and hence the higher the deathbed rank can be. This means that at Moundville (along the subordinate axis, at least), adult burials should be more lavish than those of children, and children should be accompanied by more grave goods than infants. And because subordinate ranking is also graded by gender, men and women should not be expected to have equivalent grave goods.

The *superordinate* division at Moundville is a partially hereditary ordering based on criteria other than age and sex. Among the elite (superordinate) division—people whose status was assigned at birth—some individuals will be infants, some children, and the rest adults.

In sum, Peebles and Kus predicted that the statuses should form a pyramid-shaped distribution. At the base of the pyramid are the commoners, whose statuses are determined strictly by sex and age. The next step up the social ladder consists of those few individuals with ascribed—inherited—status.

Finally, at the top will be the paramount individuals, those who enjoy all the emblems of status and rank available in the society.

Quantitative Distribution of Moundville Grave Goods

This model was tested by performing an in-depth statistical analysis on 2,053 of the best-documented burials from Moundville. Cluster IA–the supreme division–are presumably chiefs, those individuals enjoying the highest of statuses and the ultimate political authority. All males, these supremely elite were buried in large, truncated mounds, accompanied by a lavish array of material culture, including numerous Southern cult–adorned artifacts. Infants and human skulls (of individuals presumably sacrificed for the occasion) were buried as part of the Cluster IA ritual. Large copper axes found in these graves seem to symbolize the high offices held by these rulers.

Cluster IB burials, both children and adult males, were interred nearby. They also had a number of Southern cult artifacts, plus mineral-based paints, included in their grave goods. Apparently, these second-order ritual or political officers seem to have been those charged with the ceremonial application of body paint or tattoos to others. Cluster II, the final cluster of the superordinate class, included adults and children buried in cemeteries near the mounds and in **charnel houses** near the main plaza; their grave goods included chest beads, copper gorgets, and galena cubes.

Charnel house: A ritual house or chamber in which human corpses and/or isolated bones are deposited.

Hierarchically below the Cluster A elite are those of subordinate Clusters B and C (which enjoy status strictly on the basis of sex and age differences). In Cluster III, for instance, stone ceremonial axes are found only with adult males, whereas infants and children have "toy" vessels, clay "playthings," and unworked freshwater shells. Unworked bird claws, and deer and turtle bones were found only with adults. The individuals in the lowest segment, C, were buried away from the mounds and major ceremonial areas at Moundville.

Burial context appears to clarify the nature of ranking in the Moundville society. The most elite were buried in a sacred area and accompanied by symbols of their exalted status. The Moundville elite apparently lived in larger, more complex dwellings than did the commoners. Elite membership was conditioned by genealogy, and because social position was inherited within the elite, even children occupied such social positions.

Farther down the ladder, the villagers' graves also reflected their social stations in life at this level, positions conditioned largely by sex and age distinctions rather than by inheritance. Their less glamorous grave goods were distributed in a different way. Graves contained pottery vessels, bone awls, flint projectile points, and stone pipes, all of which were distributed mostly to older adults. Peebles and Kus infer that these individuals were required to *achieve*–rather than inherit–their social status. The prize artifacts for villagers went to the "self-made," those who had achieved status on their own. Over half of the Moundville graves contained commoners buried with no grave goods at all.

Peebles and Kus tried to place Moundville into a regional framework consisting of the 20-plus sites that seemed to be part of a single system, held together by a common social organization and common ritual. Part of the production of this society as a whole was used to support a number of specialized politico-religious offices, mostly associated with Moundville itself, as well as some minor ceremonial centers and villages in the hinterlands. Recruitment to these high offices was probably limited to members at the apex of the social organization. Nevertheless, bonds of kinship and reckoned genealogical relationship probably integrated the whole society.

Peebles and Kus suggest that Moundville conformed to a **chiefdom** model, characterized by a status framework with fewer valued positions than there were individuals capable of handling them. The economy was probably redistributive, with Moundville serving as a center for the regional distribution of key goods. Since the Peebles and Kus research at Moundville, ranked forms of social organization have been recognized at other Mississippian sites in Tennessee, Georgia, Oklahoma, and the lower Illinois Valley. In all cases, burial populations served as the source of inference. We will have more to say about chiefdoms later, when we consider the evolution of various social forms in some detail.

Chiefdom: A regional polity in which two or more local groups are organized under a single chief (who is the head of a ranked social hierarchy). Unlike autonomous bands and villages, chiefdoms consist of several more or less permanently aligned communities or settlements.

Alternative Interpretations of Mortuary Patterning

Several postprocessualists, including Michael Parker Pearson and Randall McGuire, have criticized this approach to past mortuary behavior. Situated, as it was, firmly within the processual agenda, the Peebles and Kus study of Moundville makes a number of implicit assumptions about the nature of social systems—how they operate and how they change. Taken together, these assumptions dictate how the social organization of an ancient society can be reconstructed from its mortuary record.

De mortuis nil nisi bonum [Say nothing but good of the dead]

KURT VONNEGUT JR., AUTHOR

There are many strengths to this approach. For one, the generalizing, systemic approach advocated by Peebles and Kus holds that evidence from a particular, target society can be grouped with data from similar societies into a larger, evolutionary framework according to the degree of organizational complexity. In addition, the available ethnographic evidence confirms that mortuary patterning alone often predicts the rest of the social pattern–such as egalitarian and ranked organization.

Nevertheless, the systemic perspective has been heavily criticized because it implies that scientists can readily divide the "whole" of the past into distinct yet interrelated subsystems. Employing a systemic premise, the Moundville study approaches mortuary data as a subsystem that reflects the overall social system.

Postprocessual critics have suggested that such reflections may not be so clear-cut after all. In the next section, we will briefly examine an example–trying to understand the social organization of the ancient Hohokam of the American Southwest–the kind of explanation that

Hohokam Archaeology on the Internet:

Hohokam Farming Systems: http://fadr.msu.ru/rodale/agsieve/txt/vol5/3/art1.html

Archaeology in Tucson (Newsletter for the Center of Desert Archaeology) contains numerous articles dealing with Hohokam archaeology: http://seamonkey.ed.asu.edu/swa/ait/ait1.html

flows from a postprocessual perspective. After that, we will return to two of the key concepts—agency and power—that inform this alternative perspective.

Life and Death Among the Hohokam

Hohokam: A long-lived cultural tradition centered in the deserts of southern Arizona and northern Sonora, Mexico. Four cultural periods subdivide the Hohokam tradition: Pioneer (A.D. 1–725), Colonial (A.D. 725–1000), Sedentary (A.D. 1000–1100), and Classic (A.D. 1100–1450).

O'odham: Native American group living in the Sonoran desert in the Gila and Salt River valleys, near modern Phoenix, Arizona. The O'odham speak a Piman language; the names "Pima" and "Papago" are commonly used to designate the O'odham people.

The Hohokam people once lived in the blistering deserts of southern Arizona and northern Sonora, Mexico. **Hohokam** is an **O'odham** (also known as Pima) Indian word meaning literally "all-used-up," but usually it is given the more generic translation of "ancient" or "old ones."

Shortly after A.D. 1, groups of part-time farmers moved into the sizzling Lower Sonoran desert. Before long, relatively large settlements sprouted, reflecting their successful experimentation with diversion dams, ditches, and levees that dramatically increased farming productivity. By A.D. 700, farming communities were prospering along the major river systems of the Phoenix Basin, and the Hohokam heartland had grown to encompass roughly 4,000 square miles. Communities at this point ranged in size from a few extended families to more than several hundred people.

Things soon intensified into still larger villages, more intensive canal irrigation, increased population size, and amplified ceremonialism. Trade networks expanded far beyond previous frontiers, funneling scarce and expensive resources to talented Hohokam artisans. Hohokam communities straddled major continental trade routes, from the California coast to the Great Plains, from the high civilizations in Mexico to the resource-rich Rocky Mountains. Intrepid Hohokam middlemen eventually bartered and transported merchandise as diverse as deer skins, seashells, turquoise, obsidian, rare minerals, finished textiles, salt, exotic feathers, and ceramics. Artistic excellence was expressed in increasingly diverse media, including stone, bone, shell, and ceramics.

The Hohokam: Egalitarian or Socially Complex?

For more than a century, archaeologists have tried to make sense of Hohokam social organization. Dozens of archaeologists have looked at architectural data, settlement pattern evidence, artifacts, and mortuary patterning. In the 1890s, Frank Hamilton Cushing interpreted Classic period Hohokam social organization as nonegalitarian (that is, ranked). Then, during the 1930s, archaeologists Harold Gladwin and Emil Haury developed a model of Hohokam society as basically egalitarian, living much like ethnohistoric Tohono O'odham communities in dispersed autonomous communities along major river margins. In the past couple of

The Tohono O'odham Nation on the Internet:

Tohono O'odham Nation Home Page gives details about conditions on the reservation, which is roughly the size of the state of Connecticut:
http://summs.la.asu.edu/tohono.html

Community Profile of the Tohono O'odham Nation Reservation contains a detailed accumulation of demographic conditions, scenic attractions, and tribal facilities:
http://www.state.az.us/ep/comm/sells.shtml

A Tohono O'odham Creation Story:
http://hanksville.phast.umass.edu/poems/Papagocreation.html

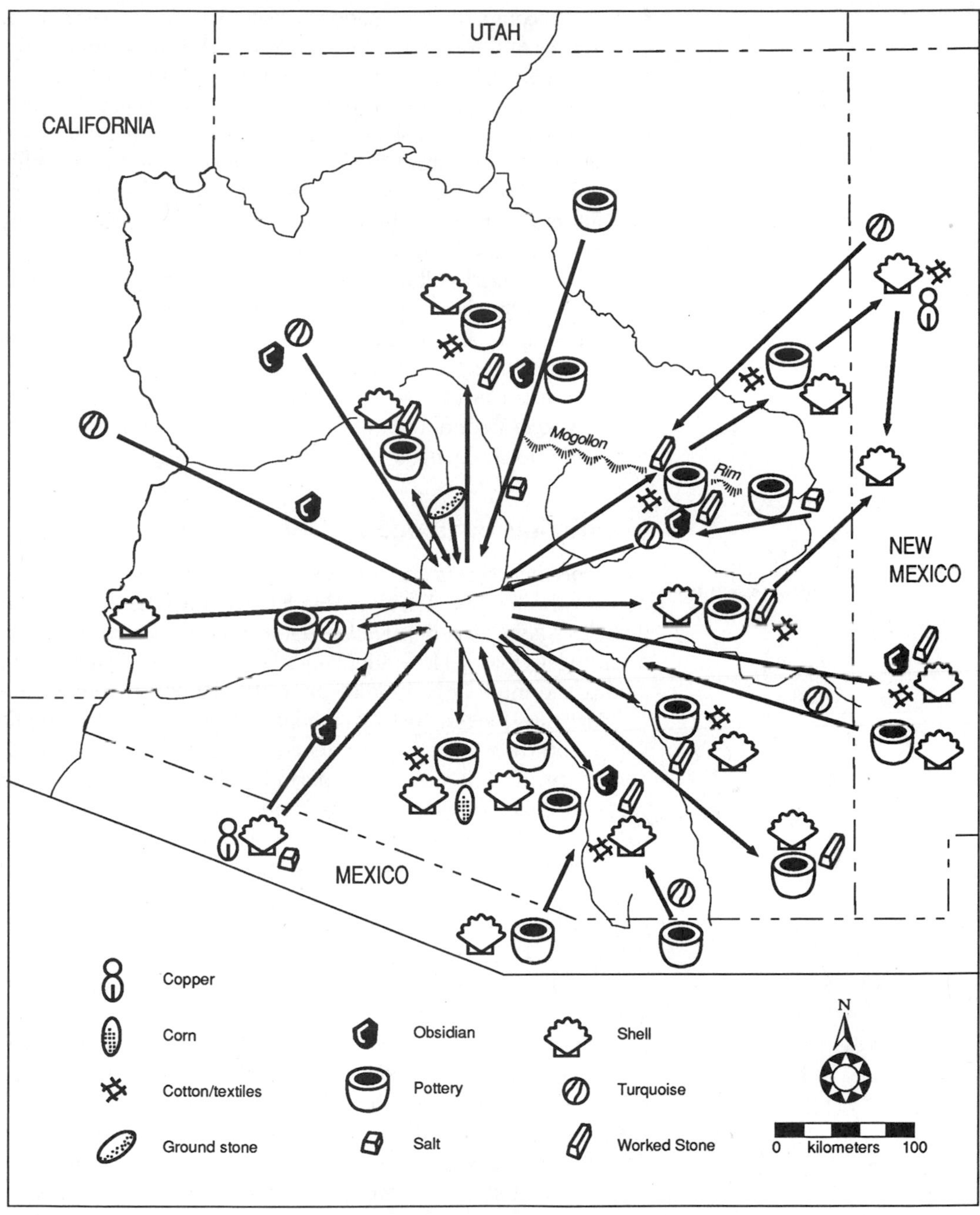

Hohokam trade networks. This network reached its peak between A.D. 800 *and* 1100.

decades, the tempo of Hohokam archaeology has accelerated dramatically and, today, several explanations of Hohokam social organization exist. Although some archaeologists still view the Hohokam in largely egalitarian terms, many others argue for greater social complexity, suggesting that Hohokam society must have been ranked, perhaps even operating at the chiefdom level. Some have argued that a privileged elite must have emerged, enjoying their wealth, living in large house clusters, and burying their dead in richly accompanied cremation burials. The Tohono O'odham people themselves have oral traditions suggesting that their ancestors were once ruled by powerful political leaders, who organized warfare on a massive scale.

Implicit in most of such models is the assumption that ancient Hohokam society should be viewed as a coherent, functioning, integrated system. This perspective derives from the basic processual agenda, which maintains that any given part of an interconnected system necessarily carries with it important implications for the rest of the system. Accordingly, any aspect of the material culture record should provide a direct, if not straightforward, reflection of the overall cultural system. Consider, for instance, mortuary patterning. Properly analyzed, these data should tell us about correlative organizations, practices, and relations within the rest of the social and economic system. In practice, this means that archaeological research has commonly attempted to isolate these various subsystems—architecture, mortuary patterning, and other material categories—and has studied them independently, without regard to the context *within the society under study.*

Conflicting Evidence in Hohokam Archaeology

With specific reference to the Hohokam at the site of La Ciudad (not far from downtown Phoenix, Arizona), Randall McGuire has rejected this systemic approach in favor of a nontypological, nonsystem approach. He employs a *contextual* view that seeks understanding through an examination of power relations and internal contradictions within Hohokam society.

McGuire looked first at Hohokam architecture (to simplify matters, we will concentrate strictly on evidence from the Colonial [A.D. 725–1000] and Sedentary [A.D. 1000–1100] periods). Extensive archaeological evidence suggests that Hohokam houses were simple structures with sidewalls and roofs of reeds, supported by a framework of posts and covered with an external earthen veneer. Sometimes, covered sheltering extensions (*ramadas*) were attached to the exterior walls. Although there is little direct evidence of what these superstructures looked like, archaeologists commonly assume that these Hohokam houses were all built of the same materials, were roughly the same shape, were relatively impermanent, and varied mostly in size only.

What do these houses tell us about Hohokam social organization?

To McGuire, the important point was the lack of any clear-cut examples of elite structures during the Colonial and Sedentary periods (although there *is* such evidence for later phases). Had such high-status residences been present, one might reasonably infer some degree of social inequality between commoners and elite during Colonial/Sedentary times. However, lacking evidence for elite dwellings, one would conclude—from an overarching *systemic* perspective—that the social organization must have been relatively egalitarian, lacking social ranking.

The mortuary evidence, however, tells a different story, one that contradicts the notion of everyday equality in Hohokam life. The Hohokam cremated their dead, then buried the ashes with appropriate grave goods. Some burials contain huge amounts of mortuary items, while others contain none. The grave goods, when present, include items that seem to have been worn by the deceased at the time of cremation (such as finely made shell bracelets, beads, and hair ornaments). Also included were utilitarian artifacts, such as stone tools and pottery vessels; some may have been personal possessions and others were perhaps offerings for use in the afterworld. There were also inclusions of shell wastage, suggesting, perhaps, craft specialization on the part of the deceased. Several Hohokam cremations contained what archaeologists have called "esoterica"—exotic goods, such as stone palettes, clay figurines, and incense burners; the consensus is that such finely worked and specialized artifacts held special meaning for the Hohokam, both in life and after death.

In the mortuary ritual, tensions between the egalitarian ideology of the Hohokam and the existing inequalities in the social order would be revealed and then mediated. The egalitarian ideology is affirmed and the social order is reproduced and legitimized.

RANDALL MCGUIRE, ARCHAEOLOGIST (STATE UNIVERSITY OF NEW YORK, BINGHAMTON)

McGuire's Contextual Approach

Taken by itself, the presence of a few very richly accompanied individuals certainly would seem to suggest the existence of real-life inequities in Hohokam life, with the elite enjoying more formalized status and differential access to economic and political power. But McGuire believes that Hohokam social organization cannot be understood from this either-or perspective. He rejects the idea that "complexity" or "stratification" can be encapsulated into a single dimension.

Instead, McGuire argues for a more *contextual approach,* in which mortuary ritual, as a manifestation of Hohokam ideology, played a role in "negotiation of power relations in Hohokam society." He views burial ritual, first of all, as embedded within the active negotiation, reproduction, and legitimization of the social order. Following a *dialectical* approach derived from Marxist theory, McGuire emphasizes the need to identify and analyze "contradictions" between various artifact classes (such as burials and architecture) and between different social categories (such as mundane and ritual; see *Marxist Approaches in Anglo-American Archaeology).*

McGuire takes exception to the view that architectural and mortuary data must have the same meaning, or even necessarily agree. Emphasizing the overall cultural landscape, McGuire believes that, for the Hohokam, houses were largely taken for granted. The built environment "forms the stage for all human action." Dwellings were simply a part of mundane, everyday reality.

But nothing about the mortuary ritual, he argues, is mundane. Death can potentially create immense emotional impact—the shock of losing a loved one, apprehension over one's own eventual death, resentment toward the supernaturals who control life/death, wariness regarding the corpse, and so forth. McGuire points out that death will always be the final rite of passage, creating stress for individuals involved and for their personal social linkages. Although the ethnographic record contains a broad range of attitudes and beliefs regarding burial rites and mortuary rituals, the event of death is rarely considered to be routine.

So, returning to the question posed earlier: Were the Colonial and Sedentary people an egalitarian or a ranked society? McGuire argues that the Hohokam were both. Whereas the everyday architecture suggests a sense of sameness and equality, the inequalities of the Hohokam social order were revealed ritually in the assemblage of mortuary items. After the cremation

IN HIS OWN WORDS

Marxist Approaches in Anglo-American Archaeology by Randall H. McGuire

The labels processual and postprocessual archaeology often lack a precise definition within archaeology, despite their frequent use as an opposition. Any attempt to characterize the diversity and richness of theory in archaeology will have to oversimplify that theory. Such contrasts are easily overdrawn and can never capture the complexities of thought that lie in the heads of individual researchers. I do not like to characterize my work as postprocessual. This label includes far too much. I would call my work Marxist.

Marxism is not a single, coherent theory of society that can be hitched to our purposes or dismissed in a few terse sentences. It is, instead, a philosophy, a tradition of thought, a mode of theoretical production, which has produced, and will produce, many theories. The theory of archaeology that I use springs from a tradition of Marxist thought that is ***dialectical*** *and historical.*

Within the great variety of theories that characterize Marxism in Anglo-American archaeology, there is a set of general principles that all, or most, of these views share:

1. *Each claims Marx as an important intellectual ancestor and as a source of inspiration. In all of these archaeologies, his work is a starting point, not an end point.*
2. *All seek to account for sociocultural change in terms of a similar theoretical and philosophical framework that puts social relations at the core of our research and seeks to break down the oppositions that bedevil our research; oppositions between mentalism and materialism, humanism and science, history and evolution, relativism and determinism.*
3. *Each treats society as a whole, a totality, that should be ultimately understood as such. They reject the idea that scholars can come to a better understanding of social process by reducing social phenomena to their parts and examining those parts.*

Dialectic: A focus on the internal relations that structure the social world, both the world of the pasts archaeologists study and the world we live in. These relations are made up of contradictions that bind individuals and groups with opposing and conflicting interests together, and because small changes in this social whole will alter the structure of relations, the whole is always in flux.

ceremony, the bone fragments and broken artifacts were gathered up and placed in the ground—disappearing from the everyday world. McGuire believes that Hohokam mortuary ritual brought the living and the dead together in a purposeful way; it revealed and mediated the tensions between an egalitarian ideal and the real-world inequities of everyday Hohokam life.

McGuire's analysis emphasizes the *social negotiation* within and between social groups, with grave goods establishing a complex of cultural debts and debits. McGuire concludes that Hohokam social organization "was too intricate to yield characterizations of evolutionary stage, level of complexity, or simple oppositions between egalitarian and ranked or achieved and ascribed status."

A Larger Postprocessual Context

The Hohokam and Moundville studies were selected because they approach past social organization from rather different angles. Operating largely from a processual perspective, Peebles and Kus made some important assumptions:

4. *All emphasize contradiction and conflict as vital features of human society and internal sources of change in those societies. As such, they reject functionalism, the notion that social phenomena can be adequately understood in terms of how they function to maintain society or allow it to adapt to an environment.*
5. *Each takes a human-centered view of history that gives human action or* ***praxis*** *some significant role in the process of history. They therefore reject any form of determinism (environmental, material, or technological) and the idea of abstract knowledge divorced from the action of people.*
6. *All recognize that our knowledge of the past is created in a social and political context, that people make knowledge. And, that this knowledge can never be merely a reflection of the reality of that past, nor should scholars simply make it up to fit our own political and social agendas.*
7. *Each shares a commitment that the power relations and structure of the modern, capitalist-dominated world is unjust and destructive to people. All advocate some form of socialism as the alternative to this system.*

These principles can be used to contrast Marxism as a way of knowing the world, as a critique of the world, and as a means for action in the world, with the other theoretical approaches current in Anglo-American archaeology.

RANDALL H. MCGUIRE is a professor of anthropology at the State University of New York, Binghamton.

- Material culture associated with the deceased—grave goods, monuments, place of burial, and so forth—should directly reflect the amalgamated social statuses (the *social persona*) in life. In effect, the grave is viewed as carrying on these various social forms after death.
- The material expressions of these composite statuses are comparable from individual to individual, from site to site, and from culture to culture.
- The differential patterning evident in these mortuary contexts reflects ranked hierarchical relations that once existed in the society under study.

Praxis: Theoretical informed practice. Through the process of praxis, salient ideas shape social, scientific, and political action, and this action alters the social, scientific, and political contexts of life. Struggle and crisis lead individuals to rethink and remake theory, and then to engage the world again, continuing the dialectic of praxis.

From this baseline, Peebles and Kus employed the inferred system of social ranking (as reflected by mortuary patterning at Moundville) to explore the nature of Mississippian social relations in general. They argued that Moundville likely operated as a *chiefdom,* with numerous local groups organized under the authority of a regional elite. The mortuary record—reflecting as it does the "fossilized terminal statuses" of the individuals at Moundville—permits archaeologists to reconstruct the nature of past social systems.

McGuire's consideration of Hohokam social organization questions these theoretical assumptions and substitutes a rather different viewpoint:

Individuals are not simple instruments in some orchestrated game and it is difficult to see how subsystems and roles can have "goals" of their own. Adequate explanations of social systems and social change must involve the individual's assessments and aims.

Ian Hodder, archaeologist (Cambridge University)

- What if the archaeological record is constituted *not* by social roles and status? What if that record is shaped instead by recurrent social practices?
- What if *social power* is central to the operation of such social systems?
- What if burial practices have been *manipulated* by the powerful to rationalize, reify, or mask existing social inequality?
- What if culture is not so *systemic* after all?

Viewed from this vantage point, burial practices may actually *contradict* other important aspects of social structure, revealing some tensions and covering up others. McGuire argues that looking for and exploring such contradictions may be the most fruitful avenue for approaching past social structures and understanding how these structures changed through time.

McGuire's research reflects the larger postprocessual critique, which has shifted debate on ancient social organization. Postprocessual critics suggest that archaeologists should look more closely at the roles of power and human agency in an attempt to understand the larger meaning of the human past. We will now look at these concepts in more detail.

The Issue of Human Agency

Agency: This is one of man's oldest riddles. How can the independence of human volition be harmonized with the fact that we are integral parts of a universe which is subject to the rigid order of Nature's laws?

Sir Arthur Eddington (1882–1944), astronomer and physicist

A key operative assumption behind the processual agenda is that human beliefs, desires, and choices are not a factor—at least not a *significant* factor—in structuring the archaeological record or in establishing important trajectories of cultural change. Relying on a *systemic view of culture,* the processual agenda assumes the existence of superhuman, "extra-somatic" forces that condition everyday life—forces over which individuals have little or no control.

A number of contemporary archaeologists have come to believe that this perspective is wrong, as it not only overemphasizes the role of adaptation, but also undervalues the power of the human mind—both today and in the past. In Ruth Tringham's language (see Chapter 17), the processual agenda reduces the people of the past into "a lot of faceless blobs."

Today, there is a heightened interest in what is termed *human agency*—the role of thoughts and decisions in shaping the evolution and structure of human society. As card-carrying humans, each of us knows—from very personal experience—that many of us do indeed think, and that we often jump into action *in the real world* as a direct result of our thoughts. The postprocessual critique decries the way in which the processual agenda has removed the individual from archaeological analysis.

The Importance of Power

[Power is] the probability that one actor within a social relationship will be in a position to carry out his own will despite resistance.

Max Weber (1864–1920), social historian

Postprocessual critics argue that processual approaches define problems and construct explanations in ways that marginalize or ignore the role of social power. The highly conservative process of socialization is thought to ensure that cultural traditions are maintained, in all societies at all social levels. Cultural change, when it occurs, is generally a response to *exterior change*—particularly environmental and/or technological change—rather than change from within.

When addressed at all, the issue of social power is largely *epiphenomenal,* less important than the larger issues of adaptation, complexity, or energy capture. So viewed, *social power* is considered largely in negative terms (as Weber's definition implies). Social science has traditionally equated power with force—the ability of a person or a social group to act in a desired manner.

By this view, power accrues mostly in formal, sociopolitical institutions. By looking, for instance, at the way societies employ sanctions, power is conceived as being set apart from society as a whole—something found in some institutions and not in others (and hence something possessed by some but not by others). The social elite has more power than the commoners. Egalitarian social groups, by their very nature, are assumed to have little power; the distribution of power becomes a social issue only with the advent of ranking.

Social power at Moundville is viewed as menacing and coercive—the compelling force that motivated commoners to construct the massive mortuary mounds and pay for the expensive symbolic riches that accompanied their elite to the afterlife. The funerary remains at Moundville are taken as directly reflecting the strength of centralized, formal leadership—the chiefs, priests, elite, and lords. Power is something embodied in a social institution. This is the processual perspective on power.

Postprocessual critics generally distance themselves from the notion that power is strictly negative or menacing. Daniel Miller and Christopher Tilley have elaborated this point, making the useful distinction between "power to" and "power over." Max Weber's power-as-domination was basically about *power over,* a negative, coercive form of social control. But this traditional view overlooks a second, more inclusive form of power—the *power* that attends all human actions.

Power to is an integral and **recursive** element in all social life. Power in this sense is not a simple commodity, something to be hoarded and parceled out in enlightened self-interest. Everyone enjoys the *power to* interact with his/her own world on a daily basis. *Power to* permeates all social life, with both positive and negative consequences. This approach recognizes human agency, the human capacity to modify or transform—which does not necessarily require or even involve *power over.*

Looking at power as a broad-based concept opens a large arena of inquiry, including (but not restricted to) the temples, residences, and luxurious graves of the elite. The inventory of power-laden social relations expands extraordinarily and becomes embedded in everyday life: husband-wife, parent-child, doctor-patient, owner-worker, and so forth.

But when the elite exert their "power to," members of the nonelite can likewise marshall a "power *not* to." *Power not to* includes an ability to resist domination, to fight back, and to circumvent authority. Open defiance—as in revolution and strikes—is the most commonly recognized form of resistance. But the so-called powerless also have at their disposal a number of more subtle weapons—foot dragging, false compliance, embezzling, feigned ignorance, slander, arson, sabotage, and so forth.

Social science has traditionally looked mostly at power in the hands of the dominators, less often at the use of power (resistance) by those dominated. But archaeologists have the ability to look beyond the temples and tombs of the powerful; an archaeological record of resistance by the "powerless" presumably exists in the sanctuaries of the weak—barrios, exploited

Power tends to corrupt, and absolute power corrupts absolutely.

LORD ACTON (1824–1902), HISTORIAN AND PHILOSOPHER

Power corrupts. Absolute power is kind of neat.

JOHN LEHMAN, FORMER U.S. SECRETARY OF THE NAVY

A consideration of ideology and power means that we are no longer able simply to "read off" the nature of past societies from material evidence. Instead the archaeological record must be understood as actively mediated and manipulated as part of the social strategies of the individuals and groups that constituted a past society.

DANIEL MILLER, ARCHAEOLOGIST (UNIVERSITY COLLEGE, LONDON), AND CHRISTOPHER TILLEY, ARCHAEOLOGIST (UNIVERSITY OF CAMBRIDGE)

Recursive: A procedure that can repeat itself indefinitely, cycling back and self-correcting.

Political power grows out of the barrel of a gun.

MAO TSE-TUNG (1893–1976), PRINCIPAL FOUNDER OF THE PEOPLE'S REPUBLIC OF CHINA

Power is the great aphrodesiac.

HENRY KISSINGER, SCHOLAR, STATESMAN, AND NOBEL LAUREATE

Classic Maya on the Internet:

The Classic Maya Calendar presents the basics of Maya calendrics, illustrating several of the date glyphs: http://www.eecis.udel.edu/~mills/maya.html

Mayan Astronomy:
http://www.astro.uva.nl/michielb/maya/astro.html

villages, lower-status households, and so forth.

This broader view of social power crops up several times in upcoming chapters, and we will examine both ends of the power spectrum—the "powerful" and the "powerless." In Chapter 16, we see how the Chavín elite derived power from control over both sacred ritual knowledge and tribute offered to regional ceremonial centers from travelers and pilgrims. In this way, religious ideology seems to have played a critical role in promoting and legitimizing profound social changes. In Chapter 18, we see how archaeologist Mark Leone analyzes power relations in the power-laden pleasure gardens of seventeenth-century Annapolis (Maryland). Chapter 19 will show how the archaeological record reflects the numerous strategies of both overt and covert resistance evident among African Americans.

Before turning to these examples, we conclude this chapter with a consideration of how power and ideology conditioned the distribution and operation of settlements in the Classic Maya lowlands of Central America.

Regional Inequities: Classic Maya Regional Settlement Hierarchies

One of America's most intensively studied civilizations is that of the Classic Maya, which flourished in the lowland forests of northern Guatemala and surrounding regions from about A.D. 250 to 900. The ancient Maya constructed immense cities characterized by monumental pyramids that supported temples, grand palaces, stone monuments with hieroglyphic texts, and lavish tombs that held the remains of royalty. There were also many lower-order religious and political centers, and scattered around these lesser sites were the hamlets of the lower-status Maya.

Maya temple mound at Tikal (Guatemala).

How these various Classic Maya sites were tied together sociopolitically has been a subject of debate for decades. Was Maya society rigidly stratified? Did the ruling Maya elite function as philosopher-kings, chiefs, or priests? Did the Classic Maya have a "middle class"? How did the ancient Maya derive their power? Over the years, archaeologists have employed a broad range of analytical techniques to decipher the sociopolitical organization of the Classic Maya.

Here we will introduce two complementary approaches to understanding the social and political world of the ancient Maya. The first is *etic,* in the sense that it reflects a scientific, "external" view of Maya administrative hierarchies. We will examine the available settlement pattern data to see what the physical layout of Maya sites might imply about administrative and ritual hierarchies—especially the way in which tribute and labor were channeled through the Maya sociopolitical system. Second, we adopt an *emic* perspective in an attempt to see how the Classic Maya themselves may have perceived their world.

Ballcourt at Copán (Honduras).

Explaining Maya Settlement Patterning

Most archaeologists agree that the major determinants of *initial* Maya settlements were land and water. Although critical to the establishment of sites, such ecological factors cannot explain the pattern of growth and spacing that Classic Maya cities later displayed. Joyce Marcus has argued that a complex set of sociopolitical factors, such as tribute demands, control of labor, ritual and administrative services, and proximity to neighboring sites, all came into play once sites had been founded. Others believe that environmental and sociopolitical factors should not be regarded as mutually exclusive.

Numerous regional archaeological surveys (of the type discussed in Chapter 4) have demonstrated a remarkable degree of regularity in Maya settlement patterning. Major regional centers, such as Copán (Honduras) and Tikal (Guatemala), contained acropolises, multiple ceremonial plazas, and a great number of carved monuments, called **stelae.** Inscribed on these monuments are royal genealogies and records of conquests. Only a few of these primary civic-ceremonial centers existed, and they are widely distributed across the Maya landscape.

Stela: A freestanding stone monument carved with hieroglyphs, commonly found at Classic Maya sites (plural: *stelae*).

Distributed around these major regional capitals are numerous smaller ("secondary") ceremonial-civic centers, which contained pyramids and palacelike residences for the local priesthood. More common still are the *village hamlets,* often little more than clusters of thatched huts occupied by groups of related families.

Central Place Theory: An Etic Approach

The abundance of datable inscriptions found on these sites clearly reveals that by A.D. 500, four major regional centers appeared to dominate the lowland Maya landscape: Copán, Tikal, Palenque (Mexico), and Calakmul (Mexico). Kent Flannery was the first to note that the secondary Maya centers seemed to be positioned about these regional capitals at remarkably uniform intervals; because natural resources are not evenly distributed across the landscape, the uniform spacing of sites suggests that social, political, and economic factors came to override strictly environmental ones in determining the location of major centers.

Central place theory: A series of theoretical models designed to explain how settlement hierarchies function around central places and how they determine demography in modern market economies.

Joyce Marcus elaborated on this notion by using so-called **central place theory** to study the apparently equidistant spacing of secondary centers around regional capitals. Central place theory was initially proposed as a series of models designed to explain how settlement hierarchies function and to determine demography within a modern market economy. Briefly stated, the locational theory suggests that a hexagon is the most efficient geometric form for the equal division of an area among a number of points. Using the hexagon as the fundamental building block, the locational theory explains the spacing of towns and cities that act as centers for the distribution of goods and services to smaller towns and the rural hinterland.

Central place theory requires several assumptions:

- Population and purchasing powers are uniformly distributed.
- Terrain is uniform and resources are uniformly distributed.
- Transport facilities are equal in all directions.
- All central places perform the same functions and serve areas of the same size.

Although these assumptions will never be completely satisfied, they do provide an idealized, theoretical model of the most economic arrangement of service centers, resulting in a hexagonal network or lattice. In such an idealized lattice, each of the major Classic Maya regional capitals was a "central place," surrounded by six secondary centers distributed with almost equidistant spacing. In several cases, the secondary centers likewise appear to have been encircled by a smaller lattice of tertiary sites.

Joyce Marcus's hypothesis suggesting how the Lowland Classic Maya organized their territory from regional capitals to outlying hamlets. Circled stars indicate the four regional capitals; circled 2's represent the secondary centers; circled 3's represent the tertiary centers. The small dots represent shifting hamlets around the tertiary centers.

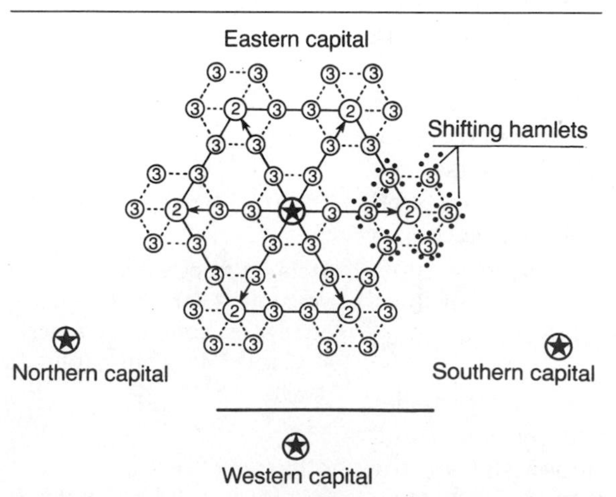

All this, of course, is only a theoretical model awaiting detailed testing. The crux of the issue is how well the actual Maya settlement pattern corresponds to the central place model.

In fact, the sites fit the hexagonal distribution remarkably well. Consider the case of Calakmul (Maya for "Place of Two Adjacent Mounds [pyramids]"). Marcus identified Calakmul as one of the four major Maya regional centers. Surrounding Calakmul are five to eight smaller sites, each almost exactly the same distance away. The Marcus model suggests that between A.D. 600 and 900 Calakmul was the "central place" of a hexagon defined by the smaller, apparently secondary sites of Naachtun, Altamira, La Muñeca, Oxpemul, Sasilha, and Uxul.

Looking farther down the line, the secondary centers themselves seem to define the central points of smaller hexagonal lattices of tertiary sites. Uxul, for example, is encircled by Discordia, Chilar, and Chumbec. Analysis at the tertiary level is hampered by incomplete archaeological surveys of the lowlands, but in the 1970s, when Marcus first set out this hierarchical explanation, the available data seemed fairly consistent with the hexagonal model.

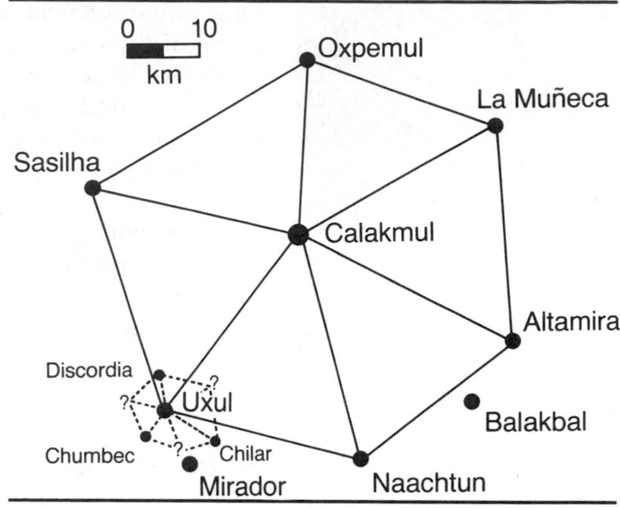

Calakmul, one of the four Maya regional capitals. Note that the six secondary centers are almost exactly the same distance from Calakmul (as predicted from central place theory).

Maya Hieroglyphs: An Emic Approach to Regional Inequity

This central place approach attempts to project what idealized settlements such as those of the Classic Maya might actually look like *on the ground*—with equidistant spacing of the secondary centers around the primary capitals. This is an etic perception, reflecting how we, as archaeologists, would rank-order the various known Classic Maya centers.

But Marcus was also interested in finding a method to discover how the Maya *themselves* may have ranked their centers, so that she could compare their hierarchy with that generated by Western scholars. An alternative (emic) approach attempted to define how each Maya center perceived itself—either subordinate to or dominant over the others. Marcus accomplished this by comparing the on-the-ground settlement hierarchy with evidence obtained from "emblem glyphs" or "place names" inscribed as **hieroglyphs** at the various regional capitals. The hieroglyphic texts on monuments at lower-order centers mentioned the "site names" of higher-order centers to which they owed allegiance.

Hieroglyph: The pictographic script in which the characters are pictorial (that is, represent recognizable objects).

The iconographic evidence seemed to support Marcus's argument that the lowland Maya had four major regional capitals. Evidence for this "quadripartite" (four-part) organization of capitals was found, for instance, on Stela A at Copán: This A.D. 731 hieroglyphic Maya text gives three clauses stating (1) "four on high," (2) the names of four capitals (Copán, Tikal, Calakmul[?], and Palenque), and (3) the four world quadrants (east, west, south, and north). Marcus noted that this evidence squares with the ethnohistoric record indicating that the sixteenth-century Maya divided their world into quadrants.

In accordance with Maya cosmology, four of these capitals were associated with the four world quadrants, regardless of their physical location. According to Marcus, "So strong was the cognized model that, despite the rise and fall of individual centers, there seem always to have been four capitals, each associated with a direction and, presumably, with a color." Significantly,

Calakmul on the Internet:

MayaQuest is a highly successful, interactive program between on-site archaeologists and school kids around the world. In 1995, more than a million kids helped lead the expedition by way of the Internet. MayaQuest provides an illustrated overview of the archaeological site: http://www.mecc.com/mayaquest.html

Maya stela at Copán (*Honduras*).

some of the stelae at secondary centers mention the emblem glyph (or site name) of the major center, Calakmul.

Such Classic Maya iconography suggests several important points about the sociopolitical organization at the time: (1) the site hierarchy changed over time; (2) at any one time, the Maya listed four centers as being "on high" or "regional capitals"; (3) the Maya view of which sites were secondary, tertiary, and quaternary did not always conform to site-size differences; (4) there was only one "regional capital" per region; (5) the Maya envisioned their realm as divided into four administrative quadrants; and (6) sites could rise in the hierarchy by establishing their independence (sometimes following a battle) and then displaying their own "site name" and setting up their own hieroglyphic monuments.

Testing the Model

To this point, we have two independent models of the Classic Maya settlement hierarchy: (1) an etic, on-the-ground model based on central place theory and (2) an emic model based on Maya cosmology and hieroglyphic place names. Since Marcus developed her model, considerable archaeological research has taken place at Classic Maya sites, and it is possible to compare her suggestions with new data, unavailable to Marcus in her earlier research.

The whole rationale behind the central place argument is this: The hexagon is the most efficient geometrical form for equally dividing such an area among a number of points. Such efficiency, it is reasoned, is important here because strong governance requires that the capital communicate quickly and effectively with its subordinate administrative centers.

Sacbeob: Ancient Maya roads that connected precincts within and between Maya cities. *Sac* means "white" or "artificial"; *beob* is the Maya term for "road."

And yet, travel within the Maya lowlands was a particular problem. During the dry season, travel was hampered by a shortage of drinking water along these routes. In the wet season, foot traffic was slowed by flooded lowlands and slippery, slick clay. Moving about in the tropical rain forests of Central America was (and remains today) anything but easy.

One solution for overland travel through the seasonally flooded areas was to build raised roadways, called ***sacbeob*** by the Maya. Although such roadways are known to exist *within* a number of Maya cities, long-distance *sacbeob* connecting major cities have rarely been recorded.

Part of the problem is the sheer difficulty in finding such roads, because the rain forest environment conspires against most forms of conventional archaeo-

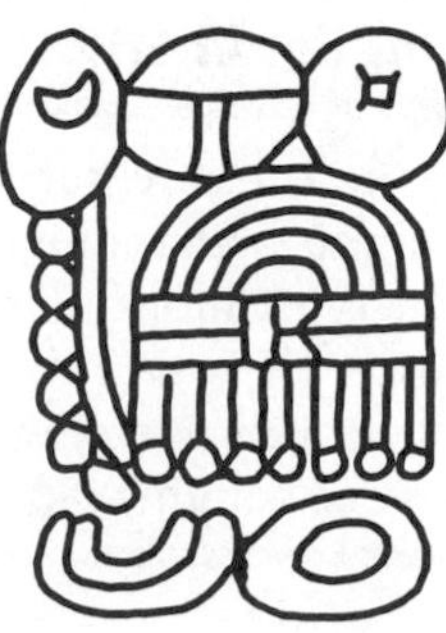

Maya emblem glyphs, each depicting a primary regional center. From left to right, they signify Copán, Tikal, Calakmul, and Palenque.

New Remote Sensing Technology Discovers Ancient Maya Road Systems

In order to test Joyce Marcus's hierarchical model, Frank Miller of the Department of Forestry at Mississippi State University began using Landsat satellite imagery to look for undiscovered Maya roads around Calakmul. By using a variety of techniques, it was possible to discriminate both roads and potential archaeological sites.

Because *sacbeob* are elevated as they cross swampy land, they support a more vigorous vegetation than the surrounding lowlands. Sometimes these vegetational differences could be directly detected from the Landsat imagery. In other cases, Miller could employ the satellite imagery to detect zones of distinctive dryness, another clue to where ancient Maya roads might lie. Although this entire operation was heavily computerized, the key to discovering Maya roads still lay with the knowledgeable interpreter, who was best capable of differentiating between the linearity of possible roads and that of geological faults and joints or other data anomalies.

In effect, remote sensing such as this remains an art, a game of probabilities based on evaluating the strength of various technical modifications. As it turned out, the probability of correctly identifying new roads at Calakmul was fairly high (somewhere between 50 percent and 80 percent). It is still necessary to follow up each suggested road by *ground-truthing*; that is, by conventional archaeological foot survey. It is also important to determine exactly when such road systems were constructed.

This much, however, is clear: Landsat imagery has proven to be an invaluable technique for finding the hidden road systems of the ancient Maya. If the search continues to be successful, then Marcus's hypothesis of Calakmul as a major Maya regional center will have been given an enormous boost. Although many Maya archaeologists were skeptical of the regional center model when it was first proposed more than 20 years ago, the additional input from remote sensing is changing their perception of Maya political organization.

logical survey. For instance, the well-known *sacbeob* at Cobá (on the peninsula of Yucatán) were discovered by intensive ground survey, supplemented by aerial photography; the knowledge of local Maya people was also invaluable.

When Marcus suggested her model of Maya sociopolitical hierarchies, relatively little was known about the site of Calakmul. Some skeptics felt that this site could not possibly have served as a major regional center during Classic Maya times.

Since then, a new, 12-year-long project of mapping and excavations at Calakmul has been undertaken, stimulated in part by Marcus's controversial suggestion. So far, archaeologists working at Calakmul have recorded more than 6,700 structures, uncovering in the process more than 100 stelae (more than any other Maya site). Not only has a complex network of canals been uncovered within the city itself, but a new network of roads has recently been discovered.

Calakmul is a key site at the center of Marcus's hypothesis regarding the Maya regional hierarchy. Marcus had hypothesized that several secondary centers should lie at a uniform distance slightly over 100 miles from Calakmul. For years, archaeologists had known that a couple of small roads existed within the city center at Calakmul. One—more than 1,500 feet long and stone lined—had been partially mapped in the 1930s; another, shorter one was discovered accidentally much later. But after Marcus's somewhat revolutionary suggestion—that Calakmul was one of four regional Maya centers and, hence, should have been connected to its dependencies by a road system—the search for new *sacbeob* was on. Two previously unknown roads, each several miles long, were sighted by archaeologists as they stood atop the elevated Structure 1 at Calakmul. This is when the search for more *sacbeob* went high-tech (see *New Remote Sensing Technology Discovers Ancient Maya Road Systems*).

Although many of the results remain preliminary, archaeologists have found a previously unknown system of roads centering at Calakmul and running outward, like spokes in a wheel. This newly discovered road system seems to connect several secondary centers with Calakmul. Some roads run farther still, perhaps linking Calakmul to even more distant dependencies. These new data, derived largely from remote sensing, would seem to support the model of large regional polities advocated by Marcus, in particular showing marked correlation between central place models and actual settlement locations.

SUMMARY This chapter dealt with social systems of the human past, defining what they were and how archaeologists study them. The basic social unit is the *group* (both residential and nonresidential), which is quite different from the network of *statuses*—the rights, duties, and privileges that define the nature of interpersonal relations. Social statuses are apportioned according to culturally determined criteria. The term *kinship* refers to the socially recognized network of relationships through which individuals are related to one another by ties of descent (real or imagined) and marriage.

We also distinguished between *sex* (the inherited and biological differences between males and females) and *gender* (a culturally constructed concept varying considerably from culture to culture).

We also delved into the way in which societies assign social statuses. *Ascribed statuses* are parceled out to individuals at birth, without regard to the characteristics of those receiving status. Societies can also allow members to *achieve* their statuses. As a result, achieved statuses remain unfilled until the necessary competition and individual effort define who gets them.

The concept of status allows us to leap from the level of the individual to that of the entire society. A society is termed *egalitarian* when the number of valued statuses is roughly equivalent to the number of persons with the ability to fill them. Such societies lack the means to fix or limit the number of persons capable of exerting power; egalitarian societies are therefore characterized by generally equal access to important resources. But in ranked societies there is an intrinsic hierarchy in which members have unequal access to basic life-sustaining resources. Egalitarian and ranked societies are often studied through the patterning in their mortuary remains, but considerable difference of opinion exists about how directly such burial associations reflect social organization.

Chapter 14

The Archaeology of Foragers: Seasons, Life Space, and Gender

PREVIEW We have already explored dozens of ways in which archaeologists are seeking to understand the diversity in hunter-gatherer lifeways. We learned what the thousands of bison bones at Olsen-Chubbuck told us about buffalo hunters 8,000 years ago on the western American Plains. We saw how George Frison is able to conduct modern experiments to learn about ancient mammoth-hunting practices. We looked at the pollen record at hunter-gatherer sites in England, Arizona, and Iraq. We looked at the genetic makeup of the first Americans, an ancient foraging society. We have seen how ethnoarchaeologists work among modern hunter-gatherers—such as the !Kung of South Africa and the Nunamiut of Alaska—in order to refine the methods by which we study ancient foraging cultures. We learned that because many foraging people pursued a highly mobile existence, archaeological survey techniques must avoid the trap of seeking the "typical" site; for most hunter-gatherers, "typical" sites do not exist.

In short, we have learned much about how modern archaeologists approach the archaeology of ancient foragers. But several important topics have yet to be addressed, and, here, we fill some of these gaps. Next, we see how to determine the "seasonality" of archaeological sites, how to define the various activity-areas within forager sites, how to employ models from evolutionary ecology to predict how foragers might behave "optimally," and how to explore the nature of gender roles in the past. In so doing, we will examine some of the newest theoretical approaches in Americanist archaeology.

Take a look at the archaeological reconstruction of Neanderthal life, shown on the next page. This is a life-sized diorama in the Hall of Human Biology and Evolution at the American Museum of Natural History (in New York City). It shows a scene from about 50,000 years ago, at the French rock shelter of Le Moustier (western France).

This classic reconstruction was devised by my colleague Ian Tattersall, who was attempting to bring the ancient Neanderthal lifeway "alive" for the modern museum-going audience (Tattersall also supervised the reconstruction of the Laetoli footprints, reproduced in Chapter 8). So far as Tattersall could tell, the appearance of the Neanderthal mannequins and the reconstructions of their activities reflected the best available archaeological information.

Life-size reconstruction of a Neanderthal family group roughly 50,000 years ago at the site of Le Moustier (France).

There is good archaeological evidence, for instance, that Neanderthals lived at least part-time in cave entrances and beneath rock overhangs like the one shown here. There are also excavated examples of Neanderthal-built shelters and cooking hearths. They lived during the second major phase of the last Ice Age, and almost certainly made clothing from hides.

In Chapter 10, we considered how archaeologists study microwear on stone tools; such studies of Neanderthal stone tools indicate that they were used in shaping wood. This is why Tattersall has shown the tall, standing Neanderthal male sharpening a wooden spear. Microwear analysis also shows that stone tools were used for butchering meat and for other domestic tasks.

The young Neanderthal female in this scene is using a stone tool to scrape a hide that she holds in her teeth. This reconstruction is also supported by microwear studies conducted on the front teeth of Neanderthal fossils, revealing evidence of heavy wear and polish, and suggesting that the teeth were used extensively in such ways.

We have only indirect means of knowing the courage and activity of the Neanderthals in the chase, through the bones of animals hunted for food which are found intermingled with the flints around their ancient hearths.

Henry Fairfield Osborne (1857–1935), paleontologist

But even with this solid scientific backup, Tattersall emphasizes the speculative aspects of the Neanderthal reconstruction (see *Reconstructing Our Foraging Ancestors* by Ian Tattersall). The anatomical details, such as hair and skin color, length, density, and distribution of hair, and the shapes of noses, lips, and ears, are all educated guesses. So are the details of the clothing. But to complete his reconstruction, Tattersall had to make some educated guesses, based on the best available evidence. Hunter-gatherer archaeology has always been like that: Take what you think you know, and do the best you can.

Not all archaeological reconstructions take place in some dramatic museum setting. More often, archaeologists reconstruct the details of past lifeways on paper—published in scientific papers and books. In fact, many such reconstructions are today produced directly as computer simulations or virtual reality packages. But regardless of medium, reconstructing aspects of the past remains a complex mix of scientific fact and educated guesswork.

In this chapter, we explore some of the ways in which archaeologists are attempting to reconstruct the life of our ancient foraging ancestors: how seasonal occupations are analyzed, how foragers carve up their life space, how foraging people decide which resources to exploit (and which to bypass), and how archaeologists are trying to understand gender relationships in the past.

IN HIS OWN WORDS

Reconstructing Our *Foraging* Ancestors by Ian Tattersall

Ancient bones are the objective evidence of biological history. From my standpoint as a paleontologist, they are vastly more informative about extinct creatures than reconstructions or models. Yet I am also a museum curator, and from that perspective I am keenly aware that nothing brings the past alive in the public's eye like a well-crafted reconstruction. For the average person, fossil bones are static things: beautiful or majestic, perhaps, but hard to imbue with the attributes of a living, breathing form.

When I was given the responsibility of curating the American Museum of Natural History's new Hall of Human Biology and Evolution, it was therefore evident to me . . . that we needed to include some reconstructions of early humans. . . . We hoped that clever sculpting and modern casting materials could provide us with a level of realism rivaling that of the spectacular dioramas of modern animals in the adjacent galleries.

What I had failed to consider, however, was the extraordinary number of awkward decisions that would become necessary as work progressed. Paleontologists have no living Neanderthal standards for comparison.

Once I would have laughed if anyone had predicted that I would spend weeks agonizing over Neanderthal eyebrows. Did they even have eyebrows? How long would untended Neanderthal beards have been? How much body hair did the men and women have? What was its color and texture? What was the skin color? All these details offered endless scope for quibbling.

You might conclude that the cumulative result of these unscientific decisions would be purely fantastic figures. Not so. Although I would not stake my life on many of the details, through careful sculpture and respect for the measured skull and body proportions, we have produced evocations of these vanished humans that bring them to life without sacrificing reasonable scientific accuracy.

IAN TATTERSALL is a curator of anthropology at the American Museum of Natural History (New York City).

Such reconstructions are important because they connect us to our remote ancestry, to our long-term human heritage. Neanderthals were foragers, as were the first human beings on earth. It is not surprising that anthropologists place such heavy emphasis on the hunters and gatherers, scavengers and fishers. After all, the foraging lifeway has dominated more than 99.9 percent of human history.

Keep in mind that all such reconstructions require that archaeologists make certain assumptions. As we will see, the nature of these assumptions must periodically be examined and reexamined. The assumptions we make, after all, tell us as much about ourselves as about the ancient ancestors we are trying to understand.

Estimating Seasonality

Mobility has always been considered a key characteristic of the foraging lifeway. But hunter-gatherers move in very different ways: Some move around a lot, others stay put. As we already saw in Chapter 4, many foraging groups can be characterized by their *seasonal round*—how they move between various locations, following key resources season by season. The Nevada Shoshone people, for instance, survived by collecting seasonally ripening plant foods, supplemented to some degree by hunting.

The seasonal round of the Shoshone people is known today because ethnographer Julian Steward spent considerable time talking to Shoshone men and women about their cultural landscape. Assuming that Steward's informants were telling him the truth, this pattern can be safely projected back in time only to the mid-nineteenth century or so. Because no earlier ethnographic or ethnohistorical accounts are available, evidence about earlier periods must be gleaned from the archaeological record.

Seasonality: An estimate of when during the year a particular archaeological site was occupied.

Seasonality studies are particularly important in archaeology because they enable investigators to deduce what time of the year various sites and resource areas were utilized. Put enough such contemporary, seasonally specific sites together, and you can reconstruct an ancient seasonal round.

Excavating and Interpreting Seasonal Diagnostics

Suppose that an archaeologist who visited us from outer space were trying to explain human history to his fellow spacelings. He might illustrate the results of his digs by a 24-hour clock on which 1 hour represents 100,000 years of real past time. If the history of the human race began at midnight, then we would now be almost at the end of our first day. We lived as hunter-gatherers for nearly the whole of that day, from midnight through dawn, noon, and sunset. Finally, at 11:54 p.m., we adopted agriculture.

JARED DIAMOND, ORNITHOLOGIST AND ECOLOGIST

Sometimes it's easy to tell the season in which a site was used. We have already seen, for instance, how Joe Ben Wheat figured out the season in which the Olsen-Chubbuck bison kill took place. Both sexes and all ages of bison were represented at Olsen-Chubbuck, with roughly 6 percent being juveniles (most of these were a month or two old, although some could not have been more than a few days old). Employing an analogy to modern American bison, Wheat estimated that the 8,000-year-old kill at Olsen-Chubbuck could have occurred as early as April or as late as August, with the best evidence suggesting a time fairly late in the calving season, probably late May or early June.

Olsen-Chubbuck is something of an ideal case, because archaeologists can rarely assume that their sites accumulated from a single event (such as ambushing a bison herd). More commonly, sites accumulated over hundreds, even thousands, of years. In fact, archaeological sites are often compared to a *palimpsest*—a parchment or tablet that has been erased and subsequently reused (sometimes multiple times). Like the palimpsest manuscript page, archaeological sites are commonly used and reused, making the assignment of "season of use" difficult.

Sometimes, plant remains can be used to estimate seasonality. The figure on the next page shows Kent Flannery's listing of the seasonal availability of important plant foods in the environment of the eastern Valley of Oaxaca (Mexico). Considerable seasonal variability is evident in this ecosystem, with some plants becoming available at the start of the rainy season (beginning in June), others toward the end of this period (around November), and still others during the dry season (in about April). By looking at deliberate caches of these wild plant foods, Flannery and his colleagues could tell something about the human utilization of Guilá Naquitz Cave.

We no longer think of the preceramic plant-collectors as a ragged and scruffy band of nomads; instead, they appear as a practiced and ingenious team of lay botanists who know how to wring the most out of a superficially bleak environment.

KENT FLANNERY, ARCHAEOLOGIST (UNIVERSITY OF MICHIGAN)

Estimating site seasonality is hardly new in archaeology. In a classic study from the 1920s, Hildegarde Howard demonstrated the potential of such noncultural remains for reconstructing lifeways by identifying the avifauna (birds) from the Emeryville Shellmound on San Francisco Bay. Howard identified several of the bones as those of cormorants, birds that bred on offshore islands in the early summer. After about a month, the nestlings moved onshore, where they were killed by prehistoric hunters. Because the bones found in the mound were those of relatively immature birds, Howard reasoned that the prehistoric hunts must have taken place between the middle of June and the end of July. Cormorant bones were found throughout the midden, leading Howard to infer that the site was occupied at least during the summer months. Howard also noted the presence of a foot bone from a young great blue heron and took it as evidence of a May occupation.

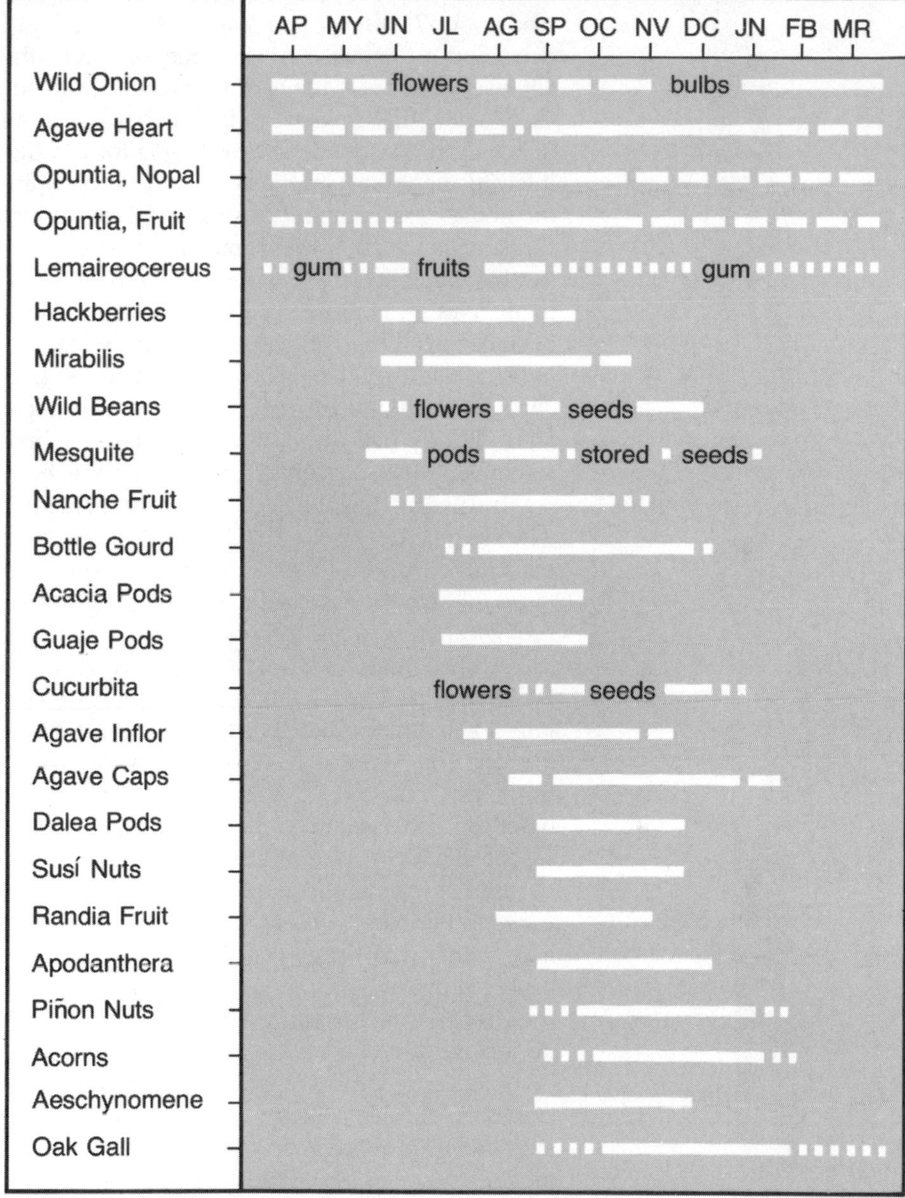

Seasonal availability of various plants in the Guilá Naquitz area, Oaxaca (Mexico). Solid lines indicate periods of peak availability; dashed or dotted lines indicate periods of occasional availability.

This single bone was used to extend the summer occupation of the site backward to include part of the spring, an example of what is now termed the *presence-absence* method of inferring seasonality. Though certainly not in conflict with the cormorant data, Howard's adding a spring component on the basis of a single bone is nevertheless a risky inference. Even if one could be certain that this bone had been introduced by humans, it seems more reasonable to require the presence of several different indicators for a given season as a basis for advancing a seasonality estimate.

Defining Seasonality at Star Carr

Several other techniques have been used to estimate the season of use in archaeological sites. J. D. G. Clark, for instance, used antlers to derive seasonal

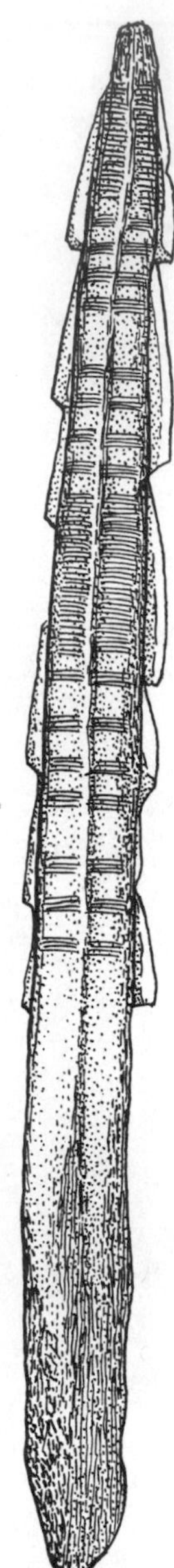

This beautifully decorated Mesolithic dagger (or spearhead) has several tiny flint flakes (microliths) set in grooves carved in the edges of a piece of deer bone.

information at Star Carr, a major Mesolithic site in northern England occupied about 7500 B.C. The major food animals at Star Carr were roe deer, red deer, and a few elk. Red deer remains were the most abundant, and virtually every red deer stag had been killed while he was still carrying his antlers. Clark knew that modern red deer carry their antlers from mid-October until late April. Assuming similar timing for red deer of 9,500 years ago, Clark inferred that Star Carr must have been occupied at least during the winter months. A great number of shed red deer antlers were also found at the site. Clark suggested that these must have been retrieved almost immediately after they had been shed; otherwise the deer themselves would have devoured them. This piece of information was taken to mean that Star Carr must have been occupied until at least early April, when red deer normally discard their antlers. The high frequency of unshed roe deer antlers also suggested an April occupation. Just when the occupation began at Star Carr was problematical. Nearly half the elk stags had antlers, indicating that they were killed sometime before December and perhaps as early as October.

In Clark's view, Star Carr was a settlement consisting of several families who occupied their site during midwinter and spring, returning to it at least once. Like Howard's work discussed earlier, Clark's excavation and interpretation of Star Carr is classic, a pioneering achievement in the application of ecological approaches to archaeology.

Archaeologist Mike Pitts, however, questioned this interpretation. Whereas Clark assumed that Star Carr was a complete Mesolithic settlement, Pitts suggested instead that the excavated area was a specialized industrial activity zone where deer antlers were worked and animal hides were processed. Critical to the argument is his rejection of red deer as dominant based on antler counts. Pitts suggests that all the deer antlers were collected specifically for the manufacture of barbed points and that mandibles instead be used for minimum number of individuals (MNI) counts. Viewed in this way, red deer do not seem to be the "key animal." This underscores the problems with the MNI approach. More important, if red deer antlers were being collected throughout the year for tool manufacture, then they should not be used for seasonal estimates. If Pitts is right, then Clark's interpretation must be incorrect.

Clark's inferences about Star Carr have also been questioned by John Andresen and his colleagues. Relying on experimental and ethnoarchaeological studies (such as those presented in Chapter 10), they reason that site formation processes label Star Carr as a hunting and butchering site, visited for very short periods at various times in the year. They also question the use of red deer antlers as a seasonal indicator, best collected when shed in April: Fewer than 40 percent of the antlers recovered had actually been shed, and even these could easily have been stored. The unshed antlers could have been acquired any time between late summer and April. Clark had argued that in order for antlers to be worked into tools, they must have been collected shortly after they dropped; otherwise, they would have been too deteriorated to serve as raw materials for tool manufacture. Andresen and his colleagues question this technological assumption, noting that shed antlers were not worked with any greater frequency than were their unshed counterparts. The investigators also emphasized that two elk skulls lacked antlers, indicating they were collected in January or later.

Several other seasonality studies rely on growth lines in marine shells. Season of death can be estimated from thin sections of these shells. Fish remains are also highly sensitive seasonal indicators. But a note of caution is required. Each technique can tell the archaeologist only when one or more animals died. The fact that some cormorants died at Emeryville in June or July is, by itself, archaeologically irrelevant. Archaeologists must be continually concerned with demonstrating that the death of a clam or a bighorn is somehow contemporaneous with (and relevant to) a specific behavioral event of interest. Without the demonstration of such relevance, the seasonal dates might tell us something about red deer or cormorant archaeology, but nothing about people.

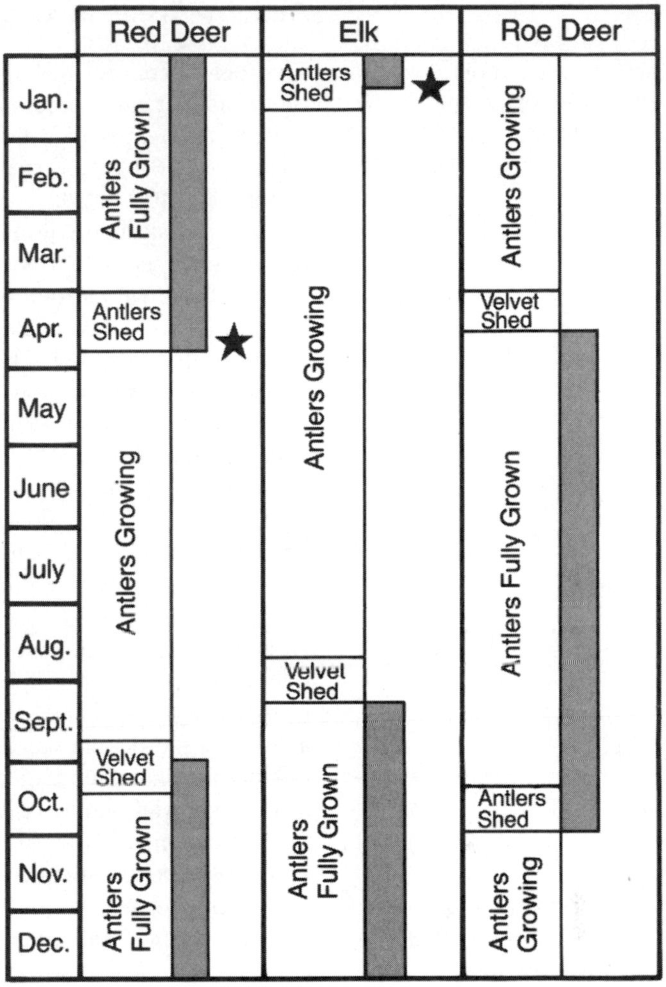

Inferred seasonal occupation of Star Carr, Yorkshire (England).

Tool Kits and Activity-Areas

Analyzing ecofacts can provide one way to isolate patterning in the archaeological record of foraging people. Another way is to look at the occurrence and spatial distribution of ancient *tool kits*—the related scattering of artifacts, waste products, and/or raw materials found in a spatially discrete assemblage. Tool kits are by no means ubiquitous in the archaeological record. In fact, for a tool kit to survive intact, the tools must be discarded nearly simultaneously and the association must not have been destroyed by postdepositional factors.

Burial Assemblages as Tool Kits

Archaeologists sometimes study prehistoric tool kits by looking at ancient burial assemblages, to see which individuals are buried with what tools. If, for instance, a human burial was found accompanied by certain function-specific artifacts, then maybe the deceased used these tools in life. Assuming this to be true, archaeologists have traditionally reconstructed ancient gender-specific roles in now-extinct societies. Today, archaeologists are increasingly reluctant to make such gender-specific assignments, unless considerably more documentation is available; we return to this tricky topic later in the chapter.

Activity-Areas at Coxcatlán Cave

Activity-area: A place within an archaeological site at which one or more specific activities (such as stone tool production or pottery manufacture) took place.

The tool-kit concept has also been used to infer intrasite (within-site) **activity-areas.** For an example, we turn to MacNeish's excavations at Coxcatlán Cave in the Tehuacán Valley of Puebla, Mexico. Initially occupied in approximately 10,000 B.C., Coxcatlán Cave continued to accumulate debris until about A.D. 1300 or so.

The physical stratigraphy of Coxcatlán Cave was quite clear, and excavators easily separated the zones of occupation. Twenty-eight living surfaces were isolated, with a total of 42 actual "occupations." During the excavation, concentrations of the artifacts, ecofacts, and features from each occupation were carefully mapped. These field data were then computer coded, and a series of living-floor maps were plotted. Look at the living-floor map produced by the Tehuacán Valley study, representing Zone XXIII of the Coxcatlán Shelter, with a key to the ecofacts and artifacts. With radiocarbon dates ranging between approximately 7200 and 6700 B.C., Zone XXIII was occupied during the Ajuereado Phase. The thickness of the floor was about 15 centimeters, and it covered almost 40 square meters.

After analyzing the artifacts, bones, and plant remains in Zone XXIII, the excavators defined three separate activity-areas. *Activity-area A* contained a variety of stone, bone, and antler artifacts. MacNeish took the presence of a fully developed deer antler to indicate a winter occupation. The abundance of bones and associated projectile points suggested that hunting was a major activity of the people who occupied Area A. The excavators suggested that butchering, skin preparation, and flintknapping may also have taken place during the brief winter visit.

This Mesolithic elk antler tool has a shaft hole and extensive ornamentation. Archaeologists don't know what purpose such artifacts served. Any guesses?

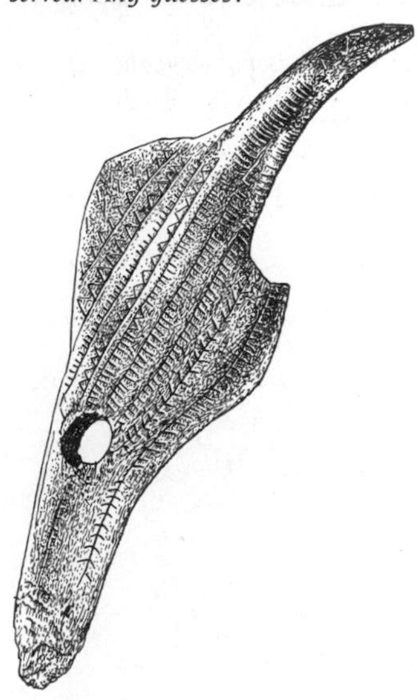

Activity-area C was to the east of A. The artifacts included sidescrapers and endscrapers, a metate, other grinding stones, flintknapping debris, and a variety of deer and cottontail bones.

Perhaps most important, however, is the storage pit (labeled Feature 35). Found in this basin-shaped depression were the leaves and seeds of *Setaria,* mesquite, and *Opuntia* (cactus). These plant remains indicate not only the food preferences of the Ajuereado occupants but also the seasonality, as this particular selection of seeds would have been available only during the spring. The associated artifacts in Area C were interpreted as resulting from a relatively short occupation by a few individuals who came to Coxcatlán Cave to perform specific tasks. The seeds and grinding stones, along with the thin scattering of animal bones and the absence of projectile points, were taken as an indication that seed collecting was the major activity. Scraping and graving tools suggest hide preparation, and the presence of a core and flakes may denote some flintknapping during the spring occupation of Area C.

Spatially intermediate between A and C is *Activity-area B.* No animal or plant remains were found, and seed-grinding tools were also absent. Area B was tentatively interpreted as being similar to A, involving hunting, skin preparation and/or butchering, woodworking, and flintknapping.

Zone XXIII of Coxcatlán Cave is only a small part of the living-floor analysis conducted for the Tehuacán Valley. MacNeish and his colleagues isolated over 75 occupations from about a dozen sites. Taken together, these

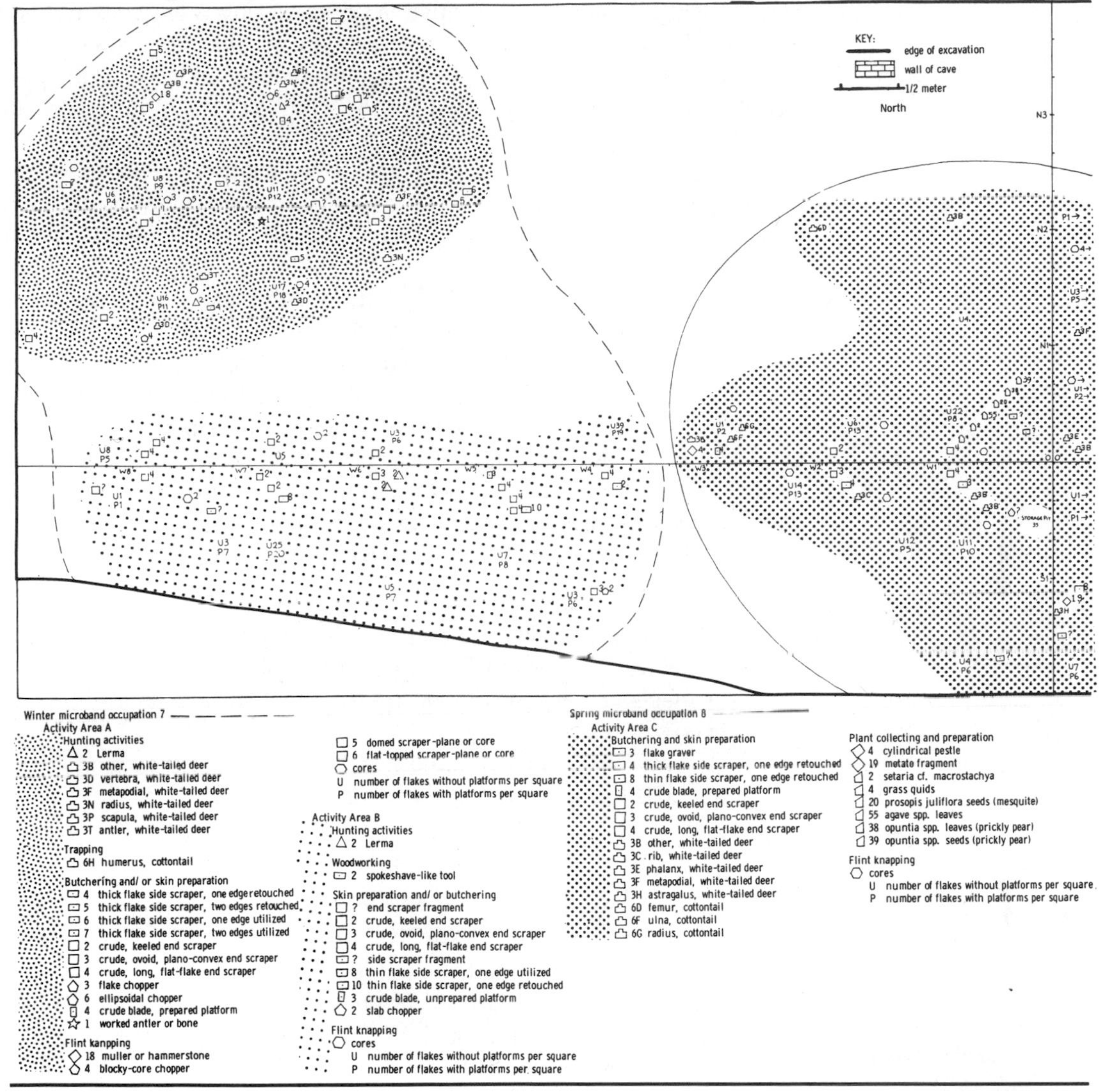

Presumed activity-areas in Zone XXIII at Coxcatlán Cave, Tehuacán Valley (Mexico), as reconstructed by Melvin Fowler and Richard MacNeish.

data allow reconstruction of the subsistence pattern, ecology, and social organization of this area over the past 12,000 years.

Archaeology Loses Some More Innocence

Truth comes out of error more readily than out of confusion.

FRANCIS BACON (1561–1626), PHILOSOPHER AND AUTHOR

Over the past couple of decades, archaeologists have looked more closely at the tacit assumptions that underpin unconstrained reconstructions, such as that for Coxcatlán Cave. Consider the issue of seasonality: Earlier in this chapter, we discussed the difficulties in seasonal estimates based on the presence/absence of "diagnostic" elements.

Today, few archaeologists are comfortable with assigning Activity-area A to "winter" simply because a fully developed deer antler was found there.

Such conclusions ignore the formation processes involved. How do we know that the Tehuacános collected antlers only in the "hardened, October–February" condition? Such a linkage requires that we understand the processes of prehistoric antler working, and we presently lack such an understanding.

And how did such a seasonally specific ecofact end up in Zone XXIII? Must humans have brought it in? How do we eliminate the agency of packrats and coyotes who live in the area today? In short, we lack the necessary bridging argument that relates the shedding of a deer antler to human behavior at Coxcatlán Cave.

The assignment of Feature 35 is more satisfactory. Multiple plant indicators (available only during the spring) were deliberately deposited by humans in a storage pit. But few contemporary archaeologists would accept the extension of this single-feature spring estimate to the entire living surface.

The MacNeish reconstruction also attempts to explain artifact and ecofact distributions as inextricably related to time-specific activity-areas. He and his colleagues expended much effort on piece-plotting artifacts to define clear-cut activity-areas; more than six dozen living-floor maps were published from the Tehuacán research, each one guided by three fundamental (and explicit) assumptions:

1. Seasonal availability of ecofacts found on a given surface is sufficient to define the season of occupation for that surface.
2. Artifacts and ecofacts found on the same surface define synchronous events.
3. Artifacts and ecofacts found nearby on the same surface were probably used in the same specific activities.

Today, not one of these assumptions is acceptable in light of available middle-range research.

It is a great temptation to define activity-areas by inspection, a temptation few of us can resist. . . . From time to time we all fall prey to what Binford (1981) has called "the Pompeii premise," a tendency to assume that prehistoric people left everything just where they used it.

KENT FLANNERY, ARCHAEOLOGIST (UNIVERSITY OF MICHIGAN)

Kent Flannery, among others, has criticized the methods used for "living-floor analysis" at Coxcatlán Cave. For one thing, the living-floor maps for Coxcatlán Cave were analyzed by simple visual inspection; when a cluster of items turned up, it was designated as an "activity-area" resulting from "hunting and trapping" or "woodworking." Such intuitive patterns of association lack any statistical means of determining which clusters are significant and which could be expected from chance association alone. How many artifacts does it take to make a cluster?

It is also unlikely that activities such as "hunting and trapping" or "plant collecting and growing" actually took place *inside* Coxcatlán Cave. More likely, these specific activities occurred elsewhere. The various "activity-specific" artifacts—projectile points, digging sticks, and so forth—were constructed to be used elsewhere. Who would stalk a deer or dig for roots *inside* a cave? More likely, all these artifacts were discarded inside Coxcatlán Cave as simple *refuse,* not "in the line of duty" for the functions they once served.

Even the distribution of the various food bones found inside Coxcatlán Cave probably does not tell us much about butchering and dismembering of carcasses. Most of the bones were probably tossed away after they had been thoroughly roasted, boiled, and split apart for bone marrow. At best, they might represent an "eating" area inside the cave. Even more likely, however, these discarded food bones were considerably moved around by domestic dogs, wild carnivores, or cave-dwelling rodents (such as packrats). In that quite-likely event, the distribution of food bones might more clearly reflect the nonhuman scavenging patterns inside the cave rather than any human behavior that once took place here.

Flannery concluded that "activity-areas" reconstructed for cave surfaces must be based not on the functions for which the artifacts were originally manufactured but on the subsequent activities that account for their being discarded on the floor.

For this reason, rigid activity-area models are now taking into account the various depositional and postdepositional processes involved in creating the archaeological record. Such approaches are briefly considered in the next section.

This conclusion in no way belittles the achievements of MacNeish and his colleagues. The Tehuacán Valley project was the epitome of 1960s hyperreconstructionist archaeology, the standard-bearer of the interdisciplinary revolution. It typifies an enthusiastic era during which archaeologists boldly penetrated new areas of ecological and anthropological interest. This research will always retain an important place in the history of Americanist archaeology. But archaeology has outgrown its age of innocence. Our present understanding of site formation processes renders many of these 1960s assumptions simplistic or downright wrong.

The Archaeology of Individual Life Space

In questioning the straightforward tool-kit/activity-area association, archaeologists have begun to appreciate the scores of factors that conspire to muddy seemingly clear-cut distinctions in the archaeological record: differential preservation, variable "use lives" of artifacts, artifact curation and periodic episodes of site cleaning, recycling, and caching–to say nothing of a host of postdepositional processes. Archaeologists, in short, have begun the tedious process of building the middle-range bridges necessary to understand spatial patterning in the archaeological record.

The Mask Site Model

Lewis Binford studied the Mask site to learn more about the way in which the archaeological record reflects human life space. In this "classic" study of ethnoarchaeology, Binford looked at the consequences of modern behavior to inform our investigations of the past.

The Mask site is a hunting stand, situated atop a north-south-oriented glacial moraine, not far from the present village of Anaktuvuk (Alaska). Here men congregate to watch for game and to plan hunting strategies once game is spotted. The site covers about 65 square meters; in the center is a cluster of five fire hearths. The differential use of the individual hearths depends on wind direction and herd movements. Tiny bone chips created while breaking

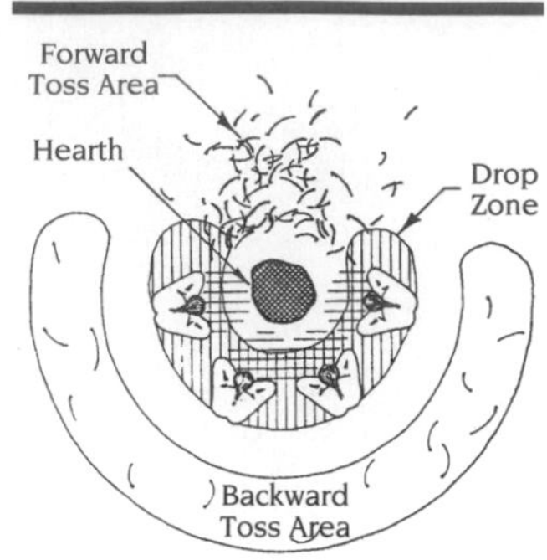

"Men's" Outside Hearth Model

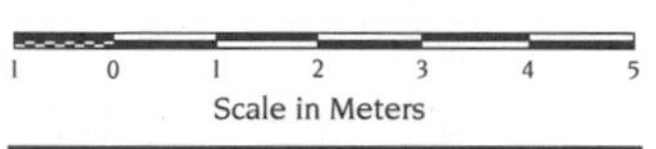

Models of drop and toss zones developed by Lewis Binford from his observations at the Mask site in Anaktuvuk Pass, Alaska.

open bones to get at the marrow are concentrated around each hearth, in an area Binford termed the *drop zone.* Similar distributions are deposited by people chipping stone tools, while sitting around a hearth. Both flakes and bone chips were left in place by the Nunamiut at the location where the stone working and marrow cracking took place. Such drop zones contain *primary refuse*—bone chips and splinters, wood shavings, and the occasional item fumbled and forgotten during the activities.

Several formation processes condition what actually ends up in the drop zone. Light or small objects are less visible and are incorporated into the archaeological record more readily, as they are less likely to be removed during cleanup. But the spatial distribution of larger pieces of bone is quite different because these larger bones are usually tossed or placed beyond the hearth area, away from where the men are working and sitting. The resultant *toss zone* is produced by a kind of "preventive maintenance" at the seating area.

Thus, the Nunamiut dispose of their debris in two different ways. They simply drop and forget the small things and toss away the larger items. At the Mask site, the residents threw sardine and pop cans away from the immediate hearth area after the contents were consumed. When Lewis Binford asked them why they disposed of their refuse in two different ways, he was asked simply, "Who wants to sit down on a large bone?"

The most obvious consequence of such behavior is that debris becomes *size sorted* in the process of discard. This size-sorting effect has been shown to operate in diverse settings, and it can be a critical factor in the site formation process. Contrary to what one expects from a rigid tool-kit/activity-area concept, item distribution can be patterned in the archaeological record strictly on the basis of size, without regard to function or derivation. Tossing behavior can, in effect, create zones of spurious intrasite association, and an uncritical use of the tool-kit and activity-area concepts can misinterpret such patterning.

The spatial configuration of the Mask site is the result of several distinct disposal modes: dropping, tossing, resting, placing, and dumping. The configuration of the drop and toss zones varies from site to site, but similar underlying factors may be operative in a wide variety of situations.

Drop Zone/Toss Zone Patterning at Gatecliff Shelter

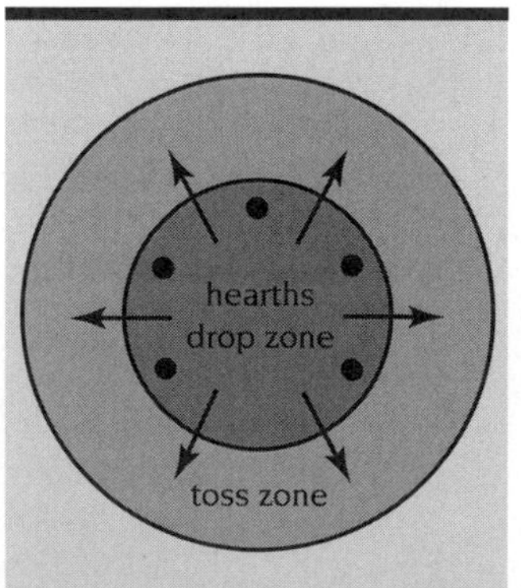

The Mask site refuse disposal model.

We used Binford's Mask site model as a general framework for examining the spatial distribution of materials at Gatecliff Shelter. A toss zone can be created in any direction, and the Mask site model operates within a full 360-degree arena. In many cases, however, directionality may be determined by cultural or natural factors. The construction of summer houses or windbreaks, for instance, has a marked effect on refuse disposal practices. At Gatecliff, the immovable rear wall tightly structures debris discard, providing a natural backdrop for all activities conducted inside the shelter.

Despite such directional constraints, the same depositional processes might be expected to occur at Gatecliff as at the Mask site, creating predictable intrasite disposal areas. The hearths still provide the focal points for cooking, eating, sleeping, tool manufacture, and repair. Similarly, a drop zone could be presumed to exist around each hearth area. But the configuration of Gatecliff Shelter might also be expected to influence the direction and configuration of the toss zone. Because debris cannot be tossed through the rear of the cave, toss zones should occur in this case outside the shelter drip line, on the apron of the cave.

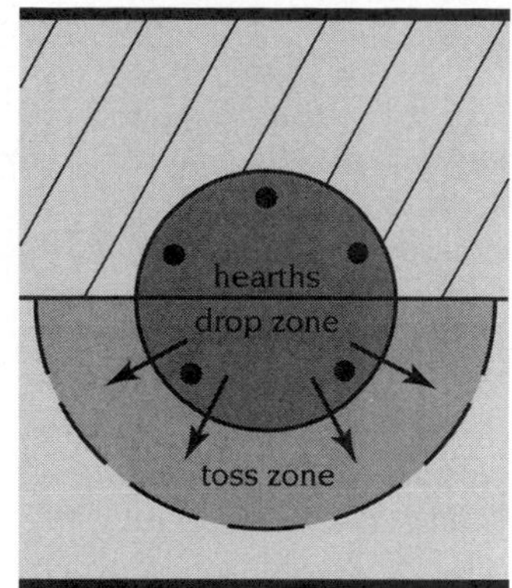

Drop zone/toss zone patterning, extrapolated from the Mask site model to a 180° version suitable for sites like Gatecliff Shelter.

Look at how the Mask site model is transposed to a setting in which the hearths are constructed within a restricted space. This derivative model provided a departure point for analyzing both the hearth positioning and the potential size sorting of debris at Gatecliff Shelter.

We plotted 36 hearths at Gatecliff and found them to be tightly patterned, in accord with the 180-degree version of the Mask site model. In effect, each cultural horizon was characterized by a distinctive "hearth line," a band of fire hearths running across the mouth of Gatecliff Shelter. These parallels were particularly striking because each horizon was capped by a layer of compact calcareous silt, varying in thickness from 6 inches to 2 feet. These silt lenses effectively sandwiched living surfaces between sterile layers, totally isolating intrasite patterning from that of earlier horizons. That is, the internal structure of each living surface was separate from every other horizon.

The distance between these hearth lines and the rear wall was almost constant at about 15 feet. So positioned, the hearths offered several advantages. A distinct work area was defined between the hearth line and the rear wall. Placement somewhat inside the drip line protected the fires from rain, snow, and wind, venting the smoke outside. In effect, each hearth created a relatively warm and smoke-free rear room, as well as a heated work and sleep area. The south-facing rear wall of the shelter absorbed heat from both hearths and sunlight.

The 16 cultural horizons at Gatecliff were also analyzed to determine how debris size sorting was manifested. It turned out that the Gatecliff debris was indeed heavily size-sorted. With the exception of Horizon 2—where bighorn sheep were butchered inside the cave—all the horizons clearly indicated that the artifacts, waste flakes, and ecofacts at the rear of the site were significantly smaller than those deposited near the drip line.

We found that debris size was the single most important factor influencing intrasite spatial patterning at Gatecliff. Regardless of raw material, stage of manufacture, potential use-life, edge attrition, and typological or functional category, the internal positioning of debris was best predicted by a single variable: weight. This finding was important because it mandates considerable caution when using the tool-kit/activity-area concept as an explanatory principle for understanding the human use of space.

Note particularly the difference in interpretation between Coxcatlán Cave and Gatecliff Shelter. At Coxcatlán, the investigators assumed (1) that artifacts and ecofacts found on the same surface were deposited at the same time and (2) that intrasite spatial patterning corresponded to specific activity sets. In our analysis of patterning at Gatecliff, we could not justify these assumptions, and for good reason. Instead, we found that size sorting was sufficient to account for nearly all the patterning present.

I suspect that similar size sorting operated at Coxcatlán Cave. Viewed from the perspective of the Mask site model, one expects that areas in the

Hunter-gatherer subsistence can be viewed profitably in terms of the same general theory now being applied by evolutionary ecologists to the study of feeding strategies. . . . The value of such theory lies in its role as a reference dimension, as a source of testable hypotheses about the organization of subsistence-related behavior in a wide range of environmental, technological, and social circumstances.

JAMES F. O'CONNELL, ARCHAEOLOGIST, AND KRISTEN HAWKES, ETHNOGRAPHER (UNIVERSITY OF UTAH)

rear of the cave should be the drop zone, whereas things found along the apron of the cave should be toss zone debris. To conduct an adequate reanalysis, it would be necessary to consider the size of the various bones, plant parts, and artifacts. But the living-floor map certainly suggests that such is the case.

Binford's work among the Nunamiut also pointed out how *artifact curation* could bias the archaeological record. Nunamiut hunters carry their artifacts around with them to such a degree that tool inventories of their sites have precious little to do with the activities that took place there. The problem for archaeologists dealing with Nunamiut sites is that there may be little relationship between the activities performed and the artifacts discarded.

Rethinking Activity-Areas and Tool Kits

Before leaving this topic, let me stress the recent difficulties with the tool-kit concept. Specifically as a result of ethnoarchaeological observations, investigators have pointed out that the "living floor" is an assumption that may not hold for many modern societies. At !Kung campsites in South Africa, for example, stone hammers and anvils are used to crack mongongo nuts, and these tools are often found in nuclear camp areas, which are also commonly littered with high concentrations of bone. But the stones have no relationship to the faunal remains. Both are physical remains of very different activities, and they occur together only fortuitously. It thus should be apparent that inferring from a single tool kit could erroneously influence the interpretation of, say, Coxcatlán Zone XXIII.

Hunter-Gatherer as Optimal Forager

Over the past few decades, archaeologists and ethnoarchaeologists have begun approaching hunter-gatherers from yet another perspective. Several investigators believe that a processual understanding of hunter-gatherers can be obtained from the larger body of developing theory in evolutionary biology. One increasingly popular method of inquiry employs **optimal foraging theory**, a broad-based theoretical perspective that attempts to develop a set of models general enough to apply to a wide range of animal species, yet rigorous and precise enough to explain the details of behavior exhibited by a particular forager.

Optimal foraging theory: A broad-based theoretical perspective employed in evolutionary biology; attempts to develop a set of models general enough to apply to a broad range of animal species, yet rigorous and precise enough to explain the details of behavior exhibited by a particular forager.

Enter Evolutionary Ecology

One relatively early effort in this direction was attempted by archaeologist Edwin Wilmsen, who proposed a generalized model of hunter-gatherer spatial organization. Beginning with the perspective of locational geography, Wilmsen borrowed a theory initially derived from observations on blackbirds (but intended to apply to the relationship between the distribution of resources and consumers in general). This biogeographic model suggested that blackbirds tend to space themselves throughout their territories according to a precise mathematical formula. Wilmsen examined how well the model seemed to account for known hunter-gatherer patterns and suggested that the revised model could be tested against archaeological evidence. Since then, several others have followed Wilmsen's lead, looking to evolutionary biology for general theoretical guidance.

Archaeologist James O'Connell proposes that the logic underlying the application of optimal foraging theory to archaeology may go something like this: Because archaeologists embrace such a huge empirical domain, a general theory of behavior may be required. Much of the archaeological record for the past several thousand years was created under conditions similar to those observed ethnographically. Provided that one exercises the cautions implicit in good archaeological practice, there is every likelihood of success in accounting for the general structure of the archaeological record in behavioral terms. Middle-range research is critical to this endeavor; mature general theory may not be.

Over the past 30 years [the framework of behavioral ecology] has proven useful in exploring behavioral variation in many living organisms, including humans. If, as many contend, the archaeological record provides systematic evidence of past human behavior and its evolution, then it should be possible to use this framework, in tandem with ethnoarchaeology, to explore it, at all times and in all places.

JAMES F. O'CONNELL

We lack the appropriate ethnographic analogies for temporally more remote segments of the archaeological record. The patterns of behavior in the remote past may be too dissimilar to those of the present to allow any acceptable linkage between the two. Optimal foraging theory may offer a partial solution to this problem. Although the patterns of behavior in the distant past may have been vastly different from those of the present, a *uniformitarian* assumption holds: The principles that shape the behavior of modern *Homo sapiens* are constant and unchanging in time and space. Evolutionary ecologists apply theory at a general level, anchored in assumptions derived from basic postulates of natural selection theory. This approach uses mathematical and graphic representations as part of the heavily scientific approach of the processual agenda.

Although neither complete nor unified, optimal foraging models are general and offer some degree of explanatory power. Today, specific applications remain provisional and directed at limited aspects of cultural systems, but because optimal foraging models are grounded in the general theory of natural selection, such models may provide a general, more unified understanding of human behavior—provided that the assumptions hold for the archaeological record and that the applications hold up under empirical scrutiny.

Perhaps the greatest appeal of optimal foraging models is their ability to bring specific testable projections of human behavior to bear on real data. Although most such "testing" has been conducted by biologists, applications to human populations have appeared in the past couple of decades. We will discuss two examples.

Looking at the pattern of archaeological work over the last 20 years, one can see a rapid turnover of ideas that come into fashion, are briefly modish, and are then ditched for their failings. The speed at which they come and go is disconcerting; when I spent a few years out of the business in the 1970s I missed one mode, optimal foraging theory, completely—it came, "failed," and it was sent on while I chanced briefly to be looking the other way.

CHRISTOPHER CHIPPINDALE, ARCHAEOLOGIST AND EDITOR

Diet-Breadth Modeling

One problem with foraging theory concerns prey choice and diet breadth. Out of the array of available things to eat, which ones should an efficient forager attempt to harvest? To answer this question, optimal foraging theorists have developed the *diet-breadth model.*

We begin with a hypothetical predator seeking prey scattered randomly throughout the environment. The idea is to specify which and how many resources this forager should pursue in order to achieve the highest net rate

Optimal foraging is no more than the long-known minimum-effort–maximum-gain economic theory as it is applicable to the study of subsistence.

Jesse D. Jennings (1909–1997), archaeologist

of energy intake. Bruce Winterhalder has outlined seven assumptions necessary in the diet-breadth model:

Currency

1. Some optimal foraging models assume that the hypothetical organism attempts to maximize its net rate of energy intake while foraging; other approaches use different currencies.

Constraints

2. Prey is encountered randomly (that is, the next kind of prey encountered is independent of the last kind encountered).
3. For a particular diet breadth, the hypothetical organism either takes a prey item or it does not (there are no "partial" preferences).
4. The "quality" of a prey type can be evaluated independently of the others in terms of its stable ranking (defined as net energy value per unit of pursuit and handling costs).
5. "Foraging" consists of two independent phases. Predators first "search" all prey jointly but then "pursue" the target prey singly.
6. The density of prey remains constant throughout the foraging interval.
7. Costs and benefits associated with resources are treated as firm expectations (without considering statistical variability).

As Winterhalder wryly notes, "Despite its appearance, this is not a paralyzing list."

O'Connell suggests that these "assumptions" can also be perceived as hypotheses, themselves subject to testing. Viewed in this way, applications of foraging models routinely use a set of hypotheses regarding (1) the goals of foraging, (2) the alternative methods of achieving these goals, (3) the costs and benefits associated with these alternative means, (4) the currencies in which these costs and benefits are to be measured, and (5) the time frame in which the goals are to be met. *If* the forager is behaving "optimally" with respect to the specified goals and *if* the currencies and so forth are correct, *then* certain predictions about behavior will follow. But if these predictions are not met, then one or more of the various hypotheses will be judged to be incorrect. Optimal foraging models, as such, are never actually tested, nor is the question of optimality (which is assumed).

The MacArthur and Pianka diet-breadth model.

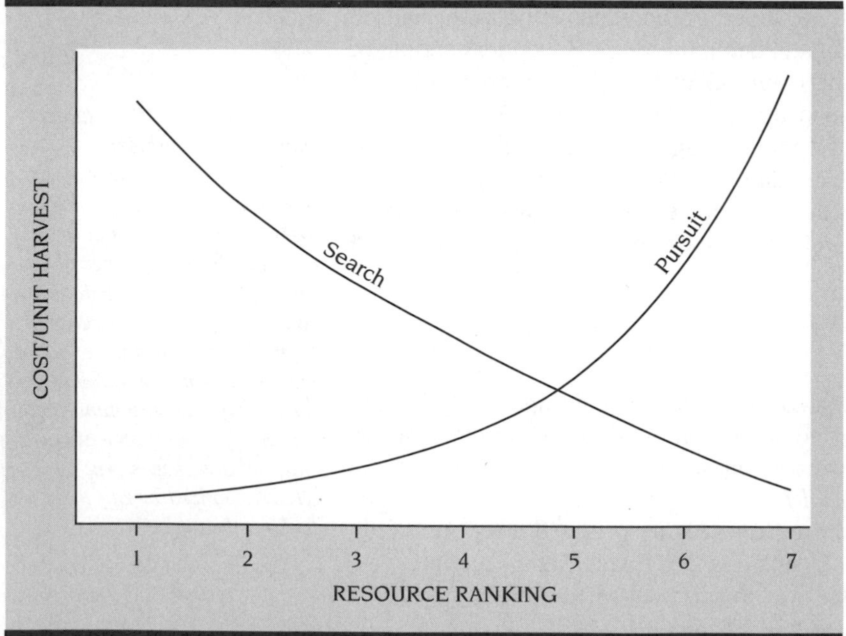

The graph illustrates the diet-breadth model. The

baseline contains the "ranked" number of resource types in the diet of our hypothetical forager, scaled according to the "currency" we mentioned. As each prey type is added to the diet, the "search" curve (i.e., the average search costs) decreases, and the "pursuit" curve (the average pursuit costs) increases. In other words, the more one searches, the more one will find; but because the prey types are rank ordered, these new additions are more difficult to capture (or less rewarding when secured). The *optimal diet breadth* occurs at the intersection of the two curves. This general format allows the investigator to project hypothetical changes when any of the environmental parameters are shifted.

When converted to its algebraic format, this model provides a set of predictions (x) about how foragers should behave under certain circumstances (y). The animal ecologist can determine the explanatory power of such projections by observing and recording behavior in a quantitative manner; ecologists working on living animal populations can simultaneously measure the state of the environment to see whether x and y covaried as the theory predicts.

Alyawara Foraging and Diet-Breadth Models

James O'Connell (an archaeologist) and Kristen Hawkes (an ethnographer) were among the first to apply the diet-breadth model to examine plant use by the modern Alyawara people of Australia. They began by asking why the Alyawara had effectively stopped eating native grass and tree seeds, foods that had been staples in the traditional diet and remain available today.

The primary goal among hunter-gatherers is to provide the basic nutritive and other raw materials necessary for the survival of the population.

ARTHUR S. KEENE, ARCHAEOLOGIST (UNIVERSITY OF MASSACHUSETTS, AMHERST)

An optimal diet model provides a series of predictions (x): If Alyawara collectors forage optimally, then the resources taken from each "patch" will depend on the relative energy return per unit of handling time and the average return from collecting in that patch. Resources yielding a return higher than the average for a patch should be included in the diet, but resources with lower returns should not. The expectations generated by these propositions were expressed in the formal algebraic terms of **kilocalories** per forager hour.

Kilocalorie: Unit used to express the amount of energy that a food provides when consumed. One calorie is the amount of heat required to raise the temperature of 1 gram of water 1 degree Celsius; a *kilocalorie* equals 1,000 calories.

Situation y in this case reflects the state of the environment–degree of rainfall, relative temperature, and, most important, geographic distribution and condition of available plant communities–at Bendaijerum (Australia) between 1974 and 1975. The covariation between y and x was monitored across a series of Alyawara foraging events observed by O'Connell. On 11 visits to the sandhills, energy returns were indeed well above average for the patch, and although several species of ripe seeds were available in these patches, they were never harvested during these particular visits because the returns from other, higher-ranked resources (roots and fruit) did not fall low enough. The seeds were collected only during a brief period after they had reached maximum size and before they had hardened, when handling time was relatively low and energy returns were correspondingly high.

People do not behave in the sense that animals behave, they act*. . . . Human social action is . . . inherently meaningful and 99% of this action has no direct survival value.*

MICHAEL SHANKS, ARCHAEOLOGIST, AND CHRISTOPHER TILLEY, ARCHAEOLOGIST (UNIVERSITY OF WALES)

O'Connell and Hawkes concluded that the predictions based on the model passed the test for plant collection in the sandhills: "Foraging behavior in this habitat is clearly consistent with the predictions of the optimal diet model." Foraging in the mulga woodland produced different results, with Alyawara foraging behavior not fitting the optimal diet prediction about the threshold at which lower-ranked resources will be collected. O'Connell and

Hawkes believe that future modeling must include cost-benefit analyses of manufacturing and maintaining processing gear. Another reason for the lack of fit between behavior and predictions in the mulga woodland could be that the returns were not accurately observed or were initially underestimated.

Using an array of such optimal foraging models, O'Connell and Hawkes effectively answered their initial research question. The Alyawara stopped eating native grass and tree seeds—even when available—because they were "too expensive" in cost-benefit terms. The researchers also were able to figure out why such food was so important in traditional times. Before the introduction of European foods, pressure on native plant resources must have been much greater, with collectors depleting certain high-ranked resources even in a good year.

Although the potential of foraging theory for archaeology was somewhat overstated by early proponents, more recent studies, such as this one by O'Connell and Hawkes, present more balanced views of both costs and benefits.

Optimal Foraging and the Archaeological Record

Applying [optimal foraging] theory presumes that the archaeological record is reasonably clear concerning what prehistoric folks did, and the task is then to explain *it. But in fact, such an assumption is almost completely wrong in many important instances.*

Eric Alden Smith, ethnographer (University of Washington)

Numerous applications of optimal foraging models to strictly archaeological data have been attempted. Shifting empirical referents from the ethnographic present to the archaeological past means that neither behavior nor environment can be directly observed. But before optimal foraging theory—or any other general theory—can be brought to bear on archaeological data, it is necessary to infer past behavior from the archaeological record and also to infer past environmental states from the paleoenvironmental record. Both records are static, and all dynamics must be inferred through middle-range linkages.

We might also point out that the process of reconstructing (or inferring) past behavior is itself often a theory-dependent endeavor. If, for instance, one wishes to reconstruct the behavior of *Homo erectus,* a theoretical framework is necessary to define the possible alternative behavioral models that could be tested archaeologically. Such theory sets the direction of research and anticipates the range of plausible results. We cannot simply dig a number of sites, reconstruct behavior, and then seek an explanation in general theoretical terms.

As you can appreciate from the preceding example, optimal foraging projections require comprehensive cultural and paleoenvironmental chronologies: One must have an accurate picture of (1) who lived where (and when) and (2) what plants and animals were (or were not) available for inclusion in the diet. We suggested earlier that archaeology has emerged from an "age of innocence," and we now require better-reasoned associations to establish reliable estimates of seasonality and annual round.

Grinding stones were once considered to equal (1) women and (2) seed collection, but we no longer assume such a relationship. Projectile points once meant "men went hunting," but (as discussed in the next section) we now realize that the relationship between gender and technology is considerably more complex. We must keep in mind that the mere presence of bones and seeds at an archaeological site is no longer considered to be valid evidence of human consumption. Rather, we must adequately document the procurement and processing strategies applied to these resources—how the seeds were processed and how such processing shows up in the archaeological record.

While middle-range research on seasonality, size sorting and intrasite patterning, tool kits and activity-areas, regional variability, taphonomy, and postdepositional modifications proceeds apace—as documented in earlier chapters—such progress carries with it the sober realization that archaeological data are more intractable than was appreciated during the first decades of the processual agenda. Granted, generating such fine-grained data is a tall order, but technological advances in archaeology—such as accelerator C-14 and stable isotope analysis of human skeletal remains—may eventually be able to fill the bill.

These are not shortcomings in optimal foraging theory but uniquely archaeological problems emerging from the specifics of the past and the immaturity of our middle-range methods of understanding. Optimal foraging models may prove to be an effective bridge for archaeologists to use to pass into the realm of general theory.

O'Connell and Hawkes argue that, if successfully applied, the perspective of evolutionary biology may provide a way to understand long-term human dietary change and land use patterns: "The value of such theory lies in its role as a reference dimension, as a source of testable hypotheses about the organization of subsistence-related behavior in a wide range of environmental, technological, and social circumstances."

There is some danger here, of course, because archaeologists are, from time to time, seduced and sidetracked by slick techniques. Some, unfortunately, think that any general theory is preferable to no theory at all, and archaeologists remain in constant peril of simply buying their theory straight off the rack.

There can be no question, however, that optimal foraging models do indeed open up potentially fruitful lines of inquiry. Either the foraging models stand up to observable behavior, or they do not. When models fail to fit behavioral reality, they can be refined or discarded. This is perhaps the greatest strength of the optimal foraging effort in anthropology.

Engendering the Foraging Past

We have often mentioned how ethnographic and ethnohistoric evidence can be used to model what the archaeological record might be expected to look like. What we haven't said—yet—is how heavily such expectations rely on methodological and theoretical assumptions. Let us conclude this discussion of hunter-gatherer archaeology by taking a look at the issue of gender bias in our understanding of the past.

To consider one sex while ignoring the other is like looking at an old family photograph in which the males occupy the foreground as distinct figures, while the females are an undifferentiated blur in the background.

LINDA REIBER AND JANE DE HART MATHEWS, HISTORIANS

We begin with a concrete example. You will remember (from Chapter 4) how we used the rich ethnographic and ethnohistorical record from the Great Basin to project a series of behavioral activities into the regional archaeological record. The idea was to design a computer simulation that would emulate behavior from a known group of people (the Western Shoshone) in a known spot (the Reese River Valley) for a known period of time (immediately prior to European contact in the area, roughly A.D. 1840).

Northern Paiute woman preparing to harvest piñon nuts in 1914 (near Fallon, Nevada).

We made a number of gender-based inferences. For one thing, we inferred that women and children harvested piñon pine nuts during the fall months because (1) several Western Shoshone women said they did this in the nineteenth century and (2) numerous eyewitnesses reported seeing Shoshone women and children doing this a few decades later. Similarly, we thought that hunting parties comprised of all-male adults stalked bighorn sheep for the same reason. We further believed that entire family groups participated in communal jackrabbit drives, once again because this is what Western Shoshone informants and ethnohistoric accounts told us. We tried to determine the gender composition of various camp and task groups for the entire seasonal round of the mid-nineteenth-century Western Shoshone people.

Unfortunately, archaeologists do not encounter camp and task groups; archaeologists recover artifacts and ecofacts. Thus it was necessary for us to assign material culture implications for each activity—once again based on appropriate ethnographic analogs. The distribution of these various artifacts and ecofacts was then projected across the target area in the central Nevada landscape. The regional randomized archaeological survey (also discussed in Chapter 5) was designed specifically to see how well these ethnographically grounded projections anticipated the archaeological record of the Reese River Valley.

At the time, it seemed to make perfect sense to employ the available ethnographic information to project human behavior into the recent past. Today, 30 years later, such inferences still make sense—provided there is direct historical continuity between the ethnographic and archaeological records.

Later in this book, we will examine a very different approach to archaeology, but one that nevertheless shares this same basic perspective on gender roles in the past. In Chapter 17, we will see how Janet Spector employed an empathetic, feminist approach at the Little Rapids site in Minnesota. After extensive ethnographic and ethnohistorical research on the Eastern Dakota people who once lived at Little Rapids, Spector felt confident in projecting many modern-day gender-specific activities onto the archaeological record of this mid-nineteenth-century Dakota site.

Clear-cut linkages between the documentary and archaeological record existed for both the Eastern Dakota and the Western Shoshone research, conducted by Spector and me, respectively—so long as we were discussing the mid-nineteenth century. But how far back in the past could we legitimately project the gender-specific ethnohistoric information? Another century (to the mid-eighteenth century)? A millennium? A million years?

The Man-the-Hunter Myth

The entire village left the next day in about 30 canoes, leaving us alone with the women and children in the abandoned houses.

Claude Levi-Strauss, anthropologist

I raise this point to highlight an increasingly important issue, that of gender bias in reconstructing the past. More than a decade ago, Margaret Conkey and Janet Spector explored this matter in some detail; their now-classic research stands as the first call for an explicit, gender-based approach to the archaeological record.

Conkey and Spector found that conventional archaeological interpretation was permeated with an unrecognized (and presumably unintentional) gender bias and **androcentrism.** They uncovered case after case of archaeologists—both male and female—projecting their own ill-defined stereotypes into the past: They criticized the then-dominant processual agenda for creating a false sense of objectivity about how gender roles are encoded in the archaeological record.

Androcentric: Characterized by or based on an exclusively masculine perspective.

The focus of the Conkey and Spector critique was the so-called *Man-the-Hunter* model of human evolution. In effect, this widespread view projected modern gender stereotypes back into the remote past: Males were typically portrayed as "stronger, more aggressive, more active, and in general more important than females [who were] . . . presented as weak, passive, and dependent."

[The Man-the-Hunter model] includes a set of assumptions about males and females—their activities, their capabilities, their relations to one another, their social position and value relative to one another, and their contributions to human evolution—that epitomize the problems of androcentrism.

MARGARET CONKEY, ARCHAEOLOGIST (UNIVERSITY OF CALIFORNIA, BERKELEY), AND JANET SPECTOR, ARCHAEOLOGIST (UNIVERSITY OF MINNESOTA)

The Man-the-Hunter model assumed a long-term continuity in gender arrangements and ideology, extending from the present back to the earliest humans. This model implied a relatively rigid division of labor along gender lines, a sort of inevitability about gender roles. Specific artifact forms were also viewed as sex-linked—weaponry for hunting was always male, plant-collecting apparatus was always female. Men always made the projectile points. Women always made the pottery. Women who are found buried with a grinding stone were assumed to have used this artifact in life. If a man was buried with the same grinding stone, it was because he manufactured it.

Conkey and Spector found most archaeologists failed to identify the sources for their assumptions and rarely tried to confirm or validate them. Archaeologists were "gendering" the past on the basis of their intrinsic, stereotypical notions about male and female roles.

This is the myth of Man-the-Hunter—drawing upon androcentric assumptions about human nature and society, with the unintended consequence of either ignoring women's activities altogether or characterizing them in secondary, subservient terms. This model overemphasizes the importance of male activities and results in "gender-exclusive" reconstructions of past human behavior.

Anybody doubting that such androcentric gender bias exists need look no farther than the neighborhood museum diorama or popular publications on archaeology. Age and gender stereotypes about our human past are everywhere—once you actually begin to recognize them.

To gauge the extent of such bias, archaeologist Diane Gifford-Gonzalez studied the way in which our ancient human ancestors were depicted in popular accounts of human evolution—in places like museum exhibits; the covers of *Time, Newsweek,* and *National Geographic* magazines; and throughout the pages of coffee table books about archaeology. She particularly looked at (1) what kinds of people were depicted and (2) what activities they were engaged in.

Gifford-Gonzalez found that roughly 85 percent of such popular characterizations showed middle-aged men; women showed up in less than half the scenes. Children and older people were rarely shown playing active, useful roles in the past. Women's work was almost always shown in patronizing, demeaning ways—the not-so-subtle message suggesting that the *real* human story depended almost wholly on men's activities. In *The Real Flintstones,* Gifford-Gonzalez discusses these sometimes humorous characterizations of our human past.

Northern Paiute burden basket: If you found this artifact in an archaeological site, would you call it a "woman's artifact?"

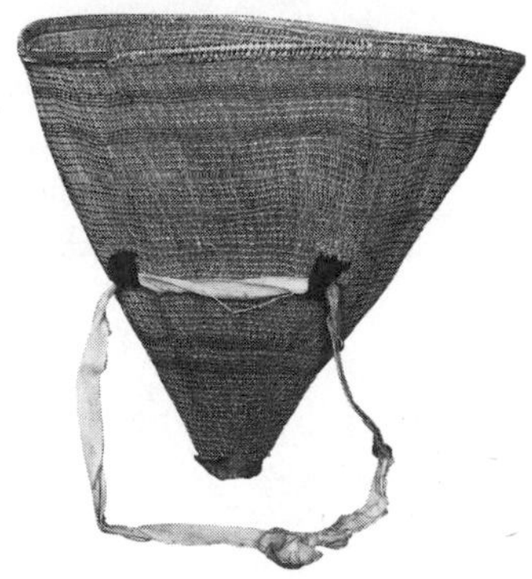

ARCHAEO-MYTHBUSTERS

The Real *Flintstones*? by Diane Gifford-Gonzalez

The Drudge:

You have probably seen her, frequenting the diorama scene at your local museum or in that coffee table book on human evolution. It's likely you've not given her a second glance, she is so much a part of the scenery. She is the Drudge-on-the-Hide; the woman on her hands and knees scraping away at the skin of a large animal, on the margins of the home camp scene. The men are usually center stage foreground, doing something interesting, while she's over there, hiding out. You usually can not see her face; she is looking down, and the artist may not have bothered to sketch in her brows or mouth. She is not talking to anyone; no one is talking to her.

Conventionalized representations such as the drudge repeat themselves through the works of various artists, their postures and actions suggesting that artists have drawn from their own fine arts traditions, rather than from ethnographically informed suggestions from their scientist collaborators. The "Drudge-on-a-Hide," for example, mimics the scullery maid scrubbing the floor in the background of the 18th century evocations of bourgeois success.

The Guy-With-a-Rock:

Another common motif, the "Guy-With-a-Rock" about to hurl a huge rock into a pit containing a large and unhappy beast (mammoth, mastodon, woolly rhino, or cave bear), suggests Herculean figures in portrayals of classical myths. Though his hunting mates sport the latest ballistic weapons, this stone-age conservative has a hefty rock as his weapon of choice from 2 million B.C. *to Holocene bison hunts in Dakota.*

The Deer-on-a-Stick:

Homecoming from a successful hunt incorporates the "Deer-on-a-Stick" motif. The massive prey portrayed in most hunt scenes shrinks to a readily transported package, hefted on a pole between two extraordinarily tidy hunters. They are never shown bringing home dismembered animal parts, nor besmirched with gore. If anyone is portrayed close to such nastiness, it's Woman, crouched on a bloody hide. Faced with the lack of fit between ethnographic data on animal butchery and these scenes, one's mind readily wanders down Freudian, rather than archaeological, corridors.

Madonna-With-Child:

The other common female motif besides the abject Drudge is the "Madonna-With-Child," a youthful woman standing with baby in arms and doing absolutely nothing. Cumulatively, illustrations of paleolithic women present a contrast to the busy lives of ethnographically documented mothers in hunter-gatherer societies. Stone Age woman's life seems to have begun with a placid but immobile young motherhood, rooted decoratively to the spot as camp life swirled about her, followed by dull and dumpy middle age, hiding out on the margins of the fun stuff (still not a whit of social interaction), followed by aged and inactive sitting and watching, waiting for the paleolithic version of the Grim Reaper to work his way up the valley. It is a wonder women learned to talk at all.

Archaeologists can readily testify to the difficulties of assigning gender or maturational stage to most of the activities portrayed, in view of humanity's global diversity in cultural practices. Yet the graphic story reaching out from the museum halls and coffee table pages treats men's and women's—and youngsters' and oldsters'—estate as foregone conclusions. When viewed cumulatively, as we would see them in our lifetimes of museum-going and reading, the vast majority of existing portrayals give us a narrow and repetitious view of prehistoric human life.

The challenge for illustrators and experts really is not to fashion politically correct portrayals of human ancestors—drawing a Guy-on-a-Hide or a Gal-With-a-Rock—nor to produce accurate but pedestrian ones—daily trips to the waterhole, perhaps.

Seeking Archaeology's Amazingly Invisible Woman

Conkey and Spector established the archaeology of gender as a focus of intense study. In several places throughout this text, we discuss how feminist archaeology is changing our perception of gender in the past. Here, we fo-

Diane Gifford-Gonzalez doing ethnoarchaeological research in Kenya. She is conducting a taphonomic study on a zebra that was killed hours earlier by lions.

As an archaeologist trained in an anthropological view of the past and a citizen of an ethnically and racially diverse nation, I believe we can serve the greater public by expanding the range of possible pasts represented in depictions of prehistoric people. I am not arguing for revising past worlds as they have conventionally been represented using a representational quota system, by which various ages, genders, and races get their fair share of prestige as defined in these works—where women hunt, men scrape hides, old folks run and dance—though all probably did a good deal of these activities. Rather, why not combine scientific rigor and creativity to offer viewers social arrangements different from any known today, or hominid species with truly different adaptations and behaviors? By picturing unexpected past worlds—inhabited not by mimics or parodies of ourselves but by those who may have been strong, successful, yet very unlike us—we might succeed in actually drawing more viewers into the real problems, possibilities, and pleasures of research on the past.

DIANE GIFFORD-GONZALEZ is professor of anthropology at the University of California, Santa Cruz.

cus on one immediate response to the Conkey-Spector critique—the attempt to develop methods and concepts to attribute gender to specific sets of material culture.

The processual agenda generally assumed the existence of "knowable" correlations between the world of material remains and particular activities, behaviors, and beliefs. It was just a matter of operationally defining the linkages between the archaeological record and the behavior that produced it. There seemed to be every reason to assume that gender is variously encoded in material remains and their spatial arrangements. Several attempts at doing this have already been discussed in this chapter.

Some archaeologists have specifically addressed the counterpoint to the Man-the-Hunter model—the apparent invisibility of women in the archaeological record. Glynn Isaac, for instance, noted that, "as long as we do not correct for the imbalance created by the durability of bone as compared with that of plant residues, studies of human evolution will always have a male bias." Embedded in Isaac's statement is, of course, the assumption that men always hunt and women always collect plant foods.

When I analyzed the artifacts from Gatecliff Shelter, I took up the same issue, speaking specifically of "The Amazingly Invisible Woman":

> There is also an important correlation between the sexual division of labor and the productive modes in hunter-gatherer society. Males tend to be highly visible in the archaeological record because many male fabrication activities involve subtractive technology [particularly stone tool manufacture]. Conversely, females make few artifacts subtractively, and their archaeological visibility suffers accordingly.
>
> Although both males and females employ additive technology, female fabrication is dominated by this self-corrective, centripetal mode of production, particularly basket making, fiber clothing manufacture, weaving, sewing, and, in some cases, pottery making. . . .
>
> Neither technology is sex specific, but there is an obvious association between the mode of technology and the sexual division of labor. Male tool kits are simply more archaeologically visible than female tool kits. This bias must be kept in mind when reconstructing the activity structure of the various Gatecliff occupational surfaces.

When this was written, Isaac and I both felt that the archaeological record of hunter-gatherers was intrinsically biased against recognizing female activities. But if we just tried hard enough, we thought, we could perhaps recover enough solid evidence to "find women in the past" after all.

Conkey and Spector addressed the same subject—the so-called invisibility of women in the archaeological record—but they attributed the problem to a pervasive androcentric bias and a host of unquestioned assumptions made by archaeologists such as myself. To them, the problem was "more the result of a false notion of objectivity and of the gender paradigms archaeologists employ than an inherent invisibility of such data. One can claim that female-related data in the archaeological record are invisible only if one makes some clearly questionable assumptions, such as the existence of an exclusive sexual division of labor."

This was an important point, which drew considerable attention as feminist archaeology matured. Writing nearly 15 years after her critique with Janet Spector, Margaret Conkey joined with Joan Gero to edit an important book entitled *Engendering Archaeology: Women and Prehistory,* published in 1991. We will recap some of the key points made in that influential volume.

The Difference Between Sex and Gender

It is critical here to clarify the difference between *sex* and *gender*. To some extent, this is merely a semantic distinction, but it also has some important attendant understandings.

The term **sex** refers strictly to the biological differences between males and females; these are the facts of biology. But **gender** is a culturally constructed concept, which may or may not emphasize biological differences. Some cultural traditions claim that male-female differences are almost completely biological, while others pay very little attention to biology.

Sex: The biological differences that distinguish males and females.

Gender: The culturally specific elaborations and meanings attached to sexual (biological) differences.

Bioarchaeology: The "Smoking Gun" of Gender Studies?

Some have suggested that attempts to engender the past should begin with the biological basics. Sex, after all, has a genetic basis. It has been argued, for instance, that the "smoking gun" of gender studies might be the actual human skeletal remains. The bones should establish, once and for all, the presence of human beings in the past, in indisputably sex-specific terms.

This is not so. It is important to note that the bones, by themselves, provide only information about sex, not gender: Gender involves the expected roles, norms, values, and relative statuses of biological males and females (at least as they were treated at the time of death). These culture-based practices can, perhaps, be understood by studying the materials accompanying human burials.

There have even been problems with deriving the biological, sex-specific information from human bones. In Chapter 12, for instance, we discussed how human remains are used to reconstruct ancient demography. We mentioned the particularly significant skeletal series recovered by Kidder at Pecos Pueblo. More than 2,000 human burials were excavated, dating from A.D. 1300 to the historic period. Surely a sex-based study of grave goods, disease, and nutrition would reveal a great deal about the respective roles of men and women at Pecos. After all, determining sex and age of human skeletons is a straightforward, "objective" technique of bioarchaeology, right?

Again, things are not so straightforward. When physical anthropologists "sexed" the skeletons from Pecos, they did so by observing certain universal characteristics of the bones, and then attributing biological femaleness and maleness. As we have seen, the operational definitions of biological "male" and "female" skeletons have not remained static through time: What to Hooton were "females" are today considered to be "males." This is because of the evolving nature of the middle-range biological research linking static skeletal remains of the past with their biological correlates.

Recently, the search for sex attribution has gone high-tech. It is now possible, at least on a limited basis, to ascribe sex on the basis of ancient DNA (using techniques discussed in Chapter 12). In one pilot study by Mark Sutton and his colleagues, human DNA was extracted from four human coprolites (desiccated feces) from archaeological sites in California and Nevada. Two of the samples are from women, one from a man (the fourth was indeterminate). When these results are expanded to much larger samples, it may eventually be possible to detect gender differences in cuisine, pharmacology, and access to certain foods in the past.

So it would seem that, despite early difficulties with linkages, bioarchaeologists will indeed provide some useful tools for projecting sex into the past. But what about the difficulties in reading the material culture record? After all, there are fundamental differences between biological and cultural correlates. When physical anthropologists "sex" skeletons, they are working from biology. In examining the material dimensions of gender, however, archaeologists are approaching culturally conditioned and culturally variable behavior. When archaeologists explore the relative locations of male and female remains in a burial mound, when they observe gender-specific "status" differences in grave goods, and when they infer male and female activity-areas in archaeological sites, they are looking at culturally and historically specific expressions of what it means to be "male" and "female" at a particular point in time and space. These are not biological givens to be assumed; they are cultural variables to be explored.

Gero on "Genderlithics": Man-the-Toolmaker?

Tools have played a decisive part in the evolution of civilization. Man's unique ability to make and use tools distinguishes him from all other creatures on earth and—half a million years ago—permitted his escape from the dark unknown of the early Pleistocene era and his survival through the glacial ages that followed.

KENNETH OAKLEY (1918–1970), ARCHAEOLOGIST

Beyond mere biology, Conkey and Gero are doubtless correct in assigning a key role to commonly unidentified assumptions regarding gender roles, gender relations, and gender ideology. Too often, researchers have depended on long-standing assumptions and stereotypes regarding women's roles: Women did most of the cooking, gardening, collecting of shellfish, and pottery manufacturing, to name but a few.

Feminist researchers challenge such assumptions. The issue of male bias is not just about ignoring and devaluing women (as when culturally specific gender stereotypes are perpetuated). Gender bias also conditions our overall views of the past. Androcentric interpretations are flawed, pure and simple. They misrepresent prehistoric cultural dynamics and obscure our understanding of past human life—of both men and women.

Nowhere in archaeology are such assumptions more deeply ingrained than in studies of stone tools. British archaeologist Kenneth Oakley once wrote a wildly successful book called *Man the Tool-maker,* first published in 1950 and reissued internationally through multiple editions. Oakley's thesis was simple: "If man is defined as the tool-making animal . . . [then] systematic making of tools implies a marked capacity for conceptual thought." That is, by looking at the axeheads, spearpoints, and the rest of the stone tool assemblage, you can monitor the "progress" of humanity.

The feminist critique suggests otherwise. Archaeologist Joan Gero recently has reconsidered the role of women in stone tool use, "deconstructing" a number of conventional archaeological interpretations—including my own (cited earlier). In her study of "genderlithics" (her term) she turned up, not surprisingly, a number of androcentric assumptions about stone tool production and use.

Tools provide a thermometer for measuring intellectual heat.

WILLIAM LAUGHLIN, ARCHAEOLOGIST (UNIVERSITY OF CONNECTICUT)

Gero challenges the Man-the-Toolmaker premise on a number of levels. For one thing, she disapproves of the use of "man" by Oakley (and many others): "'Man' is not a semantic generalization—such tools were seen, without doubt, as the products of male labor."

Gero also closely considers the meaning of the term "tool." Remember from our discussion of flintknapping (Chapter 10) some of the basic distinctions made in stone tool technology. *Tools* are the desired end products of stone tool manufacture; the Folsom and Clovis points we considered earlier are definitely "tools." Very often, flintknappers begin the process with a *core,* a piece of stone that is worked ("knapped") into tools. Finally, there is *flake,* a thin, sharp sliver of stone removed from a core during the knapping process. Flakes are usually considered to be the byproduct of stone tool manufacture, but sometime these "byproducts" themselves are utilized—the sharp flakes as cutting implements and the "cores" as instruments for bashing or battering. But use of byproducts is difficult to determine, usually requiring the microscopic techniques discussed in Chapter 10.

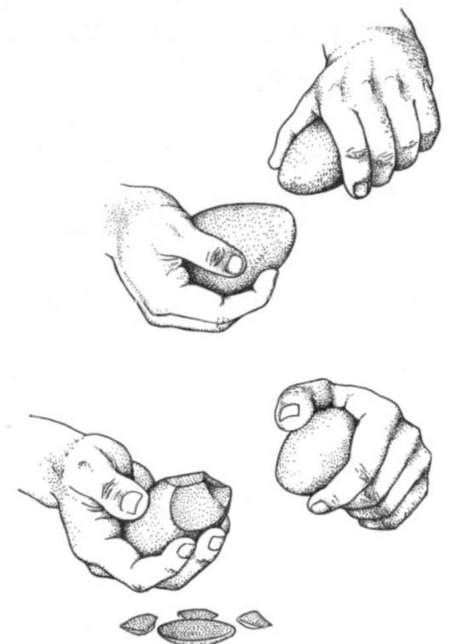

Deliberate rock-on-rock percussion produces both cores and flakes. Each can be used as-is or further knapped into more specialized kinds of implements.

In the simplest case, the toolmaker begins with some raw material (a core), removes the excess (some flakes), and ends up with a "tool." (Hint: If these terms are confusing, I suggest that you look closely at the accompanying illustrations, where each one is clearly shown.)

Conventional archaeological analysis has stressed the study of formal tools (the intentional end product of flintknapping). For years, archaeologists have simply assumed that specific tools must have specific functions: For decades, everybody "knew" that arrowheads were used for hunting and warfare, that axeheads were used for chopping wood, and that flaked stone knives were used for cutting up meat.

One unintended consequence of this traditional approach is that virtually all the "tools" ended up in male hands. Men were the hunters, the warriors, the providers, the craftsmen; men made and used most of the formal "tools." By this way of thinking, then, the study of men and their tools would lead to an understanding of humanity's "marked capacity for conceptual thought" (in Oakley's terms).

Gero disagrees. She argues that most of the implements used in the past were actually flakes (not formal tools); that is, the flakes were *end products* rather than just "byproducts" of stone tool–using economies. Gero believes that the very process of lithic analysis—of dividing stone implements into conventional "flake" and "tool" categories—has inevitably drawn the archaeologist's attention toward the completed, more sophisticated items (the "tools"). The simpler implements (the "flakes") are seen as second-rate sources of information about the past.

It is through such procedural assumptions, Gero suggests, that archaeologists introduce a lot of ill-founded, self-referential stereotypes into our understanding of the past. Her study of stone tool manufacture and use suggests that if archaeologists would concentrate on flake tools, they would discover the economic contributions of a broader, more diverse group of individuals in the past.

Joan Gero (center) in the Province of Catamarca in northwest Argentina where she is excavating an early formative archaeological site. Gero is shown with Señora Celia Chayle de Araoz (left) and her daughter, Gabriela, friends from the nearby village of Yutopian.

Where do these assumptions come from?

Gero sees an implicit, assumed androcentrism at work here. After all, she argues, virtually all modern flintknappers are male, most replicative studies are conducted by males, and ethnoarchaeological study of stone tool production is almost exclusively male. She's right: Every single flintknapper, experimenter, and ethnoarchaeologist discussed in Chapter 10—except for Ruth Tringham—is

There is no compelling biological, historical, sociological, ethnographic, ethnohistorical, or experimental reason why women could not have made—and good reason to think they probably did *make—all kinds of stone tools, in all kinds of lithic materials, for a variety of uses and contexts.*

JOAN GERO, ARCHAEOLOGIST (UNIVERSITY OF SOUTH CAROLINA)

indeed male. Gero concludes that the evidence from replicative studies in archaeology is this: "Western males generally make stone tools and women don't. . . . Modern gender ideology is underwritten by male archaeologists undertaking lithic studies that illustrate males making and using stone tools, appropriating this productive arena as male for as far back as humanity can be extended."

Gero does not mean, of course, that female archaeologists do not study stone tools—they do. Also in Chapter 10, we prominently featured Ruth Tringham's pioneering study of microwear analysis on archaeological artifacts. But, Gero notes, microwear research such as this is not considered as studying stone "tools"; Tringham analyzed a variety of flaked stone materials—mostly unmodified flakes—plus a variety of materials, such as antler, bone, wood, skin, flesh, and plant fiber.

Gero points out that today's female archaeologists—who are overrepresented in the field of microwear research—spend most of their time studying "the flake tools, the 'nonstandardized,' 'non-curated,' 'expedient' tools that are in almost all regards held to be inferior, based on contemporary values attached to time and form and ranking, and on the male-biased standards for tools that pervade lithic studies."

Gero argues, contrary to the predominant focus of males on male-defined tools, it is the stone-making and stone-using activities that are most commonly recovered in the excavation of household and village contexts. Gero points out that modern women (herself included) are often capable flintknappers. Isn't it reasonable to conclude that women of the past could also make and use stone tools?

Gero adds, significantly, "On the other hand, direct gender attribution of individual tools remains problematic; women, like men, can't easily be sought at the level of individual tool producers."

The point is this: unless one is willing to make the unyielding assumption that the sexual division of labor has remained inviolable throughout the human past, then archaeologists assuming a one-to-one correlation between artifact type and gender do so at their own risk.

Gender Attribution: Do We Really Need It?

We do not see a feminist approach to archaeology as dependent on some sort of methodological breakthrough that will suddenly render women (or even men) "archaeologically visible." Being able to "assign" certain activities or material culture to males and/or females is not the *goal; it is not an end nor is it* the *means.*

MARGARET CONKEY AND JOAN GERO

Such are the difficulties that attend attempts to link specific aspects of the archaeological record with male and/or female behaviors. But Conkey and Gero caution that such gender-attribution studies are really questions of *method* and may not be central to the thrust of feminist archaeology. Terming such methodological breakthroughs as mere "band-aids" masking a large problem, Conkey and Gero argue for a much broader research program.

As we noted in Chapter 3, many of those engaged in feminist archaeology—including Conkey and Gero—heartily endorse the major propositions of the postprocessual critique. By adopting gender as an analytical concept, they argue for a radically redefined view of prehistory and archaeological reasoning. Many of the postmodern principles we have already considered have today been incorporated as mainstays in a feminist approach to archaeology.

Viewed this way, the process of gender attribution—the linking of material culture with males and/or females—becomes another form of middle-range theory building. The postprocessual critique, which is highly critical of theory at the middle range, argues that human behavior observed in the present cannot readily be transferred into the past by reference to any single system of laws. The relevance of one observation to another must be established by a network of local understandings.

In short, many of the emerging approaches aimed at engendering the human past fit quite comfortably within the overall thrust of postmodernism in Americanist archaeology. Conkey and Gero, for instance, insist that an archaeology employing gender as a central concept must emphasize the individual as an active social agent; this important point, central to the postprocessual critique, is explored in a feminist context in Chapter 17. Like other participants in the postprocessual critique, many pursuing gender-based research reject the systematic, clinical, single-minded approaches of the past. Many also reject the etic, evolutionary, antihistorical, objective, rigidly science-based, and ethically neutral approach of the processual agenda.

The primary topics of the postprocessual critique—gender, power, ideology, text, discourse, rhetoric, writing, structure, history, and the role of the individual—are likewise central to many aspects of feminist approaches to the past.

It is important to note that gender-related studies can take on many different forms and follow several different theoretical frameworks. Although some gender studies fit quite comfortably within the postprocessual critique, that relationship is neither exclusive nor required.

SUMMARY This chapter has explored in detail the archaeology of our forager ancestry. We have seen how archaeologists figure out the seasonal movements of nonagricultural people. We have seen how tool kits, activity-areas, and drop zone/toss zone patterning have been used to understand how foragers have partitioned their life space over the millennia.

Over the past couple of decades, archaeologists have looked more closely at the tacit assumptions that underpin unconstrained seasonal, activity-area, and tool-kit reconstructions. Today, archaeologists are working more cautiously in such reconstructions, attempting to take into account the various depositional and postdepositional processes involved in creating the archaeological record.

Several archaeologists argue that a better processual understanding of hunter-gatherers can be obtained from the larger body of developing theory in evolutionary biology. One increasingly popular method of inquiry employs *optimal foraging theory,* a broad-based theoretical perspective that attempts to develop a set of models general enough to apply to a wide range of animal species, yet rigorous and precise enough to explain the details of behavior exhibited by a particular forager.

This chapter also considers the role of sex and gender in studying our foraging past. For years, archaeologists employed a "*Man-the-Hunter*" approach, assuming long-term continuity in gender arrangements and ideology, extending from the present back to the earliest humans. This model implied a relatively rigid division of labor and a sort of inevitability about gender roles: Hunting was always male, plant collecting was always female, and so forth. This model overemphasizes the importance of male activities and results in "gender-exclusive" reconstructions of past human behavior.

Many of those engaged in "engendering" the foraging past heartily endorse the major propositions of the postprocessual critique. By adopting gender as an analytical concept, they argue for a radically redefined view of prehistory and archaeological reasoning. Many of the postmodern principles we have already considered have today been incorporated as mainstays in a feminist approach to archaeology.

Chapter 15

Some Neo-Evolutionary Approaches

PREVIEW This chapter sketches some of the milestones in the long-term evolution of culture. For more than a million years, our ancestors pursued a hunting, gathering, and scavenging existence. Then, within the last 10,000 years, people began domesticating plants and animals. The farming lifeway had profound implications for human beliefs and social practices. Without an agricultural baseline, the development of large communities, urban centers, and state-level organization would never have taken place.

Here, we examine the various conceptual tools used by archaeologists to understand the evolution of human social organization. As you might anticipate, considerable diversity of opinion surrounds such large-scale questions. We will explore how these various evolutionary and neo-evolutionary perspectives came to be and how they are being modified in light of archaeology's current emphasis on understanding the role of the individual in cultural evolution.

[Evolution is] a change from an indefinite, incoherent homogeneity to a definite, coherent heterogeneity, through continuous differentiations and integrations.

Herbert Spencer (1820–1903), social philosopher

Evolution is a change from a no-howish, untalkaboutable all-alikeness to a somehowish and in-general-talkaboutable not-all-alikeness, by continuous somethingelseifications and sticktogetherations.

Thomas Penyngton Kirkman (1806–1895), mathematician (and Spencer critic)

The reasonable man adapts himself to the world; the unreasonable one persists in trying to adapt the world to himself. Therefore, all progress depends upon the unreasonable man.

George Bernard Shaw (1865–1950), playwright

With the publication of *On the Origin of Species* in 1859, Charles Darwin provided Euroamericans with new ways to view their world. Sometimes called "the book that shook the world," *On the Origin of Species* sold out on its first day of publication (and it is still in print and even available on the Internet).

As he explained in that revolutionary volume, Darwin believed that because the world's food supply is inherently inadequate, the young of any species must struggle to survive (and most of them don't). The survivors who live to foster the next generation do so because of certain naturally favored characteristics; this is the process of **natural selection.** These physical variations will be passed along to the next generation. The evolutionary process, being gradual and continuous, eventually gives rise to new species. Darwin not only introduced the notion that all organisms are descended from a common ancestor but also provided evidence that the earth with its various lifeforms is dynamic and ever changing.

Natural selection: A natural process resulting in the survival and reproductive success of individuals or groups best adjusted to their environment, leading to a perpetuation of genetic qualities best suited for a particular environment.

Although Darwin did not actually use the term *evolution,* the very last word in the first edition of *The Origin* is "evolved," and the term *evolutionary theory* will forever be associated with his name. Darwin supplied the world of science with a coherent rationale for the rich diversity of life. Although many religions of the world came to accept Darwin's view, others loathed the concept of descent with modification.

Charles Darwin.

Social Darwinism: The extension of the principles of Darwinian evolution to social phenomena. The implication is that conflict and competition between societies (and between classes of the same society) has a beneficial effect in long-term human evolution. Social Darwinism has three different premises:

Rapid elimination of "unfit" individuals benefits society.

Laissez-faire economics: A society's economic system functions best when the state keeps "hands off," allowing the fittest business enterprises to survive and the unfit to go under.

Warfare is the chief way in which natural selection operates on societies; thus warfare has had an enormous role in the rise of the state (and various other social, political, economic, and religious organizations).

[Lubbock's Pre-historic Times*] was almost certainly the most influential work dealing with archaeology published during the nineteenth century.*

BRUCE TRIGGER, ARCHAEOLOGIST (MCGILL UNIVERSITY)

The Rise and Fall of Unilinear Evolution

Darwin did more than just theorize about the diversity of life on the planet. He also provided his Euroamerican audience–unintentionally–with a scientific rationale for the then-prevalent belief in racial inequality. The so-called *social Darwinists* believed that people, like all other organisms, compete for survival and hence success in life. Those becoming rich and powerful, in this view, are the "fittest." Lower socioeconomic classes are thus "the least fit," as are the "primitive" people of the world. **Social Darwinism** suggested that human progress depends on competition, and in the nineteenth century, this theory was used to justify global imperialism, racism, and the excesses of capitalism.

Social Darwinists argued that human societies varied in their "evolutionary" status from highly evolved groups (such as Europeans) to those who differed only slightly from the advanced apes. In this view, less civilized people were also less capable intellectually and emotionally.

Early anthropology grew up in this intellectual climate. Anatomical parallels were drawn between Neanderthal crania and contemporary Australian aborigines, and some suggested cultural parallels as well. In the nineteenth-century perspective of social Darwinism, cultural evolution became a logical extension of biological evolution.

Lubbock's *Pre-historic Times*

Evolution was soon tied directly to the archaeological record. In 1865, John Lubbock–Darwin's next-door neighbor in Kent, England–published his influential *Pre-historic Times, as Illustrated by Ancient Remains, and the Manners and Customs of Modern Savages.* Widely read on both sides of the Atlantic, Lubbock's synthesis became archaeology's primary textbook.

Lubbock advocated a cross-cultural, comparative method to illustrate the life of the "paleolithic" (Old Stone Age) and "neolithic" (New Stone Age) people by reference to contemporary "primitives." Specifically, he argued that Darwinian-style natural selection had operated on ancient human societies to produce natural and cultural differences, which were closely interlinked. Cultures fell into a neat, linear continuum with Anglo-Euroamerican capitalist society being the most advanced.

Societies lacking advanced technology, Lubbock argued, were handicapped by inferior intelligence and base emotions. The message was simple: Through the process of natural selection, humanity was improving–biologically, culturally, emotionally, and intellectually. Left to their own devices, capitalist societies would prosper and improve.

The downside, of course, is that the world's primitives were doomed. In Lubbock's view, these primitives had not evolved sufficiently and no degree of remedial education could repair the damage done by millennia of natural selection. Although neither Darwin nor Lubbock advocated exploitation of non-Western people, both believed that the modern world was better off without them.

Lubbock's books passed through multiple editions. Here was scientific justification for the British colonization of the world; there was no need to worry about the rapidly declining native populations of North America, Australia, and the Pacific—it was their biological destiny. Pity that natural selection so poorly equipped them to hold off the spread of civilization, but there you are.

> **Evolution on the Internet:**
>
> ***Origin of Species*** (complete hypertext version):
> http://www.emergentmedia.com/~madsen/origin/intro.html
>
> **Biography of Charles Darwin:**
> http://oz.plymouth.edu/~biology/history/darwin.html
>
> **Down House Home Page:** Darwin's home is now a natural history museum:
> http://weber.u.washington.edu/~wcalvin/down_hse.html
>
> **Discussions of Natural Selection and Evolution:**
> http://mac246.ed.uinc.edu/edpsy-387/Bonnie-Sklar/evolution.html
> http://www.biohaven.com/biology/evol.htm
>
> **Discussions of Social Darwinism:**
> http://www.liberty.com/home/kholder/forge.html
> http://www.stile.lut.ac.uk/ngycnr/STILE/t0000015.html

Morgan's Unilinear Evolution

Lubbock's thesis sold books in America. To many, the United States was all about progress and natural destiny. Nineteenth-century Euroamerican society was held to be the culmination of human achievement. The move westward toward the Pacific was both inevitable and laudable. In Lubbock's view, Native Americans were culturally and biologically ill-equipped to resist; long-term selective pressure had doomed the Indians to extinction.

One of the most influential nineteenth-century anthropologists was Lewis Henry Morgan, a Rochester lawyer-turned-ethnologist. Echoing Lubbock's evolutionary philosophy, Morgan argued that today's institutions can be understood only by reference to how they had evolved; the present could not be understood wholly in terms of the present.

Morgan's *Ancient Society* (1877) divided the progress of human achievement into three major "ethnical periods"—savagery, barbarism, and civilization—which were subscaled into seven major categories:

1. *Lower status of savagery:* Commenced with the infancy of the human race in restricted habitats, subsisting on fruits and nuts. No such tribes survived into the historical period.
2. *Middle status of savagery:* Commenced with catching of fish and the use of fire. Humanity spread over a greater portion of the earth's surface. Exemplified by Australian aborigines and Polynesians.
3. *Upper status of savagery:* Commenced with the invention of the bow and arrow. Exemplified by the Athapascan tribes of Hudson's Bay Territory.
4. *Lower status of barbarism:* Commenced with the invention and manufacture of pottery. Exemplified by the Native American tribes of the United States east of the Missouri River.
5. *Middle status of barbarism:* Commenced with the domestication of animals in the Eastern Hemisphere, and in the Western with cultivation by irrigation and the use of adobe brick and stone in architecture. Exemplified by villages in New Mexico and Mexico.
6. *Upper status of barbarism:* Commenced with the manufacture of iron. Exemplified by Grecian tribes of the Homeric Age and Germanic tribes of the time of Caesar.

> *The institutions of man are as distinctly stratified as the earth on which he lives. They succeed each other in series substantially uniform over the globe, independent of what seem the comparatively superficial differences of race and language, but shaped by similar human nature acting through successively changed conditions in savage, barbaric, and civilized life.*
>
> LEWIS HENRY MORGAN (1818–1881), ETHNOLOGIST

> *The experience of mankind has run in nearly uniform channels; the human necessities in similar conditions have been substantially the same.*
>
> LEWIS HENRY MORGAN

7. *Status of civilization:* Commenced with the use of a phonetic alphabet and the production of literary records; divided into ancient and modern.

Unilinear cultural evolution: The belief that human societies have evolved culturally along a single developmental trajectory. Typically, such schemes depict Western civilization as the most advanced evolutionary stage.

Morgan's was only one of several schemes of **unilinear cultural evolution** to be devised during the late nineteenth century. All such schemes defined a sort of "evolutionary ladder," with both contemporary and ancient societies arrayed along it vertically. Although differing in detail, the bottom rung exemplified "savagery"—the primeval, rudimentary, and primitive. The top of evolution's ladder was reserved for various "advanced" societies, with the uppermost rung occupied by modern Western civilization, particularly that of western Europe.

"The unfit die—the fit both live and thrive."
Alas, who says so? Those who do survive.

SARAH NORCLIFFE CLEGHORN (1876–1959), AUTHOR AND POET

How "Evolution" Became a Dirty Word

In the early twentieth century, the anthropological world turned against this *ethnocentric* notion of progress (and its distinct racial overtones). Franz Boas—often called the "father of American anthropology"—and several of his students emphatically rejected cultural evolution as a worthwhile way to study the human condition. The Boasian program called for anthropologists to study a culture in all its aspects; each culture is unique, Boas argued, and should be valued as such. Cultures change in ways unique to themselves and no generalizations are possible from culture to culture. This doctrine, known as **cultural relativism**, questions the existence of any universal standard by which to judge either the degree of development or intrinsic worth of different cultures.

Cultural relativism: The view that cultures are different, with no culture better or worse than another.

Historical particularism: The view that each culture is the product of a unique sequence of developments in which chance plays a major role in bringing about change.

For Boas and others arguing for **historical particularism**, use of the comparative method was the cardinal error of the evolutionist school. Boas argued that sociocultural evolution was so complex and had taken so many diverse paths that there could have been no progressive evolution in the human past. The simplest kinds of technology (as among Australian aborigines) are today accompanied by the world's most complex forms of social organization. Boas also argued that human institutions such as slavery, private property, and the state level of government are today associated with an amazing array of concomitant sociocultural features.

Boas took a stand against evolutionary schemes that grouped all humankind into a single developmental formula. Although he did admit to some degree of regularity in history, Boas believed that the amount of regularity had been grossly exaggerated, at the expense of culturally specific, ethnographic detail. Boas believed that the patient accumulation of historical data would eventually lead to improvement of anthropological theory.

Neo-Evolutionism: What Is It?

So it was that unilinear cultural evolution fell into disfavor under the withering assault from Boas and his students. But the cultural particularism that characterized the first half of the twentieth century was in turn discredited by the mounting evidence from archaeology and ethnography showing that cultural evolution had indeed occurred.

Within a decade after Boas's death—he died while presenting an anti-racist lecture in the Men's Faculty Club at Columbia University—cultural evolution paid another visit to the halls of anthropology. Although hardly dominating anthropological explanation, so-called *neo-evolutionary* thought began in the 1950s and 1960s and continues to exert a significant influence in Americanist archaeology.

Franz Boas.

A note on terminology: Here, we use the term *neo-evolutionism* to distinguish this mid-twentieth-century movement from the earlier, nineteenth-century perspective, which is designated *unilinear evolution.* In so doing, we must note in fairness, we are ignoring Leslie White's admonition that there was no such thing as "neo-evolution"; White claimed that his own evolutionism "differed not one whit" from the earlier version. Still, for our purposes, we find it useful to retain the term *neo-evolution* to keep the nineteenth- and twentieth-century versions of evolution distinct.

Neo-evolutionism differs in some important ways from the earlier unilinear evolutionism. Earlier nineteenth-century evolutionary models emphasized the role of the individual in culture change, with gifted individuals often thought to be responsible for bettering the quality of human life (by inventing, for instance, plant and animal domestication, ceramics, metallurgy, writing, and calendrics). By contrast, neo-evolutionism accentuates the role of ecological, demographic, and/or technological determinism by stressing dynamic relationships between human cultures and the rest of the ecosystem.

Marshall Sahlins and Elman Service have clarified this semantic issue. They believe that cultural evolution is most profitably viewed at two levels. According to Sahlins and Service, "Any given system—a species, a culture or an individual—improves its chances for survival, progresses in the efficiency of energy capture, by increasing its adaptive specialization. This is **specific evolution.** The obverse is directional advance or progress stage by stage, measured in absolute terms rather than by criteria relative to the degree of adaptation to particular environments. . . . A man is higher than an armadillo. . . . This is **general evolution.**"

Specific evolution: Local history of a specific society.

General evolution: Major cultural changes that have taken place in essentially parallel ways on a global scale; many believe that this change is due largely to technological advancements.

The Law of Evolutionary Potential

Sahlins and Service also emphasize the important distinction between *cultures* and *Culture.* Specific *cultures* adapt to a unique human and natural backdrop, sometimes evolving toward increasing specialization and at other times remaining relatively unvarying for thousands of years. But *Culture*—the cumulative, worldwide, nonbiological body of wisdom—is viewed by many archaeologists as evolving from homogeneity toward heterogeneity, particularly as more technologically advanced groups expand globally at the expense of less successful cultures. Others prefer to scale *Culture* in terms of absolute magnitude and internal complexity.

With these two types of evolution in mind (global Culture and specific cultures), let us scan a particular anthropological theory that Sahlins and Service termed the *law of evolutionary potential:*

> The more specialized and adapted a form in a given evolutionary stage, the smaller its potential for passing to the next stage. . . . Specific evolutionary progress is inversely related to general evolutionary potential.

I think it would be a good idea.

MOHANDAS GANDHI (1869–1948)
[WHEN ASKED WHAT HE THOUGHT OF WESTERN CIVILIZATION]

Sahlins and Service proposed that groups with more generalized adaptations have a greater evolutionary potential (more options for change) than do groups with a highly specific adaptation. The archaeological record abounds in examples of this principle, often manifested as the ubiquitous so-called northern barbarian invasion. For example, Mexican prehistory is repeatedly punctuated by raiders from the north, who time after time overwhelmed the established state. Moving from their homeland on the frontiers of northern Mexico, the Toltecs moved south to found Tula, the city-state that ruled after the fall of classic Teotihuacán. Tula later suffered the same fate as Teotihuacán, namely, destruction at the hands of another tribal group. Not long thereafter, the Aztecs came along—also from the north (or at least so their origin story says).

Similar conquests characterize much of human history, such as the relationship of ancient Rome to Greece and the rise of modern China. These case histories have a common denominator in that, all else being equal, the most rapid evolutionary acceleration occurred among the have-nots, not within the establishment. As we will see later in this chapter, agriculture may not have arisen among the hunter-gatherer groups in ecologically favored areas but, rather, in areas of stress and competition. Plant domestication appeared initially among those in need, not among people deeply immersed in some stable, yet conservative, productive network.

The law of evolutionary potential is neither purely ethnological nor purely archaeological; it is both. As archaeological data are progressively incorporated into general anthropological theory, rigid lines continue to blur, and such generalizations become amalgamated with the "laws" governing culture.

The theory of cultural evolution, to my mind the most inane, sterile, and pernicious theory ever conceived in the history of science (a cheap toy for the amusement of big children).

BERTHOLD LAUFER (1874–1934), ARCHAEOLOGIST

Generalizations such as this are usually statistical in nature. The Sahlins-Service "law" is one of potential, not strict determinism. Nobody expects archaeological "laws" to be exact, for such statements project incompletely understood phenomena. At best, these are successive approximations to the laws of nature; one can only hope that such predictions will be correct most of the time, at least until the conditions under which the phenomena will always occur can be specified more clearly.

Neo-Evolution and the Processual Agenda

Bruce Trigger has written of a "present-mindedness" in American culture that grows out of the mistaken impression that America has somehow freed itself from the legacy of a European past. As a result, history—both as an academic discipline and as a way of knowing the past—has long been viewed with a sense of distrust in America. Henry Ford seems to have reflected a national contempt when he said simply, "History is bunk."

When we have cleared up the history of a single culture and understand the effects of environment and the psychological conditions that are reflected in it we have made a step forward, as we can then investigate how far the same causes or other causes were at work in the development of other cultures.

FRANZ BOAS (1858–1942), FATHER OF AMERICAN ANTHROPOLOGY

Archaeology's processual agenda equated history with chronology, description, and a preoccupation with irrelevant occurrences. According to the processual view, explaining solitary events would doom archaeology to remain a particularistic, nongeneralizing field. Cultural-historical objectives were considered inferior to formulating general rules of cultural behavior.

As discussed previously, processual archaeology embraced instead both cultural ecology and Leslie White's concept of culture as extrasomatic adaptation, downgrading history to a merely descriptive rather than explanatory role. Further, the neo-evolutionary perspective plays down the importance of individual human decisions in cultural change (viewing the human capacity to reason and plan as being powerfully directed by cultural focuses). Specific human decisions and specific historical sequences were not of particular interest or significance in their own right, according to neo-evolutionists.

The processual agenda, with its emphasis on adaptive processes, saw the human being as the *locus of interaction* for a variety of cultural elements. Although an individual might effect a new synthesis of these forces, human inventiveness and innovation were not seen as independent forces capable of bringing about major changes. As a neo-evolutionist, Lewis Binford believed that there was a high degree of regularity in human behavior and that ethnographic study would reveal much about aspects of past cultures not directly observable from the archaeological record.

Processual archaeology attempted to employ scientific methods for testing generalizations about human behavior across long spans of time. As Bruce Trigger has pointed out, these evolutionary leanings "encouraged a major devaluation of an already weak historical perspective in favor of an evolutionary one." Neo-evolutionists, of course, would argue that they had already taken history into account in the distinction between specific and general evolution (introduced earlier).

If History is bunk, then Archaeology is junk.

PAUL BAHN, ARCHAEOLOGIST

History as the model for archaeological investigations is . . . totally inappropriate.

LEWIS R. BINFORD, ARCHAEOLOGIST (SOUTHERN METHODIST UNIVERSITY)

I tell you the past is a bucket of ashes.

CARL SANDBURG (1878–1967), POET

A Sample Evolutionary Sequence

In order to explore how this neo-evolutionary perspective operates in modern Americanist archaeology, it will be necessary first to introduce some key terms and concepts commonly used in the discussion of social and political evolution.

Hunting and gathering bands are the least complex of human societies. Fifteen thousand years ago, virtually all our ancestors lived this way. Although few true hunter-gatherer bands survive today, they were common in many parts of the world during the nineteenth century. Hunter-gatherers survive on wild plants and animals, and often change location several times throughout the year. Most settlements number less than three dozen people, although larger aggregations occur when resources are particularly abundant.

Hunting and gathering bands are *egalitarian,* meaning they lack hereditary differences in social rank or authority. Such societies are integrated on the basis of age and gender. Leadership is informal and temporary, based mostly on age, competence, and personal magnetism. The Great Basin Shoshone are frequently cited as an example of band structure, as are the Inuit (Eskimo), South African Bushmen, and Australian Aborigines.

Were it not for the domestication of plants and animals, the entire world would still be living a hunting and gathering lifestyle. But agriculture seems to have come into being in the Near East by about 7000 B.C. New World agriculture began between 5000 B.C. and 3000 B.C. in both Mexico and Peru.

With the advent of agriculture came *autonomous village societies,* characterized by larger and more sedentary settlements. Such communities occur throughout the world and vary considerably in appearance. Although community size is generally larger than that of hunters and gatherers, autonomous village societies still lack hereditary differences in rank, and larger villages maintain no authority over smaller neighboring communities. Although everyone in such societies is equal at birth, considerable disparities in prestige can accrue during one's lifetime, and ritual privileges are often differentially distributed along gender lines. Several early-twentieth-century autonomous village societies have been well studied by ethnographers, including Pueblo Indian groups of the American Southwest, communities in highland New Guinea, and many villages in the Amazon Basin.

A third social form, *rank society,* at times evolves from autonomous villages. Here, the egalitarian ethic (downplaying success and prestige) gives way to the belief that individuals are inherently unequal at birth. Commonly, certain family groups are considered to have descended from esteemed ancestors. The closer this relationship, the greater one's hereditary rank and power. Marrying wisely becomes a way to enhance the rank of your children.

Ethnologist Robert Carneiro has pointed out that two kinds of rank societies populated the nineteenth-century world. Some, like the Kwakwaka'wakh (Kwakiutl) of the American Northwest Coast, had hereditary ranked differences, but each community was autonomous from the others.

In some societies, however, such as the Natchez (who lived along the lower Mississippi River), the smaller villages were subject to the powerful, hereditary leadership of the larger, stronger communities. These societies—large-scale ranked societies with loss of village autonomy—are called *chiefdoms.*

Powerful chiefs could bring thousands of people under their control. Such leaders and their kin differentiated themselves with a variety of symbols, including precious trade items, lavish dwellings, and prominent temples for worship by the elite. Smaller villages were vulnerable to raiding, and the vanquished were frequently converted to slaves. Warfare between rival chiefdoms was distinctly unpleasant, typically involving torture, mutilation, human sacrifice, and the taking of human trophy skulls.

Archaic state: A centralized political system found in complex societies, characterized by having a virtual monopoly on the power to coerce.

Under certain conditions, **archaic states** evolved from competing chiefdoms. The term *archaic* is used here to distinguish this ancient social form from modern industrial states, which are commonly governed by elected presidents or prime ministers.

Most archaic states operated as kingdoms, characterized by a strong and centralized government with a professional bureaucratic ruling class. These societies devalued the kinship bonds evident in less complex political forms, and the social structure was highly stratified by social class. States maintained their authority through an established legal system and the power to wage war, levy taxes, and draft soldiers. States generally had populations numbering (at least) in the hundreds of thousands, and urban centers generally exhibited a high level of artistic and architectural achievement. A state religion was generally practiced, even in areas of linguistic and ethnic diversity. The Classic Maya and the Aztecs are examples of archaic state-level organization.

Civilization: A complex urban society, with a high level of cultural achievement in the arts and sciences, craft specialization, a surplus of food and/or labor, and a hierarchically stratified social organization.

One final term needs some attention: **civilization.** In neo-evolutionism, the notion of "civilization" is closely associated with the development of the archaic state. The development of writing and keeping of bureaucratic records is commonly considered to be a characteristic of "civilized" society (but because the Inka did not have writing, this criterion is hardly ironclad). Be sure to note that when anthropologists use the term "civilization," *no value judgment is implied (in the sense of refinement or good manners).*

Later in this chapter, we will be discussing various theories that have been advanced to explain the evolution of these different social forms. Before that, however, we must examine the issue of plant and animal domestication. After all, without agriculture, there would have been no development of some of the complex social forms detailed earlier.

You can't say that civilization doesn't advance, for in every war they kill you in a new way.

WILL ROGERS (1875–1935), COWBOY PHILOSOPHER

Why Were Plants and Animals Domesticated?

Countless theories have been constructed to account for the initial efforts at domesticating plants and animals. Anthropologists of the eighteenth and nineteenth centuries were concerned largely with devising worldwide evolutionary schemes, yet they lacked the relevant archaeological data. Cultural evolutionists relied instead on analogies with contemporary "primitive societies" and linguistic evidence. As we saw, Lewis Henry Morgan in *Ancient Society* (1877) suggested that animal domestication (pastoralism) must have preceded agricultural villages throughout the Eastern Hemisphere.

When tillage begins, other arts follow. The farmers, therefore, are the founders of human civilization.

DANIEL WEBSTER (1782–1852), STATESMAN AND WORDSMITH

According to Morgan's study of "Aryan" (Indo-European) languages, plant domestication provided the most expedient way to feed the already domesticated herds: "[That] the discovery and cultivation of cereals by the Aryan family was subsequent to the domestication of animals is shown by the fact that there are common terms for these animals in the several dialects of the Aryan language, and no common terms for the cereals or cultivated plants."

Childe's Oasis Theory: Symbiosis

Through the years, a number of other theories appeared, and their evolution is instructive, indicating major avenues of thought. One of the most compelling explanations—the *oasis theory*—was devised in the 1940s by Australian-British archaeologist V. Gordon Childe. Briefly, Childe's theory held that as the Pleistocene glaciers melted (at the end of the Ice Age), the world's climate became warmer and drier. In desert areas, especially those of the Near East, finding water became the single major problem for survival. Both people and animals flocked to oases and rare desert streams in search of water, and this forced association eventually produced a *symbiotic relationship* (**symbiosis**), through time developing from mutual benefit to mutual dependence.

Symbiosis: Two dissimilar organisms living in intimate association in a mutually beneficial relationship.

Childe explained the mechanisms (processes) for the beginnings of animal domestication in fairly simple terms:

> The huntsman and his prey thus find themselves united in an effort to circumvent the dreadful power of drought. But if the hunter is also a cultivator, he will have something to offer the famished beasts: the stubble of his freshly reaped fields will afford the best grazing in the oasis. Once the grains are garnered, the cultivator can tolerate half-starved mouflons or wild oxen trespassing upon his

> garden plots. Such will be too weak to run away, too thin to be worth killing for food. Instead, man can study their habits, drive off the lions and wolves that would prey upon them, and perhaps offer them some surplus grains from his stores. The beasts, for their part, will grow tame and accustomed to man's proximity.

Clearly, in Childe's scheme, the domestication of animals was possible only after people had become successful cultivators of plants.

> *History records the names of royal bastards, but it cannot tell us the origin of wheat.*
>
> JEAN HENRI FABRE

Childe was less clear about how and where plants were initially domesticated. Childe believed, based on then-available evidence, that plants had been domesticated before animals, probably in such places as the nearby Nile Valley. The "nobler grasses"—ancient ancestors of modern wheat and barley—apparently grew in abundance on the banks of the Nile, where they were subjected to annual flooding and enrichment by the fertile alluvial soil. Childe felt that the plants of the Nile Valley were controlled by nature's perfect irrigation cycle and that it remained only for "some genius" to produce similar artificial irrigation conditions elsewhere.

Braidwood's "Hilly Flanks" Theory: Culture Was Ready for It

> *The great tragedy of Science—the slaying of a beautiful hypothesis by an ugly fact.*
>
> THOMAS HENRY HUXLEY (1825–1895), BIOLOGIST

Although Childe's explanation seemed plausible at the time, supportive data were fairly weak. The chronology for the Near East–Nile Valley was sketchy, and no archaeological evidence for early food production was available for the area.

Shortly after World War II, Robert Braidwood of the University of Chicago decided to search for some relevant data. Traveling to the foothills of Iraq, he spearheaded a series of excavations to test—in the field—various explanations regarding the origins of domestication. Braidwood obtained some of the first archaeologically relevant C-14 dates.

Braidwood's empirical results questioned the very existence of significant post-Pleistocene climatic shifts in the Near East. He and his team found that the climate had been essentially stable during the period of animal and plant domestication. These data suggested that Childe's oasis theory had to be rejected.

Braidwood proposed a new explanation, which came to be known as the "hilly flanks theory." Rather than calling on environmental change to explain the origins of agriculture in the Near East, Braidwood and his colleagues concluded instead that agriculture arose as a "logical outcome" of culture elaboration and specialization. The hunters and gatherers simply "settled in" after the end of the Pleistocene, becoming intimately familiar with their plant and animal neighbors. As culture evolved further, so did people's means of exploiting the environment. Agriculture, in this view, was merely another natural link in the long evolutionary chain.

Southwestern Asia was a logical place for this to occur because the wild plants suitable for domestication (especially wild wheat, barley, and legumes) were already growing there naturally; wild cattle, sheep, and goats also lived there (becoming the natural targets for animal domestication).

Although Childe and Braidwood used different data and reached conflicting conclusions, they agreed on the fundamental processes that triggered the initial domestication of Old World plants and animals. Both theories implicitly assumed that humanity continually seeks to improve its technology and subsistence. Whenever the proper conditions came along, it is "logical" that plants and animals would be domesticated, because domestication provided a more technologically advanced economic base.

Braidwood on the Internet:

Robert Braidwood personally summarizes results of his Joint Prehistory Project in southeastern Turkey; particularly interesting for his account of political and military problems encountered.

1992–1993 *Annual Report*:
http://www.oi.uchicago.edu/OI/AR/92-93/92-93_Prehistoric.html

1993–1994 *Annual Report*:
http://www.oi.uchicago.edu/OI/AR/93-94/93-94_Prehistoric.html

1994–1995 *Annual Report*:
http://www.oi.uchicago.edu/OI/AR/94-95/94-95/_Prehistoric.html

In effect, Childe and Braidwood were *Malthusians*, meaning that they shared the basic economic premises set forth almost 200 years ago by Thomas R. Malthus (see *Thomas Malthus: Starvation and Misery Are Inevitable*). Their Malthusian position stressed that population will grow until checked by increased death rates—caused by starvation, epidemic, warfare, civil unrest, and so forth—what Malthus collectively termed "vice and misery." But the key, underlying factor in such Malthusian arguments remains *population pressure*.

You can see why the Childe and Braidwood theories are fundamentally Malthusian in nature. Why were plants and animals domesticated? The Malthusian argument suggests that domestication occurred simply as a natural consequence of people's continual struggle to improve technology, driven by population pressure—the root cause of domestication. Because growing crops and keeping flocks are more advanced means of subsistence, people quite naturally stopped foraging to become full-time farmers and herders. Once agriculture was adopted, the human population was free to increase dramatically. The wholesale shift to domestication came to be known as the **Neolithic** Revolution.

Neolithic: The ancient period during which people began using ground stone tools, manufacturing ceramics, and relying on domesticated plants and animals—literally the "New Stone Age." This term, incidentally, was introduced by Sir John Lubbock (in 1865).

Stress Models: Domestication for Survival

The Childe and Braidwood theories assume that people will continuously attempt to increase their food supply. Yet the archaeological record clearly shows long periods of technological and economic stability. How can such stability be explained in the face of Malthusian progress?

In the past few decades, many anthropologists have become uncomfortable with Malthusian explanations. Particularly difficult to accept is the economic and ecological determinism implied by the neo-Malthusian position. Childe argued that when the climate changed, people would readily turn to domestication. Braidwood rejected Childe's notion, arguing instead that domestication arose as an evolutionary elaboration of the "settling-in" process. In both cases, cultural change was determined by environmental conditions.

Thomas Malthus: Starvation and Misery Are Inevitable

Malthusian, adj. Pertaining to Malthus and his doctrines. Malthus believed in artificially limiting population, but found that it could not be done by talking.

Ambrose Bierce (1842–1914?), journalist and writer

Thomas Robert Malthus was born into a wealthy, eighteenth-century English family, and his father, Daniel, was the embodiment of the Age of Reason, well connected in intellectual and philosophical circles. To Daniel's entire generation, the world seemed poised on the threshold of paradise: The laws of reason, they thought, would eventually eradicate all poverty, misery, and suffering.

Despite this rosy outlook, trouble lurked just down the road. These were also the years that Charles Dickens called "the best of times, the worst of times," and revolution was sweeping France. Being gentlemen of leisure, Thomas and Daniel Malthus debated the significance of the French Revolution. Father Daniel remained enthusiastic, still arguing that "reason" should be sufficient to lift humanity from darkness, superstition, and cruelty.

Young Malthus disagreed, and he brooded about the future of civilized humanity. How could society be perfected when population growth was so obviously outstripping the available resources? Their British country manor reverberated as father and son debated their positions. Finally, Thomas Malthus prepared a treatise so that he could more effectively marshal his arguments against his father. The elder Malthus was so impressed with the document that he encouraged his son to publish it, which Thomas did (anonymously) as *An Essay on the Principle of Population As It Affects the Future Improvement of Society* (1798). Five years later, Malthus published a second essay, documenting his speculations and answering his numerous critics.

Thomas Robert Malthus.

The Malthusian essays explore the relationship between human population and the resource base available to support it. The *Malthusian position* holds that because human fertility is essentially constant, the size of human populations will be governed only by changing mortality rates: Population size will grow unchecked until something dramatic happens, what Malthus termed "vice and misery"—catastrophes such as war, epidemic, or disaster. In a slightly modified form, the basic Malthusian position remains an important force in contemporary economics.

Danish economist Ester Boserup provided an appealing alternative. The Malthusian argument was essentially pessimistic—with starvation and misery rising as the human population increased toward carrying capacity. Boserup's view is more optimistic, suggesting that technological responses to increasing subsistence demands will become available or will be devised "when they are needed" (see *Ester Boserup: Technology Will Respond When Needed*).

Lewis Binford built upon Boserup's theoretical position, in which people adopt new energy sources (such as domesticated plants) only when forced to do so. In his so-called *density-equilibrium model,* Binford rejected Braidwood's

Ester Boserup: Technology Will Respond When Needed

In her influential book, *The Conditions of Agricultural Growth: The Economics of Agrarian Change Under Population Pressure* (1965), Danish economist Ester Boserup reversed the classic Malthusian equation. Unlike Malthus—who regarded population growth as a response to changing economic and ecological potential—Boserup argued that population growth is itself the autonomous or independent variable. Population growth as such is held to be a major factor in determining agricultural development and productivity.

Concerned primarily with contemporary agrarian societies, Boserup asked: What happens when the population increases? In low-density, primitive agricultural areas, excess land is available, and such societies practice slash-and-burn agriculture. People move from one plot to another, eventually coming back to the original plot. All of this occurs within a home territory. In such a system, the land is given sufficient time to replenish its resources through lengthy fallow periods. Slash-and-burn methods today support some 200 million people in Africa, Latin America, and Asia.

But as population increases, land must be used more intensively, with fallow periods becoming shorter and shorter. People must work harder as land becomes more scarce, and technology increases in the form of agricultural machinery, fertilizers, and pesticides. Boserup sees the frequency of cropping as a key variable and contends that economic systems can be viewed along a continuum. At one end is the society with excess uncultivated land; at the other extreme is the society with multi-cropped land, in which a second crop is sown as the first is reaped. Boserup believes that all forms of more intense land use can be viewed along this continuum, that population growth is the prime mover causing societies to evolve from one stage to another.

Ester Boserup.

Several archaeologists have applied Boserup's ideas to prehistoric evidence, looking at population growth as a key factor. Other investigators disagree, relying instead on more traditional Malthusian perspectives. The outlooks differ in their view of population growth: Is it a cause or an effect?

---

notion that agriculture developed because "culture was ready for it." On this point, Binford agreed with Childe's earlier argument that domestication constitutes a new **ecological niche**, one imposed by changing conditions. But whereas Childe named climatic and environmental changes as the initiating factors, Binford proposed that the true stress on these groups was pressure from other human populations.

Ecological niche: The functional role of a species within a biological community.

Specifically, population pressure was exerted by groups of people with an extremely successful Mesolithic adaptation who were occupying the same habitat, such as the Fertile Crescent. The post-Pleistocene emphasis on river and lakeside food sources (fish, shellfish, sea mammals) permitted a comparatively lavish and more sedentary existence than that of the more traditional hunter-gatherers. The competitive pressure on nonsedentary peoples must have been severe, and it is in these marginal areas, Binford suggests, that people first turned to domestication for survival.

"The long run" is nothing more than a continuous series of short runs, of nows, placed end to end.

BARBARA PRICE, ARCHAEOLOGIST

Binford's hypothesis attempted not only to explain most of the known facts but also to provide directly testable implications for further archaeological fieldwork. Specifically, Binford predicted:

1. In the optimal zones, there must have been a population increase owing to a new and efficient Mesolithic lifeway before the first domestication.
2. The earliest evidence of domestication should come not from these optimal zones where the Mesolithic lifeway functioned but, rather, in the marginal, less favored areas (as the law of evolutionary potential would suggest).
3. The material culture of the earliest Neolithic populations should be essentially similar to that of their Mesolithic neighbors.
4. There should be no circumscribed center of domestication; the process should have occurred simultaneously in several areas under population pressure.

Kent Flannery then applied Binford's "density equilibrium" model to the archaeology of the Near East. Following Binford's arguments to their logical conclusion, Flannery suggested that the "optimal" habitats should have been the centers for population growth, with the marginal areas receiving the emigrant overflow. Flannery discussed a "broad-spectrum" revolution that began about 20,000 B.C. and amounted to a major broadening of the subsistence base from mostly hunting terrestrial game to including larger amounts of fish, crabs, water turtles, mollusks, and migratory waterfowl. To Flannery, this change in subsistence was due less to post-Pleistocene climatic change than to a simple overuse of prime land. The demand for the previously ignored invertebrates, fish, waterfowl, and plant resources would have increased in precisely those "marginal" areas in which Binford believed that the initial domestication of plants occurred. Therefore, domestication occurred in these areas because the demand for other food types could not be satisfied. Flannery, like Binford, contended that the population increase (à la Boserup) could have functioned as a major factor, encouraging hunting-gathering groups to begin cultivating plant crops.

The Flannery-Binford model was roundly criticized, and both have heavily revised their earlier arguments. Some pointed out that this model lacked empirical support, as the archaeological record shows no evidence of inland migration near the early agricultural centers. Critics also pointed out that the "broad-spectrum" adaptation was not restricted to seacoasts and that agriculture actually arose earlier and in areas other than those recognized by Flannery and Binford. Even though no longer a viable theory, Binford's discussion proved to be a turning point because it tried to identify the stimuli that changed hunter-gatherer adaptations into agriculture-based lifeways.

Mark Cohen took matters one step farther by suggesting that population growth was *even more pervasive* than Boserup originally thought. Cohen posed two important questions:

1. Why would successful hunter-gatherers decide to become agricultural in the first place?
2. Why did people all around the world acquire agriculture at about the same time?

Cohen's answer was that by about 15,000 B.P. in the Old World, and 8,000–10,000 B.P. in the New World, human populations had spread out across most of the habitable landscape, basically exhausting all available strategies for garnering a living through hunter-gatherer lifestyles. The quality of life began to deteriorate as people were forced away from the desirable (but scarce) large fauna toward more plentiful, if less desirable, "secondary" resources (such as grains and tubers). In light of a continually growing human population, no options remained except agriculture—and that's what people did, by intensifying their exploitation of the more productive plant species, some of which changed genetically in the process.

Cohen's heavy reliance on population pressure has been challenged on various counts. Some assert that population pressure could not have been such an important causal factor because many people—"advanced" and "primitive"—knew how to control population levels before they reached carrying capacity. Others see population pressure as a problem restricted to relatively recent times, the result of health advances made during the Industrial Revolution.

A Selectionist Perspective

So far, we have considered relationships among (1) human sedentism, (2) population growth, and (3) resource-choice strategies. There is a good deal of debate as to which of these variables should be assigned causal priority over the other two. Childe and Braidwood argued that sedentism must have come first, followed by domestication and population growth. Those favoring the Boserup school contended that population growth was primary, with the other two variables falling into a secondary role.

There is another way to view things, by focusing instead on the underlying process of natural selection. Like the optimal foraging models discussed in Chapter 14, this approach relies heavily on Darwinian principles developed by evolutionary ecologists working in the fields of genetics, plant ecology, and, most recently, molecular plant biology.

Employing his **selectionist explanation**, the late David Rindos argued that the origins of agriculture are best understood through a consideration of the evolutionary forces at work. So viewed, plant domestication is not an evolutionary stage of cultural development, but rather a process—the result of *coevolutionary* interactions between humans and plants. **Coevolution** suggests that agricultural origins can be explained in terms of a mutual selection among components, rather than a linear cause-and-effect sequence.

Rindos asserts that the relationships between plants and people must be appreciated without recourse to either cultural adaptations or human intent. *Incidental domestication* occurs as the product of the dispersal and protection of wild plants by members of nonagricultural human societies, the direct result of human feeding behavior. Eventually, this relationship selects for certain changes in the plants involved, "preadapting" them for further domestication. Initial domestication promotes a "conservative" interaction between people and plants. The size of human populations carried by the plant communities is limited, and, in return, the rate of change in the plants is relatively low (compared with what will develop later).

Selectionist explanation: The view that human societies have evolved culturally in accord with the process governing biological evolution, namely natural selection.

Coevolution: A theory of cultural evolution suggesting that changes in social systems are best understood as mutual selection among components rather than as a linear cause-and-effect sequence. David Rindos has argued that the origins of agriculture are best understood by exploring the evolutionary forces affecting the development of domestication systems. Viewed this way, domestication is not seen as an evolutionary stage, but rather as a process; it is the result of interactions between humans and plants.

I think it unlikely that social imperatives were prime movers in transitions to agriculture. But I do not think they should be categorically ignored.

PATTY JO WATSON, ARCHAEOLOGIST (WASHINGTON UNIVERSITY)

Specialized domestication occurs as new types of plant–people interactions develop. As humans become the dispersal agents for various species of plants, these plants spread into the specific areas where humans live. In effect, a new brand of ecological succession takes place—as plants become more important to humans as food, they also become more common in places where people are living. This change is largely demographic, the effect of people changing their environment so as to benefit indirectly the domesticated plant. That is, people become so dependent on the plant communities that the survival of both is interdependent. People also begin selectively destroying various unwanted plant species around their communities, setting the stage for the development of complex agricultural systems. Full-blown *agricultural domestication* takes place when practices like weeding, irrigation, and plowing create new opportunities for plant evolution, thereby increasing the rate at which domesticated plants evolve.

Rindos's model of coevolution has been used to explain plant domestication in many parts of the world. The coevolutionary explanatory framework has the advantage of moving beyond single-factor, "prime mover" arguments. Cohen's argument, for instance, assigns strict causal priority to population growth. Under the coevolutionary approach, however, the question of which came first—population growth, plant domestication, or sedentism—becomes irrelevant.

So does the question of why humans would enter into such a coevolutionary relationship with plants. To Rindos, this is "a question without real meaning. We might as well ask why certain ants established coevolutionary relationships with fungi or certain birds with specific fruits." The coevolutionary approach holds that changes occur as a result of maximizing adaptive fitness at a particular time, in a particular place: "They were neither inevitable nor desirable, but merely happened."

Rindos completely sidesteps such issues as human intent, conscious selection, the "cultural factors" that give rise to domestication, and even the when and where of agricultural invention—focusing instead on the coevolutionary relationships that developed between and among plant and animal species. To those pursuing a processual agenda, this adaptive perspective is a welcome change.

But many contemporary archaeologists and neo-evolutionists take exception to this view. They are uncomfortable with what they see as Rindos's "slavish" adherence to a Darwinian model for cultural evolution; so viewed, human inventiveness—like genetic mutation—becomes simply another random process.

The big issue here is *human intent.* Robert Carneiro cannot believe that developing agriculturalists were oblivious to the changes happening in what they ate. Didn't those ancient Mesoamerican farmers deliberately decide that they wanted their corn cobs to be larger? Carneiro views intent as an "intermediate element" between ecological pressures and cultural outcome. Intent is always a factor, but is not likely to be the most persuasive determinant.

In the accompanying box, *Why Did People Domesticate Plants,* Kent V. Flannery goes a step farther, weighing in with the view that by ignoring human intent, Rindos and his selectionist view misses the point entirely.

IN HIS OWN WORDS:

Why Did People Domesticate Plants? by Kent V. Flannery

I have always been struck by the fact that while paleontologists most frequently ask how, *anthropologists most frequently ask* why. *Paleontologists are concerned with evolutionary mechanisms, and they try to answer the* how *question by studying the intervening fossil forms from an evolutionary transition. Anthropologists are concerned with human aspirations, with what* [David] *Rindos has called "intentionality," and they try to answer the* why *question by studying culturally patterned behavior. Paleontologists do not picture reptiles saying, "let's turn into birds," but many anthropologists do picture hunter-gatherers saying, "Let's plant those seeds on the talus slope below our cave."*

We can ignore human intentionality and concentrate on the underlying biological aspects of domestication, producing a universal model as Rindos *has recently done. The trouble is that while such a model may satisfy biologists, it often does not satisfy anthropologists: Anthropologists want cultural explanations for cultural behavior and are not usually satisfied when culture is reduced to biology. Anthropologists know that human hunter-gatherers are mammals, primates, and predators, but that is not what anthropologists find most interesting about them.*

My main worry about Rindos's *model is that, in the process of finding some analogies for agriculture elsewhere in the animal kingdom, he has concluded that human domestication of plants can be filed away as just one more case of a well-known biological process. In 1957, when I was a zoology student at the University of Chicago, that might have seemed like a great idea, but now that I am an anthropologist, I have some reservations.*

I suggest that what we have here is a classic case of scholars from two different disciplines talking past each other. Rindos, *trained as a biologist, is content with reducing domestication to a biological model that is admirably general but (by his own admission) lacks the resolution to explain the origins of agriculture in any area. He apparently does not realize that anthropologists, trained to seek explanations in terms of cultural, social, political, and economic decisions, are most interested precisely in the testable, high-resolution explanations that his model fails to provide. The fact that there are biological analogies for human behavior is as big a bore for anthropologists as human intentionality is for* Rindos.

There is no need to explore other theories attempting to account for plant and animal domestication (and, believe me, plenty of additional explanations exist). The point is not to define the exact moment that somebody first planted a seed or monkeyed around with the genetics of penned animals but, rather, to illustrate how the search for the process proceeds.

Why Did the Archaic State Arise?

In Chapter 2 we discussed in some detail how contemporary social scientists study the societal and political dynamics of cultural institutions. There were, you will remember, two basic research approaches. The synchronic procedure emphasizes the in situ analysis of functioning cultural systems. This is the basic concern of ethnographers, sociologists, economists, psychologists, and ethnoarchaeologists. Synchronic studies provide a picture of the dynamics of a system that operates at a single point in time: now. We also discussed the ways in which archaeologists can conduct synchronic studies of another time period: then. In effect, the general objective of reconstructing past lifeways is to unravel the specifics and dynamics of single societies.

The first human being who hurled an insult instead of a stone was the founder of civilization.

ATTRIBUTED TO SIGMUND FREUD (1856–1939), FOUNDER OF PSYCHOANALYSIS

Anthropology's second fundamental approach is diachronic, emphasizing the development of societies over a span of time. Although the ethnographer can justly point to the richness of the detail available in contemporary society, such studies invariably fall short in an evolutionary sense because the time factor is lacking. Of course, archaeological data lack great ethnographic detail, but archaeology can provide a chronicle of in situ cultural developments without which diachronic studies cannot proceed.

The previous section considered some theories of plant and animal domestication, one of the most important technoecological developments in the history of human evolution. We shall now turn to the evolution of sociopolitical institutions as another example of how archaeologists are working to construct general theories to account for stability and change.

What Is the Archaic State?

The *archaic state* has been defined in a number of ways over the years, and, to simplify this discussion, we will follow Kent Flannery's definition:

> The state is a type of very strong, usually highly centralized government, with a professional ruling class, largely divorced from the bonds of kinship which characterize simpler societies. It is highly stratified and extremely diversified internally, with residential patterns often based on occupational specialization rather than blood or affinal relationships. The state attempts to maintain a monopoly of force, and is characterized by true law.

Archaic states generally have powerful economic structures and often a market system. The state economy is controlled by an elite, which maintains its authority by means of a combination of law and differential access to key goods and services. Archaic states generally have populations numbering at least in the hundreds of thousands, and this population is often concentrated in large cities. Much of the population consists of economic specialists, dependent on the labor of others for subsistence. Archaic states are also known for a high level of artistic achievement, monumental architecture, and an overall state religion.

The archaic state is thus a complex form of sociopolitical organization. Ethnographers and other social scientists have studied the modern state for decades, and its dynamics are relatively well understood. But it is clear that these contemporary states are the products of a long chain of sociopolitical evolution, and how they came to be remains an unanswered question. "Archaic" archaeological states are evident throughout the world. Although contemporary ethnographic studies can satisfactorily unravel the synchronic dynamics of functioning state-level organization, no amount of study of modern states can explain its evolution. The state as we know it today is a worldwide phenomenon, with a long history preserved in the archaeological record. Only through a consideration of the archaeological evidence can an accurate diachronic study be made of societies as they developed to the state level.

> *Archaeology can supply the skeleton of state-level organization. But only the comparative ethnohistorical study of societies at different stages of cultural evolution can fill in the soft tissue.*
>
> Robert Carneiro, neo-evolutionist and ethnologist (American Museum of Natural History)

Theories about the origin of the archaic state go back to the nineteenth-century cultural evolutionists, introduced briefly in the first part of this chapter. A number of causal factors have been suggested to account for the development of the archaic state: irrigation, warfare, population growth, circumscription, trade, cooperation and competition, and the integrative power of great religions. We will sample a few such explanations.

Wittfogel's "Irrigation Hypothesis"

To see how archaeologists, as social scientists, attempt to unravel the evolution of the archaic state, we begin by looking at one of the historically important theories, Karl A. Wittfogel's *irrigation hypothesis.* As before, we are more concerned with the nature of the search than with providing the ultimate truth.

In his influential book *Oriental Despotism* (1957), Karl A. Wittfogel asserted that the mechanisms of large-scale irrigation were directly responsible for creating the archaic state. He argued that the great oriental societies (China, India, Mesopotamia) followed a radically different evolutionary course than did the societies of Western Europe and elsewhere. The archaic state evolved because of special conditions required by large-scale irrigation: the imposition of inordinately strong political controls to maintain the hydraulic works, the tendency for the ruling class to merge with the ruling bureaucracy, the close identification of the dominant religion with governmental offices, and the diminution of private property and economic initiative. Wittfogel contended that after a creative period in which the bureaucracy was begun, stagnation set in, corrupting power and creating a despotic and feudal system. Wittfogel saw the hydraulic society as an initial step to totalitarianism, and his theory of the state was clearly framed with twentieth-century cold war perspectives in mind.

According to Wittfogel's theory, the state evolved in direct response to the demands of large-scale irrigation. The need for coordinated labor, massive construction, and so forth led to increased wealth and military strength, and eventually to the powerful ruling bureaucracy that characterized state development.

Schematic diagram of Wittfogel's irrigation hypothesis for the origin of the state.

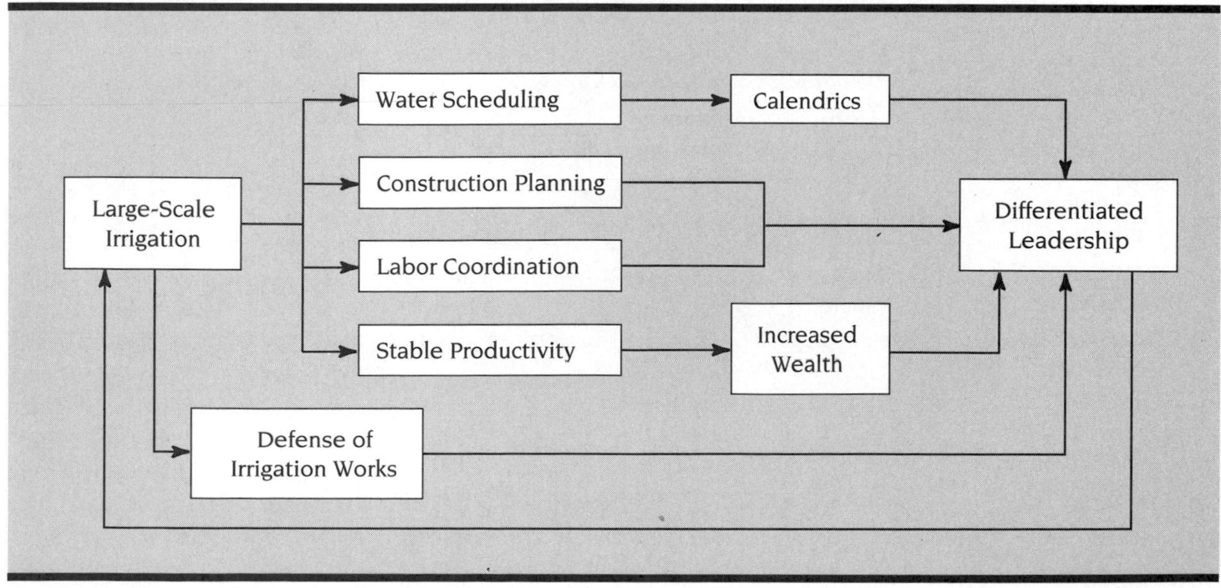

Carneiro's "Warfare and Circumscription Hypothesis"

War is the father of all things.

HERACLITUS (CA. 540–475 B.C.), PHILOSOPHER

A second explanation for the origin of the archaic state, offered by ethnologist Robert Carneiro, rests on a different initial premise, that autonomous political units never willingly surrender their sovereignty. Carneiro terms Wittfogel's irrigation hypothesis a "voluntaristic" theory, one requiring that "at some point in their history, certain peoples spontaneously, rationally, and voluntarily gave up their individual sovereignties and united with other communities to form a larger political unit deserving to be called a state." This is why he objects to the irrigation hypothesis.

Carneiro argues, instead, that egalitarian settlements will be transformed into chiefdoms, and chiefdoms into kingdoms, only when coercive force is involved, and that warfare is especially pertinent to this transformation. Of course, some tribes might agree to cooperate in times of stress, but such federations are temporary and voluntarily dissolved once the crisis has passed. Carneiro's initial premise stipulates that political change of lasting significance will come about only as the result of coercive pressure. Warfare is the only mechanism powerful enough to impose bureaucratic authority on a large scale. Thus warfare—the world's main coercive device—plays an important role in the origin of the state.

It is clear from the archaeological record, however, that warfare is considerably older and more widespread than the state. Because warfare does not invariably lead to archaic state formation, Carneiro is quick to add that, though necessary, warfare is not sufficient in itself to account for the state. According to Carneiro, it is in areas where agricultural land is at a premium—areas that are environmentally "circumscribed"—that warfare predictably leads to state formation. Competition over land arose first where arable land was restricted by natural barriers, such as mountains, deserts, or seas. The vanquished peoples had no place to flee and thus were required to submit

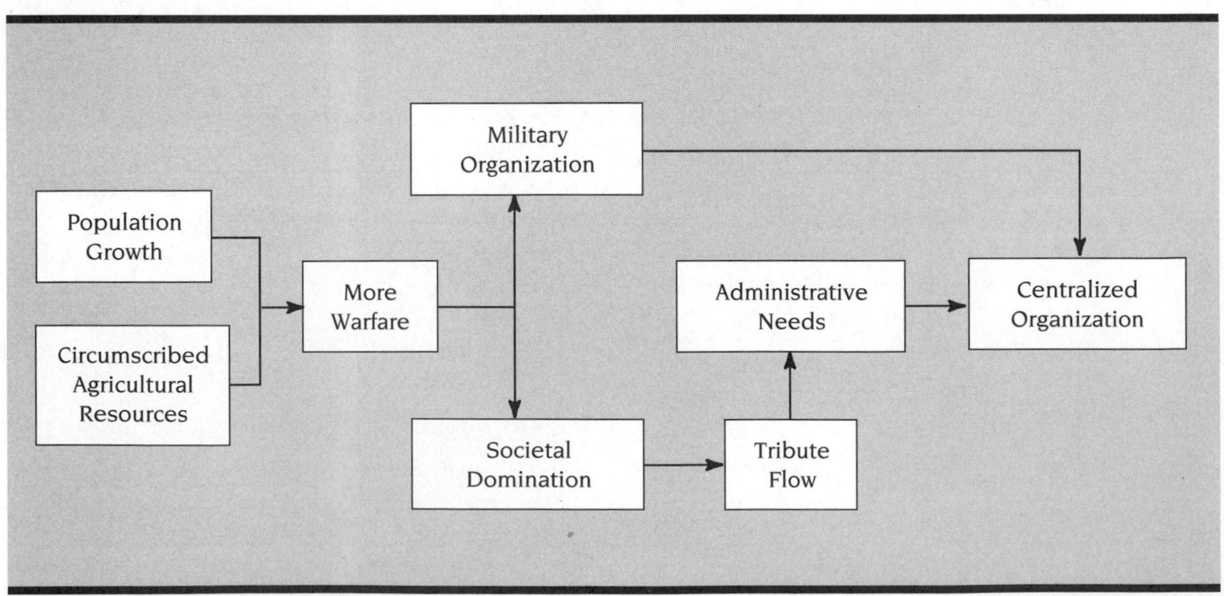

Schematic diagram of Carneiro's circumscription and warfare hypothesis for the origin of the state.

to the expanding political units of the victors. Carneiro points out that the early archaic states near the Nile, the Tigris-Euphrates (Mesopotamia), the Indus Valley, and the valleys of Mexico and Peru all evolved in areas of circumscribed agricultural land. Conversely, in areas where agricultural land was plentiful—such as in northern Europe, central Africa, and the eastern woodlands of North America—states were quite late in developing, if they did at all.

In Carneiro's circumscription theory, the combination of population growth and circumscribed agricultural resources leads to increased warfare, which in turn leads to the centralized political organization characteristic of state-level complexity.

Robert Carneiro while conducting ethnographic fieldwork among the Amahuaca (Peru). He is wading in the Inuya ("with jaguar") River.

Multicausal Theories of State Formation

Both the irrigation and circumscription hypotheses are examples of general theory in anthropology. Each proponent would claim that all else being equal, theory explains the origin of the archaic state throughout the world, at any time.

More recently, in his review of the tremendous quantity of data now relating to state-level organization in Mesopotamia, the Indus Valley, Mesoamerica, and the central Andes, Henry Wright has suggested that the regularities postulated by Wittfogel, Carneiro, and others cannot be sustained by the archaeological record, as it is now understood. Similarly, while granting that Wittfogel and Carneiro have stimulated considerable controversy and worthwhile research, Mark Cohen asserts that their theories "have 'failed' as explanations to varying degrees because localized research has failed (1) to confirm the existence of the postulated common element in areas of state formation; (2) to demonstrate its absence in other areas; or (3) to confirm its postulated role in the evolutionary process."

In the discussion dealing with the origins of agriculture, we considered Cohen's views on the role of human population pressure in the domestication of plants and animals. At this point, you might think that perhaps Mark Cohen would have jumped into the particularistic breach, to suggest his own population pressure theory to explain the origin of the archaic state.

Cohen asked a compelling question: "Why did many independent human populations begin to organize themselves hierarchically at the same time after so many millennia of egalitarian structure?" The answer to this question, according to Cohen, lies in the consequences of the abandonment of a hunting-gathering lifeway in favor of an agricultural strategy. Although agriculture potentially increased the available calories to feed human society, it also left people more vulnerable to environmental fluctuations. As such stress increased, so did the development of cultural buffering mechanisms: the development of storage systems, increased interregional trade (in both luxury and subsistence items), and the greater importance of centralized authorities who became essential to ensuring economic security.

Well aware of the possibility of "alternative pathways" to civilization, Cohen proposed two hypotheses for the origin of the state: (1) as occurring in "special environments" and (2) as an "epiphenomenon." The first explanation suggests that if population pressure-driven vulnerability to environmental

Whether or not cultural evolution has taken place is no longer an issue. Recent archaeological work on all continents documents the basic development from early small-scale societies to later complex societies. . . . Subsistence intensification, political integration, and social stratification are three interlocked processes observed again and again in historically unrelated cases. Foragers diversify and gradually adopt agriculture; villages form and integrate into regional polities; leaders come to dominate and transform social relationships.

ALLEN JOHNSON, CULTURAL ANTHROPOLOGIST (UNIVERSITY OF CALIFORNIA, LOS ANGELES), AND TIMOTHY EARLE, ARCHAEOLOGIST (NORTHWESTERN UNIVERSITY)

fluctuations is a major stimulus to political evolution, then one might expect the process of centralization to be most pronounced under conditions in which vulnerability was high.

Admitting that such explanations are problematical, Cohen decided that these environmental/ecological explanations might not account for the specific evolution of archaic states, because "there appears to be ample justification for recognizing a common set of adaptive problems as underlying the more *general* emergence of centralized governments."

Alternatively, suppose that the earliest state developed as just an *epiphenomenon*—something explainable only by historical factors. If so, then the process may reflect "random creative processes" rather than the more systematic selective processes. In short, whereas Carneiro's integrated theory relies on the potential territorial expansion of a social unit as the key factor in state formation, Cohen worries that no single "prime mover" may ever be found.

Let me mention one final theory regarding the evolution of the archaic state. Drawing on three case studies—France and Japan (both during the Middle Ages) and the Inka of the Andes—ethnologist Allen Johnson and archaeologist Timothy Earle conclude that state formation can indeed be explained on the basis of a few universal factors.

They find subsistence intensification to be a necessary, if not sufficient, cause of archaic state formation. As population grows and the landscape fills in, increased food production requires capital improvements, carefully regulated agricultural cycles, competition for prime lands, and populations sufficiently large to support a market economy. But such a society would not be economically integrated enough to attain this level of social complexity. Rather, state-level organization can develop only when two conditions are present: "high population density, with explicit needs for an overarching system of integration; and opportunities for sufficient economic control to permit the stable financing of regional institutions and to support a ruling class. Where these two sets of conditions occur together, we find the rapid expansion of the political economy and the beginning of the state."

There is ample reason to think that strongly materialist approaches are seriously incomplete. This is not to say that material factors are unimportant. But ideational factors are also much too important to be ignored, even in a first approximation. Ideology, religion, beliefs, values, socially induced emotions, and culturally conditioned perceptions of reality do not float independently of geography, geology, climate, and biology; but neither are they determined in all important aspects by material circumstances.

GEORGE COWGILL, ARCHAEOLOGIST (ARIZONA STATE UNIVERSITY)

Ideational Explanations of Cultural Evolution

To this point, we have explored several theories stressing the importance of technology and material forces in cultural evolution. The processual agenda emphasizes that significant cultural change takes place when the technoeconomic base is somehow altered. This subsistence-level change produces changes in social interaction, which in turn cause shifts in social organization. Ideological changes develop as a means to validate the new social organization. A more Darwinian view (such as Rindos developed to explain the origins of agriculture) might suggest that selective pressures operate to promote the survival of technologically more efficient social systems.

This materialistic position has the advantage that it emphasizes those aspects of cultural behavior that are most obviously subject to a few fundamental, ecological principles. In the preceding chapter, for example, we saw how archaeologists have employed *optimal foraging theory* to explain human foraging practices in terms of the general principles developed in evolutionary ecology.

Undoubtedly the desire for food has been, and still is, one of the main causes of great political events.

BERTRAND RUSSELL (1872–1970), MATHEMATICIAN AND PHILOSOPHER

As discussed in Chapter 3, the processual agenda in archaeology relies heavily on the principles of cultural materialism, a special case or subclass of Darwinian evolutionary processes. The explicit linkage of human population growth to biological evolution confers on this position a certain epistemological strength; such principles are, at least in theory, quantifiable and testable. Ideational views of causality are not so easily quantified or tested.

Archaeologists also have commonly turned to materialist explanations because of the availability of large-scale data on subsistence remains and settlement patterns, which can readily be interpreted in terms of ecology, hydraulic systems, population dynamics, and systems of exchange. Drawing on the cultural materialistic explanatory framework, each of these archaeologists has explicitly denied a causal role for ideology, which was dismissed as being *epiphenomenal*–merely legitimation of existing economic and political realities.

As such ecologically oriented archaeology proceeded, however, many came to believe that population growth and irrigation alone could not be the overriding factors in explaining cultural change. Some studies hinted that the archaeological research focus on single valleys, drainages, or other ecologically defined universes might be obscuring major interregional, interethnic patterns that were important in the rise of complex society. Further, increased chronological control demonstrated that Wittfogel's irrigation (hydraulic) hypothesis did not hold up in either the New or Old Worlds.

It is exciting to have a real crisis on your hands, when you have spent half your political life dealing with humdrum issues like the environment.

MARGARET THATCHER, FORMER PRIME MINISTER OF GREAT BRITAIN [ON THE FALKLANDS CAMPAIGN OF 1982]

Kent Flannery and Joyce Marcus have criticized the ecological approach mainly for assuming that changes in resource exploitation and population growth are the most significant factors in cultural evolution. Flannery argues for a more systemic approach, with mutual causal interactions among a wide range of variables, including not only those often considered as prime movers in the ecological approach, but also such variables as ideology and political organization (features that, from a strictly materialistic view, derive from the technoeconomic).

Within the past decade or so, archaeologists have increasingly turned to the ideas that lay behind the materials of prehistory. Some are now reversing the causal arrow to suggest that *ideology* may have provided the major stimulus driving cultural change. In several subsequent chapters, we will look in some detail at how archaeologists examine the role of ideology in the past. For now, we focus strictly on ideologically based theories that have been proposed to account for the development of state-level organization.

By **ideology,** we mean the ritual, religion, and explicit cosmology that, taken together, provide the group members with a rationale for their existence. Leslie White has characterized the extreme ideological position as follows: "Ideas come first; they are the real things; they endure forever, material objects and sensory experiences are merely imperfect and ephemeral manifestations of the ideas . . . [which] are the original seeds, the prime movers." The ideologist's basic argument is that whenever a new form of behavior is encountered, it has been immediately preceded by an idea. The best

Ideology: A systematic body of concepts and beliefs—often political, religious, and cosmological in nature—that rationalizes the existence of a cultural group.

This is something like saying that it's the crankshaft *that really drives a car, because it is what most immediately imparts movement to the wheels. But the crankshaft is an* intermediate term *between the piston-cylinder system and the wheels. It's necessary, but it is not the prime mover.*

ROBERT CARNEIRO

way to explain cultural change is to begin with ideas, and determine how they came to modify behavior.

Many critics wish to shift the focus toward ideology, stressing the role of political legitimization in early state formation. Some approaches invoke ideology as a powerful driving force in cultural change. Others moderate this view, stressing that the role of ideology is simply to reinforce and justify existing arrangements of political power and exploitive economic order.

Most contemporary ideological approaches do not explicitly reject cultural ecology or the emphasis on technoeconomic factors. Rather, they insist that *somehow,* explanations of cultural change must integrate ideology into the standard mix of ecological, economic, and political factors. As we shall see in the next chapter, Kent Flannery views ideology as a dynamic element in cultural change, operating as an information-regulating mechanism and thereby shaping a group's possible adaptive responses to the natural and social environment. For many archaeologists, this approach provides a workable common ground between idealist and materialist positions. Others disagree.

Direct historical approach: A general technique for extending knowledge of the historical period into the past. Carefully done, this procedure allows documentary evidence to be cautiously applied to archaeological data from the more ancient past, *provided* a linkage can be established between the historical and ancient cultures.

Including ideology is, of course, much easier when dealing with ethnohistoric and historically known empires; such cases rely heavily on a **direct historical approach.** These ideological arguments, however, become more tenuous and less convincing when applied to prehistoric cases.

Here, we have dealt almost exclusively with materialistic views in neo-evolution. In subsequent chapters, we will explore in detail the role of ideology in the formation of Andean civilization. After evaluating the various materialistic alternatives—particularly the Wittfogel and Carneiro hypotheses discussed earlier—Richard Burger concludes that cosmology and religion played a causal role in the origins of Chavín civilization.

Neo-Evolutionism: Pros and Cons

Neo-evolutionary theory is today in flux. Some see its stock on the rise, others declare it bankrupt. In this section, we will briefly review some of the most common criticisms of neo-evolutionism, and then look at how neo-evolutionists are modifying their approach in response to their critics.

Evolution was a key in the works of such founding fathers as Morgan . . . , but was rejected as an overt conceptual approach in the early days of this century. . . . Evolution is now returning to center stage.

ROBERT DUNNELL, ARCHAEOLOGIST (UNIVERSITY OF WASHINGTON)

Today, neo-evolutionary accounts have held sway long enough.

PHILIP KOHL, ARCHAEOLOGIST (WELLESLEY COLLEGE)

Criticisms of the Neo-Evolutionary Program

Critics of neo-evolutionism abound. Some criticisms hark back to earlier arguments advanced by Boas, who mistrusted generalizations and advocated a position of extreme cultural particularism. Others, such as Rindos and the rest of the selectionists, believe that neo-evolutionism does not go far enough. Still others, while generally sympathetic with neo-evolutionary objectives, feel that specific research methods need to be modified before the nature of cultural evolution can be understood.

Here are some of the most common criticisms of the neo-evolutionary agenda:

Neo-evolutionism relies too heavily on ecological determinism.

How else are we to deal with the undeniable cultural change from the Paleolithic to the present?

ROBERT CARNEIRO

Neo-evolutionary theory, critics point out, depends heavily on biological approaches to ecology and evolution—bodies of theory not designed to explain human symbol systems and cultural motivation. Human behavior, they argue, is too complex to be understood as simply the product of orderly evolutionary processes. Nobody will ever be able to explain the workings of culture change in general because it is impossible to predict (to *retrodict*) how specific ways of life changed in the remote past. That can be known only by studying specific sequences of development in their particularistic complexity.

Neo-evolutionism relies on simplistic typologies of evolutionary stages.

The systemic, neo-evolutionary view posits that a particular kind of economy gives rise to a particular social matrix: Egalitarian bands and tribes have reciprocal forms of exchange, chiefdoms are characterized by redistribution, and so forth.

Critics charge that such neo-evolutionary stages address culture in piecemeal fashion, without taking into account the nature of cultural diversity, sociocultural detail, and relevant historical particulars. Although some obvious correlations exist between economic systems and social organization, these simple one-to-one correlations can be challenged. They should be the focus of study, rather than procedural assumptions.

Some also feel that the use of evolutionary stages implies a set of stable social formations that, when beset by external problems (such as population growth or environmental change), simply move to the next higher stage or break down (depending on the circumstances). Archaeologist Norman Yoffee has termed this view "the stepladder" perception: Bands become tribes, which become chiefdoms, which finally become states.

Researchers, critics argue, must abandon these static ideal-type stages and explore the ways in which political actors in the past constructed and maintained polities and other sociocultural institutions. Neo-evolutionists respond that, although a single picture can be thought of as "static," a succession of them produces a motion picture.

Neo-evolutionism ignores internal social differentiation.

Some reject neo-evolutionism as an adequate model of overarching, society-wide change. Norman Yoffee, for instance, criticizes models of "holistic change" because they tie all social institutions—politics, economics, and social organization—into a single, tidy bundle. In this view, when cultural change takes place, it must occur in all institutions at the same time, in the same place, and in the same direction.

Archaeology, history, and anthropology appear as increasingly arbitrary partitions of the necessary elements of comprehensive understanding.

ANDREW SHERRATT, ARCHAEOLOGIST (ASHMOLEAN MUSEUM, OXFORD UNIVERSITY)

What is lacking in neo-evolutionary theory, critics charge, is any sense of *internal* social division. It is these very trends—intrasocial conflicts such as inequality, stratification, and incomplete social integration—that should form the heart of social evolutionary theory. Society must be analyzed in terms of independent institutional units, which combine and fragment in various patterns. There is no uniform, underlying structure as implied by the various discrete typological stages.

Neo-evolutionism demeans the role of the individual.

Yet another major objection to processual-style neo-evolutionism is that individual human beings become devalued and irrelevant. In their rejection of neo-evolutionism, postprocessual critics have championed a human-centered perspective, with an emphasis on meaning, symbolism, and social context.

The cultural framework within which we act, and which we reproduce in our actions, is historically derived, and each culture is a particular historical product. The uniqueness of cultures and historical sequences must be recognized.

Ian Hodder, archaeologist (Cambridge University)

Neo-evolutionism artificially separates history from evolution.

The neo-evolutionary perspective carefully distinguishes the culturally specific (the "historical") from the cross-culturally general (the "scientific" or "evolutionary"). Postprocessual critics reject this distinction, arguing instead that cultural change is largely dependent on culturally specific cosmologies, astronomical beliefs, art styles, religious beliefs, and other topics deliberately marginalized in the processual agenda. Many argue that the two approaches must merge into a new kind of history, regarded as somehow scientific in nature.

Some neo-evolutionists would respond: How would postprocessualists account for the emergence of *hundreds* of chiefdoms around the world in just a few millennia after the beginnings of agriculture? Is this sheer coincidence?

So fixated are post-modernists at the level of ethnography, that they have failed to fulfill ethnography's traditional obligation to ethnology. . . . For it is here, in ethnology, that broad theories are built and generalizations crafted; where the major questions of anthropology are asked and answered. Here it is that we debate . . . the invention of agriculture, . . . the rise of chiefdoms, and the development of states. What have post-modernists contributed to the solution of these great problems? Nothing. Has anyone even heard of a post-modernist theory of the origin of the state?

Robert Carneiro

The Emergent Middle Ground?

Renfrew's "two paths" highlight the problem and perhaps point to a new direction for the future. Today, a middle ground seems to be emerging on neo-evolutionism. Many believe that isolating and explaining cross-cultural generalities remains a central mission of Americanist archaeology. Many also reject the old processual assertion that *only* cross-cultural regularities are worthy of study. There is much to understand in specific historical cultural sequences; to ignore this contextual richness is to degrade and disparage major areas of human experience.

Following Renfrew, Charles Spencer has recently argued for a dual approach to neo-evolutionism. At one level, neo-evolutionism continues to seek common principles in the evolution of all civilizations. This transformational approach suggests that—regardless of specific historical contexts—the evolution of social forms involves profound and relatively rapid restructuring of administrative organization. State emergence, when it occurs, involves certain transformations that can be studied cross-culturally. Suppose that you wish, for instance, to compare the rise of the ancient Zapotec state (Valley of Oaxaca, Mexico) with, say, the lowland Classic Maya (centered at Tikal, Guatemala). If you focus strictly on contextual details—the iconography, calendrical systems, political developments, warfare histories, and so forth—then the two civilizations are not directly comparable, for each took place in very different environments, shaped by its own unique cultural and historical systems, and by a different series of human decisions.

It must simply be recognized that there are two different paths here—one toward the general and hence the comparative; the other toward the specific analysis of context and hence ultimately to the unique.

Colin Renfrew, archaeologist (Cambridge University)

To define a cross-cultural common ground, it becomes necessary to reduce the Zapotec and Classic Maya cases to their conceptual basics. This is where the stage-wise progression comes into play: the band, the chiefdom, the archaic state. These neo-evolutionist abstractions provide workable, if incomplete, characterizations of step-wise, qualitative change. To be sure, the stage-wise evolutionary sequence from bands to the archaic state factors out the role of individual actors. It is the *system*—variously comprised of population pressure, environmental change, and internal class struggle—that drove human societies into new evolutionary stages. Like all broadly generalizing approaches, this second approach has sparked, and will continue to spark, intense debate, particularly when it seems to take the humanity of the past and reduce the actors to pawns.

Just as paleontologists would find it difficult to study biological evolution without stages like "fish," "amphibian," "reptile," and "mammal," archaeologists would find it difficult to study social evolution if hunting-gathering bands, chiefdoms, and archaic states were simply lumped together as "prehistoric societies."

JOYCE MARCUS AND KENT FLANNERY, ARCHAEOLOGISTS (UNIVERSITY OF MICHIGAN)

The second part of Spencer's approach, which he terms the *gradualist* position, clearly recognizes the historical, contextual dimension. Systemic pressures, though not discounted, are balanced against the realization that all cultural events take place as a result of particular individuals' decisions.

That is, although humans have always themselves interacted with a natural environment, this interaction has been heavily conditioned by the culture they brought with them: their beliefs, cosmologies, ideologies, customs, and traditions. This relationship had a prior history, shaped partly by human decisions and partly by factors entirely out of the control of the human actors.

Human decisions, more than likely, did not attempt to overthrow the system (in revolutionary fashion). Instead, most actors operated on the basis of enlightened, if short-term, self-interest; the consequences of their decisions were not always fully realized until much later.

Sometimes, significant changes originated within the system, producing problems that the actors had to resolve. But sometimes, change is initiated by the actors operating in their own self-interest. This middle-ground approach emphasizes the diachronic interplay of system and actor.

This "dual" neo-evolutionary approach attempts to combine the *historical* with the *comparative,* to define a common ground between history and evolution. Only time will show whether this modification to neo-evolutionism is going to bear theoretical fruit.

The neo-evolutionist perspective in anthropology . . . is neither dead nor seriously ailing; with appropriate modifications it can continue to enhance our understanding of the development of complex human societies.

CHARLES SPENCER, ARCHAEOLOGIST (AMERICAN MUSEUM OF NATURAL HISTORY)

SUMMARY Although Charles Darwin did not actually use the term *evolution* in his revolutionary work *On the Origin of Species,* the term *evolutionary theory* will forever be associated with his name. Darwin not only supplied the world of science with a coherent rationale for the rich diversity of life, but he also inadvertently provided his Euroamerican audience with a scientific rationale for the then-prevalent belief in racial inequality. So-called *social Darwinists* argued that people, like all other organisms, compete for survival and hence success in life. Social Darwinism suggested that human progress depends on competition, and, in the nineteenth century, this theory was used to justify global imperialism, racism, and the excesses of capitalism. Social Darwinists also argued that human societies varied in their "evolutionary" status from highly evolved groups (such as Europeans) to those who differed only slightly from the advanced apes. In this view, less civilized people were also less capable intellectually and emotionally.

This is the climate in which early anthropology matured. Lewis Henry Morgan devised a *unilinear* scheme of cultural evolution that created a sort of "evolutionary ladder," with both contemporary and ancient societies arrayed along it vertically. Morgan's bottom rung exemplified "savagery"—the primeval, rudimentary, and primitive. The top of evolution's ladder was reserved for various "advanced" societies, with the uppermost rung occupied by modern Western civilization, particularly that of western Europe.

The early-twentieth-century anthropological world turned against this *ethnocentric* notion of progress (and its distinct racial overtones). Franz Boas and his students rejected cultural evolution as a worthwhile way to study the human condition. The Boasian program called for *cultural relativism,* which questioned the existence of any universal standard by which to judge either the degree of development or intrinsic worth of different cultures.

Archaeology's processual agenda, with its emphasis on adaptive processes, brought back an interest in evolutionary processes by focusing on the degree of regularity in human behavior. The so-called neo-evolutionary perspective views *hunting and gathering bands* as the least complex of human societies. With the advent of agriculture came *autonomous village societies,* characterized by larger and more sedentary settlements. A third social form, *rank society,* at times evolved from autonomous villages, in which the egalitarian ethic gives way to the belief that individuals are inherently unequal at birth.

In some ranked societies, smaller villages were subject to the powerful, hereditary leadership of the larger, stronger communities. These societies—large-scale ranked societies with loss of village autonomy—are called *chiefdoms.* Powerful chiefs could bring thousands of people under their control. Warfare between rival chiefdoms was distinctly unpleasant, typically involving torture, mutilation, human sacrifice, and the taking of human trophy skulls.

Under certain conditions, *archaic states* evolved from competing chiefdoms, creating centralized political systems, with a virtual monopoly on the power to coerce. Most archaic states operated as kingdoms, characterized by a strong and centralized government with a professional bureaucratic ruling class. Neo-evolutionism attempts to explain the processes behind the development of these successive sociocultural levels, from band through archaic state.

Critics of neo-evolutionism abound, raising numerous objections, including that the theory relies too heavily on ecological determinism and simplistic typologies of evolutionary stages, ignores internal social differentiation, and denies the role of the individual. Postprocessual critics argue that neo-evolutionism artificially separates history from evolution.

At present, a middle ground may be emerging through explicit recognition of two distinct pathways of cultural change, one toward the general (and hence the comparative) and the other toward the specific analysis of context (and hence ultimately to the unique). This "dual" neo-evolutionary approach attempts to combine the *historical* with the *comparative,* to define a common ground between history and evolution. Only time will show whether this modification to neo-evolutionism is going to bear theoretical fruit.

Chapter 16

Archaeology of the Human Mind: Some Cognitive Approaches

It is only when we make assumptions about the subjective meanings in the minds of people long dead that we begin to do archaeology.

IAN HODDER, ARCHAEOLOGIST (CAMBRIDGE UNIVERSITY)

Humanists must cease thinking that ecology dehumanizes history, and ecologists must cease to regard art, religion, and ideology as mere "epiphenomena" without causal significance. In an ecosystem approach to the analysis of human societies, everything which transmits information is within the province of ecology.

KENT FLANNERY, ARCHAEOLOGIST (UNIVERSITY OF MICHIGAN)

The problem is that past ideas are represented as such through symbols, which are by definition arbitrary with respect to their referents. . . . For prehistory where no such bilinguals (as in ethnography or historical archaeology) exist, how are the symbols in the archaeological text to be read?

ANTONIO GILMAN, PREHISTORIAN (CALIFORNIA STATE UNIVERSITY, NORTHRIDGE)

PREVIEW In recent years, a so-called *cognitive revolution* has swept across Americanist archaeology. Concerned with defining an "archaeology of the human mind," cognitive archaeologists have pursued a broad agenda, ranging from relatively scientific to relatively humanistic. Regardless of the methodological approach, cognitive archaeologists all seek to find out about concepts and perceptions in the past through the archaeological record. Although a huge range of human behavior falls under this category, current directions in cognitive archaeology stress the importance of ritual and religion, symbolism and iconography, and the development of human consciousness.

In this chapter and the next, we explore the sweep of modern cognitive approaches to the archaeological record and provide several examples of ongoing directions of inquiry.

When processual archaeology gained prominence in the 1960s, it fostered numerous important studies of prehistoric demography and changing settlement patterns; the origins of agricultural and irrigation technologies; and the human use of soils, plants, and animals. These approaches relied heavily on scientific methods and rigor. The focus was materialistic, with processual archaeologists believing that subsistence behavior provided the infrastructure for the rest of the cultural system.

At the outset, archaeologists framing the processual agenda were fairly optimistic that *all aspects* of the human condition were available for archaeological investigation. This upbeat assessment differed markedly from previous attitudes that stressed the limitations of archaeology and focused mostly on writing cultural history.

Throughout the 1970s and 1980s, processual archaeology remained distinctly lukewarm, if not outright hostile, toward "cognitive" approaches to the past. To many, the realm of "ideas" was too shaky and the archaeological record of these things too ambiguous to be approached in an explicitly scientific, objective manner. Others put down the cognitive aspects of culture—such as religion and ideology—as "epiphenomena" (mere dependent variables deriving from the technological and economic basics). Cognitive elements were considered to be nonessential and second-rate avenues of study.

Lewis Binford, primary architect of the processual agenda, decisively distanced himself from any form of ideological or symbolic inquiry. If processual archaeologists were to attempt a cognitive approach, Binford quipped, "We would be *paleopsychologists,* and our training equips us poorly for this role."

The early appeal of cultural materialism to Americanist archaeology is fairly easy to understand. This is a research strategy that lays theoretical priority on just those things that archaeologists are most confident of recovering from their sites—evidence about past environments, technologies, ecosystems, and economies.

Not all archaeologists accepted these notions at the time. Some felt that such heavy-handed materialism dehumanized the past. They argued that archaeologists should try to include more of the values, ideas, beliefs, and cognitive processes that make us all human. A growing cadre of archaeologists turned to an ideational emphasis in their research, examining the active role of ideology in shaping the ultimate social, and even technological, structure of societies.

This point of view was well expressed by Kent Flannery, who felt that the processual agenda was too narrow. Human ecosystems, he said, are characterized by exchanges of matter, energy, and information.

The extreme paleoecological position emphasizes the matter–energy exchange and altogether ignores the informational aspects (art, religion, ritual, writing systems, and so on). Flannery accused the cultural ecologists and cultural materialists of focusing too heavily on technological and subsistence matters: "To read what the 'ecologists' write, one would often think that civilized people only ate, excreted and reproduced."

Arguing for a more inclusive "ecosystem approach," Flannery suggested that *all* information-processing mechanisms be included in the ecological whole. The problem here, of course, is that ritual, religion, cosmology, and iconography were traditionally considered almost the exclusive province of the ethnographer. Processual archaeology lacked any established, scientifically valid procedures for dealing with such intangible phenomena.

So-called ecological, materialist attitudes certainly slowed the growth of cognitive archaeology, but some scholars remained interested in the role of cognition. By the early 1980s, several archaeologists (some of them former members of the processual camp) began developing cognitive approaches as antidotes to the heavy-handed materialism of the time.

This group began developing a way to discover an interpretive system that would (1) not rigidly preassign chronological or causal priority to economy, demography, technology, and ecology and (2) incorporate internal societal diversity, human initiative and enterprise, and ideology in theories of cultural change.

In the box *The Peace Pipe as Ritual Weapon,* we present a now-classic study in early cognitive archaeology in which Robert Hall urged archaeologists to invest as much effort in studying the "cognitive core" as they had in assessing the environmental, technological, and ecological cores. Two decades have passed since Hall's admonishment and, as he suggested, Americanist archaeology has indeed shifted toward more ideational objectives.

If archaeologists are to think themselves into the past and regard the process of inference as a species of story-telling, we shall not only lose academic credibility as scientists, but also we shall bore the public who can always find more entertaining versions of the past than archaeologists are likely to produce.

NORMAN YOFFEE, ARCHAEOLOGIST (UNIVERSITY OF MICHIGAN), AND ANDREW SHERRATT, ARCHAEOLOGIST (ASHMOLEAN MUSEUM, UNIVERSITY OF OXFORD)

There is one thing stronger than all the armies in the world: and that is an idea whose time has come.

VICTOR HUGO (1802–1885), AUTHOR

Hopewell representation of a powerful bird talon. The raw material (mica) came from North Carolina, but the finished product was found in an Ohio burial mound.

The Peace Pipe as Ritual Weapon

Writing in the late 1970s, archaeologist Robert L. Hall accused his colleagues of *econo-think*—of placing undue emphasis on the changing tactics of technological adaptation at the expense of "what it may have been that prehistoric peoples found worthwhile to live for." Hall used the *calumet*—the peace pipe—to show how a cognitive approach could broaden the horizons of archaeological investigations.

Hopewell effigy pipes (Tremper Mound, Ohio).

Hall focused on *Hopewell*, North America's first Pan-Indian religion, stretching from Mississippi to Minnesota, and from Nebraska to Virginia. During Hopewell times (between about 200 B.C. and A.D. 500), native peoples, who probably spoke different languages, were drawn together by a unifying set of symbols and ideology. Raw materials and exotic artifacts symbolic of Hopewell ideology and religion were distributed throughout a huge trade network, known as the *Hopewell Interaction Sphere*.

The most famous kind of Hopewell artifact is the *platform pipe*, often ornamented with mammals, birds, or reptiles. Using locally available pipestone, Hopewell artists fashioned these pipes, which have a decorated cylindrical bowl resting upon a straight or curved base. Nobody is quite sure what was smoked in the pipes, because tobacco is not native to the area and there is little record of its use anywhere in eastern North America prior to European contact. But whatever the Hopewell people were smoking, archaeological evidence clearly demonstrates that the pipe ritual was a critical aspect of Hopewell ceremonial life. Hundreds of pipes were found in the so-called *Mound of the Pipes* at Mound City, near Chillicothe, Ohio. Some think that this mound was a monument to a master carver of sacred pipes.

Hall argued that processual archaeologists spent so much time emphasizing economy and ecology that they entirely overlooked the symbolic and "affective" qualities of these unforgettable Hopewellian artifacts. What do they have to tell us?

Suppose we ask some questions that don't relate to economics and demography? Why, for instance, does the "peace pipe" used historically to establish friendly contact almost always take the form of a weapon? Why did the famous Hopewell pipes take the form they did?

To explore such ideational questions, Hall began with a model familiar to all. He reasoned that everyone engages in certain culturally dictated customs whose exact meaning and origin may be lost in time. For example, the rite of "toasting" originally was the sloshing and spilling together of two persons' drinks to reduce the possibility that one planned to poison the other. But how many of us who have toasted friends realize the origin of the custom? Or saluting, a custom that stems from the act of raising visors on armored helmets in order to expose the faces of the two persons encountering each other. Hall suggested that although the original function of the gestures lost their practical significance, the acts survive as elements of etiquette or protocol.

He decided to apply similar reasoning to the Hopewell platform pipes. Throughout historic times in the eastern United States, Indian tribes observed the custom of smoking a sacred tribal pipe. When the pipe was present, violence was absolutely ruled out. Moreover, the so-called peace pipe (the calumet) usually was made in a distinctive, weaponlike form. The Pawnee peace pipe, for instance, looked like an arrow. In fact, the Osage word for *calumet* translated as "arrowshaft." Hall suggested that the weaponlike appearance resulted from a specific ceremonial custom. Could it be that, at least during the period of European contact, the peace pipe symbolized a *ritual weapon*?

Hall then extended his hunch back into ancient Hopewell times (between about 1,500 and 2,200 years ago). Suppose that the distinctive Hopewell platform pipes were also ritual weapons—but made before these people knew of the bow and arrow. At that time, the most common Hopewell weapon was the *atlatl* (the spear thrower—discussed in Chapter 10).

Hall suggested that the distinctive Hopewell platform pipe symbolically represented a flat atlatl, decorated with an effigy spur. Hall observed that the animal on the bowl was almost always carved precisely where an atlatl spur would be. And the curvature of the platform seemed to correspond to the curvature on the atlatl.

These correspondences led Hall to conclude: "I see the Hopewell platform pipe as the archaeologically visible part of a transformed ritual atlatl, a symbolic weapon which in Middle Woodland times probably had some of the same functions as the calumet of historic times, itself a ritual arrow."

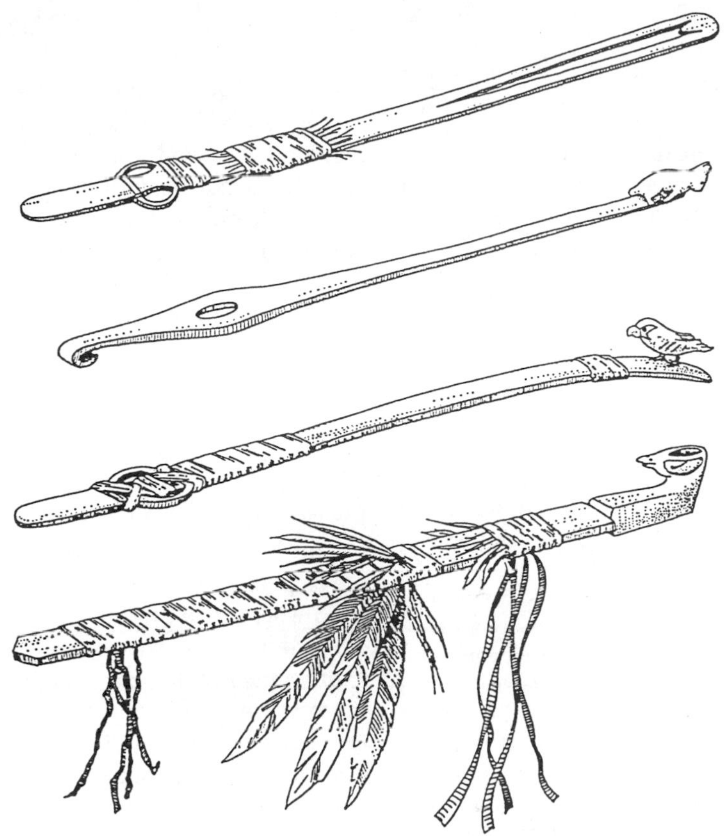

Some representations of atlatls in aboriginal North American art.

Interesting suggestion. But Hall went on to propose that the importance of the Hopewell pipe might well extend beyond mere symbolism—that the platform pipe was not merely *one of many* items exchanged between groups, but that "it may have been part of the very mechanism of exchange." And here is the potential contribution of Hall's work.

Adaptively oriented research on eastern United States prehistory has conventionally defined the Hopewell Interaction Sphere primarily in economic and environmental terms. Perhaps, by maintaining relationships between large-scale networks of ritual trading partners, far-flung Hopewell communities could have joined economic forces, looking to one another for support in lean years of drought or crop failure.

Hall suggested that a shifting away from strictly materialistic thinking—toward a new, cognitive approach—could generate a broader understanding of the Hopewell lifeway. Reasoning from historically recorded Native American analogies, Hall contended that peace pipe ceremonialism served to mediate interaction over a vast central part of the United States and Canada. Hall was not suggesting that researchers ignore the economic and political ramifications of such interaction, but he did urge archaeologists to also consider the symbolic details of Hopewellian exchange. He argued that through "peace pipe diplomacy," the Hopewell Interaction Sphere tended to reduce regional differences and promote friendly contact and communication between discrete groups.

Contemporary Approaches in Cognitive Archaeology

Cognitive archaeology: The study of all those aspects of ancient culture that are the product of the human mind: the perception, description, and classification of the universe; the nature of the supernatural; the principles, philosophies, ethics, and values by which human societies are governed; the ways in which aspects of the world, the supernatural, or human values are conveyed in art.

Cosmology: The study of the origin, large-scale structure, and future of the universe. A cosmological explanation demonstrates how the universe developed—both the totality and its constituent parts—and also what principles keep it together.

The term *cognition* refers to the act or process of knowing. Taken in its widest sense, cognition includes sensation, perception, conception, memory, reasoning, judgment, and imagination. **Cognitive archaeology**—what many would call "the archaeology of the mind"—involves the study of material remains in order to learn about religion and belief systems, symbolism and iconography, and the origins and development of human consciousness. Following the lead of Kent Flannery and Joyce Marcus, we will divide the subject matter of cognitive archaeology into four primary areas, each a product of the human mind: cosmology, religion, ideology, and iconography. Let us briefly explore each arena.

Cosmology

Every society wants to understand how its universe—its *cosmos*—works. **Cosmology** is the study of the universe as a whole—how it originated and developed, how the various parts fit together and what laws they obey, plus a glimpse at what the future of the universe holds.

We in the Western world have an ample paper trail to help us trace our evolving cosmological beliefs. Six thousand years ago, the ancients in Mesopotamia believed that the earth was at the center of the universe, with the heavenly bodies moving around it. The Greek philosopher Aristotle endorsed this notion, suggesting that the stars moved about the earth on rotating crystalline spheres.

Then, in the sixteenth century A.D., the Western world came to accept a cosmological system in which planets (including the earth) revolve in circular orbits around the sun. Today, our shared cosmology, in the form of the so-called Big Bang Theory, suggests that the universe was created in a gigantic explosion, sometime between 7 billion and 20 billion years ago.

Cognitive archaeology attempts to combine traditional analysis of past subsistence and settlement patterns with an understanding of cosmologies that operated in extinct, nonliterate societies. As we will see here and elsewhere, such cognitive approaches are generally most fruitful when the strictly archaeological evidence can be heavily augmented by relevant ethnographic and/or ethnohistoric information.

Using words to describe magic is like using a screwdriver to cut roast beef.

TOM ROBBINS, AUTHOR

Ritual and Religion

It is not likely that we will be able to "reconstruct" ancient cosmologies for . . . cultures based solely on an examination of their plant and animal remains.

KENT FLANNERY AND JOYCE MARCUS, ARCHAEOLOGISTS (UNIVERSITY OF MICHIGAN)

Broadly speaking, *religion* is a specific set of beliefs based on one's ultimate relation to the supernatural. Religion is a society's mechanism for relating supernatural phenomena to the everyday world—a set of rituals, rationalized by cosmology, that enlists supernatural powers for the purpose of achieving or preventing transformations of state in humans and nature.

Religion is universal because of the ubiquitous cultural desire to influence change in people and nature. Sometimes the objective is to effect the quickest possible transformation; sometimes the goal is to prevent an undesired change from occurring. The primary objective of religious behavior is to influence the course of this change by appeal to a supernatural power, a power quite separate from that of the muscles, the brain, or the elements of nature.

Religious beliefs are manifested in everyday life in a "program of ritual," a succession of discrete events, such as prayer, music, feasting, sacrifice, and taboos. These stereotyped sequences are the cultural mechanisms by which individuals attempt to intercede with the supernatural. It is fair to say that ritual is the fundamental religious act.

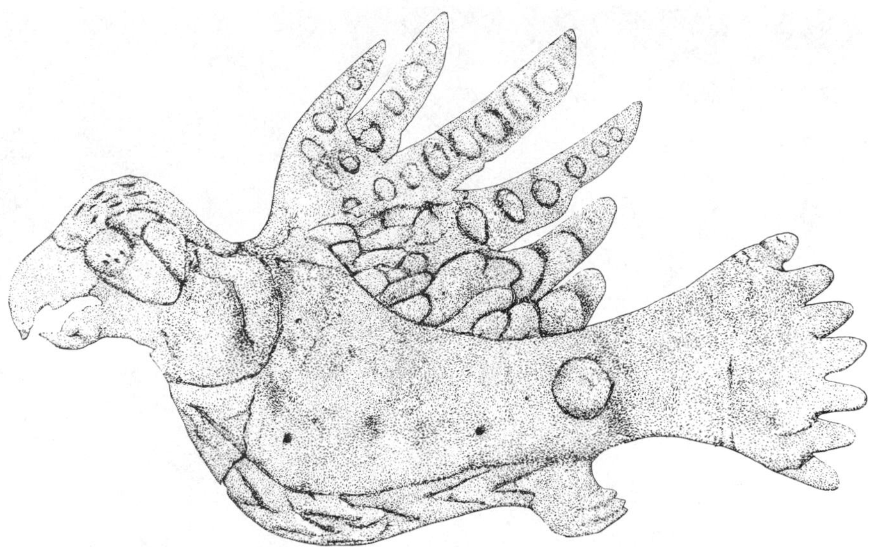

This hammered copper hawk accompanied a member of the Hopewell elite to the afterlife.

This particular definition of religion is especially relevant to archaeology because of its emphasis on ritual and its de-emphasis of the overall cosmology. Most rituals, after all, are closely related to material culture and, as such, are often represented in the archaeological record. Cosmology is quite difficult to define without recourse to documentary evidence. The analysis of past ritual behavior is thus archaeology's major contribution to the study of religion.

Ideology

Ideology is defined as a systematic body of concepts and beliefs—often political in nature—about human life or culture. Communism is an ideology, as are democracy and fascism. Ideology differs from religion because it addresses society and politics (although they certainly can overlap).

We may not be able to establish what *people thought; we can aspire to learn* how *they thought.*

Colin Renfrew, Archaeologist (Cambridge University)

The term *ideology* is used here in two distinct senses. Previously, we have discussed "ideology" in terms of the research strategy of cultural materialism (Chapter 3). In this sense, religion and ideology were viewed as "epiphenomena"—cultural add-ons with little long-term explanatory value.

Another, rather different use of "ideology" derives from the writings of Karl Marx, who believed that ideologies were counterfeit systems of political, social, and moral concepts both invented and perpetuated by ruling classes out of self-interest. In modern usage, ideology has come to carry with it this pejorative meaning: Adherents to any particular sociopolitical system are free to dismiss competing arguments as "ideologically based" (that is, false because they reflect only the ideological biases of the opponent, rather than a true state of affairs). Because this tactic can be used to argue against *any and every* ideology, the clash of modern ideologies has become strident and hot-headed, more closely resembling propaganda than rational argument.

In Chapter 18, we will explore the archaeology of ideology in some detail, with specific reference to the interrelationships of capitalism, power, and

Spear-thrower with bison licking its flank, sculpted of reindeer antler.

ideology in early Anglo-American society.

Iconography

The term *iconography* refers to the study of how people use art forms to represent their religious, political, ideological, or cosmological beliefs. Iconographic analysis covers a broad range from well-known complex systems—such as Egyptian hieroglyphs and Mayan inscriptions—to cryptic incisions on ancient stone and bone artifacts.

In the next two sections of this chapter, we will see how iconographic studies explore two very different kinds of symbolic data. We begin with iconographic research on the La Marche antler, a 14,000- to 15,000-year-old engraved artifact from the European Upper Paleolithic period, which may (or may not) contain evidence relevant to the origins of later formal systems, such as writing, arithmetic, and true calendrics.

Then we turn to the complex iconography of the Chavín horizon, earliest of the distinctive Andean civilizations of South America. In the preceding chapter, we explored some of the major theories about the evolution of state-level sociopolitical organization. Here, we examine the critical importance of Chavín iconography and cosmology in the evolution of the Andean state.

Seeking the Origins of Iconography

The problem is that the archaeologist has no direct access to the thoughts of the past, while social scientists disagree quite profoundly about the nature of thought as exhibited in the modern world.

Bruce Trigger, Archaeologist (McGill University)

Since about 1865, a steady flood of carved and incised fragments of bone and antler have been recovered from various Old World sites. Such so-called *mobiliary* artifacts seem to be a portable adjunct to the spectacular Ice Age art images and signs that adorn the walls of the ancient "sanctuary" caves in France and Spain.

For more than a century, archaeologists have attempted to ascribe meaning to the mysterious ancient engravings: counts of prey animals killed, systems of symbolic notation, mathematical conceptions of the cosmos, implied numbering system, and mnemonic support for recitations.

For the past quarter century, Alexander Marshack has examined thousands of these objects—through the lens of a binocular microscope. In his influential book *The Roots of Civilization,* Marshack discusses how his research began as a relatively straightforward search for the origins of scientific thought. To his surprise, Marshack found that near scientific thinking could be traced only to early agricultural societies, and then the trail disappeared. Largely because he felt that "something was missing," Marshack began his attempt to trace the origins of rational "processual" observations and thought earlier in time. Eventually, this quest led Marshack to personally study nearly the entire body of engraved, symbolic materials from the **Upper Paleolithic,** including the "signs" and images of animals and humans. In so doing, he pioneered a method for studying and seeking meaning in the ancient inscribed artifacts.

Upper Paleolithic: The last major division of the Old World Paleolithic, beginning about 40,000 years ago and lasting until the end of the Pleistocene (ca. 10,000 years ago). This is the period during which modern humans replaced the Neanderthals.

Magdalenian: The last major culture of the European Upper Paleolithic period (ca. 16,000–10,000 B.C.); named after the rock shelter La Madeleine, in southwestern France. Magdalenian artisans crafted intricately carved tools of reindeer bone and antler; this was also the period during which Upper Paleolithic cave art in France and Spain reached its zenith.

The La Marche Antler Under the 'Scope

Marshack's approach can be demonstrated by his analysis of an incised antler from the Upper Paleolithic site of La Marche in central France. Several hundred stone and bone artifacts were excavated here in 1937 and 1938. Most of the incised materials came from the **Magdalenian** levels, dating approximately 13,000–12,000 B.C. One of the visually less exciting pieces is a discolored, deteriorated antler fragment engraved with a series of faint marks and lines.

Three views of the La Marche antler. Note the faint, yet distinctive engravings on all sides.

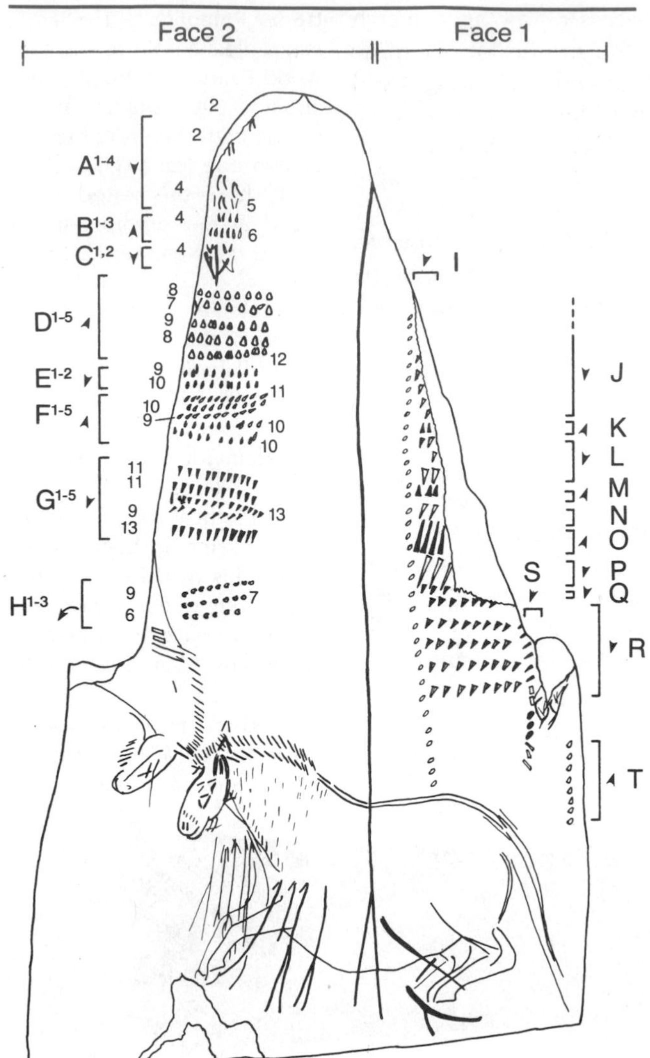

Marshack's schematic analysis of all intentional marks on both faces of the La Marche antler. Note that the engravings are broken down into sets, that several different engraving points were used, and that the totals of marks for each set have been included. Also shown are the two horses, with later engraved additions.

Early in his research, Marshack used low-power microscopy to analyze the La Marche antler. His study turned up an unsuspected complexity. Apparently, the antler had initially been fashioned as a kind of tool for straightening spear shafts. At some point, it broke and was reshaped into a flaker for finishing or resharpening stone tools.

But the functional uses for this antler tool were less interesting than the intricate engravings, barely visible on its surface. Look at the schematic rendition of the La Marche antler, particularly the two horses carved near the bottom. The unbroken horse seems to represent a pregnant mare with a rounded belly. Marshack's microscopic study suggested that this mare had three eyes, three ears, a second mane, and two backs. What's going on here?

Marshack's microscopic technique is similar to the ballistic analysis used in law enforcement. Each minute scratch is examined to determine the nature of the tool that performed the carving, and the sequence in which the marks were made. Some tools were relatively flat and blunt, and others made a deeper, more V-shaped groove. The analysis suggested that each of the mare's three ears was carved by a different stone point, presumably at different times.

The series of tiny marks covering the rest of the La Marche antler as an accumulation of sets of marks comprise a sequence of engraving that Marshack thinks is neither random nor decorative but, rather, a complex form of notation. Row H, for instance, has been inscribed by a cutting edge that flares near the top, creating an irregular angle in cross section. The marks were incised by a turning or twisting stroke, with the set angled about 15° from the baseline of the antler. By contrast, the engravings immediately above Row H are perpendicular to the axis of the antler and were each made by a single downward stroke.

Marshack's microscopic analysis suggested that numerous distinctive tool tips were used to engrave the various sets and that sometimes the antler was turned 180° to mark neighboring sets. The internal complexity of the marking suggests that the sets were accumulated through time. The two surfaces were probably carved at different times yet almost certainly within the same cultural context.

An Ancient Lunar Calendar?

But what do such ordered accumulations of marks mean? A number of hypotheses have been considered to explain engravings such as those on the

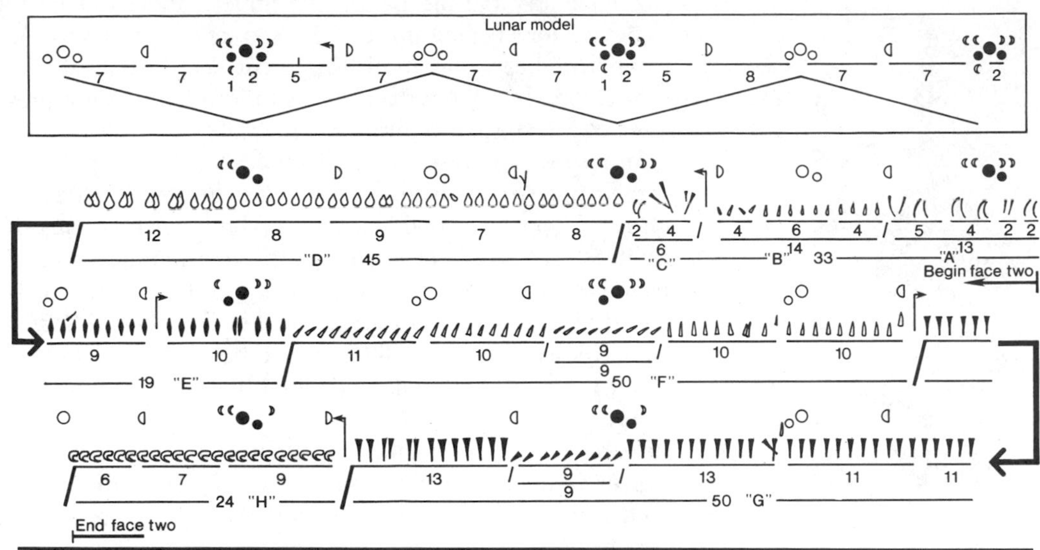

Marshack's lunar "test" of the La Marche engravings. This chart begins at the upper right and proceeds sequentially in alternative directions along each line, ending at the bottom left. One space in each 2 months (the right-angle arrow) represents zero, providing the proper total of 59 marks for 2 months in a model scaled to 60. The lettered sets, subsets, and cue marks are indicated, along with the astronomically correct observation point. The differences in the engraved points are schematically rendered.

La Marche antler. One investigator suggested that the marks are hunting tallies, and another saw a recurrent use of the number 7, a suggested early ritual number.

Marshack proposes that the marks could be recording the passage of time by observations of the moon, and he tested the La Marche marks against a lunar model. Beginning with Block A in the upper right corner, the counts are arranged sequentially, as indicated by microscopic analysis, with an overlay of modern astronomic observations. The darkened circles represent invisibility, and the white circles represent the full moon.

The fit with the lunar model was surprisingly close. Of 23 subsets of marks observable on the single face of the La Marche antler, only four (E^2, F^2, $G^{1,2}$) fail to begin or end around normal observational phases of the moon. Of these, three subsets correspond to the difficult period of the crescents and new moon, when precise observation is difficult. According to this interpretation, the marks cover a span of seven and a half months.

But why, some 14,000 years ago, would Magdalenian hunter-gatherers care about observing and recording the periodicities of the moon? Looking at ethnographic data from a range of Native American and Siberian cultures, Marshack notes that in many cases, **shamans** maintained lunar (or "month" records) of one form or another. Months were named according to their seasonal and regional significance, triggering appropriate ritual or economic responses. Marshack believes that the Upper Paleolithic notations, such as those on the La Marche antler, were also maintained by ritual specialists. If the La Marche notations began with the thaw in late March, then the notation would have ended in mid-November, at approximately the time of the first freeze or snow. Such a sequence of marking can be maintained without complex arithmetic. Marshack suggests that both the accumulation of sets and the reuse of animals on the La Marche antler argue for a "scheduled," "time-factored" cultural year, even in Upper Paleolithic times. He has supported this argument by studies of the seasonal character of many Magdalenian animal depictions.

Shaman: One who has the power to contact the spirit world through trance, possession, or visions. On the basis of this ability, the shaman invokes, manipulates, or coerces the power of the spirits for socially recognized ends—both good and ill.

Alexander Marshack.

Marshack contends that the La Marche antler could have been used as a notational device for keeping track of the sequences of moons. As we will see, this "lunar hypothesis" has received a great deal of critical attention by archaeologists. In one sense, however, this is unfortunate, as it represents but a single aspect of Marshack's innovative research.

At a different level of abstraction, Marshack is also concerned with understanding the cognitive processes and strategies involved in the making and use of all forms of Upper Paleolithic imagery. The lunar notations–if, in fact, that is what they are–represent a prewriting, prearithmetic symbol system that was related to other modes of symbolizing in these cultures. The same cultures created an elaborate iconography in the French and Spanish caves, yet these paintings involved very different symbol systems. Doubtless, there were also other forms of symboling and ritual that have not been preserved archaeologically.

Marshack thinks that the cognitive strategies utilized on the La Marche (and on other early nonarithmetical) notations differ from the records found in later settled farming villages. He maintains that the Upper Paleolithic engravings were made and used by the engraver alone as an early scheduling device. As later cultures became increasingly complex, more formal systems of record-keeping developed, leading finally to the development of true writing for agricultural, temple, and commercial uses.

Thus, at one level, Marshack is examining symbolic artifacts to determine their function within a specific cultural setting. Simultaneously, Marshack raises profound questions concerning the evolution of human cognitive and intellectual capacity. Surely an evolving notational system that spans some 25,000 years implies something about the developing cognitive powers of the people who used it. Marshack has also examined artifacts made by Neanderthals to determine whether the symbolic behaviors of those populations imply that they had language. Marshack's research has explored the extremely variable and complex range of *Homo sapiens'* capacity for art and symbol, with special emphasis on the evolution of intelligence and language.

A Call for Middle-Range Controls

When first published, nobody knew what to do with Marshack's research. He was asking new questions, generating new data, and offering new interpretations. Reactions were characteristically mixed. Many archaeologists were skeptical, suggesting that Marshack had "gone beyond the data," ignored "all likely alternative explanations," and failed to present the data necessary to support his hypotheses. But others lauded Marshack's analytical approach, using such terms as "significant breakthrough" and "breaking new ground." One investigator raved that Marshack "has come as close as any archaeologist ever to reading the mind of ancient man." Today, many would credit Marshack with an innovative effort in establishing the field of cognitive archaeology.

Regardless of individual opinion, many recognized the potential of this new analytical technique, and it was clear that Marshack had opened up an entirely new direction in cognitive archaeology. Several follow-up studies soon appeared.

As it turned out, the first of these occurred by accident. Randall White, an archaeologist at New York University, was conducting experiments with *burins,* chisel-ended stone tools common in both European and North American assemblages. White manufactured a sample of 25 burins, then conducted use-wear experimentation on fresh bone and sandstone cobbles. After examining the edge damage on the burins–the main reason for the experiment–White made a curious discovery. Quite by accident, when preparing some of the worked bone surfaces for photography, he discovered that the various burin experiments had produced some characteristic incisions on the bone. When used for scraping, the burins produced a flat, shallow, U-shaped groove; when the corner of the burin was offset and used for scraping, a characteristic V-shaped groove resulted.

Thinking that Marshack's three-part subdivision of incisions "was too good to be true," White compared his results with photomicrographs published by Marshack, to see how closely the experimental incisions compared with examples from Paleolithic portable art (like the La Marche antler). The fit was precise. White's experiments seemed to contradict Marshack's hypothesis that different observable cross sections must have been produced by different tools: White produced three characteristic cross sections with the same burin–simply held three different ways. White's burin study raised a major question about the validity of Marshack's method of analysis.

As we know from the previous chapter, modern archaeologists are increasingly concerned with assessing the degree to which their own biases impact the archaeological data they collect. White has suggested that Marshack's analytical method is essentially "internal," dependent upon unexplicit, nonreplicable criteria. How, for example, does Marshack distinguish actual, intended notation from mere decoration? Does the distinction between notation and decoration have any validity outside our own Western tradition? Marshack has argued that such discriminations are analytically apparent. White, however, has raised the now-familiar point that construction of meaning is very much a cultural matter.

That is, what if Marshack's "objective" method of microscopic analysis isn't so objective after all? Marshack expresses great confidence in his ability to identify human-made markings–defining the direction of tool movement, possible changes in tool tips, shifts in orientation of the worked object, superposition of one incision over another, and the direction and sequence of engraving–all by relying on the microscopic observation of archaeological marks. He also believes he can distinguish and discount simple random, careless, and meaningless markings from intentional incisions.

White decries Marshack's "purity of observation. For him the processes by which the marks were created are self-evident. . . . We are led to believe that Marshack's photos are indisputable depictions of reality when in fact they are *visual arguments* which can be countered by other visual arguments." White believes that different results can be produced by varying lighting conditions, magnification, and scale.

When questioned about his criteria for ascertaining notation and problems that others have had in reproducing his results, Marshack has responded that White's own microscopy and "visual arguments" are often seriously flawed even when he is making "cross-sectional" comparisons, and that

[Marshack] maintains the view that what he sees under the microscope is somehow an objective reality, never once flinching in, for example, identifying schematic images as female vulvas, or ibex heads, or fish.

RANDALL WHITE, ARCHAEOLOGIST (NEW YORK UNIVERSITY)

A priori argument: A logical assertion relating to or derived by reasoning from self-evident propositions or personal experience.

White's symboling arguments have been made largely **a priori**—before he had adequately studied the variability and complexity of the Upper Paleolithic engraving traditions.

This is basically a problem of *middle-range theory*—of linking observable archaeological data with the relevant human behavior that produced them. In Chapter 3, we discussed several experimental approaches involved in middle-level theory building. Archaeologists sometimes experimentally manufacture their own stone tools, studying how specific stoneworking techniques are translated into specific archaeologically observable evidence (such as flaking scars, breakage patterns, and leftover flake byproducts). Experimental archaeologists experiment with techniques of pottery manufacture, house construction, hunting, fishing, and plant collection, to name just a few. Remember from Chapter 10 that some of the better middle-level research involves "blind" experiments to test both the accuracy and the repeatability of archaeological technique.

Obviously there can be no complete objectivity here. To think that it can be achieved is to fool one's self, and to attempt to achieve it is to destroy a greater truth.

FREDERICA DE LAGUNA, ARCHAEOLOGIST (BRYN MAWR UNIVERSITY)

White suggests that similar rigor is necessary to lend credibility to Marshack's results. When he distinguishes human-produced marks from "natural" scratches (such as carnivore or rodent gnawing), or identifies marks made by different tool points, Marshack's inferences should be supported by a body of middle-range theory—an external understanding of how differing tools, techniques, raw materials, tool breakage patterns, and artifact surfaces affect the outcome. As we see later, White and others have recently designed a series of experiments to create bridging theory between observations and interpretation.

The La Marche Antler Revisited

Francesco d'Errico, a researcher now at the University of Bordeaux (France), has expressed similar reservations about Marshack's results, particularly his failure to describe diagnostic criteria for the microscopic analysis and the absence of replication experiments.

Attempting to provide such experimental controls and to replicate Marshack's earlier results, d'Errico recently returned to the La Marche antler. To establish a systematic protocol, d'Errico made rubber molds of critical areas of the artifact and also conducted several new experiments. Numerous experimental marks were made on various species of antler, each series with a different tool. Some marks were made on dry antler, others on water-soaked antler. Fracturing of the tool tips was noted.

The various experimental tool tips and replicated incisions were cast in rubber molds, which were then used to produce positive resin replicas that could be examined microscopically. The resulting images were computerized into density profile plots for both tools and incised lines. In this way, the experimental results could be compared with the original La Marche engravings by means of image-analysis equipment. Computerization permitted overlaying and enhancement to define continuities and changes in tool tips. Changes of tool tip and direction of working were recalculated on the basis of the experimental evidence. The idea was to use sophisticated imaging technology to eliminate investigator bias and inconsistency.

This experimentally based, painstaking analysis produced a second, independent "reading" of the various incisions on the La Marche antler. Significantly, a number of differences emerged between the analyses by Marshack and d'Errico. Sometimes, d'Errico discounted Marshack's marks as natural depressions. Other marks, previously noted as separate, were combined into a single mark. Still others were excluded as postdepositional marking or as counting errors in the earlier analysis. D'Errico concluded that the marks on the La Marche antler could have been produced by no more than seven or eight tool points (a number considerably lower than Marshack's estimate).

As in White's experiments, d'Errico's analysis questions Marshack's key assumption that such fine incising causes no appreciable wear or damage to the engraving tool. Experiments show that, particularly on dry antler, the tool breaks rather frequently. Ancillary experimental evidence further suggests that the La Marche antler may have been soaked to minimize tool breakage.

To summarize, Marshack's interpretation of the La Marche antler as a lunar record hinges on two important steps: (1) recognizing numerous tool changes among the various sets of marks (interpreted as the result of accumulations over different time spans) and (2) testing the accumulation of sets against a lunar model. D'Errico's new analysis challenges both assumptions, suggesting that an accumulation of marks over a period of time did not play a major role on the La Marche antler. Still, this conclusion does not directly preclude the possibility that the engraving represents a lunar notation. But if it did, then it must have been planned beforehand because d'Errico's analysis indicates that the antler was probably engraved in a single session.

Marshack's measured response to this criticism is instructive. On the one hand, Marshack credits d'Errico with a major technological breakthrough in the study of ancient incised materials. There is every reason to believe that d'Errico's experimental mode of engraved cross-section analysis will be widely applied (and improved upon) in future research. It is an important step in minimizing the variability between observers in such purportedly "objective" analysis.

Marshack is far less generous in his appraisal of d'Errico's reinterpretation of what the La Marche antler really means. He points out that the La Marche antler falls within a highly variable, yet continuously developing tradition of Upper Paleolithic notation. And he faults d'Errico for his failure to take this variability and development into account.

At the level of technology and the development of technical "criteria" for the study of cross sections, d'Errico's research and his recent article represents major contributions. But technology is not science.

ALEXANDER MARSHACK, ARCHAEOLOGIST (HARVARD UNIVERSITY)

When d'Errico's recounting of the La Marche accumulations failed to turn up the number 28, he rejected the notion that lunar months (of supposedly 28 days each) were being counted. Marshack responds that "I have never argued that an observational lunar notation required groups of 28, or precision in the recording of periods."

Rather than focusing on an arithmetical 28-day lunar month, Marshack argues that an observational lunar notation is not arithmetical. Instead, he suggests that only through the analysis of long sequential accumulations of sets can one test for observational correlations: The number 28 might *never* occur, but in long sequences a pattern of lunar observation would be made apparent.

To show this is true, Marshack uses d'Errico's revised counts (those obtained using engraved cross-section analysis) to show that just such a long-term sequence is evident on the La Marche antler. In his original analysis, Marshack had concluded that his counts indicated a notation for seven and a half lunar months; d'Errico's new counts of 212 marks show the period to be almost precisely seven lunar months: 212/29.5=7.18 months. Thus, Marshack argues, d'Errico's method provides even stronger support for a long-term lunar record than did his own original analysis.

We are drowning in information but starved for knowledge.

JOHN NAISBITT

Without question, d'Errico's method improves upon and "corrects" counts obtained by Marshack a quarter of a century earlier. But the meaning of the markings and the viability of the lunar hypothesis (even though the La Marche markings appear to be a notation) remains very much an open question—dependent upon additional testing and verification on other Upper Paleolithic examples. As Marshack puts it, it is clear "that study of the La Marche antler is not finished. It will have again to be 'revisited.' "

Exploring Ancient Chavín Cosmology

MYTHOLOGY, n. *The body of a primitive people's beliefs concerning its origin, early history, heroes, deities and so forth, as distinguished from the true accounts which it invents later.*

AMBROSE BIERCE (1842–1914?), JOURNALIST AND WRITER

The Chavín horizon of the central Andes has already figured twice in this text. In Chapter 11, we discussed 12,000 fragments of food bones recovered from excavations at Chavín de Huántar. Then, in Chapter 12, we saw how carbon isotope analysis could determine the degree of maize dependence of both human and animal populations living at this same site. Both studies employed a fairly conventional, materialistic perspective to flesh out ancient patterns of Andean settlement and subsistence, sometimes in great detail.

But to most archaeologists, the term *Chavín* conjures up more than llama bones and maize kernels. Chavín is commonly considered to be Peru's first highland civilization because of its stratified socioeconomic organization and achievements in metallurgy, weaving, monumental architecture, irrigation systems, and stone sculpture. For the first time, ancient Peru was united by a shared religion and technology. Chavín was the first great Andean civilization.

Chavín also left a lasting legacy in Andean ideology. Somehow the iconography evident at Chavín de Huántar established the tone of subsequent central Andean cosmology. All deities of the succeeding generations in the central Andes looked more or less like the god in the temple at Chavín de Huántar.

This decidedly ideational view differs sharply from the materialistic approaches employed earlier in discussing the bones from Chavín de Huántar. In this section, we will explore the nature of Chavín cosmology, looking in particular at the distinctive Chavín iconography that seems to have played a key role in the spread of civilization throughout the central Andes.

Every culture has devised its own way of responding to the riddle of the Cosmos. . . . There are many different ways of being human.

CARL SAGAN (1934–1996), ASTRONOMER

Seeking the Catalyst of Chavin Civilization

In Chapter 15, we considered several theories designed to explain the origins of the archaic state. Our attempt was to illustrate the diversity in opinion about this controversial subject. No single set of prior conditions or prime movers seems to explain the origin of the state in all its manifestations.

Archaeologist Richard Burger has explored many of the same models in an attempt to understand why Chavín civilization arose where and when it did, and why it was so monumentally successful in spreading across the central Andes in a relatively short period of time. Here, we recap his findings.

Wittfogel's "irrigation" hypothesis

Karl Wittfogel, you will remember, argued that state-level bureaucracies commonly arose as an integral part of agricultural irrigation management. Extensive supervision was required to coordinate and direct the operation of local canal systems. This in turn led to a concentration of administrative power to control and exploit the farming peasantry. In this view, the administration of irrigation systems paved the way for social stratification and centralized agriculture in arid lands.

Burger rejects this hypothesis for the Chavín. Irrigation systems in the central Andes, he says, were small-scale affairs, even after large, centralized states had arisen. Irrigation was a matter controlled at the community level, without the need for the irrigation bureaucracy required by the Wittfogel hypothesis.

Carneiro's "warfare and circumscription" hypothesis

Briefly stated, Robert Carneiro suggested that the state arose in areas of circumscribed population growth; after conflict occurred, the resulting class stratification and administrative needs led to state formation.

Although Carneiro used the Andean case to support his initial argument, Burger feels that sufficient archaeological evidence for warfare is lacking at major Chavín settlements. Whereas Burger grants that the processes described by Carneiro are important in other periods of Andean prehistory, he rejects the "warfare and circumscription" hypothesis as an explanation for state-level organization at Chavín de Huántar.

In fact, Burger rejects all the available materialistic, processual explanations for formation of the Chavín state. He argues instead that it was the power of cosmology and religion that accounted for the origins of Chavín civilization.

Head of a mythical Chavín priest, almost completely transformed into a feline state. The long strands of mucus running out of the nostrils suggest usage of hallucinogenic snuff.

Animal Symbolism in Chavín Iconography

Since its inception, the community of Chavín de Huántar depended on a range of highland animals, including wild deer and vicuña, plus llamas and guinea pigs. These were local beasts, probably encountered by local residents on a daily basis. Processual, materialist perspectives emphasize just these aspects of subsistence and settlement pattern at Chavín de Huántar.

The site has given its name to one of the Americas' most famous art styles—Chavín—generally thought to be the religious iconography of an expansive cult, once widespread throughout the central Andes. Symbols of the Chavín cult—derived from stone sculptures at Chavín de Huántar—were reproduced on locally made ceramics, textiles, goldwork, and stone. Some believe that Chavín art represents the pinnacle of Andean artistry.

The elaborate Chavín iconography, however, does not feature these commonplace local animals; rather, the Chavín style drew symbolic inspiration for its stylized fangs and talons, feathers and scales from the jaguar, harpy eagle, monkey, serpent, and cayman (alligator). These are all creatures native to the tropical north coast and rainforest, located several hundred miles to the east.

As Miller and Burger put it:

> The paradox of Chavín existence can . . . be seen as dividing itself along the classic lines of cultural materialistic vs. ideational views of culture. The cultural materialist examining only the fecal residue of Chavín behavior finds an emergent Andean agropastoral economy and a community filling its belly from the typical menu of highland food animals. The ideationalist, reading only the iconographic data, perceives an entirely different world at Chavín de Huántar, a cosmos inhabited by fearsome creatures entirely foreign to the daily lives of the Chavín farmer or artisan.

At first glance, all of this seems pretty obvious. After all, if you're going to myth-make about animals, do you pick something exotic and rarely seen, or do you worship something in the everyday stew pot?

Miller and Burger emphasize that the distinction between sacred and profane is not merely a matter of emphasis; it is absolute. The highland animals upon which the citizens of Chavín de Huántar depended for food and transport were *never* depicted in Chavín iconography. The locally available llama, vicuña, white-tailed deer, and the rest are entirely and conspicuously absent from the thousands of known temple sculptures, ceramics, and textiles that displayed the widespread Chavín style.

Instead, the supernaturals were imported from afar, from the distant tropical rainforest:

> The ideology of Chavín de Huántar, with its heavy emphasis on carnivorous and tropical forest fauna, can be seen as mystifying the society's source of wealth and power, rather than mapping it in metaphorical terms. . . . It seems . . . probable that the priests of Chavín de Huántar intentionally chose alien metaphors of profound mystery to fuel their spirits. . . . Caymans and jaguars were good to think, llamas were good to eat.

The entire cast of sacred characters appears to have been derived from the cloud forests and rainforest of the eastern Andean slope, if not the floodplains of Amazonia itself. These same animals—jaguar, snake, crested-eagle, and cayman—still play a prominent role in the mythology and religious symbolism of modern people of Amazonia.

Yet today in the Andean highlands, both colonial and modern Quechuan myths feature local Andean fauna, such as llama, deer, condor, fox, and hummingbird. Note the parallel pattern: Amazonian animals in modern Amazonian mythology; Andean animals in modern Andean mythology.

Not so with Chavín religious imagery—an ancient Andean mythology based on Amazonian characters. What Burger terms the "intrusive" character of Chavín symbolism extends even to agricultural crops: manioc, bottle gourd, hot peppers, and possibly peanuts—all eastern lowland crops impossible to grow in Andean environments, such as that around Chavín de Huántar.

This is the single question that has plagued all archaeologists attempting to explain the extraordinarily rapid and widespread distribution of the Chavín cult: *Why are the major animals of Chavín religious art drawn from outside the local highland environment?*

Explaining Where Chavín Cosmology Came From

Richard Burger has noted that three possibilities exist to explain this puzzling aspect of ancient Chavín cosmology. The first possibility is that the climate was radically warmer and more humid during Chavín times. If so, then maybe the lowland complex of animals—the jaguar, the cayman, the crested-eagle, and so forth—could have once lived in the highlands around Chavín de Huántar. Thanks to recent paleoenvironmental studies, it is possible to reject this climate-change model out of hand.

Several lines of independent evidence demonstrate that the climate was very similar to the modern pattern during the Chavín time period (900–200 B.C.); remember from Chapter 11 that the animal bones recovered from Chavín de Huántar belong to the same species as modern highland animals—camelids, deer, and so forth. Clearly, significant paleoenvironmental change will not explain the nature of Chavín iconography.

Perhaps, then, the lowland plant and animal complex was introduced to Chavín de Huántar by immigrants from the tropical forest. This second possibility—the migration hypothesis—was championed by Peruvian archaeologist Julio Tello, discoverer of Chavín civilization and first excavator at Chavín de Huántar (in the 1930s). More recently, this thesis was advocated by Donald Lathrap, an archaeologist at the University of Illinois, who argued that population pressure in the lowland Amazonian or Orinoco basins must have forced the early Chavín folk into the Andean highlands. According to Lathrap, the heavy Amazonian component of Chavín religious art displayed homage and deference to the ancient homeland and subsistence regime that was responsible for the initial success of the Chavín elite.

Burger questions this reconstruction. For one thing, the earliest ceramics at Chavín de Huántar—the pots made by the first occupants—show a conspicuous lack of Amazonian characteristics. If a tropical forest people had moved wholesale into the Andes, their ceramic traditions should show a direct relationship to the Amazonian homeland. But their pottery looks local rather than imported. It also seems clear that the basic high-altitude mixed agricultural subsistence pattern practiced by the pioneer population at Chavín de Huántar was not Amazonian at all; it had developed in place—in the highlands—at least a thousand years earlier. The ceramic and subsistence evidence make it highly unlikely that a tropical forest group was responsible for the lowland iconography evident on the earliest buildings at Chavín de Huántar.

For these reasons, Burger advocates a third hypothesis to explain the obvious Amazonian elements of Chavín cosmology. Emphasizing the importance of Chavín de Huántar's strategic gateway position, Burger argues that Amazonian symbolism was deliberately imported by Chavín's religious leaders, perhaps in the belief that exotic lowland people curated especially powerful esoteric knowledge. This interpretation, supported by ethnographic and ethnohistoric documentation, suggests that shamans and healers may have made pilgrimages to the distant lowlands—viewed as the powerful source of sacred knowledge, medicinal plants, and other ritual necessities. In this view, the Chavín cult imported to the Andean highlands religious knowledge from the remote exotic tropics.

Analysis of Chavín iconography provides some of the details, explaining the cult's remarkable success. Early sculptural evidence suggests that Chavín ideology held that priests had the ability to turn themselves into mythical beasts, in order to intervene with supernatural forces. Temple sculptures clearly demonstrate that, employing hallucinogenic snuff and beverages, Chavín shamans could transform themselves into jaguar or crested-eagles. Specially designed drug paraphernalia—stone mortars, bone trays, spatulas, miniature spoons, and tubes—all seem to be part of the Chavín ritual tool kit. Use of similar artifacts can be documented among modern South American people.

Burger believes that this model—based on sixteenth-century ethnohistoric sources—may explain the singular success of the Chavín cult in uniting previously unrelated cultures throughout the Andean highlands and along the Peruvian coast.

The sixteenth-century example shows how a religious network could have operated 2,000 years earlier. At the center of this regional cult was a large ceremonial complex featuring an **oracle**, accessible only to certain cult specialists. Based on the oracle's secret projections, cult members were able to provide "insider information," offering favorable intervention with the natural elements, protection against disease, and specialized knowledge concerning auspicious times for planting and harvesting.

Oracle: A shrine in which a deity reveals hidden knowledge or divine purpose.

Under this broad, regional system, local communities could establish "branch shrines" by petitioning cult headquarters and pledging support for cult ideology. If accepted, a local priest was assigned, but in return, local communities allotted agricultural lands to produce tribute and promised public labor for farming and herding. In effect, these local branches supported cult headquarters with large quantities of cotton, corn, dried fish, llamas, guinea pigs, raw materials (such as gold and obsidian), and manufactured goods (such as fine cloth).

Burger suggests that this ethnohistoric cult provides a workable model of the distinctive regional organization that characterized Chavín civilization. He believes that the oracle cult center was located at the archaeological site of Karwa, which unfortunately was looted during the 1970s. Iconographic elements—particularly stylized felines and raptorial birds—woven into textile fragments recovered from tombs at Karwa show unmistakable ties to the sculptures at Chavín de Huántar. Despite the nearly 400 miles separating the two sites, the complex elements of Chavín cosmology seem to have been transported intact, without simplification or misrepresentation.

The Role of Cosmology in Andean Civilization

This model suggests that the overall regional cult known as Chavín was subdivided into a number of localized branches, each sharing in the major elements of Chavín iconography—probably reflecting major deities—but complemented by distinctive localized elements. According to this view, the Chavín cult maintained its characteristic regional flavor, but also demonstrated a willingness to incorporate motifs and symbols significant to local constituencies.

Burger emphasizes that the long-standing interest of archaeologists in Chavín iconography has led to a deep understanding of how this distinctive civilization came to be. Had this research taken place within a strictly materialistic framework, Burger suggests, the direction would have been much different, and considerably more restricted. He stresses that interregional exchange and tribute in the form of gifts to the religious center contributed to sociocultural complexity. He also argues that the wealth which fueled the emergence of social differentiation came from selective expropriation of nonlocal resources rather than from local agricultural products.

The spread of Chavín elements (500–250 B.C.) across the central Andes happened at a turbulent time, following the collapse of many early coastal polities. An unprecedented amount of contact occurred between distant and unrelated groups, producing a previously unknown degree of sharing of ideology and technology, reinforced by the actual movement of goods and people. "Thus, the Chavín horizon can be viewed," says Burger, "as a forerunner of later attempts to forge a single Andean civilization out of the staggering diversity of local cultures."

So why did Chavín succeed where earlier attempts failed?

Relying on historical evidence from the sixteenth-century regional ceremonial complex, Burger argues that Chavín was a large-scale religious cult, transcending political and ethnic boundaries. Chavín ideology and rituals were sufficiently powerful to support a hierarchical organization, with officials overseeing local cult activities and monitoring deviation among local congregations. Although considerable regional diversity was evident throughout the reach of the Chavín cult, a degree of central authority was exerted, with tribute directed toward the center of the system. Thus, as in the model, the Chavín cult spread not because of political expansion, but because of the extension of a powerful shared cosmology, rendered visible in ritual objects and manifested through the growth of complex interregional exchange networks.

Civilization had appeared in the central Andes by about 400 B.C. According to Burger, the centers of the Chavín horizon rivaled the classic Greek cities in size and beauty: There were massive public structures with finely cut-and-polished masonry, and the settlements were home to a complex society, differentiated by both social status and economic activities.

Burger argues that this power came from the original priestly occupants of Chavín de Huántar, who focused the growing Chavín mythology on the mysterious rather than the mundane. It was these mysterious animals of the lowlands that ultimately determined the long-term success of Chavín society and economy.

> One message of Chavín art may have been that the prosperity and well-being of the community depended on maintaining the favor of forces alien to the local

habitat and daily experience, forces redolent of the powers of the distant and mysterious tropical forest. The mediation of this relationship required the services of ritual specialists.

This explanation suggests that Chavín ideology—heavily emphasizing the exotic tropical forest fauna—ritually reinforced the wealth and power of Chavín de Huántar society.

While some of the features associated with Chavín civilization had existed earlier, the pooling and reworking of ideas and their spread during the Chavín horizon led to the creation of the shared cultural consciousness in the central Andes that was Chavín's most enduring legacy.

Richard Burger, archaeologist (Yale University)

Current evidence suggests that social stratification may have first appeared in the highlands, in association with long-distance exchange—offering local leaders an unparalleled opportunity to control and manipulate the existing socioeconomic system. Burger believes that tribute supplied to regional ceremonial centers by travelers and pilgrims could have been a major source of wealth and power for newly emerging elites.

Religious ideology seems to have played a central role in promoting and legitimizing these profound sociopolitical transformations, suggesting that many of the key ingredients for social complexity existed in the central Andes prior to the Chavín horizon.

Multiple Voices From Bighorn Medicine Wheel

In this final example of cognitive approaches to archaeology, we consider Wyoming's celebrated Medicine Wheel. Today—as almost certainly in the past—this ancient stone alignment is a *sacred site,* a place for ritual and religion. Understanding the meaning of the Medicine Wheel and dozens of places like it has been a source of tremendous frustration to processual archaeologists; to date, explicitly scientific archaeology has enjoyed precious little success in explaining sacred sites of the past. But cognitive archaeology, with its more wide-open view of method and theory, promises to make more sense of places like the Medicine Wheel—provided that the archaeological community can live with the uncertainty and diversity of opinion implied in these new approaches to ancient ritual and religion.

Panorama of the Bighorn Medicine Wheel, taken in 1926.

Let us first examine some of the specific explanations that have been offered for the Medicine Wheel; then, we will briefly touch on the implications of such explanations for the shape of cognitive archaeology in the future.

What Does It Look Like?

Looking at the Bighorn Medicine Wheel, you are confronted by simplicity itself: a stone circle—the "wheel"—nearly 90 feet in diameter, astride an isolated peak 9,640 feet above sea level. Inside are 28 unevenly spaced stone "spokes," each radiating out from the central "hub," a stone **cairn** about 15 feet across. Five smaller cairns dot the periphery.

Cairn: A mound of stones. Cairns (and rock walls) are sometimes casually created in the process of clearing stones from agricultural fields. But cairns can also be deliberately constructed as an aid to navigation, as a memorial, or to mark the location of a grave.

For nearly a century, scientists have puzzled over why anybody would build this high-altitude rock alignment. The Western world first took notice of the Medicine Wheel in 1903, when an article, published by *Forest and Stream* magazine, pointed out certain similarities to the celebrated Aztec calendar stone. Before long, Chicago's Field Museum of Natural History launched an expedition to study the enigmatic rock alignment. Over the decades, several teams of archaeologists have also trekked into the Bighorn Mountains, to see the Medicine Wheel firsthand. Most came to the conclusion that the stone alignments were constructed in several stages, with some parts appearing older than others. Cultural materials recovered in association with the wheel date to the Late Prehistoric and historic periods. To this point, there seems to be little controversy.

Maybe It's a Tomb

But here consensus vanishes. Numerous hypotheses have been advanced to explain precisely who built the Medicine Wheel, and why. Some have suggested that the rock cairns were originally constructed as grave markers, each a memorial marking where a particularly powerful person died. The lines of rocks (the "spokes" of the wheel) show the different directions in which the departed ranged "on the warpath," recording in effect the war deeds of each dead chief. The rock piles at the ends of the rock lines may represent enemies killed in battle.

Maybe It Was a Vision Quest Site

Other investigators, drawing upon the rich ethnohistoric record of the Northern Plains, relate the alignment to the ancient practice of the *vision quest,* a widespread ritual seeking communication with the spirit world by a solitary individual. Although the specifics varied widely, participants were usually sequestered in remote sacred places, without food or water, praying for spiritual guidance.

The Crow people explain the Bighorn Medicine Wheel this way:

> Red Plume, a famous Crow chief of the period of Lewis and Clark, obtained his inspiration and received his medicine and the token which resulted in the application of that name by him at the Medicine Wheel. As a young man, Red Plume visited the wheel in the hope of receiving a strong medicine which would make of him a great warrior and chief. Without food, water, or clothing, he remained

> for four days and nights awaiting recognition from the spirits. On the fourth night he was approached by the three little men and one woman who inhabited the underground passage to the wheel and was conducted by them to the underground chamber. He remained there for three days and three nights and was instructed in the arts of warfare and in leading his people. He was told that the Red Eagle would be his powerful medicine and would guide him and be his protector through life. He was told to wear always upon his person as an emblem of his medicine, the soft little feather which grows upon the back above the tail of the eagle. This little red plume gave him his name. Upon his death, after many years of successful warfare and leadership, he instructed his people that his spirit would occupy the shrine at the medicine wheel which is not connected with the rim, except by an extended spoke, and that they might at all times communicate with him there.

Red Plume, also known as Long Hair, was a real person, a Crow leader who died in 1836. His visit to the Bighorns could have taken place during the late 1700s.

I don't believe in magic—a lot of superstitious hocus pocus. I'm going after a find of incredible historical significance. You're talking about the bogey-man.

INDIANA JONES (RAIDERS OF THE LOST ARK)

The Medicine Wheel is, without doubt, well suited for vision questing. Several contemporary Native American people say they have used it this way. From its lofty perch, the site commands a spectacular view of the Bighorn Basin to the west. Up-slope winds whistle through countless crevices, creating a babel of moaning and shrieking voices when air velocities are high. Some archaeological evidence suggests the rock cairns were protected by small enclosures during the early historic period, perhaps providing some modicum of shelter for those fasting, waiting, and seeking supernatural advice.

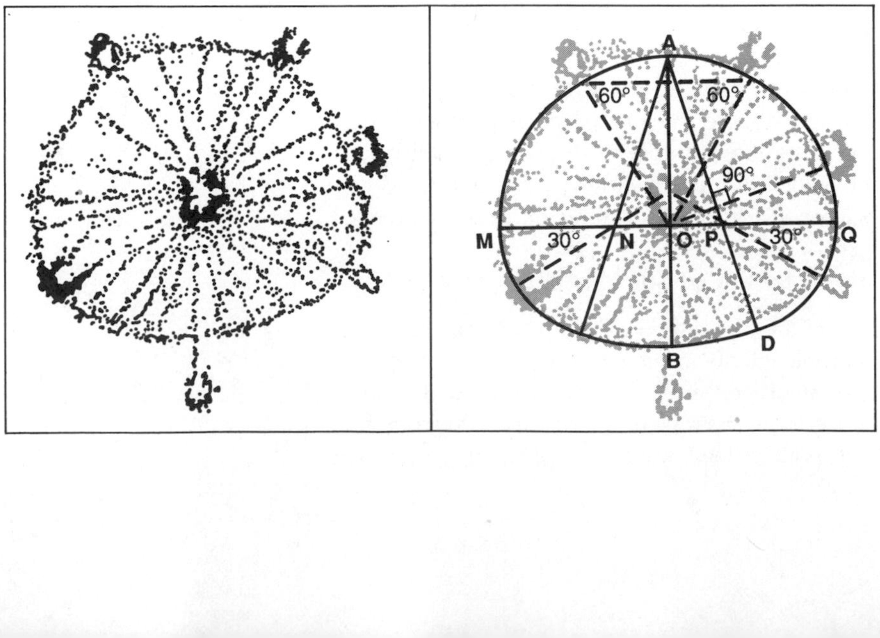

Scale drawing of the Bighorn Medicine Wheel. The spoked wheel is roughly 90 feet across, and five cairns stand about 4 feet high. Below right, a series of geometric projections have been superimposed over the Medicine Wheel, demonstrating how the overall shape closely approximates a ring made of four precise geometric arcs, each of which could be readily laid out on the ground by using stakes and ropes.

Maybe It's an Ancient Observatory

John A. Eddy set out the most highly publicized hypothesis, published in the pages of *Science* magazine more than two decades ago. An astronomer by profession, Eddy suggested—not surprisingly—that Native Americans constructed the Medicine Wheel as an outdoor astronomical observatory. Noting that selected stone cairns might once have held wooden poles, Eddy argued that these posts could have served as foresight and backsight, defining the azimuth of the rising or setting of some important celestial object (probably the sun).

Predicting significant celestial events such as the summer and winter solstices, the Medicine Wheel could have imparted powerful knowledge, useful for calendrical, ritual, or even agricultural purposes. Because of its elevation–the site is buried beneath deep snow drifts throughout the winter–Eddy focused on the summer solstice. In a dramatic, televised recreation, Eddy laid out imaginary sighting poles using a surveyor's transit, steel tape, and compass on the morning of June 20, 1972. At dawn on the day of the summer solstice, the sun rose exactly where he predicted it would.

Eddy's conclusion: Simply by observing the sunrise over the cairns at the Medicine Wheel, aboriginal astronomers could have predicted the timing of the summer solstice "with a precision of several days." After further experimentation, Eddy suggested that the additional cairns may have marked rising spots of the brightest stars in the summer dawn, stars which themselves further enhanced prediction of the coming solstice.

Skeptics have pointed out several flaws in Eddy's argument. For one thing, the Medicine Wheel lacks convincing evidence for such sighting poles. In addition, the cairns are so large that precise sighting (even with a pole) would not be possible. And even allowing for poles and precision, Eddy's astronomical argument still leaves one cairn unaccounted for.

Other investigators suggest that the Medicine Wheel was built to aid travel, the rock piles left as directional aids to newcomers. Still others believe that the floorplan of the Medicine Wheel was a two-dimensional imitation of the 28-raftered lodge built as part of the Sun Dance ceremony. Other hypotheses hold that the Medicine Wheel may have been a boundary marker, a depiction of a stone turtle, or an enduring stone marker demonstrating geometrical expertise.

The major difference between American Indian views of the physical world and Western science lies in the premise accepted by Indians and rejected by scientists: the world in which we live is alive. Many scientists believe this idea to be primitive superstition, and consequently the scientific explanation rejects any nuance of interpretation which would credit the existence of activities as having partial intelligence or sentience. American Indians look at events to determine the spiritual activity supporting or undergirding them. Science insists, albeit at a great price in understanding, that the observer be as detached as possible from the event he or she is observing. . . . Indians also know that human beings must participate in events, not isolate themselves from occurrences in the physical world.

VINE DELORIA JR., PHILOSOPHER (UNIVERSITY OF COLORADO, STANDING ROCK SIOUX)

The Medicine Wheel as a Modern Sacred Site

After a century of probing and digging, mapping and sighting, the Medicine Wheel is still, as one investigator puts it, "a well-known archaeological structure whose origin and purpose remain unexplained."

But the Medicine Wheel is much more than an archaeological site. To many contemporary Indian people, it is also a holy place, one of many sacred sites where important ceremonies are performed to this day. Sacred lands are considered to be vital to individual and tribal harmony.

And yet many of the most important sacred sites–places like the Bighorn Medicine Wheel–are being overrun each year by thousands of non-Indians: well-meaning tourists, scientific teams, and New Agers seeking a spiritual experience. There is great concern among Indians that the plants, paths, shrines, rocks, and other aspects of their sacred sites are being destroyed by the curious and the insensitive.

A coalition representing varied interests–tribal, scientific, ecological, and governmental–is attempting to protect, preserve, and respect the Bighorn Medicine Wheel. In recent years, the last section of access road has been closed to vehicular traffic, requiring visitors to travel the remaining 1.5 miles on foot. This solution minimizes the negative impact of tourism, respects the religious freedom of native people, and keeps this powerful place accessible to the many who wish to see firsthand the isolated mountain that has drawn people here for centuries.

The diversity of postprocessual archaeology and the advocacy of multiple perspectives for perceiving the past is, generally speaking, a strength; it certainly is a welcome development to the orthodoxy or dogmatic features of the new (or) processual archaeology.

PHILIP L. KOHL, ARCHAEOLOGIST (WELLESLEY COLLEGE)

For my thoughts are not your thoughts, neither are your ways my ways.

THE BIBLE

Given these diverse opinions and vested interests in the history of the Medicine Wheel, is it any puzzle that so many voices wish to be heard about its meaning? The Medicine Wheel has become a postmodern dream and a processual nightmare.

How do you study a place like this? Where is the consensus? Where is the authority? Where is the scientific objectivity? The postmodern answer is this: Indeterminacy, multivocality, and relativism will probably always thrive in places like the Medicine Wheel. Maybe it's just one of those places that defies finality.

Blueprints for the Archaeology of the Mind

The best anthropologists are those who never lose track of the importance of accurate knowledge and yet never lose track of the wonder and deep significance of the human beings with whom they work.

E. A. ANDERSON, CULTURAL ANTHROPOLOGIST (UNIVERSITY OF CALIFORNIA, RIVERSIDE)

To sum up what has been said about cognitive approaches in archaeology, we must be clear about two important points:

- Cognitive archaeology is a very hot topic.
- Considerable debate exists about how best to proceed.

As we've seen throughout these pages, the extremes are defined by processual and postmodern perspectives, with plenty of room for defining an expanding middle ground.

Some Postmodern Approaches

Progress is marked less by a perfection of consensus than by a refinement of debate. What gets better is the precision with which we vex each other.

CLIFFORD GEERTZ, INTERPRETIVE ANTHROPOLOGIST (PRINCETON UNIVERSITY)

The Medicine Wheel has brought us full circle. At the beginning of this chapter, we discussed how cognitive approaches were stifled under archaeology's processual agenda. Today, few modern anthropologists believe in absolute value neutrality and complete objectivity. Today, most philosophers of science recognize that science exists as part of culture, not outside it. Values, properly factored in, can be productive, not contaminating.

Although some persist in pursuing their version of ultimate truth—the way it *absolutely, really* was—most Americanist archaeologists are assessing the degree to which their interpretations express their own cultural biases. Few archaeologists adhere to strict empiricism—the view that data are so self-evident that the analyst can passively experience them.

With the advent of postmodernism, the debate shifted away from rigid objectivity and oppressive scientific methodologies. Postmodernism by its very nature encourages cognitive, ideational approaches to the past. In the words of one postmodern thinker, Jean-François Lyotard, consensus has become "an outmoded and suspect value."

I see the world in very fluid, contradictory, emerging, interconnected terms, and with that kind of circuitry I just don't feel the need to say what is going to happen or not happen.

JERRY BROWN, FORMER GOVERNOR OF CALIFORNIA

Postmodern views of the past replace scientific unanimity with a sense of theoretical *pluralism.* No grand synthesis is expected to emerge. According to the postprocessual critique, archaeology will come to be characterized by multiple paths toward understanding the past. A primary plank in the postmodern agenda is to learn how to live with mutually irreconcilable views about the past.

To see what these multiple pasts might look like, we need look no farther than Wyoming's renowned Medicine Wheel, an ancient stone arrangement that figures prominently in high-tech approaches to archaeology and also in long-term indigenous theology. Here on a windswept peak in Wyoming's Bighorn Mountains are played out, at times dramatically, the diverse objectives of modern science, cognitive archaeology, traditional Native American religion, and the driving forces of so-called heritage tourism in contemporary America. Like so many elements of the human past, the Medicine Wheel means many different things to many different people.

The recognition of multiple pasts is one of the undeniably positive aspects to be derived from the postprocessual critique. It has produced a new openness, an insistence on theoretical multiplicity. This perspective stands to benefit archaeology in several ways.

Often, the shortcomings of a given theory can only be appreciated from the vantage point of a competing theory. Because such competition tends to raise the level of theoretical inquiry, its existence is essential. Adequate quality control demands a deluge of diverse and conflicting theories. Theories do not just disappear on their own—they generally hang around until something "better" replaces them. So it becomes important to generate a host of diverse and contrasting theories, which can be qualified and enlarged, or rejected and replaced—all as part of the everyday archaeological process.

But good theories are hard to come by. So, to generate more theories, some researchers have suggested relaxing the methodological constraints that hinder the free-flowing generation of theories. Some archaeologists do not think this is a good idea.

Some More Scientific Approaches

Postmodern perspectives have opened many avenues of inquiry into the "archaeology of the human mind." But some self-described cognitive archaeologists—luminaries like Kent Flannery, Joyce Marcus, and Colin Renfrew—continue to advocate fairly stringent scientific controls.

Renfrew warns of the dangers inherent in "new-age archaeology," adamantly insisting that cognitive archaeology proceed only within the framework of acceptable scientific method. First, one must recognize that archaeology (re-)captures only certain, limited aspects of ancient ideas. Renfrew expresses contempt for attempting to reconstruct "worldviews" or "totalities of thought"—emphasizing the notable lack of success with which ethnographers have tried to do this (and they are working with living people whose "totality of thought" is very much intact).

Cognitive approaches can only be used when . . . the body of supporting data is sufficiently rich. When it is not so rich, cognitive archaeology becomes little more than speculation, a kind of bungee jump into the Land of Fantasy.

Kent Flannery and Joyce Marcus

Projecting ideas into the past is unfeasible within a framework of rigid, testable, fully objective science. Even without such uncompromising testability, Renfrew insists that at least one's cognitive inferences must be induced "carefully" from the data and limited to statements that can be inferred directly from those data. In this way, statements open to empirical assessment can be "distanced" from the investigator.

Flannery and Marcus deride those who employ cognitive archaeology as "a shortcut to the kind of 'armchair archaeology' that requires no fieldwork

There is at present no evidence of techniques that will allow detailed insights into culturally specific aspects of rituals—except those associated with the direct historical approach or the use of written documents.

BRUCE TRIGGER

or rigorous analysis of any kind. As a result of this shortcut, many of the worst fears of the materialists have been realized—namely that *any* fanciful mentalist speculation is allowed, so long as it is called 'cognitive archaeology.' " They worry about the numerous "idiosyncratic fantasies," which tell us more about the archaeologist in charge than the ancient culture under study. Be skeptical, they argue, when authors ask that we trust their "highly-developed intuition" rather than present acceptable evidence supporting their interpretation.

Flannery and Marcus insist that iconography is not merely some esoteric skill. Such procedures can work in concert with established subsistence and settlement perspectives, integrating the findings drawn from the natural and social sciences.

Marcus and Flannery believe that cognitive archaeology can indeed follow relatively rigorous methods, provided ample ethnohistorical and ethnographic documentation is available. Here is their four-step method for research into ancient religion:

1. Build a model from ethnohistoric documents.
2. Isolate those elements of material culture—such as temples and ritual artifacts—that are likely to be preserved archaeologically.
3. Undertake a detailed study combining ancient temple plans and an analysis of where ritual paraphernalia was found when excavated.
4. Compare and contrast the observed archaeological remains with the expected pattern derived from ethnohistory.

That's one of the great dangers of archaeology—folklore.

INDIANA JONES (RAIDERS OF THE LOST ARK)

In this way, it is possible to use the archaeological record in a relatively objective study of the past. But, they warn, if ethnohistory is lacking, "far less success should be anticipated."

SUMMARY Americanist archaeologists are increasingly concerned with defining an "archaeology of the mind." Although processual archaeology was initially optimistic that *all aspects* of the human condition were available for archaeological investigation, the proponents of processual approaches during the 1970s and 1980s were distinctly lukewarm, if not outright hostile, toward "cognitive" archaeology.

Modern cognitive archaeology is developing methods for studying all those aspects of ancient culture that are the product of the human mind: the perception, description, and classification of the universe; the nature of the supernatural; the principles, philosophies, ethics, and values by which human societies are governed; and the ways in which aspects of the world, the supernatural, or human values are conveyed in art.

For one thing, archaeologists attempt to understand *cosmology,* how various past cultures have explained their universe—how it originated and developed, how the various parts fit together and what laws they obey, plus a concern with what the future of the universe holds.

Archaeologists are also attempting to understand the past's *religions*—the specific set of beliefs based on one's ultimate relation to the supernatural. Such religious beliefs are manifested in everyday life in a "program of ritual," a succession of discrete events such as prayer, music, feasting, sacrificc, and taboos.

Ideology is defined as a systematic body of concepts and beliefs—often political in nature—about human life or culture. Communism is an ideology, as are democracy and fascism. Ideology differs from religion because it addresses society and politics (although they certainly can overlap).

To illustrate some current cognitive approaches in archaeology, we draw upon recent studies of *iconography*—the way in which people have employed art forms to represent their religious, political, ideological, or cosmological beliefs. Iconographic analysis covers a broad range from well-known complex systems—such as Egyptian hieroglyphs and Mayan inscriptions—to cryptic incisions on ancient stone and bone artifacts.

Chapter 17

Archaeology of the Mind: Some Empathetic Approaches

PREVIEW The processual agenda maintains that although the questions being asked by archaeologists may to some degree reflect contemporary social conditions, sufficient data and sound analytical procedures will ultimately produce scientifically valid statements uncontaminated by ideology or personal prejudice.

The postprocessual critique emphasizes that we live today in a postmodern world. As explained in Chapter 3, postmodernism is a dramatic shift in perception that resonates through the world's cultural, political, economic, and artistic outlooks. The postmodern view emphasizes social fragmentation and instability, decentralization and anarchy—and this includes the way archaeologists view the past.

In this chapter, we explore some empathetic ways to view the human past, attempts to reveal the intentions and thoughts of long-gone actors.

The world has always been inhabited by human beings who have always had the same passions.

NICCOLÒ MACHIAVELLI (1469–1527), POLITICAL PHILOSOPHER

Postmodernism challenges modern forms of representation, "deconstructing" these forms, critically analyzing and contextualizing the ways in which we express ourselves (in our "texts")—seeking to find out how our various rhetorical forms convey and distort reality. The postmodern movement places great emphasis on the detailed understanding of such texts, and deconstruction is the technique for doing this: looking inside one text for another, seeking meanings that were not necessarily intended by the writer, charting what is absent from a text and what is silenced by it.

Deconstructing the Archaeological Text

Archaeology shows more clearly, perhaps, than any other activity that we go out and "get" the past. The past isn't just there. The relationship between present and past is not a "given." We go and dig it up.

IAN HODDER, ARCHAEOLOGIST (CAMBRIDGE UNIVERSITY)

Because we live in a postmodern world, and because deconstruction is sometimes useful for teasing out hidden meanings, and because it is important to understand how "texts" convey our subconscious, we will now undertake a deconstruction of our own—a deconstruction of two texts written by stellar figures in Americanist archaeology. Following the lead of British archaeologist Ian Hodder, let us strip away the surface, textual forms to explore truths buried and concealed. Let us look closely at the transformation of archaeological writing over the past two centuries to see what these texts have to say about the direction of archaeological thought–in both the historic past and the very recent past.

Here, we focus on writings by Thomas Jefferson (America's first scientific archaeologist) and Lewis Binford (leading proponent of processual archaeology). In the two accompanying boxes, we have reproduced a key text from each writer.

Selecting a text from Thomas Jefferson is easy: He wrote only once about archaeology. The box is taken from the American edition of *Notes on the State of Virginia* (1787), Jefferson's only book. Arguing that Native Americans were entirely capable of constructing large-scale prehistoric monuments, Jefferson decided to excavate a burial mound located on his property. This was a major step, pioneering the basics of archaeological reporting for decades to come (see *Excavating a Virginia Burial Mound* by Thomas Jefferson).

Selecting a text by Lewis Binford was more difficult. A prolific writer, Binford has published thousands of pages in which he set out his ideas about archaeological method and theory. Here, I have selected Binford's account of his fieldwork at Hatchery West, located on the east bank of the Kaskaskia River, just east of Carlyle, Illinois. With his colleagues Sally R. Binford, Robert Whallon, and Margaret Ann Hardin, Binford described the field operations undertaken during the summer of 1963. Although each of the coauthors undoubtedly contributed to the overall narration, we will (for present purposes) treat the Hatchery West report as if it were written solely by the senior author, Lewis Binford (see *Archaeology at Hatchery West*).

The most obvious difference between these two texts is narrative *style*. Jefferson writes in the fashionable patrician–some would say flowery–timbre of his eighteenth-century contemporaries. One can easily picture the future president gripping his quill pen, guiding it carefully, taking care not to smear the fresh ink with his frilled shirt cuff. On the other hand, in a manuscript bristling with detailed measurements and lengthy tables, Binford evokes images of white lab coats and statistical methods. In places verging on the arrogant, Binford writes to set the record straight, to describe exhaustively for the reader the work at Hatchery West–"the first attempt . . . at the definition of the internal structure of an archaeological site thus far attempted in Eastern North America."

These differences in narrative style must not be allowed to obscure the authors' basic purpose. Each author is writing a scientific account, doing his best to provide readers with an enduring account of an archaeological investigation–what methods were employed, what was encountered, and what the various finds tell us about ancient people. That is, the shift in narrative style over two centuries does *not* reflect simply an increased reliance on scientific principles in archaeology. Thomas Jefferson injects his version of scientific rigor into his account, and so does Lewis Binford. Jefferson was the leading archaeologist of his time, and so is Binford.

Given their common scientific purpose, we can view these two texts as somehow reflecting the changes in serious archaeological discourse over the past two centuries.

IN HIS OWN WORDS

Excavating a Virginia Burial Mound by Thomas Jefferson (1787)

I know of no such thing existing as an Indian monument: for I would not honour with that name arrow points, stone hatchets, stone pipes, and half-shapen images. Of labour on the large scale, I think there is no remain as respectable as would be a common ditch for the draining of lands: unless indeed it be the Barrows, *of which many are to be found all over this country. . . . There being one of these in my neighbourhood, I wished to satisfy myself whether any, and which of these opinions were just. For this purpose I determined to open and examine it thoroughly. It was situated on the low grounds of the* Rivanna, *about two miles above its principal fork, and opposite to some hills, on which had been an Indian town. It was of a spheroidical form, of about forty feet diameter at the base, and had been of about twelve feet altitude, though now reduced by the plough to seven and a half, having been under cultivation about a dozen years. Before this it was covered with trees of twelve inches diameter, and round the base was an excavation of five feet depth and width, from whence the earth had been taken of which the hillock was formed. I first dug superficially in several parts of it, and came to collections of human bones, at different depths, from six inches to three feet below the surface. These were lying in the utmost confusion, some vertical, some oblique, some horizontal, and directed to every point of the compass, entangled, and held together in clusters by the earth. Bones of the most distant parts were found together, and, for instance, the small bones of the foot in the hollow of a scull, many sculls would sometimes be in contact, lying on the face, on the side, on the back, top or bottom, so as, on the whole, to give the idea of bones emptied promiscuously from a bag or basket, and covered over with earth, without any attention to their order. . . . I proceeded then to make a perpendicular cut through the body of the barrow, that I might examine its internal structure. This passed about three feet from its center, was opened to the former surface of the earth, and was wide enough for a man to walk through and examine its sides. At the bottom, that is, on the level of the circumjacent plain, I found bones; above these a few stones, brought from a cliff a quarter of a mile off, and from the river one-eighth of a mile off; then a large interval of earth, then a stratum of bones, and so on. At one end of the section were four strata of bones plainly distinguishable; at the other, three; the strata in one part not ranging with those in another. The bones nearest the surface were least decayed. No holes were discovered in any of them as if made with bullets, arrows, or other weapons. I conjectured that in this barrow might have been a thousand skeletons. Every one will readily seize the circumstances above related, which militate against the opinion, that it covered the bones only of persons fallen in battle, and against the tradition also, which would make it the common sepulchre of a town, in which the bodies were placed upright, and touching each other. Appearances certainly indicate that it has derived both origin and growth from the accustomary collection of bones, and deposition of them together; that the first collection had been deposited on the common surface of the earth, a few stones put over it, and then a covering of earth, that the second had been laid on this, had covered more or less of it in proportion to the number of bones, and was then also covered with earth, and so on. The following are the particular circumstances which give it this aspect.*

1. The number of bones. 2. Their confused position. 3. Their being in different strata. 4. The strata in one part have no correspondence with those in another. 5. The difference in the time of inhumation. 6. The existence of infant bones among them.

When deconstructing a comparable set of archaeological texts, Hodder has suggested that the real differences between archaeological writing during the late eighteenth century and that of the late twentieth century are profound and telling.

For one thing, Jefferson firmly fixes his archaeological report in time and place. The very first words of *Notes on the State of Virginia* are these: "The following notes were written in Virginia in the year 1781, and somewhat corrected and enlarged in the winter of 1782, in answer to Queries proposed to

IN THEIR OWN WORDS

Archaeology at Hatchery West by Lewis R. Binford, Sally R. Binford, Robert Whallon, and Margaret Ann Hardin (1970)

The purpose of this report is to provide a descriptive account of the cultural features recovered from Hatchery West *during the* 1963 *field season and to review some of the general results obtained from the execution of a research design aimed at obtaining as complete a picture as possible of the internal structure of an archaeological site. . . . Field procedure was guided by the assumption that an archaeological site is the fossilized remains of the operation of the extinct cultural system participated in by the past occupants of the site.* As *such the archaeological site should exhibit a complex formal-spatial structure in direct correspondence to the degree of differentiation of activities and social units performing the various activities. The job of the archaeologist is the dissection of this structure so as to recover information about the degree of activity differentiation and corresponding social context. In seeking to specify the structure of a site, one seeks to demonstrate the differential spatial clustering of implements and facilities which remain as clues to the differentiated activities conducted at the location, as well as the indicators of the cultural history for the location, insofar, as there were repeated occupations, each representing different segments of the operation of extinct cultural systems.*

Throughout the report our analysis will be directed toward the specification of the internal structure of the various archaeological components, each representative of a different phase in the cultural complex history represented at the Hatchery *site. We will hopefully be able to demonstrate, as a result of the particular controls which our data collection strategy provided, the utility of certain field techniques employed, the degree to which certain field decisions were in post hoc judgment appropriate to the accomplishment of research aims, and to evaluate our methodological assumptions in light of the first attempt to my knowledge at the definition of the internal structure of an archaeological site thus far attempted in* Eastern North America.

Lewis R. Binford is professor of anthropology at Southern Methodist University.
Sally R. Binford (1925–1995) was a professor at the University of New Mexico.
Robert Whallon is curator of Mediterranean prehistory, Museum of Anthropology, University of Michigan.
Margaret Ann Hardin is curator of anthropology at the Natural History Museum of Los Angeles County.

the Author, by a Foreigner of Distinction, then residing among us." Although Jefferson's account is, by today's standards, rather sketchy and imprecise, he clearly defines when and where his account originates.

Jefferson establishes for himself a definite place within the text. As in many texts of Jefferson's era, the author employs the first-person perspective, as if writing a letter to a friend or colleague. Jefferson tells you, the reader, about his excavations in an ancient Rivanna River mound:

"*I wished to satisfy myself . . .* "

"*I proceeded then to make a perpendicular cut . . .* "

"*I conjectured that in this barrow might have been . . .* "

Jefferson describes what he was thinking when he decided to dig here, how and where he decided to proceed, what he was looking for, and what he found.

There is no hesitation here. This is a specific sequence of events in which Jefferson himself participated. His account involves named actors and tells us

I find a certain excitement in reading these eighteenth-century reports, and a tension as one follows the process of discovery. This excitement is enhanced by the use of personal pronouns and actor-oriented accounts. . . . The understanding of the site is tied to the process of excavation itself. Hypotheses are rejected or adopted as the excavation continues. The meaning of the site is linked to the circumstances of recovery.

Ian Hodder

what they thought about what they saw. This eighteenth-century narrative style, emphasizing as it does the importance of sequence, carries with it the implication that had others dug the site using a different strategy, a different interpretation might have resulted.

Jefferson frequently warns his reader that *Notes on the State of Virginia* reflects his personal opinion, not an established fact. In the very first paragraph of the book, he warns that "the subjects are all treated imperfectly; some scarcely touch[ed] on . . . some of their imperfections may with truth be ascribed . . . to the want of information and the want of talents in the writer." In the postprocessual language of Hodder, Jefferson's narrative comes to his reader as "situated, particular, contingent, and transient."

Throughout Anglo-America, archaeology was conducted mostly by men of learning and letters. Jefferson's simple site report transmitted the sense of elevated social position to the general readership. The accuracy of archaeological interpretation at that time was judged on the basis of personal authority and privilege of the author; many such personalized eighteenth-century accounts include debate, controversy, and differing opinions about the meaning of the archaeological remains encountered. Hodder suggests that these eighteenth-century accounts include the specific actions of individuals "because power outside the text is also individual, personal, and arbitrary."

Let's turn now to the Hatchery West account, published 183 years after Jefferson's Rivanna River narrative. Throughout the twentieth century, archaeological reports changed, reflecting the shifting style in scientific documents in general; personal pronouns all but evaporate, as do named authors or actors (except, of course, on the title page). In the Hatchery West report, Binford and his colleagues write:

> "*The job of the archaeologist is the dissection of this structure . . .* "
>
> "*Field procedure was guided by the assumption . . .* "
>
> " . . . *certain field decisions were in post hoc judgment appropriate to the accomplishment of research aims . . .* "

There is clearly a sense here that research goals and excavation strategies are guided by a single, universally accepted set of guidelines. Perhaps also there is only a single possible interpretation of results, at which any careful excavator would arrive.

To be sure, the Hatchery West investigation existed in space and time: near Carlyle (Illinois) during the summer of 1963. But the description of that fieldwork is abstract, with the writer and excavator virtually disappearing—hidden within scientific convention. Throughout, the Hatchery West report employs an intrinsic, standardized narrative style, almost a descriptive code.

Typically, modern archaeological reports (such as that presenting the Hatchery West results) are organized into rigid categories that divide the artifacts and cultural features, rather than by sequence of excavation: Site Definition, Cultural Features (Structural Features, Pit Features . . .), Comparative Analysis of the Components (Domestic Architecture, Orientation of Structures . . .), and so on. Description of the actual process of archaeological fieldwork is minimized, except to note standardized techniques being employed (grid orientation, screen size, flotation method, and so forth).

Hodder suggests the following:

> How can I explain the gradual shift from the contingent and contextualised in the eighteenth century to the modern, abstract, distanced, and universal? Why do contingent conclusions appear today as unargued, dry descriptions of the self-evident? I [link] the gradual shift in writing style to changing structures of power and of the production of knowledge. In the eighteenth century, scientific authority was identified with the personal authority of individuals including lords and bishops. In the twentieth century, power in the archaeological community has been dispersed. It resides in institutions and in the public space. The authority of the text is no longer personal, but lies in the adherence to abstract codes. The self, history and uncertainty must be denied.

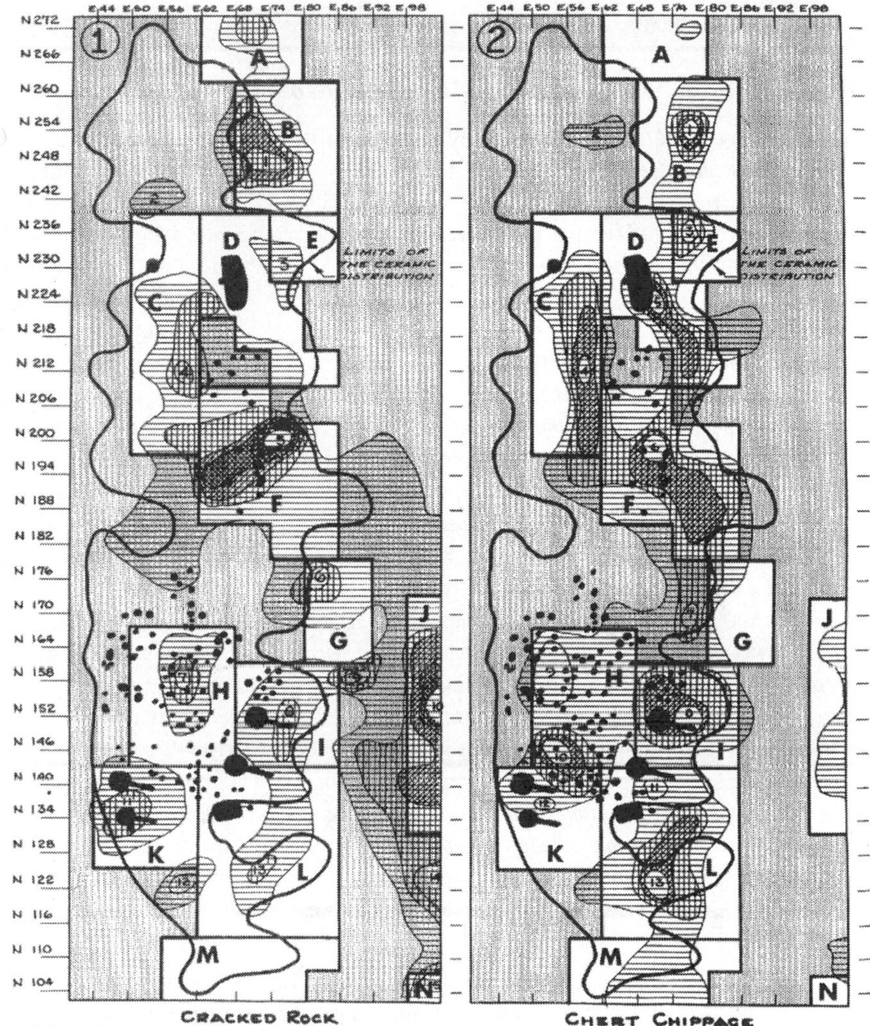

Comparative surface artifact distributions at Hatchery West, Illinois.

Hodder describes recent archaeological reports as comprising a formalized grid: "The writing has become increasingly distant, objective, impersonal and universal. We have become blind to the fact that we are writing. It appears as if self-evident data are simply described in neutral terms. The description is undated, timeless and beyond history."

The Processual Agenda: Some Unintended Consequences

Over the past three decades, processual archaeology has been firmly grounded in an adaptive, systemic approach to the past. The stated goal of processual archaeology is to create universally valid generalizations that should

IN THEIR OWN WORDS

On Getting on With Southwestern Archaeology

The following "Open Letter," recently published in the *Anthropological Newsletter*, represents one attempt to define a contemporary research agenda that avoids the polarities of both processual and postprocessual extremes.

For the past quarter-century, the US Southwest has been dominated by a school of thought known as "processual archaeology." We are Southwestern archaeologists who question many aspects of current thinking in our field and who, despite broad differences in approach, share ideas about how we may best understand the past.

The theories of processual archaeology are many and varied, but current practice in the Southwest often involves an approach we term "ecological functionalism." Under that approach, societies are assumed to be systems, in the sense that groups within a society are functionally bound to each other and do not vary with any degree of independence. As a consequence, interaction within a society is not viewed as a meaningful source of historical change. Instead, change is explained by appeal to the interaction between the entire "system" and external factors such as environmental change or independent demographic growth.

In extending the work of the past 25 years, we assume that prehistoric Southwestern societies consisted of groups that acted with varying degrees of independence and at scales ranging from that of the individual and household to that of the community and region. From this perspective, historical change springs not only from relations between societies and the environment or demographic growth, but also from relations between and within social groups. Because the checks and balances that maintain a given social order are imperfect, social relations are inherently dynamic. In acting out the relations between them, social groups change those relations—and themselves. Thus the internal dynamics of a society, far from being a passive aspect of systemic change, are a vital source of change and a point of departure for archaeological study.

In seeking to explain change, we further believe that we need to begin and end with the actual history of specific societies. Concepts like "chiefdom" or "Anasazi" may help guide our thinking, but they are not real in and of themselves. The discovery of similar patterns of behavior within different societies may lead us to postulate social models at various levels of abstraction, but such generalizations are a means, not an end. Our task is not complete until we demonstrate how those models improve our understanding

ultimately prove to be of practical value for the improvement and management of contemporary societies. Informed by the strategy of cultural materialism, processualists focused on large-scale structures and long-term dynamics, deliberately looking beyond archaeological detail and historical specifics.

Archaeology, I would say, doesn't mean nothing to me, to my religious beliefs for our tribe. My ancestors, relatives, grandmother . . . they tell you about the history of our people and it's passed on. . . . We just accept it, not accept archaeology but accept the way our past has been established and just go on trying to live that same style, however old it is . . . would say that archaeology just helps a little bit, but frankly, archaeologists don't mean nothing to me.

CECIL ANTONE (GILA RIVER TRIBE)

An Exclusion of Native American History

Like many indigenous groups, American Indians are sometimes puzzled and dissatisfied with processual archaeology's strident insistence on evolutionary, antihistorical generalizing about human behavior. The almost clinical hypothesis-testing agenda of processualism largely precluded exploration of the specific historical events of interest to many Indian groups. The unrelenting focus on ecology and adaptation effectively ignored and belittled the importance of cultural and religious tradition. Processual archaeology sent an unspoken message to American Indians: We will be using the archaeology of Native America for ends that have no special relevance to native people. Bruce Trigger has suggested that the heavy-handed pursuit of law-like generalizations created an unintended, chilling effect, "spiritually alienating" the Euroamerican archaeologist from Native American communities.

of the actual societies we study. Explanation is embedded in the history that inspires it; reducing social behavior to abstract dimensions—then ordering societies along those dimensions—does not constitute explanation.

Although we no longer emphasize a search for universal patterns abstracted from the archaeological record or for universal laws to explain them, we continue to believe in a scientific archaeology—one that moves beyond description to explanation by verifying propositions about prehistoric social behavior. Ancient societies had an existence independent of our inquiries, even if we understand their material traces only imperfectly. The objective existence of those societies—and those traces—means that our propositions about the past are testable. The decision to accept or reject explanations for specific archaeological patterns can and must be grounded in those same archaeological patterns. This implies, in turn, a continued commitment to the utmost methodological and interpretive rigor, including the further development of middle range theory.

We do not wish to establish a new "dominant paradigm" or belittle the accomplishments of Southwest archaeology over the last 25 years. Instead, we wish to define an approach by which we can add to those accomplishments. At this point we wish to stress our shared concerns: dissatisfaction with tracing all historical change to environmental or demographic roots; willingness to seek social or political mechanisms for change; and the sense that explanation means analyzing and comparing actual instances of change, not examining differences between abstractions. We also seek new ways to bring people together and begin defining an approach that is explicitly historical, yet methodologically and theoretically rigorous.

Signed,
David A. Phillips Jr. (adjunct associate professor of anthropology, University of New Mexico)
Philip Duke (professor of anthropology, Fort Lewis College)
Randall H. McGuire (professor of anthropology, State University of New York, Binghamton)
Dean J. Saitta (associate professor of anthropology, University of Denver)
Lynne Sebastian (state archaeologist, New Mexico)
David R. Wilcox (senior research archaeologist, Museum of Northern Arizona)

In sharp contrast, the postprocessual critique puts down attempts by "authority" to speak for "the other"–colonized peoples, indigenous groups and minorities, religious groups, women, and the working class–with a unified voice. Each group has a right to speak for itself, in its own voice, and have that voice accepted as authentic and legitimate. This postmodern spirit of *pluralism* has penetrated contemporary archaeology, creating a more diverse set of research objectives–expressed in a less authoritarian manner. The postprocessual critique calls for and welcomes multiple perspectives on the past.

Although there is a long history of archaeologists working with (and sometimes for) Indian tribes, the last decade has seen a dramatic increase in such interactions–archaeologists helping Native American communities establish their own archaeology programs and pursuing tribally defined archaeological objectives. Some native groups use archaeology to provide evidence relevant to land claims cases. Other Indian tribes are conducting archaeology to encourage tourism, to inform educational programs, and to preserve sacred sites on their own land. Some Native Americans are sponsoring archaeological excavations in tandem with oral history programs, retrieving a past directly relevant to tribal members. Some Indian groups welcome the postprocessual interest in Native American religion, power, authority,

There are signs that groups other than white, . . . middle class intellectuals want to write their own pasts. Other social groups in England and America, ethnic minorities and archaeologists in less-developed countries are beginning to make claims to their own archaeology.

Ian Hodder

Native American Resources on the Internet:

NativeWeb:
http://www.maxwell.syr.edu/nativeweb/

Aboriginal Super Information Hwy:
http://www.abinfohwy.ca/abinfohwy/

American Indian and Alaskan Native:
http://www.nativeweb.org/

Tribal Voice was created "to facilitate the propagation of cybertribes within the realm of cyberspace." It sponsors a PowWow page with addresses, reviews, resources, and search engines for Indian Country:
http://www.tribal.com/

For an index of available resources, see:
http://hanksville.phast.umass.edu/misc/NAresources.html

and gender roles; others question whether these are appropriate areas of study.

Indigenous groups throughout the world are defining their own connections with the past through archaeology. They want to contribute their perspectives and knowledge about their own cultures and histories, drawing on a variety of sources, including oral tradition, and knowledge of religious leaders and elders. Such inclusion and self-expression did not commonly occur under archaeology's processual agenda.

This is not to say, of course, that processualism *per se* made Indian participation impossible or that postprocessualism automatically ensures Native American participation. Indigenous people began participating in archaeology for multiple reasons, only one of which was the theoretical configuration of the field. The social/political and civil rights movements of the 1960s had a significant impact on scholarship and participation in it. Issues about the treatment of women and minorities as subjects of study and as participants in various fields emerged in tandem with the processual/postmodern dialogue.

An Exclusion of Gender-Based Inquiry

Advocates of pluralistic archaeology also argue that the processual agenda exerted a stultifying effect on gender-based research. Explanations in processual archaeology operated at the level of the cultural system, defining a focus on systemwide mechanisms—specifically those mediating adaptive responses to the environment.

This system-based approach contrasts sharply with the needs of gender-based inquiry. During the 1970s and 1980s, emerging feminist theory began to define major arenas of interest—gender identities, gender roles, and gender ideology—which were highly variable, involving ideational and symbolic components. Small wonder, then, that gender-based inquiry fell largely outside the purview of processual approaches, which, by definition, specifically focus on adaptation, demography, and technology. Gender systems were largely ignored in materialistic, processual archaeology.

Alison Wylie has argued that processual approaches made key assumptions about gender that denied (or overlooked) the relevance of women in understanding the past through the archaeological record. In its search for a single, coherent, and comprehensive ("true") understanding of the past, processual archaeology downplayed the possibility of seeking alternative perspectives that direct attention toward the activities of men and women. The postprocessual critique demonstrated (to the satisfaction of many) that the so-called value-neutral scientific approach was full of androcentric biases and assumptions.

In addition, processual archaeology—operating within a highly structured, "objective" framework—generally viewed gender-based variables as "too soft," "too subjective" to be reconstructed on the basis of archaeological data. Gender-based inquiry seemed unsuitable for properly scientific methods of hypothesis testing (an integral part of the processual agenda). Those who argued for study of the symbolic, ideational bases of gender relations were commonly put down as nonscientific and irrelevant.

Today, we find considerable variability within the emerging field of gender archaeology, and it is easy to see why feminist scholars welcomed archaeology's postprocessual critique. Although not all feminist archaeology is postprocessual in nature, many of the themes developed in feminist writing are consistent with those of the postprocessual critique: a concern with meaning and human agency, a willingness to listen to other voices, a concern with power and self-reflexive views of the past.

Putting the "I" Back in Archaeology: Defining an Empathetic Approach

The increase in gender-based studies and increasing involvement of ethnic minorities are just two examples illustrating the changing directions within Americanist archaeology. Just as some have attacked the antihistorical, generalizing, and materialist biases of processual archaeology, others have taken issue with the way in which processual approaches dismiss the role of the individual (see *On Envisioning Gender—More Than Faceless Blobs* by Ruth E. Tringham).

Archaeology is a story we tell ourselves about ourselves through meditation upon the archaeological record.

Elizabeth M. Brumfiel, archaeologist (Albion College)

In Chapter 13, we considered the importance of human agency, and the role it plays in the postprocessual critique. The debate of how best to bring individuals into theories about the past has crystalized archaeology's so-called cognitive revolution, addressed in this and the previous chapter.

Human Agency, Revisited

Some archaeologists believe that in order to reintroduce human agency into the past, we must develop a more empathetic approach, involving not only human thoughts and decisions but also such highly subjective elements as affective states, spiritual orientations, and deep-down meanings. This approach assumes that the inner experiences of individuals are worthy of study, both for their own sake and as a clue for finding meaning in the human past.

To do this, empathetic methods assume the existence of a common, shared structure behind all human experience, a structure that allows an investigator to "bridge" into the feelings, hopes, and meanings of the past. It is assumed that modern investigators and ancient target groups share similar cognitive configurations, more or less.

Empathetic explanation: A view that reconstructs not only thoughts and decisions, but also such elements as affective states, spiritual orientations, and experiential meanings.

An **empathetic explanation** of the past requires two key assumptions. First, it is necessary to assume that thoughts and decisions really *do have agency*—that is, that they are truly individual, not just reflections of some

IN HER OWN WORDS

On Envisioning Gender—More Than Faceless Blobs by Ruth E. Tringham

[In April 1988] *I was taken kicking and screaming to the conference* "Women and Production in Prehistory" *in the marshes of* South Carolina, *convinced that gender differences were not visible in the archaeological record, least of all in the architectural remains of deep prehistory, with which I was most concerned. I was moreover at a loss as to how I should rework my current research strategy to face the question of what women were doing in the houses that I was so busy studying.*

I had an "Aha" experience.

I presented a summarized version of my paper about investigating household organization and architectural remains in prehistoric southeast Europe *to the* 20 *or so participants round the table. They listened politely—the archaeologists did—and worried about the validity of the data I presented for my conclusions.*

And then someone said, "Yes, but how do you envisage these households?" It was Henrietta Moore, *I think.*

"You mean how do I imagine their composition?" thinking: Oh, *heavens, she wants me to imagine their kinship structure, but I am interested in what households* did *not what they comprised. . . .*

Henrietta said "No, *how do you envisage them going about their daily actions?"*

You can imagine, I felt quite defensive. "Archaeologists *don't do that. We don't go around envisaging people leading cows to pasture and gossiping around the household chores."*

"Yes, but what if you were allowed to do it; just relax; no one will tell. Now, *just tell us how you see them.* What *do they look like?"*

"Well," I said, "there's a house, and cows, and pigs, and garbage . . . "

"Yes, but the people, tell us about the people."

"Well . . . ," I said. And *then I realized what I saw. "I see," I said, " . . . a lot of faceless blobs."*

And then it dawned on me what she wanted me to see. That until, as an archaeologist, you can learn to give your imagined societies faces, you cannot envisage gender. Or, in somebody else's term (Conkey's?) *you cannot engender prehistory.*

And until you can engender prehistory, you cannot think of your prehistoric constructions as really human entities with a social, political, ideological, and economic life.

Ahaaaa!

Ruth E. Tringham is professor of anthropology at the University of California, Berkeley.

"superstructure" that derives directly from underlying material "forces" (as is assumed in the processual agenda). Empathetic approaches also assume that *collective* actions and shared institutions can be interpreted as the direct products of decisions and actions of past individuals.

Clearly, this is a sharp break from the processual agenda, which focuses on the cultural system that, to one degree or another, conditions all human actions. Taken together, these two assumptions provide the basis for "the cognitive revolution" in archaeology—discussed in this and the previous chapter.

What we call our data are really our own constructions of other people's constructions of what they and their compatriots are up to.

Clifford Geertz, interpretive anthropologist (Princeton University)

Reflexive Ethnography

But how do we actually introduce *agency* into our understanding of the human condition? One way, postmodernists argue, is to modify the narrative style in which anthropological findings are expressed. Not unlike Jefferson's perspective discussed earlier, modern interpretive anthropology stresses the importance of *context*—not just the context in which the subject exists, but also the context within which the observer, the ethnographer, operates. Such ethnographic inquiry is "interpretive" in that the explanatory framework is extended from the observed to the observer, from the described to the describer.

Such interpretive approaches—both in ethnography and archaeology—result directly from a postmodern perspective that challenges many current forms of representation, transcending history, political science, economics, sociology, psychology, law, art, and even architecture. Postmodern methods attempt to "deconstruct" various means of communication by critically analyzing—by *contextualizing*—how they were constructed and how they attempt to convey credibility.

The fact that archaeology is accepted by only a fraction of the world's populations, and the fact that only some questions about the past are admitted as relevant to its study of the past, suggest how deeply archaeology is embedded in a particular set of values and knowledge.

JOAN M. GERO, ARCHAEOLOGIST (UNIVERSITY OF SOUTH CAROLINA)

Today, cultural anthropologists worry about the issue of *authenticity*. For decades, ethnographic credibility has derived from a sense of "having been there," emphasizing the believability of a trained observer who has directly experienced another culture and a different language. Traditionally, such experiences were considered adequate to empower the ethnographer as a competent translator of other cultures.

Interpretive anthropologists have heavily criticized the traditional role of such "ethnographic authority," questioning in particular the anthropologist's ability to separate the observed from the observer. Modern cultural anthropology is increasingly critical of time-honored forms of ethnographic writing because they fail to relate what is being described (the people under study) to the describer (the ethnographer conducting the study). Great concern has been expressed about how various identities—one's subjects, the ethnographer, the ethnographic project itself—are negotiated in the various places that anthropologists conduct their fieldwork.

A new form of ethnographic writing has sprung up in response to this concern, emphasizing the importance of *reflexivity* by defining the role of the anthropologist in the ethnographic inquiry. **Reflexive** accounts are *self-conscious* in that they emphasize the conditions under which anthropological knowledge is produced, discarding the "naive" assumptions of objectivity and realism. Postmodern, interpretive ethnographic writing increasingly shows a sense of reflexive collaboration, in which informant and ethnographer collectively construct a text.

Reflexive: Directed to or looking back on oneself. In anthropology, a reflexive approach explicitly recognizes the interaction between the anthropologist and the culture being studied.

As George Marcus has put it, reflexive perspective requires us to replace the objective eye with the more personal "I."

Reflexive Archaeology

Similar trends can be found in modern archaeological thought. Many archaeologists have backed away from the notions of absolute objectivity and glacial impartiality. Following the lead of interpretive ethnography, archaeologists are once again putting the "I" back into their own writings.

This trend, of course, flies in the face of traditional views of scientific discourse. Although many undergraduates are still advised to remove first-person references from their technical writings, some archaeologists feel that removing the "I" effectively denies the self and the author—in effect replacing the authority of the actual archaeologist with an unwarranted brand of faceless, impersonal objectivity.

More and more, archaeologists are including in their site reports the sense of revelation and unfolding that characterizes most excavations, imposing a feeling of sequence, discovery, and surprise. As every participant in an archaeological excavation clearly realizes, the hands-on process of archaeological inquiry is neither simple nor clear-cut. Every day on a dig poses new questions to the diggers, specialists, supervisors, and site directors: Why was this wall destroyed? Is this really a house floor? Should we dig through this fire hearth to see what's below? Why was this A.D. 1200 potsherd found in a posthole that apparently dates to A.D. 600?

Some blame the disembodied, colorless character of archaeological writing for obscuring the dynamics of the archaeological process. Archaeology isn't dull. It isn't boring. And it certainly isn't self-evident. So why must modern archaeologists still present their findings in a mind numbing, prepackaged, matter-of-fact style?

Nobody is suggesting a return to eighteenth-century rhetoric. Thomas Jefferson's account of his Virginia excavations is not a model for modern site reportage. But many archaeologists are drawing upon some qualities evident in Jefferson's seminal text: a return to first-person narrative, an openness to diversity of opinion rather than consensus, an emphasis on the role of the archaeologist in conditioning the outcome. Such archaeological texts not only come alive, but also more clearly reflect how down-and-dirty archaeology is really done. As we will see later, many would also claim that this shift in narrative style reveals deeper changes in the underlying structure of archaeological thought.

[The historian] may begin by discovering the outside of an event, but it can never end there; he must always remember that the event was an action, and that his main task is to think himself into this action, to discern the thought of its agent.

R. G. COLLINGWOOD (1889–1943), HISTORIAN AND PHILOSOPHER

The ultimate aim can only be self-knowledge. In projecting ourselves into the past, critically, we come to know ourselves better.

IAN HODDER

We study history . . . in order to attain self-knowledge.

R. G. COLLINGWOOD

Thinking Yourself Into the Past

Current empathetic approaches in archaeology draw their inspiration in part from the writings of English historian and philosopher Robin George Collingwood. In his influential writings, Collingwood argued that in order to understand events in the human past, it is necessary to distinguish between the "outsider" and "insider" views of the past. The "outsider" (or etic) view, to Collingwood, could be described in terms of bodies and their movements—people participating in the observable events of the past. But the "insider" (what today we would term emic) view can be described only in terms of the thoughts once held by those people. This is the goal of an empathetic approach to the past—to penetrate the past event and actually insinuate oneself into the role the actor played in that event.

Collingwood's "from the inside" approach—attempting to get at the intentions and thoughts of actors in the past—found ready acceptance in the postprocessual critique, most notably in Ian Hodder's influential *Reading the Past*, published in 1986. Following Collingwood, Hodder argued that knowing the past is not merely the passive reception of facts; it is, rather, the discerning of the thought that took place inside the event.

According to Hodder's reading of Collingwood, archaeologists must "think themselves into the past." In the next section, we will see how Janet Spector has effectively employed one version of empathetic archaeology in her important research at the site of Little Rapids, Minnesota.

Ian Hodder on the Internet:

A Review of His Career:
http://129.215.101.2/arch/arch1/arch1/sum4ih.html

Feminist Archaeology at a Dakota Village: Janet Spector's Empathetic Approach

Janet Spector.

We further explore the empathetic approach in archaeology by looking at an important recent study by Janet Spector, a specialist in the archaeology and ethnohistory of the Great Lakes region. Like many of us, Spector decided early on to become an archaeologist. Although told that girls could not be archaeologists, she decided to study archaeology anyway, eventually becoming a professor of anthropology at the University of Minnesota.

Spector moved away from fieldwork for a while, trying instead to develop an explicitly feminist approach to archaeology. She found in the women's movement some reasons why her early anthropological training left her feeling dissatisfied. Her undergraduate courses not only ignored living Indian people—they ignored women! Americanist archaeology, Spector decided, had been produced "almost exclusively by white, middle-class men from Euroamerican societies that discriminate on the basis of sex, race, and class."

With Margaret Conkey, Spector produced an important early commentary on the impact of male-dominated thinking on archaeology (see Chapter 14 for a further discussion of her views). As she explored archaeological approaches to the study of gender, Spector was eventually drawn back to the archaeological record. Was it possible to recognize male and female roles and beliefs in actual ancient sites?

As Spector looked for someplace to examine gender relationships in the past, she came across the Little Rapids site, which had been occupied by the Eastern Dakota (or "Sioux") people sometime in the early and middle 1800s. The site had been badly damaged by relic collectors and archaeological hobbyists. Professional archaeologists had stayed away. But because a number of documentary sources, sketches, and paintings depicted life at sites like Little Rapids, and because it was located only 45 miles from her Minneapolis campus, Spector decided to work there, directing several archaeological field schools at Little Rapids. After three field seasons, she stopped excavating to analyze what had been recovered. Everything was done exactly by the book.

Dakota Village (*engraving by Seth Eastman,* 1853).

Involving Dakota People in Dakota Archaeology

As Spector wrote up her preliminary report on Little Rapids, she felt something was still lacking. Spector came to realize that, as a relatively privileged non-Indian university

WHAT'S IN A NAME?

Sioux *or* Dakota?

The term *Sioux* (pronounced "sue") is a fragment of the French/Ojibwa word *nadouessioux*. This name arose as a derogatory term (meaning "little snakes"), applied by the Ojibwas to their western "Sioux" neighbors. Although the term *Sioux* remains in common use, many contemporary tribal members resent the use of this disparaging term, preferring the more specific terms *Dakota*, *Nakota*, and *Lakota* when referring to themselves as a people and a nation.

In these pages, we will respect that request.

[Can] a non-Indian person do Indian-centered work? When men ask me if they can do feminist work, I say yes. Although not all feminists agree, I do not think a person has to be female to detect gender bias or to write from a feminist perspective. I wondered if this same principle were true for non-Indian people doing Indian studies.

Janet Spector, Archaeologist (University of Minnesota)

professor, she was in danger of doing something that had bothered her years before as an undergraduate: Inadvertently, she had been excluding exactly the people she wished to learn about.

Once she recognized the problem, she began talking to Dakota people. Initially, she encountered some resentment toward the "anthros," as the Indians called them; throughout Indian Country, many Native American people question whether archaeologists can really be trusted. But after months of discussion and site visits, Spector enlisted several Dakota people to help her understand the archaeology of their ancestral site. Excavations began again at Little Rapids, this time with the hands-on participation of members of the Wahpeton Dakota community.

Tribal members helped out by providing Dakota names for various plants and animals, and some crew members learned the rudiments of the Dakota language as they dug. During lunchtime, Dakota people led discussions about their culture and history. On Fridays, the project historian helped the groups work through the strengths and limitations of the available documentary evidence. "For the first time in my archaeological career, a project felt right. We worked as an interdisciplinary, multicultural team."

Beaded Dakota pipe bags.

Archaeology as Four-Act Theater

Spector came to view her archaeology in a different light. Although she continued to dig according to the standard scientific operating procedures, the style of her archaeology changed. As she researched the archaeological and ethnohistoric record of Little Rapids, Spector found herself trying to transcend the detail of the archaeological and written records. "I sometimes imagine being transported into the past by a bilingual, bicultural, bitemporal guide—a Dakota person willing and able to explain to me his or her view of the area's politics, tensions, and interactions."

With her imagined guide, Spector began approaching Little Rapids as drama or theater.

The drama began with Spector's experience of finding the site itself—an elusive objective further obscured by dense ground cover and buzzing mosquitoes. Then there were the stresses and amusement of organizing each field season—assembling the crew, raising the necessary funds, worrying about the weather, and the dozen other details that make or break an excavation.

Dakota people with horse-drawn travois (Indians Travelling *by Seth Eastman,* 1853).

Day after day, the crew fell into the rhythm typical of all digs. Arrive early, split into small teams, digging and taking notes. Get together at lunch and talk about the finds. Work all afternoon digging or doing labwork, then finally break off. During the day, the excavators would speculate about what had taken place on this or that part of the site, why artifacts had been left where they were found, how the nineteenth-century Dakota people felt living there: "Did they watch the darkening skies some days as we did, hoping to finish our work before a thunderstorm struck? Was their community life, like ours, punctuated by summer romances and interpersonal tensions, or were such relationships a product of our particular time and place only?"

As on all digs, the excavation at Little Rapids was tedious, but the anticipation of an unexpected find kept everyone on their toes. The discovery process at Little Rapids also included searching through written documents, so considerable "unearthing" took place in libraries and archives as well.

Nearly 100 students and volunteers participated in the dig at Little Rapids. Each person played a different role. Janet Spector saw herself as the "project's director, producer, teacher, and writer." Others helped as teachers and supervisors. Beginners became old hands and often returned as interns to supervise and teach others.

Spector came to see the various activity areas at Little Rapids as "acts," each presenting different takes on the past that had played out there. "Act I" was a summer lodge, "Act II" was the community dump, and so forth. Problems arose in "Act III"—the presumed dance area. After excavations had been completed here, Spector's team applied for permission from the Minnesota Intertribal Board for further testing in the suspected dance area. A non-Dakota board member objected strongly. Spector found that "to them, a dance area—even a suspected one—was sacred and, like a burial place, should not be disturbed." Respecting these views, Spector shifted focus elsewhere. More and more, archaeologists are conflicted by episodes like this. Spector noted: "Do I wish we might have had a chance to follow these tantalizing leads? Yes. Would I knowingly dig in sacred areas? No."

The site was the set for past human actions, emotions, and conflicts: the plot was activated by "the dig," which was a story in itself. The artifacts, like stage props, were material cues of time, place, and culture last used by people living more than a century earlier and brought to life again when twentieth-century excavators touched them.

Janet Spector

Like casts in community theater productions, crew members varied considerably in their talent and tolerance for the work. Some people loved digging and found the materials we unearthed fascinating. . . . Others quickly found the digging tedious. They hated the blisters, sore muscles, and sweat and became preoccupied with the earthworms, mosquitoes, gnats, snakes, poison ivy, and other distractions common to most digs.

Janet Spector

Archaeology in the Active Voice

The archaeologist is digging up, not things, *but* people.

Sir Mortimer Wheeler (1890–1976), archaeologist

Although the archaeologist's writing style is intentionally depersonalized and object centered, it still conveys feelings. Boring, tedious, and confusing-to-read descriptions of awls affect readers, who inevitably transfer their feelings to the people who once made or used the tools. . . . Why do archaeologists write dense technical reports in esoteric language instead of lively cultural studies?

Janet Spector

When it came time to publish the results, Spector wrestled with the meaning of what she had found. Although conducted according to thoroughly modern standard scientific procedures, the Little Rapids project had also been strongly conditioned by Spector's own changing perceptions of archaeology. The dig itself was part of the story, and so was the world around it.

In the fall of 1991, as Spector was writing up the Little Rapids materials, the Atlanta Braves baseball team finally made it to the World Series. Three months later, professional football's Washington Redskins played in the Superbowl. That year, Indian people across the country were protesting being used as sport mascots, further highlighting tensions between themselves and the dominant Euroamerican community. To Spector, this was a repetition—150 years later—of the confrontation evident in the archaeological record at Little Rapids.

Maybe if the American public knew more about Indian cultural roots and sensibilities, she thought, they would better understand why being considered a sport mascot is so offensive to Indian people, why so many Native Americans object to the way they have been portrayed in movies, on television, and in the rest of American pop culture.

Spector felt a growing need to communicate with others what she had learned about this abandoned Wahpeton Dakota community. She wanted to highlight women's activities and the relationship between men and women. And she also wanted to draw Dakota voices and perspectives into her story.

Dakota people lived in skin lodges like this in their winter camps (Dakota Encampment *by Seth Eastman,* 1853).

One particular find captured her imagination: the deer antler handle of an awl (and its iron tip found nearby). From her ethnohistoric research, Spector knew that nineteenth-century Dakota women used such awls for working hides into moccasins, bags, and clothing. Although buried for more than a century, this particular awl was remarkably well preserved, with traces of red pigment still evident in the decorations along the edge. Because it was not broken or worn out, Spector felt that it must somehow have been lost (rather than deliberately thrown away). She became intrigued with the woman who once had owned it.

I turned my attention to a small antler handle, delicately inscribed with a series of dots and lines. I felt certain that a Wahpeton woman had once used that tool at Little Rapids and that its inscriptions conveyed a great deal about her accomplishments to those who understood their meaning.

JANET SPECTOR

This simple yet elegant artifact came to symbolize for Spector what she was learning from doing archaeology at Little Rapids. She wanted to communicate that knowledge to others. But how?

Archaeologists, of course, describe things all the time. Using the standard archaeological typologies and language, such metal awls would be grouped into a series of carefully defined, objective categories according to size, material, spatial and temporal distribution. Sometimes, observations might be made about how traditional forms of technology fared after Euroamerican contact. Spector, like all archaeologists, had previously employed such approaches in her own archaeology. But she had grown tired of these bland, impersonal terms.

She also came to believe that neutral, monotonous descriptions unintentionally carry with them negative messages about Indian people and culture. She worried, for instance, that such descriptions inadvertently assumed that European-produced tools were somehow "more important" than those produced by Indian people. She even felt that seemingly value-neutral descriptions reflected nineteenth-century European social theory, creating divisions that do not accurately describe Native American life, either today or in the past. Spector further objected to the way that standard archaeological description minimizes the role of actual people.

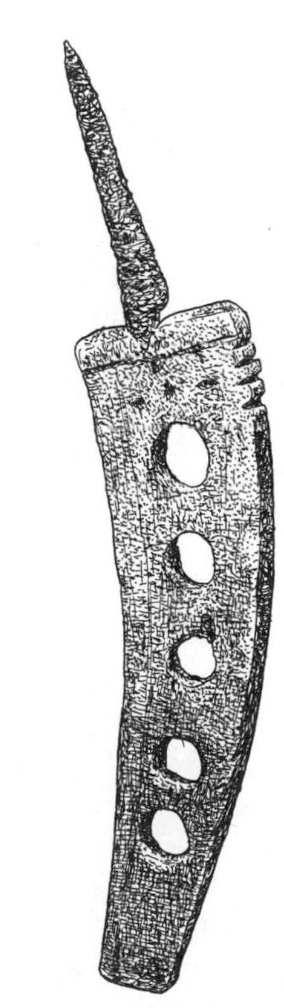

The awl from Little Rapids.

This simple artifact communicated something to Spector, and she wanted to communicate her feelings to others. To do this, she described the awl from Little Rapids in a different way. She wrote instead an imaginative reconstruction of Mazaokiyewin, the young Dakota woman who Spector envisioned had lost the awl in a rainstorm; later it was swept up and discarded in the dump (see *What This Awl Means*). Although Spector made up the specific circumstances about the awl, Mazaokiyewin was a real person (grandmother to one of the Dakota women who worked with Spector at Little Rapids). Such narratives, while still uncommon, are one way of injecting more humanistic perspectives into archaeology.

Many of the details in *What This Awl Means* derive from solid ethnohistoric research. Although at first the inscriptions on the handle held no meaning for her, Spector later learned that Dakota women, in the way men kept war records, kept count of their accomplishments. Reflecting their ambition to excel, women recorded the number of robes and tipis they completed by incising dots along the handles of their elkhorn tools.

Spector describes her feelings when she discovered what the awl inscriptions may have actually meant. It was "like cracking a code or being able to read some ancient, previously undeciphered text for the first time. . . . The awl inscriptions provided a kind of access to the people at Little Rapids that I had never before imagined possible."

What This Awl Means *is an eloquent restoration of women's voices: the voice of the female archaeologist and that of the woman who used the awl. Together they tell an important story.*

JANET CATHERINE BERLO, ARCHAEOLOGIST (UNIVERSITY OF MISSOURI, ST. LOUIS)

IN HER OWN WORDS

What This Awl Means by Janet Spector

The women and children of Inyan Ceyaka Atonwan (Little Rapids) had been working at the maple sugar camps since Istawicayazan wi (the Moon of Sore Eyes, or March). At the same time, most of the men had been far from the village trapping muskrats. When Wozupi wi (the Moon for Planting, or May) came, 15 households eagerly reunited in their bark lodges near the river.

One day some villagers brought their tanned furs and maple sugar to the lodge of Jean Baptiste Faribault. He lived among them a few months each year with his Dakota wife, Pelagie. In exchange for furs and maple sugar, Faribault gave them glass beads, silver ornaments, tin kettles, and iron knives, awl tips, axes, hatchets, and hoes for their summer work.

Mazomani (Iron Walker) and Hazawin (Blueberry Woman) were proud of their daughter, Mazaokiyewin (Woman Who Talks to Iron). The day after visiting Faribault, they had given her some glass beads and a new iron awl tip. The tip was the right size to fit into the small antler handle that Hazawin had given Mazaokiyewin when she went to dwell alone at the time of her first menses. Mazaokiyewin used the sharp-pointed awl for punching holes in pieces of leather before stitching them together with deer sinew. Though young, she had already established a reputation among the people at Inyan Ceyaka Atonwan for creativity and excellence in quillwork and beadwork.

Mazaokiyewin's mother and grandmothers had taught her to keep a careful record of her accomplishments, so whenever she finished quilling or beading moccasins, she remembered to impress a small dot on the fine awl handle that Hazawin had made for her. When Mazaokiyewin completed more complicated work, such as sewing and decorating a buckskin dress or pipe bag, she formed diamond-shaped clusters of four small dots which symbolized the powers of the four directions that influenced her life in many ways. She liked to expose the handle of this small tool as she carried it in its beaded case so that others could see she was doing her best to ensure the well-being of their community.

When she engraved the dots into her awl handle, she carefully marked each one with red pigment, made by boiling sumac berries with a small root found in the ground near the village. Dakota people associated the color red with women and their life forces. Red also represented the east, where the sun rose to give knowledge, wisdom, and understanding. Red symbolized Mazaokiyewin's aspirations to these qualities.

When the designated day in Wasuton wi arrived, Mazomani led the people in the medicine dance near the burial place of their ancestors. Members of the medicine lodge danced within an enclosed oval area, separated from the audience by a low, hide-covered fence.

One hot day following the dance, Mazaokiyewin gathered together all of the leatherwork she had finished since returning to Inyan Ceyaka Atonwan after the spring hunting and sugaring seasons. Now, Mazaokiyewin eagerly anticipated the quilling contest and feast called by a woman of a neighboring household to honor a family member. Mazaokiyewin knew she had produced more beaded and quilled articles than most of the community's young women, and she looked forward to bringing recognition to her parents and grandparents.

She started uphill carrying the *miniapahatapi* (skin water bags) carefully, but near the quilling-contest lodge she slipped on the muddy path where water had pooled in the driving rain. As she struggled to regain her footing without dropping the bags, the leather strap holding her awl in its case broke, and the small awl dropped to the ground. It fell close to one of the cooking fires outside the lodge entrance.

Mazaokiyewin did not miss her awl that day, because as soon as she entered the lodge with the water, the host of the contest took her hand and escorted her to the center of the crowd. The host had already counted each woman's pieces and distributed a stick for each. Mazaokiyewin had accumulated more sticks than all but three older women. The host then led the four to the place of honor in the lodge and gave them their food first to honor their accomplishments. Later, the results of this contest would be recorded for all to see on the hides lining the walls of the lodge. This pleased Hazawin and Mazomani.

The heavy rain that day had scattered debris over the village, and on the day after the quilling contest and medicine dance, people joined together to clean up the encampment. Using old hides and baskets, they carried off loads of fallen branches, wet fire ash and charcoal, and the remains of the feast to the community dump above the slough. Somehow, Mazaokiyewin's small awl was swept up and carried off with other garbage from the quilling contest. It disappeared in the dump as the villagers emptied one basketload after another on top of it.

Beaded Dakota pouches.

Later, the loss of the awl saddened Mazaokiyewin and Hazawin, but they knew the handle was nearly worn out, and both realized it was more a girl's tool than a woman's. Mazaokiyewin was almost a woman ready to establish her own household, no longer a child of her mother's lodge. It was time to put aside her girl-tools, she knew, but she had intended to keep this awl. Its finely incised dots and engraved lines showed how well she had learned adult tasks, and she took as much pleasure in displaying it as her mother did in watching others admire it.

The following day, they packed the equipment that the family would need over the next several months. As they assembled their hide-working tools, they spoke again of Mazaokiyewin's missing awl. They realized that their feeling of loss was not simply about that one small tool. Instead, as fall approached and they prepared to leave Inyan Ceyaka Atonwan, they had troubling premonitions about the future.

IN HER OWN WORDS

On *Archaeology and Empathy* by Janet Spector

Until now, when I wrote about [archaeological] sites and objects, I felt no connection with the past, my own or that of the people whose cultural landscapes I unearthed. Writing "What This Awl Means," a story about a Dakota girl who lost a carved awl handle a century and a half ago, brought back thoughts and feelings I had experienced as a young girl drawn to archaeology. As I learned about the discipline—and, especially how to write about archaeology for academic readers—I found myself increasingly distanced from the question that had fascinated me since childhood: What was life like for people in the past? While composing the awl story in place of the standard archaeological report or scholarly article, I was reminded of my original reasons for wanting to be an archaeologist. The motives are empathetic—a longing to discover essences, images, and feelings of the past—not detached, distanced, objective.

It took me a long time to reconnect with the past.

I began studying archaeology in 1962 as a freshman at the University of Wisconsin at Madison, but I found the subject much less interesting than I had expected. This disappointed me, since I had decided in the ninth grade to become an archaeologist, despite having been told that girls could not be archaeologists and not knowing what it took to become one. With a few exceptions the readings in undergraduate courses bored me. I learned from these courses that archaeologists apparently considered artifact classification more important than the people who had made the tools, about whom very little was said. The archaeology I was taught was objective, object oriented, and objectifying.

For almost a decade of summers I excavated at Indian sites in Wisconsin, [but] neither professors of archaeology nor authors of archaeology texts suggested that we might get closer to these people by studying contemporary Indian languages, religions, or philosophies. They implied that too much time had elapsed, too much change had occurred, too much history separated people from their pasts. People occupied these "prehistoric" sites long before traditional Indian culture had "disintegrated" through contact with Europeans. Contemporary Indians were disconnected from their ancestors. But no one I knew ever bothered to ask Indian people about these notions.

["What This Awl Means"] incorporate[s] voices and viewpoints other than my own—those of the Dakota people, as well as the fur traders, officials, explorers, and missionaries that the Indians encountered, sometimes in harmony but more often in conflict. Throughout I have tried to convey the turmoil of times and avoid the rhetoric of archaeology that frequently obscures the people being studied.

Shaping my work are the ongoing tensions between archaeologists and Indian people. These conflicts exemplify the archaeological premise that the past shapes the present. A viewpoint archaeologists less often acknowledge is that the present shapes our rendering of the past.

The young Dakota woman whom Janet Spector writes about was our grandmother. Having worked with Janet on the Little Rapids Project, I respect her sensitivity; for us to be involved as Wahpeton people, was really special.

CAROLYNN SCHOMMER, WAHPETON DAKOTA WOMAN

When she began the Little Rapids project, Spector wanted to bring a feminist perspective to archaeology. She would counteract the long-standing male biases and focus on the role of women and the importance of gender in shaping the encounter between Dakota and Euroamerican people at Little Rapids. But as the project unfolded, she found herself increasingly aware of her own privilege by race and by profession. Although she still wished for a time machine, Spector became increasingly concerned with linking her archaeological finds at Little Rapids to the lives of Dakota people who had once lived there. This is why, as she began to write up her findings at the Little Rapids site, Spector decided to abandon the strictly scientific, "lifeless" format of the standard archaeological site report.

As we saw earlier, many ethnographers have become concerned with the political implications of their writing and reporting style. Many sociocultural anthropologists have dropped their detached, descriptive tone in favor of new and more varied styles that portray the people being studied more vividly and more empathetically. Although such concerns are rarely expressed out loud by archaeologists, Spector decided to find a better way to convey what the archaeology of Little Rapids meant to her (see *On Archaeology and Empathy* by Janet Spector).

SUMMARY Postmodern approaches to archaeology have challenged various forms of representation and communication, "deconstructing" and critically analyzing the ways in which archaeologists express themselves. The goal is to look inside archaeological communications, to seek meanings that were not necessarily intended by the writer, to determine what is absent from the archaeological text and what is silenced by it.

Examples of archaeological writings of Thomas Jefferson and Lewis Binford are compared here. Following the lead of British archaeologist Ian Hodder, we strip away the surface, textual forms to explore truths buried and concealed, to see what these texts have to say about the archaeological thought in both the historic past and the very recent past.

In this exercise, we see a processual approach to archaeology with the stated goal of creating universally valid generalizations that should ultimately prove to be of practical value for the improvement and management of contemporary societies. But an unintended consequence of this approach has been an unspoken message sent to Indian Country: We will be using the archaeology of Native America for ends that have no special relevance to native people. In some cases, the heavy-handed pursuit of law-like generalizations created an unintended, spiritual alienation of Euroamerican archaeologists from Native American communities.

By contrast, postprocessual approaches have affirmed the right of each special interest group—colonized peoples, indigenous groups and minorities, religious groups, women, and the working class—to speak for themselves, in their own voice, with that voice accepted as authentic and legitimate. The current spirit of theoretical pluralism characterizes contemporary archaeology and has curated a more diverse set of research objectives, expressed in a less authoritarian manner. The increase in gender- and ethnic-based studies underscores the changing directions within Americanist archaeology.

Some archaeologists believe that in order to reintroduce human agency into the past, more empathetic approaches should be employed, involving not only human thoughts and decisions but also such highly subjective elements as affective states, spiritual orientations, and deep-down meanings. This approach assumes that the inner experiences of individuals are worthy of study, both for their own sake and as a clue for finding meaning in the human past.

Chapter 18

Historical Archaeology: Exploring Capitalism and Power in Anglo-America

We think of historical archaeology as one of the most democratic of the social sciences.

KATHLEEN DEAGAN, HISTORICAL ARCHAEOLOGIST (FLORIDA MUSEUM OF NATURAL HISTORY)

PREVIEW Up to now, we have glimpsed nearly a dozen cases of historical archaeology in action: Kathleen Deagan's long-term research at St. Augustine, Schliemann's monumental quest for the historic city of Troy, my own search for Mission Santa Catalina, the ground-penetrating radar exploration of Japanese burial mounds, tree-ring dating of a Viking queen's grave, C-14 dating of the Shroud of Turin, Bill Rathje's archaeology-of-us Garbage Project, Betsy Reitz's reconstruction of foodways in Spanish Florida, reconstruction of California's Gold Rush cuisine, phytolith analysis of Thomas Jefferson's garden, and the use of molecular archaeology to identify Russia's missing royal family.

Basically, we've drawn upon selected aspects of historic-period contexts to illustrate some more general points about how archaeologists do what they do. But in all this talk about historical archaeology, something is still missing. We have yet to deal with historical archaeology *per se:* What is it? How is it defined? How does it differ from prehistoric archaeology? Is historical archaeology a branch of anthropology, or history, or what?

In this and the next chapter, historical archaeology—as a defined entity—becomes our specific focus. I want you to understand why the field of historical archaeology has become one of the most vigorous aspects of Americanist archaeology. We'll also show you how (and why) historical archaeologists have taken a major leadership role in crafting archaeological theory for the future.

Historic-period sites have been investigated for a very long time. Several of the pioneering archaeologists discussed in Chapter 1 worked on historic-period materials, digging in the classical sites of Greece, Rome, and the Holy Lands. They employed complementary written and archaeological records to understand the past.

The hardest part is getting this thing off the ground.

ATTRIBUTED TO THE WRIGHT BROTHERS (BY J. C. HARRINGTON, "FATHER" OF HISTORICAL ARCHAEOLOGY IN AMERICA)

The Rise of Historical Archaeology in America

The first *bona fide* historical archaeology in America took place only about 150 years ago. James Hall, a trained civil engineer, was a direct descendant of Miles Standish, who arrived with the Pilgrim fathers aboard the *Mayflower* in 1620 and eventually became a leader in Plymouth Colony. Wanting to learn more about his celebrated ancestor, Hall located the foundations of the Standish homestead in Duxbury, Massachusetts, and, in 1853, he conducted detailed excavations there.

Plimoth Plantation on the Internet:

Plimoth Plantation includes a virtual tour of the plantation:
http://www.media3.com/plymouth/plant.htm

Plymouth: Its History and People provides a historical overview and details about individual Puritan settlers:
http://www.media3.com/plymouth/history.htm

For more than a century, Hall's fieldnotes and artifact collection from the Standish house remained unknown to anybody but immediate family members. In the 1960s, however, they surfaced in Mexico and were soon brought to the attention of James Deetz, a historical archaeologist working at Plymouth Plantation. As he looked over the surviving materials, Deetz was astonished at the high quality of Hall's 1853 excavation.

Hall had carefully gridded the site and established datum points to maintain vertical control. A meticulous site map had been prepared. As he dug, Hall attempted to recover artifacts in situ, plotting the location of each on the master site map. Hall even made notes recording various stratigraphic relationships within the house ruin. After the excavation, Hall cataloged each artifact, carefully numbering each find. In short, Hall's 1853 excavation technique measures up quite nicely with today's standards of acceptable archaeological practice (as set out in Chapter 6).

The Pilgrim Fathers landed on the shores of America and fell upon their knees. Then they fell upon the aborigines.

Attributed to H. L. Mencken (1880–1956), journalist and writer

Almost simultaneously, a second pioneering exploration in historical archaeology was taking place in Canada, under very different circumstances. In 1855, Father Félix Martin, a Jesuit priest from Montreal, was awarded a commission by the Canadian government to explore and excavate the site of Ste. Marie, Georgian Bay (near Midland, Ontario).

Sainte Marie was a tiny mission outpost founded in 1639 to bring Christianity to the local Huron Indians. Although they were 800 miles west of their supply base in Quebec, the missionaries enjoyed some success and several left the mission proper to work with surrounding Huron communities. But during the winter of 1648–1649, the Huron villages in this area came under attack from raiding Iroquois war parties. As the villages were being destroyed, the resident Jesuit priests refused to flee and several died martyrs' deaths. In March, the surviving priests abandoned Mission Sainte Marie. Although it had lasted only a decade, Sainte Marie became a sacred place in Christian history, what archaeologist Kenneth Kidd would later describe as "the pulsating heart of French missionary effort in America."

It is for this reason that Father Martin went to Sainte Marie in 1855. Seeking to establish a personal link to his own Jesuit past, Martin identified the location of the site, mapped and described the ruins, painted several watercolors, and conducted limited excavations. Years later, the Jesuit Order purchased the site to encourage its preservation and make it available for religious pilgrimages. Today, the Martyrs Shrine Church stands nearby, honoring both the Jesuit missionaries and the Christian Huron people who once lived there.

The site of Sainte Marie . . . will always remain a place of prime significance to Canadians. Foremost of all, it is hallowed ground to Roman Catholics, for here lived the first Canadian martyrs to their religion.

Kenneth E. Kidd (1906–1994), archaeologist (Royal Ontario Museum)

Together, Martin's exploration of Sainte Marie and Hall's work on the Miles Standish house signaled the beginning of serious historical archaeology

Sainte Marie on the Internet:

Sainte-Marie Among the Hurons, sponsored by the Wyandote Nation, sketches the history of the mission and discusses current activities at the Sainte-Marie Among the Hurons Historical Park, which has a living history exhibit and canoe tours:
http://www.sfo.com/~denglish/wynaks/wn_stmar.htm

North American Martyrs (1642–1649), sponsored by the Jesuit Order, discusses the martyrdom of various Canadian martyrs commemorated at the Martyrs Shrine, near the site of Sainte Marie:
http://www.udmercy.edu/htmls/Jesuits/saints.na.html

See also **Midland Tourism:**
http://mss.scbe.on.ca/midland.htm

in America, defining a first-rate methodological baseline that would win high praise from historical archaeologists working on both sites more than a century later.

These two mid-nineteenth-century digs also incorporated two important themes that would ultimately distinguish and define the field of historical archaeology. First, both excavators were motivated by a dynamic and personal connection to their own past—Hall to his Pilgrim heritage and Father Martin to the legacy of his martyred Jesuit brothers. For both men, the past had a special relevance to the present.

Both excavators also seem to have been familiar with the documentary sources relating to their dig sites. Before looking to the archaeology of their respective sites, they had some knowledge of what to expect: where to dig, what to look for, and generally what kind of material record they should encounter—expectations derived from basic historical sources. By themselves, however, these historical sources were incomplete and not entirely satisfying. Encountering the archaeological record itself—the physical remains of the past—induced Martin and Hall to undertake excavations of their own.

Historical archaeology . . . the study of human behavior through material remains, for which written history in some way affects its interpretation.

KATHLEEN DEAGAN

So what is historical archaeology? Although a profusion of definitions exist, the early excavations by Hall and Martin basically defined the field. As reflected in Kathleen Deagan's more formal definition, historical archaeology looks at material remains from past societies that also left behind some form of written documentation ("history") about themselves.

Developing Historical Archaeology: Just a "Handmaiden to History"?

The archeological scientist digs
to find
Within apparent chaos from the
past,
Hidden order in the refuse man
has left behind.
Explanation of the pattern lies
In answer to the question "why?"
Creatively invented in the scien-
tific mind.

STANLEY SOUTH, HISTORICAL ARCHAEOLOGIST (UNIVERSITY OF SOUTH CAROLINA)

Historical archaeology, as a discipline, has undergone a number of transformations since the days of Martin and Hall. During the first half of the twentieth century, historical archaeologists labored mostly to supplement the historical record of the past. In the words of Ivor Noël Hume (the long-time director of the archaeological program at Colonial Williamsburg, Virginia), the proper role of historical archaeology was to serve as a "handmaiden to history"; the historic site archaeologist became "a new breed—he is actually a historian with a pen in one hand and a trowel in the other."

This perspective is particularly evident in those massive, continuing projects closely linked to historic reconstruction and restoration. When you go to public places such as Plimoth Plantation (Massachusetts), Colonial Williamsburg, Little Bighorn (Montana), and Fort Michilimackinac (Michigan), you should know that extensive archaeology has been conducted here, specifically to recover the data necessary to restore and interpret the sites. Such projects in historical archaeology began in America in the 1940s and 1950s, concentrating on a very few selected sites, particularly houses of the rich and famous, forts, and other military sites.

Colonial Williamsburg served as a model for this early-stage historical archaeology. At first, the digging at Williamsburg was done mostly by architectural historians, concerned with exposing historic-period building foundations; they didn't dig very carefully and showed little interest in the trash middens and smaller structures that would captivate archaeological interest later on. Once they had exhausted the historic documents, historical archaeologists generally followed the example of their prehistoric colleagues in developing independent, artifact-based methods for dating sites and components.

Curious visitors experience something of what life was like in seventeenth-century colonial America by visiting Plimoth Plantation (Massachusetts).

Historical Archaeology Goes Processual

Things changed in the 1960s. Some archaeologists, trained on prehistoric sites, realized that they could refine their archaeological methods and theories by working in the contexts of verifiable historical controls. During this period several archaeologists began looking at historic-period material culture to refine dating techniques and to explore the nature of **acculturation** and culture change.

Acculturation: Major cultural changes that people are required to make in the aftermath of intensive, firsthand contact between societies.

About the same time, historical archaeology was propelled to adopt the thriving processual agenda. Early on, Lewis Binford clearly saw that historical archaeology would readily fit beneath the umbrella of processual archaeology. Binford himself had excavated at Fort Michilimackinac, an eighteenth-century French-British frontier site on Mackinac Island, Michigan. He believed that his generalizing, processual objectives could readily be pursued on historic-period sites, if only historical archaeologists would recognize the importance of transcending their own particularistic objectives.

Stanley South helped the transition along. In his influential book *Method and Theory in Historical Archeology* (1977), South laid out in punctilious detail how

Historical Archaeology on the Internet:

Society for Historical Archaeology Home Page includes a general statement about what historical archaeology is all about, what the society does, some job listings, and an excellent guide to graduate programs: http://www.azstarnet.com/~sha/

Stanley South excavating a sixteenth-century Spanish colonial pottery kiln at Santa Elena (South Carolina).

Welcome historic sites archaeology to the science of archaeology.

LEWIS R. BINFORD (IN HIS FOREWORD TO STANLEY SOUTH'S METHOD AND THEORY IN HISTORICAL ARCHEOLOGY)

Archaeologists dealing with data from historic sites must synthesize beyond the ruin-specific level if they are to address themselves to questions involving past cultural systems instead of merely past cultural ruins.

STANLEY SOUTH

Here the melting pot stands open—if you're willing to get bleached first.

BUFFY SAINTE-MARIE, NATIVE AMERICAN SINGER, ACTRESS, AND ACTIVIST

the processual agenda should be translated into the field of historical archaeology. He argued that historical archaeologists should work within an explicitly evolutionary framework, employ logically grounded scientific methods, apply quantitative methods of pattern recognition, and—above all—formulate the findings of historical archaeology as timeless, spaceless generalizations about the human condition.

Mainstream historical archaeology soon distanced itself from what Noël Hume once called a "Barnum and Bailey" stress on the "oldest," "largest," and "most historically significant" sites—focusing instead on the larger social context. By looking beyond the lives of the rich and famous, historical archaeology began a phase of what has been called "backyard archaeology." One particularly important direction was the focus on historically disenfranchised groups in our own culture—what has been termed "archaeology of the people without history"—attempting to uncover the archaeological roots of African American and Asian American cultures, Native Americans during the historic period, and Hispanic American Creoles. There is a distinct parallel to W. W. Taylor's message four decades ago, when he urged Mayan archaeologists to transcend the hierarchical and the grandiose, and to get on with the anthropology of "real" people.

Some of this research has called into question the "melting-pot" interpretation of America's past. Both James Deetz and Robert Schuyler contend that the evolution of American society largely involved the systematic exclusion of non-Anglo groups from mainstream Anglo-American society. They argue that such bias is generally unknown because conventional historical records are incomplete and distorted when dealing with racial minorities. Yet in other cases, as at St. Augustine, Kathleen Deagan has argued that the "melting-pot" model seems a rather accurate reflection of the way in which Hispanic American society functioned in the New World.

In one sense, historical archaeologists have an advantage because they can enhance their shovel work with documentary records: In many cases, the effects of ethnic affiliation, income, religion, occupation, family composition, economic network, and political restrictions can be taken as givens and need not be inferred directly from the archaeological record. One particularly effective result of processual research in historical archaeology has been the study of trading relations, religious conversion, and racial intermarriage—all important acculturative processes.

Although many historical archaeologists continued to believe that augmenting specific culture histories should be the primary objective of historical archaeology, others joined Stanley South in maintaining that such research is merely a necessary first step toward more important goals. For one thing, the business of "culture resource management" in the 1970s and 1980s created a boom in historical archaeology (see also Chapter 20). In many parts of the country, it blossomed into a massive program, comparable in funding and popularity to prehistoric archaeology. In years past, this research would have been mostly done by those trained initially in history or architecture; however, more recent research has been conducted largely by those whose major academic ties are to anthropology.

By the 1980s, a large segment of historical archaeologists saw themselves as sharing an anthropological perspective with the rest of Americanist archaeology. Viewed on this broader scale, historical archaeology may pertain to the entire range of human behavior: spoken word, written word, preserved behavior, and observed behavior. There was little doubt that historical archaeology was perceived by most practitioners as a subdiscipline of anthropology (a good thing, as most contemporary historical archaeologists received the bulk of their training in departments of anthropology).

America is like a melting pot. The people at the bottom get burned, and the scum floats to the top.

CHARLIE KING

Since 1950, I have watched historical archaeology grope its way from a condition of near chaos to the status of an established discipline with a rapidly maturing methodology.

EDWARD B. JELKS, ARCHAEOLOGIST (ILLINOIS STATE UNIVERSITY)

Historical Archaeology Connects With the Postprocessual Critique

Historical archaeology has also proved to be extremely fertile ground for postprocessual interests in culture-specific historical contexts. Postprocessual approaches require a more "situated" archaeology—a view of the past more closely attuned to contextual specifics. So-called text-aided archaeology became a logical focus for postprocessual studies because of the wealth of documentary evidence available with which to contextualize the archaeological record. This was a call to project oneself into the particular contexts of the past, to discover the significance and meaning of particular past actions. The study of the symbolic meaning of material remains also proceeds much more comfortably in the text-aided context, where independent confirmation or disconfirmation can be found in the documentary record.

The quest for historical sites investigations takes us to every community in North America as a viable and useful discipline.

JOHN L. COTTER, ARCHAEOLOGIST (UNIVERSITY OF PENNSYLVANIA)

Bruce Trigger has pointed out that most successful symbolic studies lie in the field of historical archaeology, concluding that "the cultural specific (emic) meaning of artefacts that cannot be embraced by the direct historical approach may forever lie beyond the realm of scientific study." We have already seen numerous examples of the use of historical archaeology for understanding these emic meanings, such as Janet Spector's powerful study of gender relations among a nineteenth-century Eastern Dakota people. Her analysis of "what this awl means" would have been considerably less convincing had she been working on the archaeology of Paleo-Indian people living 12,000 years ago, without benefit of ethnographic or ethnohistoric documentation or the rich oral tradition of living descendants.

Archaeology, as we know it today, was a product of the Industrial Revolution, the formation of capitalist class relations, the rise of modern nationalism, and Enlightenment thought.

THOMAS C. PATTERSON, ARCHAEOLOGIST (TEMPLE UNIVERSITY)

Viewing material culture as a "text" is difficult because multiple readings are always possible and because no informant can be consulted to clarify meaning. But in the world of historical archaeology, at least written documentation (and sometimes oral tradition) can be called upon to determine which interpretations are more appropriate than others and which explanation best fits the data.

[Historical archaeology] is the archaeology of the spread of European societies worldwide, beginning in the fifteenth century, and their subsequent development and impact on native peoples in all parts of the world.

JAMES DEETZ, HISTORICAL ARCHAEOLOGIST (UNIVERSITY OF VIRGINIA)

Postprocessual critics have also argued that mainstream archaeology should be more politically aware and involved. After all, their argument goes, the internal political structure of archaeology itself mediates the larger political effect of the discipline, determining what kind of research is pursued, who is empowered to pursue these objectives, what standard of adequacy constrains this investigation, and, therefore, what conception of the past will be acceptable as archaeological knowledge.

Some have argued that processual archaeology itself has played a rationalizing role for Western, technological society. In this view, processualism is

Redefining the Relationship Between Material Culture and Documentary Evidence

Historical archaeologists have traditionally linked the documentary and archaeological records in rather unsatisfactory ways. For a long time, the documentary record was viewed as a kind of literary time machine—the archaeologist dug first and then sifted through the documents to see what things meant. Alternatively, one could begin by writing document-based history and then excavate to fill in the gaps and add detail.

Either way, archaeological and documentary records have been treated as somehow linked, with one field being dependent on the other. Any unexpected finding or inconsistency between the archaeological and documentary evidence was commonly labeled as "an exception" or "an anomaly" and promptly discarded, thereby quashing any hope of fresh insight. This has been the traditional approach in historical archaeology.

But James Deetz, Mark Leone, and Parker Potter have suggested that historical documentation can be more profitably viewed as another kind of experimental or ethnoarchaeological input—as a way of building *independent* middle-range expectations for the material culture record. As discussed in Chapter 11, an ethnoarchaeologist, for instance, can use the "economic anatomy" of a given species to assess samples of bones—both observed ethnographically and recovered archaeologically. Neither sample is "correct" or "superior." Each framework has its own biases and frame of reference. Insight is gained by understanding the "ambiguity" between the two independent records.

Leone and Potter suggest that historical archaeologists should employ this same middle-range framework by viewing the archaeological and documentary records *as equally valid yet independent lines of evidence*. Rather than discarding differences in the record as "exceptions" or "noise," we should look for "ambiguities" between the historical and archaeological evidence, recognizing that the unexpected differences between the two will continue to expand our knowledge.

not an objective, scientific approach to the past, but rather a cleverly disguised use of a special interpretation of the past to rationalize the present. The criticism here is that processualists have failed to acknowledge that their scientific program serves a political role within today's society.

The often-stated political aims of the postprocessual critique usually emphasize the goal of emancipating the individual. One way to accomplish this is to expose those ideologies that systematically mask the contradictions within society and manipulate them to effect change.

In fact, some archaeologists sympathetic to the postprocessual program, such as Mark Leone, believe that employing Deetz's definition of historical archaeology (instead of Deagan's broader definition, cited earlier) more properly focuses attention specifically on European colonialism and its effects on the indigenous peoples of the world. The postprocessual emphasis on power, for instance, meshes easily with historical archaeology's ample record of developing capitalist society in America and elsewhere.

Despite all the calls for political awareness . . . archaeologists are unaware of being entangled in the social relations they describe.

MARK LEONE, ARCHAEOLOGIST (UNIVERSITY OF MARYLAND)

These diverse threads, taken together, comprise archaeology's postprocessual critique–the call for increased political awareness, multiple views of the past, an explicit concern with power relations, more humanistic approaches, and the symbolic meaning of the past–and all fit quite comfortably with the text-aided and culturally connected complexion of historical archaeology. This diversity in approach makes historical archaeology one of the most exciting and rapidly growing subfields in all of Americanist archaeology (see *Redefining the Relationship Between Material Culture and Documentary Evidence*).

Evolving American Worldviews

Having said something about the development and changing character of historical archaeology, we will now shift gears to bring in an extended example illustrating how contemporary historical archaeologists actually work.

Here, we will look at the archaeology of Colonial America, with a particular emphasis on shifting power relations and the development of capitalist culture during the eighteenth century. As we shall see, ongoing excavations are challenging traditional views of Colonial America, bringing to light new archaeological evidence that documents the rise of inequality and popular resistance to the dominant economic order. We will also see some methods archaeologists are using to ask both how and why the past was organized the way it was.

The most important facts historical archaeology can reveal to us about America's past are those that cannot be discovered and replicated any other way.

KATHLEEN DEAGAN

Aboveground Archaeology in Middle Virginia

As John Cotter and others have observed, when historical archaeologists have expanded their theoretical horizons, they have expanded their database as well. For one thing, "aboveground" archaeology—analyzing unburied material culture such as architecture and landscapes—became fair game. In this section, we explore an intriguing attempt to understand the meaning of late-eighteenth- and early-nineteenth-century houses in Virginia. Although this study slightly postdates the Colonial American focus, its innovative methods of analysis will carry through the rest of the chapter.

The archaeology of historical sites has led to "above-ground archaeology"—the recognition, analyzing, and conservation of artifacts and the documentation, written and oral, that may be associated with them and with historical features.

JOHN L. COTTER, ARCHAEOLOGIST (UNIVERSITY OF PENNSYLVANIA)

Folklorist Henry Glassie has argued that historians too often overemphasize the written record, neglecting the important evidence available from surviving material culture. Thus Glassie adopted a *structural* perspective in historical archaeology. Before looking at his findings, it is necessary to glance briefly at the basics of **structuralism**, an approach to understanding human culture.

Structuralism: A movement in anthropology, particularly associated with Claude Levi-Strauss. Structuralism seeks to analyze social relationships in terms of highly abstract relational "structures" commonly expressed in a logical symbolism.

The objective of *structural analysis* is to discover the basic principles of the human mind as reflected in major cultural domains—myth, art, kinship, and language. Structural approaches emphasize the importance of shared cultural symbols as cumulative creations of the mind. To anthropologist Claude Levi-Strauss, primary architect of the structural view, the real world could always be reduced to mental structure. The underlying logic of thought was always *binary*—in this way, the human mind is like a modern computer—relying on two-way contrasts (such as inside/outside, nature/culture, or male/female). These symbolic polarities run throughout the fabric of a culture. In fact, because such binary contrasts operate in all cultures, this fundamental dualism is a cultural constant, not a variable.

Glassie's adaptation of a structural approach led him to 100 superficially similar farmhouses in Louisa and Goochland counties, an area called "Middle"

Virginia because it is wedged between the Tidewater area of Chesapeake Bay and the Appalachian Mountains.

On Privacy and Individualism

Glassie began by asking how alike these houses really were and, more important, why? Glassie found that the culture, as reified in these 100 houses, was so heavily patterned that he could generate a "grammar" detailing how Middle Virginia houses were thought of *by the people who built them.* Based on structural binary principles, this explicit set of structural binary rules defined the various ways of combining architectural elements (doors, windows, latches, and chimneys) with variations in size, shape, and room arrangements. In effect, Glassie's grammar attempted to reflect the decisions made by a builder in planning and erecting any given house.

Glassie's rules attempt to reflect the mind-set of a Middle Virginia architect. We see 15 oppositional structures–intellect/emotion, private/public, and so forth–as they existed in the Virginia Piedmont during the late eighteenth and early nineteenth centuries. The earliest dominant opposition for each

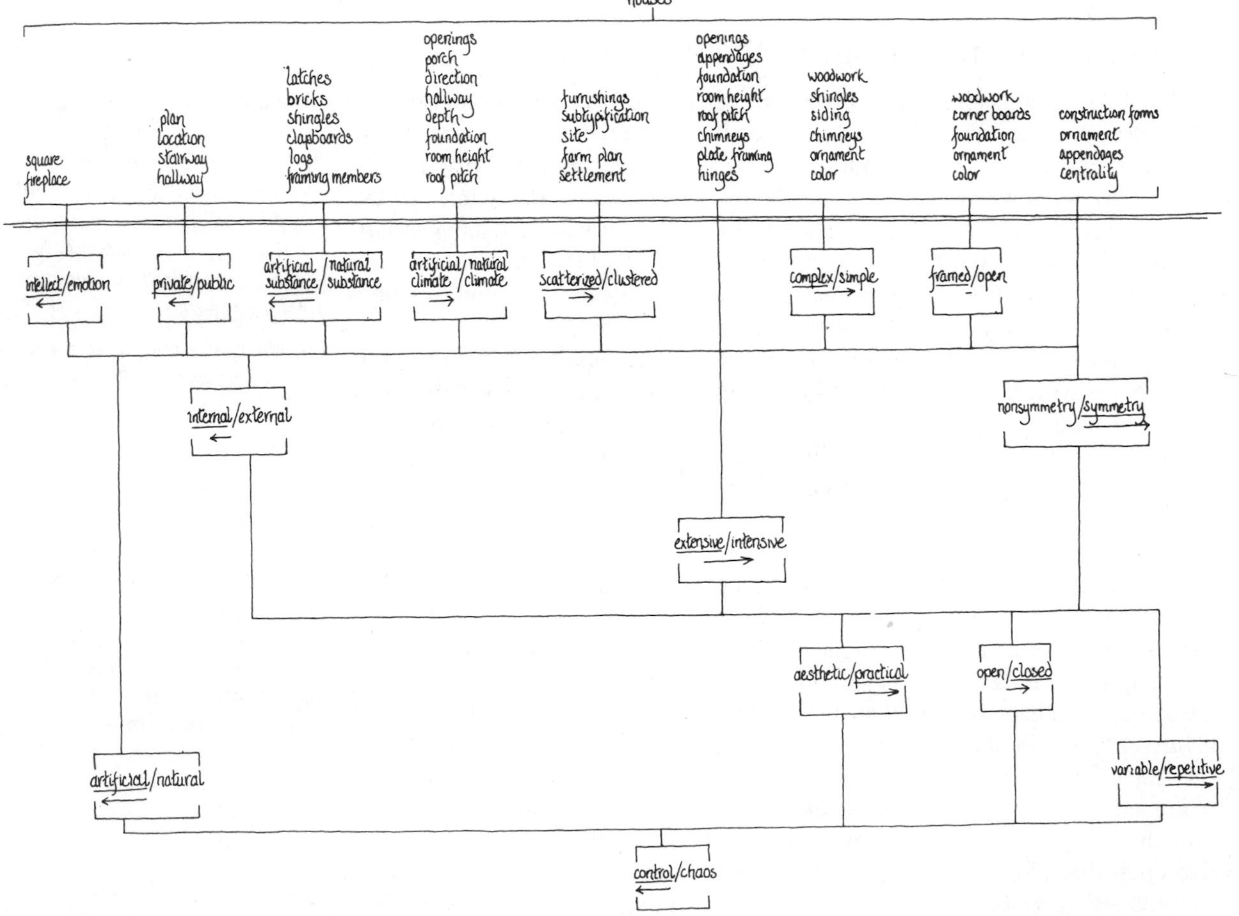

Glassie's "architecture of design" for understanding Middle Virginia houses. Above the double line are listed observable phenomena under study. Below the line is Glassie's structural interpretation of the architect's mind—a guide for past decision making. The underlined term in the binary opposition is the one that was dominant at the earliest time. Arrows indicate the direction of change from about 1760 on.

pair is illustrated, plus the direction of change from 1760 on. Along the top of the diagram is the architectural reflection of each opposition; the shifting dichotomy from scattered to clustered, for instance, is reflected in furnishings, farm plan, and settlement pattern.

With these emic rules in hand, Glassie discovered a trend toward privacy. In about 1760, the basic structural layout of houses shifted toward a geometric symmetry that, Glassie concluded, reflected an increase in the need for privacy, repetition, and control. According to Glassie, this increasingly individual expression was

> accompanied by a contraction of the culture: the dominance of fewer house types, less variation within types once the fully symmetrical design had been achieved, and a diminishing of the inventory of detail and decoration. Houses once red, yellow, and white became white. . . . Windows once had twelve, fifteen or eighteen lights; they came to have only twelve.

For Glassie, the trend toward eighteenth-century individualism led to freedom for only a few, and increasing fear for most. This change in worldview occurred during a mid-eighteenth-century economic crisis, a depression in the tobacco market. All except the most wealthy farmers felt the strain, and social stratification developed among rural white farmers. As people struggled to increase their individualism—to achieve "control"—they increasingly withdrew behind less ornamental façades, painted in whites rather than warmer colors.

Individual vigor was withdrawn from community-spirited projects and invested instead in abstract ideas, such as "racial superiority, nationalism or artificial symmetrical order." Glassie concluded that these houses expressed and allowed greater *control* over post-Revolutionary circumstances in Middle Virginia, an environment that appeared to be haphazard and uncontrollable (see *On the Importance of Artifacts* by Henry Glassie).

They left no writing, but they did leave all those houses.

HENRY GLASSIE, FOLKLORIST (UNIVERSITY OF PENNSYLVANIA)

About five years ago I suddenly discovered a whole new world which wasn't even buried at all. It was all around me. It was called houses and cemeteries, and automobiles, and they're perfectly legal: you can do some pretty groovy things with hub caps and hood ornaments just as much as you can with pre-Columbian ceramics.

JAMES DEETZ, ARCHAEOLOGIST (UNIVERSITY OF VIRGINIA)

America's Georgian Mind-Set: How It Came to Be

Heavily influenced by Glassie's study of Middle Virginia architecture, James Deetz set out to see whether the same cognitive pattern could be found in Colonial New England. Using a much broader range of data covering a considerably longer time span, Deetz found that the earlier group-oriented lifeway had been replaced by the spirit of individualism, just as in Virginia.

Deetz (the archaeologist) and Glassie (the folklorist) both emphasized the reconstruction of "rules" (or *cognitive patterns*) behind expressions of material culture, and both drew heavily on structuralist methods. Deetz's vision for historical archaeology was to transcend behavioral and environmental factors in order to view material culture in terms of its original cognitive state. The early British colonists arrived in New England with what Deetz termed a *medieval mind-set* that encouraged a group-oriented, corporate, and relatively undifferentiated lifestyle (see *Structural Approaches to Archaeology* by James Deetz).

In about 1660, however, another mind-set—the **Georgian order**—came to dominate the Anglo-American Colonial and early national times. As

Georgian order: A worldview (ca. 1660/1680–1820), arising in the European Age of Reason and implying that the world has a single, basic immutable order. Using the powers of reason, people can discover what that order is, and, knowing this, can control the environment as they wish. The Georgian order is informed by the rise of scientific thought and by the balance and order in Renaissance architecture and art.

IN HIS OWN WORDS

On the Importance of Artifacts by Henry Glassie

There are documents, government reports, and small books from which a little can be learned, but there is not enough to allow a historian to write about this area [Middle Virginia]—or about the many other areas that are like it primarily in being unknown. If this land and the people who made it have no place in the historical record, then the worth of the study of history must be called sharply into question. The written primary sources are too scanty, but there are fences in the forest and silent old houses set back from the roads. They are decaying and difficult to decipher, they demand tiring work in the field and complicated analysis, but they can be made to reveal the information upon which a strengthened historiography could be based. With brave exceptions, though, historians pass by such sources without a look. History moves on, leaving this land, like almost everywhere else, and these people, like almost everyone else, out of account.

Two diseases have crippled and nearly killed the silent artifact as a source for history. Most historians, it seems, continue to view the artifact as only an illustrative adjunctive to the literary narrative. Perhaps when the elite is studied, this is not an unintelligent course of research. A knowledge of Thomas Jefferson might be based on his writings and only supplemented by a study of Monticello, but for most people, such as the folks who were chopping farms out of the woods a few miles to the east while Jefferson was writing at his desk, the procedure must be reversed. Their own statements, though made in wood or mud rather than ink, must take precedence over someone else's possibly prejudiced, probably wrong, and certainly superficial comments about them. The historian's benign neglect of silent artifacts and their people is a reasonable, if shallowly reasoned, response to the way that artifacts have most often been studied—obsessively, that is, as ends in themselves. Some archaeologists stop work when their findings are listed in site reports, and some connoisseurs not only persist in treating the artifact as a unique wonder rather than as a material manifestation of culture, they even eliminate from scrutiny the things that do not measure up to their own taste. Maybe some of these things are "bad," but most of them are "good" things that the connoisseur has failed to understand. The decision to eliminate some artworks from study makes as much sense as would the choice by the historian to read only books with pretty bindings or to study only old documents calligraphed in a lovely hand. Any artifact that can be provided with association in space and time, either by being accompanied by a document or better—as with gravestones or buildings—by being set into the land, is a valuable source of a great quantity of information.

cultural conservatism set in, people gradually drifted away from mother England to form more regionally differentiated folk cultures. During this critical period, Deetz argues, Georgian attitudes created material culture correlates, patterns that became increasingly individualistic, often differentiated through symmetry and tripartite divisions.

- *Architecture:* Medieval house architecture, for instance, decreed only one or two rooms, arranged along asymmetrical floor plans. In these rooms all domestic activities took place, from sleeping and eating, to working and socializing. But with the Georgian worldview, houses became functionally structured and compartmentalized, with more balanced floor plans.
- *Ceramics:* Pottery also reflected the shift in early American "foodways." The medieval mind-set was characterized by plain, utilitarian earthen-

James Deetz on the Internet:

Deetz Summarizes His Research Interests:
http://www.virginia.edu/~anthro/deetz.html

IN HIS OWN WORDS

Structural Approaches to Archaeology by James Deetz

The causes of the transformation of specific sectors of the physical world—be they gravestones, dishes, clothing, or houses—seem relatively easy to identify but may be difficult to explain. To say that tastes, values, or simple preference changed and produced a new form merely points to a cause and an effect, but does not explain what activated the causes (e.g., why did tastes change?). A more powerful explanatory tool might be found in the still controversial school of structural anthropology, which has incurred the distrust of many social scientists, who charge that it is non-positivist and cannot be subjected to scientific methods of proof, and that it has little predictive value. Yet structuralism holds the promise of providing an explanation for change in the physical world in toto, of explicating relationships between changes in seemingly unrelated categories of material culture, and of relating these transformations to changes in attitudes and worldview.

In simplest terms, structuralism holds that human thought is organized and functions according to a universally shared complex of oppositional structures that are mediated differently by different cultures, or by the same culture at different times. Although such a proposition is unprovable—we may or may not think in binary terms—it may provide a model that has heuristic value. As Glassie states, "At least binary thinking has aided in theory building." These oppositional pairs are believed to structure subconscious thought and thus affect all of human behavior as it is seen at the observable particularistic level. Accordingly, similar changes taking place in the same direction and at the same time in otherwise unrelated sectors of culture are attributable to changes in the nature of the mediation of underlying oppositional structures. For example, the shift from many colors to white seen not only in houses but also in gravestones and ceramics [in New England] at the end of the eighteenth century might result from the strong mediation of the complex-simple opposition in the direction of simplicity, and the strong mediation of the opposition between artificial and natural in the direction of artificiality. Rather than seek an explanation of why houses, or gravestones, or dishes are made white by the century's end, we should look for an explanation of the underlying shift in mediation of the oppositional structures in question.

ware, reflecting the dependence on dairying. Food was served directly from the cooking pot and consumed from "trenchers," wooden trays that were usually shared with one or more "trencher mates." During this period, ceramics played a small role in food consumption.

Puritanism: The haunting fear that someone, somewhere, may be happy.

H. L. Mencken (1880–1956), JOURNALIST AND SATIRIST

The Georgian worldview provided a stark contrast. Not only did creamware and pearlware–products of the Industrial Revolution–become common, but they also were purchased as a matched set of plates and teacups. This "new Georgian order" established a one-plate–one-person commonality, reflecting the existence of individuals around the family table.

Whereas the medieval worldview emphasized the natural, the Georgian mind-set became increasingly artificial. Before the Industrial Revolution, people relied on natural colored earthenwares, reflecting their earthy origins. But Georgian ceramics became progressively whiter as technology improved.

- *Mortuary Art:* Gravestones also became white, replacing earlier green, black, blue, and red markers. Also the backs were sculpted smooth like the fronts, "denying their origin in the native stone." The messages written on these gravestones offered Deetz his most eloquent *entrée* into the shifting mind-sets of early America. Death during Medieval times reminded survivors of their own mortality, and,

The tiny ship that dropped anchor in Plymouth harbor in the December cold of 1620 carried a precious cargo. Its 102 passengers, Englishmen who had come to the New World for a variety of reasons, brought with them a blueprint–in their minds–for recreating the culture they had left behind.

James Deetz

accordingly, gravestones displayed the "death's head," and the stones said simply "Here lies . . . " or "Here lies buried . . . ." But the typical inscription changed to "In memory of . . . ," and the urn and willow motif was used as a "symbol of commemoration." This is also reflected in the epitaphs, which began to praise the worldly achievements of individuals. To Deetz, these changes indicated a "secularization" of religion.

- *Food Preparation:* Medieval diners usually attacked their meat in joints, "showing in part at least the vestiges of the anatomy of the beast from which they came." But structured Georgian "foodways" were dominated by artificially segmented cuts of meat. Archaeologically, this shift is seen as the shift from chopping bones to sawing them.
- *Refuse Disposal:* These shifting mind-sets can also be inferred from the change in trash disposal. During the early Medieval days, trash was simply tossed out of doors and windows, creating a sheet of refuse that allowed domestic animals like pigs and chickens to scavenge for leftovers. But by the mid-eighteenth century, the Georgian New Englander's mind-set dictated a more orderly method for disposing of trash, and people began digging square pits up to 7 feet deep. The frequency of chamber pots also skyrocketed with this transition, reflecting a desire for increased privacy.

Summarizing the conceptual linkages between Middle Virginia and New England, Deetz emphasizes the disappearance of shared seating and shared utensils at mealtime, and the appearance of the very personal burial motifs on New England gravestones. Simpler ceramic forms replaced more complex ones. More complex pottages and stews gave way to discrete foodstuffs. The shift to symmetry reflected in central hall houses throughout the Anglo-American world is seen as reflecting the emergence of the individual and the material culture appropriate to that concept.

To arrive at his synthesis of these conceptual changes in New England, Deetz used the same structural oppositions employed by Glassie in describing Middle Virginia housing: intellect/emotion, private/public, artificial/natural substance, scattered/clustered, extensive/intensive, complex/simple, framed/open, and nonsymmetry/symmetry. Each of these was thought to fall under a larger opposition—order/chaos or culture/nature.

The Georgian Order: Why Did It Evolve?

Deetz took Glassie's notions on Virginia architecture and refined them on the basis of New England archaeology. He defined the emergence of the Georgian mind-set in New England culture as a movement characterized by intellect (rather than emotion), privacy, refined substances, orientation toward internal matters, and increasing subdivision to maintain control. But as Mark Leone and his colleagues working at Historic Annapolis (Maryland) asked: Control over what?

By employing a postprocessual, "critical" approach to human behavior, Leone and his colleagues have taken Deetz's ideas a step farther—examining not only the operation of the Georgian worldview, but also how and why it came to be.

Since 1981, the Historic Annapolis Foundation has been working with Leone and his research team based at the University of Maryland, College Park. Conducting what is literally an exercise in "backyard archaeology," they have spent decades excavating in basements and backyards, beneath parking lots and pavements throughout Annapolis. In so doing, they are looking at material culture—floor plans, dishes, façades, architectural statements, silverware, furniture, gardens, the above- and below-ground remnants—attempting to establish the relevance of eighteenth-century Annapolis to ourselves and the way we view our own past.

By looking at the derivation of some mundane, taken-for-granted aspects of contemporary life, Leone is attempting to demonstrate that our modern way of life is not inevitable. Our past had its origins and its reasons for being. And because of this history, our past is open to question and challenge. In this explicitly postprocessual approach, Leone is trying to demonstrate the degree to which our history is often "constructed"—written and presented for contemporary purposes.

Because of the explicit political agenda behind Leone's work at Annapolis, it is important that you understand the theoretical perspective being employed. Leone is working within a framework called *critical theory.* As applied to archaeology, critical theory emphasizes the importance of archaeologists' understanding of the specific contexts within which they work *(self-reflection)* and the notion that all knowledge is situated (and hence serves special interests). This explanatory premise assumes, from the outset, that domination is a central element of modern capitalist society (see *Critical Theory in Historical Archaeology*).

"Critical" in this sense means that the relations between the assumptions and discoveries of a scholarly discipline and its ties to modern life become a central concern and are subject to examination, automatically relating the questions, methods, and discoveries of a science like anthropology to those of the anthropologist's own culture. Critical theorists seek simultaneously to explain the social world, to criticize it, and to empower their audience to deal with it more productively through advocating change (critical theory never advocates violence).

Capitalism and Power in Historic Annapolis

We now return to the specifics of capitalism and power in colonial America. Remember that Deetz attempted to relate material culture in New England to the cognitive structures that produced it. But Deetz was largely concerned with describing and defining thought patterns; according to Leone, Deetz was not concerned with ultimate origins, not trying to find out why American patterns existed and why today is—or is not—their product. Leone departs from Deetz by looking at the "recursive" quality of material culture. The Georgian order and its local adaptation in Maryland are related to the penetration of merchant capitalism and the crises it created. In effect, the Annapolis group

The oppressed are allowed once every few years to decide which particular representatives of the oppressing class are to represent and repress them.

Karl Marx (1818–1883), Political Philosopher

Critical Theory in Historical Archaeology

Critical theory refers to a series of attempts to adapt ideas from Karl Marx to an understanding of events and circumstances of twentieth-century life that Marx did not anticipate. It rejects violence as a valid means for change, assuming instead that explicit knowledge of our condition will facilitate the necessary change. "Critical" analysis automatically subjects the questions, methods, and discoveries of a discipline to questions about the scholar's own culture. Beginning in the 1920s, such critical theory has been applied to a variety of intellectual endeavors, including law, history, decorative arts, literature, geography, museum studies, and, of course, anthropology.

Critical theory, which has become one of the major branches of the postprocessual critique, has attracted a loyal and vocal following, particularly among historical archaeologists. Critical theory, along with several other approaches to archaeology, highlights the importance of taking archaeology to the public. To understand how critical theory works in Americanist archaeology—and how it differs from the other available perspectives—you must understand three important points.

First, *critical theory emphasizes the "reflexive" aspects of culture*. Rather than assuming that people simply bear their culture passively, the critical theorist views culture from an *interactive* (or *recursive*) perspective, assuming that people actively create, use, modify, and manipulate their symbolic capabilities to rework the world they live in. In this reflexive sense, material culture is viewed not merely as a reflection of economics, social organization, or ideology, but rather as an instrument to create meaning and order in one's world. Critical theorists recognize a distinctive relationship between the present and the past, assuming this relationship to be economic and political. Who owns the artifacts of the past? Who controls their disposition? For what purposes do archaeologists interpret the past?

The second point is that *critical theory emphasizes meaning*. Like other ideational perspectives, critical

redefined capitalism, not as an economic system, but, in a larger sense, as an all-encompassing culture. The Georgian order was important because it facilitated the arrival and success of capitalism.

Annapolis has been a small community since it was founded in about 1650. It became the capital of Maryland in 1695, later experiencing a "golden age" of wealth and fame that peaked between about 1760 and the end of the American Revolution. In a move designed to symbolically subordinate the military to civil authority, George Washington came to Annapolis to resign his command of the Continental army. The Treaty of Paris, which officially ended the American Revolution, was also signed there. During the early days of the United States, even though Annapolis remained the state capital, the international commercial and industrial potential of nearby Baltimore attracted many of its wealthiest residents. Although the United States Naval Academy moved to Annapolis in 1845, the nineteenth century signaled what has been called an era of "gentle eclipse" for Annapolis. The 1950s saw the beginning of a commercial revival based on yachting, tourism, and new highways that defined Annapolis as a suburb of Washington, D.C., and Baltimore, less than 30 miles away.

Two decades ago, Leone and his team began applying their critical approach to the archaeology of the Chesapeake region. They consciously de-

theory rejects the *doctrine of infrastructural determinism* (discussed in Chapter 3). Whereas ecological, economic, demographic, and technological considerations are not excluded, they are encompassed by and subordinated to an analysis of the social—and particularly political—organization of production. Unlike the cultural materialists, critical theorists do not dismiss cultural beliefs and native categories as irrelevant to the "real" or objective operations of a society.

Critical theorists retain a role for the materialist tradition. Although rejecting the cultural materialist's ranked order of causal relationships, critical theory welcomes advances in our understanding of the natural environment, economy, demography, and technology and suggests that such conditions lead to social contradictions, conflicts, and exploitation. Ideology, in effect, "hides" or "masks" such internal, inevitable contradictions, preventing active conflict and ensuring continued operation of the cultural system. Ideology, in this sense, acts within a stratified or class society to reproduce inequality without serious resistance, violence, or revolution.

Critical theory attempts to offer a place for everything, refusing to partition inquiries into material relations and "ideology." In a sense, critical theory attempts to mediate between the hard-line etic, "scientific" materialists and the "soft" emic, subjective ideationalists.

Finally, *critical theory critiques the function of the past and our knowledge of it*. Critical archaeology asserts the active role of the past in a society that studies it. The past, whether viewed through archaeology, the print and video media, myth, or museums, becomes an active vehicle for communicating and composing meaning. The critical archaeologist argues, in the Marxist tradition, that history will always be produced to serve class interests. Exploring the political uses of archaeology produces a more conscious perception of the social function of archaeology, and requires that archaeologists address the past for the greater social benefit as defined through a materialist critique.

constructed the ideology behind the historical development of Annapolis and its environs: Why did some people become rich? Why were some poor? What was the relationship between the two? How did the American Revolution affect these inequalities?

Over the years, Leone and his colleagues developed a "theory of power" to explain the growth of Chesapeake society under the European and American systems. By 1720, a class structure had developed in which a few families of the gentry controlled most of the wealth. The social position of the rest of the population—poorer whites, Native and African Americans—remained the same before and after the American Revolution.

The Power Garden: Landscape Archaeology as Ideology

Leone has employed the principles of landscape architecture to explore Glassie's and Deetz's concept of the Georgian order. Leone's specific objective—once again from the perspective of critical theory—was to learn how gardens were conceptualized and what role they played in eighteenth-century life in Maryland.

Photograph of the William Paca garden (Annapolis).

Consider the case of the formal gardens that existed in Annapolis during the late eighteenth century. Best known is the 2-acre garden of William Paca—a signer of the Declaration of Independence—which illustrates how eighteenth-century aristocrats strove to demonstrate the power of Reason over Nature. The garden, once described as "the most elegant in Annapolis," was originally built in the 1760s, behind a large, five-part Georgian mansion, with façade and floor plan exhibiting bilateral symmetry. Perceived from Deetz's perspective of the Georgian worldview, this house could be taken as reflecting the ideas of the person as an individual, the afterlife as a specific reward for personal behavior while alive, privacy, the segregation of different everyday activities from one another, and the segregation of the members of the family.

The garden likewise is Georgian, with a central axis, a straight, broad path descending through four sets of steps as one leaves the house, dividing the space into two parts. These steps lead down over a series of small terraces, creating the same visual effect as that of a Georgian façade or floor plan: bilateral symmetry.

The garden survived into the early twentieth century, when it was destroyed to make room for a 200-room hotel. When the hotel was torn down in 1968, Stanley South excavated in and around the standing house. Historical archaeologists then moved into the garden area, first testing and then excavating large areas. Original wall footings, documenting the terraces (which could be seen in profile), were found; thus, the garden's basic topography became available. Trenching and examination of the profiles showed a canal and pond at the bottom of the garden, surrounded by a natural garden (or "wilderness") in the lowest third of the garden. Foundations for a central pavilion and springhouse, and footings for a bridge over the ponds were discovered, and 125 paleobotanical samples were recovered from the wet fill. These archaeological data were combined with a few period descriptions, plus a contemporary portrait of William Paca with the garden as background. The pavilion, bathhouse, springhouse, and Chinese Chippendale bridge all have been restored. Today, the Paca garden is open to the public as both an archaeologically based reconstruction and a horticultural experiment.

You show me a capitalist, I'll show you a bloodsucker.

MALCOLM X (1946–1952),
RELIGIOUS LEADER

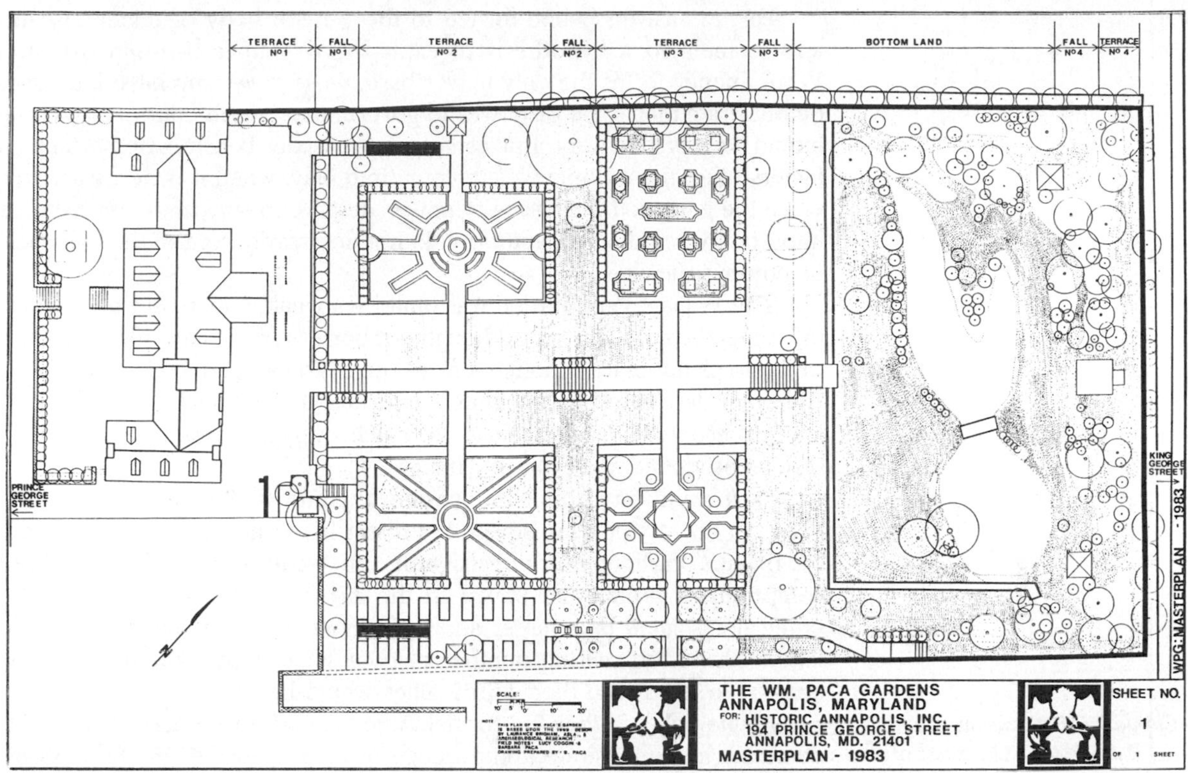

The outlines of the William Paca garden, including the basic subdivisions and the shape of the pond, are archaeologically derived—but the terraces are conjectural, as are the positions of most of the plantings. The Paca garden slopes about 16.5 feet from left to right.

Leone first visited the garden in the early 1980s, and his impressions remained the "touchstone" for his subsequent archaeological analyses. He later wrote, "As I began to walk through the garden from the top, which is 16 feet higher than the bottom, which is 150 feet away, I found it difficult to tell distances; I felt I was being controlled, as paths, precise borders, openings, stairs, and objects that had to be stepped over operated everywhere to control me. This sensation was especially true regarding sight."

Is this simply the impact of fastidious design? Or is it Paca's expression of the natural order, putting each natural thing—each tree and shrub—into its proper place?

After studying two other large gardens in Annapolis, Leone synthesized what he believed to be the rules behind the design. The Paca garden was constructed as a volume, following the laws of perspective and using baroque rules for creating optical illusions: Convergent or divergent lines of sight (to make distances appear shorter or longer, depending on the specific need in each garden) were created, and rows of beds or shrubs were formed into trapezoids and focal points (rather than strictly parallel lines) to manipulate the view. "The gardens are three-dimensional spaces built consciously using rules which were well understood to create illusions for those who walked through them."

But why the illusion? And why would such Anglo-American gardens proliferate just before the American Revolution and then disappear—like the rest of Georgian material culture—during the early nineteenth century?

For an answer, Leone turned to the general body of materialist theory and formulated a hypothesis to explain governance through ostentation. When money forms the only power base, those governing have little need to demonstrate their right or power to govern; they are in control and certainly intend to stay that way. But ostentatious display becomes important when factors other than simple wealth come into play, when it is necessary to convince the governed that those in power deserve to stay there. *Show* becomes important when those in authority do not necessarily control the purse strings or power structure.

The William Paca garden was built by a wealthy man, but one who lived in a time of contradictions. Although not born to particular affluence, he married into plenty of it. Although a slave owner, he argued for the Bill of Rights. Although descended from planters and tied to merchants, he grew up and lived in economic circumstances in which everyone around him was facing serious economic and political change.

Paca could have built his garden anytime during his lifetime, but he chose to do so when his power to protect his wealth was being diminished by Britain. Parliamentary restrictions on trade and local office holding compromised profits and power in the 1760s. Paca was socially and economically isolated by a larger and even more difficult-to-control slave population, plus an increasing number of poor white farmers and day laborers, anxious to learn who their future allies would be.

Capitalism is the astounding belief that the most wickedest of men will do the most wickedest of things for the greatest good of everyone.

JOHN MAYNARD KEYNES (1883–1946), ECONOMIST

Leone believes that the formal Anglo-American gardens were built deliberately to demonstrate a knowledge of–and control over–the laws of nature. Paca was trying to create the illusion that either (1) he still retained the power over his own wealth or (2) he should be granted new, American-based political clout to do so. In this perspective, the garden was not a statement of what existed. The Paca garden was ideology, an "adjunct to power" at a time when the wealth and prestige of his class were being undermined and diminished.

The Paca garden illustrates the same underlying principles that defined the layout of the town of Annapolis as a whole. These street patterns and placement of buildings still survive and dominate daily life in the city. This archaeological study of Paca's garden reveals that perspective and its power to invite attention are still actively used to manage relations of power in the city today. The relations between the prominence of the state capitol, the isolation of the U.S. Naval Academy, and the invisibility of the black community are all managed through the spatial principles exhibited in Paca's garden. Together, historical archaeological and critical theory illustrate the origins of modern–and exploitative–social relations that continue to the present.

While it will always be true that archeologists need to communicate effectively among themselves, it is now abundantly clear that unless they also communicate effectively with the general public . . . all else will be wasted effort.

CHARLES R. MCGIMSEY III AND HESTER A. DAVIS, ARCHAEOLOGISTS (ARKANSAS ARCHAEOLOGICAL SURVEY)

Taking Critical Theory Public: Touring Historic Annapolis Then and Now

As discussed in Chapter 3, anthropology in the postmodern era has become increasingly concerned with understanding how American culture and capitalism shape present-day anthropological interpretations, and how anthropology can discover the origins of the interpretations. Ethnographers have begun to take local history into account, to situate their work within the contemporary environment.

Similarly, archaeology's postprocessual critique has called attention to the important role played by local politics in archaeological interpretation—and particularly interpretation within the field of historical archaeology. Whereas such postmodern thought has deeply influenced the trajectory of British and European archaeology, Americanist archaeology has largely resisted the notion that contemporary political realities play a major role in conditioning archaeological interpretation.

Historic Annapolis on the Internet:

Historic Annapolis provides an overview of facilities and attractions:
http://www.umcp.umd.edu/CampusMaps/Annapolis/Welcome.html

Guided Sightseeing Tours has an extensive listing, including historical garden, architecture, and archaeology tours:
http://umcp.umd.edu/CampusMaps/Annapolis/Guided_Tours.html

Critical theorists argue that the proper role of the historian is to unearth the beginnings of contemporary class-based ideologics—distortions that rationalize forms of exploitation, such as slavery, sexism, and racism. Applied to historical archaeology, such theory suggests that once a repressed people can be shown a past in which things were different, they can use this knowledge to change the inequities of the present. By this view, the responsible historian (and historical archaeologist) should form alliances with members of oppressed classes and work toward social change to better the workers' condition. To the critical theorist, capitalism is a negative social force that should be confronted.

Leone's research at historical Annapolis was grounded in the belief that archaeologists and historians should "stand up" against the oppressive excesses of capitalism. In other words, it was not enough for archaeologists simply to learn about abuse of power in the past; it was essential that this knowledge be brought forward into the present.

The call for historical archaeology to become more political comes from two directions. As archaeology becomes more public, individual archaeologists are increasingly called upon to interpret their findings for "the general public." Such interpretation takes many forms—traditional museum exhibits, outdoor history museums, site-specific tourist facilities, and television and other media interpretations of "the past." But the problem immediately surfaces—which and whose past?

Consider the case of Annapolis, where historic preservation has played a major role in the commercial renaissance of the city. Annually, more than 1 million people visit Annapolis, a city of only about 32,000 people. As in many other small, historic towns, local residents work hard to protect those things that attract visitors.

The encapsulated history of Annapolis has been peddled to generations of tourists who buy guidebooks, listen to tour guides, and saunter through the historic-house museums. Prominent are references to the ultimate first

Tourists learning about the archaeology of Annapolis.

tourist, none other than George Washington himself. Discussing his nearly 20 dozen visits, conventional Annapolis history played up the social and domestic aspects of Washington's jaunts into the city—going to the racetrack, attending social events and plays, and visiting a host of friends and family members. In effect, the image of Washington-in-Annapolis largely mirrored the profile of just the sort of visitor that Annapolis wanted to attract—the high-end tourist with some money to spend, but without an attitude.

Through the lens of critical theory, however, archaeologist Parker Potter noticed something interesting about the tourism process. As the tourists poured through, they were presented the history of Annapolis as a collection of disconnected units from different time periods and institutions. History-for-the-tourist was left in the hands of diverse groups and institutions, some overlapping, some in competition. Potter realized that Annapolis thus had no unified history to connect the different parts of the city. Black and white populations were presented as unconnected, as were the histories of the city of Annapolis and the Naval Academy.

I raise the need for historical archaeology to be more involved with the politics that sustains it. . . . Such political involvement will provide a more coherent justification for our concern with forgotten, anonymous, and unknown peoples, who are the exploited and suppressed members of classes.

MARK LEONE

A historical archaeology concerned with capitalism, investigating the roots of those who have been denied pasts and explaining why they are here now in the condition in which they find themselves . . . [links] past impoverishment to its continuation in the present.

MARK LEONE

As written and presented by whites, black history (viewed from the nineteenth century) was considered to be separate from white history (presented from the eighteenth-century perspective). Slavery was not seen as an antecedent to relationships between contemporary groups.

In other words, a series of separations forced history into opposing compartments:

- eighteenth century versus nineteenth century
- white versus black
- historic district versus Naval Academy
- residents versus visitors

Potter, working with Leone and others, designed an on-site program for the 5,000 to 10,000 visitors who stopped by each year. Tourists visiting Historic Annapolis often have a chance to walk through the ongoing archaeological excavations. Well-prepared guides are available to explain what the archaeologists are doing, and why they are doing it.

Did Critical Theory Fall Short at Annapolis?

The site excursions were enormously popular with tourists and residents in Annapolis, and they seemed to rally the city's support to protect the archaeological sites of Annapolis. But in regard to social change, both Leone and Potter were frustrated with the results. Potter believed that the Archaeology in Annapolis tour program failed "to affect life in Annapolis. . . . Public archaeological interpretation presented through site tours may not be the best way to build an archaeological practice, if the goal of such a practice is to inspire social change." "As far as I can tell," Leone has written, "[the tours] changed consciousness not at all. . . . We were speaking to the wrong audience."

It is the politics of class that accounts for the absence of immigrants, children, women, slaves, and free African Americans in the models of social behavior that are created through historical narratives. This politics not only suppresses the exploited themselves, but their histories as well, leaving historical archaeology as their means of finding a voice.

MARK LEONE

For a historical archaeology of capitalism to be fruitful, Leone realized, "there would have to be a dialogue with those who see knowledge about themselves as a way of dealing with their own oppression or victimization." This was disappointing in a sense because it suggested that critical theory—as a strategy for effecting social change (its avowed goal)—might not work as intended (at least not by itself).

On reflection, Leone still believed that the Archaeology in Annapolis program had successfully explored the histories of the white residents who lived there (even if the white tourists to Annapolis did not seem to pick up on the message to "stand up against capitalism"). But he also realized that in its early stages, the archaeology program had overlooked a major portion of the city by not explicitly addressing the historic African American experience through archaeology.

This realization led Leone and the public programming effort at Annapolis in another direction—into the contemporary African American community of Annapolis. "Black people want to know how they got to be here now. White people, on the other hand, do not want such knowledge."

The dialogue between Annapolis archaeologists and the African American community immediately raised three related questions:

- Was there, indeed, any way to tell whether archaeological material was associated with African Americans?
- Does the African American community care about that record? (Some important questions: Can you tell us about freedom, not just about slavery? Is there anything left from Africa?)
- What would an African American historical archaeology look like?

Faced with this entirely new direction, Leone realized, "We ourselves had to admit we did not know the answers."

So began a new interchange at Annapolis, between white archaeologists and African Americans. No longer was the archaeologist the "teacher," with the community serving only as "listener." In this dialogue, all participants defined themselves as professionals, informants, scholars, students, and fundraisers. Everyone involved, according to Leone, admitted ignorance on some topics, but also expressed a willingness to learn.

In the next chapter, we will explore the topic of African American archaeology in some detail. As we shall see, African American communities have become actively involved in a number of archaeological programs

Archaeology in Annapolis demonstrates the promise of critical theory for historical archaeology. As an experiment, the project is neither so unsuccessful that nobody should ever try it again nor so successful that it need never be tried again.

PARKER POTTER, ARCHAEOLOGIST (NEW HAMPSHIRE DIVISION OF HISTORICAL RESOURCES)

across the country. It is an important new direction because it shows how archaeology has become a way for the previously silenced and disenfranchised to learn about and express their own history.

SUMMARY *Historical archaeology* looks at material remains from past societies that also left behind some form of written documentation ("history") about themselves. So defined, the first *bona fide* historical archaeology in America took place only about 150 years ago. During the first half of the twentieth century, historical archaeologists labored mostly to supplement historical records, serving as a kind of "handmaiden to history." This perspective is particularly evident in massive reconstruction and public interpretive projects, such as Plimoth Plantation, Colonial Williamsburg, and the Little Bighorn battlefield. Such projects tended to concentrate on a very few selected sites, particularly houses of the rich and famous, forts, and other military sites.

Things changed in the 1960s, when some processual archaeologists realized that they could refine their archaeological methods and theories by working in the contexts of verifiable historical controls. Mainstream historical archaeology soon distanced itself from the "Barnum and Bailey" emphasis on the "oldest," "largest," and "most historically significant" sites—looking instead at the larger social context. In the 1960s, historical archaeology began doing what has been called "backyard archaeology," including a focus on historically disenfranchised groups in our own culture. The so-called archaeology of the people without history is attempting to uncover the archaeological roots of African American and Asian American cultures, Native Americans during the historic period, and Hispanic American Creoles.

Historical archaeology has also been fertile ground for postprocessual interests in culture-specific historical contexts. Postprocessual approaches require a more "situated" archaeology—a view of the past more closely attuned to contextual specifics. "Text-aided" archaeology became a logical focus for postprocessual studies because of the wealth of documentary evidence available with which to *contextualize* the archaeological record. The study of the symbolic meaning of material remains also proceeds much more comfortably in the text-aided context, where independent confirmation or disconfirmation can be found in the documentary record. In the world of historical archaeology, written documentation (and sometimes oral tradition) can be called upon to determine which interpretations are more appropriate than others and which explanation best fits the data.

Historical archaeology is today one of the most rapidly expanding and exciting directions in Americanist archaeology.

Chapter 19

Historical Archaeology: Digging up African America

PREVIEW This chapter develops an in-depth case study in historical archaeology. We delve into the rapidly developing field of African American archaeology. Not only are we learning about a largely unknown chapter of American history, but we are also seeing an increased involvement of well-trained African American people in the archaeology of their own cultural heritage.

According to Theresa Singleton, a leader in this new field, the archaeological study of slavery and of black-occupied sites–increasingly referred to as *African American archaeology*–is defined as the deliberate use of material culture to interpret African American life.

Although the field of African American archaeology remains in its infancy, with a still-developing theoretical framework, several promising directions have emerged for understanding the archaeological record of slavery: What were the actual living conditions of those who were enslaved? What status differences can be identified within the plantation communities? What can we learn about the interplay between the dominant planters and the difficult-to-see slave resistance? What can archaeology contribute to the development of African American cultural identity?

We didn't land on Plymouth Rock. Plymouth Rock landed on us.

MALCOLM X (1925–1965), RELIGIOUS LEADER

The archaeology of African American people, particularly the study of slavery, has grown rapidly over the past two decades and today has become a major new horizon for Americanist archaeology. Numerous social, political, and intellectual forces spurred the origin and growth of African American archaeology: black activism, passage of historic preservation legislation, emergence of an archaeological interest in the immigrant ethnic groups of America, and the increased use of archaeology in the public interpretation of historic sites (such as plantations). In this chapter, we explore some major current directions in the rapidly expanding field of African American archaeology.

History and the "Silk Pants Patriots"

Colonial Williamsburg (Virginia) is one of the world's most famous history museums. It consists of more than 500 buildings, 88 of which are claimed

IN HER OWN WORDS

Choosing a Name for the Africans Abroad by Cheryl White

Since the mobilization of African peoples to the Western Hemisphere, a host of labels and titles have been used to define us. The desire to assimilate and to be recognized in a land other than our own, keeps afloat the age-old question "Who am I?"

This search for identity has led us to cling to transient ethnic logos that are indicative of the Eurocentrism that is, more often than not, the template for our own approach to self-definition.

Over the course of history there has been much creative jargon used to disassociate peoples of the African **Diaspora** *from their place of origin. "Negroes," "coloreds," "blacks," "Afro-Americans," and finally the politically correct term of the moment, "African Americans."*

Which do I pick to represent me?

Black, the term most commonly used to describe the dark pigmented people of the world, seems somehow to imply meanings of gloomy, pessimistic, dismal, sullen, or even hostile. Negro is the Spanish/Portuguese variation of the word black. The many hyphenated conjectures, simply by their syntax, automatically contort my identity in the eyes of white America. Some would interpret still further, by calling themselves "Americanized Africans" or "peoples of African descent living in America" (I personally prefer the latter). In the nineties, we hear "The New African," whatever that means. But however you shuffle these complementary terms, they still resonate of European colonization.

To name ourselves is to define ourselves. To define ourselves brings about a heightened recognition of our place in the world. If we can recognize and understand our geographical origin and its place in history, we bring to the table a richer and more holistic perception of identity that extends beyond rhetorical antics.

Now that "multiculturalism" has become the buzzword of the nineties, a greater emphasis is placed on the need to categorize. It is easy to get lost in the sea of misnomers and believe the rhetoric that promotes disintegration.

So much time is spent thinking of what we should call each other that we lose sight of the commonsense tactics needed to live among one another: to recognize each person as a human being and acknowledge his or her contribution to the world at large. There is no reason why anyone, "black" or "white," should have to succumb to frivolous titles.

But, if I had to choose, I would want to be acknowledged for the place of my origin. No hyphenations, no subtext, as an African pure and simple.

CHERYL WHITE is a technical assistant in the North American Archaeology Laboratory, American Museum of Natural History, New York City.

Diaspora: The settling of scattered colonies of people far from their ancestral homeland.

The destiny of the colored American . . . is the destiny of America.

FREDERICK DOUGLASS (1817–1895), ABOLITIONIST AND WRITER

to be "originals . . . restored" to their mid-eighteenth-century condition. The rest are "reconstructions," new buildings constructed in a style to blend in with the historical flavor of this museum-city. The more than 1 million people who visit Colonial Williamsburg annually are presented with a daunting array of interpreted "history," and the museum encourages visitors to stay for several days in order to "experience" the range of what is being offered.

From the beginning of its renaissance as a tourist destination, Colonial Williamsburg stood as a deliberate monument to the spirit and values of the American Revolution. Aided in great measure by John D. Rockefeller Jr., the restoration process rescued an architectural style and a handicraft tradition, both of which were judged to be tasteful and virtuous. The overriding message, at least until recently, was a patriotic one.

Survey data generated in-house by Colonial Williamsburg gives a pretty clear picture of who, over the past three decades, has been going there: They are affluent, mostly white, well educated, and geographically far-flung. One insider's joke has it that the museum is basically a "Republican Disneyland."

But repeat visitors to Colonial Williamsburg will have noted a dramatic shift in the exhibitions, reflecting equally dramatic shifts in the underlying philosophies governing these exhibits. During recent decades, officials at Colonial Williamsburg have been increasingly criticized for focusing almost entirely on the colonial elite. The product, some argued, was a version of American history that was too "genteel" to be taken seriously. Taking such criticism to heart, the staff at Colonial Williamsburg have deliberately shifted their emphasis toward a more multicultural perspective, designed to make "slaves, women, children, and just plain, ordinary people more conspicuous than they used to be in the Williamsburg story."

Colonial Williamsburg on the Internet:

Colonial Williamsburg Home Page provides an overview of history, events, a visitor's guide, educational resources, and the mission of the Colonial Williamsburg Foundation: http://www.history.org/welcome.html

Gateway Guides: Seasonal Programs and Special Tours: http://www.gateway-va.com/pages/guides/wmburg/seasonal.htm

Since the late 1970s, some effort has indeed been directed toward female and working-class histories. But the major thrust of the current revisionism has been directed at "the other half," meaning the African American community that once made up literally half of the eighteenth-century population of Colonial Williamsburg.

Today's visitor to Colonial Williamsburg encounters African American history at nearly every turn, particularly in the numerous special programs, tours, and performances. In *The Other Half Tour,* for instance, visitors can join a 90-minute walking tour that plays out what life was like for the slaves and free blacks who lived in eighteenth-century Colonial Williamsburg.

Colonial Williamsburg has always, justifiably, prided itself on the accuracy of the history portrayed here; and high-quality authenticity was relatively easy to ensure in the case of the so-called silk pants patriots—legendary elders such as George Washington, Thomas Jefferson,

Visitors in Colonial Williamsburg.

WHAT'S IN A NAME?

African American Archaeology

As Cheryl White notes in her article, considerable ambivalence and apprehension surround the issue of *Choosing a Name for the Africans Abroad*. While recognizing the broad range of existing opinions, in these pages we will follow the usage of Theresa A. Singleton in discussing current trends in the field of *African American archaeology*.

and Patrick Henry. Ample written records exist documenting their activities and their beliefs. In many cases, the surviving artifacts and inventories of personal estates allow interpreters to speak directly about the lives of these important personages. The Colonial Williamsburg tours have always included a wealth of accurate detail about these specific individuals—particularly the white Anglo-Saxon landowners, and occasionally their dependents.

But with the new emphasis on black history at Colonial Williamsburg, a major interpretive problem arises: What, exactly, are the facts of the African American experience? Are there any facts at all (or just informed opinions)?

Black history was not well recorded at the time. And yet, recreating the totality of slave life requires a wealth of detail to be credible: Where did the slaves sleep? What did they wear? What and where did they eat? Unless such details can be supplied, the reconstruction of African American history runs the risk of appearing somehow impoverished, "less real" than the contemporary white American history.

Here is where the archaeology comes in. As noted in the preceding chapter, historical archaeology has become known, in part, as the archaeology of the "people without history," capable of telling tales of the poor and the powerless. Particularly over the past decade, archaeologists have excavated an array of slave artifacts, leading to a much richer understanding of plantation life.

The History of Plantation Archaeology

After four hundred years of slave labor, we have some back pay coming.

MALCOLM X

Plantation archaeology seems to have begun in 1931, at Mount Vernon (Virginia), Washington's plantation home. In his role as director of research and restoration at Mount Vernon, Morley Jeffers Williams—a landscape architect—wanted to know where the various structural remains were on the property, so he conducted extensive and systematic archaeological testing. Although hardly up to contemporary standards, these excavations did permit the reconstruction of the first president's residence and kicked off the study of plantation archaeology, as we now know it.

Several other plantations were explored during this period, including Thomas Jefferson's Monticello. But—consistent with the broader goals of historical archaeology—this early phase of research was usually conducted to assist with the restoration and preservation of places like Williamsburg,

Plymouth, and Jamestown. The excavations were undertaken to find out the general layout and configuration of the plantation and the location and identity of structures, and to delineate special activity areas. Basically, the notion here was to supplement the existing historical record of a site in order to derive a narrative of what had happened there. Generally, the enslaved African Americans living there were incidental to the primary story line. As Charles Orser has described the work, it was "archaeology at a plantation, rather than plantation archaeology."

Slave archaeology began in the late 1960s when Charles Fairbanks (University of Florida) initiated his explorations of coastal plantations in Georgia and Florida. Fairbanks was the first to study explicitly the institution of slavery from the archaeological record. He emphasized the richness and diversity of America's heritage, departing from the traditional "melting pot" theme. Fairbanks and his students set out to dispel myths concerning the biological and cultural inferiority of black Americans that were being used to legitimize continued segregation and discrimination.

Today, the field of African American archaeology is a growth industry, the roots of which can be traced directly to these early archaeological studies of plantation slavery.

Jefferson's Dilemma: Plantation Archaeology at Monticello

Visitors motoring up the serpentine driveway to Thomas Jefferson's Monticello are first struck by the world famous architecture, the vast gardens, and glimpses of mountains in the sprawling Virginia countryside. Walking through Monticello, polite guides provide the visitor with ample (and at times, seemingly endless) details about the life of Thomas Jefferson—the third president, the architect, the statesman (and archaeologist).

When a man becomes a public trust, he should consider himself as public property.

THOMAS JEFFERSON (1743–1826), PROMINENT SLAVEOWNER

Until recently, you didn't hear much about Thomas Jefferson the slave owner. In the days when Jefferson lived at Monticello, the approach to the main house was called Mulberry Row; it was lined by 19 buildings—the houses and workshops of Jefferson's slaves, hired laborers, artisans, and indentured servants. The mansion at Monticello still stands, attracting tourists by the thousands, yet all but one of the structures along Mulberry Row have vanished.

On Slavery: [It's like holding] the wolf by the ears, and we can neither hold him nor safely let him go. Justice is in one scale, self-preservation in the other.

THOMAS JEFFERSON

Historical archaeologists working at Monticello have brought Mulberry Row back to life. Supported in part by the Thomas Jefferson Memorial Foundation, William Kelso and his crew have, for several years, been excavating at Mulberry Row with the specific aim of understanding the patterns of slavery in the antebellum American South.

West portico and lawn at Monticello.

Jefferson had mixed feelings about slavery. Whereas he regarded the institution of slavery as preeminently brutal and immoral—and although he personally favored the abolition of all slavery—as a politician, he realized that this solution would not be acceptable in the late-eighteenth-century United States. Jefferson had a plan to emancipate all slaves, but he also doubted whether the two races could successfully create a biracial society, and so he favored a plan to transport free blacks back to Africa or elsewhere.

Fort Mose: Colonial America's Black Fortress of Freedom

The stereotypical image of Blacks in Colonial history has been that of servitude alone. In fact, free Blacks had a very active role in La Florida's Colonial history. Fort Mose is a symbol of Black freedom in Colonial America, and that's an image we don't get much of in the history books.

KATHLEEN DEAGAN, ARCHAEOLOGIST (FLORIDA MUSEUM OF NATURAL HISTORY)

African American archaeology is not exclusively focused on slavery. Yet another perspective on African American history was achieved through the discovery of Fort Mose, 50 miles south of the Georgia-Florida border. Here, archaeologist Kathleen Deagan and her colleagues at the University of Florida have found concrete evidence of the first legally sanctioned, free African American community in the country.

Beginning with the founding of Charles Towne by the British in 1670, Spain employed free Africans to further its colonial objectives by having them populate and hold territories vulnerable to foreign encroachment. Both free and slave Africans were also used in military operations, a black militia having been established in St. Augustine. By 1673, the Spanish Crown declared that all escaped fugitives from British plantations were to be granted sanctuary and, eventually, freedom in Spanish Florida "so that by their example and by my liberality, others will do the same." Like so many episodes in African American history, the story of Fort Mose is incompletely known, a forgotten footnote to mainstream American history.

Deagan found the lost site of Fort Mose in 1986, and her excavations have provided an opportunity to reexamine the role of African Americans in colonial history. She is particularly interested in the effect of freedom on the blacks of Fort Mose. How much did they adapt to Spanish ways? Did they attempt to revive their African heritage?

Recognizing the relevance of the Fort Mose research, the state of Florida was quick to help out. State Representative Bill Clark, who sponsored the bill helping to finance the archaeology, has called Deagan's discovery of Fort Mose "a major historical find for black people." To Clark, himself an African American, the excavations demonstrate that "blacks were never content to be slaves. . . . These are America's first freedom fighters."

These liberal sympathies notwithstanding, Jefferson owned a slave force sometimes numbering more than 200 people. We know from surviving documents that unlike many other slaveowners of his time, Jefferson felt obligated to protect his slaves from ruthless treatment and to provide more than merely adequate clothing and housing. Jefferson claimed never to require more of his slaves than would be required of free laborers.

With this as background, Kelso and his crew began digging at Mulberry Row in 1980 to learn more about the living and working conditions of Jefferson's slaves. Working from an insurance plat of 1796, Kelso suspected that Jefferson had done away with the "barracks" approach to slave housing, introducing single-family dwellings at Monticello. Although few ruins were visible, Kelso soon found by exploratory excavation that the subsurface record of Mulberry Row was relatively undisturbed.

Kelso found not only that Jefferson seems to have improved the quality of slave housing but also that a significant diversity in housing existed at any particular time. Whereas some slaves lived in spartan, dirt-floored log cabins

Kathleen Deagan (center) and Florida State Representative Bill Clark (left) work with the excavation team to recover minute archaeological evidence at Fort Mose, Florida.

only 12 by 14 feet, their neighbors lived in comfortable stone houses twice that size, with stone and brick fireplaces, wooden flooring, and neoclassical façades complete with elevated pediments.

It also seems likely that the residents of Mulberry Row were the house servants and artisans who enjoyed a considerably better standard of living than, say, the field hands, who lived in other settlements farther down the mountain. Even along Mulberry Row, there was probably a social hierarchy, with butlers and favorite cooks maintaining a better standard of living than maids or laundresses. The archaeological findings tend to confirm this pattern. Although pig, cow, and deer bones recovered came mostly from poorer cuts of meat, more long-bone fragments turned up at one particular (higher-status?) house than at others, where bones from the less meaty parts were found. Some were also ground up, suggesting the use of meat in stews.

Excavations at the apparently higher-status building also turned up a huge, high-quality ceramic assemblage dating around 1770 to 1800. Some 289 vessels were recovered, mostly representing 30 different forms and 36

The whole commerce between master and slave is a perpetual exercise of the most boisterous passings, the most unremitting despotism on the one part, and degrading submissions on the other.

THOMAS JEFFERSON

Excavating slave dwellings built during Jefferson's lifetime at Monticello. Evident in this picture are the remains of building "l," the storehouse (foreground), building "m," the smokehouse-dairy (center), and the rebuilt walls of an 1809 stone house (background).

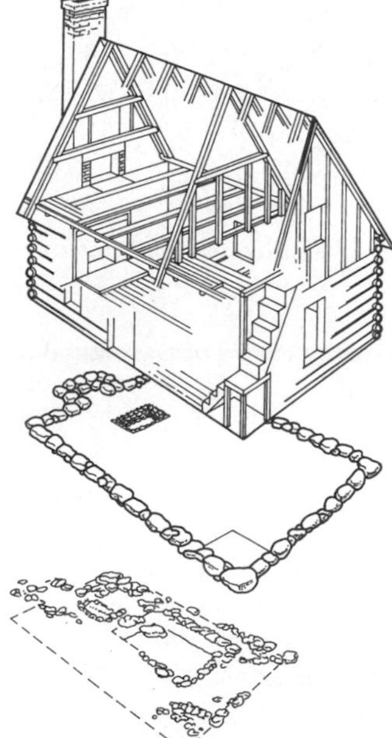

Artist's reconstruction of slave housing at Monticello. This figure shows a view of a slave cabin at Bremo Recess Plantation (Virginia) superimposed over the archaeological plan of a similar structure (servant's house "o") excavated at Monticello.

different types. Clearly such tableware was no longer suitable for use in the main house because the edges were cracked or chipped. Did the slaves living in the "higher-status" house dine and drink from this rather elegant ware?

Social Status in Antebellum Georgia

Historical archaeologists working along coastal Georgia and northern Florida have noted even greater diversity within the slave communities. Excavating at Cannon's Point Plantation, on St. Simons Island (Georgia), John Solomon Otto worked in several dwelling sites formerly occupied by people of three distinctly different racial and legal status groups.

At the bottom of the social pyramid were the black slaves, essentially without legal status. In return for their labor in the fields, slaves received rations of food and clothing, gifts of some household articles, and housing. The overseers, free whites, supervised the field workers and were paid modest salaries and provided with housing. Held in low esteem by the plantation employers, overseers had minimal job security and dignity, whereas the plantation managers enjoyed considerably more social and economic success.

Otto excavated dwelling sites from each socioeconomic and racial category and found the status differences to be clear-cut. Perhaps as a symbol of racial solidarity, the overseers lived in relatively comfortable houses, more closely resembling those of planters than slaves.

The future is the only kind of property that masters willingly concede to slaves.

ALBERT CAMUS (1913–1960), AUTHOR

The food remains reflected a further racial and legal differentiation among these three groups. Although all groups supplemented their diet with wild mammals, fish, and turtles, the slave population was much more dependent on wild taxa than were either the white overseers or the planters.

Food preparation also varied according to subordinate and elite status differences. The plantation owners, waited on by domestic slaves, often enjoyed roasts and steaks served on transfer-printed platters, and seafood- and meat-based soups served in tureens. Food bones recovered from these contexts showed mostly saw marks on the scapulae, ribs, and vertebrae of large mammal bones, indicating that the carcasses had been carefully butchered to produce regular cuts and joints for the planter's table.

But because they had less time for such elaborate food preparation, overseers and slaves commonly dined on one-pot meals that could be left simmering for hours. These meals were often served in bowls, and the ceramic inventory reflects this difference. Food bones recovered from slave and overseer quarters often have axe and knife marks because the bones were often cleaved open to increase available nourishment; no saw marks are present because the bones were mostly used in stews.

Although archaeologists have had some success at reconstructing slave diets, the measurement of nutritional adequacy remains the subject of considerable debate. Few nutritional studies (of the kind discussed in Chapter 12) have been performed on slave remains, and so investigators have relied heavily on contemporary documentation that suggests that malnutrition was rampant in some places. The archaeological data confirm this, indicating that despite the opportunity to supplement their diet with wild foodstuff, slaves appear to have been consistently undernourished. The caloric intake from the core diet of slaves has been estimated to be about 2,350 calories. By comparison, it has been estimated that adult males expend more than 6,000 calories per day while performing moderate work.

Men would rather be starving and free than fed in bonds.

PEARL S. BUCK (1892–1973), NOVELIST

Public Archaeology: Interpreting Carter's Grove Plantation

Nowhere is the interplay between plantation archaeology and the interpretation of black history more evident than at Carter's Grove, a James River plantation 8 miles from the historic area in Colonial Williamsburg. First opened to the public in 1969, the early exhibits at Carter's Grove provided basically a decorative arts tour of the mansion, the great house of Carter Burwell, completed in 1753. The house became a symbol of Burwell's wealth and prominence in Virginia Colony. Visitors can peer inside the famous "Refusal Room," where marriage proposals from George Washington and Thomas Jefferson were allegedly refused by indifferent Southern belles—convinced, we are told,

If men and women are in chains, anywhere in the world, then freedom is endangered everywhere.

JOHN F. KENNEDY (1917–1963), 35TH PRESIDENT OF THE UNITED STATES

Visitors taking the tour of the Carter's Grove Plantation.

that these two men would "never amount to anything." The Big House, like so many such mansions, is "a glorious, living monument to an elegant age, irretrievably lost," at least so reads the Internet promotion of Carter's Grove.

But because this mansion is owned and managed by the Colonial Williamsburg Foundation, Carter's Grove was also subjected to criticisms of elitism and an infatuation with silk pants patriots. As the facility matured, several questions arose about the most appropriate way to present the diverse history contained at the Carter's Grove plantation complex:

> Should the mansion be restored to its original 1755 condition (or should the "more popular" Colonial Revival style be maintained)?
>
> How should the results of the well-publicized excavation of the nearby site of seventeenth-century Martin's Hundred be presented? (After all, people had read about the dig in the pages of *National Geographic;* yet when they came to Carter's Grove, all they saw was a barren field with some stakes indicating the defensive perimeter of the site.)
>
> And, trickiest of all, how to present the working eighteenth-century plantation, known to have functioned almost literally within the shadow of the Big House?

By the mid-1980s, a major decision had been made: The on-site interpretation would embrace the entire four centuries of life known to have been played out here. No attempt would be made to restore the Carter's Grove property to a single era or year.

But there was to be an important exception: the plantation outbuildings. Because of the overarching emphasis on interpreting black history at Colonial Williamsburg, a decision was made to create an on-site display of slavery at Carter's Grove plantation.

The first step was to conduct systematic archaeological excavations at the supposed site of the slave quarters. Archaeologists soon discovered a foundation—a "footprint"—of an eighteenth-century outbuilding that appeared to have served as slave housing. They also found a series of shallow pits, believed to be root cellars similar to those commonly found in slave quarters elsewhere in Virginia. The buildings were (re)constructed on the spot.

Today Carter's Grove has blossomed into a full-scale exhibit complex, presenting four centuries of history through three interrelated components: an eighteenth-century Georgian mansion ("the Big House"), a reconstruction of Martin's Hundred and Wolstenholme Towne (an administrative center established in 1619 and largely destroyed in an Indian uprising of 1622), plus a recently excavated and reconstructed eighteenth-century slave quarter. Near the complex is the Winthrop Rockefeller Archaeology Museum, a 7,000-square-foot, contemporary, single-level museum built on a knoll overlooking the James River, just north of the Carter's Grove Mansion.

Visitors to Carter's Grove begin at the reception center where, armed with a descriptive brochure, they are invited to view an introductory slide show and work through a small orientation exhibition. After learning something about the local Algonquian Indians and their predecessors, visitors proceed into the reconstructed slave quarter where they are greeted by African American interpreters, dressed in period clothing, who provide a third-person interpretation of slave life and guide visitors through the reconstructed buildings and associated yards.

The interpreters cover a broad range of topics about working routines, slave resistance, foodways, punishment, and life expectancy. At one point, the barbarity of the slave trade is illustrated by audience volunteers, arranged to show the "loose" and "tight" packing used on slave ships.

Although located on the site where the archaeological investigations took place, the Carter's Grove complex is not intended as a literal reconstruction. Rather, it is a compilation based on documentary and on-site archaeological information and extensive comparative research. The Carter's Grove reconstruction is intended both to show what a typical Chesapeake slave quarter looked like and also to provide an interpretive resource suitable for the overall needs of Colonial Williamsburg's educational programs. For the first time in the six decades of historical interpretation at Colonial Williamsburg, slave buildings have been deliberately constructed to show the public what slavery was like.

And what are the visitors told?

One story deals with the conflict implied by the elite and everyday architectures seen at Carter's Grove. Terrence Epperson has argued that this spatial patterning reflects the underlying racial ideology. In effect, he argues, the exclusion of slave dwellings from the formal landscape is a reflection of the planter's domination over that landscape and its architecture. Enslaved people, however, resisted such domination by creating their own outdoor spaces, hidden from the watchful eye of planters or overseers. Epperson uses Carter's Grove to show how this works: Slaves added back doors to their dwellings, providing access to an open space shielded by other dwellings on all sides. Within these exclusive, hidden spaces, enslaved people maintained some control over their own actions.

As in all other forms of domination, successful slavery was characterized by a fundamental contradiction. There was the exclusionary impulse represented by the need to create the "Other" as different and alien. On the other hand, that "Other" must also be incorporated into a single social and cultural

Uncovering Buried African Connections

We are seeing not a history of oppression, but a history of responses to oppression, discovered through archaeology.

MARK LEONE, ARCHAEOLOGIST (UNIVERSITY OF MARYLAND)

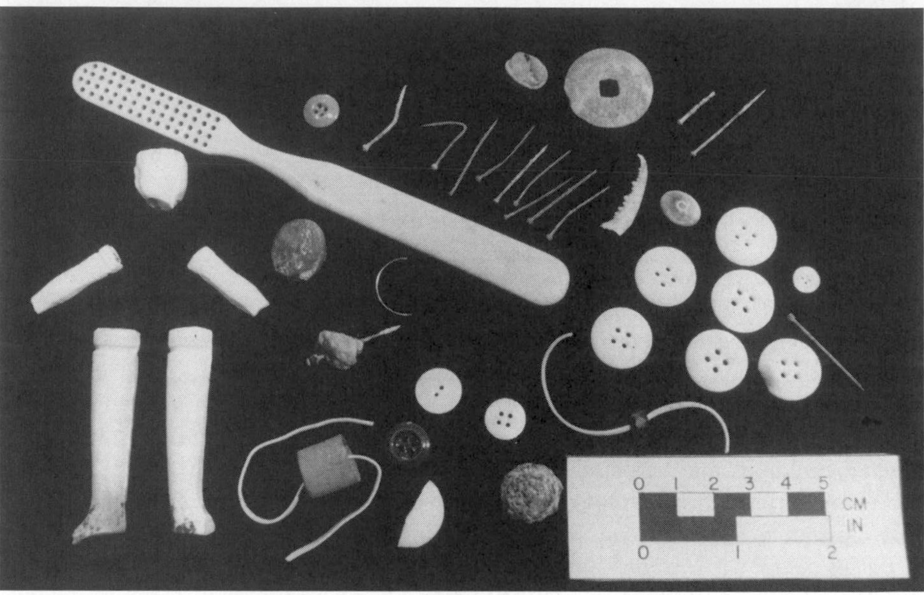

These artifacts from a Slayton House cache may symbolize the spirits of the ancestors.

While excavating in the ground-floor workrooms of the Slayton House, a four-story, brick row house erected in 1774 in downtown Annapolis, Mark Leone and his team of historical archaeologists made an important discovery about the culture of enslaved African Americans. Unexpectedly, they found several **caches,** buried there in the nineteenth century by slave inhabitants, containing brass pins, buttons and beads, a crab claw, a brass ring and bell, and the arms and legs of a small doll.

Because the slaves living in the Slayton House worked in the ground-floor kitchen and laundry, it seems likely that these artifacts were buried as ritual bundles, a part of *hoodoo*, the term most commonly applied to the ritual practices of this "traditional religion."

The artifacts probably represented the spirits of ancestors and reflect the religious practices of slaves using their African heritage: seeking protection from cruel slaveowners, attempting to cast healing spells, and expressing hope for the future.

Such practices were conducted in secret. Although living in America, these enslaved people clearly retained African traditions while also usually becoming fervent Christians. Such continuities and amalgams are rarely reflected in the contemporaneous histories of the time, which are almost universally written from the dominant, white perspective.

Leone and his students are increasingly focusing their work on sites in historic Annapolis that document how slaves maintained at least part of their African identity in a white-dominated society. Today, in excavations such as Leone's in Annapolis and those in the African Burial Ground in New York City, archaeologists are finding evidence of African American lifeways, going back as far as those of the European colonists, but rarely documented in American history books.

When slaves are brought over or were born here or sold to different owners, they didn't forget the beliefs they were brought up with. We're finding the evidence more often now because we are aware of it.

LYNN D. JONES, ARCHAEOLOGIST (UNIVERSITY OF MARYLAND)

system of domination. Compare, for example, the perceived need for severe and sometimes brutal discipline to "keep the slaves in line" (the exclusionary impulse) with the common practice of imposing the slaveholder's English name upon recently arrived African slaves (an incorporating aspect of domination).

The incorporative motive can clearly be seen in the planter's efforts to impose what Terrence Epperson terms "a disciplinary grid" on the Carter's Grove slave quarters: The spacing, alignment, and even the appearance of the façade were carefully designed to incorporate these quarters into the formal landscape of the plantation. In this sense, the slaveowner living in the Big House viewed the enslaved workers as part of "my family," effectively asserting that slavery was a natural extension of the plantation patriarch's overall authority. And yet, it was also important to manipulate this landscape to exclude the slave families from view (and hence from consciousness).

Layout of the slave reconstruction at Carter's Grove Plantation.

Here then, at Carter's Grove, can be seen the fundamental conflict within which slavery operated in Tidewater Virginia: In effect, the slaves must be closely controlled, but they must simultaneously be invisible. The slave complex consists of a cluster of buildings and associated outdoor area, located about 800 feet northwest of the Big House mansion. The entire complex is partially screened by topography and a row of trees from the gaze of those inside the Big House. Here is the exclusionary aspect of the formal plantation space.

Cache: A hiding place for concealing and preserving provisions, implements, or other important possessions.

The slave buildings have been reconstructed using eighteenth-century methods and materials. First, there is a log corn crib, which was generally kept locked (access being controlled by the plantation owner or slave foreman). Then there is a fairly large, one-room foreman's house, a reconstruction of a 1770s single-family residence of an enslaved foreman and his family. The somewhat elevated status of this household is shown in several ways: The house is built closest to the mansion, on a slightly elevated rise. A fairly neat rectangular yard is attached.

This is the only instance in the Carter's Grove reconstruction where an intact slave family is shown living together, within a single architectural space.

This type of research is the closest we can come to time travel, going back and asking our ancestors about their lives. Sometimes I think we're sitting at the feet of our ancestors. It's one thing to have chronicles and documents about one's ancestors, it's another thing to be in the presence of the actual remains.

MICHAEL L. BLAKEY, BIOARCHAEOLOGIST (HOWARD UNIVERSITY)

The interiors are sparsely furnished with objects, such as gourds and ceramic vessels, found in archaeological investigations or listed in contemporary accounts. The foreman's cabin contains a greater variety of household items, suggesting that he and his family had greater access to goods and money.

The interpreters spend considerable time explaining the difficult position of the enslaved foreman in the plantation hierarchy, something like being "between a rock and a hard place." Required to carry out the wishes of the owner, the overseer was mistrusted by other slaves. But if he failed to obey the slaveowner, he and his family could be harshly punished, possibly through the sale of his wife and/or children. Overseers were, however, rewarded for good service with better housing and more household goods. Although hardly luxurious, the foreman's house was comparable to those lived in by non-slaveowners of the eighteenth century.

Because the slave quarters are the first major exhibits encountered by most visitors at Carter's Grove, they effectively define the rest of the experience. By viewing life from the perspective of the enslaved, not the enslavers, the audience is introduced to the lifeways of African Americans as enslaved people. From this viewpoint, the plantation is not simply a landscape owned and controlled by a white planter. It is a community in which blacks are numerically dominant, and an environment in which they exert an influence whenever possible.

The interpretation notes that, at the insistence of the owner, the façade of this log cabin is rigidly symmetrical and oriented toward the river (at the same angle as the mansion). Although separate, the slave buildings are also tightly integrated into the plantation nucleus. The message comes through loud and clear: There are very definite limits upon the cultural autonomy of those living in these slave dwellings.

The Archaeology of New York's African Burial Ground

Nineteenth-century engraving depicting an African being auctioned into slavery in Dutch New Amsterdam.

The bones of 427 enslaved Africans, interred by their own community and forgotten for centuries, were discovered beneath a parking lot in downtown New York City in 1991.

The isle of Manhattan is a long way from the land of cotton, and few today remember that colonial New York was former slave territory. Too often recalled as an exclusively southern institution, slavery was deeply ingrained in the economy of the colonial North as well. That story is being told in excavations at New York's African Burial Ground.

Slavery in Old New York?

The narrative begins in 1626, when the Dutch West India Company unloaded its first shipment of enslaved Africans in New Amsterdam (today's New York City): 11 young men from what today is the Congo-Angola region of southwestern Africa. Two years later, the Dutch imported three African women "for the comfort of the company's Negro men." The Dutch at the time were experiencing a labor shortage in their colonies, and they found slave labor to be the answer to building and maintaining the colony.

Some scholars argue that the Dutch system was less repressive than later systems. They point out that a few slaves had more rights than New Amsterdam's Jews, who were forbidden from owning land or serving in the militia. Under the Dutch, the Africans were permitted to intermarry with whites, attend white churches, own property, and enjoy the same status as whites in court.

According to this view, the Dutch practiced half-freedom, with true slavery not being introduced until 1664, when the Dutch ceded Manhattan to the British. At that time, the population of enslaved Africans made up about 40 percent of New Amsterdam's total population.

A 35- to 40-year-old woman with her child, interred at the African Burial Ground. Both probably died during childbirth, or shortly thereafter.

But there can be no mistaking the intention of the British, who continued to import slaves during the first half of the eighteenth century. Everywhere one looked in colonial New York, there were toiling slaves—loading and unloading ships on the waterfront, building the streets, and erecting the buildings to house this bustling port city, crowded onto the southern end of Manhattan.

On the eve of the American Revolution, New York City had the largest number of enslaved Africans of any English colonial city except for Charleston, South Carolina. In fact, New York City had the highest proportion of slaves to Europeans of any northern settlement. Despite the lily-white perspectives found in most American history books, it is clear that the African population had a significant hand in the building of colonial New York.

Eighteenth-century New York followed a policy of "mortuary apartheid," meaning that African burial in Manhattan's churchyards was strictly prohibited. Left without a place to bury their dead, New York's African population eventually established a cemetery on a deserted tract of land lying just outside the city's protective wooden palisade (the "wall" of modern "Wall Street" fame). There, from roughly 1712 to 1790, somewhere between 10,000 and 20,000 people, mostly black, but also a few lower-class whites, were buried. A 1755 map of downtown New York clearly shows the "Negro Burial Ground," covering perhaps five city blocks.

Some scholars question 1712 as the appropriate beginning date for the cemetery. Because Africans had lived in the area since at least 1624, some burials could easily have taken place earlier. To African American historian Christopher Moore, the date 1712 is significant only because that is when "the first European noticed that blacks were burying their dead."

It was not until 1827 that New York finally abolished slavery altogether. In the meantime, African American populations had abandoned the downtown area, moving northward in New York City. Over the subsequent decades, the Negro Burial Ground was slowly swallowed up by urban expansion. By the late twentieth century, Manhattan's forgotten African cemetery lay buried beneath 20 feet of fill, a scant two blocks north of New York's City Hall.

This is the most important African archaeological site in the United States. . . . A people's identity is largely historical. What we know about ourselves is primarily connected with the past. How we developed here is important to how we believe in ourselves and look to the future.

MICHAEL L. BLAKEY

IN HIS OWN WORDS

Bioarchaeology of the African Burial Ground by Michael L. Blakey

The African Burial Ground in New York City is the earliest and largest African cemetery in North America. Originally located just outside the walls of the colonial city, enslaved and free Africans used the cemetery beginning sometime in the seventeenth century and continuing until 1794.

Public and scientific controversy began when part of the site was uncovered in 1991. African Americans sought to stop archaeological excavation and building construction. They wanted to establish a fitting memorial and to determine for themselves whether research should be conducted. Rising protests, town meetings, and lobbying efforts were mounted by the African American "descendant community" in order to assure proper treatment of their ancestors.

The Sankofa, a well-known West African symbol found on a coffin lid at the African Burial Ground.

One set of concerns that involved the African Burial Ground had to do with the politics of the past. Eurocentric distortions and omissions of African and African American anthropology and history have been persistently cited by black scholars and activists as far as the mid-nineteenth century.

The very existence of an African Burial Ground in colonial New York raised the issue of false historical representation. The vast majority of educated Americans had learned that there was little if any African presence in New York during the colonial period, and that the northern American colonies had not engaged in the practice of slavery. The Burial Ground helped show that these notions comprised a kind of national myth. Africans arrived in New York and its Dutch predecessor, New Amsterdam, from the beginning; they had represented 15 to 40 percent of these colonies and had labored in most aspects of the building of the city and its economy. The majority of these people had been enslaved until Emancipation Day in 1827. In an attempt to insure a fair and empowering interpretation of the past, African Americans were determined to include scholars from their own communities prominently in any research that might be done on the site. This site constituted one of the few means of restoring lost pages of American history that might reveal untold dimensions of African American identity.

I organized a research team consisting of anthropologists, historians, geneticists, and other scientists who had previous experience in the study of both African American and African archaeology and biology. Based at Howard University (the nation's leading African American research university), the research group prominently includes African American and African scholars who shared many of the descendant community's concerns. Following partly from the African American tradition of "scholar activism" and partly from anthropological approaches to "public engagement," Howard anthropologists and their consultants involved the community in discussions of their proposed research design. They assumed that descendant or culturally affiliated persons should have the right to determine whether research was sufficiently worthwhile as to amount to something more than desecration of the cemetery.

Through public meetings, researchers described their methods for restoring the lost history of the enslaved

Archaeology Can Be Contentious

But the Negro Burial Ground was not destined to lie undisturbed. In 1990, the city of New York sold the property to the General Services Administration

Africans who were buried there. The community introduced their own research questions and thoughts about how the site should be interpreted. This community feedback was incorporated in the research design, so long as the integrity of the scientific method remained intact. The result was a better and more meaningful research project that was not only acceptable to the descendant community, but which they had become part of.

There were now two types of client: an ethical client *(descendant or culturally affiliated communities) and a* business client *(the federal government, responsible for funding the project's research). While responsible for satisfying the legal requirements of its business client, the research team took on responsibility for seeing that agreements made with its ethical client were carried out. One such agreement was the return of skeletons for reburial and memorialization once the important data had been gathered. Thus, scientific, cultural, spiritual, or religious treatments of the cemetery would complement its significance rather than compete.*

The details of our study are facts that many African Americans are anxious to examine. The comprehensive anthropological research will not be completed until the year 2000. So far, much has already been learned from the skeletal remains being studied in Howard's Cobb Laboratory. We have reconstructed, measured, documented, and analyzed most of the 400 remains.

The skeletons tell a story of high infant and childhood mortality and morbidity. About 50 percent of the population died before reaching 12 years of age. Workloads of the African Burial Ground population were excessive. Most men and women have enlarged muscle attachments as well as lesions from torn muscles and ligaments. Some skeletons show cranial and spinal fractures related to heavy work and load bearing that sometimes caused their deaths. The low frequency of dental growth defects in adults (which record malnutrition and disease during childhood) when compared with other Northern and Southern African American sites, suggests a more favorable way of life in West or Central Africa prior to being brought to New York.

Although few artifacts remain, one woman was found wearing a string of glass and cowrie shell beads around her waist. In what is today Ghana and Benin, such beads would have been given as a wedding present. The coffin lid of one man's burial had an elaborate heart-shaped design made of brass tacks. One likely possibility being explored is the Asanti adinkra symbol "Sankofa," which means, "look to the past to inform decisions about the future."

The New York African Burial Ground tells us that archaeology, physical anthropology, and history are often important in the minds of everyday people. Whether as a basis for defining national and group identity, the elucidation of processes leading to current social conditions, or as a guide to the future, disciplines that construct the past do so within the context of broader cultural and political meanings.

It is important for a community to be empowered to evaluate its own past, for better or worse, and to honor that past in ways that are meaningful for it. African Americans are certainly not singular in these respects. Indigenous people in many parts of the world are advocating control of their cultural patrimony, including sacred archaeological sites and skeletal remains curated by museums. National legislation has begun to protect those rights for Native Americans.

Working with the remains of the dead also means having an impact on living communities that are affiliated with the dead. Archaeologists and skeletal biologists who work with archaeological populations are well served when they have had "holistic" training in the history, ethnography, ethics, and even the political issues of living communities. These issues mark the terrain often entered when digging for the past.

MICHAEL L. BLAKEY is associate professor and curator of anthropology at Howard University.

(GSA), the arm of the U.S. government responsible for constructing and maintaining federal buildings. The GSA had grand plans to build a 34-story office tower at 290 Broadway—complete with an adjacent four-story pavilion on the parking lot area—to house the United States attorney's office, a regional office of the Environmental Protection Agency, and a district office of the Internal Revenue Service. Although administrators knew at the time that the GSA pavilion was slated to rise directly above a colonial cemetery, they seriously underestimated its extent and the extraordinary degree of burial preservation.

Black folks wanted to hear what a black scientist would say about this situation. There is a level of trust for our own institutions that does not exist for European American institutions.

MICHAEL L. BLAKEY

As we will discuss in the next chapter, the United States has an elaborate legal framework to protect its archaeological resources—particularly those lying on federal land. Part of this legislation requires that an environmental impact statement be filed before any construction can begin. Archaeologists and historians routinely participate in preparing such impact statements. The archaeological firm retained for the 290 Broadway historical inventory correctly noted that the "Negro Burial Ground" appeared on historical maps of the area, and probably lay nearby. But, recognizing the long-standing construction history of the site, the impact statement concluded that the digging of nineteenth- and twentieth-century basements had probably obliterated any human remains within the historical boundaries of the cemetery. Although the environmental impact statement did note that a portion of the old cemetery might have survived intact beneath an old alleyway, nobody expected much in the way of human remains to surface when construction began at 290 Broadway.

Still, because there remained a possibility of finding significant archaeological deposits in the construction zone, federal law required that exploratory archaeological excavation be undertaken. Suspecting that only a handful of human bones might turn up, a team of archaeologists began the small-scale excavations in September 1991. Right away, they found human bone—not just a few scattered burials, but dozens (then hundreds) of intact human burials.

The unexpectedly productive excavations at 290 Broadway began interfering with construction schedules. Worried that the archaeology might delay the $276 million project, the GSA insisted that the archaeologists work faster, excavating skeletons 10 and 12 hours a day, 7 days a week. Laboratory crew members were reassigned to field excavation duty—anything to speed things up.

At this point, word of the new finds got out to New York's African American community. Here, lying 16 to 28 feet below the modern street level, some 427 skeletons had been found from the long-forgotten Negro Burial Ground (soon termed the "African Burial Ground" by community representatives). African American leaders were concerned that there was no community involvement in the 290 Broadway project. As one citizen put it, "If it was an African find, we wanted to make sure that it was interpreted from an African point of view." The GSA countered that appropriate notification had been made, as mandated by law: "We didn't include the Harlem community board because the project isn't in Harlem, it's in lower Manhattan."

I cried. . . . You hear all about these archaeological and scientific terms and you say to yourself "This is very interesting." But until you get down there and you see what the bodies look like—you see the skeletons of the children laying in the earth—then you realize that these are people.

NOEL POINTER, JAZZ MUSICIAN [COMMENTING ON HIS FIRST VISIT TO THE AFRICAN BURIAL GROUND]

The situation reached a flash point when a backhoe operator, excavating for the tower's foundation, destroyed several of the burials. Once word of the destruction leaked out, large-scale protests ensued, culminating in a one-day blockade of the site, shutting down all construction on the GSA tower project.

These excavations and the subsequent laboratory analysis drew nationwide attention. To some, the debate surrounding the African Burial Ground excavations became a "microcosm of the issues of racism and economic exploitation confronting New York City."

The GSA eventually commissioned an advisory committee—comprised of historians, anthropologists, museum professionals, architects, attorneys, clergy, government officials, and concerned community members—to represent the interests of the African descendant community at large.

There were, naturally, differences of opinion about how the remains should be treated. Some in the African American community felt that archaeological investigations were disrespectful, adding the insult of grave robbing to the injury of slavery. Others believed that a thorough yet respectful scientific study of the skeletons was not only a way of honoring the dead, but also of restoring them to their rightful place in American history.

Eventually, a working consensus was forged. A research team, headed by Dr. Michael L. Blakey, was chosen to carry out a 5-year research program on the remains, at Howard University's Cobb Biological Anthropology Laboratory. Bringing in Dr. Blakey was a popular decision. Having received his Ph.D. in biological anthropology at the University of Massachusetts, Amherst, he had an established track record in bioarchaeology, including important work at the First African Baptist Cemetery in Philadelphia. Not insignificantly, Dr. Blakey is an African American employed by the nation's premier black research university. Blakey's active participation became an overt symbol to the African descendant community that their wishes were indeed being considered. In an article written specifically for this text, Blakey describes his involvement in the project and presents some of the preliminary findings of his bioarchaeological analysis (see *Bioarchaeology of the African Burial Ground* by Michael L. Blakey).

Supported by then Mayor David N. Dinkins (New York City's first African American mayor), the African descendant community became actively involved in the preservation, dedication, and management of the cemetery site. It soon became clear that the GSA plans for the proposed federal building would have to be modified.

African American Archaeology on the Internet:

African Burial Ground news:
http://www.afrinet.net/~hallh/abg.html

African-American Archaeology is the newsletter of the African-American Archaeology Network:
http://www.ilinks.net/~newsouth.html

Bibliography: Slavery and African-American History:
http://www.monticello.org/Matters/Bibliography/slavery.html

See also:
http://earth.library.pitt.edu/%7Ehilmlib/afro/afamerican.html

Michael L. Blakey.

The African Burial Ground Today

Eventually, so that the site could be appropriately memorialized, all plans to erect the four-story pavilion were scrubbed. On February 25, 1993, the New York City Landmarks Commission designated the site the African Burial Ground and the Commons Historical District. Later that year, the African Burial Ground achieved National Historic Landmark status.

A Yoruba priestess, and Hru Ankh Ra Semahj Se Ptah, a Kemet priest, pass a newborn child back and forth over a recently-excavated grave at the African Burial Ground. This West African burial custom symbolizes the continuation of life.

Visitors are flocking to the African Burial Ground from around the world; at last count, more than 30,000 people had seen historical slide presentations and participated in laboratory tours and site visits. Some visitors have come all the way from Africa. Mme. Albertina Sisilu, at the time the only elected black member of parliament in South Africa, visited the African Burial Ground in late 1994. In a separate, private ceremony, a Yoruba priestess and a Kemet priest reenacted a West African burial ceremony while the excavations were still in progress, passing a newborn back and forth across the open excavation pits to symbolize the continuation of life (see *Ghanaian Chiefs Visit the African Burial Ground*).

Today, the visitor to 290 Broadway is confronted by a striking memorial mosaic created by artist Roger Brown. Across the bottom is row after row of human skulls, a graphic reminder of those still buried in the African Burial Ground. Above are honeycombed portraits of the multiple races that today populate New York City. Along the top are stylized depictions of such New York landmarks as the Brooklyn Bridge and the Empire State Building.

Nearby, on the façade of the Federal Office Building, stands the Clyde Lynds relief sculpture "America Song," which combines reinforced concrete and stainless steel with fiber optic light in a tribute to those still buried below.

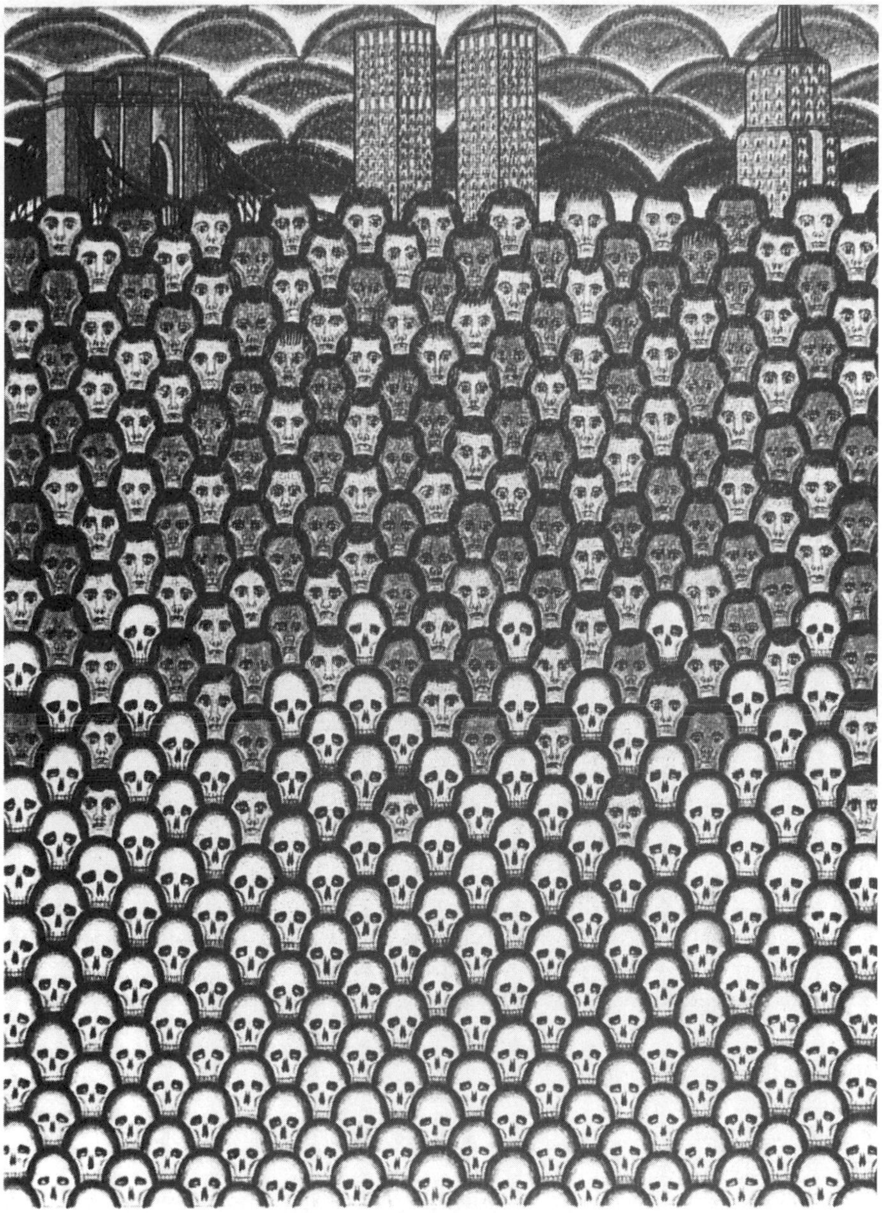

Guided tours and videotapes of the African Burial Ground project are now available through the Office of Public Education and Interpretation of the African Burial Ground, which is actively engaged in bringing the findings to a broader public. Public educators deliver slide presentations both on- and off-site. Symposia and workshops are held to discuss the significance of the African Burial Ground, and a quarterly newsletter keeps the community apprised of the ongoing research programs. The African Burial Ground Archival Center screens related films and sponsors internships and volunteer programs. Sherrill D. Wilson, an anthropologist of African American descent who directs this program, notes that the sudden involvement of black scholars was "very revolutionary. . . . [Such scholarship] is going to set a precedent for what happens to African burial grounds in the future and how African heritage will be viewed by the public."

The Roger Brown Mosaic, erected in Foley Square, directly above the African Burial Ground (New York).

This episode, which began with the straightforward archaeological excavations at an eighteenth-century cemetery, evolved into a story about African American empowerment, a watershed occurrence in the larger struggle of descendant communities attempting to reclaim their heritage.

Above all, it is a chilling reminder that New York City has been free soil for less than half of its history.

Ghanaian Chiefs Visit the African Burial Ground

Archaeology of the African Burial Ground resonates in the African homeland, where slavery is not a simple subject. The labor of captive people was once an important part of the African agricultural economy, and a byproduct of warfare. Although Europeans transformed the traditional practice of African slavery, some African chiefs and merchants profited mightily from the slave trade.

African American tourists are now visiting these former slaving areas of Africa, partly as a search for roots, and partly in the spirit of reconciliation. Today, Asante leaders are admitting that the greatness of their kingdom must be attributed in part to the profits and power gained from the former slave trade.

During the summer of 1995, a royal delegation of West African chiefs visited both the African Burial Ground and the Biological Anthropology Laboratory at Howard University. Their purpose was one of atonement and reunification, both to affirm the cultural and spiritual ties between Africans and African Americans, and to symbolically ask forgiveness for the misdeeds of past African rulers who helped sustain the transatlantic slave trade by selling people.

Michael Blakey told his African visitors that the remains are "of the very people who are your uncles and your aunts." The Ghanaian chiefs examined the bones closely, and then conducted an African libation ceremony to the beat of traditional African drums and percussion instruments. As one member of the delegation describes it:

> [We] all put on mourning clothes as if we were going to a funeral. . . . Everything that happened was very solemn. . . . We felt that these were our people who have been buried here, they could be our sisters, brothers, our great-grandfathers and great-grandmothers. The libation that I poured was to ask for forgiveness from them, so that they should accept our pleading for forgiveness.

Nana Odenoho Oduro Namapau II, president of the National House of Chiefs of Ghana, also spoke of what he saw:

> This is clear evidence, indeed, [that] these are our brothers and sisters who were enslaved. Normally when we go to a cemetery, we go home to have a day of mourning. I want to declare this a day of mourning for African people. We have come to say we are sorry our forefathers took part in this unfortunate thing [slavery]. We say enough is enough. We want African-Americans to come home to build their own country.

The historical research and physical analysis of the bones of our ancestors will challenge the very foundations of what is known about the African presence in Colonial New York. Basically, history books depict little or no African presence in Colonial New York. There is a great need for firsthand accounts of what some of the social, cultural, and economic conditions were like for Africans who were among the founders of New Amsterdam and Early New York.

Sherrill D. Wilson, urban anthropologist (African Burial Ground)

The Future of African American Archaeology

The field of African American archaeology is in its infancy, still developing theoretical frameworks to advance the inquiry beyond the previous, mostly descriptive approach. According to Theresa Singleton, four major elements hold particular promise for understanding the archaeological record of slavery:

- living conditions under slavery
- status differences within the plantation community
- interplay of planter dominance and slave resistance
- formation of African American cultural identity

In her view, no amount of theory building will correct the major drawback in this growing field: the lack of attention to African American perspectives (see *Why Are So Few African-Americans Doing African-American Archaeology?* by Theresa A. Singleton).

IN HER OWN WORDS

Why Are So Few African-Americans Doing African-American Archaeology? by Theresa A. Singleton

. . . [B]y concentrating on ethnic minorities that are both culturally and physically distinct from the white majority in the United States, archaeologists inadvertently created an ethnic archaeology of the Other. The results, combined with the fact that the archaeological profession in this country is almost totally white, have produced a study of ethnicity that more often reflects the perspectives of its investigators than the perspectives of those being investigated—an outcome that is the exact opposite of what this research was intended to do. Such realities are difficult to face and when raised are highly controversial, but archaeologists are beginning to address these concerns. . . .

The fact that too few of the archaeologists engaged in this research are African-Americans is only part of the problem. A far more serious problem is that African-Americans are rarely involved in this research in any substantive way. Most discussions concerning the involvement of blacks in African-American archaeology consider blacks only as consumers of this research, rather than as part of the research process. Input from African-Americans should also be considered in generating questions to be investigated and in the interpretation of the results.

The development of an African-American archaeology that is informed by African-American perspectives should involve the following: First, it should expand on the existing African-American resources used in archaeological studies. Many archaeologists use WPA [Depression-era] narratives, but other comparable material such as the antebellum autobiographies of African-Americans or other scholarly creative writings of African-Americans are rarely used. Second, it should establish stronger alliances between archaeologists and African-Americanists. This research interest began isolated from the work of African-Americanists, but there is no reason that it should continue within this vacuum. Although individual archaeologists work with African-Americanists, these collaborations have not resulted in formal research and training programs. Finally, it should include as part of the project the particular black community in which the research is being undertaken. These communities should not be viewed only as activists for or consumers of an archaeological product; they are contributors to an ongoing dialogue that maximizes the interpretative potential of the archaeological record. Only when archaeologists begin to realize that the inclusion of African-Americans is an asset to this research will African-American archaeology cease to be just another anthropological discourse of an Other.

Theresa Singleton.

THERESA A. SINGLETON is curator of anthropology at the National Museum of Natural History, Smithsonian Institution.

SUMMARY Theresa Singleton, a leader in the developing field of *African American archaeology,* emphasizes the deliberate use of material culture to interpret African American life. The archaeology of African American people has today become a major new horizon for Americanist archaeology. Several contemporary forces have contributed to the emergence of this exciting new field: the emergence of black activism, the legislative emphasis on historic preservation (particularly in urban America), the stepped-up emphasis on American ethnicity, and the realization that archaeologists need to be more involved in the public interpretation of historic period artifacts.

This chapter has focused on a few key sites to illustrate the current state of African American archaeology. At Virginia's Colonial Williamsburg, for instance, officials and historians have responded to criticism for focusing almost entirely on the colonial elite. The product, some argued, was too sanitized, too "genteel." More recent public programming at Colonial Williamsburg has shifted emphasis toward a more multicultural perspective, with slaves, women, children, and "just plain, ordinary people" playing a more conspicuous role in the Williamsburg story.

African American archaeology is studying explicitly the institution of slavery from the material record, emphasizing the richness and diversity of America's heritage and downplaying the traditional "melting pot" theme.

Just down the James River from Colonial Williamsburg is Carter's Grove plantation. Although early interpretations emphasized strictly the "silk pants" aspects of history, recent excavations in the slave areas tell other stories. For the first time in the six decades of historical interpretation at Colonial Williamsburg, slave buildings have been deliberately constructed to show the public what slavery was like. The interpreters cover a broad range of topics about working routines, slave resistance, foodways, punishment, and life expectancy.

We have also highlighted the recent archaeological exploration of New York City's African Burial Ground, a long-forgotten burial place for thousands. Perhaps more than any other site discussed in this book, the African Burial Ground illustrates the interplay of science, community involvement, ethnic pride, and sociopolitical reality. A team of bioarchaeologists, under the direction of Michael Blakey, are still studying excavated remains from the African Burial Ground. Blakey emphasizes the importance of the impact of the dead on the living descendant communities, and the continuities of African traditions that were imported by the enslaved on their involuntary journeys to America.

African American archaeology is helping these traditions to survive.

Chapter 20

The Business of Archaeology: Caring for America's Cultural Heritage

PREVIEW Americanist archaeology has a very practical role in modern society, and this chapter describes how that business works. America has come to recognize that her common cultural heritage is under threat from the demands of contemporary life. As transportation systems improve, the past is paved over. As new houses and hospitals are erected, the debris of the past is carted away in dump trucks. As power lines go up, sites are bulldozed.

A trade-off is taking place here. Most people would enjoy an improved transportation system, better hospitals, more efficient electrical service. But in the process, America is losing important parts of her cultural heritage. Developers are not evil people, and neither are those wishing to preserve the past. This is a dilemma facing both urbanized nations and developing countries: What part of our past must we save, and what part can we do without?

This chapter discusses some of the ways in which archaeologists are helping to preserve our common cultural heritage. It also describes, in practical terms, how most participants in Americanist archaeology are currently making a living.

Archaeology is now a worldwide operation: and there are more archaeologists working today than in the total sum of all previous generations.

ANDREW SHERRATT, ARCHAEOLOGIST (ASHMOLEAN MUSEUM, UNIVERSITY OF OXFORD)

Many countries, including the United States, are attempting to resolve the conflicting goals of economic development and heritage preservation by creating laws and regulations to protect the past. The sum total of these statutes and the methods for their execution have come to be known as *cultural resource management.*

What Is Cultural Resource Management (CRM)?

Cultural resource management (CRM) exists today at two levels. In one sense, looking out for the global heritage is just one more way of protecting an endangered worldwide environment. CRM in this larger context meshes readily with other efforts designed to comply with current environmental requirements, including legislation protecting endangered species, wetlands, water and air quality, and timber and minerals.

Cultural Resource Management on the Internet:

Internet Resources for Heritage Conservation, Historic Preservation and Archaeology is an extensive and important overview, including journals, newsgroups, essay texts, indexes, images, databases, and FAQs (Frequently Asked Questions):
http://www.cr.nps.gov/ncptt/irg/welcome.html

Preserve/Net is a resource for preservationists, planners, and architects:
http://www.preservenet.cornell.edu/preserv1.html

The American Cultural Resources Association (ACRA) Home Page contains plenty of information, including links to archaeology, historic preservation, and history:
http://www.mindspring.com/~wheaton/ACRA.html

SHPO List provides the names and addresses of all state historic preservation offices:
http://www.cr.nps.gov/pad/shpolist.html

Preserve/Net Index lists information on preservation education, conferences, employment, and organizations. The PNLS aids lawyers, activists, and owners in understanding the laws relating to preservation:
http://www.preservenet.cornell.edu/

Federal Preservation Forum:
http://www.ca.blm.gov/cdd/fpforum.html

The roots of environmentalism in America extend back to such nineteenth-century writers as Henry David Thoreau, John Muir, and Ernest Thompson Seton. They and many others inspired readers to take an interest in the natural world around them and to heed the increasing human impact on that landscape.

Some, appalled at the needless slaughter of the Great Plains bison in the late nineteenth century, started the movement to save the continent's wildlife. Others, called to action by the 1864 publication of George Perkins Marsh's widely read *Man and Nature,* became concerned with wholesale environmental degradation around the world.

President Theodore Roosevelt was particularly concerned about Marsh's plea that disturbed environments be allowed to heal naturally, or be restored by specific conservation management plans. Roosevelt insisted that large areas of forest and grazing land be set aside in the United States, to protect timber supplies *for future use and development.* At the same time, John Muir, founder of the Sierra Club, argued for leaving large tracts of western lands untouched *for their long-term aesthetic values.* These two often-conflicting philosophies remain with us today.

In the 1960s and 1970s, a large portion of the American public—many aroused by Rachel Carson's *Silent Spring* (1962)—recognized that wilderness and wildlife refuges alone could not stem the tide of pollution. In the mid-1960s there were demonstrations such as Earth Day, and thousands of people chanted non sequiturs like "Save the Ecology," or displayed bumper stickers proclaiming "I'm for Ecology." The voter appeal of these popular movements was not lost on the legislators and many of them became "conservationists," too. In fact, sufficient power came down on the side of the ecologists for laws to be drafted protecting the *nonrenewable resources* of the nation.

Largely as a result of such efforts, in 1970, the U.S. Congress established the Environmental Protection Agency (EPA) to protect and maintain the environment for future generations. The initial charge was to control and lessen air and water pollution, noise pollution, and pollution by radiation, pesticides, and other toxic agents. In the late 1980s, the mission of the EPA was expanded to include problems of global warming and environmental change.

In Wildness is the preservation of the world.

HENRY DAVID THOREAU (1817–1862), AUTHOR AND ENVIRONMENTALIST

But what are these so-called nonrenewable resources? Most people think of redwoods and whooping cranes and baby seals. Others think of energy-related assets, such as oil, coal, and uranium. But most legislators have a legal background, and in the course of legally defining national resources, they realized that properties of historic value must be included as well. After all, they reasoned, how many Monticellos do we have? Should archaeological sites be considered to be national resources as well?

As a result of this legislation, archaeological sites were included in the ecological legislation of the late 1960s and the 1970s, and are now considered **cultural resources,** to be legally protected just like redwoods, whooping cranes, and shale-oil fields.

Cultural resources: Physical features, both natural and human made, associated with human activity. These would include sites, structures, and objects possessing significance in history, architecture, or human development. Cultural properties are unique and nonrenewable resources.

Obviously, cultural resource management is only a small part of today's concern with saving the planet. And, it must be stressed, archaeology is only part of CRM efforts (although, in terms of dollars spent, archaeology is a *major* part of the program). Archaeology, in this context, is part of a multidisciplinary, applied effort that draws on the expertise of cultural anthropologists, historians, architectural historians, historical architects, landscape architects, engineers, archivists, and many others to help respect the integrity and relevance of the past. Cultural resource management is concerned with all kinds of historic buildings and structures (such as bridges), artifacts, documents, and, of course, archaeological sites. For decades, cultural resource managers shared in the responsibilities of identifying, evaluating, preserving, managing, and treating these resources.

CRM legislation has defined a new philosophy of governmental decision making, requiring that environmental and cultural variables be considered side by side with technological and economic benefits when planning future construction. These new requirements have created a market for thousands of archaeological contracts, which produce reports detailing the nature of the archaeological resources endangered and how a project's impact should be mitigated.

The immediate result of federal legislation has been to spotlight the need for accurate information regarding archaeological sites. Sometimes the federal agencies have the resources to undertake such studies, but more commonly the agencies contract with academic institutions, museums, archaeological contracting firms, and qualified private individuals to prepare the required reports. Although hard numbers are difficult to find, it has been estimated that at least 90 percent of all archaeological research in the United States is today contract-related.

The nature of *conservation archaeology,* or cultural resource management, has been changing in recent years. Environmental impact mitigation no longer means merely finding a few sites that might be nice to dig. Federal agencies are now taking steps to locate at least the major archaeological sites of value in areas that are under the agency's control. The archaeological sites discovered are then evaluated against a recent set of federal standards known as the Criteria of Eligibility for the National Register of Historic Places.

Our ideals, laws, and customs should be based on the proposition that each generation in turn becomes the custodian rather than the absolute owner of our resources—and each generation has the obligation to pass this inheritance on to the future.

ALDEN WHITMANN

Defining Archaeological Significance

Archaeologists use the term *significant* in two very different ways. Usually, archaeologists follow common English usage: "Blackwater Draw might be the

ARCHAEO-MYTHBUSTERS

Must All *Archaeologists* Be *Macho* Men?

Americanist archaeology is struggling to escape the myths promulgated by movies and television. As everyone knows, Hollywood archaeologists are pistol-packing, hard-drinking professors who circle the globe seeking ancient treasure, braving the occult and political intrigue, muttering "To hell with the mummy's curse."

These mythical macho men are accompanied by buxom yet plucky research assistants—always young, female, and foxy. Together, they are academic but death defying as they oversee their crew of a thousand sweating, cursing, rebellious natives. They usually have a treasure map.

The history of our field does reveal a glimmer of truth in the stereotype. Archaeologists do, from time to time, carry guns. Fieldwork has sometimes been hazardous. Some archaeologists drink too much. And one or two even have worked as CIA spies.

Although today's reality is quite different, many myths persist. In this book, we have tried to explode several of the most common fictions:

Indiana Jones in Raiders of the Lost Ark — portrayed by actor Harrison Ford *— artfully personified a world of stereotypes regarding archaeologists.*

- The truth is that most Americanist archaeologists are not professors; in this chapter, we see that the vast majority of archaeologists in this country make their living protecting America's cultural heritage, not by teaching or working in museums.
- Archaeologists are actively seeking the hands-on participation of native people—not just as laborers or informants, but as active participants in research and applied archaeological projects. Native people are increasingly receiving high-level professional training and several are today employed as full-time archaeologists.
- Americanist archaeology is not just for macho men. Although archaeology has traditionally been a male-dominated venture, the numbers of men and women pursuing advanced training in archaeology today are nearly equal, and perhaps one-quarter of all fully employed archaeologists in America are female.

most significant Paleo-Indian site in North America." *Significant* in this case is basically equivalent to "consequential" or "intriguing."

But many contemporary archaeologists also use *significant* in a second, legalistic way. Federal laws and regulations protecting archaeological resources apply *only* to "significant" archaeological sites. If an archaeological site is not "significant," the law says it will not get studied or sampled, excavated or protected. It is this second, more specialized usage that requires some explanation.

National Register of Historic Places on the Internet:

Information About the National Register:
http://www.cr.nps.gov/nr/bulletins/nr16_pre.html/toc

See also:
http://interoz/com/lubbock/ar22.html

http://129.252.216.12/hpfs3.html

http//www.cr.nps.gov/nr/welcome.htm

http://www.cr.nps.gov/nr/nrcollec.html

Significance and the National Register of Historic Places

To understand how an archaeological site becomes "significant" in the legal sense, we must begin with the *National Historic Preservation Act (NHPA).* Passed into law in 1966, the NHPA establishes the framework within which Americanist archaeology today must operate.

According to the National Historic Preservation Act, an archaeological site is considered "significant" if it is included on (or eligible for) the **National Register of Historic Places,** a listing of "significant" historic and prehistoric properties, including districts, sites, buildings, structures, and objects. Such a site must meet one or more of the following four criteria:

National Register of Historic Places: A list of significant historic and prehistoric properties, including districts, sites, buildings, structures, and objects.

- association with important events or patterns of events in history, prehistory, or culture
- association with important people in the past
- possession of distinctive characteristics of a class, school of architecture, etc.
- known or likely to contain data important in history or prehistory

Legal "significance"—defined as suitability for the National Register—is based strictly on these four principles. In effect, a site is considered "significant" if it contributes answers to important archaeological problems or humanistic interests. Management concerns—such as what is to be done with the property—are irrelevant here.

If getting something listed on the National Register sounds difficult, it is. Before a property can be declared to be "significant," a so-called Section 106 review must be undertaken. The Section 106 process attempts to resolve conflicts between preservation of historic properties and contemporary land uses. In one form or another, this review is also what provides most Americanist archaeologists with their livelihoods.

Section 106 of the National Historic Preservation Act requires that federal agencies must consult with relevant cultural resource managers about the effects of their "actions" on **"historical properties."** By "action," the legislation means modifications to the landscape, such as constructing buildings, drilling wells, building roads, or conducting military exercises. By "historical property," the law means something included in (or eligible for) the National Register.

Historical property: Defined by the National Historic Preservation Act as any property included in or eligible for the National Register of Historic Places.

Archaeologists involved with cultural resource management are responsible for setting out ways to determine which sites are significant, and which are not. The guiding principles for CRM treatment of archaeological properties require that research questions be specifically defined, supported by scholarly argument and references:

- Archaeological research must be linked to the ability to address significant questions about the past.
- The importance of archaeological sites is proportional to their ability to contribute to the study of important research problems.
- Because not all research problems are equally important, neither are all archaeological properties.
- Treatment of an archaeological property depends on its value for research, balanced against other public values.

Sometimes, archaeologists feel conflicted in making such judgments. Suppose that a proposed interstate highway route will obliterate a particular archaeological site. It is your duty as the consulting archaeologist to figure out whether this given site is significant, according to the criteria spelled out in the National Historic Preservation Act.

Here is where your archaeological judgment and experience come into play. If you think that this site contains unique artifacts, then it's probably significant. Or if it could contribute to our understanding of regional chronology or regional settlement and subsistence systems or to an understanding of how key resources are procured, then it's also probably significant, and you must make a case according to the National Register criteria.

But suppose that the new interstate will destroy many other, smaller surface sites. As you do your archaeological survey of the proposed right-of-way, you discover these small sites, record them, and collect the artifacts from them. In some cases, you excavate a few small test pits. As an archaeologist, you must once again make up your mind whether these "lesser" sites are eligible for the National Register. If they are eligible, then they are protected by legislation. If they are not, they are written off in the eyes of the law.

Significance: Yours or Mine?

It will always be impossible to save everything. As you can see, CRM archaeologists must make critical judgments about what to protect, and what to lose. It is a responsibility that archaeologists take very seriously. Good archaeology results when the system works properly. But, alas, the system does not always work.

Some archaeologists are bothered by the two meanings of *significant* because the substantive and legal meanings of this term are often at odds. Many of the techniques discussed in the first third of this book are designed to extract ever more information from a distant past that is no longer available for direct observation. As we noted in the discussion of surface archaeology (Chapter 4), even a simple scatter of stone tools can be significant in this sense.

In the framework of the National Register definition, however, significance is determined according to rigid criteria, primarily historical and architectural. For years, research-oriented archaeologists—working both in academic and in CRM settings—have worried about writing off as "insignificant" a site that could someday answer an important research question that has yet to be asked. Certainly, what may not seem significant today, given what today's archaeology knows, may someday prove to be highly significant in light of future advances. To what degree are the compliance requirements of CRM—that is, the identification and preservation of significant archaeological data—actually skewing the archaeological record for future researchers?

The opposite case is also a problem: Is the current CRM system capable of striking a balance between resource management needs and problem-oriented archaeological research? Archaeologists sometimes fret over the millions of dollars being spent on sites that have legal significance, but seem to be inconsequential archaeologically. Some would prefer to collect a kind of tax from developers in exchange for agreeing to ignore the archaeological record. Such a tax could go into a fund that would support work on truly important sites that perhaps are not protected (private land) or not studied because they are far outside transportation corridors and so forth—and hence escape the CRM process.

Although such a plan would indeed support archaeology on some truly important sites, it remains controversial. Why, the developer might ask, should I pay an archaeology tax to fund research someplace else? And who is to decide what's truly important in archaeology anyway? Many CRM archaeologists criticize the present system of competitive bidding, in which contracts are awarded to the lowest bidder (often without any consideration of the qualifications of the archaeologists involved). Others remain unconvinced that control by a cartel of "good" archaeologists would improve things much.

Yet another problem exists here. Despite such obvious conflicts between academic and applied interests, the CRM legislation was framed by a consortium of professional archaeologists, historians, architects, and lawmakers, who hammered out the current definition of *significance* in the National Register sense. This is the definition enshrined in today's legislation and the one in everyday use in CRM-style archaeology.

But critics believe that the current approach to significance, while perhaps adequately serving the archaeological community, falls flat in the real world. The National Register definition, as we have seen, simply assumes that significance is *inherent* in historic properties.

But what if significance lies instead in the eye of the beholder? Roger Anyon and T. J. Ferguson, both professional archaeologists with extensive experience working with native people in the American Southwest, see major problems with *significance* when applied to sites in Indian Country. In *Contrasting Views of "Significance" at Zuni Pueblo,* they point out some of the conflicts between the CRM-driven archaeological perspective and that of Zuni people.

The Structure of CRM in America

Many governments around the world claim outright ownership of all archaeological resources in their territory. But the situation is different in the United States, where archaeological sites on private land generally are the

WHO OWNS THE PAST?

Contrasting Views of "Significance" at Zuni Pueblo by Roger Anyon and T. J. Ferguson

There are no absolute or philosophical truths that explain the past.

EZRA ZUBROW, ARCHAEOLOGIST (STATE UNIVERSITY OF NEW YORK, BUFFALO)

Cultural resources management (CRM) in the USA is conducted under a patchwork of legal and regulatory mandates promulgated by people educated, working, and living in a Euroamerican cultural milieu—rather than being informed by Zuni values. The differing cultural views of archaeological sites and of human burials are instructive.

As viewed by archaeologists, and enshrined in federal regulatory language, archaeological sites are valued for their potential to inform about the past: sites are abandoned inanimate things from which information can be extracted.

As viewed by Zunis, archaeological sites are an essential link to the land, their ancestors, their culture and traditions: sites embody life forces. Religious offerings made when sites were established and lived in, and when they were left during the tribe's migrations, still have power and significance in present day Zuni religion. Zunis have no concept of sites having been abandoned. Ancestral spirits continue to reside in these places, the stewards of the land that provide a temporal link to present day Zuni.

Archaeologists view human remains as they do sites: things holding information about population structure, diet, disease, genetics, burial practices, and so forth. To Zunis, human burials are on a journey: each person passes through four stages during their journey of existence, of which the life that we know is only the first. Each human burial is at some point along the latter three stages of that life journey, completed only when the skeletal remains have finally disintegrated into the earth. No human burial should be disturbed; disrupting the journey that each individual must complete has unimagined consequences for both the deceased and the living.

In general, the Euroamerican view of cultural resources is restrictive, limiting them to archaeological remains and to those places actively used today in a cultural tradition. These small "cultural islands" within the larger landscape have a fixed significance. For Zunis cultural resources are any tangible or intangible aspect of the world that has meaning, regardless of when it was last active in any ceremony. Cessation of ritual activities at a shrine or disused trail for hundreds of years does not diminish its present cultural significance. Nor are cultural resources bounded for Zunis. How can one bound and separate a spring at which a deer drinks from the ancestral archaeological sites this deer visits to pay its respect to the spirits inhabiting that site?

In the Zuni view the entire landscape is a cultural resource, with no fixed boundaries and no fixed significance. Temporal and spatial contexts define meaning and significance, and these may change—for example, by time of year, by virtue of the conduct of a particular ceremony, or depending upon the landscape scale within which it is viewed.

ROGER ANYON and T. J. FERGUSON work for Heritage Resources Management Consultants, a private company in Tucson, Arizona, that is dedicated to assisting Indian tribes and governmental agencies manage cultural resources.

Until recently, American archaeology was an example of what many people think of as an ivory tower profession. Confined almost exclusively to the halls of academia, employment opportunities for archaeologists were rather limited.

ALLEN G. PASTRON, ARCHAEOLOGIST

legal and exclusive property of the landowner (and hence are subject to no external control). There are exceptions, of course, such as federally assisted projects involving private property, or, in some states, abandoned cemeteries and unmarked burials. But in most cases, archaeological resources on private property are privately owned, and hence unprotected.

In contrast, archaeological sites located on federal land are legally protected by an elaborate network of federal legislation, policies, and regulations. Protection on state-owned jurisdictions varies considerably, with the overall protection ranging somewhere between the firm control exercised over federal lands and the negligible safeguards offered sites on private lands.

Federal authority for protection of archaeological resources tends to be fragmented and decentralized. Most federal agencies employ their own CRM personnel. Some of the largest—such as the Forest Service, Army Corps of Engineers, and the Bureau of Land Management (BLM)—maintain multimillion-dollar annual budgets devoted to CRM planning, compliance, and public education. Both the National Park Service and the Advisory Council on Historic Preservation have overarching preservation responsibilities, but no single agency oversees the entire archaeological operation.

Faron Nastacio, a Zuni tribal member, takes a tree-ring sample from a historic structure at Ojo Caliente, as part of a large-scale dendrochronology on the Zuni Indian Reservation.

This decentralized approach to federal CRM offers some advantages, because it requires little coordination between agencies (often a stumbling block both in the United States and in other countries). But the truth is that some agencies take on their preservation responsibilities with a real sense of stewardship, while others seem content merely to carry out the letter of the law. Federal agencies also commonly find themselves seriously underfunded. A fairly recent survey indicated, for instance, that less than 10 percent of all federal lands had even been inventoried for archaeological resources.

In a recent overview, Ricardo Elia has found contemporary CRM archaeology in the United States to be "highly idiosyncratic and beset with many problems." He highlights, for instance, the difficulties in conducting adequate archaeological surveys and creating workable site inventories. The results are disappointing and difficult to compare area to area. Although millions are being spent annually, still more millions are required to build an adequate regional base. Despite the avowed interest in conserving sites, too many are still being excavated (when they could readily have been kept intact). And Elia finds that during such excavations, sampling percentages are still distressingly low. It is not uncommon in some areas, for instance, to have sites completely destroyed after less than a 10 percent sampling. Not only the overall lack of CRM funding, but also competitive bidding for contracts seems to guide many such decisions.

Ironically, the CRM field has produced a whole generation of archaeologists who, while paying lip service to the conservation ethic, have grown accustomed to consenting to the destruction of substantial percentages of significant archaeological sites.

Ricardo J. Elia, Archaeologist (Boston University)

Despite its problems and growing pains, CRM is today the most influential force in Americanist archaeology. Increasing numbers of young archaeologists are being hired in the private and government sectors, while the number of more traditional teaching and museum-based jobs has stabilized or even begun to shrink. This means that the raw bulk of archaeological work being done has shifted from the academic side to the private and government sectors.

The Need for Professional Standards in Archaeology

Americanist archaeology has rapidly evolved from a relatively small "academic" discipline to one with a major daily impact on the public. As

Archaeological Societies on the Internet:

Society for American Archaeology Home Page:
http://www.saa.org/

Society of Professional Archaeology Home Page:
http://www.smu.edu/~anthrop/sopa.html

Society for Historical Archaeology Home Page:
http://www.azstarnet.com/~sha/

economic development programs of all types bring about increased land disturbance, archaeologists have assumed the responsibility for representing the public interest in avoiding or at least mitigating the adverse effects of such development on the archaeological record.

This realization brings us to one of the most serious, yet least discussed, aspects of CRM in Americanist archaeology: the lack of effective quality control. According to Elia, "there has long been an awareness that CRM archaeology, despite relatively abundant funding, often results in work of poor quality. . . . Much of the basic work that is being done, the research, data acquisition, analysis, interpretation and reporting, is often mediocre, and some is downright incompetent." Part of the problem stems from a lack of specific training in conducting CRM-related archaeology, and also from the competitive bidding process, which often results in the selection of low-bidding archaeological consultants (who are sometimes incompetent).

With greater public involvement has come the need for an accepted code of archaeological ethics and standards of performance, backed up by an effective method of policing transgressors. Unfortunately, shoddy archaeological work exists, causing problems for both the archaeological profession and for the public it serves.

Over the past several decades, many archaeologists (and the professional organizations that represent them) have devoted considerable attention to developing a higher degree of professionalism. Although basic standards do exist, the leading archaeological organizations have not enforced them.

One step in this direction was taken in 1976 by the Society of Professional Archeologists (SOPA), which established a set of codified ethics, standards of performance, and proven grievance procedures. But SOPA's effectiveness has been undermined by a lack of direct support from major archaeological organizations and particularly by the failure of large numbers of professional archaeologists to subscribe to its more rigorous ethics and standards.

Recently, representatives of the four major associations overseeing Americanist archaeology—the Society for American Archaeology, the Society of Professional Archeologists, the Society for Historical Archaeology, and the Archaeological Institute of America—have moved to establish and maintain registration requirements, a code of ethics, standards of performance, and grievance procedures for the practice of archaeology.

Whether this initiative will be fruitful remains to be seen, but it is imperative that those in the profession of Americanist archaeology agree to adhere to basic professional ethics and standards.

CRM Archaeology as a Career

Within a period of two decades or so, CRM has radically transformed the practice of Americanist archaeology, particularly with respect to career op-

Pampered Archaeologists?

Careers magazine recently listed "anthropologist/archaeologist" as one of America's "25 Most Pampered Jobs: The Appeal of Perk Power." Anthropologists/archaeologists had it pretty cushy, the article said, because "workers in this field are usually assigned large, private offices and have regular access to administrative aids."

But what really sent our profession over the top, according to *Careers* magazine, were the "perks" associated with anthropological/archaeological fieldwork—free or subsidized housing, meals, and transportation provided at no cost.

When was the last time, we wonder, that our intrepid *Careers* reporter was "pampered" with a steady diet of stale peanut-butter-and-jelly sandwiches, overindulged by a summer in a soggy sleeping bag, and coddled by riding to work in the back of an uncovered pickup truck?

Hello! Get out much?

portunities, funding sources, and guiding philosophy. In 1981, the annual funding for CRM was estimated to be about $300 million, involving 2,000 full-time CRM staff in federal and state agencies, with another 250 academic and nonprofit institutions and 500 private firms, employing perhaps 4,000 full-time staff, providing CRM services on a contract basis.

I don't see how you could regret a career in anthropology. . . . Even if you don't make anthropology your major field of endeavor, the background in anthropology is perfect for so many other professions.

MARJORIE F. LAMBERT, ARCHAEOLOGIST (SCHOOL OF AMERICAN RESEARCH)

Although nobody seems certain just how much money is being spent on CRM today, it far exceeds the early 1980s level and outstrips funding available for more traditional academic and institutional research archaeology. By way of comparison, two of the largest sponsors of archaeological research, the National Science Foundation and the Wenner-Gren Foundation, spent only $3.4 million for archaeological research in 1991.

In this context, the conservation archaeologist acts as the contact point between the government (required by statute to protect archaeological sites) and various developers and other interested parties wishing to modify the environment. So positioned, it is the responsibility of the CRM archaeologist to ensure compliance with the broad and sometimes confusing range of federal, state, local, and other national laws, regulations, standards, guidelines, and procedures, as well as international conventions and recommendations and standards of professional practice.

People participate in CRM archaeology in a variety of ways. Some work strictly in the field, others only in the lab, some in museums, some in offices with a phone glued to their ear and a computer fused to their lap. A few focus their efforts on teaching conservation values to the general public and to children, in hopes that CRM will not have such an uphill struggle in the future.

Today's CRM archaeologists are tackling, on a daily basis, the future of the past: What does America's archaeological record really consist of? What must we study and protect for future benefit? What can we live without?

All archaeologists are aware that sites are vanishing at an unprecedented rate. But it is the archaeologist specializing in CRM who must wrestle with the implications of this fact on a day-to-day basis.

The Status of Women in Archaeology

I asked a Burmese why women, after centuries of following their men, now walk ahead. He said there were many unexploded land mines since the war.

ROBERT MUELLER

Like all social scientists, American archaeologists will always remain creatures of their own culture. Throughout this text, we have explored how contemporary attitudes toward race, politics, religion, and gender color our specific interpretations of the past. In this chapter, as we focus on the "business of archaeology," it makes sense to examine how Western cultural biases have influenced the degree to which women participate in this profession.

Traditional Americanist archaeology has, without question, been a male-dominated venture. Chapter 1 sketched the history in terms of eight forebears, and not until we reached the 1970s could a woman, Kathleen Deagan, be selected to represent the field. My choice of America's premier archaeologists reflects somewhat my own view of the profession and also the fact that for decades women were excluded from Americanist archaeology. And the written histories of the field necessarily reflect this bias.

Previously, Mary Ann Levine noted that although women have been participating archaeologists for more than a century, their contributions have largely been overlooked (see *Archaeology's Unrecognized Working Women* by Mary Ann Levine, Chapter 1). According to Levine, "archeology's nearly forgotten foremothers . . . did not face an unconditionally prohibitive environment, [but] their involvement in Americanist archeology was limited and circumscribed."

As a science which accepted the psychic unity of mankind, anthropology was kinder to women. . . . This professional tradition of liberality has not been complete or unblemished. . . . Women have been made more welcome than in other professions, but not unequivocally.

MARGARET MEAD (1901–1978), ANTHROPOLOGIST

The first generation of women working in archaeology was a small group, including several women who were sufficiently affluent to afford a career in archaeology, where they served mostly as unpaid and loosely affiliated fieldworkers. Cynthia Irwin-Williams has emphasized the contributions of Sophie Schliemann in her husband's successful search for the legendary city of Troy (see *The Hidden Contributions of Sophie Schliemann* by Cynthia Irwin-Williams, Chapter 2): "Although thoroughly overshadowed by her flamboyant husband, Sophie was recognized as the more diligent, careful, and perseverant of the two. What records were made of the excavations were largely the result of her efforts."

During the nineteenth century, access to formal training in archaeology for women was severely limited, fieldwork opportunities almost nonexistent, and publication outlets nil. These women are not well represented in the written histories of the field.

A second generation of female archaeologists appeared in the 1920s. A number of women, such as Florence Hawley Ellis, received first-rate archaeological training and made significant contributions to the archaeological literature (see *Fieldwork 1920s-Style at Chetro Ketl* by Florence Hawley Ellis, Chapter 8). Several women even broke into the formal ranks of university-level teaching.

But women interested in archaeology continued to face substantial obstacles in the 1930s and 1940s, and their career advancement was still seriously hampered by gender-based status discrimination. Most archaeologists get their first taste of fieldwork in academic-based field schools. Although some archaeological field schools admitted women in the 1920s, it was not until the early 1970s that "mixed" digs became commonplace. Documented cases exist in which a male archaeologist attempted to undermine publications by his female colleague, and a senior male professor insisted that a female junior faculty member fetch his lunch daily. Also on the record is a statement by a senior male archaeologist suggesting that women were better suited to laboratory work because it closely resembled housework. One prominent male archaeologist felt that women were an "unreliable element" in archaeological field crews because they were likely to get married (and hence disappear); apparently unmarried men were not a problem—if they did get married, their wives could always serve as unpaid lab assistants.

Anthropology, like all professions, has myths—one of these myths is that women have been welcomed in the profession because they were needed. It would be more accurate to say that they were tolerated in certain areas because they were useful and at times even respected.

Nancy Parezo, anthropologist (University of Arizona)

Such gender bias was evident everywhere in archaeology's past. The first annual meeting of the Society for American Archaeology (SAA)—still the most conspicuous professional organization representing Americanist archaeologists—was held in Pittsburgh in 1935. Of the 42 members presented for election as "fellows" of the new society, only four were women. The presidency of the SAA remained exclusively male until 1958, when H. Marie Wormington was elected to the office, and several women have since served as president. It was also true of the Society for Historical Archaeology, which, since its founding in 1967, has elected nearly 30 presidents, six of whom have been women—Kathleen Gilmore (1978), Kathleen Deagan (1985), Mary Beaudry (1989), Julia Costello (1991), Elizabeth Reitz (1994), and Donna Seifert (1995).

[Gender bias] makes for a kind of "do or die" point of view. The result for me was that I began to do individual independent research much earlier than people who found it easier to join large projects. Exclusion from the mainstream opportunities led to a fierce determination to do it on my own.

Cynthia Irwin-Williams (1936–1990), archaeologist

The late H. Marie Wormington, a pioneer in the field of Paleo-Indian archaeology, attributed much of the earlier bias against women in archaeology to the mistaken beliefs that "women could not withstand the rigors of the field" and that marriage and childbearing would preclude devotion to an archaeological career. As she noted dryly, "Activities by many archaeologists, who are women, have amply demonstrated that this is not the case."

I always published under my initials, H. M. Wormington. The director of the museum felt nobody would read a book written by a woman.

Hannah Marie Wormington (1914–1994), archaeologist

A relatively recent volume entitled *Equity Issues for Women in Archeology* (1994) assessed the current situation. In their conclusion, Sarah M. Nelson and Margaret C. Nelson made some pertinent observations:

> Recent estimates suggest that women comprise about 20 percent of fully employed archaeologists in America. Today, the proportion may be even higher, and many female archaeologists are quite successful and making significant contributions to the field.
>
> Compared with a decade or two ago, a much higher proportion of the graduate and undergraduate students specializing in archaeology are women. The numbers of men and women pursuing advanced training in archaeology today are nearly equal; women are apparently enjoying equivalent levels of success in school, as measured by research performance, funding, and publication. Many believe that "times have changed."

Maybe so, but there remain some disturbing trends. For one thing, women seem to drop out of graduate school at a higher rate than men. A larger proportion of women also disappear from the job pool after they complete their degrees. This may suggest, at least in part, a tendency for more women to make nonacademic career choices than men. But such "choices" may reflect not only decisions in favor of spouse and family, but also lowered career expectations in academic or other archaeological careers.

Being a woman anthropologist isn't easy, but it's better than being a physicist.

Nancy Parezo

Even after completion of graduate training, women assume proportionately fewer leadership positions, publish fewer books, receive fewer research grants, and generally receive less recognition for their work. Women are still underrepresented in senior positions in archaeology. One result of this is that young women deciding on career directions have few female role models.

We have come a long way from the days when many male archeologists would not take women into the field, when some women students were treated merely as toys for male faculty, when women were ineligible for tenure-track positions in archeology at "elite" institutions. But inequities remain, both individual and societal, and old behaviors are difficult to eradicate.

SARAH M. NELSON, ARCHAEOLOGIST (UNIVERSITY OF DENVER), AND MARGARET C. NELSON (STATE UNIVERSITY OF NEW YORK, BUFFALO)

Anthropologists Nancy Parezo and Susan Bender describe the "chilly climate" in which female professional archaeologists sometimes work: male-dominated, male-controlled, and male-oriented. Recent research suggests that in some cases, the work of female archaeologists has been marginalized, their voices not heard, their work considered trivial. Analysis of these data suggests that the differentials between men and women are societal, not individual. Women are still sometimes discouraged, given the cold shoulder through various subtle attitudes and such behaviors as stereotyping, devaluation, exclusion, isolation, tokenism, and outright sexual harassment. In the academic world, chilly climates result in slower rates of promotion, lower pay scales, and in the more subtle practice of ignoring the work of women whenever similar ideas originate with a male author.

In sum, it is clear that women today still enjoy a lower status than men in archaeology, reflected in lower income and lower prestige. Nelson and Nelson suggest the following strategies that could change this picture in the future:

- Encourage women to pursue archaeology as a career.
- Increase the number and percentage of women in managerial and administrative roles.
- Encourage women to become more visible through publication and original research.
- Work to change the dysfunctional stereotypes still operating in the professional cultures of archaeology.

As Nelson and Nelson put it, "Giving women their due improves working conditions for everyone."

This leads us to one final point. As several archaeologists (including Joan Gero, Mary Whelan, and Margaret Conkey) have emphasized, the inclusion of female archaeologists in the Americanist mainstream involves more than "just add women and stir." We are not simply seeing women coming in and doing the same thing as the men.

Women still face a great many barriers to full participation [in archeology]. As much as we might wish for the issue to disappear, . . . "gender is still an issue in archeology" . . . [and] while some gains have been made, equity is not a fact of life for most women archeologists.

SARAH M. NELSON AND MARGARET C. NELSON

The field of Americanist archaeology is necessarily changing as a result of integrating a distinctive group of people (women) because all of us reflect—to one degree or another—our own cultural experience when we interpret the past. Women's experiences are different from men's because women occupy a different place in American society than men do. The theoretical diversity in Americanist archaeology is closely linked with our ability to encourage diversity among the participants in the field—be they women, Native Americans, black Americans, or other previously disenfranchised ethnic groups.

Educating Our Cultural Resource Managers

A quarter century has passed since cultural resource management burst onto the archaeological scene; today, CRM provides archaeologists with several hundred million dollars in funding, and thousands of people make their living doing CRM archaeology. And yet, many archaeologists feel that the professional training of CRM personnel simply does not measure up.

There seems to be a problem with the way many archaeology students are being trained. Today, a curious dichotomy exists in employment opportunities: Although fewer jobs are available in academic institutions, highly desirable senior positions in CRM firms sometimes go vacant due to the lack of sufficiently trained and experienced applicants.

Robert Elston.

Many believe that American universities and colleges are not preparing their archaeology graduates with the tools they need to be effective in the world of cultural resource management. Although many such institutions offer a course or two on some aspect of CRM archaeology, only a handful (of the hundreds of colleges and universities that teach archaeology) offer specialized CRM programs at the M.A. level. Doctorate programs in cultural resource management do not exist. The unhappy result is that most CRM archaeologists get their early experience as "on the job training."

As principal and director of research at Intermountain Research (a consulting archaeology firm based in Silver City, Nevada), Robert Elston has supervised nearly 600 archaeological projects and has personally hired hundreds of fledgling archaeologists to help him out, both in the field and in the lab. Take a look at the box *On Getting a Practical Archaeological Education,* in which Elston communicates his experiences, and provides some down-to-earth advice for those thinking of entering the field.

CRM archaeology is a viable career option, in both the private and public sectors. The demand for trained people is greater than it ever has been. Although traditional archaeological skills are necessary, the individual's repertoire must be broadened with business and management skills as well.

Protecting the Past for the Future

When enough people become concerned about our cultural resources, legislative indifference to their protection and proper management will not be tolerated.

George Frison, archaeologist (University of Wyoming)

Talk to any archaeologist in America and sooner or later the subject of *pothunting* will come up. It's reached epidemic proportions and is getting worse.

Charles S. Koczka, former senior special agent for the U.S. Customs Service, has estimated that illegal trafficking in antiquities may today be second only to the drug trade in international crime. David Pendergast, a field archaeologist with extensive experience, thinks that the well-organized looting crews operating in Belize today are "larger than any ever mustered by archaeologists." Unless site destruction can be curbed soon, the future of the past is dim indeed (see *Stop Those Pothunters–They're Stealing America's Masterpieces!* by U.S. Senator Pete V. Domenici).

"Pothunting" means all kinds of damage done to archaeological sites in the interests of artifact collecting, commercial trafficking in artifacts, and plain hell raising.

Thomas F. King, consultant in historic preservation

The museum community has been surprisingly slow to condemn the looting of archaeological sites and the marketing of illegally obtained antiquities. Nevertheless, responsible museums today uniformly refuse to accept

IN HIS OWN WORDS

On Getting a Practical Archaeological Education by Robert G. Elston

From my perspective as an employer of archaeologists, there is a tendency for postgraduate anthropology programs to skimp on course work emphasizing practice (field and laboratory methods), and to completely ignore the need for managerial skills or knowledge of the system in which archaeology is conducted. These deficiencies often are justified by assuming students eventually will "pick it up if they need it." This was perhaps a viable strategy when virtually all archaeologists taught in universities, but large numbers of archaeologists now are employed in nonacademic jobs. Consequently, a person with a fresh M.A. or Ph.D. in anthropology may go directly to an agency or contracting firm unprepared for work in full-time research or management. Archaeologists going to academic jobs may be ill-equipped to deal with bureaucracies, ethics, project management, and technical aspects of archaeological research.

Archaeologists with advanced degrees, especially those working in contract firms, are expected to assume leadership and management roles. To the extent new archaeologists have any management experience, it usually has involved supervising field crews, but different skills and knowledge are called for in organization and direction of laboratory work and writing, proposal preparation, and interaction with bureaucracies, clients, and proponents. At the least, students can be guided to the Business Administration library and texts concerned with work group dynamics, conflict resolution, and project management. . . . It is important for new archaeologists to understand the critical nature of deadlines in agency, and especially, contract archaeology. After funding, performance schedules constitute the single most significant constraint on quality of performance and economic viability.

Descriptive and expository writing is essential for all archaeologists, yet few just out of school write well; most have never edited another's manuscript. Graduate archaeologists must understand the purpose of a research design and understand how a good research design is constructed. *This means they must also know something of contemporary theoretical and methodological approaches in archaeology. I often find inadequate technical training among applicants for staff level jobs, particularly with regard to writing and editing, computer skills, quantitative analysis, use of technologically advanced equipment, and in geomorphology, soils and stratigraphy. Dirt is the scaffolding of the archaeological record. A competent archaeologist knows the genesis and transformations of soil in landscapes, and can describe them.*

Academic colleagues often tell me that there are so many other demands on student time made by core Anthropology curricula, that courses teaching the essential crafts of archaeology are difficult to introduce into existing graduate anthropology programs. But this is exactly the point. As archaeology becomes increasingly professionalized, higher proportions of postgraduates are following nonacademic careers where the broadest possible anthropological education has less value than specific skills needed to practice contemporary archaeology. If core curricula are not adjusted to acknowledge this reality, anthropology programs cannot serve the needs of graduates, the public, or the discipline.

Robert G. Elston is principal and director of research at Intermountain Research, an archaeological consulting firm based in Silver City, Nevada.

artifacts illegally imported from the country of origin; the more circumspect also decline to display illegitimate artifacts. At the American Museum of Natural History, for instance, curators are explicitly forbidden by the Trustees from authenticating or appraising any artifacts. The Museum Shop refuses to sell antiquities in any form, and *Natural History* magazine will not accept advertising for antiquities, regardless of how acquired.

As the museum community is increasingly drawn into active participation in conservation efforts, maintenance of biodiversity, and investigating

IN HIS OWN WORDS

Stop Those Pothunters—They're Stealing America's Masterpieces! by Pete V. Domenici

With unfortunate frequency, thieves break into some noted art museum and steal works of art. News of the heist is relayed around the world through television, radio, newspapers, and magazines. Invariably, the theft is described as "sensational," and commentators bemoan the loss of these treasured cultural objects. . . .

Yet where is the concern of the public and the media about the cultural thievery that is being committed every week across our land? On public lands across our nation, pothunters and other archaeological looters are digging through ancient Indian pueblos, historic Spanish shipwrecks, and the graves of Civil War soldiers and Native Americans, then stealing artifacts for a collection or sale.

Like an art heist, the theft of archaeological artifacts . . . deprives the public of an opportunity to study and enjoy objects that are part of our shared cultural heritage.

Just as we are outraged by the theft of masterpieces from museums, we must also be outraged by the theft of our nation's archaeological artifacts.

PETE V. DOMENICI is a U.S. senator from the state of New Mexico and author of the Archaeological Resources Protection Act of 1979.

global climate change, it would seem worthwhile to alert the public about ongoing site destruction and potential losses of human heritage. Still, when was the last time you saw an exhibition that even mentioned the evils of archaeological thievery and art smuggling?

While we tend to think of [archaeological] looting as a phenomenon that occurs outside the United States, the scale of looting inside this country is massive.

JAMES ADOVASIO, ARCHAEOLOGIST (MERCYHERST COLLEGE)

One commendable exception was an exhibit called "Stolen Treasures—Missing Links" mounted by the National Geographic Society in Washington, D.C. It consisted of 500 pre-Columbian pieces seized by American customs in the previous 2 years. After touring eight major museums nationwide, the artifacts were returned to Peru as part of a bilateral agreement to return such property recovered at U.S. borders. We need more exhibits of this sort.

Looting and site vandalism continue to be major problems threatening Americanist archaeology. Sometimes, due to lack of legislation, the commercial mining of both terrestrial and underwater sites for artifacts is completely legal. Moreover, the sheer magnitude of federal holdings—millions of acres where looting and vandalism are strictly illegal—makes it virtually impossible to patrol and protect them. The U.S. Government Accounting Office estimates that of the 2 million archaeological sites presently recorded in the American Southwest, at least one-third have already been looted, to some degree. The House subcommittee investigating such things puts the number much higher—between 50 percent and 90 percent.

The looting of archaeological sites is also a major concern of Indian people because, in many cases, it is the Native American past that is being vandalized. Listen to what Katherine Saubel (a member of the Cahuilla tribe and president of Southern California's Malki Museum) has to say about looting of her ancestral sites:

> As children we were taught not to do things that were going to be dishonoring the future, the past, ancient people. And they would say: "Never pick up anything, never pick up something that belongs to another culture and always

IN HER OWN WORDS

Avocational Archaeology Groups—A Secret Weapon for Site Protection by Hester A. Davis

It is important to set down some definitions so that readers will understand what is meant by "avocational archaeologists." The term has often been used synonymously with the term "amateur archaeologists," and presumably is to differentiate these people from "professional archaeologists," on the one hand, and "artifact dealers" and "grave robbers," on the other. And then there are "collectors" and "relic hunters": those who do not profess to be "archaeologists," as the term is usually used, but who are quick to point out that they do not destroy sites, as do grave robbers and vandals.

There is, perhaps, another way of looking at the semantics of this universe of people: there are archaeologists and there are nonarchaeologists, and the basic distinction is that of attitude toward the resources. Archaeologists consider sites and artifacts as sources of information; nonarchaeologists consider sites as sources of artifacts.

The greatest potential for greater site protection is through statewide avocational groups. The secret weapon held by these organizations is their ability to influence their own members, politicians, landowners, teachers, school children, and even pothunters. By their very numbers and the fact of their organization, avocational archaeological societies should be the real advocates for site protection, in the most contemporary use of that term.

Avocational archaeological groups have the greatest potential for making a real difference in which sites and how many sites are protected in the future. All archaeologists, in my use of the term, must coordinate, communicate, organize nationally, and become proprotection. Legislation protecting unmarked graves must hit hard on the looters and vandals; ordinances at the local level must become commonplace. The names and faces of archaeological organizations speaking for less wanton destruction must be on educational television and the evening news.

There are probably four or five times as many avocational archaeologists as there are professional ones. There are probably dozens more avocational archaeological organizations than there are professional ones. Since their interests are supposed to be the same, they must all become strong active advocates for site protection, from the individual site where the shopping center is going in, to the national historic landmarks still in private ownership.

HESTER A. DAVIS is state archaeologist, Archaeological Survey, Fayetteville, Arkansas.

respect that, and never take it home." And now that is one of the problems that we are facing. People go out and "pot-hunt." Some of the people who are interested in Indian artifacts go out and deliberately dig up things and destroy data [that] a professional archaeologist would get a lot of information from that area. The pot-hunters are not just grabbing at dead things, they are destroying history. Because things are missing the archaeologist then has a hard time putting things together from the past. I think people should be aware of that, not only because it is our own history but it is everyone's in the United States. I think that we should help one another protect these things.

I got my rights and this is a free country. I pay taxes and I can dig there if I want to—I've been doing it for years . . . I got my rights! If I can't dig here I might as well go to Russia.

AN ADMITTED ARCHAEOLOGICAL LOOTER INTERVIEWED AT BIG CYPRUS NATIONAL PRESERVE

Numerous federal and private agencies have taken aggressive antilooting measures, such as site monitoring, fencing, and more diligent law enforcement. The highly successful Adopt a Site program pairs motivated avocational archaeologists with particularly vulnerable sites that need protection (see *Avocational Archaeology Groups—A Secret Weapon for Site Protection* by Hester A. Davis).

SUMMARY America is losing major parts of her cultural heritage and archaeologists are today helping decide which parts of the past we can save, and which parts we can do without.

Cultural resource management (CRM), in a broad sense, is a multidisciplinary, applied effort that draws on the expertise of cultural anthropologists, historians, architectural historians, historical architects, landscape architects, engineers, archivists, and many others to help respect the integrity and relevance of the past. Cultural resource management is concerned with all kinds of historic buildings and structures (such as bridges), artifacts, documents, and, of course, archaeological sites.

Conservation archaeologists are actively involved in the governmental decision making that requires environmental and cultural variables be considered side by side with technological and economic benefits when planning future construction. The immediate result of federal legislation has been to spotlight the need for accurate information regarding archaeological sites.

Cultural resource management is today the most influential force in Americanist archaeology. The raw bulk of archaeological work being done has shifted from the academic side to the private and government sectors. Today, perhaps 90 percent of all archaeological research in the United States is related to providing such information about sites, on a contract-related basis.

People participate in CRM archaeology in a variety of ways. Some work mostly in the field, others work largely in the lab, some focus their efforts on teaching conservation values to the general public and to children.

Compared with a decade or two ago, a much higher proportion of the graduate and undergraduate students specializing in archaeology are women. The numbers of men and women pursuing advanced training in archaeology today are nearly equal; women are apparently enjoying equivalent levels of success in school. Today, women comprise perhaps one quarter of the fully employed archaeological work force in America. Some experience a "chilly climate" finding the field to be male-dominated, male-controlled, and male-oriented. Others believe that "times have changed."

Today's applied archaeologists are tackling, on a daily basis, the future of the past: What does America's archaeological record really consist of? What must we study and protect for future benefit? What can we live without?

Chapter 21

Archaeology's Unfinished Business: Challenges at the Millennium

PREVIEW Throughout the first 20 chapters, I've told you many stories, trying to give you a graphic, yet realistic picture of what Americanist archaeology is all about. Here, in this concluding chapter, I want to leave you with just a few more stories, but these are more serious.

Although this chapter addresses our knowledge of the past—the stuff that archaeology's made of—it's a little different from earlier chapters because it's mainly concerned with the uses of archaeological knowledge—today and tomorrow, next year and the next millennium. These are stories whose endings are still being written.

Any suggestion that archaeology is a unified, monolithic field is erroneous.

EZRA ZUBROW, ARCHAEOLOGIST (STATE UNIVERSITY OF NEW YORK, BUFFALO)

Archaeology was once widely regarded as some sort of backward extension of recorded history, offered as some kind of shadowy reconstruction of the past. Today, rather suddenly, archaeology seems relevant *and relevant in a very international way.*

COLIN RENFREW, ARCHAEOLOGIST (CAMBRIDGE UNIVERSITY)

As we approach the millennium, Americanist archaeology faces some monumental challenges:

- Is archaeology "relevant" to the modern world?
- Are archaeologists grave robbers?
- Whose past is it, anyway?

In this final chapter, as we address these issues, you will find more questions than answers.

Archaeological Science: Pure or Applied?

Pure (basic) science: Systematic research directed toward acquisition of knowledge for its own sake.

Anthropology is usually perceived as a **pure science**, as the systematic pursuit of knowledge for its own sake. And it is true that anthropologists, like many other scientists, are commonly motivated more by intellectual curiosity than by the practical applications of what they learn. Anthropologists have traditionally looked for answers to the larger, holistic questions regarding the human condition: How, where, and when did humanity arise? What is the relative importance of nature and nurture? How (and why) did the major social institutions evolve? These are large-scale questions about the basic nature of the human condition, issues without immediate practical application or "relevance."

Basic research is what I am doing when I don't know what I am doing.

WERNHER VON BRAUN (1912–1977), ROCKET SCIENTIST

Of course, throughout the history of science, many discoveries made initially as "pure science" have turned out to have practical as well as theoretical significance—and this is true of both the "hard" and the social sciences.

For decades, anthropologists have attempted to "apply" their findings to practical ends (**applied science**). During World World II, for instance, some American anthropologists volunteered their services in the war effort. Several of them collaborated on "national character" studies—detailed memoranda on European and Asian countries, attempting to characterize peoples who were either allies or enemies, or lived in enemy-occupied territory. These anthropologists eventually evolved their own way of working—the so-called cultures at a distance approach—working with knowledgeable people in the United States, to generalize about countries unvisitable because of wartime conditions.

One of the best-known culture at a distance studies was conducted by Ruth Benedict. At the time a recognized authority on American Indians, Benedict temporarily left her professorship at Columbia to join the Bureau of Overseas Intelligence of the U.S. War Department (1943–1946). She was eventually to take on a study of Japanese national character, providing information that would ultimately prove critical for Allied forces occupying Japan during the postwar period.

Like the rest of anthropology, archaeology is trying to "apply" some of its knowledge to the modern world. In Chapter 10, we heard Bill Rathje declare how much we still have to learn about the material culture of our own society; his Garbage Project attempts to bring a century of archaeological experience to bear on relevant issues of modern society. In the same chapter, we saw how archaeologists are helping to manufacture obsidian scalpels—using ancient flintknapping technology—to assist surgeons of the future in perfecting more precise and faster healing surgical incisions. And in the preceding chapter, we saw how archaeologists—working as cultural resource managers—are participating in a massive, multidisciplinary effort to preserve important aspects of our common global heritage.

In the next two sections, we will explore additional frontiers of applied archaeological research.

Ruth Benedict (1887–1948).

Applied science: Research to acquire the knowledge necessary to solve a specific, recognized problem.

Why does this magnificent applied science which saves work and makes life easier bring us so little happiness? The simple answer runs: because we have not yet learned to make sensible use of it.

Albert Einstein (1879–1955), physicist

Unfortunately, there is still a strong but erroneous opinion in some circles that practical anthropology is fundamentally different from theoretical or academic anthropology. The truth is that science begins with application. . . . What is application in science and when does "theory" become practical? When it first allows us a definite grip on empirical reality.

Bronislaw Malinowski (1884–1942), anthropologist

Forensic Archaeology

In my first year as a curator at the American Museum of Natural History, I received an odd telephone call—from a Sergeant McTigue of the New York City bomb squad. At the time, McTigue was assigned to solve a series of New York City subway bombings. Nearly a dozen such attacks had occurred, killing one person and injuring several others. McTigue suspected that a political protest group was behind the bombings, and he had even identified a prime suspect ("I know the creep who's doin' it.").

Before he could make an arrest, however, McTigue had to establish that, in fact, a crime had been committed. Otherwise, "the perp's [perpetrator's] lawyer will claim that it was a natural gas explosion, and we can't prove otherwise." To clinch his case, McTigue needed to produce the "smoking gun"—in this case, parts of the actual detonating device that had triggered the explosion. Knowing this, McTigue kept sorting through the debris left by each underground explosion. But he never could find what he was looking for. So "the perps" remained free to bomb again, which they did with alarming regularity.

As he was investigating yet another ruined subway station, McTigue finally admitted (to himself) that he didn't really know what he was doing. He was a cop trained in standard law enforcement techniques. What did he know about bomb debris? Once he made this admission, the next step was easy: If he (McTigue) wasn't an expert in sorting through trash and debris, who was? Why, that's what archaeologists do, right?

This was the logical connection that brought McTigue to my office. He explained the problem to me in simple terms: Suppose that we treat each crime scene as if it were an ancient archaeological site. What are the systematic, standardized techniques that archaeologists use to recover their data?

So there, right in my office, McTigue and I spent the next 3 hours working our way through Basic Archaeology 101: how to establish a three-dimensional grid system and datum point, how to map in surface finds, how to systematically remove archaeological strata, how to use sifters and flotation devices to recover tiny bits of important artifacts, how to take proper notes, how to photograph and draw archaeological exposures, how to catalog and store the finds. McTigue was a motivated student, taking notes, making drawings of our various sifting devices, and copying down brand names of the "correct" digging tools. Armed with this new investigative strategy, McTigue thanked me and took off.

A couple of days later, there was the good sergeant with his bomb squad buddies on the 6 o'clock news. They were quickly, yet efficiently, digging and measuring, photographing and sifting amidst the ruins of the latest subway station bombing. Except for being a little older (and also heavily armed), they looked not much different from any other novices on their first "dig class." After a week or two, I got a call from Sergeant McTigue, and sure enough, they'd found the detonating device they were looking for. An arrest was quickly made, and New York's subway bombings came to an end.

Forensic archaeology: The application of archaeological and bioarchaeological knowledge for legal purposes.

This was my first experience with **forensic archaeology**—using established archaeological techniques to assist law enforcement agencies. I was surprised at the connection, but as I asked around, I soon learned that many other archaeologists had similar experiences, working closely with police departments, county coroners, medical examiners, and even private investigators. Over the years, I've advised the New York City Police Department on a variety of matters—from tracking down the source of illegally sold antiquities to using remote sensing technology to map and explore a gangland graveyard on Staten Island.

Archaeologists as Crime Busters

Theories come and go, but fundamental data always remain the same.

Mary Leakey (1913–1996), archaeologist

Today, several archaeological organizations regularly conduct seminars and workshops for law enforcement personnel. More than a decade ago, for example, the Oklahoma City Police Academy recognized the need to train its crime investigators in thorough and rigorous approaches to evidence. Each year, the academy sends its trainees to an archaeological field program designed and taught by members of the Oklahoma Archeological Survey. There,

Clea Koff, forensic archaeologist working with a team from the Physicians for Human Rights, excavating human remains from a mass grave in the former Yugoslavia.

the archaeologists teach the police trainees how to read a soil profile, how to probe the ground to find subsurface pits, how to read topographic maps and county soil reports, how to find and map potential surface evidence. They learn some basic identification skills, such as distinguishing between human and animal bones.

The Oklahoma City program places particular emphasis on the detection and analysis of human burials. Months before the instruction is to take place, Oklahoma Archeological Survey members take animal bones, old clothing, and simulated crime "evidence" to prepare a series of mock crime scenes. Each synthetic "site" is carefully mapped as it is created. Months later, the Police Academy trainees are asked to find the "graves," establish systematic grid systems, then carefully expose and examine the "body," recording the "skeleton's" position and all associated evidence.

Both students and teachers learn from the experience. Working in teams of four to six officers, trainees are graded on how well their grave maps compare with the "originals" prepared by the archaeology instructors. In this way, the Police Academy personnel improve their skills in detection and collection of forensic evidence. The archaeologists also learn something about how the bones and artifacts change position and condition in the months between construction of the mock grave and the subsequent excavation. They also can see how long it takes for freshly excavated ground to settle and for

IN HER OWN WORDS

The Journey of a Young Forensic Anthropologist by Clea Koff

My first experience with archaeology was at the age of 10, digging around in my backyard to find the dead bird I had buried the previous winter. I found the bird and an old hairpin. Years later, on a college-level archaeological dig in the Greek countryside, we found Athenian coins, stone foundations, and one human skeleton.

This was my first exposure to human bones and it was a profound experience. I became curious about what the bones could tell us about people, about how they lived and died.

About this time, I read a book describing how forensic anthropologists were helping investigate human rights abuses in Latin America, not only helping to return the remains of missing persons to their families, but also providing evidence to prosecute criminals. This application inspired me to take more classes in anthropology, archaeology, and human osteology at the University of Arizona. As part of my training, I helped the county medical examiner identify human remains and completed the Armed Forces Institute of Pathology/National Museum of Health and Medicine course in Forensic Anthropology.

I was particularly inspired by reading about the application of forensic anthropology to the investigation of human rights violations in Latin America where the result was both the return of missing persons to their families for proper burial as well as providing evidence for clandestine criminal acts. I vowed to become a part of this effort wherever possible.

In 1996, I joined a team of forensic experts brought together by Physicians for Human Rights to work on behalf of the United Nations International Criminal Tribunals for Rwanda and the Former Yugoslavia, the international bodies prosecuting war criminals for genocide and crimes against humanity in those two countries. Our job was to locate, exhume, and analyze human remains from mass graves to provide evidence of the decedents' age, sex, and cause of death. For 6 months, I helped analyze five mass graves, each holding from 30 to over 400 remains. We worked long hours under the protection of military guards, and often lived in military compounds.

However, working at mass grave sites has a legacy that goes beyond the mandate of the tribunals to hold accountable those responsible for these crimes. For example, after the exhumation and analysis at the first site in Rwanda, Kibuye, was completed, a "Clothing Day" was convened. It was publicized on the radio that our team would be display-

vegetation to mask a new grave. Sometimes, this evidence has even proved useful for the archaeology instructors in their own research on late prehistoric camps and villages.

The Archaeology of Mass Disaster

Archaeologists are sometimes asked to work with forensic investigators on actual crime scenes of much larger magnitude. Recently, for instance, professional archaeologists joined investigatory teams from the United Nations to explore the sites of alleged massacres of civilians in Croatia, El Salvador, and Rwanda.

The violence in Rwanda began in April 1994, shortly after Rwandan president Juvenal Habyarimana was killed in an airline crash. Within months, more than half a million people had been killed in Rwanda. Seeking to determine whether these deaths resulted from civil war or genocide, United Nations investigators authorized archaeological investigations at key sites in central Rwanda.

One such excavation took place at Home St. Jean, where an estimated 4,000 to 6,000 people were killed. The Midwest Archeological Center (a *ing clothing from the grave, and we asked survivors to view the clothing in the hopes of providing leads to probable identifications. This day was important as it was our first opportunity to interact with survivors of this particular massacre.*

I shall never forget one woman. She looked as though she was in her fifties, wearing a traditional kanga *(a large, printed piece of cloth worn wrapped around the body) over a knit shirt. She was a dignified woman who held her head high, as though not wanting to be involved in this sordid business, but having no choice.*

She recognized one of the jackets on display and assented to an interview about the clothing. I asked her for her name and to whom she thought the jacket belonged. She gave a man's name, adding that he could still be alive, having removed his jacket at some point and lent it to someone who was subsequently killed at Kibuye.

I then asked her if she knew if this man had any surviving relatives. Yes, she replied, he'd had a sister. I asked for the sister's name and she gave one, pointedly not looking at me. The name sounded familiar, so I flipped back to the first page of the witness statement and there was that name. It was her name. She was talking about her brother.

As this dawned on me, my eyes shifted to that dirty, empty jacket baking in the sun. I thought of her brother and of my brother, and what I would feel if that thing that had come out of a mass grave looked like my brother's jacket. I couldn't look her in the eye at first, so I looked at her hands—one hand on her purse and one hand grasping her other arm, holding herself together.

I finally looked at her face, unable to talk. Her eyes brimmed ever-so-slightly with tears as she looked out into the distance. I looked where she was looking and saw nothing. I wanted to apologize, to hug her, but I had no protocol. So I just capped my pen, and put my hand on her forearm. She said nothing, I said nothing, but she held her head high. As I held that woman's arm I had a true sensation of being on the continuum of history for the Rwandans affected by the genocide.

We are irretrievably part of their process of healing. I continue to try to understand and articulate this phenomenon.

CLEA KOFF is presently a graduate student in forensic anthropology.

branch of the U.S. National Park Service) was called in to assist in the investigations at the massacre site. Working with forensic specialists, the archaeological team conducted a three-stage investigation:

1. *Initial documentation:* Following standard archaeological procedures, the archaeologists carefully mapped the site, establishing datum points and employing a computerized mapping program. The team photographer recorded all 23 buildings at the scene.
2. *Recovery of surface evidence:* After the arrival of forensic bioarchaeologists, the archaeological team recorded the presence of surface skeletal materials and walked transects to determine the site's boundaries. All skeletal remains were numbered, photographed in situ, then removed and analyzed.
3. *Excavation of mass graves:* This preliminary reconnaissance revealed six potential mass graves, and archaeologists began working on the largest. Once the stratigraphy of the area was determined through hand excavation of several test trenches, the overburden was removed with a backhoe. Human remains were exposed by standardized archaeological procedures, photographed, mapped, and then removed from the grave.

Forensic Archaeology on the Internet:

Physicians for Human Rights actively recruits qualified archaeological volunteers to assist in documenting human rights abuses throughout the world:
http://www.friends-partners.org/oldfriends/ccsi/csusa/internal/phys4hr.htm

List of Related Sites:
gopher://gopher.igc.apc.org5000/11/int/phr

Forensic Anthropology Bibliography:
http://ruralnet.marshall.edu/users/pritche1/bones.htm

So You Want to Be a Forensic Anthropologist?
http://taylor.anthro.umt.edu/studguid/forensic.htm

American Board of Forensic Anthropology Inc. Home Page:
http://www.csuchico.edu/anth/ABFA/

Several hundred remains were recovered using these procedures, making this one of the largest exhumations ever conducted in the investigation of human rights violations. Autopsies were conducted to determine sex, age, kind of trauma, and cause of death.

The meticulous archaeological documentation provided critical evidence for the United Nations tribunal, which quickly handed down numerous indictments. As one of the investigating archaeologists noted, "Sound archaeological documentation [added] materially in making a strong case both in the court of the International Tribunal for Rwanda and the court of public opinion."

Beyond providing legalistic evidence, archaeologists also exposed and documented associated material culture (particularly items of clothing) to assist relatives in identifing the remains. DNA testing is also scheduled to match victims with their surviving relatives. (See *The Journey of a Young Forensic Anthropologist* by Clea Koff.)

Archaeologists are playing an increasingly important role in the investigation and documentation of human rights abuses. *Physicians for Human Rights* (100 Boylston St., S-702, Boston, MA 02116, 617-695-0041, e-mail: phrusa@igc.apc.org) has been particularly active in this field. In addition to sponsoring the archaeological investigations of genocide in Rwanda, Physicians for Human Rights has examined grave sites in Bosnia, and recovered remains from illegal political executions in Honduras and elsewhere.

Rediscovering Ancient Agricultural Technology

We suspect that unless archaeologists find ways of making their research increasingly relevant to the modern world, the modern world will find itself increasingly capable of getting along without archaeologists.

JOHN FRITZ AND FRED PLOG (1944–1992), ARCHAEOLOGISTS

Many ancient techniques for growing and storing foodstuffs have fallen into disuse; many are forgotten and simply lost to modern people. Yet some of these techniques were developed in places ill-suited for agriculture and would be of value today.

As human populations expand, they are forced to move into areas of marginal utility. Throughout the world, peasant populations are using increasingly marginal land as populations expand and as wealthier farmers and agricultural corporations claim exclusive use of prime farmland. In addition, intensive agricultural practices sometimes lead to severe degradation of soil and water, making even highly desirable farmland less productive.

The Importance of Ancient Crops

Seasonally inundated (pampa) landscape near Huatta (Peru), showing pre-Hispanic and rehabilitated raised fields (in the center of the photograph). The darker areas are field platforms and the lighter parts are canals between the fields. Located approximately 12,500 feet above sea level, these agricultural features were constructed between 800 B.C. and A.D. 1400.

Modern scholars from many disciplines are expressing alarm at the reduction in the genetic diversity of cultivated agricultural crops. As the world's population continues to expand, we are relying on fewer domesticated species to feed an increasing global population. Some programs to introduce highly productive new cultivars have led to the extinction of various indigenous food sources, which not only were well adapted to local environments, but which stored the genetic diversity critical to develop new varieties.

As a direct result, both governmental and nongovernmental agencies have launched efforts to preserve traditional varieties of plants before these crops become extinct. To date, emphasis has been on extant species, but some archaeologists believe that extinct species might also hold potential to help preserve or even increase the overall genetic diversity of the world's food supply—*if* these "extinct" plants can be brought back to life with the help of the archaeological record (see *The Phoenix Phenomenon,* Chapter 11).

Today, some formerly cultivated crops survive only as native (or "wild") plants. The archaeological record clearly demonstrates that such species were formerly cultivated—and could be again. As research on early plant domestication continues, archaeologists and plant geneticists are expanding the list of plants known to have been cultivated by ancient populations.

It is now established, for instance, that ancient Native American populations cultivated a broad range of native species, including sunflower, Jerusalem artichoke, and marshelder.

> *Given the current environmental devastation caused by contemporary agricultural practices in Amazonia, a study of the pre-Hispanic agricultural technologies capable of supporting dense populations is of critical importance. These systems may provide alternative and less destructive strategies for sustainable development in the wetlands of Amazonia and other endangered tropical environments.*
>
> CLARK L. ERICKSON, ARCHAEOLOGIST (UNIVERSITY OF PENNSYLVANIA)

Reviving "Antiquated" Technology

Throughout Peru and Bolivia, there is ample evidence of vast expanses of former croplands during pre-Hispanic times that are all but abandoned today. Between 50 percent and 75 percent of the ancient Inka agricultural terraces are no longer in use. Some archaeologists suggest that along the Peruvian coastline, up to 40 percent more farmland was irrigated in pre-Conquest times than today.

Some pre-Hispanic technologies have been completely forgotten, such as the circular field basins *(qochas)* of the high Andes. In other places, practices such as sunken gardens in coastal areas of high groundwater and systems of raised fields in waterlogged areas are used today only on the most limited basis.

Ancient Agricultural Technology on the Internet:

http://www.sas.upenn.edu/~cerickso/applied.html

Several teams of archaeologists have been studying these ancient Andean agricultural systems, with an eye toward reintroducing selected aspects of these extinct technologies. Clark Erickson, working from aerial photographs of the Lake Titicaca area (along the Peru–Bolivia border), identified a large series of ancient raised fields along the lake margin. Today, we know that more than 200,000 acres of the low-lying land near Lake Titicaca had once been converted into raised agricultural platforms.

Subsequent archaeological excavations revealed that, starting about 3,000 years ago, farmers dug a series of parallel canals and piled the earth between them to form long, low mounds roughly 3 feet high, 15 to 30 feet wide, and up to 300 feet long. These artificial canals not only provided moisture during drought periods, but the organic-rich muck periodically dredged from the canals was used to fertilize the fields (reducing or even eliminating the need for "fallow" periods between plantings). Pollen analysis shows that potatoes and quinoa (a high-altitude, protein-rich grain) were grown in these artificially raised gardens.

Experiments based on the archaeological findings show that the water in the canals running between the raised surfaces also served as heat sinks, collecting warmth during the day and slowly releasing it at night; temperatures around the crops were about 2° higher than in the surrounding area, both reducing frost damage and extending the length of the growing season. The larger the area of the raised fields, the greater was the environmental impact.

Clark Erickson (on the right) and Wilma Winkler Velarde (Bolivian project co-investigator, seated on left) meeting with local farmers in Bermeo (Bolivia) to discuss construction of experimental raised fields as part of the research on ancient agriculture of the Bolivian Amazon.

In another part of the Lake Titicaca basin, the ancient city of Tiwanaku began to expand, and an increased demand for agricultural products led ancient farmers to create an almost entirely artificial landscape in the Tiwanaku hinterland. Slopes were artificially terraced and raised fields created in the valleys. During the wet season, water was collected in the hills in modified natural gullies and transported in aqueducts across the plain and into the lake.

Quechua farmers from the Andean community of Huatta reconstructing raised field patterns in the seasonally flooded plain around Lake Titicaca (Peru). This reconstructed agricultural system is based on both indigenous knowledge systems and intensive archaeological research on ancient field patterns. The retaining wall and platform (on the left) are made of sod blocks and the archaeologically excavated canal appears on the right.

This delicate highland environment has been badly damaged by modern agricultural technology, which is heavily conditioned by modern social, political, and economic factors. Farmers barely get by, and malnutrition is rampant. But applied archaeologists believe that traditional, pre-Hispanic technologies provide workable alternatives for reversing this situation. For instance, experimental raised field farming provides potato yields twice those of plots using conventional (modern) techniques. And because of the heat sink effect, the loss of potatoes and other Andean crops due to frost is minimal.

This ancient technology appears to be cost effective. Several large-scale agribusiness experiments in this area have required huge investments in capital and were often directed at producing cash crops instead of subsistence-level farming. By contrast, projects involving ancient technologies typically target the villagers themselves, rather than working down from the top. Moreover, raised field agriculture employs native crops and tools, eliminating the need to import seed, chemicals, or machinery. The only real cost is human labor. In effect, an entire agricultural system, abandoned before the arrival of the first Europeans, is being tried out by the local community (see *Ancient Andean Engineers Feed Modern Peru Populations*).

Erickson is cautiously optimistic when evaluating the results of these experiments. Some communities participate freely, others do not. Some of those interested initially abandon the experiment later on. The reintroduced technology seems to catch on best for family-based agricultural fields, with more resistance turning up in community-owned fields. And, of course, the modern sociopolitical situation is much different from that of the past, when agricultural technology and productivity were rigidly controlled by the Andean state. Today, the failure to adapt or continue raised field agriculture may not be due to problems in technology, but rather to other sociopolitical constraints.

The saddest aspect of life right now is that science gathers knowledge faster than society gathers wisdom.

ISAAC ASIMOV
(1920–1992), WRITER

What is being argued here is not a naive romantic "return to the past," but a plea for the need to investigate and experiment with past agricultural systems as potentially viable alternative models for rural development.

CLARK L. ERICKSON

Archaeology and America's Sacred Sites

One way or another, virtually all archaeological research depends on public support. Some of this support comes directly from universities, museums, and

Ancient Andean Engineers Feed Modern Peru Populations

During 500 years, we have lost more than 70% of the productive capacity of these terraces. The Spanish were so dumb that instead of doing innovations with traditional things that were adequate to our conditions, they imported.

ELIAS MUJICA, PERUVIAN ARCHAEOLOGIST

Near the ancient Inka capital of Cuzco, an ancient pre-Columbian canal has been rehabilitated to provide water to the abandoned Inka terraces. According to archaeologist Ann Kendall, terraces renovated in the 1980s provide the highest productivity available. Inspired by this pilot project, Peruvian villagers are today reconstructing other canal systems.

Modern hydraulic engineers marvel at the precise way the ancient canals were constructed. To keep the water from racing down precipitous grades and causing damage, ancient Inka (and pre-Inka) builders installed protruding stones in the walls and floors of the canals; they also built zigzags and doglegs into steep sections. In this way, they slowed the water flow before it could damage canals or erode the fields.

Clark Erickson has heard an interesting anecdote about this. Apparently, after the canals were renovated by Andean peasants, a wealthy landowner "found" the deed to the land and took it over for himself.

One recent project in Cuzco attempted to speed the restoration process by using concrete on the old canals. But because concrete is subject to damage by earthquakes, slope slippage, and water pressure, it was soon abandoned in favor of the traditional earth-stone-clay building method, which was not only cheaper, but also more flexible (and hence more durable).

Some archaeologists estimate that before the Spanish conquest, the agricultural terrace system in Peru might have covered 2.5 million acres. Over the past decade, governmental and private groups have assisted in the restoration of these ancient canal systems.

Near the fabled Inkan site of Machu Picchu, the long-abandoned terrace system is still in ruins. But archaeologists are working with local farmers to restore the canals and plant the terraces with crops. According to archaeologist Elias Mujica, "The only way to preserve them is to give them the function they had, make them productive."

federal, state, or local government agencies. The American public also supports archaeology indirectly—through benefits (including tax deductions) offered by governments to patrons and nonprofit agencies. Particularly within the past decade, responsible archaeologists have recognized the importance of returning to the public some of the benefits and insights—that is, the archaeological knowledge—that have been derived from such public support.

In the sections that follow, we examine some of the ways in which archaeologists are attempting to "take their message public." As you will see, archaeologists increasingly find it necessary to deal with several different public sectors. Some are anxious to hear what the archaeologists have to say; others are less enthusiastic (and a few are downright hostile).

Refighting the Battle of the Alamo

Before we explore these important questions more deeply, let us shift our attention to another of America's sacred sites—the Alamo.

In 1836, a Mexican force of perhaps 4,000 soldiers commanded by Antonio López de Santa Anna reached the outskirts of San Antonio, Texas. The Anglo-American garrison, numbering 187 men under the command of Col. William Travis, withdrew to the Alamo. For 13 days, the Texans withstood siege until Mexican troops breached the walls and killed the Alamo defenders.

Public Archaeology on the Internet:

Time Traveler: Where the Future Meets the Past is a brand new kind of archaeology, designed for the broadest possible audience. Although most Internet sites cater to professional archaeologists and their students, *Time Traveler* is designed as an informal magazine about the past for the casual browser and interested lay person. It includes magazine, newsletter, and forum segments, which provide travel information, fieldwork opportunities, job listings, and upcoming events in the world of archaeology. At this writing, *Time Traveler* is undergoing a trial period. If it survives, it will provide an important new way to bring archaeology to an interested public.
http://www.ucsb.edu/anth/graduate/personalpages/dKennett/tt.html

See also:
http://www.usd.edu/anth/pubed.html

Today's textbooks commonly pay homage to this heroic episode in the Texan war of independence against Mexico. As one historian put it, the courageous trio, Travis, Bowie, and Crockett, shed their blood upon "a holy altar." Their martyrs' death is commonly praised as a strategic and well-executed military move, a sacrifice that successfully delayed Mexican forces and ultimately set up a glorious victory for Texas at the subsequent Battle of San Jacinto, where Santa Anna was roundly defeated. The victorious battle cry became "Remember the Alamo!"

And remember it we have. Enshrined in the dominant American folklore, the Alamo remains one of America's most cherished cultural icons. According to frontier ideology, Americans arriving in Texas brought with them a culture capable of transforming the wilderness into a productive part of the United States of America. The birth of Texas, it is written, was made possible by the death of the Alamo defenders. For many, the Alamo remains a symbolic confirmation that the spread of Anglo-Texan culture across the American Southwest had been predestined by God Almighty. Many a Texan ranks the Alamo alongside Lexington and Concord in terms of historical significance.

But for many Texans of Hispanic descent, the Alamo has long been a recurring bad dream, reinforcing the exclusion of Hispanic populations from any honorable role in Texas history. More than half of San Antonio's current population is Hispanic, and many have challenged the traditional heroic image of the Alamo. Some voices demand that the Hispanic people be assigned a more positive and significant role in the history of the American Southwest.

The Alamo, they point out, began as a small-scale Spanish mission long before it became an Anglo-Texan shrine. Known as *Mission San Antonio de Valero,* it was established to bring Christianity to the local Indian population. By this view, a handful of brave and unarmed friars attempted to bring their own brand of civilization to the untamed Texas wilderness. They had no interest in storming sturdy fortresses. They were men of peace, whose goal was to save souls (but see the next section for a very different, Native American perspective on the American mission past).

What does all this have to do with archaeology? Plenty.

Our historic battlefields remain our battlegrounds. They are still where we fight the social and political Other, but with images and words rather than with guns. Here we create boundaries between "us" and "them" with identities born from historic individuals, identities inherited by entire groups in current society. Our battle sites, in being the origin of these images, become our most hallowed ground and the object of patriotic pilgrimages.

HOLLY BREACHLEY BREAR, ANTHROPOLOGIST (GEORGE MASON UNIVERSITY)

I looked upon the Mexicans as scarce more than apes.

NOAH SMITHWICK, EARLY ANGLO-AMERICAN SETTLER IN TEXAS

Archaeology for Kids on the Internet:

The DIG Project is a simulation curriculum in which kids invent their own ancient civilization, artifacts, symbols, and values; it includes lessons on "what makes a culture": http://www.ed.gov/pubs/edreformstudies/edtech/dig.html

Newton's Apple provides a general archaeology site: http://ericir.syr.edu/projects/newton/

Curriculum and Lesson Plans (K–12 sources): http://execpc.com/~dboals/k-12.html

Diana Nemorens is the Web page describing scientific and archaeological reconstruction of a Roman ship: http://www.virtual-pc.com/orontes/index.html

Exploring Ancient World Cultures: http://eawc.evansville.edu

See also:
http://www.execpc.com/~dboals/arch.html
http://www.csun.edu/~hcedu013/

Some representatives of San Antonio's Hispanic community believe that additional research should be conducted at the Alamo—archaeological research that emphasizes *not* the short-lived 1836 battle, but rather the eighteenth-century mission period. Archaeologist Anne Fox (University of Texas, San Antonio) agrees. She has a deep and longstanding interest in the Spanish missions of Texas and believes that further excavations in and around the Alamo would shed important new light on this little known chapter of San Antonio history.

But there is a problem. The Daughters of the Republic of Texas (DRT) are the state-appointed custodians of the Alamo, its archaeological record and extensive archives on Texas history. For years, the DRT discouraged, even stonewalled, research into the Alamo-as-mission; they believed that mission-period research detracted from the true historical significance of the Alamo as "the cradle of Texas liberty."

Anthropologist Holly Breachley Brear has analyzed the social and political situation surrounding the modern Alamo. According to Brear, archaeologists like Fox threaten the current political structure in San Antonio. Although that attitude has softened somewhat in recent years, in the eyes of the DRT members, it is those "thirteen days to glory" that still constitute the primary significance of the Alamo. Brear argues that if the DRT were to recognize the historical significance of the earlier mission period, or to honor the Mexican soldiers who fought in the Battle of the Alamo, they would threaten the sociopolitical power balance in modern San Antonio. They would be empowering an ethnic group directly descended from the "enemy" at the Alamo.

In addition, any strategy for understanding the mission period would require excavations reaching far beyond the boundary of the state-owned property at the Alamo. As archaeologists sought to locate and expose the foundations of the mission compound, their excavations extended well into the predominantly city-owned portion of the Alamo Plaza. Clearly, these new physical and conceptual boundaries better serve the Hispanic community's broader interest in the site and undermine the DRT's narrow focus on Alamo-as-battlefield. Many politically active Hispanics are encouraging broadscale archaeological research and public interpretation of the Alamo-as-mission to highlight peaceful Hispanic origins within the state of Texas.

Culture with a capital C *involves the civilization-versus-wilderness distinction; it is cultivated gardens, fine arts, and elegant homes. But culture with a lowercase* c *is ethnicity, which seemingly can be bought and sold at the Mercado in downtown San Antonio.*

HOLLY BREACHLEY BREAR

Fox finds the apprehensiveness of the DRT toward mission research troublesome. But she is also critical of anybody who attempts to keep the animosity between early Texans and Mexicans alive in the late twentieth cen-

WHAT'S IN A NAME?

Hispanic and Anglo

Numerous pejoratives have been applied to people of Latin American descent living north of Mexico. For years, the terms *Puerto Rican* (mostly in the eastern United States) and *Mexican* (in the western United States) were routinely applied—usually in a derogatory sense—without regard to country of birth. Largely to avoid such negative connotations, the term *Hispanic* has come into common usage (as in the U.S. census).

But considerable disagreement persists about such terminology. In parts of the American West, the term *Chicano* implies a sense of cultural and ethnic pride. In Texas and elsewhere in the American Southwest, people usually use the term *Hispanic* to distingish themselves or others as people related in some way to Mexico, Spain, Cuba, or another country with Spanish as the primary language. In our discussion of San Antonio and the Alamo, we use the word *Hispanic* (which conforms with local usage).

People living in the American West also use *Anglo* to distinguish white, English-speaking people from those of Hispanic descent. Interestingly, although those on the Anglo side of the dichotomy do not often refer to themselves publicly as such, there is no commonly self-applied term. In fact, in San Antonio and elsewhere, "Anglo" is often used by Hispanics to designate "The Other" in a fairly emotionally charged sense.

Obviously, such terms tend to be vague, incompletely sorted out, and heavily value-laden.

The fish trap exists because of the fish: once you've gotten the fish, you can forget the trap. . . . Words exist because of meanings: once you've gotten the meanings, you can forget the words.

CHUANG-TZU (4TH CENTURY B.C.), PHILOSOPHER AND TEACHER

tury. Fox believes that archaeologists should "just wait and watch and put in a word when asked, trying to keep out of the fray and maintain a reputation for not taking sides except to provide the historical facts."

Archaeologists digging and interpreting American historic sites such as the Alamo also face considerable pressure from tourist expectations. The Alamo attracts visitors mostly because of the famous 1836 battle. When archaeologists like Anne Fox excavate there, the public can expect to read about their finds in tomorrow's newspaper. The dig itself becomes a tourist attraction.

Such excavations are always in danger of threatening prevailing ideology. During the 1988 field season at the Alamo, one reporter from an Austin newspaper complained that the archaeologists working on mission-period remains outside the Alamo "seemed to be drawing as much reverent attention from the tourists as the indoor exhibits on David Crockett, William Travis, and the other heroes of 1836." The problem is clear: Archaeologists allowed to dig at the Alamo are supposed to find the concrete evidence of the known past–that is, the 1836 past.

Similar problems plague the serious historian seeking to conduct meaningful research elsewhere in the Hispanic Southwest. As David Weber, a distinguished historian of the Spanish Borderlands, points out, some of the most cherished morsels of Alamo lore simply have no basis in historic fact (see *Texas-Sized Mythology About the Alamo*).

If we had some way to measure it, I think that it might be proved that more ink than blood has been spilled over the Texas Revolution in general, and the Alamo in particular.

DAVID J. WEBER, HISTORIAN (SOUTHERN METHODIST UNIVERSITY)

ARCHAEO-MYTHBUSTERS

Texas-Sized Mythology About the Alamo

The great difference between Texas and every other American state in the 20th century was that Texas had a history. Other American regions merely had records of development.

T. R. Fehrenbach, historian

As historian David Weber has noted, somewhere along the line, the legend of the Alamo "moved out of the earthly realm of reality into the stratosphere of myth." Here is what happens to some of the more cherished pieces of Alamo lore when they are brought back down to earth:

Myth: William Barrett Travis is supposed to have traced a line in the dirt and said something like: "Those of you who are willing to stay with me and die with me, cross that line."

Fact: There is no convincing evidence that Travis ever uttered this famous speech or drew such a line. In fact, many military historians have concluded that the defense of the Alamo is best characterized in terms of indecision and fatigue.

Legend: The battle slogan of Colonel Travis at the Alamo was "Victory or Death."

Fact: True enough, but Travis was no deliberate martyr. He said "Victory or Death" only at the beginning of the siege, when he fully expected to win and live. He thought that victory was immediately at hand, so long as reinforcements arrived; they never came.

Legend: The most holy of the divine trinity at the Alamo, Davy Crockett, who, according to one well-respected account, arrived there "in his foxskin [*sic*] cap . . . with old Betsy cradled in his arms, appeared bigger than life itself. He was just the tonic needed at the right time." Today, replicas of Crockett's coonskin cap are the single biggest seller in the Alamo gift shop. And, sure enough, entombed in a glass case on display at the Alamo, there she is—Old Betsy herself.

Fact: Old Betsy wasn't at the Alamo for the famous 1836 battle. Crockett left her in Tennessee. Sometime later, the rifle was transported to Texas for display in the Alamo museum.

Legend: The fearless Alamo defenders fought to their last breath, only to perish beneath a human tidal wave of Mexican soldiers.

Fact: Davy Crockett and a half dozen other Alamo defenders were probably captured by Mexican troops and then, on orders from Santa Anna, executed. Even worse, some contemporary accounts suggest that Crockett and the others may even have—horrors!—*surrendered*.

Legend: We'll never know exactly what happened at the Alamo; after all, nobody who fought there survived.

Fact: Actually, there were lots of survivors—at least a couple of thousand soldiers in the victorious Mexican army. But their recorded observations have sometimes been denigrated in Anglo-Texas history. After all, these are "enemy" accounts.

The story goes that when Senator John F. Kennedy visited the Alamo, he was surrounded by large crowds and asked his host, Maury Maverick, if they might escape the crush by going out the back door. "There is no back door," Maverick is said to have replied, "that's why there were so many heroes."

When serious students of Texas history turn to the evidence contained in the Mexican accounts of the battle, they are sometimes publicly reviled. One Texas newspaper termed Hispanic perspectives on Alamo history "a commie plot to trash our heroes." Another writer–from Crockett's home state of Tennessee–questioned the manhood of the historian involved, describing him as a "gutless wonder."

Fortunately, such extreme positions have softened in recent years. A new generation of DRT members shows an increasing interest in telling a more complete story of the Alamo. Although they still emphasize the 1836 battle,

The Alamo.

today they present a more evenhanded view. For one thing, recent historical research has emphasized the role of local Hispanics who sided with the Texan "heroes." In so doing, they highlight the dilemma of the local Hispanic populace, forced to choose sides (and the number of them who steadfastly refused to do so). As time passes, the various extreme positions are moderating, downplaying fractious dichotomies such as "heroes" and "enemies."

Such are the tensions surrounding America's sacred sites. When archaeologists excavate and interpret their findings, they are increasingly faced with pressure and conflict from the various public constituencies. The world of archaeology is only beginning to appreciate the ramifications and conflicts involved when multiple versions of ultimate reality are taken to the American public.

The newer battles at the Alamo reflect something of the tension between various present-day ethnic groups for control of the past. For many conservative Anglos, the Alamo is hallowed ground, a place where their ancestors perished trying to fight off the Mexican peril. For some of today's Hispanic population, the Alamo is better seen as a place of peace, where brave, unarmed men of God brought their own version of civilization, toiling to save wayward American Indian souls. It is the pacific mission heritage, the argument goes, that reflects a more accurate picture of the Hispanic past in Texas.

California's Simulated Mission Past

These frontier churches strung along the California coast like so many beads in a rosary stood for spiritual foundations as impressive as those suggested by the rooster-vaned spires of Massachusetts. One need not be a Catholic . . . to feel the power of the missions as historical monuments or to internalize them as symbolic elements of great use to the present.

KEVIN STARR, HISTORIAN (UNIVERSITY OF SAN FRANCISCO)

Spanish missions, of course, were hardly restricted to Texas soil. Some mission sites are conspicuous features of the modern landscape: Mission San Javier del Bac (outside of Tucson) and the string of missions near San Antonio. Other missions, such as Santa Catalina de Guale, survive strictly as below-the-ground archaeological remains. But regardless of present condition, the dozens of Spanish missions that remain are some of America's most vivid reminders of this country's Hispanic patrimony.

In fact, it's downright impossible to escape this mission heritage. On one San Diego street alone, you'll find Mission Transmission sharing a warehouse with Mission Valley Pool and Spas–right next door to the Old Mission Deli. Not far away is the Padre Trail Inn (at the corner of Mission and Friars Roads),

California Mission Archaeology on the Internet:

California Missions Resources includes an interactive field trip and a brief overview of each mission:
http://www.santacruz.k12.ca.us/vft/missions.html

See also:
http://tqd.advanced.org/3615/

bordering on the Friars Mission subdivision. A major league baseball team—the San Diego Padres—plays right down the street. But, the crass mission message aside, California's mission system comprises one of the most powerful and visible connections to the archaeological record of the American west.

Growing up (as I did) in California, the first archaeological site I ever visited was Mission Santa Clara de Asís, just south of San Francisco Bay. I was 12 years old when my mother took me there, and I still remember the experience: It was the first time that the dull, boring textbook history actually came alive for me. That first visit to Mission Santa Clara inspired me to visit all 21 of the California missions (and, ultimately, to study archaeology in college).

Unknowingly, I'd joined a long line of mission pilgrims, each seeking out that ancient mission past that *was* California. Sure, some of it is schlocky and overcommercialized today. To visit California's missions, you must elbow your way past the gift shops stocked with typical mission mementos—my personal favorite is the "Just a Swallow from Capistrano" shotglass. But the hassle is worth it. Once inside, you can experience the real thing: the adobe churches, the somber graveyards, the mission gardens—here is hands-on history. This is the old California, the way it really was.

Like other California mission pilgrims for more than a century, I was eventually drawn to San Carlos Borromeo—"Mission Carmel"—the mission headquarters and home of Father Junípero Serra, venerable patriarch of California's mission heritage.

Today's history-minded tourist can visit Father Junípero Serra's cell, the bedroom where he died at Mission San Carlos Borromeo on August 28, 1784. Hanging on a nail is Serra's authentic iron-and-braided wire "discipline," his penitential scourge. Few have any inkling that this legendary locale is but a simulated reality, completely reconstructed from ruins in 1937.

Mission Carmel was everything I'd hoped it would be. I could see why President Dwight D. Eisenhower came here in 1956. Small wonder that, 4 years later, U.S. Senator (and Democratic presidential candidate) John F. Kennedy insisted on celebrating his forty-third birthday by attending Mass in the old Mission Carmel church. Easy to see why Ronald Reagan would eventually borrow Father Serra's original mission Bible for his swearing-in ceremony as governor of California.

Reagan would later salute Father Serra as "one of the heroes of our land.

This is what Father Serra's "cell" and the rest of the convento wing of Mission Carmel actually looked like in the 1920s, before extensive reconstruction. The cross marks the approximate location of Serra's room.

His tireless work for the Indians of California . . . remains a shining page in our history. His missions stand as a monument." So compelling was the California mission heritage that it could readily span the political, social, and even religious agendas separating presidents Eisenhower, Kennedy, and Reagan.

Like every California school kid, I knew about Father Serra, and I lined up with the rest of the tourists to see his personal bedroom (what the Franciscans call his "cell"). In this very room (on Saturday, August 28, 1784), a devoted Father Francisco Palóu brought the weary Serra a cup of broth. As he later recorded in his diary, Father Palóu heard Serra whisper: "Now, let us go to rest." It was *siesta* time and when Palóu returned, he found Serra "asleep in the Lord . . . his body showing no other sign of death than the cessation of breathing."

You can imagine my shock when I learned, years later, that Father Serra's cell at Mission Carmel is a complete fake—a total reconstruction, without archaeological or historical integrity. Take a look at the pictures: During the 1920s, the adobe walls of Father Serra's cell had melted down to barely waist high. The original "cell" had disappeared. Where I stood was a complete fabrication, a modern counterfeit. Sure, Serra's original Bible was there, but it rested on a reconstructed wooden bench in a completely simulated setting—reconstructed for the benefit of tourists.

What had happened here? I came to Carmel to experience the "original" California missions and their history. Why had one of the most celebrated places in California's history books been transformed into a Hollywood set?

To answer this question, you must situate the California missions in the socioeconomic climate of a century ago. Southern California was caught up in the great western land boom. Hundreds of thousands of easterners were moving westward and many of the old mission sites became nuclei for rapidly expanding late-nineteenth-century settlements. Real estate promoters cleverly associated the concept of "Spanish" with an easygoing, relaxed, fun-loving lifestyle—a semitropical fantasy attainable by any hardworking Anglo willing to settle in sunny California.

The mission ruins themselves became the architectural reification of a larger, more pervasive "Mediterranean analogy" that swept across late-nineteenth-century southern California. The missions drew in the newly arrived Anglo-Americans, attracted to what they were told was the aristocratic life of

Most beautiful of the California missions, San Carlos Borromeo exerts a romantic spell over all who visit it. In its setting against sea and river, its fair gardens, the solid competence of its vaulted ceiling—in all these things it tells the viewer that here stands the work of men with the mind and heart to design with integrity and warmth.

SUNSET MAGAZINE

The missions are, next to our climate and its consequences, the best capital Southern California has.

CHARLES FLETCHER LUMMIS (1859–1928), AUTHOR AND EDITOR

Protestant that I am, I . . . walked again past the old Catholic Mission. The last swallows were wheeling home, and the sparrows in the ivy were sleepily querulous. The fading light lingered on the crumbling cornices, and the tile-capped belfry rose peacefully into the clear dusk of the sky. After all, age is a kind of sacrament.

J. Smeaton Chase (British tourist in late-nineteenth-century California)

leisure of the not-so-remote Hispanic past. The Californian land boom was an antiquarian odyssey, a sentimental passage through the relics and ruins of the dimly remembered past. Almost overnight, California's mission sites became places of pilgrimage (and, for some, bait to lure easterners westward). They remain so today.

But late-nineteenth-century California had a big problem: its sanctified sites were falling apart. And the hordes of tourists to the missions expedited matters by chipping away tons of adobe remembrances.

A movement to "rescue" the California missions began in the late 1880s when, despite considerable anti-Catholic sentiments, the missions took on a significance far beyond their religious affiliation.

Enterprising California boosters felt that the unadulterated mission ruins—no matter how romantic—were too remote and confusing for an everyday audience. If California was to eulogize a glorious pre-Anglo, Hispanic past—and, in the process, chisel out its unique regional identity—then the missions must be quickly restored "so that they could be read more easily by a popular audience."

I did it the way they would have done it if they'd had a little money.

Henry John Downie, Mission Carmel Curator

And restore them they did. The emphasis soon shifted from preservation to restoration, resulting in what architectural historians have termed "elaborate misinterpretations of history." As the missions were variously restored, a highly romantic conception of the Spanish period was cultivated, primarily for the benefit of the incoming tide of tourists.

Many of the earlier reconstructions were poorly researched and conducted with little understanding of the archaeological realities. The best were well-meaning fabrications, conducted with great enthusiasm and widespread support; the worst were revisionist muddling.

The sweeping restorations at Mission Carmel were the handiwork of Henry Downie. A cabinetmaker by profession, Downie turned a temporary job of repairing Carmel statuary in 1931 into a lifetime position as restorer-curator and would-be archaeologist. To his credit, Downie doggedly tracked down many of the mission's original furnishings, and installed them permanently. He also distinguished himself through his conscientious effort to ensure that historical reconstructions were accurate.

However well-intentioned, in three decades Downie single-handedly reconfigured Carmel and several other missions, rendering future archaeological examinations problematic. This kind of well-meaning, if theatrical approach to restoration will always remain a mixed blessing for serious students of history because without appropriate archaeological input, the integrity of both buried deposits and aboveground architecture is inevitably destroyed. In California, fanciful enhancements were all too common, and that problem persists today.

For future archaeologists, these reconstructions will likely provide more information on the restorers than on the past they were trying to depict.

Leo Barker, archaeologist (Golden Gate National Recreational Area), and Julia Costello, consulting archaeologist

This is an issue facing all who wish to "take archaeology to the American public": So much of our past has already been reconstructed and, in the process, interpreted. As so commonly happens with tourism-directed restorations around the globe, only the more spectacular, elite archaeological sectors are restored—the temples, the pyramids, the king's tomb. In California, "mission" is commonly equated with "church," and early restorers universally emphasized the latest colonial construction, to the exclusion of earlier forms and attendant structures. Only rarely is the restoration extended to other important structures around the quadrangle—the *convento,* the women's quarters, the workshops, and the storerooms.

Such restorations inflate the white, Catholic, European aspects of mission life. The surrounding, "lower status" structures of the Indian *ranchería* are usually ignored. Although Franciscan graves are carefully marked and venerated, mission reconstructions never identify individual Indian graves. Most Indians were apparently interred in mass graves; some, such as those at San Juan Bautista, are not marked at all. This progressive Europeanization of California's missions denigrates, if not eliminates, Indians in the mission context.

No reasonable person can argue that the California Indians in any way benefited from a colonization scheme that confiscated their land and resources; uprooted entire villages; forced them to migrate to the feudalistic mendicant estates on the coast; subjected them to daily floggings, forced labor, and wholesale sexual assaults on their wives and daughters; and resulted in the deaths of thousands of innocent men, women, and children.

ED D. CASTILLO, HISTORIAN (SONOMA STATE UNIVERSITY) AND MEMBER OF THE CAHUILLA TRIBE

Considerable damage has been done to California's missions by overzealous restorers and revisionists. Not only has such misguided overrestoration resulted in the unwarranted destruction of archaeological deposits, but the simulated realities of lush gardens and romanticized architecture have contributed numerous misinterpretations of history. The importance of high-quality historical and archaeological research has never been fully realized, and mission exhibitions still contribute to the near invisibility of Native Americans in California's past. Too often, contemporary mission exhibits attempt to present themselves as bona fide heirlooms of the past—and many succeed in giving that false impression.

Fortunately, there are exceptions. Mission San Francisco Solano, located on the central plaza of downtown Sonoma, is a textbook example of how restorations *should be and can be* presented to the public. Like so many missions, Solano passed through a series of hands after secularization, serving variously as a barn and a blacksmith's shop. By the late 1960s, only a portion of the padre's quarters remained as original construction. The rest is twentieth-century reconstruction.

What sets this mission above its contemporaries is that Mission Solano explicitly owns up to what it is—a heavily reconstructed interpretation of the past. This disclaimer is not subtle; immediately after entering the *convento,* all visitors run squarely into an impossible-to-overlook sign, warning in boldface:

> Reconstruction of this mission and many others throughout the state was done around the first years of this century. Often accomplished without the benefit of historical or archeological research, these reconstructions were based on romanticized paintings and accounts of the 19th century. Occasionally walls appeared or disappeared in these paintings and sketches. The reconstructions would reflect this misinformation.

Nearby are a dozen photographs and period sketches of various attempts at reconstructing Mission Solano. Other prominent exhibit cases show how archaeology was conducted here, and how archaeologists interpreted what they found. Another caption, highly visible as one enters the chapel, explains the extent of restoration, and discusses the evidence leading to the specific reconstructions.

The state of California has done a first-rate job presenting this reconstructed mission to the public. Only the most obtuse visitor could leave Sonoma Mission State Historical Park thinking she or he had observed the authentic, unrestored nineteenth-century Mission Solano—although I am certain that some still do.

The days of the padres shimmered in a golden haze of mingled myth and memory, free of fanaticism and injustice, their cruelty and pain forgotten. No matter that the mission system itself was founded on ambiguity: the enforced enclosure of the Indians. No matter that the Spanish soldiers hunted them in the hills like so much prey and drove them down into the mission compounds like so much cattle. There, in churchly captivity, the majority of them declined . . . from the trauma of having their way of life and their tribal places so cruelly taken away.

KEVIN STARR

Heritage Tourism on the Internet:

In several chapters, we have provided Internet information about visiting specific sites mentioned in the text. Here are two more links for those interested in seeing our archaeological heritage firsthand:

Links to the Past is a nifty U.S. government program, with clickable images of historic places, structures, and landscapes; history; archaeology; museum collections; preservation programs; national parks; and grants. Take a virtual tour of a national park!
http://www.cr.nps.gov

UNESCO World Heritage List is a compilation of the most important archaeological resources on the planet:
http://www.cco.caltech.edu/~salmon/world.heritage.html

Taking Archaeology Public: Not an Easy Call

When we are talking about the Alamo or Mission Carmel, tourism is a given. America's sacred sites comprise an important element in our national identity. American pride will always motivate people to visit such places, to experience the power of the place for themselves. Closing the Alamo to tourists would be sacrilegious to Anglo-Americans, for whom such historic touchstones provide information about our national, heroic roots. The Hispanic community also wishes to see people visit the Alamo, but they want to present a very different message there. Archaeologists have a role to play for both constituencies.

It's very important that we visit each other's worlds.

LORI VILLAMIL

Tourism at Wyoming's Bighorn Medicine Wheel (discussed in Chapter 16) raises a rather different set of concerns. To many Indian people, this remains a holy place, one of many sacred sites where important ceremonies are performed to this day. Sacred lands are considered to be vital to individual and tribal harmony.

And some of the most important sacred sites, including the Bighorn Medicine Wheel, are being overrun each year by thousands of non-Indians: well-meaning tourists, teams of archaeologists, and New Agers seeking a spiritual experience. There is great concern in Indian Country that the plants, paths, shrines, rocks, and other aspects of sacred sites are being destroyed by the curious and the insensitive.

Many North American archaeologists would agree that the Bighorn Medicine Wheel is one of America's more intriguing ancient sites. With its spectacular setting and puzzling past, the Medicine Wheel seems to be a natural for the heritage tourist. Or is it? Should tourists be encouraged to visit the Bighorn Medicine Wheel?

How do archaeologists balance the dual concerns of bringing American archaeology to the interested public while respecting the wishes of the descendant populations still involved with many of those sites?

Let me sketch two different approaches to this problem, once again returning to the Bighorn Medicine Wheel as a concrete example. Today, two popular guidebooks attempt to bring North American archaeology to an interested traveling public. In *America's Ancient Treasures,* Franklin Folsom and Mary Etling Folsom describe thousands of archaeological museums and sites available for tourist visitation. They provide a first-rate, encyclopedic overview, one designed "to open doors to those who are curious and who want to dig metaphorically into the past." Another book, my own *Exploring Ancient Native America,* attempts to do the same thing, but employs a more selective, more personalized and thematic framework. Both books are designed to educate the traveler about the ancient Native American past. Both also ac-

How would you like it if I took my picnic basket, my family and dog into your church while you were praying?

WILLIAM TALLBULL, NORTHERN CHEYENNE ELDER

knowledge the sometimes conflicting aims of archaeological research and traditional American Indian religious beliefs.

The Folsoms considered this issue carefully, and decided to exclude the Medicine Wheel from *America's Ancient Treasures.* After consulting with representatives at the American Indian Rights Fund, they declined either to discuss the site or to provide directions for visitation. Instead, they simply wrote: "[The Bighorn Medicine Wheel] is sacred to Native Americans who worship there. They request that visitors stay away and do not invade their privacy." This position reflects a sensitivity to native interests. The Folsoms made a good decision.

At about the same time, I struggled with precisely the same issue—but came to the opposite conclusion. In *Exploring Ancient Native America,* I spent eight pages describing the Bighorn Medicine Wheel in some detail, discussing several possible explanations of its origin and use, and providing precise directions for tourists wishing to get there.

Like the Folsoms, I consulted various native people, and my conversations elicited a broad range of opinion. Some expressed the view that sacred sites should never be visited by the non-Indian public. Others saw no particular problem with tourists visiting such sites. After all, they pointed out, places like the Medicine Wheel are already visited by thousands of non-Indians every year; no single author can hope to stem this flood of visitation. The key issue, they pointed out, was to educate the public about native values and to be certain that such sacred sites are protected from looting and despoliation.

I do not claim that archaeology should be coherent, integrated, unified. . . . If there is to be a new consensus it is that we accept to live with diversity.

IAN HODDER, ARCHAEOLOGIST (CAMBRIDGE UNIVERSITY)

I was still undecided about whether to include the Medicine Wheel when I discussed the matter with the late William Tallbull, a Northern Cheyenne elder with a deep and long-lasting personal relationship to the Medicine Wheel. Tallbull was an important part of a coalition of tribal, scientific, ecological, and government agencies, cooperating to assure that the Medicine Wheel would be protected, preserved, and respected. He supported the Forest Service's decision to keep the site open to the public, but with the last 1.5 miles of the access road closed to vehicular traffic. Tourists were still permitted to visit the site, but were required to cover the remaining distance on foot. In his view, this solution minimized the negative impacts of tourism while maintaining the religious freedom of the native people (himself included) who worshiped there.

To Tallbull, education remained a key consideration. He also felt it important to keep the site accessible to anybody who wished to experience the power of the place. After all, people have been drawn to this isolated mountaintop for centuries, and Tallbull believed it inappropriate to exclude anybody. Not only did he encourage me to include the Bighorn Medicine Wheel in *Exploring Ancient Native America,* but he offered to write an accompaniment to my own discussion (see *Archaeological Sites or Sacred Places? A Native American Perspective* by William Tallbull). In his perspective, sacred sites offer an important opportunity for teaching tolerance and respect. In my discussion of the Medicine Wheel, I also included a lengthy poem in which Suzan Shown Harjo (Cheyenne/Hodulgee Muscogee) spoke eloquently about the importance of respecting sacred ground throughout Indian Country.

Which approach is "correct"? As we take American archaeology to the public, what should we do about sacred sites?

IN HIS OWN WORDS

Archaeological Sites or Sacred Places? A Native American Perspective by William Tallbull

To the Indigenous Peoples of North America, the archaeological sites found on North American soil are not "archaeological" sites. They are sites where our relatives lived and carried out their lives.

Sacred Sites such as the Medicine Wheel and Medicine Mountain are no different. To Native Americans they are living cultural sites from which help comes when "The People" needed or need help. They were/are places where tribal peoples went in times of famine and sickness, in periods of long drought when animals would leave, or in more current times when tribes are being torn apart by politics, alcohol, or other abuses.

The men make a pledge to go and vision quest at these places, seeking help. As we leave to go to these sites, our every breath is a prayer. We follow the path to the sites; observing a protocol that has been in place for thousands of years. The Native American approaching these sites must stop four times from the beginning of his or her journey to arrival at the site. A trip to a Sacred Site was/is not done just for curiosity, but only after much preparation and seeking.

Many blessings have come to "The Peoples" in this way. Many tribes have received covenants (bundles) from these sites. Some Tribes still carry the bundles that were received from a certain mountain or site. These are considered no different than the covenants given Moses or the traditional law that went with it.

When Native Peoples have been blessed by a site or area, they go back to give thanks and leave offerings whenever they get a chance. These should be left undisturbed and not handled or tampered with.

Today many of our people are reconnecting with these sites after many years of being denied the privilege of practicing our own religion at these very sacred areas. In the past, trips were made in secret and hidden from curious eyes.

If you go to see a Sacred Site, remember you are walking on "holy ground," and we ask that you respect our culture and traditions. If you come to a site that is being used for a religious purpose, we hope you will understand.

The late WILLIAM TALLBULL was an elder of the Northern Cheyenne tribe.

I don't know.

I certainly have no quibble with the Folsoms' decision to exclude the Medicine Wheel; they did so for exactly the right reasons. But I'm also glad that I included it, juxtaposed with the personal perspectives on this site from two prominent Indian people.

Whether we are considering the Medicine Wheel, Mission Carmel, or the Alamo, it is impossible for archaeologists to escape the central issue: Whose past is it, anyway?

In the next section, let's confront this difficult issue head on.

Some Ethical Challenges: Who Owns the Past?

Prehistoric: Belonging to an early period and a museum.

AMBROSE BIERCE (1842–1914?), JOURNALIST AND WRITER

Ambrose Bierce had it about right—until very recently. Many of the world's great museums already had huge collections in Bierce's day. Despite a late-twentieth-century "birth of conscience" regarding the expropriation of antiquities from other countries, museum stockpiles have continued to expand.

It was in the museums of natural history and ethnology that many of us bumped firsthand into the non-Western world. Through the high-security glass, we peered at our first Mayan stelae, saw an Egyptian mummy, and stared down at our first pygmy manniken. Hermetically sealed cases displayed seemingly endless rows of originals—Chinese jades, deadly Amazonian blowguns, and ingenious Eskimo harpoons.

Through the decades, museums have shown the "civilized world" how vast, complex, and varied the human experience has been. To urbanite and rural fair goer alike, exhibit halls have served up what people around the world were really like. Although television might capture better images, only a museum could flaunt the real thing.

Now, many of the world's people want their real things back. Although research and exhibition still dominate a curator's daily life, the corridors of today's museums echo with a strange new jargon: repatriation of patrimony, restriction of imports and exports, and rights retained by concerned parties. In many ways, today's archaeology museums are under siege, and the ground rules governing museum collections are still rapidly changing.

The Rosetta Stone.

Some Iroquois people are asking for the return of their False Face masks. Some Australian aboriginals are demanding back their skeletons. Some New Zealand Maoris insist that mummified "trophy heads" be taken off display in museums halfway around the globe. In one form or another, each is requesting that control over objects of cultural significance be **repatriated** to them.

Repatriate: To restore or return control to the rightful place of origin, allegiance, or citizenship.

An early chapter in the repatriation story was written, of all places, in Iceland, where legal, political, diplomatic, and social pressure ultimately forced the controversial 1971 return by Denmark of the *Flateyjarbók* and *Codex Reguis,* the most valuable manuscript treasures of Iceland's medieval literature. Although opposition arose at every turn, Icelandic self-respect and pride ultimately won out over Danish jurisprudence.

Few people know of Iceland's triumph. Many more are aware of the tiff surrounding the world famous Elgin Marbles—or, as Greek nationals more correctly term them, the Parthenon Marbles. By whatever name, this 247-foot-long frieze of marble sculptures, lifted by Lord Elgin nearly two centuries ago from the Parthenon in downtown Athens (Greece), is today ensconced in the Duveen Gallery of the British Museum. Without question, the marbles have become the subject of the most famous and most controversial request for cultural repatriation.

The museum remains the major institutional connection between archaeology as a discipline and the wider society. . . . Here one can visit the past, but it is a past which is not at all relevant to most interest-groups in society. In their present structure, museums serve by and large to distance and disenfranchise people from their past. The transformation of museums must play an important role in archaeology that is practised as a form of social and political action.

CHRISTOPHER TILLEY, ARCHAEOLOGIST

The late Greek minister of culture Melina Mercouri argued that these sculptures symbolize Greece itself, that they constitute part of Greece's psychological landscape. Sir David Wilson, dogged director of the British Museum, countered that *any* such return—and most particularly that of the Elgin Marbles—smacks of "cultural fascism."

While recognizing that world history reveals an "intricate web of universal plunder" and "the cannibalization of cultures" (see *The Sordid Tale of Priam's Treasure*), a growing chorus of concerned scholars urge that certain kinds of objects should be returned immediately to their countries of origin. Citing both logical and legal grounds, they argue that museums within the world's developing countries should own *some* of the objects in the national museums of the West, that *some* of the Benin bronzes should find their way into African museums, and that the **Rosetta stone**—clearly collected as a spoil of war—should be on display in Cairo rather than in London.

Rosetta stone: A black basalt stone found in 1799 that bears an inscription in three languages. By working from Greek texts, scholars were able to decipher the ancient Egyptian hieroglyphs.

The larger debate over "who owns the past" has taken a number of curious turns recently. Superficially, the dispute reflects the predictable split between "haves" and "have-nots," but much more is involved than an

WHO OWNS THE PAST?

The Sordid Tale of Priam's Treasure

You will remember (from Chapter 2) the tale of how, in the spring of 1873, Heinrich and Sophie Schliemann discovered and excavated *Priam's Treasure*—the Trojan gold hoard that became one of archaeology's richest and most celebrated treasure troves. Although art historians and archaeologists continue to debate it, recent research dates the "Treasure of Priam" artifacts to 2200 B.C. (or older), about 1,000 years prior to Homeric Troy. Schliemann accepted this conclusion before his death. While this much seems certain, subsequent events surrounding Priam's Treasure (prosaically, or more accurately, known as "Treasure A") have created a web of intrigue and a stir in international politics that continue to make headlines today.

At first, the Schliemanns hid the thousands of gold pieces—the necklaces, earrings, buttons, and beads—from the on-site Turkish guards, whose duty it was to inspect all finds. Turkish law at the time required that half the artifacts remain in the national museum at Constantinople. From its hiding place beneath the Schliemanns' bed, the booty was packed into suitcases, labeled as personal possessions, and shipped directly to Athens. In this way, Schliemann avoided the required inspection by Turkish officials.

Once in Athens, Schliemann hid the treasure in a secret storehouse. Only on selected days, such as Greek holidays, would he risk transporting any of the illicit artifacts. Little by little, the objects were cleaned, repaired, and photographed for publication. Eight thousand gold beads were strung into two necklaces, one of 11 strands, the other of 13. Schliemann even photographed Sophie modeling the diadem, earrings, and one of the necklaces from Priam's Treasure. Contrary to modern protocol among professional archaeologists, Schliemann regarded these priceless artifacts as his personal property, and these underhanded dealings made it easy for his enemies to accuse him of looting and privateering.

Schliemann presented his find to the Prussian government in 1881, and Priam's Treasure went on exhibit in the Berlin Museum for Early History. For years, the treasure was considered one of the world's greatest archaeological discoveries.

Then Priam's Treasure disappeared. Toward the end of World War II, as British planes began bombing Berlin, curators removed the collection from exhibition and hid it away. In early 1945, with Allied invasion imminent, various art and archaeological treasures were dispersed to castles, mine shafts, and monasteries throughout the German countryside to avoid capture. Although many of these treasures were indeed seized by the invading Red Army, the "Treasure of Priam" simply vanished.

Several scholars-turned-sleuths tried to track the whereabouts of Schliemann's missing treasure by examining hundreds of thousands of wartime diaries, official accounts, and soldiers' letters from the front—but to no avail. For nearly five decades, not a single gold bead from Priam's Treasure surfaced. Rumors abounded: It was bombed, or melted down, or confiscated, or stolen.

Then, after the Soviet Union crumbled, in August 1993, the Russian minister of culture announced that the "Treasure of Priam" had been found in deep storage at Moscow's Pushkin Museum. It had been seized in Berlin by Soviet troops and shipped to Moscow along with other art treasures claimed as spoils of war.

There is no question that the artifacts are indeed the same ones found by the Schliemanns in 1873. Many of the objects in Russia still bear Berlin museum labels, and match pre-war catalog descriptions.

Today, museums around the world are anxious to exhibit the newly rediscovered Trojan treasure. But before any such exhibit can be planned, the issue of ownership must be resolved. Most scholars express disinterest in where the treasure is ultimately stored—so long as the artifacts are available for study by all qualified persons.

But the politicians feel otherwise. Russian Republic president Boris Yeltsin announced a willingness to discuss mutual repatriation of wartime booty and, after lengthy negotiations, the German and Russian governments promised to do their best to return artworks stolen from each other in World War II. Some Russian nationalists howled, insisting that all art treasures removed from Germany be kept as reparation for Nazi war crimes. Others point out that since Germany has many fewer Russian treasures, the Germans should pay a cash settlement to make up the difference in value.

At various times, the United Kingdom, Germany, Greece, Turkey, and Russia have all claimed the Trojan gold. As this is being written, Russia and Germany are still negotiating as to the ownership. There are some in Russia who want to establish a museum for the trophy treasures, and keep it there. If this works out to Russia's satisfaction, the gold may go on an international tour. Proposed stops include Greece, Turkey, and the United Kingdom—but, significantly, *not* Germany.

Heinrich Schliemann's 1875 illustration of the "Treasure of Priam," one of the world's greatest archaeological finds.

This plan enraged Turkish officials, who threatened to file a suit to claim the gold as their own. Because of current political animosities, the Turks don't want Priam's Treasure inside Greece. For its part, Greece is planning its exhibit in Schliemann's old home (in Athens), and it emphatically contests the Turkish claim. Repatriation claims on Priam's Treasure have also been made by heirs of Frank Calvert, Schliemann's contemporary and rival, who some consider to be "the unheralded discoverer of Troy."

Should the artifacts stay in Moscow, be returned to Germany, or go back where they were found?

Who owns the Treasure of Priam, anyway?

Archaeology Museums on the Internet:

Hotlist of Museums lists dozens of science, natural history, and other relevant institutions:
http//sln.fi.edu/tfi/hotlists/museums.html

international game of "finders–keepers." Underlying and crosscutting such intuitive dichotomies is a complex set of conflicting claims and counterclaims, sometimes between the claimants themselves.

Whose World, Whose Heritage?

There is, some feel, an encroaching sense of "pan-ism." Seeking to defend the British Museum's claim to the Elgin Marbles, the Parliamentary Assembly of the Council of Europe passed a resolution stressing "the unity of the European cultural heritage." In effect, this quickening "pan-European perspective" was employed to vindicate strictly British privilege. In their ultimately futile attempt to retain the Icelandic manuscripts, a band of Danish university lecturers had claimed that the texts were more properly viewed as a "pan-Scandinavian treasure." That the manuscripts happened to be written in Icelandic, they argued, was mere historical happenstance. Some would argue that a similar "pan-Indian" mandate is at work to justify claims in complex issues of reburial of Native American skeletal remains, and repatriation of items of cultural heritage. In each case, a covering "pan-ism" is interjected to warrant exclusive access to the past, too often ignoring the diverse and even fractious communities actually represented.

Archaeology museums are sometimes viewed as interested only in retaining their collections—getting the most artifacts and sitting on them. Such institutions need to demonstrate how the interrelated objectives of collecting, conserving, and disseminating can serve the greater public, both at home and abroad. Museums can indeed serve a global, increasingly pluralistic community, if they are willing to accept the challenge.

Most modern archaeologists reject the demand for universal repatriation; taken to their illogical extreme, these arguments would insist that every Picasso painting hang in Spain, that all of da Vinci's creations be repatriated to Italy, and that every archaeological artifact be returned to its country of origin.

The living are responsible for the dead, and the dead—often seen not as being really "dead" but as transformed, and still powerful—must be treated with respect.

THOMAS F. KING, ARCHAEOLOGIST

Suppose, as many paleoanthropologists believe, that we are all descended from a single, very early African population. If all the world's population is actually descended from one African "Eve" (as discussed in Chapter 12), do we all "own" any artifact of the human past that is more than 200,000 years old? And what would such ownership mean? Certainly not the right to go to Africa and, on our own, dig up million-year-old skulls—the African countries where such remains are found are too conscious of their importance to the history of humanity to allow most of us anywhere near them. For this reason, African nations closely control access to their ancient archaeological record. But perhaps we all have the right to make an interpretation of their meaning.

Consider the archaeological site of L'Anse au Meadows, a Viking settlement in Newfoundland, radiocarbon dated to about A.D. 900. Does L'Anse au Meadows "belong" to the Canadian people because the site is on Canadian

L'Anse au Meadows, a 1,000-year-old Viking site on the northern tip of Newfoundland (Canada).

soil? Or does the site "belong" to modern Scandinavians, whose ancestors lived there?

And what about actress Shirley MacLaine, who claims (quite sincerely from all accounts) that she's a reincarnated Inka princess. Should we seriously consider negotiating with Ms. MacLaine if she were to launch a "repatriation" claim for Inka gold held by museums?

Although some such claims are clearly frivolous or hypothetical, many are not. Some of the complex issues behind the repatriation question can be illustrated by recent legislation in the United States. In the following section, we explore some of the legal and ethical implications for Americanist archaeology.

The Surgeon General is anxious that our collection of Indian crania, already quite large, should be made as complete as possible.

MADISON MILLS, SURGEON (UNITED STATES ARMY, 1868)

Are Archaeologists Grave Robbers?

If you desecrate a white grave, you wind up sitting in prison. But desecrate an Indian grave, you get a Ph.D. The time has come for people to decide: Are we Indians part of this country's living culture or are we just here to supply museums with dead bodies?

WALTER ECHO-HAWK (PAWNEE), CIVIL RIGHTS ATTORNEY

In 1988, the Senate Select Committee on Indian Affairs was told by the American Association of Museums that 43,306 individual Native American skeletons were held in 163 United States museums. Native American representatives pointed out that although Indian people represent less than 1 percent of the U.S. population, their bones comprise more than 54 percent of the skeletal collection in the Smithsonian Institution. Many senators were shocked.

This testimony spurred the Senate into action and brought an end to decades of wrangling that pitted museums, universities, and federal agencies against Native American tribes. In 1990, Congress passed and President

What, Exactly, Is NAGPRA?

Although not widely discussed by the general public, NAGPRA resonated throughout Indian Country. Without doubt, NAGPRA is a milestone in Indian and white relations. A significant triumph for Indian people, **NAGPRA** is important human rights legislation that permits the living to exercise traditional responsibilities toward the dead. NAGPRA also rocked the world of Americanist archaeology, forever changing the way we do business.

The NAGPRA legislation:

- protects Indian graves on federal and tribal lands
- recognizes tribal authority over treatment of unmarked graves
- prohibits the commercial selling of native dead bodies
- requires an inventory and repatriation of human remains held by the federal government and institutions that receive federal funding
- requires these same institutions to return inappropriately acquired sacred objects and other important communally owned property to native owners

When addressing the issue of cultural repatriation, NAGPRA specifically defines three basic kinds of material culture:

funerary object: something placed with a human body or made to contain human remains at the time of burial

sacred objects: specific ceremonial objects necessary for current practice of traditional Native American religions

cultural patrimony: something that was once owned by the entire tribe (rather than by an individual), and thus was considered "inalienable" at the time it left the tribe's possession

NAGPRA requires that all universities and museums receiving federal money must summarize and inventory such objects. Once the items have been identified, the museum community is required to consult with appropriate Native American representatives regarding the "expeditious return" of these funerary objects, sacred materials, and items of cultural patrimony.

NAGPRA: The Native American Graves Protection and Repatriation Act of 1990, devised to protect Native American burial sites and to return certain kinds of religious materials removed from Indian land. Most Indian people view this statute as an important initial step in reversing the transgression against Native Americans over the past 500 years.

George Bush signed into law a piece of landmark legislation called the *Native American Graves Protection and Repatriation Act–NAGPRA* for short (see *What, Exactly, Is NAGPRA?*).

The new legislation has mandated an intensive and continuing interaction between museum and tribal representatives. At first, these interactions were colored with mutual mistrust and apprehension. For decades, many Native American people had felt uncomfortable visiting public museums where their cultural heritage was on display. Some Indian people saw NAGPRA as placing them on equal footing with museum and university officials. Other Native American representatives believed that NAGPRA unfairly favored the museum community, hindering native people in gaining control over materials that rightfully belong to them (and which never, in their view, should have left Indian land in the first place).

The museums, for their part, are wary of dissolving collections long held in the public trust; such behavior is contrary to every museum charter. Many museum collections contain pieces specifically commissioned for exhibit and for study purposes. Museums would argue that, far from robbing native people of their heritage, ethnographers and archaeologists attempted to preserve this heritage for the future and the common good.

After the initial period of discomfort, however, many members of both museum and tribal communities began to take a more positive view, looking on NAGPRA as a way to foster new collaboration and cooperation in the preservation of Native American traditions and scholarship. A number of repatriations have already taken place, with museum and tribal representatives working toward the common goal of "doing the right thing." A number of tribal museums have already opened, sometimes with the help and cooperation of the museum establishment.

NAGPRA on the Internet:

Repatriation and Reburial Issues are monitored here, including a legal summary, consideration of case studies, ethics codes, state laws, organizations, bibliographies, and articles:
http://www.usd.edu/anth/repat.html

NAGPRA, of course, covers not only cultural artifacts, but also human skeletal remains. Not unexpectedly, this issue has touched off considerable controversy and ill feeling. The Native American community has become deeply involved in deciding what to do about the thousands of remains that resulted from the nineteenth-century practice of collecting Indian bones and skulls. For archaeologists, NAGPRA has become one of the major cultural resource management issues of the day.

When human remains are displayed in museums or historical societies, it is never the bones of white soldiers or the first European settlers that came to this continent that are lying in glass cases. It is Indian remains. The message that this sends to the rest of the world is that Indians are culturally and physically different and inferior to non-Indians. By any definition, this is racism.

DANIEL K. INOUYE, U.S. SENATOR

Reburying the Dead

A century ago, this basic issue—esteem for the dead—underlay much of the resistance shown by native people to their forcible removal from their traditional lands. For instance, when federal troops forced Cherokee and Choctaw people to move from their southeastern U.S. homeland to Oklahoma, some families dug up and took the bones of their relatives along on the bitter Trail of Tears. The ancestral bones were reburied after arrival in Oklahoma.

At the very basic level, there is complete agreement: All archaeologists, no matter how concerned with preservation of scientific evidence, agree that the bones of known relatives should be returned to demonstrable descendants. The disagreement comes over what is "demonstrable," and the specifics of the NAGPRA legislation are still being hammered out.

Despite strong feelings on both sides of the reburial issue, Indian groups and archaeologists are beginning to define common ground here as well. Several recent cases show how this newly emergent sense of cooperation works.

Some tribes do not wish to deal directly with human remains at all. The Eastern Shoshone people on the Wind River Reservation in Wyoming do not wish their ancestral remains repatriated because they question the accuracy of museum records. The Zuni people have asked that the skeletons removed from tribal lands remain under museum curation. The Chumash people of California, while quite concerned about the issue, have also elected not to request repatriation of their tribal human remains held in museum collections.

How would you feel if your grandmother's grave were opened and the contents were shipped back east to be boxed and warehoused with 31,000 others . . . and itinerant pothunters were allowed to ransack her house in search of "artifacts" with the blessing of the U.S. government? It is sick behavior. It is un-Christian. It is punishable by law.

WILLIAM TALLBULL

To many Native Americans, the collecting of their ancestors' bones and bodies by museums is a source of pain and humiliation—the last stage of a conquest that had already robbed them of their lands and destroyed their way of life.

DOUGLAS PRESTON, AUTHOR

In one noteworthy case of cooperation, Smithsonian scientists and a delegation of Blackfeet representatives worked out a resolution for problems raised by 15 skulls sent from the Blackfeet reservation to the Army Medical College in 1892. The Blackfeet people were concerned because of the open hostilities that had existed between their ancestors and neighboring groups in the late nineteenth century. What if enemy skulls had been misidentified as Blackfeet a century ago?

In order to avoid an unacceptable mixing of spirits, they asked for assurances that only legitimate Blackfeet remains were being returned for reburial. Accordingly, bioarchaeologists at the Smithsonian conducted a battery of tests on the presumed Blackfeet remains in their collections, returning only those thought conclusively to be Blackfeet. These remains were subsequently reinterred in Montana, where a monument was erected on the Blackfeet reservation in their honor.

We don't expect everyone to share our beliefs, but it doesn't take the wisdom of Solomon to understand that our dead deserve to rest in peace. . . . All we're asking for is a little common decency. . . . We're not asking for anything but to bury our dead.

WALTER ECHO-HAWK

Considerably more controversy surrounded the case of "Buhla," accidentally discovered in 1989 during a gravel pit operation at Buhl, Idaho (hence the name). Although the lower extremities had been mostly destroyed by a rock crusher, Buhla's skull and most of the upper skeletal bones were recovered relatively intact.

In those days (before NAGPRA), this unexpected find fell under the jurisdiction of Idaho's Graves Protection Act that required notification of the state archaeologist and consultation with the appropriate local Indian group, in this case, the Shoshone-Bannock people living on the Fort Hall Indian Reservation.

The Shoshone-Bannock Tribal Council was entirely reasonable in its approach, permitting physical analysis and radiocarbon dating of the remains. The physical anthropologist studying the skeleton determined that "Buhla" was a female roughly 18 to 20 years old at death. She stood about 5 feet 2 inches tall.

But the radiocarbon evidence surprised everyone: Buhla had died roughly 10,765 years ago. Hers was one of the oldest skeletons ever found in the Americas.

It is most unpleasant work to steal bones from a grave, but what is the use, someone has to do it.

FRANZ BOAS (1858–1942), FATHER OF AMERICAN ANTHROPOLOGY

This is when the controversy arose. Tribal elders had become increasingly concerned about the lengthy time required for the analysis. At one point, a full 3 years after the bones had been discovered, Buhla's wandering, frustrated spirit was blamed for a recent death on the reservation. The Shoshone-Bannock Tribal Council insisted that the remains be immediately reburied at a secret location, and this was done.

Some archaeologists were incensed. Buhla was one of the most ancient Paleo-Indian skeletons ever found in the Americas, and she had been reburied before any detailed chemical or DNA studies could be attempted. Part of the problem was legal because, unlike NAGPRA (and most relevant state legislation), Idaho's law did not require that any degree of cultural affiliation be established between the ancient remains and the local Native American tribe. Some archaeologists questioned the authority of Shoshone-Bannock tribal members over Paleo-Indian remains. One archaeologist fumed: "[This law] certainly puts Idaho in the front ranks of anti-intellectual politicians who can't tell the difference between relatives and paleontological fossils."

Clement Meighan, then senior archaeologist at UCLA and outspoken critic of NAGPRA, went even farther, arguing that the Shoshone-Bannock people were "throwing away one of the two or three major finds in the New World. . . . [Buhla] was around 5,000 years old before the pyramids of Egypt were built, [and] repatriation is a loaded and improper term because it implies that you're giving something back to people who own it. They don't own it, and never did."

At issue here, of course, is our perception of human skeletal remains. Meighan's argument, and he is supported by a number of sympathetic archaeologists, is based on the long-standing social policy in America that emphasizes the common heritage of the citizenry. So viewed, the scientific community is responsible for understanding the human condition of all, including Indian people, ancient and living. By removing cultural materials from museums and reburying skeletal remains, selected elements of the common heritage are being removed from the public domain. A vocal minority views NAGPRA and the repatriation effort as the blatant destruction of archaeological collections. They urge archaeologists to stand up for their rights and duties as scientists. This argument holds that as scientists, archaeologists are bound to an ethical system requiring honest reporting and preservation of the evidence. Repatriation and reburial efforts are viewed as "censorship," undermining the ability of scientists to inspect the work of others for errors and misinterpretations—a procedure basic to all modern science.

Since we commonly proclaim that archaeological collections are unique and irreplaceable, how can we ever justify the conscious and acquiescent destruction of our data?

CLEMENT MEIGHAN, ARCHAEOLOGIST (UNIVERSITY OF CALIFORNIA, LOS ANGELES)

Fifty years from now, Meighan argues, people will look back at NAGPRA and condemn the archaeological and museum communities for their shortsightedness, for caving in to political and religious demands and allowing the destruction of irreplaceable scientific materials.

It is disturbing to see skeletal collections . . . reburied. From the viewpoint of a skeletal biologist this is similar to burning the books in our libraries.

WILLIAM BASS, PHYSICAL ANTHROPOLOGIST (UNIVERSITY OF TENNESSEE)

Some archaeologists share Meighan's view that human remains are vital scientific data and should be kept in the public domain. Other archaeologists—and most Indian people—feel otherwise.

Seeking Some Common Ground

Many, perhaps even most, in America's archaeological community seek to define a middle ground in the reburial and repatriation dispute. Passing judgment on anybody's values or beliefs is tricky business. But so long as people with very different religious beliefs and cultural backgrounds must coexist, some such assessment cannot be avoided. One of the key challenges for those charged with managing America's cultural resources is to find accommodation between the scientific and ethnic concerns (see *Digging Afognak*).

NAGPRA is merely one example of the worldwide concern with conflicting heritage claims and the issues of intellectual property rights. The issue revolves around ownership of the past—not just the objects of the past, but also the broader perceptions of that past. Similar questions about ownership arise from those advocating the "radical archaeology" agendas discussed earlier. Is not all "scientific," "objective" archaeology really just the imposition of Western ideals and dominant ideology upon minority people?

Scientifically oriented archaeologists respond: Suppose that we accept American Indian, Black African, or Maori views of their own past as legitimate? How then can we deny those who believe in "crackpot archaeology" or the role of ancient astronauts in creating the great monuments of the past?

Digging Afognak: Native American Archaeologists Go to Work

Storm waves, vandalism, and time itself are working to destroy the archaeological record. Dig Afognak *is part of a community-wide effort to regain, restore, and carry forward the light of our culture.*

THE ALUTIIQ PEOPLE

Shauna Lukin (Alutiiq) excavates the floor of a 600-year-old house built by her ancestors at Settlement Point, Kodiak Island (Alaska).

If you'd visit *Dig Afognak*, you would see a fairly typical archaeological field scene: people crouched over, working with trowels and tape measures. They are mapping ancient house floors and exposing long-buried depostis of trash. As on digs anywhere in the world, the archaeologists are taking notes, making maps, and carefully collecting bits of bone and stone, shell and charcoal.But if you look closer, there is one big difference between *Dig Afognak* and the typical excavation. Here, in Alaska's remote Kodiak archipelago, native people are working as equal partners with trained archaeologists, exploring continuities of Alutiiq culture, and sharing that information with others—particularly the next generation of native people.

What's in a Name? The term *Alutiiq* is today widely used as the English term for both the native people of Kodiak Island and their language.

Things have not always been rosy between the archaeologists and the Alutiiq people, however. Several Kodiak Island village elders still remember an archaeological dig in the 1930s, when a famed Smithsonian Institution anthropologist—Ales Hrdlicka (pronounced *hrr*-LICH-*ka*)—dug up one of their ancient burial grounds (which had been used for about 3,000 years until it was abandoned about A.D. 1500). Some elders, who were present during Hrdlicka's dig, still call him "hard liquor."

This was the largest single-site dig ever conducted in Alaska. Hrdlicka excavated several hundred graves and removed thousands of associated artifacts. This collection comprised more than 5 percent of the Smithsonian's holdings in physical anthropology.

From Hrdlicka's strictly scientific perspective, the Kodiak Island bones and artifacts were an important cultural resource from which anthropologists could reconstruct millennia of the cultural and biological history of Alaska's native peoples.

But the descendants of these same people were still living there, and they remember Hrdlicka as a man who respected neither the living nor the dead of Kodiak Island. The Alutiiq people did not share Hrdlicka's commitment to scientific discovery, and they deeply resented the fact that hundreds of their ancestors had been dug up and shipped more than 7,000 miles away, to be stored on the shelves of some remote museum.

This resentment simmered for decades until, in the late 1980s, the people of Kodiak Island requested that the bones and funerary objects be returned to the community for reburial.

This simple request for repatriation—which has been termed "a watershed event in the history of social science"—forced curators and archaeologists to confront the knotty ethical and moral problems inherent in their treatment of Native American burial grounds.

The Smithsonian Institution immediately refused the request, pointing to the scientific importance of the collection and questioning the relationship between the modern people of Kodiak Island and those buried in the ancient cemetery. The Tribal Council took offense at this knee-jerk response, and continued to press for return of the collection.

After years of controversy, the Smithsonian Institution eventually agreed to return several hundred human skeletons and funerary objects to the Kodiak Island peoples. In the fall of 1991, priests from the Russian Orthodox Church officiated at the reburial ceremony. Village elders sang hymns in the Alutiiq, Russian, and English languages. Leaders from the tribal council and Smithsonian Institution spoke as the remains were returned to the Kodiak soil.

This was a curious situation. On the one hand, the native community argued (successfully) for the return of archaeological and skeletal materials from the Smithsonian Institution. At the same time, however, these same villagers were encouraging and even supporting archaeological research—at the very same site.

While the repatriation struggle was going on, Amy Steffian (then a graduate student at the University of Michigan) requested permission to dig further at Hrdlicka's site. She and her colleagues argued that archaeological research could provide important clues about modern Alutiiq identity. Native community leaders not only granted her permission to excavate, but they even offered to help out with a research grant from the Kodiak Area Native Association's bingo fund.

Today, Steffian serves as curator of the Alutiiq Museum, an outgrowth of the Kodiak Area Native Association's Center and Heritage program. This program was founded in 1987 to develop an islandwide strategy of archaeological research and to promote educational programs on Alutiiq culture, language, and arts. Eight native corporations today fund and govern the Alutiiq Museum; they also oversee their own archaeological research projects, employing professional archaeologists to work with crews of native people. The Alutiiq Museum curates the resulting collections and displays key artifacts in a native-governed repository. In fact, the artifacts repatriated from Hrdlicka's excavation are today stored and available for study in the Alutiiq Museum.

The museum also provides professional and technical support to the *Dig Afognak* archaeological program, which is organized and staffed through the Afognak Native Corporation. *Dig Afognak* offers the opportunity to live and work with native people in the remote wilderness of the Kodiak archipelago, a 20-minute floatplane ride from the city of Kodiak.

Shawn Dickson (Sioux), mapping artifacts at a Russian workstation on Afognak Island (Alaska).

Dig participants live in heated platform tents, dine in a large field kitchen, and bathe in a native-style sauna. For more information on *Dig Afognak*, visit their Web site at http://www.afognak.com.

The founding of the museum and the growth of archaeological programs have produced new career opportunities for native people. Alutiiq people have long participated in local excavations and have more recently been employed as archaeological laboratory technicians. Many of the Alutiiq students involved in the archaeology program are now pursuing college degrees in history and anthropology.

Through *Dig Afognak*, Alutiiq people are participating in the administration of both an archaeological project and a major tourism venture. They have been responsible for designing the program, staffing the field camp, and conducting hands-on archaeological research.

Our hearts were deeply touched by the work of our ancestors, and we determined that we needed to take responsibility for the excavation of the many sites located on our Native lands. . . . To make the research circle complete, we decided to take the step of inviting the interested public, people like yourself, to join us as a Dig Afognak *participant.*

The Alutiiq People

In truth, the answers to such difficult questions are fundamentally political. In most countries, science is still associated with a position of moral authority. Traditionally at least, scientists have been our teachers, and most people accepted most of their statements most of the time. For the greater part of this century, the world has believed in its scientists because they can make concrete predictions and demonstrate the consequences of their conclusions.

If, however, we do not accept the basic premises upon which scientific reasoning is founded, then none of the rest is acceptable. This is the position of some Christians for whom the Bible is literally true: They know the world was created 6,000, not millions of years ago, so human evolution is quite unacceptable. Many Native American people firmly believe in their own traditions that document their eternal presence in America. They reject scientific claims that Indian people are descended from the migrants who traveled across the Bering Strait from Asia.

Ownership of the past is thus impossible to divorce from our beliefs about it and who should write about it. There can be no single answer to such questions.

Archaeology at the Millennium

Today, I suspect that many (perhaps even most) archaeologists are sympathetic to the multiple voices being heard in modern archaeology. Most would agree that it's a good thing to have increased Native American participation in national archaeology meetings (even if some don't like the specific messages being delivered). Most archaeologists are glad that, increasingly, female voices are being included in the profession, their contributions openly recognized and rewarded (although some are uncomfortable with specific views being expressed by some feminists). And I also think that the upsurge of interest in such areas as African American and Hispanic American archaeology is a vital new direction in the field. These are all important new voices in the Americanist archaeology at the millennium.

But there is a real question about the degree to which postmodern thought has penetrated the American psyche. To be sure, there is an increased level of tolerance for other opinions within the academic world of professional archaeology, the rest of social science, and the humanities. But how much of this is strictly academic fad and fancy?

As archaeology becomes increasingly inclusive, as previously disenfranchised groups are empowered and their voices heard, as power is more broadly and more democratically distributed, what is the message for the American public?

Will we continue to hear about the "death of authority"—or only the "death of *your* authority"? Will the new openness remain open, or will we experience the same old intolerance of different ideas, with only the power shifted from the traditional "haves" to the "have-nots"? The widespread call for multiple voices and diverse perspectives does not necessarily ensure tolerance for opinions that differ from one's own. Will the new inclusiveness turn out to be just a warmed-over version of the old exclusionism—dressed up in a different mix of racial, sexual, economic, and ideological dogma?

Archaeologists have special responsibilities here—not only to recover and interpret evidence of the human past, but also to ensure that the past is not used for malevolent purposes in the present. This is not an easy task because it requires that individual archaeologists balance and sort out the sometimes conflicting realities.

This, it seems, is perhaps the greatest challenge facing the archaeologists of the twenty-first century.

Don't let it end like this. Tell them I said something.

LAST WORDS OF FRANCISCO "PANCHO" VILLA (1878–1923), MEXICAN REVOLUTIONARY LEADER

SUMMARY One way or another, virtually all archaeological research depends on public support. Particularly within the last decade, responsible archaeologists have recognized the importance of returning to the public some of the benefits and insights—that is, the archaeological knowledge—that have been derived from such public support.

Although archaeology is conventionally perceived as a "pure" science, many today realize that archaeology impacts the daily life of many, and archaeologists are increasingly trying to find meaningful ways of addressing their many publics.

Some archaeologists and bioarchaeologists are involved in *forensic archaeology* by working with law enforcement officials, providing training in the recovery and analysis of material remains, and generating firsthand evidence to be presented in courts of law.

Others are involved in rediscovering and reintroducing ancient agricultural technologies. Some are trying to bring back indigenous food sources that were not only well adapted to local environments, but that stored the genetic diversity critical to develop new varieties.

"Taking archaeology public" has become an extremely important—and sometimes volatile—aspect of American archaeology at the millennium. Archaeologists increasingly find it necessary to deal with several different public sectors. Some of these are anxious to hear what the archaeologists have to say; others are less enthusiastic (and a few are downright hostile). This chapter considered the various messages implicit in the archaeology of places like the Alamo, the Californian missions, and the Bighorn Medicine Wheel.

The chapter concluded with a look at the overall issue of "Who Owns the Past?", a storyline followed throughout the book. After considering a number of international repatriation claims, we examined in some detail the impact of recent U.S. legislation addressing the relationship between archaeological research and Native American communities.

As archaeologists face the next millennium, they have increasingly important and sensitive responsibilities—not only to recover and interpret evidence of the human past, but also to ensure that the past is not used for inappropriate purposes in the present.

Bibliography

Abbott, James T., and Charles D. Frederick. 1990. Proton magnetometer investigations of burned rock middens in West-Central Texas: Clues to formation processes. *Journal of Archaeological Science* 17: 535–545.

Abrams, Elliot M. 1989. Architecture and energy: An evolutionary perspective. *Archaeological Method and Theory* 1: 47–87.

Abruzzi, William. 1982. Ecological theory and ethnic differentiation among human populations. *Current Anthropology* 23(1): 13–35.

Adams, Karen R., and Robert E. Gasser. 1980. Plant microfossils from archaeological sites: Research considerations and sampling techniques and approaches. *The Kiva* 45(4): 293–300.

Adams, William Y. 1988. Archaeological classification: Theory versus practice. *Antiquity* 62(234): 40–56.

Adams, William Y., and Ernest W. Adams. 1991. *Archaeological Typology and Practical Reality: A Dialectical Approach to Artifact Classification and Sorting.* Cambridge: Cambridge University Press.

Addington, Lucile R. 1986. *Lithic Illustration: Drawing Flaked Stone Artifacts for Publication.* Chicago: University of Chicago Press.

Adkins, Lesley, and Roy A. Adkins. 1989. *Archaeological Illustration.* Cambridge: Cambridge University Press.

Adler, Michael A. (Ed.). 1996. *The Prehistoric Pueblo World: A.D. 1150–1350.* Tucson: University of Arizona Press.

Adler, Michael A., Todd Van Pool, and Robert D. Leonard. 1996. Ancestral Pueblo population aggregation and abandonment in the North American Southwest. *Journal of World Prehistory* 10(3): 375–438.

Adovasio, J. M., and Ronald C. Carlisle. 1988. Some thoughts on cultural resource management archaeology in the United States. *Antiquity* 62(234): 72–87.

Adovasio, J. M., J. Donahue, and R. Stuckenrath. 1990. The Meadowcroft Rockshelter radiocarbon chronology 1975–1990. *American Antiquity* 55(2): 348–354.

Aitken, M. J. 1989. Luminescence dating: A guide for non-specialists. *Archaeometry* 31(2): 147–159.

———. 1990. *Science-Based Dating in Archaeology.* London: Longman.

Aldenderfer, Mark. 1993. Ritual, hierarchy, and change in foraging societies. *Journal of Anthropological Archaeology* 12(1): 1–40.

Allen, K. M. S., S. W. Green, and E. B. W. Zubrow (Eds.). 1990. *Interpreting Space: GIS and Archaeology.* London: Taylor and Francis.

Allen, Susan Heuck. 1995, May/June. In Schliemann's shadow: Frank Calvert, the unheralded discoverer of Troy. *Archaeology* 48(3): 50–57.

Ambler, J. Richard. 1989. *The Anasazi: Prehistoric People of the Four Corners Region.* 4th ed. Flagstaff: Museum of Northern Arizona Press.

Ambrose, W. R. 1976. Intrinsic hydration rate dating of obsidian. In R. E. Taylor (Ed.), *Advances in Obsidian Glass Studies* (pp. 81–105). Park Ridge, NJ: Noyes Press.

Ammerman, A. J. 1981. Surveys and archaeological research. *Annual Review of Anthropology* 10: 63–88.

Anderson, E. N. 1995. Keeping the anthropological bird aloft. *Anthropology Newsletter* 36(9): 2.

Anderson, James E. 1965. Human skeletons from Tehuacan. *Science* 148: 496–497.

Andresen, John M., Brian F. Byrd, Mark D. Elson, Randall H. McGuire, Ruben G. Mendoza, Edward Staski, and J. Peter White. 1981. The deer hunters: Star Carr reconsidered. *World Archaeology* 13(1): 31–46.

Anon. 1989. Archeology and the Oklahoma City Police Training Academy. *Newsletter, Oklahoma Archeological Survey* 8(4): 1.

Anon. 1992, April. Idaho chucks oldest American. *American Committee for Preservation of Archaeological Collections, Newsletter:* 1.

Anon. 1995a, November 19. A little green shoot sprouts from a seed 1,288 years old. *The New York Times.*

Anon. 1995b, September 1. DNA identified Czar's bones. *The Richmond Times Dispatch.*

Anon. 1996. *Annual Report.* Santa Fe: School of American Research.

Anyon, Roger, and T. J. Ferguson. 1995. Cultural resources management at the Pueblo of Zuni, New Mexico, USA. *Antiquity* 69: 913–930.

Arden, H. 1989. Who owns our past? *National Geographic Magazine* 175(3): 376–392.

Arnold, Bettina. 1992, July/August. The past as propaganda. *Archaeology* 45(4): 30–37.

Arnold, Jeanne E. 1993. Labor and the rise of complex hunter-gatherers. *Journal of Anthropological Archaeology* 12(1): 75–119.

Ascher, Robert, and Charles H. Fairbanks. 1971. Excavation of a slave cabin: Georgia, U.S.A. *Historical Archaeology* 5: 3–17.

Ashmore, Wendy, and Robert J. Sharer. 1995. *Discovering Our Past: A Brief Introduction to Archaeology.* 2d ed. Mountain View, CA: Mayfield Publishing.

Avery, T. E., and T. R. Lyons. 1981. *Remote Sensing: Aerial and Terrestrial Photography for Archaeologists.* Washington, DC: National Park Service, Supplement 7.

Babcock, Barbara A. 1982. Ritual undress and the comedy of self and other: Bandelier's *The Delight Makers.* In Jay Ruby (Ed.), *A Crack in the Mirror: Reflexive Perspectives in Anthropology* (pp. 187–203). Philadelphia: University of Philadelphia Press.

Babcock, Barbara A., and Nancy J. Parezo. 1988. *Daughters of the Desert: Women Anthropologists and the Native American Southwest 1880–1980.* Albuquerque: University of New Mexico Press.

Bacus, Elisabeth A., Alex W. Barker, Jeffrey D. Bonevich, Sandra L. Dunavan, J. Benjamin Fitzhugh, Debra L. Gold, Nurit S. Goldman-Finn, William Griffin, and Karen M. Mudar (Eds.). 1993. *A Gendered Past: A Critical Bibliography of Gender in Archaeology.* Technical Report 25. Ann Arbor: University of Michigan, Museum of Anthropology.

Bahn, Paul G. 1987. Getting blood from stone tools. *Nature* 330: 14.

———. 1989. *Bluff Your Way in Archaeology.* London: Ravette Books Limited.

——— (Ed.). 1992. *Collins Dictionary of Archaeology.* Glasgow: HarperCollins Publishers.

Baillie, M. G. L. 1995. *A Slice Through Time: Dendrochronology and Precision Dating.* London: Batsford.

Bamforth, Douglas B. 1986. A comment on "functional variability in an assemblage of endscrapers." *Lithic Technology* 15: 61–64.

Bamforth, Douglas B., and Albert C. Spaulding. 1982. Human behavior, explanation, archaeology, history, and science. *Journal of Anthropological Archaeology* 1(2): 179–195.

Bandelier, Adolph. 1883. A visit to the aboriginal ruins in the Valley of the Rio Pecos. *Papers of the Archaeological Institute of America* (American Series) 1(2): 34–133.

———. [1890] 1971. *The Delight Makers: A Novel of Prehistoric Pueblo Indians.* San Diego: Harcourt Brace Jovanovich.

———. 1890. Final report of investigations among the Indians of the Southwestern United States, carried on mainly in the years from 1880 to 1885, Part I. *Papers of the Archaeological Institute of America* (American Series III). Cambridge, MA.

———. 1892. Final report of investigations among the Indians of the Southwestern United States, carried on mainly in the years from 1880 to 1885, Part II. *Papers of the Archaeological Institute of America* (American Series IV). Cambridge, MA.

———. 1966. *The southwestern journals of Adolph F. Bandelier, 1880–1882.* Edited and annotated by Charles H. Lange and Carroll Riley. Albuquerque: University of New Mexico Press.

———. 1975. *The southwestern journals of Adolph F. Bandelier, 1885–1888.* Edited and annotated by Charles H. Lange, Carroll Riley, and Elisabeth M. Lange. Albuquerque: University of New Mexico Press.

Bandelier, Adolph, and Edgar L. Hewett. 1937. *Indians of the Rio Grande Valley.* Albuquerque: University of New Mexico Press.

Banning, E. B., and L. A. Pavlish. 1978. Direct detection in radiocarbon dating. *Journal of Field Archaeology.* 5(4): 480–483.

Bannister, Bryant. 1962. The interpretation of tree-ring dates. *American Antiquity* 27(4): 508–514.

———. 1970. Dendrochronology. In Don Brothwell and Eric Higgs (Eds.), *Science in Archaeology: A Survey of Progress and Research.* 2d ed. (pp. 191–205). New York: Praeger.

Bannister, Bryant, and William J. Robinson. 1975. Tree-ring dating in archaeology. *World Archaeology* 7(2): 210–225.

Bapty, Ian, and Tim Yates (Eds.). 1990. *Archaeology After Structuralism: Post-Structuralism and the Practice of Archaeology.* London and New York: Routledge.

Barbour, Warren T. D. 1994, Spring. Musings on a dream deferred. *Federal Archaeology Report:* 12–13.

Barker, Leo R., and Julia Costello (Eds.). 1992. *The Archaeology of Alta California.* New York: Garland Publishing.

Barnett, William K., and John W. Hoopes (Eds.). 1995. *The Emergence of Pottery: Technology and Innovation in Ancient Societies.* Washington, DC: Smithsonian Institution Press.

Beaudry, Mary C. (Ed.). 1988. *Documentary Archaeology in the New World.* Cambridge: Cambridge University Press.

Beck, Charlotte (Ed.). 1994. *Dating in Exposed and Surface Contexts.* Albuquerque: University of New Mexico Press.

Beck, Lane Anderson (Ed.). 1995. *Regional Approaches to Mortuary Analysis.* New York: Plenum Press.

Behrensmeyer, Anna K., and Susan M. Kidwell. 1985. Taphonomy's contributions to paleobiology. *Paleobiology* 11(1): 105–119.

Bell, James A. 1994. *Reconstructing Prehistory: Scientific Method in Archaeology.* Philadelphia: Temple University Press.

Bender, Barbara. 1975. *Farming in Prehistory.* New York: St. Martin's Press.

———. 1978. Gatherer-hunter to farmer: A social perspective. *World Archaeology* 10(2): 204–222.

———. 1993. Cognitive archaeology and cultural materialism. *Cambridge Archaeological Journal* 3(2): 257–260.

Benditt, J. 1989. Molecular archaeology: DNA from a 7,000-year-old brain opens new vistas in prehistory. *Scientific American* 261: 25–26.

Benedict, Ruth. 1948. Anthropology and the humanities. *American Anthropologist* 50(4, part 1): 585–593.

Bennett, C. L., R. P. Beukens, M. R. Clover, H. E. Gove, R. B. Liebert, A. E. Litherland, K. H. Purser, and W. E. Sondheim. 1977. Radiocarbon dating using electrostatic accelerators: Negative ions provide the key. *Science* 198: 508–510.

Berger, R. 1979. Radiocarbon dating with accelerators. *Journal of Archaeological Science* 6: 101–104.

Berlo, Janet Catherine. 1993. Review of *What This Awl Means* by Janet D. Spector. *American Indian Culture and Research Journal* 17(3): 244–248.

Betancourt, Julio L., Thomas R. Van Devender, and Paul S. Martin (Eds.). 1990. *Packrat Middens: The Last 40,000 Years of Biotic Change.* Tucson: University of Arizona Press.

Bettinger, Robert L. 1980. Explanatory/predictive models of hunter-gatherer adaptation. In Michael B. Schiffer (Ed.), *Advances in Archaeological Method and Theory.* Vol. 3 (pp. 189–255). New York: Academic Press.

———. 1987. Archaeological approaches to hunter-gatherers. *Annual Review of Anthropology* 16: 121–142.

———. 1991. *Hunter-Gatherers: Archaeological and Evolutionary Theory.* New York: Plenum Press.

Bevan, Bruce W. 1983. Electromagnetics for mapping buried earth features. *Journal of Field Archaeology* 10(1): 47–54.

Bevan, Bruce W., and J. Kenyon. 1975. Ground-penetrating radar for historical archaeology. *MASCA Newsletter* 11(2): 2–7.

Bevan, Bruce W., David G. Orr, and Brooke S. Blades. 1984. The discovery of the Taylor house at the Petersburg National Battlefield. *Historical Archaeology* 18(2): 64–74.

Bigham, Gary N. 1973. Zone of influence—Inner continental shelf of Georgia. *Journal of Sedimentary Petrology* 43(1): 207–214.

Binford, Lewis R. 1962a. A new method of calculating dates from kaolin pipe stem samples. *Southeastern Archaeological Conference Newsletter* 9(2): 19–21.

———. 1962b. Archeology as anthropology. *American Antiquity* 28: 217–225.

———. 1964. A consideration of archaeological research design. *American Antiquity* 29(4): 425–441.

———. 1965. Archaeological systematics and the study of cultural process. *American Antiquity* 31(2): 203–210.

———. 1967. Smudge pits and hide smoking: The use of analogy in archaeological reasoning. *American Antiquity* 32(1): 1–12.

———. 1968a. Archeological perspectives. In Sally R. Binford and Lewis R. Binford (Eds.), *New Perspectives in Archeology* (pp. 5–32). Chicago: Aldine.

———. 1968b. Post-Pleistocene adaptations. In Sally R. Binford and Lewis R. Binford (Eds.), *New Perspectives in Archeology* (pp. 313–341). Chicago: Aldine.

———. 1968c. Some comments on historical versus processual archaeology. *Southwestern Journal of Anthropology* 24(3): 267–275.

———. 1972a. *An Archaeological Perspective.* New York: Seminar Press.

———. 1972b. The "Binford" pipe stem formula: A return from the grave. *The Conference on Historic Site Archaeology Papers* 6: 230–253.

———. 1973. Interassemblage variability—The Mousterian and the "functional" argument. In Colin Renfrew (Ed.), *The Explanation of Culture Change: Models in Prehistory* (pp. 227–254). London: Duckworth.

———. 1977a. Foreword to *Method and Theory in Historical Archeology,* by Stanley South. New York: Academic Press.

——— (Ed.). 1977b. *For Theory Building in Archaeology.* New York: Academic Press.

———. 1978a. Dimensional analysis of behavior and site structure: Learning from an Eskimo hunting stand. *American Antiquity* 43(3): 330–361.

———. 1978b. *Nunamiut Ethnoarchaeology.* New York: Academic Press.

———. 1980. Willow smoke and dogs' tails: Hunter-gatherer settlement systems and archaeological site formation. *American Antiquity* 45(1): 4–20.

———. 1981. *Bones: Ancient Men and Modern Myths.* New York: Academic Press.

———. 1982. The archaeology of place. *Journal of Anthropological Archaeology* 1(1): 5–31.

———. 1983a. *In Pursuit of the Past: Decoding the Archaeological Record.* London: Thames and Hudson.

——— (Ed.). 1983b. *Working at Archaeology.* New York: Academic Press.

———. 1984. *Faunal Remains From Klasies River Mouth.* Orlando, FL: Academic Press.

———. 1986. An Alyawara day: Making men's knives and beyond. *American Antiquity* 51(3): 547–562.

———. 1987a. Data, relativism, and archaeological science. *Man* 22(3): 391–404.

———. 1987b. Researching ambiguity: Frames of reference and site structure. In Susan Kent (Ed.), *Method and Theory for Activity Area Research: An Ethnoarchaeological Approach* (pp. 449–512). New York: Columbia University Press.

———. 1989a. *Debating Archaeology.* San Diego: Academic Press.

———. 1989b. Science to seance, or processual to "post-processual" archaeology. In *Debating Archaeology* (pp. 27–40). San Diego: Academic Press.

———. 1989c. Review of Hodder, *Reading the Past: Current Approaches to Interpretation in Archaeology.* In *Debating Archaeology* (pp. 69–71). San Diego: Academic Press.

Binford, Lewis R., Sally R. Binford, Robert Whallon, and Margaret Ann Hardin. 1970. *Archaeology at Hatchery West.* Memoirs of the Society for American Archaeology, no. 24. Washington, DC: Society for American Archaeology.

Binford, Lewis R., and James F. O'Connell. 1984. An Alyawara day: The stone quarry. *Journal of Anthropological Research* 40(3): 406–432.

Binford, Lewis R., and J. A. Sabloff. 1982. Paradigms, systematics, and archaeology. *Journal of Anthropological Research.* 38(2): 137–153.

Binford, Sally R., and Lewis R. Binford (Eds.). 1968. *New Perspectives in Archeology.* Chicago: Aldine.

Bingham, Hiram. 1914. Bandelier. *The Nation* 98(2543, March 26): 328–329.

Bintliff, John. 1991. Post-modernism, rhetoric, and scholasticism at TAG: The current state of British archaeological theory. *Antiquity* 65(247): 274–278.

———. 1993. Why Indiana Jones is smarter than the post-processualists. *Norwegian Archaeological Review* 26(2): 91–100.

Bird, Junius. 1980. Comments on sifters, sifting, and sorting procedures. In Martha Joukowsky, *A Complete Manual of Field Archaeology* (pp. 165–170). Englewood Cliffs, NJ: Prentice Hall.

Blakey, Michael L. 1995. Race, nationalism, and the Afrocentric past. In *Making Alternative Histories: The Practice of Archaeology and History in Non-Western Settings* (pp. 213–228). Santa Fe, NM: School of American Research Press.

Blanton, Dennis B. 1995. The case for CRM training in academic institutions: The many faces of CRM. *Bulletin of the Society for American Archaeology* 13(4): 40–41.

Blanton, Richard E. 1976. The role of symbiosis in adaptation and sociocultural change in the Valley of Mexico. In Eric R. Wolf (Ed.), *The Valley of*

Mexico: Studies in Pre-Hispanic Ecology and Society (pp. 181–201). Albuquerque: University of New Mexico Press.

———. 1978. *Monte Albán: Settlement Patterns at the Ancient Zapotec Capital.* New York: Academic Press.

Blanton, Richard E., Gary M. Feinman, Stephen A. Kowalewski, and Peter N. Peregrine. 1996. A dual-processual theory for the evolution of Mesoamerican civilization. *Current Anthropology* 37(1): 1–14.

Blegen, Carl. 1963. *Troy and the Trojans.* London: Frederick A. Praeger.

Boakyewa, Ama Badu. 1995, January 1. African Burial Ground and Five Points Archaeological Projects. Press release. Office of Public Education and Information, African Burial Ground.

Boas, Franz. [1888] 1940. *Race, Language and Culture.* New York: Macmillan.

Bocquet-Appel, J., and C. Masset. 1982. Farewell to paleodemography. *Journal of Human Evolution* 11: 321–333.

Bohannan, Paul. 1965. *Social Anthropology.* New York: Holt, Rinehart and Winston.

Bohannan, Paul, and Mark Glazer (Eds.). 1988. *High Points in Anthropology.* 2d ed. New York: Knopf.

Bonde, Niels, and Arne Emil Christensen. 1993. Dendrochronological dating of the Viking Age ship burials at Oseberg, Gokstad, and Tune, Norway. *Antiquity* 67: 575–583.

Bonnichsen, Robson, and Alan L. Schneider. 1995, May/June. Ancient hair, and the DNA embedded in it, might reveal when and how the Americas were settled—but not if some Native Americans can help it. *The Sciences*: 27–31.

Bonnichson, Jim. 1990. Studying ancient American DNA. *Mammoth Trumpet* 6 (1): 1,3,6.

Borofsky, Robert (Ed.). 1994. *Assessing Cultural Anthropology.* New York: McGraw-Hill.

Boserup, Ester. 1965. *Conditions of Agricultural Growth; the Economics of Agrarian Change Under Population Pressure.* Chicago: Aldine.

Bowman, Sheridan. 1990. *Radiocarbon Dating.* Berkeley: University of California Press.

———. 1994. Using radiocarbon: An update. *Antiquity* 68(261): 838–843.

Boyd, Mark F., Hale G. Smith, and John W. Griffin. 1951. *Here They Once Stood: The Tragic End of the Apalachee Missions.* Gainesville: University of Florida Press.

Boyd, Robert, and Peter J. Richerson. 1985. *Culture and the Evolutionary Process.* Chicago: University of Chicago Press.

Braidwood, Robert J. 1959. Archeology and the evolutionary theory. In *Evolution and Anthropology: A Centennial Appraisal* (pp. 76–89). Washington, DC: Anthropological Society of Washington.

Braun, David P. 1985. Absolute seriation: A time-series approach. In Christopher Carr (Ed.), *For Concordance in Archaeological Analysis: Bridging Data Structure, Quantitative Technique, and Theory* (pp. 509–539). Kansas City, MO: Westport.

Bray, Tamara L., and Thomas W. Killion (Eds.). 1994. *Reckoning With the Dead: The Larsen Bay Repatriation and the Smithsonian Institution.* Washington, DC: Smithsonian Institution Press.

Bray, Warwick. 1990. Agricultural renascence in the high Andes. *Nature* 345(6274): 385.

Brear, Holly Breachley. 1995. *Inherit the Alamo: Myth and Ritual at an American Shrine.* Austin: University of Texas Press.

Brew, John Otis. 1946. Archaeology of Alkali Ridge, Southeastern Utah. *Papers of the Peabody Museum of American Archaeology and Ethnology,* no. 21.

Brewer, Douglas J. 1992. Zooarchaeology: Method, theory, and goals. In M. B. Schiffer (Ed.), *Archaeological Method and Theory.* Vol. 4 (pp. 195–244). Tucson: University of Arizona Press.

Brigham, Clarence S. 1937. Clarence Bloomfield Moore. *Proceedings of the American Antiquarian Society* (1936) 46: 13–14.

Brody, J. J. 1990. *The Anasazi: Ancient Indian People of the American Southwest.* New York: Rizzoli.

———. 1991. *Anasazi and Pueblo Painting.* Albuquerque: University of New Mexico Press.

Bronitsky, G. (Ed.). 1989. *Pottery Technology: Ideas and Approaches.* Boulder, CO: Westview Press.

Brooks, A. S., P. E. Hare, J. E. Kokis, G. H. Miller, R. D. Ernst, and F. Wendorf. 1990. Dating Pleistocene archeological sites by protein diagenesis in ostrich eggshell. *Science* 248: 60–64.

Browman, David L. 1981. Isotopic discrimination and correction factors in radiocarbon dating. In Michael B. Schiffer (Ed.), *Advances in Archaeological Method and Theory.* Vol. 6 (pp. 241–295). New York: Academic Press.

Browman, David L., and Douglas R. Givens. 1996. Stratigraphic excavation: The first "new archaeology." *American Anthropologist* 98(1): 1–17.

Brown, Ian W. 1978. James Alfred Ford: The man and his works. *Southeastern Archaeological Conference,* Special Publication no. 4.

Brown, James A. 1976. The Southern cult reconsidered. *Midcontinental Journal of Archaeology* 1(2): 115–135.

Brown, Peter Lancaster. 1976. *Megaliths, Myths and Men: An Introduction to Astroarchaeology.* New York: Harper & Row.

Brown, Shelby. 1993. Feminist research in archaeology: What does it mean? Why is it taking so long? In Nancy Sorkin Rabinowitz and Amy Richlin (Eds.), *Feminist Theory and the Classics* (pp. 238–271). New York: Routledge.

Brown, Terence A., R. G. Allaby, K. A. Brown, and M. K. Jones. 1993. Biomolecular archaeology of wheat: Past, present and future. *World Archaeology* 25(1): 64–73.

Brown, Terence A., and Keri A. Brown. 1992. Ancient DNA and the archaeologist. *Antiquity* 66(250): 10–23.

Brumfiel, Elizabeth M. 1996. The quality of tribute cloth: The place of evidence in archaeological argument. *American Antiquity* 61(3): 453–462.

Bruner, Edward M. 1994. Abraham Lincoln as authentic reproduction: A critique of postmodernism. *American Anthropologist* 96(2): 397–415.

Bryant, Vaughn M., Jr., and Stephen A. Hall. 1993. Archaeological palynology in the United States: A critique. *American Antiquity* 58(2): 277–286.

Bryant, Vaughn M., Jr., and Richard G. Holloway. 1983. The role of palynology in archaeology. In Michael B. Schiffer (Ed.), *Advances in Archaeological Method and Theory.* Vol. 6 (pp. 191–224). New York: Academic Press.

Buck, Bruce A. 1982. Ancient technology in contemporary surgery. *The Western Journal of Medicine* 136: 265–269.

Buikstra, Jane E., and Della C. Cook. 1980. Paleopathology: An American account. *Annual Review of Anthropology* 9: 433–470.

Buikstra, Jane E., and L. Konigsberg. 1985. Paleodemography: Critiques and controversies. *American Anthropologist* 87: 316–333.

Buikstra, Jane E., and James H. Mielke. 1985. Demography, diet, and health. In Robert I. Gilbert, Jr., and James H. Mielke (Eds.), *The Analysis of Prehistoric Diets* (pp. 359–422). New York: Academic Press.

Burch, Ernest S., Jr., and Linda J. Ellanna (Eds.). 1994. *Key Issues in Hunter-Gatherer Research.* Oxford: Berg Publishers.

Burger, Richard L. 1992. *Chavín and the Origins of Andean Civilization.* London: Thames and Hudson.

Burger, Richard L., and Nikolaas J. van der Merwe. 1990. Maize and the origin of highland Chavín civilization: An isotopic perspective. *American Anthropologist* 92: 85–95.

Burgh, Robert F. 1950. Comment on Taylor's *A Study of Archeology. American Anthropologist* 52(1): 114–117

Buurman, Janneke, and Jan Peter Pals. 1994. Palaeoethnobotany: What's in a name? Review of "Phytoarchaeology" by Robert R. Brooks and Dieter Johannes; "New light on early farming" by Jane M. Renfrew; and "Progress in Old World palaeoethnobotany" ed. by Willem van Zeist, Krystyna Wasylikowa, and Karl-Ernst Behre. *Antiquity* 68:471–473.

Butzer, Karl W. 1982. *Archaeology as Human Ecology: Method and Theory for a Contextual Approach.* Cambridge: Cambridge University Press.

Calder, William M., III, and David A. Traill. 1986. *Myth, Scandal, and History: The Heinrich Schliemann Controversy and a First Edition of the Mycenaean Diary.* Detroit: Wayne State University Press.

Caldwell, Joseph. 1959. The new American archaeology. *Science* 129(3345): 303–307.

Carbone, Victor A., and Bennie C. Keel. 1985. Preservation of plant and animal remains. In Robert I. Gilbert and James H. Mielke (Eds.), *The Analysis of Prehistoric Diets* (pp. 1–19). New York: Academic Press.

Carmichael, David L., Jane Hubert, Brian Reeves, and Audhild Schanche (Eds.). 1994. *Sacred Sites, Sacred Places.* One World Archaeology, vol 23. London: Routledge.

Carneiro, Robert L. 1970a. A quantitative law in anthropology. *American Antiquity* 35(4): 492–494.

———. 1970b. A theory of the origin of the state. *Science* 169: 733–738.

———. 1973a. Classical evolution. In Raoul Naroll and Frada Naroll (Eds.), *Main Currents in Cultural Anthropology* (pp. 57–121). Englewood Cliffs, NJ: Prentice Hall.

———. 1973b. The four faces of evolution: Unilinear, universal, multilinear, and differential. In John J. Honigmann (Ed.), *Handbook of Social and Cultural Anthropology.* Chicago: Rand McNally.

———. 1988. The circumscription theory: Challenge and response. *American Behavioral Scientist* 31(4): 497–511.

———. 1992. The role of natural selection in the evolution of culture. *Cultural Dynamics* 5(2): 113–140.

———. 1995. Godzilla meets new age anthropology: Facing the post-modernist challenge to a science of culture. *Europaea* 1(1): 3–22.

Carney, Heath J., Michael W. Binford, Alan L. Kolata, Ruben R. Marin, and Charles R. Goldman. 1993. Nutrient and sediment retention in Andean raised-field agriculture. *Nature* 364: 131–133.

Carpenter, Edmund. 1991. Repatriation policy and the Heye Collection. *Museum Anthropology* 15(3): 15–18.

Carr, Christopher. 1977. A new role and analytical design for the use of resistivity surveying in archaeology. *Mid-Continental Journal of Archaeology* 2(2): 161–193.

———. 1982. *Handbook on Soil Resistivity Surveying: Interpretation of Data From Earthen Archaeological Sites.* Evanston, IL: Center for American Archeology Press.

Carr, Christopher, and Jill E. Neitzel (Eds.). 1995. *Style, Society, and Person: Archaeological and Ethnological Perspectives.* New York: Plenum Press.

Carrithers, Michael. 1990. Is anthropology art or science? *Current Anthropology* 31(3): 263–282.

———. 1992. *Why Humans Have Culture: Explaining Anthropology and Social Diversity.* Oxford: Oxford University Press.

Cashdan, Elizabeth (Ed.). 1990. *Risk and Uncertainty in Tribal and Peasant Economies.* Boulder, CO: Westview Press.

Casteel, Richard W. 1977. Characterization of faunal assemblages and the minimum number of individuals determined from paired elements: Continuing problems in archaeology. *Journal of Archaeological Science* 4(2): 125–134.

Ceram, C. W. 1971. *The First American: A Story of North American Archaeology.* New York: Harcourt Brace Jovanovich.

Cerroni-Long, E. L. 1996. Human science. *Anthropology Newsletter* 37(1): 50, 52.

Chaffee, Scott D., Marian Hyman, Marvin W. Rowe, Nancy J. Coulam, Alan Schroedl, and Kathleen Hogue. 1994. Radiocarbon dates on the All American Man pictograph. *American Antiquity* 59(4): 769–781.

Chaplin, R. E. 1971. *The Study of Animal Bones From Archaeological Sites.* London: Seminar Press.

Chase, A. F., D. Z. Chase, and H. W. Topsey. 1988. Archaeology and the ethics of collecting. *Archaeology* 41(1): 56–60, 87.

Chase, J. Smeaton. 1913. *California Coast Trails: A Horseback Ride From Mexico to Oregon.* Boston: Houghton Mifflin.

Childe, V. Gordon. 1951a. *Man Makes Himself.* New York: New American Library.

———. 1951b. *Social Evolution.* New York: Henry Schuman.

Chippindale, Christopher. 1993. Ambition, deference, discrepancy, consumption: The intellectual background of a post-processual archaeology. In Norman Yoffee and Andrew Sherratt (Eds.), *Archaeological Theory: Who Sets the Agenda?* (pp. 27–36). Cambridge: Cambridge University Press.

Christenson, Andrew L. 1989. *Tracing Archaeology's Past: The Historiography of Archaeology.* Carbondale: Southern Illinois University Press.

Church, Tim. 1994. *Lithic Resource Studies: A Sourcebook for Archaeologists.* Special Publication no. 3. Lithic Technology. Department of Anthropology, University of Tulsa, Oklahoma.

Claassen, Cheryl (Ed.). 1992. *Exploring Gender Through Archaeology: Selected Papers From the 1991 Boone Conference.* Monographs in World Archaeology, no. 11. Madison, WI: Prehistory Press.

———. 1994. *Women in Archaeology.* Philadelphia: University of Pennsylvania Press.

Clark, Anthony. 1990. *Seeing Beneath the Soil: Prospecting Methods in Archaeology.* London: Batsford.

Clark, Donavan L. 1964. Archaeological chronology in California and the obsidian hydration method: Part 1. *Archaeological Survey Annual Report* (pp. 139–225). Los Angeles: University of California.

Clark, J. D. G. 1954. *Excavations at Star Carr, an Early Mesolithic Site at Seamer, Near Scarborough, Yorkshire.* Cambridge: Cambridge University Press.

———. 1972. Star Carr: A case study in bioarchaeology. *McCaleb Module in Anthropology,* no. 10. Reading, MA: Addison-Wesley Modular Publications.

Clarke, David L. 1968. *Analytical Archaeology.* London: Methuen.

———. 1972. Archaeology: The loss of innocence. *Antiquity* 47: 6–18.

———. 1979. *Analytical Archaeologist: Collected Papers of David L. Clarke.* Edited by his colleagues. New York: Academic Press.

Cleere, Henry (Ed.). 1989. *Archaeological Heritage Management in the Modern World.* London: Unwin Hyman.

———. 1993. Managing the archaeological heritage. *Antiquity* 67: 400–402.

Clifford, James. 1988. *The Predicament of Culture: Twentieth Century Ethnography, Literature, and Art.* Cambridge: Harvard University Press.

Clifford, James, and George E. Marcus (Eds.). 1986. *Writing Culture: The Poetics and Politics of Ethnography.* Berkeley: University of California Press.

Cobb, Charles R. 1993. Archaeological approaches to the political economy of nonstratified societies. In M. B. Schiffer (Ed.), *Archaeological Method and Theory.* Vol. 5 (pp. 43–100). Tucson: University of Arizona Press.

Cohen, Mark Nathan. 1977. *The Food Crisis in Prehistory: Overpopulation and the Origins of Agriculture.* New Haven: Yale University Press.

———. 1981. The ecological basis of New World state formation: General and local model building. In Grant D. Jones and Robert R. Kautz (Eds.), *The Transition to Statehood in the New World* (pp. 105–122). Cambridge: Cambridge University Press.

Cohen, Mark Nathan, and George J. Armelagos (Eds.). 1984. *Paleopathology at the Origins of Agriculture.* Orlando, FL: Academic Press.

Coles, John M. 1973. *Archaeology by Experiment.* New York: Scribner's.

Colley, Sarah M. 1990. The analysis and interpretation of archaeological fish remains. In M. B. Schiffer (Ed.), *Archaeological Method and Theory.* Vol. 2 (pp. 207–253). Tucson: University of Arizona Press.

Collingwood, Robin George. 1939. *An Autobiography.* Oxford: Oxford University Press.

Conkey, Margaret W. 1980. The identification of prehistoric hunter-gatherer aggregation sites: The case of Altamira. *Current Anthropology* 21(5): 609–630.

———. 1982. Boundedness in art and society. In Ian Hodder (Ed.), *Symbolic and Structural Archaeology* (pp. 115–128). Cambridge: Cambridge University Press.

———. 1991. Does it make a difference? Feminist thinking and archaeologies of gender. In *The Archaeology of Gender* (pp. 24–33). Proceedings of the 22nd Annual Chacmool Conference. Calgary: University of Calgary Archaeological Association.

Conkey, Margaret W., and Joan M. Gero. 1991. Tensions, pluralities, and engendering archaeology: An introduction to women and prehistory. In Joan M. Gero and Margaret W. Conkey (Eds.), *Engendering Archaeology: Women and Prehistory* (pp. 3–30). Oxford: Basil Blackwell.

Conkey, Margaret W., and Christine A. Hastorf (Eds.). 1990. *The Uses of Style in Archaeology.* Cambridge: Cambridge University Press.

Conkey, Margaret W., and Janet Spector. 1984. Archaeology and the study of gender. In Michael B. Schiffer (Ed.), *Advances in Archaeological Method and Theory.* Vol. 7 (pp. 1–38). Orlando, FL: Academic Press.

Connor, Melissa. 1996. The archaeology of contemporary mass graves. *Bulletin of the Society of American Archaeology* 14(4): 6, 31.

Conrad, Geoffrey W. 1981. Cultural materialism, split inheritance, and the expansion of ancient Peruvian empires. *American Antiquity* 46(1): 3–26.

Conrad, Geoffrey W., and Arthur A. Demarest. 1984. *Religion and Empire: The Dynamics of Aztec and Inca Expansionism.* Cambridge: Cambridge University Press.

Conyers, Lawrence B. 1995. The use of ground-penetrating radar to map the buried structures and landscape of the Ceren site, El Salvador. *Geoarchaeology* 10(4): 275–299.

Cook, Karen. 1993. Bones of contention. *The Village Voice* 38(18): 23–27.

Cook, Robert E. 1981. Pin cherry perceptions. *Natural History Magazine* 90(11): 96–102.

Cook, S. F., and Robert F. Heizer. 1965. Studies on the chemical analysis of archaeological sites. *University of California Publications in Anthropology,* Vol. 2.

Cordell, Linda S. 1984. *Prehistory of the Southwest.* Orlando, FL: Academic Press.

———. 1994. *Ancient Pueblo Peoples.* Montreal: St. Remy Press; Washington, DC: Smithsonian Books.

Cornwall, I. W. 1956. *Bones for the Archaeologist.* London: Phoenix House.

Costin, Cathy Lynne, and Timothy Earle. 1989. Status distinction and legitimation of power as reflected in changing patterns of consumption in late prehispanic Peru. *American Antiquity* 54(4): 691–714

Cotter, John L. 1994. Beginnings. In Stanley South (Ed.), *Pioneers in Historical Archaeology: Breaking New Ground* (pp. 15–25). New York: Plenum Press.

Cotterell, Brian, and Johan Kamminga. 1990. *Mechanics of Pre-Industrial Technology.* Cambridge: Cambridge University Press.

Courty, M. A., P. Goldberg, and R. Macphail. 1989. *Soils and Micromorphology in Archaeology.* Cambridge: Cambridge University Press.

Cowan, C. Wesley, and Patty Jo Watson (Eds.). 1992. *The Origins of Agriculture: An International Perspective.* Washington, DC: Smithsonian Institution Press.

Cowgill, George L. 1975a. On the causes and consequences of ancient and modern population changes. *American Anthropologist* 77: 505–525.

———. 1975b. Population pressure as a non-explanation. In A. Swelund (Ed.), *Population Studies in Archaeology and Biological Anthropology: A Symposium* (pp. 127–131). *Society of American Archaeology Memoir,* no. 33.

———. 1988. Comment on "Ecological theory and cultural evolution in the Valley of Oaxaca" by William T. Sanders and Deborah L. Nichols. *Current Anthropology* 29(1): 54–55.

Crabtree, Don E. 1966. A stoneworker's approach to analyzing and replicating the Lindenmeier Folsom. *Tebiwa* 9: 3–39.

———. 1968. Mesoamerican polyhedral cores and prismatic blades. *American Antiquity* 33(4): 446–478.

———. 1979. Interview. *Flintknappers' Exchange* 2(1): 29–33.

Crabtree, Pam J. 1990. Zooarchaeology and complex societies: Some uses of faunal analysis for the study of trade, social status, and ethnicity. In M. B. Schiffer (Ed.), *Archaeological Method and Theory.* Vol. 2 (pp. 155–205). Tucson: University of Arizona Press.

Crader, Diana C. 1990. Slave diet at Monticello. *American Antiquity* 55(4): 690–717.

Creer, Kenneth M. 1977. Geomagnetic secular variations during the last 25,000 years: An interpretation of data obtained from rapidly deposited sediments. *Geophysical Journal of the Royal Astronomical Society* 48(1): 91–109.

Cronin, C. 1962. An analysis of pottery design elements, indicating possible relationships between three decorated types. In Paul S. Martin et al. (Eds.), *Chapters in the Prehistory of Eastern Arizona. Fieldiana Anthropology I* 53: 105–114.

Cronyn, J. M. 1990. *The Elements of Archaeological Conservation.* London: Routledge.

Crown, Patricia L., and W. James Judge (Eds.). 1991. *Chaco and Hohokam: Prehistoric Regional Systems in the American Southwest.* Santa Fe: School of American Research Press.

Crumley, Carole. 1976. Toward a locational definition of state systems of settlement. *American Anthropologist* 78(1): 59–73.

Cullen, Tracey. 1995. Women in archaeology: Perils and progress. Review of *Equity Issues for Women in Archeology* edited by M. C. Nelson, S. M. Nelson, and A. Wylie; and *Women in Archaeology* edited by C. Claassen. *Antiquity* 69: 1042–1045.

Dale, W. S. A. 1987. The shroud of Turin: Relic or icon? In H. H. Andersen and S. T. Picraux (Eds.), *Nuclear Instruments and Methods in Physics Research: Section B, Beam Interactions With Materials and Atoms.* Proceedings of the Fourth International Symposium on Accelerator Mass Spectrometry B29: 187–192.

D'Altroy, Terence N. 1992. *Provincial Power in the Inka Empire.* Washington, DC: Smithsonian Institution Press.

Dancey, William S. 1981. *Archaeological Field Methods: An Introduction.* Minneapolis: Burgess.

D'Andrade, Roy G. 1995. *The Development of Cognitive Anthropology.* Cambridge: Cambridge University Press.

Daniel, Glyn. 1962. *The Idea of Prehistory.* Baltimore: Penguin Books.

———. 1976. *A Hundred and Fifty Years of Archaeology.* Cambridge: Harvard University Press.

——— (Ed.). 1981. *Towards a History of Archaeology.* New York: Thames and Hudson.

Daniel, Glyn, and Christopher Chippindale (Eds.). 1989. *The Pastmasters: Eleven Modern Pioneers of Archaeology.* London: Thames and Hudson.

Daniel, Glyn, and Colin Renfrew. 1988. *The Idea of Prehistory.* Edinburgh: University of Edinburgh Press.

Dark, K. R. 1995. *Theoretical Archaeology.* Ithaca: Cornell University Press.

David, Nicholas, and Jonathan Driver. 1989. *The Next Archaeology Workbook.* Philadelphia: University of Pennsylvania Press.

Davis, Carolyn O'Bagy. 1995. *Treasured Earth: Hattie Cosgrove's Mimbres Archaeology in the American Southwest.* Tucson: Sanpete Publications and Old Pueblo Archaeology Center.

Davis, Hester A. 1991. Avocational archaeology groups: A secret weapon for site protection. In George S. Smith and John E. Ehrenhard (Eds.), *Protecting the Past* (pp. 175–180). Boca Raton, FL: CRC Press.

Davis, Jonathan O. 1978. Quaternary tephrochronology of the Lake Lahontan area. *Nevada Archaeological Survey Research Paper,* no. 7.

———. 1983. Geology of Gatecliff Shelter: Sedimentary facies and Holocene climate. In "The archaeology of Monitor Valley: 2. Gatecliff Shelter" by David Hurst Thomas. *Anthropological Papers of the American Museum of Natural History* 59(1): 64–87.

Davis, Mary B. (Comp.). 1987. *Field Notes of Clarence B. Moore's Southeastern Archaeological Expeditions, 1891–1918: A Guide to the Microfilm Edition.* Bronx, NY: Huntington Free Library, Museum of the American Indian.

Davis, Simon J. M. 1987. *The Archaeology of Animals.* New Haven: Yale University Press.

Day, Petra. 1993. Preliminary results of high-resolution palaeoecological analyses at Star Carr, Yorkshire. *Cambridge Archaeological Journal* 3(1): 129–140.

Deagan, Kathleen. 1973. Mestizaje in colonial St. Augustine. *Ethnohistory* 20(1): 55–65.

———. 1978a. Cultures in transition: Fusion and assimilation among the Eastern Timucua. In Jerald Milanich and Samuel Proctor (Eds.), *Tacachale: Essays on the Indians of Florida and Southeastern Georgia During the Historic Period* (pp. 89–119). Gainesville: University Press of Florida.

———. 1978b. The material assemblage of 16th century Spanish Florida. *Historical Archaeology* 12: 25–50.

———. 1980. Spanish St. Augustine: America's first "melting pot." *Archaeology* 33(5): 22–30.

———. 1981. Downtown survey: The discovery of 16th century St. Augustine in an urban area. *American Antiquity* 46(3): 626–634.

———. 1982. Avenues of inquiry in historical archaeology. In Michael B. Schiffer (Ed.), *Advances in Archaeological Method and Theory*. Vol. 5 (pp. 151–177). New York: Academic Press.

———. 1983. *Spanish St. Augustine: The Archaeology of a Colonial Creole Community*. New York: Academic Press.

———. 1987. *Artifacts of the Spanish Colonies of Florida and the Caribbean, 1500–1800*. Vol. 1, *Ceramics, Glassware, and Beads*. Washington, DC: Smithsonian Institution Press.

———. 1988. Neither history nor prehistory: The questions that count in historical archaeology. *Historical Archaeology* 22(1): 7–12.

———. 1991. Historical archaeology's contributions to our understanding of early America. In Lisa Falk (Ed.), *Historical Archaeology in Global Perspective* (pp. 97–112). Washington, DC: Smithsonian Institution Press.

——— (Ed.). 1995. *Puerto Real: The Archaeology of a Sixteenth-Century Spanish Town in Hispaniola*. Gainesville: University Press of Florida.

———. 1996. Colonial transformation: Euro-American cultural genesis in the early Spanish-American colonies. *Journal of Anthropological Research* 52(2): 135–160.

Deagan, Kathleen, and Jane Landers. n.d. Excavating Fort Mose: A free black town in Spanish Florida. In Theresa Singleton (Ed.), *Studies in African American Archaeology*. Charlottesville: University of Virginia Press, forthcoming.

Deagan, Kathleen, and Darcie MacMahon. 1995. *Fort Mose: Colonial America's Black Fortress of Freedom*. Gainesville: University Press of Florida/Florida Museum of Natural History.

Dean, Jeffrey S. 1970. Aspects of Tsegi phase social organization: A trial reconstruction. In William A. Longacre (Ed.), *Reconstructing Prehistoric Pueblo Societies* (pp. 140–174). Albuquerque: University of New Mexico Press.

———. 1978a. Independent dating in archaeological analysis. In Michael B. Schiffer (Ed.), *Advances in Archaeological Theory and Method*. Vol. 1 (pp. 223–255). New York: Academic Press.

———. 1978b. Tree-ring dating in archeology. *University of Utah Miscellaneous Anthropological Papers*, no. 24, 99: 129–163.

Deetz, James. 1977a. *In Small Things Forgotten: The Archaeology of Early American Life*. Garden City, NY: Anchor Books.

———. 1977b. Material culture and archaeology—What's the difference? In Leland Ferguson (Ed.), *Historical Archaeology and the Importance of Material Things* (pp. 9–12). Society for Historical Archaeology, Special Publication Series, no. 2.

———. 1983. Scientific humanism and humanistic science: A plea for paradigmatic pluralism in historical archaeology. *Geoscience and Man* 23(29): 27–34.

———. 1988. Material culture and worldview in colonial Anglo-America. In Mark Leone and Parker Potter (Eds.), *The Recovery of Meaning: Historical Archaeology in the Eastern United States* (pp. 219–233). Washington, DC: Smithsonian Institution Press.

———. 1991. Introduction: Archaeological evidence of sixteenth- and seventeenth-century encounters. In Lisa Falk (Ed.), *Historical Archaeology in*

Global Perspective (pp. 1–9). Washington, DC: Smithsonian Institution Press.

de Laguna, Frederica. 1957. Some problems of objectivity in ethnology. *Man* 57(228): 179–182.

Deloria, Vine, Jr. 1992a. Indians, archaeologists, and the future. *American Antiquity* 57(4): 595–598.

———. 1992b. Afterword. In Alvin M. Josephy, Jr. (Ed.), *America in 1492: The World of the Indian Peoples Before the Arrival of Columbus* (pp. 429–443). New York: Knopf.

———. 1993. Sacred lands. *Winds of Change* 8(4): 30–37.

———. 1995. *Red Earth, White Lies: Native Americans and the Myth of Scientific Fact.* New York: Scribner's.

Del Pozzo, Giovanna. 1989. Mummy DNA fragment identified. *Nature* 339(June 8): 431–432.

Demarest, Arthur A. 1989. Ideology and evolutionism in American archaeology: Looking beyond the economic base. In C. C. Lamberg-Karlovsky (Ed.), *Archaeological Thought in America* (pp. 89–102). Cambridge: Cambridge University Press.

Demarest, Arthur A., and Geoffrey W. Conrad (Eds.). 1992. *Ideology and Pre-Columbian Civilizations.* Santa Fe: School of American Research Press.

DeNiro, Michael J. 1987. Stable isotopy and archeology. *American Scientist* 75(2): 182–191.

DeNiro, Michael J., and S. Epstein. 1981. Influence of diet on the distribution of nitrogen isotopes in animals. *Geochimica de Cosmochimica Acta* 45: 341–351.

DeNiro, Michael J., and Margaret J. Schoeniger. 1983. Stable carbon and nitrogen isotope ratios of bone collagen: Variations within individuals, between sexes, and within populations raised on monotonous diets. *Journal of Archaeological Science* 10(3): 199–203.

DePratter, Chester B., and James D. Howard. 1977. History of shoreline changes determined by archaeological dating: Georgia Coast, U.S.A. *Technical Papers and Abstracts, Gulf Coast Association of Geological Societies* 27: 252–258.

d'Errico, Francesco. 1995. A new model and its implications for the origin of writing: The La Marche antler revisited. *Cambridge Archaeological Journal* 5(2): 163–206.

DeSalle, Rob, and David Grimaldi. 1994. Very old DNA. *Current Opinion in Genetics and Development* 4: 810–815.

Deuel, Leo. 1969. *Flights Into Yesterday: The Story of Aerial Archaeology.* New York: St. Martin's Press.

———. 1977. *Memoirs of Heinrich Schliemann.* New York: Harper & Row.

Diamond, Jared. 1988. The golden age that never was. *Discover* 9(12): 70–79.

Dibble, Harold L. 1987. Measurement of artifact provenience with an electronic theodolite. *Journal of Field Archaeology* 14(2): 249–254.

Dickerson, James. 1993, August. Murders from the past. *Omni* 15(10): 50–54, 56–57, 82.

Dillehay, Tom D. 1989. *Monte Verde: A Late Pleistocene Settlement in Chile.* Washington, DC: Smithsonian Institution Press.

Dillehay, Tom D., and David J. Meltzer (Eds.). 1991. *The First Americans: Search and Research.* Boca Raton, FL: CRC Press.

Dillon, Brian D. (Ed.). 1989. *Practical Archaeology: Field and Laboratory Techniques and Archaeological Logistics.* Archaeological Research Tools 2. Los Angeles: Institute of Archaeology, University of California.

Dimbleby, Geoffrey W. 1977. *Ecology and Archaeology.* London: Arnold.

Divale, William Tulio, and Marvin Harris. 1976. Population, warfare, and the male supremacist complex. *American Anthropologist* 78(3): 521–538.

Domenici, Pete V. 1991. Preface B. In George S. Smith and John E. Ehrenhard (Eds.), *Protecting the Past* (pp. v–vi). Boca Raton, FL: CRC Press.

Doran, Glen H., David N. Dickel, William E. Ballinger, Jr., O. Frank Agee, Philip J. Laipis, and William W. Hauswirth. 1986. Anatomical, cellular and molecular analysis of 8,000-yr-old human brain tissue from the Windover archaeological site. *Nature* 323: 803–806.

Dorn, R. I., P. B. Clarkson, M. F. Nobbs, L. L. Loendorf, and D. S. Whitley. 1992. New approach to the radiocarbon dating of rock varnish, with examples for drylands. *Annals of the Association of American Geographers* 82(1): 136–151.

Douglass, Andrew Ellicott. 1929. The secret of the Southwest solved by talkative tree rings. *National Geographic* 56(6): 736–770.

Douglass, Frederick. 1950. The claims of the Negro ethnologically considered: Address delivered at Western Reserve College, July 12, 1854. In Philip S. Foner (Ed.), *The Life and Writings of Frederick Douglass.* Vol. 2, *Pre–Civil War Decade 1850–1860* (pp. 289–309). New York: International Publishers.

Doyel, David E. 1991. Hohokam exchange and interaction. In Patricia L. Crown and W. James Judge (Eds.), *Chaco and Hohokam: Prehistoric Regional Systems in the American Southwest* (pp. 225–252). Santa Fe: School of American Research Press.

Drennan, Robert D. 1976. A refinement of chronological seriation using nonmetric multidimensional scaling. *American Antiquity* 41(3): 290–302.

Dreyfus, Hubert, and Paul Rabinow. 1983. *Michel Foucault: Beyond Structuralism and Hermeneutics.* Chicago: University of Chicago Press.

Duke, Philip, and Michael C. Wilson (Eds.). 1995. *Beyond Subsistence: Plains Archaeology and the Postprocessual Critique.* Tuscaloosa: University of Alabama Press.

Dunnell, Robert C. 1970. Seriation method and its evaluation. *American Antiquity* 35(3): 305–319.

———. 1971. *Systematics in Prehistory.* New York: Free Press.

———. 1979. Trends in current Americanist archaeology. *American Journal of Archaeology* 83(4): 437–449.

———. 1980. Evolutionary theory and archaeology. In Michael B. Schiffer (Ed.), *Advances in Archaeological Method and Theory.* Vol. 3 (pp. 35–99). New York: Academic Press.

———. 1982a. Americanist archaeological literature: 1981. *American Journal of Archaeology* 86: 509–529.

———. 1982b. Science, social science, and common sense: The agonizing dilemma of modern archaeology. *Journal of Anthropological Archaeology* 38: 1–25.

———. 1985. Americanist archaeology in 1984. *American Journal of Archaeology* 89: 585–611.

———. 1986a. Five decades of American archaeology. In David J. Meltzer, Don D. Fowler, and Jeremy A. Sabloff (Eds.), *American Archaeology Past and Future: A Celebration of the Society for American Archaeology 1935–1985* (pp. 23–49). Washington, DC: Smithsonian Institution Press.

———. 1986b. Methodological issues in Americanist artifact classification. In Michael B. Schiffer (Ed.), *Advances in Archaeological Method and Theory.* Vol. 9 (pp. 149–207). New York: Academic Press.

———. 1989. Aspects of the application of evolutionary theory in archaeology. In C. C. Lamberg-Karlovsky (Ed.), *Archaeological Thought in America* (pp. 35–49). Cambridge: Cambridge University Press.

Dunnell, Robert C., and William S. Dancey. 1983. The siteless survey: A regional scale data collection strategy. In Michael B. Schiffer (Ed.), *Advances in Archeological Method and Theory.* Vol. 6 (pp. 267–287). New York: Academic Press.

Durham, William. 1981. Overview: Optimal foraging analysis in human ecology. In Bruce Winterhalder and Eric Alden Smith (Eds.), *Hunter-Gatherer Foraging Strategies: Ethnographic and Archaeological Analyses* (pp. 218–232). Chicago: University of Chicago Press.

———. 1990. Advances in evolutionary culture theory. *Annual Review of Anthropology* 19: 187–210.

———. 1992. Applications of evolutionary culture theory. *Annual Review of Anthropology* 21: 331–355.

Earle, Timothy K. (Ed.). 1991. *Chiefdoms: Power, Economy, and Ideology.* Cambridge: Cambridge University Press.

Earle, Timothy K., Terence D'Altroy, Cathy LeBlanc, Christine Hastorf, and Terry Levine. 1980. Changing settlement patterns in the Yanamarca Valley, Peru. Los Angeles: Institute of Archaeology, University of California, *Journal of New World Archaeology* 4(1).

Earle, Timothy K., Terence D'Altroy, Christine Hastorf, Catherine Scott, Cathy Costin, Glenn Russell, and Elsie Sandefur. 1987. *Archaeological Field Research in the Upper Mantaro, Peru, 1982–1983: Investigations of Inka Expansion and Exchange.* Monograph 28. Los Angeles: Institute of Archaeology, University of California.

Earle, Timothy K., and Robert W. Preucel. 1987. Processual archaeology and the radical critique. *Current Anthropology* 28(4): 501–538.

Easton, Donald F. 1981. Schliemann's discovery of "Priam's Treasure": Two enigmas. *Antiquity* 55: 179–183.

Ebert, James I. 1984. Remote sensing applications in archaeology. In Michael B. Schiffer (Ed.), *Advances in Archaeological Method and Theory.* Vol. 7 (pp. 293–362). New York: Academic Press.

———. 1992. *Distributional Archaeology.* Albuquerque: University of New Mexico Press.

Echo-Hawk, Roger C., and Walter R. Echo-Hawk. 1994. *Battlefields and Burial Grounds: The Indian Struggle to Protect Ancestral Graves in the United States.* Minneapolis: Lerner.

Echo-Hawk, Walter (Ed.). 1992. Special Issue: Repatriation of American Indian remains. *American Indian Culture and Research Journal* 16(2): 1–200.

Eddy, Frank, Dale R. Lightfoot, Eden A. Welker, Layne L. Wright, and Dolores C. Torres. 1996. Air photographic mapping of San Marcos Pueblo. *Journal of Field Archaeology* 23(1): 1–13.

Eddy, John A. 1974. Astronomical alignment of the Big Horn medicine wheel. *Science* 184(4141): 1035–1043.

———. 1977. Medicine wheels and Plains Indian astronomy. In Anthony F. Aveni (Ed.), *Native American Astronomy* (pp. 147–169). Austin: University of Texas Press.

Ehrenberg, Ralph E. 1987. *Scholars' Guide to Washington, D.C. for Cartography and Remote Sensing Imagery.* Washington, DC: Smithsonian Institution Press.

Ehrenreich, Robert M., Carole L. Crumley, and Janet E. Levy (Eds.). 1995. Heterarchy and the analysis of complex societies. *Archeological Papers of the American Anthropological Association,* no. 6.

Eichler, Margrit, and Jeanne Lapoint. 1985. *On the Treatment of the Sexes in Research.* Ottawa: Social Sciences and Humanities Research Council of Canada.

Eisele, J. A., D. D. Fowler, G. Hanes, and R. A. Lewis. 1995. Survival and detection of blood residues on stone tools. *Antiquity* 69: 36–46.

Elia, Ricardo J. 1993. U.S. cultural resource management and the ICAHM charter. *Antiquity* 67: 426–438.

Elkins, James. 1996. On the impossibility of close reading: The case of Alexander Marshack. *Current Anthropology* 37(2): 185–226.

Elliott, Melinda. 1995. *Great Excavations.* Santa Fe: School of American Research Press.

Ellis, Florence Hawley. 1983. Foreword to *The Architecture and Dendrochronology of Chetro Ketl, Chaco Canyon, New Mexico,* ed. by Stephen H. Lekson. Reports of the Chaco Center, no. 6. Albuquerque: Division of Cultural Research, National Park Service.

Ellis, G. Lain, Glenn A. Goodfriend, James T. Abbott, P. E. Hare, and David W. Von Endt. 1996. Assessment of integrity and geochronology of archeological sites using amino acid racemization in land snail shells: Examples from central Texas. *Geoarchaeology* 11(3): 189–213.

Elster, H., E. Gil-Av, and S. Weiner. 1991. Amino acid racemization of fossil bone. *Journal of Archaeological Science* 18: 605–617.

Elston, Robert G. 1992. Archaeological research in the context of cultural resource management: Pushing back in the 1990s. *Journal of California and Great Basin Anthropology* 14(1): 37–48.

Emerson, Thomas E., and Lewis, R. Barry (Eds.). 1991. *Cahokia and the Hinterlands: Middle Mississippian Cultures of the Midwest.* Urbana: University of Illinois Press.

Englestadt, Ericka. 1991. Images of power and contradiction: Feminist theory and post-processual archaeology. *Antiquity* 65: 502–514.

Epperson, Terrence W. 1990. Race and the disciplines of the plantation. *Historical Archaeology* 24(4): 29–36.

Erickson, Clark L. 1988. Raised field agriculture in the Lake Titicaca Basin: Putting ancient agriculture back to work. *Expedition* 30(3): 8–16.

———. 1992a. Applied archaeology and rural development: Archaeology's potential contribution to the future. *Journal of the Steward Anthropological Society* 20(1, 2): 1–16.

———. 1992b. Prehistoric landscape management in the Andean highlands: Raised field agriculture and its environmental impact. *Population and Environment* 13(4): 285–300.

———. 1993. The social organization of prehispanic raised field agriculture in the Lake Titicaca Basin. In V. L. Scarborough and B. L. Isaac (Eds.), *Research in Economic Anthropology: Economic Aspects of Water Management in the Prehistoric New World.* Supplement 7: 369–426. Greenwich, CT: JAI Press.

———. 1994. Methodological considerations in the study of ancient Andean field systems. In Naomi F. Miller and Kathryn L. Gleason (Eds.), *The Archaeology of Garden and Field* (pp. 111–152). Philadelphia: University of Pennsylvania Press.

———. 1995. Archaeological methods for the study of ancient landscapes of the Llanos de Mojos in the Bolivian Amazon. In Peter W. Stahl (Ed.), *Archaeology in the Lowland American Tropics: Current Analytical Methods and Applications* (pp. 66–95). Cambridge: Cambridge University Press.

Ericson, J. E. 1975. New results in obsidian hydration dating. *World Archaeology* 7(2): 151–159.

Evans, Clifford. 1968. (Obituary of) James A. Ford, 1911–1968. *American Anthropologist* 70(6): 1161–1167.

Ezzo, Joseph A., Clark Spencer Larsen, and James H. Burton. 1995. Elemental signatures of human diets from the Georgia Bight. *American Journal of Physical Anthropology* 98: 471–481.

Faegri, K., P. E. Kaland, and K. Krzywinski. 1989. *Textbook of Pollen Analysis.* 4th ed. New York: Wiley.

Fagan, Brian M. 1994. *Quest for the Past: Great Discoveries in Archaeology.* 2d ed. Prospect Heights, IL: Waveland Press.

Fairbanks, Charles H. 1977. Backyard archaeology as research strategy. *The Conference on Historic Site Archaeology Papers* 11: 133–139.

———. 1984. Plantation archaeology of the southeastern coast. *Historical Archaeology* 18:1–14.

Falk, Lisa (Ed.). 1991. *Historical Archaeology in Global Perspective.* Washington, DC: Smithsonian Institution Press.

Farnsworth, Paul, James E. Brady, Michael J. DeNiro, and Richard S. MacNeish. 1985. A reevaluation of the isotopic and archaeological reconstructions of diet in the Tehuacan Valley. *American Antiquity* 50(1): 102–116.

Feder, Kenneth L. 1995. *Frauds, Myths, and Mysteries: Science and Pseudoscience in Archaeology.* 2d ed. Mountain View, CA: Mayfield.

———. 1996. *The Past in Perspective: An Introduction to Human Prehistory.* Mountain View, CA: Mayfield.

Fedick, Scott L. 1995. Indigenous agriculture in the Americas. *Journal of Archaeological Research* 3(4): 257–303.

Fedigan, Linda Marie. 1986. The changing role of women in models of human evolution. *Annual Review of Anthropology* 15: 25–66.

Fehrenbach, T. R. 1968. *Lone Star: A History of Texas and the Texans.* New York: Macmillan.

Feinman, Gary M., and Linda M. Nicholas. 1990. Settlement and land use in ancient Oaxaca. In Joyce Marcus (Ed.), *Debating Oaxaca Archaeology.* Ann Arbor: University of Michigan, Museum of Anthropology, *Anthropological Papers* 84: 71–114.

Ferguson, Leland B. 1987. J. C. Harrington Medal in Historical Archaeology: Stanley A. South, 1987. *Historical Archaeology* 21(2): 1–5.

———. 1992. *Uncommon Ground: Archaeology and Early African America, 1650–1800.* Washington, DC: Smithsonian Institution Press.

Ferguson, T. J. 1996. Native Americans and the practice of archaeology. *Annual Review of Anthropology* 25: 63–79.

———. n.d. Native Americans and the practice of archaeology. *Annual Review of Anthropology.* In press.

Fiedel, Stuart J. 1996. Blood from stones? Some methodological and interpretive problems in blood residue analysis. *Journal of Archaeological Science* 23(1): 139–147.

Findlow, Frank J., Victoria C. Bennett, Jonathon E. Ericson, and Suzanne P. De Atley. 1975. A new obsidian hydration rate for certain obsidians in the American Southwest. *American Antiquity* 40(3): 344–348.

Fish, Suzanne K., and Stephen A. Kowalewski (Eds.). 1990. *The Archaeology of Regions: A Case for Full-Coverage Survey.* Washington, DC: Smithsonian Institution Press.

Fisher, Deborah L., Mitchell M. Holland, Lloyd Mitchell, Paul S. Sledzik, Allison Webb Wilcox, Mark Wadhams, and Victor W. Weedn. 1993. Extraction, evaluation, and amplification of DNA from decalcified and undecalcified United States Civil War bone. *Journal of Forensic Sciences* 38(1): 60–68.

Fladmark, Knud R. 1978. *A Guide to Basic Archaeological Field Procedures.* Burnaby, British Columbia: Department of Archaeology, Simon Fraser University.

Flannery, Kent V. 1965. The ecology of early food production in Mesopotamia. *Science* 147(3663): 1247–1255.

———. 1966. The postglacial "readaptation" as viewed from Mesoamerica. *American Antiquity* 31(6): 800–805.

———. 1967a. Culture history vs. cultural process: A debate in American archaeology. *Scientific American* 217(2): 119–121.

———. 1967b. Vertebrate fauna and hunting patterns. In Douglas S. Byers (Ed.), *The Prehistory of the Tehuacan Valley.* Vol. 1 (pp. 132–177). Austin: University of Texas Press.

———. 1969. Origins and ecological effects of early domestication in Iran and the Near East. In P. J. Ucko and G. W. Dimbleby (Eds.), *The Domestication and Exploitation of Plants and Animals* (pp. 73–100). Chicago: Aldine.

———. 1972. The cultural evolution of civilizations. *Annual Review of Ecology and Systematics* 3: 399–426.

———. 1973a. Archeology with a capital S. In Charles L. Redman (Ed.), *Research and Theory in Current Archeology* (pp. 47–53). New York: Wiley and Sons.

———. 1973b. The origins of agriculture. *Annual Review of Anthropology* 2: 271–310.

——— (Ed.). 1976. *The Early Mesoamerican Village.* New York: Academic Press.

———. 1977. A setting for cultural evolution: Review of *The Valley of Mexico: Studies in Prehispanic Ecology and Society. Science* 196: 759–761.

———. 1982. The golden Marshalltown: A parable for the archeology of the 1980s. *American Anthropologist* 84(2): 265–278.

——— (Ed.). 1986. *Guilá Naquitz: Archaic Foraging and Early Agriculture in Oaxaca, Mexico.* Orlando, FL: Academic Press.

———. 1995. *Prehistoric Social Evolution: Research Frontiers in Anthropology.* Needham Heights, MA: Simon and Schuster.

Flannery, Kent V., and Joyce Marcus. 1976. Formative Oaxaca and the Zapotec cosmos. *American Scientist* 64(4): 374–383.

———. 1993. Cognitive archaeology. *Cambridge Archaeological Journal* 3(2): 260–270.

Flannery, Kent V., Chris L. Moser, and Silvia Maranca. 1986. The excavation of Guilá Naquitz. In Kent V. Flannery (Ed.), *Guilá Naquitz: Archaic Foraging and Early Agriculture in Oaxaca, Mexico* (pp. 65–95). Orlando, FL: Academic Press.

Flannery, Kent V., and Marcus C. Winter. 1976. Analyzing household activities. In Kent V. Flannery (Ed.), *The Early Mesoamerican Village* (pp. 34–44). New York: Academic Press.

Fleming, Stuart. 1977. *Dating Techniques in Archaeology.* New York: St. Martin's Press.

———. 1979. *Thermoluminescence Techniques in Archaeology.* New York: Oxford University Press.

Flenniken, J. Jeffrey. 1978. Reevaluation of the Lindenmeier Folsom: A replication experiment in lithic technology. *American Antiquity* 43(3): 473–480.

———. 1981. Replicative systems analysis: A model applied to the vein quartz artifacts from the Hoko River site. *Laboratory of Anthropology Reports of Investigations,* no. 59. Pullman: Washington State University.

———. 1984. The past, present, and future of flintknapping: An anthropological perspective. *Annual Review of Anthropology* 13: 187–203.

Fletcher, Roland. 1977. Settlement studies. In David L. Clarke (Ed.), *Spatial Archaeology* (pp. 47–162). New York: Academic Press.

Folan, William J., Joyce Marcus, and W. Frank Miller. 1995. Verification of a Maya settlement model through remote sensing. *Cambridge Archaeological Journal* 5(2): 277–301.

Foley, Robert. 1981. Off-site archaeology: An alternative approach for the short-sited. In Ian Hodder, Glynn Isaac, and Norman Hammond (Eds.), *Pattern of the Past: Studies in Honour of David Clarke* (pp. 157–183). Cambridge: Cambridge University Press.

Folsom, Franklin, and Mary Elting Folsom. 1993. *America's Ancient Treasures.* 4th ed. Albuquerque: University of New Mexico Press.

Ford, James Alfred. 1949. Cultural dating of prehistoric sites in the Virú Valley, Peru. Pt. 2 of "Surface survey of the Virú Valley, Peru" by James Alfred Ford and Gordon R. Willey. *Anthropological Papers of the American Museum of Natural History* 43(1).

———. 1952. Measurements of some prehistoric design developments in the southeastern states. *Anthropological Papers of the American Museum of Natural History* 44(3).

———. 1954. The type concept revisited. *American Anthropologist* 56(1): 42–54.

———. 1957. A quantitative method for deriving cultural chronology. *Pan American Union, Technical Manual,* I. (Reprinted as *University of Missouri, Museum of Anthropology, Museum Brief,* no. 9.)

———. 1962. *A quantitative method for deriving cultural chronology.* Washington, DC: Pan American Union, Technical Manual, I.

———. 1969. A comparison of formative cultures in the Americas: Diffusion or the psychic unity of man? *Smithsonian Contributions to Anthropology,* vol. 2.

Ford, James Alfred, and Clarence H. Webb. 1956. Poverty Point, a late Archaic site in Louisiana. *Anthropological Papers of the American Museum of Natural History* 46(1): 1–140.

Ford, James Alfred, and Gordon R. Willey. 1941. An interpretation of the prehistory of the eastern United States. *American Anthropologist* 43(3): 325–363.

Ford, Richard I. 1973. Archeology serving humanity. In Charles L. Redman (Ed.), *Research and Theory in Current Archeology* (pp. 83–93). New York: Wiley.

———. 1979. Paleoethnobotany in American archaeology. In Michael B. Schiffer (Ed.), *Advances in Archaeological Method and Theory.* Vol. 2 (pp. 285–336). New York: Academic Press.

Fotiadis, M. 1994. What is archaeology's "mitigated objectivism" mitigated by? Comments on Wylie. *American Antiquity* 59(3): 545–555.

Fowler, Don D. 1982. Cultural resources management. In Michael B. Schiffer (Ed.), *Advances in Archaeological Method and Theory.* Vol. 5 (pp. 1–50). New York: Academic Press.

———. 1986. Conserving American archaeological resources. In David J. Meltzer, Don D. Fowler, and Jeremy A. Sabloff (Eds.), *American Archaeology: Past and Future: A Celebration of the Society for American Archaeology 1935–1985* (pp. 135–162). Washington, DC: Smithsonian Institution Press.

Fowler, Melvin L., and Richard S. MacNeish. 1972. Excavations in the Coxcatlán locality in the alluvial slopes. In Richard S. MacNeish, Melvin L. Fowler, Angel Garcia Cook, Frederick A. Peterson, Antoinette Nelken-Terner, and James A. Neely (Eds.), *The Prehistory of the Tehuacan Valley* (pp. 219–340). Austin: University of Texas Press.

Fox, Richard G. (Ed.). 1991. *Recapturing Anthropology: Working in the Present.* Santa Fe: School of American Research Press.

Fradkin, Arlene. 1980. Hog jowls and coon meat: An analysis of faunal remains from the Hampton Plantation, St. Simons Island, Georgia. *Southeastern Archaeological Conference Bulletin* 22: 57–59.

Fried, Morton H. 1967. *The Evolution of Political Society.* New York: Random House.

Friedman, Irving. 1983. Obsidian hydration dating update. *American Antiquity* 48(3): 544–547.

Friedman, Irving, and Robert L. Smith. 1960. A new dating method using obsidian. Pt. 1: The development of the method. *American Antiquity* 25(4): 476–522.

Friedman, Irving, and Fred W. Trembour. 1978. Obsidian: The dating stone. *American Scientist* 66(1): 44–51.

Friedman, Irving, Fred W. Trembour, Franklin L. Smith, and George I. Smith. 1994. Is obsidian hydration dating affected by relative humidity? *Quaternary Research* 41: 185–190.

Frisbie, Theodore R. 1975. A biography of Florence Hawley Ellis and bibliography of Florence Hawley Ellis. In Theodore R. Frisbie (Ed.), Collected Papers in Honor of Florence Hawley Ellis. *Papers of the Archaeological Society of New Mexico* 2: 1–11, 12–21.

———. 1991. Florence Hawley Ellis, 1906–1991. *Kiva* 57(1): 93–97.

Frison, George C. 1984. Avocational archaeology: Its past, present, and future. In E. L. Green (Ed.), *Ethics and Values in Archaeology* (pp. 184–193). New York: Free Press.

———. 1989. Experimental use of Clovis weaponry and tools on African elephants. *American Antiquity* 54(4): 766–784.

———. 1993. North American high plains paleo-Indian hunting strategies and weaponry assemblages. In Olga Soffer and N. D. Praslov (Eds.), *From Kostenki to Clovis: Upper Paleolithic-Paleo-Indian Adaptations* (pp. 237–249). New York: Plenum.

Frison, George C., and Bruce A. Bradley. 1980. *Folsom Tools and Technology at the Hanson Site, Wyoming.* Albuquerque: University of New Mexico Press.

Fritts, H. C. 1976. *Tree Rings and Climate.* New York: Academic Press.

Fritz, Gayle J. 1990. Multiple pathways to farming in precontact eastern North America. *Journal of World Prehistory* 4(4): 387–435.

Fritz, John M. 1978. Paleopsychology today: Ideational systems and human adaptation in prehistory. In Charles L. Redman, Mary Jane Berman, Edward V. Curtin, William T. Laughorne, Jr., Nina M. Versaggi, and Jeffrey C. Wanser (Eds.), *Social Archaeology: Beyond Subsistence and Dating* (pp. 37–59). New York: Academic Press.

Fritz, John M., and Fred T. Plog. 1970. The nature of archaeological explanation. *American Antiquity* 35(4): 405–412.

Gable, Eric, and Richard Handler. 1996. After authenticity at an American heritage site. *American Anthropologist* 98(3): 568–578.

Gable, Eric, Richard Handler, and Anna Lawson. 1992. On the uses of relativism: Fact, conjecture, and black and white histories at Colonial Williamsburg. *American Ethnologist* 19(4): 791–805.

Gabriel, Kathryn. 1991. *Roads to Center Place: A Cultural Atlas of Chaco Canyon and the Anasazi.* Boulder: Johnson Books.

Gacs, Ute, Aisha Khan, Jerrie McIntyre, and Ruth Weinberg (Eds.). 1989. *Women Anthropologists: Selected Biographies.* Urbana: University of Illinois Press.

Gaines, Patrice. 1995, August 3. Bones of forebears. *The Washington Post.*

Galloway, Patricia (Ed.). 1989. *The Southeastern Ceremonial Complex: Artifacts and Analysis.* Lincoln: University of Nebraska Press.

Gamble, C. S., and W. A. Boismier (Eds.). 1991. *Ethnoarchaeological Approaches to Mobile Campsites.* Ann Arbor: International Monographs in Prehistory.

Gardin, J. C. 1980. *Archaeological Constructs: An Aspect of Theoretical Archaeology.* Cambridge: Cambridge University Press.

Garrison, Ervan G., James G. Baker, and David Hurst Thomas. 1985. Magnetic prospection and the discovery of Mission Santa Catalina de Guale, Georgia. *Journal of Field Archaeology* 12(3): 299–313.

Gathercole, Peter, and David Lowenthal (Eds.). 1990. *The Politics of the Past.* One World Archaeology series. London: Unwin Hyman.

Geertz, Clifford. 1973. *The Interpretation of Cultures.* New York: Basic Books.

———. 1983. *Local Knowledge: Further Essays in Interpretive Anthropology.* New York: Basic Books.

———. 1984. Distinguished lecture: Anti anti-relativism. *American Anthropologist* 86(2): 263–278.

Gero, Joan M. 1983. Gender bias in archaeology: A cross-cultural perspective. In Joan Gero, David M. Lacy, and Michael L. Blakey (Eds.), *The Socio-Politics of Archaeology* (pp. 51–57). *University of Massachusetts Department of Anthropology Research Report,* no. 23.

———. 1985. Socio-politics and the woman-at-home ideology. *American Antiquity* 50(2): 342–350.

———. 1988. Gender bias in archaeology: Here, then and now. In Sue V. Rosser (Ed.), *Resistance of the Science and Health Care Professions to Feminism.* Elmsford, NY: Pergamon Press.

———. 1989. Stylistic information in stone tools: How well do lithics measure up? In Robin Torrence (Ed.), *Time, Energy, and Stone Tools* (pp. 92–105). Cambridge: Cambridge University Press.

———. 1991a. Genderlithics: Women's roles in stone tool production. In Joan M. Gero and Margaret W. Conkey (Eds.), *Engendering Archaeology: Women and Prehistory* (pp. 163–193). Oxford: Basil Blackwell.

———. 1991b. Gender divisions of labor in the construction of archaeological knowledge. In *The Archaeology of Gender* (pp. 96–102). Proceedings of the 22nd Annual Chacmool Conference. Calgary: The University of Calgary Archaeological Association.

Gero, Joan M., and Margaret W. Conkey (Eds.). 1991. *Engendering Archaeology: Women and Prehistory.* Oxford: Basil Blackwell.

Gibbon, Guy. 1989. *Explanation in Archaeology.* Oxford: Basil Blackwell.

Gibbons, Ann. 1991. A "new look" for archaeology. *Science* 252: 918–920.

———. 1993. An array of science from mitochondrial Eve to EUVE. *Science* 259: 1249–1250.

Gibbs, Liv. 1987. Identifying gender representation in the archaeological record: Contextual study. In Ian Hodder (Ed.), *The Archaeology of Contextual Meanings* (pp. 79–89). Cambridge: Cambridge University Press.

Gibson, Alex M., and Ann Woods. 1990. *Prehistoric Pottery for the Archaeologist.* Leicester, England: Leicester University Press.

Giddings, J. L. 1961. Cultural continuities of Eskimos. *American Antiquity* 27(2): 155–173.

———. 1966. Cross-dating the archaeology of northwestern Alaska. *Science* 153(3732): 127–135.

Gifford, Diane P. 1981. Taphonomy and paleoecology: A critical review of archaeology's sister disciplines. In Michael B. Schiffer (Ed.), *Advances in Archaeological Method and Theory.* Vol. 4 (pp. 365–438). New York: Academic Press.

Gifford-Gonzalez, Diane. 1993. You can hide, but you can't run: Representation of women's work in illustrations of paleolithic life. *Visual Anthropology Review* 9(1): 23–40.

———. 1995. The real Flintstones? What are artists' depictions of human ancestors telling us? *Anthro Notes, National Museum of Natural History Bulletin for Teachers* 17(3): 1–9.

Gilbert, B. Miles. 1980. *Mammalian Osteology.* Laramie, WY: Modern Printing.

Gilbert, Robert I., Jr., and James H. Mielke (Eds.). 1985. *The Analysis of Prehistoric Diets.* Orlando, FL: Academic Press.

Gilchrist, Roberta. 1991. Women's archaeology? Political feminism, gender theory and historical revision. *Antiquity* 65: 495–501.

———. 1994. *Gender and Material Culture: The Archaeology of Religious Women.* London: Routledge.

Gill, David W. J. 1995. Archaeology on the World Wide Web. *Antiquity* 69(264): 626–630.

Gilman, Antonio. 1987. Comment on "Processual archaeology and the radical critique" by T. K. Earle and R. W. Preucel. *Current Anthropology* 28(4): 515–516.

———. 1989. Marxism in American archaeology. In C. C. Lamberg-Karlovsky (Ed.), *Archaeological Thought in America* (pp. 63–73). Cambridge: Cambridge University Press.

Givens, Douglas R. 1992. *Alfred Vincent Kidder and the Development of Americanist Archaeology.* Albuquerque: University of New Mexico Press.

Glassie, Henry. 1975. *Folk Housing in Middle Virginia.* Knoxville: University of Tennessee Press.

Glover, I., and D. Griffiths (Eds.). 1989. Ceramic technology. *World Archaeology* 21(1).

Goffer, Zvi. 1980. *Archaeological Chemistry: A Sourcebook on the Applications of Chemistry to Archaeology.* New York: Wiley.

Goldschmidt, Walter. 1960. *Exploring the Ways of Mankind.* New York: Holt, Rinehart and Winston.

———. 1983. Review of *Beyond the Myths of Culture: Essays in Cultural Materialism,* ed. Eric B. Ross. *American Anthropologist* 85(3): 695–698.

Goldstein, Lynn, and Keith Kintigh. 1990. Ethics and the reburial controversy. *American Antiquity* 55(33): 585–591.

Good, Diane L. 1989. Birds, beads and bells: Remote sensing of a Pawnee sacred bundle. *Kansas State Historical Society, Anthropological Series,* no. 15.

Goodenough, Ward H. 1965. Rethinking "status" and "role": Toward a general model of the cultural organization of social relationships. In Michael Banton (Ed.), *The Relevance of Models for Social Anthropology* (pp. 1–24). ASA Monographs, no. 1. New York: Praeger.

———. 1994. Toward a working theory of culture. In Robert Borofsky (Ed.), *Assessing Cultural Anthropology* (pp. 262–273). New York: McGraw-Hill.

Goodman, Dean. 1994. Ground-penetrating radar simulation in engineering and archaeology. *Geophysics* 59(2): 224–232.

Goodman, Dean, and Yasushi Nishimura. 1993. A ground-radar view of Japanese burial mounds. *Antiquity* 67: 349–354.

Goodman, Dean, Y. Nishimura, T. Uno, and T. Yamamoto. 1994. A ground radar survey of medieval kiln sites in Suzu City, Western Japan. *Archaeometry* 36: 317–326.

Gould, Richard A. 1966. Archaeology of the Point St. George site, and Tolowa prehistory. *University of California Publications in Anthropology,* vol. 4.

Gove, H. E. 1987. Turin workshop on radiocarbon dating the Turin shroud. *Nuclear Instruments and Methods in Physics Research* B29(1, 2): 193–195.

Graham, Martha. 1994. *Mobile Farmers: An Ethnoarchaeological Approach to Settlement Organization Among the Rarámuri of Northwestern Mexico.* International Monographs in Prehistory, Ethnoarchaeological Series 3. Ann Arbor, Michigan.

Grauer, Anne L. (Ed.). 1995. *Bodies of Evidence: Reconstructing History Through Skeletal Analysis.* New York: Wiley-Liss.

Grayson, Donald K. 1973. On the methodology of faunal analysis. *American Antiquity* 38(4): 432–440.

———. 1978. Minimum numbers and sample size in vertebrate faunal analysis. *American Antiquity* 43(1): 53–65.

———. 1979. On the quantification of vertebrate archaeofaunas. In Michael B. Schiffer (Ed.), *Advances in Archaeological Method and Theory.* Vol. 2 (pp. 199–237). New York: Academic Press.

———. 1983. *The Establishment of Human Antiquity.* New York: Academic Press.

———. 1984. *Quantitative Zooarchaeology: Topics in the Analysis of Archaeological Faunas.* Orlando, FL: Academic Press.

———. 1986. Eoliths, archaeological ambiguity, and the generation of "middle-range" research. In David J. Meltzer, Don D. Fowler, and Jeremy A. Sabloff (Eds.), *American Archaeology Past and Future: A Celebration of the Society of American Archaeology 1935–1985* (pp. 77–133). Washington, DC: Smithsonian Institution Press.

Grayson, Donald K., and David Hurst Thomas. 1983. Seasonality at Gatecliff Shelter. In "The archaeology of Monitor Valley: 2. Gatecliff Shelter" by David Hurst Thomas. *Anthropological Papers of the American Museum of Natural History* 59(1): 434–438.

Green, Ernestine L. (Ed.). 1984. *Ethics and Values in Archaeology.* New York: Free Press.

Greenburg, D. W. 1926. Sheridan's historic settings. *The Midwest Review* 7(10): 50–69ff, 71, 90.

Greenfield, Jeanette. 1989. *The Return of Cultural Treasures.* Cambridge: Cambridge University Press.

Greenlee, Bob. 1995. *Life Among the Ancient Ones: Two Accounts of an Anasazi Archaeological Research Project.* Boulder: Hardscrabble Press.

Grey, Don. 1963. Big Horn medicine wheel site, 48BH302. *Plains Anthropologist* 8(19): 27–40.

Griffin, James B. 1943. *The Fort Ancient Aspect: Its Cultural and Chronological Position in Mississippi Valley Archaeology.* Ann Arbor: University of Michigan Press.

Griffin, Martha M., and Vernon J. Henry. 1984. Historic changes in the mean high water shoreline of Georgia, 1857–1982. *Georgia Department of Natural Resources Bulletin* 98.

Grimaldi, David. 1993, June. Forever in amber. *Natural History* 59–61.

Grimaldi, David, and Rob DeSalle. 1994. The scientific romance with amber. In G. D. Rosenberg and D. L. Wolberg (Eds.), *Dino Fest: Proceedings of a Conference for the General Public.* Paleontological Society Special Publication, no. 7. Knoxville: University of Tennessee Press.

Griset, Suzanne (Ed.). 1986. Pottery of the Great Basin and adjacent areas. *University of Utah Anthropological Papers,* no. 111.

Gryba, Eugene M. 1988. A Stone Age pressure method of Folsom fluting. *Plains Anthropologist* 33(119): 53–66.

Gulliford, Andrew. 1996. Bones of contention: The repatriation of Native American human remains. *The Public Historian* 18(4): 119–143.

Gumerman, George J. (Ed.). 1991. *Exploring the Hohokam: Prehistoric Desert Peoples of the American Southwest.* Albuquerque: University of New Mexico Press.

Haag, William G. 1968. (Obituary of) James Alfred Ford, 1911–1968. *The Florida Anthropologist* 21(1): 31–33.

Habermas, J. 1987. *The Philosophical Discourse of Modernity.* Oxford: Oxford University Press.

Hagelberg, Erika. 1993, August/September. DNA from archaeological bone. *The Biochemist:* 17–22.

Hall, Robert L. 1977. An anthropocentric perspective for eastern United States prehistory. *American Antiquity* 42(4): 499–518.

Hammond, George P., and Edgar F. Goad. 1949. *A Scientist on the Trail: Travel Letters of A. F. Bandelier, 1880–1881.* Berkeley, CA: Quivira Society.

Hammond, Philip C. 1974. Archaeometry and time: A review. *Journal of Field Archaeology* 1(3/4): 329–335.

Handler, Jerome. 1979. Plantation slavery on Barbados, West Indies. *Archaeology* 32(4): 45–52.

Handler, Jerome, and Frederick Lange. 1978. *Plantation Slavery in Barbados: An Archaeological and Historical Investigation.* Cambridge: Harvard University Press.

Handsman, Russell G., and Mark P. Leone. 1989. Living history and critical archaeology in the reconstruction of the past. In Valerie Pinsky and Alison Wylie (Eds.), *Critical Traditions in Contemporary Archaeology: Essays in the Philosophy, History and Socio-Politics of Archaeology* (pp. 117–135). Cambridge: Cambridge University Press.

Handt, Oliva, Martin Richards, Marion Trommsdorff, Christian Kilger, Jaana Simanainen, Oleg Georgiev, Karin Bauer, Anne Stone, Robert Hedges, Walter Schaffner, Gerd Utermann, Bryan Sykes, and Svante Pääbo. 1994. Molecular genetic analyses of the Tyrolean ice man. *Science* 264: 1775–1778.

Hanson, Lee H., Jr. 1972. A few cents more. *The Conference on Historic Site Archaeology Papers* 4(1): 2–15.

Hantman, Jeffrey L., and Gary Dunham. 1993, May/June. The enlightened archaeologist. *Archaeology:* 44–49.

Harbert, Nancy, and Jeanne McDowell. 1991, January 14. This land is their land. *Time:* 18–19.

Harding, Sandra. 1991. *Whose Science? Whose Knowledge? Thinking From Women's Lives.* Ithaca: Cornell University Press.

Harjo, Suzan Shown. 1993. Foreword to *North American Indian Landmarks: A Traveler's Guide,* by George Cantor. Detroit: Visible Ink Press.

Harner, Michael J. 1970. Population pressure and the social evolution of agriculturalists. *Southwestern Journal of Anthropology* 26(1): 67–86.

Harp, Elmer, Jr. 1975. *Photography in Archaeological Research.* Albuquerque: University of New Mexico Press.

Harper, K. T., and G. M. Alder. 1970. Appendix I: The macroscopic plant remains of the deposits of Hogup Cave, Utah, and their paleoclimatic implications. In C. Melvin Aikens, *Hogup Cave. University of Utah Anthropological Papers* 93: 215–240.

———. 1972. Paleoclimatic inferences concerning the last 10,000 years from a resampling of Danger Cave, Utah. In Don D. Fowler (Ed.), Great Basin cultural ecology: A symposium. *Desert Research Institute Publications in the Social Sciences* 8: 13–23.

Harrington, Jean C. 1954. Dating stem fragments of seventeenth and eighteenth century clay tobacco pipes. *Quarterly Bulletin: Archaeological Society of Virginia* 9(1).

———. 1994. From architraves to artifacts: A metamorphosis. In Stanley South (Ed.), *Pioneers in Historical Archaeology: Breaking New Ground* (pp. 1–14). New York: Plenum Press.

Harrington, Spencer P. M. 1991, May/June. The looting of Arkansas. *Archaeology* 44(3): 22–30.

———. 1993, March/April. Bones and bureaucrats. *Archaeology* 46(2): 28–38.

Harris, David R. 1972. The origins of agriculture in the tropics. *American Scientist* 60: 180–193.

———. 1994. Agricultural origins, beginnings and transitions: The quest continues. *Antiquity* 69(261): 873–877.

Harris, David R., and Gordon C. Hillman (Eds.). 1989. *Foraging and Farming: The Evolution of Plant Exploitation.* London: Unwin Hyman

Harris, E. 1989. *Principles of Archaeological Stratigraphy.* 2d ed. New York: Academic Press.

Harris, Marvin. 1968a. Comments. In Sally R. Binford and Lewis R. Binford (Eds.), *New Perspectives in Archeology* (pp. 359–361). Chicago: Aldine.

———. 1968b. *The Rise of Anthropological Theory.* New York: Thomas Y. Crowell.

———. 1979. *Cultural Materialism: The Struggle for a Science of Culture.* New York: Random House.

———. 1985. *Good to Eat: Riddles of Food and Culture.* New York: Simon and Schuster.

———. 1991. Anthropology: Ships that crash in the night. In Richard Jessor (Ed.), *Perspectives on Social Science: The Colorado Lectures* (pp. 70–114). Boulder: Westview Press.

———. 1993. *Culture, People, Nature: An Introduction to General Anthropology.* 6th ed. New York: HarperCollins.

———. 1994. Cultural materialism is alive and well and won't go away until something better comes along. In R. Borofsky (Ed.), *Assessing Cultural Anthropology* (pp. 62–76). New York: McGraw-Hill.

Harris, Marvin, and Eric B. Ross (Eds.). 1987. *Food and Evolution: Toward a Theory of Human Food Habits.* Philadelphia: Temple University Press.

Harrison, Peter D. 1981. Some aspects of preconquest settlement in southern Quintana Roo, Mexico. In Wendy Ashmore (Ed.), *Lowland Maya Settlement Patterns* (pp. 259–286). Albuquerque: University of New Mexico Press.

Harrison, Peter D., and B. L. Turner II. 1978. *Pre-Hispanic Maya Agriculture.* Albuquerque: University of New Mexico Press.

Harvey, David. 1989. *The Condition of Postmodernity: An Enquiry Into the Origins of Cultural Change.* Cambridge, MA: Blackwell.

Hassan, Fekri A. 1975. Determination of the size, density and growth rate of hunting-gathering populations. In S. Polgar (Ed.), *Population, Ecology and Social Evolution.* The Hague: Mouton.

———. 1981. *Demographic Archaeology.* New York: Academic Press.

Hassan, I. 1985. The culture of postmodernism. *Theory, Culture and Society* 2(3): 119–132.

Hasten, Linda L. 1995. *Archaeology, 1995/96: Annual Editions.* Guilford, CT: Dushkin Publishing Group.

Hastorf, Christine A., and Sissel Johannessen. 1991. Understanding changing people/plant relationships in the prehispanic Andes. In Robert W. Preucel (Ed.), *Processual and Postprocessual Archaeologies: Multiple Ways of Knowing the Past* (pp. 140–155). Southern Illinois University at Carbondale, Center for Archaeological Investigations, Occasional Paper, no. 10.

Hastorf, Christine A., and Virginia S. Popper (Eds.). 1988. *Current Paleoethnobotany: Analytical Methods and Cultural Interpretations of Archaeological Plant Remains.* Chicago: University of Chicago Press.

Hather, Jon G. (Ed.). 1994. *Tropical Archaeobotany: Applications and New Developments.* London: Routledge.

Haury, Emil W. 1950. *The Stratigraphy and Archaeology of Ventana Cave, Arizona.* Albuquerque: University of New Mexico Press; Tucson: University of Arizona Press.

———. 1962. HH-39: Recollections of a dramatic moment in Southwestern archaeology. *Tree-Ring Bulletin* 24(3–4): 11–14.

———. 1976. *The Hohokam, Desert Farmers & Craftsmen: Excavations at Snaketown, 1964–1965.* Tucson: University of Arizona Press.

Haury, Emil W., E. B. Sayles, and William W. Wasley. 1959. The Lehner mammoth site, southeastern Arizona. *American Antiquity* 25: 2–30.

Haviland, William A. 1994. *Anthropology.* 7th ed. Fort Worth: Harcourt Brace College Publishers.

Hawkes, Jaquetta. 1967. God in the machine. *Antiquity* 41(163): 174–180.

Hawkes, Kristen, and James F. O'Connell. 1985. Optimal foraging models and the case of the !Kung. *American Anthropologist* 87(2): 401–405.

Hawkes, Kristen, James F. O'Connell, and N. Blurton Jones. 1987. Hardworking Hadza grandmothers. In R. Foley and V. Standen (Eds.), *Comparative Socioecology of Mammals and Man.* London: Basil Blackwell.

Hawkesworth, Mary E. 1989. Knowers, knowing, known: Feminist theory and claims of truth. *Signs: Journal of Women in Culture and Society* 14(3): 533–557.

Hawley, Florence M. 1934. The significance of the dated prehistory of Chetro Ketl, Chaco Canyon, New Mexico. *University of New Mexico Bulletin,* Monograph Series 1(1). Albuquerque: University of New Mexico Press.

———. 1937. Reversed stratigraphy. *American Antiquity* 4: 297–299.

Hay, Richard I., and Mary D. Leakey. 1982. The fossil footprints of Laetoli. *Scientific American* 246(2): 50–57.

Hayden, Brian. 1979. *Palaeolithic Reflections: Lithic Technology and Ethnographic Excavation Among Australian Aborigines.* Atlantic Highlands, NJ: Humanities Press.

———. 1981a. Research and development in the Stone Age: Technological transitions among hunter-gatherers. *Current Anthropology* 22(5): 519–548.

———. 1981b. Subsistence and ecological adaptations in modern hunter-gatherers. In Robert S. O. Harding and Geza Teleki (Eds.), *Omnivorous Primates* (pp. 344–421). New York: Columbia University Press.

———. 1987. *Lithic Studies Among the Contemporary Highland Maya.* Tucson: University of Arizona Press.

———. 1990. Nimrods, piscators, pluckers, and planters: The emergence of food production. *Journal of Anthropological Archaeology* 9: 31–69.

———. 1992. Observing prehistoric women. In Cheryl Claassen (Ed.), *Exploring Gender Through Archaeology: Selected Papers From the 1991 Boone Conference.* Monographs in World Archaeology, no. 11 (pp. 33–47). Madison, WI: Prehistory Press.

Hayden, Brian, and Aubrey Cannon. 1984. The structure of material systems: Ethnoarchaeology in the Maya highlands. *Society of American Archaeology Papers,* no. 3.

Hedges, R. E. M., and J. A. J. Gowlett. 1986. Radiocarbon dating by accelerator mass spectrometry. *Scientific American* 254(1): 100–107.

Heighton, Robert F., and Kathleen A. Deagan. 1972. A new formula for dating kaolin clay pipestems. *The Conference on Historic Site Archaeology Papers* 6(2): 220–229.

Henderson, Julian (Ed.). 1989. *Scientific Analysis in Archaeology and Its Interpretation.* Los Angeles: UCLA Institute of Archaeology.

Henry, Donald O., and George H. Odell (Eds.). 1989. *Alternative Approaches to Lithic Analysis.* Archaeological Papers of the American Anthropological Association, no. 1. Washington, DC: American Anthropological Association.

Herrmann, Bernd, and Susanne Hummell (Eds.). 1994. *Ancient DNA: Recovery and Analysis of Genetic Material From Paleontological, Archaeological, Museum, Medical, and Forensic Specimens.* New York: Springer-Verlag.

Hester, Thomas R., Harry J. Shafer, and Kenneth L. Feder. 1997. *Field Methods in Archaeology.* 7th ed. Mountain View, CA: Mayfield.

Hill, Andrew. 1979a. Butchery and natural disarticulation: An investigatory technique. *American Antiquity* 44: 739–744.

———. 1979b. Disarticulation and scattering of mammal skeletons. *Paleobiology* 5(3): 261–274.

Hill, Andrew, and Anna Kay Behrensmeyer. 1984. Disarticulation patterns of some modern East African mammals. *Paleobiology* 10(3): 366–376.

Hill, James N. 1991. Archaeology and the accumulation of knowledge. In Robert W. Preucel (Ed.), *Processual and Postprocessual Archaeologies: Multiple Ways of Knowing the Past* (pp. 42–53). Center for Archaeological Investigations, Occasional Paper, no. 10. Carbondale: Southern Illinois University.

Hill, James N., and R. K. Evans. 1972. A model for classification and typology. In David L. Clarke (Ed.), *Models in Archaeology* (pp. 231–273). London: Methuen.

Hill, James N., and Richard H. Hevly. 1968. Pollen at Broken K Pueblo: Some new interpretations. *American Antiquity* 33(2): 200–210.

Hill, Jane. 1995. Science in anthropology: A perspective from linguistic anthropology. *Anthropology Newsletter* 36(7): 20.

Hobbs, Hulda R. 1940, June. Bandelier in the Southwest. *El Palacio* 47: 121–136.

Hodder, Ian. 1982a. *Symbols in Action: Ethnoarchaeological Studies of Material Culture.* Cambridge: Cambridge University Press.

——— (Ed.). 1982b. *Symbolic and Structural Archaeology.* Cambridge: Cambridge University Press.

———. 1985. Postprocessual archaeology. In Michael B. Schiffer (Ed.), *Advances in Archaeological Method and Theory.* Vol. 8 (pp. 1–26). Orlando, FL: Academic Press.

———. 1986. *Reading the Past: Current Approaches to Interpretation in Archaeology.* Cambridge: Cambridge University Press.

———. 1989a. Post-modernism, post-structuralism and post-processual archaeology. In Ian Hodder (Ed.), *The Meaning of Things.* One World Archaeology, no. 6 (pp. 64–78). London: Unwin Hyman.

———. 1989b. Writing archaeology: Site reports in context. *Antiquity* 63(239): 268–274.

———. 1990. Archaeology and the post-modern. *Anthropology Today* 6(5): 13–15.

———. 1991a. Postprocessual archaeology and the current debate. In Robert W. Preucel (Ed.), *Processual and Postprocessual Archaeologies: Multiple Ways of Knowing the Past* (pp. 30–41). Center for Archaeological Investigations, Occasional Paper, no. 10. Carbondale: Southern Illinois University.

———. 1991b. Interpretive archaeology and its role. *American Antiquity* 56(1): 7–18.

———. 1995. *Theory and Practice in Archaeology.* London: Routledge.

Hodder, Ian, Michael Shanks, Alexandra Alexandri, Victor Buehli, John Carman, Jonathan Last, and Gavin Lucas (Eds.). 1995. *Interpreting Archaeology: Finding Meaning in the Past.* London and New York: Routledge.

Hodge, Frederick Webb. 1914. Bandelier obituary. *American Anthropologist* 16(2): 349–358.

———. 1932. Biographical sketch and bibliography of Adolphe Francis Alphonse Bandelier. *New Mexico Historical Review* 7(4): 353–370.

Hoffman, Ellen. 1993, December. Saving our world's heritage. *Omni* 52–54, 58, 60–61.

Holliday, Vance T. (Ed.). 1992. *Soils in Archaeology: Landscape Evolution and Human Occupation.* Washington, DC: Smithsonian Institution Press.

Holloway, Marguerite. 1995. The preservation of the past. *Scientific American* 272(5): 98–101.

Holly, Gerald A., and Terry A. Del Bene. 1981. An evaluation of Keeley's "Microwear approach." *Journal of Archaeological Science* 8: 337–352.

Hooton, Earnest Albert. 1930. *The Indians of Pecos Pueblo: A Study of Their Skeletal Remains.* Papers of the Phillips Academy Southwestern Expedition 4. New Haven: Yale University Press.

Horai, Satoshi, Rumi Kondo, Yuko Nakagawa-Hattori, Seiji Hayashi, Shunro Sonoda, and Kazuo Tajima. 1993. Peopling of the Americas, founded by four major lineages of mitochondrial DNA. *Molecular Biological Evolution* 10(1): 23–47.

Horgan, John. 1996a. *The End of Science: Facing the Limits of Knowledge in the Twilight of the Scientific Age.* Reading, MA: Addison-Wesley.

———. 1996b, July 16. Science set free from truth. *The New York Times:* A-11.

Howard, Hildegarde. 1929. The avifauna of Emeryville shellmound. *University of California Publications in Zoology* 32:301–394.

Howells, W. W. 1960. Estimating population numbers through archaeological and skeletal remains. In R. F. Heizer and S. F. Cook (Eds.), *The Application of Quantitative Methods in Archaeology.* Viking Fund Publications in Anthropology, no. 28 (pp. 158–185). Chicago: Quadrangle.

Hoyt, John H., and John R. Hails. 1967. Pleistocene shoreline sediments in coastal Georgia: Deposition and modification. *Science* 155: 1541–1543.

Hoyt, John H., and Vernon J. Henry, Jr. 1971. Origin of capes and shoals along the southeastern coast of the United States. *Geological Society of America Bulletin* 82: 59–66.

Hu, Q., P. E. Smith, N. M. Evensen, and D. York. 1994. Lasing in the Holocene: Extending the ^{40}Ar-^{39}Ar laser probe method into the ^{14}C age range. *Earth and Planetary Science Letters* 123: 331–336.

Huss-Ashmore, Rebecca, Alan H. Goodman, and George J. Armelagos. 1982. Nutritional inference from paleopathology. In Michael B. Schiffer (Ed.), *Advances in Archaeological Method and Theory.* Vol. 5 (pp. 395–474). New York: Academic Press.

Hutchinson, Dale, and Clark Spencer Larsen. 1988. Determination of stress episode duration from linear enamel hypoplasias: A case study from St. Catherines Island, Georgia. *Human Biology* 60(1): 93–110.

Hyslop, John. 1984. *The Inka Road System.* Orlando: Academic Press.

Irwin-Williams, Cynthia. 1990. Women in the field: The role of women in archaeology before 1960. In G. Kass-Simon and Patricia Farnes (Eds.), *Women of Science: Righting the Record* (pp. 1–41). Bloomington: Indiana University Press.

Isaac, Glynn L. 1978. The food-sharing behavior of protohuman hominids. *Scientific American* 238(4): 90–108.

Jacobi, R. M. 1978. Northern England in the eighth millennium BC: An essay. In Paul Mellars (Ed.), *The Early Post-Glacial Settlement of Northern Europe* (pp. 295–332). London: Duckworth.

Jamieson, Ross W. 1995. Material culture and social death: African-American burial practices. *Historical Archaeology* 29(4): 39–58.

Jefferson, Thomas. 1787. *Notes on the State of Virginia.* London: John Stockdale (reprinted Chapel Hill: University of North Carolina Press, 1954).

Jelks, Edward B. 1988. Optimal foraging and the division of labor. *American Anthropologist* 90: 130–136.

———. 1994. Frizzens of brass, alas. In Stanley South (Ed.), *Pioneers in Historical Archaeology: Breaking New Ground* (pp. 189–195). New York: Plenum Press.

Jennings, Jesse D. 1994. *Accidental Archaeologist: Memoirs of Jesse D. Jennings.* Salt Lake City: University of Utah Press.

Johnson, Allen W., and Timothy Earle. 1987. *The Evolution of Human Societies: From Foraging Group to Agrarian State.* Stanford, CA: Stanford University Press.

Johnson, George. 1996, October 22. Indian tribes' creationists thwart archaeologists. *The New York Times.*

Johnson, Gregory A. 1972. A test of the utility of central place theory in archaeology. In P. J. Ucko, R. Tringham, and G. W. Dimbleby (Eds.), *Man, Settlement and Urbanism* (pp. 769–785). London: Duckworth.

———. 1975. Locational analysis and Uruk local exchange systems. In Jeremy A. Sabloff and C. C. Lamberg-Karlovsky (Eds.), *Ancient Civilization and Trade* (pp. 285–339). Albuquerque: University of New Mexico Press.

Johnson, Jay K. (Ed.). 1993. *The Development of Southeastern Archaeology.* Tuscaloosa: University of Alabama Press.

Johnston, R. B. 1961. Archaeological application of the proton magnetometer in Indiana (U.S.A.). *Archaeometry* 4: 71–72.

Josephy, Alvin M., Jr. 1982. *Now That the Buffalo's Gone.* New York: Knopf.

Joukowsky, Martha. 1980. *A Complete Manual of Field Archaeology: Tools and Techniques of Field Work for Archaeologists.* Englewood Cliffs, NJ: Prentice Hall.

Judge, W. James, James I. Ebert, and Robert K. Hitchcock. 1975. Sampling in regional archaeological survey. In James W. Mueller (Ed.), *Sampling in Archaeology* (pp. 82–123). Tucson: University of Arizona Press.

Jull, A. J. T., D. J. Donahue, and P. E. Damon. 1996. Factors affecting the apparent radiocarbon age of textiles: A comment on "Effects of fires and biofractionation of carbon isotopes on results of radiocarbon dating of old textiles: The Shroud of Turin" by D. A. Kouznetsov et al. *Journal of Archaeological Science* 23: 157–160.

Katzenberg, M. Anne, Henry P. Schwarcz, Martin Knyf, and F. Jerome Melbye. 1995. Stable isotope evidence for maize horticulture and paleodiet in southern Ontario, Canada. *American Antiquity* 60(2): 335–350.

Keegan, William F. 1986. The optimal foraging analysis of horticultural production. *American Anthropologist* 88(1): 92–107.

———. 1992. *The People Who Discovered Columbus: The Prehistory of the Bahamas.* Gainesville: University Press of Florida.

Keeley, Lawrence H. 1974. Technique and methodology in microwear studies: A critical review. *World Archaeology* 5(3): 323–336.

———. 1980. *Experimental Determination of Stone Tool Uses: A Microwear Analysis.* Chicago: University of Chicago Press.

Keeley, Lawrence H., and M. H. Newcomer. 1977. Microwear analysis of experimental flint tools: A test case. *Journal of Archaeological Science* 4: 29–62.

Keene, Arthur S. 1979. Economic optimization models and the study of hunter-gatherer subsistence settlement systems. In C. Renfrew and K. Cooke (Eds.), *Transformations: Mathematical Approaches to Culture Change* (pp. 369–404). New York: Academic Press.

Keesing, Roger M. 1994. Theories of culture revisited. In Robert Borofsky (Ed.), *Assessing Cultural Anthropology* (pp. 301–310). New York: McGraw-Hill.

Kehoe, Alice B., and Thomas F. Kehoe. 1973. Cognitive models for archaeological interpretation. *American Antiquity* 38(2): 150–154.

Kelley, Jane Holden, and Marsha P. Hanen. 1988. *Archaeology and the Methodology of Science.* Albuquerque: University of New Mexico Press.

Kelly, Robert L. 1995. *The Foraging Spectrum.* Washington, DC: Smithsonian Institution Press.

Kelso, William M. 1982. Jefferson's garden: Landscape archaeology at Monticello. *Archaeology* 35(4): 38–45.

———. 1984. Landscape archaeology: A key to Virginia's cultivated past. In Robert P. Maccubbin and Peter Martin (Eds.), *British and American Gardens in the Eighteenth Century* (pp. 159–169). Williamsburg, VA: Colonial Williamsburg Foundation.

———. 1986. Mulberry Row: Slave life at Thomas Jefferson's Monticello. *Archaeology* 39(5): 28–35.

Kemeny, John G. 1959. *A Philosopher Looks at Science.* New York: Van Nostrand Reinhold.

Kent, Susan. 1987. Parts as wholes: A critique of theory in archaeology. In Susan Kent (Ed.), *Method and Theory for Activity Area Research: An Ethnoarchaeological Approach* (pp. 513–546). New York: Columbia University Press.

Kidd, Kenneth E. 1949. *The Excavation of Ste Marie I.* Toronto: University of Toronto Press.

———. 1994. The Phoenix of the North. In Stanley South (Ed.), *Pioneers in Historical Archaeology: Breaking New Ground* (pp. 49–65). New York: Plenum Press.

Kidder, Alfred V. 1924. *An Introduction to the Study of Southwestern Archaeology.* New Haven: Yale University Press.

———. 1928. The present state of knowledge of American history and civilization prior to 1492 (pp. 749–753). Paris: International Congress of History, Oslo, 1928, Compte Rendu.

———. 1960. Reminiscences in Southwest archaelogy, I. *Kiva* 25: 1–32.

Kidder, Alfred V., and Samuel J. Guernsey. 1921. Basket-maker caves of northeastern Arizona. *Papers of the Peabody Museum of American Archaeology and Ethnology* 8(2).

Kidder, Alfred V., Jesse D. Jennings, and Edwin M. Shook. 1946. *Excavations at Kaminaljuyu, Guatemala.* Washington, DC: Carnegie Institution of Washington Publication no. 561.

King, Thomas F. 1991. Some dimensions of the pothunting problem. In George S. Smith and John E. Ehrenhard (Eds.), *Protecting the Past* (pp. 83–92). Boca Raton, FL: CRC Press.

Klejn, L. S. 1977. A panorama of theoretical archaeology. *Current Anthropology* 18: 1–42.

———. 1982. *Archaeological typology.* Translated by P. Dole. British Archaeological Reports, International Series, no. 153. Oxford B. A. R.

Klesert, Anthony L. 1992. A view from Navajoland on the reconciliation of anthropologists and Native Americans. *Human Organization* 51(1): 17–22.

Klesert, Anthony L., and Alan S. Downer (Eds.). 1990. Preservation on the reservation: Native Americans, Native American lands and archaeology. *Navajo Nation Papers in Anthropology,* no. 26.

Klesert, Anthony L., and Shirley Powell. 1993. A perspective on ethics and the reburial controversy. *American Antiquity* 58(2): 348–354.

Klotz, Irving M. 1996. Postmodernist rhetoric does not change fundamental scientific facts. *The Scientist* 10(15): 9.

Kluckhohn, Clyde. 1964. *Mirror for Man: The Relation of Anthropology to Modern Life.* 7th ed. Greenwich, CN: Fawcett Publications.

Knapp, A. Bernard. 1996. Archaeology without gravity: Postmodernism and the past. *Journal of Archaeological Method and Theory* 3(2): 127–158.

Knuttson, K., and R. Hope. 1984. The application of acetate peels in lithic usewear analysis. *Archaeometry* 26: 49–61.

Koch, Christopher P. (Ed.). 1989. *Taphonomy: A Bibliographic Guide to the Literature.* Orono, ME: Center for the Study of the First Americans.

Kohl, Philip L. 1984. Force, history and the evolutionist paradigm. In Matthew Spriggs (Ed.), *Marxist Perspectives in Archaeology* (pp. 127–134). Cambridge: Cambridge University Press.

———. 1993. Limits to a post-processual archaeology (or, the dangers of a new scholasticism). In Norman Yoffee and Andrew Sheratt (Eds.), *Archaeological Theory: Who Sets the Agenda?* (pp. 13–19). Cambridge: Cambridge University Press.

Kolata, Alan L., and Charles Ortloff. 1989. Thermal analysis of Tiwanaku raised field systems in the Lake Titicaca Basin of Bolivia. *Journal of Archaeological Science* 16: 233–263.

Konigsberg, Lyle W., and Jane E. Buikstra. 1995. Regional approaches to the investigation of past human biocultural structure. In Lane Anderson Beck (Ed.), *Regional Approaches to Mortuary Analysis* (pp. 191–219). New York: Plenum Press.

Kosso, P. 1991. Method in archaeology: Middle-range theory as hermeneutics. *American Antiquity* 56(4): 621–627.

Kottak, Conrad Philip. 1991. *Anthropology: The Exploration of Human Diversity.* 5th ed. New York: McGraw-Hill.

Kouznetsov, Dmitri A., Andrey A. Ivanov, and Pavel R. Veletsky. 1996. Effects of fires and biofractionation of carbon isotopes on results of radiocarbon dating of old textiles: The shroud of Turin. *Journal of Archaeological Science* 23: 109–121.

Kowalewski, Stephen A. 1990a. Merits of full-coverage survey: Examples from the Valley of Oaxaca, Mexico. In Suzanne K. Fish and Stephen A. Kowalewski (Eds.), *The Archaeology of Regions: A Case for Full-Coverage Survey* (pp. 33–85). Washington, DC: Smithsonian Institution Press.

———. 1990b. Scale and complexity: Issues in the archaeology of the Valley of Oaxaca. In Joyce Marcus (Ed.), *Debating Oaxaca Archaeology.* Ann Arbor: Museum of Anthropology, University of Michigan. *Anthropological Papers,* 84: 207–270.

Kraft, John C., Ilhan Kayan, and Oguz Erol. 1980. Geomorphic reconstructions in the environs of ancient Troy. *Science* 209(4458): 776–782.

Krieger, Alex D. 1944. The typological concept. *American Antiquity* 9(3): 271–288.

Kroeber, Alfred L., and Clyde Kluckhohn. 1952. Culture: A critical review of concepts and definitions. *Papers of the Peabody Museum of American Archaeology and Ethnology,* no. 47(1).

Kroll, Ellen M., and T. Douglas Price (Eds.). 1991. *The Interpretation of Archaeological Spatial Patterning.* New York: Plenum Press.

Kvamme, Kenneth L. 1989. Geographic information systems in regional archaeological research and data management. In M. B. Schiffer (Ed.), *Archaeological Method and Theory.* Vol. 1 (pp. 139–204). Tucson: University of Arizona Press.

Lahren, Larry, and Robson Bonnichsen. 1974. Bone foreshafts from a Clovis burial in southwestern Montana. *Science* 186: 147–149.

Lamberg-Karlovsky, C. C. (Ed.). 1989. *Archaeological Thought in America.* Cambridge: Cambridge University Press.

Lambert, Patricia M. 1993. Health in prehistoric populations of the Santa Barbara Channel Islands. *American Antiquity* 58(3): 509–522.

Lambert, Patricia M., and Phillip L. Walker. 1991. Physical anthropological evidence for the evolution of social complexity in coastal Southern California. *Antiquity* 65(249): 963–973.

Landon, David B. 1996. Feeding colonial Boston: A zooarchaeological study. *Historical Archaeology* 30(1).

Lange, Charles H., and Carroll L. Riley. 1996. *Bandelier: The Life and Adventures of Adolph Bandelier.* Salt Lake City: University of Utah Press.

Lange, Frederick W., and Jerome S. Handler. 1985. The ethnohistorical approach to slavery. In Theresa A. Singleton (Ed.), *The Archaeology of Slavery and Plantation Life* (pp. 15–32). Orlando, FL: Academic Press.

Larsen, Clark Spencer. 1987. Bioarchaeological interpretations of subsistence economy and behavior from human skeletal remains. In Michael B. Schiffer (Ed.), *Advances in Archaeological Method and Theory.* Vol. 10 (pp. 339–445). Orlando, FL: Academic Press.

———. 1995. Biological changes in human populations with agriculture. *Annual Review of Anthropology* 24: 185–213.

———. 1997. *Bioarchaeology: Interpreting Behavior From the Human Skeleton.* Cambridge: Cambridge University Press.

Larsen, Clark Spencer, and David Hurst Thomas. 1982. The anthropology of St. Catherines Island: 4. The St. Catherines period mortuary complex. *Anthropological Papers of the American Museum of Natural History* 57(4): 271–342

Lathrap, Donald W. 1973. Gifts of the cayman: Some thoughts on the subsistence basis of Chavín. In Donald W. Lathrap and Jody Douglas (Eds.), *Variation in Anthropology* (pp. 91–105). Urbana: Illinois Archaeological Survey.

———. 1977. Our father the cayman, our mother the gourd: Spinden revisited, or a unitary model for the emergence of agriculture in the New World. In Charles A. Reed (Ed.), *Origins of Agriculture* (pp. 713–751). The Hague: Mouton.

———. 1985. Jaws: The control of power in the early nuclear American ceremonial center. In C. B. Donnan (Ed.), *Early Ceremonial Architecture in the Andes* (pp. 241–267). Washington, DC: Dumbarton Oaks Research Library and Collection.

Laughlin, William S. 1968. Hunting: An integrative biobehavioral system and its evolutionary importance. In Richard Lee and Irven DeVore (Eds.), *Man the Hunter* (pp. 304–320). Chicago: Aldine.

Layton, Robert (Ed.). 1989. *Who Needs the Past? Indigenous Values and Archaeology.* One World Archaeology Series. London: Unwin Hyman.

Leakey, Mary. 1984. *Disclosing the Past.* Garden City: Doubleday.

Leakey, Mary, and J. M. Harris (Eds.). 1987. *Laetoli: A Pliocene Site in Northern Tanzania.* Oxford: Clarendon Press.

Lee, Richard B., and Irven DeVore. 1968. *Man the Hunter.* Chicago: Aldine.

Lees, Susan H. 1994. Irrigation and society. *Journal of Archaeological Research* 2(4): 361–378.

Legge, A. J., and P. A. Rowley-Conwy. 1988. *Star Carr Revisited.* London: Centre for Extra-Mural Studies, Birkbeck College, University of London.

Lekson, Stephen H. 1986. *Great Pueblo Architecture of Chaco Canyon.* Albuquerque: University of New Mexico Press.

Lenihan, Daniel J. 1993, November. Damming the past. *Natural History* 102(11): 41–46.

Lentz, D. L. 1991. Maya diets of the rich and poor: Paleoethnobotanical evidence from Copan. *Latin American Antiquity* 2(3): 269–287.

Leonard, Robert D., and George T. Jones. 1987. Elements of an inclusive evolutionary model for archaeology. *Journal of Anthropological Archaeology* 6(3): 199–219.

Leone, Mark P. 1984. Interpreting ideology in historical archaeology: Using the rules of perspective in the William Paca garden in Annapolis, Maryland. In Daniel Miller and Christopher Tilley (Eds.), *Ideology, Power, and Prehistory* (pp. 25–36). Cambridge: Cambridge University Press.

———. 1986. Symbolic, structural, and critical archaeology. In David J. Meltzer, Don D. Fowler, and Jeremy A. Sabloff (Eds.), *American Archaeology Past and Future: A Celebration of the Society for American Archaeology 1935–1985* (pp. 415–438). Washington, DC: Smithsonian Institution Press.

———. 1987. Rule by ostentation: The relationship between space and sight in eighteenth-century landscape architecture in the Chesapeake region of Maryland. In Susan Kent (Ed.), *Method and Theory for Activity Area Research: An Ethnoarchaeological Approach* (pp. 604–633). New York: Columbia University Press.

———. 1988a. The Georgian order as the order of merchant capitalism in Annapolis, Maryland. In Mark P. Leone and Parker B. Potter (Eds.), *The Recovery of Meaning: Historical Archaeology in the Eastern United States* (pp. 235–261). Washington, DC: Smithsonian Institution Press.

———. 1988b. The relationship between archaeological data and the documentary record: Eighteenth century gardens in Annapolis, Maryland. *Historical Archaeology* 22(1): 29–35.

———. 1995. A historical archaeology of capitalism. *American Anthropologist* 97(2): 251–268.

Leone, Mark P., Paul R. Mullins, Marian C. Creveling, Laurence Hurst, Barbara Jackson-Nash, Lynn D. Jones, Hannah Jopling Kaiser, George C. Logan, and Mark S. Warner. 1995. Can an African-American historical archaeology be an alternative voice? In Ian Hodder, Michael Shanks, Alexandra Alexandri, Victor Buchli, John Carman, Jonathan Last, and Gavin Lucas (Eds.), *Interpreting Archaeology: Finding Meaning in the Past* (pp. 110–124). London: Routledge.

Leone, Mark P., and Parker B. Potter, Jr. 1992. Legitimation and the classification of archaeological sites. *American Antiquity* 57(1): 137–145.

Leone, Mark P., Parker B. Potter, Jr., and Paul A. Shackel. 1987. Toward a critical archaeology. *Current Anthropology* 28(3): 283–302.

Leone, Mark P., and Neil Asher Silberman. 1995. *Invisible America: Unearthing Our Hidden History.* New York: Henry Holt.

Leone, Mark P., Jennifer Stabler, and Anna-Marie Burlaga. n.d. A street plan for hierarchy in Annapolis: An analysis of State Circle as a geometric form. In Paul Shackel, Paul Mullins, and Mark Warner (Eds.), *Annapolis Pasts.* Knoxville: University of Tennessee Press. In press.

Leroi-Gourhan, Arlette. 1975. The flowers found with Shanidar IV, a Neanderthal burial in Iraq. *Science* 190(4214): 562–564.

Levine, Mary Ann. 1994. Creating their own niches: Career styles among women in Americanist archaeology between the wars. In Cheryl Claassen (Ed.), *Women in Archaeology* (pp. 9–40). Philadelphia: University of Pennsylvania Press.

Levy, Clifford J. 1993, August 13. Study to examine bones from blacks' burial site. *The New York Times.*

Lewarch, Dennis E., and Michael J. O'Brien. 1981. The expanding role of surface assemblages in archaeological research. In Michael B. Schiffer (Ed.), *Advances in Archaeological Method and Theory.* Vol. 4 (pp. 297–342). New York: Academic Press.

Lewin, Roger. 1992. Mitochondria tell the tale of migrations to America. *New Scientist* 133(1809): 16.

———. 1993. Genes from a disappearing world. *New Scientist* 138(1875): 25–29.

———. 1994. Human origins: The challenge of Java's skulls. *New Scientist* 142(1924): 36–40.

Liebowitz, Harold, and Robert L. Folk. 1980. Archaeological geology of Tel Yin'am, Galilee, Israel. *Journal of Field Archaeology* 7(1): 23–42.

Lightfoot, Kent G. 1995. Culture contact studies: Redefining the relationship between prehistoric and historical archaeology. *American Antiquity* 60(2): 199–217.

Lipe, William D. 1995. The archeology of ecology. *Federal Archaeology* 8(1): 8–13.

Lister, Adrian M. 1994. Ancient DNA: Not quite *Jurassic Park. Trends in Ecology and Evolution* 9(3): 82–84.

Lister, Robert H., and Florence C. Lister. 1981. *Chaco Canyon: Archaeology and Archaeologists.* Albuquerque: University of New Mexico Press.

Little, Barbara J. (Ed.). 1992. *Text-Aided Archaeology.* Boca Raton, FL: CRC Press.

Little, Elizabeth A., and Margaret J. Schoeninger. 1995. The Late Woodland diet on Nantucket Island and the problem of maize in coastal New England. *American Antiquity* 60(2): 351–368.

Lofstrom, Ted, Jeffrey P. Tordoff, and Douglas C. George. 1982. A seriation of historic earthenwares in the Midwest, 1780–1870. *The Minnesota Archaeologist* 41(1): 3–29.

Long, A., and Bruce Rippeteau. 1974. Testing contemporaneity and averaging radiocarbon dates. *American Antiquity* 39(2): 205–215.

Long, William R. 1993, August 24. Old canals carry hope to Andes. *Los Angeles Times.*

Longacre, William A. (Ed.). 1991. *Ceramic Ethnoarchaeology.* Tucson: University of Arizona Press.

Longacre, William A., and James M. Skibo (Eds.). 1994. *Kalinga Ethnoarchaeology: Expanding Archaeological Method and Theory.* Washington, DC: Smithsonian Institution Press.

Loy, Thomas H. 1983. Prehistoric blood residues: Detection on tool surfaces and identification of species of origin. *Science* 220(4602): 1269–1271.

Loy, Thomas H., and B. L. Hardy. 1992. Blood residue analysis of 90,000-year-old stone tools from Tabun Cave, Israel. *Antiquity* 66(250): 24–35.

Loy, Thomas H., Rhys Jones, D. E. Nelson, Betty Meehan, John Vogel, John Southon, and Richard Cosgrove. 1990. Accelerator radiocarbon dating of human blood proteins in pigments from Late Pleistocene art sites in Australia. *Antiquity* 64(242): 110–116.

Lubbock, Sir John. 1865. *Pre-historic Times, As Illustrated by Ancient Remains, and the Manners and Customs of Modern Savages.* London: Williams and Norgate.

———. 1869. *Pre-historic Times.* 2d ed. London: Williams and Norgate.

———. 1870. *The Origin of Civilization and the Primitive Condition of Man: Mental and Social Conditions of Savages.* London: Longmans, Green.

Lukacs, John R., and Lori L. Minderman. 1992. Dental pathology and agricultural intensification from Neolithic to Chalcolithic periods at Mehrgarh (Baluchistan, Pakistan). In C. Jarrige, *South Asian Archaeology, 1989.* Monographs in World Archaeology, no. 14 (pp. 167–179). Madison, WI: Prehistory Press.

Lukacs, John R., D. H. Retief, and Jean-Francois Jarrige. 1985, Spring. Dental disease in prehistoric Baluchistan. *National Geographic Research* 1(2): 184–197.

Lukacs, John R., Michael Schultz, and Brian E. Hemphill. 1989. Dental pathology and dietary patterns in Iron Age northern Pakistan. In P. Sorensen and K. Frifelt (Eds.), *South Asian Archaeology 1985* (pp. 475–496). London: Curzon Press.

Lummis, Charles F. 1914, April/May. Death of Bandelier, an irreparable loss. *El Palacio* 1(6, 7): 1, 3, 4.

Lyman, R. Lee. 1987. Archaeofaunas and butchery studies: A taxonomic perspective. In Michael B. Schiffer (Ed.), *Advances in Archaeological Method and Theory*. Vol. 10 (pp. 249–337). New York: Academic Press.

———. 1994. *Vertebrate Taphonomy*. Cambridge: Cambridge University Press.

Lynott, Mark J., and Alison Wylie. 1995. *Ethics in American Archaeology: Challenges for the 1990s*. Special Report, Society for American Archaeology.

Lyon, Edwin A. 1996. *A New Deal for Southeastern Archaeology*. Tuscaloosa: University of Alabama Press.

Lyons, T. R., and T. E. Avery. 1984. *Remote Sensing: A Handbook for Archaeologists and Cultural Resource Managers*. Washington, DC: National Park Service, U.S. Department of the Interior.

Lyotard, Jean François. 1984. *The Postmodern Condition: A Report on Knowledge*. Translated by G. Bennington and B. Massumi. Minneapolis: University of Minnesota Press.

MacMahon, Darcie, and Kathleen Deagan. 1996, September/October. Legacy of Fort Mose. *Archaeology:* 54–58.

MacNeish, Richard S. 1964. Ancient Mesoamerican civilization. *Science* 143(3606): 531–537.

———. 1967. A summary of the subsistence. In Douglas S. Byers (Ed.), *The Prehistory of the Tehuacan Valley*. Vol. 1, *Environment and Subsistence* (pp. 290–309). Austin: University of Texas Press.

———. 1978. *The Science of Archaeology?* North Scituate, MA: Duxbury Press.

———. 1992. *The Origins of Agriculture and Settled Life*. Norman: University of Oklahoma Press.

MacNeish, Richard S., Melvin L. Fowler, Angel Garcia Cook, Frederick A. Peterson, Antoinette Nelken-Terner, and James A. Neely (Eds.). 1972. *The Prehistory of the Tehuacan Valley*. Vol. 5, *Excavations and Reconnaissance*. Austin: University of Texas Press.

Majewski, Teresita, and Michael J. O'Brien. 1987. The use and misuse of nineteenth-century English and American ceramics in archaeological analysis. In Michael B. Schiffer (Ed.), *Advances in Archaeological Method and Theory*. Vol. 11 (pp. 97–210). New York: Academic Press.

Malinowski, Bronislaw. 1945. In P. Kaberry (Ed.), *The Dynamics of Culture Change: An Inquiry Into Race Relations in Africa*. New Haven: Yale University Press.

Mansfield, Victor N. 1980. The Bighorn Medicine Wheel as a site for the vision quest. *Archaeoastronomy Bulletin* 3(2): 26–29.

Maples, William R., and Michael Browning. 1994. *Dead Men Do Tell Tales*. New York: Doubleday.

Marcus, George E. 1994. After the critique of ethnography: Faith, hope, and charity, but the greatest of these is charity. In Robert Borofsky (Ed.), *Assessing Cultural Anthropology* (pp. 40–54). New York: McGraw-Hill.

Marcus, George E., and Michael M. J. Fischer. 1986. *Anthropology as Cultural Critique: An Experimental Moment in the Human Sciences*. Chicago: University of Chicago Press.

Marcus, Joyce. 1973. Territorial organization of the lowland Classic Maya. *Science* 180(4089): 911–916.

———. 1974. Reply to Romanov and Hammond. *Science* 183: 876–877.

———. 1976. *Emblem and State in the Classic Maya Lowlands: An Epigraphic Approach to Territorial Organization.* Washington, DC: Dumbarton Oaks.

———. 1983. Lowland Maya archaeology at the crossroads. *American Antiquity* 48(3): 454–488.

——— (Ed.). 1990. *Debating Oaxaca Archaeology.* Ann Arbor: Museum of Anthropology, University of Michigan. *Anthropological Papers,* no. 84.

———. 1992. *Mesoamerican Writing Systems: Propaganda, Myth, and History in Four Ancient Civilizations.* Princeton: Princeton University Press.

Marcus, Joyce, and Kent Flannery. 1996. *Zapotec Civilization.* London: Thames and Hudson.

Marquardt, William H. 1978. Advances in archaeological seriation. In Michael B. Schiffer (Ed.), *Advances in Archaeological Method and Theory.* Vol. 1 (pp. 257–314). New York: Academic Press.

Marshack, Alexander. 1976. Implications of the Paleolithic symbolic evidence for the origin of language. *American Scientist* 64(2): 136–145.

———. 1989. Evolution of the human capacity: The symbolic evidence. *Yearbook of Physical Anthropology* 32: 1–34.

———. 1991. *The Roots of Civilization: The Cognitive Beginnings of Man's First Art, Symbol and Notation.* Revised and expanded. Mount Kisco, NY: Moyer Bell.

———. 1995a, July/August. Images of the Ice Age. *Archaeology:* 28–36, 38–39.

———. 1995b. Methodology and the search for notation among engraved pebbles of the European Late Palaeolithic. *Antiquity* 69(266): 1049–1051.

———. 1996. A Middle Paleolithic symbolic composition from the Golan Heights: The earliest known depictive image. *Current Anthropology* 37(2): 357–365.

Marshack, Alexander, and Francesco d'Errico. 1996. The La Marche antler revisited. *Cambridge Archaeological Journal* 6(1): 99–118.

Martin, Debra L., Alan H. Goodman, and George J. Armelagos. 1985. Skeletal pathologies as indicators of quality and quantity of diet. In Robert I. Gilbert and James H. Mielke (Eds.), *The Analysis of Prehistoric Diets* (pp. 227–279). Orlando: Academic Press.

Martin, John F. 1985. Optimal foraging theory: A review of some models and their applications. *American Anthropologist* 85: 612–629.

Martin, Paul S. 1954. Comments on "Southwestern archaeology: Its history and theory" by Walter W. Taylor. *American Anthropologist* 56: 570–572.

Martin, Paul S., and David A. Gregory. 1973. Prehistoric and contemporary problems. In Paul S. Martin and Fred Plog (Eds.), *The Archaeology of Arizona: A Study of the Southwest Region* (pp. 361–368). Garden City, NY: Doubleday/Natural History Press.

Martin, Paul S., and Fred Plog (Eds.). 1973. *The Archaeology of Arizona: A Study of the Southwest Region.* Garden City, NY: Doubleday/Natural History Press.

Martin, William A., James E. Bruseth, and Robert J. Huggins. 1991. Assessing feature function and spatial patterning of artifacts with geophysical remote-sensing data. *American Antiquity* 56(4): 701–720.

Maschner, Herbert Donald Graham (Ed.). 1996. *Darwinian Archaeologies.* New York: Plenum Press.

Masco, Joseph. 1996. Competitive displays: Negotiating genealogical rights to the potlatch at the American Museum of Natural History. *American Anthropologist* 98(4): 837–852.

Mason, Owen K., and Stefanie L. Ludwig. 1990. Resurrecting beach ridge archaeology: Parallel depositional records from St. Lawrence Island and Cape Krusenstern, Western Alaska. *Geoarchaeology* 5(4): 349–373.

Matson, R. G. 1991. *The Origins of Southwestern Agriculture.* Tucson: University of Arizona Press.

Maynard Smith, J. 1978. Optimization theory in evolution. *Annual Review of Ecology and Systematics* 9: 31–56.

Mazess, Richard B., and D. W. Zimmermann. 1966. Pottery dating from thermoluminescence. *Science* 152(3720): 347–348.

McAlister, George A. 1988. *Alamo—The Price of Freedom: A History of Texas.* San Antonio: Docutex.

McDonald, William A. 1967. *Progress Into the Past: The Rediscovery of Mycenaean Civilization.* New York: Macmillan.

McDougall, I. 1990. Potassium-argon dating in archaeology. *Science Progress* 74: 15–30.

McEwan, Bonnie G. (Ed.). 1993. *The Spanish Missions of La Florida.* Gainesville: University Press of Florida.

McGimsey, C. R., III, and H. A. Davis. 1977. *The Management of Archaeological Resources: The Airlie House Report.* Special publication of the Society for American Archaeology.

McGuire, Randall H. 1992a. *A Marxist Archaeology.* San Diego: Academic Press.

———. 1992b. *Death, Society, and Ideology in a Hohokam Community.* Boulder: Westview Press.

———. 1993. Archaeology and Marxism. In M. B. Schiffer (Ed.), *Archaeological Method and Theory.* Vol. 5 (pp. 101–157). Tucson: University of Arizona Press.

McGuire, Randall H., and Robert Paynter (Eds.). 1991. *The Archaeology of Inequality.* Oxford: Basil Blackwell.

McGuire, Randall H., and Michael B. Schiffer (Eds.). 1982. *Hohokam and Patayan: Prehistory of Southwestern Arizona.* New York: Academic Press.

McManamon, Francis P. 1984. Discovering sites unseen. In Michael B. Schiffer (Ed.), *Advances in Archaeological Method and Theory.* Vol. 7 (pp. 223–292). New York: Academic Press.

———. 1991. The many publics for archaeology. *American Antiquity* 56(1): 121–130.

———. 1992. Managing America's archaeological resources. In LuAnn Wandsnider (Ed.), *Quandaries and Quests: Visions of Archaeology's Future* (pp. 25–40). Carbondale: Southern Illinois University, Center for Archaeological Investigations, Occasional Paper, no. 20.

———. 1994. Changing relationships between Native Americans and archaeologists. *Historic Preservation Forum* 8(2): 15–20.

McManamon, Francis P., Patricia C. Knoll, Ruthann Knudson, George S. Smith, and Richard C. Waldbauer (Comps.). 1993. *The Secretary of the Interior's Report to Congress: Federal Archeological Programs and Activities.* Washington, DC: Departmental Consulting Archeologist Archeological Assistance Program, National Park Service, Dept. of the Interior.

McMillon, Bill. 1991. *The Archaeology Handbook: A Field Manual and Resource Guide.* New York: John Wiley and Sons.

McNutt, Charles H. 1973. On the methodological validity of frequency seriation. *American Antiquity* 38: 45–60.

Meggers, Betty J. 1971. *Amazonia: Man and Nature in a Counterfeit Paradise.* Chicago: Aldine.

Mehrer, Mark W. 1995. *Cahokia's Countryside: Household Archaeology, Settlement Patterns, and Social Power.* DeKalb: Northern Illinois University Press.

Mehringer, Peter J. 1977. Great Basin late-Quaternary environments and chronology. In Don Fowler (Ed.), Models and great basin prehistory: A symposium. *Desert Research Institute Publications in the Social Sciences* 12: 113–167.

———. 1986. Prehistoric environments. In Warren L. D'Azevedo (Ed.), *Handbook of North American Indians.* Vol. 11 (pp. 31–50). Washington, DC: Smithsonian Institution Press.

Mehringer, Peter J., Eric Blinman, and Kenneth L. Peterson. 1977. Pollen influx and volcanic ash. *Science* 198(4314): 257–261.

Mehringer, Peter J., and Vance Haynes. 1965. The pollen evidence for the environment of early man and extinct mammals at the Lehner mammoth site, southeastern Arizona. *American Antiquity* 31(1): 17–23.

Meighan, Clement W. 1976. Empirical determination of obsidian hydration rates from archaeological evidence. In R. E. Taylor (Ed.), *Advances in Obsidian Glass Studies* (pp. 106–119). Park Ridge, NJ: Noyes Press.

———. 1992. Some scholars' views on reburial. *American Antiquity* 57(4): 704–710.

Meltzer, David J. 1989. Why don't we know when the first people came to North America? *American Antiquity* 54(3): 471–490.

———. 1993, October. Coming to America. *Discover:* 90–97.

———. 1995. Clocking the First Americans. *Annual Review of Anthropology* 24: 21–45.

Meltzer, David J., Don D. Fowler, and Jeremy A. Sabloff (Eds.). 1986. *American Archaeology Past and Future: A Celebration of the Society for American Archaeology 1935–1985.* Washington, DC: Smithsonian Institution Press.

Messenger, Phyllis (Ed.). 1989. *The Ethics of Collecting Cultural Property: Whose Culture? Whose Property?* Albuquerque: University of New Mexico Press.

Metcalfe, D., and K. Heath. 1990. Microrefuse and site structure: The hearths and floors of the Heartbreak Hotel. *American Antiquity* 55(4): 781–796.

Meyer, Karl E. 1993, November/December. The hunt for Priam's treasure. *Archaeology:* 26–32.

———. 1995, July/August. Who owns the spoils of war? *Archaeology:* 46–52.

Michels, Joseph W. 1973. *Dating Methods in Archaeology.* New York: Seminar Press.

Miksicek, Charles H. 1987. Formation processes of the archaeobotanical record. In Michael B. Schiffer (Ed.), *Advances in Archaeological Method and Theory.* Vol. 10 (pp. 211–247). New York: Academic Press.

Miller, Daniel, and Christopher Tilley. 1984. *Ideology, Power and Prehistory.* Cambridge: Cambridge University Press.

Miller, George R., and Richard L. Burger. 1995. Our father the cayman, our dinner the llama: Animal utilization at Chavín de Huántar, Peru. *American Antiquity* 60(3): 421–458.

Miller, Gifford H., Peter B. Beaumont, A. J. T. Jull, and Beverly Johnson. 1992. Pleistocene geochronology and palaeothermometry from protein diagenesis in ostrich eggshells: Implications for the evolution of modern humans. *Philosophical Transactions of the Royal Society of London* B337: 149–157.

Milner, George R., Eve Anderson, and Virginia G. Smith. 1991. Warfare in late prehistoric west-central Illinois. *American Antiquity* 56(4): 581–603.

Minnis, Paul E. 1981. Seeds in archaeological sites: Sources and some interpretive problems. *American Antiquity* 46(1): 143–152.

Mithen, Steven. 1989. Evolutionary theory and post-processual archaeology. *Antiquity* 63(240): 483–494.

———. 1990. *Thoughtful Foragers: A Study of Prehistoric Decision Making.* Cambridge: Cambridge University Press.

———. 1995. Palaeolithic archaeology and the evolution of mind. *Journal of Archaeological Research* 3(4): 305–332.

Mobley, Charles M. 1980. Demographic structure of Pecos Indians: A model based on life tables. *American Antiquity* 45(3): 518–530.

Monastersky, Richard. 1990. Reopening old wounds. *Science News* 137(3): 40–42.

———. 1994. Fingerprints in the sand. In Aaron Podolefsky and Peter J. Brown, *Applying Anthropology: An Introductory Reader,* 3d ed. (pp. 90–93). Mountain View, CA: Mayfield Publishing.

Monks, Gregory G. 1981. Seasonality studies. In Michael B. Schiffer (Ed.), *Advances in Archaeological Method and Theory.* Vol. 4 (pp. 177–240). New York: Academic Press.

Moore, Clarence B. 1905. Certain aboriginal remains of the Black Warrior River. *Journal of the Academy of Natural Sciences of Philadelphia.* Second Series, 13: 123–244.

———. 1907. Moundville revisited. *Journal of the Academy of Natural Sciences of Philadelphia,* Second Series, 13: 337–405.

Moore, Kenneth (Ed.). 1987. *Waymarks: The Notre Dame Inaugural Lectures in Anthropology.* Notre Dame, IN: University of Notre Dame Press.

Moore, P. D., J. A. Webb, and M. E. Collinson. 1991. *Pollen Analysis.* Oxford: Blackwell Scientific.

Morell, Virginia. 1993. Anthropology: Nature-culture battleground. *Science* 261: 1798–1802.

———. 1994. An anthropological culture shift. *Science* 264: 20–22.

Morgado, Martin J. 1987. *Junipero Serra's Legacy.* Pacific Grove, CA: Mount Carmel.

Morgan, Lewis Henry. [1877] 1963. *Ancient Society.* E. Leacock (Ed.), New York, Meridian Books; World Publishing.

Morren, George E. B., Jr. 1984. Warfare on the highland fringe of New Guinea: The case of the mountain Ok. In R. Brian Ferguson (Ed.), *Warfare, Culture, and Environment* (pp. 169–207). Orlando: Academic Press.

Morris, Ann Axtell. 1933. *Digging in the Southwest.* New York: Doubleday, Doran.

Morris, Craig. 1995. Airborne archeology. *Natural History* 104(12): 70–72.

Morris, Craig, and Adriana von Hagen. 1993. *The Inka Empire and Its Andean Origins.* New York: Abbeville Press.

Morris, Ian. 1991. The archaeology of ancestors: The Saxe/Goldstein hypothesis revisited. *Cambridge Archaeological Journal* 1(2): 147–168.

Moss, Emily. 1983. *The Functional Analysis of Flint Implements–Pincevent and Pont d'Ambon: Two Case Studies From the French Final Palaeolithic.* British Archaeological Reports, International Series, no. 177.

Mudar, Karen. 1978. The effects of socio-cultural variables on food preferences in early 19th century Detroit. *The Conference on Historic Site Archaeology Papers* 12: 323–329.

Mueller, James W. 1974. The use of sampling in archaeological survey. *Society for American Archaeology Memoir,* no. 28.

——— (Ed.). 1975. *Sampling in Archaeology.* Tucson: University of Arizona Press.

Murra, John V. 1994. John Hyslop, 1945–1993. *Andean Past* 4: 1–7.

Murray, Tim. 1996. Coming to terms with the living: Some aspects of repatriation for the archaeologist. *Antiquity* 70(267): 217–220.

National Park Service. 1995, Fall/Winter. Special Report: The Native American Graves Protection and Repatriation Act. *Federal Archeology.*

Neary, John. 1993, September/October. Project sting. *Archaeology:* 52–59.

Neff, Hector. 1992. Ceramics and evolution. In M. B. Schiffer (Ed.), *Archaeological Method and Theory.* Vol. 4 (pp. 141–194). Tucson: University of Arizona Press.

Nei, Masatoshi. 1992. Age of the common ancestor of human mitochondrial DNA. *Molecular Biology and Evolution* 9(6): 1176–1178.

Nelson, Nels C. 1909. Shellmounds of the San Francisco Bay region. *University of California Publications in American Archaeology and Ethnology* 7(4): 310–356.

———. 1914. Pueblo ruins of the Galisteo Basin, New Mexico. *Anthropological Papers of the American Museum of Natural History* 15(1).

———. 1916. Chronology of the Tano Ruins, New Mexico. *American Anthropologist* 18(2): 159–180.

Nelson, Margaret C., Sarah M. Nelson, and Alison Wylie (Eds.). 1994. Equity issues for women in archeology. *Archeological Papers of the American Anthropological Association,* no. 5.

Nelson, Sarah M., and Alice B. Kehoe (Eds.). 1990. Powers of observation: Alternative views in archaeology. *Archeological Papers of the American Anthropological Association,* no. 2.

Nelson, Sarah M., and Margaret C. Nelson. 1994. Conclusion. In M. C. Nelson, S. M. Nelson, and A. Wylie (Eds.), Equity issues for women in archeology. *Archeological Papers of the American Anthropological Association* 5: 229–235.

Neuman, Robert W. 1984. *An Introduction to Louisiana Archaeology.* Baton Rouge: Louisiana State University Press.

Newcomer, M. H., and L. H. Keeley. 1979. Testing a method of microwear analysis with experimental flint tools. In Brian Hayden (Ed.), *Lithic Use-Wear Analysis* (pp. 195–205). New York: Academic Press.

Nicholas, Lynn H. 1994. *The Rape of Europa: The Fate of Europe's Treasures in the Third Reich and the Second World War.* New York: Knopf.

Nixon, Lucia. 1994. Gender bias in archaeology. In Leonie J. Archer and Susan Fischler (Eds.), *Women in Ancient Societies: An Illusion of the Night* (pp. 1–23). Basingstoke: Macmillan Press.

Noble, David Grant (Ed.). 1984. *New Light on Chaco Canyon.* Santa Fe: School of American Research Press.

———. 1991a. *Ancient Ruins of the Southwest: An Archaeological Guide.* Rev. ed. Flagstaff: Northland Publishing.

——— (Ed.). 1991b. *The Hohokam: Ancient People of the Desert.* Santa Fe: School of American Research Press.

Noël Hume, Ivor. 1964. Archaeology: Handmaiden to history. *The North Carolina Historical Review* 41(2): 214–225.

———. 1969a. *Archaeology and Wetherburn's Tavern.* Williamsburg: Colonial Williamsburg Foundation.

———. 1969b. *Historical Archaeology.* New York: Knopf.

———. 1970. *A Guide to Artifacts of Colonial America.* New York: Knopf.

———. 1976. *A Guide to Artifacts of Colonial America.* New York: Knopf.

Oakley, Kenneth P. 1959. *Man the Tool-maker.* 4th ed. Chicago: University of Chicago Press.

———. 1968. *Frameworks for Dating Fossil Man.* 2d ed. Chicago: Aldine.

O'Brien, Michael J., and Thomas D. Holland. 1990. Variation, selection, and the archaeological record. In Michael B. Schiffer (Ed.), *Archaeological Method and Theory.* Vol. 2 (pp. 31–79). Tucson: University of Arizona Press.

O'Connell, James F. 1987. Alyawara site structure and its archaeological implications. *American Antiquity* 51: 74–108.

———. 1995. Ethnoarchaeology needs a general theory of behavior. *Journal of Archaeological Research* 3(3): 205–255.

O'Connell, James F., and Kristen Hawkes. 1981. Alyawara plant use and optimal foraging theory. In Bruce Winterhalder and Eric Alden Smith (Eds.), *Hunter-Gatherer Foraging Strategies: Ethnographic and Archaeological Analyses* (pp. 99–125). Chicago: University of Chicago Press.

———. 1984. Food choice and foraging sites among the Alyawara. *Journal of Anthropological Research* 40(4): 504–535.

Odell, George Hanley (Ed.). 1996. *Stone Tools: Theoretical Insights Into Human Prehistory.* New York: Plenum Press.

Odell, George Hanley, and F. Odell-Vereecken. 1980. Verifying the reliability of lithic use-wear assessments by "blind tests": The low power approach. *Journal of Field Archaeology* 7: 87–120.

Ofori-Ansa, Kwaku. 1995. Identification and validation of the Sankofa symbol. *Update: Newsletter of the African Burial Ground and Five Points Archaeological Projects* 1(8): 3.

Olsen, Stanley J. 1960. Post-cranial skeletal characters of *Bison* and *Bos*. *Papers of the Peabody Museum of American Archaeology and Ethnology* 35(4).

———. 1964. Mammal remains from archaeological sites, part 1: Southeastern and southwestern United States. *Papers of the Peabody Museum of American Archaeology and Ethnology* 61(1).

———. 1968. Fish, amphibian, and reptile remains from archaeological sites, part 1: Southeastern and southwestern United States. *Papers of the Peabody Museum of American Archaeology and Ethnology* 61(2).

———. 1973. Mammal remains from archaeological sites, part 1: Southeastern and southwestern United States. *Papers of the Peabody Museum of Archaeology and Ethnology* 56(1).

Orlove, Benjamin S. 1980. Ecological anthropology. *Annual Review of Anthropology* 9: 235–273.

Orme, B. (Ed.). 1982. *Problems and Case Studies in Archaeological Dating.* Devon: University of Exeter.

Orser, Charles E., Jr. 1984. The past ten years of plantation archaeology in the southeastern United States. *Southeastern Archaeology* 3: 1–12.

———. 1991. The continued pattern of dominance: Landlord and tenant on the postbellum cotton plantation. In Randall H. McGuire and Robert Paynter (Eds.), *The Archaeology of Inequality* (pp. 40–54). Oxford: Basil Blackwell.

———. 1995. *A Historical Archaeology of the Modern World.* New York: Plenum.

——— (Ed.). 1996. *Images of the Recent Past: Readings in Historical Archaeology.* Walnut Creek, CA: Altamira Press.

Orser, Charles E., Jr., and Brian M. Fagan. 1995. *Historical Archaeology.* New York: HarperCollins.

Ortner, Donald J., and Walter G. J. Putschar. 1985. *Identification of Pathological Conditions in Human Skeletal Remains.* Washington, DC: Smithsonian Institution Press.

Orton, Clive, Paul Tyers, and Alan Vince. 1993. *Pottery in Archaeology.* Cambridge: Cambridge University Press.

O'Shea, John M. 1984. *Mortuary Variability: An Archaeological Investigation.* Orlando: Academic Press.

Ovenden, Michael W., and David A. Rodger. 1981. Megaliths and medicine wheels. In Michael Wilson, Kathie L. Road, and Kenneth J. Hardy (Eds.), Megaliths to medicine wheels: Boulder structures in archaeology. *Proceedings of the Eleventh Annual Chacmool Conference* (pp. 371–386). Calgary: The Archaeological Association of the University of Calgary.

Pääbo, Svante. 1993, November. Ancient DNA: Genetic information that had seemed lost forever turns out to linger in the remains of long-dead plants and animals. *Scientific American:* 87–92.

Palkovich, Ann M. 1983. A comment on Mobley's "Demographic structure of Pecos Indians." *American Antiquity* 48(1): 142–147.

Parezo, Nancy J. (Ed.). 1993. *Hidden Scholars: Women Anthropologists and the Native American Southwest.* Albuquerque: University of New Mexico Press.

Parezo, Nancy J., and Susan Bender. 1994. From glacial to chilly climate: A comparison between archeology and socio-cultural anthropology. In M. C. Nelson, S. M. Nelson, and A. Wylie (Eds.), *Equity Issues for Women in Archeology* (pp. 73–81). *Archeological Papers of the American Anthropological Association,* no. 5.

Parker Pearson, Michael. 1982. Mortuary practices, society and ideology: An ethnoarchaeological study. In Ian Hodder (Ed.), *Symbolic and Structural Archaeology* (pp. 99–113). Cambridge: Cambridge University Press.

———. 1995. Return of the living dead: Mortuary analysis and the New Archaeology revisited. *Antiquity* 69(266): 1046–1048.

Parmalee, Paul W. 1985. Identification and interpretation of archaeologically derived animal remains. In Robert I. Gilbert and James H. Mielke (Eds.), *The Analysis of Prehistoric Diets* (pp. 61–95). New York: Academic Press.

Parrington, Michael. 1983. Remote sensing. *Annual Review of Anthropology* 12: 105–124.

Parsons, Jeffrey R. 1990. Critical reflections on a decade of full-coverage regional survey in the Valley of Mexico. In Suzanne K. Fish and Stephen A. Kowalewski (Eds.), *The Archaeology of Regions: A Case for Full-Coverage Survey* (pp. 7–31). Washington, DC: Smithsonian Institution Press.

Pastron, Allen G. 1994. Opportunities in cultural resources management. In Aaron Podolefsky and Peter J. Brown (Eds.), *Applying Anthropology: An Introductory Reader* (pp. 86–89). Mountain View, CA: Mayfield Publishing.

Patterson, Thomas C. 1971. The emergence of food production in central Peru. In Stuart Struever (Ed.), *Prehistoric Agriculture* (pp. 181–207). New York: Natural History Press.

———. 1990. Some theoretical tensions within and between the processual and postprocessual archaeologies. *Journal of Anthropological Archaeology* 9(2): 189–200.

———. 1991. Who did archaeology in the United States before there were archaeologists and why? Preprofessional archaeologies of the nineteenth century. In Robert W. Preucel (Ed.), *Processual and Postprocessual Archaeologies: Multiple Ways of Knowing the Past* (pp. 242–250). Carbondale: Southern Illinois University, Center for Archaeological Investigations, Occasional Paper, no. 10.

———. 1994. *The Theory and Practice of Archaeology: A Workbook.* 2d ed. Englewood Cliffs, NJ: Prentice Hall.

———. 1995. *Toward a Social History of Archaeology in the United States.* Fort Worth: Harcourt Brace.

Paynter, Robert. 1989. The archaeology of equality and inequality. *Annual Review of Anthropology* 18: 369–399.

Paynter, Robert, and Randall H. McGuire. 1991. The archaeology of inequality: Material culture, domination, and resistance. In Randall H. McGuire and Robert Paynter (Eds.), *The Archaeology of Inequality* (pp. 1–27). Oxford: Basil Blackwell.

Peacock, James. 1994. Challenges facing the discipline. *Anthropology Newsletter* 35(9): 1, 5.

Pearsall, Deborah M. 1982. Phytolith analysis: Applications of a new paleoethnobotanical technique in archeology. *American Anthropologist* 84(4): 862–870.

Pearsall, Deborah M., and Dolores R. Piperno. 1990. Antiquity of maize cultivation in Ecuador: Summary and reevaluation of the evidence. *American Antiquity* 55(2): 324–337.

Peck, Mary. 1994. *Chaco Canyon: A Center and Its World.* Santa Fe: Museum of New Mexico Press.

Peebles, Christopher S. 1971. Moundville and surrounding sites: Some structural considerations of mortuary practices II. In James A. Brown (Ed.), *Approaches to the Social Dimensions of Mortuary Practices. Society for American Archaeology Memoir* 25: 68–91.

———. 1977. Biocultural adaptation in prehistoric America: An archeologist's perspective. In Robert L. Blakely (Ed.), *Biocultural Adaptation in Prehistoric America* (pp. 115–130). *Southern Anthropological Society Proceedings*, no. 11. Athens: University of Georgia Press.

———. 1981. Archaeological research at Moundville: 1840–1980. *Southeastern Archaeological Conference Bulletin* 24: 77–81.

———. 1987. Moundville from 1000 to 1500 A.D. as seen from 1840 to 1985 A.D. In Robert D. Drennan and Carlos A. Uribe (Eds.), *Chiefdoms in the Americas* (pp. 21–41). Lanham, MD: University Press of America.

Peebles, Christopher S., and Susan M. Kus. 1977. Some archaeological correlates of ranked societies. *American Antiquity* 42: 421–448.

Pendleton, Michael W. 1983. A comment concerning testing flotation recovery rates. *American Antiquity* 48(3): 615–616.

Percy, George. 1976. The use of a mechanical earth auger at the Torreya Site, Liberty County, Florida. *Florida Anthropologist* 29(1): 24–32.

Perkins, Dexter, and Patricia Daly. 1968. A hunter's village in Neolithic Turkey. *Scientific American* 219: 96–106.

Phillips, David A., Philip Duke, Randall H. McGuire, Dean J. Saitta, Lynne Sebastian, and David R. Wilcox. 1994, March. An open letter to Southwestern archaeologists. *Anthropology Newsletter* 35(3): 15–16.

Phillips, E. D. 1964. The Greek vision of prehistory. *Antiquity* 38(151): 171–186.

Phillips, James L., and James A. Brown (Eds.). 1983. *Archaic Hunters and Gatherers in the American Midwest.* New York: Academic Press.

Phillips, Philip, and James A. Brown. 1978. *Pre-Columbian Shell Engravings From the Craig Mound at Spiro, Oklahoma. Part 1.* Cambridge, MA: Peabody Museum Press.

———. 1984. *Pre-Columbian Shell Engravings From the Craig Mound at Spiro, Oklahoma. Part 2.* Cambridge: Peabody Museum of Archaeology and Ethnology.

Pinsky, Valerie, and Alison Wylie (Eds.). 1995. *Critical Traditions in Contemporary Archaeology: Essays in the Philosophy, History and Socio-Politics of Archaeology.* Albuquerque: University of New Mexico Press.

Piperno, Dolores R. 1984. A comparison and differentiation of phytoliths from maize and wild grasses: Use of morphological criteria. *American Antiquity* 49(2): 361–383.

———. 1987. *Phytolith Analysis: An Archaeological and Geological Perspective.* San Diego: Academic Press.

Pitts, Mike. 1979. Hides and antlers: A new look at the gatherer-hunter site at Star Carr, North Yorkshire, England. *World Archaeology* 11(1): 32–42.

Plog, Stephen, Fred Plog, and Walter Wait. 1978. Decision making in modern surveys. In Michael B. Schiffer (Ed.), *Advances in Archaeological Method and Theory.* Vol. 1 (pp. 383–421). New York: Academic Press.

Podolefsky, Aaron, and Peter J. Brown. 1994. *Applying Anthropology: An Introductory Reader.* 3d ed. Mountain View, CA: Mayfield Publishing.

Pollard, Mark. 1989, January 21. Archaeology in ruins? *New Scientist:* 52–55.

Pope, Saxton T. 1974. Hunting with Ishi–the last Yuana Indian. *Journal of California Anthropology* 1(2): 152–173.

Potter, Parker B., Jr. 1994. *Public Archaeology in Annapolis: A Critical Approach to History in Maryland's Ancient City.* Washington, DC: Smithsonian Institution Press.

Powell, Mary Lucas. 1985. The analysis of dental wear and caries for dietary reconstructions. In R. I. Gilbert, Jr., and J. H. Mielke (Eds.), *The Analysis of Prehistoric Diets* (pp. 307–338). Orlando: Academic Press.

———. 1988. *Status and Health in Prehistory: A Case Study of the Moundville Chiefdom.* Washington, DC: Smithsonian Institution Press.

Powell, Mary Lucas, Patricia S. Bridges, and Ann Marie Wagnes Mires (Eds.). 1991. *What Mean These Bones? Studies in Southeastern Bioarchaeology.* Tuscaloosa: University of Alabama Press.

Powell, Shirley, Christiana Elnora Garza, and Aubrey Hendricks. 1993. Ethics and ownership of the past: The reburial and repatriation controversy. In Michael B. Schiffer (Ed.), *Archaeological Method and Theory.* Vol. 5 (pp. 1–42). Tucson: University of Arizona Press.

Powledge, Tabitha M., and Mark Rose. 1996, September/October. The great DNA hunt. *Archaeology:* 36–44.

Preston, Douglas J. 1986. *Dinosaurs in the Attic: An Excursion Into the American Museum of Natural History.* New York: St. Martin's Press.

———. 1989, February. Skeletons in our museums' closets. *Harper's Magazine* 278(1665): 66–75.

Preucel, R. W. (Ed.). 1991. *Processual and Postprocessual Archaeologies: Multiple Ways of Knowing the Past.* Carbondale: Southern Illinois University, Center for Archaeological Investigations, Occasional Paper, no. 10.

———. 1995. The postprocessual condition. *Journal of Archaeological Research* 3(2): 147–175.

Price, Barbara J. 1982. Cultural materialism: A theoretical review. *American Antiquity* 47(4): 709–741.

Price, T. Douglas (Ed.). 1989. *The Chemistry of Prehistoric Human Bone.* Cambridge: Cambridge University Press.

Price, T. Douglas, and James A. Brown. 1985. Aspects of hunter-gatherer complexity. In T. Douglas Price and James A. Brown (Eds.), *Prehistoric Hunter-Gatherers: The Emergence of Cultural Complexity* (pp. 3–20). New York: Academic Press.

Price, T. Douglas, and Gary M. Feinman. 1993. *Images of the Past.* Mountain View, CA: Mayfield Publishing.

——— (Eds.). 1995. *Foundations of Social Inequality.* New York: Plenum Press.

Price T. Douglas, and Anne Birgitte Gebauer (Eds.). 1995. *Last Hunters–First Farmers: New Perspectives on the Prehistoric Transition to Agriculture.* Santa Fe: School of American Research Press.

Price, T. Douglas, and Gitte Gebauer. 1996. *Adventures in Fugawiland! A Computer Simulation in Archaeology.* 2d ed. Mountain View, CA: Mayfield Publishing.

Purdy, Barbara A. 1996. *How to Do Archaeology the Right Way.* Gainesville: University Press of Florida.

Quimby, George I. 1994. Historical archaeology as I saw it: 1935–1970. In Stanley South (Ed.), *Pioneers in Historical Archaeology: Breaking New Ground* (pp. 113–124). New York: Plenum Press.

Raab, L. Mark, and Albert C. Goodyear. 1984. Middle-range theory in archaeology: A critical review of origins and applications. *American Antiquity* 49(2): 255–268.

Radin, Paul. 1942. *The Unpublished Letters of Adolphe F. Bandelier Concerning the Writing and Publication of* The Delight Makers. El Paso: Carl Hertzog.

Ralph, Elizabeth K., and Mark C. Han. 1966. Dating of pottery by thermoluminescence. *Nature* 210(5033): 245–247.

———. 1969. Potential of thermoluminescence in supplementing radiocarbon dating. *World Archaeology* 1(2): 157–169.

Ramenofsky, Ann F. 1987. *Vectors of Death: The Archaeology of European Contact.* Albuquerque: University of New Mexico Press.

Ramsey, Christopher Bronk. 1995. *OxCal Program 2.18.* Oxford Radiocarbon Accelerator Unit. Oxford: Oxford University.

Rankin-Hill, Lesley M., and Michael L. Blakey. 1994. W. Montague Cobb (1904–1990): Physical anthropologist, anatomist, and activist. *American Anthropologist* 96(1): 74–96.

Rapp, George, and John A. Gifford (Eds.). 1985. *Archaeological Geology.* New Haven: Yale University Press.

Rapp, George, and Susan C. Mulholland (Eds.). 1992. *Phytolith Systematics: Emerging Issues.* New York: Plenum Press.

Rathje, William L. 1971. The origin and development of lowland Classic Maya civilization. *American Antiquity* 36(3): 275–285.

———. 1975. Le projet du garbage 1975: Historic trade-offs. Paper presented at the annual meeting of the American Anthropological Association, San Francisco.

———. 1984. The garbage decade. *American Behavioral Scientist* 28(1): 9–29.

———. 1991, May. Once and future landfills. *National Geographic* 25: 116–134.

Rathje, William L., and Wilson W. Hughes. 1975. The garbage project as a nonreactive approach: Garbage in . . . garbage out. In H. W. Sinaiko and L. A. Broedling (Eds.), *Perspectives on Attitude Assessment: Surveys and Their Alternatives.* Manpower Research and Advisory Services, Smithsonian Institution, Technical Report, no. 2.

Rathje, William L., W. W. Hughes, D. C. Wilson, M. K. Tani, G. H. Archer, R. G. Hunt, and T. W. Jones. 1992. The archaeology of contemporary landfills. *American Antiquity* 57(3): 437–447.

Rathje, William L., and Michael McCarthy. 1977. Regularity and variability in contemporary garbage. In Stanley South (Ed.), *Research Strategies in Historic Archeology* (pp. 261–286). New York: Academic Press.

Rathje, William L., and Michael B. Schiffer. 1982. *Archaeology.* New York: Harcourt Brace Jovanovich.

Redman, Charles L. 1991. In defense of the seventies–The adolescence of New Archeology. *American Anthropologist* 93(2): 295–307.

Reiber, Linda, and Jane de Hart Mathews. 1982. Refocusing the past: Women in American history. *History News* 34: 40–41.

Reitz, Elizabeth J., and C. Margaret Scarry. 1985. Reconstructing historic subsistence with an example from sixteenth-century Spanish Florida. *Society of Historical Archaeology, Special Publication Series,* no. 3.

Reneau, S. L., T. M. Oberlander, and C. D. Harrington. 1991. Accelerator mass spectrometry radiocarbon dating of rock varnish: Discussion and reply. *Geological Society of America Bulletin* 103: 310–314.

Renfrew, Colin. 1972. *The Emergence of Civilisation: The Cyclades and the Aegean in the Third Millennium* B.C. London: Methuen.

———. 1979. *Problems in European Prehistory.* Edinburgh: Edinburgh University Press.

———. 1982a. Explanation revisited. In C. Renfrew, M. J. Rowlands, and B. A. Segraves (Eds.), *Theory and Explanation in Archaeology* (pp. 1–23). New York: Academic Press.

———. 1982b. *Towards an Archaeology of the Mind: An Inaugural Lecture Delivered Before the University of Cambridge on 30 November 1982.* Cambridge: Cambridge University Press.

———. 1983. Foreword to *Pursuit of the Past: Decoding the Archaeological Record* by Lewis R. Binford. New York: Thames and Hudson.

———. 1984. *Approaches to Social Archaeology.* Cambridge: Harvard University Press.

———. 1992. Archaeology, genetics and linguistic diversity. *Man* 27: 445–478.

———. 1993. Cognitive archaeology: Some thoughts on the archaeology of thought. *Cambridge Archaeological Journal* 3(2): 248–250.

———. 1994. What's new in archaeology? In Aaron Podolefsky and Peter J. Brown (Eds.), *Applying Anthropology: An Introductory Reader* (pp. 82–85). 3d ed. Mountain View, CA: Mayfield Publishing.

Renfrew, Colin, and Paul Bahn. 1996. *Archaeology: Theories, Methods, and Practice.* 2d. ed. London: Thames and Hudson.

Renfrew, Colin, and Stephen Shennan (Eds.). 1982. *Ranking, Resource and Exchange.* Cambridge: Cambridge University Press.

Renfrew, Colin, and Ezra B. W. Zubrow (Eds.). 1994. *The Ancient Mind: Elements of Cognitive Archaeology.* Cambridge: Cambridge University Press.

Reyman, J. E. (Ed.). 1992. *Rediscovering Our Past: Essays on the History of American Archaeology.* Brookfield, VT: Avebury.

Rice, Prudence M. 1987. *Pottery Analysis: A Sourcebook.* Chicago: University of Chicago Press.

———. 1996a. Recent ceramic analysis: 1. Function, style, and origins. *Journal of Archaeological Research* 4(2): 133–163.

———. 1996b. Recent ceramic analysis: 2. Composition, production, and theory. *Journal of Archaeological Research* 4(3): 165–202.

Rick, John W. 1987. Dates as data: An examination of the Peruvian preceramic radiocarbon record. *American Antiquity* 52(1): 55–73.

———. 1996. Total stations in archaeology. *Bulletin of the Society for American Archaeology* 14(4): 24–27.

Riding In, James. 1992. With ethics and morality: A historical overview of imperial archaeology and American Indians. *Arizona State Law Journal* 24(1): 11–34.

Ridings, Rosanna. 1996. Where in the world does obsidian hydration dating work? *American Antiquity* 61(1): 136–148.

Riley, D. N. 1987. *Air Photography and Archaeology.* London: Duckworth.

Rindos, David. 1984. *The Origins of Agriculture: An Evolutionary Perspective.* Orlando, FL: Academic Press.

———. 1989a. Diversity, variation and selection. In R. D. Leonard and G. T. Jones (Eds.), *Quantifying Diversity in Archaeology* (pp. 13–23). Cambridge: Cambridge University Press.

———. 1989b. Undirected variation and the Darwinian explanation of culture change. In M. B. Schiffer (Ed.), *Archaeological Method and Theory.* Vol. 1 (pp. 1–46). Tucson: University of Arizona Press.

Roberts, Charlotte A., and Keith Manchester. 1995. *The Archaeology of Disease.* 2d ed. Ithaca: Cornell University Press.

Roberts, David. 1993, December. "Reverse Archaeologists" are tracing the footsteps of a cowboy-explorer. *Smithsonian* 24(9): 28–38.

———. 1996. *In Search of the Old Ones: Exploring the Anasazi World of the Southwest.* New York: Simon and Schuster.

Rogers, Juliet, and Tony Waldron. 1989. Infections in paleopathology: The basis of classification according to most probable cause. *Journal of Archaeological Science* 16: 611–625.

Roosevelt, Anna Curtenius. 1980. *Parmana: Prehistoric Maize and Manioc Subsistence Along the Amazon and Orinoco.* New York: Academic Press.

Rose, Jerome C., Thomas J. Green, and Victoria D. Green. 1996. NAGPRA is forever: Osteology and the repatriation of skeletons. *Annual Review of Anthropology* 25: 81–103.

Rose, Mark. 1993, November/December. What did Schliemann find—and where, when, and how did he find it? *Archaeology* 46(6): 33–36.

Rosenau, Pauline Marie. 1992. *Post-Modernism and the Social Sciences: Insights, Inroads, and Intrusions.* Princeton: Princeton University Press.

Rosenberg, Michael. 1994. Pattern, process, and hierarchy in the evolution of culture. *Journal of Anthropological Archaeology* 13: 307–340.

Ross, Eric B. 1980. Patterns of diet and forces of production: An economic and ecological history of the ascendancy of beef in the United States diet. In Eric B. Ross (Ed.), *Beyond the Myths of Culture* (pp. 181–225). New York: Academic Press.

Ross, Jane Bennett. 1980. Ecology and the problem of tribe: A critique of the Hobbesian model of preindustrial warfare. In Eric B. Ross (Ed.), *Beyond the Myths of Culture* (pp. 33–60). New York: Academic Press.

Rossignol, Jacqueline, and LuAnn Wandsnider (Eds.). 1992. *Space, Time, and Archaeological Landscapes.* New York: Plenum Press.

Rothschild, Bruce M., and Larry D. Martin. 1993. *Palaeopathology: Disease in the Fossil Record.* Boca Raton, FL: CRC Press.

Rothschild, Nan A. 1990. *New York City Neighborhoods: The 18th Century.* San Diego: Academic Press.

Rouse, Irving. 1960. The classification of artifacts in archaeology. *American Antiquity* 25(3): 313–323.

———. 1967. Seriation in archaeology. In Carrol L. Riley and Walter W. Taylor (Eds.), *American Historical Anthropology: Essays in Honor of Leslie Spier* (pp. 153–195). Carbondale: Southern Illinois University Press.

Rovner, Irwin. 1983. Plant opal phytolith analysis: Major advances in archaeobotanical research. In Michael B. Schiffer (Ed.), *Advances in Archaeological Method and Theory.* Vol. 6 (pp. 225–266). New York: Academic Press.

———. 1987. Plant opal phytoliths: A probable factor in the origins of agriculture. In Linda Manzanilla (Ed.), *Studies in the Neolithic and Urban Revolutions* (pp. 103–119). B.A.R. International Series 349.

———. 1988. Macro- and micro-ecological reconstruction using plant opal phytolith data from archaeological sediments. *Geoarchaeology* 3(2): 155–163.

Rowe, John Howland. 1965. The renaissance foundations of anthropology. *American Anthropologist* 67(1): 1–20.

Ruff, Christopher B. 1981. A reassessment of demographic estimates for Pecos Pueblo. *American Journal of Physical Anthropology* 54: 147–151.

Russell, Steve. 1995. The legacy of ethnic cleansing: Implementation of NAGPRA in Texas. *American Indian Culture and Research Journal* 19(4): 193–211.

Ryder, M. L. 1969. *Animal Bones in Archaeology.* Oxford: Blackwell Scientific Publications.

Sabins, Floyd F., Jr. 1996. *Remote Sensing: Principles and Interpretation.* 3d ed. New York: W. H. Freeman.

Sabloff, Jeremy A., Lewis R. Binford, and Patricia A. McAnany. 1987. Understanding the archaeological record. *Antiquity* 61: 203–209.

Sahlins, Marshall D., and Elman R. Service. 1960. *Evolution and Culture.* Ann Arbor: University of Michigan Press.

Saitta, Dean J. 1992. Radical archaeology and middle-range methodology. *Antiquity* 66: 886–897.

Salmon, Merrilee H. 1982. *Philosophy and Archaeology.* New York: Academic Press.

Salmon, Merrilee H., and Wesley C. Salmon. 1979. Alternative models of scientific explanation. *American Anthropologist* 81(1): 61–74.

Salwen, Bert, and Sarah T. Bridges. 1977. Cultural differences and the interpretation of archaeological evidence: Problems with dates. *Researches and Transactions of the New York State Archaeological Association* 17(1): 165–173.

Sanders, John, and Peggy Sanders. 1986. Archaeological Graphic Services remote mapping system. *Advances in Computer Archaeology* 3: 40–55.

Sanders, William T., and Deborah L. Nichols. 1988. Ecological theory and cultural evolution in the Valley of Oaxaca. *Current Anthropology* 29(1): 33–80.

Sanders, William T., Jeffrey R. Parsons, and Robert S. Santley. 1979. *The Basin of Mexico: Ecological Processes in the Evolution of a Civilization.* New York: Academic Press.

Sanders, William T., and Barbara J. Price. 1968. *Mesoamerica: The Evolution of a Civilization.* New York: Random House.

Sassaman, Kenneth E. 1992. Lithic technology and the hunter-gatherer sexual division of labor. *North American Archaeologist* 13(3): 249–262.

———. 1993. *Early Pottery in the Southeast: Tradition and Innovation in Cooking Technology.* Tuscaloosa: University of Alabama Press.

Schiffer, Michael B. 1972. Archaeological context and systemic context. *American Antiquity* 37(2): 156–165.

———. 1976. *Behavioral Archeology.* New York: Academic Press.

———. 1977. Toward a unified science of the cultural past. In Stanley South (Ed.), *Research Strategies in Historical Archeology* (pp. 13–40). New York: Academic Press.

———. 1987. *Formation Processes of the Archaeological Record.* Albuquerque: University of New Mexico Press.

Schiffer, Michael B., and William L. Rathje. 1973. Efficient exploitation of the archeological record: Penetrating problems. In Charles L. Redman (Ed.), *Research and Theory in Current Archeology* (pp. 169–179). New York: Wiley.

Schiffer, Michael B., James M. Skibo, Tamara C. Boelke, Mark A. Neupert, and Meredith Aronson. 1994. New perspectives on experimental archaeology: Surface treatments and thermal response of the clay cooking pot. *American Antiquity* 59(2): 197–217.

Schliemann, Heinrich. 1875. *Troy and Its Remains.* New York: Scribner, Welford and Armstrong.

———. 1880. *Ilios: The City and Country of the Trojans.* London: Murray.

———. 1884. *Troja: Results of the Latest Researches.* New York: Harper.

Schmidt, Peter R., and Thomas C. Patterson (Eds.). 1995. *Making Alternative Histories: The Practice of Archaeology and History in Non-Western Settings.* Santa Fe: School of American Research Press.

Schoelwer, Susan P. 1985. *Alamo Images: Changing Perceptions of a Texas Experience.* Dallas: DeGolyer Library and Southern Methodist University Press.

Schommer, Carolynn. 1993. Comment on back cover of *What This Awl Means* by Janet D. Spector. St. Paul: Minnesota Historical Society Press.

Schuchhardt, C. 1891. *Schliemann's Excavations.* Translated by Eugénie Sellers. London: Macmillan.

Schulz, Peter D., and Sherri M. Gust. 1983a. Faunal remains and social status in 19th century Sacramento. *Historical Archaeology* 17(1): 44–53.

———. 1983b. Relative beef cut prices in the late 19th century: A note for historic sites faunal analysts. *Pacific Coast Archaeological Society Quarterly* 19(1): 12–18.

Schuyler, Robert. 1976. Images of America: The contribution of historical archaeology to national identity. *Southwestern Lore* 42(4): 27–39.

Schwimmer, Brian. 1996. Anthropology on the Internet: A review and evaluation of networked resources. *Current Anthropology* 37(3): 561–568.

Scollar, Irwin. 1969. Some techniques for the evaluation of archaeological magnetometer surveys. *World Archaeology* 1(1): 77–89.

Scollar, Irwin, A. Tabbagh, A. Hesse, and I. Herzog (Eds.). 1990. *Archaeological Prospecting and Remote Sensing.* Cambridge: Cambridge University Press.

Scott, Elizabeth M. (Ed.). 1994. *Those of Little Note: Gender, Race, and Class in Historical Archaeology.* Tucson: University of Arizona Press.

Sebastian, Lynne. 1992. *The Chaco Anasazi: Sociopolitical Evolution in the Prehistoric Southwest.* New Studies in Archaeology. Cambridge: Cambridge University Press.

Seifert, Donna J. (Ed.). 1991. Gender in Historical Archaeology. *Historical Archaeology* 25(4).

Service, Elman. 1971. *Primitive Social Organization: An Evolutionary Perspective.* 2d ed. New York: Random House.

———. 1975. *Origins of the State and Civilization: The Process of Cultural Evolution.* New York: Norton.

Shackel, Paul A. 1993. *Personal Discipline and Material Culture: An Archaeology of Annapolis, Maryland, 1695–1870.* Knoxville: University of Tennessee Press.

———. 1996. *Culture Change and the New Technology: An Archaeology of the Early American Industrial Era.* New York: Plenum Press.

Shackel, Paul A., and Barbara J. Little (Eds.). 1994. *Historical Archaeology of the Chesapeake.* Washington, DC: Smithsonian Institution Press.

Shackley, Steven. 1995, March. Relics, rights and regulations. *Scientific American*: 115.

Shanks, Michael. 1992. *Experiencing the Past: On the Character of Archaeology.* London: Routledge.

Shanks, Michael, and Christopher Tilley. 1987a. *Reconstructing Archaeology: Theory and Practice.* Cambridge: Cambridge University Press.

———. 1987b. *Social Theory and Archaeology.* Albuquerque: University of New Mexico Press.

———. 1992. *Re-Constructing Archaeology: Theory and Practice.* 2d ed. London: Routledge.

Shapiro, Gary. 1984. A soil resistivity survey of 16th-century Puerto Real, Haiti. *Journal of Field Archaeology* 11(1): 101–110.

———. 1987. Archaeology at San Luis: Broad-scale testing, 1984–1985. *Florida Archaeology,* no. 3.

Shea, John J. 1987. On accuracy and relevance in lithic use-wear analysis. *Lithic Technology* 16(2–3): 44–50.

Sheets, Payson D. (Ed.). 1983. *Archeology and Volcanism in Central America: The Zapotitán Valley of El Salvador.* Austin: University of Texas Press.

———. 1987. Dawn of a new Stone Age in eye surgery. In Robert J. Sharer and Wendy Ashmore (Eds.), *Archaeology: Discovering Our Past* (pp. 230–231). Mountain View, CA: Mayfield Publishing.

———. 1992. *The Cerén Site: A Prehistoric Village Buried by Volcanic Ash in Central America.* Fort Worth: Harcourt Brace Jovanovich.

Sheets, Payson D., and Donald K. Grayson. 1979. *Volcanic Activity and Human Ecology.* New York: Academic Press.

Sheets, Payson D., K. Hirth, F. Lange, F. Stross, F. Asaro, and H. Michel. 1990. Obsidian sources and elemental analyses of artifacts in southern Mesoamerica and the northern intermediate area. *American Antiquity* 55(1): 144–158.

Sheets, Payson D., and Brian R. McKee (Eds.). 1994. *Archaeology, Volcanism, and Remote Sensing in the Arenal Region, Costa Rica.* Austin: University of Texas Press.

Sheets, Payson D., and Tom Sever. 1988, November/December. High-tech wizardry. *Archaeology* 41(6): 28–35.

Sherratt, Andrew. 1993. The relativity of theory. In Norman Yoffee and Andrew Sherratt (Eds.), *Archaeological Theory: Who Sets the Agendu?* (pp. 119–130). Cambridge: Cambridge University Press.

Shipp, E. R. 1992, August 9. Black cemetery yields wealth of history. *The New York Times.*

Shippee, Robert. 1932. Lost valleys of Peru: Results of the Shippee-Johnson Peruvian expedition. *Geographical Review* 22(4): 562–581.

Shott, Michael J. 1996. An exegesis of the curation concept. *Journal of Anthropological Research* 52(3): 259–280.

Shreeve, James. 1992, September. The dating game. *Discover* 13(9): 76–83.

———. 1994. *Erectus* rising. *Discover* 15(9): 80–89.

Singleton, Theresa A. (Ed.). 1985. *The Archaeology of Slavery and Plantation Life.* Orlando, FL: Academic Press.

———. 1993. Carter's Grove: The Winthrop Rockefeller Archaeology Museum, Wolstenholme Towne, the slave quarter and the mansion: Long-term exhibitions at Colonial Williamsburg. *American Anthropologist* 95(2): 525–528.

———. 1995. The archaeology of slavery in North America. *Annual Review of Anthropology* 24: 119–140.

Singleton, Theresa A., and M. Bograd. 1995. The archaeology of the African diaspora in the Americas. *Columbian Quincentenary Series Guides to the Archaeological Literature of the Immigrant Experience in America, no. 2.* Glassboro, NJ: Society for Historical Archaeology.

Skibo, James M., William H. Walker, and Axel E. Nielsen (Eds.). 1995. *Expanding Archaeology.* Salt Lake City: University of Utah Press.

Smith, Bruce D. (Ed.). 1990. *The Mississippian Emergence.* Washington, DC: Smithsonian Institution Press.

———. 1992. *Rivers of Change: Essays on Early Agriculture in Eastern North America.* Washington, DC: Smithsonian Institution Press.

———. 1995. *The Emergence of Agriculture.* New York: Scientific American Library.

Smith, Charles C. 1994, Fall. In the presence of ancestors. *Massachusetts:* 10–13.

Smith, Eric Alden. 1983. Anthropological applications of optimal foraging theory: A critical review. *Current Anthropology* 24(5): 625–651.

———. 1985. On the logic and application of optimal foraging theory: A brief reply to Martin. *American Anthropologist* 87: 645–648.

———. 1991. *Inujjuamiut Foraging Strategies: Evolutionary Ecology of an Arctic Hunting Economy.* New York: Aldine de Gruyter.

Smith, Eric Alden, and Bruce Winterhalder. 1981. New perspectives on hunter-gatherer socioecology. In Bruce Winterhalder and Eric Alden Smith (Eds.), *Hunter-Gatherer Foraging Strategies: Ethnographic and Archeological Analyses* (pp. 1–12). Chicago: University of Chicago Press.

——— (Eds.). 1992. *Evolutionary Ecology and Human Behavior.* New York: Aldine de Gruyter.

Smith, George S., and John E. Ehrenhard (Eds.). 1991. *Protecting the Past.* Boca Raton, FL: CRC Press.

Smith, Laurajane. 1994. Heritage management as postprocessual archaeology? *Antiquity* 68(259): 300–309.

Smith, Phillip E. L. 1976. *Food Production and Its Consequences.* Menlo Park, CA: Cummings.

Smith, Phillip E. L., and T. Cuyler Young, Jr. 1972. The evolution of early agriculture and culture in greater Mesopotamia: A trial model. In Brian Spooner (Ed.), *Population Growth: Anthropological Implications* (pp. 1–59). Cambridge: MIT Press.

Snodgrass, Anthony. 1995. Betrayer of truth: Review of *Schliemann of Troy: Treasure and Deceit* by David A. Traill. *Nature* 378: 113–114.

Sobel, Mechal. 1987. *The World They Made Together: Black and White Values in Eighteenth-Century Virginia.* Princeton: Princeton University Press.

Sobolik, Kristin D. (Ed.). 1994. *Paleonutrition: The Diet and Health of Prehistoric Americans.* Carbondale: Southern Illinois University, Center for Archaeological Investigations, Occasional Paper, no. 22.

Society for American Archaeology. 1991. Archaeology . . . Is gender still an issue? *Bulletin of the Society for American Archaeology* 9(1).

Solecki, Ralph S. 1971. *Shanidar: The First Flower People.* New York: Knopf.

South, David B. 1972. Mean ceramic dates, median occupation dates, red ant hills and bumble bees: Statistical confidence and correlation. *The Conference on Historic Site Archaeology Papers* 6: 164–174.

South, Stanley A. 1977a. *Method and Theory in Historical Archeology.* New York: Academic Press.

——— (Ed.). 1977b. *Research Strategies in Historical Archaeology.* New York: Academic Press.

———. 1988. Santa Elena: Threshold of conquest. In Mark P. Leone and Parker B. Potter (Eds.), *The Recovery of Meaning: Historical Archaeology in the Eastern United States* (pp. 27–71). Washington, DC: Smithsonian Institution Press.

———. 1994a. The archaeologist and the crew: From the mountains to the sea. In Stanley South (Ed.), *Pioneers in Historical Archaeology: Breaking New Ground* (pp. 165–187). New York: Plenum Press.

——— (Ed.). 1994b. *Pioneers in Historical Archaeology: Breaking New Ground.* New York: Plenum Press.

Spaulding, Albert C. 1953. Statistical techniques for the discovery of artifact types. *American Antiquity* 18: 305–313.

———. 1960. The dimensions of archaeology. In G. E. Dole and R. L. Carneiro (Eds.), *Essays in the Science of Culture in Honor of Leslie A. White* (pp. 437–456). New York: Thomas Y. Crowell.

———. 1968. Explanation in archeology. In Sally R. Binford and Lewis R. Binford (Eds.), *New Perspectives in Archeology* (pp. 33–39). Chicago: Aldine.

———. 1977. On growth and form in archaeology: Multivariate analysis. *Journal of Anthropological Research* 33: 1–15.

———. 1985. Fifty years of theory. *American Antiquity* 50(2): 301–308.

———. 1988. Distinguished lecture: Archeology and anthropology. *American Anthropologist* 90(2): 263–271.

Spector, Janet D. 1983. Male/female task-differentiation among the Hidatsa: Toward the development of an archeological approach to the study of gender. In Patricia Albers and Beatrice Medicine (Eds.), *The Hidden Half: Studies of Plains Indian Women* (pp. 77–99). Lanham, MD: University Press of America.

———. 1993. *What This Awl Means: Feminist Archaeology at a Wahpeton Dakota Village.* St. Paul: Minnesota Historical Society Press.

Spector, Janet D., and Mary K. Whelan. 1989. Incorporating gender into archaeology courses. In Sandra Morgen (Ed.), *Gender and Anthropology: Critical Reviews for Research and Teaching* (pp. 65–94). Washington, DC: American Anthropological Association.

Spencer, Charles. 1990. On the tempo and mode of state formation: Neoevolutionism reconsidered. *Journal of Anthropological Archaeology* 9(1): 1–30.

———. 1993. Human agency, biased transmission, and the cultural evolution of chiefly authority. *Journal of Anthropological Archaeology* 12: 41–74.

———. 1994. Factional ascendance, dimensions of leadership, and the development of centralized authority. In E. M. Brumfiel and J. W. Fox (Eds.), *Factional Competition and Political Development in the New World* (pp. 31–43). Cambridge: Cambridge University Press.

Spencer-Wood, Suzanne M. 1991a. Toward a feminist historical archaeology of the construction of gender. In *The Archaeology of Gender* (pp. 234–244). Proceedings of the 22nd Annual Chacmool Conference. Calgary: The University of Calgary Archaeological Association.

———. 1991b. Toward an historical archaeology of materialistic domestic reform. In Randall H. McGuire and Robert Paynter (Eds.), *The Archaeology of Inequality* (pp. 231–286). Oxford: Basil Blackwell.

Speth, John D., and Gregory A. Johnson. 1976. Problems in the use of correlation for the investigation of tool kits and activity areas. In Charles E. Cleland (Ed.), *Cultural Change and Continuity: Essays in Honor of James Bennett Griffin* (pp. 35–57). New York: Academic Press.

Spielmann, Katherine A. (Ed.). 1995. The archaeology of gender in the American Southwest. *Journal of Anthropological Research* 51(2): 91–191.

Spielmann, Katherine A., Margaret J. Schoeninger, and Katherine Moore. 1990. Plains-Pueblo interdependence and human diet at Pecos Pueblo, New Mexico. *American Antiquity* 55(4): 745–765.

Spier, Leslie. 1917. An outline for a chronology of Zuñi ruins. *Anthropological Papers of the American Museum of Natural History* 18(3): 207–331.

———. 1931. N. C. Nelson's stratigraphic technique in the reconstruction of prehistoric sequences in southwestern America. In S. A. Rice (Ed.), *Methods in Social Science* (pp. 275–283). Chicago: University of Chicago Press.

Stafford, T. W., Jr., A. J. T. Jull, T. H. Zabel, D. J. Donahue, R. C. Duhamel, K. Brendel, C. V. Haynes, Jr., J. L. Bischoff, L. A. Payen, and R. E. Taylor. 1984. Holocene age of the Yuha burial: Direct radiocarbon determinations by accelerator mass spectrometry. *Nature* 308: 446–447.

Stahl, Ann B. 1995. Has ethnoarchaeology come of age? *Antiquity* 69(263): 404–407.

Stahl, Peter W. 1996. Holocene biodiversity: An archaeological perspective from the Americas. *Annual Review of Anthropology* 25: 105–126.

Stahle, David W., and Daniel Wolfman. 1985. The potential for archaeological tree-ring dating in eastern North America. In Michael B. Schiffer (Ed.), *Advances in Archaeological Method and Theory*. Vol. 8 (pp. 279–302). New York: Academic Press.

Staley, David P. 1993. The antiquities market. *Journal of Field Archaeology* 20(3): 347–355.

Stallings, W. S., Jr. 1939. *Dating Prehistoric Ruins by Tree-Rings*. Santa Fe: Laboratory of Anthropology Bulletin no. 8.

Stark, Barbara L. 1986. Origins of food production in the New World. In David J. Meltzer, Don D. Fowler, and Jeremy A. Sabloff (Eds.), *American Archaeology Past and Future: A Celebration of the Society for American Archaeology 1935–1985* (pp. 277–321). Washington, DC: Smithsonian Institution Press.

Stark, Miriam T. 1993. Re-fitting the "cracked and broken facade": The case for empiricism in post-processual ethnoarchaeology. In Norman Yoffee and Andrew Sherratt (Eds.), *Archaeological Theory: Who Sets the Agenda?* (pp. 93–104). Cambridge: Cambridge University Press.

Starr, Kevin. 1985. *Inventing the Dream: California Through the Progressive Era*. New York: Oxford University Press.

Staski, Edward, and Jonathan Marks. 1992. *Evolutionary Anthropology: An Introduction to Physical Anthropology and Archaeology*. Fort Worth: Harcourt Brace Jovanovich.

Steadman, David W. 1995. Prehistoric extinctions of Pacific island birds: Biodiversity meets zooarchaeology. *Science* 267: 1123–1131.

Steen-McIntyre, Virginia. 1985. Tephrochronology and its application to archaeology. In George Rapp, Jr., and John A. Gifford (Eds.), *Archaeological Geology* (pp. 265–302). New Haven: Yale University Press.

Stein, Julie K. 1987. Deposits for archaeologists. In Michael B. Schiffer (Ed.), *Advances in Archaeological Method and Theory*. Vol. 11 (pp. 337–395). New York: Academic Press.

——— (Ed.). 1992. *Deciphering a Shell Midden*. San Diego: Academic Press.

Stephens, David W., and John R. Krebs. 1986. *Foraging Theory*. Princeton: Princeton University Press.

Steponaitis, Vincas P. 1983. *Ceramics, Chronology, and Community Patterns: An Archaeological Study at Moundville*. New York: Academic Press.

Steponaitis, Vincas P., and J. P. Brain. 1976. A portable differential proton magnetometer. *Journal of Field Archaeology* 3(4): 455–463.

Sterngold, James. 1993, May 24. Emperor's buried secrets: No digging allowed. *The New York Times:* A4.

Stevens, William K. 1988, November 22. Scientists revive a lost secret of farming. *The New York Times*.

Steward, Julian H. 1938. Basin-plateau aboriginal sociopolitical groups. Washington, DC: Bureau of American Ethnology Bulletin no. 120.

———. 1954. Types of types. *American Anthropologist* 56(1): 54–57.

Stiebing, William H., Jr. 1994. *Uncovering the Past: A History of Archaeology.* New York: Oxford University Press.

Stoltman, James B. 1973. The southeastern United States. In James E. Fitting (Ed.), *The Development of North American Archaeology: Essays in the History of Regional Traditions* (pp. 117–150). University Park: Pennsylvania State University Press.

Stone, Anne C., and Mark Stoneking. 1993. Ancient DNA from a Pre-Columbian Amerindian population. *American Journal of Physical Anthropology* 92: 463–471.

Stoneking, Mark. 1994. In defense of "Eve"—a response to Templeton's critique. *American Anthropologist* 96(1): 131–141.

Straus, Lawrence G. 1990. Underground archaeology: Perspectives on caves and rockshelters. In M. B. Schiffer (Ed.), *Archaeological Method and Theory.* Vol. 2 (pp. 255–304). Tucson: University of Arizona Press.

Struever, Stuart. 1968. Flotation techniques for the recovery of small-scale archaeological remains. *American Antiquity* 33(3): 353–362.

Stuckenrath, R. 1977. Radiocarbon: Some notes from Merlin's diary. *Annals of the New York Academy of Science* 288: 181–188.

Stuiver, Minze, and Paula J. Reimer. 1993. Extended ^{14}C database and revised CALIB 3.0 ^{14}C age calibration program. *Radiocarbon* 35(1): 215–230.

Sunset editors. 1979. *The California Missions: A Complete Pictorial History and Visitor's Guide.* Menlo Park, CA: Lane Publishing Company.

Sutton, Mark Q., and Brooke S. Arkush. 1996. *Archaeological Laboratory Methods: An Introduction.* Dubuque, IA: Kendall/Hunt Publishing.

Sutton, Mark Q., Minnie Malik, and Andrew Ogram. 1996. Experiments on the determination of gender from coprolites by DNA analysis. *Journal of Archaeological Science* 23(2): 263–267.

Swanson, Earl (Ed.). 1975. *Lithic Technology: Making and Using Stone Tools.* The Hague: Mouton.

Swisher, C. C., III, G. H. Curtis, T. Jacob, A. G. Getty, and A. Suprijo Widasmoro. 1994. Age of the earliest known hominids in Java, Indonesia. *Science* 263: 1118–1121.

Swisher, Karen. 1989, October 3. Skeletons in the closet. *Washington Post.*

Szathmary, Emöke J. E. 1993. Genetics of aboriginal North Americans. *Evolutionary Anthropology* 1(6): 202–220.

Tainter, Joseph A. 1983. Settlement behavior and the archaeological record: Concepts for the definition of "archaeological site." *Contract Abstracts and CRM Archaeology* 3(2): 130–132.

Talalay, Lauren E. 1994, May/June. Indiana Joans. *Archaeology:* 60–63.

Tallbull, William. 1994. Archaeological sites or sacred places? Native American perspective. In David Hurst Thomas, *Exploring Ancient Native America* (pp. 238–239). New York: Macmillan.

Tattersall, Ian. 1992, August. Evolution comes to life. *Scientific American:* 80–87.

———. 1995. *The Last Neanderthal: The Rise, Success, and Mysterious Extinction of Our Closest Human Relatives.* New York: Macmillan.

Taylor, R. E. 1985. The beginnings of radiocarbon dating in *American Antiquity:* A historical perspective. *American Antiquity* 50(2): 309–325.

———. 1987a. AMS 14-C dating of critical bone samples: Proposed protocol and criteria for evaluation. In H. H. Andersen and S. T. Picraux (Eds.), *Nuclear Instruments and Methods in Physics Research: Section B, Beam Interactions With Materials and Atoms.* Proceedings of the Fourth International Symposium on Accelerator Mass Spectrometry, B29: 159–163. Ontario, Canada.

——. 1987b. *Radiocarbon Dating: An Archaeological Perspective.* New York: Academic Press.

Taylor, R. E., Austin Long, and Renee S. Kra (Eds.). 1992. *Radiocarbon After Four Decades: An Interdisciplinary Perspective.* New York: Springer-Verlag.

Taylor, R. E., and Ian Longworth (Eds.). 1975. Dating: New methods and new results. *World Archaeology* 7(2).

Taylor, R. E., and Clement W. Meighan (Eds.). 1978. *Chronologies in New World Archaeology.* New York: Academic Press.

Taylor, R. E., L. A. Payen, C. A. Prior, P. J. Slota, Jr., R. Gillespie, J. A. J. Gowlett, R. E. M. Hedges, A. J. T. Jull, T. H. Zabel, D. J. Donahue, and R. Berger. 1985. Major revisions in the Pleistocene age assignments for North American skeletons by C-14 accelerator mass spectrometry: None older than 11,000 C-14 years B.P. *American Antiquity* 50(1): 136–140.

Taylor, Walter W. 1948. A study of archeology. *American Anthropological Association, Memoir,* 69.

———. 1954. Southwestern archaeology, its history and theory. *American Anthropologist* 56: 561–570.

———. 1972. Old wine and new skins: A contemporary parable. In Mark P. Leone (Ed.), *Contemporary Archaeology* (pp. 28–33). Carbondale: Southern Illinois University Press.

Tello, J. C. 1943. Discovery of the Chavín culture in Peru. *American Antiquity* 9(1): 135–160.

Teltser, Patrice A. (Ed.). 1995. *Evolutionary Archaeology: Methodological Issues.* Tucson: University of Arizona Press.

Templeton, Alan R. 1993. The "Eve" hypotheses: A genetic critique and reanalysis. *American Anthropologist* 95(1): 51–72.

———. 1994. "Eve": Hypothesis compatibility versus hypothesis testing. *American Anthropologist* 96(1): 141–147

Thomas, David Hurst. 1969. Great Basin hunting patterns: A quantitative method for treating faunal remains. *American Antiquity* 34(4): 392–401.

———. 1972a. A computer simulation model of Great Basin Shoshonean subsistence and settlement patterns. In David L. Clarke (Ed.), *Models in Archaeology* (pp. 671–704). London: Methuen.

———. 1972b. Western Shoshone ecology: Settlement patterns and beyond. In Don D. Fowler (Ed.), Great Basin Cultural Ecology, a Symposium. *Desert Research Institute Publications in the Social Sciences* 8: 135–153.

———. 1973. An empirical test for Steward's model of Great Basin settlement patterns. *American Antiquity* 38(2): 155–176.

———. 1976. *Figuring Anthropology: First Principles of Probability and Statistics.* New York: Holt, Rinehart and Winston.

———. 1978. The awful truth about statistics in archaeology. *American Antiquity* 43(2): 231–244.

———. 1981. How to classify the projectile points from Monitor Valley, Nevada. *Journal of California and Great Basin Anthropology* 3(1): 7–43.

———. 1983a. The archaeology of Monitor Valley: 1. Epistemology. *Anthropological Papers of the American Museum of Natural History* 58(1): 1–194.

———. 1983b. The archaeology of Monitor Valley: 2. Gatecliff Shelter. *Anthropological Papers of the American Museum of Natural History* 59(1): 1–552.

———. 1986. Contemporary hunter-gatherer archaeology in America. In David J. Meltzer, Don D. Fowler, and Jeremy A. Sabloff (Eds.), *American Archaeology Past and Future: A Celebration of the Society of American Archaeology 1935–1985* (pp. 237–276). Washington, DC: Smithsonian Institution Press.

———. 1987. The archaeology of Mission Santa Catalina de Guale: 1. Search and discovery. *Anthropological Papers of the American Museum of Natural History* 63(2): 47–161.

———. 1988a. Saints and soldiers at Santa Catalina: Hispanic designs for colonial America. In Mark P. Leone and Parker B. Potter (Eds.), *The Recovery of Meaning in Historic Archaeology* (pp. 73–140). Washington, DC: Smithsonian Institution Press.

———. 1988b. The archaeology of Monitor Valley: 3. Survey and additional excavation. *Anthropological Papers of the American Museum of Natural History* 66(2): 131–633.

———. 1993. The archaeology of Mission Santa Catalina de Guale: Our first 15 years. In Bonnie G. McEwan (Ed.), *The Missions of La Florida* (pp. 1–34). Gainesville: University Press of Florida.

———. 1994. *Exploring Ancient Native America: An Archaeological Guide.* New York: Macmillan.

———. 1995. Spanish missions: Ideology and space at Santa Catalina. In Mark P. Leone and Neil Asher Silberman (Eds.), *Invisible America: Unearthing Our Hidden History* (pp. 66–67). New York: Henry Holt.

Thomas, David Hurst, and Robert L. Bettinger. 1976. Prehistoric piñon ecotone settlements of the upper Reese River Valley, central Nevada. *Anthropological Papers of the American Museum of Natural History* 53(3): 263–366.

Thomas, Kenneth (Ed.). 1990. Soils and early agriculture. *World Archaeology* 22(1).

——— (Ed.). 1996. Zooarchaeology: New approaches and theory. *World Archaeology* 28(1).

Thompson, Robert S., and Eugene M. Hattori. 1983. Packrat (*Neotoma*) middens from Gatecliff Shelter and Holocene migrations of woodland plants. In David Hurst Thomas, The archaeology of Monitor Valley: 2. Gatecliff Shelter. *Anthropological Papers of the American Museum of Natural History* 59(1): 157–167.

Tilley, Christopher. 1990. *Reading Material Culture.* Oxford: Basil Blackwell.

Tindale, Norman B. 1985. Australian aboriginal techniques of pressure-flaking stone implements: Some personal observations. In Mark G. Plew, James C. Woods, and Max G. Pavesic (Eds.), *Stone Tool Analysis: Essays in Honor of Don E. Crabtree* (pp. 1–33). Albuquerque: University of New Mexico Press.

Tolstikov, Vladimir, and Mikhail Treister. 1996. *The Gold of Troy: Searching for Homer's Fabled City.* New York: H. N. Abrams.

Torroni, Antonio, Theodore G. Schurr, Chi-Chuan Yang, Emöke J. E. Szathmary, Robert C. Williams, Moses S. Schanfield, Gary A. Troup, William C. Knowler, Dale N. Lawrence, Kenneth M. Weiss, and Douglas C. Wallace. 1991. Native American mitochondrial DNA analysis indicates that the Amerind and the Nadene populations were founded by two independent migrations. *Genetics* 130: 153–162.

Traill, David A. 1996. *Schliemann of Troy: Treasure and Deceit.* New York: St. Martin's Press.

Trigger, Bruce G. 1970. Aims in prehistoric archaeology. *Antiquity* 44(173): 26–37.

———. 1980a. *Gordon Childe: Revolutions in Archaeology.* New York: Columbia University Press.

———. 1980b. Archaeology and the image of the American Indian. *American Antiquity* 45(4): 662–676.

———. 1981a. Archaeology and the ethnographic present. *Anthropologica* 23(1): 3–17.

———. 1981b. Giants and pygmies: The professionalization of Canadian archaeology. In Glyn Daniel (Ed.), *Towards a History of Archaeology* (pp. 69–84). London: Thames and Hudson.

———. 1989a. *A History of Archaeological Thought.* Cambridge: Cambridge University Press.

———. 1989b. Comments on archaeology in the 1990s. *Norwegian Archaeological Review* 22(1): 28–31.

———. 1991. Post-processual developments in Anglo-American archaeology. *Norwegian Archaeological Review* 24: 65–76.

———. 1993. Marxism in contemporary western archaeology. In M. B. Schiffer (Ed.), *Archaeological Method and Theory.* Vol. 5 (pp. 159–200). Tucson: University of Arizona Press.

———. 1995. Expanding middle-range theory. *Antiquity* 69(264): 449–458.

Tringham, Ruth. 1991. Households with faces: The challenge of gender in prehistoric architectural remains. In Joan M. Gero and Margaret W. Conkey (Eds.), *Engendering Archaeology: Women and Prehistory* (pp. 93–131). Oxford: Basil Blackwell.

Tunnell, C. 1977. Fluted projectile point production as revealed by lithic specimens from the Adair-Steadman site in northwest Texas. In Eileen Johnson (Ed.), Paleoindian lifeways. Lubbock: West Texas Museum Association, Texas Tech University. *The Museum Journal* 17: 140–168.

Tuohy, Donald R., and L. Kyle Napton. 1986. Duck decoys from Lovelock Cave, Nevada, dated by 14-C accelerator mass spectrometry. *American Antiquity* 51(4): 813–816.

Turnbaugh, William, and Sarah Peabody Turnbaugh. 1977. Alternative applications of the mean ceramic date concept for interpreting human behavior. *Historical Archaeology* 11: 90–104.

Turner, Christy G., II. 1979. Dental anthropological indications of agriculture among the Jomon people of central Japan, pt. 10: Peopling of the Pacific. *American Journal of Physical Anthropology* 51(4): 619–636.

Tuttle, Russell, D. Webb, E. Weidl, and M. Baksh. 1990. Further progress on the Laeotoli trails. *Journal of Archaeological Science* 17(3): 347–362.

Tyler, Stephen A. 1986. Post-modern ethnography: From document to the occult to occult document. In James Clifford and George E. Marcus (Eds.), *Writing Culture: The Poetics and Politics of Ethnography* (pp. 122–140). Berkeley: University of California Press.

Tylor, Edward Burnett. 1871. *Primitive Culture.* Vols. 1 and 2. London: Murray.

———. 1889. On a method of investigating the development of institutions, applied to laws of marriage and descent. *Journal of the Royal Anthropological Institute* 18: 245–272.

Ubelaker, Douglas. 1990. Review of "Birds, beads and bells: Remote sensing of Pawnee sacred bundle" by Diane L. Good. *Plains Anthropologist* 35(128): 213–214.

U'mista Culture Centre. 1983. *Box of Treasures.* Film. Directed by Dennis Wheeler, narrated by Gloria Cranmer Webster. Alert Bay, Canada: U'mista Cultural Centre.

Upham, Steadman (Ed.). 1990. *The Evolution of Political Systems: Sociopolitics in Small-Scale Sedentary Societies.* Cambridge: Cambridge University Press.

Valladas, H., H. Cachier, P. Maurice, F. Bernaldo de Quiro, J. Clottes, V. Cabrera Valdés, P. Uzquiano, and M. Arnold. 1992. Direct radiocarbon dates for prehistoric paintings at the Altamira, El Castillo and Niaux caves. *Nature* 357: 68–70.

van der Merwe, Nikolaas J. 1982. Carbon isotopes, photosynthesis, and archaelogy. *American Scientist* 70: 596–606.

van der Plicht, Johannes. 1993. The Groningen Radiocarbon Calibration Program. *Radiocarbon* 35(1): 231–237.

Van Devender, Thomas R. 1977. Holocene woodlands in the southwestern deserts. *Science* 198: 189–192.

Van Devender, Thomas R., and W. G. Spaulding. 1979. Development of vegetation and climate in the southwestern United States. *Science* 204: 701–710.

Van Gerven, Dennis P., and George Armelagos. 1983. "Farewell to paleodemography?" Rumors of its death have been greatly exaggerated. *Journal of Human Evolution* 12: 353–360.

Van Gerven, Dennis P., Susan Guise Sheridan, and William Y. Adams. 1995. The health and nutrition of a medieval Nubian population. *American Anthropologist* 97(3): 468–480.

Vaughan, Patrick C. 1985. *Use-Wear Analysis of Flaked Stone Tools.* Tucson: University of Arizona Press.

Verano, John W., and Douglas H. Ubelaker (Eds.). 1992. *Disease and Demography in the Americas.* Washington, DC: Smithsonian Institution Press.

Victor, Katharine L., and Mary C. Beaudry. 1992. Women's participation in American prehistoric and historical archaeology: A comparative look at the journals *American Antiquity* and *Historical Archaeology.* In Cheryl Claassen (Ed.), *Exploring Gender Through Archaeology: Selected Papers From the 1991 Boone Conference.* Monographs in World Archaeology, no. 11 (pp. 11–21). Madison, WI: Prehistory Press.

Villablanca, Francis X. 1994. Evolutionary analysis: 3. Spatial and temporal aspects of populations revealed by mitochondrial DNA. In Bernd Herrmann and Susanne Hummel (Eds.), *Ancient DNA: Recovery and Analysis of Genetic Material From Paleontological, Archaeological, Museum, Medical, and Forensic Specimens* (pp. 31–58). New York: Springer-Verlag.

Vivian, R. Gwinn. 1990. *The Chacoan Prehistory of the San Juan Basin.* San Diego: Academic Press.

Vizenor, Gerald. 1990. *Crossbloods: Bone Courts, Bingo, and Other Reports.* Minneapolis: University of Minnesota Press.

von Frese, R. R. B., and V. E. Noble. 1984. Magnetometry for archaeological exploration of historical sites. *Historical Archaeology* 18(2): 38–53.

Wagner, Gail E. 1982. Testing flotation recovery rates. *American Antiquity* 47(1): 127–132.

Wahlgren, Erik. 1986. *The Vikings and America.* London: Thames and Hudson.

Walde, Dale, and Noreen D. Willows (Eds.). 1991. *The Archaeology of Gender.* Proceedings of the 22nd Annual Chacmool Conference. Calgary: The University of Calgary Archaeological Association.

Walker, Phillip L. 1986. Porotic hyperostosis in a marine-dependent California Indian population. *American Journal of Physical Anthropology* 69: 345–354.

Wall, Diane diZerega. 1994. *The Archaeology of Gender: Separating the Spheres in Urban America.* New York: Plenum Press.

Ward, R. G. W. (Ed.). 1987. Applications of tree-ring studies: Current research in dendrochronology and related subjects. *BAR International Series,* no. 333.

Wardle, H. Newell. 1929. Wreck of the archaeological department at the Academy of Natural Sciences of Philadelphia. *Science* 70(1805): 119–121.

———. 1956. Clarence Bloomfield Moore (1852–1936). *Bulletin of the Philadelphia Anthropological Society* 9(2): 9–11.

Wardwell, Allen. 1986. *Ancient Eskimo Ivories of the Bering Strait.* New York: Hudson Hills Press.

Waring, A. J., Jr., and Preston Holder. 1945. A prehistoric ceremonial complex in the southeastern United States. *American Anthropologist* 47(1): 1–34.

Waselkov, Gregory A. 1979. Zumwalt's Fort: An archaeological study of frontier process in Missouri. *The Missouri Archaeologist* 40: 1–129.

Wason, Paul K. 1994. *The Archaeology of Rank.* Cambridge: Cambridge University Press.

Waters, Michael R. 1992. *Principles of Geoarchaeology: A North American Perspective.* Tucson: University of Arizona Press.

Watson, Patty Jo. 1973. The future of archeology in anthropology: Cultural history and social science. In Charles L. Redman (Ed.), *Research and Theory in Current Archeology* (pp. 113–124). New York: Wiley.

———. 1974. Flotation procedures used on Salts Cave sediments. In Patty Jo Watson (Ed.), *Archeology of the Mammoth Cave Area* (pp. 107–108). New York: Academic Press.

———. 1976. In pursuit of prehistoric subsistence: A comparative account of some contemporary flotation techniques. *Midcontinental Journal of Archaeology* 1(1): 77–100.

———. 1986. Archaeological interpretation, 1985. In David J. Meltzer, Don D. Fowler, and Jeremy A. Sabloff (Eds.), *American Archaeology Past and Future: A Celebration of the Society of American Archaeology 1935–1985* (pp. 439–457). Washington, DC: Smithsonian Institution Press.

———. 1995. Archaeology, anthropology, and the culture concept. *American Anthropologist* 97(4): 683–694.

Watson, Richard A. 1991. What the New Archaeology has accomplished. *Current Anthropology* 33: 275–291.

Wauchope, Robert. 1965. (Obituary of) Alfred Vincent Kidder, 1885–1963. *American Antiquity* 31(2, pt. 1): 149–171.

Webb, Clarence H. 1968. (Obituary of) James Alfred Ford, 1911–1968. *Texas Archaeological Society Bulletin* 38: 135–146.

Weber, David J. 1988. Refighting the Alamo: Mythmaking and the Texas Revolution. In David J. Weber, *Myth and the History of the Hispanic Southwest: Essays by David J. Weber* (pp. 133–151). Albuquerque: University of New Mexico Press.

Weberman, A. J. 1971. The art of garbage analysis. *Esquire* 5(456): 113–117.

Webster, Gloria Cranmer. 1991. The contemporary potlatch. In Aldona Jonaitis (Ed.), *Chiefly Feasts: The Enduring Kwakiutl Potlatch* (pp. 227–250). Seattle: University of Washington Press; New York: American Museum of Natural History.

Weiner, Daniel H. 1995, Spring. NAGPRA: Legal burden or historic opportunity? *The World of Tribal Arts.*

Welch, Paul D., and C. Margaret Scarry. 1995. Status-related variation in foodways in the Moundville chiefdom. *American Antiquity* 60(3): 397–419.

Wendorf, Fred. 1987. The advantages of AMS to field archaeologists. In H. H. Andersen and S. T. Picraux (Eds.), *Nuclear Instruments and Methods in Physics Research: Section B, Beam Interactions With Materials and Atoms.* Proceedings of the Fourth International Symposium on Accelerator Mass Spectrometry B29: 155–158. Ontario, Canada.

Weymouth, John W. 1986. Geophysical methods of archaeological site surveying. In Michael B. Schiffer (Ed.), *Advances in Archaeological Method and Theory.* Vol. 9 (pp. 311–395). Orlando, FL: Academic Press.

Weymouth, John W., and Robert Huggins. 1985. Geophysical surveying of archaeological sites. In George R. Rapp, Jr., and J. Gifford (Eds.), *Archaeological Geology* (pp. 191–235). New Haven: Yale University Press.

Whallon, Robert E., Jr. 1973. Spatial analysis of occupation floors: I. Application of dimensional analysis of variance. *American Antiquity* 38(3): 266–278.

———. 1974a. Working with the "new paradigm." *Reviews in Anthropology* 1(1): 25–33.

———. 1974b. Spatial analysis of occupation floors: II. The application of nearest neighbor analysis. *American Antiquity* 39(1): 16–34.

———. 1986. A spatial analysis of four occupation floors at Guilá Naquitz. In Kent V. Flannery (Ed.), *Guilá Naquitz: Archaic Foraging and Early Agriculture in Oaxaca, Mexico* (pp. 369–384). Orlando, FL: Academic Press.

Whallon, Robert E., Jr., and James A. Brown (Eds.). 1982. *Essays on Archaeological Typology.* Evanston, IL: Center for American Archaeology Press.

Wheat, Joe Ben. 1972. The Olsen-Chubbuck site: A Paleo-Indian bison kill. *Society for American Archaeology Memoir* no. 26.

Wheeler, Mortimer. 1954. *Archaeology From the Earth.* Oxford: Oxford University Press (Clarendon).

Whelan, Mary K. 1995. Beyond hearth and home on the range: Feminist approaches to Plains archaeology. In Philip Duke and Michael C. Wilson (Eds.), *Beyond Subsistence: Plains Archaeology and the Postprocessual Critique* (pp. 46–65). Tuscaloosa: University of Alabama Press.

White, Leslie A. 1949. *The Science of Culture.* New York: Grove Press.

———. 1959. *The Evolution of Culture.* New York: McGraw-Hill.

———. 1975. *The Concept of Cultural Systems.* New York: Columbia University Press.

White, Murray. 1996, November 11. A matter of gravity. *The New Yorker:* 36–38.

White, Randall. 1982. The manipulation of burins in incision and notation. *Canadian Journal of Anthropology* 2: 129–135.

———. 1992. Beyond art: Toward an understanding of the origins of material representation in Europe. *Annual Review of Anthropology* 21: 537–564.

———. 1994. Review of *The Roots of Civilization* by Alexander Marshack. *American Antiquity* 59(2): 392–393.

———. 1996. Comment. *Current Anthropology* 37(2): 218–220.

White, Theodore E. 1953. A method of calculating the dietary percentage of various food animals utilized by aboriginal peoples. *American Antiquity* 18(4): 396–398.

———. 1954. Observations on the butchering technique of some aboriginal peoples, nos. 3, 4, 5, and 6. *American Antiquity* 19(3): 254–264.

White, Tim D. 1991. *Human Osteology.* San Diego: Academic Press.

———. 1992. *Prehistoric Cannibalism at Mancos 5MTUMR-2346.* Princeton: Princeton University Press.

Whitley, David S. 1992. Prehistory and post-positivist science: A prolegomenon to cognitive archaeology. In M. B. Schiffer (Ed.), *Archaeological Method and Theory.* Vol. 4 (pp. 57–100). Tucson: University of Arizona Press.

Whittaker, John C. 1994. *Flintknapping: Making and Understanding Stone Tools.* Austin: University of Texas Press.

Wilford, John Noble. 1996a, January 16. Archaeologists rally to defend a suspect giant. *The New York Times.*

———. 1996b, August 27. Slave artifacts under the hearth. *The New York Times:* C1, C7.

Willey, Gordon R. 1967. (Obituary of) Alfred Vincent Kidder. *National Academy of Sciences Biographical Memoirs*. Vol. 39 (pp. 292–322). New York: Columbia University Press.

———. 1969. (Obituary of) James Alfred Ford, 1911–1968. *American Antiquity* 34(1): 62–71.

———. 1976. Mesoamerican civilization and the idea of transcendence. *Antiquity* 50(199/200): 205–215.

Willey, Gordon R., and Philip Phillips. 1958. *Method and Theory in American Archaeology*. Chicago: University of Chicago Press.

Willey, Gordon R., and Jeremy A. Sabloff. 1993. *A History of American Archaeology*. 3d ed. New York: Freeman.

Williams, Barbara. 1981. In *Breakthrough: Women in Archaeology*. New York: Walker.

Williams, Leonard, David Hurst Thomas, and Robert Bettinger. 1973. Notions to numbers: Great Basin settlements as polythetic sets. In Charles L. Redman (Ed.), *Research and Theory in Current Archeology* (pp. 215–237). New York: Wiley.

Williams, Stephen. 1991. *Fantastic Archaeology: The Wild Side of North American Prehistory*. Philadelphia: University of Pennsylvania Press.

Willis, E. H. 1969. Radiocarbon dating. In Don Brothwell and Eric Higgs (Eds.), *Science in Archaeology* (pp. 46–57). London: Thames and Hudson.

Wilmsen, Edwin N. 1973. Interaction, spacing behavior, and the organization of hunting bands. *Journal of Anthropological Research* 29(1): 1–31.

Wilshusen, Richard H., and Glenn D. Stone. 1990. An ethnoarchaeological perspective on soils. *World Archaeology* 22(1): 104–114.

Wilson, David. 1974. *The New Archaeology*. New York: Knopf.

——— (Ed.). 1980. *The Northern World: The History and Heritage of Northern Europe AD 400–1100*. New York: H. N. Abrams.

Wilson, Michael, Kathie L. Road, and Kenneth J. Hardy (Eds.). 1981. *Megaliths to Medicine Wheels: Boulder Structures in Archaeology*. Proceedings of the Eleventh Annual Chacmool Conference. Calgary, Alberta: Department of Archaeology, University of Calgary.

Wing, Elizabeth S., and Antoinette B. Brown. 1979. *Paleonutrition: Method and Theory in Prehistoric Foodways*. New York: Academic Press.

Winterhalder, Bruce. 1981. Optimal foraging strategies and hunter-gatherer research in anthropology: Theory and models. In Bruce Winterhalder and Eric Alden Smith (Eds.), *Hunter-Gatherer Foraging Strategies* (pp. 13–35). Chicago: University of Chicago Press.

———. 1987. The analysis of hunter-gatherer diets: Stalking an optimal foraging model. In Marvin Harris and Eric B. Ross (Eds.), *Food and Evolution: Toward a Theory of Human Food Habits*, (pp. 311–339). Philadelphia: Temple University Press.

Winterhalder, Bruce, and Eric Alden Smith (Eds.). 1981. *Hunter-Gatherer Foraging Strategies: Ethnographic and Archaeological Analyses*. Chicago: University of Chicago Press.

Wintle, Ann G. 1996. Archaeologically relevant dating techniques for the next century. *Journal of Archaeological Science* 23(1): 123–138.

Wissler, Clark. 1914. A pioneer student of Ancient America (Bandelier obituary). *El Palacio* 1 (6, 7): 8.

———. 1917. The new archaeology. *The American Museum Journal* 17(2): 100–101.

Wittfogel, Karl A. 1957. *Oriental Despotism: A Comparative Study of Total Power.* New Haven: Yale University Press.

Wolf, Eric R. 1982. *Europe and the People Without History.* Berkeley: University of California Press.

Woodbury, Nathalie F. S. 1992, March. When my grandmother is your database: Reactions to repatriation. *Anthropology Newsletter:* 6, 22.

Woodbury, Richard B. 1954. Review of *A Study of Archeology* by Walter W. Taylor. *American Antiquity* 19: 292–296.

———. 1960. Nels C. Nelson and chronological archaeology. *American Antiquity* 25(3): 400–401.

———. 1973. *Alfred V. Kidder.* New York: Columbia University Press.

———. 1993. *Sixty Years of Southwestern Archaeology: A History of the Pecos Conference.* Albuquerque: University of New Mexico Press.

Wormington, H. M. 1981. Foreword to *Breakthrough: Women in Archaeology* by Barbara Williams. New York: Walter.

Wright, Henry T. 1977. Toward an explanation of the origin of the state. In James N. Hill (Ed.), *Explanation of Prehistoric Change* (pp. 215–230). Albuquerque: University of New Mexico Press.

———. 1986. The evolution of civilizations. In David J. Meltzer, Don D. Fowler, and Jeremy A. Sabloff (Eds.), *American Archaeology Past and Future: A Celebration of the Society for American Archaeology 1935–1985* (pp. 323–365). Washington, DC: Smithsonian Institution Press.

Wright, Henry T., and Gregory A. Johnson. 1975. Population, exchange, and early state formation in southwestern Iran. *American Anthropologist* 77(2): 267–289.

Wylie, Alison. 1991a. Feminist critiques and archaeological challenges. In *The Archaeology of Gender.* Proceedings of the 22nd Annual Chacmool Conference (pp. 17–23). Calgary: The University of Calgary Archaeological Association.

———. 1991b. Gender theory and the archaeological record: Why is there no archaeology of gender? In Joan M. Gero and Margaret W. Conkey (Eds.), *Engendering Archaeology: Women and Prehistory* (pp. 31–54). Oxford: Basil Blackwell.

———. 1992. The interplay of evidential constraints and political interests: Recent archaeological research on gender. *American Antiquity* 57(1): 15–35.

———. 1994. On "capturing facts alive in the past" (or present): Response to Fotiadis and to Little. *American Antiquity* 59(3): 556–560.

Wynn, J. C. (Ed.). 1986. Special issue: Geophysics in archaeology. *Geophysics* 51(3): 533–639.

Yarnell, Richard A. 1974. Intestinal contents of the Salts Cave mummy and analysis of the initial Salts Cave flotation series. In Patty Jo Watson (Ed.), *Archaeology of the Mammoth Cave Area* (pp. 109–112). New York: Academic Press.

———. 1982. Problems of interpretation of archaeological plant remains of the Eastern Woodlands. *Southeastern Archaeology* 1(1): 1–7.

Yellen, John E. 1976. Settlement patterns of the !Kung: An archaeological perspective. In R. B. Lee and I. DeVore (Eds.), *Kalahari Hunter-Gatherers* (pp. 47–72). Cambridge: Harvard University Press.

———. 1977. *Archaeological Approaches to the Present: Models for Reconstructing the Past.* New York: Academic Press.

Yentsch, Anne Elizabeth, and Mary C. Beaudry (Eds.). 1992. *The Art and Mystery of Historical Archaeology: Essays in Honor of James Deetz.* Boca Raton, FL: CRC Press.

Yesner, David. 1981. Archaeological applications of optimal foraging theory: Harvest strategies of Aleut hunter-gatherers. In Bruce Winterhalder and Eric A. Smith (Eds.), *Hunter-Gatherer Foraging Strategies: Ethnographic and Archaeological Analyses* (pp. 148–170). Chicago: University of Chicago Press.

Yoffee, Norman. 1993. Too many chiefs? (or, safe texts for the '90s). In Norman Yoffee and Andrew Sherratt (Eds.), *Archaeological Theory: Who Sets the Agenda?* (pp. 60–78). Cambridge: Cambridge University Press.

Yoffee, Norman, and George L. Cowgill (Eds.). 1988. *The Collapse of Ancient States and Civilizations.* Tucson: University of Arizona Press.

Yoffee, Norman, and Andrew Sherratt (Eds.). 1993a. *Archaeological Theory: Who Sets the Agenda?* Cambridge: Cambridge University Press.

———. 1993b. Introduction: The sources of archaeological theory. In Norman Yoffee and Andrew Sherratt (Eds.), *Archaeological Theory: Who Sets the Agenda?* (pp. 1–9). Cambridge: Cambridge University Press.

Ziegler, Alan C. 1973. Inference from prehistoric faunal remains. *Addison-Wesley Module in Anthropology,* no. 43.

Zihlman, Adrienne. 1981. Women as shapers of the human adaptation. In Frances Dahlberg (Ed.), *Woman the Gatherer* (pp. 75–120). New Haven: Yale University Press.

Bibliographic Essay

In this bibliographic essay, I will lead you through a prodigious body of archaeological literature. This listing includes sources and citations for many of the direct quotes used in the text. I also present the primary sources (that I drew upon directly in my narrative) and suggest ancillary materials to amplify my presentation.

But before we turn to the specifics, I'd like to mention briefly a few important books that I've found especially appropriate for accompanying my own text in the classroom. One useful adjunct is Thomas Patterson's *The Theory and Practice of Archaeology: A Workbook* (1994), which provides a dozen detailed problems, illustrating the workings of archaeological reasoning. *The Next Archaeology Workbook* by Nicholas David and Jonathan Driver (1989) provides various datasets for students to use in applying archaeological method and theory. I also like Price and Gebauer's (1996) *Adventures in Fugawiland!,* an interactive computer program that gives a feeling of what it's like to excavate sites and study archaeological data. Linda L. Hasten (1995) has compiled an animated series of articles that bring diverse approaches to contemporary archaeology to life. For an excellent overview of archaeological fieldwork, I highly recommend the seventh edition of *Field Methods in Archaeology* (Hester et al., 1997). I also like *Archaeological Laboratory Methods: An Introduction* by Mark Q. Sutton and Brooke S. Arkush (1996).

Preface

Specific quotes and citations:

"Scientists are not mere . . ." (Horgan 1996: 5)
"Archaeology was not practiced . . ." (Spaulding 1985: 307)

Chapter 1

I strongly recommend Bruce Trigger's *A History of Archaeological Thought* (1989a) as a theoretically informed overview of worldwide archaeology and its history. Additional important sources include *The Idea of Prehistory* by Glyn Daniel and Colin Renfrew (1988) and Donald K. Grayson's *The Establishment of Human Antiquity* (1983); see also Daniel (1976), Daniel and Chippindale (1989), and Stiebing (1994). For a glimpse of the major archaeological site discoveries throughout the world, see Fagan (1994), and Price and Feinman (1993).

A History of American Archaeology by Willey and Sabloff (1993) is a major synthesis. For a contrasting view, see Patterson's (1995) social history of United States archaeology, which situates archaeological theory and practice within its intellectual roots and contexts; see also the papers in the Fiftieth Anniversary Issue of *American Antiquity* (1985), Christenson (1989), Johnson (1993), Lyon (1996), Meltzer et al. (1986), Reyman (1992), and Woodbury (1993).

On Thomas Jefferson: The key source is *Notes on the State of Virginia* (Jefferson 1787); for evaluations of Jefferson's contributions to archaeology, see Hantman and Dunham (1993), Kelso (1982, 1986), and Willey and Sabloff (1993, chapter 2).

On Clarence B. Moore: Moore published 21 large volumes, mostly in the *Journal of the Academy of Natural Science of Philadelphia* (see, for example, Moore 1905, 1907). These monographs were amply illustrated, often with detailed photographs (Moore himself was an award-winning photographer). Even today, these publications remain valuable references for archaeologists working on the mortuary complex of the prehistoric American Southeast. For more on Moore, see Brigham (1937), M. Davis (1987), Neuman (1984: 38–40), Stoltman (1973), and Wardle (1929, 1956).

On Nels Nelson: His most important publications are Nelson (1909, 1914, and 1916). For critical discussions of Nelson's stratigraphic technique, see Browman and Givens (1996), Willey and Sabloff (1993, chapter 3), and Woodbury (1960); Nelson's experiences with the Central Asiatic expedition are discussed by Preston (1986, chapter 8).

On Alfred V. Kidder: A complete bibliography is published in Wauchope (1965), and selected writings by Kidder appear in Woodbury (1973); some of his most significant publications are Kidder (1924, 1928), Kidder and Guernsey (1921), and Kidder, Jennings, and Shook (1946). Givens (1992) discusses Kidder's role in the development of Americanist archaeology and Woodbury's (1973) biography is also an important source. Walter Taylor's (1948) monograph takes a decidedly less positive tone; see also W. Taylor (1954), Trigger (1989a), Wauchope (1965), and Willey (1967).

On James A. Ford: His most important writings include Ford and Willey (1941), Ford (1949, 1954, 1957, 1969), and Ford and Webb (1956); see also Brown (1978), Evans (1968), Haag (1968), Stoltman (1973), Webb (1968), Willey (1969), and Willey and Sabloff (1993, esp. chapters 4 and 5).

On Walter W. Taylor: His classic book is, of course, *A Study of Archeology* (Taylor 1948); see also Taylor (1954, 1972). For assessments of Taylor's work, see Binford (1972a: 541), Burgh (1950), Martin (1954), Trigger (1989a, chapters 7 and 8), Willey and Sabloff (1993, chapters 5 and 6), and Woodbury (1954).

On Lewis Binford: His important books include *New Perspectives in Archeology* (Binford and Binford 1968); *For Theory Building in Archaeology* (1977b); *Nunamiut Ethnoarchaeology: A Case Study in Archaeological Formation Processes* (1978b); *Bones: Ancient Men and Modern Myths* (1981); *In Pursuit of the Past: Decoding the Archaeological Record* (1983a); and *Faunal Remains From Klasies River Mouth* (1984). Binford has collected his scientific papers into three additional books (valuable not only for the articles but also for his retrospective comments about each): *An Archaeological Perspective* (1972a), *Working at Archaeology* (1983b), and *Debating Archaeology* (1989a); see also Binford (1962b, 1964, 1965, 1967, 1968c, 1973, 1980, 1982). For some views on Binford and his *processual agenda,* see Daniel and Renfrew (1988, chapter 9), Flannery (1967a), Harris (1968a), Hodder (1985, 1986, 1991), Leone (1987), Redman (1991), Renfrew (1983), Trigger (1989a, chapter 8), Watson (1991), and Willey and Sabloff (1993, chapter 6).

On the various "New Archaeologies": See Wissler (1917), and Caldwell (1959).

On Kathleen Deagan: Important writings include Deagan (1973, 1978a, 1978b, 1980, 1981, 1988, 1991, 1996), and her books: *Spanish St. Augustine: The Archaeology of a Colonial Creole Community* (1983), *Artifacts of the Spanish Colonies of Florida and the Caribbean, 1500–1800. Vol. 1, Ceramics, Glassware, and Beads* (1987), *Puerto Real: The Archaeology of a Sixteenth-Century Spanish Town in Hispaniola* (1995), and *Fort Mose: Colonial America's Black Fortress of Freedom* (with Darcie MacMahon, 1995).

On the contributions of women to Americanist archaeology: See *Hidden Scholars: Women Anthropologists and the Native Southwest* (Parezo 1993), and *Daughters of the Desert: Women Anthropologists and the Native American Southwest 1880–1980* (Babcock and Parezo 1988). See also Claassen (1994), Gacs et al. (1989), O'Bagy (1995), and Victor and Beaudry (1992).

Specific quotes and citations:

"Archaeology is a collection . . ." (Dunnell 1989: 9)
"The ancient Greeks . . ." (Rowe 1965: 2)
"Archaeology is rather like . . ." (Bahn 1989: 5)
"We may perhaps . . ." (Daniel 1962: 19)
"Archaeology in Canada . . ." (Trigger 1981b: 80)
"When we go back . . ." (Daniel 1981: 10)
Use of *Americanist archaeology* follows Dunnell (1979).
"Archaeologists typically ignore . . ." (Spector 1993: 30)
"Do not be discouraged . . ." (Harjo 1993: xliii)
"People have a . . ." (Hill 1991: 45)

"Each age has its archaeology . . ." (Renfrew 1982b)
The Pan-Scientific Approach to Archaeology is reproduced with permission from Kidder (1928: 753).
The Goals of Archaeology is reproduced with permission from Ford (1952: 317–318).
Archaeology's Unrecognized Working Women is reproduced with permission from Levine (1994: 11–12).
The Challenge of Archaeology is reproduced with permission from Binford (1983a: 19, 23).
"It wouldn't be any fun . . ." (quoted in Babcock and Parezo 1988: 147)
On the Potential of Historical Archaeology is reproduced with permission from Deagan (1982: 170–171).

Chapter 2

Some general sources on anthropological theory include Bohannan and Glazer (1988), Borofsky (1994), Carrithers (1990, 1992), D'Andrade (1995), Geertz (1973, 1983, 1984), Harris (1968b, 1993), Haviland (1994), and Kottak (1991).

The culture concept in anthropology and archaeology: Watson (1995) is a very important source; see also Binford (1962b), Flannery (1982), Goodenough (1994), Keesing (1994), Kroeber and Kluckhohn (1952), Taylor (1948, chapter 4), and White (1959: 8, 38–39).
On the methodology of science: Paul Horgan's *The End of Science* (1996a) contains interviews with the world's best scientists, asking them about what they do, why they do it, and what science will look like in the future.
Science in archaeology: The best single source relating archaeology to its scientific framework is Bell's *Reconstructing Prehistory: Scientific Method in Archaeology* (1994). Gibbon's *Explanation in Archaeology* (1989) and Patty Jo Watson's (1986) synthesis are likewise important, as is Merrilee Salmon's *Philosophy and Archaeology* (1982); see also Bamforth and Spaulding (1982), Binford (1977b), Dunnell (1982a), Flannery (1973a), Grayson (1986), Kelley and Hanen (1988), Kemeny (1959), Raab and Goodyear (1984), Salmon and Salmon (1979), Schiffer (1976, esp. chapter 2), South (1977a, esp. chapters 1, 2, and 8), and Spaulding (1968). For some practical applications of scientific methods in archaeology, see Goffer (1980) and Henderson (1989).
On early plant domestication in the New World: Important volumes include Cowan and Watson's *The Origins of Agriculture: An International Perspective* (1992), *The Evolution of Plant Exploitation* (Harris and Hillman (1989), *The Origins of Agriculture* by Rindos (1984), and Smith's *Rivers of Change* (1992); see also Cohen (1977), Cohen and Armelagos (1984), Fedick (1995), Flannery (1966, 1973b, 1986), Fritz (1990), Larsen (1995), MacNeish (1992), Matson (1991), Price and Gebauer (1995), Stark (1986), and Thomas (1990).

Schliemann on Hissarlik (Troy): See *Troy and Its Remains* (1875), *Ilios: The City and Country of the Trojans* (1880), and *Troja: Results of the Latest Researches* (1884); see also Schuchhardt (1891).

More contemporary approaches to Mycenaean archaeology (including Troy): Blegen (1963), Kraft et al. (1980), McDonald (1967), and Renfrew (1972).

On Schliemann, the controversial archaeologist: For a rather unsavory view of Schliemann, see Calder and Traill (1986) and Traill (1996). Schliemann has been defended by Easton (1981), Deuel (1977), Snodgrass (1995), and Wilford (1996).

On humanistic approaches to anthropology and archaeology: See Benedict (1948), Carrithers (1990), Deetz (1983), and Spector (1983, 1993). A particularly informative dialogue on the interrelationship between scientific and humanistic approaches in anthropology can be found in the 1995–1996 issue of *Anthropological Newsletter* (published by the American Anthropological Association).

On Bandelier's scientific humanism: Lange and Riley (1996) provide the best biographical source on Adolph Bandelier; see also Bandelier (1883, [1890] 1971, 1890, 1892), Bingham (1914), Hammond and Goad (1949), Hobbs (1940), Hodge (1914, 1932), Lummis (1914), Roberts (1996), and Wissler (1914).

Specific quotes and citations:

"Man is an animal and . . ." (Meggers 1971: 4)
"a messy, bumbling . . ." (Cerroni-Long, 1996: 52)
"There is no other field . . ." (quoted in Morell 1993: 1802)
"The 21st century should be . . ." (Peacock, 1994: 1)
"As a University of Chicago . . ." (Watson 1995: 283)
"Culture . . . taken in its . . ." (Tylor 1871: 1)
What's in a Name? Who Are We? is reproduced from label copy of the exhibition of *Chiefly Feasts* at the American Museum of National History; see also Masco (1996: 839).
"A lot of people . . ." (quoted in U'mista Culture Centre, 1983)
"Today, anyone may attend . . ." (Webster 1991; 232)
"As this work progresses . . ." (Orlove 1980: 262)
"The problem of creativity . . ." (Spaulding 1988: 264)
"It is quite true that . . ." (Spaulding 1988: 264)
"The philosophers of science . . ." (Renfrew 1984: 18)
"more a rape . . ." (McDonald 1967: 17)
"large copper article . . ." (Schliemann 1875: 323)
"unfortunately, in 1871 and 1872 . . ." (Schliemann 1875: 347–348)
The Hidden Contributions of Sophie Schliemann is reproduced with permission from Irwin-Williams (1990: 6).
"I have excavated . . ." (Schliemann 1875: 349–352)
"the question is now decided . . ." (Schuchhardt 1891: 18)
"[Schliemann] found a whole series . . ." (Bahn 1989: 56)
"Labeling a theory . . ." (Bell 1994: 23)

"No one is more convinced than I am . . ." (Benedict 1948: 587)
"[Anthropology is] the most humanistic . . ." (U. Leonard Moss, quoted by Hill, 1995: 20)
"In retrospect, I believe my archaeological goals . . ." (Quimby 1994: 113)
"Science and humanism . . ." (Anderson 1995: 2)
"I have known many scholars . . ." (Lummis 1971: xxvi)
"How long this drudging day . . ." (quoted in White 1940: 194)
"I am dirty . . ." (quoted in White 1940: 212–213)
"My relations with the Indians . . ." (Bandelier and Hewett 1937: 248)
"Bandelier with his usual . . ." (Kidder 1924: 88)
"I was prompted to perform the work . . ." (Bandelier 1971: xxi)
"We anthropologists . . ." (quoted in Anonymous 1996: 14)
"We have . . . unsettled the Romantic School . . ." (Bandelier letter of 1888, quoted in Radin 1942: xi)
In His Own Words: Bringing Tyuonyi's Past Alive is reproduced from Bandelier (1971: 3, 4, 5, 485, 486, 488, 489).
"The descriptions of manners . . ." (Bandelier 1971: xxi–xxii)
"The material that Bandelier gathered . . ." (Ceram 1971: 66)
"Nor, I should add . . ." (Babcock 1982: 195)
"I divide scientific and humanistic approaches . . ." (Lekson, personal communication)
"[*The Delight Makers*] will always be . . ." (Lummis 1971: xxvii)
"Any theoretical discussions or speculations . . ." (Bandelier 1892: 577)

Chapter 3

This chapter relies on Trigger's (1989a) discussion of levels of theory in archaeology; see also Binford (1981), Clarke (1979), Gardin (1980), Harris (1968a, 1979), Klejn (1977), Raab and Goodyear (1984), and Spaulding (1960).

On cultural materialism: Marvin Harris gave the name to this approach, but the roots run much deeper; for a general introduction, see *The Rise of Anthropological Theory* (Harris 1968b), *Cultural Materialism: The Struggle for a Science of Culture* (Harris 1979), and *Food and Evolution: Toward a Theory of Human Food Habits* (Harris and Ross 1987); see also "Anthropology: Ships that crash in the night" (Harris 1991), *Culture, People, Nature* (Harris 1993), and "Cultural materialism is alive and well and won't go away until something better comes along" (Harris 1994). For some ethnological applications of this approach, see Abruzzi (1982), Divale and Harris (1976), Harris (1985), Harris and Ross (1987), Morren (1984), E. Ross (1980), and J. Ross (1980).

Some archaeological applications of cultural materialism: Harrison and Turner (1978), MacNeish (1964, 1967), Sanders et al. (1979), Sanders and Price (1968), and Wright and Johnson (1975).

Some criticisms of the cultural materialistic approach: Bender (1978), Blanton (1976), Conrad (1981), Conrad and Demarest (1984), Cowgill (1975b),

Drennan (1976), Flannery (1972, 1977), Flannery and Marcus (1976), Hodder (1982b), and Willey (1976).

What's up with postmodernism? The most accessible introduction is Harvey's *The Condition of Postmodernity* (1989); other important works include Habermas (1987), Harding (1991), Hassan (1985), Hawkesworth (1989), and Lyotard (1984).

On postmodern (interpretive) anthropology: Writing culture: Clifford (1988), Clifford and Marcus (1986), Dreyfus and Rabinow (1983), Fox (1991), Geertz (1983, 1984), Marcus and Fischer (1986), Rosenau (1992), and Tyler (1986).

Critiques of postmodern approaches: Bruner (1994), Carneiro's (1995) "Godzilla meets new age anthropology: Facing the post-modernist challenge to a science of culture," and Harris (1994); see also Klotz (1996).

Archaeology's postprocessual critique: Ian Hodder has been the most vocal and prolific postprocessual critic. His more influential books and articles include "Postprocessual archaeology" (1985), *Reading the Past: Current Approaches to Interpretation in Archaeology* (1986), "Post-modernism, post-structuralism and post-processual archaeology" (1989a), "Archaeology and the post-modern" (1990), "Postprocessual archaeology and the current debate" (1991a), *Theory and Practice in Archaeology* (1995), and *Interpreting Archaeology: Finding Meaning in the Past* (Hodder et al. 1995). For additional discussions of processual approaches, see Bapty and Yates (1990), Duke and Wilson (1995), Earle and Preucel (1987), Knapp (1996), Kosso (1991), Nelson and Kehoe (1990), Leone (1986), Patterson (1990), Preucel's "The postprocessual condition" (1995), Schmidt and Patterson (1995), Shanks and Tilley's *Reconstructing Archaeology: Theory and Practice* (1987a) and *Social Theory and Archaeology* (1987b), Shanks (1992), Tilley's *Reading Material Culture* (1990), and Whitley (1992).

On "guarded objectivity" in archaeology: Brumfiel (1996), Hodder (1991b), Fotiadis (1994), Stark (1993), Watson and Fotiadis (1990), and Wylie (1992, 1994).

Some critics of the postprocessual critique: Binford (1987a, 1989b, 1989c), Bintliff (1991), and Watson (1991).

Some more balanced assessments of contemporary archaeological theory: Bell (1994), Dark (1995), Lamberg-Karlovsky (1989), Preucel (1991), Skibo et al. (1995), Trigger (1989a, 1991), and Yoffee and Sherratt (1993a).

Bandelier as a postmodernist is discussed in Babcock (1982); see also the references listed in Chapter 2. For more on Uncas and the surviving Mohegan people, see Josephy (1982: 72).

Specific quotes and citations:

"I cannot remember exactly . . ." (Harvey 1989)

"We are now in the process . . ." (quoted in Harvey 1989: 9)

The table "Some Binary Contrasts . . ." is taken from Hassan (1985: 123–124) and Harvey (1989, table 1.1).

"Postmodernism swims, even wallows . . ." (Harvey 1989: 44)

"There's a Chinese curse . . ." (quoted in Morell 1994: 1798)

"Scientific thought is now . . ." (Tyler 1986: 123)
"We once had in our . . ." (quoted in Morell 1994: 1801)
"There was always . . ." (quoted in Morell 1994: 1798)
"[Human evolution is a] sexist . . ." (quoted in Morell 1993: 1801)
"If the . . . scientists . . ." (Kohl 1993: 13)
"Some very different intellectual . . ." (Renfrew 1993: 248)
"Scientific methods of study . . ." (Leonc 1995: 253)
Archaeology and the Modern/Postmodern Dialogue is reproduced, in part, from White (1996).
"The aim of archaeology . . ." (Hodder 1991a: 30)
"All of the fashionable adjectives . . ." (Spaulding 1988: 269)
"The frustrating thing . . ." (Schiffer, personal communication)
"Published in 1890 . . ." (Babcock 1982: 188)
"Beyond the much-repeated words . . ." (Babcock 1982: 190)
"[*The Delight Makers*] failed to attract . . ." (Jovanovich 1991: xvii)
" . . . hideous, often obscene clowns or jesters . . ." (Bandelier 1890: 296)
"nearly naked black and white apparitions . . ." (Babcock 1982: 191)
"disgusting creatures . . . in full ritual undress" (quoted in Babcock 1982: 188)
"During [the dancing] the skirmishers . . ." (Bandelier 1966: 199–200)
"Bandelier was neither the first . . ." (Babcock 1982: 192)
"Well, white man . . ." (quoted in Babcock 1982: 192)
In His Own Words: The Multiple Voices of Adolph Bandelier is reproduced with permission from Babcock (1982: 192, 193, 196, 200, 201, 202).
"I am getting tired . . ." (Bandelier 1975: 288)
"There is far greater continuity . . ." (Kohl 1993: 19)
"I have always regarded . . ." (Trigger 1989a: xiv)
In His Own Words: On Multiple Perspectives in Archaeology is reproduced with permission from Preucel (1991: 14).

Chapter 4

The importance of regional archaeology and sampling at a regional level is discussed by Ammerman (1981), C. Beck (1994), Binford (1964), Dunnell (1985), Dunnell and Dancey (1983), Ebert (1984, 1992), Judge, Ebert, and Hitchcock (1975), Lewarch and O'Brien (1981), Mueller (1974, 1975), Plog, Plog, and Wait (1978), Rossignol and Wandsnider (1992), and Thomas (1978, 1986).

On the Inka Road: Hyslop (1984), and Morris and von Hagen (1993). For more on John Hyslop, see Murra (1994).
Surface archaeology of the Reese River Valley: The best overall summary of this research is given in Thomas (1973, 1988b); see also Thomas (1972a, 1972b), Thomas and Bettinger (1976), and Williams et al. (1973).
Mission Santa Catalina de Guale (Georgia): Thomas (1987, 1988a, 1993, 1995). For more on the archaeology of the mission system in Spanish Florida, see McEwan (1993). For discussions of power auger survey in

archaeology, see Deagan (1980, 1981), McManamon (1984), Percy (1976), and Shapiro (1987).

On the archaeology of the Valley of Oaxaca (Mexico): An enormously important contribution is *Zapotec Civilization* (Marcus and Flannery 1996). The archaeological survey of this area is specifically discussed in Blanton (1978), Blanton et al. (1996), Feinman and Nicholas (1990), Flannery (1976), and Kowalewski (1990a, 1990b), plus additional papers in Marcus (1990). For some dissenting views, see Sanders and Nichols (1988).

On full-coverage archaeological survey: Fish and Kowalewski (1990), especially the contribution by Parsons (1990).

Specific quotes and citations:

What Archaeological Survey Was Like in 1907 is reproduced from Kidder (1960: 12).

"And luck does play . . ." (Noël Hume 1964: 217)

Finding a Place to Dig—That Old "MacNeish" Luck is reproduced with permission from MacNeish (1978: 14–15).

"The simplest way to find sites . . ." (Bahn 1989: 16)

"Simply walking around . . ." (Noël Hume 1969)

Exploration Archaeology on the Inka Road is reproduced with permission from Hyslop (1984: 3–11).

"Fieldwork requires both . . ." (quoted in Babcock and Parezo 1988: 39)

"alluviation, erosion . . ." (Kowalewski 1990a: 80)

What Does "Full-Coverage" Survey Mean? is reproduced with permission from Parsons (1990: 11–12).

Chapter 5

Weymouth (1986) provides an important overview of remote sensing in archaeology; see also Avery and Lyons (1981), A. Clark (1990), Ebert (1984), Gibbons (1991), Lyons and Avery (1984), Martin et al. (1991), McManamon (1984), Parrington (1983), Pollard (1989), Sabins (1996), Scollar et al. (1990), and Wynn (1986). For discussions on the overall potential of noninvasive archaeology, see Binford (1980: 9), Dunnell and Dancey (1983), Foley (1981), Tainter (1983), and Thomas (1987). Availability of remote sensing imagery is discussed by Ehrenberg (1987); see also Drager and Ireland (1986). Gibbons (1991) discusses how remote sensing technology has been used to look for early hominid remains. Remote sensing of Plains Indian medicine bundles is discussed by Diane Good (1989); see also Ubelaker (1990).

On the search for Mission Santa Catalina: See Thomas (1987). Some results and interpretations also appear in Thomas (1988a, 1993) and Garrison et al. (1985).

On proton magnetometers in archaeology: Abbott and Frederick (1990),

Johnston (1961), Scollar (1969), Steponaitis and Brain (1976), von Frese and Noble (1984), and Weymouth (1986).

Using GIS in archaeology: Kvamme (1989), and Allen et al. (1990).

On high-altitude imagery: General sources include Deuel (1969), Harp (1975), and Riley (1987). Lindbergh's early aerial surveys are discussed by Ann Axtell Morris (1933). Eddy et al. (1996) discuss use of air photography for archaeological site mapping.

On ancient roads of Chaco Canyon: Crown and Judge (1991), Gabriel (1991), and Lyons and Avery (1984).

On the Shippee-Johnson expeditions: Morris (1995), and Shippee (1932).

More on the archaeology of ancestral Pueblo people: Adler (1996), Adler et al. (1996), Ambler (1989), Brody (1990, 1991), Cordell (1984, 1994), Lekson (1986), Noble (1984, 1991), Peck (1994), Roberts (1996), Sebastian (1992), and Vivian (1990); see also T. White's (1992) controversial study of cannibalism among ancestral Puebloan populations.

On soil resistivity in archaeology: Bevan (1983), Carr (1977, 1982), Shapiro (1984), Weymouth (1986), and Weymouth and Huggins (1985).

On ground-penetrating radar studies of Japanese burial mounds: Goodman (1994), Goodman and Nishimura (1993), and Goodman, Nishimura, and Yamamoto (1994); see also Sterngold (1993). Bevan and Kenyon (1975) provide a detailed discussion for archaeologists, outlining the theory behind ground-penetrating radar surveys; see also Bevan et al. (1984), and Weymouth (1986).

The Cerén site: Conyers (1995), and Sheets (1983, 1992); the Arenal project is described in Sheets and McKee (1994).

Specific quotes and citations:

"Ideally, we should . . ." (Binford 1964: 437)

"began to perceive . . ." (Sheets 1992: 12)

High-Tech Wizardry is reproduced, with permission, from Sheets and Sever (1988: 28).

"Every professional . . ." (quoted in Sterngold 1993)

Chapter 6

Several handbooks describe current approaches to archaeological fieldwork. Among the best sources are *Practical Archaeology: Field and Laboratory Techniques and Archaeological Logistics* (Dillon 1989), *The Archaeology Handbook: A Field Manual and Resource Guide* (McMillon 1991), and *Field Methods in Archaeology* (Hester et al. 1997); see also Dancey (1981), Fladmark (1978), and Joukowsky (1980). Although thoroughly dated, Wheeler's *Archaeology From the Earth* (1954) provides the flavor of what digging was like in the good old days of archaeological imperialism. Elliott's *Great Excavations* (1995) details several important digs in the American Southwest. Stanley South (1977a, chapter 8) draws on his extensive experience to provide some guidelines for excavating historic period sites; Noël Hume (1969) covers the same ground, but with a rather different emphasis. Straus (1990) discusses the archaeology of caves and rockshelters around the world.

John Rick (1996) has recently discussed the use of high-tech distance measuring instruments on archaeological sites. Dibble (1987) describes the setup he used for automated measurement in the La Quina excavations; see also Sanders and Sanders (1986).

Flotation techniques in archaeology: Flannery (1976: 104–105), Pendleton (1983), Reitz and Scarry (1985: 12–13), Struever (1968), Wagner (1982), Watson (1974, 1976), and Yarnell (1974).

Specific quotes and citations:

"When I excavate . . ." (Spector 1993: 1)
"Excavated sites . . ." (Binford 1983a: 109)
"My fieldwork . . ." (quoted in Babcock and Parezo 1988: 143)
"The major flaw . . ." (Schiffer 1987: 356)
"Field Archaeologists dig up . . ." (Bahn 1989: 15)
"technofunctional . . ." (Rathje and Schiffer 1982: 194)
"The sifters utilized . . ." (Bird 1980: 165)
Who Really Dug Guilá Naquitz? is reproduced with permission from Flannery (1986: 65–67).
"Of course we are all . . ." (Noël Hume 1973: 6)
"Once I discovered there was such a thing . . ." (quoted in Babcock and Parezo 1988: 151)

Chapter 7

For a discussion of the theory behind chronological studies in contemporary archaeology, see Dean (1978a), Hammond (1974), Rick (1987), and Schiffer (1972). For a discussion of various new and innovative dating techniques, see Shreeve (1992) and Wintle (1996). Other solid general sources on chronology in archaeology include Fleming (1977), Michels (1973), Oakley (1968), Orme (1982), Taylor and Longworth (1975), and Taylor and Meighan (1978).

Dendrochronology: Important overviews include Baillie (1995), Bannister and Robinson (1975), Dean (1978b), Fritts (1976), Stahle and Wolfman (1985), and Ward (1987). Classic discussions of dendrochronology can be found in Bannister (1962, 1970) and Stallings (1939); closing "The Gap" is discussed by Douglass (1929), Haury (1962), and Morris (1933). The example from Betatakin is based on Dean (1970). "Dating the Oseberg ship burial" derives from Bonde and Christensen (1993).

Radiocarbon dating in archaeology: Bowman (1990) is a user-friendly and up-to-date introduction to the subject. Another useful overview is Taylor's (1987b) *Radiocarbon Dating: An Archaeological Perspective,* emphasizing particularly the collaboration between archaeologist and radiocarbon lab; see also Adovasio et al. (1990), Aitken (1990), Bowman (1994),

Taylor (1985), and Taylor et al. (1992). The statistics attached to radiocarbon dates are discussed by Long and Rippeteau (1974), and Thomas (1976, chapter 10).

AMS dating: Hedges and Gowlett (1986) provide a particularly readable summary of new developments in accelerator dating; see also Banning and Pavlish (1978), Bennett et al. (1977), Berger (1979), Browman (1981), and Wendorf (1987). For discussions of dating early human skeletons in the New World, see Stafford et al. (1984), Taylor (1987a), and Taylor et al. (1985). AMS dating of the Lovelock Cave duck decoy is discussed by Tuohy and Napton (1986). Loy et al. (1990) discuss the AMS dating of ancient blood residues. For progress in AMS dating of rock art, see Chaffee et al. (1994), Dorn et al. (1992), Reneau et al. (1991), and Valladas et al. (1992).

Computer programs for calibrating radiocarbon dates: The *OxCal Program* from Oxford University (Ramsey 1995), the *Calib* program from the University of Washington (Stuiver and Reimer 1993), and the Groningen Radiocarbon Calibration Program (van der Plicht 1993).

On dating the Shroud of Turin: Dale (1987), Gove (1987), Kouznetsov et al. (1996), and Jull et al. (1996).

On obsidian hydration: The Government Mountain–Sitgreaves Peak study is based on research by Findlow et al. (1975). For a consideration of obsidian hydration and sourcing, see Ambrose (1976), D. Clark (1964), Ericson (1975), Friedman (1983), Friedman and Smith (1960), Friedman and Trembour (1978), Friedman et al. (1994), Meighan (1976), Michels (1973, chapter 13), Michels and Tsong (1980), Ridings (1996), and Sheets et al. (1990).

On thermoluminescence dating: Aitken (1989, 1990), Fleming (1979), Mazess and Zimmerman (1966), Ralph and Han (1966, 1969), and Rice (1987).

On argon-argon dating: The redating of Java man is discussed by Swisher et al. (1994); see also Shreeve (1994) and Lewin (1994). For more information on the potassium-argon and argon-argon techniques, see Hu et al. (1994) and McDougall (1990).

On protein dating of ancient ostrich eggshells: See Brooks et al. (1990), Ellis et al. (1996), Elster et al. (1991), and Miller et al. (1992).

Chapter 8

For a general overview of geoarchaeology, I highly recommend *Principles of Geoarchaeology: A North American Perspective* (Waters 1992); other important sources include Butzer (1982), Courty et al. (1989), Dimbleby (1977), Harris (1989), Holliday (1992), Rapp and Gifford (1985), Stein (1987, 1992), and Wilshusen and Stone (1990).

On the Laetoli footprints: The stratigraphy at Laetoli is described in Leakey and Harris (1987); the footprints themselves are analyzed by Tuttle et al. (1990). For a popularized account, see Hay and Leakey (1982) and Leakey (1984).

Using volcanic ashes to date archaeological sites (tephrachronology): See Sheets and Grayson (1979) and Steen-McIntyre (1985). For specifics about the Mount Mazama eruption, see Davis (1978, 1983), Mehringer (1986), and Mehringer et al. (1977).

The index fossil concept in archaeology: Nelson's use of diagnostic artifacts and ersatz stratigraphy are discussed by David Browman and Douglas Givens in "Stratigraphic excavation: The first 'new archaeology'" (1996); see also Kidder (1924: 94–129), Nelson (1914, 1916), Spier (1917, 1931), and Woodbury (1960).

Reverse stratigraphy at Chetro Ketl: Hawley (1934, 1937). For more on the career of Florence Hawley Ellis, see Babcock and Parezo (1988: 125–129), Claassen (1994), Frisbie (1975, 1991), Gacs et al. (1989), and Irwin-Williams (1990: 21–26).

Geoarchaeology of Cape Krusenstern: Giddings (1961, 1966). The original beach ridge archaeology and radiocarbon chronology at Cape Krusenstern are critically evaluated by Mason and Ludwig (1990).

Geoarchaeology of the Georgia and southeastern Atlantic coastline: Bigham (1973), DePratter and Howard (1977), Griffin and Henry (1984), Hoyt and Hails (1967), and Hoyt and Henry (1971).

Specific quotes and citations:

"They are the most remarkable . . ." (quoted in Price and Feinman 1993: 11)
"Stratum 22, Rubble . . ." (Thomas 1983b: 55–56)
"I performed this work . . ." (Nelson 1916: 165)
"Dedication to anthropology . . ." (quoted in Babcock and Parezo 1988: 125)
"Chaco Canyon offered . . ." (Lister and Lister 1981: 95)
Fieldwork 1920s-Style at Chetro Ketl is quoted from Ellis (1983).
"The suggestion looked . . ." (Hawley 1937: 298)
"Unhappily we can scarcely say . . ." (Hawley 1937: 298–299)

Chapter 9

Some general sources on the theory behind chronology building in archaeology: Adams (1988), Adams and Adams (1991), Binford (1965), Binford and Sabloff (1982), Dean (1978a), Dunnell (1971, 1986a), Hammond (1974), Hill and Evans (1972), Klejn (1982), Spaulding (1977), Thomas (1981), and Whallon and Brown (1982). For some classical views of classification in archaeology, see Brew (1946: 44–66), Ford (1954), Krieger (1944), Rouse (1960), Spaulding (1953), and Steward (1954). For some guidelines to archaeological laboratory procedures, see Cronyn (1990) and Dillon (1989). For discussions on the meaning of "style" in archaeology, see Carr and Neitzel (1995) and Conkey and Hastorf (1990).

Contemporary approaches for analyzing archaeological ceramics: Barnett and Hoopes (1995), Bronitsky (1989), Gibson and Woods (1990), Glover and Griffiths (1989), Longacre (1991), Neff (1992), Orton et al. (1993), and Rice (1987, 1996a, 1996b).

Seriation in archaeology: Braun (1985), Dunnell (1970), Ford (1962), Marquardt (1978), McNutt (1973), and Rouse (1967).

Pipe stem dating: The initial work was conducted by Harrington (1954), then refined by Binford (1962a, 1972b); see also Hanson (1972), Heighton and Deagan (1972), Noël Hume (1976: 296–301), Lofstrom et al. (1982), Majewski and O'Brien (1987: 170–172), Salwen and Bridges (1977), D. South (1972), S. South (1972, 1977a: chapter 7), Turnbaugh and Turnbaugh (1977), and Waselkov (1979).

Specific quotes and citations:

"Artifacts themselves are not important . . ." (quoted in Babcock and Parezo 1988: 151)
"The exact meaning . . ." (Griffin 1943: 340)
"*Discs*—Of the twenty-four . . ." (Haury 1950: 329)
"Taxonomy in archeology . . ." (Taylor 1948: 148)
"1. *Form, Size, etc.*— . . ." (Nelson 1916: 168)
"Peculiar kind of pottery . . ." (Nelson 1916)
"We need more rather than fewer . . ." (Brew 1946: 65)
"Seriation is a deceptively simple . . ." (Marquardt 1978: 257)
"like slats of a venetian blind" (Ford 1962: 42)
"arrange and rearranged . . ." (Ford 1962: 42)
"In making use of this dating device . . ." (Harrington 1954: 8)
"in all probability, therefore, . . ." (Noël Hume 1976: 41)
"a date after which . . ." (Noël Hume 1970: 8)
"the cornerstone of all . . ." (Noël Hume 1970: 11)
"Stan used to come up to . . ." (quoted in Ferguson 1987: 5)
"an archaeological unit possessing . . ." (Willey and Phillips 1958: 22)
" . . . for a time . . ." (Jennings 1994: 270)

Chapter 10

Specific case studies considered here can be found in Chaplin (1971), Frison (1989), Gould (1966), Hawkes, O'Connell, and Blurton Jones (1987), Heizer and Clewlow (1968), Liebowitz and Folk (1980), Perkins and Daly (1968), and White (1953, 1954). For a recent study of fiber-tempered ceramics in the American Southeast, see Sassaman (1993). Basin Shoshone ceramics are discussed by Griset (1986).

Schiffer on formation processes: Michael Schiffer has been a driving force behind the recognition and explicit study of formation processes. *Behavioral Archaeology* (1976) remains critical to an understanding of modern archaeology, and *Formation Processes of the Archaeological Record* (1987) synthesizes the basic principles; see also Schiffer (1972, 1977).

On middle-range research in archaeology: The basics of middle-range research were set out by Lewis Binford (1977b, 1981, 1983a, and 1987b); see also Grayson (1986), Hayden and Cannon (1984), Kosso (1991), O'Connell (1995), Raab and Goodyear (1984), Sabloff et al. (1987), Salmon (1982), Thomas (1983a, 1986), Trigger (1989a, 1995), and Willey and Sabloff (1993).

On ethnoarchaeology: Binford (1986), Binford and O'Connell (1984), Gamble and Boismier (1991), Graham (1994), Hayden (1979, 1987), Longacre (1991), Longacre and Skibo (1994), O'Connell (1995), Saitta (1992), Stahl (1995), Stark (1993), Tindale (1985), and Wilshusen and Stone (1990).

The tool-kit concept in archaeology: Whallon (1973, 1974a, 1986), Yellen (1977), Binford (1983a: 238–239; 1987b), Schiffer (1972), and Schiffer and Rathje (1973).

Archaeology's Garbage Project: An overview of the Garbage Project is provided by Rathje (1984, 1991); see also Rathje (1974), Rathje and McCarthy (1977), Rathje and Schiffer (1982), and Rathje et al. (1992).

On experimental archaeology: Cotterell and Kamminga (1990), and Schiffer et al. (1994).

Some guidelines for illustrating stone tools: Addington (1986), and Adkins and Adkins (1989).

On the experimental replication of stone tools: John Whittaker's (1994) *Flintknapping: Making and Understanding Stone Tools* has been called the new "bible" on the subject, and I agree. He presents a balanced, well-reasoned introduction to the making of stone tools, of interest to both amateur and professional students of the human past. Odell's (1996) *Stone Tools* presents several new, theory-based approaches to lithic analysis and its relationship to human behavior. For more on flintknapping, see Addington (1986), Buck (1982), Church (1994), Crabtree (1966, 1979), Flenniken (1978, 1981, 1984), Frison and Bradley (1980), Gryba (1988), Henry and Odell (1989), Sheets (1987), Swanson (1975), and Tunnell (1997).

Use-wear studies of lithic artifacts: Some sources on "low-power" microscopic methods are Hayden (1979), Odell (1979, 1981a), and Vaughan (1985: 19–23). On the "high-power" microscopic methods, see Holly and Del Bene (1981), Keeley (1974, 1980: 63–82), Keeley and Newcomer (1977), Moss (1983), and Newcomer and Keeley (1979). Other studies employing "blind testing" are Bamforth (1986), Knuttson and Hope (1984), Odell and Odell-Vereecken (1980), and Shea (1987).

Specific quotes and citations:

"Behavior is the first thing . . ." (quoted in Monastersky 1990: 41)
"this information awaits further . . ." (Liebowitz and Folk 1980: 33)
"the Tel Yin'am pavement . . ." (Liebowitz and Folk 180: 32)
"The old-timers never put . . ." (Gould 1966: 43)
"the aim of such analysis . . ." (Whallon 1973: 266)
"Plausibility does not render . . ." (Binford 1983a: 75)
Why I Began Doing Ethnoarchaeology is quoted with permission from Binford (1983a: 98, 100–101).

"the focus on fauna . . ." (Binford 1978b: 451)
"Show me a neighborhood's . . ." (Rathje 1991: 130)
"the many rock magazines . . ." (Weberman 1971: 114)
"a rip-off, a threat . . ." (Rathje and Hughes 1975: 154)
"Because we know so little . . ." (Rathje 1991: 128)
Garbage and Our Future is quoted with permission from Rathje (1991: 134).
"if we are making such a large . . ." (Rathje 1991: 120)
"everybody's favorite villain . . ." (Rathje 1991: 122)
"Those of us in the Garbage Project . . ." (Rathje et al. 1992: 445)
"To make arrows properly . . ." (quoted in Pope 1994: 164)
"They take the stick . . ." (quoted in Crabtree 1968: 449)
"Damn! That's sharp!" (Whittaker 1994: 243)
The quotations cited in the sidebar are derived from Crabtree (1979).
"My experiments in flintknapping . . ." (Crabtree 1966: 3)
"applying this sort of accidental . . ." (Keeley and Newcomer 1977: 34)
"The Clovis projectile point . . ." (Frison 1993: 241)

Chapter 11

The archaeology of the Olsen-Chubbuck site is discussed by Joe Ben Wheat (1972). The faunal remains from Smoky Creek Cave are presented by Thomas (1969). Consideration of sixteenth-century diet in Spanish Florida is taken from Reitz and Scarry (1985). The California Gold Rush example comes from Shulz and Gust (1983a, 1983b).

Some general sources on zooarchaeology: Grayson's *Quantitative Zooarchaeology* (1984) reviews the basic assumptions, procedures, and analytical techniques of zooarchaeology in detail. A special issue of *World Archaeology* (K. Thomas 1996) contains several papers about contemporary zooarchaeology; see also Brewer (1992), Carbone and Keel (1985), Colley (1990), Crabtree (1990), S. Davis (1987), Parmalee (1985), Reitz and Scarry (1985), and Wing and Brown (1979).

Manuals to help archaeologists identify nonhuman bones: Casteel (1977), Chaplin (1971), Cornwall (1956), Gilbert (1980), Olsen (1960, 1964, 1968, 1973), and Ryder (1969).

On the concept of minimum number of individuals: Flannery (1967b: 157), Grayson (1973, 1978, 1979, 1984), and Ziegler (1973).

On taphonomy: The best single source is Lee Lyman's *Vertebrate Taphonomy* (1994). Another highly useful source is *Taphonomy: A Bibliographic Guide to the Literature* (Koch 1989); see also Lyman (1987), Behrensmeyer and Kidwell (1985), Hill (1979a, 1979b), and Hill and Behrensmeyer (1984).

Faunal remains in historic-period sites: Fradkin (1980), Landon (1996), Mudar (1978), and Reitz and Scarry (1985).

On the zooarchaeology of Chavín de Huántar: See Miller and Burger's excellent article entitled "Our father the cayman, our dinner the llama: Animal utilization at Chavín de Huántar, Peru" (1995). For an overview of the

Chavín culture, see *Chavín and the Origins of Andean Civilization,* by Richard L. Burger (1992).

Studying ancient plant remains from archaeological sites: Janneke Buurman and Jan Peter Pals (1994) discuss *Palaeoethnobotany: What's in a Name?* Another important resource is *Current Paleoethnobotany: Analytical Methods and Cultural Interpretations of Archaeological Plant Remains,* edited by Christine Hastorf and Virginia S. Popper (1988); see also Adams and Gasser (1980), Carbone and Keel (1985), Ford (1979), Hather (1994), Lentz (1991), Miksicek (1987), Minnis (1981), Pearsall and Piperno (1990), Reitz and Scarry (1985), Smith (1985), and Yarnell (1982).

Plant remains in Great Basin archaeological sites: Harper and Alder (1970, 1972), and Mehringer (1977).

The Phoenix Phenomenon: See Anonymous (1995a); see also R. Cook (1981).

Some general sources on palynology: Bryant and Hall (1993) provide a thorough critique of archaeological applications of palynology in the United States; see also Bryant and Holloway (1983), Faegri et al. (1989), and Moore et al. (1991).

Palynology at Star Carr: See Clark (1954, 1972). Legge and Rowley-Conwy (1988) provide support for a summer occupation of the site. Day (1993) reports new research on both micro- and macroscopic plant remains that suggests the possibility of year-round activity; see also Chapter 14 discussion.

Palynology at Lehner Ranch: See Mehringer and Haynes (1965). The archaeology of Lehner Ranch is discussed by Haury et al. (1959).

Palynology at Lost Trail Pass Bog: Mehringer et al. (1977).

Palynology of Shanidar Cave: Leroi-Gourhan (1975), Miksicek (1987), and Solecki (1971).

Palynology at Broken K Pueblo: Hill and Hevly (1968).

On the analysis of phytoliths from archaeological context: See Pearsall (1982, Piperno (1984, 1987), Rapp and Mulholland (1992), and Rovner (1983, 1987, 1988). Kelso (1984) provides additional background on the archaeology of Monticello.

Analysis of pack rat nest contents for reconstructing past environments: The best single source is Betancourt et al., *Packrat Middens: The Last 40,000 Years of Biotic Change* (1990); see also Thompson and Hattori (1983), Van Devender (1977), and Van Devender and Spaulding (1979).

"Reading the fuel": See Hastorf and Johannessen (1991). For additional information on the Upper Montaro Valley Archaeological Project, see Costin and Earle (1989), D'Altroy (1992), and Earle et al. (1980, 1987).

Specific quotes and citations:

"Bones are documents . . ." (Wheeler 1954: 192)

Ancient Bison Hunting at Olsen-Chubbuck is reproduced with permission from Wheat (1972: 1–2).

"What are all those bones . . ." (quoted in Lyman 1994: 161)

"It is necessary . . ." (quoted in Lyman 1994: 223)

"When I started my studies . . ." (Lyman 1994: xxiii)
"Only a small part . . ." (quoted in Lyman 1994: 1)
"The study of pollen is . . ." (Bahn 1989: 27)
"Wood and trees in the Andes . . ." (Hastorf and Johannessen 1991: 141)
"several dimensions of meaning . . ." (Hastorf and Johannessen 1991: 154)

Chapter 12

A major new contribution is Larsen's (1997) *Bioarchaeology: Interpreting Behavior From the Human Skeleton.* The general field of bioarchaeology has also been recently reviewed by Grauer (1995), and Larsen (1995), and in White's *Human Osteology* (1991); see also Buikstra and Cook (1980), Cohen and Armelagos (1984), Gilbert and Mielke (1985), Huss-Ashmore et al. (1982), Konigsberg and Buikstra (1995), Lambert (1993), Lambert and Walker (1991), Larsen (1987), Lukacs and Minderman (1992), Martin et al. (1985), Milner et al. (1991), Ortner and Putschar (1985), Powell et al. (1991), Sobolik (1994), van Gerven et al. (1995), Walker (1986), and Zimmerman and Kelley (1982).

On stable isotope analysis: Ezzo et al. (1995), Katzenberg et al. (1995), Little and Schoeninger (1995), Price (1989), Sillen et al. (1989), and Spielmann et al. (1990); for a relatively nontechnical general overview, see van der Merwe (1982) and DeNiro (1987). The Tehuacán Valley study was conducted by DeNiro and Epstein (1981) and Farnsworth et al. (1985); see also Anderson (1965), DeNiro and Schoeniger (1983), and MacNeish (1967). The Chavín de Huántar study is reported by Burger and van der Merwe (1990).

Bioarchaeological investigation of "stress": Huss-Ashmore et al. (1982), Hutchison and Larsen (1988), Martin et al. (1985), Powell (1985), and Turner (1979).

On the archaeology of ancient disease: Roberts and Manchester (1995), Rogers and Waldron (1989), and Rothschild and Martin (1993).

On the relationship of agriculture to human health: Larsen (1987, 1995), Lukacs et al. (1985), Lukacs et al. (1989), and Lukacs and Minderman (1992).

On paleodemography: Verano and Ubelaker (1992) is a particularly important source; see also Bocquet-Appel and Masset (1982), Buikstra and Konigsberg (1985), Buikstra and Mielke (1985), Larsen (1987), Ramenofsky (1987), and Van Gerven and Armelagos (1983). Primary data and initial interpretations of the Pecos population are presented by Hooton (1930), Mobley (1980), Palkovich (1983), and Ruff (1981); see also Howells (1960); Spielmann et al. (1990) report on stable isotope studies of this population.

On molecular archaeology: Svante Pääbo (1993) provides an excellent and nontechnical overview of the potential for analyzing ancient DNA recovered in long-dead plants and animals; for other nontechnical introductions, see Benditt (1989), Brown and Brown (1992), Herrmann and

Hummell (1994), and Powledge and Rose (1996). For some specific applications of molecular archaeology, see Del Pozzo (1989) on the subject of DNA fragments identified in mummified human remains. Handt et al. (1994) evaluate the DNA structure of the famous Tyrolean ice man; Doran et al. (1986) discuss the cellular and molecular composition of the 8,000-year-old human brain tissue recovered at the Windover site in Florida; see also Hagelberg (1993), and Villablanca (1994). Additional sources on molecular archaeology include Bonnichson (1990), Brown et al. (1993), and Grauer (1995). Bonnichsen and Schneider (1995) discuss the recovery of ancient hair from archaeological sites, and its potential for DNA analysis. Fisher et al. (1993) discuss DNA analysis of Civil War–era skeletal remains.

The case of the missing Russian czar: The best single reference is Maples and Browning (1994); see also Dickerson (1993).

On the African "Eve" hypothesis: Gibbons (1993), Nei (1992), Stoneking (1994), and Templeton (1993, 1994).

On the archaeology of DNA and the first Americans: See Dillehay (1989), Dillehay and Meltzer (1991), Horai et al. (1993), Lewin (1992), Meltzer (1989, 1993, 1995), Stone and Stoneking (1993), Szathmary (1993), and Torroni et al. (1991); on the relationship between archaeology, genetics, and linguistic diversity, see Renfrew (1992a) and Meltzer (1995).

On the Human Genome Project: Lewin (1993).

On the Jurassic Park scenario: Grimaldi and DeSalle (1994) discuss the "scientific romance with amber" and its role in analysis of very ancient DNA; see also DeSalle and Grimaldi (1994), Grimaldi (1993), and Lister (1994).

On the recovery and analysis of ancient human blood: Eisele et al. (1995), Fiedel (1996), Loy (1983), Loy et al. (1990), and Loy and Hardy (1992).

Specific quotes and citations:

"I am convinced . . ." (quoted in Ross 1992: 119)
"I stood by . . ." (cited in Maples and Browning 1994: 243)
"A great murder mystery . . ." (as cited in Anonymous 1995b)
"Beyond any reasonable doubt . . ." (as cited in Anonymous 1995b)
"Short of the Last Judgment . . ." (Maples and Browning 1994: 267)
"People are hair factories . . ." (Bonnichsen and Schneider 1995: 27)
"It's over for Eve . . ." (quoted in Gibbons 1993: 1249)
"The antiquity of the first Americans . . ." (Meltzer 1995: 21)
"The Bering Strait theory . . ." (Deloria 1992b: 433)
"Even as intelligent a man . . ." (Momaday 1996)
"Ultimately, the question . . ." (Meltzer 1995: 32)
"[The Human Genome Project is] a 21st-century . . ." (as cited in Lewin 1993: 27)

Indigenous Person From Papua, New Guinea . . . is taken from a news release issued by the Rural Advancement Foundation International (October 4, 1995).

Chapter 13

The definitions of social organization and social status are based on Bohannan (1965), Goldschmidt (1960, 1983), Goodenough (1965), and Service (1971). The sex-and-gender discussion follows Conkey and Spector (1984) and Gero (1988); see also the references in Chapter 14.

Some key references on Moundville: Peebles and Kus (1977) provide the basic model distinguishing between ranked and egalitarian systems; see also Peebles (1971, 1977, 1981, 1987), Powell (1988), Steponaitis (1983), and Welch and Scarry (1995).

More on Mississippian archaeology: Emerson and Lewis (1991), Mehrer (1995), and Smith (1990).

On the Southern Cult (or Southeastern Ceremonial Complex): J. A. Brown (1976), Galloway (1989), Phillips and Brown (1978, 1984), and Waring and Holder (1945).

On the archaeology of social status and inequity: McGuire and Paynter (1991) and Price and Feinman (1995) present diverse perspectives about the origins and operation of social inequality in the human past; see also Cobb (1993), Costin and Earle (1989), Ehrenreich et al. (1995), Flannery (1995), Gilman (1989), Paynter (1989), Renfrew and Shennan (1982), Upham (1990), and Wason (1994).

Life and death among the Hohokam: The discussion is based on Randall McGuire's *A Marxist Archaeology* (1992a); see also McGuire (1992b).

More on Hohokam archaeology: Crown and Judge (1991), Gumerman (1991), Haury (1976), McGuire and Schiffer (1982), and Noble (1991b).

On Marxist approaches in archaeology: McGuire (1993) and Trigger (1993).

How archaeologists approach ancient mortuary behavior: Beck (1995), McGuire (1992a: chapter 7), Morris (1991), O'Shea (1984), Parker Pearson (1982, 1995), and Peebles (1971).

The archaeology of power: Costin and Earle (1989), Mehrer (1995), and Miller and Tilley (1984).

Classic Maya regional settlement hierarchies: Some key references include Folan et al. (1995) and Marcus (1973, 1974, 1976, 1983); see also Flannery (1972), Harrison (1981; 274), and Rathje (1971).

Other applications of central place theory in archaeology: Clarke (1968), Crumley (1976), Flannery (1972), and G. Johnson (1972, 1975).

Specific quotes and citations:

"The structure of a society . . ." (Goldschmidt 1960: 266)

"Gender . . ." (Conkey and Gero 1991: 8)

"In the mortuary ritual . . ." (McGuire 1992a: 206)

Marxist Approaches in Anglo-American Archaeology is reproduced with permission from McGuire (1992a: 1–2, 9, 83–84).

"Individuals are not simple . . ." (Hodder 1982b: 5)

"A consideration of ideology and power . . ." (Miller and Tilley 1984: vii)

Chapter 14

Robert Kelly's (1995) *The Foraging Spectrum* is the best single source for understanding modern research on foraging populations. Other important sources include Mithen's (1990) now-classic volume on *Thoughtful Foragers,* and Bettinger's (1991) *Hunter-Gatherers: Archaeological and Evolutionary Theory;* see also Aldenderfer (1993), Arnold (1993), Burch and Ellanna (1994), and Gamble and Boismier (1991). The papers in Lee and DeVore (1968) provide an important historical perspective. On the problems of Neanderthal reconstructions, see Tattersall (1992, 1995).

On understanding seasonality: The listing of seasonally available plant foods near Guilá Naquitz is based on Flannery (1986: chapter 18). Howard (1929) discussed seasonality in the Emeryville Shellmound. Seasonality at Star Carr was first considered by Clark (1954), with subsequent critiques by Andresen et al. (1981), Jacobi (1978), and Pitts (1979); see also Day (1993). Some additional references on seasonality include Grayson and Thomas (1983), and Monks (1981).

On the archaeology of life space: The papers in Kent (1987) provide a well-balanced and diversified approach to activity areas; see also Fletcher (1977), Kroll and Price (1991), Metcalfe and Heath (1990), Speth and Johnson (1976), and Whallon (1973, 1974b). Activity areas at Coxcatlán Cave derive from Fowler and MacNeish (1972); see also MacNeish et al. (1972). The critique draws on Flannery (1986). The Mask Site model of individual life space is derived by Binford (1978a). For other discussions of size-sorting effects, see O'Connell (1987) and Yellen (1976). The application of this model to Gatecliff Shelter is discussed in Thomas (1983b).

On engendering the foraging past: The two landmark sources are "Archaeology and the study of gender" (Conkey and Spector 1984) and *Engendering Archaeology: Women and Prehistory* (edited by Gero and Conkey, 1991). Other important sources include Brown (1993), Claassen (1992, 1994), Conkey (1991), Cullen (1995), Fedigan (1986), Jochim (1988), Gero (1983, 1985), Gibbs (1987), Gilchrist (1994), Hayden (1981b, 1992), Nixon (1993), Seifert (1991), Spencer-Wood (1991), Spielmann (1995), Tringham (1991), Walde and Willows (1991), Whelan (1995), and Wylie (1991). To see the relationship between postprocessual archaeology and feminist theory, see Engelstad (1991), Gilchrist (1991), and Wylie (1992). The persistence of gender stereotypes is effectively and humorously addressed by Diane Gifford-Gonzalez (1993, 1995). Bacus et al. (1993) provide a critical bibliography of gender in archaeology. Spector and Whelan (1989) provide guidelines for incorporating gender into archaeology courses. A special issue of the *Bulletin of the Society for American Archaeology* (1991) asks "Is Gender Still an Issue?" *The Man-the-Hunter Myth* discussion is based in part on Conkey and Spector (1984). The "Genderlithics" discussion is based on Gero (1991a); see also Gero (1991b) and Sassaman (1992). The possibility of determining gender from coprolites is presented by Sutton et al. (1996).

On optimal foraging approaches: Smith and Winterhalder (1992) and Cashdan (1990) include some important contributions, and Bettinger (1980) provides an early, programmatic statement for archaeologists (see also

Bettinger 1987); Eric Alden Smith (1983) wrote a balanced, discriminating piece on the same topic. See also Durham (1981), O'Connell and Hawkes (1984), Smith and Winterhalder (1981, 1985), and Winterhalder (1981, 1987). *Foraging Theory* (Stephens and Krebs 1986) is a general treatment of the subject; for a discussion of the concept of optimization, see Maynard Smith (1978). Alyawara foraging is discussed by O'Connell and Hawkes (1981, 1984); see also Jochim (1988), Keegan (1986, 1992), Martin (1985), Smith (1983, 1991), Winterhalder (1981), Winterhalder and Smith (1981), and Yesner (1981).

Specific quotes and citations:

Reconstructing Our Foraging Ancestors is reproduced with permission from Tattersall (1992: 80, 84, 87).
"Suppose that an archaeologist . . ." (quoted in Podolefsky and Brown 1994: 102–103).
"We no longer think . . ." (Flannery 1968: 67)
"It is a great temptation . . ." (Flannery 1986: 322)
"Hunter-gatherer subsistence . . ." (O'Connell and Hawkes 1981: 116)
"Over the past 30 years . . ." (O'Connell 1995: 233)
"Looking at the pattern . . ." (Chippindale 1993: 33)
"Optimal foraging is no more . . ." (Jennings 1994: 271)
"Despite its appearance . . ." (Winterhalder 1987: 316)
"The primary goal . . ." (Keene 1979: 370)
"People do not behave . . ." (Shanks and Tilley 1992: 55–56)
"Foraging behavior in this habitat . . ." (O'Connell and Hawkes 1981: 109)
"Applying [optimal foraging] theory . . ." (quoted in Thomas 1986: 257)
"The value of such theory . . ." (O'Connell and Hawkes 1981: 116)
"To consider one sex . . ." (Reiber and Mathews 1982: 41)
"The entire village . . ." (quoted by Eichler and Lapointe 1985: 11, and Wylie 1991b: 38)
"[The Man-the-Hunter model] includes a set of . . ." (Conkey and Spector 1984: 7)
The Real Flintstones? is quoted with permission from Gifford-Gonzalez (1995: 1–2).
"as long as we do not correct for . . ." (Isaac 1978: 102)
"There is also an important correlation . . ." (Thomas 1983b: 439–440)
"more the result of a false notion . . ." (Conkey and Spector 1984: 6)
"Tools have played . . ." (Oakley 1959, book jacket)
"Tools provide a thermometer . . ." (Laughlin 1968: 318)
"If man is defined . . ." (Oakley 1959: 5)
"'Man' is not a semantic . . ." (Gero 1991a: 164)
"Western males generally make . . ." (Gero 1991a: 168)
"There is no compelling . . ." (Gero 1991a: 176)
"the flake tools . . ." (Gero 1991a: 169)
"On the other hand, direct gender attribution . . ." (Gero 1991a: 176)
"We do not see a feminist approach . . ." (Conkey and Gero 1991: 11)

Chapter 15

For a general overview of archaeology's neo-evolutionary directions, see Marcus and Flannery (1996), Maschner (1996), Spencer (1990, 1993, 1994), and Trigger (1989a, chapters 4 and 8). Other important references include Abrams (1989), Binford (1967, 1968a), Boyd and Richerson (1985), Carneiro (1970a, 1970b, 1973a, 1973b, 1988), Dunnell (1980), Durham (1990, 1992), Earle (1991), Ehrenreich et al. (1995), Flannery (1965, 1969, 1972, 1973b), Fried (1967), Harris (1968b, chapters 6, 7, 22, 23), Johnson and Earle (1987), Lees (1994), Leonard and Jones (1987), Mithen (1989), Neff (1992), Rindos (1984), Rosenberg (1994), Stanley and Marks (1992), Trigger (1980a), Wright (1977, 1986), Yoffee and Cowgill (1988), and Yoffee and Sherratt (1993a).

Some classic sources include Boserup (1965), Braidwood (1959), Childe (1951a and 1951b), Cohen (1977, 1981), Morgan (1877), Lubbock (1865, 1869, 1870), Sahlins and Service (1960), Service (1975), White (1949, 1959, 1975), and Wittfogel (1957).

Some models deriving from Boserup's work: Cohen (1977), Flannery (1969, 1973b, 1986), Harner (1970), D. R. Harris (1972), Patterson (1971), P. E. L. Smith (1976), and P. E. L. Smith and Young (1972).

Some criticisms of the population pressure approach: Bender (1975), Cowgill (1975a), Dunnell (1979, 1982b), Hassan (1975, 1981), Hayden (1981a), Price and Brown (1985: 14), and Roosevelt (1980).

On the origins of agriculture: Binford (1968b), Cowan and Watson (1992), Fedick (1995), Harris (1994), Hayden (1990), MacNeish (1992), Matson (1991), Price and Gebauer (1995), Smith (1995), and Thomas (1990).

On selectionist approaches to neo-evolutionary archaeology: Dunnell (1989), O'Brien and Holland (1992), Rindos (1984, 1989a, 1989b), and Teltser (1995).

Some cognitive and ideological approaches to evolution: Demarest (1989), Flannery and Marcus (1993), Hodder (1982a), and Marcus and Flannery (1996); for a concentrating view, see Carneiro (1992).

For a critical view of neo-evolutionary theory: Kohl (1993), Trigger (1989a: chapter 8), Yoffee (1993), and Yoffee and Sherratt (1993a).

Specific quotes and citations:

"[Lubbock's *Pre-historic Times*] was . . ." (Trigger 1989a: 114)
"The institutions of man . . ." (Tylor 1889: 269)
"The experience of mankind . . ." (Morgan [1877] 1963: 7)
"Any given system . . ." (Sahlins and Service 1960: 94–95)
"The more specialized . . ." (Sahlins and Service 1960: 97)
"When we have cleared up . . ." (Boas [1888] 1940: 279)
"If History is bunk . . ." (Bahn 1989: 5)
"History as the model . . ." (Binford 1987a: 401)
"encouraged a major devaluation . . ." (Trigger 1989: 24)
". . . the discovery and cultivation . . ." (Morgan [1877] 1963: 23)
"The huntsman and his prey . . ." (Childe 1951a: 67–68)

"'The long run' . . ." (Price 1982: 716)
"a question without real meaning . . ." (Rindos 1984: 141)
"They were neither inevitable . . ." (Rindos 1984: 141)
Why Did People Domesticate Plants? is quoted, with permission, from Flannery (1986: 5, 14, 16).
"The state is a type of very strong . . ." (Flannery 1972: 403–404)
"Archaeology can supply the skeleton . . ." (Robert Carneiro, personal communication, June 1996)
"at some point in their history . . ." (Carneiro 1970a: 733)
"Why did many independent . . ." (Cohen 1977)
"there appears to be ample . . ." (Cohen 1981: 121–122)
"high population density . . ." (Johnson and Earle 1987: 270)
"Whether or not cultural evolution . . ." (Johnson and Earle 1987: 4)
"There is ample reason . . ." (Cowgill 1988: 54)
"This is something like . . ." (Robert Carneiro, personal communication, June 1996)
"Today, neo-evolutionary accounts . . ." (Kohl 1984: 129)
"How else are we to deal . . ." (Robert Carneiro, personal communication, June 1996)
"Archaeology, history, and anthropology . . ." (Sherratt 1993: 123)
"So *fixated* are post-modernists . . ." (Carneiro 1995: 14–15)
"It must simply be recognized . . ." (Renfrew 1982: 21)
"Just as paleontologists would . . ." (Marcus and Flannery 1996: 30)
"The neo-evolutionist perspective . . ." (Spencer 1990: 23)

Chapter 16

Some key references include Renfrew's groundbreaking *Towards an Archaeology of the Mind* (1982b) and Mithen's now-classic volume on *Thoughtful Foragers* (1990). Two important reference volumes are Renfrew and Zubrow's (1994) *The Ancient Mind: Elements of Cognitive Archaeology,* and *Archaeology: Theories, Methods, and Practice* (Renfrew and Bahn 1996, esp. chapter 10); see also Bender (1993), Demarest and Conrad (1992), Earle (1991), Flannery and Marcus (1993), Fritz (1978), Marcus (1992), Mithen (1995), and Renfrew (1993). *Peace Pipe a Ritual Weapon* is based on Hall (1977).

On Marshack's work on the origins of iconography: The best general source is Marshack's revised edition of *The Roots of Civilization: The Cognitive Beginnings of Man's First Art, Symbol and Notation* (1991); see also Marshack (1976, 1989, 1995b, 1996, in press). A more popular overview is available in "Images of the Ice Age" (Marshack 1995a).

Some criticisms of Marshack's research: James Elkins's "On the impossibility of close reading: The case of Alexander Marshack" (1996) is a literary critique, but the article is equally important for the appended comments by a range of interested scholars; see also d'Errico (1995), and White (1982, 1992, 1994).

Exploring ancient Chavín cosmology: Burger's *Chavín and the Origin of Andean Civilization* (1992) is a key resource here, as is Morris and von Hagen (1993); see also Miller and Burger (1995). For earlier views on Chavín, see Lathrap (1973, 1977, 1985), and Tello (1943).

Multiple voices from the Bighorn medicine wheel: Eddy (1974, 1977); see also the edited volume by Michael Wilson et al. (1981). Deloria (1993) presents a passionate defense of protecting sacred land in Indian Country; see also various papers in Carmichael et al. (1994), Grey (1963), and Mansfield (1980).

Specific quotes and citations:

"It is only when . . ." (Hodder 1986: 7)
"Humanists must cease thinking . . ." (Flannery 1972: 400)
"The problem is that past ideas . . ." (Gilman 1987: 516)
"If archaeologists are to think . . ." (Yoffee and Sherratt 1993: 6)
"We would be *paleopsychologists* . . ." (Binford 1987a)
"To read what the 'ecologists' . . ." (Flannery 1972: 400)
"what it may have been . . ." (Hall 1977)
"I see the Hopewell platform pipe . . ." (Hall 1977: 504–505)
"It is not likely . . ." (Flannery and Marcus 1993: 262)
"We may not be able . . ." (Renfrew 1993: 249)
"The problem is that the archaeologist . . ." (Trigger 1989a: 378)
"[Marshack] maintains the view . . ." (White 1994: 392)
"purity of observation . . ." (White 1996: 219)
"Obviously there can be no . . ." (de Laguna 1957: 181)
"At the level of technology . . ." (Marshack 1996: 39)
"I have never argued . . ." (Marshack 1996: 36)
"that study of the La Marche . . ." (Marshack 1996: 39)
"The paradox of Chavín . . ." (Miller and Burger 1995: 453–454)
"The ideology of Chavín de Huántar . . ." (Miller and Burger 1995: 454)
"Thus, the Chavín horizon . . ." (Burger 1992: 184)
"One message of Chavín . . ." (Miller and Burger 1995: 454)
"While some of the features . . ." (Burger 1992: 226)
"Red Plume, a famous Crow chief . . ." (Greenburg 1926: 66)
"The major difference . . ." (Deloria 1995: 55)
"The diversity of postprocessual . . ." (Kohl 1993: 14)
"The best anthropologists are those . . ." (Anderson 1995: 2)
"Progress is marked less . . ." (Geertz 1973: 29)
"Cognitive approaches can only be used . . ." (Flannery and Marcus 1993: 261)
"There is at present no evidence . . ." (Trigger 1989a: 342)

Chapter 17

This section, in places, follows the useful discussions by Bell (1994, chapter 8), Hodder (1989b), and Trigger (1980b). The phrase "unintended consequence" is taken from Wylie (1991b); the notion of replacing the objective eye with the personal "I" comes from Marcus (1994: 45). For more on the humanistic tradition of Bandelier, I recommend Greenlee's (1995) account of his personal experience with ancestral Puebloan archaeology.

Specific quotes and citations:

"Archaeology shows more clearly . . ." (Hodder 1991a: 31)
"the first attempt . . ." (Binford et al. 1970: 1)
Excavating a Virginia Burial Mound is quoted from Jefferson (1787: 97–100).
Archaeology at Hatchery West is quoted from Binford et al. (1970: 1).
"I find a certain excitement . . ." (Hodder 1989b: 270)
"because power outside the text . . ." (Hodder 1989b: 270)
"How can I explain . . ." (Hodder 1989b: 272)
"The writing has become . . ." (Hodder 1989: 271)
In Their Own Words: On Getting on With Southwestern Archaeology is reproduced with permission from Phillips et al. (1994).
"Archaeology, I would say . . ." (quoted in Quick 1985: 103–104)
"There are signs . . ." (Hodder 1984: 3–31)
"Archaeology is a story . . ." (Brumfiel 1987: 513)
On Envisioning Gender–More Than Faceless Blobs is quoted with permission from Tringham (1991: 93–94).
"What we call our data . . ." (Geertz 1973: 9)
"The fact that archaeology . . ." (Gero 1989: 97)
"The ultimate aim . . ." (Hodder 1986: 101–102)
"We study history . . ." (Collingwood 1939: 114)
"almost exclusively by white . . ." (Spector 1993: 7)
"[Can] a non-Indian person . . ." (Spector 1993: 13)
"For the first time . . ." (Spector 1993: 15)
"I sometimes imagine being . . ." (Spector 1993: 65)
"Did they watch . . ." (Spector 1993: 89)
"The site was the set for past . . ." (Spector 1993: 79)
"Like casts in community theater . . ." (Spector 1993: 85)
"to them, a dance area . . ." (Spector 1993: 121)
"The archaeologist is digging up . . ." (Chippindale 1993: 28)
"Although the archaeologist's writing . . ." (Spector 1993: 33)
"I turned my attention . . ." (Spector 1993: 18)
"*What This Awl Means* . . ." (Berlo 1993: 247)
"like cracking a code . . ." (Spector 1993: 38–39)
What This Awl Means is quoted with permission from Spector (1993: 19–29).
On Archaeology and Empathy is quoted with permission from Spector (1993: 1–18).
"The young Dakota woman . . ." (Schommer 1993)

Chapter 18

Here are some key and relatively new contributions to historical archaeology: the volume honoring the contributions of James Deetz (Yentsch and

Beaudry 1992), Leone and Silberman's *Invisible America* (1995), and Little's *Text-Aided Archaeology* (1992); see also Beaudry (1988), Deagan (1988, 1991, 1995), Deetz (1977a, 1991), Falk (1991), Handsman and Leone (1989), Kelso and Most (1990), Landon (1996), Lightfoot (1995), Seifert (1991), Shackel (1996), South (1977a, 1977b, 1994a), and Wall (1994). On America-as-melting-pot, see Deagan, (1980), Deetz (1977a), and Schuyler (1976). This chapter draws on examples from Deetz (1977a, 1983) and Glassie (1975). The discussion of the Paca Garden relies on Leone (1984, 1987, 1988a, 1988b).

On the beginnings of Americanist historical archaeology: Deetz (1977: 29–30) describes Hall's early excavation of the Standish house, the story of Sainte Marie is told by Kidd (1949), and the development of "backyard archaeology" is discussed by Fairbanks (1977). See also Ascher and Fairbanks (1971), Fairbanks (1984), Orser and Fagan (1995: chapter 2), and South (1994b).

On the archaeology of Annapolis and the Chesapeake region: For a summary of new directions in the historical archaeology of the Chesapeake region, see Leone et al. (in press), Potter (1994), Shackel (1994), and Shackel and Little (1994).

On critical theory in historical archaeology: A key resource is Mark Leone's "A historical archaeology of capitalism" (1995), and the papers in Pinsky and Wylie (1995); see also Leone et al. (1987) and McGuire (1992a: 36–39).

Specific quotes and citations:

"We think of historical archaeology . . ." (Deagan 1991: 1100)
"The hardest part . . ." (quoted in Harrington 1994: 5)
"the pulsating heart of . . ." (Kidd 1994: 49)
"The site of Sainte Marie . . ." (Kidd 1994: 60)
"Historical archaeology . . ." (Deagan 1982: 153)
"Handmaiden to History . . ." (from title of Noël Hume's 1964 article)
"a new breed . . ." (Noël Hume 1964: 215)
"The archaeological scientist . . ." (South 1977a: 1)
"Welcome historic sites archaeology . . ." (Binford 1977b: xii)
"Archaeologists dealing with data . . ." (South 1994: 165)
"Barnum and Bailey . . ." (Noël Hume 1969: 10)
"archaeology of the people without history . . ." (from the title of Wolf's 1982 book)
"Since 1950, I have watched . . ." (Jelks 1994: 189)
"The quest for historical sites . . ." (Cotter 1994: 15)
"the cultural specific (emic) . . ." (Trigger 1989b: 31)
"Archaeology, as we know it . . ." (Patterson 1991: 242)
"[Historical archaeology] is . . ." (Deetz 1991: 1)
"Despite all the calls . . ." (Leone 1995: 251)
"The most important facts . . ." (Deagan 1991: 110)
"The archaeology of historical sites . . ." (Cotter 1994: 22)
"They left no writing . . ." (Glassie 1975: 178)
"accompanied by a contraction . . ." (Glassie 1975: 182–184)

On the Importance of Artifacts is quoted with permission from Glassie (1975: 7, 12).
Structural Approaches to Archaeology is quoted with permission from Deetz (1988: 221, 222).
"The tiny ship . . ." (Deetz 1983: 33)
"As I began to walk . . ." (Leone 1988b: 32)
"The gardens are three-dimensional . . ." (Leone 1988b: 32)
"While it will always be true . . ." (McGimsey and Davis 1977: 89)
"I raise the need for historical archaeology . . ." (Leone 1995: 251)
"A historical archaeology . . ." (Leone 1995: 251)
"It is the politics of class . . ." (Leone 1995: 251)
"to affect life in . . ." (Leone 1995: 261)
"Black people want to know . . ." (Leone 1995: 262)
"We ourselves had to admit . . ." (Leone 1995: 262)
"Archaeology in Annapolis . . ." (Potter 1994)

Chapter 19

Some key resources in African American archaeology include Deagan and MacMahon (1995), Ferguson's *Uncommon Ground* (1992), Lange and Handler (1985), Leone et al. (1995), MacMahon and Deagan (1996), Scott (1994), and Singleton (1985, 1995); see also Barbour (1994), Blakey (1995), Jamieson (1995), Orser (1984, 1991, 1995), Orser and Fagan (1995), Rankin-Hill and Blakey (1994), and Sobel (1987). Singleton and Bograd (1995) have published a bibliographic guide to the literature of the African diaspora. Slave diets at Monticello are discussed by Crader (1990).

On the Colonial Williamsburg and Carter's Grove reconstructions: Barbour (1994), Epperson (1990), Gable et al. (1992), Gable and Handler (1996), Handler (1979), Handler and Lange (1978), and Singleton (1993).
On the archaeology of the African Burial Ground: Cook (1993), Gaines (1995), Harrington (1993), Levy (1993), Rothschild (1990), and Smith (1994). For more on American slave life, see Douglas (1950). Ofori-Ana (1995) discusses the meaning of the Sankofa symbol.

Specific quotes and citations:

Choosing a Name for the Africans Abroad was written specifically for this chapter by Cheryl White.
The title *Fort Mose: Colonial America's Black Fortress of Freedom* is taken from Deagan and MacMahon (1995).
"The stereotypical image . . ." (quoted in *Northeast Florida Advocate,* March 16, 1987)
"so that by their example . . ." (quoted by Deagan and Landers, in press)
Quotes in *Uncovering Buried African Connections* are taken from Wilford (1996).
"This type of research . . ." (Smith 1994: 10)

"for the comfort of the company's Negro men . . ." (quoted in Harrington 1993: 30)

"the first European . . ." (quoted in K. Cook 1993)

"This is the most important . . ." (quoted in Shipp 1992)

Bioarchaeology of the African Burial Ground was written specifically for this chapter by Michael L. Blakey.

"Black folks wanted to hear . . ." (Smith 1994: 13)

"If it was an African . . ." (quoted in Harrington 1993: 34)

"We didn't include . . ." (quoted in Harrington 1993: 33)

"I cried . . ." (quoted in Shipp, 1993)

"microcosm of the issues . . ." (cited in Harrington 1993: 30)

"very revolutionary . . ." (quoted in Harrington 1993: 38)

The account of the Ghanaian chiefs' visit is based on Gaines (1995).

"The historical research . . ." (quoted in Boakyewa 1995: 3)

Why Are So Few African-Americans Doing African-American Archaeology? is quoted with permission from Singleton (1995).

Chapter 20

On the practice of cultural resource management: See Adovasio and Carlisle (1988), Anyon and Ferguson (1995), D. Blanton (1995), Cleere (1989, 1993), Elia (1993), Elston (1992), Fowler (1982, 1986), Klesert and Downer (1990), Leone and Potter (1992), McManamon (1991, 1992), McManamon et al. (1993), Podolefsky and Brown (1994), and Smith (1994). The Advisory Council on Historic Preservation has produced numerous manuals for resource managers (esp. 1988, 1989).

On women as working archaeologists: Babcock and Parezo (1988), Claassen (1992, 1994), Cullen (1995), Irwin-Williams (1990), Nelson et al. (1994), Parezo (1993), and Williams (1981).

On looters and pothunters: Staley (1993) details some problems with the antiquities market, and Neary (1992) tells of a government sting operation to nab looters of archaeological materials; see also Harrington (1991), Hoffman (1993), Holloway (1995), Lenihan (1993), and Messenger (1989).

On the importance of avocational archaeology: H. Davis (1991), Frison (1984), and Roberts (1993).

Specific quotes and citations:

"Archaeology is now . . ." (Sherratt 1993: 119)

Contrasting Views of "Significance" at Zuni Pueblo is reproduced with permission from Anyon and Ferguson (1995: 913–915).

"There are no absolute . . ." (Zubrow 1989: 44)

"Until recently, American . . ." (Pastron 1994: 86)

"Ironically, the CRM field . . ." (Elia 1993: 431)

Pampered Archaeologists is based on an article that appeared in the 1988 Holiday issue of *Careers* magazine.

"I don't see how . . ." (quoted in Babcock and Parezo 1988: 130)
"As a science which . . ." (Mead 1960: 5)
"Anthropology, like all professions . . ." (Parezo 1993: 363)
"[Gender bias] makes for a . . ." (quoted in Williams 1981: 9)
"women could not withstand . . ." (Wormington 1981: v)
"Activities by many archaeologists . . ." (Wormington 1981: v)
"I always published . . ." (Wormington in Parezo 1993: 5)
"Being a woman . . ." (Parezo 1993: 363)
The phrase "chilly climate" is taken from Parezo and Bender (1994).
"We have come a long way . . ." (Nelson and Nelson 1994: 230)
"Giving women their due . . ." (Nelson and Nelson 1994: 235)
"Women still face . . ." (Nelson and Nelson 1994: 229)
"When enough people become . . ." (Frison 1984: 190)
"'Pothunting' means all kinds . . ." (King 1991: 83)
On Getting a Practical Archaeological Education is quoted with permission from Elston (1992: 43–44).
Stop Those Pothunters . . . is reproduced with permission from Domenici (1991).
"While we tend to think . . ." (quoted in Monastersky 1994: 91)
"As children we were taught . . ." (Saubel 1994)
Avocational Archaeology Groups is reproduced with permission from Davis (1991).
"I got my rights . . ." (quoted in Smith and Ehrenhard 1991: 19)

Chapter 21

On ethics in archaeology: The papers published by Lynott and Wylie (1995) cover a range of ethical concerns for the 1990s; see also Chase et al. (1988), Green (1984), and Messenger (1989).

Archaeological approaches to biodiversity and understanding modern ecosystems: Diamond (1988), Lipe (1995), Stahl (1996), and Steadman (1995).

On the use of ancient agricultural technology: Bray (1990), Carney et al. (1993), Erickson (1988, 1992a, 1992b, 1993, 1994, 1995), and Kolata and Ortloff (1989); this chapter also draws on discussions in Long (1993) and Stevens (1988).

On archaeology and the Alamo: Brear (1995), and Weber (1988).

On who owns the past: Arden (1989), Bray and Killion (1994), Gathercole and Lowenthal (1990), Goldstein and Kintigh (1990), Greenfield (1989), Layton (1989), Messenger (1989), Murray (1996), and Powell et al. (1993).

On Troy and Schliemann: The catalog of the Treasure of Priam's first world tour has been published by Tolstikov and Treister (1996); see also Allen (1995), Meyer (1993, 1995), Nicholas (1994), Rose (1993), Snodgrass (1995), Traill (1996), and Wilford (1996).

On the Native American Graves and Protection Act: Some of the key sources include Carpenter (1991), Deloria (1992a, 1995), Echo-Hawk and Echo-Hawk (1994), Ferguson (1996), Gulliford (1996), Klesert (1992), Klesert and Powell (1993), McManamon (1994), Meighan (1992), Morell (1994), Preston (1989), Riding In (1992), Rose et al. (1996), Russell (1995), Shackley (1995), Weiner (1995), and Woodbury (1992). Special issues of *American Indian Culture and Research Journal* (Echo-Hawk 1992) and *Federal Archeology* (National Park Service 1995) are devoted to NAGPRA discussions.

Specific quotes and citations:

"Any suggestion that archaeology . . ." (Zubrow 1989: 45)
"Archaeology was once widely regarded . . ." (Renfrew 1994: 82)
"Unfortunately, there is still . . ." (Malinowski 1945)
"Theories come and go . . ." (quoted in *The New York Times,* December 23, 1996: 69)
The Journey of a Young Forensic Anthropologist was written specifically for this chapter by Clea Koff.
"Sound archaeological documentation . . ." (Connor 1996: 31)
"We suspect that . . ." (Fritz and Plog 1970: 412)
"Given the current environmental . . ." (Erickson 1995: 95)
"What is being argued here . . ." (Erickson 1992: 12)
"During 500 years . . ." (quoted in Long 1993)
"The only way . . ." (quoted in Long 1993)
"Our historic battlefields . . ." (Brear 1995: 1)
"I looked upon . . ." (quoted in Weber 1988: 142)
"Culture with a capital *C* . . ." (Brear 1995: 196)
I gratefully acknowledge the assistance of Mr. Anibal Rodriguez in preparing *What's in a Name? Hispanic and Anglo.*
"just wait and watch . . ." (Anne Fox, personal communication, August 1996)
"seemed to be drawing . . ." (Brear 1995: 146)
"If we had some way to measure it . . ." (Weber 1988: 133)
"The great difference . . ." (Fehrenbach 1968: 711)
"moved out of the earthly . . ." (Weber 1988: 135–136)
"in his foxskin [*sic*] cap . . ." (McAlister 1988: 140)
"a commie plot . . ." (quoted in Weber 1988: 137)
"The story goes . . ." (quoted in Schoelwer 1985: 115, and Weber 1988: 138)
"These frontier churches . . ." (Starr 1985: 85)
"one of the heroes . . ." (quoted in Morgado 1987: 145)
"Most beautiful of the California missions . . ." (*Sunset* editors 1979: 83)
"The missions are . . ." (cited in Starr 1985: 85)
"Protestant that I am . . ." (Chase 1913: 223)
"so that they could be read . . ." (Gebhard 1980: 138)
"elaborate misinterpretations of history" (Gebhard and Winter 1985: 27)
"For future archaeologists . . ." (Barker and Costello 1992: xvi)
"No reasonable person can argue . . ." (Castillo 1989: 378, 392)
"The days of the padres . . ." (Starr 1985: 58)
"Reconstruction of this mission . . ." (signpost at Mission Solano, Sonoma, California)
"How would you like it . . ." (quoted in Harbert and McDowell 1991: 19)

"to open doors to those . . ." (Folsom and Folsom 1993: 251)
"[The Bighorn Medicine Wheel] is sacred . . ." (Folsom and Folsom 1993: 251)
"I do not claim . . ." (Hodder 1991a: 31–32)
Archaeological Sites or Sacred Places? A Native American Perspective is reproduced with permission from Tallbull (1994: 238–239).
"The museum remains . . ." (Tilley 1989: 113)
"the unheralded discoverer . . ." (Allen 1995)
"The living are responsible . . ." (quoted in Gulliford 1996: 122)
"The Surgeon General . . ." (quoted in Gulliford 1996: 119)
"If you desecrate a white grave . . ." (quoted in Vizenor 1990)
"How would you feel . . ." (quoted in Swisher, 1989)
"To many Native Americans . . ." (Preston 1989: 67)
"We don't expect everyone . . ." (quoted in Preston 1989: 75)
"It is most unpleasant work . . ." (quoted in Preston 1989: 70)
"[This law] certainly puts Idaho . . ." (Anon. 1992: 1)
"throwing away one of the . . ." (quoted in Gulliford 1996: 134)
"Since we commonly proclaim . . ." (Meighan 1992: 705)

Illustration Credits

5 Courtesy American Museum of Natural History.
9 Courtesy American Museum of Natural History.
10 Courtesy American Museum of Natural History.
11 Courtesy Harvard University and Robert Neuman.
11 Courtesy Robert Neuman.
12 Courtesy American Museum of Natural History.
13 Courtesy Faith Kidder Fuller and Douglas R. Givens.
15 Courtesy Faith Kidder Fuller.
17 Courtesy American Museum of Natural History and Junius Bird.
20 Courtesy Walter W. Taylor.
21 Courtesy American Museum of Natural History; photograph by Deborah Mayer O'Brien.
24 Courtesy Kathleen Deagan; photograph by Bill Ballenberg.
36 Courtesy American Museum of Natural History.
38 Courtesy American Museum of Natural History.
39 Courtesy American Museum of Natural History.
44 Courtesy Richard S. MacNeish.
46 Courtesy Richard S. MacNeish and the University of Texas Press.
47 After Kemeny (1959: 86).
48 Courtesy American Museum of Natural History.
53 Courtesy American Museum of Natural History.
55 Courtesy American Museum of Natural History.
60 Courtesy Museum of New Mexico (9127); photograph by Robert Benecke.
61 After Bandelier (1883: Plate VI).
63 Courtesy School for American Research.
72 Courtesy Marvin Harris.
82 Courtesy Universal Press Syndicate.
89 Courtesy Museum of New Mexico (134736).
91 Courtesy Museum of New Mexico (41548).
96 Courtesy Faith Fuller Kidder and the School of American Research.
99 Courtesy American Museum of Natural History; photograph by the author.
101 Courtesy American Museum of Natural History; photograph by the author.
102 Courtesy American Museum of Natural History.
104 After Steward (1938: figure 8); drawing by Dennis O'Brien.
108 After Thomas (1973: figure 6); drawing by Dennis O'Brien.
116 Courtesy American Museum of Natural History; photograph by Dennis O'Brien.
117 (top) Drawing by Dennis O'Brien.
117 (bottom) Courtesy American Museum of Natural History; photograph by Deborah Mayer O'Brien.
119 (top) After Deagan (1980: 23); drawing by Dennis O'Brien.
119 (bottom) Courtesy Kathleen Deagan.
120 Drawing by Dennis O'Brien.
122 Drawing by Dennis O'Brien.
123 Courtesy American Museum of Natural History.
124 After Marcus and Flannery (1996: figure 10); drawing by Diana Salles.
131 After Boyd et al. (1951); courtesy of the University Press of Florida.
135 Courtesy American Museum of Natural History; photograph by Dennis O'Brien.
136 (top) Courtesy School of American Research (130198).
136 (bottom) Courtesy American Museum of Natural History.
138 (top) Courtesy American Museum of Natural History.
138 (bottom) Courtesy American Museum of Natural History.
140 Courtesy American Museum of Natural History; drawing by Dennis O'Brien.
142 Courtesy American Museum of Natural History.
145 Courtesy Payson Sheets.
146 Courtesy Payson Sheets.
147 Courtesy Payson Sheets.
149 Courtesy Payson Sheets and *Archaeology*.
150 Courtesy Dean Goodman.
151 Courtesy Dean Goodman.
152 Courtesy Dean Goodman.
158 Courtesy American Museum of Natural History; photograph by Dennis O'Brien.
159 After Thomas (1983b: figure 8). Courtesy American Museum of Natural History; drawing by Dennis O'Brien.
160 Courtesy American Museum of Natural History; photograph by Susan L. Bierwirth.
161 Courtesy American Museum of Natural History; drawing by Dennis O'Brien.
162 Courtesy American Museum of Natural History; drawing by Dennis O'Brien.
163 Courtesy American Museum of Natural History; photograph by Susan L. Bierwirth.
164 Drawing by Dennis O'Brien.

165 Courtesy Patty Jo Watson and the Cave Research Foundation.
167 Courtesy Universal Press Syndicate Company.
168 After Flannery (1986: figure 5.2); courtesy Kent V. Flannery.
170 Courtesy American Museum of Natural History; photograph by Deborah Mayer O'Brien.
171 Photograph by the author.
173 Courtesy American Museum of Natural History; photograph by Clark Spencer Larsen.
178 (top) Courtesy University of Arizona.
178 (bottom) Courtesy American Museum of Natural History.
179 Drawing by Dennis O'Brien.
181 (top) Courtesy Jeffrey S. Dean and the Laboratory of Tree-Ring Research, University of Arizona.
181 (bottom) After Dean (1970: figure 13); drawing by Dennis O'Brien.
182 Courtesy University Museum of National Antiquities, Oslo, Norway.
183 (top) After Wilson (1980: 141); drawing by Diana Salles.
183 (bottom) Courtesy University Museum of National Antiquities, Oslo, Norway.
184 Courtesy North American Syndicate.
187 Courtesy Rainer Berger and the University of California, Los Angeles.
188 After Taylor (1987b); drawing by Dennis O'Brien.
189 Courtesy American Museum of Natural History.
192 After Stuiver and Reimer (1993); courtesy of the University of Washington.
193 After Stuiver and Reimer (1993); courtesy of the University of Washington.
194 Courtesy National Museum of the American Indian.
195 Courtesy Frank J. Findlow.
197 Courtesy the Holy Shroud Guild.
198 Drawing by Dennis O'Brien.
203 Drawing by Diana Salles.
206 Courtesy Universal Press Syndicate Company.
207 Courtesy American Museum of Natural History; photograph by Susan L. Bierwirth.
208 Courtesy American Museum of Natural History.
211 Courtesy American Museum of Natural History.
213 After Thomas (1983b: figure 22); drawing by the author and Nicholas Amorosi.
215 Courtesy American Museum of Natural History; photograph by Susan L. Bierwirth.
217 Courtesy American Museum of Natural History.
218 Courtesy American Museum of Natural History.
219 Courtesy Faith Kidder Fuller.
221 Courtesy Museum of New Mexico (29747).
222 Courtesy American Museum of Natural History.
224 After Giddings (1966: figures 3 and 4). Courtesy National Oceanic and Atmospheric Administration and the American Association for the Advancement of Science.
225 After Wardwell (1986: figure 9); drawing by Diana Salles.
226 After Wardwell (1986: figure 131); drawing by Diana Salles.
236 After Haury (1950: 29); drawing by Dennis O'Brien.
238 Courtesy American Museum of Natural History; drawing by Nicholas Amorosi.
240 Courtesy American Museum of Natural History; photograph by Craig Chesek.
241 Courtesy American Museum of Natural History; photographs by Craig Chesek.
242 (top) Courtesy American Museum of Natural History; drawing by Dennis O'Brien.
242 (bottom) Courtesy American Museum of Natural History; photograph by Craig Chesek.
243 Courtesy American Museum of Natural History; photograph by Craig Chesek.
245 After Thomas (1983b: figure 66). Courtesy American Museum of Natural History; drawing by Dennis O'Brien.
246 After Mayer-Oakes (1955: figure 15); drawing by Dennis O'Brien.
247 After Ford (1952: figure 15). Courtesy American Museum of Natural History; drawing by Nicholas Amorosi.
248 After Ford (1957: figure 4). Courtesy American Museum of Natural History; drawing by Nicholas Amorosi.
249 Modified from Noël Hume (1976: figure 97); drawing by Dennis O'Brien.
250 After Harrington (1954); drawing by Dennis O'Brien.
251 (top) Courtesy Museo del Prado, Madrid.
251 (bottom) Courtesy the Print Collection, Miriam and Ira D. Wallach Division of Art, Prints, and Photographs. The New York Public Library, Astor, Lenox and Tilden Foundation.
252 After Deagan (1987: figure 6.2); drawing by Dennis O'Brien.
253 Courtesy American Museum of Natural History.
260 Courtesy Donald R. Tuohy and the Nevada State Museum.
263 Courtesy Michael Schiffer.
270 Courtesy James F. O'Connell.
272 Courtesy James F. O'Connell.
274 After Yellen (1977: figure 12); drawing by Dennis O'Brien.

277 Courtesy William Rathje.
278 Courtesy William Rathje.
285 (top) Courtesy American Museum of Natural History; photograph by R. Wanamaker.
285 (bottom) Courtesy Universal Press Syndicate Company.
286 Courtesy American Museum of Natural History; drawing by Diana Salles.
287 Drawing by Dennis O'Brien.
288 Drawing by Dennis O'Brien.
289 (top) Courtesy Bruce Bradley and the Crow Canyon Archaeological Center.
289 (bottom) Courtesy American Museum of Natural History.
291 Courtesy C. William Clewlow.
292 (top) Courtesy Ruth Tringham.
292 (bottom) Courtesy American Museum of Natural History.
295 (top) After Lahren and Bonnichsen (1974); drawing by Diana Salles.
295 (bottom) Courtesy American Museum of Natural History; photograph by Anibal Rodriguez.
296 Drawing by Diana Salles.
301 Courtesy Joe Ben Wheat and the University of Colorado.
302 Courtesy American Museum of Natural History; photograph by Lyntou Gardinier.
304 (top) Courtesy American Museum of Natural History; photograph by C. Reed Jr.
304 (bottom) Drawing by Diana Salles.
306 (top) After Thomas (1969: figure 1).
306 (bottom) Courtesy American Museum of Natural History.
311 Courtesy Elizabeth Reitz.
314 After Schulz and Gust (1983a, figures 1 and 2); drawing by Dennis O'Brien.
316 Photograph by John Rick.
317 (top) Courtesy American Museum of Natural History.
317 (bottom) After Miller and Burger (1995: figure 4); courtesy of the authors and the Society for American Archaeology.
318 Courtesy American Museum of Natural History; photograph by John Bigelow Taylor.
320 After Miller and Burger (1995: figure 11); courtesy of the authors and the Society for American Archaeology.
324 Courtesy American Museum of Natural History; photograph by Winston Hurst.
329 After Mehringer and Haynes (1966: figure 8); drawing by Dennis O'Brien.
330 After Mehringer et al. (1977: figure 3); drawing by Dennis O'Brien.
331 Courtesy Ralph Solecki.
334 Courtesy Susan Mulholland.
335 Courtesy Massachusetts Historical Society.
336 After Kelso (1984: figure 31); courtesy William Kelso and the Thomas Jefferson Memorial Foundation.
338 After Hastorf and Johannessen (1991); courtesy Christine Hastorf.
339 After Hastorf and Johannessen (1991); courtesy Christine Hastorf.
341 After Hastorf and Johannessen (1991); courtesy Christine Hastorf.
346 Drawing by Dennis O'Brien.
347 Courtesy American Museum of Natural History.
348 After Farnsworth et al. (1985: figure 1); drawing by Dennis O'Brien.
349 Courtesy American Museum of Natural History; photograph by John Bigelow Taylor.
353 Courtesy Clark Spencer Larsen; photograph by Barry Stark.
354 After Mobley (1980: figure 1); drawing by Dennis O'Brien.
356 (top) Courtesy Corbis-Bettman.
356 (bottom) Courtesy Corbis-Bettman.
357 Courtesy William R. Maples.
375 Courtesy Margaret Conkey; photograph by J. Clottes.
378 After Moore (1905: 109).
379 Drawing by Diana Salles.
380 After Moore (1905: figures 114, 115, 117, 118; Moore 1907: figures 57–61); drawing by Dennis O'Brien.
381 After Peebles and Kus (1977: figure 3).
385 After Doyel (1991); drawing by Dennis O'Brien.
392 Courtesy American Museum of Natural History.
393 Courtesy American Museum of Natural History.
394 After Marcus (1976: figure 1.12); drawing by Dennis O'Brien.
395 After Marcus (1976: figure 1.15); drawing by Dennis O'Brien.
396 (top) Courtesy American Museum of Natural History.
396 (bottom) Drawings by Diana Salles.
400 Courtesy American Museum of Natural History; photograph by Craig Chesek.
403 After Flannery (1986: figure 18.1); drawing by Dennis O'Brien.
404 Drawing by Diana Salles.
405 After Clark (1954: figure 5); drawing by Dennis O'Brien.
406 Drawing by Diana Salles.
407 After Fowler and MacNeish (1972: figure 104); courtesy Richard S. MacNeish and the University of Texas Press.

410 (top) After Binford (1983b: figure 89); courtesy Lewis Binford and Thames and Hudson.
410 (bottom) After Thomas (1983b: figure 221); drawing by Dennis O'Brien.
411 After Thomas (1983b: figure 222); drawing by Dennis O'Brien.
414 After Winterhalder (1987: figure 2.2); drawing by Dennis O'Brien.
418 Courtesy American Museum of Natural History; photograph by Robert Lowie.
419 Courtesy American Museum of Natural History.
421 Courtesy Diane Gifford-Gonzalez; photograph by Michael J. Mehlman.
425 (top) Drawing by Diana Salles.
425 (bottom) Courtesy Joan Gero.
430 Courtesy American Museum of Natural History.
433 Courtesy American Museum of Natural History.
440 Courtesy American Museum of Natural History.
441 Courtesy Ester Boserup.
449 Courtesy Robert Carneiro.
459 Drawing by Diana Salles.
460 Courtesy American Museum of Natural History; drawing by Dennis O'Brien.
461 After Hall (1977: figure 2); drawing by Dennis O'Brien.
463 Drawing by Diana Salles.
464 Courtesy American Museum of Natural History.
465 Photograph by Alexander Marshack.
466 Drawing by Dennis O'Brien.
467 Drawing by Dennis O'Brien.
468 Photograph by Alexander Marshack.
478 Courtesy American Heritage Center, University of Wyoming.
480 After Ovenden and Rodger (1981); drawing by Dennis O'Brien.
491 After Binford et al. (1970); courtesy Lewis Binford and the Society for American Archaeology.
499 (top) Courtesy Janet Spector.
499 (bottom) Courtesy American Museum of Natural History.
500 Courtesy American Museum of Natural History; photograph by R. E. Dahlgren.
501 Courtesy American Museum of Natural History.
502 Courtesy American Museum of Natural History.
503 Drawing by Diana Salles.
505 Courtesy American Museum of Natural History.
511 Courtesy Plimoth Plantation.
512 Courtesy Stanley South and the Institute of Archaeology and Anthropology, University of South Carolina.
516 After Glassie (1975); courtesy University of Tennessee Press.
524 Courtesy Maryland Historical Society, Baltimore.
525 Courtesy Mark Leone and the Historic Annapolis Foundation.
528 Courtesy Parker Potter.
533 Courtesy Colonial Williamsburg Foundation.
535 Courtesy American Museum of Natural History.
537 Courtesy Kathleen Deagan.
538 (top) After Kelso (1986: figure 6); courtesy William Kelso and the Archaeological Institute of America.
538 (bottom) After Kelso (1986: figure 3); drawing by Dennis O'Brien.
540 Courtesy Colonial Williamsburg.
542 Courtesy Mark Leone.
543 Courtesy Colonial Williamsburg.
544 Courtesy The Granger Collection.
545 Courtesy African Burial Ground and U.S. General Services Adminstration.
546 Drawing by Diana Salles.
549 Courtesy Michael L. Blakey and Howard University College of Medicine; photograph by Jeffrey John Fearing.
550 Courtesy Chester Higgins Jr.
551 Photograph by the author.
553 Courtesy Theresa Singleton.
558 Courtesy Lucasfilm, Ltd; photograph by Keith Hamshere.
563 Courtesy Barbara Mills.
569 Courtesy Robert Elston.
577 Photograph courtesy Clea Koff and Physicians for Human Rights.
581 Courtesy Craig Erickson.
582 Courtesy Craig Erickson.
583 Courtesy Craig Erickson.
589 Photograph by the author.
590 Courtesy Bell Magazine Agency, Monterey, California.
591 Courtesy California Section, California State Library.
597 Courtesy American Museum of Natural History.
599 Courtesy American Museum of Natural History.
601 Photograph by the author.
606 Courtesy the Alutiiq Museum photoarchives; photograph by Patrick Saltonstall.
607 Courtesy the Alutiiq Museum photoarchives; photograph by Richard Lee.

Index